Integrated Marketing Communications in Advertising and Promotion

Terence A. **Shimp**
University of South Carolina

SOUTH-WESTERN
CENGAGE Learning™

Australia • Brazil • Japan • Korea • Mexico • Singapore • Spain • United Kingdom • United States

SOUTH-WESTERN
CENGAGE Learning™

Integrated Marketing Communications in Advertising and Promotion, 8e

Terence A. Shimp

Vice President of Editorial, Business: Jack W. Calhoun

Vice President/Editor-in-Chief: Melissa S. Acuna

Acquisitions Editor: Mike Roche

Sr. Developmental Editor: Susanna C. Smart

Marketing Manager: Mike Aliscad

Content Project Manager: Corey Geissler

Media Editor: John Rich

Production Technology Analyst: Emily Gross

Frontlist Buyer, Manufacturing: Diane Gibbons

Production Service: PrePressPMG

Sr. Art Director: Stacy Shirley

Internal Designer: Chris Miller/cmiller design

Cover Image: Shutterstock

Permission Aquistion Manager/Photo: Deanna Ettinger

Permission Aquistion Manager/Text: Mardell Glinski Schultz

For product information and technology assistance, contact us at
Cengage Learning Customer & Sales Support, 1-800-354-9706

For permission to use material from this text or product,
submit all requests online at **www.cengage.com/permissions**
Further permissions questions can be emailed to
permissionrequest@cengage.com

Library of Congress Control Number: 2008939395

ISBN 13: 978-0-324-66531-4

ISBN 10: 0-324-66531-8

Cengage Learning International Offices

Asia
cengageasia.com
tel: (65) 6410 1200

Australia/New Zealand
cengage.com.au
tel: (61) 3 9685 4111

Brazil
cengage.com.br
tel: (011) 3665 9900

India
cengage.co.in
tel: (91) 11 30484837/38

Latin America
cengage.com.mx
tel: +52 (55) 1500 6000

UK/Europe/Middle East/Africa
cengage.co.uk
tel: (44) 207 067 2500

Represented in Canada by Nelson Education, Ltd.
nelson.com
tel: (416) 752 9100/(800) 668 0671

For product information: **www.cengage.com/international**
Visit your local office: **www.cengage.com/global**
Visit our corporate website: **www.cengage.com**

Printed in China
1 2 3 4 5 6 7 12 11 10 09

Dedication

I dedicate this 8th edition of Integrated Marketing Communications in Advertising and Promotion *to all of my family members, past and present. The depth of my love and gratitude for all of you is immeasurable. I also acknowledge the inspiration and support I have received through the years from my faculty colleagues and Ph.D. students, many of whom honored me to a degree they cannot possibly realize when they traveled from around the country and surprised me with a marvelous retirement party.*

brief contents

Preface xv
About the Author 1

Part 1 Integrated Marketing Communications: Processes, Brand Equity, and Marcom's Role in Introducing New Brands 2

1 Overview of Integrated Marketing Communications 4
2 Marketing Communications Challenges: Enhancing Brand Equity, Influencing Behavior, and Being Accountable 32
3 Facilitating the Success of New Brands 60

Part 2 The Fundamental Marcom Decisions: Targeting, Positioning, Objective Setting, and Budgeting 94

4 Targeting 96
5 Positioning 126
6 Objective Setting and Budgeting 154

Part 3 Advertising Management 178

7 Overview of Advertising Management 180
8 Effective and Creative Advertising Messages 206
9 Message Appeals and Endorsers 240
10 Measuring Advertising Message Effectiveness 280
11 Advertising Media: Planning and Analysis 316
12 Traditional Advertising Media 358
13 Internet Advertising 392
14 Other Advertising Media 420

Part 4 Sales Promotion Management 442

15 Sales Promotion and the Role of Trade Promotions 444
16 Sampling and Couponing 480
17 Premiums and Other Promotions 508

Part 5 Other Marcom Tools 532

18 Marketing-Oriented Public Relations and Word-of-Mouth Management 534
19 Event and Cause Sponsorships 560
20 Signage and Point of Purchase Communications 574

Part 6 Marcom Constraints 602

21 Ethical, Regulatory, and Environmental Issues 604

Glossary 639
Name Index 645
Subject Index 650

contents

Preface xv
About the Author 1

Part 1

Integrated Marketing Communications: Processes, Brand Equity, and Marcom's Role in Introducing New Brands 2

Chapter 1

Overview of Integrated Marketing Communications 4

Marcom Insight: Appealing to Youth and Reinvigorating a Brand Image: State Farm's nowwhat.com Campaign 5
Introduction 6
The Tools of Marketing Communications 7
The Integration of Marketing Communications 8
Why Integrate? 8 • IMC Skeptics 9 • IMC and Synergy 9 • And Now a Definition of IMC 10
Key IMC Features 10
Key Feature #1: The Consumer or Business Customer Must Represent the Starting Point for All Marketing Communications Activities 10

Global Focus: *Creating a Pepsi Commercial in China* 12

Key Feature #2: Use Any and All Marcom Tools That Are Up to the Task 13

IMC Focus: *The Laundry Hanger as an Advertising Touch Point* 15

Key Feature #3: Multiple Messages Must Speak with a Single Voice 16 • Key Feature #4: Build Relationships Rather Than Engage in Flings 17 • Key Element #5: Don't Lose Focus of the Ultimate Objective: Affect Behavior 18 • Obstacles to Implementing the Key IMC Features 20
The Marketing Communications Decision-Making Process 20
Fundamental Marcom Decisions 21 • Marcom Implementation Decisions 23 • Marcom Outcomes 26 • Program Evaluation 27
Summary 27
Appendix 28
Discussion Questions 29
End Notes 30

Chapter 2

Marketing Communications Challenges: Enhancing Brand Equity, Influencing Behavior, and Being Accountable 32

Marcom Insight: When Polls Fail to Reveal the Complete Picture 33
Introduction 34
Brand Equity 34
A Firm-Based Perspective on Brand Equity 35 • A Customer-Based Perspective on Brand Equity 36 • Enhancing Brand Equity 41

IMC Focus: *Neuromarketing and the Case of Why Coca-Cola Outsells Pepsi* 43

What Benefits Result from Enhancing Brand Equity? 46

Global Focus: *The World's Perception of America* 47

Characteristics of World-Class Brands 48
Affecting Behavior and Achieving Marcom Accountability 50
Difficulty of Measuring Marcom Effectiveness 51 • Assessing Effects with Marketing Mix Modeling 53

IMC Focus: *Harley-Davidson—An Iron Horse for Rugged Individualists, Including Females!* 54
Summary 55

Discussion Questions 55
End Notes 56

Chapter 3

Facilitating the Success of New Brands 60

Marcom Insight: First the Taurus, Next the Five Hundred, and then Taurus's Return 61
Introduction 62
Marcom and Brand Adoption 62
Brand Characteristics That Facilitate Adoption 64

Global Focus: *Washing Machines for the Masses in Brazil, China, and India* 65

Quantifying the Adoption-Influencing Characteristics 69
Brand Naming 71
What Constitutes a Good Brand Name? 71

IMC Focus: *A Musical Toothbrush That Encourages Children to Brush Longer* 74

The Brand-Naming Process 77 • The Role of Logos 79
Pacakaging 81
Packaging Structure 81 • Evaluating the Package: The VIEW Model 84 • Quantifying the VIEW Components 87 • Designing a Package 88
Summary 89
Discussion Questions 90
End Notes 91

Part 2

The Fundamental Marcom Decisions: Targeting, Positioning, Objective Setting, and Budgeting 94

Chapter 4

Targeting 96

Marcom Insight: Reaching Teens by Appealing to Cheerleaders 97
Introduction 98
Behaviorgraphic Targeting 98
Online Behavioral Targeting 100 • Privacy Concerns 101
Psychographic Targeting 101
Customized Psychographic Profiles 102 • General Purpose Psychographic Profiles 102
Geodemographic Targeting 106
Demographic Targeting 107

Global Focus: *General Electric's Targeting Indians with Ultrasound Machines* 108

The Changing Age Structure 109

IMC Focus: *College Students: An Inviting Target for Odor-Fighting Products* 114

The Ever-Changing American Household 117 • Ethnic Population Developments 118

IMC Focus: *A Special Beverage for Latino Consumers, Clamato* 121

Summary 122
Discussion Questions 123
End Notes 124

Chapter 5

Positioning 126

Marcom Insight: "McBucks": It's Not the McDonald's You've Always Known 127
Introduction 128
Positioning in Theory: A Matter of Creating Meaning 128
The Meaning of Meaning 129 • Meaning Transfer: From Culture to Object to Consumer 129
Positioning in Practice: The Nuts and Bolts 131
Benefit Positioning 134

IMC Focus: *Not Lovely, but Successful* 135

Global Focus: *The Symbolism of Certifying Products as Fair Traded* 136

Attribute Positioning 137 • Repositioning a Brand 137
Implementing Positioning: Know Thy Consumer 140
The Consumer Processing Model (CPM) 141 • The Hedonic, Experiential Model (HEM) 147

Summary 149
Discussion Questions 150
End Notes 151

Chapter 6

Objective Setting and Budgeting 154

Marcom Insight: Impressive Results Produced by Spending Big on Cavemen Characters and a Talking Gecko 155
Introduction 156
Setting Marcom Objectives 156
The Hierarchy of Marcom Effects 157
IMC Focus: *This Cat(fight) Is a Dog* 160
Requirements for Setting Suitable Marcom Objectives 162 • Should Marcom Objectives Be Stated in Terms of Sales? 164
Marcom Budgeting 166
Budgeting in Theory 166
Global Focus: *The Top-25 Global Marketers' Advertising Spending* 167
Budgeting in Practice 169
Summary 175
Discussion Questions 176
End Notes 176

Part 3

Advertising Management 178

Chapter 7

Overview of Advertising Management 180

Marcom Insight: Is Advertising Rocket Science? 181
Introduction 182
The Magnitude of Advertising 183
Global Focus: *Which Source of Product Information Do Consumers Most Trust?* 184
Advertising-to-Sales Ratios 185 • Advertising Effects Are Uncertain 185
Advertising Functions 188
Informing 188 • Influencing 188
IMC Focus: *A National Advertising Effort for Starbucks* 189
Reminding and Increasing Salience 189 • Adding Value 190 • Assisting Other Company Efforts 190
The Advertising Management Process 190
Managing the Advertising Process: The Client Perspective 191 • The Role of Advertising Agencies 192 • Agency Compensation • 194
Ad-Investment Considerations 195
The Case for Investing in Advertising 196 • The Case for Disinvesting 196 • Which Position Is More Acceptable? 197
Summary 202
Discussion Questions 202
End Notes 203

Chapter 8

Effective and Creative Advertising Messages 206

Marcom Insight: Perhaps the Greatest TV Commercial of All Time 207
Introduction 208
Creating Effective Advertising 208
Creativity: The CAN Elements 209 • Getting Messages to "Stick" 210 • Illustrations of Creative and Sticky Advertising Executions 213
Global Focus: *Why Dump an Extraordinarily Successful Ad Compaign?* 215
Advertising Successes and Mistakes 217
Constructing a Creative Brief 219
IMC Focus: *How Well Do You Know Advertising Slogans?* 222
Alternative Styles of Creative Advertising 223
Unique Selling Proposition Creative Style 223 Brand Image Creative Style 224 • Resonance Creative Style 225 • Emotional Creative Style 225 • Generic Creative Style 225 • Preemptive Creative Style 226 • Section Summary 227
Means-End Chaining and the Method of Laddering as Guides to Creative Advertising Formulation 228
The Nature of Values 228 • Which Values Are Most Relevant to Advertising? 229

• *Advertising Applications of Means-End Chains: The MECCAS Model 230 • Identifying Means-End Chains: The Method of Laddering 233 • Practical Issues in Identifying Means-End Chains 234*
Corporate Image and Issue Advertising 234
Corporate Image Advertising 235 • Corporate Issue (Advocacy) Advertising 235
Summary 236
Discussion Questions 236
End Notes 237

Chapter 9

Message Appeals and Endorsers 240

Marcom Insight: The Use of Humor and Comparisons in Advertising **241**
Introduction 242
Enhancing Consumers' Motivation, Opportunity, and Ability to Process Advertisements 242
Motivation to Attend to Messages 244 • Motivation to Process Messages 246 • Opportunity to Encode Information 246 • Opportunity to Reduce Processing Time 247 • Ability to Access Knowledge Structures 247 • Ability to Create Knowledge Structures 247 • Section Summary 250
The Role of Celebrity Endorsers in Advertising 250
Endorser Attributes: The TEARS Model 251 • Endorser Selection Considerations: The "No Tears" Approach 254
Global Focus: *Two Unknowns (to Americans) Connect in China* 255
The Role of Q Scores 257
The Role of Humor in Advertising 258
Appeals to Consumer Fears 260
Fear Appeal Logic 260 • Appropriate Intensity 260 • The Related Case of Appeals to Scarcity 261
Appeals to Consumer Guilt 262
The Use of Sex in Advertising 262
What Role Does Sex Play in Advertising? 263 • The Potential Downside of Sex Appeals in Advertising 263
Subliminal Messages and Symbolic Embeds 264
Why It Is Unlikely That Subliminal Advertising Works 265
The Functions of Music in Advertising 267
IMC Focus: *Subliminal Priming and Brand Choice* 268
The Role of Comparative Advertising 269
Is Comparative Advertising More Effective? 270 • Considerations Dictating the Use of Comparative Advertising 271
Summary 272
Discussion Questions 272
End Notes 273

Chapter 10

Measuring Advertising Message Effectiveness 280

Marcom Insight: What Makes a Commercial Watchable? **281**
Introduction to Advertising Research 282
It's Not Easy or Inexpensive 282 • What Does Advertising Research Involve? 282
IMC Focus: *Testing TV Commercials in Prefinished Form* 283
Industry Standards for Message Research 284 • What Do Brand Managers and Ad Agencies Want to Learn from Message Research? 286
Two General Forms of Message Research 286
Qualitative Message Research 287 • Quantitative Message Research 287
Measures of Recognition and Recall 289
Starch Readership Service 289
Global Focus: *Is What's Good for Vodka Good for Tequila?* 292
Bruzzone Tests 293 • Day-After Recall Testing 295
Measurement of Emotional Reactions 297
Neuroscience and Brain Imaging 298 • Self-Report Measurement 298 • Physiological Testing 298
Measures of Persuasion 299
*The Ipsos-ASI Next*TV method 300 • The ARS Persuasion Method 300*
Measures of Sales Response (Single-Source Systems) 302
ACNielsen's ScanTrack 302 • IRI's BehaviorScan 303
Some Major Conclusions about Television Advertising 304
Conclusion 1—All Commercials Are Not Created Equal: Ad Copy Must Be Distinctive 305 • Conclusion 2—More Is Not Necessarily Better: Weight Is Not Enough 306 • Conclusion 3—All Good Things Must End: Advertising Eventually Wears Out 310 • Conclusion 4—Do Not Be

Stubborn: Advertising Works Quickly or Not at All 311
Summary 311
Discussion Questions 312
End Notes 313

Chapter 11

Advertising Media: Planning and Analysis 316

Marcom Insight: Is Super Bowl Advertising Worth the Expense? 317
Introduction 318
Some Useful Terminology: Media versus Vehicles 318 • Messages and Media: A Hand-in-Glove Relation 318
Global Focus: *Searching for Media Options around the Globe* 318
Selecting and Buying Media and Vehicles 319
The Media-Planning Process 320
Selecting the Target Audience 321
Specifying Media Objectives 322
Reach 322
IMC Focus: *Do Mac Owners' Personalities Match the Mac Character's Personality?* 323
Frequency 324 • Weight 326 • Continuity 333 • Recency Planning (a.k.a. The Shelf-Space Model) 335 • Cost Considerations 339 • The Necessity of Making Tradeoffs 340
Media-Scheduling Software 341
Hypothetical Illustration: A One-Month Magazine Schedule for the Esuvee-H 343
Review of Media Plans 346
The Diet Dr Pepper Plan 346 • Saab 9–5's Media Plan 348 • Olympus Camera Media Plan 350
Summary 354
Discussion Questions 355
End Notes 356

Chapter 12

Traditional Advertising Media 358

Marcom Insight: Is TV Advertising Declining in Effectiveness? 359
Introduction 360
Some Preliminary Comments 360
Newspapers 360
Buying Newspaper Space 361 • Newspaper Advertising's Strengths and Limitations 362
Magazines 363
Buying Magazine Space 363 • Magazine Advertising's Strengths and Limitations 366 • Magazine Audience Measurement 367 • Using Simmons and MRI Reports 368 • Customized Magazines 371
Radio 371
Buying Radio Time 372 • Radio Advertising's Strengths and Limitations 372 • Radio Audience Measurement 374
Television 375
Television Programming Dayparts 375 • Network, Spot, Syndicated, Cable, and Local Advertising 376 • Television Advertising's Strengths and Limitations 379
IMC Focus: *The Rising Cost of Super Bowl Advertising* 381
Global Focus: *Place-Shifting TV Viewing* 383
Infomercials 383 • Brand Placements in Television Programs 384 • Television Audience Measurement 385
Summary 388
Discussion Questions 388
End Notes 389

Chapter 13

Internet Advertising 392

Marcom Insight: Gains for Online Advertising Are Losses for Traditional Media 393
Introduction 394
The Two i's of the Internet: Individualization and Interactivity 394 • The Internet Compared with Other Ad Media 395 • Internet Advertising Formats 396
Web Sites 397
Display or Banner Ads 398
Click-through Rates 398 • Standardization of Banner-Ad Sizes 399
Rich Media: Pop-Ups, Interstitials, Superstitials, and Video Ads 399
Video Ads and Webisodes 400
Blogs, Podcasts, and Social Networks 400
IMC Focus: *Web Videos for Johnson's Baby Lotion* 401
Blogs 401 • Podcasts 402 • Social Networks 403
E-mail Advertising 403

Global Focus: *Nescafé's Viral E-mail Effort in Argentina* 404
Opt-In E-mailing versus Spam 404 • E-mail Magazines (E-zines) 405 • Wireless E-mail Advertising 406 • The Special Case of Mobile Phones 407
Global Focus: *Cell Phone Advertising in India* 408
Search Engine Advertising 409
The Fundamentals of Search Engine Advertising 409 • Purchasing Keywords and Selecting Content-Oriented Web Sites 410 • SEA Is Not without Problems 412
Advertising via Behavioral Targeting 413
Measuring Internet Ad Effectiveness 414
Metrics for Measuring Internet Ad Performance 414
Summary 415
Discussion Questions 416
End Notes 417

Chapter 14

Other Advertising Media 420

Marcom Insight: Some Definitions Encapsulating This Chapter 421
Introduction 422
Direct Advertising via Postal Mail 422
Illustrations of Successful P-mail Campaigns 423
Global Focus: *How a Major Production Mistake Turned into a Huge Direct Mailing Success* 423
P-mail's Distinctive Features 425 • Who Uses P-Mail and What Functions Does It Accomplish? 426 • The Special Case of Catalogs and Audiovisual Media 427 • The Use of Databases 428
Brand Placements in Movies and TV Programs 431
Brand Placements in Movies 432 • Brand Placements in TV Programs 433
Yellow-Pages Advertising 434
Distinguishing Features of Yellow-Pages Advertising 434
Video-Game Advertising (a.k.a. Advergaming) 435
Measuring Video-Game Audiences 435
IMC Focus: *Profile of the Online Gaming Community* 435
Cinema Advertising 436
Potpourri of Alternative Advertising Media 436
Summary 438
Discussion Questions 439
End Notes 440

Part 4

Sales Promotion Management 442

Chapter 15

Sales Promotion and the Role of Trade Promotions 444

Marcom Insight: It's a Matter of Power—Nike versus Foot Locker 445
Introduction 446
The Nature of Sales Promotion 446
IMC Focus: *"Cheap Seats" and Free Eats* 447
Promotion Targets 447
Increased Budgetary Allocations to Promotions 448
Factors Accounting for the Shift 448 • A Consequence of the Increase: New Accounting Rules 452
What Are Sales Promotion's Capabilities and Limitations? 454
What Promotions Can Accomplish 454 • What Promotions Cannot Accomplish 458
The Role of Trade Promotions 459
Trade Promotions' Scope and Objectives 460 Ingredients for a Successful Trade Promotion Program 460
Global Focus: *An Altered Organization at Procter & Gamble to Better Manage Trade Promotion Spending* 461
Trade Allowances 462
Major Forms of Trade Allowances 462 • Undesirable Consequences of Off-Invoice Allowances: Forward Buying and Diverting 466
Efforts to Rectify Trade Allowance Problems 468
Everyday Low Pricing (EDLP) 468 • Pay-for-Performance Programs 470 • Customizing Promotions: Account-Specific Marketing 471

Generalizations about Promotions 472

Generalization 1: Temporary retail price reductions substantially increase sales—but only in the short term 472 • Generalization 2: The greater the frequency of deals, the lower the height of the deal spike 474 • Generalization 3: The frequency of deals changes the consumer's reference price 474 • Generalization 4: Retailers pass through less than 100 percent of trade deals 474 • Generalization 5: Higher-market-share brands are less deal elastic 475 • Generalization 6: Advertised promotions can result in increased store traffic 475 • Generalization 7: Feature advertising and displays operate synergistically to influence sales of discounted brands 475 • Generalization 8: Promotions in one product category affect sales of brands in complementary and competitive categories 476 • Generalization 9: The effects of promoting higher- and lower-quality brands are asymmetric 476

Summary 476

Discussion Questions 477

End Notes 478

Chapter 16

Sampling and Couponing 480

Marcom Insight: The Use of On-Campus Promotions to Influence Students' Purchase Behavior 481

Introduction 482

Why Use Consumer Promotions? 482 • Brand Management Objectives and Consumer Rewards 483 • Classification of Promotion Methods 485

Sampling 486

IMC Focus: *Sampling Food and Beverage Products with Taste Strips* 487

Major Sampling Practices 488 • When Should Sampling Be Used? 491

Global Focus: *Introducing Oreos to China* 492

Sampling Problems • 492

Couponing 493

Couponing Background 493 • Point-of-Purchase Couponing 496 • Mail- and Media-Delivered Coupons 498 • In- and On-Pack Coupons 499 • Online Couponing 500 • The Coupon Redemption Process and Misredemption 501

The Role of Promotion Agencies 503

The Rise of the Online Promotion Agency 503

Summary 503

Discussion Questions 504

End Notes 505

Chapter 17

Premiums and Other Promotions 508

Marcom Insight: The Use of Promotions to Nurture Customer Loyalt 509

Introduction 510

Premiums 510

Free-with-Purchase Premiums 511 • Mail-In Offers 511 • In-, On-, and Near-Pack Premiums 512

Global Focus: *Barq's Root Beer and Russian Knickknacks* 513

Self-Liquidating Offers 513 • Phone Cards 514

IMC Focus: *A Super-Successful Self-Liquidating Premium Promotion* 514

What Makes a Good Premium Offer? 515

Price-Offs 515

Federal Trade Commission Price-Off Regulations 515

Bonus Packs 516

Games 516

Avoiding Snafus 516

Rebates and Refunds 517

Phantom Discounts 518 • Rebate Fraud 518

Sweepstakes and Contests 520

Sweepstakes 520 • Contests 521 • Online Sweeps and Contests 522

Continuity Promotions 522

Overlay and Tie-In Promotions 523

Overlay Programs 523 • Tie-In Promotions 523

Retailer Promotions 524

Retail Coupons 524 • Frequent-Shopper Programs 525 • Special Price Deals 525 • Samples and Premiums 525

Evaluating Sales Promotion Ideas 526

A Procedure for Evaluating Promotion Ideas 526 • Postmortem Analysis 527

Summary 529

Discussion Questions 530

End Notes 531

Part 5

Other Marcom Tools 532

Chapter 18

Marketing-Oriented Public Relations and Word-of-Mouth Management 534

Marcom Insight: Rats in KFC/Taco Bell Restaurant 535
Introduction 536
MPR versus Advertising 536
Marketing-Oriented Public Relations (MPR) 537
Proactive MPR 537 • Reactive MPR 538 • Crisis Management 542
The Special Case of Rumors and Urban Legends 543
What Is the Best Way to Handle a Rumor? 545
Word-of-Mouth Influence 545
IMC Focus: *Two Cases of Contamination Rumors: Aspartame and Plastic Water Bottles* 546
Global Focus: *Create a False Blog and Go to Jail* 547
Strong and Weak Ties 547 • The Role of Opinion Leaders in WOM Dissemination 548 • Prevent Negative WOM 548
Creating Buzz 549
Some Anecdotal Evidence 549 • Formal Perspectives on Buzz Creation 551
Summary 555
Discussion Questions 556
End Notes 557

Chapter 19

Event and Cause Sponsorships 560

Marcom Insight: Unilever's Sponsorship of NASCAR 561
Introduction 562
Event Sponsorship 563
Selecting Sponsorship Events 563
IMC Focus: *Big Brown (the Thoroughbred Racehorse) and UPS* 565
Creating Customized Events 565 • Ambushing Events 566 • Measuring Success 566
Cause Sponsorships 567
Global Focus: *The Product RED CRM Program* 568
The Benefits of CRM 569 • The Importance of Fit 570 • Accountability Is Critical 570
Summary 571
Discussion Questions 571
End Notes 572

Chapter 20

Signage and Point of Purchase Communications 574

Marcom Insight: Shopping Cart Advertising 575
Introduction 576
On-Premise Business Signage 576
Types of On-Premise Signs 576 • The ABCs of On-Premise Signs 577 • Seek Expert Assistance 577
Out-of-Home (Off-Premise) Advertising 578
Forms of Billboard Ads 578
Global Focus: *Billboard Advertising Trends in BRIC Countries* 579
Buying Billboard Advertising 581 • Billboard Advertising's Strengths and Limitations 581 • Measuring Billboard Audience Size and Characteristics 583 • A Case Study of Billboard Effectiveness 584 • Other Forms of OOH Advertising 585
Point-of-Purchase Advertising 586
The Spectrum of P-O-P Materials 586 • What Does P-O-P Accomplish? 587 • P-O-P's Influence on Consumer Behavior 588
IMC Focus: *The Growth of In-Store TV* 589
Evidence of In-Store Decision Making 591 • Evidence of Display Effectiveness 595 • The Use and Nonuse of P-O-P Materials 597 • Measuring In-Store Advertising's Audience 598
Summary 598
Discussion Questions 599
End Notes 600

Part 6

Marcom Constraints 602

Chapter 21

Ethical, Regulatory, and Environmental Issues 604

Marcom Insight:: Battle of the Sweeteners 605

Introduction 606

Ethical Issues in Marketing Communications 606

The Ethics of Targeting 607
Ethical Issues in Advertising 610
Ethical Issues in Public Relations 614
Ethical Issues in Packaging and Branding 615
Ethical Issues in Sales Promotions 615

IMC Focus: *A Rigged Promotion for Frozen Coke 616*

Ethical Issues in Online Marketing 616
Fostering Ethical Marketing Communications 617

Regulation of Marketing Communications 618

When Is Regulation Justified? 618 • Regulation by Federal Agencies 620 • Regulation by State Agencies 624 • Advertising Self-Regulation 624

Environmental Marketing Communications 626

Green Marketing Initiatives 626

Global Focus: *Environmentally Sustainable Consumption in 14 Countries* 627

Guidelines for Green Marketing 631

Summary 632

Discussion Questions 633

End Notes 634

Glossary 639

Name Index 645

Subject Index 650

preface

Responding to a Dynamic World

The field of marketing communications is ever changing. Brand managers continually attempt to gain advantage over competitors and endeavor to achieve larger market shares and profits for the brands they manage. Marketing communications, or *marcom* for short, is just one element of the marketing mix, but advertising, sales promotions, marketing-oriented public relations, and other marcom tools are performing increasingly important roles in firms' quest to achieve financial and nonfinancial goals. Marcom practitioners are confronted with the rising costs and challenges of placing ads in traditional advertising media (television, magazines, etc.). It is for these reasons that advertising and promotion budgets are beginning to shift away from traditional media and toward the Internet as a means of both accessing difficult-to-reach groups (e.g., college-age consumers) and providing an economically viable option for conveying advertising messages and promotional offers.

Marketing communicators realize now more than ever that they must be held financially accountable for their advertising, promotion, and other marcom investments. As companies seek ways of communicating more effectively and efficiently with their targeted audiences, marketing communicators are continually challenged. They must use communication methods that will break through the clutter, reach audiences with interesting and persuasive messages that enhance brand equity and drive sales, and assure firms that marcom investments yield an adequate return on investment. In meeting these challenges, companies increasingly embrace a strategy of integrated marketing communications whereby all marcom elements must be held accountable for delivering consistent messages and influencing action.

Focus of the Text

Whether students are taking this course to learn more about the dynamic nature of this field or as part of planning a career in advertising, sales promotion, or other aspects of marketing, *Integrated Marketing Communications in Advertising and Promotion* will provide them with a contemporary view of the role and importance of marketing communications. The text emphasizes the importance of integrated marketing communications (IMC) in enhancing the equity of brands, and provides thorough coverage of all aspects of an IMC program: advertising, sales promotion, packaging and branding strategies, point-of-purchase communications, marketing-oriented public relations, word-of-mouth buzz creation, and event- and cause-oriented sponsorships. These topics are made even more accessible in this edition through expanded use of examples and applications. And of course, the text covers appropriate academic theories and concepts to provide formal structure to the illustrations and examples.

Integrated Marketing Communications in Advertising and Promotion is intended for use in undergraduate or graduate courses in marketing communications, advertising, promotion strategy, promotion management, or other courses with similar concentrations. Professors and students alike should find this book substantive but highly readable, eminently current but also appreciative of the evolution of the field. Above all, this eighth edition blends marketing communications practice in its varied forms with research and theory. Throughout its previous seven editions, the attempt has been made to balance coverage in examining marketing communications both from the consumer's and the marketer's vantage points. This edition focuses more than ever on managerial aspects of marketing communications and also gives increased attention to business-to-business-oriented marketing communications.

Changes and Improvements in the Eighth Edition

The eighth edition of *Integrated Marketing Communications in Advertising and Promotion* reflects many changes beyond those just described. The textbook has been thoroughly updated to reflect the following:

- State-of-the-art coverage of major academic literature and practitioner writings on all aspects of marketing communications. These writings are presented at an accessible level to students and illustrated with examples and special inserts—*Marcom Insight* features, *IMC Focus* boxes, and *Global Focus* inserts.
  - ***Marcom Insight***—Each chapter opens with a Marcom Insight that corresponds to the thematic coverage of the chapter, piques students' interest, and illustrates the content to follow.
  - ***IMC Focus***—Each chapter includes features that illustrate key IMC concepts by using real-company situations that showcase how various aspects of marketing communications are put into practice.
  - ***Global Focus***—These features enhance the text's global perspective and spotlight international applications of marcom principles.
- This edition of *Integrated Marketing Communications in Advertising and Promotion* has expanded from 20 to 21 chapters. Many of the chapters have been substantially rewritten or rearranged to reflect a more logical progression of material coverage. The following updates and improvements are reflected in this new edition:
  - Chapter 1 expands its coverage of IMC fundamentals and also provides a model of the marcom process that structures the text as well as provides a useful framework for comprehending the strategic and tactical aspects of marketing communications.
  - Marcom's role in enhancing brand equity and influencing behavior receives updated treatment in Chapter 2. The chapter emphasizes the importance of achieving marcom accountability and includes discussion of return on marketing investment and efforts to measure marcom effectiveness.
  - Chapter 3 is a revision of the previous edition's Chapter 7—moved for better flow of coverage—and focuses on marcom's role in facilitating the success of new brands. The chapter devotes substantial coverage to the role of brand naming and packaging. In addition to other substantive changes, Chapter 3 removes coverage of word-of-mouth influence and shifts that material to a new Chapter 18 that deals exclusively with marketing-oriented public relations and word-of-mouth management.
  - Chapters 4 through 6 focus on the fundamental marcom decisions that are based on the marcom-process model introduced in Chapter 1. These chapters include detailed coverage of marcom targeting (Chapter 4), positioning (Chapter 5), and objective setting and budgeting (Chapter 6). Chapter 4 includes a thorough update of demographic facts and figures, Chapter 5 integrates the coverage of positioning with fundamentals of consumer behavior and the concept of meaning creation, and Chapter 6 augments discussion of marcom budgeting.

- Chapter 7, in its overview of advertising management, examines the role of messages, media, and measurement. The chapter devotes major coverage to the advertising management process and also presents a perspective on the case for investing or disinvesting in advertising.
- Chapter 8 lays out the fundamentals and importance of advertising creativity.
- Chapter 9 examines (1) specific forms of creative messages (e.g., humor, appeals to fear and guilt, sex appeals) and (2) endorser factors that influence message processors' motivation, opportunity, and ability to process ad messages.
- Chapter 10 provides expanded and improved coverage of measures of advertising effectiveness.
- Chapter 11 treats media planning and analysis in detail and provides a common set of concepts, terms, and metrics for describing the specific media that are covered in Chapters 12 through 14.
- Chapter 12 analyzes traditional ad media (newspapers, magazines, radio, and TV) and updates this coverage.
- Chapter 13 covers Internet advertising. This chapter is especially current in its treatment of search engine advertising, wireless forms of Internet advertising, and the role of blogs and social networks as potentially viable advertising media.
- Chapter 14 investigates "other" forms of ad media, including direct mail and database marketing, videogame advertising (adver-gaming), brand placements in movies and TV programs, cinema advertising, and a potpourri of other ad media.
- Chapter 15 introduces sales promotions and explores in detail trade-oriented promotions. The chapter also presents a series of generalizations regarding trade-promotion effectiveness.
- Chapters 16 and 17 deal with consumer-oriented forms of sales promotions. Chapter 16 covers sampling and couponing. Chapter 17 examines all remaining forms of consumer promotions—premiums, price-offs, bonus packs, games, rebates and refunds, sweepstakes and contests, continuity promotions, overlay and tie-in promotions, and retailer promotions.
- Chapter 18 is a new chapter that combines material that the seventh edition treated separately in Chapters 7 and 20. Specifically, the chapter combines marketing-oriented public relations with the related topic of word-of-mouth management.
- Chapter 19 exclusively covers event sponsorships and cause-related marketing, topics previously covered together with marketing-oriented public relations in the seventh edition's Chapter 20.
- Chapter 20 is a unique chapter that explores topics often neglected or receiving minimal coverage in most advertising and marcom texts: on-premise business signage, out-of-home (off-premise) advertising, and in-store point-of-purchase advertising.
- Chapter 21, which was Chapter 3 in the seventh edition, provides in-depth coverage of ethical issues in marketing communications along with marcom-related regulatory and environmental issues. Expanded coverage is devoted to environmental issues in view of growing emphasis on global warming and sustainability.

A Premier Instructional Resource Package

The resource package provided with *Integrated Marketing Communications in Advertising and Promotion,* eighth edition, is specifically designed to meet the needs of instructors facing a variety of teaching conditions and to enhance students' experience with the subject. We have addressed both the traditional and the innovative classroom environments by providing an array of high quality and technologically advanced items to bring a contemporary, real-world feel to the study of advertising, promotion, and integrated marketing communications.

- Instructor's Manual. This comprehensive and valuable teaching aid includes the Resource Integration Guide, a list of chapter objectives, chapter summaries, detailed chapter outlines, teaching tips, and answers to discussion questions. The *Instructor's Manual* for this edition is revised by Renee J. Fontenot of Georgia College & State University.
- Test Bank. The Test Bank, revised by Patricia Kennedy of the University of Nebraska at Lincoln, provides testing items for instructors' reference and use. It has been thoroughly revised and contains over 1,500 multiple-choice, true/false, and essay questions in varying levels of difficulty.
- ExamView™ Testing Software. ExamView™ is a computerized testing program that contains all of the questions in the printed test bank. **ExamView™ Testing Software** is an easy-to-use test creation software compatible with Microsoft Windows. Instructors can add or edit questions, instructions, and answers, and they can select questions by previewing them onscreen, selecting them randomly, or selecting them by number. Instructors can also create and administer quizzes online, whether over the Internet, a local area network (LAN), or a wide area network (WAN).
- PowerPoint® Presentation. The PowerPoint® package, revised by Charlie T. Cook, Jr., of the University of West Alabama, covers all of the material found in the textbook in addition to outside supplemental examples and materials.
- Video Package. The video package provides a relevant visual teaching tool for the classroom. Each video segment gives students the opportunity to apply what they are learning to real-world situations and enables instructors to better illustrate concepts. Companies such as Timberland, Tower Records, Pfizer, and Radio Shack are featured.

Comprehensive Web Site

Visit the text Web site at www.cengage.com/international to find instructor's support materials and study resources to help students practice and apply the concepts they learned in class.

Instructor Resources

- Downloadable **Instructor's Manual** and **Test Bank** files available in Microsoft Word and Adobe Acrobat format.
- Downloadable **PowerPoint® Presentations**

Student Resources

Product Support Site www.cengage.com/international

- **Online Interactive quizzes** for each chapter are available to those students who would like extra study material. After each quiz is submitted, automatic feedback tells the students how they scored and what the correct answers are to the questions they missed. Students are then able to email their results directly to their instructor.
- **Flashcards** pulled from the key terms in the text help students study the vocabulary covered in the text.

Acknowledgments

I sincerely appreciate the thoughtful comments from the colleagues who recommended changes and improvements for this edition. Previous editions also have benefited from the many useful comments from the following reviewers, friends, and acquaintances, whose affiliations may have changed:

Craig Andrews, *Marquette University*
Charles S. Areni, *Texas Tech University*
Guy R. Banville, *Creighton University*
Ronald Bauerly, *Western Illinois University*
M. Elizabeth Blair, *Ohio University*
Barbara M. Brown, *San Jose State University*
Gordon C. Bruner II, *Southern Illinois University*
Chris Cakebread, *Boston University*
Newell Chiesl, *Indiana State University*
Bob D. Cutler, *Cleveland State University*
Robert Dyer, *George Washington University*
Denise Essman, *Drake University*
P. Everett Fergenson, *Iona College*
James Finch, *University of Wisconsin, LaCrosse*
George R. Franke, *University of Alabama*
Linda L. Golden, *University of Texas, Austin*
Stephen Grove, *Clemson University*
Ronald Hill, *Villanova University*
Clayton Hillyer, *American International College*
Robert Harmon, *Portland State University*
Stewart W. Husted, *Lynchburg College*
Patricia Kennedy, *University of Nebraska, Lincoln*
Susan Kleine, *Bowling Green State University*
Russell Laczniak, *Iowa State University*
Geoffrey Lantos, *Bentley College*
Monle Lee, *Indiana University, South Bend*
William C. Lesch, *University of North Dakota*
J. Danile Lindley, *Bentley College*
Wendy Macias, *University of Georgia*
Therese A. Maskulka, *Lehigh University*
John McDonald, *Market Opinion Research*
Gordon G. Mosley, *Troy State University*
John Mowen, *Oklahoma State University*
Darrel D. Muehling, *Washington State University*
Darrel Muehling, *Washington State University*
Kent Nakamoto, *Virginia Tech University*
D. Nasalroad, *Central State University*
Nusser Raajpoot, *Central Connecticut State University*
Cindy Raines, *University of Tennessee*

Jayanthi Rajan, *University of Connecticut*
Edward Riordan, *Wayne State University*
Alan Sawyer, *University of Florida*
Stanley Scott, *Boise State University*
Douglas Stayman, *Cornell University*
Jeff Stoltman, *Wayne State University*
Linda Swayne, *University of North Carolina, Charlotte*
John A. Taylor, *Brigham Young University*
Kate Ternus, *Century College*
Carolyn Tripp, *Western Illinois University*
Karen Faulkner Walia, *Long Beach City College*
Josh Wiener, *Oklahoma State University*
Liz Yokubison, *College of DuPage*

My appreciation extends to a number of former Ph.D. students—my friends, who have shared their experiences in using the textbook and have provided valuable suggestions for change: Avery Abernethy, Auburn University; Craig Andrews, Marquette University; Mike Barone, University of Louisville; Paula Bone, West Virginia University; Tracy Dunn, Benedict College; Ken Manning, Colorado State University; David Sprott, Washington State University; Elnora Stuart, University of South Carolina Upstate; and Scott Swain, Boston University.

I also wish to express my sincere appreciation to two special friends. First, to Professor Jack Lindgren, University of Virginia, for his contributions to the previous editions, and second, to my colleague at the University of South Carolina, Professor Satish Jayachandran, for his invaluable suggestions on prior editions.

Finally, I very much appreciate the excellent work of the Cengage team for their outstanding efforts in bringing to fruition this eighth edition. I especially appreciate the support and guidance of Susan Smart; the extensive production management by Corey Geissler; the valuable copyediting by Maggie Sears; the encouragement of Mike Roche and Melissa Acuña; the marketing efforts of Mike Aliscad; the contributions of the many hands that touched the book; and finally, the creativity of the technology group in preparing the Web site and its contents.

Terence A. Shimp
Distinguished Professor Emeritus
University of South Carolina
October 2008

about the author

Terence A. Shimp

Terence A. Shimp received his doctorate from the University of Maryland and taught for four years at Kent State University before moving to the University of South Carolina, where he was a faculty member for 29 years. While at the University of South Carolina, Shimp was the W. W. Johnson Distinguished Foundation Fellow and for 12 years was the Chair of the Marketing Department in the Moore School of Business. He now is Distinguished Professor Emeritus but continues to research, write, teach occasionally, and work with Ph.D. students.

Shimp earned a number of teaching awards during his career, including the Amoco Foundation Award that named him the outstanding teacher at the University of South Carolina in 1990. He has published widely in the areas of marketing, consumer behavior, and advertising. His work has appeared in outlets such as the *Journal of Consumer Research, Journal of Marketing Research, Journal of Marketing, Journal of Advertising, Journal of Advertising Research, Journal of Consumer Psychology,* and the *Journal of Public Policy and Marketing.* "A Critical Appraisal of Demand Artifacts in Consumer Research," published with Eva Hyatt and David Snyder in the *Journal of Consumer Research,* received that journal's award for the top article published during the period 1990–1992. "Endorsers in Advertising: The Case of Negative Celebrity Information," co-authored with Brian Till, was named the outstanding article published in 1998 in the *Journal of Advertising.* Shimp was the 2001 recipient of the American Academy of Advertising's lifetime award for outstanding contributions to research in advertising. He was elected Fellow of the Society for Consumer Psychology in 2003.

Shimp is past president of the Association for Consumer Research and past president of the *Journal of Consumer Research* policy board. For many years, he served on the editorial policy boards of premier journals such as the *Journal of Consumer Research, Journal of Consumer Psychology, Journal of Marketing, Marketing Letters, Journal of Public Policy & Marketing,* and the *Journal of Advertising.* He has represented the Federal Trade Commission and various state agencies as an expert witness in issues concerning advertising deception and unfairness.

CHAPTERS

1

Overview of Integrated Marketing Communications

2

Marcom's Communications Challenges: Enhancing Brand Equity, Influencing Behavior, and Being Accountable

3

Facilitating the Success of New Brands

Part 1

Integrated Marketing Communications: Processes, Brand Equity, and Marcom's Role in Introducing New Brands

Part One introduces students to the fundamentals of integrated marketing communications (IMC). *Chapter 1* overviews IMC and discusses the importance of marketing communications (marcom). The chapter emphasizes the need for integrating the various marketing communication elements (advertising, sales promotions, event marketing, etc.) rather than treating them as separate and independent tools. The payoff from an IMC approach is synergy—multiple tools working together to achieve more positive communication results than do the tools used individually. The chapter describes five key IMC features and presents a model of the marcom decision-making process. This integrative framework postulates the marcom program as consisting of a set of fundamental decisions (about targeting, positioning, etc.) and a series of implementation decisions that determine program outcomes with regard to enhancing brand equity and affecting behavior. The final model component is program evaluation, which entails measuring the results of communications activities, providing feedback, and taking corrective action.

Chapter 2 explains how IMC enhances brand equity, influences behavior, and achieves accountability. A brand equity model conceptualizes brand equity from the customer's perspective and shows how equity is enhanced by elevating brand awareness and creating brand associations. It is explained that marcom's eventual challenge is to influence customer behavior and ultimately to affect a brand's sales volume and revenue, and the return on marketing investment is discussed.

Chapter 3 looks at marcom's role in achieving acceptance for new products and how marketing communicators facilitate product adoption and diffusion. Chapter 3 also provides detailed descriptions of the initial elements responsible for a brand's image: brand name, logo, and package. This section explores the requirements for a good brand name, the steps involved in arriving at a good name, and the role of logos. Also presented is a useful framework that describes the visual, informational, emotional, and functional features that determine packaging success.

1

Overview of Integrated Marketing Communications

State Farm is a large and highly successful insurance company, indeed the largest insurer of homes and automobiles in the United States. Company research revealed, however, that State Farm was considered a brand for older consumers and had limited appeal to 18-to-25-year-olds. Hence, the challenge: How could the State Farm brand name be reinvigorated to appeal to this youthful age group?

Marketing research determined that the State Farm brand was well respected among this younger age group, but, at the same time, they considered the brand basically irrelevant for their financial needs. The solution: State Farm and its advertising agency devised an integrated marketing communication program, called the *Now What?* campaign, to target 18-to-25-year-olds. Included in the multipronged campaign were TV and print advertisements, direct mail pieces, a dedicated Web site, and a kickoff event at the Lollapalooza music festival in Chicago—a truly multifaceted, integrated marketing communications campaign. One TV spot, for example, depicted a young man installing a room air conditioner on a hot day and then, ever-so-briefly, enjoying the cool air pumped out by his new A/C unit. Then, to his great dismay, the improperly installed A/C fell out of the window and landed on his car parked below. The screen then morphed into the words … nowwhat.com.

This particular TV spot, like others in the campaign, illustrates dilemmas faced by young consumers when bad things happen that require an insurance solution. In a similar magazine ad, a car is shown sticking out of the side of a building. Beside it is the key phrase, nowwhat.com, which serves to link together all advertising executions in the ongoing campaign to reach out to young consumers. Additionally, direct mail pieces, such as one illustrating the rear end of a car that was crushed by another vehicle, were mailed to hundreds of thousands of prospects in the 18-to-25 age group. The mailer stated: "Find out how to straighten out a mess like this before it puts a dent in your wallet at nowwhat.com/crushed."

Interestingly, none of the TV or print executions revealed the State Farm brand name; this was information acquired only after interested consumers went to the nowwhat.com Web site. A company spokesperson explained this strategy as one that allowed ad receivers to mentally pose the question: "If [the scenario depicted in the ad] happened to me, where would I go [for a solution]?" The ad campaign thus had the potential to engage consumers who heretofore considered the product somewhat irrelevant to their needs, but who could readily imagine being confronted with a problem requiring an insurance solution.

Early results indicated that the campaign was enjoying considerable success. The nowwhat.com site was

© State Farm Mutual Automobile Insurance Company 2005. Used by permission

receiving 10,000 to 20,000 or more hits per day, and comments about the campaign were generally very positive on blogs written by and appealing to the targeted age group of 18-to-25 year olds. The campaign's success can be attributed in large part to the fact that the various advertising messages did not attempt to oversell State Farm, but rather were designed to capture attention with humorous, slice-of-life executions that would heighten curiosity and give young consumers good reason to seek additional information from the nowwhat.com Web site.

Source: Adapted from Deborah L. Vence, "Better Coverage," *Marketing News,* January 15, 2007, 13–14.

Chapter Objectives

After reading this chapter you should be able to:

1. Appreciate the practice of marketing communications and recognize the marcom tools used by practitioners.
2. Describe the philosophy and practice of integrated marketing communications (IMC).
3. Understand the five key features of IMC.
4. Recognize the activities involved in developing an integrated communications program.
5. Identify obstacles to implementing an IMC program.
6. Understand and appreciate the components contained in an integrative model of the marcom decision-making process.

>>Marcom Insight:

Appealing to Youth and Reinvigorating a Brand Image: State Farm's nowwhat.com Campaign

Introduction

All firms employ marketing communications (marcom) to one degree or another, and it doesn't matter whether their efforts are directed at consumers—i.e., people like you and me in our day-to-day consumption activities—or focused on customers of other businesses. Consider the following examples of integrated marketing communications (IMC) programs. The first example is in a business-to-consumer (B2C) context, the second is in a business-to-business (B2B) environment, and the third represents a marcom program that is directed at both consumers and business customers.

When Buick introduced its Rainier sports utility vehicle (SUV), it needed a marcom program that would create awareness for the Rainier and enhance the image of the Buick name. These tasks were accomplished with an integrated program combining online and TV advertising along with an appealing sales promotion. Hiring Tiger Woods as endorser of the Buick line of vehicles made the job easier. A series of five-minute films featuring this famous golfer were available at Buick's Web site (http://www.buick.com). With a 30-second commercial that was widely aired on network and cable stations, Buick encouraged consumers to visit its Web site. Visitors to the site were able to enter a contest that provided winners an opportunity to play a round of golf with Tiger and a chance to win a Rainier vehicle. Two million unique visitors were drawn to Buick's Web site only two months after initiating this program, and awareness of the Rainer SUV increased by 70 percent while positive perceptions of Buick rose by 122 percent.[1]

An integrated communications program undertaken by General Electric (GE) illustrates a successful B2B application of integrated marketing communications. With an objective of increasing awareness among business customers that GE is a company that does more than manufacture light bulbs and appliances, GE's advertising agency initiated an integrated campaign titled "Imagination at Work" to establish that GE also is successful in producing wind power, security systems, and jet engines, among other products. The intensive ad campaign involved a combination of TV, print (ads in business publications such as *Business Week, Forbes,* and *Fortune*), and online advertising. For example, a clever TV advertisement dramatically illustrated that GE produces jet engines by showing a vintage Wright Brothers–era airplane equipped with a modern GE jet engine. The integrated campaign, which was conducted in Europe as well as in the United States, was fabulously successful in changing business customers' perceptions of GE. Post-campaign research revealed that perceptions of GE as an innovative company increased by 35 percent, opinions of GE as offering high-tech solutions increased by 40 percent, and perceptions of it as being dynamic increased by 50 percent. By any standard, this was a highly successful integrated campaign that combined multiple communication elements to alter perceptions of GE positively.[2]

© Doug Murray/Icon SMI /Newscom

AT&T, upon its acquisition by SBC Communications, undertook an extensive IMC campaign to introduce the new brand to consumers, to business customers, and to government audiences. Under the banner, "Your World Delivered," the "new" AT&T was introduced to these diverse audiences along with a redesigned corporate logo. The campaign objective was to establish that the two companies, SBC and AT&T, had merged and that the combined company was to be known as AT&T. The "Your World Delivered" tagline was used to convey that the new AT&T is an innovative company that delivers on its promises and improves people's lives. The global IMC program included extensive TV, magazine, and online advertising. AT&T also sponsored such events as Dick Clark's New Year's Rockin' Eve, the Winter Olympics, soccer's World Cup, football's Cotton Bowl Classic, and golf's Pebble Beach tournament. This integrated campaign achieved, in less than one full year, a threefold increase in unaided brand awareness of the AT&T name and a fourfold increase in unaided advertising awareness.[3]

The Tools of Marketing Communications

As the preceding examples illustrate, marketing communications is a critical aspect of companies' overall marketing missions and a major determinant of their successes or failures. As noted in the introduction, all organizations—whether firms involved in B2B exchanges, companies engaged in B2C marketing, or organizations delivering not-for-profit services (museums, symphony orchestras, charitable organizations, etc.)—use various marketing communications tools to promote their offerings and achieve financial and nonfinancial goals.

The primary forms of marketing communications include traditional mass media advertising (TV, magazines, etc.); online advertising (Web sites, opt-in e-mail messages, text messaging, etc.); sales promotions (samples, coupons, rebates, premium items, etc.); store signage and point-of-purchase communications; direct-mail literature; public relations and publicity releases; sponsorships of events and causes; presentations by salespeople; and various collateral forms of communication devices. Table 1.1 provides a complete listing of marketing

table 1.1

The Tools of Marketing Communications

1. Media Advertising • TV • Radio • Magazines • Newspapers 2. Direct Response and Interactive Advertising • Direct mail • Telephone solicitation • Online advertising 3. Place Advertising • Billboards and bulletins • Posters • Transit ads • Cinema ads 4. Store Signage and Point-of-Purchase Advertising • External store signs • In-store shelf signs • Shopping cart ads • In-store radio and TV	5. Trade- and Consumer-Oriented Promotions • Trade deals and buying allowances • Display and advertising allowances • Trade shows • Cooperative advertising • Samples • Coupons • Premiums • Refunds/rebates • Contests/sweepstakes • Promotional games • Bonus packs • Price-off deals	6. Event Marketing and Sponsorships • Sponsorship of sporting events • Sponsorship of arts, fairs, and festivals • Sponsorship of causes 7. Marketing-Oriented Public Relations and Publicity 8. Personal Selling

Source: Adapted from Figure 1.1 in Kevin Lane Keller, "Mastering the Marketing Communications Mix: Micro and Macro Perspectives on Integrated Marketing Communication Programs," *Journal of Marketing Management* 17 (August, 2001), 823–851.

communication elements. Collectively, these communication tools and media constitute what traditionally has been termed the *promotion* component of the marketing mix. (You will recall from your introductory marketing course that the "marketing mix" includes four sets of interrelated decision areas: *product, price, place,* and *promotion,* or the "4Ps.")

Although the "4P" characterization has led to widespread use of the term *promotion* for describing communications with prospects and customers, *marketing communications* is the expression most marketing practitioners and many educators prefer. We will use *marketing communications*—or, for short, marcom—throughout this text to refer to the collection of advertising, sales promotions, public relations, event marketing, and other communication devices that are identified in Table 1.1. The text covers all of these topics except personal selling, which is better treated in a stand-alone course devoted exclusively to that topic.

The Integration of Marketing Communications

Mountain Dew is a well-known brand that is consumed by millions of predominately young, active, outdoor-oriented consumers and is the fourth highest selling soft-drink brand in the United States. On the market for more than 50 years, Mountain Dew is positioned as a brand that stands for fun, exhilaration, and energy—FEE for short. Brand managers have been consistent over time and across communication media in maintaining the FEE theme that represents the brand's core meaning—its positioning. Various advertising media, event sponsorships, and consumer promotions have been employed over the years to trumpet the brand's core meaning. The brand managers of Mountain Dew use network TV commercials as well as local TV and radio spots to appeal to the brand's target audience.

Event sponsorships provide another major communication medium for Mountain Dew, which has sponsored leading alternative sports competitions such as the Dew Action Sports Tour (extreme sports tournament), the Summer and Winter X Games, and the Mountain Dew Vertical Challenge (a series of ski and snowboard races held at various resorts in the northeastern and western United States). In addition to these prominent sponsorships, Mountain Dew also hosts a variety of smaller events that draw audiences as small as 5,000 people. Appealing giveaway items (T-shirts, videos, branded snowboards and mountain bikes, etc.) are distributed at these events to generate excitement and foster positive connections between the Mountain Dew brand and its loyal consumers.

Much of Mountain Dew's continued success is attributable to its brand managers' dedication to presenting consistent messages about the brand, both over time and across communication media. By contrast, many companies treat the various communication elements—advertising, sales promotions, public relations, and so on—as virtually separate activities rather than as integrated tools that work together to achieve a common goal. Personnel responsible for advertising sometimes fail to coordinate adequately their efforts with individuals in charge of sales promotions or publicity. The lack of integration was more prevalent in the past than the present, but many brands still suffer from poorly integrated marketing communications programs.

Why Integrate?

The logic underlying integration seems so clear and compelling that the student may be wondering: What's the big deal? Why haven't firms practiced IMC all along? Why is there reluctance to integrate? Good questions, all, but what sounds reasonable in theory is not always easy to put into practice.[4] Organizations traditionally have handled advertising, sales promotions, point-of-purchase displays, and other communication tools as virtually separate practices because different units within organizations have specialized in separate aspects of marketing communications—advertising, *or* sales promotions, *or* public relations, and so on—rather than having generalized knowledge and experience with all communication tools. Furthermore, outside suppliers (such as advertising agencies, public relations agencies, and sales promotion agencies) also have tended to specialize in single facets of marketing communications rather than to possess expertise across the board.

There has been a reluctance to change from this single-function, specialist model due to managerial parochialism (e.g., advertising people sometimes view the world exclusively from an advertising perspective and are blind to other communication traditions) and for fear that change might lead to budget cutbacks in their areas of control (such as advertising) and reductions in their authority and power. Advertising, public relations, and promotion agencies also have resisted change due to reluctance to broaden their function beyond the one aspect of marketing communications in which they have developed expertise and built their reputations.

In recent years a number of advertising agencies have expanded their roles by merging with other companies or creating new departments that specialize in the growth areas of sales promotions, marketing-oriented public relations, event sponsorship, and direct marketing. Many firms, including suppliers of marketing communication services, along with their brand-manager clients, have increasingly adopted an integrated approach to their communication activities.

IMC Skeptics

Some suggest that IMC is little more than a management fashion that is short lived.[5] There is evidence to the contrary, however, which suggests that IMC is not fleeting but rather has become a permanent feature of the marketing communications landscape around the world and in many different types of marketing organizations.[6] In the final analysis, the key to successfully implementing IMC is that brand managers must closely link their efforts with outside suppliers of marcom services (such as ad agencies), and both parties must be committed to assuring that all communication tools are carefully and finely integrated.[7]

Although there is movement toward increased implementation of IMC, not all brand managers or their firms are equally likely to have adopted IMC. In fact, experienced managers are more likely than novice managers to practice IMC. Firms involved in marketing services (rather than products) and B2C (versus B2B) companies are more likely to practice IMC. More sophisticated companies also are likely adherents to IMC.[8]

IMC and Synergy

IMC is a goal worth pursuing because using multiple communication tools in conjunction with one another can produce greater results than tools used individually and in an uncoordinated fashion. That is, multiple methods combined can yield more positive communication results than do the same tools used individually or in an uncoordinated manner. There is a *synergistic effect* of using multiple well-coordinated marcom tools. A study of Levi Strauss' Dockers brand of khaki pants illustrated this value of synergy.[9] Using sophisticated analytical techniques, researchers determined that the use of both TV and print advertisements produced a synergistic effect on sales of pants that was significantly additional to the individual effects of each advertising medium. Another study demonstrated that TV and online advertising used in conjunction produced positive synergistic effects that were additional to each medium's individual effects. TV and online advertising used together produced more attention, more positive thoughts, and higher message credibility than did the sum of the two media when used individually.[10]

And Now a Definition of IMC

Proponents of IMC have provided slightly different perspectives on this management practice, and not all educators or practitioners agree on the precise meaning of IMC. Notwithstanding these differences, a working definition is in order. The following definition reflects this text's position on the topic.

> **IMC** *is a communications process that entails the planning, creation, integration, and implementation of diverse forms of marcom (advertisements, sales promotions, publicity releases, events, etc.) that are delivered over time to a brand's targeted customers and prospects. The goal of IMC is ultimately to influence or directly affect the behavior of the targeted audience. IMC considers all touch points, or sources of contact, that a customer/prospect has with the brand as potential delivery channels for messages and makes use of all communications methods that are relevant to customers/prospects. IMC requires that all of a brand's communication media deliver a consistent message. The IMC process further necessitates that the customer/prospect is the starting point for determining the types of messages and media that will serve best to inform, persuade, and induce action.*[11]

Key IMC Features

Inherent in the definition of integrated marketing communications are several essential features that provide the philosophical foundation for this practice. These features are listed in Table 1.2 and require detailed discussion hereafter. It is important to note before proceeding that these elements are interdependent and that there is no particular order of importance suggested by the listing in Table 1.2. It also is essential for you to recognize that all five features are critical to both understanding the philosophy of IMC and appreciating what must be accomplished to implement this philosophy into practice. These five features *do* warrant your committing them to memory.

Key Feature #1: The Consumer or Business Customer Must Represent the Starting Point for All Marketing Communications Activities

This feature emphasizes that the marcom process must *start with the customer or prospect* and then work back to the brand communicator in determining the most appropriate messages and media to employ for informing, persuading, and

table 1.2

Five Key Features of IMC

1. Start with the customer or prospect.
2. Use any form of relevant contact or touch point.
3. Speak with a single voice.
4. Build relationships.
5. Affect behavior.

inducing customers and prospects to act favorably toward the communicator's brand. The IMC approach avoids an "inside-out" approach (from company to customer) in identifying communication vehicles and instead starts with the customer ("outside-in") to determine those communication methods that will best serve customers' information needs and motivate them to purchase the brand.

Consumers in Control

It is widely acknowledged that marketing communications are governed by a key reality: The consumer increasingly wants to be in control! Marcom practitioners must accept the fact that marketing communications must be *consumer-centric.* A respected advertising pundit has characterized this new marcom reality in these terms:

> *The fact is, people care deeply—sometimes perversely—about consumer goods.... What they don't like is being told what they should care about or when they should be caring.... This may be culturally difficult for advertisers to accept, having spent two centuries trying to browbeat/seduce captive audiences. But take heart. Once the consumer is in the driver's seat, he or she will often cheerfully drive right in your direction.*[12]

There are numerous signs that consumers control when, how, and where they devote their attention to marcom messages. Technological developments such as digital video recorders (e.g., TiVo), MP3 players (e.g., iPods), and high-tech cell phones (e.g., iPhones) have enabled consumers to enjoy television programs, music, podcasts, and other forms of entertainment when and where they want. As such, consumers have the ability to pay attention to advertising messages, or to ignore them! The Internet and the digital world allow consumers to seek the information about product services that they want—via online searches, blogging, emailing, text messaging, and social networking in outlets such as Facebook, MySpace, and YouTube—rather than being mere captives of the messages that marketing communicators want them to receive. (See the *Global Focus* insert for a marcom program in China that puts consumers in control.)

Consumers not only passively receive marcom messages, but now they are active participants in creating messages via consumer-generated media such as those noted immediately above. Does this idea of consumer-generated media and consumer-centric marketing mean that consumers no longer attend to TV commercials or to magazine or newspaper advertisements? Well, of course not, as you can prove by reflecting on your own experiences with these media and the ads placed in them. It does mean, however, that consumers—particularly younger consumers who were born and raised in the digital era—can actively acquire information about the brands they favor rather than depend on the passive receipt of unwanted information received at inopportune times.

Reduced Dependence on the Mass Media

Many marketing communicators now realize that communication outlets other than the mass media often better serve the needs of their brands. The objective is to contact customers and prospects effectively using touch points that reach them where, when, and how they wish to be contacted. Mass media advertising is not always the most effective or cost-efficient avenue for accomplishing this objective. Television and radio programs and magazine and newspaper pages (collectively, the mass media) are not always the most engaging contexts in which to place marketing messages. It is for this reason that marketing communicators are increasingly using event sponsorships, the Internet, mobile advertising, and other digital media as contexts in which to place their messages. Illustrative of the move toward Internet advertising, Nike—in a move that shocked the advertising community—dropped its ad agency of 25 years because it was dissatisfied with the

global focus

Creating a Pepsi Commercial in China

In an effort to reach out to China's Internet-savvy youth and to engage their interest in Pepsi, the marketers of this soft drink brand created the Pepsi Creative Challenge contest. Consumers were invited to develop a TV spot that would star Jay Chow (also spelled Chou), who is a superstar in the entertainment business throughout Asia.

Contest entrants were instructed to submit scripts for a commercial with a maximum of 200 words. Other consumers who logged on to a Web site then read and scored the submitted scripts. A panel consisting of Pepsi executives and Mr. Chow then selected the best five ideas from among the 100 highest-scoring entries during each two-week period. At the end of six weeks, 15 finalists were identified. The 15 scripts were posted on the Web site, and interested consumers then voted for the best script. The winner received $12,500 and an opportunity to participate in the production of the commercial. The remaining 14 finalists earned $1,250 cash prizes for their efforts and were invited to attend the party launching the new commercial.

As indicated by a Pepsi executive, the response was extremely positive with more than 27,000 commercial scripts submitted. A marketing researcher stated that "The reason why digital interactive marketing campaigns like the Pepsi Creative Challenge work is that they add value by creating a mechanism for consumers to get involved." Of course, "getting involved" is simply another way of saying that consumers'control over advertising content is increasing—in China as elsewhere around the globe.

SOURCES: Adapted from Normandy Madden, "Consumers to Create Pepsi Spot in China," *Advertising Age*, June 5, 2006, 15; "Wharton's Take on the Internet in China," April 17, 2007, http://www.edelmanapac.com/edelman/blog/2007/04/17/Whartons-Take-on-the-Internet-in-China.html (accessed July 4, 2007).

agency's lack of digital expertise.[13] In actuality, many advertising agencies have been slow to adapt to advertisers' increasing use of the Internet and are understaffed with employees who possess digital expertise and experience.[14]

Although advertising in the digital media is increasing rapidly, this does not mean that mass media advertising is unimportant or in threat of extinction. The point instead is that other communication methods must receive careful consideration *before* mass media advertising is automatically assumed to be *the* solution. It is easy to build the case, in fact, that brand managers should turn to alternative means of marketing communication as the option of first choice rather than automatically defaulting to mass media advertising.

In addition to the growth of the Internet and other digital media as viable alternatives to mass media, many brand managers and their agencies have reduced the role of TV in their marcom budgeting because TV advertising is not as effective or cost-efficient as it once was. TV audiences are more fragmented than in prior years and relatively fewer consumers can be reached by the advertising placed on any particular program. Moreover, other advertising and nonadvertising tools often are superior to TV in achieving brand managers' objectives. For example, Unilever's brand of Wisk detergent was historically advertised heavily on TV. Wisk®'s brand managers devised a media plan that minimized TV in the ad budget in lieu of using online media to reach people where "their passions get them dirty." Specifically, banner ads were placed on targeted Web sites where consumers were learning more about their passions (ie: Foodies on Foodnetwork.com®, do-it-yourselfers on DIY.com®, etc.) and other touch points directed consumers to a Wisk® Web site where further information was provided. Tag line: Wisk®. Your passions get your dirty. Our power gets you clean.[15]

In the spirit of reducing dependence on TV advertising, McCann Worldgroup, a highly respected advertising agency, has developed the concept of a *media-neutral approach* when counseling its clients in selecting appropriate marcom tools.

© Courtesy of WISK®, Unilever United States, Inc.

This approach requires that the brand marketer first identify the goal(s) a marcom program is designed to accomplish (building brand awareness, creating buzz, influencing behavior, etc.) and then determine the best way to allocate the marketer's budget.[16] This media-neutral approach is perfectly in accord with our earlier discussion about selecting the most appropriate communication tool given the task at hand.

Takeaway from Key IMC Feature #1: *Learn the media preferences and lifestyles of your customers/prospects so you know the best contexts (media, events, etc.) in which to reach them with your brand messages. In short, take an outside-in approach. Recognize and adapt to the fact that consumers are increasingly in control of their media choices for acquiring information about brands.*

Key Feature #2: Use Any and All Marcom Tools That Are Up to the Task

To appreciate fully this second key IMC feature, it will be useful to draw an analogy between the tools available to marketing communicators (which include advertising, sales promotions, sponsorships, and the others illustrated in Table 1.1) and those used by people in craft industries such as carpentry, plumbing, and automobile repair. Each of these craftspeople possesses a toolbox that is filled with gear of different sorts. A carpenter's toolbox, for example, contains items such as hammers, pliers, screwdrivers, drills, sanding equipment, fasteners, and so on. When given a new construction or repair job, carpenters turn to those tools that are most appropriate for the task at hand. In other words, some tools are more appropriate for particular purposes than are others. A carpenter can pound a nail with the blunt end of a screwdriver, but a hammer can do the job more efficiently. Such is the case with marketing communications: not all tools (again, advertising, sales promotions, sponsorships, etc.) are equally effective for all jobs. Rather, a truly professional marketing communicator selects the best tools for the job. The toolbox metaphor is a good way of thinking about what a professional marketing communicator must do.

Touch Points and 360-Degree Branding

Now, as applied to marketing communications, IMC practitioners need to be receptive to using all forms of *touch points,* or *contacts,* as potential message delivery channels. **Touch point** and **contact** are used here as interchangeable terms to mean any message medium capable of reaching target customers and presenting the brand in a favorable light. The key feature of this IMC element is that it reflects a willingness on the part of brand communicators to use any communication outlets (i.e., touch points or contacts) that are appropriate for reaching the target audience. Marketing communicators who practice this principle are not pre-committed to any single medium or subset of media. Rather, the challenge and related opportunity are to select those communication tools that are best at accomplishing the specific objective that has been established for the brand at a particular point in time.

In many respects, this amounts to surrounding present or prospective customers with the brand message at every possible opportunity and allowing them to use whatever information about the brand they deem most useful.[17] This notion of surrounding the customer or prospect with a brand's marcom messages is labeled *360-degree branding,* a phrase that suggests that a brand's touch points should be everywhere the target audience is. A marketing manager for Ford trucks put it this way: "We want to be everywhere that makes sense for our customer. We go to the places they are."[18]

Toyota Motor Sales U.S.A. and its advertising agency Saatchi & Saatchi illustrate the use of a multiple–touch point strategy during their introduction of the Yaris subcompact automobile.[19] In an effort to reach a market of 18-to-34-year-olds, Toyota's ad agency promoted the Yaris in branded entertainment venues that reached Yari's youthful age-group target. The multiple–touch point strategy included the following elements: (1) A series of 26 mobile-phone episodes that were spun off the TV program *Prison Break;* each two-minute "mobisode" was preceded by a 10-second advertisement for the Yaris. (2) An Internet contest had consumers create their own three-minute TV commercials for the Yaris under the theme "What would you do with your Yaris?" (3) Yaris was the title sponsor in specially designed video games. (4) Yaris was featured in various sponsored events such as the South by Southwest Music festival held in Austin, Texas. (5) Finally, the subcompact Yaris was integrated into the TV comedy show, *Mad TV,* through a series of sketches that were built around the car.

© Emile Wamsteker/Bloomberg News /Landov

In general, brand touch points include numerous possibilities, as illustrated by the following examples:

- MasterCard provided complimentary snacks, games, puzzles, and movie headphones on select American Airlines flights during the busy Christmas holiday season.
- Brand managers at Procter & Gamble placed the Tide detergent logo on napkin dispensers in pizza shops and cheesesteak shops in Boston and Philadelphia. These napkin dispensers held napkins imprinted with the Tide logo and the message "Because napkins are never in the right place at the right time."
- JELL-O pudding was promoted by affixing stickers with the JELL-O name to bananas—one product

(bananas) was used as a contact channel for reaching consumers about another (JELL-O).

- In New York City, ads are placed on large vinyl sheets that cover scaffolding at construction sites. These ads sometimes extend for an entire city block and serve to convey the advertiser's message in prominent and dramatic fashion.
- Germany's Puma brand of athletic footwear promoted itself during soccer's World Cup hosted in Japan by spotlighting its new brand of Shudoh soccer cleats at sushi restaurants in major cities around Asia and Europe. The shoes were encased in stylish displays made of bamboo and glass and placed on tables.
- Hershey Foods Corporation, makers of Hershey's Kisses among many other items, designed a huge display rising 15 stories high in New York City's Times Square district.
- BriteVision designed a unique touch point in the form of advertisements on coffee sleeve insulators that protect coffee drinkers from burning their hands.
- By partnering with the owner of 125 shopping malls, 20th Century Fox devised a creative solution to movie marketing. Under an exclusive deal, new movies from 20th Century Fox were advertised on huge banners in mall garages, on tray liners in restaurants, and elsewhere in malls.
- An outdoor media company in Denmark devised a creative way to reach consumers with advertising messages. The company gave parents free use of

IMC >> i.m.c. focus

The Laundry Hanger as an Advertising Touch Point

Reaching large numbers of men with advertising messages is often difficult because most ad media are fragmented; that is, they appeal to relatively small groups of people who share common interests but fail to reach large numbers whose interests are highly diverse and thus do not watch the same TV programs, read the same magazines, listen to the same radio programs, and so on. It is for this reason that advertisers and their agencies are continuously seeking media alternatives that can make contact with difficult-to-reach consumers. Enter the mundane laundry hanger as a novel point of contact.

A small New York company, Hanger Network, is generating interest from some major advertisers who are constantly searching for unique ways to reach consumers economically. Hanger Network's advertising proposition is straightforward: It arranges with laundry-supply firms to make and distribute laundry hangers carrying advertising messages for distribution in dry cleaners throughout the United States. For example, the marketers of Mitchum deodorant used hangers as part of a multimedia campaign for its new brand of men's deodorant named Smart Solid. Smart Solid is positioned as a brand that won't leave a white residue on clothing as do other antiperspirants. Hanger ads for this brand carried a variety of taglines such as "You won't find white residue on a Mitchum Man's shirt," "Chilidog stains are another story," and "A Mitchum Man doesn't wear his emotions on his sleeve, or his deodorant." Prior to fully committing to hanger advertising, Mitchum pretested hanger ads in two cities and experienced double-digit growth in consumer brand awareness and purchase intentions by the completion of the pretest. The decision to expand the campaign in other markets was a no-brainer based on these impressive results.

Hanger Network's ads have been used in approximately 40 percent of the 25,000 dry cleaning outlets in the United States. There have been some problems that need to be worked out, but it is likely that hanger advertising has a future. But, although it has potential to achieve advertisers' needs, it isn't an inexpensive form of advertising. In fact, the price is around $45 for every thousand hangers that carry an ad, which on a cost-per-thousand basis is more expensive even than advertising during some high-profile sporting events on television!

SOURCES: Adapted from Suzanne Vranica, "Marketers Try Hanging Out at Dry Cleaners," *The Wall Street Journal Online,* March 12, 2007, http://online.wsj.com (accessed March 12, 2007).

high-quality baby carriages (i.e., buggies or strollers) that carried the names of corporate sponsors on the sides.

- Another creative touch point is described in the *IMC Focus* insert.

The foregoing illustrations hopefully have made it clear that adherents to IMC are not tied to any single communication method (such as mass media advertising on television and in magazines) but instead use whatever touch points and contact methods best enable the communicator to deliver brand messages to targeted audiences. The IMC objective is to reach the target audience efficiently and effectively using touch points that are appropriate. The chair and chief executive officer of Young & Rubicam, a major Madison Avenue ad agency, succinctly yet eloquently captured the essence of the foregoing discussion when stating, "At the end of the day, [marcom agencies] don't deliver ads, or direct mail pieces, or PR and corporate identity programs. We deliver results."[20]

Not All Touch Points Are Equally Engaging

In concluding this section, it is important to emphasize that not all touch points are equally effective—a comment that is somewhat obvious but requires elaboration nonetheless. Marketing communicators have learned that the identical message has differential impact depending on the medium that carries the message. To state it another way, the context in which a marketing message appears influences the impact that the message has. Contexts, or touch points, that are more relevant and involving enhance message effectiveness. For example, a message received in context of a highly relevant Internet site stands a stronger likelihood of positively influencing consumers than the identical message carried, say, in a low-interest TV program. There is, in other words, a synergistic effect between message medium (contact or touch point) and message content.

This notion that context matters, that not all touch points are equally effective, has been termed *engagement* by marcom practitioners. We will move on to other key features of IMC at this point but return to the concept of engagement at various points throughout the text.

Takeaway from Key IMC Feature #2: *Use all touch points that effectively communicate the brand message. Surround customers/prospects with the message, but not to the point of being irritatingly present.*

Key Feature #3: Multiple Messages Must Speak with a Single Voice

Inherent in the philosophy and practice of IMC is the demand that a brand's assorted communication elements must strive to present the same message and convey that message consistently across diverse points of contact. Marketing communications must, in other words, *speak with a single voice.* Coordination of messages and media is absolutely critical to achieving a strong and unified brand image and moving consumers to action. Failure to closely coordinate all communication elements can result in duplicated efforts or, worse, contradictory brand messages.

A vice president of marketing at Nabisco fully recognized the value of speaking with a single voice when describing her intention to integrate all the marketing communication contacts for Nabisco's Oreo brand of cookies. This executive captured the essential quality of "single voicing" when stating that, under her leadership, "whenever consumers see Oreo, they'll be seeing the same message."[21] A general manager at Mars, Inc., maker of candy products, expressed a similar sentiment when stating, "We used to look at advertising, PR, promotion plans, each piece as separate. Now every piece of communication from package to Internet has to reflect the same message."[22]

In general, the single-voice principle involves selecting a specific positioning statement for a brand. A **positioning statement** is the key idea that encapsulates what a brand is intended to stand for in its target market's mind and then consistently delivers the same idea across all media channels. IMC practitioners such as Oreo's vice president of marketing and Mars, Inc.'s general manager know it is critical that they continually convey the same message on every occasion where the brand comes into contact with the target audience. A framework presented later in the chapter will further discuss the important role of positioning, and Chapter 5 will cover the topic of positioning in detail as it applies in an advertising context.

Takeaway from Key IMC Feature #3: *All touch points must present a unified message that is based on the brand's positioning strategy, or, in other words, communicate with a "single voice."*

Key Feature #4: Build Relationships Rather Than Engage in Flings

Successful marketing communication requires building relationships between brands and their consumers/customers. A **relationship** is an enduring link between a brand and its customers. Successful relationships between customers and brands lead to repeat purchasing and, ideally, loyalty toward a brand.

The value of customer retention has been compared to a "leaky bucket," the logic of which is nicely captured in the following quote:

> *As a company loses customers out of the leak in the bottom of the bucket, they have to continue to add new customers to the top of the bucket. If the company can even partially plug the leak, the bucket stays fuller. It then takes fewer new customers added to the top of the bucket to achieve the same level of profitability. It's less expensive and more profitable to keep those customers already in the bucket. Smart business people realize that it costs five to 10 times more to land a new customer than to keep a customer they already have. They also recognize that increasing the number of customers they keep by a small percentage can double profits.*[23]

Loyalty Programs

One well-known method for building customer relations is the use of *loyalty programs,* which also are called frequency or ambassador programs. Loyalty programs are dedicated to creating customers who are committed to a brand and encouraging them to satisfy most of their product or service needs from offering organizations.[24] Airlines, credit card companies, hotels, supermarkets, and many other businesses provide customers with bonus points—or some other form of accumulated reward—for their continued patronage.

© Jeffrey Coolidge/Stone/Getty Images

For example, to encourage its customers to use its debit/gift card and to remain loyal purchasers, the Caribou Coffee chain developed an incentive whereby consumers who used the Caribou Card and spent at least $1.50 per visit over 10 visits would receive a $4 credit on their Caribou Card.[25] The Pizza Hut food chain encouraged repeat purchasing from its customers by promoting a fee-based program in which customers paid an annual fee of $14.99; in return, they received an initial free large pizza and an additional free pizza every month if they placed two orders per month. This program enabled Pizza Hut to retain its best customers and keep them from switching their loyalties to other pizza makers.[26]

In step with the consumer-centric movement discussed in the context of key IMC feature #1, loyalty programs are increasingly being designed so that consumers are in control of how their reward points are used rather than restricting them to using the points only in a manner directed by the brand manager. As a case in point, Canada's Air Miles Reward Program enables its frequent fliers to use their reward miles for shopping at over 100 sponsors and allows them to acquire movie tickets, electronic merchandise, Walt Disney World tickets, gift cards, and literally hundreds of other product options of their choosing.[27]

Experiential Marketing Programs

Another way relationships between brands and customers are nurtured is by creating brand experiences that make positive and lasting impressions. This is done by creating special events or developing exciting venues that attempt to build the sensation that a sponsoring brand is relevant to the consumer's life and lifestyle. For example, Toronto-based Molson beer conducted the Molson Outpost campaign that took 400 sweepstakes winners on a weekend escapade of outdoor camping and extreme activities such as mountain climbing. Lincoln automobiles, a sponsor of the US Open tennis tournament, converted an unused building at the USTA National Tennis Center into a complex that immersed visitors in the history of tennis. The building featured soundstages, faux docks with real water, and images of the evolution of tennis around the world. Some 30,000 leads were obtained from people interested in Lincoln automobiles, prompting Lincoln's marketing communications coordinator to comment that "experiential marketing is permeating our entire marketing mix."[28]

Takeaway from Key IMC Feature #4: *Because it is more economical to maintain current customers than to recruit new ones, use marcom programs that encourage repeat purchasing and enhance brand loyalty whenever possible.*

Key Element #5: Don't Lose Focus of the Ultimate Objective: Affect Behavior

A final IMC feature is the goal of *affecting the behavior* of the target audience. This means that marketing communications must do more than just influence brand awareness or enhance consumer attitudes toward the brand. Instead, successful IMC requires that communication efforts be directed at encouraging some form of behavioral response. The objective, in other words, is to *move people to action.* An advertising campaign for a political candidate has not succeeded by simply increasing name recognition and getting people to like the candidate; rather, success is determined by whether or not people vote for the candidate—voting is the desired behavior. An advertising campaign that reminds people of the tragedy in New Orleans following Hurricane Katrina is ineffective if it merely gets people to feel sorry for the plight of New Orleans' residents; rather, effectiveness is demonstrated by people contributing money to a hurricane relief fund—financial contributions are the desired behavior. A marcom program for a brand is similarly ineffective if people learn about the brand and have favorable thoughts/feelings toward it but fail to purchase it in the quantities necessary to justify the marcom expenditures—purchasing is the desired behavior.

To better understand IMC's behavior-affecting objective, consider the situation faced by producers of natural food products. Research conducted to gauge consumers' feelings about 10 natural products (free-range chickens, organic fruits, etc.) revealed that natural products had a good image but not many people were buying them. Only 6 percent of the sampled consumers had purchased free-range chickens during the year preceding the survey, yet 43 percent thought that

Courtesy www.adbusters.org

free-range chickens were superior to conventional chickens.[29] This is a classic illustration of buyer behavior not following directly from attitudes. In a case such as this, the goal of marketing communications would be to convert these good feelings toward natural products into product consumption—it does little good to have consumers like your product but not buy it.

A similar challenge confronts antismoking proponents. Although most people understand intellectually that smoking causes cancer, emphysema, and other ailments, these same people often think that cancer and other problems will happen to smokers other than themselves. Hence, antismoking ads may serve to make people aware of the problems associated with smoking, but such campaigns are ineffective if people continue to smoke. The IMC goal in such a case is to develop more compelling advertisements that influence smokers to discontinue this practice. A creative approach other than the standard smoking-is-bad-for-you message is needed to redirect behavior. Appeals to normative influences (e.g., "smoking is uncool") may represent a superior tack in the antismoking initiative to reduce this unhealthy practice, particularly among teenagers.

We must be careful not to misconstrue this point. An IMC program must be judged, *ultimately,* in terms of whether it influences behavior; but it would be simplistic and unrealistic to expect an action to result from every communication effort. Prior to purchasing a new brand, consumers generally must be made aware of the brand and its benefits and be influenced to have a favorable attitude toward it. Communication efforts directed at accomplishing these intermediate, or pre-behavioral, goals are fully justified. Yet eventually—and preferably sooner than later—a successful marcom program must accomplish more than encouraging consumers to like a brand or, worse, merely familiarizing them with its existence. This partially explains why sales promotions and direct-to-consumer advertising are used so extensively—both practices typically yield quicker results than other forms of marketing communications such as advertising.

Takeaway from Key IMC Feature #5: *Marcom's goal is ultimately to affect the behavior of the target audience. Don't be satisfied with the mere achievement of intermediate goals such as creating brand awareness and positively affecting attitudes. Keep the eye on the prize, which is ultimately to move the target audience to action.*

Obstacles to Implementing the Key IMC Features

Brand managers typically use outside suppliers, or specialized services, to assist them in managing various aspects of marketing communications. These include advertising agencies, public relations firms, sales promotion agencies, direct-advertising firms, and special-event marketers. Herein is a major reason why marketing communication efforts often do not meet the ideals previously described. Integration requires tight coordination among all elements of a marcom program. However, this becomes complicated when different specialized services operate independently of one another.

Perhaps the greatest obstacle to integration is that few providers of marketing communication services have the far-ranging skills to plan and execute programs that cut across all major forms of marketing communications. Advertising agencies, which traditionally have offered a greater breadth of services than do other specialists, are well qualified to develop mass media advertising campaigns; most, however, do not also have the ability to conduct direct-to-customer advertising, and even fewer have departments for sales promotions, special events, and publicity campaigns. Although many advertising agencies have expanded their services and full-service agencies have emerged, IMC awaits major changes in the culture of marketing departments and service providers before it becomes a reality on a large scale. In the final analysis, although most marketers consider themselves proponents of IMC, a major challenge facing brand marketers and their agencies is assuring that all marcom tools used in a particular marketing execution are consistently executed.[30]

Marketing communication suppliers such as advertising agencies, sales promotion firms, and public relations agencies have historically offered a limited range of services. Now it is increasingly important for suppliers to offer multiple services—which explains why some major advertising agencies have expanded their offerings beyond just advertising services to include sales promotion assistance, public relations, direct marketing, and event marketing support. In fact, brand managers can turn to "full-service" agencies that supply all forms of marcom and not just advertising, sales promotion, or publicity per se.

The Marketing Communications Decision-Making Process

So far we have discussed the importance of tightly integrating all marcom elements such that a unified message is delivered wherever the customer or prospect comes into contact with the brand. This section presents a framework that will provide a useful conceptual and schematic structure for thinking about the types of practical decisions that marketing communicators make. The framework is presented in Figure 1.1. It is very important at this time that you scan and achieve a basic understanding of the model components in preparation for the following discussion, which fleshes out the model's skeleton.

Figure 1.1 conceptualizes the various types of brand-level marcom decisions and the outcomes desired from those decisions. It will be noted that the model consists of a set of fundamental decisions, a set of implementation decisions, and program evaluation. The model in Figure 1.1 shows that *fundamental decisions* (targeting, positioning, setting objectives, and budgeting) influence *implementation decisions* regarding the mixture of communications elements and the determination of messages, media, and momentum. The expected *outcomes* from these decisions are enhancing brand equity and affecting behavior. Subsequent to the implementation of the marcom decisions, *program evaluation*—in the form of

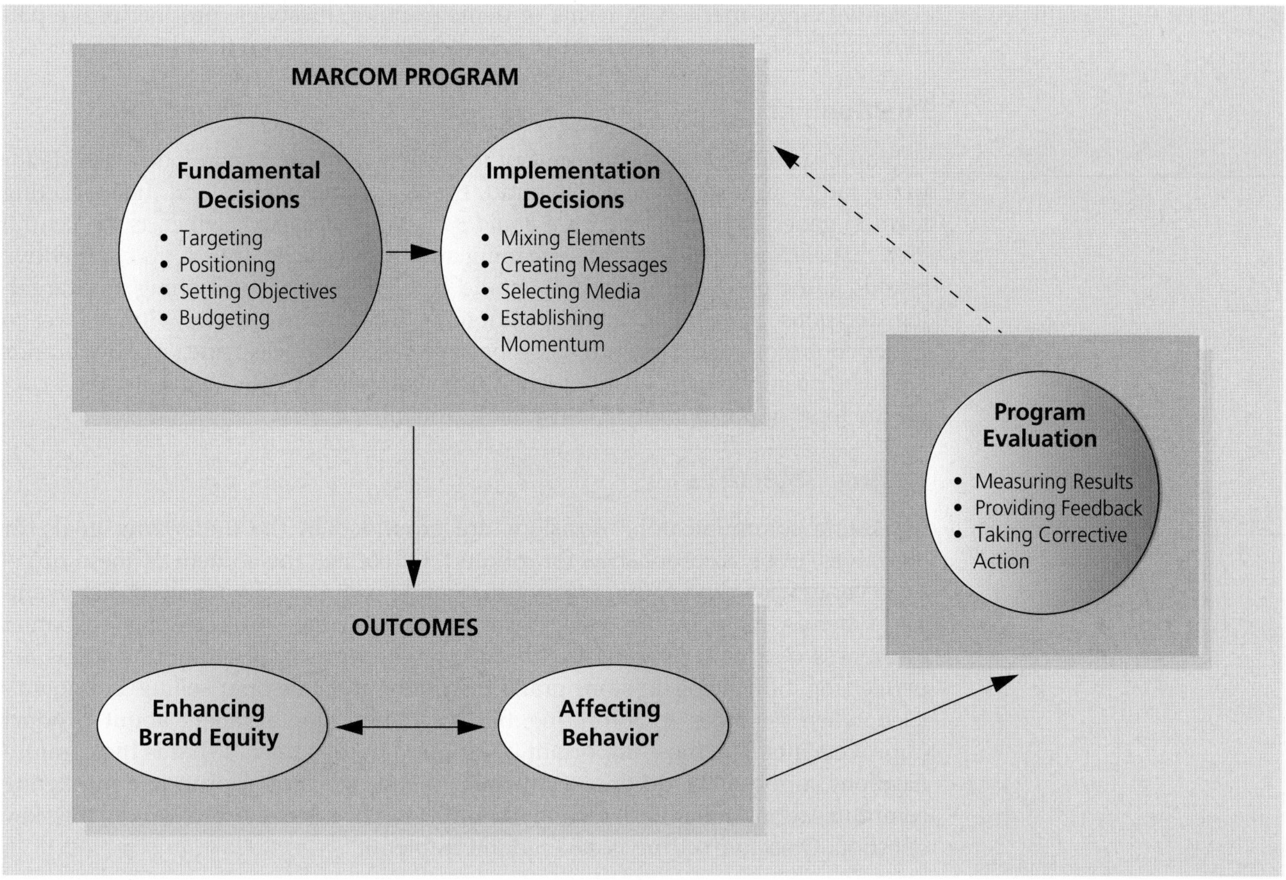

Figure 1.1

Making Brand-Level Marcom Decisions and Achieving Desired Outcomes

measuring the results from marcom efforts, providing feedback (see dashed arrow in Figure 1.1), and taking corrective action—is essential to determining whether outcomes match objectives. Corrective action is required when performance falls below expectations.

The objective of marketing communications is to enhance *brand equity* as a means of moving customers to *favorable action toward the brand*—that is, trying it, repeat purchasing it, and, ideally, becoming loyal toward the brand. Enhancing equity and affecting behavior depend, of course, on the suitability of all marketing-mix elements—e.g., product quality and price level—and not just marcom per se. Marcom efforts nonetheless play a pivotal role by informing customers about new brands and their relative advantages and by elevating brand images.

As will be fully developed in the following chapter, brand equity is enhanced when consumers become familiar with the brand and hold favorable, strong, and perhaps unique associations in memory about the brand. A brand has no equity if consumers are unfamiliar with it. Once consumers have become aware of a brand, the amount of equity depends on how favorably they perceive the brand's features and benefits as compared to competitive brands and how strongly these views are held in memory.

Fundamental Marcom Decisions

Targeting

Targeting lets marketing communicators deliver messages more precisely and prevent wasted coverage to people falling outside the intended audience. Hence, selection of target segments is a critical step toward effective and efficient marketing communications for both B2B and B2C companies. Companies identify potential target markets in terms of demographics, lifestyles, product usage patterns, and geographic considerations. Targeting is covered in detail in Chapter 4.

Positioning

A brand's position represents the key feature, benefit, or image that it stands for in the target audience's collective mind. Brand communicators and the marketing team in general must decide on a *brand positioning statement*, which is the central idea that encapsulates a brand's meaning and distinctiveness vis-à-vis competitive brands in the product category. It should be obvious that positioning and targeting decisions go hand in hand: positioning decisions are made with respect to intended targets, and targeting decisions are based on a clear idea of how brands are to be positioned and distinguished from competitive offerings. Chapter 5 covers the topic of positioning in considerable detail.

Setting Objectives

Marketing communicators' decisions are grounded in the underlying goals, or objectives, to be accomplished for a brand. Of course, the content of these objectives varies according to the form of marketing communications used. For example, whereas mass media advertising is ideally suited for creating consumer awareness of a new or improved brand, point-of-purchase communications are perfect for influencing in-store brand selection, and personal selling is unparalleled when it comes to informing B2B customers and retailers about product improvements. The most important question to pose is this: "What is the communications supposed to do or accomplish?"[31] The choice of appropriate marketing communications tools and media naturally flows from the answer to this key question. Objective setting is covered in Chapter 6.

Budgeting

Financial resources are budgeted to specific marcom elements to accomplish desired objectives. Companies use different budgeting procedures in allocating funds to marketing communications managers and other organizational units. At one extreme is *top-down budgeting (TD),* in which senior management decides how much each subunit receives. At the other extreme is *bottom-up budgeting (BU),* in which managers of subunits (such as at the product category level) determine how much is needed to achieve their objectives; these amounts are then combined to establish the total marketing budget.

Most budgeting practices involve a combination of top-down and bottom-up budgeting. For example, in the *bottom-up/top-down process (BUTD),* subunit managers submit budget requests to a chief marketing officer (say, a vice president of marketing), who coordinates the various requests and then submits an overall budget to top management for approval. The *top-down/bottom-up process (TDBU)* reverses the flow of influence; top managers first establish the total size of the budget and then divide it among the various subunits. Research has shown that combination budgeting methods (BUTD and TDBU) are used more often than the extreme methods (TD or BU). The BUTD process is by far the most frequently used, especially in firms where marketing departments have greater influence than finance units.[32] Budgeting is covered in Chapter 6 along with objective setting.

A Concluding Mantra

Mantra is a Hindu word meaning incantation or recitation (of a song, word, statement, or passage). The following statement serves as a mantra to capture the preceding discussion of fundamental marcom decisions. It is my strong encouragement to you, the reader of this text, to commit this mantra to memory and to turn to it as a constant point of reference whenever you are in a capacity that requires you to make some form of marcom decision. You regularly should pose questions to yourself—and to your colleagues—such as these: Is our brand clearly positioned? Is our communication directed to a specific target? What specific objective is our advertising (or sales promotion, or event, etc.) attempting to accomplish? Is our proposed strategy within the budget available, or do we need to request more budget?

> **A Commit-to-Memory Mantra:** *All marketing communications should be: (1) directed to a particular target market, (2) clearly* positioned, *(3) created to achieve a* specific objective, *and (4) undertaken to accomplish the objective* within budget constraint.

Marcom Implementation Decisions

The fundamental decisions just described are conceptual and strategic. Comparatively, the implementation decisions are practical and tactical. Here is where the proverbial rubber hits the road. Marcom managers must make various implementation decisions in the pursuit of accomplishing brand-level objectives and achieving the brand's positioning and targeting requirements. Initially they must choose how best to integrate, or mix, the various communications elements to achieve objectives toward the target market and within budget constraint. Then they must decide what types of messages will accomplish the desired positioning, which media are appropriate for delivering messages, and what degree of momentum is needed to support the media effort. Please refer again to Figure 1.1 to obtain a view of the "forest" prior to examining specific "trees."

Mixing Elements

A fundamental issue confronting all companies is deciding exactly how to allocate resources among the various marketing communications tools. For B2B companies, the mixture typically emphasizes, in the following order of budgeting importance, direct mail, online marketing, trade shows, brand advertising, and telemarketing.[33] For consumer goods marketers, mixture decisions are, in many respects, more complicated because greater options are available. The issue boils down in large part to a decision of how much to allocate to advertising and to sales promotions. (Note: In keeping with practitioner convention, the word *promotion* hereafter will be used interchangeably with *sales promotion.*) The trend during the past two decades has been toward greater expenditures on promotions and fewer on advertising.

Is there an *optimum mixture* of expenditures between advertising and promotion? There is not, unfortunately, because the marketing communications–mix decision constitutes an *ill-structured problem.*[34] This means that for a given level of expenditure, there is no way of determining the mathematical optimum allocation between advertising and promotion that will maximize revenue or profit. Two major factors account for this inability to determine a mathematically optimum mix. First, advertising and promotions are somewhat interchangeable—both tools can accomplish some of the same objectives. Hence, it is impossible to know exactly which tool or combination of tools is better in every situation. Second, advertising and promotions produce a synergistic effect—their combined results are greater than what they would achieve individually. This makes it difficult to determine the exact effects that different combinations of advertising and sales promotion might generate.

Although it is impossible to determine a mathematically optimum mixture of advertising and promotion expenditures, a satisfactory mixture can be formulated by considering the differing purposes of each of these marcom tools. A key strategic consideration is whether short- or long-term schemes are more important given a brand's life-cycle stage and in view of competitive realities. An appropriate mixture for mature brands is likely to be different from the mixture for brands recently introduced. New brands require larger investment in promotions such as couponing and sampling to generate trial purchases, whereas mature brands might need proportionately greater advertising investment to maintain or enhance a brand's image.

Brand equity considerations also play a role in evaluating a satisfactory combination of advertising and promotions. Poorly planned or excessive promotions can damage a brand's equity by cheapening its image. If a brand is frequently placed on sale or if some form of deal (price-offs, discounts) is regularly offered, consumers will delay purchasing the brand until its price is reduced. This can cause the brand to be purchased more for its price discount than for its nonprice attributes and benefits (Figure 1.2).

The matter of properly mixing advertising and promotion is aptly summarized in the following quote:

> *As one views the opportunities inherent in ascertaining the proper balance between advertising and promotion, it should be quite clear that both should be used as one would play a pipe organ, pulling out certain stops and pushing others, as situations and circumstances change. Rigid rules, or continuing application of inflexible advertising-to-promotion percentages, serve no real purpose and can be quite counterproductive in today's dynamic and ever-changing marketing environment. A short-term solution that creates a long-term problem is no solution at all.*[35]

The "short-term solution" refers to spending excessive amounts on promotion to create quick sales while failing to invest sufficiently in advertising to build a brand's long-term equity. That is, excessive promotions can rob a brand's future. An appropriate mixture involves spending enough on promotions to ensure sufficient sales volume in the short term while simultaneously spending enough on advertising to ensure the growth or preservation of a brand's equity position.

Creating Messages

A second implementation decision is the creation of messages in the form of advertisements, publicity releases, promotions, package designs, and any other form of marcom message. Subsequent chapters will address specific message issues relating to each marcom tool. Suffice it to say at this point that systematic (versus ad hoc) decision making requires that message content be dictated by the brand's positioning strategy and aligned with the communications objective for the designated target audience.

Selecting Media

All marketing communications messages require an instrument, or medium, for transmission. Although the term *media* is typically applied to advertising (television, magazines, radio, Internet, etc.), the concept of *media* is relevant to all marcom tools. For example, personal sales messages can be delivered via face-to-face communications or by telemarketing; these media alternatives have different costs and effectiveness. Point-of-purchase materials are delivered via in-store signs, electronically, musically, and otherwise. Each represents a different medium.

Detailed discussions of media are reserved for specific chapters later in the text. Advertising media are discussed in particular detail, and considerable attention also is devoted to the media of consumer promotions. At the risk of redundancy it is important to note again that media decisions are determined in large measure by the fundamental decisions previously made regarding choice of target audience, positioning strategy, type of objectives to be achieved, and how much is to be budgeted to a brand during each budgeting period.

WM. WRIGLEY JR. COMPANY

Figure 1.2

A Buy-One-Get-One-Free Promotion

Establishing Momentum

The word *momentum* refers to an object's force or speed of movement—its impetus. A train has momentum as it races down the tracks, a spacecraft has momentum as it is launched into orbit, a hockey player has momentum when skating past the defensive opposition, a student has momentum when making good progress on a term paper after delaying getting started. Marketing communications programs also have, or lack, momentum. Simply developing an advertising message, creating a buzz-generating viral campaign, or releasing publicity is insufficient. The effectiveness of each of these message forms requires both a sufficient amount of effort and continuity of that effort. This is the meaning of momentum as it relates to marketing communications. Insufficient momentum is ineffective at best and a waste of money at worst.

Critical to the concept of momentum is the need to sustain an effort rather than starting advertising for a while, discontinuing it for a period, reinstating the advertising, stopping it again, and so on. In other words, some companies never create or sustain momentum because their marketplace presence is inadequate. "Out of sight, out of mind" is probably more relevant to brands in the marketplace than to people. We generally do not forget our friends and family, but today's brand friend is tomorrow's stranger unless it is kept before our consciousness. Because consumers make hundreds of purchase decisions in many different product categories, continual reminders of brand names and their benefits are required if these brands are to stand a strong chance of becoming serious purchase candidates.

Toyota Motor Corporation had available in stock on one occasion only a 16-day supply of the fast-selling Camry. Yet it launched a major advertising campaign aggressively encouraging consumers to purchase Camrys. Critics declared that it was unwise for Toyota to advertise when insufficient product was available to fulfill orders. In response, the vice president of Toyota Motor Sales, U.S.A., asserted that even when demand is strong, it is important "to keep your momentum in the marketplace going."[36] This executive obviously appreciates the value of achieving and maintaining a brand's momentum. Many marketing communicators and higher-level managers do not. For example, advertising is one of the first items cut during economic downturns, even when, by continuing to advertise, the advertised brand could gain market share over brands that have suspended or severely slashed their ad budgets.

Marcom Outcomes

Referring back to our conceptual framework for marketing communications decisions, it can be seen that the outcomes from a marcom program are twofold: enhancing brand equity and affecting behavior. Figure 1.1 displays a double-headed arrow between these outcomes, which signifies that each outcome influences the other. If, say, an advertising campaign for a new brand generates brand awareness and creates a positive brand image, consumers may be inclined to try the new brand. In such a situation, the brand's equity has been enhanced, and this in turn has affected consumer behavior toward the brand. In similar fashion, a promotion for the new brand, such as a free sample, may encourage consumers to initially try and then subsequently purchase the brand (Figure 1.2). A positive experience with the brand may lead to positive brand perceptions. In this situation, a promotion affected consumer behavior, which in turn enhanced the promoted brand's equity.

As established previously, a fundamental IMC principle is that marcom efforts must ultimately be gauged by whether they *affect behavior*. Sales promotion is the marcom tool most capable of directly affecting consumer behavior. However, excessive reliance on promotions can injure a brand's reputation by creating a low-price and perhaps low-quality image. It is for this reason that marketing communicators often seek first to enhance a brand's equity as a foundation to influencing behavior. Indeed, much if not most marcom efforts are designed to enhance brand equity. We thus need to explore fully the concept of brand equity and understand what it is and how it can be influenced by marcom efforts. We will examine this topic in detail in Chapter 2.

Program Evaluation

After marketing communications objectives are set, elements selected and mixed, messages and media chosen, and programs implemented and possibly sustained, program evaluation must take place. This is accomplished by measuring the results of marcom efforts against the objectives that were established at the outset. For a local advertiser—say, a sporting goods store that is running an advertised special on athletic shoes for a two-day period in May—the results are the number of Nike, Reebok, Adidas, and other brands sold. If you tried to sell an old automobile through the classified pages, the results would be the number of phone inquiries you received and whether you ultimately sold the car. For a national manufacturer of a branded product, results typically are not so quick to occur. Rather, a company invests in point-of-purchase communications, promotions, and advertising and then waits, often for weeks, to see whether these programs deliver the desired sales volume.

Regardless of the situation, it is critical to evaluate the results of marcom efforts. Throughout the business world there is increasing demand for *accountability,* which requires that research be performed and data acquired to determine whether implemented marcom decisions have accomplished the objectives they were expected to achieve. Results can be measured in terms of behavioral impact (such as increased sales) or based on communication outcomes.

Measures of *communication outcomes* include brand awareness, message comprehension, attitude toward the brand, and purchase intentions. All of these are communication (rather than behavioral) objectives in the sense that an advertiser has attempted to communicate a certain message argument or create an overall impression. Thus, the goal for an advertiser of a relatively unknown brand may be to increase brand awareness in the target market by 30 percent within six months of starting a new advertising campaign. This objective (a 30 percent increase in awareness) would be based on knowledge of the awareness level prior to the campaign's debut. Post-campaign measurement would then reveal whether the target level was achieved.

It is essential to measure the results of all marcom programs. Failure to achieve targeted results prompts corrective action (see the dashed arrow in Figure 1.1). Corrective action might call for greater investment, a different combination of communications elements, revised creative strategy, different media allocations, or a host of other possibilities. Only by systematically setting objectives and measuring results is it possible to know whether marcom programs are working as well as they should and how future efforts can improve on the past.[37]

Summary

This opening chapter has overviewed the fundamentals of IMC and provided a framework for thinking about all aspects of marcom decision making. IMC is an organization's unified, coordinated effort to promote a consistent brand message through the use of multiple communication tools that "speak with a single voice." One of several key features of IMC is the use of all sources of brand or company contacts as potential message delivery channels. Another key feature is that the IMC process starts with the customer or prospect rather than the brand communicator to determine the most appropriate and effective methods for developing persuasive communications programs. Consumers are increasingly in control of marketing communications both in their active choice of which media outlets to attend and by generating their own brand-related communications—via podcasting, blogging, and creating messages on community-based sites such as MySpace, YouTube, and Facebook.

This chapter has provided a model of the marcom process to serve as a useful integrative device for better structuring and understanding the topics covered throughout the remainder of the text. The model (Figure 1.1) includes three components: a marcom program consisting of fundamental and implementation decisions, outcomes (enhancing brand equity and affecting behavior), and program evaluation. Fundamental decisions include choosing target markets, establishing a brand positioning, setting objectives, and determining a marcom budget. Implementation decisions involve determining a mixture of marketing communications tools (advertising, promotions, events, point-of-purchase efforts, etc.) and establishing message, media, and momentum plans. These decisions are evaluated by comparing measured results against brand-level communications objectives.

As author of eight editions of this text over the past quarter century, it is my sincere hope that this introductory chapter has piqued your interest and provided you with a basic understanding of the many topics you will be studying while reading this text and participating in classroom lectures and discussions. Marketing communications truly is a fascinating and dynamic subject. It combines art, science, and technology and allows the practitioner considerable latitude in developing effective ways to skin the proverbial cat. It will serve you well throughout your studies and into your marketing career to remain ever mindful of the key elements of IMC described in this chapter. Organizations that truly succeed in their marcom pursuits must accept and practice these key elements.

Because the field of marketing communications involves many forms of practice, a number of specialty trade associations have evolved over time. The following appendix overviews, in alphabetical order, some of the more influential associations in the United States. Internet sites are provided to facilitate your search for additional information about these organizations. (Many countries other than the United States have similar associations. Interested students might want to conduct an Internet search to identify similar associations in a country of interest.)

Appendix

Some Important U.S. Trade Associations in the Marcom Field:

Advertising Research Foundation (ARF, http://www.arfsite.org)—ARF is a nonprofit association dedicated to increasing advertising effectiveness by conducting objective and impartial research. ARF's members consist of advertisers, advertising agencies, research firms, and media companies.

American Association of Advertising Agencies (AAAA, http://www.aaaa.org)—The Four *A*s, as it is referred to conversationally, has the mission of improving the advertising agency business in the United States by fostering professional development, encouraging high creative and business standards, and attracting first-rate employees to the advertising business.

Association of Coupon Professionals (ACP, http://www.couponpros.org)—This coupon-redemption trade association strives to ensure coupons as a viable promotional tool and to improve coupon industry business conditions.

Association of National Advertisers (ANA, http://www.ana.net)—Whereas the AAAA serves primarily the interests of advertising agencies, ANA represents the interests of business organizations that advertise regionally and nationally. ANA's members collectively represent over 80 percent of all advertising expenditures in the United States.

Direct Marketing Association (DMA, http://www.the-dma.org)—DMA is dedicated to encouraging and advancing the effective and ethical use of direct marketing. The association represents the interests of direct marketers to the government, media, and general public.

Incentive Manufacturers and Representatives Alliance (IMRA, http://www.imraorg.net)—Members of IMRA are suppliers of premium merchandise. The association serves these members by promoting high professional standards in the pursuit of excellence in the incentive industry.

Internet Advertising Bureau (IAB, http://www.iab.net)—IAB's mission is to help online, Interactive broadcasting, email, wireless and Interactive television media companies increase their revenues.

Mobile Marketing Association (MMA, http://www.mmaglobal.com)—The Mobile Marketing Association (MMA) is a global association dedicated to stimulating the growth of mobile marketing and its associated technologies.

Point-of-Purchase Advertising International (POPAI, http://www.popai.org)—This trade association serves the interests of advertisers, retailers, and producers/suppliers of point-of-purchase products and services.

Promotional Products Association International (PPAI, http://www.ppa.org)—PPAI serves the interests of producers, suppliers, and users of promotional products. The businesses PPAI represents used to be referred to as the specialty advertising industry, but promotional products is the term of current preference.

Promotion Marketing Association (PMA, http://www.pmalink.org)—PMA's mission is to foster the advancement of promotion marketing and facilitate better understanding of promotion's role and importance in the overall marketing process.

Discussion Questions

1. One key feature of IMC is the emphasis on affecting behavior and not just its antecedents (such as brand awareness or favorable attitudes). For each of the following situations, indicate the specific behavior(s) that marketing communications might attempt to affect: (a) your university's advertising efforts, (b) a professional baseball team's promotion for a particular game, (c) a not-for-profit organization's efforts to recruit more volunteers, and (d) Gatorade's sponsorship of a volleyball tournament.
2. Assume you are in charge of fund-raising for an organization on your campus—a social fraternity or sorority, a business fraternity, or any other such organization. It is your job to identify a suitable project and to manage the project's marketing communications. For the purpose of this exercise, identify a fund-raising project idea and apply the subset of the model involving fundamental decisions. In other words, explain how you would position your fund-raising project, whom you would target, what objective(s) you would set, and how much (ballpark figure) you would budget for marcom efforts.
3. The following quote from an advertising executive appeared in the chapter in the section under key IMC feature #2: "At the end of the day, [marcom agencies] don't deliver ads, or direct mail pieces, or PR and corporate identity programs. We deliver results." Explain what you think this executive meant in making this statement.
4. Explain the concept of *momentum* and offer an account as to why momentum is important for a specific brand of your choosing.
5. Explain the meaning of "360-degree branding." What are the advantages and potential disadvantages of such a practice?
6. Why do you think that the trend in marcom budgeting is toward increased expenditures on promotions and reduced advertising spending?
7. Based on your experiences and those of close friends with whom you discuss such matters, what might be the future role of social networking outlets (e.g., MySpace, Facebook, and YouTube) in disseminating brand information? On the basis of your experience, is most brand-related information that appears on these sites positive or negative?
8. What is the distinction between top-down (TD) and bottom-up (BU) budgeting? Why is BUTD used in companies that are more marketing oriented, whereas TDBU is found more frequently in finance-driven companies?
9. What steps can marketing communicators take to allow consumers to exercise their control of when, where, and how they receive brand messages? Provide specific examples to support your answer.
10. Brand positioning and targeting also are necessarily interdependent. Explain this interdependency and provide an example to support your point.
11. Explain what it means to say that the consumers are in control of marketing communications. Provide an example from your own experience that supports the contention that marcom is becoming increasingly consumer-centric.
12. Objectives and budgets are necessarily interdependent. Explain this interdependency and construct an illustration to support your point.
13. The combined use of different marcom tools—such as advertising a brand on TV along with sponsoring an event—can produce a synergistic effect for a brand. What does the concept of synergy mean in this context? Provide a practical illustration of how two or more marcom tools when used in combination are capable of

producing results greater than the sum of their individual contributions.

14. Assume you are in charge of advertising a product that is marketed specifically to college students. Identify seven contact methods (include no more than two forms of mass media advertising) you might use to reach this audience.
15. Explain how your college or university uses marketing communications to recruit students.

End Notes

1. This description is adapted from Jean Halliday, "Buick Builds Buzz for SUV On-, Off-Line," *Advertising Age,* August 11, 2003, 34.
2. Kate Maddox, "Special Report: Integrated Marketing Success Stories," BtoBonline.Com, June 7, 2004, http://www.btobonline.com (accessed June 7, 2004).
3. Kate Maddox, "Integrated Marketing Success Stories," *BtoB,* August 14, 2006, 28–29.
4. Bob Hartley and Dave Pickton, "Integrated Marketing Communications Requires a New Way of Thinking," *Journal of Marketing Communications* 5 (June 1999), 97–106; Philip J. Kitchen, Joanne Brignell, Tao Li, and Graham Spickett Jones, "The Emergence of IMC: A Theoretical Perspective," *Journal of Advertising Research* 44 (March 2004), 19–30.
5. Joep P. Cornelissen and Andrew R. Lock, "Theoretical Concept or Management Fashion? Examining the Significance of IMC," *Journal of Advertising Research* 40 (September/October 2000), 7–15. For counterpositions, see Don E. Schultz and Philip J. Kitchen, "A Response to 'Theoretical Concept or Management Fashion?'" *Journal of Advertising Research* 40 (September/October 2000), 17–21; Stephen J. Gould, "The State of IMC Research and Applications," *Journal of Advertising Research* 40 (September/October 2000), 22–23.
6. Don E. Schultz and Philip J. Kitchen, "Integrated Marketing Communications in U.S. Advertising Agencies: An Exploratory Study," *Journal of Advertising Research* 37 (September/October 1997), 7–18; Philip J. Kitchen and Don E. Schultz, "A Multi-Country Comparison of the Drive for IMC," *Journal of Advertising Research* 39 (January/February 1999), 21–38.
7. Stephen J. Gould, Andreas F. Grein, and Dawn B. Lernan, "The Role of Agency-Client Integration in Integrated Marketing Communications: A Complementary Agency Theory-Interorganizational Perspective," *Journal of Current Issues and Research in Advertising* 21 (spring 1999), 1–12.
8. These findings are based on research by George S. Low, "Correlates of Integrated Marketing Communications," *Journal of Advertising Research* 40 (May/June 2000), 27–39.
9. Prasad A. Naik and Kalyan Raman, "Understanding the Impact of Synergy in Multimedia Communications," *Journal of Marketing Research* 40 (November 2003), 375–388.
10. Yuhmiin Chang and Esther Thorson, "Television and Web Advertising Synergies," *Journal of Advertising* 33 (summer 2004), 75–84.
11. This definition is the author's adaptation of one developed by members of the marketing communications faculty at the Medill School, Northwestern University. The original definition was reprinted in Don E. Schultz, "Integrated Marketing Communications: Maybe Definition Is in the Point of View," *Marketing News,* January 18, 1993, 17.
12. Bob Garfield, "The Chaos Scenario 2.0: The Post Advertising Age," *Advertising Age,* March 26, 2007, 14.
13. Suzanne Vranica, "On Madison Avenue, a Digital Wake-up Call," *The Wall Street Journal Online,* March 26, 2007, http://online.wsj.com (accessed March 26, 2007).
14. Brian Steinberg, "Ogilvy's New Digital Chief Discusses Challenges," *The Wall Street Journal Online,* April 4, 2007, http://online.wsj.com (accessed April 4, 2007).
15. Weber Shandwick, 919 Third Avenue, New York, NY, 10022.
16. Lisa Sanders, "'Demand Chain' Rules at McCann," *Advertising Age,* June 14, 2004, 6.
17. David Sable, "We're Surrounded," *Agency* (spring 2000), 50–51.
18. Amy Johannes, "A Cool Moves Front," *Promo,* August 2006, 21.
19. Marc Graser, "Toyota Hits Touch Points as It Hawks Yaris to Youth,"*Advertising Age,* May 1, 2006, 28.
20. Peter A. Georgescu, "Looking at the Future of Marketing," *Advertising Age,* April 14, 1997, 30.
21. Judann Pollack, "Nabisco's Marketing VP Expects 'Great Things,'" *Advertising Age,* December 2, 1996, 40.
22. Stephanie Thompson, "Busy Lifestyles Force Change," *Advertising Age,* October 9, 2000, s8.
23. This quote is from author Vicki Lenz as cited in Matthew Grimm, "Getting to Know You," *Brandweek,* January 4, 1999, 18.
24. The importance of creating committed customers is verified empirically in Peter C. Verhoef, "Understanding the Effect of Customer Relationship Management Efforts on Customer Retention and Customer Share Development," *Journal of Marketing* 27 (October 2003), 30–45.
25. Amy Johannes, "Coffee Perks," *Promo,* September 2006, 41.
26. Samar Farah, "Loyalty Delivers," *Deliver,* September 2006, 10–15.
27. Amy Johannes, "Top of Wallet," *Promo,* July 2007, 20–22.
28. Dan Hanover, "Are You Experienced?" *Promo,* February 2001, 48.
29. Leah Rickard, "Natural Products Score Big on Image," *Advertising Age,* August 8, 1994, 26.

30. A survey of over 200 marketing professionals found that both brand marketers and agencies consider consistency of execution the major challenge to integrating marcom strategies. See Claire Atkinson, "Integration Still a Pipe Dream for Many," *Advertising Age,* March 10, 2003, 1, 47.
31. Don E. Schultz, "Relax Old Marcom Notions, Consider Audiences," *Marketing News,* October 27, 2003, 8.
32. Nigel F. Piercy, "The Marketing Budgeting Process: Marketing Management Implications," *Journal of Marketing* 51 (October 1987), 45–59.
33. Carol Krol, "DMA: Direct Response Gets Largest Share of B-to-B Marketing," *BtoB,* May 7, 2007, 3.
34. Thomas A. Petit and Martha R. McEnally, "Putting Strategy into Promotion Mix Decisions," *The Journal of Consumer Marketing* 2 (winter 1985), 41–47.
35. Joseph W. Ostrow, "The Advertising/Promotion Mix: A Blend or a Tangle," *AAAA Newsletter,* August 1988, 7.
36. Quoted in Sally Goll Beatty, "Auto Makers Bet Campaigns Will Deliver Even If They Can't," *The Wall Street Journal Online,* October 13, 1997, http://online.wsj.com (accessed October 13, 1997).
37. Tim Ambler, *Marketing and the Bottom Line: The New Metrics of Corporate Wealth* (London: Pearson Education Limited, 2000), especially Appendix A.

2

Marketing Communications Challenges: Enhancing Brand Equity, Influencing Behavior, and Being Accountable

Marketing researchers and pollsters are constantly surveying people about their likes and dislikes, their voting intentions, their thoughts about which actors should win Academy Awards, and on and on. Needless to say, pollsters also investigate consumers' thoughts and feelings toward brands. Harris Interactive, the world's twelfth largest market research firm, conducts an annual poll that requests American consumers to indicate which brands they consider best. A recent poll involved online interviews with nearly 2,400 adults. Interviewees were asked a single question: "We would like you to think about brands or names of products and services you know. Considering everything, which three brands do you consider the best?" Interviewees were, in other words, asked to spontaneously identify up to three brands that they personally regarded as the "best." Results from the poll identified the following 10 brands as those most often mentioned as best:[1]

Brand	Ranking
Coca-Cola	1
Sony	2
Toyota	3
Dell	4
Ford	5
Kraft Foods	6
Pepsi-Cola	7
Microsoft	8
Apple	9
Honda	10

Critics of this form of one-question polling suggest that such polls are not true indicators of the equity of a brand. Ford Motors, for one example, is anything but one of the world's best brands when "best" is based on objective indicators such as profitability, market share, sales growth, and consumer confidence. How could an exciting, innovative brand such as Apple be beaten out by eight other brands, including those that are basically resting on past laurels (think Ford, Dell, etc.)?

It would seem that this "best brands" survey is more a measure of brand awareness than of brand equity and reflects past achievements rather than current performance.[2] In other words, when asked to spontaneously identify the three best brands that come to mind, many respondents, especially in reply to an online survey, would mention those brands that come easiest and quickest to mind. Yet this top-of-mind recall, though certainly a good indicator of brand

© Richard Levine/Alamy

awareness, is not equivalent to a measure of a brand's strength, value, or equity. This chapter discusses in detail the concepts of brand awareness and brand equity, and upon completing your reading of this material you will fully appreciate why mere awareness is a necessary but insufficient indicator of brand equity.

Chapter Objectives

After reading this chapter you should be able to:

1. Explain the concept of brand equity from both the company's and the customer's perspectives.
2. Describe the positive outcomes that result from enhancing brand equity.
3. Appreciate a model of brand equity from the customer's perspective.
4. Understand how marcom efforts must influence behavior and achieve financial accountability.

>>Marcom Insight:

When Polls Fail to Reveal the Complete Picture

Introduction

The previous chapter introduced the philosophy and practice of integrated marketing communications (IMC) and then presented a framework for thinking about all aspects of the marcom process. You will recall that this framework included four components: (1) a set of fundamental decisions (targeting, positioning, etc.), (2) a group of implementation decisions (mixing elements, creating messages, etc.), (3) two types of outcomes resulting from these decisions (enhancing brand equity and affecting behavior), and (4) a regimen for evaluating marcom results and taking corrective action. This chapter focuses on the third component in this framework, namely, the desired outcomes of marcom efforts.

The basic issues addressed are these: What can marketing communicators do to enhance the equity of their brands and, beyond this, affect the behavior of their present and prospective customers? Also, how can marketing communicators justify their investments in advertising, sales promotions, and other marcom elements and demonstrate financial accountability? The chapter first discusses the concept of brand equity and explores this topic from both company and customer perspectives. A following section then addresses the importance of affecting behavior, including a discussion of accountability.

Brand Equity

A **brand** exists when a marketing entity—i.e., a product, a retail outlet, a service, or even a geographical place such as an entire country, region, state, or city—receives its own name, term, sign, symbol, design, or any particular combination of these elements as a form of identification. Without a recognizable brand, a product is but a mere commodity. Many marcom experts are of the mind-set that all products can be branded. One observer has even claimed that the word "commodity" is an open admission of marketing bankruptcy.[3]

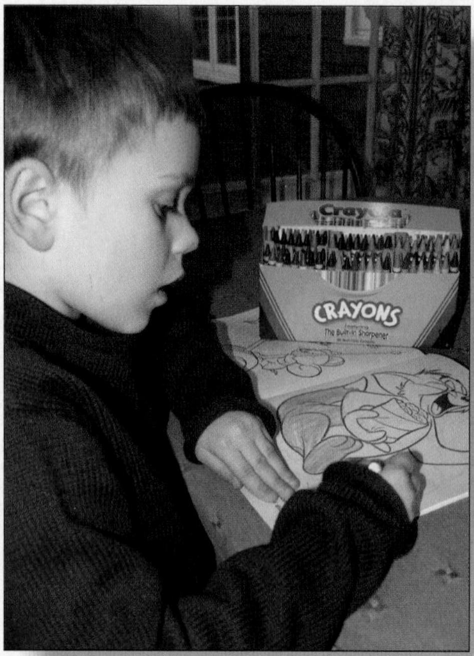

© Susan Van Etten

But a brand is more than *just* a name, term, symbol, and so on. A brand is everything that one company's particular offering stands for in comparison to other brands in a product category. A brand represents a set of values that its marketers, senior company officials, and other employees consistently embrace and communicate for an extended period.[4] For example, Volvo is virtually synonymous with safety; Crayola crayons stand for fun; Absolut vodka encapsulates hipness; Harley-Davidson embodies freedom and rugged individualism (see *IMC Focus*); Sony represents high quality and dependability; Chanel No. 5 means eloquence; Toyota's Prius personifies environmental consciousness; and Rolex watches represent master craftsmanship and sophistication. Each of these brands has embraced and communicated a particular set of values. All of these brands possess high equity because consumers believe these brands have the ability and willingness to deliver on their brand promises.[5]

The concept of *brand equity* can be considered both from the perspective of the organization that owns a brand and from the vantage point of the customer. We will devote more discussion to brand equity from the customer perspective, but it will be useful to initially examine the concept from the standpoint of the marketing organization that owns a brand.

A Firm-Based Perspective on Brand Equity

The firm-based viewpoint of brand equity focuses on outcomes extending from efforts to enhance a brand's *value* to its various stakeholders. As the value, or equity, of a brand increases, various positive outcomes result. These include (1) achieving a higher market share, (2) increasing brand loyalty, (3) being able to charge premium prices, and (4) earning a revenue premium.[6] The first two outcomes are straightforward and require no further discussion. Simply put, higher-equity brands earn greater levels of customer loyalty and achieve higher market shares. The third outcome, being able to charge premium prices, means that a brand's elasticity of demand becomes less elastic as its equity increases. Phrased differently, brands with more equity can charge higher prices than brands with less equity. Consider household brands of paint, such as the Sears brand versus the Martha Stewart or Ralph Lauren brands. The quality differential between the Sears brand and the designer brands likely is considerably less than is the premium-price differential that the designer brands command. This price differential is brand equity in action.

The fourth outcome, namely, earning a revenue premium, is an especially interesting result of achieving higher levels of brand equity. **Revenue premium** is defined as the revenue differential between a branded item and a corresponding private-labeled item. With revenue equaling the product of a brand's net price × volume, a branded good enjoys a revenue premium over a corresponding private-label item to the degree it can charge a higher price and/or generate greater sales volume. In equation form, the revenue premium for brand *b* compared to a corresponding private-label item, *pl,* is as follows:

$$\text{(2.1)} \quad \textbf{Revenue premium}_b = (\textbf{volume}_b)(\textbf{price}_b) - (\textbf{volume}_{pl})(\textbf{price}_{pl})$$

It has been demonstrated that grocery brands possessing higher equity generate higher revenue premiums. In turn, there is a strong positive correlation between the revenue premiums brands enjoy and the market shares they realize.[7] The ability to charge higher prices and generate greater sales volume is due in large part to marcom efforts that build favorable images for well-known brands. In other words, many private-label brands—which are items that carry the names of retail outlets—possess levels of quality that are equivalent to manufacturers' national brands; nevertheless, many consumers prefer the more expensive national brands and buy them regularly rather than purchasing less expensive private brands. These national brands thus enjoy a revenue premium because they possess higher equity, which is a tribute to effective marcom efforts.

Finally, another form of firm-based brand equity is somewhat akin to the notion of revenue premium just described. We might label this unique form "taste-premium" brand equity. Only a single published study has documented this unique form of equity, so it would be inappropriate to treat this distinctive type of brand equity with the same stature as the four well-established forms that were previously described.

The fast-food chain McDonald's was the focus of a study involving the taste perceptions of a sample of preschool children from low-income backgrounds.[8] The study design had the children taste two versions each of five products (hamburger, chicken nugget, french fries, milk/apple juice, and carrot). In one version (the McDonald's-packaging version), each product was presented to the preschool children in a package with McDonald's packaging graphics. In the second version (the plain-white-packaging version), the same products were presented in packages absent McDonald's identification. (Note that this plain-white version might be roughly equated with the private-label brands in the case of the revenue-premium form of brand equity.) With the exception of carrots, which are not sold at McDonald's restaurants, all other items were actual McDonald's products,

table 2.1

Children's Taste Preferences (In percents)

Food or Drink Item	Preferred McDonald's Version	Thought the Two Versions Tasted the Same or Gave No Answer	Preferred the Plain-white Version	P-value*
Hamburger	48.3%	15.0%	36.7%	.33
Chicken nugget	59.0	23.0	18.0	<.001
French fries	76.7	10.0	13.3	<.001
Milk or apple juice	61.3	17.7	21.0	<.001
Carrot	54.1	23.0	23.0	.006

*The probability level based on a test of significant difference among the percentages. P-values of .05 or less are conventionally considered statistically significant.

regardless of whether they were presented to the children in McDonald's packages or in the plain-white packages. After tasting both versions of each product, the preschoolers were instructed to indicate whether they (1) had no preference between the two versions, (2) preferred the taste of the McDonald's version, or (3) preferred the taste of the plain-white version. It is important to note that research assistants didn't actually ask children whether they preferred the McDonald's version or the plain-white version, but rather simply had them identify which item they liked more, the food/drink located on the left or right side of the tray on which the two versions were placed.

Table 2.1 presents study results in terms of three percentages for each of the five products: (1) the percentage of children who considered the food/drink item with the McDonald's packaging to taste the best, (2) the percentage who thought the two versions tasted the same or gave no answer when asked "Tell me if they taste the same, or point to the food (drink) that tastes the best to you," and (3) the percentage who considered the food/drink item in the plain-white packaging to taste the best.

The percentages in Table 2.1 make it clear that the participating preschoolers preferred the taste of all five food and drink items when they were tasted in the context of McDonald's packaging graphics over the identical food/drink items when tasted in the context of plain-white packaging graphics. The percentage of children preferring McDonald's french fries was a whopping 76.7 percent. Even for carrots, which is not a McDonald's menu item, 54.1 percent considered the sampled carrot better tasting when it was served in a McDonald's package versus the 23.0 percent who preferred the carrot when served in a plain-white package.

These results convincingly indicate brand equity in action. Simply placing products in well-identified McDonald's packaging led children to regard these items to be superior tasting in comparison to identical items in plain-white packages. Moreover, additional analyses revealed that preference for the McDonald's (versus plain-white) version of the food/drink items was especially strong among those children who lived in homes with more television sets and who more frequently ate food from McDonald's. As will be indicated in the following section on consumer-based brand equity, these results demonstrate the role that the speak-for-itself and message-driven approaches play in enhancing a brand's equity.

A Customer-Based Perspective on Brand Equity

From the perspective of the customer—whether a B2B customer or a B2C consumer—a brand possesses equity to the extent that people are familiar with the brand and have stored in memory favorable, strong, and unique brand associations.[9] **Associations** (or, more technically, mental associations) are the particular thoughts and feelings that consumers have linked in memory with a particular brand, much in the same fashion that we hold in memory thoughts and feelings about other people. For example, what thoughts/feelings come immediately to mind when you think of your best friend? You undoubtedly associate your friend with certain features, strengths, and perhaps frailties. Likewise, brands are linked in our memories with specific thought-and-feeling associations.[10]

Another way of thinking about brand equity is that it consists of two forms of brand-related knowledge: *brand awareness* and *brand image.* Subsequent coverage of customer-based brand equity describes in detail each of these two aspects of brand knowledge and builds the discussion around Figure 2.1. It will be useful before reading on to thoroughly examine this figure.

Brand Awareness

Brand awareness is an issue of whether a brand name comes to mind when consumers think about a particular product category and the ease with which the name is evoked. Stop reading for a moment and consider all the brands of toothpaste that come immediately to your mind.

For students in the United States, Crest and Colgate probably came to mind immediately, because these brands are the market share leaders among American brands of toothpaste. Perhaps you also thought of Aquafresh, Mentadent, and Arm & Hammer insofar as these brands also obtain a large share of toothpaste purchases. But did you consider Close-Up, Pepsodent, or Aim? Maybe so; probably not. These brands are not as widely known or frequently purchased as are their more successful counterparts. As such, they have lower levels of awareness than, say, Colgate and Crest. Now repeat the same exercise for brands of athletic

Figure 2.1

A Customer-Based Brand Equity Framework

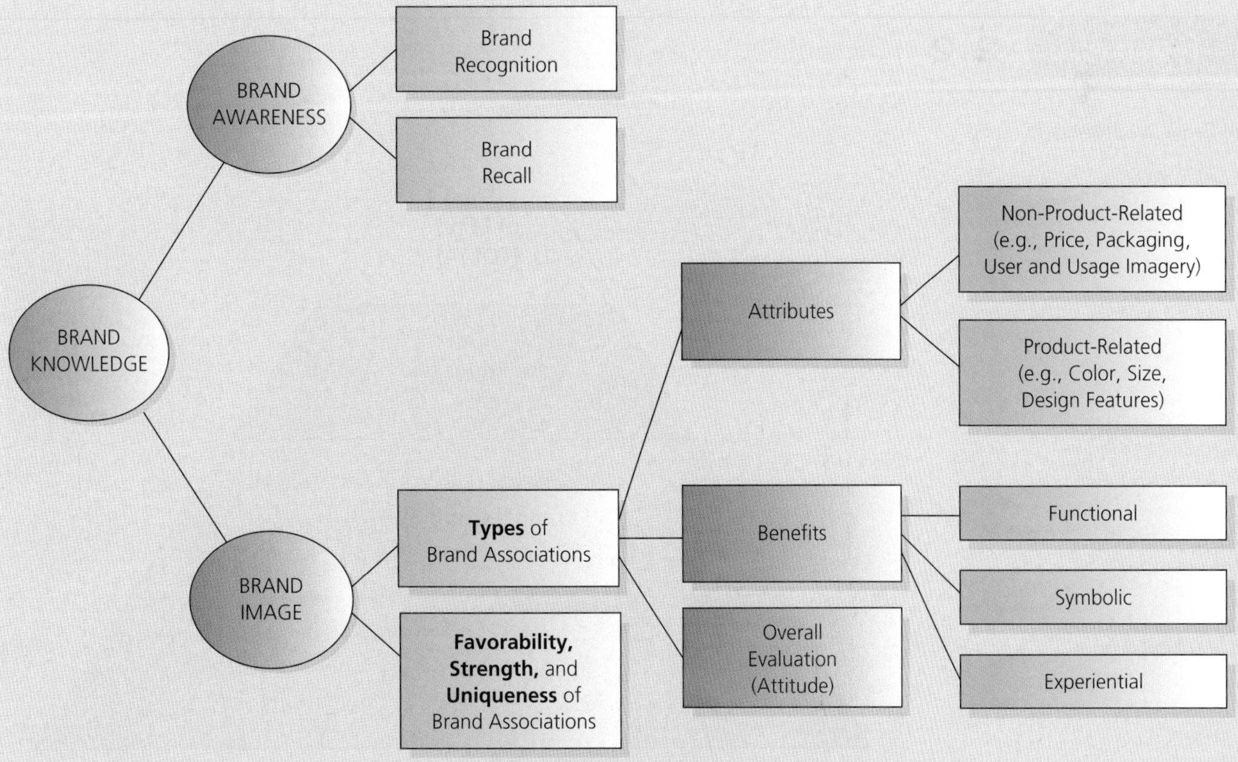

Source: Adapted from Kevin Lane Keller, "Conceptualizing, Measuring, and Managing Customer-Based Brand Equity," *Journal of Marketing* 57 (January 1993), 7.

footwear. Your short list probably contains Nike, Reebok, Adidas, and maybe New Balance. What about K-Swiss, Vans, Converse, Puma, and Asics? Again, these latter brands possess lower levels of awareness for most people and, as such, have less equity vis-à-vis a brand such as Nike.

Brand awareness is the basic dimension of brand equity. From the vantage point of an individual consumer, a brand has no equity unless the consumer is at least aware of the brand. Achieving brand awareness is the initial challenge for new brands. Maintaining high levels of brand awareness is the task faced by all established brands.

Figure 2.1 shows two levels of awareness: brand recognition and recall. *Brand recognition* reflects a relatively superficial level of awareness, whereas *brand recall* indicates a deeper form. Consumers may be able to identify a brand if it is presented to them on a list or if hints/cues are provided. However, fewer consumers are able to retrieve a brand name from memory without any reminders. It is this deeper level of awareness—brand recall—to which marketers aspire. Through effective and consistent marcom efforts, some brands are so well known that virtually every living person of normal intelligence can recall the brand. For example, if asked to mention names of luxury automobiles, most people would include Mercedes-Benz on the list. Asked to name brands of athletic footwear, most people would mention Nike, Reebok, and perhaps Adidas.

The marcom imperative is to move brands from a state of unawareness, to recognition, on to recall, and ultimately to top-of-mind awareness (TOMA). This pinnacle of brand-name awareness (i.e., TOMA status) exists when your company's brand is the first brand that consumers recall when thinking about brands in a particular product category. Figure 2.2 illustrates this brand-awareness progression, from an absence of brand awareness (unaware of brand) to TOMA status.

figure 2.2

The Brand Awareness Pyramid

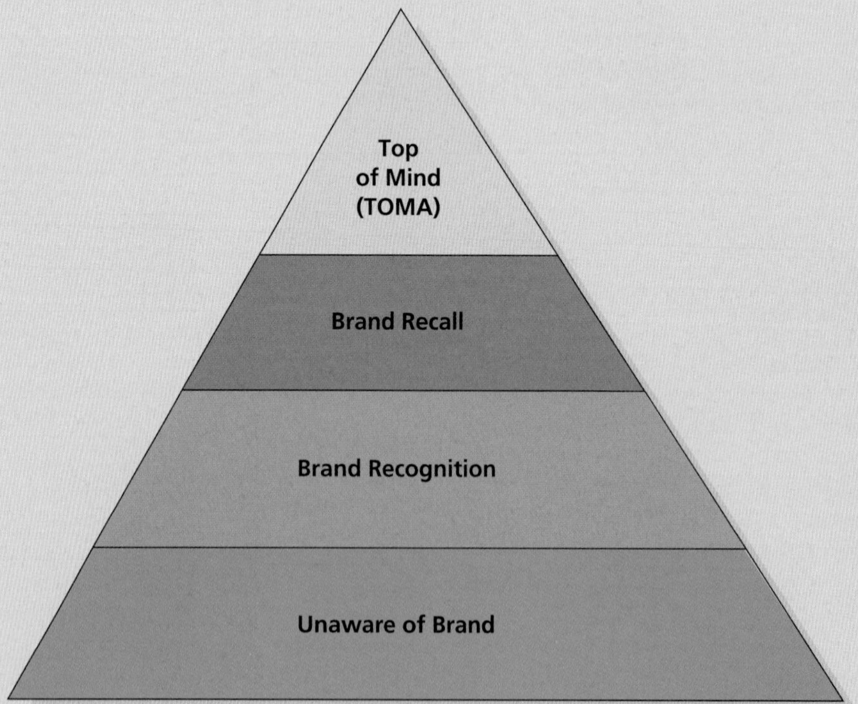

Source: David A. Aaker, *Managing Brand Equity* (New York: Free Press, 1991), 62.

Brand Image

The second di[illegible] of consumer-based brand knowledge is a brand's image. [illegible]**nage** represents the associations that are activated in mem[illegible]n people think about a particular brand. As shown in Figure 2.1, these associations can be conceptualized in terms of *type, favorability, strength,* and *uniqueness.*

© PRNewsFoto/McDonald's

To illustrate these points, it will be helpful to consider a specific brand and the associations that a particular consumer has stored in memory for this brand. (It will be instructive to refer back to Figure 2.1 before reading the following description.) Consider the case of Henry and the McDonald's fast-food chain. Now a 27-year-old college graduate living in Chicago, Henry has been eating at McDonald's since he was two years old. He can be described as a lifelong lover of fast food and of McDonald's in particular. His mouth virtually salivates (à la Pavlov's dog) when the name McDonald's is mentioned. He vividly remembers going to a McDonald's in his home town with his parents and siblings. Nothing was more enjoyable than going to their local McDonald's on a cool autumn day after raking leaves and doing other chores. Ronald McDonald, the golden arches, and the pungent smell of burgers and fries are some of the thoughts that immediately enter his mind. He especially loves McDonald's fries and considers them superior to those available in other chains. As he has become more mature and health conscious, he is especially pleased that McDonald's fries now are free of trans fats. He also likes the simple décor that is common to McDonald's. And he can't forget all of the good times that he and his high school friends had when enjoying each other's company after school or following football and basketball games. To this day Henry loves McDonald's. About the only thing he dislikes is the fact that clerks sometimes are poorly trained, inefficient, and not particularly friendly.

All of these thoughts and feelings represent *types* of associations in Henry's memory about McDonald's. All of these associations, with the exception of occasional mediocre service and rude employees, represent *favorable* links with McDonald's as far as Henry is concerned. These associations are held *strongly* in Henry's memory. Some of the associations are *unique* in comparison to other fast-food chains. Only McDonald's has golden arches and Ronald McDonald. No other fast-food chain has, in Henry's mind, fries that taste nearly as good as McDonald's.

From this illustration and in the context of the specific elements portrayed in Figure 2.1, we can see that Henry associates McDonald's with various *attributes* (e.g., golden arches) and *benefits* (e.g., great tasting fries), and that he possesses an overall favorable evaluation, or *attitude,* toward this brand. These associations for Henry are held strongly and are favorable and somewhat unique. McDonald's would love to have millions of Henrys in its market, which it undoubtedly does. To the extent that Henry is typical of other consumers, it can be said that McDonald's has high brand equity. In contrast to McDonald's, many brands have relatively little equity. This is because consumers are (1) only faintly aware of these brands or, worse yet, are completely unaware of them or (2) even if aware, do not hold strong, favorable, and unique associations about these brands.

Although a brand's image is based on a variety of associations that consumers have developed over time, brands—just like people—can be thought of as having their own unique personalities. Research has identified five personality dimensions that describe most brands: sincerity, excitement, competence, sophistication, and ruggedness.[11] That is, brands can be described as possessing some degree of each of these dimensions, ranging from "the dimension doesn't describe the brand at all" to "the dimension captures the brand's essence." For example, one brand may be regarded as high in sincerity and competence but low in sophistication, excitement, and ruggedness. Another brand may epitomize sophistication and excitement but be regarded as lacking in all other dimensions.

© B.M.Uz / Alamy

The five brand-related personality dimensions are described and illustrated as follows. Bear in mind that each illustration attempts to capture a single personality dimension when in fact brands, like people, are multifaceted with respect to their personality characteristics.

1. **Sincerity**—This dimension includes brands that are perceived as being down-to-earth, honest, wholesome, and cheerful. Sincerity is precisely the personality that Disney has imbued in its brand.
2. **Excitement**—Brands scoring high on the excitement dimension are perceived as daring, spirited, imaginative, and up-to-date. The Apple iPhone perhaps epitomized this personality dimension when it was introduced in 2007 amid much fanfare and even consumer frenzy, as purchasers sought to be among the first to own this unique cell phone.

© Stefan Sollfors / Alamy

3. **Competence**—Brands scoring high on this personality dimension are considered reliable, intelligent, and successful. In the automobile category, few brands are perceived as more competent than Toyota. Toyotas are not particularly exciting or rugged, but consumers regard them as reliable and competent. J.D. Power, an organization that surveys automobile owners to assess levels of satisfaction, annually reports that Toyota is at or near the top of satisfaction ratings. This, of course, is due to the brand's overall success and reliability.
4. **Sophistication**—Brands that are considered upper class and charming score high on the sophistication

dimension. Luxury automobiles, jewelry items, expensive perfume, and high-end kitchen appliances are just some of the many product categories that include brands that score high on the sophistication scale. In the jewelry category, for example, Rolex and Cartier are well-known sophisticated brands.

5. **Ruggedness**—Rugged brands are thought of as tough and outdoorsy. L.L. Bean and Patagonia typify retailers that offer brands regarded as rugged and outdoorsy. In the automobile category, the Honda Element, with its appeal to young, outdoor-oriented consumers, is another example of a brand that would score high on the ruggedness dimension.

© John-Mark Odero / Alamy

Enhancing Brand Equity

In general, efforts to enhance a brand's equity are accomplished through the initial choice of positive brand identity (that is, via the selection of a good brand name and logo) but mostly through marketing and marcom programs that forge favorable, strong, and unique associations with the brand in the consumer's mind. It is impossible to overstate the importance of efforts to enhance a brand's equity. Brands that are high in quality and represent good value potentially possess high equity, but effective and consistent marcom efforts are needed to build on and maintain brand equity.

A favorable brand image does not happen automatically. Sustained marketing communications are generally required to create favorable, strong, and perhaps unique associations about the brand. For example, it could be claimed that one of the world's greatest brands, Coca-Cola, is little more than colored sugar water. This brand nevertheless possesses immense brand equity because its managers are ever mindful of the need for continual advertising executions that sustain the Coca-Cola story and build the image around the world. In the United States alone, the Coca-Cola Company in a recent year commanded 43 percent of the carbonated soft-drink market, which totals over $50 billion in revenue. Coke Classic (Coke) held an individual brand share of nearly 18 percent, whereas its nearest competitor, Pepsi, had about an 11 percent share.[12] Consumers don't buy this "colored sugar water" merely for its taste; they instead purchase a lifestyle and an image when selecting Coke over other available brands. It is effective advertising, exciting sales promotions, creative sponsorships, and other forms of marketing communications that are responsible for Coca-Cola's positive image and massive market share. Coca-Cola outperforms Pepsi not

Rolex Watch U.S.A., Inc.

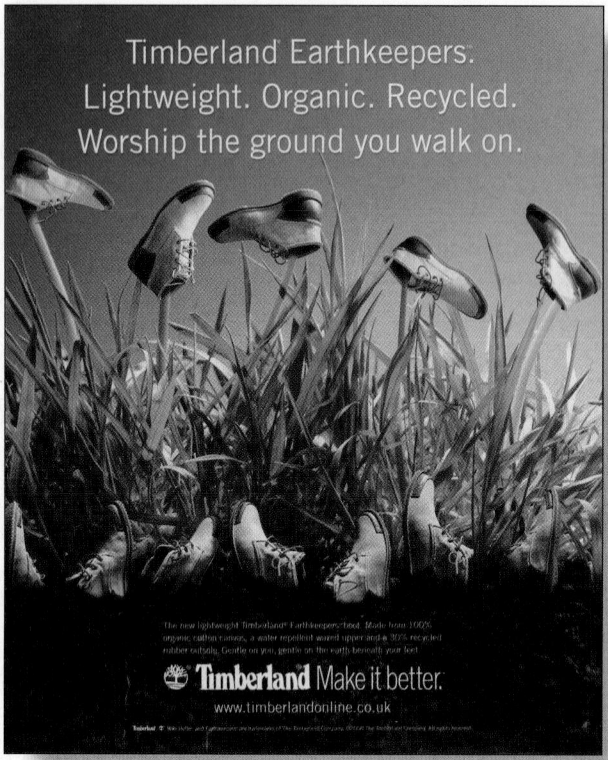

Image courtesy of The Advertising Archives

because Coke is necessarily a better tasting product, but because it has developed a more positive image with greater numbers of consumers. For a fascinating review of evidence supporting this contention, read the *IMC Focus* insert and its discussion of a new technology called neuroscience and its application in commerce, where it is referred to as neuromarketing.

What actions can be taken to enhance a brand's equity? Because a brand's equity is a function of the favorability, strength, and uniqueness of associations held in consumers' memories—as previously detailed in the context of Figure 2.1—the simple answer is to forge stronger, more favorable, and unique associations. But this begs the question of how this is to be accomplished. In actuality, associations are created in a variety of ways, some of which are initiated by marketers (e.g., via advertising) and others that are not.[13] The following discussion identifies three ways by which brand equity may be enhanced and labels these the (1) speak-for-itself approach, (2) message-driven approach, and (3) leveraging approach.

Enhancing Equity by Having a Brand Speak for Itself

As consumers, we often try brands without having much, if any, advance knowledge about them. Consumers form favorable (or perhaps unfavorable) brand-related associations merely by consuming a brand absent any significant brand knowledge prior to the usage experience. In effect, the brand "speaks for itself" in informing consumers of its quality, desirability, and suitability for satisfying their consumption-related goals. Consumers learn how good (or bad) brands are and what benefits they are capable (or incapable) of delivering by trying and using the products. It is apparent that in the speak-for-itself approach, marketing communicators play a limited role other than by, perhaps, creating attractive point-of-purchase materials or appealing sales promotions that motivate consumers to try a brand.

Enhancing Equity by Creating Appealing Messages

Marcom practitioners in their various capacities can build (or attempt to build) positive brand-related associations via the dint of repeated claims about the features a brand possesses and the benefits it delivers. This type of brand-equity-building can be thought of as the "message-driven approach." Such an approach is effective if marcom messages are creative, attention getting, believable, and memorable. Needless to say, the speak-for-itself and message-driven approaches need not be independent; that is, consumers' associations related to a particular brand result both from what they've learned firsthand about a brand through usage and what they've acquired through exposure to the brand's marcom messages.

Enhancing Equity via Leveraging

A third equity-building strategy that increasingly is being used is "leveraging."[14] Brand associations can be shaped and equity enhanced by having a brand tie into, or leverage, positive associations that already are contained in the world of people, places, and things. That is, the culture and social systems in which consumers learn about brands and how marketing communications take place are loaded with

IMC >> i.m.c. focus

Neuromarketing and the Case of Why Coca-Cola Outsells Pepsi

Coca-Cola (Coke) and Pepsi are two well-known carbonated beverages that have been marketed for over 100 years. These brands have been locked in fierce battles for decades, described sometimes as "the cola wars." One sensational battle began in 1975 when Pepsi sponsored a national taste test to determine which brand, Coke or Pepsi, was regarded as better tasting. Following this testing, Pepsi undertook an advertising campaign (called the "Pepsi Challenge") that directly compared Pepsi with Coke and claimed the research evidence (i.e., so-called "blind" taste tests) revealed that consumers prefer Pepsi over Coke. If in fact Pepsi is a better tasting beverage than Coke, why is Coca-Cola the higher selling and more popular beverage? For an answer, let's enter the world of neuromarketing and the technology of brain imaging.

Neuromarketing is a specific application of the field of brain research called neuroscience. Neuroscientists study activation of the brain to outside stimuli with the use of brain scanning machines that take functional magnetic resonance images (fMRIs) when individuals visually or otherwise employ their senses upon exposure to stimuli.[16] Brain scans with fMRI machines reveal which areas of the brain are most activated in response to external stimuli. With this brief description in mind, we can describe research conducted by a neuroscientist at the Baylor College of Medicine in Texas, research that might be described as the "21st Century Pepsi Challenge."

The scientist, Read Montague, performed this newfangled Pepsi Challenge by scanning the brains of 40 study participants after they tasted intermittent squirts of Pepsi and Coke. When "blind" as to which brand they were tasting, Pepsi came out the clear winner. That is, the reward center of the brain, the ventral putamen, revealed a much stronger preference for Pepsi versus Coke when study participants were unaware of which brand they had tasted. However, this result flip-flopped when Montague altered the testing procedure by telling participants the name of the brand they were about to taste. Now a different region of the brain was more activated and Coca-Cola was the winner in this nonblind taste test. In particular, activation in the medial prefrontal cortex—an area of the brain associated with cognitive functions such as thinking, judging, preference, and self-image—revealed that participants now preferred Coke. In short, with blind taste tests, Pepsi was the winner. With nonblind tests, Coke prevailed. What's going on?

The apparent answer is a difference in brand images, with Coke possessing the more attractive image earned through years of effective marketing and advertising effort. When participants knew they were tasting Coke, their preference for that brand was mediated by past experiences and positive associations of the brand matching their self-images—as reflected in the activation of the medial prefrontal cortex. When clueless of brand identity, the "raw" reward center of the brain, the ventral putamen, revealed Pepsi to be the winner, presumably because it is a somewhat better tasting soft drink. Most interesting is the fact that Coca-Cola's marcom efforts have enabled that brand to rise to the top. Past ad campaigns such as "It's the Real Thing," "I'd Like to Buy the World a Coke," and "Have a Coke and a Smile" have possibly resonated more positively with consumers than has Pepsi's marketing, which has concentrated more on aligning that brand with, as it turned out, ill-advised celebrities such as Michael Jackson and Britney Spears. In sum, this "21st century Pepsi Challenge" further demonstrates the importance of effective marcom efforts and the role that a positive brand image plays in determining brand equity and influencing consumer choices.

SOURCES: Edwin Colyer, "The Science of Branding," *Brandchannel*, March 15, 2004, http://brandchannel.com. (accessed March 22, 2004); Clive Thompson, "There's a Sucker Born in Every Medial Prefrontal Cortex," *The New York Times*, October 26, 2003, http://rickross.com (accessed July 20, 2004); David Wahlberg, "Advertisers Probe Brains, Raise Fears," *The Atlanta Journal-Constitution*, February 1, 2004, http://cognitiveliberty.org (accessed July 20, 2004); Melani Wells, "In Search of the Buy Button," *Forbes.com*, September 1, 2003, http://forbes.com (accessed July 20, 2004); "The Cola Wars: Over a Century of Cola Slogans, Commercials, Blunders, and Coups," http://geocities.com/colacentury (accessed July 21, 2004).

meaning. Through socialization, people learn cultural values, form beliefs, and become familiar with the physical manifestations, or artifacts, of these values and beliefs. The artifacts of culture are charged with meaning, which is transferred from generation to generation. For example, the Lincoln Memorial and Ellis Island are signs of freedom to Americans. To Germans and many other people throughout the world, the now-crumbled Berlin Wall signified oppression and hopelessness. Comparatively, yellow ribbons signify crises and hopes for hostage release and the safe return of military personnel. Pink ribbons signal support for breast cancer victims. Red ribbons have grown into an international symbol of solidarity on AIDS. The Black Liberation flag with its red, black, and green stripes—representing blood, achievement, and the fertility of Africa—symbolizes civil rights.

Marketing communicators draw meaning from the *culturally constituted* world (i.e., the everyday world filled with signs and artifacts such as the preceding examples) and transfer that meaning to consumer goods. Marketing communicators engage in *meaning transfer* when they connect a consumer good with a representation of the culturally constituted world. "The known properties of the culturally constituted world thus come to reside in the unknown properties of the consumer good and the transfer of meaning from world to [consumer] good is accomplished."[15]

Stated alternatively, this account says that marketing communicators *leverage* meaning and create associations for their brands by connecting them with other objects that already possess well-known meaning. Figure 2.3 portrays how brands leverage associations by forming connections with (1) other brands, (2) places, (3) things, and (4) people. There are numerous ways for leveraging favorable brand associations, and Figure 2.3 is a good starting point for appreciating these options. (It will be beneficial to study Figure 2.3 before reading on.)

Figure 2.3

Leveraging Brand Meaning from Various Sources

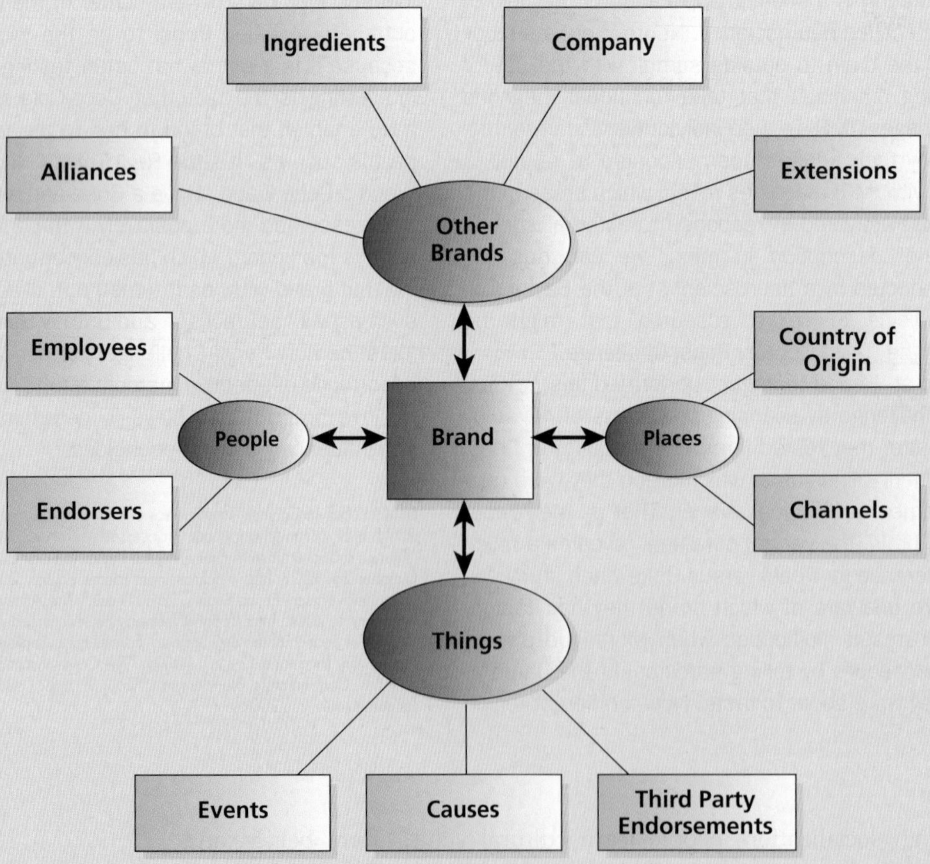

Source: Kevin Lane Keller, "Brand Synthesis: The Multidimensionality of Brand Knowledge," *Journal of Consumer Research* 29 (March 2003), 598. By permission of the University of Chicago Press.

© Susan Van Etten

Leveraging Associations from other Brands Among other forms of leveraging, Figure 2.3 shows how a brand can leverage associations from *other brands.* In recent years two brands often enter into an alliance that potentially serves to enhance both brands' equity and profitability. You need only look at your bank card (e.g., Visa) to see that it likely carries the name of an organization such as your college or university. The two have entered into an alliance, or a co-branding relation, for their mutual benefit. Your college or university perhaps aligns itself with other organizations by naming academic buildings and athletic facilities for the organization that provides financial support.

Examples of branding alliances are virtually endless, many of which you have observed as an everyday participant in the marketplace. The common theme is that brands entering into alliances do so on grounds that their images are similar, that they appeal to the same market segment, and that the co-branding initiative is mutually beneficial. The most important requirement for successful co-branding is that brands possess a *common fit* and that the combined marcom efforts maximize the advantages of the individual brands while minimizing the disadvantages.[17] It has been demonstrated that alliances are most effective when both partners experience increased equity from forming a partnership.[18]

Ingredient branding is a special type of alliance between branding partners. For example, Lycra, a brand of spandex from DuPont, initiated a multimillion-dollar global advertising effort to increase consumer ownership of jeans made with Lycra. Along the lines of the "Intel Inside" campaign, Lycra's advertising featured Lycra jeans by Levi Strauss, Diesel, DKNY, and other jean manufacturers. DuPont began this campaign in an effort to differentiate itself from cheaper unbranded spandex from Asia.[19] Other well-known instances of ingredient branding include various ski-wear brands that prominently identify the Gore-Tex fabric from which they are made and cookware makers that tout the fact that their skillets and other cookware items are made with DuPont's Teflon nonstick coating. Although ingredient branding is in many instances beneficial for both the ingredient and "host" brands, a potential downside for the host brand is that the equity of the ingredient brand might be so great that it overshadows the host brand. This situation would arise, for example, if skiers knew that their ski jacket was made of Gore-Tex fabric but they had no awareness of the company that actually manufactured the jacket.

Leveraging Associations from People Beyond leveraging a brand's image by associating itself with another brand, Figure 2.3 points out that a brand can leverage its equity by aligning itself with *people,* such as its own employees or endorsers. A later chapter discusses the role of endorsers in detail, so nothing more will be said at this time other than to note that brand associations with endorsers can be fabulously successful (think Michael Jordan and Gatorade) or potentially disastrous (think Michael Vick after his indictment on dog-fighting charges and the brands that dropped their relationships with hot-potato haste—Nike, Reebok, the trading card company Upper Deck, and Rawlings).

Leveraging Associations from Things Other forms of leveraging include associating a brand with *things* such as events (e.g., sponsorship of the World Cup soccer championship) and causes (e.g., sponsorship of a save-Darfur rally). Again, no further discussion is devoted to these topics at this point given that Chapter 19 describes these forms of association in depth.

Leveraging Associations from Places Finally, a brand's equity can be leveraged by being associated with *places* such as the channel in which a brand is distributed or a country image (labeled country of origin in Figure 2.3). Imagine, for example, the difference in a brand's image—holding everything else constant, such as product quality and price—if a brand were carried in a mass merchandise store, such as Wal-Mart, compared to being distributed in a high-end department store. In which store would the brand be regarded more positively?

Leveraging a brand by emphasizing its *country of origin* is a potentially effective way to enhance the brand's equity.[20] For example, brands with German and Swiss heritage often are perceived around the globe as being high in craftsmanship. Japanese electronic products are regarded as unparalleled in innovativeness, quality, and dependability.

How important is a brand's country of origin in affecting its brand equity and determining its commercial success? Frankly, there is no simple answer and the research on this issue is mixed.[21] No doubt, some consumer segments place greater importance on a brand's country of origin than do others. Older consumers, for example, are generally more concerned with where a brand comes from than are their more youthful counterparts, who are more comfortable living in a global world and buying products based on considerations other than where they are made. In fact, research has shown that American college students are somewhat clueless as to where the brands they consume originate.[22] For example, just 4.4 percent of 1,000 students knew that Nokia cell phones are made in Finland (53 percent thought Nokia to be Japanese), and just 8.9 percent knew LG cell phones are from Korea. Nearly 50 percent thought that Adidas clothing is from the United States rather than its true home country, Germany. Motorola, a long-established American brand, was misperceived to be Japanese by more than 40 percent of respondents.

When a brand leverages its country of origin, the potential exists for the brand to benefit from this association or possibly to suffer if the country is perceived in a less than positive light. It obviously is in brand marketers' best interest that their countries of origin are perceived favorably. The *Global Focus* insert provides a look at how the world perceives the United States.

What Benefits Result from Enhancing Brand Equity?

One major by-product of efforts to increase a brand's equity is that consumer *brand loyalty* might also increase.[24] Indeed, long-term growth and profitability are largely dependent on creating and reinforcing brand loyalty. The following quote from two respected marketing practitioners sums up the nature and importance of brand loyalty:

> *While marketers have long viewed brands as assets, the real asset is brand loyalty. A brand is not an asset. Brand loyalty is the asset. Without the loyalty of its customers, a brand is merely a trademark, an ownable, identifiable symbol with little value. With the loyalty of its customers, a brand is more than a trademark. A trademark identifies a product, a service, a corporation. A brand identifies a promise. A strong brand is a trustworthy, relevant, distinctive promise. It is more than a trademark. It is a trustmark of enormous value. Creating and increasing brand loyalty results in a corresponding increase in the value of the trustmark.*[25]

Research has shown that when firms communicate unique and positive messages via advertising, personal selling, promotions, events, and other means, they are able to differentiate their brands effectively from competitive offerings and insulate themselves from future price competition.[26]

Marketing communications plays an essential role in creating positive brand equity and building strong brand loyalty. However, this is not always accomplished with traditional advertising or other conventional forms of marketing

global focus

The World's Perception of America

Strange as it may seem, nations themselves can be thought of as brands. That is, people form mental associations of nations that are equivalent to "brand" images. Firms marketing their products under the banner—the country of origin—of a particular nation are thus affected by how positive or negative that country's image is. Many countries actively market themselves with the goal of forging favorable and strong associations in the minds of people around the world. Regardless of whether a country actively markets itself, however, people nevertheless form associations based on that county's business climate, its international relations, its attractiveness as a tourist location, and so on.

A British market research firm has developed a Nations Brand Index (NBI) as a barometer of global opinion toward a large number of countries around the globe.[23] Each business quarter the NBI researchers poll over 25,000 people around the world on their perceptions of over 35 countries. Survey respondents are asked questions about each country in six areas:

1. **Exports**—their level of satisfaction with products and services produced in that country.
2. **People**—their thoughts and feelings about the people in the country based on questions such as "How much would you like to have a close friend from [name of country]?"
3. **Governance**—their perceptions of whether the country can be trusted to make responsible decisions and to uphold international peace and security.
4. **Tourism**—their perceptions of a country's natural beauty and historical heritage and the likelihood of visiting the country if money were no obstacle.
5. **Culture and Heritage**—their perceptions of a country's cultural heritage and feelings about its contemporary culture, such as its music, art and literature, sporting excellence, and film quality.
6. **Immigration and Investment**—their willingness to live and work in a country for an extended period and their perceptions of whether the country would be a good place to pursue further education.

A nation's "brand" image is the sum of its scores on these six dimensions. The most recent NBI results resulted in the following set of overall rankings:

Overall ranking	Country	Overall ranking	Country	Overall ranking	Country
1	United Kingdom	15	New Zealand	29	India
2	Germany	16	Ireland	30	Mexico
3	Canada	17	Belgium	31	South Korea
4	France	18	Portugal	32	South Africa
5	Switzerland	19	Brazil	33	Tibet
6	Australia	20	Iceland	34	Turkey
7	Italy	21	Russia	35	Malaysia
8	Sweden	22	China	36	Estonia
9	Japan	23	Argentina	37	Latvia
10	Netherlands	24	Czech Republic	38	Israel
11	United States	25	Hungary	39	Indonesia
12	Spain	26	Poland	40	Iran
13	Denmark	27	Singapore		
14	Norway	28	Egypt		

SOURCE: Simon Anholt, "The Anholt Nation Brands Index Special Report, Q1 2007," http://www.nationbrandindex.com (accessed August 3, 2007).

In this version of the NBI, the United States is ranked eleventh among the 40 countries evaluated. Although the United States performs very well in four (exports, people, tourism, and investment and immigration) of the six dimensions, it suffers in the two remaining areas (cultural heritage and governance). Many people

(**Continued**)

global focus (Continued)

outside the United States regard America as relatively uncultured, and the poor performance on the governance dimension is hardly surprising given the widespread opposition to the war in Iraq, the U.S. government's recent record on treatment of enemy combatants (think Abu Ghraib and Guantanamo Bay), its saber-rattling posture toward Iran and North Korea, and so on.

A country's image, like any brand image, is not immutable but can be changed by the actions of its leaders and its people. The actions of government can be perceived by the people of another country as sensitive and respectful of their culture or arrogant and ignorant of cultural differences—thus personifying the caricature of "the ugly American" that was captured a half-century ago in a book and subsequent film with the same name. Likewise, the actions of people, when traveling internationally, can be perceived as appreciative and respectful of the countries they visit, or, instead, as boorish. In sum, it is important as a matter of international relations and economics that a country have a positive image. Each of us has a role to play in this regard by the people we choose to lead us and by the behavior we display when traveling abroad.

communications. For example, Starbucks, the virtual icon for upscale coffee, does very little advertising, yet this brand has a near cult-like following. Nevertheless, Starbuck's chairman voiced concern that efforts to grow sales and profits—e.g., introducing breakfast items in some stores and replacing conventional espresso makers with automatic machines—may have damaged Starbuck's reputation for providing a unique consumption experience.[27]

An ex-CEO and chairman of PepsiCo provides us with a fitting section conclusion in the following implicit description of the importance of that company's efforts to build the equity of its brands:

> *In my mind the best thing a person can say about a brand is that it's their favorite. That implies something more than simply they like the package, or the taste. It means they like the whole thing—the company, the image, the value, the quality, and on and on. So as we think about the measurements of our business, if we're only looking at this year's bottom line and profits, we're missing the picture. We should be looking at market share, but also at where we stand vis-à-vis our competitors in terms of consumer awareness and regard for our brands. You always know where you stand in the [profit and loss statement] because you see it every month. But what you need to know, with almost the same sense of immediacy, is where you stand with consumers and your customers.*[28]

Characteristics of World-Class Brands

Some brands have such exceptional brand equity that they deserve the label "world class." The well-known EquiTrend survey by the market research firm Harris Interactive is conducted biannually and includes responses from more than 25,000 consumers who collectively, not individually, rate over 1,000 brands. Each respondent evaluates each of 80 brands in terms of (1) whether he or she is *familiar* with the brand, (2) how good the brand's *quality* is, and (3) whether he or she would *consider purchasing* the brand. These three scores then are combined to form a *brand equity* score for each brand, with a theoretical range from zero to 100.[29] Brands receiving high equity scores are well known, perceived as high quality, and are likely purchase candidates.

The most recent EquiTrend survey reveals the 10 brands in Table 2.2 as the overall highest equity brands. Many of these brands regularly appear in EquiTrend's top-10 rankings. Brands that receive high equity scores based on EquiTrend's measure tend to make straightforward promises to consumers and deliver on these promises over extended periods. In short, these brands possess high brand equity because they are well known and possess strong and favorable associations in consumers' memories.

table 2.2

Top Ten World-Class Brands Overall (Among 1,030 total brands included in EquiTrend's Spring 2006 survey)

Brand	Rank	Equity Score
Reynolds Wrap Aluminum Foil	1	80.8
Ziploc Food Bags	2	79.1
Hershey's Milk Chocolate Bars	3	78.1
Kleenex Facial Tissues	4	78.0
Clorox Bleach	5	78.0
WD-40 Spray Lubricant	6	77.7
Heinz Ketchup	7	77.5
Ziploc Containers	8	77.2
Windex Glass Cleaner	9	76.9
Campbell's Soups	10	76.6

Source: Spring 2006 EquiTrend brand study by Harris Interactive, http://www.harrisinteractive.com/news/allnewsbydate.asp?NewsID=1063 (accessed July 26, 2007).

Another brand-ranking analysis is undertaken annually by Interbrand, which ranks the 100 top global brands.[30] Its brand-ranking method is based on calculating (1) the percentage of a company's revenue that can be credited to a brand, (2) the strength of a brand in terms of influencing customer demand at the point of purchase, and (3) the ability of the brand to secure continued customer demand as a result of brand loyalty and repurchase likelihood. Only those brands that provide public financial data (thus excluding private companies) and that secure at least one third of their revenues from international operations are potential candidates for inclusion in Interbrand's rankings of "best global brands." This latter factor accounts for why some of the brands included in Table 2.2, which consists entirely of American brands, are not also included in Interbrand's top-20 list. Table 2.3 lists the top 20 "best brands" based on Interbrand's analysis in one recent year.

table 2.3

Interbrand's Top 20 Global Brands, 2007

Rank	Brand	Country of Origin	Brand Value ($mil)
1	Coca-Cola	US	65,324
2	Microsoft	US	58,709
3	IBM	US	57,091
4	GE	US	51,569
5	Nokia	Finland	33,696
6	Toyota	Japan	32,070
7	Intel	US	30,954
8	McDonald's	US	29,398
9	Disney	US	29,210
10	Mercedes	Germany	23,568
11	Citi	US	23,443
12	Hewlett-Packard	US	22,197
13	BMW	Germany	21,612
14	Marlboro	US	21,283
15	American Express	US	20,827
16	Gillette	US	20,415
17	Louis Vuitton	France	20,321
18	Cisco	US	19,099
19	Honda	Japan	17,998
20	Google	US	17,837

Source: Interbrand Report, "Best Global Brands 2007," http://www.interbrand.com/best_brands_2007.asp.

Affecting Behavior and Achieving Marcom Accountability

When discussing in Chapter 1 the principles underlying IMC, one major point of emphasis was that marcom efforts should be directed, ultimately, at affecting behavior rather than merely enhancing equity. Creating brand awareness and boosting brand image serve little positive effect unless individuals ultimately make purchases or engage in some other form of desired behavior—by "behavior" we mean that the customer takes some *action* such as contributing to a charitable organization, discontinuing smoking, voting for a political candidate, staying on a diet plan, attending a concert, working on a term project rather than contemplating its start, and so on. All of these behaviors, or acts, contrast with pre-behavioral cognitions or emotions whereby one merely thinks that doing something is a good idea or feels good about the prospect of doing something. The proof of the behavioral pudding is in the *action*.

Marcom's eventual challenge is to influence behavior, whatever the nature of that behavior might be. To simplify the following discussion we will hereafter refer to behavior only in the context of business organizations rather than talking about many different forms of behavior. From this perspective, behavior essentially equates to purchase behavior. Purchase behavior is, of course, a customer-based concept (i.e., customers buy, or purchase products and services). From the marketer's standpoint, desired behavior from customers corresponds to sales volume and revenue, with revenue representing the monetized equivalent of sales volume (i.e., volume × net price = revenue). Looked at in this manner, marcom's objective is ultimately to affect sales volume and revenue.

The effect of marcom, or of its specific elements such as advertising, can thus be gauged in terms of whether it generates a reasonable revenue return on the marcom investment. This idea of return on investment, which is well known to anyone who has taken a basic course in accounting, finance, or managerial economics, is referred to in marketing circles as **return on marketing investment (ROMI).** In a world of increased accountability, as discussed in Chapter 1, it is imperative that marketing people in all capacities, including marcom practitioners, demonstrate that additional investments in, say, advertising yield returns that meet or exceed alternative applications of corporate funds. Chief executive officers (CEOs) as well as chief marketing officers (CMOs) and chief financial officers (CFOs) are increasingly asking, "What's my ROMI?" The vast majority of marketing executives consider the measurement of marketing performance an important priority, and marketing academics along with practitioners are actively involved in devising ways to measure marketing performance so as to achieve financial accountability for marketing actions.[31] Two primary motivations underlie this increased focus on measuring marketing performance, as explained in the following quote:

> *First, greater demands for accountability on the marketing function from the CEO, the Board, and other executives mandate a greater focus on measurement. For a CMO to truly command an equal seat at the executive table, a CMO must define and deliver quantitative measurements for the corporation. And these metrics must be clearly and convincingly communicated to the appropriate audiences. A second, perhaps equally important driver is the imperative for a CMO to get better at what they do. As the budget battles become more frequent and uncomfortable, a CMO can make marketing a more effective organization only by measuring and understanding what is working and what isn't.*[32]

Difficulty of Measuring Marcom Effectiveness

Though most marketing executives agree that measuring marketing performance is critically important, at the present time relatively few organizations are doing a sophisticated job. This is not because marketing executives are uninterested in determining what aspects of their marcom efforts are or are not working most effectively; rather, the problem resides with the difficulty of measuring marcom effectiveness. Several reasons account for this complexity: (1) obstacles in identifying an appropriate measure, or metric, of effectiveness; (2) complications with getting people throughout the organization to agree that a particular measure is the most appropriate; (3) snags with gathering accurate data to assess effectiveness; and (4) problems with determining the exact effect that specific marcom elements have on the measure that has been selected to indicate effectiveness.

Choosing a Metric

An initial problem is one of determining which specific measures (also called *metrics*) should be used to judge marcom effectiveness. Prior to discussing the importance of selecting the right metric(s) in a marcom context, it will be insightful to view the choice of metric in evaluating a baseball pitcher's performance. At the end of the season, how does one gauge whether a pitcher has had a successful season? One often used metric is the pitcher's won-loss record. But that metric is imperfect inasmuch as a pitcher might do well individually—say, give up only three runs on average per game—but still have a relatively mediocre win-to-loss ratio because his poor-hitting team was unable to produce many runs. Another possible metric to gauge a pitcher's performance is earned run average (ERA), which measures how many runs a pitcher is responsible for giving up during an average nine-inning game. An ERA of 6.00, for example, indicates that opposing teams averaged two thirds of a run per inning against a pitcher during a typical nine-inning game.

ERA is a useful metric, but baseball specialists use additional metrics for judging a pitcher's performance. Another metric is walks plus hits divided by innings pitched (WHIP). This metric also is flawed insofar as it counts extra-base hits (i.e., doubles, triples, and home runs) as equivalent to singles and walks.[33] For this reason a superior metric to measure pitcher performance is bases per batter, or BPB. This measure sums the number of hits and walks a pitcher has allowed during the course of a season and then adds one extra point for each double, two extra for each triple, and three extra for each homer. This sum, or grand total bases (GTB), is divided by the number of batters a pitcher has faced to yield the pitcher's BPB for the season.[34] The lower a BPB score, the better a pitcher has done in minimizing the number of bases given up to opposing teams.

This digression to baseball is relevant to marketing by establishing that regardless of what performance domain is being judged, various metrics are available; however, not all metrics are equally good for judging how well someone has performed. Let's return to the business world for additional discussion of metrics.

Consider, for example, the case of an automobile company that has increased its annual marcom budget for a particular model by 25 percent over the previous year's budget. The company will advertise this particular model using a combination of TV, magazine, and online advertising. It also will sponsor a professional golf tournament and have a presence at several other sporting and entertainment events. Moreover, it will use an attractive rebate program to encourage consumers to buy sooner rather than postpone purchases. What metric(s) should the company use to gauge the effectiveness of its marcom efforts? Possible options include changes in *brand awareness* before and after the aggressive marcom program is undertaken, improved *attitudes* toward the automobile model, increased *purchase intentions*, and larger *sales volume* compared to last year's performance. None of these options is without problems. For example, awareness is a good measure of marcom effectiveness only if increases in awareness translate in some known proportion to sales increases; likewise, improved attitudes and purchase intentions are suitable measures only if they predictably turn into increased sales in the current or subsequent accounting periods. And sales itself is an imperfect measure, since marcom efforts in the current accounting period may not improve sales volume measurably until a later period. In short, there typically is no perfect metric by which marcom effectiveness can be judged. All measures/metrics are flawed in some way, though some (such as BPB in the above baseball illustration) are superior to others (such as WHIP).

The difficulty of determining how best to measure marketing's return on investment is illustrated by a recent study that the Association of National Advertisers (ANA) conducted on its membership.[35] In response to a key question asking respondents to identify which metric is closest to their company's definition of marketing ROI, more than 15 versions of ROMI were revealed. It is evident from this study that companies differ widely in their concept of how to measure ROMI. The five metrics in most frequent usage are these: (1) incremental sales revenue generated by marketing activities (66 percent of respondents identified this metric), (2) changes in brand awareness (57 percent), (3) total sales revenue generated by marketing activities (55 percent), (4) changes in purchase intention (55 percent), and (5) changes in attitudes toward the brand (51 percent).[36] (The percentages sum to greater than 100 because some companies use multiple metrics.) It also is noteworthy that three of the leading metrics (i.e., changes in brand awareness, attitudes, and purchase intentions) do not even involve sales revenue but instead are based on pre-sales diagnostics.

Gaining Agreement

As is generally the case when intelligent people representing different organizational interests are asked to select a particular solution to a problem, consensus is lacking. This is not because people are necessarily uncooperative; rather, individuals from different backgrounds and with varied organizational interests often see their "world" differently or operate with varying ideas of what best indicates suitable performance. Whereas finance people are inclined to view things in terms of *discounted cash flows* and *net present values* of investment decisions, marketing executives have historically tended to use measures of brand awareness, image, and equity to indicate success.[37] Hence, arriving at a suitable system for measuring marcom performance requires gaining agreement from different company officials, who likely have different views regarding how performance should be assessed.

Collecting Accurate Data

Whatever the measure chosen, any effort to meaningfully assess marcom performance necessitates having data that are reliable and valid. Returning to the automobile illustration, suppose that sales volume is the metric used to judge the effectiveness of this year's marcom efforts. It would seem a simple matter to accurately assess how many units of the automobile model have been sold during the present fiscal period. However, some of the units sold this year are residual orders from last. Also, a number of the units sold are fleet sales to companies that are entirely independent of the marcom efforts directed to consumers. How sales should be calculated can also be problematic, given the difference between units sold to dealers and units moved through to end-user consumers. All in all, collecting accurate data is no slam dunk.

Calibrating Specific Effects

Our hypothetical automobile company will employ several marcom tools (various advertising media, several events, and periodic rebates) to "move" automobiles to consumers. Ultimately, brand managers and other marketing executives are interested in knowing more than just the overall effectiveness of the marcom program. They also need to identify the relative effectiveness of individual program elements in order to make better decisions in the future about how best to allocate resources. This is, perhaps, the most complicated problem of all. How much relative effect does each program element have on, say, sales volume compared to the effects of other elements? A technique called *marketing mix modeling* is increasingly being used for this purpose.

Assessing Effects with Marketing Mix Modeling

To understand and appreciate the nature and role of marketing mix modeling (MMM), let's return to our example of the automobile marketer that increased its marcom budget for a particular model by 25 percent over the previous year's budget. To advertise and promote the brand, the following marcom tools were used: (1) advertising via TV, magazine, and online media; (2) sponsorship of a professional golf tournament along with several other sporting and entertainment events; and (3) use of an attractive rebate program to encourage consumers to buy now rather than later.[38]

Each of these activities can be thought of as individual *elements* constituting the brand's marcom mix. The issue that marketing mix modeling addresses is this: what effect did each of these elements have in affecting this automobile model's sales volume in a prior period? Marketing mix modeling employs well-known econometric statistical techniques (e.g., multivariate regression analysis) to estimate the effects that the various advertising, promotion, and other marcom elements have in driving sales volume. Though it is beyond the scope of this text to offer a technical explanation of regression analysis or of other more sophisticated analytic techniques used in MMM, the conceptual underpinnings are straightforward. Let us demonstrate this approach using the following multivariate regression equation:

$$(2.2) \quad Y_i = \beta_0 + \beta_1 X_{1i} + \beta_2 X_{2i} + \beta_3 X_{3i} + \beta_4 X_{4i} + \beta_5 X_{5i} + \beta_6 X_{6i}$$

where:

Y_i = The number of automobiles sold during the period of analysis, designated as period i

X_{1i} = TV advertising expenditures (designated as element 1) during the ith period

X_{2i} = Magazine advertising expenditures (element 2) in the ith period

X_{3i} = Online advertising expenditures (element 3) in the ith period

X_{4i} = Amount spent sponsoring the golf tourney (element 4) in the ith period

X_{5i} = Amount spent sponsoring other, minor events (element 5) in the ith period

X_{6i} = Amount spent on rebates (element 6) during the ith period

β_0 = Baseline sales without any advertising or promotions

$\beta_1, \beta_2, \beta_3, \beta_4, \beta_5, \beta_6$ = Estimates of the individual effects the various advertising and promotion elements had on sales.

In order to employ marketing mix modeling, a relatively long series of longitudinal data is required. The data for each period would include the level of sales

IMC >> i.m.c. focus

Harley-Davidson—An Iron Horse for Rugged Individualists, Including Females!

Brand managers at Harley-Davidson Motor Co. ran a magazine ad several years ago that captured the essence of this company's famous motorcycles. The ad depicted a driverless Harley-Davidson motorcycle on an open road in the American West in a fashion reminiscent of a wild mustang in a similar scene. The ad's headline declared, "Even Cows Kick Down the Fence Once in a While," and was supported with copy stating:

> It's right there in front of you, Road, wind, country. A Harley-Davidson motorcycle. In other words, freedom. A chance to live on your own terms for a while ... Anyone who's been there knows: Life is better on the outside.

This advertising message was subtle but clear: if you cherish freedom, independence, and perhaps a sense of being a kindred spirit with others of like mind, then Harley-Davidson is the motorcycle for you. The cowboy spirit was encapsulated in this positioning, which tacitly equated Harley motorcycles with horses. (Harley-Davidson equals "iron horse.") Potential purchasers of Harley motorcycles probably as youngsters envisioned themselves riding horses in America's Old West.[39]

What makes Harley-Davidson motorcycles such a unique and strong brand, indeed a brand of virtual iconic status? Informed observers and students of brand marketing would suggest that Harley, more so than most brands, has a deep emotional connection with present and prospective owners.[40] As captured in the previous description of a Harley advertisement, the brand has been marketed as and has virtually become synonymous with American culture and values of personal freedom, rebelliousness, and rugged individualism.[41] Harley also has created a sense of brand community among owners of its brand, who share strong comradeship.[42] In fact, when Harley celebrated its 100th anniversary, over 250,000 individuals from around the world came to Milwaukee, Wisconsin, to participate in the big party. Needless to say, few brands anywhere in the world have such loyal and devoted followers.

An especially interesting aspect of Harley's consumer community is that it has become increasingly female—American women are a fast-growing segment of the motorcycle business, with annual purchases exceeding 100,000 cycles![43] Nearly one in eight sales of Harley motorcycles is to women, which is attributable in large part to Harley's concerted effort to appeal to the female segment. For example, its dealers hold "garage parties," organized gatherings at which dealer representatives inform women about Harley-Davidson motorcycles, appeal to their dreams of owning a motorcycle, and attempt to reduce their fears.[44]

during that period (Y_i) along with corresponding advertising, promotion, and sponsorship expenditures for each program element (X_{1i} through X_{6i}). Imagine, for example, that our hypothetical automobile company records weekly sales and has meticulous records of precisely how much is spent weekly on each advertising and promotion element for a period of two full years. Records of this sort would produce a set of 104 observations (52 weeks × 2 years), which would provide a sufficient number of observations to produce reliable parameter estimates for the various program elements.

The analytic aspect of marketing mix modeling yields statistical evidence regarding the relative effects that each program element has had in influencing sales of this particular automobile model. Managers learn from such analysis which elements are outperforming others and can use this statistical information to shift budgets from program element to element. Obviously, more effective elements would in the future receive relatively greater budgets vis-à-vis the less effective elements.

Marketing mix modeling has been used off and on for nearly a quarter century, but current use is at a high point with leading marketers such as Procter & Gamble (P&G) and the Clorox Company benefiting greatly from the use of this analytic approach. In one recent year, for example, P&G's application of MMM resulted in that firm's changing how it spent more than $400 million of its advertising and promotion budget.[45] Based on its modeling, P&G substantially increased its advertising budget. Comparatively, Clorox's use of MMM led it to shift some money away from advertising into promotions. The important point is that each application of marketing mix modeling is based on a unique set of marketing circumstances. What's good for the goose (say, P&G) is not necessarily good for the gander (say, Clorox). One solution does not, in other words, fit all.

Marketing mix modeling is widely used by consumer packaged goods (CPG) companies such as P&G and Clorox, but it also is being used increasingly by non-CPG companies in the B2C environment and also by B2B companies. Any company can employ the techniques of marketing mix modeling provided it maintains (or can purchase from syndicated sources) sales data on a period-by-period basis as well as meticulous records of its expenditures on a period-by-period basis for all of its advertising, promotion, and other marcom elements. The example we've been working with for the automobile model is actually simplistic in that a full marketing mix analysis would consider not just expenditures on, say, a particular advertising medium such as television but would disaggregate the data for specific types of TV expenditures (e.g., network TV versus cable) and even different day parts (daytime, prime time, etc.). The finer, or more disaggregated, the data, the better analysts can determine which specific marketing mix elements are most and least effective in driving sales.

Summary

This chapter discussed the nature and importance of brand equity. The concept of brand equity is described as the value in a brand resulting from high brand-name awareness and strong, favorable, and perhaps unique associations that consumers have in memory about a particular brand. Marcom efforts play an important role in enhancing brand equity. Enhanced equity, in turn, bolsters consumer brand loyalty, increases market share, differentiates a brand from competitive offerings, and permits charging relatively higher prices. The chapter also discussed the importance of not restricting the assessment of marcom performance to brand equity measures only, but of also considering whether marcom efforts have influenced behavior. By examining the effect that marcom has on behavior, it is possible to gauge financial accountability and thus better equip marketing communicators when they request increased budgets from CFOs. The technique of marketing mix modeling provides an analytic method for assessing the effectiveness of individual marcom elements and for determining how budgets should be shifted among program elements.

Discussion Questions

1. Compare and contrast the speak-for-itself and message-driven approaches to enhancing brand equity.
2. Assume that your college or university has had difficulty getting nonstudent residents in the local community to attend football games. Your school's athletic director requests that an organization you belong to (say, a local chapter of the American Marketing Association) develop an advertising program that is to be targeted to local residents to encourage them to attend football games. What measures/metrics

could you use to assess whether the advertising program you developed has been effective? How might you assess the ad campaign's ROMI?

3. Provide several examples of co-branding or ingredient branding other than those presented in the chapter.
4. Why is demonstrating accountability an imperative for marcom practitioners?
5. When discussing brand equity from the firm's perspective, it was explained that as the equity of a brand increases, various positive outcomes result: (1) a higher market share, (2) increased brand loyalty, (3) ability to charge premium prices, and (4) capacity to earn a revenue premium. Select a brand you are particularly fond of and explain how its relatively greater equity compared to a lesser brand in the same product category is manifest in terms of each of these four outcomes.
6. What does it mean to say that marketing communications should be directed, ultimately, at affecting behavior rather than merely enhancing equity? Provide an example to support your answer.
7. Provide examples of brands that in your opinion are positioned in such a way as to reflect the five personality dimensions: sincerity, excitement, competence, sophistication, and ruggedness.
8. Describe the leveraging strategy for enhancing brand equity. Take a brand of your choice and, referring to Figure 2.3, explain how that brand could build positive associations, thereby enhancing its equity, by linking itself to (a) places, (b) things, (c) people, and (d) other brands. Be specific.
9. An ex-CEO of PepsiCo was quoted in the text as saying, "In my mind the best thing a person can say about a brand is that it's their favorite." Identify two brands that you regard as your favorites. Describe the specific associations that each of these brands hold for you and thus why they are two of your favorites.
10. What are your reactions to the application of neuroscience to marketing (neuromarketing) that was described in the *IMC Focus*? Do you consider this technique ethical? Do you fear that with the knowledge obtained from its application marketers will be able to manipulate consumers?
11. Using the framework in Figure 2.1, describe all personal associations that the following brands hold for you: (a) Harley-Davidson motorcycles, (b) Hummer vehicles, (c) Red Bull energy drink, (d) *The Wall Street Journal* newspaper, (e) entertainer Paris Hilton, and (f) the Prius hybrid automobile.
12. Select a brand of vehicle (automobile, truck, motorcycle, SUV, etc.) and with this brand describe the type, favorability, strength, and uniqueness of brand associations that you hold in memory for this brand.
13. With reference to the Marketing Insight segment that opened the chapter and in view of the detailed section on brand equity later in the chapter, explain why brand awareness is a necessary but insufficient indicator of brand equity.

End Notes

1. The Harris Poll #71, Harris Interactive, July 17, 2007, http://consumerist.com/consumer/branding/coca+cola-is-the-best-brand-microsoft-beats-apple-279388.php (accessed July 25, 2007).
2. Matthew Creamer, "Is Your Brand the Best? What Polls Really Mean," *Advertising Age*, July 23, 2007, 1.
3. Statement made by Terry O'Connor as cited in Bob Lamons, "Brand Power Moves BASF Past Commodity," *Marketing News*, March 15, 2004, 6.
4. Jacques Chevron, "Unholy Grail: Quest for the Best Strategy," *Brandweek*, August 11, 2003, 20.
5. Brand credibility includes dimensions of expertise, or ability, and trustworthiness, or willingness to consistently deliver on brand promises. See Tülin Erdem and Joffre Swait, "Brand Credibility, Brand Consideration, and Choice," *Journal of Consumer Research* 31 (June 2004), 191–198.
6. Arjun Chaudhuri and Morris B. Holbrook, "The Chain of Effects from Brand Trust and Brand Affect to Brand Performance: The Role of Brand Loyalty," *Journal of Marketing* 65 (April 2001), 90; Peter Doyle, *Value-Based Marketing: Marketing Strategies for Corporate Growth and Shareholder Value* (Chichester, England: John Wiley & Sons, 2000), 300.
7. Kusum L. Ailawadi, Donald R. Lehmann, and Scott A. Neslin, "Revenue Premium as an Outcome Measure of Brand Equity," *Journal of Marketing* 67 (October 2003), 1–17.
8. Thomas N. Robinson, Dina L. G. Borzekowski, Donna M. Matheson, and Helena C. Kraemer, "Effects of Fast

Food Branding on Young Children's Taste Preferences," *Archives of Pediatric & Adolescent Medicine* 161 (2007), 792–797.
9. Kevin Lane Keller, "Conceptualizing, Measuring, and Managing Customer-Based Brand Equity," *Journal of Marketing* 57 (January 1993), 2.
10. A useful method for identifying brand associations is available in Deborah Roedder John, Barbara Loken, Kyeongheui Kim, and Alokparna Basu Monga, "Brand Concept Maps: A Methodology for Identifying Brand Association Networks," *Journal of Marketing Research* 43 (November 2006), 549–563.
11. Jennifer L. Aaker, "Dimensions of Brand Personality," *Journal of Marketing Research* 34 (August 1997), 347–356. See also, Jennifer Aaker, Susan Fournier, and S. Adam Brasel, "When Good Brands Do Bad," *Journal of Consumer Research* 31 (June 2004), 1–16.
12. "Special Issue: All-Channel Carbonated Soft Drink Performance in 2005," *Beverage Digest* 48 (March 8, 2006).
13. This and subsequent comments in this section are adapted from Kevin Lane Keller, "Brand Synthesis: The Multidimensionality of Brand Knowledge," *Journal of Consumer Research* 29 (March 2003), 595–600.
14. Ibid.
15. Grant McCracken, "Culture and Consumption: A Theoretical Account of the Structure and Movement of the Cultural Meaning of Consumer Goods," *Journal of Consumer Research* 13 (June 1986), 74.
16. For a more technical but readable discussion of the fMRI device, see the Appendix in Carolyn Yoon, Angela H. Gutchess, Fred Feinberg, and Thad A. Polk, "A Functional Magnetic Resonance Imaging Study of Neural Dissociations between Brand and Person Judgments," *Journal of Consumer Research* 33 (June 2006), 31–40.
17. Cited in Kevin Lane Keller, *Strategic Brand Management: Building, Measuring, and Managing Brand Equity* (Upper Saddle River, NJ: Prentice Hall, 1998), 285. For excellent theoretical treatments of this issue, see C. Whan Park, Sung Youl Jun, and Allan D. Shocker, "Composite Branding Alliances: An Investigation of Extension and Feedback Effects," *Journal of Marketing Research* 33 (November 1996), 453–466; and Bernard L. Simonin and Julie A. Ruth, "Is a Company Known by the Company It Keeps? Assessing the Spillover Effects of Brand Alliances on Consumer Brand Attitudes," *Journal of Marketing Research* 35 (February 1998), 30–42.
18. Ed Lebar, Phil Buehler, Kevin Lane Keller, Monika Sawicka, Zeynep Aksehirli, and Keith Richey, "Brand Equity Implications of Joint Branding Programs," *Journal of Advertising Research* 45 (December 2005), 413–425.
19. Sandra Dolbow, "DuPont Lycra Stretches Out Into Jeans," *Brandweek*, July 2, 2001, 8.
20. For further reading, see Terence A. Shimp, Saeed Samiee, and Thomas J. Madden, "Countries and Their Products: A Cognitive Structure Perspective," *Journal of the Academy of Marketing Science* 21 (1993), 323–330.
21. See, for example, Saeed Samiee, Terence A. Shimp, and Subhash Sharma. "Brand Origin Recognition Accuracy: Its Antecedents and Consumers' Cognitive Limitations" *Journal of International Business Studies* 36 (2005), 379–397.
22. "New National Research Study: It's from Where? College Students Clueless on Where Favorite Brands Come From," Anderson Analytics, May 24, 2007, http://www.andersonanalytics.com (accessed July 31, 2007); Beth Snyder Bulik, "Ditch the Flags; Kids Don't Care Where You Come From," *Advertising Age*, June 4, 2007, 1, 59.
23. Simon Anholt, "Anholt Nation Brands Index: How Does the World See America," *Journal of Advertising Research* 45 (September 2005), 296–304; Simon Anholt, "The Anholt Nation Brands Index Special Report, Q1 2007" http://www.nationbrandindex.com (accessed August 3, 2007).
24. For sophisticated discussions of the relationship between brand equity and brand loyalty, consult the following sources: Tülin Erdem and Joffre Swait, "Brand Equity as a Signaling Phenomenon," *Journal of Consumer Psychology* 7, 2 (1998), 131–158; Chaudhuri and Holbrook, "The Chain of Effects from Brand Trust and Brand Affect to Brand Performance: The Role of Brand Loyalty."
25. Larry Light and Richard Morgan, *The Fourth Wave: Brand Loyalty Marketing* (New York: Coalition for Brand Equity, 1994), 11.
26. William Boulding, Eunkyu Lee, and Richard Staelin, "Mastering the Mix: Do Advertising, Promotion, and Sales Force Activities Lead to Differentiation?" *Journal of Marketing Research* 31 (May 1994), 159–172.
27. Janet Adamy, "Starbucks Chairman Says Trouble May Be Brewing," *The Wall Street Journal Online*, February 23, 2007 (accessed February 24, 2007).
28. "The PepsiCo Empire Strikes Back," *Brandweek*, October 7, 1996, 60.
29. Press release from Harris Interactive, June 20, 2006, http://www.harrisinteractive.com (accessed July 26, 2007).
30. Interbrand Report, "Best Global Brands 2007," http://www.interbrand.com/best_brands_2007.asp (accessed August 3, 2007).
31. For example, see Sunil Gupta, Donald R. Lehmann, and Jennifer Ames Stuart, "Valuing Customers," *Journal of Marketing Research* 41 (February 2004), 7–18; Roland T. Rust, Katherine N. Lemon, and Valarie A. Zeithaml, "Return on Marketing: Using Customer Equity to Focus Marketing Strategy," *Journal of Marketing* 68 (January 2004), 109–127; "Measures and Metrics: The Marketing Performance Measurement Audit," The CMO Council, June 9, 2004.
32. The CMO Council, "Measures and Metrics: The Marketing Performance Measurement Audit," June 9, 2004, 3.
33. For readers unfamiliar with the game of baseball, there are four bases on a baseball field. The objective for an offensive team is to have its hitters move around all four bases and thus score a run. Batters (a.k.a. hitters) move to first base when they get a single or are walked by the pitcher, to second base when they get a double, to third base with a triple, and all the way to home plate—thus scoring a run—when hitting a home run.
34. Allen St. John, "The Best at Keeping Batters Off Base," *The Wall Street Journal Online*, http://online.wsj.com (accessed

August 3, 2007). Note that this article uses the acronym BABE instead of BPB to signify bases per batter.
35. Hillary Chura, "Advertising ROI Still Elusive Metric," *Advertising Age,* July 26, 2004, 8.
36. Ibid.
37. The *net present value (NPV)* of an investment represents the present, or discounted, value of future cash inflows minus the present value of the investment. The related concept of *discounted cash flow* expresses the value of future cash flows in present dollars. For example, if a firm's cost of borrowing money is 10 percent, then $100 that will not be received for three years is worth in current value only about $75. That is, if you invested $75 today and received 10 percent interest on this investment, in three years it would grow in value to $100. The concept of discounted cash flow simply reverses this logic and examines what a future flow of cash is worth in today's dollars. If this remains unclear, please go online and identify a source that discusses the concept of *time value of money.*
38. The example given here focuses only on marketing communication elements. In actuality, a full-blown MMM would include all elements of a brand's marketing mix (e.g., price, distribution channels) and not just marcom elements.
39. For a fascinating ethnographic analysis of Harley-Davidson owners and more detail on the Harley-as-horse metaphor, see John W. Schouten and James H. McAlexander, "Subcultures of Consumption: An Ethnography of the New Bikers," *Journal of Consumer Research* 22 (June 1995), 43–61.
40. Some of the following comments are adapted from James D. Speros, chief marketing officer at Ernst & Young and chair of the Association of National Advertisers, in "Why the Harley Brand's So Hot," *Advertising Age,* March 15, 2004, 26.
41. For an interesting treatment of rugged individualism in a marketing/advertising context, see Elizabeth C. Hirschman, "Men, Dogs, Guns, and Cars," *Journal of Advertising* 32 (spring 2003), 9–22.
42. For further reading on brand communities, see Albert M. Muniz Jr. and Thomas C. O'Guinn, "Brand Community," *Journal of Consumer Research* 27 (March 2000), 412–432.
43. Clifford Krauss, "Harley Woos Female Bikers," *The New York Times Online,* July 25, 2007, http://www.nytimes.com (accessed July 25, 2007).
44. Ibid.
45. Jack Neff, "P&G, Clorox Rediscover Modeling," *Advertising Age,* March 29, 2004, 10.

3

Facilitating the Success of New Brands

The Ford Taurus, introduced in 1986, was one of the most successful models in the history of Ford automobiles. During its first 20 years of production—from 1986 to 2006, when production was temporarily suspended—Ford sold more than 7.5 million Taurus vehicles. Between 1992 and 1996, Taurus was the best selling automobile in the United States, alhough by 1997 it was overtaken by the Toyota Camry and thereafter continued to lose substantial market share to foreign competitors including the Camry and the Honda Accord. Ford executives decided to discontinue production of the Taurus in 2006, at which time the Ford Five Hundred entered the market in lieu of the Taurus.

In retrospect, it was obvious that Ford executives had made a bad decision. The Taurus was an automobile with a very high level of consumer awareness and generally a positive image—the ingredients for positive brand equity (recall discussion in the previous chapter). The Five Hundred, by comparison, was a new model that enjoyed zero brand awareness when introduced. In fact, after two years on the market the Five Hundred was unable to achieve the level of brand awareness necessary for the brand to realize a high level of sales success. In addition to the Five Hundred's limitations, many loyal Ford consumers felt betrayed that the Taurus, a vehicle they much admired and enjoyed, was no longer available. The Ford Motor Company was thus confronted with a double-whammy situation: unhappy Taurus owners and a new model—the Five Hundred—that was unlikely to recruit many new customers to Ford Motors.

Then, in 2007, a new chief executive officer, Alan Mulally, took over at Ford. One of his initial decisions was to dump the Five Hundred and resurrect the Taurus in its place. Mulally believed it would take many years for the Five Hundred to reach the level of brand equity that the Taurus had gained during its 20-year run as a top American automobile. The new Taurus, like the Five Hundred model it replaced, will compete in a more upscale market than did the earlier-generation Taurus, whose competition was mid-level vehicles such as the Accord and Camry. Only time will tell whether the new Taurus will achieve anywhere near the level of success it enjoyed during its prior incarnation. One certainty, however, is that marketers of the Taurus will have to invest heavily in marketing communications in order to reintroduce this once-proud automobile successfully and to re-teach the marketplace that the new Taurus is a much different (i.e., bigger, better) vehicle than was the earlier-generation Taurus.

Sources: Renée Alexander, "Ford Taurus—Dead Bull?" July 2, 2007, http://www.brandchannel.com (accessed July 2, 2007); "Ford Taurus," http://en.wikipedia.org/wiki/Ford_Taurus (accessed August 11, 2007).

© Drive Images/Alamy

Chapter Objectives

After reading this chapter you should be able to:

1. Appreciate marcom's role in facilitating the introduction of new brands.
2. Explain the innovation-related characteristics that influence adoption of new brands.
3. Understand the role performed by brand names in enhancing the success of new brands.
4. Explain the activities involved in the brand-naming process.
5. Appreciate the role of logos.
6. Describe the various elements underlying the creation of effective packages.

>>Marcom Insight:

First the Taurus, Next the Five Hundred, and then Taurus's Return

Introduction

Introducing new brands is critical for achieving continued growth and long-term success, and this chapter examines general factors that influence the likelihood of new brands being accepted in the marketplace and their successful economic lives. Also examined are considerations involved in developing brand names and designing packages, both of which play key roles in influencing the initial success of new brands and the sustained success of mature brands.

Introducing a stream of new brands is absolutely essential to most companies' long-term growth. But despite the huge investments and concerted efforts in introducing new brands, many are never successful. Although it is impossible to pinpoint the exact percentage of unsuccessful new brands, failure rates typically range between 35 and 45 percent, and the rate may be increasing.[1] This chapter will explain the job marketing communications plays in facilitating the successful introduction of new brands, and, particularly, it will emphasize the role performed by brand names, logos, and packages in achieving successful outcomes for new (and established) brands.

Marcom and Brand Adoption

The acceptance of new ideas, including new brands, has traditionally been referred to as *product adoption,* although the emphasis here will be with respect to specific brands rather than entire product categories. We initiate this discussion by conceptualizing the process by which consumers and B2B customers become aware of new brands, undertake trial purchases of these brands, and, possibly, become repeat purchasers.[2] The notions of trial and repeat purchase are particularly apt for inexpensive consumer packaged goods, but even expensive durable goods like automobiles are tried via test-drives and repeat purchased at longer inter-purchase rates than characterize consumer goods. Likewise, products purchased by B2B customers also are subject to being tried and repeat purchased.

The model in Figure 3.1, termed the Brand Adoption Process, indicates—with circles—the three main stages through which an individual becomes an adopter of a new brand. These stages are the awareness, trier, and repeater classes, with the term class referring to a group, or category, of consumers and customers who occupy the same stage with respect to whether they are simply aware of a brand, have tried it, or are repeat purchasers of that brand. The blocks surrounding the circles are mostly marcom tools that play a role in moving consumers from initial awareness, through trial, and ultimately to becoming repeat purchasers. Please note these tools are designated (in parentheses) as being used primarily in the B2C or B2B domains, or both.

The advertisement in Figure 3.2 for Fruit$_2$O, a brand from Kraft Foods, will facilitate the subsequent discussion. The original Fruit$_2$O brand was a fruit-flavored water beverage that came in eight flavors (raspberry, grape, lemon, etc.). Kraft Foods subsequently extended the product line with four versions of vitamin-enhanced fruit-flavored water beverages, named Immunity, Energy, Hydration, and Relaxation—each containing different vitamin enhancements. For example, Fruit$_2$O Immunity (Figure 3.2) contains antioxidants and vitamin A; Fruit$_2$O Energy has caffeine and B vitamins.

The first step in facilitating adoption is to make consumers aware of a product's existence. Figure 3.1 illustrates four determinants of the **awareness class:** free samples and coupons, trade shows and personal selling, advertising, and distribution. The first three of these are distinctly marcom activities; the fourth, distribution, is closely allied in that point-of-purchase materials and shelf placement are aspects

figure 3.1

Model of the Brand Adoption Process

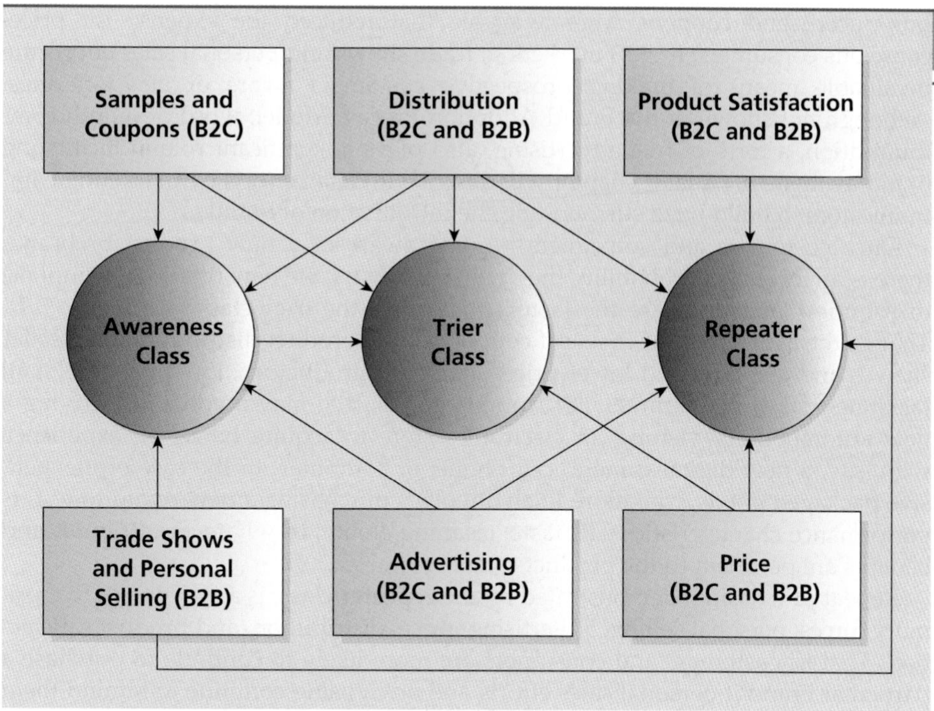

of a brand's distribution. Successful introduction of new brands typically requires an effective advertising campaign, widespread distribution backed up with point-of-purchase materials, and, in the case of inexpensive packaged goods, extensive sampling and couponing. $Fruit_2O$, for example, was sampled extensively when

Figure 3.2

Advertisement Illustrating the Brand Adoption Process

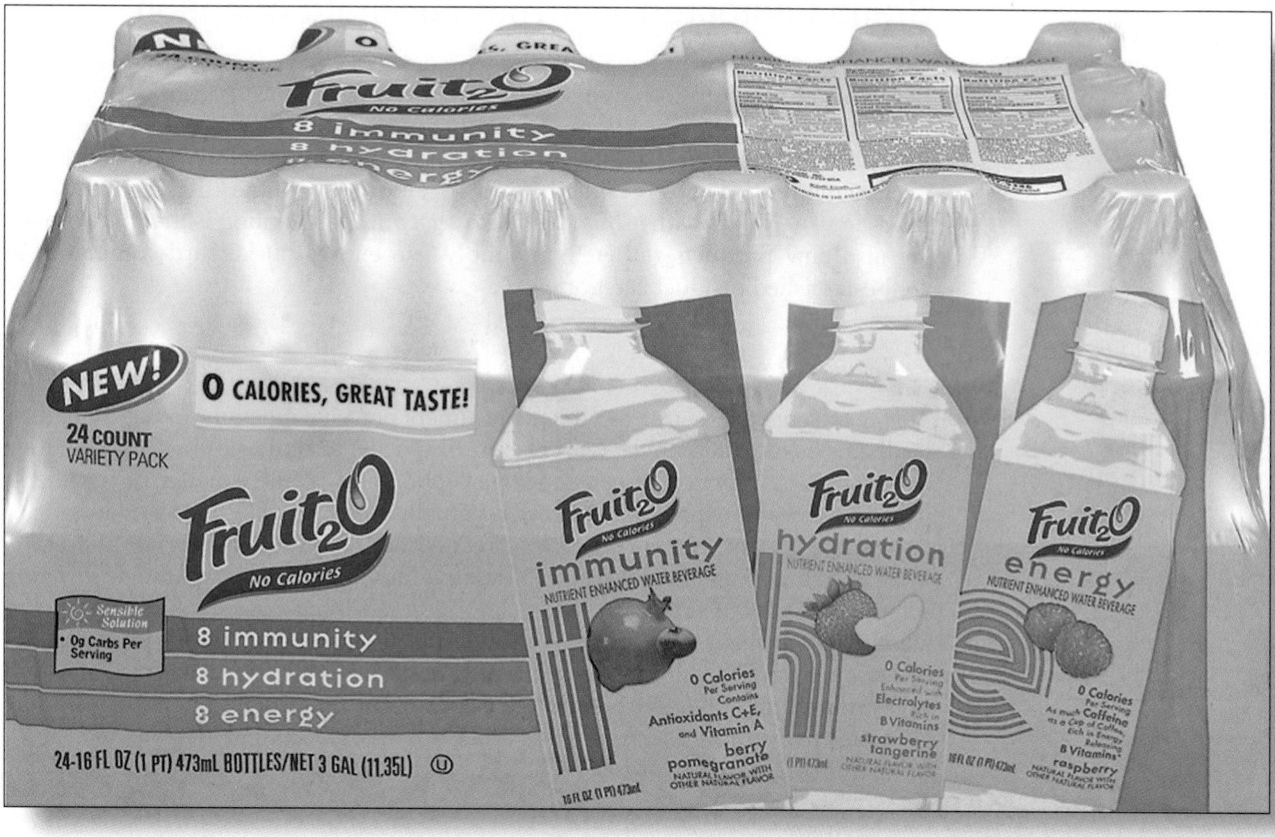

introduced, and coupons were available that reduced the expense for price-conscious consumers. In B2B marketing, trade shows and personal sales efforts are invaluable means of making prospective customers aware of new offerings. Although not shown in the Brand Adoption Process Model, word-of-mouth communication, a form of free advertising, also plays a significant role in facilitating brand awareness. (A later chapter will describe in detail efforts by marketing communicators to build buzz surrounding the introduction of brands.)

Once customers and consumers become aware of a new product or brand, there is an increased probability they will actually try the new offering.[3] Coupons, distribution, and price are the factors that affect the **trier class** (see Figure 3.1). That is, the availability of cents-off coupons, wide product distribution on retailer shelves and displays, and lower prices (such as introductory, low-price offers) all facilitate trial of new brands. For durable goods, trial may involve test-driving a new automobile or visiting an electronics store to acquire hands-on experience with, say, a new digital camera, cell phone, or computer. In the case of inexpensive packaged goods, trial more likely involves purchasing a new brand to test its performance characteristics—its taste, cleaning ability, or whatever attributes and benefits are pertinent to the product category.

Repeat purchasing, demonstrated by the **repeater class,** is a function of five primary forces: personal selling, advertising, price, distribution, and product satisfaction. That is, customers and consumers are more likely to continue to purchase a particular brand if personal sales efforts and advertising continue to remind them about the brand, if the price is considered reasonable, if the product or service is easily accessed, and if product quality is deemed satisfactory. On this last point, it is undeniable that marcom efforts are critical to boosting repeat purchasing, but they cannot make up for poor product performance. Consumer satisfaction with a brand is the major determinant of repeat purchasing. Consumers typically will not stick with brands that fail to live up to expectations.

Brand Characteristics That Facilitate Adoption

Discussion to this point has identified marcom tools that affect product adoption. Explanation now turns to five brand-related characteristics that influence consumers' attitudes toward new brands and hence their likelihood of adopting them. These are a brand's: (1) relative advantage(s), (2) compatibility, (3) complexity, (4) trialability, and (5) observability.[4] It is important to note that the discussion refers to new *brands,* rather than new *products,* but the intention is that new brands are also new products rather than simply late entries by laggard companies in well-established product categories.

Relative Advantage

This represents the degree to which consumers perceive a new brand as being better than existing alternatives with respect to specific attributes or benefits. **Relative advantage** is a function of consumer perception and is not a matter of whether a new brand in a new product category is actually better by objective standards.

Relative advantage is positively correlated with an innovation's adoption rate. That is, the greater an innovation's relative advantage(s) compared to existing offerings, the more rapid the rate of adoption, all other considerations held constant. (Conversely, a new brand's relative disadvantage(s)—high price, difficulty of learning how to use a new product, and so on—will retard the rate of adoption.) In general, a relative advantage exists to the extent that a new brand offers (1) better performance compared to other options, (2) savings in time and effort, or (3) immediacy of reward.

global focus

Washing Machines for the Masses in Brazil, China, and India

Millions of people throughout the developing world wash clothes the old-fashioned way: either with washboards and soap or with machines that are not fully automatic. (Most readers of this text never have seen such a machine, but the author and his contemporaries remember seeing their mothers wash the laundry in electric-powered machines that required individual items be manually "fed" through rollers to remove excess water prior to hanging the items on lines for drying.) This still is how it is done in much of the world. But Whirlpool Corp. has designs on changing the model of how people do their laundry. The secret to success is designing fully automatic washing machines that are functional and aesthetically appealing, yet affordable for the masses to purchase them. These relative advantages over traditional (non-automatic washer) solutions to doing the laundry will likely yield huge profits for Whirlpool in its global undertaking to alter laundry-washing behavior.

Whirlpool has designed a machine named Ideale for distribution in Brazil, China, India, and other developing countries. The retail price is in the range of $150–$200, compared with the average automatic washer in the United States, priced at nearly $500. About one quarter of Brazilian households have automatic washing machines, whereas the penetration levels in China and India are less than 10 percent. Importantly, Whirlpool has designed its washing machines to fit uniquely the consumption habits and preferences in each country. For example, in Brazil consumers are in the habit of washing floors beneath furniture and appliances; accordingly, the Ideale for Brazil was made to stand high on four legs. Also, because Brazilian homemakers want to see the machine operate, Whirlpool equipped the Ideale with a transparent, acrylic lid. In China, families often have shelves above their washers, so the tops of Whirlpool machines for that country were designed to be foldable. Also, because space constraints in China mean that many families locate their appliances in the living room, it was important that the washing machine for consumers in that country be aesthetically appealing. In India, washers often are placed in a position of pride in the home but are moved around the house; thus, washing machines for that market have caster wheels for easy mobility. Color preferences also vary from country to country. In Brazil, the Ideale comes only in white because Brazilians associate white with cleanliness. But Chinese dislike white appliances because they show dirt and grime, so Whirlpool produces light blue and gray machines for consumers in that country. Consumers in India can choose from white, blue, or green machines.

SOURCES: Adapted from Miriam Jordan and Jonathan Karp, "Machines for the Masses," *The Wall Street Journal Online*, December 9, 2003, http://online.wsj.com.

Consider the following illustrations of relative advantages (also see the *Global Focus* insert for another illustration of relative advantages for washing machines in developing countries):

- Digital cameras allow photographers the opportunity to view images prior to committing them to hard-copy photographs. Moreover, these images can be transmitted electronically in digitized form, thus avoiding the expense, hassle, and time associated with snail mailing photographs.
- The sweetener brand Splenda affords consumers the distinct relative advantage of tasting like sugar but being calorie free.
- Hybrid automobiles (such as the Toyota Prius) offer meaningful relative advantages in the form of being more fuel efficient and environmentally friendly than conventional, fully gasoline-fueled automobiles.
- Flat-screen, plasma TVs take up less space, weigh less, and provide better resolution than conventional televisions. This technology is expensive for most consumers, which explains the slow rate of adoption in households, but bars and

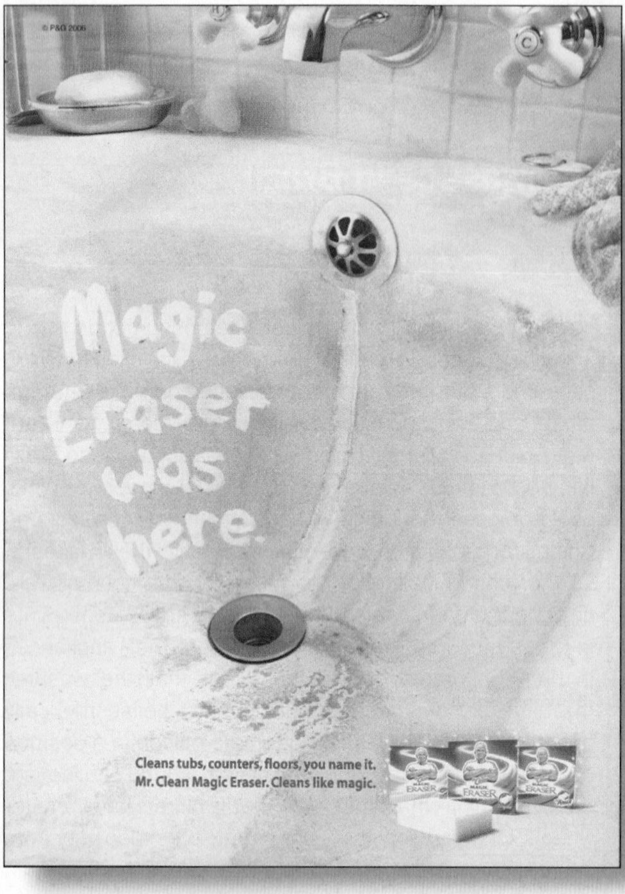

Figure 3.3

Advertisement Illustrating Relative Advantage

restaurants shifted in droves from conventional to flat-screen TVs, and households are now doing the same as prices come down.

- Brands in the so-called quick clean category have exploded in recent years. This includes items such as Procter & Gamble's Swiffer, which is a home mopping system that allows the consumer to mop hard surfaces easily by placing dirt-grabbing electrostatic sheets on pads that are attached to mop handles. Procter & Gamble's Mr. Clean Magic Eraser (Figure 3.3) illustrates another quick-clean brand that offers distinct relative advantages over more traditional cleaning products.
- MP3 players such as the Apple iPod offer huge music storage capacity and portability. It is little wonder that iPod's success has generated a slew of competitors.
- Unilever introduced a product long desired by parents: less drippy popsicles. Named Slowmelt Pops, these specially formulated popsicles reduce melting and dripping and stay on the stick longer.
- And finally, Nintendo's video game called Wii has the relative advantage of permitting game players to be physically active as they swing a virtual tennis racket, engage in a boxing match, or perform a variety of other virtual activities that require a level of physical exertion—and hence involvement with whatever game is being played—rarely matched by the role a game player performs in passive video games.

Compatibility

The degree to which an innovation is perceived to fit into a person's way of doing things is termed **compatibility.** In general, a new brand is more compatible to the extent that it matches consumers' needs, personal values, beliefs, and past consumption practices. Incompatible brands are those that are perceived as incongruent with how people have learned to satisfy their consumption needs. For example, although horse meat is an alternative to beef in European countries such as Belgium, France, Italy, and Spain, it is hard to imagine North American consumers converting from their deeply ingrained preference for beef to this lean, sweet-tasting alternative.

Consider also the traditional manner by which wine bottles have been "corked." For hundreds of years, real cork—which is the outer bark of oak trees—has provided the stopper material for wine bottles. Alternatives to real cork are beginning to serve as substitutes, including plastic stoppers and even twist-off metal caps. Although these newer types of stoppers are as effective as cork (and may even be superior because they cannot contaminate wine with the sometimes musty smell of cork), many traditionalists consider non-cork stoppers unacceptable. In many people's minds, cork stands for fine wine, whereas wines plugged with non-cork stoppers are considered cheap substitutes. A survey of members of the U.S. wine trade (restaurateurs, hotel wine buyers, etc.) revealed that these experts believe their customers think that non-cork enclosures cheapen a bottle of wine, and that the reason consumers prefer cork enclosures is simply a matter of tradition rather than performance.[5] In another words, non-cork enclosures lack compatibility with how many consumers and wine aficionados deem a wine bottle should be "corked."

Generally speaking, adoption rapidity is increased with greater compatibility. Innovations that are compatible with consumers' existing situations are less risky, more meaningful, and require less effort to incorporate into one's consumption lifestyle. Hybrid automobiles probably will experience a relatively slow rate of adoption because the idea of a combined gasoline and electric, or hybrid, automobile is somewhat incompatible with consumers' concept of how an automobile should be energized. However, with the rapid rise of gasoline prices, consumers have become more accepting of hybrid automobiles because of their lower operating cost.

Sometimes the only way to overcome perceptions of incompatibility is through heavy advertising to convince consumers that a new way of doing things truly is superior to an existing solution. Consider the case of Parmalat and other brands of ultra-high-temperature (UHT) milk, which is a heat-treated product that lasts up to six months on the shelf and tastes the same as "regular" milk. Shelf-stable milk is standard fare throughout much of Europe and Latin America with market shares of well over 50 percent in many countries. In the United States, however, sales of UHT are negligible. Italy's Parmalat brand entered the massive U.S. market with plans to change America's preference to shelf-stable milk. However, after more than a decade on the U.S. market, Parmalat's market share pales in comparison to sales of refrigerated milk. The problem is one of incompatibility: Americans are wedded to refrigerated milk. Parmalat, along with other UHT producers, will have to advertise heavily to influence large numbers of American consumers to purchase UHT milk regularly instead of the conventional refrigerated variety. Of course, because success breeds further success, brands that suffer from images of incompatibility often do not have sufficient funds to overcome their status.

Makers of soy "milk" also have recognized that they must advertise aggressively to overcome incompatibility problems. Although soy drinks possess the relative advantage of being healthier than traditional cow's milk, many consumers eschew purchasing soy drinks due to thoughts that a product made from a vegetable would probably taste strange and ruin, rather than enhance, the taste of milk-related products such as cereal. In an attempt to overcome incompatibility problems, makers of soy milk brands such as Silk and Great Awakenings have increased their ad budgets in the hopes of attracting new users to the category.

Complexity

Complexity refers to an innovation's degree of perceived difficulty. The more difficult an innovation is to understand or use, the slower the rate of adoption. As unlikely as it may seem in the 21st century, personal computers when first available were adopted slowly because many homeowners perceived them as too difficult to understand and use. The adoption of programmable TVs with hard drives (e.g., TiVo) also has been slower than expected, likely because many consumers fear they will be unable to use the technology successfully.

The success of Apple's iMac in the late 1990s attests to the value of making product use simple. The iMac was virtually an instant success, selling about one quarter of a million units in the first six weeks after launch and becoming one of the hottest products on the market during the holiday season. Although a very good personal computer, the iMac's retail price at $1,299 was, if anything, at a premium level compared to functionally competitive PCs. Indeed, in terms of specifications, the original iMac was nothing exceptional, with only 32MB of RAM, a 4GB hard drive, and a 233-MHz processing chip. However, the iMac's design was special. With a choice of five novel colors, translucent case, one-piece unit, rounded (versus angular) shape, and pre-installed software, the iMac was unlike any other personal computer. Beyond its unique design, the iMac was perhaps the most user-friendly computer to ever hit the market. Essentially, the user simply had to plug it in and turn it on—no setup, no hassle. This perhaps explains why nearly one third of the iMac buyers were first-time computer owners who apparently believed that the iMac did not exceed their threshold for complexity.

Trialability

The extent to which an innovation can be used on a limited basis prior to making a full-blown commitment is referred to as **trialability.** In general, new brands that lend themselves to trialability are adopted at a more rapid rate. Trialability is tied closely to the concept of perceived risk. Test-driving new automobiles, eating free food products at local supermarkets, and trying out a new golf driver before purchasing it illustrate trial behaviors. The trial experience serves to reduce the consumer's risk of being dissatisfied with a product after having permanently committed to it through an outright purchase. As will be discussed in detail in a later chapter, sampling is an incomparable promotional method for encouraging trial by reducing the risk that accompanies spending money on a new, untried product.

© Getty Images for John Deere

Facilitating trial is typically more difficult with durable products than with inexpensive packaged goods. Automobile companies allow consumers to take test-drives, but what do you do if you are, say, a computer manufacturer or a lawn mower maker? If you are creative, you do what companies like Apple Computer and John Deere did in novel efforts to give people the opportunity to try their products. Apple developed a "Test Drive a Macintosh" promotion that gave interested consumers the opportunity to try the computer in the comfort of their own homes for 24 hours at no cost. John Deere offered a 30-day free test period during which prospective mower purchasers could try the mower and then return it, no questions asked, if not fully satisfied. British-based Land Rover initiated a unique money-back offer to encourage purchases of Land Rover's Discovery Series II SUV model. Prospective buyers could drive the new SUV for 30 days or 1,500 miles and then return it for a full refund if they were dissatisfied with its performance.

Observability

Observability is the degree to which the user of a new brand or other people can observe the positive effects of new-product usage. The more a consumption behavior can be sensed (seen, smelled, etc.), the more observable, or visible, it is said to be. Thus, wearing a new perfume with a subtle fragrance is less "visible" than adopting an avant-garde hairstyle, and driving an automobile with a new type of engine is less visible than driving one with a unique body design such as a BMW Mini Cooper or a Hummer. In general, innovations that are high in observability lend themselves to rapid adoption if they also possess relative advantages, are compatible with consumption lifestyles, and so on. Products whose benefits lack observability are generally slower in adoptability.[6]

The important role of product observability is illustrated by Nike's long-standing use of showing the technology in its athletic shoes such as its Shox brand. Highly visible inserts in the heels of shoes convey the benefits of stability, cushioning, and increased lift through tiny shock absorbers that provide spring. Nike could design its shoes so that the shock absorbers are concealed from observation; instead, the company made the feature conspicuous by "exposing the technology" and, in so doing, provided itself with the easily communicable point that Nike shoes enable greater leaping ability than do competitive brands. Nike's exposing-the-technology practice recognizes that consumers are more likely to adopt a new product when its advantages are observable.

The importance of observability perhaps explains why Dell introduced its Inspiron notebook computers in eight colors not normally associated with this product category (e.g., pink, yellow, green, and red; see Figure 3.4). With languishing sales and slow growth, Dell created a new organizational unit that brought together personnel from industrial design, engineering, and marketing with the purpose of enabling Dell to respond to consumer trends quickly and to introduce a continuous stream of exciting new products.[7]

Because status from brand ownership is one form of consumption advantage, albeit an advantage high in symbolism rather than functionality, it perhaps is not surprising that many well-known clothing brands plaster their apparel items with prominent brand names and logos that are observable to the world. Consumers have become walking billboards for designer brands, a case of observability incarnate.

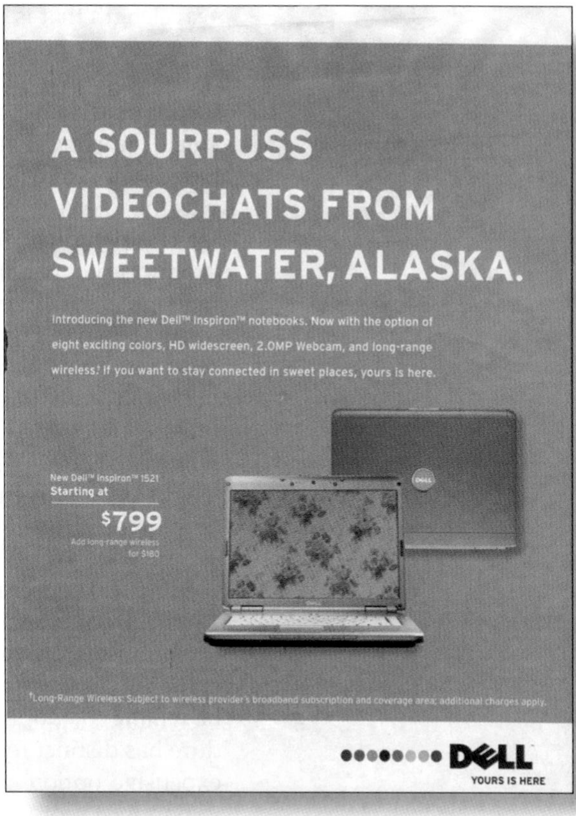

Figure 3.4

Advertisement Illustrating Observability

Quantifying the Adoption-Influencing Characteristics

To this point we have described each of the five factors that influence the likelihood that a new brand will be adopted and the rate at which adoption will occur. It would be useful to go beyond mere description and have a procedure whereby the five characteristics could be quantified on a case-by-case basis to determine whether a proposed product concept stands a good chance of being successful. Figure 3.5 illustrates a procedure for accomplishing this goal. Each of the five characteristics is rated, first in terms of its *importance* in determining the success of a proposed new product and then with respect to how well the new brand performs on each characteristic, its *evaluation score.*

For illustration purposes, consider the issue of hair removal. Many women (and some men) go to doctors and salons to have unwanted hair removed by a laser procedure. It is estimated that professional hair removal in the United States commands annual revenues in excess of $2.5 billion.[8] Hair removal via the laser procedure stunts the growth of hair follicles by using light at a frequency and

figure 3.5

Hypothetical Illustration of Quantifying the Adoption-Influencing Characteristic

Characteristic	Importance (I)*	Evaluation (E)†	I × E
Relative advantage(s)	5	5	25
Compatibility	3	3	9
Complexity	4	−2	−8
Trialability	5	−1	−5
Observability	1	0	0
Total Score	NA	NA	21

*Importance is rated on a scale with values ranging from zero to five. A rating of zero would indicate that a specific characteristic has no importance in this particular case. Higher positive values indicate progressively increasing levels of importance.

†Evaluation is rated on a scale with values ranging from minus five to five. A rating of zero, the midpoint of the scale, would indicate that the proposed new product performs neither favorably or unfavorably on the characteristic at hand; negative values indicate poor performance, with minus five representing the worst possible performance; positive values indicate favorable performance, with five representing the best possible performance.

wavelength that is absorbed by the follicles but not by the surrounding skin tissue. Imagine how popular such a procedure would be if a product were available for *in-home use.* Or would it? Well, Gillette, a company famous for its razors and blades is betting that such a product will be highly demanded. Gillette has teamed up with a small company, Palomar Medical Technologies Inc., to develop an in-home laser-based hair-removal product. Palomar pioneered the field of laser hair removal and was the first company to obtain approval from the Food and Drug Administration for removing hair by such a procedure.[9] Although an in-home laser hair-removal product is not commercially available yet, we will assume it is and apply the model in Figure 3.5 to quantify the success potential of such a product.

As shown in Figure 3.5, relative advantages and trialability are judged to be the most important considerations in determining the success of this new laser product, both with importance ratings of five. This in-home hair-removal product must compete against conventional hair-removal procedures (e.g., shaving legs with blades or applying a chemical substance) in terms of ease of hair removal, length of effectiveness, and amount of effort and pain involved. The proposed new brand (let's call it LaserGillette, for convenience) must possess these *relative advantages* vis-à-vis existing hair-removal products if it stands any chance of succeeding. Likewise, it is maximally important that potential purchasers be able to try the product in advance of actually purchasing it, so *trialability* also receives an importance score of five. *Compatibility,* however, is considered to be of only moderate importance (a score of three) insofar as potential users of LaserGillette may be willing to adopt a somewhat radical new method of removing hair if the procedure has distinct relative advantages that justify what undoubtedly will be a more expensive option compared to conventional methods. *Complexity of use,* with an importance score of four, is considered a very important determinant of product adoption inasmuch as many potential users would be reluctant to switch from their present hair-removal procedure, say shaving, if the laser procedure is perceived as being difficult to use. Finally, *observability* receives an importance score of only one in that product adoption does not involve others seeing how well the product works because this is mostly a private matter that is best ascertained by the product user.

With importance ratings determined, we can turn to the evaluation of LaserGillette on each of the five adoption-influencing characteristics. On relative advantages, this new brand is assessed to have the highest possible score, a five. The arithmetic product of its importance rating multiplied by its evaluation score results in LaserGillette receiving a combined relative advantage score ($I \times E$) of 25 points on this single dimension. Because the product is not drastically different than other hair-removal procedures (all involve moving an object, such as a razor, over the skin), its compatibility evaluation score is a three, which thus produces a combined $I \times E$ score of 9 points. It can be seen in Figure 3.5, however, that LaserGillette scores on the negative side with respect to both complexity and trialability. The product is perceived as being somewhat difficult to learn to use and cannot be tried prior to purchase other than by viewing a product-in-use video that is available at the point of purchase. Because observability is not really at issue, LaserGillette's $I \times E$ score on this dimension is 0. The total score, as shown in Figure 3.5, is a 21. Based on its past new-product introduction efforts, let us assume that Gillette has learned that all brands with scores of 18 or higher typically are successful when introduced to the market. Hence, with a total score of 21, it is likely that LaserGillette will be a success.

Although this illustration is hypothetical, the point is that it is possible to quantify the five adoption determining factors and arrive at a total score that indicates the likelihood that a new product will succeed. Models such as this are invariably somewhat subjective, but a brand management team along with its various marcom agencies should be able to make these judgments with some degree of reliability. Obviously, consumer research also can be applied to determine how prospective members of the target audience rate a proposed new brand on each characteristic and how important they consider each characteristic to be in their decision to adopt. Brand managers can build spreadsheets and play around with the numbers in the process of ascertaining what changes may be needed in order to increase the odds that a new product will succeed. For example, because Laser-Gillette is not evaluated favorably in terms of its trialability, the brand management team may seriously consider devising an in-store procedure that allows prospective users to try the product in a safe and hygienic manner.

Brand Naming

Choosing an appropriate brand name is a crucial decision, largely because that choice can influence early trial of a new brand and affect future sales volume. Indeed, brand names have been described as the "cerebral switches" that activate images in target audiences' collective minds.[10] Research has shown that even children (as young as 3 or 4) are aware of brand names and that by the age of 10 or so the brand name takes on conceptual significance whereby children think about brand names as more than simply another product feature. In other words, the name takes on a "life of its own," and children judge brands on the basis of their acquired reputations and evaluate people in terms of what brands they own.[11] A product's brand name plays a major role in determining its immediate success upon introduction and its sustained prosperity as it matures.

It is worth mentioning at this point that the name chosen for a new brand is an especially important decision. A new brand can succeed in spite of being saddled with a "bad" name, but the odds of success are boosted if the brand has an effective name. Good brand names evoke feelings of trust, confidence, security, strength, durability, speed, status, and many other desirable associations. The name chosen for a brand: (1) affects the speed with which consumers become aware of the brand, (2) influences the brand's image, and (3) thus plays a major role in brand equity formation. Achieving consumer awareness of a brand name is the critical initial aspect of brand equity enhancement. Brand name awareness has been characterized as the gateway to consumers' more complicated learning and retention of associations that constitute a brand's image.[12] Through brand names, a company can create excitement, elegance, exclusiveness, and influence consumers' perceptions and attitudes.[13]

What Constitutes a Good Brand Name?

This is a complex question that precludes a straightforward answer. To gain perspective, let us twist the question around and pose it in these terms: What determines whether a person's name is a good name? (Please think about this for a moment before reading on.) As you pondered this question, you likely arrived quickly at the conclusion that people's names differ dramatically and that no simple rule can answer whether a person's name is good. Perhaps you also entertained the notion that whether a person's name is "good" depends in large part on whether it "fits" the person's size, personality, and sociodemographic characteristics. Quite simply, there are many ways to have a good name, either for a person or for a brand.

Let us consider an actual brand name and the logic that went into choosing that name. In 2006 Microsoft introduced a music and video player to compete against brands such as Apple's iPod and named the brand Zune. Actually, Zune became the brand name for the media player itself and for Microsoft's hardware and Internet media store named the Zune Marketplace, which enables customers to acquire songs, movies, TV programs, and software. Why the name Zune? As is generally the case when picking a name for a new brand, Microsoft selected a company that specializes in brand naming—Lexicon Branding Inc. in this case—for the purpose of creating a name. Lexicon's chief executive justified the choice of the Zune name when offering the following comments to a *Wall Street Journal* reporter:[14]

- The letter "Z" connotes an aura of strength and reliability and, in the English language, is among the most alive and energetic sounds.
- The branding objective was to find a short word, because short words are easier for people to pronounce and remember, and a short word would reflect the small size of Microsoft's media player.
- In choosing the Zune name, Lexicon Branding considered upward of 4,500 candidate names. Over the course of three months, Zune ultimately won out as the "best" name.
- In addition to suggesting strength, reliability, and energy, the name Zune was selected due to its ring of familiarity, as, for example, the easy leap one makes in moving from the word "tune" to Zune.
- Finally, a top marketing executive at Microsoft indicated that they wanted a brand name that would sound active and could be used both as a verb and a noun, as, for example, does the name Google.

Beyond this single name choice, marketing practitioners and researchers have attempted to specify factors that determine brand name quality. Although the accumulated knowledge is nowhere close to the point of identifying scientific principles, there is general agreement that brand names should satisfy several fundamental requirements. First, a good brand name should distinguish the brand from competitive offerings. Second, it should facilitate consumer learning of desirable brand associations by describing or suggesting brand attributes or benefits. Third, it is important that the name achieve compatibility with the brand's desired image and with its product design and packaging. Fourth, it is useful for the name to be memorable and easy to pronounce and spell.[15] Finally, although not discussed subsequently as a fifth requirement, another important consideration is the suitability of the brand name for marketing a brand in multiple countries. Ideally, a brand name would satisfy requirements one through four equally well in all countries in which the brand is marketed. Needless to say, most brand names fail to satisfy this ideal. For example, it has been suggested that the Zune name is reminiscent of a Hebrew profanity word. Although that prospect has been contested, the possibility that the name may evoke a profanity may diminish the Zune's success potential in Israel and other markets with large Jewish populations.

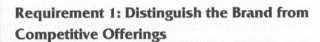

© Deborah Law/ Newscom

Requirement 1: Distinguish the Brand from Competitive Offerings

It is desirable for a brand to have a unique identity, something that clearly differentiates it from competitive brands. Failure to distinguish a brand from competitive offerings creates confusion and increases the chances that consumers will not remember the name or mistakenly select another brand. Clinique selected the name Happy to suggest precisely that feeling for its perfume brand, a name choice that is striking in its differentiation from the usually sexually suggestive names chosen for perfumes such as Passion, Allure, and Obsession.

In the low-fare airline category, brand marketers have come up with unique names such as Ted

Airlines, Song, Spirit Airlines, and JetBlue Airways—unique names that provide each airline with a distinct identity. Compare these names with the stodgy monikers that historically dominated the U.S. airline industry, names such as United, Continental, TWA, Delta, American, Northwest, Southwest, and so on. The new airline names seem intent on conveying brand personalities that suggest these airlines deliver something more than mere functionality. Moreover, all are memorable and easy to pronounce (see requirement #4).

Rather than using brand names to differentiate themselves from competitors, some marketers attempt to hitchhike on the success of other brands by using names similar to better-known and more respected brands. However, the Federal Trademark Dilution Act of 1995 protects owners of brand names and logos from other companies using the identical or similar names. (In legal terms, brand names and logos are referred to as *trademarks.*) The objective of this legislation is to protect trademarks from losing their distinctiveness.[16] Trademark infringement cases occur with some regularity in the United States, and stealing well-known brand names is widely practiced in some newly emerging market economies such as China.

Requirement 2: Facilitate Consumer Learning of Brand Associations

As described in Chapter 2, when discussing customer-based brand equity, a brand's image represents the *associations* that are activated in memory when people think about a particular brand. It is desirable that marcom efforts create associations that are favorable, strong, and perhaps unique. A brand name can facilitate consumers' learning brand associations by specifically describing or suggesting a brand's key attributes or benefits. In other words, a brand name lets consumers know what to expect from a brand, and also performs the all-important function of enabling consumers to recall important information about the brand. That is, brand names serve as *memory cues* that facilitate recall of product attributes and benefits and also predict product performance.[17]

Post-it (notepads), I Can't Believe It's Not Butter (margarine), I Can't Believe It's Not Chicken (a faux-chicken soy-based product), Healthy Choice (low-fat foods), Huggies (diapers), and Crocs (rubber shoes) illustrate brand names that do outstanding jobs in describing (or suggesting; see later discussion) their respective products' attributes or benefits. Consider also the name Liquid-Plumr, which is the brand name for a liquid product that is poured into sinks to open clogged drainage pipes. The name implies that the product is virtually like having your own plumber, without, of course, incurring the expense and inconvenience of hiring an actual plumber. The *IMC Focus* insert describes a very interesting product that has a brand name, Tooth Tunes, that clearly describes that brand's key product attribute/benefit.

Let us also ponder some of the brand names used in the cell phone category. Some names give the impression of technical sophistication by using a combination of letters and numerals. Examples include Samsung's M300, Sony Ericsson's W300, and LG's VX series (VX5300, VX8300, VX8550, and VX9900). Then there are cell phone names that describe or suggest specific brand features or benefits. These include the Samsung Hue (multiple faceplates available in different colors), the Samsung Sync (suggesting clear communications, or synchronization between caller and receiver), the Motorola RAZR (suggesting a small, razor-thin phone), Apple's iPhone (indicating an ability to access the Internet), and LG's enV (a truncated version of the word "envy," to suggest that others will envy the owner of this brand).

Brand Name Suggestiveness. Transmeta Corp., a manufacturer of computer chips that competes against the much larger Intel and its Pentium class of products, introduced a super-efficient chip designed for laptop computers. This new chip

IMC >> i.m.c. focus

A Musical Toothbrush That Encourages Children to Brush Longer

Moms and dads routinely have to remind their children to brush their teeth. With sufficient encouragement (coercion?), kids comply. But because most children consider brushing an undesirable task, the tendency is to spend too little time brushing and not doing a thorough job. Enter Tooth Tunes, the descriptive brand name of a product from Hasbro that encourages children to spend more time brushing, in fact, up to the dentist-recommended two full minutes. Tooth Tunes is a power toothbrush that plays pop songs lasting two minutes using a technology called dentamandibular sound transduction. The music cannot be heard outside the head, either by users or nonusers, and, to encourage good brushing technique, the songs sound best when kids use an up-and-down brushing stroke. Children push a button on the toothbrush; a minicomputer starts playing the song; and sound waves are transported from the front teeth, to the jawbone, and then to the inner ear.

Each Tooth Tunes brush comes loaded with a single song, with over 20 songs available from leading artists that appeal to children's musical tastes, such as Hillary Duff's *Wake Up,* the Black Eyed Peas' *Let's Get It Started,* Destiny Child's *Survivor,* and *Get 'cha Head in the Game* from the *High School Musical* movie. Tooth Tunes brushes are not inexpensive, with each being priced around $10. Hasbro hopes that kids will want to rotate the songs they listen to and thus encourage (pester?) their parents to purchase multiple brushes. Most kids couldn't care less about the expense, so their payback to parents who coerced them to brush their teeth is to coerce their parents to purchase yet another Tooth Tunes brush, which certainly is a desirable outcome from Hasbro's perspective.

Sources: Adapted from Jack Neff, "Now There's Music for Molars," *Advertising Age,* October 23, 2006, 12, http://www.hasbro.com/toothtunes (accessed August 21, 2007).

promised to extend laptop usage without battery recharge for many hours beyond the standard two or three hours enabled by conventional chips. Transmeta named the new chip Crusoe after the famous fictional character Robinson Crusoe. This brand name suggests (to anyone familiar with the Robinson Crusoe story) that a laptop powered with a Crusoe chip permits a "stranded" user to continue working for many hours without access to an electrical outlet. Although the name–benefit relation is a bit abstract in this case, it would be expected that Crusoe readily suggests a stranded-usability benefit to most prospective laptop purchasers.

Researchers have carefully examined the issue of brand name suggestiveness. *Suggestive* brand names are those that imply particular attributes or benefits in the context of a product category. Crusoe is a suggestive brand name. So is Healthy Choice for food products, intimating that this brand is low in fat content and calories. The name Outback for Subaru's SUV suggests a product that is durable and rugged—capable of taking on the challenge of the famous Australian outback. Ford Explorer is a name that suggests adventure for prospective purchasers of pickup trucks seeking the thrill of off-road driving. LG's enV suggests that owners of this cell phone will be envied by others. The name Crocs (rubber shoes) suggests that this brand is appropriate for wear in or around water as well as on land and is as tough as a crocodile's skin.

Suggestive brand names facilitate consumer recall of advertised benefit claims that are consistent in meaning with the brand names.[18] Suggestive names reinforce in consumers' memories the association between the name and the semantically related benefit information about the brand.[19] Conversely, these same suggestive names may reduce the recallability of benefit claims after a brand has been repositioned to stand for something different than its original meaning.[20]

Made-Up Brand Names. To convey key brand attributes/benefits, brand name developers sometimes create names rather than select names from actual words found in dictionaries. Microsoft's Zune, as noted previously, is a made-up name. Many automobile brand names currently in use or used in the past are made-up names, including Acura, Altima, Geo, Lexus, Lumina, and Sentra. These names were created from *morphemes,* which are the semantic kernels of words. For example, Compaq, which now has merged with Hewlett-Packard, combined two morphemes (com and paq) and in so doing suggested the product benefit of a compact computer. The automobile name Acura is a derivative of "accurate" and suggests precision in product design and engineering. The name Lexus, by comparison, appears to be an entirely made-up name that does not suggest any particular product feature or benefit.

Sound Symbolism and Brand Naming. Research is increasingly showing that sound symbolism plays a major role in determining how consumers react to brand names and form judgments about brands.[21] Individual sounds, called *phonemes,* are the basis for brand names. Not only do phonemes serve to form syllables and words but also they provide meaning about a brand through a process of *sound symbolism.*[22] Consider, for example, the use of "front" vowels in brand names (i.e., vowels such as *e* as in "bee" and *a* as in "ate") compared to "back" vowels (vowels such as *ü* as in "food" and *o* as in "home"). Research has demonstrated that brand names that include front vowels (versus back vowels) convey attribute qualities such as smallness, lightness, mildness, thinness, femininity, weakness, and prettiness.[23]

A study using ice cream as the target product created the names Frosh and Frish for an allegedly new brand. These names differ only with respect to their phonetic sounds, with Frosh and Frish based on *ä* (a back vowel) and *i* (a front vowel) sounds, respectively. The study determined that the name Frosh conveyed more positive brand attribute associations and more favorable brand evaluations than did Frish. The study further revealed that the effect of brand name sound symbolism occurred in an effortless, automatic fashion without cognitive involvement. In other words, these brand names had differential effects on perceptions and evaluations of allegedly new brands of ice cream, but participants in the research were unaware that their judgments were based on sound symbolism. Nonetheless, it was this sound symbolism that led research participants to evaluate more favorably Frosh versus Frish ice cream.

Requirement 3: Achieve Compatibility with a Brand's Desired Image and with Its Product Design or Packaging

It is essential that the name chosen for a brand be compatible with a brand's desired image and also with its design or packaging. Suppose, for example, that you wanted to name a brand of all-natural foods that have no artificial colors, flavorings, or preservatives along with a line of organic produce that has been grown with no synthetic fertilizers or pesticides. What would you name that brand? The Florida-based supermarket chain, Publix, chose the name GreenWise for its private-label collection of earth-friendly food items—a name compatible with the image desired. Many grocers have health food sections with their own brands (see Figure 3.6). Healthy Choice is an ideal name for a category of fat-free and low-fat food items targeted toward weight- and health-conscious consumers. The name suggests the consumer has a choice and that Healthy Choice is the right one.

Another name that fits well with a desired brand image is Swerve, which was Coca-Cola's now deceased milk-based drink aimed at children and teens. The dictionary meaning of the word *swerve* is to make an abrupt turn in movement or direction. Prospective users of Swerve were thus promised a drink that was out of the ordinary and that would make them part of a "movement"—perhaps away

figure 3.6

There are many image-compatible brands in health food sections of grocery stores

from ordinary soft drinks. In a sense, this name suggested that drinking milk is a "cool" thing. Swerve's packaging graphics reinforced the name by displaying a grinning cow in dark glasses, suggesting a hip brand for young people who desire their own identity and perhaps march to their own drummer. However, even a good brand name cannot save a product that fails to appeal to its intended target audience. For reasons unknown to this writer, Coca-Cola discontinued the Swerve brand after only about three years on the market.

Requirement 4: Be Memorable and Easy to Pronounce

Finally, a good brand name is easy to remember and pronounce. Although shortness is not an essential ingredient for a good name, many brand names are short, one-word names that facilitate ease of memory and pronunciation (Tide, Bold, Shout, Edge, Bounce, Cheer, Swatch, Smart, Zune, Crocs, etc.). Probably few words are as memorable as those learned in early childhood, and among the first words learned are animal names. This likely explains marketers' penchant for using animals as brand names; for example, automobile companies have used names such as Mustang, Thunderbird, Bronco, Cougar, Lynx, Skyhawk, Skylark, Firebird, Jaguar, and Ram. In addition to their memorability, animal names conjure up vivid images. This is very important to the marketing communicator because concrete and vivid images facilitate consumer information processing. Dove soap, for example, suggests softness, grace, gentleness, and purity. Ram (for Dodge trucks) intimates strength, durability, and toughness.

In coming up with memorable names, companies often take liberties with standard dictionary spellings. For example, Campbell's (of soup fame) introduced a line of energy drinks aimed at young adults. The name chosen for the brand was Invigor8. This name obviously is a derivative of invigorate, which literally means to feel with life and energy. This is an excellent name for the desired brand image (requirement #3) and is also memorable and easy to pronounce. The spelling, which substitutes the numeral 8 for the suffix ate, gives the name a special distinctiveness and yet enables easy pronunciation. Interestingly, it also is likely that Campbell's, which makes the well-known juice drink, V8, is attempting to leverage off the equity in that mature brand in a very subtle way. Whatever the case, Invigor8 is a captivating brand name. The use of this name is supported by research showing that names with unusual spellings enhance consumer recall and recognition, which probably explains why LG named its cell phone enV rather than Envy and Motorola named its phone RAZR rather than Razor.[24]

Some Exceptions to the "Rules"

The previous discussion has identified four guidelines for brand naming (and also mentioned a fifth, although it—compatibility across cultures—was not discussed in detail). The observant student will note, however, that some successful brand names seem entirely at odds with the "rules." First, some brands become successful in spite of their names. (Analogously, some people achieve prominence even though their names may not be the ones they personally would have chosen.) The first brand in a new product category can achieve tremendous success regardless of its name if the brand offers customers distinct advantages over alternative solutions to their problems. Second, in all aspects of life there are exceptions to the rules, even in brand naming.

A third major exception to the "rules" is that brand managers and their brand name consultants sometimes intentionally select names that, at inception, are virtually meaningless. For example, the word lucent in Lucent Technologies was selected because for most people this word has relatively little meaning and few associations—the *empty-vessel philosophy* of brand naming. The empty-vessel expression implies that when a name does not have much preexisting meaning, subsequent marketing communications are able to create the exact meaning desired without contending with past associations already accumulated in people's memories. In other words, rather than selecting a name already rich in meaning and filled with associations, there are advantages to using a relatively neutral name that a marcom campaign can endow with intended meaning.

The Brand-Naming Process

Brand naming involves a rather straightforward process as determined by a survey of over 100 product and brand managers who represent both B2C and B2B products. Figure 3.7 lists the steps, and the following discussion describes each.

Step 1: Specify Objectives for the Brand Name

As with all managerial decisions, the initial step is to identify the objectives to be accomplished. Most managers are concerned with selecting a name that will successfully position the brand in the minds of the target audience, provide an appropriate image for the brand, and distinguish it from competitive brands.[25] As

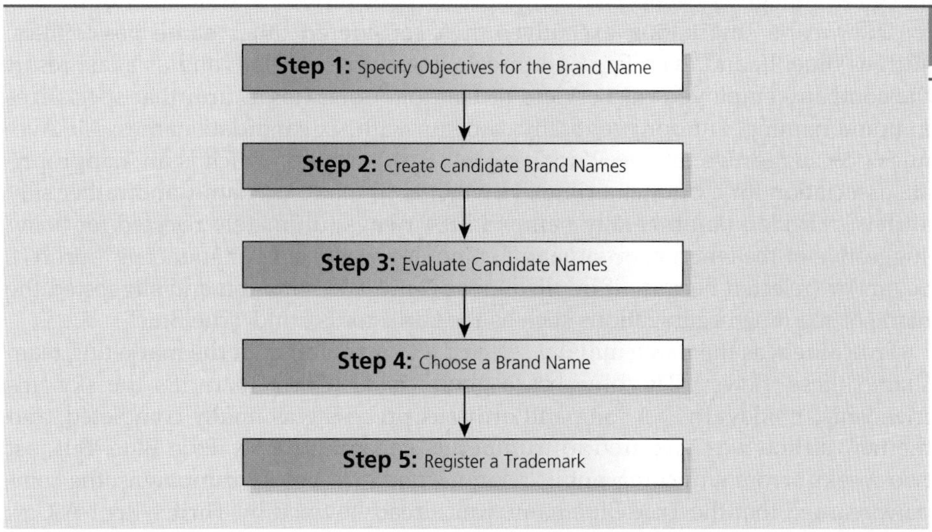

figure 3.7

The Brand-Naming Process

previously described, the name Zune for Microsoft's media player was selected to be a short name that connoted energy, strength, and reliability.

Step 2: Create Candidate Brand Names

Brand name candidates often are selected using creative-thinking exercises and brainstorming sessions. Companies frequently use the services of naming consultants to generate candidate names, as was the case in the selection of JetBlue, Verizon, Accenture, and Lucent. The survey of product and brand managers noted previously determined that nearly 50 candidate names were created for each brand-naming assignment.[26]

Step 3: Evaluate Candidate Names

The many names generated are evaluated using criteria such as relevance to the product category, favorability of associations conjured up by the name, and overall appeal. Product and brand managers consider it critical that names be easily recognized and recalled.

Step 4: Choose a Brand Name

Managers use the criteria noted in steps 1 and 3 to select a final name from the candidate field. In many firms this choice is a matter of subjective judgment rather than the product of rigorous marketing research. For example, the airline name JetBlue was chosen subjectively based on hunch and insight.[27] JetBlue's chief executive and his associates were uncertain what they wanted in a name for their new airline, but they were absolutely certain what they did not want—namely, they didn't want (1) a geographic destination such as Southwest or Northeast; or (2) a made-up word such as brand names popular in automobile marketing (e.g., Lexus and Acura).

The marketing team at "New Air," which was the operating name for the airline while awaiting the selection of a permanent name, considered numerous name possibilities, including New York Air, Gotham, Taxi, the Big Apple, Imagine Air, Yes!, and Fresh Air. Taxi was the name that had the greatest appeal to a top marketing executive, who thought that the name had "a New York feel" and would enable a unique plane design with yellow and black checkering on the tails of planes (reminiscent of the look of New York City's Checker Cabs). The name Taxi eventually was rejected, however, because in its verb usage, taxi describes what planes do on runways, and the Federal Aviation Administration rejected this usage for a brand name. Also, some feared that New York City taxi cabs had a negative image associated with high prices, poor service, and unsafe rides.

"New Air's" marketing executives then considered other name possibilities, such as Blue, It, and even Egg. All three names were rejected, and as a last resort the company employed the services of Landor Associates, a firm that specializes in brand naming. Landor eventually came up with six candidate names: Air Avenues (too suggestive of New York's swank Park Avenue, which is an inappropriate association for a budget airline); Hiway Air (a made-up name, and rather silly at that); Air Hop (another silly name); Lift Airways (ultimately rejected for being suggestive of the emergency situation embodied in the similar sounding "airlift"); Scout Air (rejected because it implied an adventure destination and suggested the name of scouting organizations such as the Girl Scouts); and True Blue.

True Blue was the name initially selected. A key member of the marketing team shared these views: "The blue has a good visual aspect to it. It's the sky, it's friendship, it's loyalty." A long and arduous process was finally completed, and the new airline was prepared to trumpet its engaging name, True Blue. But just two weeks before launching public relations and advertising campaigns, the company learned that the True Blue name was already owned by Thrifty-Rent-A-Car, which had copyrighted the name for use in a customer service program. (Parenthetically, the fact that the name was already owned had escaped Landor's legal analysis, much to the dismay of this respected brand-naming company.) Just one week before announcing the new airline, a member of the marketing team recommended the name JetBlue. Everyone agreed that the name would work, and New Air became JetBlue Airways—a fledgling airline that may become a mainstay of American airline service.

Step 5: Register a Trademark

Most companies apply for trademark registration. Some companies submit only a single name for registration, whereas others submit multiple names (on average, five names). One survey found that three names are rejected for every registered name.[28]

The Role of Logos

Related to the brand name is a graphic design element called a brand logo. These design elements, or logos, can be thought of as a shorthand way of identifying a brand. For identifying their brands, companies use logos with or without brand names.[29] Not all brand names possess a distinct logo, but many do. Figure 3.8 presents a collection of six famous logos, ones that are readily recognizable to millions of people around the globe. For example, the Nike swoosh is virtually as famous as the company name, as are the logos for Shell Oil, Coca-Cola, and the other brands shown in Figure 3.8. Consumers learn these logos and easily recognize the brands on which the logos are emblazoned. (To test this, take a moment and visualize the logos for each of the following well-known brands: Pepsi, Ralph Lauren's Polo, Tommy Hilfiger clothing, Starbucks coffee, Mercedes-Benz automobiles, Toyota automobiles, Arm & Hammer baking soda, and Cracker Jack popcorn.)

Logo designs are incredibly diverse, ranging from highly abstract designs to those that depict nature scenes and from very simple to complex depictions. Generally, good logos (1) are recognized readily, (2) convey essentially the same meaning to all target members, and (3) evoke positive feelings.[30] Although logos undoubtedly perform valuable communication roles and influence brand equity via their effect both on brand awareness and image, published research on logos is surprisingly absent. However, an important study determined that the best

figure 3.8

Famous Logos

Chevrolet © Copyright 2008 GM Corp. Used with permission, GM Media Archive; Saturn © Copyright 2008 GM Corp. Used with permission, GM Media Archive; Mastercard © MasterCard/Via Bloomberg News./Landov; Nike © AP Images/PRNewsFoto/Nike; Shell © AP Images/PRNewsFoto/Shell Oil Company; Coca-Cola © HO/AFP/Getty Images/Newscom

Figure 3.9

Cingular's Logo

strategy for enhancing the likeability of a logo is to choose a design that is moderately elaborate rather than one that is too simple or too complex. Also, natural designs (as opposed to abstract illustrations) were found to produce more favorable consumer responses.[31] Cingular's heavily advertised logo perhaps represents an illustration of a logo that achieves the goal of being neither too simple nor too complex. Cingular, a major company in the wireless industry, invested heavily in selecting the simple yet distinct icon shown in Figure 3.9. Before Cingular merged with AT&T, whose own logo is also shown in Figure 3.9, personnel at Cingular referred affectionately to their icon as "Jack," apparently due to its similarity to the object in the old-fashioned children's game of jacks.

Updating Logos

Because logos become dated over time, companies occasionally update logos to be more attuned with the times. For example, the logo representing General Mills' Betty Crocker brand is a created person named Betty Crocker. Betty Crocker has represented this brand for more than 85 years, and during this time has undergone a variety of changes. Figure 3.10 displays the four most recent incarnations of Betty Crocker. The current version, which was introduced in 1996 in celebration of Betty Crocker's 75th birthday, is a digitally morphed amalgam of the photos of 75 women.

Many other brands routinely update their logos. The URL presented in the following footnote provides a useful source for reviewing logo changes for a number of well-known brands such as Adidas, BP, Google, IBM, John Deere, Nike, Sony, and Yamaha.[32]

Courtesy of General Mills Archives

figure 3.10

The Changing Faces of Betty Crocker

Packaging

A brand's package is, of course, the container that both protects and helps sell the product. Products available on store shelves are most always bottled, boxed, or packaged in some other manner. As the term package is used in the present context, beverage bottles and cereal boxes are packages; so are the jewel boxes for CDs and DVDs, the boxes in which new shoes are contained, and so on. Marcom specialists appreciate the crucial communications role performed by brand packaging, which has given rise to expressions such as, "Packaging is the least expensive form of advertising," "Every package is a five-second commercial," "The package is a silent salesman," and "The package is the product."[33] Packaging performs key communication and sales roles at the point of purchase inasmuch as shoppers spend an incredibly short amount of time—roughly 10 to 12 seconds—viewing brands before moving on or selecting an item and placing it in the shopping cart.[34]

The growth of supermarkets, mass merchandisers (such as Wal-Mart and Target) and other self-service retail outlets has necessitated that the package perform marketing functions beyond the traditional role of containing and protecting the product. The package also serves to (1) draw attention to a brand, (2) break through competitive clutter at the point of purchase, (3) justify price and value to the consumer, (4) signify brand features and benefits, (5) convey emotionality, and (6) ultimately motivate consumers' brand choices. Packaging is particularly important for differentiating homogenous or unexciting brands from available substitutes by working uninterruptedly to say what the brand is, how it is used, and what it can do to benefit the user.[35] In short, packages perform a major role in enhancing brand equity by creating or fortifying brand awareness and building brand images via conveying functional, symbolic, and experiential benefits (recall the brand equity model presented in Chapter 2).

Packaging Structure

A package communicates meaning about a brand via its various symbolic components: color, design, shape, size, physical materials, and information labeling.[36] These components taken together represent what is referred to as the *packaging structure.* These structural elements must interact harmoniously to evoke within buyers the set of meanings intended by the brand marketer. The notion underlying good packaging is *gestalt.* That is, people react to the unified whole—the gestalt—not to the individual parts.

The following sections describe various package structure components. Because these descriptions are more anecdotal than scientific, you should find these characterizations thought provoking but certainly not definitive. Interested students will want to add personal examples to the lists of illustrations for each of the following packaging components.

The Use of Color in Packaging

Packaging colors have the ability to communicate various cognitive and emotional meanings to prospective buyers.[37] Research has convincingly demonstrated the important role that color plays in affecting our senses. For example, in one study researchers altered the shade of pudding by adding food colors to create dark brown, medium brown, and light brown "flavors." In actuality, the pudding was identical in all three versions, namely vanilla flavor. However, the research revealed that all three brown versions were perceived as tasting like chocolate. Moreover, the dark brown pudding was considered to have the best chocolate flavor and to be the thickest. The light brown pudding was perceived to be the creamiest, possibly because cream is white in color.[38] This study, although not conducted in a packaging context per se, certainly holds implications for the use of color in package design.

The strategic use of colors in packaging is effective because colors affect people psychologically and emotionally. For example, the so-called high-wavelength colors of red, orange, and yellow possess strong excitation value and induce elated mood states.[39] *Red* is often described in terms such as active, stimulating, energetic, and vital. Brands using this as their primary color include Close-Up (toothpaste), Tylenol (medicine), Coca-Cola (soft drink), and Pringles (potato chips). *Orange* is an appetizing color that is often associated with food. Popular food brands using orange packaging include Wheaties (cereal), Uncle Ben's (rice), Sanka (coffee), Stouffer's (frozen dinners), and Kellogg's Mini-Wheats (cereal). *Yellow,* a good attention getter, is a warm color that has a cheerful effect on consumers. Cheerios (cereal), Kodak (film), Mazola (corn oil), and Pennzoil (motor oil) are just a few of the many brands that use yellow packages.

Green connotes abundance, health, calmness, and serenity. Green packaging is sometimes used for beverages (e.g., Heineken beer, 7-Up, Sprite, and Mountain Dew), often for vegetables (e.g., Green Giant), most always for mentholated products (e.g., Salem cigarettes), and for many other products (Irish Spring deodorant soap, Fuji film, etc.). Green also has come to stand for environmentally friendly products and as a cue to consumers of reduced-fat, low-fat, and fat-free products (e.g., Healthy Choice products). *Blue* suggests coolness and refreshment. Blue is often associated with laundry and cleaning products (e.g., Downy fabric softener and Snuggle dryer sheets) and skin products (e.g., Nivea skin lotion, Noxzema skin cream). Finally, *white* signifies purity, cleanliness, and mildness. Gold Medal (flour), Special K (cereal), Dove (body lotion), and Pantene (shampoo) are a few brands that feature white packages.

In addition to the emotional impact that color brings to a package, using polished reflective surfaces and color schemes employing white and black or silver and gold can add elegance and prestige to products. Cosmetic packages often use gold (e.g., Revlon's MoistureStay Lipcolor) or metallic silver packages (e.g., Almay Sheer makeup).

It is pertinent to note that the meaning of color varies from culture to culture. The comments made here are based on North American culture and are not necessarily applicable elsewhere. Readers from other cultures should identify exceptions to these comments and illustrate packages that do not adhere to North American color usage. Interestingly, a Web site presents results from a global survey that has been conducted for more than a decade on the meanings particular colors convey. Over 30,000 people have taken the survey and identified the colors they associate with particular meanings. For example, what colors suggest the following meanings or emotions to you: dignity, happiness, dependability, high quality, and power? To see what others think and to take the survey yourself, go to http://express.colormatters.com/colorsurvey/. For additional information about color symbolism, review the Web site presented in the following footnote.[40]

Design and Shape Cues in Packaging

Design refers to the organization of the elements on a package. An effective package design is one that permits good eye flow, provides the consumer with a point of focus, and conveys meaning about the brand's attributes and benefits. Package designers bring various elements together to help define a brand's image. These elements include—in addition to color—shape, size, and label design.

One way of evoking different feelings is through the choice of the slope, length, and thickness of lines on a package. *Horizontal lines* suggest restfulness and quiet, evoking feelings of tranquility. There appears to be a physiological reason for this reaction—it is easier for people to move their eyes horizontally than vertically; vertical movement is less natural and produces greater strain on eye muscles than horizontal movement. *Vertical lines* induce feelings of strength, confidence, and even pride. Energizer (batteries), Aquafresh (toothpaste), and Jif (peanut butter) all feature vertical lines in their package designs. One can even think of an athletic uniform as a package of sorts, and vertical lines sometimes appear on uniforms (think, for example, of the New York Yankees' uniform with its famous pinstripes). *Slanted lines* suggest upward movement to most people in the Western world, who read from left to right and thus view slanted lines as ascending rather than descending. Armor All (automobile polish), Gatorade (power drink), and Dr. Pepper (soft drink) use slanted lines in their package designs.

Shapes, too, arouse certain emotions and have specific connotations. Generally, round, curving lines connote femininity, whereas sharp, angular lines suggest masculinity. A package's shape also affects the apparent volume of the container. In general, if two packages have the same volume but a different shape, the taller of the two will appear to hold a greater volume inasmuch as height is usually associated with volume.

For rectangular-shaped packages, research has established that the various ratios among the height, width, and depth dimensions of these packages (e.g., the ratio of the box's height to its width) play a role in affecting consumers' brand choices.[41] This may seem strange, but mathematicians, architects, artists, and others have observed that the rectangular ratio of approximately 1.62 is "golden" and has appeared in the building blocks of the Great Pyramids, the Parthenon's façade, and in some master paintings.[42] Certain ratios in rectangular-shaped objects appear to promote perceptions of harmony, balance, and even beauty. In a consumer context, researchers studied actual brand packages in four grocery product categories—cereals, cookies, soaps, and detergents—and determined that the ratios of the sides of the boxes predicted the brands' market shares. This evidence suggests that the shape of a package is a strategic decision that requires careful consideration and marketplace testing. In short, a box is more than a mere container. It also is a receptacle loaded with subtle information and cues of product attractiveness and perhaps even quality.

Packaging Size

Many product categories are available in several product sizes. Soft drinks, for example, come in 8-, 12-, and 24-ounce bottles, 1-, 1.5-, and 2-liter containers, and in 6-, 12-, and 24-unit packs. Manufacturers offer different-sized containers to satisfy the unique needs of various market segments, to represent different usage situations, and to gain more shelf space in retail outlets. An interesting issue arises from the consumer's perspective with regard to the size of the container. In particular, does the amount of product consumption vary depending on the size of the container? For example, do consumers consume more content from a large package than a smaller version? Preliminary research on this matter reveals a tendency for consumers to indeed consume more content from larger packages. One reason for this behavior is that consumers perceive they gain lower unit prices from larger than smaller packages.[43] This finding is not universal across all products, however, because consumption for some products (such as laundry bleach or vitamins) is relatively invariant. Research also has revealed that packages with unusual shapes are perceived as containing larger quantities compared to more conventional packages, even when these latter packages are taller. The reason is that the unusual- or irregular-shaped packages draw more attention from consumers, and because there is a tendency for larger packages to draw more attention than smaller ones, consumers' judgments of volume are biased when attending to irregularly shaped packages. That is, because both larger packages and irregularly shaped ones command greater attention, consumers somehow subconsciously associate irregular shapes with containing larger quantities.[44]

Physical Materials in Packaging

Another important consideration is the materials that make up a package. Increased sales and profits often result when upgraded packaging materials are used to design more attractive and effective packages. Packaging materials can arouse consumer emotions, usually subconsciously. Packages constructed of metal evoke feelings of strength, durability, and, perhaps undesirably, coldness. Plastic packages connote lightness, cleanliness, and perhaps cheapness. Materials that are soft such as velvet, suede, and satin are associated with femininity. Foil can be used to convey a high-quality image and provoke feelings of prestige. Beverage products such as beers and sparkling wines often use foil with the apparent intent of appearing high end. Finally, wood sometimes is used in packages to arouse feelings of masculinity.

Evaluating the Package: The VIEW Model

A number of individual features have been discussed with regard to what a package communicates to buyers, but what exactly constitutes a good package? Although, as always, no single response is equally suitable across all packaging situations, four general features can be used to evaluate a particular package: visibility, information, emotional appeal, and workability, or VIEW.[45]

V=Visibility

Visibility signifies the ability of a package to *attract attention* at the point of purchase. The objective is to have a package stand out on the shelf yet not be so garish that it detracts from a brand's image. Brightly colored packages are especially effective at gaining the consumer's attention. Novel packaging graphics, sizes, and shapes also enhance a package's visibility and thus serve to draw the consumer's attention.

Many brands in product categories such as soft drinks, cereal, and candy alternate packages throughout the year with special seasonal and holiday packaging as a way of attracting attention in addition to fitting in with the season. By aligning the brand with the shopping mood fitting the season or holiday, companies provide consumers with an added reason for selecting the specially packaged brand over more humdrum brands that never vary their package design. The heart-shaped package for the Whitman's Sampler (Figure 3.11) is an attractive, attention-gaining, and romance-conveying package design that is perfect for Valentine's Day.

I=Information

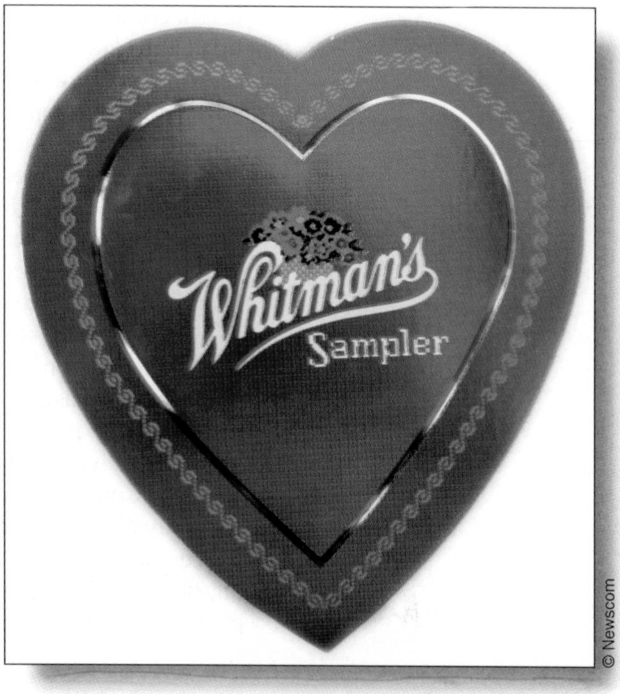

Figure 3.11

An Effective Seasonal Package Design

This second element of the VIEW model deals with various forms of product information that are presented on packages (e.g., product ingredients, usage instructions, claimed benefits, nutritional information, and product warnings). The objective is to provide the right type and quantity of information without cluttering the package with excessive information that could interfere with the primary message or cheapen the look of the package.

Package labels play an influential role in affecting consumer purchase behavior. For example, research has demonstrated that presenting graphic visuals on cigarette packages for purposes of conveying the negative health consequences of smoking results in more people intending to quit smoking and willing to encourage other smokers to quit.[46] Research also has determined that low-fat labels on food products have the perverse effect of increasing food intake by up to 50 percent compared to foods not labeled as low-fat.[47] This increased food consumption occurs for normal-weight consumers mostly with foods perceived as being relatively healthy, but for overweight people it increases their consumption of all foods. The reasons underlying this low-fat labeling and increased-food-intake relationship are twofold: (1) low-fat labels lead people to believe that products are lower in calories than they actually are, and (2) consumers' guilt as a result of overeating is reduced when consuming foods labeled as low-fat. Some people, when eating foods labeled as low-fat, infer that ingesting greater quantities is okay without considering that such foods may have lower levels of fat content but not meaningfully fewer calories. These people consequently overeat but without experiencing the guilt of so doing.

In some instances, putting a short, memorable slogan on a package is a wise marketing tactic. Slogans on packages are best used when a strong association has been built between the brand and the slogan through extensive and effective advertising. The slogan on the package, a concrete reminder of the brand's advertising, can facilitate the consumer's retrieval of advertising content and thereby enhance the chances of a trial purchase. This practice of putting an advertising slogan on a package to tie in with media advertising takes advantage of a psychological principle known as *encoding specificity*. In Chapter 20, when discussing the role of point-of-purchase communications, we will describe this principle in detail.

E=Emotional Appeal

The third component of the VIEW model, emotional appeal, concerns a package's ability to evoke a desired feeling or mood. Package designers attempt to arouse feelings such as elegance, prestige, cheerfulness, and fun through the use of color, shape, packaging materials, and other devices. Packages for some brands contain virtually no emotional elements and emphasize instead informational content, whereas packages of other brands emphasize emotional content and contain very little information. Heinz ketchup's packaging well illustrates the emotional value of packaging. Heinz, like other brands in this category, had always been packaged in glass bottles. Then the company began packaging ketchup in plastic containers. Both the bottles and the plastic containers were relatively blah, however. In an appeal to children, who consume the majority of all ketchup in the United States, Heinz eventually designed an emotionally appealing, fun-oriented package with bright coloring and a multihued, striped design. Children love the different ketchup colors (red, green, and purple) and the similarly colored packages.

What determines whether information or emotion is emphasized in a brand's package? The major determinant is the nature of the product category and the underlying consumer behavior involved. If consumers make brand-selection decisions based on objectives such as obtaining the best buy or making a prudent choice, then packaging must provide sufficient concrete information to facilitate the consumer's selection. When, however, product and brand selections are made in the pursuit of amusement, fantasies, or sensory stimulation, packaging must contain the requisite emotional content to activate purchase behavior.

This discussion should not be taken as suggesting that all packaging emphasizes either information or emotion. Although the packaging of brands in some categories does emphasize one or the other, there are many product categories where it is necessary for packaging to blend informational and emotional content so as to appeal simultaneously to consumers' rational and symbolic needs. Cereal is a case in point. Consumers require nutritional information to select from among the dozens of available brands intelligently, and research indicates that consumer choice in the cereal category is indeed influenced by nutritional components such as protein, fat, fiber, sodium, sugar, and vitamins and minerals.[48] Cereal choice also is driven by emotional factors—wholesomeness, nostalgia, excitement, and so on.

W=Workability

The final component of the VIEW model, workability, refers to how a package functions rather than how it communicates. Several workability issues are prominent: (1) does the package protect the product contents, (2) does it facilitate easy storage on the part of both retailers and consumers, (3) does it simplify the consumer's task in accessing and using the product, (4) does it protect retailers against unintentional breakage from consumer handling and from pilferage, and (5) is the package environmentally friendly?

Figure 3.12

Dutch Boy's Easy-to-Hold/Open/Pour Paint Container

Courtesy Dutch Boy Paints

Numerous packaging innovations in recent years have enhanced workability. These include pourable-spout containers for motor oil and sugar; easy-pour containers (such as for Heinz ketchup); microwaveable containers for many food items; zip-lock packaging for cheese and other food items; single-serving bags and boxes; food in tubes (e.g., yogurt, applesauce, and pudding); slimmer 12-packs of beer and soft drinks that take up less room in refrigerators; and easy-to-hold/open/pour paint containers (see Figure 3.12).

The introduction of Go-Gurt yogurt for children illustrates how a "workable" package can alter consumer behavior and increase sales. Because eating yogurt from a standard container minimally requires the availability of a spoon, children and teens were not consuming yogurt at school. Hence, standard yogurt packaging essentially restricted sales of yogurt to adults and to the relatively few children and teens willing to take a spoon to school. Marketing executives at General Mills' Yoplait division developed a simple but profitable solution to this problem when they introduced the Go-Gurt brand of yogurt in a tube. In its first year after introduction, Go-Gurt garnered national sales in excess of $100 million and nearly doubled the proportion of yogurt users under the age of 19 to about one in six. The choice of Go-Gurt as the brand name facilitated product adoption by signifying that the tube contained yogurt and suggesting that the brand was to be consumed on the go.[49] Yoplait has also developed a similar yogurt-in-a-tube product for adults called Yoplait Express.

Companies also have developed "smart packages" that include magnetic strips, bar codes, and electronic chips that can communicate with appliances, computers, and consumers. For example, packages of microwaveable foods eventually will be programmed to "tell" microwaves how long the food item should be cooked. Procter & Gamble (P&G) has tested a smart-package program that is designed to send information about a product sale to a computer database as soon as a customer removes a P&G brand from the shelf. Small computer chips attached to the package send a signal to the store shelf, which contains printed circuit boards. The objective is, of course, to provide the company with immediate sales data that will facilitate its supply chain management.[50]

A host of packaging innovations have served to increase what might be called environmental workability. Many of the changes have involved moves from plastic to recyclable paper packages; for example, many fast-food chains eliminated the use of foam packaging, and other firms have transformed their packages from plastic to cardboard containers. Another significant environmental initiative has been the increase in spray containers as substitutes for ozone-harming aerosol cans. It is undeniable, however, that too many packages are environmentally wasteful by using excessive amounts of cardboard, plastic, and other packaging materials—all of which end up in landfills and most of which generate excessive amounts of climate-warming carbon dioxide in their manufacture. Companies need to do more work to reduce the amount of packaging materials that are used to enclose and protect their brands.

Quantifying the VIEW Components

In conclusion, most packages do not perform well on all the VIEW criteria, but packages need not always be exemplary on all four VIEW components because the relative importance of each criterion varies from one product category to another. Emotional appeal dominates for some products (e.g., perfume), information is most important for others (e.g., staple food items), while visibility and workability are generally important for all products in varying degrees. In the final analysis, the relative importance of packaging requirements depends, as always, on the particular market and the competitive situation.

Although we have provided straightforward descriptions of the four VIEW components, it would be useful to go beyond mere description and have a procedure whereby the components could be quantified on a case-by-case basis to determine whether a new package proposal stands a good chance of being successful. Figure 3.13 illustrates a procedure for accomplishing this goal and applies it to the new type of paint container that was presented in Figure 3.12. Similar to what was done in quantifying the five adoption-determining characteristics (Figure 3.5), each VIEW component could be rated first in terms of its *importance* in determining the suitability of a proposed new package and then with respect to how well the new package performs on each component, its *evaluation score.* Applying this straightforward multiplicative model to the Dutch Boy paint container generates a hypothetical set of importance and evaluation scores. Because workability is considered the most important VIEW component for this particular packaging application and because the new container for Dutch Boy paint is evaluated as performing "at the max" on this component, this new packaging design receives a highly adequate total score of 49. It should be apparent that the importance scores for each packaging component will change from packaging situation

figure 3.13

Hypothetical Illustration of Quantifying the VIEW Model Components.

VIEW Component	Importance (I)*	Evaluation (E)†	I × E
Visibility	3	4	12
Information	2	5	10
Emotional Appeal	2	1	2
Workability	5	5	25
Total Score	NA	NA	49

*Importance is rated on a scale with values ranging from zero to five. A rating of zero would indicate that a specific packaging component has no importance in this particular case. Higher positive values indicate progressively increasing levels of importance.

†Evaluation is rated on a scale with values ranging from minus five to five. A rating of zero, the midpoint of the scale, would indicate that the proposed new package performs neither favorably nor unfavorably on the characteristic at hand; negative values indicate poor performance, with minus five representing the worst possible performance; positive values indicate favorable performance, with five representing the best possible performance.

to situation, and that the evaluation scores will differ for different prototype package designs that are under consideration. A simple model of this sort is not intended to make what ultimately is a subjective decision but rather to structure one's thinking in arriving at such a decision.

Designing a Package

Because package design is so critical to a brand's success, a systematic approach is recommended. Figure 3.14 provides a five-step package design process. The subsequent discussion describes each step.[51]

Step 1: Specify Brand-Positioning Objectives

This initial stage requires that the brand management team specify how the brand is to be positioned in the consumer's mind and against competitive brands. What identity or image is desired for the brand? For example, when Pfizer Inc. developed Listerine PocketPaks, a dissolvable breath-strip product containing Listerine mouthwash, the objective was to design a package that was both functional and aesthetically appealing. Specifically, the package was designed such that oral care could be provided outside the home, be easily transportable, and be accessible by men and women in a variety of situations.[52] The brand name, PocketPaks, describes perfectly how the package was designed literally to fit in a person's pants or jacket pocket.

figure 3.14

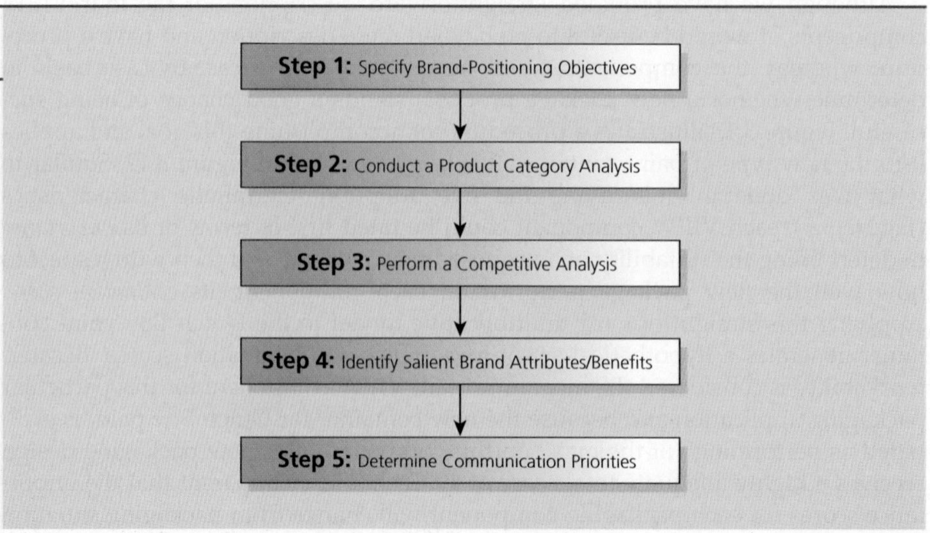

The Package Design Process

Step 2: Conduct a Product Category Analysis

Having established what the brand represents (step 1) and thus what the packaging must convey, it is essential to study the product category and related categories to determine relevant trends or anticipated events that would influence the packaging decision. The point, in other words, is that to be forewarned is to be forearmed.

Step 3: Perform a Competitive Analysis

Armed with knowledge about competitors' use of packaging colors, shapes, graphical features, and materials, the package designer is thus prepared to create a package that conveys the desired image (step 1) yet is sufficiently unique and differentiating (step 2) to capture consumer attention.

Step 4: Identify Salient Brand Attributes or Benefits

As noted earlier, research reveals that shoppers spend an incredibly short amount of time—roughly 10 to 12 seconds—viewing brands before moving on or selecting an item. It is imperative, therefore, that the package not be too cluttered with information and that it feature benefits that are most important to consumers. A general rule for displaying brand benefits on a package is, "The fewer, the better."[53] To be effective as a communication device, a package must emphasize one or two really key brand benefits rather than being cluttered with a list of benefits that will not capture consumers' attention or influence their purchase decisions.

Step 5: Determine Communication Priorities

Having identified the most salient brand benefits (step 4), the package designer at this phase of the process must establish verbal and visual priorities for the package. Although perhaps three benefits may have been identified in step 4 as essentially equal in importance, the designer must prioritize which of the three is to capture the greatest visual or verbal attention on the package. This is a very tough decision because it is tempting to devote equal attention to all important brand benefits. It is critical that the package designer acknowledge that the package "advertisement" at the point of purchase occurs in an incredibly cluttered environment for a very short duration. Acknowledging this fact makes it much easier to devote package space to the most important brand benefit.

Summary

The continual introduction of new brands is critical to the success of most business organizations. Marketing communications can facilitate the brand-adoption process by communicating a new brand's relative advantages, showing how it is compatible with consumers' existing purchase preferences and values, reducing real or perceived complexity, enhancing the brand's communicability, and making it easy to try.

The brand name is the single most important element found on a package and plays an influential role in determining whether new brands succeed. The brand name works with package graphics and other product features to communicate and position the brand's image. The brand name identifies the product and differentiates it from others on the market. A good brand name can evoke feelings of trust, confidence, security, strength, durability, speed, status, and many other desirable associations. A good brand name must satisfy several fundamental requirements: it must describe the product's benefits, be compatible with the product's image, and be memorable and easy to pronounce. A major section in this chapter was devoted to a five-step process for selecting a brand name. Another section discussed the nature and role of brand logos.

The package is perhaps the most important component of the product as a communications device. It reinforces associations established in advertising, breaks through competitive clutter at the point of purchase, and justifies price and value to the consumer. Package design relies on the use of symbolism to support a brand's image and to convey desired information to consumers. A number of package cues are used for this purpose, including color, design, shape, brand name, physical materials, and product information labeling. These cues must interact harmoniously to evoke within buyers the set of meanings intended by the marketing communicator. Package designs can be evaluated by applying the VIEW model, which contains the elements of visibility, information, emotional appeal, and workability. A concluding section described a five-step process for package design.

Discussion Questions

1. Based on your personal experience in using cell phones, propose a design for a new cell phone that, in your view, would make it a success among consumers in your age group. Based on the new attributes/benefits that your proposed cell phone would possess, provide a brand name for the phone and justify your rationale for this name.
2. Considering just the workability component of the VIEW model, provide illustrations of several packages that, in your opinion, represent higher or lower levels of workability.
3. Perform the same exercise as in question 4, but now develop a brand name for a new brand of soy milk. Perhaps the best-known brand in this category is Silk, which obviously is a conjunction of soy and milk.
4. Choose a grocery product category and analyze the various brands in this category in terms of their packaging features designed to attract consumers' attention. Identify the packaging features that make some brands in this category more or less attention-gaining than others.
5. Select a product category of personal interest and analyze the brand names for three competitive brands in that category. Analyze each brand name in terms of the fundamental requirements that were described in the chapter. Order the three brands according to which has the best, next best, and worst brand name. Support your ranking with specific reasons.
6. Analyze the packaging structure for a brand of your choice. Describe why this brand's structure is effective for the product category and for the brand name chosen.
7. Assume you work for a company that is in the business of creating brand names for clients. One of your clients is a major automobile company. This company is in the process of introducing a new hybrid automobile to compete against Toyota's Prius. Your task is to develop a name for this new automobile, either a real dictionary-word name or a made-up name along the lines of Lexus or Acura. Present and justify your choice of brand name.
8. Identify several brand logos other than those illustrated in this chapter and indicate why, in your view, these are effective logos.
9. Pick a new brand of your choice and describe in detail how that brand satisfies, or fails to satisfy, the following success requirements: relative advantages, compatibility, communicability, trialability, and observability. Note: For the purposes of this assignment, it is better to select a brand that represents an innovative product category rather than a simple extension of an established category.
10. Select a packaged-goods product category, and apply the VIEW model to three competitive brands within that category. Define all four components of the model, and explain how each applies to your selected product. Then use the following procedures to weigh each component in the model in terms of your perception of its relative packaging importance for your chosen product category:
    a. Distribute 10 points among the four components, with more points signifying more importance and the sum of the allocated points totaling exactly 10. (This weighting procedure involves what marketing researchers refer to as a constant sum scale.)
    b. Next, evaluate each brand in terms of your perception of its performance on each packaging component by assigning a score from 1 (does not perform well) to 10 (performs extremely well). Thus, you will assign a total of 12 scores: four for each VIEW component for the three different brands.
    c. Combine the scores for each brand by multiplying the brand's performance on each

component by the weight of that component (from step a) and then summing the products of these four weighted scores.

d. The summed score for each of your three chosen brands will reflect your perception of how good that brand's packaging is in terms of the VIEW model—the higher the score, the better the packaging in your opinion. Summarize the scores for the three brands for an overall assessment of each brand's packaging.

11. What determines whether a new product or service has relative advantages over competitive offerings? Identify the relative advantages of each of the following: disposable cameras, hybrid automobiles, plasma TVs. Given that each of these products also has relative disadvantages compared to competitive products, present a general statement (i.e., a statement with universal applicability) that would explain why consumers are willing to adopt new products even though they almost invariably have relative disadvantages.

12. SUVs have names such as the Ford Explorer, Chevy Blazer, Mercury Mountaineer, Lincoln Navigator, Subaru Forester, Mazda Navajo, Infinity QX-4, Honda Passport, Jeep Wrangler, Oldsmobile Bravada, Toyota Highlander, and so on. Suppose you worked for an automobile company and that your company developed an SUV that was marketed as safer than other SUVs. What would you name this new vehicle? What is your rationale for this name?

13. Sugar-substitute products have been available for years. The two historically leading brands in this category are Equal (blue package) and Sweet'N Low (pink package). A yellow-packaged product named Splenda was the latest artificial sweetener introduced and is now the market-share leader. The company that markets this brand claims that it is "made from sugar, so it tastes like sugar." Using Splenda for illustration, explain the process by which marketing variables can influence consumers to become part of the awareness, trier, and repeater classes for this brand (refer to Figure 3.1).

14. A Boston diamond wholesaler developed a special way to cut diamonds that gives diamonds perfect symmetry and extra sparkle. The wholesaler developed a viewing device (called the proportion scope) that allows consumers to see a diamond with eight perfect hearts and eight arrows when they peer through the scope. The inventor of this specially cut diamond gave his gems the brand name Hearts on Fire. Evaluate this name by applying concepts from the chapter. Propose an alternative name.

End Notes

1. William Boulding, Ruskin Morgan, and Richard Staelin, "Pulling the Plug to Stop the New Product Drain," *Journal of Marketing Research* 34 (February 1997), 164.
2. The following discussion is adapted from Chakravarthi Narasimhan and Subrata K. Sen, "New Product Models for Test Market Data," *Journal of Marketing* 47 (winter 1983), 13, 14.
3. A sophisticated and thorough empirical analysis of factors influencing the probability the people will undertake trial purchases of consumer packaged goods is provided by Jan-Benedict E. M. Steenkamp and Katrijn Gielens, "Consumer and Market Drivers of the Trial Probability of New Consumer Packaged Goods," *Journal of Consumer Research* 30 (December 2003), 368–384.
4. Everett M. Rogers, *Diffusion of Innovations*, 5th ed. (New York: Free Press, 2003).
5. Becky Ebenkamp, "Survey Says: Put a Cork in It!" *Brandweek*, March 6, 2006, 18.
6. For further discussion of the role of observability, see Robert J. Fisher and Linda L. Price, "An Investigation into the Social Context of Early Adoption Behavior," *Journal of Consumer Research* 19 (December 1992), 477–486.
7. Christopher Lawton, "Dell's Colorful Designs for Customers," http://online.wsj.com, June 26, 2007 (accessed June 27, 2007).
8. Shari Roan, "Laser Hair Removal Is Coming to the Home," http://www.courier-journal.com, August 2, 2007 (accessed August 14, 2007).
9. "Palomar Medical and Gillette Sign Agreement to Develop a Home-Use, Light-Based Hair Removal Device for Women," http://www.prnewswire.com, February 19, 2007 (accessed August 14, 2007).
10. Rob Osler, "The Name Game: Tips on How to Get It Right," *Marketing News*, September 14, 1998, 50.
11. Gwen Bachmann Achenreiner and Deborah Roedder John, "The Meaning of Brand Names to Children: A Developmental Investigation," *Journal of Consumer Psychology* 13, no. 3 (2003), 205–219.
12. Joseph W. AlbaJ. Wesley Hutchinson, and John G. Lynch, "Memory and Decision Making," in *Handbook of Consumer Behavior*, ed. Thomas S. Robertson and Harold H. Kassarjian (Englewood Cliffs, NJ: Prentice Hall, 1991), 1–49.
13. France Leclerc, Bernd H. Schmitt, and Laurette Dubé, "Foreign Branding and Its Effects on Product

Perceptions and Attitudes," *Journal of Marketing Research* 31 (March 1994), 263–270.

14. Mark Boslet, "It's Alive! It's Also Small, Simple: The Ideas behind the Name 'Zune,'" http://online.wsj.com, November 16, 2006 (accessed November 16, 2006).
15. These requirements represent a summary of views from a variety of sources, including Kevin Lane Keller, *Strategic Brand Management: Building, Measuring, and Managing Brand Equity* (Upper Saddle River, NJ: Prentice Hall, 1998), 136–140; Allen P. Adamson, *Brand Simple* (New York: Palgrave MacMillan, 2006), chapter 7; Daniel L. Doden, "Selecting a Brand Name That Aids Marketing Objectives," *Advertising Age*, November 5, 1990, 34; and Walter P. Margulies, "Animal Names on Products May Be Corny, but Boost Consumer Appeal," *Advertising Age*, October 23, 1972, 77.
16. For excellent coverage of trademark infringement, review the following sources: Jeffrey M. Samuels and Linda B. Samuels, "Famous Marks Now Federally Protected Against Dilution," *Journal of Public Policy & Marketing* 15 (fall 1996), 307–310; Daniel J. Howard, Roger A. Kerin, and Charles Gengler, "The Effects of Brand Name Similarity on Brand Source Confusion: Implications for Trademark Infringement," *Journal of Public Policy & Marketing* 19 (fall 2000), 250–264.
17. Chris Janiszewski and Stijn M. J. Van Osselaer, "A Connectionist Model of Brand-Quality Associations," *Journal of Marketing Research* 37 (August 2000), 331–350.
18. Kevin Lane Keller, Susan E. Heckler, and Michael J. Houston, "The Effects of Brand Name Suggestiveness on Advertising Recall," *Journal of Marketing* 62 (January 1998), 48–57. See also J. Colleen McCracken and M. Carole Macklin, "The Role of Brand Names and Visual Clues in Enhancing Memory for Consumer Packaged Goods," *Marketing Letters* 9 (April 1998), 209–226; and Richard R. Klink, "Creating Brand Names with Meaning: The Use of Sound Symbolism," *Marketing Letters* 11, no. 1 (2000), 5–20.
19. Sankar Sen, "The Effects of Brand Name Suggestiveness and Decision Goal on the Development of Brand Knowledge," *Journal of Consumer Psychology* 8, no. 4 (1999), 431–454.
20. Keller et al., "The Effects of Brand Name Suggestiveness on Advertising Recall." However, for an alternative perspective, see Sen "The Effects of Brand Name Suggestiveness and Decision Goal."
21. For example, Richard R. Klink, "Creating Brand Names with Meaning: The Use of Sound Symbolism," *Marketing Letters* 11 (February 2000), 5–20; and Eric Yorkston and Geeta Menon, "A Sound Idea: Phonetic Effects of Brand Names on Consumer Judgments," *Journal of Consumer Research* 31 (June 2004), 43–51.
22. Yorkston and Menon, "A Sound Idea," 43.
23. Klink, "Creating Brand Names with Meaning."
24. Tina M. Lowrey, L. J. Shrum, and Tony M. Dubitsky, "The Relation between Brand-Name Linguistic Characteristics and Brand-Name Memory," *Journal of Advertising* 32 (fall 2003), 7–18. See also Dawn Lerman and Ellen Garbarino, "Recall and Recognition of Brand Names: A Comparison of Word and Nonword Name Types," *Psychology & Marketing* 19 (July/August 2002), 621–639. This latter article provides preliminary evidence that created brand names (i.e., nonword names) generate higher recognition scores than do brand names that are based on actual words.
25. Chiranjeev Kohli and Douglas W. LaBahn, "Observations: Creating Effective Brand Names: A Study of the Naming Process," *Journal of Advertising Research* 37 (January/February 1997), 67–75.
26. Ibid., 69.
27. This description is adapted from Rebecca Johnson, "Name That Airline," *Travel & Leisure*, October 1999, 159–164; Bonnie Tsui, "JetBlue Soars in First Months," *Advertising Age*, September 11, 2000, 26; "JetBlue Airways Open for Business" (Company Press Release), January 11, 2000, http://www.jetblue.com/learnmore/pressDetail.asp?newsId=10 (accessed January 11, 2000).
28. Kohli and LaBahn, 73.
29. When brand names are used, logos are set in any of a multitude of typefaces. Typeface design can have a substantial impact on the impressions formed when viewing a logo. Fascinating research on this issue is provided by Pamela W. Henderson, Joan L. Giese, and Joseph A. Cote, "Impression Management Using Typeface Design," *Journal of Marketing* 68 (October 2004), 60–72.
30. Pamela W. Henderson and Joseph A. Cote, "Guidelines for Selecting or Modifying Logos," *Journal of Marketing* 62 (April 1998), 14–30. This article is must reading for anyone interested in learning more about logos.
31. Henderson and Cote, "Guidelines for Selecting or Modifying Logos."
32. http://worldsbestlogos.blogspot.com/2007/08/adobe-systems-logo-history.html.
33. Some of these phrases were mentioned in Michael Gershman, "Packaging: Positioning Tool of the 1980s," *Management Review* (August 1987), 33–41.
34. Peter R. Dickson and Alan G. Sawyer, "The Price Knowledge and Search of Supermarket Shoppers," *Journal of Marketing* 54 (July 1990), 42–53; John Le Boutillier, Susanna Shore Le Boutillier, and Scott A. Neslin, "A Replication and Extension of the Dickson and Sawyer Price-Awareness Study," *Marketing Letters* 5 (January 1994), 31–42.
35. John Deighton, "A White Paper on the Packaging Industry," Dennison Technical Papers, December 1983, 5.
36. An interesting article about package meaning is available in Robert L. Underwood and Julie L. Ozanne, "Is Your Package an Effective Communicator? A Normative Framework for Increasing the Communicative Competence of Packaging," *Journal of Marketing Communications* 4 (December 1998), 207–220.
37. For an in-depth treatment of the role of color in packaging and other forms of marketing communications, see Lawrence L. Garber, Jr., and Eva M. Hyatt, "Color as a Tool for Visual Persuasion," in *Persuasive Imagery: A Consumer Response Perspective*, eds. Linda M. Scott and Rajeev Batra (Mahwah, NJ: Lawrence Erlbaum, 2003), 313–336.

38. Gail Tom, Teresa Barnett, William Lew, and Jodean Selmants, "Cueing the Consumer: The Role of Salient Cues in Consumer Perception," *The Journal of Consumer Marketing* 4 (spring 1987), 23–27.
39. This comment and parts of the following discussion are based on statements appearing in Joseph A. Bellizzi, Ayn E. Crowley, and Ronald W. Hasty, "The Effects of Color in Store Design," *Journal of Retailing* 59 (spring 1983), 21–45.
40. For information about color symbolism, go to http://www.colormatters.com/brain.html.
41. Priya Raghubir and Eric A. Greenleaf, "Ratios in Proportion: What Should the Shape of the Package Be?" *Journal of Marketing* 70 (April 2006), 95–107.
42. Ibid., 96.
43. Brian Wansink, "Can Package Size Accelerate Usage Volume?" *Journal of Marketing* 60 (July 1996), 1–14.
44. Valerie Folkes and Shashi Matta, "The Effect of Package Shape on Consumers' Judgments of Product Volume: Attention as a Mental Contaminant," *Journal of Consumer Research* 31 (September 2004), 390–401.
45. Dik Warren Twedt, "How Much Value Can Be Added through Packaging," *Journal of Marketing* 32 (January 1968), 61–65.
46. Jeremy Kees, Scot Burton, J. Craig Andrews, and John Kozup, "Tests of Graphic Visuals and Cigarette Package Warning Combinations: Implications for the Framework Convention on Tobacco Control," *Journal of Public Policy & Marketing* 25 (fall 2006), 212–223.
47. Brian Wansink and Pierre Chandon, "Can 'Low-Fat' Nutrition Labels Lead to Obesity?" *Journal of Marketing Research* 43 (November 2006), 605–617.
48. George Baltas, "The Effects of Nutrition Information on Consumer Choice," *Journal of Advertising Research* 41 (March/April 2001), 57–63.
49. Sonia Reyes, "Groove Tube," *Brandweek's Marketers of the Year* insert, October 16, 2000, M111–M116.
50. Greg Dalton, "If These Shelves Could Talk," *The Industry Standard,* April 2, 2001, 49–51.
51. This discussion is adapted from Herbert M. Meyers and Murray J. Lubliner, *The Marketer's Guide to Successful Package Design* (Chicago: NTC Business Books, 1998), 55–67.
52. Catherine Arnold, "Way Outside the Box," *Marketing News,* June 23, 2003, 1315.
53. Meyers and Lubliner, *The Marketer's Guide to Successful Package Design,* 63.

CHAPTERS

4

Targeting

5

Positioning

6

Objective Setting and Budgeting

Part 2

The Fundamental Marcom Decisions: Targeting, Positioning, Objective Setting, and Budgeting

Part Two builds a foundation for understanding the nature and function of marketing communications by providing practical and theoretical overviews of four fundamental marcom decisions: targeting, positioning, objective setting, and budgeting. *Chapter 4* introduces targeting as the key element in effective marketing communications. The chapter focuses on four sets of audience-defining characteristics that singularly or in combination influence how people respond to marcom programs: behaviorgraphics, psychographics, demographics, and geodemographics. Each of these characteristics is discussed in detail, with major emphasis on: (1) the population age structure, (2) the changing household composition (e.g., increases in the number of single-person households), and (3) ethnic population developments.

Chapter 5 deals with brand positioning from the marcom practitioner's vantage point and also examines positioning from the consumer's perspective. The positioning statement is described as the central idea that encapsulates a brand's meaning and distinctiveness and explains that a good positioning statement must reflect a brand's competitive advantage and motivate customers to action. Potential starting points for developing positioning statements are then discussed as well as the topic of brand repositioning. Detailed attention is devoted to how consumers process marcom information. Particular detail is applied to describing the marcom activities necessary to promote consumer attention, comprehension, and learning of marcom messages.

Chapter 6 completes the treatment of fundamental marcom decisions by examining objective setting and budgeting. The importance of setting objectives is initially discussed and a framework called the hierarchy of effects explains how the choice of marcom objective rests with knowing where on the hierarchy members of the target audience are located. Requirements for setting suitable marcom objectives are detailed. Next to be addressed is the issue of whether marcom objectives should be formulated based on sales or presales (communication) goals. Marcom budgeting is subsequently covered with treatment of how budgets should be established in theory and practical budgeting methods are discussed in detail. Separate sections cover four budgeting methods: percentage-of-sales budgeting, objective-and-task budgeting, budgeting via the competitive parity method (with detailed treatment of share of voice and share of market assessments), and budgeting via the affordability method.

4

Targeting

Teenagers are a notoriously difficult-to-reach target group. This is because many teens rarely read newspapers and magazines, and their TV, radio, and online preferences are highly divergent. Because it is difficult to reach teenagers with traditional mass media channels, marketers are constantly on the lookout for nontraditional, cost-effective ways to connect with this evasive target audience. One creative approach some marketers are using is to appeal to the broader group of high school students by reaching out to assemblages of cheerleaders who attend cheerleading camps and other events. Cheerleaders often are very popular in high school, and their use of particular brands can influence a much wider group of teenagers through the power of word-of-mouth.

Procter & Gamble, the huge consumer-products company located in Cincinnati, Ohio, is one of the major participants at cheerleading events. At these events, P&G distributes free samples of products and assists cheerleaders in areas such as providing nutritional information and having makeup artists offer tips for applying P&G's CoverGirl line of cosmetics. Many other companies also distribute samples and coupons at cheerleading events in hopes that this influential group will return to their schools as ambassadors for marketers' new and mature brands.

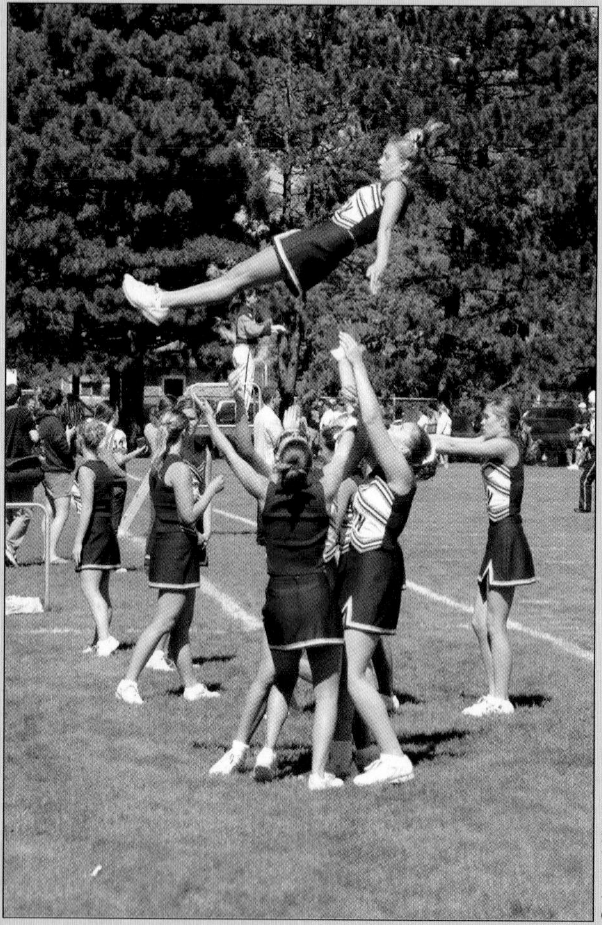

© dmac / Alamy

SOURCE: Adapted from Brian Steinberg, "Gimme an Ad! Brands Lure Cheerleaders," *The Wall Street Journal Online*, http://online.wsj.com April 19, 2007 (accessed April 19, 2007).

Chapter Objectives

After reading this chapter you should be able to:

1. Appreciate the importance of targeting marketing communications to specific consumer groups and realize that the targeting decision is the initial and most fundamental of all marcom decisions.
2. Understand the role of behaviorgraphics in targeting consumer groups.
3. Describe the nature of psychographic targeting.
4. Appreciate major demographic developments such as changes in the age structure of the population and ethnic population growth.
5. Explain the meaning of geodemographics and understand the role for this form of targeting.
6. Recognize that any single characteristic of consumers—whether their age, ethnicity, or income level—likely is not solely sufficient for sophisticated marcom targeting.

>>Marcom Insight:

Reaching Teens by Appealing to Cheerleaders

Introduction

This chapter expands the discussion of targeting that was introduced in Chapter 1. You will recall that Chapter 1 provided a model of the marcom process and described various forms of "fundamental" and "implementation" decisions. The section on fundamental decisions concluded with the following mantra:

> *All marketing communications should be: (1) directed to a particular* target market, *(2) clearly* positioned, *(3) created to achieve a* specific objective, *and (4) undertaken to accomplish the objective* within budget constraint.

Targeting specific audiences can be considered the starting point for all marcom decisions. Thus, the purpose of this chapter is to describe how marcom practitioners target prospective customers. Targeting allows marketing communicators to deliver their messages precisely and prevent wasted coverage on people falling outside the targeted market. Targeting thus implies efficiency of effort. Not to target is equivalent to shooting a basketball wildly in the air without directing it toward the hoop. It is difficult enough to connect on a shot from a 20-foot distance when that is one's intent. Imagine how unlikely you are to make a shot if you don't consciously concentrate on a specific target. Such is the case when marcom efforts fail to concentrate on a specific audience.

This chapter focuses on four sets of consumer characteristics that singularly or in combination influence what people consume and how they respond to marketing communications: behaviorgraphics, psychographics, demographics, and geodemographics. Note that "graphics," the suffix for each of these consumer characteristics, is a term that refers to *measurable characteristics* of target audiences. The prefix to each type of targeting represents *how* the audience is measured. Specifically, *behaviorgraphics* represents information about the audience's behavior—in terms of past purchase behavior or online search activity—in a particular product category or set of related categories. *Psychographics* captures aspects of consumers' psychological makeup and lifestyles including their attitudes, values, and motivations. *Demographics* reflect measurable population characteristics such as age, income, and ethnicity. And *geodemographics* is based on demographic characteristics of consumers who reside within geographic clusters such as ZIP Code areas and neighborhoods.

Subsequent sections are devoted to all four groups of audience-defining characteristics. First, however, it will be useful to distinguish the four general targeting methods in terms of two considerations: (1) how easy or difficult it is to obtain data (i.e., *measure*) the characteristic on which a targeting decision is to be made, and (2) how *predictive* the characteristic is of consumer choice behavior. The graph presented in Figure 4.1 lays these two considerations out as the vertical (measurement ease) and horizontal (behavior predictability) dimensions. It thus can be seen that demographic data is relatively easy to obtain but that demographic information is the least predictive of consumer choice behavior. At the other extreme, behaviorgraphic data are relatively difficult and/or expensive to procure but are highly predictive of choice behavior. Geodemographic and psychographic data fall between these extremes. The discussion proceeds from the most (behaviorgraphics) to the least predictive indicator of behavior (demographics).

Behaviorgraphic Targeting

Let's move forward 10 years and imagine that you are a successful entrepreneur who owns a really cool store located in a trendy area. Your establishment appeals primarily to professionals and white-collar workers. From the very start

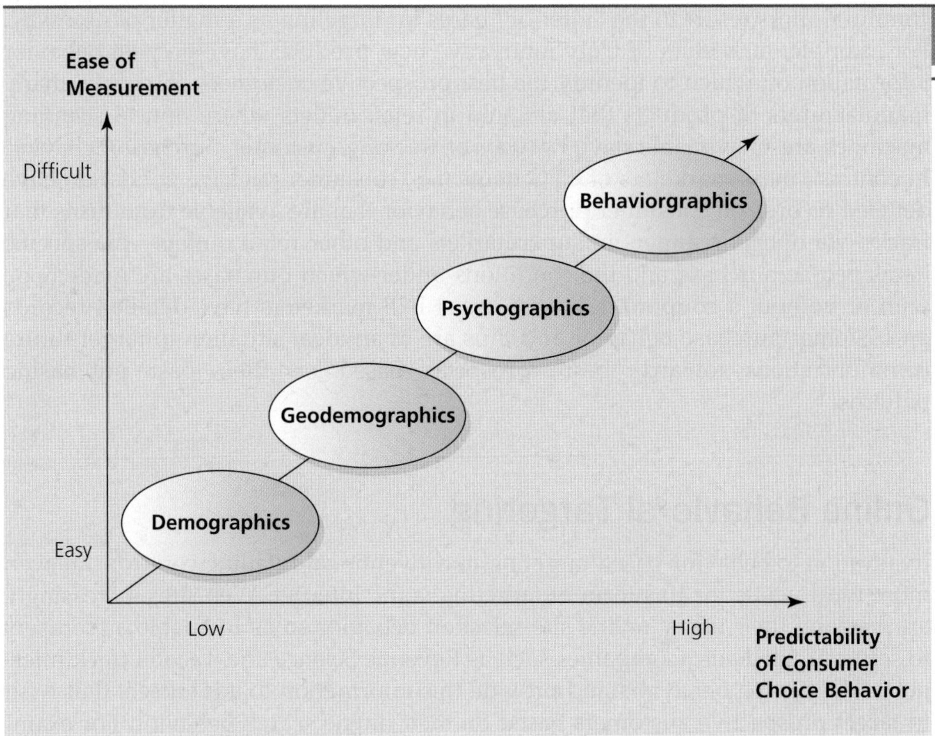

figure 4.1

Classification of Four General Targeting Characteristics

of your business five years ago, you have maintained impeccable records on every customer's purchases. You know precisely when they have purchased, what items they have selected, and how much they have spent. Now let us suppose that you are going to run a sale on a certain line of merchandise and will announce this sale via a combination of postal mail and e-mail. Although you could send postal announcements to all of your customers, you want to be more efficient in your selection so as not to waste money on reaching less viable prospects.

How would you make the targeting decision? In actuality, you have no need to target based on customers' demographic characteristics (say, by selecting just those between the ages of 25 and 39) or their psychographic profiles because you have an even better basis for making the selection decision. In particular, you know whether they have made past purchases of the specific merchandise line that you are discounting. Thus, based on customers' past behavior profiles you know which people are likely to be responsive to a sale on items that they have or have not previously purchased. Accordingly, you send sales announcements to all customers who have previously purchased the merchandise in question. By focusing on their past behavior, you have increased the odds that your mail advertising will receive a good return on your marketing investment and that you will not have wasted ad dollars by directing sale announcements to prospects unlikely to respond to discounts on merchandise they typically do not purchase.

The previous scenario, albeit simplistic, describes the essence of behaviorgraphic targeting: namely, that this form of targeting is based on how people behave (with respect to a particular product category or class of related products) rather than in terms of their attitudes and lifestyles (psychographics), their age, income, or ethnicity (demographics), or where they live (geodemographics). Behaviorgraphics provide the best basis for targeting marcom messages to customers insofar as the best predictor of someone's future behavior is his or her past behavior. Frankly, there is little need to target customers using any of the nonbehavioral bases for targeting if behaviorgraphic details are available. However, in some marcom situations behaviorgraphic information is not available, and marketing communicators resort to the "inferior" bases for targeting as a matter of necessity. For example, marketers of truly innovative new products have no past behavior information on which to identify the best prospective customers. Similarly, many manufacturers of products that are sold in retail outlets where optical scanning machines are unavailable have no way of tracking customer purchase behavior. In contrast, mass marketers of CPG items (i.e., consumer package goods) do have detailed records on consumer purchase behavior that are available from firms that track—via optical scanners in supermarkets and other retail outlets—the specific items people purchase and the conditions under which purchases are made (e.g., with or without a coupon). Likewise, most B2B marketers have detailed records on customer purchase behavior and thus are in an ideal situation to target future communications toward "best" prospects based on their past purchasing patterns.

Online Behavioral Targeting

In addition to behavior-based targeting in conventional retailing contexts, an even more ideal venue for this form of targeting is the Internet. Web sites increasingly are tracking their users' online site-selection behavior so as to enable advertisers to serve targeted ads. Companies such as Revenue Science and Tacoda track Internet users' surfing behaviors and provide this information to advertisers that wish to target prospective customers based on their online search behavior. For example, suppose a manufacturer of golfing equipment (a company such as Calloway Golf Company) wishes to reach the best prospects for purchasing its newest driver—a club likely to cost $300 or more. Turning to a company such as Revenue Science or Tacoda, Calloway would request the provider to identify prospective customers who spend a lot of time visiting golf-related Web sites. With knowledge of these individuals, it is technologically simple (by inserting "cookies" on computers that identify Web users' site-selection behavior) to place ads for Calloway's new driver on sites visited by these "golf surfers"—golf-related or otherwise. The essence of online behavioral targeting is thus a matter of directing online advertisements to just those individuals who most likely are interested—as indicated by their online site-selection behavior—in making a purchase decision for a particular product category.

A basic axiom of targeted marketing communications is to "aim where the ducks are flying." In other words, rather than shooting a gun wildly in the air and hoping that a duck might pass by, a duck hunter increases his or her odds of downing a duck if he or she refrains from shooting until flying ducks have been identified. But not all marcom practitioners heed this advice. Behaviorgraphics is a targeting approach that embodies the aim-where-the-ducks-are-flying axiom.

American Airlines employed the service of Revenue Science to identify best prospects for placing online ads. People who visited Web sites containing travel articles were pinpointed on the assumption that these individuals likely traveled on business at least occasionally. Ads for American Airlines were accordingly placed on the Web site of *The Wall Street Journal* (http://online.wsj.com) whenever individuals identified as business travelers visited this Web site. This behavioral targeting campaign enjoyed considerable success.[1]

To promote Aquafina Alive, a new brand of low-calorie vitamin-enhanced water, Pepsi-Cola employed the services of Tacoda to identify the best Web sites for reaching health-conscious consumers. Tacoda, which tracks a network of 4,000 sites, followed for a month the traffic to Web sites featuring healthy lifestyles. Pop-up ads for Aquafina Alive were then placed on the best of these sites for reaching health-conscious people. The results of the ad campaign revealed that in comparison with previous campaigns, Pepsi realized a threefold increase in the number of people clicking on the Aquafina Alive ads.[2]

Privacy Concerns

As typically is the case, technological advances in marketing bring with them increased ability to serve consumers but also at the risk of invading privacy. Applied in the context of online behavior targeting, Web surfers are increasingly more likely to be served with ads for products that are most relevant to their interests. However, this advantage comes at the expense that companies such as Revenue Science and Tacoda have access to our Internet search behavior *without our approval or knowledge*. What's the harm? It's easy to argue on either side of the issue. On the plus side, to be targeted with only those ads that we are most likely interested in is a good thing. On the other side, who wants Big Brother overlooking what we do? Would you want someone observing, if they could, every TV program you viewed during the course of a year? Probably not. Here then is the same issue as it applies to the Internet. Do you want commercial firms tracking your surfing behavior? As always in life, there are tradeoffs to be made.

Psychographic Targeting

Historically, marketers based their targeting decisions almost exclusively on their audiences' demographic characteristics—considerations such as the market's age, gender, income level, and race/ethnicity. Sophisticated practitioners eventually realized, however, that demographic information tells only part of the story about consumers' buying preferences, media-usage habits, and purchase behaviors. It is for this reason that marketing communicators also began investigating consumers' psychographic characteristics to obtain a richer understanding of how best to influence consumers to respond favorably to marcom efforts.

Consider, for example, how you might go about identifying target customers if you were marketing to prospective cruise-line travelers. Demographic information such as age and income undoubtedly would play some role in defining appropriate audiences; that is, you might expect somewhat older individuals (35-plus) and those with average or higher incomes to be prime prospects. But not everyone in the same age or income categories would be equally responsive to, say, advertisements for cruises to the Caribbean. Not all baby boomers and elderly consumers are good candidates for cruises; only those boomers and elders who are members of two particular psychographic segments—"pampered relaxers" and "global explorers"—are prime prospects for cruising.[3]

In general, **psychographics** refers to information about consumers' attitudes, values, motivations, and lifestyles as they relate to buying behavior in a particular product category. For example, a psychographic study of sports utility vehicles (SUVs) would assess the types of activities owners of SUVs participate in (e.g., camping and fishing, tailgating at sporting events, hauling lawn care items and do-it-yourself building materials) and measure their values and attitudes toward issues related to owning or not owning an SUV (e.g., how much value they place on safety, their views toward the environment, and their need for control). This information would be useful in designing advertising messages and selecting appropriate media outlets.

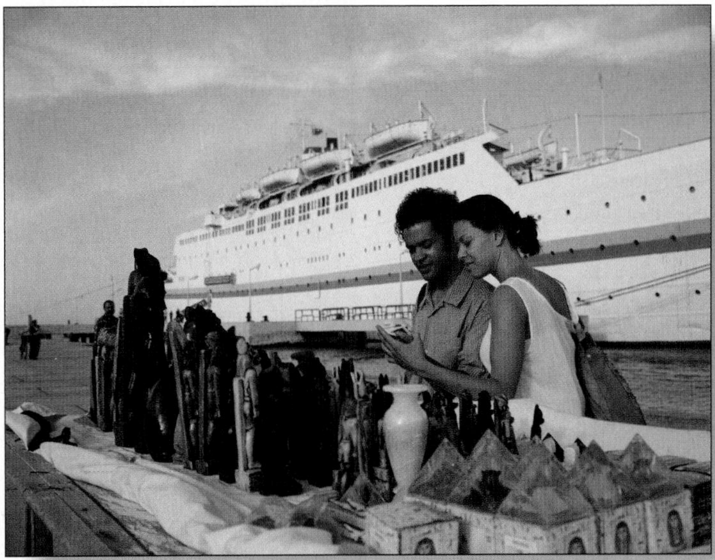

Customized Psychographic Profiles

Numerous marketing research firms conduct psychographic studies for individual clients. These studies are typically customized to the client's specific product category. The questionnaire items included in a customized psychographics study are selected in view of the unique characteristics of the product category. Table 4.1 presents a set of illustrative statements that were included in a psychographic study of consumers' banking practices. Survey respondents answered these statements in terms of how strongly they agreed or disagreed with each. Researchers then analyzed the results and, based on responses to these items, were able to categorize the 1,000 respondents into four psychographic groups—"worried traditionalists," "bank loyalists," "secured investors," and "thrifty bankers." It was determined that people classified into these groups differed substantially in terms of various banking behaviors.[4] The regional bank that sponsored this study used these results to better serve all four segments by designing new services appropriate for each and communicating differently to customers in each group. For example, communications aimed at "worried traditionalists" emphasized safety and security, whereas rate of return received greater emphasis in communications targeted to "secured investors."

General Purpose Psychographic Profiles

In addition to psychographic studies that are customized to a client's particular needs, brand managers can purchase "off-the-shelf" psychographic data from services that develop psychographic profiles of people independently of any particular product or service. One of the best known of these is the Yankelovich MindBase psychographic segmentation scheme. Yankelovich's MindBase consists of eight general segments and 32 specific subsegments. Table 4.2 summarizes the eight general MindBase segments and labels these with descriptive terms such as "I am Expressive," "I am Rock Steady," and "I am Sophisticated." Direct marketers and other marketing communicators can use these profiles for designing creative advertising campaigns that best match the attitudes, values, and lifestyles of their target audiences.

A second well-known psychographic segmentation scheme is SRI Consulting Business Intelligence's (SRIC-BI's) VALS™ system. The U.S. VALS segmentation scheme places American adult consumers into one of eight segments based on psychological characteristics that are related to purchase behavior and several key demographic variables such as age and household income. Japan VALS and U.K.

table 4.1

Illustrative Statements Used In a Banking-Related Psychographic Study

• A local bank is more likely to lend me money. • Bankers don't know as much as brokers about investments. • I rely on a banker's advice about managing money. • My debt is too high. • I'd never consider an account at a bank that doesn't have an ATM.	• A long-term relationship with a bank is more important than price. • All banks are the same. • I prefer a fixed price for all services provided to me. • I always shop around for the best deal. • I enjoy going to the lobby to do my banking business.	• There is never enough time to study all the financial alternatives. • I worry about saving enough money for the future. • I'd rather invest in Mutual Funds than CDs.

Source: James W. Peltier, John A. Schibrowsky, Don E. Schultz, and John Davis, "Interactive Psychographics: Cross-Selling in the Banking Industry," *Journal of Advertising Research* 42 (March/April 2002), Table 1. Reprinted from the *Journal of Advertising Research*, © Copyright 2002, by the Advertising Research Foundation.

table 4.2

Yankelovich MindBase Segments

I am Expressive my motto is *Carpe Diem* I live life to the fullest and I'm not afraid to express my personality. I'm active and engaged and I embody a true "live in the now" attitude with a firm belief that the future is limitless and that I can be or do anything I put my mind to.
I am Driven my motto is *Nothing Ventured, Nothing Gained* I'm ambitious with a drive to succeed both personally and professionally. I think of myself as self-possessed and resourceful, and I'm determined to show the world I'm on top of my game in all I do, from career ambitions to family, home, and my social life.
I am At Capacity my motto is *Time is of the Essence* My life is very busy and I'm looking for control and simplification. I am a demanding and vocal consumer, and I'm looking for convenience, respect, and a helping hand so I can devote more of my time to the important things in life.
I am Rock Steady my motto is *Do the Right Thing* I think of myself as a positive individual. I draw energy from my home and family. I'm dedicated to living an upstanding life and I listen to my own instincts in terms of making thoughtful decisions in my personal life and in the marketplace.
I am Down to Earth my motto is *Ease on Down the Road* I'm cruising down life's path at my own pace, seeking satisfaction where I can. I'm looking to enhance my life, stretch myself to try new things, and treat myself through novel experiences and products along the way.
I am Sophisticated my motto is *Sense and Sensibility* I am intelligent, upstanding and I have an affinity for the finer things in life. I also have high expectations both for myself and for the companies I give my business. I am dedicated to doing a stellar job at work but I balance my career dedication with a passion for enriching experiences.
I Measure Twice my motto is *An Ounce of Prevention* I'm a mature individual and I like to think of myself on a life path to actualization and fulfillment. I live a healthy, active life. I'm dedicated to ensuring that my future is both secure and highly rewarding and vitalized.
I am Devoted my motto is *Home is Where the Heart is* I'm traditional and rooted in the comforts of home. Some would say my beliefs are conventional, but they make sense to me. I'm spiritual and content with my life. I like things the way they have always been and I don't need novelty for novelty's sake or newfangled technology.

Source: Yankelovich MindBase /Segments, http://www.yankelovich.com/index.php?option=com_content&task=category&sectionid=21&id=42&Itemid=88. Yankelovich © 2005.

VALS are available for understanding consumers in those countries. (You can determine your segmentation grouping by answering the questions on a survey available at http://www.sric-bi.com/VALS/presurvey.shtml.)

Figure 4.2 presents the eight VALS segments. The horizontal dimension in this figure represents individuals' *primary motivations,* whether in terms of their pursuit of ideals, their need for achievement, or drive to self-express. The vertical dimension reflects individuals' *resources* as based on their educational accomplishments, income levels, health, energy, and consumerism. For example, as can be gleaned from Figure 4.2, "Thinkers" and "Believers" both are motivated by the pursuit of ideals, but "Thinkers" have greater financial resources than "Believers."

figure 4.2

The 8 VALS Segments

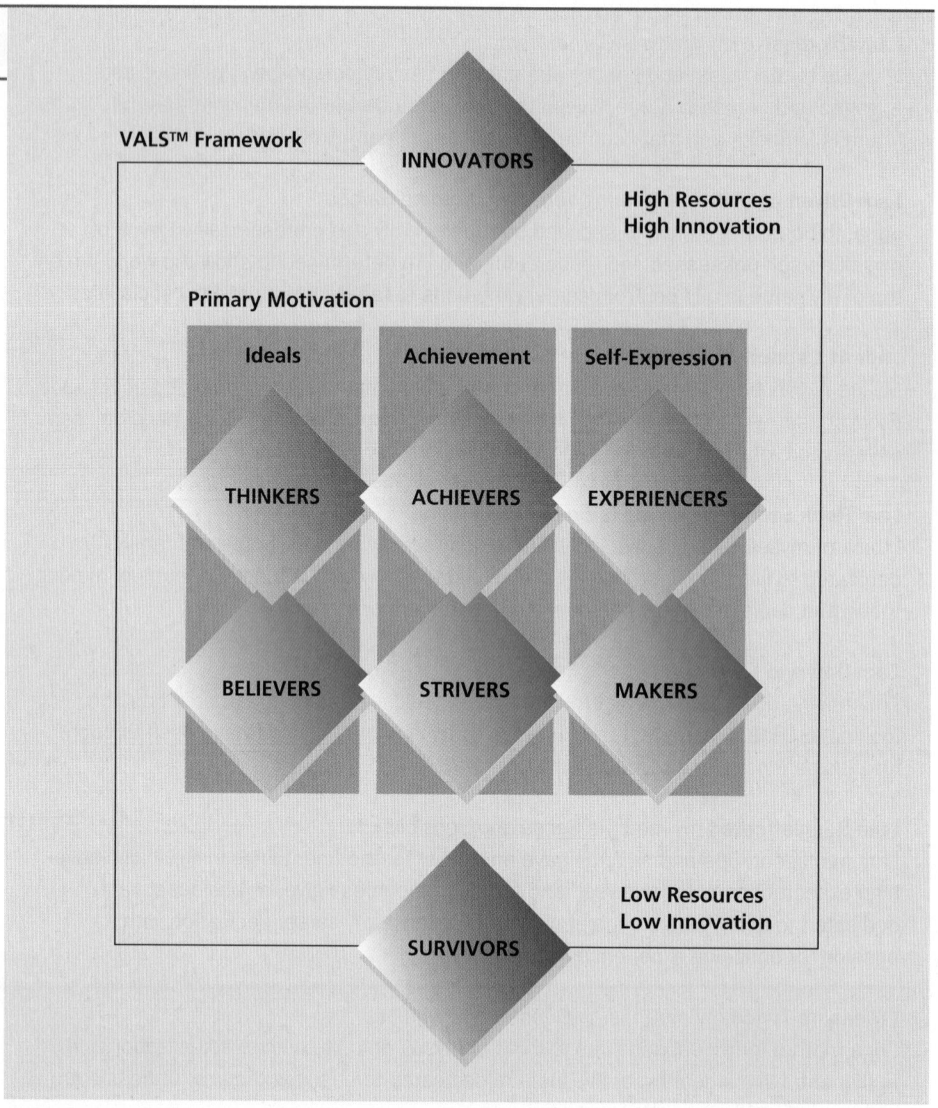

Similarly, both "Experiencers" and "Makers" are driven by the need for self-expression, but "Makers" have fewer resources than "Experiencers." Each of the eight segments in the VALS framework is now described.[5]

Innovators *are successful, sophisticated, take-charge people with high self-esteem. Because they have such abundant resources, they exhibit all three primary motivations (i.e., ideals, achievement, and self-expression) in varying degrees. They are change leaders and are the most receptive to new ideas and technologies. Innovators are very active consumers, and their purchases reflect cultivated tastes for upscale, niche products and services.*

Thinkers *are motivated by ideals. They are mature, satisfied, comfortable, and reflective people who value order, knowledge, and responsibility. They tend to be well educated and actively seek out information in the decision-making process. They are well informed about world and national events and are alert to opportunities to broaden their knowledge. Thinkers have a moderate respect for the status quo institutions of authority and social decorum, but are open to consider new ideas. Although their incomes allow them many choices, Thinkers are conservative, practical consumers; they look for durability, functionality, and value in the products they buy.*

Believers, *like Thinkers, are motivated by ideals. They are conservative, conventional people with concrete beliefs based on traditional, established codes: family, religion, community, and the nation. Many Believers express moral codes that are deeply rooted and literally interpreted. They follow established routines, organized in large part around home, family, community, and social or religious organizations to which they belong. As consumers, Believers are predictable; they choose familiar products and established brands. They favor American products and are generally loyal customers.*

Achievers, *who are motivated by the desire for achievement, have goal-oriented lifestyles and a deep commitment to career and family. Their social lives reflect this focus and are structured around family, their place of worship, and work. Achievers live conventional lives, are politically conservative, and respect authority and the status quo. They value consensus, predictability, and stability over risk, intimacy, and self-discovery. With many wants and needs, Achievers are active in the consumer marketplace. Image is important to Achievers; they favor established, prestige products and services that demonstrate success to their peers. Because of their busy lives, they are often interested in a variety of time-saving devices.*

Strivers *are trendy and fun loving. Because they are motivated by achievement, Strivers are concerned about the opinions and approval of others. Money defines success for Strivers, who don't have enough of it to meet their desires. They favor stylish products that emulate the purchases of people with greater material wealth. Many see themselves as having a job rather than a career, and a lack of skills and focus often prevents them from moving ahead. Strivers are active consumers because shopping is both a social activity and an opportunity to demonstrate to peers their ability to buy. As consumers, they are as impulsive as their financial circumstance will allow.*

Experiencers *are motivated by self-expression. As young, enthusiastic, and impulsive consumers, Experiencers quickly become enthusiastic about new possibilities but are equally quick to cool. They seek variety and excitement, savoring the new, the offbeat, and the risky. Their energy finds an outlet in exercise, sports, outdoor recreation, and social activities. Experiencers are avid consumers and spend a comparatively high proportion of their income on fashion, entertainment, and socializing. Their purchases reflect the emphasis they place on looking good and having "cool" stuff.*

Makers, *like Experiencers, are motivated by self-expression. They express themselves and experience the world by working on it—building a house, raising children, fixing a car, or canning vegetables—and have enough skill and energy to carry out their projects successfully. Makers are practical people who have constructive skills and value self-sufficiency. They live within a traditional context of family, practical work, and physical recreation and have little interest in what lies outside that context. Makers are suspicious of new ideas and large institutions such as big business. They are respectful of government authority and organized labor, but resentful of government intrusion on individual rights. They are unimpressed by material possessions other than those with a practical or functional purpose. Because they prefer value to luxury, they buy basic products.*

Survivors *live narrowly focused lives. With few resources with which to cope, they often believe that the world is changing too quickly. They are comfortable with the familiar and are primarily concerned with safety and security. Because they must focus on meeting needs rather than fulfilling desires, Survivors do not show a strong primary motivation. Survivors are cautious consumers. They represent a very modest market for most products and services. They are loyal to favorite brands, especially if they can purchase them at a discount.*

To determine the best prospective customer target for a new product or service, a company's product design team could work with the SRIC-BI consulting group. Imagine, for example, that an automobile manufacturer is interested in gauging receptivity to an innovative new automobile design. A series of focus groups could be held where each group is composed of just one VALS type (for example, one focus group comprised of Innovators, another group comprised of Achievers, etc.). Generally, each VALS type responds differently to diverse product feature and benefit sets. Getting focus group feedback by VALS type would allow the new product team to select as the target the consumer group that responds most positively to the new design concept. Having a clearly defined target and a clear understanding of their preferences and needs would enable the design team to focus its work effectively. Later in the process, knowledge of the VALS target would assist marketing communicators in how best to position their products and which creative appeals would be most effective.

Geodemographic Targeting

The word geodemographic is a conjunction of *geography* and *demography,* which beautifully describes this form of targeting. The premise underlying geodemographic targeting is that people who reside in similar areas, such as neighborhoods or postal ZIP Code zones, also share demographic and lifestyle similarities. Hence, knowing where people live also provides some information regarding their general marketplace behaviors. Several companies have developed services that delineate geographical areas into common groups, or clusters, wherein reside people with similar demographic and lifestyle characteristics. These companies (and their services, in parentheses) include CACI (ACORN), Donnelly Marketing (ClusterPlus), Experian (MOSAIC), Claritas (PRIZMNE), and SRIC-BC (GeoVALS™). The following section describes Claritas' PRIZMNE system of geodemographic profiling. Geodemographic clustering systems have been developed in many countries other than the United States, including Canada, most countries in Western Europe, some African countries, Australia, and Japan.[6]

PRIZMNE is an acronym in which PRIZM stands for *P*otential *R*ating *I*ndex by ZIP *M*arkets and NE represents the "new evolution" of Claritas' original segmentation system. The PRIZMNE classification system delineates every neighborhood in the United States into one of 66 clusters based on an analysis of neighborhoods' demographic characteristics. These characteristics include variables such as educational attainment, race/ethnicity, predominant age range, occupational achievement, and type of housing (e.g., owned versus rented). Sophisticated statistical analysis of these demographic characteristics has enabled Claritas to identify 66 groups, or clusters, of neighborhoods that share similar demographic profiles. Each cluster is labeled with a colorful and descriptive term. Illustrative names include "Upper Crust," "Big Fish, Small Pond," "Bohemian Mix," "Country Casuals," "White Picket Fences," "Heartlanders," "Suburban Pioneers," and "City Roots." Let us briefly characterize three of these clusters to give you a sense of how the clusters are characterized.[7]

Bohemian Mix captures a collection of young, mobile urbanites who represent the nation's most liberal lifestyles. Bohemian Mixers are a blend of young singles and couples, students and professionals, Hispanics, Asian-Americans, African-Americans, and whites. They are disproportionately likely to be early adopters who are quick to attend the latest movie, frequent the newest nightclub, or adopt the most up-to-date laptop. Bohemian Mix households represent nearly 2 percent of all U.S. households. The average occupant of a Bohemian Mix household is less than 35 years old; has an income of about $50,000; likely is unmarried; rents an apartment or lives in a high-rise; is college educated; and is employed as a professional or in a white-collar position. He or she is not defined by any particular race or ethnicity.

White Picket Fences represents those households at the middle of the U.S. socioeconomic ladder. People living in these households are predominantly young, middle-class, and married with children—a stereotypical American household of previous generations. Now, however, rather than being almost exclusively white, "White Picket Fencers" reflect ethnic diversity with large numbers of African-American and Hispanic households. Households such as these represent slightly over 1 percent of all U.S. households. The average occupant of a White Picket Fence household falls in the age range of 25 to 44, has an income of around $48,000, is married with children, has some college education, and works in a variety of jobs ranging from blue- to white-collar occupations.

Suburban Pioneers includes neighborhoods where occupants live eclectic lifestyles and includes a mix of young singles, recently divorced, and single parents who have moved into older, inner-ring suburbs. They reside in aging homes and garden-style apartment buildings. The mix of African-American, Latino, and white residents work in mostly blue-collar jobs and live a working-class lifestyle. The average occupant of Suburban Pioneer households is under age 45, earns an income around $33,000, and has a high school education or less. Just over 1 percent of U.S. households fall into this cluster.

Many major marketers use PRIZMNE, Donnelly's ClusterPlus, or another geodemographic clustering service to help them with important marcom decisions. Selecting geographical locales for narrowcasting television advertisements and identifying appropriate households for direct mailings are just two marcom decisions that are facilitated by the availability of geodemographic data. Needless to say, geodemographic data are extremely useful for other marketing purposes such as deciding where to locate new stores.

If you would like to know how the neighborhood in which you grew up or resided would be classified by the PRIZMNE system, enter "You Are Where You Live" into Google or another search engine. Click on the URL to which you are directed, and when you arrive at this site submit your home neighborhood's five-digit ZIP Code. You will see the major clusters that characterize your own neighborhood. For foreign nationals studying in the United States, you might want to enter your college or university's ZIP Code to identify how the surrounding neighborhood is classified. Students in countries outside the United States should go online to identify whether your country has a PRIZM system in place. See the *Global Focus* insert for discussion of a form of geodemographic targeting that was used in marketing ultrasound machines to rural doctors in India.

Demographic Targeting

This section examines three major demographic aspects that have considerable relevance for marcom practitioners: (1) the age structure of the population (e.g., children, Generations X and Y, and baby boomers); (2) the changing household composition (e.g., the increase in the number of single-person households); and (3) ethnic population developments. The focus is, necessarily, exclusively on characteristics of the U.S. population. Although the same considerations are relevant elsewhere, the particulars are country specific. Interested readers from countries outside the United States can obtain detailed demographic information from a government agency that is equivalent to the U.S. Census Bureau, which is a division of the Department of Commerce. Before examining features of the U.S. population, it will be helpful to place these topics in context by first examining population growth and geographic distribution of the world and U.S. populations.

global focus

General Electric's Targeting Indians with Ultrasound Machines

General Electric (GE) has been extremely successful in selling ultrasound machines throughout India, including in small, rural villages. An ultrasound scan can cost as little as $8, which in rural areas equates to a week's wages. As scans have become affordable to the vast majority of Indians, their usage has aggravated a long-standing social problem, namely, Indian parents' preference for boy babies. This preference extends from the fact that having girls is an expensive proposition because parents of daughters are obligated to make dowry payments at marriage. (Dowry is the historical practice of requiring a bride's parents to make payments to the groom's family as a condition of marriage. Grooms often demand large monetary payments or expect gifts of farm animals, electronic products, furniture, or other cash-equivalent items.) Although GE and its Indian partner Winpro Ltd. have been emphatic in insisting that ultrasound machines are not to be used for gender determination, the reality is that this is how the machines are often used. It is estimated that hundreds of thousands of female fetuses are aborted annually. The female-to-male ratio has steeply declined from 945 girls for every 1,000 boys in 1991 to 927 girls per 1,000 boys a decade later. In some parts of India, the ratio is below 800.

GE's success in selling ultrasound machines in India is attributable to its successful targeting of small-town doctors at affordable prices. Well aware of the social problems created by the ready availability of ultrasound machines, GE has demanded affidavits from customers that they will not use the machines for gender-determination purposes. These measures have resulted in some lost sales volume for GE, but the problem nonetheless remains. This situation represents a classic case where sound marketing strategy and good targeting practices have resulted in offsetting advantages and disadvantages: On the one hand, the ready availability of ultrasound machines, particularly in rural areas where healthcare suffers, has been beneficial by making childbirth safer; on the other hand, the machines are used for the wrong reasons by some doctors.

SOURCE: Adapted from Peter Wonacott, "India's Skewed Sex Ratio," *The Wall Street Journal Online*, April 18, 2007, http://online.wsj.com (accessed April 18, 2007).

At the time of this writing, the total population of human beings on the earth is estimated to be approximately 6.67 billion people. (For a daily update on the projected world and U.S. populations, go to http://www.census.gov/main/www/popclock.html.) The world population is expected to grow to approximately 8 billion people by the year 2025 and 9 billion by 2050. Table 4.3 provides a list of the world's 25 largest countries as of 2007; it can be seen that both China and India have populations exceeding 1 billion people with a huge drop off to the next largest country—the United States—with an estimated population of approximately 301 million. (Please note that projections of population size vary somewhat depending on the source, because estimators use slightly different assumptions about fertility rates, longevity levels, and other factors that enter into the equation.)

A particularly interesting aspect of the U.S. population is the ancestral diversity of its residents. Known as a melting pot, the United States has attracted immigrants from throughout the world, thus making the country an amalgam of people whose ancestors had different cultures and backgrounds. Many immigrants to the United States now arrive from Latin America, Asia, and Eastern Europe, although historically most came from Western European countries. This is shown in Table 4.4, which portrays the percentage of the U.S. population claiming their ancestral roots. Interestingly, slightly over 7 percent of the U.S. population now

table 4.3

World's 25 Largest Countries as of 2007

Rank	Country	Population	Rank	Country	Population
1.	China	1,321,851,888	14.	Germany	82,400,996
2.	India	1,129,866,154	15.	Egypt	80,335,036
3.	United States	301,139,947	16.	Ethiopia	76,511,887
4.	Indonesia	234,693,997	17.	Turkey	71,158,647
5.	Brazil	190,010,647	18.	Congo (Kinshasa)	65,751,512
6.	Pakistan	164,741,924	19.	Iran	65,397,521
7.	Bangladesh	150,448,339	20.	Thailand	65,068,149
8.	Russia	141,377,752	21.	France	63,718,187
9.	Nigeria	135,031,164	22.	United Kingdom	60,776,238
10.	Japan	127,433,494	23.	Italy	58,147,733
11.	Mexico	108,700,891	24.	Korea, South	49,044,790
12.	Philippines	91,077,287	25.	Burma (Myanmar)	47,373,958
13.	Vietnam	85,262,356			

Source: http://www.census.gov/cgi-bin/ipc/idbrank.pl, U.S. Census Bureau, International Database.

refer to themselves simply as "Americans," which is up from 5 percent in 1990.[8] In other words, many American residents do not acknowledge any particular ancestry—possibly in part due to pride and also in view of the hybrid character of Americans' ancestries.

The Changing Age Structure

One of the most dramatic features of the American population is its relentless aging. The median age of Americans was 28 in 1970, 30 in 1980, 33 in 1990, 36 in 2000, and is projected to be about 38 by 2025. Table 4.5 presents population figures distributed by age group. The following sections examine major age groupings of the U.S. population and the implications these hold for marcom efforts. Discussion proceeds from the youngest age cohort, preschoolers, to the elderly. First, however, it will be helpful to overview the epochal event—namely, the baby boom—that has affected future generations and the general trend toward an ever-aging population.

table 4.4

Largest Ancestral Groups of U.S. Residents

Ancestry	Percentage of U.S. Population
German	15.2%
Irish	10.8
African-American	8.8
English	8.7
American	7.2
Mexican	6.5
Italian	5.6
Polish	3.2
French	3.0
American Indian	2.8
Scottish	1.7
Dutch	1.6
Norwegian	1.6
Scotch-Irish	1.5
Swedish	1.4

Source: "A County-by-County Look at Ancestry," *USA Today*, July 1, 2004, 7A. Reprinted with permission.

table 4.5

Population of the United States by Age Group, as of 2006

Age	Population (millions)	Percent of Total
Children and Teens (<20)		
Under 5	20.42	6.8
5–9	19.71	6.6
10–14	20.63	6.9
15–19	21.32	7.1
Total	**82.08**	**27.35**
Young Adults (20–34)		
20–24	21.11	7.0
25–29	20.71	6.9
30–34	19.71	6.6
Total	**61.53**	**20.51**
Middle Agers (35–54)		
35–39	21.19	7.1
40–44	22.48	7.5
45–49	22.80	7.6
50–54	20.48	6.8
Total	**86.95**	**28.98**
Olders (55–64)		
55–59	18.22	6.1
60–64	13.36	4.5
Total	**31.58**	**10.52**
Elders (65–74)		
65–69	10.38	3.5
70–74	8.54	2.8
Total	**18.92**	**6.31**
The Very Old (75+)		
75–79	7.38	2.5
80–84	5.67	1.9
85+	5.96	2.0
Total	19.01	6.34
Total U.S. Population	**300.07**	**100%**

Source: Year Age Groups for the United States, Population Division, U.S. Census Bureau, May 17, 2007.

Demographers (people who study demographic trends) termed the birth of around 77 million Americans between 1946 and 1964 the **baby-boom generation.** This population-boom period following the end of World War II (in 1945) persisted for nearly two decades. Using 2009 as a point of reference, the youngest person classified as a "boomer" would be 45, and the oldest baby boomer would be 63. Effects of the baby boom (and subsequent bust) have been manifested in the following major population developments:

1. The original baby boomers created a mini baby boom as they reached childbearing age. As shown in Table 4.5, the number of children and teenagers in the United States totaled about 82 million in 2006.
2. Due to a low birthrate from the mid-1960s through the 1970s (prior to the time when most baby boomers were of childbearing age), relatively few babies were born. There now are proportionately fewer young adults (ages 20 to 34) than there were in prior generations.
3. The number of middle-agers (ages 35 to 54) has increased dramatically, totaling nearly 87 million Americans as of 2006. This maturing of the baby boomers has been one of the most significant demographic developments marketers faced.

Children and Teenagers

The group of young Americans age 19 and younger has fallen dramatically from 40 percent of the population in 1965 (during the baby-boom heyday) to slightly over 27 percent of the population in 2006. Yet this remains a substantial group, with over 80 million occupants. (See Table 4.5 for specific breakdowns by age group—i.e., under 5, 5 to 9, 10 to 14, and 15 to 19.)

Marketers typically refer to children ages 4 through 12 as "kids" to distinguish this cohort from toddlers and teenagers. Children in this broad grouping either directly spend or influence the spending of billions of dollars worth of purchases each year. Aggregate spending by kids or on behalf of this age group roughly doubled every decade in the 1960s, 1970s, and 1980s, and tripled in the 1990s.

Preschoolers Preschool-age children, age 5 or younger, represent a cohort that has grown substantially in recent years. More babies were born in the United States in 1990 (4.2 million) than at any time since the baby boom peak of 4.3 million babies born in 1957. Marketers of toys, furniture items, clothing, food, and many other products and services routinely appeal to the parents of these children, or, on occasion, directly to the kids themselves.

Elementary-school-age children This group includes children ages 6 to 11. These children directly influence product purchases and indirectly influence what their parents buy. Children in this group influence their parents' choice of clothing and toys and even the brand choice of products such as toothpaste and food products, as Figure 4.3 illustrates. Advertising and other forms of marketing communications aimed at young children, or their families, have increased substantially in recent years. Numerous new products annually hit the shelves to cater to kids' tastes. For example, Mattel, which is known for its line of Hot Wheels toy cars, has extended the brand into the area of marketing skateboards, snowboards, and extreme-sports apparel under the Hot Wheels name. The Walt Disney Company introduced the Disney Dream Desk PC, a computer and monitor combo where the monitor is shaped in the form of Mickey Mouse ears. Marketers are increasingly reaching these young consumers, especially girls, via online virtual communities. The Barbie Girls site, for example, has millions of registered users.[9] (To learn more about how children are socialized as consumers and develop understanding of advertising, the reader is encouraged to examine the articles identified in the following footnote.)[10]

Figure 4.3

An Appeal to Preschoolers' Parents

© AP Images/PRNewsFoto/Disney Consumer Products

Tweens A category of children that marketers have dubbed "tweens"—not quite kids nor yet teenagers—is an age cohort actively involved in consumption. Tweens are usually classified as children between the ages of 8 and 12. Tweens generally have well-formed ideas about what brands they like and dislike and are largely influenced by their peers to own those products and brands that are considered "cool." Retailers such as Limited Too gear much of their marcom efforts at garnering tweens' growing desire for fashionable clothing items (https://www.limitedtoo.com).

An important study of tweens (including also some teens age 13 and 14) examined their materialistic values and how these values relate to a variety of demographic variables, purchase-related behaviors, and involvement with advertisements and promotions.[11] To measure *materialism*—which includes the desire to buy and own products, the enjoyment of these items, and the desire for money that enables the acquisition of products—the researchers developed a measure called the "youth materialism scale" (the YMS). Participants responded to 10 statements with response options ranging from "disagree a lot" to "agree a lot." Illustrative statements include "I'd rather spend time buying things than doing almost anything else"; "I really enjoy going shopping"; and "When you grow up, the more money you have, the happier you are." Based on a national sample of U.S. households, nearly 1,000 youths between the ages of 9 and 14 completed the YMS and answered a number of other questions. The researchers statistically correlated scores on the YMS with these other measures and produced the following set of illustrative findings:

1. Boys are more materialistic than girls.
2. Youths from lower income households are more materialistic.
3. Highly materialistic youths shop more frequently.
4. Highly materialistic youths show a greater interest in new products.
5. Highly materialistic youths are: (a) more likely to watch TV commercials, (b) more likely to ask parents to buy products because they've seen them on TV, (c) more responsive to celebrity endorsements, (d) more likely to exert pressure on their parents to purchase products, (e) inclined to want more spent on them for Christmas and birthdays, and (f) prone to like school less and to have somewhat poorer grades.

Teenagers Consumers in this age group, totaling in the United States over 25 million 13- to 19-year-olds, have tremendous earning power and considerable influence in making personal and household purchases.[12] Teenagers often are referred to as members of the *Millennial Generation* or *Generation Y* (in contrast to the generation that preceded it—Generation X—which is discussed in a following section). It is important to note that there is no single definition of when people were born into the millennial generation, and no single time span is universally accepted. To avoid overlap with the generation that preceded it, Generation X (defined in this book as the generation born between 1965 and 1981), we will consider **Generation Y** to be the generation of people who were born from 1982 to 1996. Thus, as of 2009, Gen Yers would include all people between the ages of 13 and 27, or approximately 60 million Americans. The present discussion focuses just on the subset of teenagers who are members of this millennial generation.

A study by Teenage Research Unlimited, which follows teen trends and attitudes, estimated that American teenagers spend more than $150 billion annually.[13] Teenagers have purchasing influence and power far greater than ever, which accounts for the growth of marcom programs aimed at this group. For example, Hewlett-Packard changed its back-to-school computer marketing strategy from efforts to appeal to parents with price-oriented ads placed in conventional media to the use of humor appeals placed in online media that reach teenagers.[14]

Teenagers are noted for being highly conformist, narcissistic, and fickle consumers. These characteristics pose great opportunities and yet challenges for marketing communicators. An accepted product can become a huge success when the teenage bandwagon selects a brand as a personal mark of the in-crowd. However, today's accepted product or brand can easily become tomorrow's passé item.

It is said that teenagers don't like to be "marketed to." As with all consumers, it is important that marketing communicators provide useful information, but teens would rather acquire the information themselves—such as on the Internet or from friends—rather than having it imposed on them. Marcom personnel thus walk a precarious plank in communicating useful information to teens while avoiding being overbearing. The Internet is an obvious communication medium

figure 4.4

An Appeal to Teenagers

© Rob Brimson/Taxi/Getty Images

for reaching teens. Social networking sites such as MySpace and Facebook have become particularly effective venues for influencing the consumer behavior of teens and young adults. The *IMC Focus* insert offers one illustration of a creative marcom initiative on Facebook.

Young Adults

Scholarly treatment of this age cohort, commonly referred to as **Generation X,** identifies it as Americans born between 1961 and 1981.[15] However, to avoid overlap with the baby boom generation (1946 to 1964) and Gen Y (1982 to 1996), it is convenient to define this age cohort as people born between 1965 and 1981. Hence, as of 2009, Gen X constituted over 65 million Americans in the age category from 28 to 44. Because Gen Xers were born immediately after the baby boom, which ended in 1964, this group also is referred to as *baby busters.* The labels do not end there, however. Gen X has been subjected to more clichés than any group in history, most of which are deprecatory: slackers, cynics, whiners, grunge kids, and hopeless. As is typically the case when a group is stereotyped, these labels characterize only a subset of Gen Xers and are much too general to begin to capture the complexity of this group and the differences among its occupants.

One well-known marketing research firm has classified Gen Xers into four groups based on their attitudinal profiles: Yup & Comers, Bystanders, Playboys, and Drifters. *Yup & Comers* have the highest levels of education and income and account for approximately 28 percent of Gen Xers. They tend to focus on intangible rewards rather than material wealth and are confident about themselves and their futures. This clearly is not a group of people who fit the stereotypical labels attached to Gen X. *Bystanders* represent nearly 37 percent of Gen Xers and consist predominantly of female African-Americans and Hispanics. Although their disposable income is relatively low, this subsegment of Gen Xers has a flair for fashion and loves to shop. *Playboys* is a predominantly white, male group accounting for almost 19 percent of the Gen X cohort. Playboys adhere to a "pleasure before duty" lifestyle and are self-absorbed, fun loving, and impulsive. *Drifters* constitute the

IMC >> i.m.c. focus

College Students: An Inviting Target for Odor-Fighting Products

Imagine the worst dorm room you ever encountered: A dirty, cluttered, smelly, disgusting space filled with uneaten food items, dirty clothes, empty beer bottles, and perhaps even a pet. Your dorm room (or apartment) is likely much cleaner and less smelly than the hypothetical "disaster" just described. Nonetheless, with immense pressures on your time and the likelihood of two or more students occupying the same room, it is probable that your room is not as clean or as odor free as you may desire. Like millions of other college students, you are a good candidate for odor-fighting products while living in a dorm, fraternity/sorority building, or off-campus apartment.

One maker of such products, Procter & Gamble, recently began marketing its Febreze line of products explicitly to college students, which, in the United States alone, number 18 million potential customers! Realizing that reaching college students via conventional mass media such as television and magazines would be too costly and ineffective, P&G and its advertising agency opted for an online campaign using the Facebook social-networking site as the pivotal medium. An interactive Web site (http://whatstinks.com/home.jsp) was developed and housed within Facebook. The site uses humor designed to appeal to college students, and includes features such as a video game (the "Dank Game") where players armed with a bottle of Febreze take aim at dirty laundry items. In addition to the Web site, campus tours were designed in which improvisational actors conducted interactive performances with students and queried them about things in their lives that stink. All in all, this campaign is a clever way to target a previously untapped group of consumers who represent a large and viable audience for Febreze products.

SOURCE: Adapted from Rupal Parekh, "Febreze Sniffs Out New Target: Dorm Dwellers," *Advertising Age*, October 29, 2007, 12.

smallest subset at 16 percent of Gen Xers. This group is closest to the Gen X stereotype. They are frustrated with their lives, are among the least educated, seek security and status, and choose brands that offer a sense of belonging and self-esteem.[16]

These groupings make it apparent that contrary to their stereotypical portrayal, Gen Xers are not monolithic. The generalizations are incorrect and by and large unfair. As a group they are no more cynical, disenfranchised, or whiney than most people. Marketing communications directed to Gen Xers must use appeals targeted to specific subgroups such as Yup & Comers rather than stereotypes that do not adequately reach any subsegment.

Once again it is important to emphasize that the Gen X age cohort, however labeled, is not a unified group in terms of demographics or lifestyle preferences and should not be misconstrued as a single group for targeting marcom messages. Indeed, the four groupings just described are themselves simplifications, but they do offer some refinement of the general differences among the more than 65+ million Americans who have been simplistically collapsed into a single category.

Middle-Aged and Mature Consumers

Although somewhat arbitrary, we can think of **middle age** as starting at age 35 and ending at 54, at which point maturity is reached. Actually, there is some disagreement over the dividing point between middle age and maturity. Sometimes a 65-and-over classification is used, because age 65 normally marks retirement.

In this text we will use the U.S. Census Bureau's designation, which classifies **mature people** as those who are 55 and older.

Middle-aged As of 2006 there were roughly 87 million Americans between the middle ages of 35 and 54 (see Table 4.5). These individuals represent two generations of people: younger baby boomers and older Gen Xers. The following discussion focuses on baby boomers, or "boomers" for short, because Generation X already has been discussed.

As mentioned previously, the baby boom encompassed approximately 77 million Americans born immediately after World War II in 1946 and through the year 1964. This broad group of people, the so-called *baby-boom generation,* offers tremendous potential for many marketers. What makes boomers such an attractive target group is that they are relatively affluent and thus represent a good general target for second homes, quality vehicles, investments (insurance, real estate, and securities), travel, self-help products, cosmetic surgery, and grown-up "toys" like golfing equipment, automobiles with convertible tops (the average convertible buyer is 50 years old),[17] and motorcycles—Harley-Davidson's best customers are middle-aged men, and the typical buyer has an average age of 46.[18] Given their relative affluence, baby boomers also represent an attractive target for a variety of "luxury" goods. For example, appliance maker Whirlpool appeals to affluent boomers who want the very best appliance quality with a line of items named Whirlpool Gold. And luxury skin-care marketers have experienced revenue growth by introducing high-priced antiaging products such as L'Oreal's Absolue.

Moreover, just because baby boomers are aging does not necessarily mean they are getting psychologically old or are significantly altering their consumption patterns from a younger age.[19] Rather, there are indications that baby boomers are retaining many of their more youthful consumption habits and, in a sense, are unwilling to change. For example, the rather dramatic increase in purchases of hair-color products by baby boomers reflects this tendency for boomers to prolong youth and to gravitate toward products that support their youth obsession. Manufacturers of health-care items, cosmetics, exercise machines, and food products have actively appealed to baby boomers' passion for remaining in youthful shape. Figure 4.5 represents an appeal to baby boomers who are concerned about their sex appeal even though their bodies are changing. The double entendre use of the word "hotter" in this ad demonstrates the physiological effect that menopause can have while simultaneously appreciating that consumers in this stage of life can remain physically attractive, or, in the vernacular, "hot."

Because boomers represent the "epicenter of society," advertisers will march in lockstep with this group and continue to reflect their characteristics and appeal to their purchase interests and needs.[20] For example, athletic-footwear makers such as New Balance cater to baby boomers by offering shoes that come in wider widths than just the medium-size option offered in the past. Even

Figure 4.5

An Appeal to Female Baby Boomers

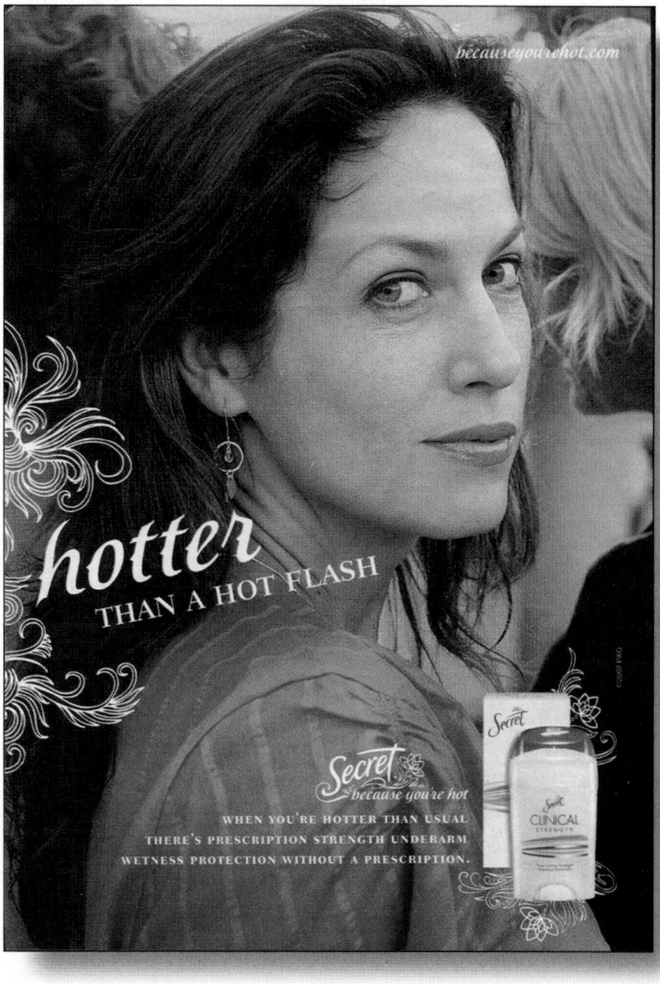

© Ronnie Kaufman/Blend Images/Jupiterimages

the makers of the high-energy drink, Red Bull, well known for its appeal to teens and young adults, now targets British golfers—many of whom are 40 or older—by making the product available in course shops, restaurants, and hotels across Britain.[21]

An important point of clarification is needed before concluding this section and moving on to the next age group. It is tempting to think of baby boomers as a monolithic group of people who think alike, act the same, and purchase identical products. Such an impression would be erroneous. Baby boomers do not represent a true market segment in the strictest sense of this term. That is, just because millions of Americans share one commonality (being born between 1946 and 1964), this does not mean they are virtual clones of one another. Within this age cohort, there are distinct differences among people with respect to chronological age, subjective age, vitality, income, ethnicity, lifestyle choices, and product/brand preferences. Hence, although it is convenient to speak of baby boomers as a single group, it would be a mistake to conclude they represent an actionable market segment. It is important to appreciate the fact that meaningful and profitable marcom targeting efforts typically require that audience members share a combination of demographic, lifestyle, and possibly geographical characteristics; broad groupings such as "baby boomers" are much too crude to satisfy the characteristics of a meaningful market segment.

In sum, baby boomers are a significant age cohort and en masse represent a powerful economic force, but they do not constitute a sufficient basis for targeting marcom programs. Thus, for example, the marketers of L'Oreal Absolue should not consider their target to be all boomers but rather only the subset of people in this age category who have indulgent personalities (a psychographic trait) and sufficient incomes to afford an expensive product.

Mature Consumers Turning to mature consumers (also called seniors), in 2006 there were nearly 70 million U.S. citizens age 55 or older, representing approximately 23 percent of the total U.S. population. In other words, nearly one quarter of all Americans are senior citizens. Historically, many marketers have ignored mature consumers or have treated this group in unflattering ways by focusing on "repair kit products" such as dentures, laxatives, and arthritis remedies.[22] Not only are mature consumers numerous but also they are wealthier and more willing to spend than ever before. Mature Americans control nearly 70 percent of the net worth of all U.S. households.

People age 65 and older are particularly well off, having the highest discretionary income (i.e., income unburdened by fixed expenses) and the most assets of any age group. The number of people in this 65-plus age category is huge, totaling about 38 million in 2006, which represents nearly 13 percent of the total population.

A variety of implications accompany marcom efforts directed at mature consumers. In advertising aimed at this group, it is advisable to portray them as active, vital, busy, forward looking, and concerned with looking attractive and being romantic. Advertisers now generally appeal to seniors in a flattering fashion such as using attractive models to represent clothing, cosmetics, and other products that had been the exclusive advertising domain of youthful models.

It is important to reiterate that just because mature consumers share a single commonality (i.e., age 55 or older), they by no means represent a homogeneous market segment. Indeed, the Census Bureau divides people age 55 and older into three distinct age segments: 55 to 64 (olders); 65 to 74 (elders); and 75 and over (the very old) (see Table 4.5). On the basis of age alone, consumers in each of these groups differ—sometimes dramatically—in terms of lifestyles, interest in the marketplace, reasons for buying, and ability to spend. Moreover, it is important to realize that age alone is not the best indicator of how an individual lives or what role consumption plays in that lifestyle. In fact, research has identified four groups of mature consumers based on a combination of health and self-image characteristics. The results of a national mail survey of over 1,000 people age 55 and older led to the classification of seniors into four groups: Healthy Hermits, 38 percent; Ailing Outgoers, 34 percent; Frail Recluses, 15 percent; and Healthy Indulgers, 13 percent.[23] Brief descriptions follow.

- Healthy Hermits, although in good health, are psychologically withdrawn from society. They represent a good market for various services such as tax and legal advice, financial services, home entertainment, and do-it-yourself products. Direct mail, the Internet, and print advertising are the best media for reaching this group.
- Ailing Outgoers are diametrically opposite to Healthy Hermits. Although in poor health, they are socially active, health conscious, and interested in learning to do new things. Home health care, dietary products, planned retirement communities, and entertainment services are some of the products and services this group most desires. They can be reached via the Internet and through select mass media tailored to their positive self-image and active, social lifestyle.
- Frail Recluses are withdrawn socially and are in poor health. Various health and medical products and services, home entertainment, and domestic assistance services (e.g., lawn care) can be successfully marketed to this group via mass media advertising.
- Healthy Indulgers are vigorous, relatively wealthy, and socially active. They are independent and want the most out of life. Mature consumers in this group represent a good market for financial services, leisure/travel entertainment, clothes, luxury goods, and high-tech products and services. They are accessible via in-store promotions, direct mail, specialized print media, and the Internet.

The Ever-Changing American Household

A household represents an independent housing entity, either rental property (e.g., a single room or an apartment) or owned property (a mobile home, condominium, or house). As of 2006, there were approximately 114.4 million households in the United States, of which 77.4 million (68 percent) were family households (i.e., two or more related people occupying the household) and 37 million (32 percent) nonfamily households. The average household size across all 114.4 million American households was 2.5 people.[24]

Households are growing in number, shrinking in size, and changing in character. The traditional American family—that is, married couples with children younger than 18—represents less than one third of all U.S. households, whereas in 1960 such families constituted nearly 50 percent. The number of new households has grown twice as fast as the population, while household size has declined. In 1950, families constituted nearly 90 percent of all households, whereas in 2006 fewer than 70 percent were family units.[25]

The changing composition of the American household has tremendous implications for marketing communicators, perhaps especially advertisers. Advertising has to reflect the widening range of living situations that exist. This is particularly true in the case of households with a single occupant. Singles and unrelated couples or friends living together represent a large and ever-growing group. Many advertisers make special appeals to the buying interests and needs of singles, appealing in food ads, for example, to such needs as ease and speed of preparation, maintenance simplicity, and small serving sizes. Reaching singles requires special media-selection efforts because singles tend not to be big prime-time television viewers but are skewed instead toward the late fringe hours (after 11 p.m.), are disproportionately more likely than the rest of the population to view cable television, and are disproportionately heavy magazine readers. Many magazines cater to the interests of singles, and TV programs are produced to represent their actual or idealized lifestyles—programs such as *The Office, Lost, Gossip Girl, How I Met Your Mother, Two and a Half Men, Friends,* and *Sex and the City* (these latter two programs remain on TV in syndication but no longer are being produced.)

Ethnic Population Developments

America has always been a melting pot. It became even more so in recent decades. The largest ethnic groups in the United States are Hispanics and African-Americans. Ethnic minorities now represent nearly one of three people in the United States. In recognition of the growing role of ethnic groups, the following sections examine population developments and marcom implications for African-Americans, Hispanics, and Asian-Americans.

A few background statistics will set the stage for these discussions. First, based on a projection from the U.S. Census Bureau's last census, the American population as of 2010 is projected to be distributed in the following fashion:[26]

White, not Hispanic	64.3%
Hispanic, of any race	15.3
Black, not Hispanic	12.9
Asians	4.6
Others*	2.9
Total	100%

*Includes American Indians, native Hawaiians, Pacific Islanders, native Alaskans, and people of mixed race.

Non-Hispanic whites' share of the U.S. population is projected to decline from 64.3 percent of the total population in 2010 to just 50 percent by 2050.[27] The implication is obvious: marketers and marketing communicators need to devise marcom strategies that meet ethnic groups' unique wants/needs because ethnicity plays an important role in directing consumer behavior.[28] Table 4.6 provides a picture of the major ethnic groups' population representation in the United States

Table 4.6

Ethnic Groups' Population Representation in the United States, 2000–2050 (in millions)

Ethnic Group	2000	2010	2020	2030	2040	2050
African-American	35.82* (12.7%)	40.45 (13.1%)	45.37 (13.5%)	50.44 (13.9%)	55.88 (14.3%)	61.36 (14.6%)
Hispanic**	35.62 (12.6%)	47.76 (15.5%)	59.76 (17.8%)	73.06 (20.1%)	87.59 (22.3%)	102.56 (24.4%)
Asian	10.68 (3.8%)	14.24 (4.6%)	17.99 (5.4%)	22.58 (6.2%)	27.99 (7.1%)	33.43 (8.0%)
Total population (major ethnic groups)	82.12 (29.1%)	102.45 (33.2%)	123.12 (36.7%)	146.1 (40.2%)	171.5 (43.7%)	197.4 (47.0%)
Total U.S. Population	282.13	308.94	335.81	363.58	391.95	419.85

*To be read: there were 35.82 million African-Americans in the United States as of 2000, which constituted approximately 12.7 percent of the total population.
**Includes Hispanics of any race.

Source: U.S. Census Bureau, 2004, "U.S. Interim Projections by Age, Sex, Race, and Hispanic Origin," http://www.census.gov/ipc/www/usinterimproj.

from 2000 through 2050. The following sections provide more details for the three major ethnic groups: African-Americans, Hispanics (Latinos), and Asian-Americans. Remaining ethnic groups (e.g., American Indians and Pacific Islanders) are important to the cultural fiber of the United States but represent relatively limited economic forces due to their relative small sizes.

African-Americans

Non-Hispanic African-Americans are projected to constitute approximately 40.5 million individuals as of 2010, or slightly more than 13 percent of the U.S. population (see Table 4.6). African-Americans are characterized more by their common heritage than by skin color—a heritage based on a beginning in slavery, a history of discrimination, limited housing opportunities, and, historically, only partial participation in many aspects of the majority culture.[29] Although this situation has changed for the better, there remain distinct differences between the majority white culture and blacks, differences that are manifest in the marketplace.

Four reasons explain why African-Americans are attractive consumers for many companies: (1) the average age of black Americans is considerably younger than that for whites; (2) African-Americans are geographically concentrated, with approximately three fourths of all blacks living in just 16 states (California, Texas, Illinois, Louisiana, Alabama, Georgia, Florida, South Carolina, North Carolina, Maryland, Michigan, Ohio, Pennsylvania, Virginia, New York, and New Jersey); (3) African-Americans tend to purchase prestige and name-brand products in greater proportion than do whites; and (4) the total spending power of African-Americans is considerable, totaling nearly $800 billion in one recent year.[30]

These impressive figures notwithstanding, many companies make no special efforts to communicate with African-Americans. This is unwise because research indicates blacks are responsive to advertisements placed in black-oriented media and to ads that make personalized appeals by using African-American models and contexts with which blacks can identify, such as the advertisement in Figure 4.6. Major corporations are increasingly developing marcom programs for communicating with black consumers. By one account, some of the American corporations that do the best job in communicating with African-American consumers include Altria Group, Ford Motor, General Motors, Procter & Gamble, and Wal-Mart.[31]

Although greater numbers of companies are realizing the importance of directing special marcom efforts to African-Americans, it is important to emphasize that black consumers do not constitute a single market any more than do whites. African-Americans exhibit diverse purchasing behaviors according to their lifestyles, values, and demographics. Therefore, companies must use different advertising media, distribution channels, advertising themes, and pricing strategies as they market to the various subsegments of the African-American population.

Figure 4.6

African-American Models Appeal to African American Consumers

© Image courtesy of The Advertising Archives

Hispanic Americans (Latinos)

The U.S. Latino[32] population grew from only 4 million in 1950 to an expected population of nearly 48 million in 2010 and now is America's largest minority with a slight edge over African-Americans in share of the total U.S. population.[33] Latinos in the United States will constitute about one quarter of the total population by 2050 (see Table 4.6) and presently constitute a population of nearly 40 million residents—a number greater than Canada's entire population! The largest percentage of Latinos are Mexican Americans—about 70 percent—but large numbers of Puerto Rican Americans, Latin Americans from Central and South America, and Cuban Americans also reside in the United States.

Hispanic Americans have historically been concentrated in a relatively few states such as California, Texas, New York, Florida, Illinois, Arizona, and New Jersey. However, Latinos are becoming increasingly mobile and have begun to fan out from the few states in which they originally concentrated. Table 4.7 provides information pertinent to the top 10 Hispanic markets in the United States. Table 4.7 shows that Latinos represent the majority or near-majority of the total population in several large U.S. cities. In Los Angeles, for example, there are over eight million Latinos representing about 47 percent of that city's population.

Marketing communicators in the past devoted insufficient attention to Hispanic Americans, but their attention has increased substantially since the Census Bureau announced a 58 percent increase in the number of Hispanic Americans between 1990 and 2000. Yet companies advertise to Latinos much less than their market size would justify. Research has shown that the frequency of Hispanics' appearances in television advertising is considerably less than their proportion of the population.[34] Many companies are increasingly shifting more of their budgets into media that reach Latino consumers, but it would appear that marketers in large part are underspending in efforts targeted toward this large and growing segment of the U.S. population.[35]

Marketing communicators need to be aware of several important points when attempting to reach Latino consumers: Because a large percentage of Hispanics use primarily Spanish media, it is important to target messages to some (but not all) Latinos using Spanish-speaking media. A key in designing effective advertising for Hispanics is to advertise to them in their dominant language.[36] Because approximately half of Hispanic Americans speak only or mostly Spanish at home, reaching these consumers requires the use of Spanish. However, for Hispanics who are English dominant, as are many younger Latinos, it obviously makes greater sense to use English in advertising copy that reflects their values and culture.

It is critical to recognize that Latinos do not represent a single, unified market. There are strong intraethnic differences among Cubans, Mexicans, and Puerto

table 4.7

Top 10 U.S. Hispanic Markets (estimates as of 2006)

Rank	Market	Hispanic Population	Hispanic % of Total Market Population
1	Los Angeles	8,421,500	46.7
2	New York	4,389,600	20.7
3	Miami-FL*	2,141,800	48.6
4	Chicago	1,922,700	19.5
5	Houston	1,913,000	33.6
6	San Francisco	1,665,300	23.7
7	Dallas-Fort Worth	1,588,000	24.5
8	Phoenix-Prescott	1,228,400	26.6
9	San Antonio	1,192,000	53.8
10	McAllen, Texas	1,115,400	94.0

*FL = Fort Lauderdale

Source: "Hispanic Fact Pack, 2007 Edition," *Advertising Age's Annual Guide to Hispanic Marketing and Media* (New York: Crain Communications Inc., July 23, 2007), 46.

IMC >> i.m.c. focus

A Special Beverage for Latino Consumers, Clamato

Clamato, the name representing the conjoining of clam and tomato, is a tomato juice containing a hint of clam along with celery, onions, and spices. Many American consumers have never tried the product or dislike it due to the difficulty of drinking juice tinged with clams. Although available on supermarket shelves for over 25 years, the brand basically languished until its marketer, Mott's, concentrated its entire marketing budget on the Latino market. Why? Because Latino consumers somehow have the impression that Clamato juice is an aphrodisiac. Although Mott's makes no claims as to Clamato's powers, advertising refers obliquely to the brand's appeal with the tagline "Clamato le pone sabor al momento" (Clamato adds flavor to the moment).

Leveraging this (mis)perception among Latino consumers, Mott's undertook an integrated campaign that involved TV and radio advertisements, outdoor signage, and in-store promotions in major Hispanic markets. In a special appeal to Mexican Americans, who constitute about 70 percent of U.S. Latinos, Mott's developed a phone card promotion whereby cards with free minutes for calls to Mexico were given away when consumers purchased 64-ounce bottles of Clamato. These IMC efforts have driven a substantial sales increase since Mott's began the Hispanic initiative for Clamato.

And of further interest, Anheuser-Busch recently developed a brand named Chelada that consists of a mixture of Budweiser (or Bud Light) with Clamato juice along with salt and lime flavoring. These two new versions of Chelada—regular and light—will come in 24-ounce cans.

SOURCE: Adapted from Gabriel Sama, "Appeal of Clamato Isn't Just Its Taste," *The Wall Street Journal Online*, October 21, 2003, http://online.wsj.com (accessed October 21, 2003). The section on Chelada is from BrewBlog, http://www.brewblog.com/brew/2007/02/ab_readies_chel.html (accessed November 9, 2007).

Ricans that necessitate unique appeals be directed to each Latino group. Moreover, as with all general groupings, there are huge differences within each group in terms of English-speaking ability, length of residence in the United States (and thus degree of acculturation), level of income, and so on. It is erroneous to speak of a Hispanic market, a Mexican market, or any other crude lumping of people who share their descent as a single defining factor.

Some prominent companies—Coca-Cola, Pepsi, Procter & Gamble, Sears, McDonald's, Dunkin' Donuts, Best Buy, Toyota, Anheuser-Busch, to name a few—are now investing heavily in Hispanic-oriented advertising and event sponsorships that reach Latinos in their local communities and often in celebratory moods. Sponsoring Cinco de Mayo events, for example, is beginning to take on the same proportion as putting commercial support behind St. Patrick's Day celebrations. For an interesting appeal to the Latino market, see the *IMC Focus* insert about the marketing of Clamato and a new brand of beer that contains Clamato juice, Chelada.

Asian-Americans

Asians in the United States represent many nationalities: Asian Indians, Chinese, Filipino, Japanese, Korean, Vietnamese, and others. Asian-Americans have been heralded as the newest "hot" ethnic market. The demographics support this optimistic outlook. By 2010 approximately 14 million Asians will be living in the United States; that number will increase to over 33 million by 2050 (see Table 4.6).

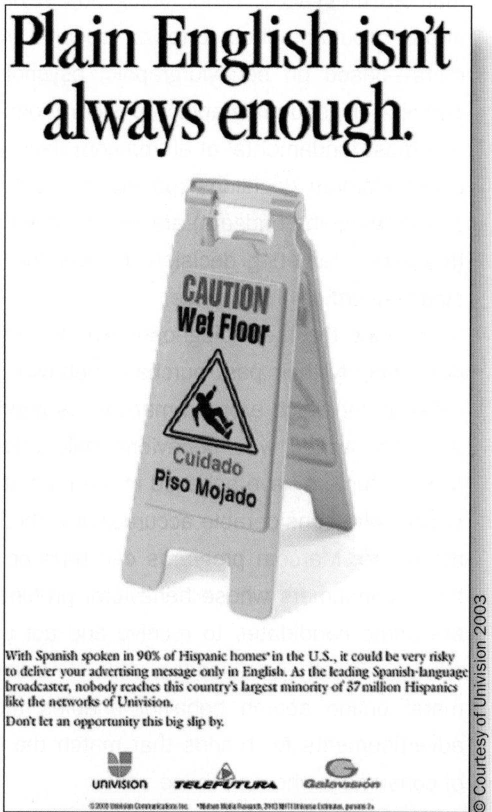

Plain English isn't always enough.
CAUTION
Wet Floor
Cuidado
Piso Mojado
With Spanish spoken in 90% of Hispanic homes* in the U.S., it could be very risky to deliver your advertising message only in English. As the leading Spanish-language broadcaster, nobody reaches this country's largest minority of 37 million Hispanics like the networks of Univision.
Don't let an opportunity this big slip by.
univision
TELEFUTURA
Galavisión

© Courtesy of Univision 2003

The largest Asian groups in the United States are of Chinese and Asian Indian descent, both with populations of about 2.5 million. Asian-Americans on average are better educated, have higher incomes, and occupy more prestigious job positions than any other segment of American society.

It is important to emphasize that just as there is no single African-American or Hispanic market, there certainly is no single Asian-American market. Moreover, unlike other ethnic groups, such as Hispanics, who share a similar language, Asian-Americans speak a variety of languages. Among Asian nationalities there are considerable differences in product choices and brand preferences. Even within each nationality there are variations in terms of English-language skills and financial well-being. Many Asian-Americans do not speak English fluently, and quite a few live in homes where no adults speak any English.

Some firms have been successful in marketing to specific Asian groups by customizing marketing programs to their values and lifestyles rather than merely translating Anglo programs. Mainstream marketers have available various media options for targeting Asian-Americans: Asian-language radio stations are now burgeoning in areas where large concentrations of Asians live, and direct marketing via postal mail is an outstanding medium for micromarketing to specific groups of Asian-Americans. The Internet also is a valuable medium for reaching Asian-Americans inasmuch as this group represents a disproportionately high group of online users in comparison to other groups of Americans, including the majority white population.

Summary

This chapter has emphasized the importance of targeting marcom messages. Determining how a brand's marcom efforts should be directed toward specific groups of consumers—based on behaviorgraphic, psychographic, demographic, or geodemographic considerations—is the initial and most fundamental of all marcom decisions. All subsequent marcom decisions (positioning, setting objectives, and determining budgets) are inextricably intertwined with this initial, targeting decision. Hence, the targeting decision is of critical importance.

Perhaps the most diagnostic way to target consumers is to identify their past purchase behavior in the product category for which a brand manager is making a targeting decision. Armed with behaviorgraphic information about how customers have behaved in the past, it is possible to project with considerable accuracy how they will behave in the future. Marcom programs can thus be aimed toward those consumers whose behavioral profiles indicate they are prime candidates to receive and act upon advertisements and other messages. Also, knowledge of consumers' online search behavior enables the targeting of advertisements for brands that match the characteristics of consumers who visit those sites.

Marketing communicators also target customers using knowledge about their activities, interests, and opinions (or, collectively, their lifestyles) to better understand what people want and how they are likely to respond to advertising, direct mail, and other forms of marketing communications. The term psychographics describes this form of targeting. Customized studies are conducted to identify psychographic segments directly applicable to the marketer's product category and brand, but syndicated research systems such as SRI's VALS system also provide useful information for making important marcom decisions. The VALS system classifies people into one of eight groups based on a combination of their self-orientation and resources.

Another basis for targeting consumers is geodemographics. This form of targeting basically identifies clusters of consumers who reside in neighborhoods where residents share similar demographic characteristics and related lifestyles. Donnelly's ClusterPlus and Claritas' PRIZMNE are two well-known and respected clustering systems that identify meaningful groupings of geographical units such as ZIP Code areas. The section on geodemographics covered the PRIZMNE and indicated that this clustering system delineates the population into 66 groups that are labeled with catchy names such as Bohemian Mix, Country Casuals, Suburban Pioneers, and City Roots. Geodemographic information is especially useful when making direct marketing decisions, selecting retail outlets, or spotting broadcast advertisements in select markets.

The final section of the chapter reviewed three major demographic developments: (1) the age structure of the U.S. population, (2) the changing American household, and (3) ethnic population developments. Some of the major demographic developments discussed include (1) the progressive aging of the U.S. population from an average age of 33 in 1990 to an expected average age of 38 by 2025, (2) the increase in the percentage of single American adults, and (3) the explosive growth of ethnic minorities, particularly Latinos.

Discussion Questions

1. Most readers of this text fall either in the Gen X or Gen Y age categories. Just because you share this commonality with all other Gen Xers or Gen Yers, does this one piece of information about you and your cohorts represent a sufficient basis on which a marcom practitioner might aim its advertising efforts?
2. Identify magazine advertisements that reflect appeals to at least three of the eight VALS groups. Describe in as much detail as possible the neighborhood in which you were raised. Come up with a label (similar to the PRIZMNE cluster names) that captures the essence of your neighborhood.
3. Demographers tell us that U.S. households are growing in number and shrinking in size. What specific implications do these changes hold for companies that manufacture and market products such as appliances, consumer electronics, and automobiles?
4. Based on your personal background and using the VALS system, how would you categorize most of the adults with whom you and your family associate?
5. Having read the section on the size of the world and U.S. populations, update the figures presented in the text, which were current as of June 2008, by going to http://www.census.gov/main/www/popclock.html.
6. What are your views on targeting products to kids, i.e., children between the ages of 4 and 12? Aside from your personal views, discuss the issue of targeting to children from two additional perspectives: first, that of a brand manager who is responsible for the profitability of a child-oriented product, and second, from the viewpoint of an ethicist. Imagine what each of these parties might say about the practice of targeting products to children.
7. To which of the VALS segments do you belong? (Go to http://www.sric-bi.com/VALS/presurvey.shtml.)
8. When we discussed the mature market, it was noted that advertising aimed at this group should portray them as vital, busy, forward looking, and attractive or romantic. Interview several mature consumers and coalesce their views on how they perceive advertising directed at them and their peers. Your interview results along with those from fellow students should lead to an interesting class discussion.
9. If you were to design a psychographic study for a new chain of lower-priced coffee stores that are planned to compete against Starbucks, what lifestyle characteristics (i.e., people's interests, values, and activities they participate in) might you consider as indicative of whether they might be interested in your new stores?
10. Assume you are brand manager of a food product that is consumed by all Americans—blacks, whites, Hispanics, Asians, and others. You are considering running an extended advertising campaign on prime-time television that uses Latino actors and appeals to Latino consumers. Aside from cost considerations, what reservations might you have about this type of campaign?
11. In what sense is online behavioral targeting a potential invasion of privacy?
12. Explain the reasons for the relentless aging of the U.S. population, and discuss some implications this will have on marketing and marketing communications in the foreseeable future.
13. In your own words, explain how online behavioral targeting works.
14. African-American, Latino, and Asian-American consumers do not signify three homogeneous markets; rather, they represent many markets composed of people who merely share a common ethnicity and/or language. Explain.
15. In what sense is behaviorgraphic information about customers more diagnostic of their future purchase behavior than is, say, demographic information?

End Notes

1. Kris Oser, "Targeting Web Behavior Pays, American Airlines Study Finds," *Advertising Age,* May 17, 2004, 8.
2. Emily Steel, "How Marketers Hone Their Aim Online," *The Wall Street Journal Online,* June 19, 2007, http://online.wsj.com (accessed June 19, 2007).
3. Carol M. Morgan and Doran J. Levy, "Targeting to Psychographic Segments," *Brandweek,* October 7, 2002, 18–19.
4. James W. Peltier, John A. Schibrowsky, Don E. Schultz, and John Davis, "Interactive Psychographics: Cross-Selling in the Banking Industry," *Journal of Advertising Research* 42 (March/April 2002), 7–22.
5. These descriptions are from http://www.sric-bi.com/VALS/types.shtml.
6. Michael J. Weiss, *The Clustered World: How We Live, What We Buy, and What It All Means About Who We Are* (Boston: Little, Brown and Company, 2000).
7. The following descriptions and data are based on documentation provided by Claritas, Inc., in materials sent to the author by Susan Fuller, Account Executive, dated June 16, 2004.
8. "A County-by-County Look at Ancestry," *USA Today,* July 1, 2004, 7A.
9. Emily Bryson York, "The Hottest Thing in Kids Marketing? Imitating Webkinz," *Advertising Age,* October 8, 2007, 38.
10. Deborah Roedder John, "Consumer Socialization of Children: A Retrospective Look at Twenty-Five Years of Research," *Journal of Consumer Research* 26 (December 1999), 183–213; Elizabeth S. Moore and Richard J. Lutz, "Children, Advertising, and Product Experiences: A Multimethod Inquiry," *Journal of Consumer Research* 27 (June 2000), 31–48.
11. Marvin E. Goldberg, Gerald J. Gorn, Laura A. Peracchio, and Gary Bamossy, "Understanding Materialism among Youth," *Journal of Consumer Psychology* 13, no. 3 (2003), 278–288.
12. For an academic treatment on the topic, see Sharon E. Beatty and Salil Talpade, "Adolescent Influence in Family Decision Making: A Replication with Extension," *Journal of Consumer Research* 21 (September 1994), 332–341; and Kay M. Palan and Robert E. Wilkes, "Adolescent-Parent Interaction in Family Decision Making," *Journal of Consumer Research* 24 (September 1997), 159–169.
13. Becky Ebenkamp, "Youth Shall Be Served," *Brandweek,* June 24, 2002, 21.
14. Beth Snyder Bulik, "Forget the Parents: HP Plans to Target Teenagers Instead," *Advertising Age,* July 30, 2007, 8.
15. William Strauss and Neil Howe, *Generations: The History of America's Future, 1584–2069* (New York: William Morrow and Company, Inc., 1991). For a less technical treatment written by an advertising person, see Karen Ritchie, *Marketing to Generation X* (New York: Lexington Books, 1995).
16. Yankelovich Partners, cited in "Don't Mislabel Gen X," *Brandweek,* May 15, 1995, 32, 34.
17. Michelle Higgins, "Cushier Convertibles for Aging Boomers," *The Wall Street Journal Online,* September 1, 2004, http://online.wsj.com (accessed September 1, 2004).
18. Margaret G. Zackowitz, "Harley's Midlife Crisis," *National Geographic,* August 2003.
19. For an interesting discussion of subjective (versus chronological) age and its role in influencing consumer behavior, see George P. Moschis and Anil Mathur, "Older Consumer Responses to Marketing Stimuli: The Power of Subjective Age," *Journal of Advertising Research* 46 (September 2006), 339–346.
20. The "epicenter of society" expression is attributed to Fred Elkind, an executive with the Ogilvy & Mather advertising agency, and cited in Christy Fisher, "Boomers Scatter in Middle Age," *Advertising Age,* January 11, 1993, 23.
21. Hannah Karp, "Red Bull Aims at an Older Crowd," *The Wall Street Journal Online,* June 7, 2004, http://online.wsj.com (accessed June 7, 2004).
22. The expression "repair kit" is from Charles D. Schewe, "Marketing to Our Aging Population: Responding to Physiological Changes," *The Journal of Consumer Marketing* 5 (summer 1988), 61–73.
23. The research was performed by George P. Moschis and is reported in "Survey: Age Is Not Good Indicator of Consumer Need," *Marketing Communications,* November 21, 1988, 6. See also George P. Moschis and Anil Mathur, "How They're Acting Their Age," *Marketing Management* 2, no. 2 (1993), 40–50.
24. All statistics in this paragraph are from the U.S. Census Bureau, Current Population Survey, Table HH-1, Households by Type: 1940 to Present. Internet release date: March 27, 2007 (accessed November 8, 2007).
25. http://www.census.gov/population/www/socdemo/hh-fam.html#ht. Table FM-1, Families by Presence of Own Children, Under 18: 1950 to Present, (accessed November 8, 2007).
26. U.S. Census Bureau, 2004, "U.S. Interim Projections by Age, Sex, Race, and Hispanic Origin," http://www.census.gov/ipc/www/usinterimproj (accessed November 8, 2007).
27. Ibid.
28. See Douglas M. Stayman and Rohit Deshpande, "Situational Ethnicity and Consumer Behavior," *Journal of Consumer Research* 16 (December 1989), 361–371; and Cynthia Webster, "Effects of Hispanic Ethnic Identification on Marital Roles in the Purchase Decision Process," *Journal of Consumer Research* 16 (September 1994), 319–331.
29. This characterization is based on James F. Engel, Roger D. Blackwell, and Paul W. Miniard, *Consumer Behavior,* 8th ed. (Fort Worth: The Dryden Press, 1995), 647.
30. Deborah L. Vence, "Mix It Up," *Marketing News,* October 15, 2006, 19.

31. Lisa Sanders, "How to Target Blacks? First, You Gotta Spend," *Advertising Age,* July 3, 2006, 19.
32. Hispanic is a government-invented term that encompasses people of Spanish or Latin American descent or Spanish-language background. Many people of Latin American descent prefer to be referred to as Latinos.
33. U.S. Census Bureau, 2004, "U.S. Interim Projections by Age, Sex, Race, and Hispanic Origin."
34. "Hispanic Characters Remain Scarce on Prime-Time TV," *The Wall Street Journal Online,* June 24, 2003, http://online.wsj.com (accessed June 24, 2003).
35. Dana James, "Many Companies Underspend in Segment," *Marketing News,* October 13, 2003, 6.
36. Sigfredo A. Hernandez and Larry M. Newman, "Choice of English vs. Spanish Language in Advertising to Hispanics," *Journal of Current Issues and Research in Advertising* 14 (fall 1992), 35–46.

5

Positioning

When the name McDonald's comes to mind, you, like most people, likely entertain thoughts of the golden arches, Ronald McDonald, french fries, Big Macs, clerks with attitudes, and so on. Similarly, when you call to mind the chain of Starbucks stores, you probably think of strong-tasting coffee and expensive specialty drinks such as espressos, lattes, cappuccinos, and mochas. But what would be your view of McDonald's if it sold specialty coffee drinks (lattes, cappuccinos, etc.), and how would you regard Starbucks if it offered sandwiches and other non-dessert breakfast items?

Well, Starbucks has indeed experimented in some stores with nontraditional breakfast items, food products typically associated more with fast food chains than with coffee shops. Perhaps of far greater interest is the move by McDonald's into specialty coffee drinks. McDonald's has added specialty coffee drinks to the menus of about 800 of its over 13 thousand U.S. stores, and intends to expand the specialty drinks to all of its U.S. stores by 2009. Because quick service will be mandatory to McDonald's success (in comparison to the more relaxed atmosphere at Starbucks), McDonald's will use push-button machines to produce

© AP Images/Dick Whipple

specialty coffee drinks in a single step. It is expected that these beverages at McDonald's will be priced about 50 cents less than at Starbucks.

One may wonder: Why would McDonald's move in this direction? Needless to say, Starbucks has been hugely successful in pioneering the mass distribution of specialty coffee drinks in the U.S. and beyond and now is ripe for competitive efforts to steal market share. It is estimated that about 20 percent of Americans daily drinks some form of espresso-based coffee, and the market is expected to grow at an annual rate of 4 percent for the next several years. On top of this, the profit margins for specialty coffees are extremely attractive in comparison to most of McDonald's menu items. The incentives are large for McDonald's to move in this direction. The president of McDonald's USA says that the objective is to transform his company into a beverage destination, and that McDonald's convenience, speed of service, and value will make that chain a formidable player in the specialty coffee business.

There's one major problem in McDonald's thrust into this new business: Many franchise owners strongly oppose the initiative in view of the estimated $100,000 investment required to cover renovations and the cost of new equipment. Franchisees are concerned that there is little customer interest in buying specialty coffee drinks at McDonald's and that it will take them years to recoup their investment. On the other hand, corporate officials estimate that offering specialty coffee products will boost individual stores' annual revenue by approximately $125,000.

Sources: Janet Adamy, "McDonald's Is Poised for Lattes," March 1, 2007, ***The Wall Street Journal Online*** (accessed November 21, 2007); Ashley M. Heher, "Big Mac, Fries and a Latte?" November 19, 2007, *ABC News Online* (accessed November 21, 2007).

Chapter Objectives

After reading this chapter you should be able to:

1. Appreciate the concept and practice of brand positioning.
2. Explain that positioning involves the creation of meaning and that meaning is a constructive process involving the use of signs and symbols.
3. Give details about how brand marketers position their brands by drawing meaning from the culturally constituted world.
4. Describe how brands are positioned in terms of various types of benefits and attributes.
5. Explicate two perspectives that characterize how consumers process information and describe the relevance of each perspective for brand positioning.

>>Marcom Insight:

"McBucks": It's Not the McDonald's You've Always Known

Introduction

This chapter is about brand positioning. A brand's **positioning** represents the key feature, benefit, or image that it stands for in the target audience's collective mind. Brand communicators and the marketing team in general must identify a *positioning statement,* which is the central idea that encapsulates a brand's meaning and distinctiveness vis-à-vis competitive brands. It should be obvious that positioning and targeting decisions—the subject of Chapter 4—go hand in hand: Positioning decisions are made with respect to intended targets, and targeting decisions are based on a clear idea of how brands are to be positioned and distinguished from competitive offering.

Returning to the *Marketing Insights* vignette at the chapter beginning, the two brands featured, McDonald's and Starbucks, have historically had straightforward brand positions. McDonald's is known for its limited menu of value-based items and its family-oriented atmosphere where children and their parents can enjoy meals in relatively look-alike stores that are adorned with golden arches and Ronald McDonald statutes. Starbucks, by comparison, caters to a more upscale target audience consisting mostly of businesspeople, professionals, and students, but also has a clear positioning as an outlet for high-quality specialty coffee drinks and a venue where customers can leisurely drink coffee while chatting with friends, surfing the Internet, or reading a book, magazine, or newspaper. Both McDonald's and Starbucks are appropriately positioned for their respective target audiences.

Positioning in Theory: A Matter of Creating Meaning

Fundamental to the concept and practice of positioning is the idea of *meaning.* This section discusses the nature of meaning using a perspective known as semiotics. **Semiotics,** broadly speaking, is the study of signs and the analysis of meaning-producing events.[1] The important point of emphasis is that the semiotics perspective sees meaning as a *constructive process.* That is, meaning is determined both by the message source's choice of communication elements and, just as importantly, by the receiver's unique social-cultural background and mind-set at the time he or she is exposed to a message. In other words, meaning is not thrust upon consumers; rather, consumers are actively involved in constructing meaning from marcom messages, meaning that may or may not be equivalent to what the communicator intended to convey. The marcom goal is, of course, to do everything possible to increase the odds that consumers will interpret messages exactly as they are intended.

The fundamental concept in semiotics is the *sign,* the noun counterpart to the verb *signify.* (Singers sing; runners run; dancers dance; and signs signify!) Marketing communications in all its various forms uses signs in the creation of messages. When reading the word *sign,* you probably think of how this word is used on an everyday basis—such as road signs (stop, yield, danger, or directional signs), store signs, signs announcing a car or home for sale, and signs of less tangible concepts such as happiness (the happy face sign). The general concept of sign encompasses these everyday notions but includes many other types of signs, including words, visualizations, tactile objects, and anything else that is perceivable by the senses and has the potential to communicate meaning to the receiver, who in semiotics terms is also referred to as an interpreter.

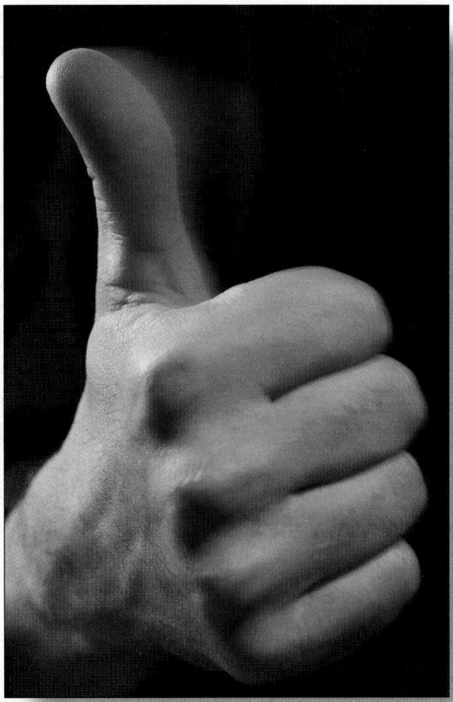
© Photodisc/Getty Images

Figure 5.1

The Thumbs-Up Sign

Formally, a **sign** is something physical and perceivable that signifies something (the *referent*) to somebody (the *interpreter*) in some *context.*[2] The dollar sign ($), for example, is understood by many people throughout the world as signifying the currency of the United States (as well as the currencies of Australia, Canada, Hong Kong, New Zealand, and several other countries). The thumbs-up sign (Figure 5.1) signifies a positive reaction to or appraisal of an action or event. For example, movie critics sometimes signify that they like a new movie by displaying an upward thumb sign. Parents display the thumbs-up when their children perform well in artistic or athletic events. Interestingly, the upward thumb in the Middle East signifies an entirely different meaning than in the West; it represents a crass expression not unlike the middle-finger sign in the West. This difference in sign usage anticipates the following discussion, which explains that meaning is contained in the person and not the sign per se; in other words, meaning is both idiosyncratic and context dependent—meaning is *constructed*!

The Meaning of Meaning

Although we use signs to share meaning with others, the two terms (*signs* and *meanings*) are not synonymous.[3] Signs are simply stimuli that are used to evoke an intended meaning in another person. But words and nonverbal signs do not have meanings per se; instead, *people have meanings for signs.* Meanings are internal responses people hold for external stimuli. Many times people have different meanings for the same words or gestures, as all of us have experienced when, say, attempting to explain something to someone from a different background or culture. It follows from these points that meanings are *not* contained in a marcom message per se but rather are perceived by the message receiver. Thus, the challenge when positioning a brand is to make sure consumers interpret as intended the signs the marketing communicator used.

This desirable outcome is most likely accomplished when signs are common to both the sender's and the receiver's fields of experience. A field of experience, also called the *perceptual field,* is the sum total of a person's experiences that are stored in memory. The larger the overlap, or commonality, in their perceptual fields, the greater the likelihood that signs will be interpreted by the receiver/interpreter in the manner intended by the sender. Effective communication is severely compromised when, for example, marketing communicators use words, visualizations, or other signs that customers do not understand. This is especially problematic when developing communication programs for consumers in other cultures.

Up to this point we have referred to meaning in the abstract. Now a definition is in order. **Meaning** can be thought of as the *thoughts and feelings* that are evoked within a person when presented with a sign in a particular *context.*[4] It should be clear that meaning is internal, rather than external, to an individual. Meaning, in other words, is subjective and highly context dependent. Again, meaning is not imposed upon us, but rather is constructed by the interpreter of signs, such as consumers who daily are barraged with hundreds of advertisements and other marcom messages.

Meaning Transfer: From Culture to Object to Consumer

The culture and social systems in which marketing communications take place are loaded with meaning. Through socialization, people learn cultural values, form beliefs, and become familiar with the physical manifestations, or artifacts, of these values and beliefs. The artifacts of culture are charged with meaning, which is transferred from generation to generation. For example, the Lincoln Memorial and Ellis Island are signs of freedom to Americans. To Germans and many other people throughout the world, the now-crumbled Berlin wall signified oppression and hopelessness. Comparatively, yellow ribbons signify crises and hopes for hostage release and the safe return of military personnel. Pink ribbons signal support for breast cancer victims. Red ribbons have grown into an international symbol of solidarity on AIDS. The Black Liberation flag with its red, black, and green stripes—representing blood, achievement and the fertility of Africa—symbolizes civil rights.

Marketing communicators, when in the process of positioning their brands, draw meaning from the *culturally constituted world* (i.e., the everyday world filled with artifacts such as the preceding examples) and transfer that meaning to their brands. Advertising is an especially important instrument of meaning transfer and positioning. The role of advertising in transferring meaning has been described in this fashion:

> *Advertising works as a potential method of meaning transfer by bringing the consumer good and a representation of the culturally constituted world together within the frame of a particular advertisement.... The known properties of the culturally constituted world thus come to reside in the unknown properties of the consumer good and the transfer of meaning from world to [consumer] good is accomplished.*[5]

When exposed to an advertisement (or any other form of marcom message), the consumer is not merely drawing information from the ad but is actively involved in assigning meaning to the advertised brand.[6] Stated alternatively, the consumer approaches advertisements as texts to be interpreted.[7] (Note that the term *text* refers to any form of spoken or written words and images, which clearly encompasses advertisements.) To demonstrate the preceding points, take into account the following advertising illustrations.

Consider first an advertisement for the Honda Accord that was created some years ago when American consumers were suspicious of Japanese-made automobiles and perhaps even considered it un-American to buy something other than an American model. Shortly after the Honda Motor Company began producing automobiles in the United States, it undertook a print advertising campaign to convey that four out of five Accords sold in America are manufactured in the United States. Beyond stating this fact in the ad copy, the two-page advertisement presented large photos of five icons of American culture: a hamburger, cowboy boots, an oversized bicycle (not like the sleek, Asian or European racing bikes), a baseball, and a jazz ensemble. By associating itself with these well-known symbols of American consumer culture, Honda pulled meaning from the "culturally constituted world" of its target audience consumers, most of whom would immediately recognize the five icons as uniquely American. The obvious intent was subtly to convey the meaning to consumers that the Accord, embedded as it was among the five icons of American popular culture, is made in America and thus is itself American. If Honda's advertising agency had made such a claim in stark, verbal form ("Honda *is* an American automobile!"), most readers would have doubted the claim, fully realizing that the Honda is of Japanese origin. But by presenting the message at a nonverbal level and merely via association with American icons, consumers probably were somewhat inclined to accept the Honda Accord as at least quasi-American.

Consider also the two advertisements for V8 vegetable juice in Figure 5.2 that embed this brand in the context of health and fitness symbols—one ad showing bottles of V8 juice as ear plugs on a stethoscope and the other displaying multiple bottles of V8 juice arranged into the shape of a zipper. The suggestion is that V8,

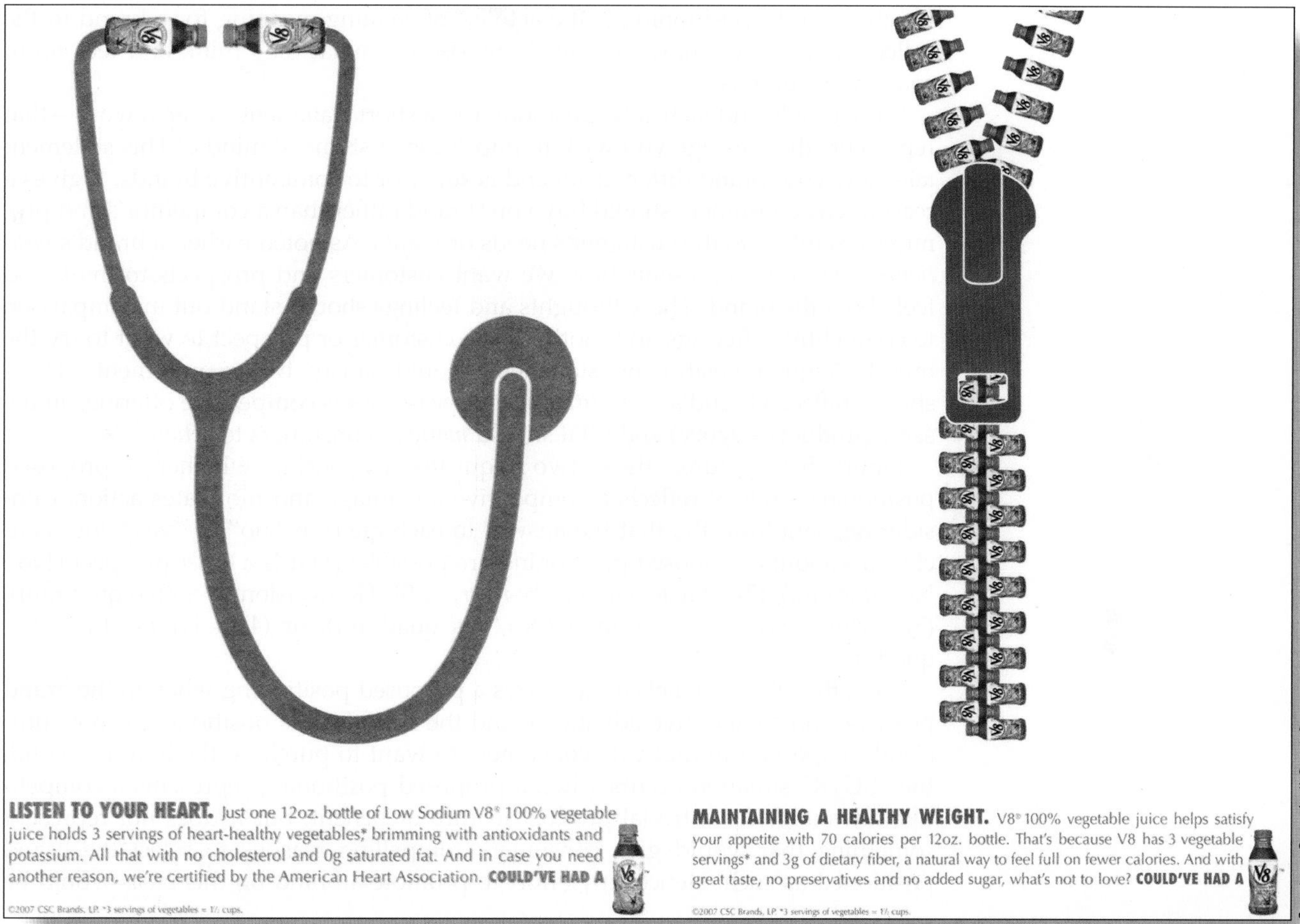

V8
LISTEN TO YOUR HEART. Just one 12oz. bottle of Low Sodium V8® 100% vegetable juice holds 3 servings of heart-healthy vegetables,* brimming with antioxidants and potassium. All that with no cholesterol and 0g saturated fat. And in case you need another reason, we're certified by the American Heart Association. COULD'VE HAD A V8
©2007 CSC Brands, LP. *3 servings of vegetables = 1½ cups.
MAINTAINING A HEALTHY WEIGHT. V8® 100% vegetable juice helps satisfy your appetite with 70 calories per 12oz. bottle. That's because V8 has 3 vegetable servings* and 3g of dietary fiber, a natural way to feel full on fewer calories. And with great taste, no preservatives and no added sugar, what's not to love? COULD'VE HAD A V8
©2007 CSC Brands, LP. *3 servings of vegetables = 1½ cups.

Courtesy Campbell Soup Company

Figure 5.2
V8 Advertisements Illustrating Contextual Meaning

which is made with 100 percent vegetable juice, is good for the heart and also the waist. Thus, once again we see an advertiser using well-known symbols to draw meaning from the "culturally constituted world" and attempt to transfer that meaning to the advertised brand.

Positioning in Practice: The Nuts and Bolts

Brand positioning is an essential preliminary activity to developing a successful marcom program. By having a clear positioning statement, the brand management team is committed to conveying a consistent message in all forms of marcom messages. Positioning is both a useful conceptual notion and an invaluable strategic tool.

Conceptually, the term *positioning* suggests two interrelated ideas. First, the marketing communicator wishes to create a specific meaning for the brand and have that meaning firmly lodged in the consumer's memory (think of this as "positioned in" the consumer's mind). Second, the brand's meaning in consumers' memories stands in comparison to what they know and think about competitive brands in the product or service category (think of this as "positioned against" the competition). Positioning thus involves two interrelated actions: positioning a brand *in* (the consumer's mind) and *against* (competitive positioning strategies).

In other words, positioning is the activity of creating meaning for a brand in the collective minds of consumers in comparison to what they think and feel about competitive brands.

Strategically and tactically, positioning is a short statement—even a word—that represents the message you wish to imprint in customers' minds.[8] This statement tells how your brand differs from and is superior to competitive brands. It gives a reason why consumers should buy your brand rather than a competitor's and promises a solution to the customer's needs or wants. As noted earlier, a brand's *positioning statement* represents how we want customers and prospects to think and feel about the brand. These thoughts and feelings should stand out in comparison to competitive offerings and motivate the customer or prospect to want to try the brand. A good positioning statement should satisfy two requirements: (1) It should reflect a brand's *competitive advantage* (vis-à-vis competitive offerings in the same product category) and (2) it should *motivate* consumers to *action*.[9]

Figure 5.3 captures these two requisites by posing whether a proposed positioning strategy reflects a competitive advantage and motivates action. Considering, simplistically, that the answer to each query is "no" or "yes," four conclusions about a proposed positioning are possible: (1) it is a *Loser* prospect (No/No quadrant); (2) a *Swimming-up-the-river*, or SUTR, decision (Yes/No quadrant); (3) a *Promote-competitors* option (No/Yes quadrant); or (4) a *Winner* (Yes/Yes quadrant).

First, the "Loser" label characterizes a proposed positioning wherein the brand possesses no competitive advantage and the basis for the positioning is not sufficiently important to motivate consumers to want to purchase the brand. Second, the "SUTR" situation occurs when a proposed positioning represents a competitive advantage for a trivial product feature or benefit, but it does not represent something that would give consumers compelling reasons to select the brand positioned as such. Hence, any effort to promote a brand on this basis would be

figure 5.3

Outcomes of Proposed Positioning

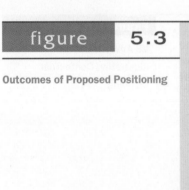

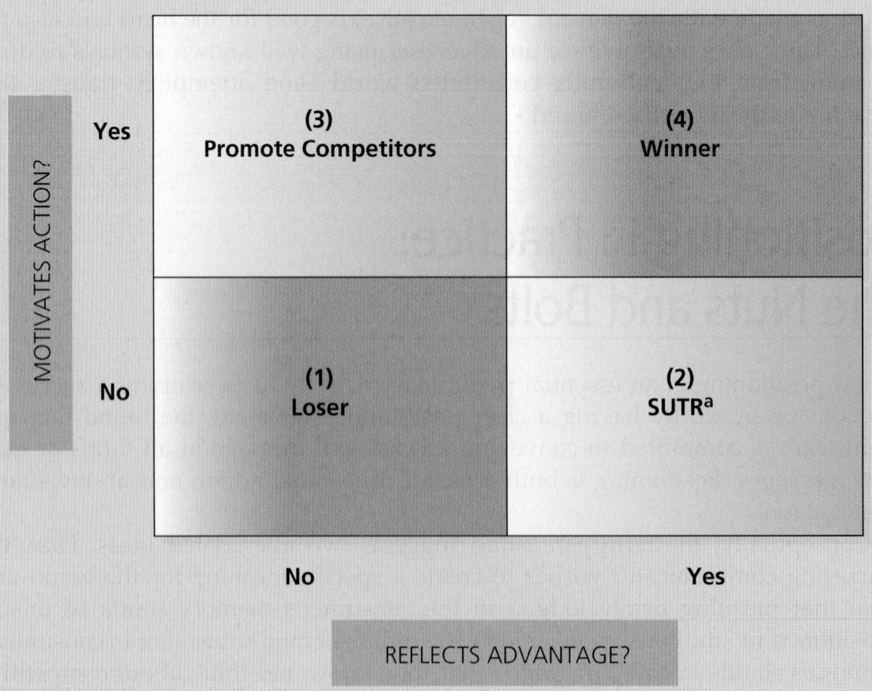

a Swimming up the river.

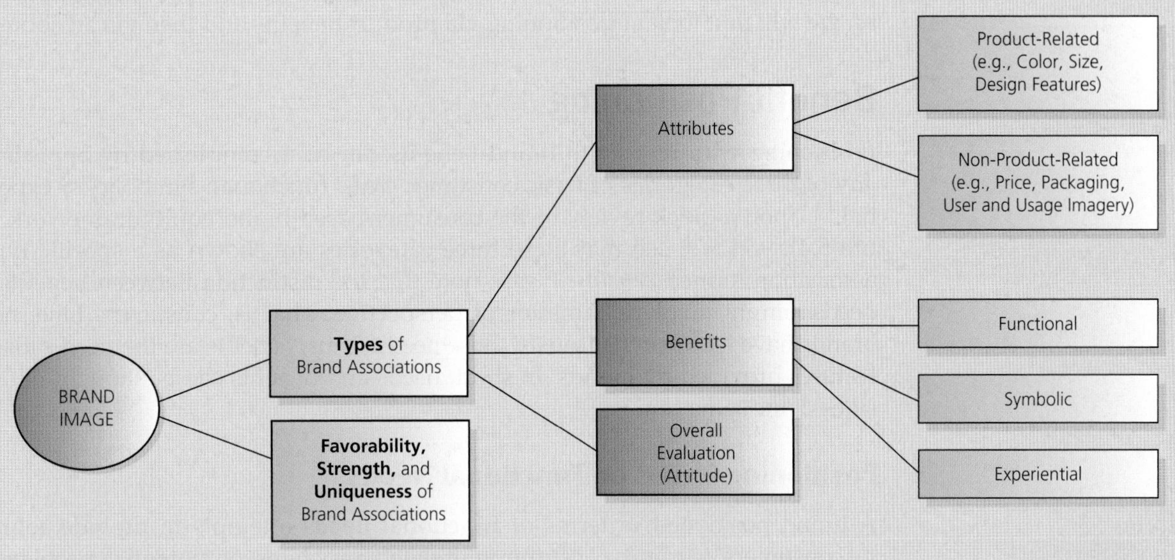

SOURCE: Adapted from Kevin Lane Keller, "Conceptualizing, Measuring, and Managing Customer-Based Brand Equity," *Journal of Marketing* 57 (January 1993), 7.

Figure 5.4

A Framework for Brand Positioning

tantamount to attempting to swim up the river (i.e., against the current)—hard work will be expended but little progress will be made. Third, the "Promote Competitors" description characterizes a positioning statement that does not reflect a competitive advantage but does represent an important reason for making brand selection decisions in the product category. Hence, any effort to position "our" brand on this basis would essentially serve to aid other brands that do have a competitive advantage with respect to a particular product feature or benefit. Finally, the "Winner" label characterizes a situation where we have positioned our brand on a product feature or benefit for which we have an advantage over competitors and which gives consumers a persuasive reason for trying our brand. When considering how best to position a brand, it is essential to appraise objectively and hypercritically whether a proposed positioning affords "your" brand a competitive advantage and whether this advantage is important enough to encourage consumers to at least make a trial purchase of your brand.

To make this idea of positioning even more concrete, let us call on the customer-based brand equity framework discussed in Chapter 2. For present purposes, it will be useful to reproduce the *brand image* part of the brand equity framework as a useful graphic for expanding our discussion of brand positioning. As can be seen in Figure 5.4, a brand's image consists of types, favorability, strength, and uniqueness of brand associations. Our focus for now will be limited to the *types* of brand associations. Please notice in Figure 5.4 that types of associations include brand attributes, benefits, and an overall evaluation of, or attitude toward, the brand. Brand *attributes* include product-related and non-product-related features. Non-product-related attributes would include, for example, a brand's price, consumer perceptions of the type of people who own the brand (user imagery), and the occasions when the brand would be appropriately used (usage imagery). Brand *benefits* consist of ways by which a brand satisfies customers' needs and wants and can be classified as functional, symbolic, or experiential.

With Figure 5.4 and the previous terminology in mind, we now can pursue the options available to marketing communicators for positioning their brands. Generally speaking, we can position a brand by focusing on product *attributes* or *benefits.* Because benefits provide B2C consumers or B2B customers with more compelling reasons for selecting a particular brand than do product attributes per se, we will first look at positioning via product benefits and then via attributes.

Benefit Positioning

Positioning with respect to brand benefits can be accomplished by appealing to any of three categories of basic consumer *needs:* functional, symbolic, or experiential.[10] Upon a quick review of the consumer-based brand equity framework (Figure 5.4), you will see that these three categories are shown as a specific type of association termed *benefits.* Please note that the distinction between benefits and needs simply involves a matter of perspective. That is, consumers have needs; brands have features that satisfy those needs. Thus, benefits are the need-satisfying features provided by brands. In short, needs and benefits can be thought of as flip sides of the same coin.

Positioning Based on Functional Needs

A brand positioned in terms of **functional needs** attempts to provide solutions to consumers' current consumption-related problems or potential problems by communicating that the brand possesses specific benefits capable of solving those problems. Appeals to functional needs are the most prevalent form of brand-benefit positioning. In B2B marketing, for example, salespeople typically appeal to their customers' functional needs for higher-quality products, faster delivery time, or better service. Consumer goods marketers also regularly appeal to consumers' needs for convenience, safety, good health, cleanliness, and so on, all of which are functional needs that can be satisfied by brand benefits. For example, the Crocs brand (see Figure 5.5) appeals to consumers' desire for lightweight, comfortable, and odor-resistant footwear. The *IMC Focus* insert offers further details about this brand.

Figure 5.5

Croc Advertisement Illustrating Appeal to Functional Needs

Positioning Based on Symbolic Needs

Other brands are positioned in terms of their ability to satisfy nonfunctional, or symbolic, needs. Positioning in terms of symbolic needs attempts to associate brand ownership with a desired group, role, or self-image. Appeals to **symbolic needs** include those directed at consumers' desire for self-enhancement, group membership, affiliation, altruism, and other abstract need states that involve aspects of consumption not solved by practical product benefits. (See the *Global Focus* insert for discussion of the growing importance of appeals to consumers using claims that agricultural products are "fair traded.") Marketers in categories such as personal beauty products, jewelry, alcoholic beverages, cigarettes, and motor vehicles frequently appeal to symbolic needs.

Positioning Based on Experiential Needs

Consumers' **experiential needs** represent their desires for products that provide sensory pleasure, variety, and, in a few product circumstances, cognitive stimulation. Brands positioned toward experiential needs are promoted as being out of the ordinary and high

IMC >> i.m.c. focus

Not Lovely, but Successful

Crocs is a brand of footwear widely worn by young and old alike. Many people own multiple pairs of the somewhat clumsy-looking shoes that are made from a plastic-like foam resin. And for every product owner, there are several other people who wouldn't be caught dead wearing Crocs. Regardless of your personal view, the fact is that Crocs became a successful brand very quickly. The Colorado-based company was founded in 2002 by three buddies who took frequent boating trips together. While sailing in the Caribbean on one occasion, one of the trio wore a pair of foam clogs he had purchased in Canada. Favorable response from others encouraged the three buddies to start their own company to market a footwear item they named Crocs. They purchased the product from a Canadian company that had proprietary rights to the foam resin from which Crocs are formed. This resin, called Croslite, is lightweight, anti-bacterial, and foot-forming. After adding a strap to the back of the original clogs, the partners started selling Crocs at boat shows and at other events that attracted potential purchasers. It wasn't long before word-of-mouth influence resulted in a rapid increase in sales and widespread distribution in many different types of retail outlets.

After realizing sales of only $1 million in 2003, by 2007 Crocs generated sales of more than $800 million from shoes sold in over 40 countries! Much of the brand's success is due to its fulfilling consumers' functional needs for a comfortable and an easy-to-care-for footwear item—slip them on and hose them off when they get dirty. The brand's phenomenal achievements also can be attributed to creative marketing that has affiliated Crocs with universities, professional sports teams, and other high-equity associations. In a sense, when purchasing Crocs the consumer purchases a functional product that is laden with emotional connection to, say, your own university.

SOURCES: Vivian Manning-Schaffel, "Crocs–Still Rocking," http://www.brandchannel.com, August 27, 2007 (accessed November 19, 2007); Evelyn M. Rusli, "Crocs Is Still a Buy," http://www.forbes.com, November 12, 2007 (accessed November 20, 2007).

in sensory value (looking elegant, feeling wonderful, tasting or smelling great, sounding divine, being exhilarating, and so on) or rich in the potential for cognitive stimulation (exciting, challenging, mentally entertaining, and so on). The Dove advertisement (Figure 5.6) represents this brand's traditional positioning as an especially flavorful chocolate candy (Seduction by Chocolate). Consumers are promised the experience of tasting a special product ("A chocolate experience like no other").

It is important to recognize that brands often offer a mixture of functional, symbolic, and experiential benefits. It has been argued that successful positioning requires a communication strategy that entices a *single type* of consumer need (functional, symbolic, or experiential) rather than attempting to be something for everyone.[11] According to this argument, a brand with a generic (multiple-personality) image is difficult to manage because it: (1) competes against more brands (those with purely functional, purely symbolic, purely experiential, and mixed images); and (2) may be difficult for consumers to understand readily what it stands for and what its defining characteristics are. This argument, although based on sound logic, is *not* irrefutable. In fact, a reasonable counterargument holds that a brand positioned as having, say, both functional qualities and symbolic appeal has the potential of recruiting prospective users who desire different things from the product category. Hence, according to this counterperspective, a "multipersonality" positioning allows consumers to read into the brand precisely what they are seeking.

Figure 5.6

Dove Advertisement Illustrating Appeal to Experiential Needs

global focus

The Symbolism of Certifying Products as Fair Traded

Most consumers know that agricultural commodities often are imported from other countries rather than grown and harvested domestically. Yet, most people go to their local grocery stores or supermarkets with little awareness that agricultural workers in other countries often are paid dreadfully low wages and farm owners have difficulty earning a profit. Poor wage rates and minuscule profits, if not losses, are largely due to the economics of growing commodity products. Coffee, for example, is grown in Latin American countries such as Brazil and Colombia and also is harvested in African countries and, ever increasingly, Vietnam. In most years, coffee supply exceeds demand, and anyone familiar with basic economics knows that the effect of this imbalance is falling prices. Intense competition has forced prices and wages down to the point where growers have difficulty making a living and workers are hard-pressed to feed their families. On the other hand, low coffee prices benefit retailers and consumers in countries that import low-priced coffee. The situation, in other words, is not win-win but rather one where businesses and consumers in economically advantaged economies gain at the expense of growers and workers in developing economies. Is there a resolution to this imbalance? Perhaps there is; please read on.

The resolution is not the competitive marketplace, because the economics of supply-demand disequilibrium inevitably lead to further lowering of commodity prices. Hence, the only way possible for commodity growers and workers to receive higher profits and wages is some form of "artificial" intervention—that is, for forces other than the economics of supply and demand to come into play. This has happened, in fact, because many consumers in advanced economies are willing to pay higher prices so poor workers and growers are able to survive. These consumers have been given the label "LOHAS" consumers, which stands for "lifestyles of health and sustainability." About one third of adults in the United States, or around 50 million people, are classified as LOHAS according to a recent study.

But even if a consumer is LOHAS inclined, how does one know which products to purchase? Increasingly, commodity products such as coffee, grapes, mangos, pineapples, and others are labeled with stickers bearing "Fair Trade Certified." This label means that workers in developing economies receive higher wages and benefits for their efforts than the supply-demand disequilibrium would normally dictate. Large retail chains such as McDonald's, Dunkin' Donuts, and Starbucks offer fair-traded coffee, and many supermarkets are carrying more commodity products with the fair-trade label. Another label being used to signify fair trading is "Rainforest Alliance Certified." Procter & Gamble's coffee products carry this label.

The LOHAS movement reveals that consumers' symbolic needs—the sense of being fair and socially responsible—sometimes trump their functional need to pay the lowest possible prices. This form of altruism enables workers and farm owners in poor countries to sustain an existence and to continue to grow and harvest products their economies depend on. Fair trading achieves more of a win-win outcome than the rich-countries-win/poor-countries-lose situation previously prevailing.

Source: Adapted from Katy McLaughlin, "Is Your Grocery List Politically Correct?" *The Wall Street Journal Online*, February 17, 2004. For additional information on fair trade and fair-traded products and organizations see http://en.wikipedia.org/wiki/Fair_trade.

Which argument is more correct? The only viable conclusion is that whether a single or multitype positioning is more effective depends on the competitive circumstances and consumer dynamics that are involved in a particular situation. What works best for a brand in one product category does not necessarily work as well for another brand in a different category. As academics like to say, it's an empirical q, which means that no single logical account or theoretical explanation is available to resolve the issue. Trial and error experience and marketing research evidence are the final arbiters.

Attribute Positioning

A brand can be positioned in terms of a particular attribute or feature, provided that the attribute represents a competitive advantage and can motivate customers to purchase that brand rather than a competitive offering. Product attributes, as shown in Figure 5.4, can be distinguished as either *product-related* or *non-product-related.*

Product-Related

Sleeker product design, superior materials, and more color options are just a few of the virtually endless attributes that can provide the foundation for positioning a brand. If your brand has a product advantage, flaunt it, especially if the advantage is something that consumers truly desire in the product category and will motivate them to action. For example, in an appeal to people who are concerned with product safety, the advertisement for the Toyota Highlander (Figure 5.7) claims that no other vehicle in the Highlander's category has more standard safety features. This is a distinct product-related positioning directed to consumers who are concerned about their personal safety and, perhaps especially, the well-being of "precious cargo" such as children and grandchildren.

Non-Product-Related: Usage and User Imagery

A brand positioned according to the image associated with how it is used, its *usage imagery,* depicts the brand in terms of specific, and presumably unique, usages that become associated with it. For example, advertisers sometimes position SUVs and passenger trucks in terms of their seemingly unique ability to go "off road" and traverse rough terrain. Such advertisements create the impression that only the advertised brand is capable of forging streams, climbing hills, and navigating other tough-to-travel areas.

Brands also can be positioned in terms of the kind of people who use them. This *user imagery* thus becomes the brand's hallmark; the brand and the people who are portrayed as using it become virtually synonymous. Positioning a brand via user imagery thus amounts to associating the brand with icon-like representations of the kind of people who are portrayed in advertisements as typical users of the brand. Consider the Ralph Lauren advertisement in Figure 5.8. The ad says little about the wide line of apparel items carried by this retailer. The ad's most prominent feature is the attractive model who reflects Ralph Lauren's positioning of a typical owner of its merchandise. In a sense, Ralph Lauren apparel and this image of a typical user are indivisible. This is an intelligent positioning for a product category such as apparel because purchase decisions are based as much on projecting a desired image as on fulfilling a functional need.

Repositioning a Brand

There are points in a brand's life cycle where brand managers need to alter what the brand stands for in order to enhance the brand's competitiveness. Consider the following illustration of successful repositioning in a B2B context. MeadWestvaco Corporation is a leading global producer of packaging products, coated and specialty papers, and other items. One of its many products is a printing paper that was once branded under the name TexCover II. Although an excellent product providing consistent performance, TexCover II held just the fifth largest market share in its category and generated annual revenues of less than $40 million.

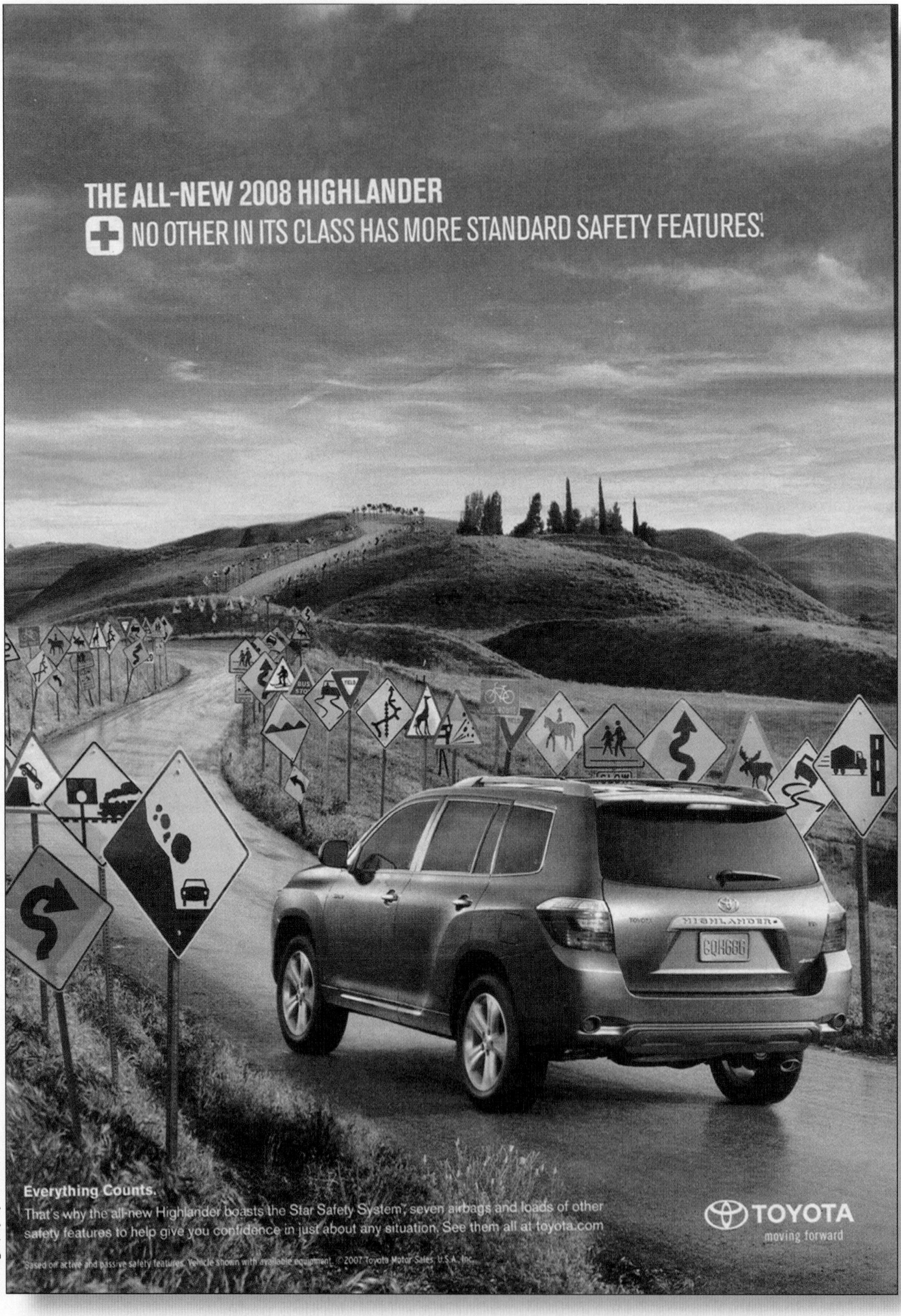

Photography by Mark Ku

Figure 5.7

Highlander Advertisement Illustrating Product-Related Attribute Positioning

Because the brand was under-performing despite its excellent quality and reputation for dependable performance, an advertising agency, the Mobium Creative Group, was hired to pump up TexCover II's performance.

A few words about the Mobium Creative Group will be helpful prior to describing the strategy the group devised for repositioning TexCover II. Unlike most B2B agencies, which are known for being relatively unexciting, if not outright boring, Mobium prides itself on being a rather wacky creative shop. For example, its opening Web page (http://www.mobium.com) states, "buddy, can you paradigm," which is a clever takeoff on the depression-era expression—"buddy, can you spare a dime?"—that captures the plea of the impoverished asking for a little help from their more well-off brethren. Mobium's paradigm expression suggests that this is what this creative agency is all about, creating new paradigms for its clients. In fact, the agency's fundamental and non-traditional value system and business model is captured on its Web site (http://www.mobium.com/work) in terms that characterize business customers as driven by emotions as well as logic. The Mobium Creative Group is, then, positioning its creative work as out of the ordinary compared with other B2B-oriented advertising and branding agencies.

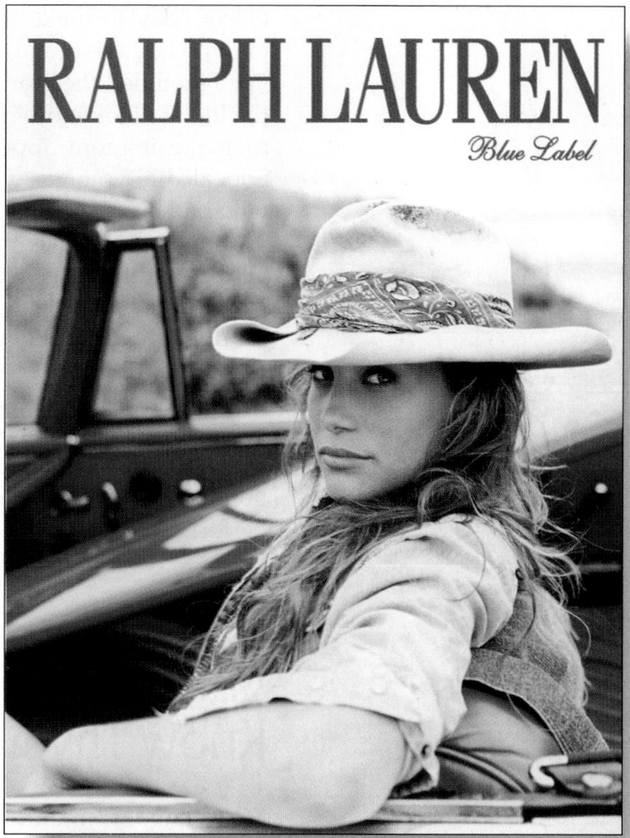

Figure 5.8

Ralph Lauren Advertisement Illustrating Positioning Based on User Imagery

With this backdrop in mind, Mobium set about the task of repositioning the line of TexCover II printing paper. Mobium made a major strategic shift by changing the brand name to the catchy name Tango and positioning the brand as "always performing." The name Tango is easy to remember, although it is not naturally related to the attributes or benefits of printing paper. The newly named brand's positioning strategy ("always performing") was reinforced through a series of attention-gaining advertisements that cleverly illustrated this positioning in a humorous and captivating manner.

These marcom innovations resulted in a first-year revenue increase of 27 percent. Despite an industry-wide recession, Tango's revenues continued to climb. In a period of just four years, this B2B brand increased its total revenue by $126 million on a marcom investment of only $2 million! This obviously represents a huge return (greater than 6,000 percent) on a modest marcom investment and demonstrates how success can be achieved when a brand is properly positioned, cleverly named, and adequately supported.[12]

Another instance of repositioning involves Oil of Olay, a decades-old line of skin-care products. Created in World War II as a lotion to treat burns, Procter & Gamble (P&G) purchased the brand from Richardson-Vicks in 1985 and developed the brand into a major line of skin-care products with revenues exceeding $500 million annually. However, over the years the brand eventually became a bit outdated. P&G's consumer research revealed that many young women considered the brand more appropriate for older women than for themselves. Young women also did not like the idea of using what they considered to be a greasy skin-care product. Although in actuality Oil of Olay is not greasy, apparently the word *oil* in the Oil of Olay brand name suggested just such an unpleasant product characteristic to young women who had never actually tried the brand. Based on this illuminating research evidence, P&G's brand management team repositioned

Oil of Olay to make it more appealing to younger women. Several steps were undertaken. First, without any fanfare so as not to bring attention to the change, P&G modified the brand name from Oil of Olay to simply Olay. They also altered the logo to look more modern and reduced the amount of writing on the package to make it more appealing to younger consumers. The new name and look appealed to younger women without alienating baby boomers and older women who had been Oil of Olay's core consumers.

Brands sometimes must be repositioned in order to grow and prosper. Oil of Olay's mature image was unappealing to millions of younger consumers who also were turned off by the thought of using what they imagined to be a greasy, oily product. By dropping *Oil* from the name and updating the packaging, P&G reinvigorated this old, successful brand. Interestingly, the name Olay, which originally was made up by the chemists who developed the product, is a surprisingly good name when marketing the product globally. The word is easily pronounced in most languages and hints at being of Spanish origin with its similar pronunciation to the Spanish word *olé,* which is a shout of approval to a bullfighter or other performer.[13]

Implementing Positioning: Know Thy Consumer

Marketing communicators direct their efforts toward influencing consumers' brand-related *beliefs, attitudes, emotional reactions,* and *choices.* Ultimately, the objective is to encourage consumers to choose "our" brand rather than a competitive offering. To accomplish this goal, marketing communicators design advertising messages, promotions, packages, brand names, sales presentations, and other forms of brand-related messages—all of which are designed to drive home the brand's meaning, its positioning. This section looks at positioning from the consumer's perspective by examining how individuals receive and are influenced by marcom messages.

The discussion is based on different perspectives about how consumers process marcom information and ultimately use this information to choose from among the alternatives available in the marketplace. We will label these the *consumer processing model (CPM)* and the *hedonic, experiential model (HEM).* From a consumer-processing perspective (CPM), information processing and choice are seen as rational, cognitive, systematic, and reasoned.[14] In the hedonic, experiential perspective (HEM), in contrast, emotions in pursuit of fun, fantasies, and feelings drive consumer processing of marcom messages and behavior.[15]

A very important point needs to be emphasized before discussing each framework: consumer behavior is much too complex and diverse to be captured perfectly by two extreme models. You should think of these as bipolar perspectives that anchor a continuum of possible consumer behaviors—ranging, metaphorically speaking, from the "icy-blue cold" CPM perspective to the "red-hot" HEM perspective (see Figure 5.9). At the CPM end of the continuum is consumer behavior that is based on *pure reason*—cold, logical, and rational. At the HEM end is consumer behavior based on *pure passion*—hot, spontaneous, and perhaps even irrational. Between these extremes rests the bulk of consumer behavior, most of which is not based on pure reason or pure passion and is neither icy blue cold nor red hot. Rather, most behavior ranges, again in metaphorical terms, from cool to warm. In the final analysis, we will examine the rather extreme perspectives of consumer behavior but recognize that often both perspectives are applicable to understanding how and why consumers behave as they do.

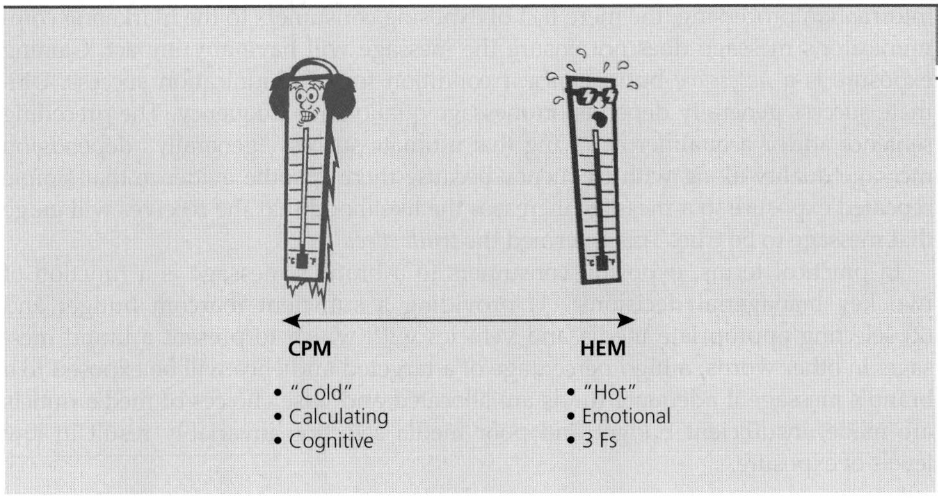

figure 5.9

Comparison of the CPM and HEM Models

The Consumer Processing Model (CPM)

The information-processing situation consumers face and the corresponding communication imperatives for marketing communicators have been described in these terms:

> *The consumer is constantly being bombarded with information which is potentially relevant for making choices. The consumer's reactions to that information, how that information is interpreted, and how it is combined or integrated with other information may have crucial impacts on choice. Hence, [marketing communicators'] decisions on what information to provide to consumers, how much to provide, and how to provide that information require knowledge of how consumers process, interpret, and integrate that information in making choices.*[16]

The following sections discuss consumer information processing in terms of a set of interrelated stages.[17] Although marcom efforts play an important role in affecting all stages of this process, we will focus exclusively on the first six stages because the last two (decision making and action) are determined by all marketing-mix elements and not by marketing communications per se:

Stage 1: Being *exposed* to information
Stage 2: Paying *attention*
Stage 3: *Comprehending* attended information
Stage 4: *Agreeing* with comprehended information
Stage 5: *Retaining* accepted information in memory
Stage 6: *Retrieving* information from memory
Stage 7: *Deciding* from alternatives
Stage 8: *Acting* on the basis of the decision

Stage 1: Being Exposed to Information

The marketing communicator's fundamental task is to deliver messages to consumers, who, it is expected, will process the messages, understand the brand positioning, and, if the positioning is congenial with the consumer's preference structure, undertake the course of action advocated by the marketer. By definition, **exposure** simply means that consumers come in contact with the marketer's message (they see a magazine ad, hear a radio commercial, notice an Internet banner, and so on). Although exposure is an essential preliminary step to subsequent stages of information processing, the mere fact of exposing consumers to the marketing communicator's message does not ensure the message will have any impact. Gaining exposure is a *necessary* but *insufficient* condition for communication success. Ultimate success generally depends on message quality and frequency. The preceding sentence added a qualifier in saying that ultimate success "generally" depends on message quality along with frequency because there is some evidence that simple repeated exposure to a message increases the likelihood that the receiver will judge that message to be true. This is termed the *truth effect.*[18]

In practical terms, exposing consumers to a brand's message is a function of two key managerial decisions: (1) providing a sufficient marcom budget and (2) selecting appropriate media and vehicles with which to present a brand message. In other words, a high percentage of a targeted audience will be exposed to a brand's message if adequate funds are allocated and wise choices of media outlets are made; insufficient budget and poor media selection invariably result in low levels of exposure.

Stage 2: Paying Attention

Laypeople use the expression "paying attention" in reference to whether someone is really listening to and thinking about what a speaker (such as a teacher) is saying, or whether his or her mind is wandering off into its own world of thought. For psychologists, the term *attention* means fundamentally the same thing. **Attention,** in its formal use, means to focus cognitive resources on and think about a message to which one has been exposed. Actually, consumers pay attention to just a small fraction of marcom messages. This is because the demands placed on our attention are great (we are virtually bombarded with advertisements and other commercial messages), but information-processing *capacity is limited.* Effective utilization of limited processing capacity requires that consumers selectively allocate mental energy (processing capacity) only to messages that are *relevant and of interest to current goals.*

For example, once their initial curiosity is satisfied, most people who are *not* in the market for a new automobile, especially a luxury brand such as a Mercedes Benz, would pay relatively little attention to an ad listing detailed comments about the Mercedes Benz because the product has little relevance to them. In contrast, people who are anxious to purchase a luxury automobile would likely devote *conscious attention* to an advertisement for, say, a Mercedes Benz because it would hold a high level of relevance to their interests. Notice that "conscious attention" is emphasized in the previous sentence. This is to distinguish this deliberate, controlled form of attention from an *automatic* form of relatively superficial attention that occurs when, for example, an individual reacts to a loud noise even when the source of the noise holds little, if any, personal relevance.[19]

How can attention selectivity be avoided? The short answer is that marketing communicators can most effectively gain the consumer's attention by creating messages that truly appeal to their needs for product-relevant information. The likelihood that consumers will pay attention to an advertisement or other form of marcom message also is increased by creating messages that are novel, spectacular, aesthetically appealing, eye catching, and so forth. We will delay further discussion of these attention-gaining strategies until a subsequent chapter, at which point we will detail ways to augment consumers' motivation to attend brand messages.

In sum, attention involves allocating limited processing capacity in a selective fashion. Effective marketing communications are designed to activate consumer interests by appealing to those needs that are most relevant to the target audience. This is no easy task; marcom environments (stores, advertising media, noisy offices during sales presentations) are inherently cluttered with competitive stimuli and messages that also vie for the prospective customer's attention, and it is well-known that *clutter* reduces message effectiveness.[20]

Stage 3: Comprehension of What Is Attended

To comprehend is to understand and create meaning out of stimuli and symbols. Communication is effective when the meaning, or positioning, a marketing communicator intends to convey matches what consumers actually extract from a message. The term **comprehension** often is used interchangeably with *perception;* both terms refer to *interpretation.* Because people respond to their perceptions of the world and not to the world as it actually is, the topic of comprehension, or perception, is one of the most important subjects in marketing communications.[21]

The perceptual process of interpreting stimuli is called **perceptual encoding.** Two main stages are involved. **Feature analysis** is the initial stage whereby a receiver examines the basic features of a stimulus (such as size, shape, color, and angles) and from this makes a preliminary classification. For example, we are able to distinguish a motorcycle from a bicycle by examining features such as size, presence of an engine, and the number of controls. Lemons and oranges are distinguishable by their colors and shapes. The second stage of perceptual encoding, **active synthesis,** goes beyond merely examining physical features. The *context* or situation in which information is received plays a major role in determining what is perceived and interpreted, or, in other words, what meaning is acquired. Interpretation results from combining, or synthesizing, stimulus features with expectations of what should be present in the context in which a stimulus is perceived. For example, a synthetic fur coat placed in the window of a discount clothing store (the context) is likely to be perceived as a cheap imitation; however, the same coat, when attractively merchandised in an expensive boutique (a different context) might now be considered a high-quality, stylish garment.

© Courtesy of John Jonik

Figure 5.10

Humorous Illustration of Selective Perception

The important point is that consumers' comprehension of marketing stimuli is determined by stimulus features and by characteristics of the consumers themselves. Expectations, needs, personality traits, past experiences, and attitudes toward the stimulus object all play important roles in determining consumer perceptions. Due to the subjective nature of the factors that influence our perceptions, comprehension is often idiosyncratic, or peculiar to each individual. Figure 5.10 provides a humorous, albeit revealing, illustration of the idiosyncrasy of perception. *The Investigation* illustrates that each individual's personal characteristics and background influence how he or she perceives the man in the middle. Please examine this figure carefully, and in so doing you will develop an enhanced appreciation of how one's personal characteristics and background influence his or her perceptions.

A classic statement regarding the idiosyncratic nature of perception is offered in the following quote:

> *We do not simply "react to" a happening or to some impingement from the environment in a determined way (except in behavior that has become reflexive or*

habitual). We [interpret and] behave according to what we bring to the occasion, and what each of us brings to the occasion is more or less unique.[22]

This quote is from an analysis of fan reaction to a heatedly contested football game between Dartmouth and Princeton universities back in 1951. The game was highly emotional and arguments and fights broke out on both sides. Interestingly, fan reaction to the dirty play divided along team loyalties. Dartmouth fans perceived Princeton players as the perpetrators; Princeton fans considered Dartmouth players to be at fault. That is, what fans experienced and how they interpreted events depended on their view of who were the "good guys." In short, our individual uniqueness conditions what we see!

An individual's *mood* also can influence his or her perception of stimulus objects. Research has found that when people are in a good mood they are more likely to retrieve positive rather than negative material from their memories; are more likely to perceive the positive side of things; and, in turn, are more likely to respond positively to a variety of stimuli.[23] Advertisers are well aware of this, at least intuitively, when they use techniques such as humor and nostalgia to put message receivers in a good mood.

Miscomprehension People sometimes *misinterpret* or *miscomprehend* messages so as to make them more consistent with their existing beliefs or expectations. This typically is done unconsciously; nonetheless, distorted perception and message miscomprehension are common. Miscomprehension of marcom messages occurs primarily for three reasons: (1) messages are themselves sometimes misleading or unclear, (2) consumers are biased by their own preconceptions and thus "see" what they choose to see, and (3) processing of advertisements often takes place under time pressures and noisy circumstances. The moral is clear: Marketing communicators cannot assume that consumers interpret messages in the manner intended, thus message testing is absolutely imperative before investing in print space, broadcast time, or other media outlets. Also, it is important that marcom messages be repeated so as to assure that most viewers and readers eventually understand the marketer's intended meaning.

Stage 4: Agreement with What Is Comprehended

A fourth information-processing stage involves the matter of whether the consumer *agrees with* (i.e., accepts) a message argument that he or she has comprehended. It is crucial from a marcom perspective that consumers not only comprehend a message but also that they agree with the message (as opposed to countering it or rejecting it outright). Comprehension alone does not ensure that the message will change consumers' attitudes or influence their behavior. Understanding that an advertisement is attempting to position a brand in a certain way is not tantamount to accepting that message. For example, we may clearly understand when a retailer advertises itself as providing outstanding service, but we would not agree with that positioning if we personally have experienced something less than this level of service from that retailer.

Agreement depends on whether the message is *credible* (i.e., believable, trustworthy) and whether it contains information and appeals that are *compatible with the values* that are important to the consumer. For example, a consumer who is more interested in the symbolic implications of consuming a particular product than in acquiring functional value is likely to be persuaded more by a message that associates the advertised brand with a desirable group than one that talks about mundane product features. Using endorsers who are perceived as trustworthy is another means of enhancing message credibility. Credibility also can be boosted by structuring believable messages rather than making unrealistic claims.

Stages 5 and 6: Retention and Search and Retrieval of Stored Information

These two information-processing stages, *retention* and *search and retrieval,* are discussed together because both involve *memory* factors. The subject of memory is a complex topic, but these complexities need not concern us here because our interest in the topic is considerably more practical.[24]

From a marcom perspective, memory involves the related issues of what consumers remember (recognize and recall) about marketing stimuli and how they access and retrieve information when in the process of choosing among product alternatives. The subject of memory is inseparable from the process of learning, so the following paragraphs first discuss the basics of memory, then examine learning fundamentals, and finally emphasize the practical application of memory and learning principles to marketing communications.

Elements of Memory Memory consists of long-term memory *(LTM);* short-term, or working, memory *(STM);* and a set of sensory stores *(SS).* Information is received by one or more sensory receptors (sight, smell, touch, and so on) and passed to an appropriate SS, where it is rapidly lost (within fractions of a second) unless attention is allocated to the stimulus. Attended information is then transferred to STM, which serves as the center for current processing activity by integrating information from the sense organs and from LTM. *Limited processing capacity* is the most outstanding characteristic of STM; individuals can process only a finite amount of information at any one time. An excessive amount of information will result in reduced recognition and recall. Furthermore, information in STM that is not thought about or rehearsed will be lost from STM in about 30 seconds or less.[25] (This is what happens when you get a phone number from a telephone directory but then are distracted before you have an opportunity to dial the number. You must refer to the directory a second time and then repeat the number to yourself—rehearse it—so that you will not forget it again.)

Information is transferred from STM to LTM, which cognitive psychologists consider to be a virtual storehouse of unlimited information. Information in LTM is organized into coherent and associated cognitive units, which are variously called *schemata, memory organization packets,* or *knowledge structures.* All three terms reflect the idea that LTM consists of associative links among related information, knowledge, and beliefs. A diagram of the concept of a knowledge structure is illustrated in Figure 5.11. This representation captures one baby boomer's memory structure for the Volkswagen Beetle, a car she first owned during her college years in the late 1960s and repurchased in 2008 to celebrate her 61st birthday.

The marketing communicator's challenge is to provide positively valued information that consumers will store in LTM and that will be used at some later time to influence the choice of "our" brand over competitive options. There is a good reason why information communicated about a brand *must* achieve long-term memory storage and be readily retrievable from memory. Namely, the point at which a consumer is exposed to information about a brand typically is separated in time—sometimes by months—from the occasion at which the consumer needs to access and use the information to make a purchase decision. Marketing communicators continually attempt to alter consumers' long-term memories, or knowledge structures, by facilitating consumer *learning* of information that is compatible with the marketer's interest.

Types of Learning Two primary types of learning are relevant to marcom efforts.[26] One form is *strengthening of linkages* between the marketer's brand and some feature or benefit of that brand. Metaphorically, the marketing communicator wishes to build mental "ropes" (rather than flimsy strings) between a brand and its positive features and benefits. The objective is, in other words, to position

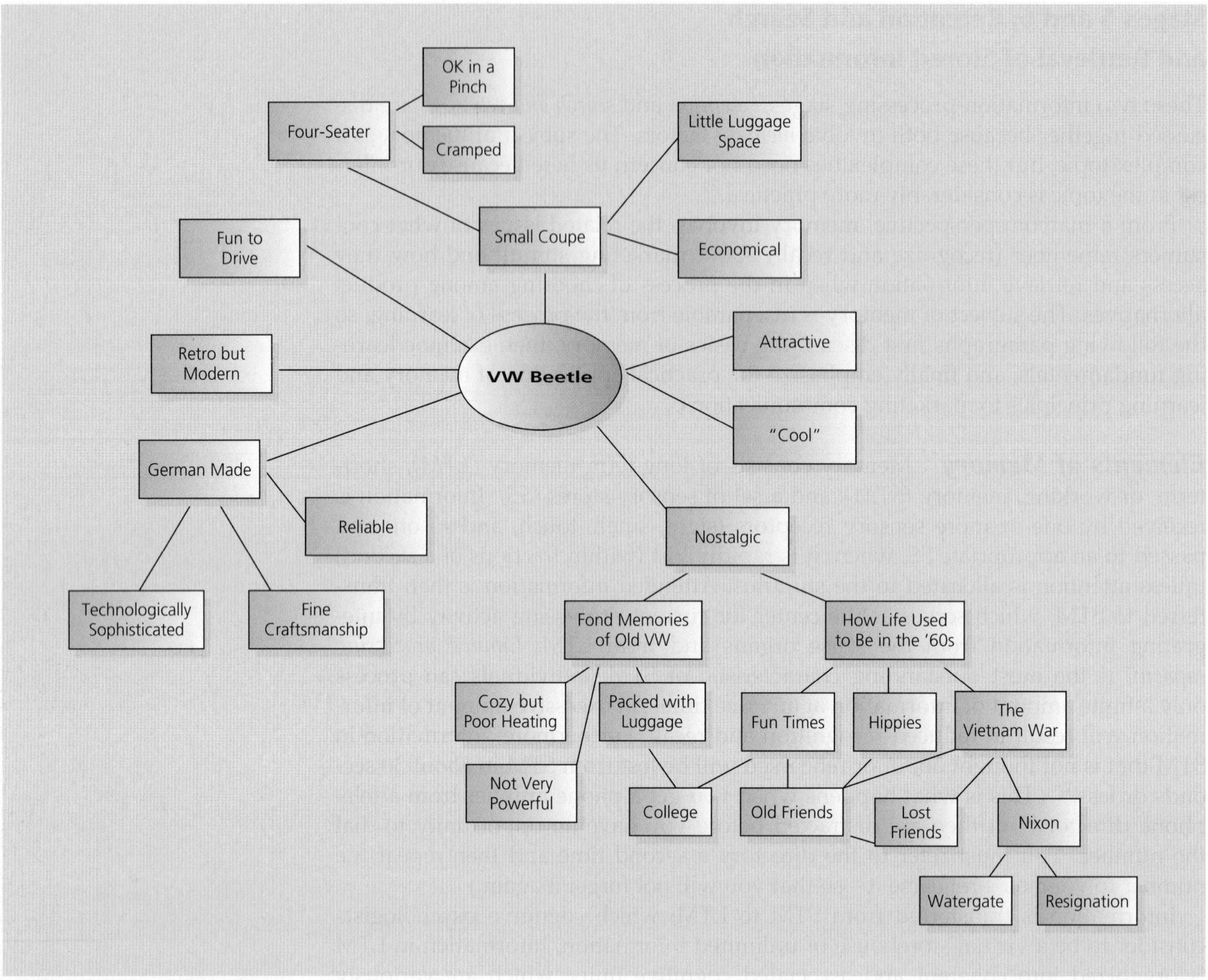

Figure 5.11

Consumer's Knowledge Structure for the Volkswagen Beetle

the brand's essence securely in the consumer's memory. In general, linkages are strengthened by *repeating* claims, being *creative* in conveying a product's features, and presenting claims in a *concrete* fashion. For example, the ad for Philadelphia Extra Light cream cheese (Figure 5.12) compares this brand to a feather and also connects it with an image of an opening of the heavens as concrete metaphorical representations that the brand is as light in fat content (only 6% fat) as the proverbial feather and that it is "heavenly" good. The marketers of Philadelphia Extra Light cream cheese have attempted to build the strong linkage in consumers' minds that although this is a healthy brand it nonetheless tastes good.

Marketing communicators facilitate a second form of learning by *establishing entirely new linkages.* Returning to our discussion of brand equity back in Chapter 2, the present notion of establishing new linkages is equivalent to the previously discussed idea of enhancing brand equity by building strong, favorable, and perhaps unique associations between the brand and its features and benefits. Hence, the terms *linkage* and *association* are interchangeable in this context. Both involve a relation between a brand and its *features and benefits that are stored in a consumer's memory.*

Search and Retrieval of Information Information that is learned and stored in memory only impacts consumer choice behavior when it is searched and retrieved. Precisely how retrieval occurs is beyond the scope of this chapter.

Suffice it to say that retrieval is facilitated when a new piece of information is linked, or associated, with another concept that is itself well known and easily accessed. This is precisely what the brand management and ad agency team for Philadelphia Extra Light cream cheese has attempted to accomplish by using a feather as a metaphorical representation that the brand is light in fat content. It is much easier for people to retrieve the concrete idea of a feather as emblematic of lightness than it is to salvage from memory the abstract semantic concept that Philadelphia Extra Light cream cheese is low in fat content. *Dual-coding theory* offers an explanation.

According to dual-coding theory, pictures are represented in memory in verbal as well as visual form, whereas words are less likely to have visual representations.[27] In other words, pictures and visuals (versus words) are better remembered because pictures are especially able to elicit mental images. Research has shown that information about product attributes is better recalled when the information is accompanied with pictures than when presented only as prose.[28] The value of pictures is especially important when verbal information is itself low in imagery.[29]

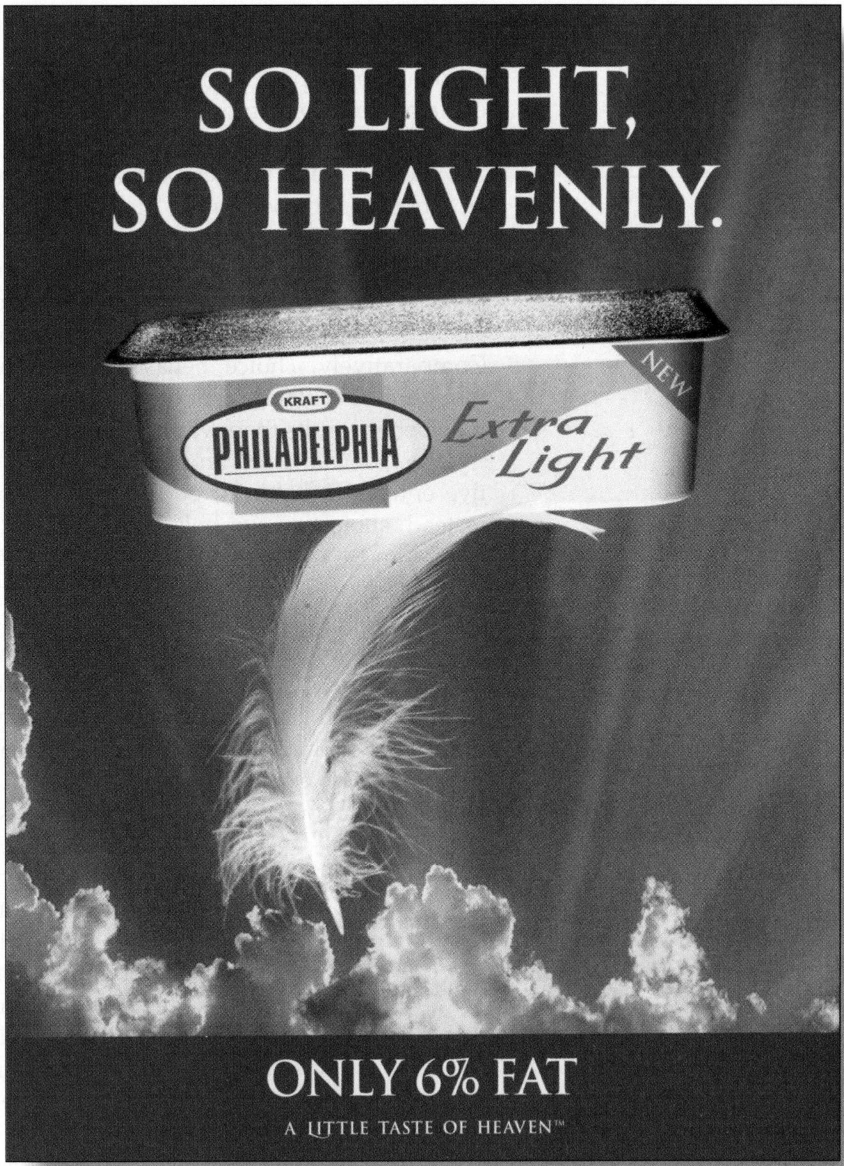

© Image courtesy of The Advertising Archives

Figure 5.12

Illustration of an Effort to Strengthen a Linkage between a Brand and Its Benefits

A CPM Wrap-Up

A somewhat detailed account of consumer information processing has been presented. As noted in the introduction, the CPM perspective provides an appropriate description of consumer behavior when that behavior is deliberate, thoughtful, or, in short, highly cognitive. Much consumer behavior is of this nature. Then again, behavior also is motivated by emotional, hedonic, and experiential considerations. Therefore, we need to consider the HEM perspective and the implications this model holds for marketing communicators and brand positioning.

The Hedonic, Experiential Model (HEM)

It again is important to emphasize that the *rational* consumer processing model (CPM) and the *hedonic, experiential* model (HEM) are *not* mutually exclusive. Indeed, there is impressive evidence that individuals comprehend reality by these rational and experiential processes operating interactively with one another, with their relative influence contingent on the nature of the situation and the amount of emotional involvement—the greater the emotional involvement, the greater the influence of experiential processes.[30] Hence, the HEM model probably better explains how consumers process information when they are carefree and happy and confronted with positive outcomes.[31]

Whereas the CPM perspective views consumers as pursuing such objectives as "obtaining the best buy," "getting the most for their money," and "maximizing utility," the HEM viewpoint recognizes that people often consume products for the sheer fun of it or in the pursuit of amusement, fantasies, or sensory stimulation.[32] Product consumption from the hedonic perspective results from the *anticipation* of having fun, fulfilling fantasies, or having pleasurable feelings. Comparatively, choice behavior from the CPM perspective is based on the thoughtful evaluation that the chosen alternative will be more functional and provide better results than will the alternatives.

Thus, viewed from an HEM perspective, products are more than mere objective entities (a bottle of perfume, a stereo system, a can of soup, etc.) and are, instead, subjective symbols that precipitate *feelings* (e.g., love, pride) and promise *fun* and the possible realization of *fantasies,* the three Fs noted in Figure 5.9. Products most compatible with the hedonic perspective include the performing arts (e.g., opera and modern dance), the so-called plastic arts (e.g., photography and crafts), popular forms of entertainment (e.g., movies and rock concerts), fashion apparel, sporting events, leisure activities, and recreational pursuits.[33] It is important to realize, however, that any product—not just these examples—may have hedonic and experiential elements underlying its choice and consumption. For example, a lot of pleasant feelings and fantasizing are attached to thinking about purchasing a product such as skis, an automobile, a bicycle, or furniture. Even Procter & Gamble, which historically has been noted for its matter-of-fact advertising style, altered its emphasis on performance claims for Tide detergent and focused more on the emotions associated with clean, fresh laundry.

The differences between the HEM and CPM perspectives hold meaningful implications for marcom practice. Whereas verbal stimuli and rational arguments designed to position a brand and to affect consumers' product knowledge and beliefs are most appropriate in CPM-oriented marcom efforts, the HEM approach emphasizes nonverbal content or emotionally provocative words and is intended to generate images, fantasies, and positive emotions and feelings. For example, the Subaru Outback, an four-wheel drive vehicle, can attribute much of its success in America to an advertising campaign that used Paul Hogan (a.k.a. Crocodile Dundee) as the spokesperson for the brand by capitalizing on his image as a fearless, charming, and down-to-earth hero from the Australian Outback. This famous advertising campaign achieved success for the Subaru Outback by creating an emotional connection between consumers and the brand.[34]

The advertisement for the Nissan Altima Coupe (Figure 5.13) exemplifies the HEM approach to advertising. This advertisement provides little information about product attributes and functional benefits other than to say "True performance." Rather, the ad in its striking simplicity appeals directly to the emotions of

Figure 5.13

Illustration of an HEM-Oriented Advertisement

fun and exhilaration by shaping mini-versions of the Nissan Altima Coupe into the form of a running shoe. The consumer in seeing this ad need not expend any thought; emotion and fantasy are front and center—this automobile will achieve "true performance," which is to be interpreted in whatever terms an individual consumer wishes to interpret that expression. Comparatively, had the brand management team for the Nissan Altima Coupe decided that a CPM approach would have been more beneficial for the brand, then the advertising campaign would have featured specific product attributes and benefits in an attempt to appeal to the target audience's more rationale needs and wants.

The prior discussion and examples have emphasized advertising, but it should be apparent that the differences between the CPM and HEM perspectives apply as well to other forms of marketing communications. A salesperson, for example, may emphasize product features and tangible benefits in attempting to make a sale (CPM approach), or he or she may attempt to convey the fun, fantasies, and pleasures that prospective customers can enjoy with product ownership. Successful salespeople employ both approaches and orient the dominant approach to the consumer's specific personality and needs. That is, successful salespeople know how to adapt their presentations to different customers—it is hoped, of course, that they are doing it honestly and maintaining standards of morality.

Finally, no single positioning strategy, whether aimed at CPM or HEM processing, is effective in all instances. What works best depends on the specific nature of the product category, the competitive situation, and the character and needs of the target audience. Returning to the fundamentals of positioning, brands can be positioned to appeal to *functional* needs, which is congenial with the CPM perspective, or to *symbolic* or *experiential* needs, which is more harmonious with the HEM approach.

Summary

This chapter introduced the concept and practice of brand positioning and described it as representing the key feature, benefit, or image that a brand stands for in the target audience's collective mind. A positioning statement is the central idea that encapsulates a brand's meaning and distinctiveness vis-à-vis competitive brands. Because meaning is fundamental to positioning, the chapter introduced the notion of semiotics and described meaning production as a process in which consumers are actively involved in constructing meaning from marcom messages, meaning that may or may not be equivalent to what the communicator intended to convey. It was further described that the fundamental concept in semiotics is the sign, which is something physical and perceivable that signifies something (the referent) to somebody (the interpreter) in some context. It further was explained that marcom practitioners, when in the process of positioning their brands, draw meaning from the culturally constituted world (i.e., the everyday world filled with artifacts) and transfer that meaning to their brands.

The chapter clarified that a good positioning statement must satisfy two requirements: (1) reflect a brand's competitive advantage (vis-à-vis competitive offerings in the same product category) and (2) motivate consumers to action. In the context of these two considerations, four possible outcomes from an attempted brand positioning were identified: the positioning is a potential "loser," a "winner," a "swimming-up-the-river" proposition, or a "promotes-competitors" prospect.

Detailed discussion was devoted to the various ways brands can be positioned. The options included benefit positioning—where a brand is positioned in terms of functional, symbolic, or experiential needs—and attribute positioning. This latter form includes positioning based on product-related features or in terms of usage or user imagery.

The chapter also described the fundamentals of consumer-choice behavior. Two relatively distinct perspectives on choice behavior were presented: the consumer processing model (CPM) and the hedonic, experiential model (HEM). The CPM approach views the consumer as an analytical, systematic, and logical decision maker. According to this perspective, consumers are motivated to achieve desired goals. The CPM process involves attending to, encoding, retaining, retrieving, and integrating information so that a person can achieve a suitable choice among consumption alternatives. Brands positioned to be in tune with the CPM process emphasize logical arguments and functional features over emotion and symbolism. Comparatively, the HEM perspective views consumer-choice behavior as resulting from the pursuit of fun, fantasy, and feelings. Thus, some consumer behavior is based predominantly on emotional considerations rather than on objective, functional, and economic factors. The distinction between the CPM and HEM views of consumer choice is important for marketing communicators. The techniques and creative strategies for affecting consumer-choice behavior clearly are a function of the prevailing consumer orientation.

Discussion Questions

1. Some magazine advertisements show a picture of a product and mention the brand name, but have virtually no verbal content except, perhaps, a single statement about the brand. Locate an example of this type and explain what meaning you think the advertiser is attempting to convey. Ask two friends to offer their interpretations of the same ad, and then compare their responses to determine the differences in meaning that these ads have for you and your friends. Draw a general conclusion from this exercise.
2. Some experts claim that countries, states, and municipalities can be positioned just like other "products" for purposes of attracting tourism dollars. If you are a U.S. resident, explain how you would position your home state to enhance its ability to attract more tourists. If you are a foreign national, explain how you would promote your country, or a region of your country, to attract more tourists.
3. How is your favorite brand of athletic footwear (Adidas, Nike, Reebok, etc.) positioned?
4. Figure 5.11 presents a consumer's knowledge structure for the Volkswagen Beetle. Construct your knowledge structure for the one automobile you most covet owning.
5. A reality of marketing communications is that the same sign often means different things to different people. Provide an example from your own personal experience in which a sign has had different meanings for diverse people. What are the general implications for marketing communications?
6. Explain each of the following related concepts: perceptual encoding, feature analysis, and active synthesis. Using a consumer packaged good of your choice, explain how package designers for this brand have used concepts of feature analysis in designing the package.
7. How does your college or university position itself? If you were responsible for coming up with a new positioning, or repositioning, for your college or university, what would that be? Justify your choice.
8. All marketing communications environments are cluttered. Explain what this means and provide several examples. Do not restrict your examples to advertisements.
9. As a brand manager, assume you have decided to promote your brand on the basis of an attribute that is very important to consumers but for which your brand has no advantage over competitive offerings. In the context of Figure 5.3, explain the likely outcome of this positioning effort.
10. Explain why attention is highly selective and what implication selectivity holds for brand managers and their advertising agencies.
11. In Chapter 2 you read about "leveraging" (refer to Figure 2.3) as one of the ways by which brand associations are created. Relate that discussion to the concept of imbuing a brand with meaning by pulling existing meaning from the "culturally constituted world."
12. When discussing exposure as the initial stage of information processing, it was claimed that gaining exposure is a necessary but insufficient condition for success. Explain.
13. Meaning creation, according to the semiotics perspective, is a constructive process. Explain what this means and illustrate your understanding with a personal example.

End Notes

1. For in-depth treatments of semiotics in marketing communications and consumer behavior, see David Glen Mick, "Consumer Research and Semiotics: Exploring the Morphology of Signs, Symbols, and Significance," *Journal of Consumer Research* 13 (September 1986), 196–213; Eric Haley, "The Semiotic Perspective: A Tool for Qualitative Inquiry," in *Proceedings of the 1993 Conference of the American Academy of Advertising,* ed. Esther Thorson (Columbia, Mo.: The American Academy of Advertising, 1993), 189–196; and Birgit Wassmuth et al., "Semiotics: Friend or Foe to Advertising?" in *Proceedings of the 1993 Conference of the American Academy of Advertising,* ed. Esther Thorson (Columbia, Mo.: The American Academy of Advertising, 1993), 271–276. For interesting applications of a semiotic analysis, see Morris B. Holbrook and Mark W. Grayson, "The Semiology of Cinematic Consumption: Symbolic Consumer Behavior in *Out of Africa,*" *Journal of Consumer Research* 13 (December 1986), 374–381; Edward F. McQuarrie and David Glen Mick, "On Resonance: A Critical Pluralistic Inquiry into Advertising Rhetoric," *Journal of Consumer Research* 19 (September 1992), 180–197; Linda M. Scott, "Understanding Jingles and Needledrop: A Rhetorical Approach to Music in Advertising," *Journal of Consumer Research* 17 (September 1990), 223–236; and Teresa J. Domzal and Jerome B. Kernan, "Mirror, Mirror: Some Postmodern Reflections on Global Advertising," *Journal of Advertising* 22 (December 1993), 1–20. For an insightful treatment on "deconstructing" meaning from advertisements and other marketing communications, see Barbara B. Stern, "Textual Analysis in Advertising Research: Construction and Deconstruction of Meanings," *Journal of Advertising* 25 (fall 1996), 61–73.
2. This description is based on John Fiske, *Introduction to Communication Studies* (New York: Routledge, 1990), and Mick, "Consumer Research and Semiotics," 198.
3. The subsequent discussion is influenced by the insights of David K. Berlo, *The Process of Communication* (San Francisco: Holt, Rinehart & Winston, 1960), 168–216.
4. This interpretation is adapted from Roberto Friedmann and Mary R. Zimmer, "The Role of Psychological Meaning in Advertising," *Journal of Advertising* 17, no. 1 (1988), 31; and Robert E. Klein III and Jerome B. Kernan, "Contextual Influences on the Meanings Ascribed to Ordinary Consumption Objects," *Journal of Consumer Research* 18 (December 1991), 311–324.
5. Grant McCracken, "Culture and Consumption: A Theoretical Account of the Structure and Movement of the Cultural Meaning of Consumer Goods," *Journal of Consumer Research* 13 (June 1986), 74.
6. For further discussion, see Grant McCracken, "Advertising: Meaning or Information," in *Advances in Consumer Research,* vol. 14, ed. Melanie Wallendorf and Paul F. Anderson (Provo, Utah: Association for Consumer Research, 1987), 121–124.
7. Edward F. McQuarrie and David Glen Mick, "Visual Rhetoric in Advertising: Text-Interpretive, Experimental, and Reader-Response Analyses," *Journal of Consumer Research* 26 (June 1999), 37–54; Linda M. Scott, "The Bridge from Text to Mind: Adapting Reader-Response Theory to Consumer Research," *Journal of Consumer Research* 21 (December 1994), 461–480.
8. Kevin J. Clancy and Peter C. Krieg, *Counter-Intuitive Marketing: Achieve Great Results Using Uncommon Sense* (New York: Free Press, 2000), 110.
9. Ibid., 111.
10. C. Whan Park, Bernard J. Jaworski, and Deborah J. MacInnis, "Strategic Brand Concept-Image Management," *Journal of Marketing* 50 (October 1986), 136. The following discussion of functional, symbolic, and experiential needs/benefits adheres to Park et al.'s conceptualizations.
11. For further discussion of this point, see ibid.
12. This description is based on Bob Lamons, "Marcom Proves Itself a Worthy Investment," *Marketing News,* June 9, 2003, 13.
13. Adapted from Emily Nelson, "Procter & Gamble Tries to Hide Wrinkles in Aging Beauty Fluid," *The Wall Street Journal Online,* May 16, 2000, http://online.wsj.com.
14. What is being called the *consumer processing model* (CPM) is more conventionally called the *consumer information processing* (CIP) model. CPM is chosen over CIP for two reasons: (1) It is nominally parallel to the HEM label and thus simplifies memory, and (2) the term *information* is too limiting inasmuch as it implies that only verbal claims (information) are important to consumers and that other forms of communications (e.g., nonverbal statements) are irrelevant. This latter point was emphasized by Esther Thorson, "Consumer Processing of Advertising," *Current Issues & Research in Advertising* 12, ed. J. H. Leigh and C. R. Martin, Jr. (Ann Arbor: University of Michigan, 1990), 198–199.
15. Elizabeth C. Hirschman and Morris B. Holbrook, "Hedonic Consumption: Emerging Concepts, Methods, and Propositions," *Journal of Marketing* 46 (summer 1982), 92–101; Morris B. Holbrook and Elizabeth C. Hirschman, "The Experiential Aspects of Consumption: Consumer Fantasies, Feelings, and Fun," *Journal of Consumer Research* 9 (September 1982), 132–140.
16. James B. Bettman, *An Information Processing Theory of Consumer Choice* (Reading, Mass.: Addison-Wesley, 1979), 1.
17. William J. McGuire, "Some Internal Psychological Factors Influencing Consumer Choice," *Journal of Consumer Research* 4 (March 1976), 302–319.
18. Scott A. Hawkins and Stephen J. Hoch, "Low-Involvement Learning: Memory without Evaluation," *Journal of Consumer Research* 19 (September 1992), 212–225.
19. For an excellent treatment of this distinction as well as a broader perspective on factors determining consumer

attention, comprehension, and learning of advertising messages, see Klaus G. Grunert, "Automatic and Strategic Processes in Advertising Effects," *Journal of Marketing* 60 (October 1996), 88–102.

20. Paul Surgi Speck and Michael T. Elliott, "The Antecedents and Consequences of Perceived Advertising Clutter," *Journal of Current Issues and Research in Advertising* 19 (fall 1997), 39–54. In addition to being disliked by consumers, advertising clutter has also been shown to have undesirable effects for the advertising community, at least in the case of magazine circulation. See Louisa Ha and Barry R. Litman, "Does Advertising Clutter Have Diminishing and Negative Returns?" *Journal of Advertising* 26 (spring 1997), 31–42.
21. A thorough discussion of comprehension processes is provided by David Glen Mick, "Levels of Subjective Comprehension in Advertising Processing and Their Relations to Ad Perceptions, Attitudes, and Memory," *Journal of Consumer Research* 18 (March 1992), 411–424.
22. Albert H. Hastorf and Hadley Cantril, "They Saw a Game: A Case Study," *Journal of Abnormal & Social Psychology* 49 (1954), 129–134.
23. Alice M. Isen, Margaret Clark, Thomas E. Shalker, and Lynn Karp, "Affect, Accessibility of Material in Memory, and Behavior: A Cognitive Loop," *Journal of Personality and Social Psychology* 36 (January 1978), 1–12; Meryl Paula Gardner, "Mood States and Consumer Behavior: A Critical Review," *Journal of Consumer Research* 12 (December 1985), 281–300.
24. Several valuable sources for technical treatments of memory operations are available in the advertising and marketing literatures. See Bettman, "Memory Functions," *An Information Processing Theory of Consumer Choice,* chap. 6; James B. Bettman, "Memory Factors in Consumer Choice: A Review," *Journal of Marketing* 43 (spring 1979), 37–53; Andrew A. Mitchell, "Cognitive Processes Initiated by Advertising," in *Information Processing Research in Advertising,* ed. R. J. Harris (Hillsdale, N.J.: Lawrence Erlbaum Associates, 1983), 13–42; Jerry C. Olson, "Theories of Information Encoding and Storage: Implications for Consumer Research," in *The Effect of Information on Consumer and Market Behavior,* ed. A. A. Mitchell (Chicago: American Marketing Association, 1978), 49–60; Thomas K. Srull, "The Effects of Subjective Affective States on Memory and Judgment," in *Advances in Consumer Research,* vol. 11, ed. T. C. Kinnear (Provo, Utah: Association for Consumer Research, 1984); and Kevin Lane Keller, "Advertising Retrieval Cues on Brand Evaluations," *Journal of Consumer Research* 14 (December 1989), 316–333.
25. Richard M. Shiffrin and R. C. Atkinson, "Storage and Retrieval Processes in Long-Term Memory," *Psychological Review* 76 (March 23, 1969), 179–193.
26. Mitchell, "Cognitive Processes Initiated by Advertising."
27. Allan Paivio, "Mental Imagery in Associative Learning and Memory," *Psychological Review* 76 (May 1969), 241–263; John R. Rossiter and Larry Percy, "Visual Imaging Ability as a Mediator of Advertising Response," in *Advances in Consumer Research,* vol. 5, ed. H. Keith Hunt (Ann Arbor: Association for Consumer Research, 1978), 621–629.
28. Michael J. Houston, Terry L. Childers, and Susan E. Heckler, "Picture-Word Consistency and the Elaborative Processing of Advertisements," *Journal of Marketing Research* 24 (November 1987), 359–369.
29. H. Rao Unnava and Robert E. Burnkrant, "An Imagery-Processing View of the Role of Pictures in Print Advertisements," *Journal of Marketing Research* 28 (May 1991), 226–231.
30. Veronika Denes-Raj and Seymour Epstein, "Conflict between Intuitive and Rational Processing: When People Behave against Their Better Judgment," *Journal of Personality and Social Psychology* 66, no. 5 (1994), 819–829.
31. Ibid.
32. Hirschman and Holbrook, "Hedonic Consumption."
33. Ibid., 91.
34. For a fascinating discussion of the Subaru Outback advertising campaign, see Sal Randazzo, "Subaru: The Emotional Myths behind the Brand's Growth," *Journal of Advertising Research* 46 (March 2006), 11–17.

6

Objective Setting and Budgeting

You likely have seen TV commercials advertising Geico, one of the major companies that sell automobile insurance. You may recall Geico's commercials with a talking, Australian-accented gecko. And who could forget those ads that featured sophisticated cavemen who were insulted—in a parody on political correctness—by "insensitive" offenders who implied that some action was "so easy, a caveman could do it." Both the gecko and cavemen commercials can be judged impressively in terms of their creativity, but that is not the issue that will be emphasized in this section. Highlighted instead is the vast amount of money budgeted by Geico in these TV commercials and the success achieved.

The top four automobile insurance companies—State Farm, Allstate, Progressive, and Geico—compete in a highly aggressive environment where price wars to lure new customers are common. Clever and frequent advertising is an alternate route by which competitors in this industry fight over new customers. And Geico, despite having the fourth largest market share, has been the leading advertiser among these top-four automobile insurance providers. Indeed, in 2006 Geico invested slightly over $500 million in advertising—which was nearly double the level of advertising by any of its competitors—and cumulatively between 2001 and 2006 it invested over $2 billion in advertising!

This massive investment has paid dividends for Geico. It now enjoys a very high level of advertising awareness—that is, over 90 percent of surveyed consumers indicate that that they have seen or heard a Geico ad within the past year. The nearest competitor in terms of ad awareness is State Farm at 80 percent. But beyond creating awareness, Geico is the only brand in the auto insurance category to obtain double-digit growth in brand share, a climb of approximately 13 percent in its share of total auto insurance business. Also, Geico is the top brand in terms of new-customer acquisition. Needless to say, these impressive gains by Geico have prompted State Farm and other competitors to elevate their own levels of advertising spending. The Geico case

OUTLASTED DINOSAURS AND THE ICE AGE, BUT CAN THEY SURVIVE YOUR PREJUDICE?
Sadly, negative stereotypes and characterizations of Cavemen continue to persist. You've seen them, portrayals of Cavemen as inarticulate and dim-witted. Cartoons showing Cavemen wearing animal skins and carrying thick wooden clubs. That was over 300,000 years ago! We are the fathers of modern-day tools and weaponry and still you depict us carrying sticks!
Recently, GEICO Auto Insurance has been running a series of print and TV ads that completely perpetuate a negative stereotype — that Cavemen are unsophisticated simpletons, that we have inferior intelligence. The slogan for their website, geico.com, is "So easy a caveman can do it." This could not be more insensitive or offensive.
We hope you'll join us in our fight for respect. Cavemen are smart, thoughtful, intelligent, cognitive, ambitious, social beings. We may not look like you, but we are just like you.
UPWITHCAVEMEN
Cavemen are people too.℠

Courtesy of GEICO

illustrates unmistakably that creative advertising backed with sufficient advertising budget can accomplish various marcom objectives such as increasing awareness, attracting new customers, and boosting market share.

Sources: Adapted from Mya Frazier, "Geico's Big Spending Pays Off, Study Says," *Advertising Age,* June 26, 2007, http://adage.com (accessed June 27, 2007).

Chapter Objectives

After reading this chapter you should be able to:

1 Understand the process of marcom objective setting and the requirements for good objectives.

2 Appreciate the hierarchy-of-effects model and its relevance for setting marcom objectives.

3 Comprehend the role of sales as a marcom objective and the logic of vaguely right versus precisely wrong thinking.

4 Know the relation between a brand's share of market (SOM) and its share of voice (SOV) and the implications for setting an advertising budget.

5 Understand the various rules of thumb, or heuristics, that guide practical budgeting.

>>Marcom Insight:

Impressive Results Produced by Spending Big on Cavemen Characters and a Talking Gecko

Introduction

Returning again to the model of the marcom process provided in Chapter 1, you will recall that the framework described various forms of "fundamental" and "implementation" decisions. We continue with this theme as it relates specifically to advertising objective setting and budgeting. These activities, along with targeting (the subject of Chapter 4) and positioning (Chapter 5), are the bedrock of all subsequent marcom decisions. Marcom strategy built on a weak foundation is virtually guaranteed to fail. Intelligent objectives and an adequate budget are critical for success. Let us not forget the mantra introduced in Chapter 1:

> *All marketing communications should be (1) directed to a particular* **target market,** *(2) clearly* **positioned,** *(3) created to achieve a* **specific objective,** *and (4) undertaken to accomplish the objective* **within budget constraint.**

This chapter culminates the discussion of fundamental marcom decisions by examining objective setting and budgeting. Both topics have been treated in the past mostly from the perspective of advertising rather than marcom in general. However, because the issues are similar regardless of the form of marketing communications, in this chapter we will pull from the advertising literature and apply it to all forms of marketing communications.

This chapter argues that objective setting and budgeting decisions must be formal and systematic rather than haphazard. Both topics represent key decisions that set the stage for the subsequent set of "implementation" decisions, which include the choice of messages, media, mixture of marcom elements, and the achievement of a continuous message presence, or momentum. (Please note that these four "implementation" decisions, along with the "fundamental" decisions, were introduced in the model of the marcom process in Chapter 1. It would be useful to review this model in Figure 1.1 [p. 21] to reacquaint yourself with the overall scope of marcom strategy.)

Setting Marcom Objectives

Marcom objectives are goals that the various marcom elements aspire to achieve individually or collectively during a scope of time such as a business quarter or fiscal year. Objectives provide the foundation for all remaining decisions. Later chapters detail the objectives that each component of the marcom mix is designed to accomplish; for present purposes it will suffice merely to list an illustrative set of objectives that communicators hope to accomplish using different marcom tools. Alongside each objective, in brackets, are the marcom tools most suitable for accomplishing that objective:

- Facilitate the successful introduction of new brands (brand naming and packaging, advertising, sales promotions, word-of-mouth buzz generation, and point-of-purchase [P-O-P] displays).
- Build sales of existing brands by increasing the frequency of use, the variety of uses, or the quantity purchased (advertising and sales promotions).
- Inform the trade (wholesalers, agents or brokers, and retailers) and consumers about brand improvements (personal selling and trade-oriented advertising).
- Create brand awareness (advertising, packaging, and P-O-P messages).
- Enhance a brand's image (brand naming and packaging, advertising, event sponsorship, cause-oriented marketing, and marketing-oriented public relations [PR]).
- Generate sales leads (advertising).

- Persuade the trade to handle the manufacturer's brands (trade-oriented advertising and personal selling).
- Stimulate point-of-purchase sales (brand naming and packaging, P-O-P messages, and external store signage).
- Increase customer loyalty (advertising and sales promotions).
- Improve corporate relations with special interest groups (marketing-oriented PR).
- Offset bad publicity about a brand or generate good publicity (marketing-oriented PR).
- Counter competitors' communications efforts (advertising and sales promotions).
- Provide customers with reasons for buying immediately instead of delaying a purchase (advertising and sales promotions).

The objectives that marketing communications in its various forms must accomplish are varied, but regardless of the substance of the objective, there are three major reasons why it is essential that objectives be established *prior to* making the all-important implementation decisions regarding message selection, media determination, and how the various marcom elements should be mixed and maintained:[1]

1. *Achieving management consensus:* The process of setting objectives literally forces top marketing executives and marcom personnel to agree on the course that a brand's marcom strategy will take for the following planning period as well as the tasks it is to accomplish for a specific brand. As such, objectives provide a formalized expression of management consensus.
2. *Guiding subsequent marcom decisions:* Objective setting guides the budgeting, message, and media aspects of a brand's marcom strategy. Objectives determine how much money should be spent and suggest guidelines for the kinds of message strategy and media choice needed to accomplish a brand's marketing communications objectives.
3. *Providing standards:* Objectives provide standards against which results can be measured. As will be detailed later, good objectives set precise, quantitative yardsticks of what a marcom program hopes to accomplish. Subsequent results can then be compared with these standards to determine whether the effort accomplished what it was intended to do.

The Hierarchy of Marcom Effects

A full appreciation of marcom objective setting requires that we first look at the process of communications from the customer's perspective. A framework called the hierarchy of effects is appropriate for accomplishing this understanding. The hierarchy framework reveals that the choice of marcom objective depends on the target audience's degree of experience with the brand prior to commencing a marcom campaign.[2]

The **hierarchy-of-effects** metaphor implies that for marketing communications to be successful, the various marcom elements must advance consumers through a series of psychological stages, much in the way a person climbs a ladder—one step, then another, and another, until the top of the ladder is reached. A variety of hierarchy models have been formulated, all of which are predicated on the idea that the marcom elements, if successful, move people from an initial state of unawareness about a brand to eventually purchasing that brand.[3] Intermediate stages in the hierarchy represent progressively closer steps to brand purchase. The hierarchy in Figure 6.1 goes a step further by establishing brand loyalty as the top step on the ladder.[4] Please examine Figure 6.1 carefully before reading on.

figure 6.1

Hierarchy of Marcom Effects

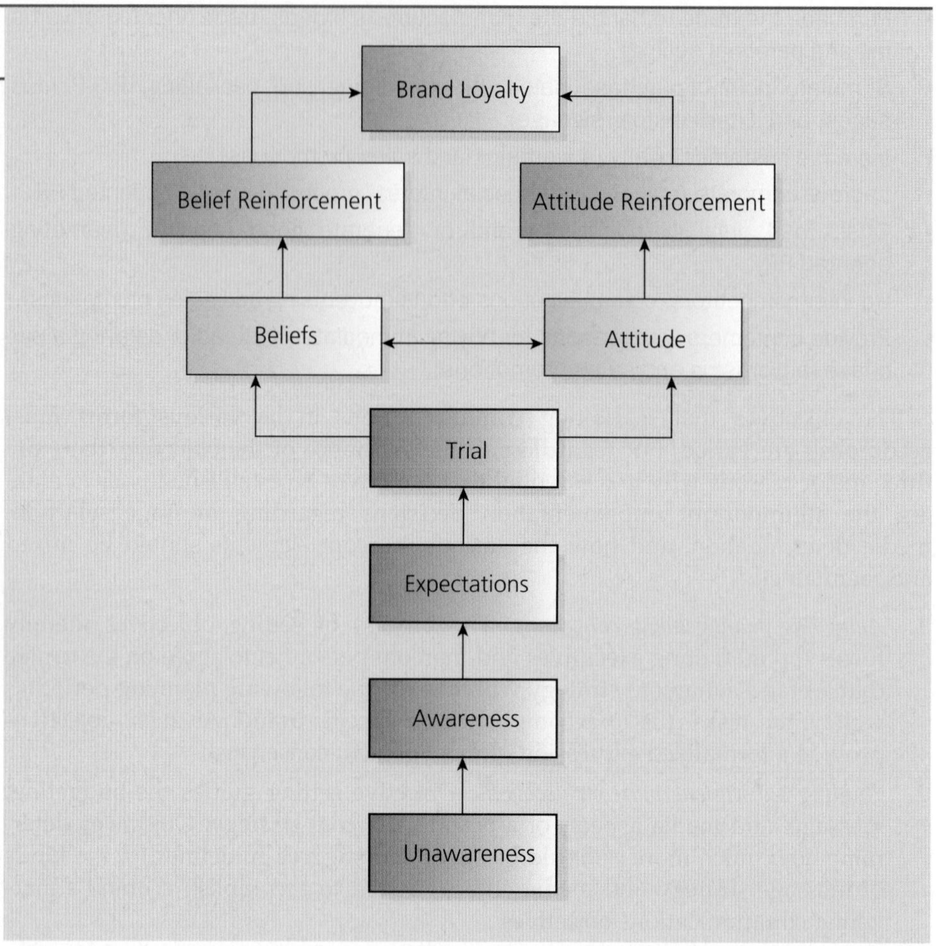

The meaning of each of these stages, or hierarchy steps, is best understood by examining an actual advertisement. Consider the ad in Figure 6.2 for a brand called Pegetables. A quick glance at this ad indicates that this product somehow is related to pets. On closer reading one can see that the brand name, Pegetables, represents a combination of the "p" in pet and the word "vegetables" without the "v"—in other words, vegetables for pets. It is a simple product indeed, but it provides us with an apt illustration of how the various marcom elements can work in concert to move consumers through the hierarchy stages.

Advancing Consumers from Unawareness to Awareness

When first introduced to the market, consumers were initially unaware of Pegetables's existence and of its special features (many no doubt remain unaware). The initial marcom imperative, therefore, is to make consumers aware that there is a product such as Pegetables. In general, creating awareness is essential for new or unestablished brands. Unless consumers are aware of a brand, that brand cannot be a member of their set of viable purchase alternatives. Of all the marcom tools, advertising (via mass media or otherwise) generally is the most effective and efficient method for quickly creating brand awareness. Sometimes advertising agencies place excessive emphasis on building brand awareness by creating zany ads with offbeat humor or using blatant sex appeals. However, please read the *IMC Focus*, which describes a case where creating awareness did not assure that consumers will move further up the hierarchy toward purchasing the brand and potentially becoming loyal repeat purchasers.

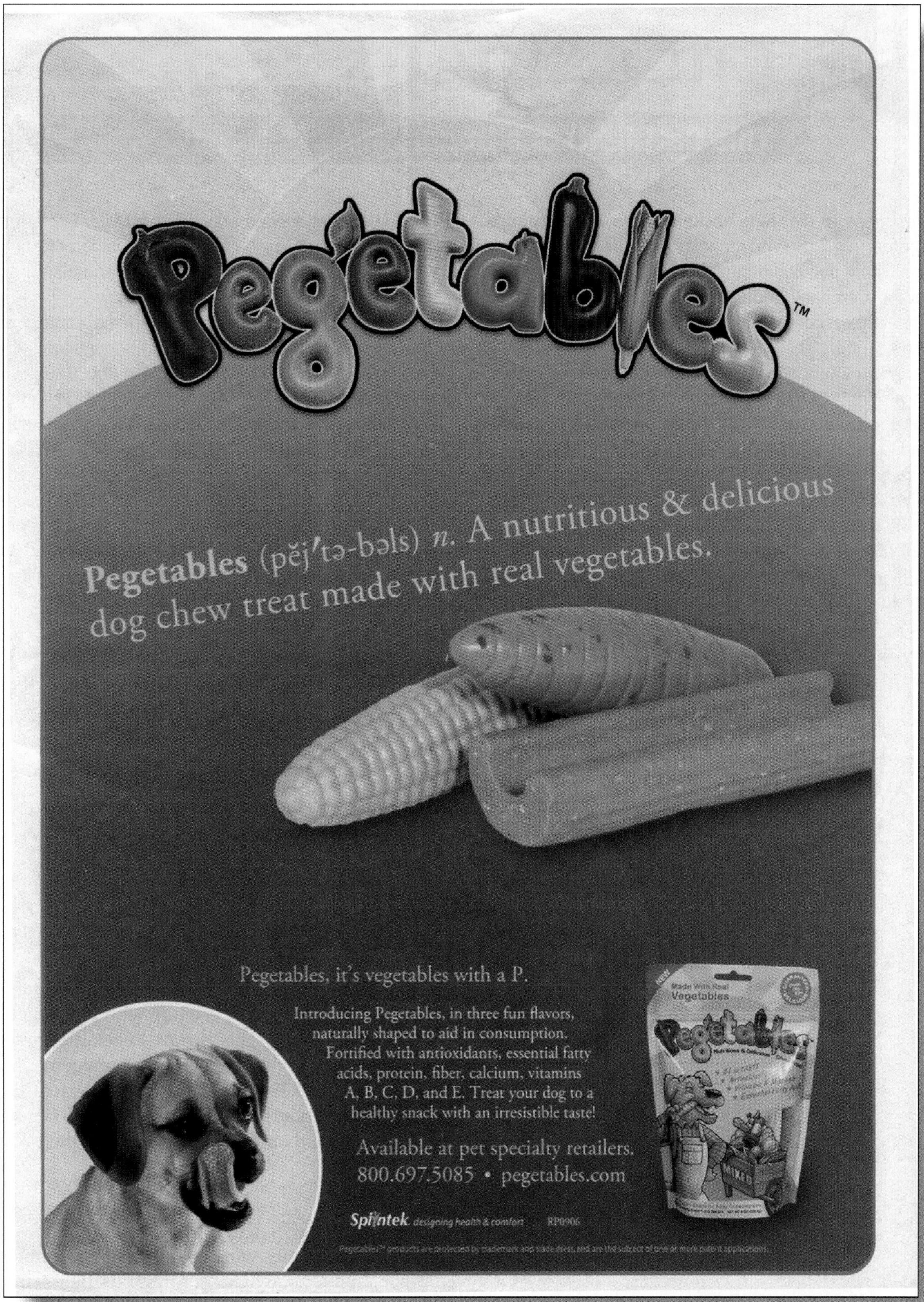

Courtesy of Pegetables

Figure 6.2

Advertisement Illustrating Hierarchy of Marcom Effects

IMC >> i.m.c. focus

This Cat(fight) Is a Dog

In response to diet fads eschewing the intake of carbohydrates (e.g., the Atkins and South Beach diets) that were highly popular during the early 2000s, the Miller Brewing Company undertook an aggressive advertising campaign by comparing Miller Lite against Anheuser-Busch's Bud Light. Using humorous but hard-hitting TV ads, Miller Lite's advertisements attempted to persuade consumers that that brand should be their preferred choice because it contains only one-half the carbohydrate content of Bud Light. This campaign had a substantial impact on Miller Lite's market share, which rose while Bud Light's share declined.

But prior to this particular ad campaign, Miller had attempted to boost sales of Miller Lite by running a campaign with blatant sex appeal. The campaign was dubbed "Catfight" based on the campaign's initial spot in which two scantily clad women fought and shed clothing over whether Miller Lite tastes great or is less filling. A series of additional spots presented sexy women in confrontational scenes arguing over Miller Lite's relative merits. The campaign generated considerable buzz as well as controversy in feminist circles and elsewhere for its treatment of women as sex objects.

However, of primary relevance in the context of the present discussion is the fact that, although brand awareness of Miller Lite increased during the Catfight campaign, actual sales declined by 3 percent. In a meeting with financial analysts who track the performance of Miller's various brands, the president of Miller Lite had this to say about the ad campaign in a retrospective analysis: "Awareness is not the problem, but actual [purchase] consideration is the problem and challenge and opportunity. We want to ensure that the [advertising] spend we put behind the brand is leading toward actual consideration and not just continuing to build awareness."

SOURCE: Hillary Chura, "Miller Loses 'Catfight,' Buzz Doesn't Lift Lite," *Advertising Age*, June 2, 2003, 3, 51.

Creating an Expectation

Mere brand name awareness generally is insufficient to get people to buy a brand, particularly when consumers already possess a solution to a consumption-related problem or remain unaware that a solution is available. Advertising and other marcom elements must instill in consumers an expectation of what product benefit(s) they will obtain from buying and experiencing a brand. It should be noted that an expectation from the consumer's perspective is based on how the brand has been positioned, which was the subject of Chapter 5.

In the case of Pegetables, consumers are basically promised that Pegetables is a delicious-tasting and nutritious snack for dogs that is made with real vegetables (see the corn-, carrot-, and celery-shaped items). This is how Pegetables has been positioned, and this is the expectation that Pegetables's brand management team wishes to implant in the target audience's collective mind. To the extent consumers develop this expectation, they may undertake trial purchases of Pegetables to learn for themselves (based on whether their pets seem to enjoy the product) whether it lives up to its promise.

Encouraging Trial Purchases

Sales promotions and advertisements sometimes work together to encourage trial purchases, often by influencing consumers to switch from brands they currently are purchasing. As the name suggests, a trial purchase is just that: The consumer tries a brand for the first time. Because most advertisements can simply hope to entice, enthuse, and whet one's appetite—or, in general, create expectations—a more compelling mechanism is required for generating trial purchases. And, indeed, this is the role of the sales promotions component of marketing communications. Free samples and coupons are particularly effective devices for getting consumers to try new brands of packaged goods. In the case of expensive durable products, major price discounts and rebate offers are effective in encouraging a form of trial behavior such as test-driving automobiles.

Forming Beliefs and Attitudes

Upon trying a brand for the first time, the consumer will form beliefs about its performance. With respect to Pegetables, the beliefs may be thoughts such as, "My dog really likes these snacks, and, because they are made with real vegetables, they must be good for him." These beliefs, in turn, form the basis for developing an overall attitude toward the brand. Beliefs and attitudes are mutually reinforcing, as illustrated by the double-headed arrow linking these two elements in Figure 6.1. If Pegetables lives up to the pet owner's expectations, the attitude toward that brand most likely will be positive; however, the attitude can be expected to be somewhat ambivalent or even negative if the brand fails to satisfy the expected benefit that motivated the trial purchase.

Reinforcing Beliefs and Attitudes

Once brand-specific beliefs and attitudes are formed as the *outcome from firsthand product usage experience,* subsequent marketing communications serve merely to reinforce the consumers' beliefs and attitudes that resulted from trying the product. In Figure 6.1 this is referred to as belief reinforcement and attitude reinforcement. The reinforcement objective is accomplished when a marketing communicator sticks with a particular promise and promotes this point repeatedly.

Accomplishing Brand Loyalty

As long as the brand continues to satisfy expectations and a superior brand is not introduced, the consumer may become a brand-loyal purchaser. This is the ultimate objective, because, as has been mentioned, it is much cheaper to retain present customers than it is to prospect continuously for new ones.[5]

Brand loyalty is the top rung on the hierarchy of marcom effects (Figure 6.1). Loyalty is not a guaranteed outcome, however. Strong brand loyalty occasionally develops. For example, some consumers always purchase the same brand of cola; others forever smoke the same brand of cigarette; and there are those who use the same brand of deodorant, toothpaste, shampoo, or even automobile. In many other instances, however, the consumer never forms a strong preference for any brand. Rather, the consumer continually shifts his or her allegiance from one brand to the next, constantly trying, trying, and trying but never developing a strong commitment to any particular brand. Consumer behavior can be like dating; some people "play the field" but never commit.

Brand loyalty is a goal to which the marketing communicator aspires. Obtaining the consumer's loyalty necessitates meeting the consumer's needs better than competitive brands and continuing to communicate the brand's merits to reinforce the consumer's brand-related beliefs and attitudes. (See Figure 6.1 as a graphic reminder of this point.) It is interesting to note, however, that the various marcom elements may be in conflict toward the goal of accomplishing brand loyalty. Whereas advertising has the desirable long-run effect of making consumers less price sensitive and more brand loyal, sales promotions can reduce loyalty by effectively "training" consumers to be price sensitive and thus inclined to switch among brands to avail themselves of price discounts.[6]

Section Summary

It should be apparent from this discussion of marcom's hierarchy of effects that the objective for a brand's marcom program at any point in time depends on where in the hierarchy consumers are located. Although individual consumers inevitably will be at different levels of the hierarchy, the issue is one of where most consumers are located. For example, if research reveals that the vast majority of the target audience remains unaware of the brand, then creating awareness is of uppermost importance. If, however, most members of the target audience know of the brand but are unclear what it stands for, then the marcom task becomes one of designing messages that build an expectation capable of motivating consumers to try the brand.

Requirements for Setting Suitable Marcom Objectives

A marcom objective is a specific statement about a planned execution in terms of what a marcom program is intended to accomplish at a point in time. That goal is based on knowledge of where on the hierarchy of effects members of the target audience are located; knowledge of the current, or anticipated, competitive situation in the product category; and the problems that the brand must confront or the opportunities that are available.

The specific content of a marcom objective depends entirely on the brand's unique situation. Hence, it is not feasible to discuss objective content without having current details (such as those provided by marketing research) about the competitive context. We can, however, describe the requirements that all good objectives must satisfy. Let us start by clarifying that not all objectives are well stated. Consider the following examples:

Example A: The objective next business quarter for Brand X is to realize increased sales.

Example B: The objective next business quarter for Brand X is to elevate overall brand awareness from the present level of 60 percent to 80 percent.

These extreme examples differ in two important respects. First, example B is obviously more specific. Second, whereas example A deals with a sales objective, example B involves a presales goal (increase awareness). The sections that follow describe the specific criteria that good objectives must satisfy.[7] We will return to examples A and B in the process of presenting these criteria, which are listed in Figure 6.3.

Objectives Must Include a Precise Statement of Who, What, and When

Objectives must be stated in precise terms. At a minimum, objectives should specify the target audience (who), indicate the specific goal—such as awareness level—to be accomplished (what), and indicate the relevant time frame over which the objective is to be achieved (when). For example, the marcom campaign

figure 6.3

Criteria That Good Marcom Objectives Must Satisfy

- Include a precise statement of who, what, and when
- Be quantitative and measurable
- Specify the amount of change
- Be realistic
- Be internally consistent
- Be clear and in writing

for Pegetables (Figure 6.2) might include an objective such as: (1) "Within four months from the beginning of the advertising campaign, research should show that 25 percent of all dog owners are aware of the Pegetables name"; (2) "Within six months from the beginning of the campaign, research should show that at least 50 percent of the target audience who now are aware of the Pegetables name know that this brand is a vegetable-based snack treat for dogs"; or (3) "Within one year from the beginning of the campaign, at least 5 million households should have tried Pegetables."

Returning to the two hypothetical objectives (A versus B), example B represents the desired degree of specificity and, as such, would give brand managers something meaningful to direct their efforts toward and provide a clear-cut benchmark for assessing whether the marcom campaign has accomplished its objective. Example A, by comparison, is much too general. Suppose sales have actually increased by 2 percent during the course of the campaign. Does this mean the campaign was successful since sales have in fact increased? If not, how much increase is necessary for the campaign to be regarded as a success?

Objectives Must Be Quantitative and Measurable

This requirement demands that ad objectives be stated in quantitative terms so as to be measurable. A nonmeasurable objective for Pegetables would be a vague statement such as, "Marketing communications should enhance consumers' knowledge of Pegetables." This objective lacks measurability because it fails to specify the product benefit of which consumers are to possess knowledge.

Objectives Must Specify the Amount of Change

In addition to being quantitative and measurable, objectives must specify the amount of change they are intended to accomplish. Example A (to increase sales) fails to meet this requirement. Example B (to increase awareness from 60 percent to 80 percent) is satisfactory because it clearly specifies that anything less than a 20 percent awareness increase would be considered unsuitable performance.

Objectives Must Be Realistic

Unrealistic objectives are as useless as having no objective at all. An unrealistic objective is one that cannot be accomplished in the time allotted to the proposed marcom campaign. For example, a brand that has achieved only 15 percent consumer awareness during its first year on the market could not realistically expect a small marcom budget to increase the awareness level to, say, 45 percent next year.

Objectives Must Be Internally Consistent

Objectives set for a particular element of a marcom program must be compatible (internally consistent) with objectives set for other marcom components. It would be incompatible for a manufacturer to proclaim a 25 percent reduction in sales force while simultaneously stating that the advertising and sales promotion objective is to increase retail distribution by 20 percent. Without adequate sales force effort, it is doubtful that the retail trade would give a brand more shelf space.

Objectives Must Be Clear and in Writing

For objectives to accomplish their purposes of fostering communication and permitting evaluation, they must be stated clearly and in writing so that they can be disseminated to marcom personnel who will be held responsible for seeing that the objectives are accomplished.

Should Marcom Objectives Be Stated in Terms of Sales?

We can broadly distinguish two types of marcom objectives: sales versus pre-sales objectives. *Pre-sales objectives* are commonly referred to as *communication objectives,* with the term *communication* derived from efforts to communicate outcomes that will increase the target audience's brand awareness, enhance their attitudes toward the brand, shift their preference from competitors' brands to our brand, and so on. Comparatively, using *sales* as the goal for a particular advertising campaign means that the marcom objective literally is to increase sales by a specified amount. Marcom practitioners and educators have traditionally rejected the use of sales as an appropriate objective. However, a relatively recent perspective asserts that influencing sales should *always* represent the objective of any marcom effort.

The following discussion first presents the traditional view on this matter (favoring a pre-sales, or communications, objective) and then introduces the heretical position (preferring a sales objective). In the manner of Hegelian dialectic—that is, stating a thesis, identifying its opposite (antithesis), and then offering a synthesis of positions—we will present the traditional and heretical views as thesis and antithesis, respectively, and follow these with a synthesis of positions.

The Traditional View (Thesis)

This view asserts that using sales as the objective for a branded product's marcom effort is unsuitable for two major reasons. First, a brand's sales volume during any given period is the consequence of a host of factors in addition to advertising, sales promotions, and other elements of the marcom program. These include the prevailing economic climate, competitive activity, and all the marketing mix variables used by a brand—its price level, product quality, distribution strategy, and so forth. It is virtually impossible, according to the traditional view, to determine precisely the role advertising or other marcom elements have had in influencing sales in a given period, because marketing communications is *just one of many possible determinants* of a brand's sales volume.

A second reason that sales response is claimed to represent an unsuitable marcom objective is that marcom's effect on sales is typically delayed, or *lagged.* For example, advertising during any given period does not necessarily influence sales in the current period but may influence sales during later periods. On the one hand, advertising for a particular automobile model this year may have limited effect on some consumers' purchasing behavior because these consumers are not presently in the market for a new automobile. On the other hand, this year's advertising can influence consumers to select the advertised model next year when they *are* in the market. Thus, advertising may have a decided influence on consumers' brand awareness, product knowledge, expectations, attitudes, and, ultimately, purchase behavior, but this influence may not be evident during the period when the effect of advertising on sales is measured.

Advocates of the traditional view thus argue that it is misguided to use sales as the goal for a particular marcom effort. Their view, fundamentally, is that it is idealistic to set sales as the objective because marcom's exact impact on sales cannot be accurately assessed.

The Heretical View (Antithesis)

Conversely, some marcom authorities contend that marketing communicators should always state objectives in terms of sales or market share gains and that failure to do so is a cop-out. The logic of this nontraditional, or heretical, view is that marcom's purpose is not just to create brand awareness, convey copy points, influence expectations, or enhance attitudes but also to generate sales. Thus, according to this position it is always possible to measure, if only vaguely and

Objective-Setting Issue	Alternative Possibilities
• Choice of Objective	Chosen objective is *Right* or *Wrong*
• Accuracy of Measurement	Accuracy is *Precise* or *Vague* (i.e., Imprecise)

figure 6.4

The Logic of Vaguely Right versus Precisely Wrong Thinking

imprecisely, marcom's effect on sales. Pre-sales, or communication, objectives such as increases in brand awareness are claimed to be "precisely wrong," in contrast to sales measures that are asserted to be "vaguely right."[8]

To better understand the logic of this *vaguely right* versus *precisely wrong* thinking (or VR versus PW for short), we need to examine closely the constituent oppositional elements: right versus wrong and precise versus vague (see Figure 6.4). First, the issue of *right* versus *wrong* concerns the choice of marcom objective. The heretical view contends that a sales objective is the right objective and that any other objective is wrong. Second, the issue of *precise* versus *vague* refers to the ability to measure accurately whether the marcom program has accomplished its objective.

With a communication objective such as brand awareness, it can be determined with relative certainty that any registered change in brand awareness that has occurred since the onset of a marcom campaign is due primarily to the marcom effort. Hence, the amount of influence that, say, advertising has had on brand awareness can be measured *relatively precisely.* However, as described previously, because many factors influence a brand's sales level, the effect that advertising and the other marcom tools have had on sales can be measured only somewhat crudely, imprecisely, or, in other words, *vaguely.*

Thus, the VR versus PW perspective makes the very important point that marketing communicators, and perhaps especially their agencies, might be deceiving themselves into thinking that, for example, an advertising campaign is effective when it leads to increases in consumer awareness or some other pre-sales objective. Adherents to the VR versus PW perspective argue that marcom is not successful unless sales and market share are increasing. Thus, if marcom's sole accomplishment is to create higher awareness levels or bolster brand images, but not to increase sales or market share, then such effort is ineffective.

An Accountability Perspective (Synthesis)

Although there is no simple resolution as to whether the traditional or heretical view is more correct, one thing is certain: Companies and their chief executives and financial officers are increasingly demanding greater *accountability* from marcom programs. Increasing pressure has been placed on agencies to develop campaigns that produce bottom-line results—increases in sales, in market share, and higher returns on investment (ROI). Although it is difficult to measure the precise effect marketing communications have on sales, in a climate of increased demands for accountability, it is critical that advertisers and other marketing communicators measure, as best they can, whether the marketing communications program during a particular financial period has increased a brand's sales, market share, and ROI.

Importantly, this is *not* to say that efforts should not also be made to assess whether marcom affects pre-sales goals such as improving brand awareness, driving home copy points, and augmenting attitudes and intentions. The point, instead, is that the measurement of effects should *not stop* with these measures. Awareness, for example, is a suitable substitute for sales only if there is a direct transformation of enhanced awareness levels into increased sales. This, unfortunately, is rarely the case. A marcom campaign may increase brand awareness by a substantial amount but have limited impact on sales (recall the discussion of the Miller Lite "Catfight" ad campaign in the *IMC Focus* insert). As such, brand managers should not permit agencies to mislead them into thinking that a campaign has been successful just because brand awareness has improved.

Returning to the hierarchy of marcom effects, increased awareness will lead to sales gains only if other rungs on the ladder have been traversed. In sum, the assessment of effectiveness should include, but not be restricted to, pre-sales goals. Setting sales as the objective of a marcom campaign ensures that this ultimate goal will not be neglected.

Marcom Budgeting

Establishing a budget is, in many respects, the most important marcom decision. Budgeting is a critical decision inasmuch as marcom endeavors such as advertising are typically very expensive. (The substantial investment in marketing communications is illustrated in the *Global Focus* insert, which identifies advertising spending by the top-25 global marketers.) Moreover, the implications of spending too little or too much are considerable. If too little is invested in marketing communications, sales volume will not achieve its potential and profits will be lost. If too much is spent, unnecessary expenses will reduce profits.

Of course, the dilemma brand managers face is determining what spending level is "too little" or how much is "too much." As with most marketing and business decisions, the "devil is in the doing"! Budgeting is not only one of the most important marcom decisions but also it is one of the most complicated, as will be demonstrated in the following discussion of how—in theory—advertising budgets should be set if the objective is to maximize profits. In order to simplify the following discussion, we will restrict the focus just to advertising. Note, however, that the comments about budgeting for advertising apply, in principle, to all marcom elements.

Budgeting in Theory

Budgeting for advertising or other marcom elements is, in theory, a simple process, provided one accepts the premise that the best (optimal) level of any investment is the level that *maximizes profits.* This assumption leads to a simple rule for establishing advertising budgets: Continue to invest in advertising as long as the marginal revenue from that investment exceeds the marginal cost.

© Plush Studios/ Photodisc/ Getty Images

Some elaboration is needed on this clear-cut rule. According to basic economics, marginal revenue (MR) and marginal cost (MC) are the changes in the total revenue and total cost, respectively, that result from a change in a business factor (such as advertising) that affects the levels of total revenue and cost. The profit-maximization rule is a matter of straightforward economic logic: Profits are maximized at the point where MR = MC. At any investment level below this point (where MR > MC), profits are not maximized because at a higher level of advertising investment more profit remains to be earned. Similarly, at any level above this point (where MC > MR), there is a marginal loss. In practical terms, this means that advertisers should continue to increase their advertising investments as long as every dollar of investment yields more than a dollar in revenue.

It is evident from this simple exercise that setting the advertising budget is a matter of answering a

global focus

The Top-25 Global Marketers' Advertising Spending

Advertising expenditures around the globe are huge. As shown in the following list, the top-25 global marketers alone spent over $57 billion on advertising in a recent year. These are all well-known companies whose products and services are available around the world. The huge American company, Procter & Gamble, leads the way with global advertising expenditures exceeding $8.5 billion, but even the smallest advertiser among these top 25 (News Corp.) spent over $1 billion advertising its services.

Rank	Advertiser	Headquarters	Ad Spend (in $ millions)
1	Procter & Gamble Co.	Cincinnati, OH	$8,522
2	Unilever	London/Rotterdam	4,537
3	General Motors Corp.	Detroit, MI	3,353
4	L'Oreal	Clichy, France	3,119
5	Toyota Motor Corp.	Toyota City, Japan	3,098
6	Ford Motor Co.	Dearborn, MI	2,869
7	Time Warner	New York, NY	2,136
8	Nestle	Vevey, Switzerland	2,114
9	Johnson & Johnson	New Brunswick, NJ	2,025
10	DaimlerChrysler	Auburn Hills, MI/Stuttgart, Germany	2,003
11	Honda Motor Co.	Tokyo	1,910
12	Coca-Cola Co.	Atlanta	1,893
13	Walt Disney Co.	Burbank, CA	1,755
14	GlaxoSmithKline	Brentford, Middlesex, U.K.	1,754
15	Nissan Motor Co.	Tokyo	1,670
16	Sony Corp.	Tokyo	1,620
17	McDonald's Corp.	Oak Brook, IL	1,611
18	Volkswagen	Wolfsburg, Germany	1,609
19	Reckitt Benckiser Slough	Berkshire, U.K.	1,550
20	PepsiCo	Purchase, N.Y.	1,530
21	Kraft Foods	Northfield, IL	1,513
22	Danone Group	Paris	1,297
23	General Electric Co.	Fairfield, CT	1,253
24	Yum Brands	Louisville, KY	1,178
25	News Corp.	New York, NY	1,104

SOURCE: "Global Marketers: Top 100," Advertising Age, November 19, 2007, 4.

series of *if-then* questions—*if* $X are invested in advertising, *then* what amount of revenue will be generated? Because budgets are set before the actual observance of how sales respond to advertising, this requires that the if-then questions be answered *before the fact.* (Analogously, this would be equivalent to predicting how many fish one will catch on a given day based simply on knowing the number of lures in that person's fishing box.) But this is where the complications begin. To employ the profit-maximization rule for budget setting, the advertising decision maker must know the *sales-to-advertising response function* for every brand for which a budgeting decision will be made. Because such knowledge is rarely available, theoretical (profit-maximization) budget setting is an ideal that is generally impractical in the real world of advertising decision making. To appreciate this point fully we need to elaborate on the concept of a sales-to-advertising (S-to-A) response function.

The **sales-to-advertising response function** refers to the relationship between money invested in advertising and the response, or output, of that investment in terms of revenue generated. As with any mathematical function, the S-to-A function maps the relationship between an "output" (in this case, sales revenue) to each meaningful level of an "input" (advertising expenditures). Table 6.1 demonstrates a hypothetical S-to-A response function by listing a series of advertising expenditures and the corresponding revenue yielded at each ad-expenditure level. Marginal costs, revenues, and profits also are presented (columns C through E).

Consider that our hypothetical decision maker is contemplating spending anywhere between $1,000,000 and $5,000,000 in advertising a brand during a particular period. Column A in Table 6.1 lists a range of possible advertising expenditures that increase in $500,000 increments starting at $1,000,000 and ending at $5,000,000. Assume, for convenience sake, that it is somehow possible to know precisely how much revenue will be generated at each level of advertising. Column B presents the various levels of sales in response to advertising. If you were to graph the relation between columns A and B, you would see that sales respond slowly to advertising until ad expenditures increase above $2,000,000, at which point sales revenue jumps considerably, especially at $3,000,000 invested in advertising. Thereafter, sales response to advertising tapers off substantially. It is easy to determine the level of marginal profit by simply subtracting the marginal cost at each level of advertising from the corresponding marginal revenue. The point of profit maximization is realized at an advertising investment of $4,000,000 where MR = MC = $500,000. Any ad investment below that amount continues to yield marginal profit, whereas any investment above $4,000,000 results in a marginal loss. Based on this illustration you should now fully understand the profit-maximization stated previously, namely that profits are maximized at the point where MR = MC.

If in fact marcom personnel could accurately estimate the S-to-A response function (columns A and B in Table 6.1), then setting the advertising budget to maximize profits would represent the proverbial "piece of cake." However, because the S-to-A response function is influenced by a multitude of factors (such as the creativity of advertising execution, the intensity of competitive advertising efforts, the overall quality of the brand's marketing mix, the state of the economy at the time advertising is undertaken, etc.) and not solely by the amount of advertising investment, it is difficult to know with any certainty what amount of sales a particular level of advertising expenditure will generate. In other words, under most circumstances it is extremely difficult, if not impossible, to derive anything approximating an accurate S-to-A response function.

table 6.1

Hypothetical Sales-to-Advertising Response Function

(A) Advertising Expenditures ($)	(B) Sales Response ($)	(C) Marginal Cost ($)	(D) Marginal Revenue ($)	(E) Marginal Profit (MR–MC)
1,000,000	5,000,000	NA	NA	NA
1,500,000	5,750,000	500,000	750,000	250,000
2,000,000	6,500,000	500,000	750,000	250,000
2,500,000	7,500,000	500,000	1,000,000	500,000
3,000,000	10,000,000	500,000	2,500,000	2,000,000
3,500,000	10,600,000	500,000	600,000	100,000
4,000,000	11,100,000	500,000	500,000	0
4,500,000	11,500,000	500,000	400,000	–100,000
5,000,000	11,800,000	500,000	300,000	–200,000

Hence, if an S-to-A response function is unknown prior to when a budgeting decision is to be made, then a total revenue curve cannot be constructed, and, in turn, marginal revenue cannot be derived at each level of ad investment. In short, applying profit-maximization budgeting requires information that rarely is available. This approach to budgeting represents a theoretical ideal but an infeasible tactic. Necessarily, marcom budget setters turn to more practical approaches for establishing budgets—methods that do not assure profit maximization but that are easy to work with and have the semblance, if not the substance, of being "correct."

Budgeting in Practice

Given the difficulty of accurately predicting sales response to advertising, companies typically set budgets by using judgment, applying experience with analogous situations, and using rules of thumb, or *heuristics.*[9] Although criticized because they do not provide a basis for advertising budget setting that is directly related to the profitability of the advertised brand, these heuristics continue to be widely used.[10] The practical budgeting methods most frequently used by both B2B companies and consumer goods firms in the United States, Europe, and even in China are the percentage-of-sales, objective-and-task, competitive parity, and affordability methods.[11]

Percentage-of-Sales Budgeting

In using the **percentage-of-sales method,** a company sets a brand's advertising budget by simply establishing the budget as a fixed percentage of *past* (e.g., last year's) or *anticipated* (e.g., next year's) sales volume. Assume, for example, that a company has traditionally allocated 3 percent of anticipated sales to advertising and that the company projects next year's sales for a particular brand to be $100,000,000. Its advertising budget would thus be set at $3,000,000.

A survey of the top 100 consumer goods advertisers in the United States found that slightly more than 50 percent employ the percentage-of-anticipated-sales method and 20 percent use the percentage-of-past-sales method.[12] This is to be expected, since budget setting should logically correspond to what a company expects to do in the future rather than being based on what it accomplished in the past.

What percentage of sales revenue do most companies devote to advertising? Actually, the percentage is highly variable. For example, among approximately 200 different types of products and services, the highest percentage of sales devoted to advertising in a recent year was the wood household furniture industry, which invested 18.4 percent of sales to advertising. Some other categories with double-digit advertising-to-sales ratios were transportation services (16.9 percent); distilled and blended liquor (16.8 percent); food products (11.9 percent); rubber and plastic footwear (11.7 percent); and dolls and stuffed toys (10.9 percent). Most product categories average less than 5 percent advertising-to-sales ratios. In fact, the average advertising-to-sales ratio across nearly 200 categories of B2C and B2B products and services was *3.1 percent.*[13]

Criticism of Percentage-of-Sales Budgeting The percentage-of-sales method is frequently criticized as being illogical. Critics argue that the method reverses the logical relationship between sales and advertising. That is, the true ordering between advertising and sales is that advertising causes sales, meaning that the level of sales is a function of advertising: *Sales = f (Advertising).* Contrary to this logical relation, implementing the percentage-of-sales method amounts to reversing the causal order by setting advertising as a function of sales: *Advertising = f (Sales).*

By this logic and method, when sales are anticipated to increase, the advertising budget also increases; when sales are expected to decline, the budget is reduced.

Applying the percentage-of-sales method leads many firms to reduce advertising budgets during economic downswings. However, rather than decreasing the amount of advertising, it may be wiser during these times to increase advertising to prevent further sales erosion. When used blindly, the percentage-of-sales method is little more than an arbitrary and simplistic rule of thumb substituted for what needs to be a sound business judgment. Used without justification, this budgeting method is another application of precisely wrong (versus vaguely right) decision making, as was discussed in the context of setting marcom objectives.

In practice, most sophisticated marketers do not use percentage of sales as the sole budgeting method. Instead, they employ the method as an initial pass, or first cut, for determining the budget and then alter the budget forecast depending on the objectives and tasks to be accomplished, the amount of competitive ad spending, and the availability of funds.

The Method of Objective-and-Task Budgeting

The **objective-and-task method** is generally regarded as the most sensible and defendable advertising budgeting method. In using this method, advertising decision makers—or those in any other marcom capacity—must specify what role they expect advertising (or some other marcom element) to play for a brand and then set the budget accordingly. The role is typically identified in terms of a communication objective (e.g., increase brand awareness by 20 percent) but could be stated in terms of expected sales volume or market share (e.g., increase market share from 15 to 20 percent).

The objective-and-task method is the advertising budget procedure used most frequently by both B2C and B2B companies. Surveys have shown that over 60 percent of consumer goods companies and 70 percent of B2B companies use this budgeting method.[14] The following steps are involved when applying the objective-and-task method:[15]

1. The first step is to establish specific *marketing objectives* that need to be accomplished, such as sales volume, market share, and profit contribution.

   Consider the marketing and advertising challenge in the United States that faced Volkswagen (VW). Although this once-vaunted automobile company had achieved huge success in the 1960s and 1970s with its VW Beetle, by the mid-1990s VW was confronted with what perhaps was its final opportunity to recapture the American consumer, who had turned to other imports and domestic models because VW had not kept up with what Americans wanted.[16] Sales of its two leading brands, the Golf and Jetta, had dropped by about 50 percent each compared with sales in prior years. VW's marketing objective (not to be confused with its specific advertising objective, which is discussed next) was, therefore, to increase sales of the Golf and Jetta models substantially and its overall share of the U.S. automobile market—from a low of only about 21,000 Golfs and Jettas to a goal of selling 250,000 VW models in the near future.

2. The second step in implementing the objective-and-task method is to assess the *communication functions* that must be performed to accomplish the overall marketing objectives.

   VW had to accomplish two communication functions to realize its rather audacious marketing objective. First, it had to increase consumers' awareness of the Golf and Jetta brand names substantially, and, second, it had to establish an image for VW as a company that offers "honest, reliable, and affordable cars." In short, VW had to enhance the Golf's and Jetta's brand equities.

3. The third step is to *determine advertising's role in the total communication mix* in performing the functions established in step 2.

© picturesbyrob/Alamy

Given the nature of its products and communication objectives, advertising was a crucial component in VW's mix.

4. The fourth step is to establish specific advertising goals in terms of the levels of *measurable communication response* required to achieve marketing objectives.

   VW might have established goals such as (1) increase awareness of the Jetta from, say, 45 percent of the target market to 75 percent; and (2) expand the percentage of survey respondents who rate VW products as high quality from, say, 15 percent to 40 percent. Both objectives are specific, quantitative, and measurable.

5. The final step is to *establish the budget* based on estimates of expenditures required to accomplish the advertising goals.

   In view of VW's challenging objectives, the decision was made to invest approximately $100 million in an advertising campaign in hopes of gaining higher brand awareness, enhancing the company's image among American consumers, and, ultimately, substantially increasing sales of VW products. The chief executive officer of VW's advertising agency explained that the advertising challenge was "to come up with hard, clear, product-focused ads that give car buyers the kind of information they need to make an intelligent choice."

In sum, the objective-and-task method of advertising budgeting is aptly named in that it is based on first establishing a clear *objective* that advertising (or another marcom element) is designed to accomplish and then identifying the *tasks* that advertising must perform in order to achieve the designated objective. The overall advertising budget can then be determined by costing out the amount of money needed to accomplish the identified tasks. In short, establish an objective → identify the tasks that need to be performed to achieve the objective → and identify the costs that will be required to accomplish the tasks. The end result from this straightforward approach is an advertising budget that is based on a systematic process rather than the consequence of arbitrariness or the application of a formulaic convention such as applying a standard percentage of sales.

Budgeting via the Competitive Parity Method

The **competitive parity method** sets the budget by examining what competitors are doing. A company may learn that its primary competitor is devoting 10 percent of sales to advertising and then adjust its percentage of advertising for its own brand. Armed with information on competitors' spending, a company may decide not merely to match but also to exceed the expenditures that competitors are committing to advertising. This is precisely what Geico did (see *Marcom Insight* at beginning of chapter) when it decided to vastly outspend its competitors in the auto insurance industry in order to attract new users and build market share. Interestingly, research has shown that companies that spend heavily on advertising can signal to customers that their brands are of high quality. Indeed, this advertising behavior has been compared to the signaling that occurs in a biological context when animals (like peacocks) have what amount to wasteful characteristics (such as a peacock's impressive tail feathers) that signal their exceptional biological fitness. Evidence suggests that heavy advertising expenditures might serve a brand in an analogous fashion.[17]

The importance of paying attention to what competitors are spending on advertising (or on any other marcom element) cannot be overemphasized. To appreciate

table 6.2

Advertising Spend, SOV, and SOM for Top-10 Wireless Phone Brands

Brand	Ad Spend (in $ million)	SOV	SOM
Verizon	$644.2	25.94	24.3
Cingular	411.3	16.56	18.4
AT&T	522.4	21.04	14.8
Sprint	477.9	19.24	9.5
Nextel	160.0	6.44	6.4
Alltell	53.3	2.15	5.6
VoiceStream	203.7	8.20	4.7
U.S. Cellular	8.6	0.35	2.9
Leap	1.9	0.08	0.3
Western	0	0.00	1.0
Totals	$2,483.3	100.00	87.9*

*SOM does not sum to 100 because these data include just the top-10 wireless phone brands.

Source: Reprinted with permission from the June 24, 2002 special edition of *Advertising Age*. Copyright, Crain Communication Inc., 2002.

this point fully, it is necessary to understand the concepts of **share of market (SOM)** and **share of voice (SOV)** and their relationship. These concepts relate to a single product category and consider each brand's revenues and advertising expenditures during, say, a fiscal year compared to the total revenues and ad expenditures in the category. The ratio of one brand's revenue to total category revenue is that brand's SOM. Similarly, the ratio of a brand's advertising expenditures (its "ad spend") to total category advertising expenditures is that brand's SOV.

SOV and SOM generally are correlated: Brands having larger SOVs also generally realize larger SOMs. For example, Tables 6.2 and 6.3 list the advertising expenditures, the SOVs, and the SOMs for the top-10 wireless phone brands (Table 6.2) and the top-10 beer brands (Table 6.3) in one recent year. The correlation between the shares of market and voice for these brands is apparent. That is, brands with larger shares of market typically have larger shares of voice. This does not mean, however, that SOV causes SOM. In fact, the relationship between SOV and SOM is bidirectional: A brand's SOV is partially responsible for its SOM. At the same time, brands with larger SOMs can afford to achieve higher SOVs, whereas smaller-share brands often are limited to relatively small SOVs.

The SOM-SOV relationship is a jousting match of sorts between competitors. If large market share brands reduce their SOVs to levels that are too low, they are vulnerable to losing market share to aggressive competitors (such as VoiceStream

table 6.3

Advertising Spend, SOV, and SOM for Top-10 Beer Brands

Brand	Ad Spend (in $ million)	SOV	SOM
Bud Light	$ 93.6	16.64	16.7
Budweiser	131.7	23.41	16.3
Coors Light	121.4	21.58	8.1
Miller Lite	102.9	18.29	7.7
Natural Light	0.1	0.02	4.0
Busch	9.4	1.67	3.7
Corona Extra	31.9	5.67	3.0
Busch Light	0.1	0.02	2.7
Miller High Life	21.8	3.87	2.6
Miller Genuine Draft	49.7	8.83	2.6
Totals	$562.6	100.00	67.4*

*SOM does not sum to 100 because these data include just the top-10 beer brands.

Source: Reprinted with permission from the June 24, 2002 special edition of *Advertising Age*. Copyright, Crain Communications Inc., 2002.

Wireless in Table 6.2). Conversely, if brands with relatively small market shares (such as Coors Light and Miller Lite in Table 6.3) become too aggressive, the leading brands (Anheuser-Busch's Bud Light and Budweiser) are forced to increase their advertising expenditures to offset the challenge.

Four General SOM/SOV Situations Figure 6.5 provides a framework for evaluating whether a brand should increase or decrease its advertising expenditures in view of its share of market (horizontal axis) and of the competitor's share of voice (vertical axis).[18] Although there are numerous possible relations in this two-dimensional space, we can simplify the discussion by considering just four general situations, which in Figure 6.5 are the quadrants, or cells, labeled A, B, C, and D. Advertising budgeting implications for each situation are as follows:

- *Cell A:* In this situation, your brand's SOM is relatively low and your competitor's SOV is relatively high. Corona Extra in Table 6.3 exemplifies this situation when compared with Budweiser. The recommendation is that the advertiser should consider decreasing ad expenditures and find a niche that can be defended against other small-share brands.
- *Cell B:* Your SOM in this situation is relatively high and your competitor has a high SOV. This characterizes Bud Light in Table 6.3 vis-à-vis Coors Light and Miller Lite. Bud Light probably should increase its advertising expenditures to defend its present market share position. Failure to do so likely would result in a share loss to these aggressive competitors.
- *Cell C:* In this situation, your SOM is low and your competitor's SOV also is low. Nextel and Alltell in Table 6.2 appear to occupy such a relationship. The general recommendation in such a situation is to attack the low-SOV competitor aggressively with a *large SOV premium* vis-à-vis that competitor. This appears to be the tact that Nextel has taken by spending three times more than Alltell. In other words, this is a good opportunity to wrest market share from a moribund or complacent competitor.
- *Cell D:* In this situation, you have the attractive position of holding a high market share, but your competitor is nonaggressive and has a relatively low SOV. Hence, it is possible for you to retain your present large share by *maintaining only a modest advertising spending premium* over your competitor.

figure 6.5

The SOV Effect and Ad Spending Implications

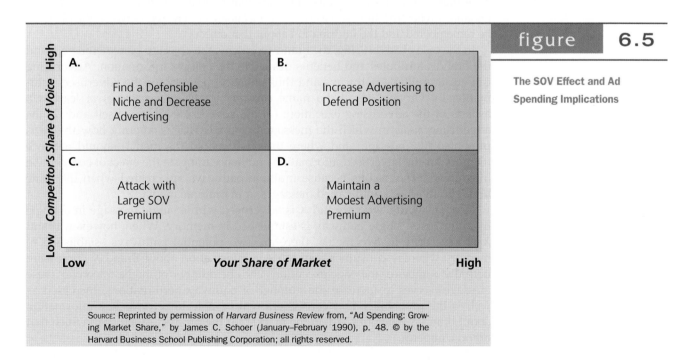

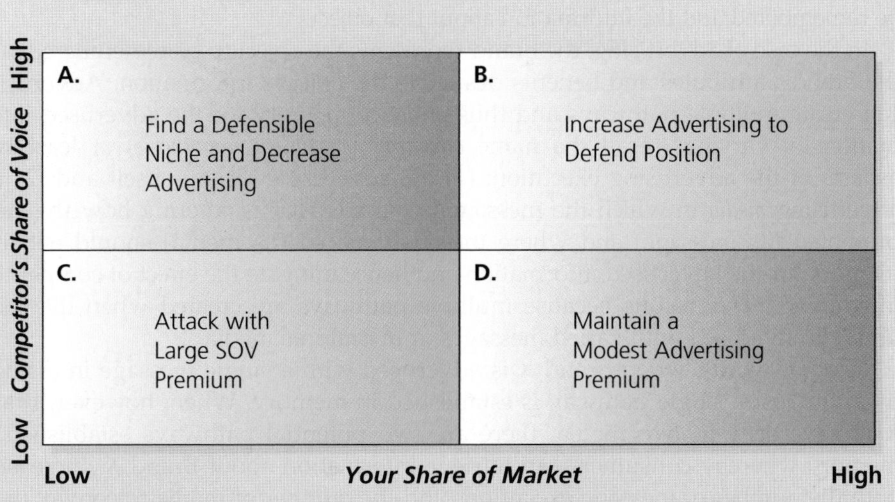

SOURCE: Reprinted by permission of *Harvard Business Review* from, "Ad Spending: Growing Market Share," by James C. Schoer (January–February 1990), p. 48. © by the Harvard Business School Publishing Corporation; all rights reserved.

These are guidelines for determining a brand's advertising budget rather than hard-and-fast rules. The general point to be stressed is that advertising budgets—as well as budgets for all other marcom elements—must be set with knowledge of what competitors are doing.[19] This is because the opportunity for growth in market share or the challenge to maintain an existing share position depends in large part on the quality and effectiveness of competitive efforts. Moreover, brand managers should generally set budgets on a market-by-market basis rather than nationally because the competitive warfare actually takes place in the individual markets.

The Role of Competitive Interference It is essential to set advertising budgets with an eye to the actions of competitors. This is especially important given that a brand's advertising must compete for the consumer's recall with the advertising from competitive brands, a situation of potential *competitive interference.* If "your" brand were the only one advertising in a particular product category, it probably could get by with a substantially smaller ad budget than what is necessitated when competitors also are aggressively advertising their brands. Merely increasing advertising expenditures does *not* guarantee a substantial impact on augmenting a brand's sales volume.[20]

There are reasons to expect that established brands in a product category are less susceptible to the interference from competitive advertising than are less-established and relatively unfamiliar brands. This explains why established brands' SOMs tend to exceed their advertising SOVs, whereas unestablished brands' SOVs often exceed their SOMs.[21] Unfamiliar brands that compete in an environment of advertising clutter are, in effect, at a competitive disadvantage in conveying their points of uniqueness vis-à-vis established brands, although even established brands suffer from the effects of competitive interference.[22] It follows that because relatively small-share brands are disadvantaged by competitive advertising, they need to avoid heavily cluttered, traditional media and perhaps turn to alternative marcom tools—such as using event marketing, viral marketing and other buzz-generating methods, or any of a number of nontraditional (alternative) advertising media.

Overcoming competitive interference is not just a matter of spending more but rather one of *spending more wisely.* A psychological theory called the encoding variability hypothesis explains how advertisers can be smarter spenders.[23] (The term *encoding* refers to transferring information into memory.) The **encoding variability hypothesis,** in its barest details, contends that people's memory for information is enhanced when multiple *pathways,* or connections, are created between the object to be remembered and the information about that object.

In the case of advertising, the brand represents the object to be remembered, and the brand's attributes and benefits designate the object's information. Advertising can create multiple pathways and thus enhance memory for the advertised information by varying (recall the name *encoding variability hypothesis*) at least two aspects of the advertising execution: (1) the advertising *message* itself and (2) the advertising *media* in which the message is placed. That is, altering how the ad is presented (its message) and where the ad is placed (its media) should enhance memory for the advertised information and hence mitigate the effect of competitive interference. This results because multiple pathways are created when the same brand is advertised with varied messages or in multiple media.

In other words, when Brand X is advertised with a single message in a single medium, just a single pathway is established in memory. When, however, Brand X is advertised in two media, there are two potential pathways established in memory whereby consumers can retrieve information about Brand X. Increasing both the number of message executions and the number of media to convey these messages serves to increase the number of pathway permutations. Increased as well is the probability that consumers will be able to retrieve key information about Brand X when they are in the market for the product category in which that brand competes.

This completes the discussion of the competitive parity "method" of setting advertising budgets. Comments have been somewhat extensive because the effectiveness of your brand's advertising is directly affected by the magnitude and quality of competitive efforts. Larger market share brands tend to gain more from their advertising efforts than do their small-share counterparts, who have difficulty overcoming the competitive clutter of their bigger adversaries. Regardless of a brand's SOM situation, it is absolutely imperative constantly to "scope out" competitive marcom spending to ensure the competition is not increasing its foothold and that you are investing adequately in your own brand.

Budgeting via the Affordability Method

In the so-called **affordability method,** a firm spends on advertising only those funds that remain after budgeting for everything else. In effect, when this "method" is used, advertising, along with other marcom elements, are relegated to a position of comparative insignificance (vis-à-vis other investment options) and are implicitly considered relatively unimportant to a brand's present success and future growth. There are times when marcom funds simply are in short supply due to extreme sales slowdowns. At such times, product and brand managers behave rationally when severely cutting back on their advertising spending or other marcom investments. Yet, in many competitive marketing situations it is critical that marcom personnel fight the tendency of financial planners to treat marcom expenditures as an unnecessary evil. The challenge is for brand managers to demonstrate that advertising and other marcom initiatives do, in fact, produce results. Absent compelling evidence, it is understandable when financial officials allocate funds for advertising as a virtual afterthought.

Section Summary

Most advertising budget setters combine two or more methods rather than depending exclusively on any one heuristic. For example, an advertiser may have a fixed percentage-of-sales figure in mind when starting the budgeting process but subsequently adjust this figure in light of anticipated competitive activity, funds availability, and other considerations.

Moreover, brand managers often find it necessary to adjust their budgets during the course of a year, keeping expenditures in line with changing conditions in the marketplace. Many advertisers operate under the belief that they should "shoot when the ducks are flying." In other words, it is logical to spend most heavily on advertising and on other marcom elements during periods when marketplace circumstances and the competitive situation warrant heavy expenditures. Rather than spending based on a fixed budget that was predetermined months in advance, it makes greater to sense to adjust the budget to accommodate current circumstances. In short, marcom expenditures should be based on current circumstances rather than determined before knowing what the marketplace conditions are that warrant increases or decreases in ad budgets.

Summary

This chapter detailed marcom objective setting and budgeting. Advertising objective setting depends on the pattern of consumer behavior and information that is involved in the particular product category. Toward this end, an introductory section presented a hierarchy-of-effect model of how consumers respond to marcom messages and discussed the implications for setting objectives. Requirements for developing effective objectives were discussed. A final section described the arguments both promoting and opposing the use of sales volume as the basis for setting objectives.

The chapter concluded with an explanation of the marcom budgeting process. The budgeting decision is one of the most important decisions and also one of the most difficult. The complication arises with the difficulty of determining the sales-to-advertising response function. In theory, budget setting is a simple matter, but the theoretical requirements are generally unattainable in practice. For this reason, practitioners use various rules of thumb (heuristics) to assist them in arriving at satisfactory, if not optimal, budgeting decisions. Percentage-of-sales budgeting and objective-and-task methods are the dominant budgeting heuristics, although maintaining competitive parity and not exceeding funds availability are other relevant considerations when setting budgets.

Discussion Questions

1. It can be argued that creating an expectation is the most important function many advertisements and other marcom messages perform. Provide examples of two magazine advertisements that illustrate advertisers' attempts to create expectations. Offer explanations of what expectations the advertisers are attempting to forge in their audiences' minds.
2. Chapter 5 was devoted to the topic of marcom positioning. Offer an explanation of the similarity between the concepts of positioning and creating expectations.
3. Apply the hierarchy-of-marcom-effects framework (Figure 6.1) to explain the evolution of a relationship between two people, beginning with dating and culminating in a wedding.
4. Repeat question 3, but use a relatively obscure brand as the basis for your application of Figure 6.1. Along the lines of the Pegetables illustration (Figure 6.2), identify a relatively unknown brand and explain how marcom efforts must attempt to move prospective customers through the various hierarchy stages.
5. What reasons can you give for certain industries investing considerably larger proportions of their sales in advertising than other industries?
6. Compare the difference between precisely wrong and vaguely right advertising objectives. Give an example of each.
7. Some critics contend that the use of the percentage-of-sales budgeting technique is illogical. Explain.
8. Explain how an advertising budget setter could use two or more budgeting heuristics in conjunction with one another.
9. In your own words, explain why it is extremely difficult to estimate sales-to-advertising response functions.
10. Established brands' shares of market tend to exceed their advertising shares of voice, whereas unestablished brands' SOVs often exceed their SOMs. Using the concept of competitive interference as your point of departure, explain these relationships.
11. Construct a picture to represent your understanding of how the encoding variability hypothesis applies in an advertising context. Use an actual brand for illustration purposes.

End Notes

1. Charles H. Patti and Charles F. Frazer, *Advertising: A Decision-Making Approach* (Hinsdale, Ill.: Dryden Press, 1988), 236.
2. Some claim that hierarchy models poorly represent the advertising process. See William M. Weilbacher, "Point of View: Does Advertising Cause a 'Hierarchy of Effects?'" *Journal of Advertising Research* 41 (November–December 2001), 19–26; William M. Weilbacher, "Weilbacher Comments on 'In Defense of Hierarchy of Effects,'" *Journal of Advertising Research* 42 (May–June 2002), 48–49; and William M. Weilbacher, "Point of View: How Advertising Affects Consumers," *Journal of Advertising Research* 43 (June 2003), 230–234. For an alternative view, see Thomas E. Barry, "In Defense of the Hierarchy of Effects: A Rejoinder to Weilbacher," *Journal of Advertising Research* 42 (May–June 2002), 44–47. Although the hierarchy model attributes excessive influence to advertising per se, the model does represent a reasonable representation of the effects that all marcom elements have working collectively.
3. For thorough discussions, see Demetrios Vakratsas and Tim Ambler, "How Advertising Works: What Do We Really Know," *Journal of Marketing* 63 (January 1999), 26–43; Thomas E. Barry, "The Development of the

Hierarchy of Effects: An Historical Perspective," *Current Issues and Research in Advertising,* vol. 10, ed. James H. Leigh and Claude R. Martin, Jr. (Ann Arbor: Division of Research, Graduate School of Business Administration, University of Michigan, 1987), 251–296; Ivan L. Preston, "The Association Model of the Advertising Communication Process," *Journal of Advertising* 11, no. 2 (1982), 3–15; and Ivan L. Preston and Esther Thorson, "Challenges to the Use of Hierarchy Models in Predicting Advertising Effectiveness," in *Proceedings of the 1983 Convention of the American Academy of Advertising,* ed. Donald W. Jugenheimer (Lawrence, Kans.: American Academy of Advertising, 1983).

4. Adapted from Larry Light and Richard Morgan, *The Fourth Wave: Brand Loyalty Marketing* (New York: Coalition for Brand Equity, American Association of Advertising Agencies, 1994), 25.
5. For further reading on the nature and role of brand loyalty, see Richard L. Oliver, "Whence Consumer Loyalty?" *Journal of Marketing* 63 (special issue 1999), 33–44; and Arjun Chaudhuri and Morris B. Holbrook, "The Chain of Effects from Brand Trust and Brand Affect to Brand Performance: The Role of Brand Loyalty," *Journal of Marketing* 65 (April 2001), 81–93.
6. Carl F. Mela, Sunil Gupta, and Donald R. Lehmann, "The Long-Term Impact of Promotion and Advertising on Consumer Brand Choice," *Journal of Marketing Research* 34 (May 1997), 248–261.
7. The following discussion is influenced by the classic work on advertising planning and goal setting by Russell Colley. His writing, which came to be known as the DAGMAR approach, set a standard for advertising objective setting. See Russell H. Colley, *Defining Advertising Goals for Measured Advertising Results* (New York: Association of National Advertisers, 1961).
8. Leonard M. Lodish, *The Advertising and Promotion Challenge: Vaguely Right or Precisely Wrong?* (New York: Oxford University Press, 1986), chap. 5.
9. Gary L. Lilien, Alvin J. Silk, Jean-Marie Choffray, and Murlidhar Rao, "Industrial Advertising Effects and Budgeting Practices," *Journal of Marketing* 40 (January 1976), 21.
10. J. Enrique Bigné, "Advertising Budgeting Practices: A Review," *Journal of Current Issues and Research in Advertising* 17 (fall 1995), 17–32; Fred S. Zufryden, "How Much Should Be Spent for Advertising a Brand?" *Journal of Advertising Research* (April/May 1989), 24–34.
11. The extensive use of the percentage-of-sales and objective-and-task methods in an industrial context has been documented by Lilien et al., "Industrial Advertising Effects," while support in a consumer context is provided by Kent M. Lancaster and Judith A. Stern, "Computer-Based Advertising Budgeting Practices of Leading U.S. Consumer Advertisers," *Journal of Advertising* 12, no. 4 (1983), 6. A thorough review of the history of advertising budgeting research is provided in Bigné, "Advertising Budget Practices." For information on advertising budgeting in China, see Gerard Prendergast, Douglas West, and Yi-Zheng Shi, "Advertising Budgeting Methods and Processes in China," *Journal of Advertising* 35, no. 3 (2006), 165–176.
12. Lancaster and Stern, "Computer-Based Advertising."
13. These data are based on research by Schonfeld & Associates and published by that company in "Advertising Ratios & Budgets," 2006.
14. Charles H. Patti and Vincent J. Blasko, "Budgeting Practices of Big Advertisers," *Journal of Advertising Research* 21 (December 1981), 23–29; Vincent J. Blasko and Charles H. Patti, "The Advertising Budgeting Practices of Industrial Marketers," *Journal of Marketing* 48 (fall 1984), 104–110. See also C. L. Hung and Douglas C. West, "Advertising Budgeting Methods in Canada, the UK and the USA," *International Journal of Advertising* 10, no. 3 (1991), 239–250.
15. Adapted from Lilien et al., "Industrial Advertising and Budgeting," 23.
16. This description is based on Kevin Goldman, "Volkswagen Has a Lot Riding on New Ads," *The Wall Street Journal,* January 31, 1994, B5.
17. Tim Ambler and E. Ann Hollier, "The Waste in Advertising Is the Part That Works," *Journal of Advertising Research* 44 (December 2004), 375–389. See also Amna Kirmani, "The Effect of Perceived Advertising Costs on Brand Perceptions," *Journal of Consumer Research* 17 (September 1990), 160–171.
18. Adapted from James C. Schroer, "Ad Spending: Growing Market Share," *Harvard Business Review* 68 (January/February 1990), 48. See also John Philip Jones, "Ad Spending: Maintaining Market Share," *Harvard Business Review* 68 (January/February 1990), 38–42.
19. For a slightly different perspective on how the relationship between competitors affects ad budgeting, see Boonghee Yoo and Rujirutana Mandhachitara, "Estimating Advertising Effects on Sales in a Competitive Setting," *Journal of Advertising Research* 43 (September 2003), 310–321.
20. Leonard M. Lodish, Magid Abraham, Stuart Kalmenson, Jeanne Livelsberger, Beth Lubetkin, Bruce Richardson, and Mary Ellen Stevens, "How T.V. Advertising Works: A Meta-Analysis of 389 Real World Split Cable T.V. Advertising Experiments," *Journal of Marketing Research* 32 (May 1995), 125–139.
21. Jones, "Ad Spending: Maintaining Market Share."
22. Robert J. Kent and Chris T. Allen, "Competitive Interference Effects in Consumer Memory for Advertising: The Role of Brand Familiarity," *Journal of Marketing* 58 (July 1994), 97–105; Robert J. Kent, "How Ad Claim Similarity and Target Brand Familiarity Moderate Competitive Interference Effects in Memory for Advertising," *Journal of Marketing Communications* 3 (December 1997), 231–242. For evidence that established brands suffer from competitive interference, see Anand Kumar and Shanker Krishnan, "Memory Interference in Advertising: A Replication and Extension," *Journal of Consumer Research* 30 (March 2004), 602–611.
23. H. Rao Unnava and Deepak Sirdeshmukh, "Reducing Competitive Ad Interference," *Journal of Marketing Research* 31 (August 1994), 403–411.

CHAPTERS

7
Overview of Advertising Management

8
Effective and Creative Advertising Messages

9
Message Appeals and Endorsers

10
Measuring Advertising Message Effectiveness

11
Advertising Media: Planning and Analysis

12
Traditional Advertising Media

13
Internet Advertising

14
Other Advertising Media

Part 3
Advertising Management

Part Three includes eight chapters that examine various facets of advertising management. *Chapter 7* presents fundamentals about the role and importance of advertising, provides advertising-to-sales ratios for various industries, and describes the functions that advertising performs. The chapter then overviews the advertising management process from the perspective of clients, and examines the role of advertising agencies in assisting clients. It also discusses financial aspects of advertising.

Chapter 8 delves into the creative aspect of the advertising management process. Discussed are general requirements for producing effective advertising messages and the role of creativity, with emphasis on originality and appropriateness. Corporate image and issue advertising is the final topic covered in this chapter.

Chapter 9 examines the use of various message appeals in advertising and the role of endorsers. Initial coverage focuses on advertisers' efforts to enhance consumers' motivation, opportunity, and ability to process ad messages.

Chapter 10 deals with the assessment of ad message effectiveness, discussing industry standards for message research and the types of information a brand management team and its ad agency desire from this form of research.

Chapter 11 provides thorough treatment of the four major activities involved in media planning and analysis: target audience selection, objective specification, media and vehicle selection, and media-buying activities. In-depth discussion focuses on media selection, and cost considerations.

Chapter 12 provides an analysis of traditional advertising media with primary attention to evaluating the unique characteristics and strengths/weaknesses of four major media: newspapers, magazines, radio, and television.

Chapter 13 covers the use of the Internet as an advertising medium, including the magnitude of online advertising and its dramatic growth potential. The chapter ends with discussion of the choice of metrics for assessing effectiveness.

Chapter 14 covers a variety of "other" advertising media: direct forms, postal-mail advertising (p-mail), and indirect forms such as yellow-pages advertising, videogame advertising, brand placements in movies and other media, cinema advertising, and other alternative media.

7

Overview of Advertising Management

With reference to performing a simple task, people often use the expression, "It's not rocket science." Rocket science serves as a comparison point to other activities because for many of us it represents the epitome of complexity. How scientists are able to propel rockets and their passengers to the moon, for example, literally boggles the mind. The enormity of this feat and its essential confluence of mathematical brilliance, mechanical sophistication, and computer wizardry is nothing short of amazing. The complexity of getting people safely into outer space and back exceeds the ordinary person's ability to grasp this accomplishment. Rocket science is not an undertaking fit for those who are ill trained to participate in the pursuit of overcoming the forces of nature and the limits of science.

What does this have to do with advertising? Well, a marketing and advertising practitioner, Sam Hill, has made the bold claim that "advertising is rocket science."[1] In keeping with the rocket science analogy, it is tempting to dismiss this assertion summarily and label its claimant a "space cadet." But let's evaluate whether there is any truth to Hill's statement.

His contention, more specifically, is that advertising, like rocket science, is itself a very complex activity. It is tempting to retort immediately, "Anyone can create an advertisement, so in what sense is advertising complex?" Unlike rocket science—which necessitates that its practitioners receive advanced academic degrees in physics, mathematics, computer science, and engineering—people with no formal training in advertising can create ads. If anyone can do it, how complex can it be?

The complexity is not in creating an ad per se; rather, it is in creating a successful advertising campaign. A successful campaign requires a confluence of the right message delivered to a targeted audience via appropriate advertising media. But accomplishing this is no easy task in view of the ever-changing competitive situation and evolving consumer tastes and preferences. The advertising milieu is, in short, more dynamic than the environment confronted by rocket scientists. Whereas the workings of gravity, mechanics, and computing can be reduced to highly predictable accounts and captured in mathematical equations, the

© Photodisc/Getty Images

landscape for advertising is continually shifting with numerous factors coming into play. And the target of any advertising effort—that is, the consumer—is inherently complex and unpredictable. According to Hill, "The customer is pulling one way, the client is pushing another and the competitors are shifting this way or that. One little mistake and hundreds of millions of dollars of advertising becomes nothing more than a bathroom break during halftime."[2] The complexity of advertising is nicely summed up as follows:

> *The truth is that in many ways advertising is harder than rocket science. It's news when a rocket launch fails. It's news when an ad campaign launch succeeds.*[3]

Chapter Objectives

After reading this chapter you should be able to:

1. Understand the magnitude of advertising and the percentage of sales revenue companies invest in this marcom tool.
2. Appreciate that advertising can be extraordinarily effective but that there is risk and uncertainty when investing in this practice.
3. Recognize the various functions that advertising performs.
4. Explore the advertising management process from the perspective of clients and their agencies.
5. Understand the functions agencies perform and how they are compensated.
6. Explore the issue of when investing in advertising is warranted and when disinvesting is justified.
7. Examine advertising elasticity as a means for understanding the contention that "strong advertising is a deposit in the brand equity bank."

>>Marcom Insight:

Is Advertising Rocket Science?

Introduction

This chapter introduces the first major IMC tool—*advertising*—and presents the fundamentals of advertising management. An initial section looks at the magnitude of advertising in the United States and elsewhere. The second major section explores the advertising management process, describes the functions of advertising, and examines the role of advertising agencies. A concluding section provides a detailed discussion of the arguments favoring investments in advertising and counterarguments regarding circumstances when it is advisable to disinvest. This section also explores the concept of advertising elasticity and compares it with price elasticity to determine the circumstances when a brand manager should either increase advertising expenditures or reduce prices.

First, however, it will be useful to define the topic of this and the seven subsequent chapters specifically so as to make a clear distinction between advertising and other forms of marketing communications.

> *Advertising is a paid, mediated form of communication from an identifiable source, designed to persuade the receiver to take some action, now or in the future.*[4]

The word *paid* in this definition distinguishes advertising from a related marcom tool, public relations, that secures unpaid space or time in media due to the news value of the public relations content. The expression *mediated communication* is designed to distinguish advertising, which typically is conveyed (mediated) via print and electronic media, from person-to-person forms of communication, including personal selling and word of mouth. Finally, the definition emphasizes that advertising's purpose is to *influence action,* either presently or in the future. The idea of influencing action is in keeping with the fifth key IMC feature presented back in Chapter 1: The ultimate objective of any form of marketing communications is to affect behavior rather than merely its precursors such as the levels of consumers' brand awareness and the favorability of their attitudes toward the advertised brand.

Companies that market their brands to final consumers undertake most advertising (B2C advertising). Consumer packaged goods companies are especially heavy advertisers in the B2C arena, but service providers (e.g., wireless telephone service) and consumer durables (e.g., automobiles) are heavy advertisers as well. Some companies that market to other companies rather than directly to consumers also are heavy advertisers (B2B advertising). Much of their advertising takes place in trade magazines that appeal to the special interests of practitioners who are prospects for the B2B advertiser's products. Interestingly, however, B2B advertisers also use traditional consumer media (e.g., television) to reach audiences that do not typically subscribe to trade publications. As an illustration, consider a television advertising campaign by a company that is unknown to most people except those in the industry. The company, Parker Hannifin, is an industrial firm that manufactures hoses, valves, and other such products. Several years ago the marketing department at Parker Hannifin undertook a TV advertising campaign, which was the first in the company's long history.

Advertisements for Parker Hannifin products were placed on cable television programs that appeal to engineers, who represent the target audience for the company's products. These included TLC's *Junkyard Wars* (a program showing clever people building machines from discarded items) and the History Channel's *Modern Marvels* (a program focusing on technology feats). The campaign was designed to increase engineers' awareness of the Parker Hannifin name and to make the name more salient such that Parker Hannifin would come to mind when a valve- or hose-purchasing need arose.

Interestingly, the campaign used humor to convey its point, which is a relatively atypical appeal in B2B advertising. In one TV spot, for example, two engineer-type

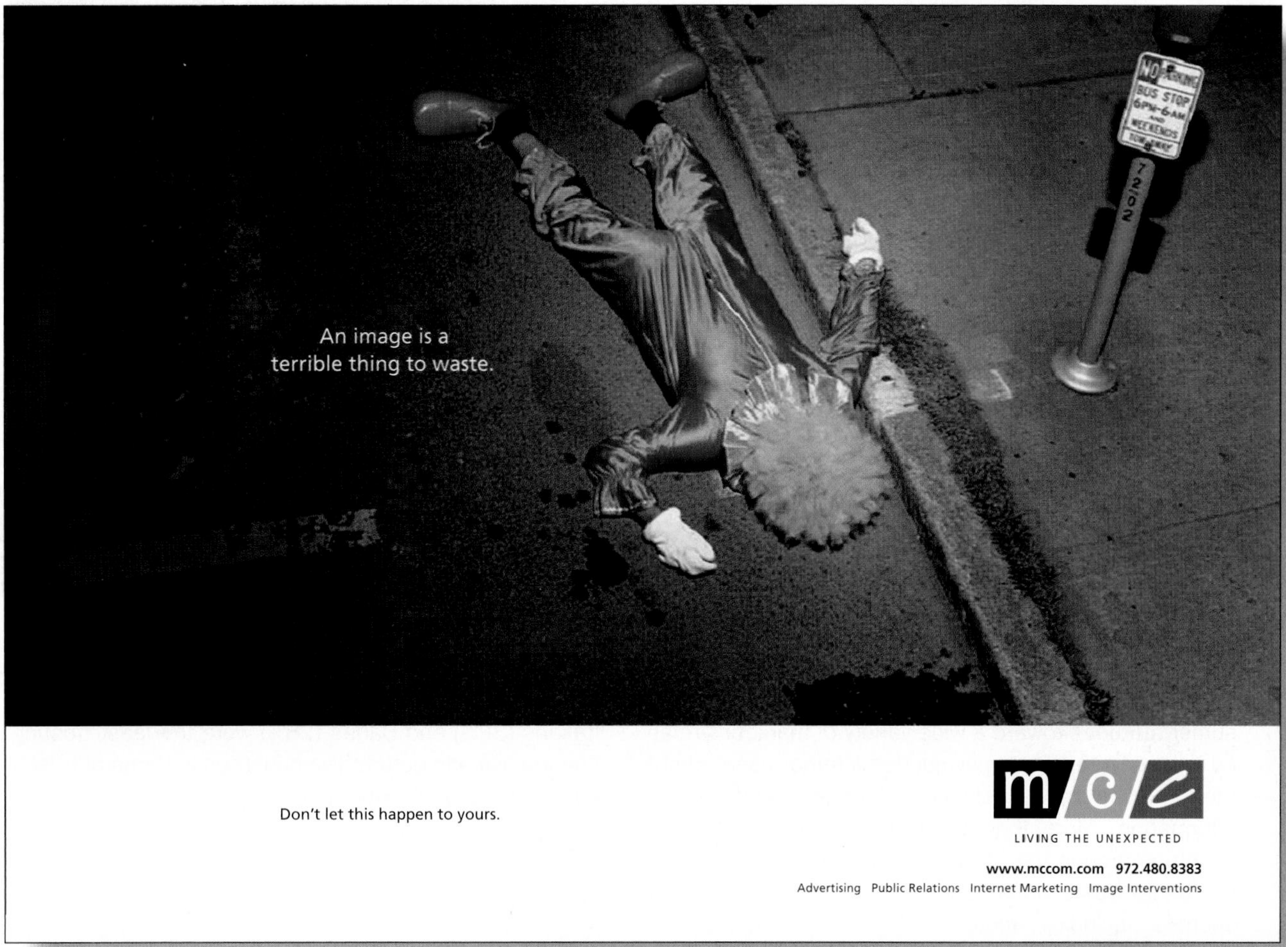

An image is a
terrible thing to waste.
Don't let this happen to yours.
m/c/c
LIVING THE UNEXPECTED
www.mccom.com 972.480.8383
Advertising Public Relations Internet Marketing Image Interventions

© M/C/C Dallas, TX

Figure 7.1

Example of the Use of Humor in B2B Advertising

characters are seated at a sushi bar and appear to be flirting with two attractive women at the other end of the bar. As one of the women uses chopsticks to lift a piece of sushi to her lips, an engineer asks his colleague, "Do you see what I see?" And the other responds, "Oh yeah." This brief dialogue is punctuated by the scene changing to a research lab where a robotic arm is shown lifting a lobster out of a tank. The connection between the sushi bar scene and the research lab is made clear when the campaign's tagline appears on the screen: "Engineers see the world differently." Parker Hannifin's campaign celebrates engineers and engineering feats, and in so doing hopes to increase the odds that real (not TV) engineers will be more likely to recommend the use of the company's products.[5]

The point of this example is that advertising is undertaken by all sorts of firms, and not just consumer goods companies. Hence, the lessons covered in this and the remaining advertising chapters are broadly applicable to all firms.

The Magnitude of Advertising

Advertising expenditures in the United States were estimated to have exceeded \$294 billion in 2008.[6] This amounts to nearly \$1,000 in advertising for each of the approximately 300 million men, women, and children living in the United States. Ad spending in the United States has for many years averaged approximately 2.2 percent of the country's gross domestic product.[7] Needless to say, advertising in the United States is serious business, to say the least!

Advertising spending is also considerable in other major industrialized countries, but not nearly to the same magnitude as in the United States. Global ad spending outside the United States totaled approximately $360 billion in 2008.[8] It is notable that ad spending in developing countries—particularly the so-called BRIC nations (Brazil, Russia, India, and China)—is growing at a much more rapid rate than in the United States and elsewhere around the globe.[9] See the *Global Focus* insert for a discussion of consumers' trust in advertising around the globe and how advertising-related trust compares with consumers' trust in information received from fellow consumers.

global focus

Which Source of Product Information Do Consumers Most Trust?

Nielsen, an influential global marketing research firm, conducts an online survey biannually that assesses consumer attitudes toward a wide variety of marketing-related issues. A recent survey queried Internet users about their trust in various sources of product and service information. More than 26,000 participants from 47 countries around the world were asked to indicate how much they trusted information received from 13 different sources, including traditional ad media (TV, newspapers, magazines, and radio), online ads, and recommendations from other consumers.

The percentages of respondents indicating that they somewhat trusted or completely trusted each source of information are as follows:

Recommendations from consumers	78%
Newspapers	63%
Consumer opinions posted online	61%
Brand Web sites	60%
Television	56%
Magazines	56%
Radio	54%
Brand sponsorships	49%
Email I signed up for	49%
Ads before movies	38%
Search engine ads	34%
Online banner ads	26%
Text ads on mobile phones	18%

The results of this survey are abundantly clear: Global consumers have greater faith in information from fellow consumers than from traditional ad media, and even less so from online ads and mobile ads. Overall trust in advertising, regardless of source, varies greatly across countries. Filipinos and Brazilians were the most trusting of all forms of advertising (tied at 67% trust), whereas Italians (32%) and Danes (28%) were the least trusting. The top five and bottom five countries in terms of trust in advertising are as follows:

Top Five

Philippines	67%
Brazil	67%
Mexico	66%
South Africa	64%
Taiwan	63%

Bottom Five

Latvia	38%
Germany	35%
Lithuania	34%
Italy	32%
Denmark	28%

It is apparent from these findings that consumers vary widely around the globe in terms of their trust (or lack of trust) in different sources of product and service information. It comes as little surprise that information received from other consumers is the most trusted inasmuch as we actively select such information in comparison to advertisements that typically are thrust upon us whether or not we are interested in receiving such information. Especially surprising is the wide differential among countries in terms of their faith in advertising. The low levels of trust among European consumers are particularly intriguing.

SOURCE: The Nielsen Company, "Trust in Advertising: A Global Nielsen Consumer Report," October 2007.

Some companies in the United States spend more than $2 billion annually to advertise their goods and services. In a recent year Procter & Gamble spent $4.89 billion advertising its products in the United States; AT&T, $3.34 billion; General Motors, $3.29 billion; Time Warner, $3.08 billion; Verizon, $2.82 billion; Ford Motor Company, $2.57 billion; GlaxoSmithKline, $2.44 billion; Walt Disney, $2.32 billion; Johnson & Johnson, $2.29 billion; and Unilever, $2.09 billion.[10] Table 7.1 lists these firms along with others that constitute the 50 top-spending U.S. advertisers in a recent year. As can be seen, even the U.S. government (ranked number 29) advertised to the tune of $1.13 billion. The government's advertising goes to such efforts as drug control, the U.S. Postal Service, Amtrak rail services, anti-smoking campaigns, and military recruiting.

Advertising-to-Sales Ratios

As pointed out in Chapter 6, in a recent year the average advertising-to-sales ratio across nearly 200 categories of B2C and B2B products and services was *3.1 percent.* That is, on average, the advertising spend for companies in the United States is approximately 3 cents out of every dollar of sales revenue. Table 7.2 provides greater detail by illustrating ad-to-sales ratios for companies that compete in six industries—automotive, computers and software, drugs, food, personal care items, and telecom service. Advertising as a percentage of sales for these select product categories ranges from a low of 1.3 percent (for IBM) to a high of 29.9 percent for Estee Lauder in the personal care industry. It also can be observed in Table 7.2 that for most companies the ad-to-sales ratio is in the range of 2 to 10 percent.

Perusal of this table also reveals that smaller competitors in each industry typically invest relatively larger percentages of their sales revenues in advertising. This is because companies with smaller market shares generally have to spend relatively heavily on advertising in order to be competitive, and thus the ad-to-sales ratios are higher because the sales base is relatively small compared with bigger competitors. A final notable observation is that the category average ad-to-sales ratio for personal care products, at 22.05 percent, is substantially higher than the corresponding averages for the remaining product categories. This is because personal care items often are sold less on the basis of product performance and more in terms of image, which requires greater advertising support to convey the desired impression. As an industry practitioner once claimed, "In the factory we make cosmetics; in the store [as well as in advertisements], we sell hope."[11]

Advertising Effects Are Uncertain

Advertising is costly and its effects often uncertain. It is for these reasons that many companies think it appropriate at times to reduce advertising expenditures or to eliminate advertising entirely. Marketing managers—and perhaps especially chief financial officers—sometimes consider it unnecessary to advertise when their brands already are enjoying great success. Companies find it particularly seductive to pull funds out of advertising during economic downturns—every dollar not spent on advertising is one more dollar added to the bottom line. For example, during the economic downturn in 2001 and the impending recession late that year—propelled in part by the economic fallout from the terrorist attacks on the World Trade Center and the Pentagon—advertising expenditures in the United States declined between 4 percent and 6 percent. Declines of this magnitude had not been seen in the United States since the Great Depression of the late 1920s and early 1930s.[12]

Such behavior implicitly fails to recognize that advertising is not just a current expense (as the term is used in accounting parlance) but rather is an investment. Although businesspeople fully appreciate the fact that building a more efficient production facility is an investment in their company's future, many of these same people often think that advertising can be dramatically reduced or even eliminated

table 7.1

Top 50 Spenders in U.S Advertising, 2006 ($ million)

Rank	Company	Headquarters	Ad Expenditures
1	Procter & Gamble Co.	Cincinnati	$4,898.0
2	AT&T	San Antonio, Texas	3,344.7
3	General Motors Corp.	Detroit	3,296.1
4	Time Warner	New York	3,088.8
5	Verizon Communications	New York	2,821.8
6	Ford Motor Co.	Dearborn, Mich.	2,576.8
7	GlaxoSmithKline	Brentford, Middlesex, U.K.	2,444.2
8	Walt Disney Co.	Burbank, Calif.	2,320.0
9	Johnson & Johnson	New Brunswick, N.J.	2,290.5
10	Unilever	London/Rotterdam	2,098.3
11	Toyota Motor Corp.	Toyota City, Japan	1,995.3
12	Sony Corp.	Tokyo	1,994.0
13	DaimlerChrysler	Auburn Hills, Mich./ Stuttgart, Germany	1,952.2
14	General Electric Co.	Fairfield, Conn.	1,860.2
15	Sprint Nextel Corp.	Reston, Va.	1,775.2
16	McDonald's Corp.	Oak Brook, Ill.	1,748.3
17	Sears Holdings Corp.	Hoffman Estates, Ill.	1,652.8
18	L'Oreal	Clichy, France	1,456.3
19	Kraft Foods	Northfield, Ill.	1,423.2
20	Macy's	Cincinnati	1,361.2
21	Honda Motor Co.	Tokyo	1,350.8
22	Bank of America Corp.	Charlotte, N.C.	1,334.4
23	Nissan Motor Co.	Tokyo	1,328.9
24	PepsiCo	Purchase, N.Y.	1,322.7
25	Nestle	Vevey, Switzerland	1,315.0
26	News Corp.	New York	1,244.5
27	J.C. Penney Co.	Plano, Texas	1,162.3
28	Target Corp.	Minneapolis	1,156.9
29	U.S. Government	Washington	1,132.7
30	Home Depot	Atlanta	1,118.1
31	Pfizer	New York	1,104.9
32	Berkshire Hathaway	Omaha, Neb.	1,093.4
33	Wyeth	Madison, N.J.	1,076.8
34	Wal-Mart Stores	Bentonville, Ark.	1,072.6
35	JPMorgan Chase & Co.	New York	1,062.5
36	Novartis	Basel, Switzerland	1,052.2
37	Estee Lauder Cos.	New York	1,031.3
38	Merck & Co.	Whitehouse Station, N.J.	1,024.2
39	Citigroup	New York	1,012.2
40	AstraZeneca	London	1,005.3
41	Viacom	New York	934.1
42	Schering-Plough Corp.	Kenilworth, N.J.	931.5
43	American Express Co.	New York	928.7
44	General Mills	Minneapolis	920.5
45	Microsoft Corp.	Redmond, Wash.	912.2
46	Yum Brands	Louisville, Ky.	902.0
47	Dell	Round Rock, Texas	882.5
48	Best Buy Co.	Richfield, Minn.	878.7
49	Capital One Financial Corp.	McLean, Va.	863.7
50	Lowe's Cos.	Mooresville, N.C.	838.5

Source: "100 Leading National Advertisers," *Advertising Age*, June 25, 2007, S–4.

table 7.2

Advertising-to-Sales Ratios for Select Product Categories

Industry & Company	U.S. Revenue ($ million)	U.S. Advertising ($ million)	Ad/Sales Ratio (%)
Automotive			
Volkswagen	18,262	419	2.3
DaimlerChrysler	79,899	1,952	2.4
General Motors	129,041	3,296	2.6
Toyota	77,692	1,995	2.6
Honda	51,648	1,351	2.6
Ford	81,155	2,577	3.2
Nissan	39,153	1,329	3.4
Category Average			**2.73**
Computers & Software			
IBM	39,511	517	1.3
Dell	36,100	883	2.4
Hewlett-Packard	32,244	829	2.6
Microsoft	29,730	912	3.1
Apple	9,307	384	4.1
Category Average			**2.70**
Drugs			
Abbott Laboratories	11,995	374	3.1
Sanofi-Aventis	12,456	463	3.7
Pfizer	25,822	1,105	4.3
Bayer	9,723	554	5.7
Eli Lilly	8,599	561	6.5
Novartis	14,998	1,052	7.0
Bristol-Myers Squibb	9,729	691	7.1
Merck	13,808	1,024	7.4
Johnson & Johnson	29,775	2,290	7.7
Astra Zeneca	12,449	1,005	8.1
Wyeth	11,054	1,077	9.7
GlaxoSmithKline	18,961	2,444	12.9
Schering-Plough	4,192	931	22.2
Category Average			**8.11**
Food			
ConAgra	10,279	366	3.6
Nestle	24,889	1,315	5.3
Kraft	20,931	1,423	6.8
General Mills	9,803	920	9.4
Kellogg	7,349	765	10.4
Campbell Soup	5,120	564	11.0
Category Average			**7.75**
Personal Care			
Unilever	17,222	2,098	12.2
Procter & Gamble	29,462	4,898	16.6
L'Oreal	4,942	1,456	29.5
Estee Lauder	3,446	1,031	29.9
Category Average			**22.05**
Telecom			
Qwest	13,923	362	2.6
Verizon	88,144	2,822	3.2
Sprint Nextel	41,028	1,775	4.3
Deutsche Telekom	17,124	815	4.8
AT&T	63,055	3,345	5.3
Category Average			**4.04**

Source: Adapted from "U.S. Company Revenue Per Advertising Dollar," *Advertising Age*, June 25, 2007, S–14.

when financial pressures call for cost-cutting measures. However, an ex–chief executive officer at Procter & Gamble—one of the world's largest advertisers—drew the following apt analogy between advertising and exercise:

> *If you want your brand to be fit, it's got to exercise regularly. When you get the opportunity to go to the movies or do something else instead of working out, you can do that once in a while—that's [equivalent to] shifting funds into [sales] promotion. But it's not a good thing to do. If you get off the regimen, you will pay for it later.*[13]

This viewpoint is captured further in the advice of a vice president at Booz Allen Hamilton, a major consulting agency, when asked what great companies such as Procter & Gamble, Kellogg, General Mills, Coca-Cola, and PepsiCo have in common. All these companies, in his opinion, are aware that *consistent investment spending* is the key factor underlying successful advertising. "They do not raid their budgets to ratchet earnings up for a few quarters. They know that advertising should not be managed as a discretionary variable cost."[14] This point should remind you of our discussion in Chapter 1 regarding the importance of establishing momentum for marcom efforts. Advertising momentum is like exercise. Stop exercising and you will lose conditioning and probably gain weight. Stop advertising and your brand likely will lose some of its equity and market share as well.

Advertising Functions

Many business firms as well as not-for-profit organizations have faith in advertising. In general, advertising is valued because it is recognized as performing five critical communications functions: (1) informing, (2) influencing, (3) reminding and increasing salience, (4) adding value, and (5) assisting other company efforts.[15]

Informing

One of advertising's most important functions is to publicize brands.[16] That is, advertising makes consumers aware of new brands, educates them about a brand's distinct features and benefits, and facilitates the creation of positive brand images. Because advertising is an efficient form of communication capable of reaching mass audiences at a relatively low cost per contact, it facilitates the introduction of new brands and increases demand for existing brands, largely by increasing consumers' *top-of-mind awareness* (*TOMA*) for established brands in mature product categories.[17] Advertising performs another valuable information role—both for the advertised brand and the consumer—by teaching new uses for existing brands. This practice, termed *usage expansion advertising,* is typified by the following illustrations:[18]

- Campbell's soup, which is typically eaten for lunch and during other informal eating occasions, was advertised as being suitable for eating during formal family dinners or even at breakfast.
- Gatorade, which originally was used during heavy athletic activity, was advertised for replenishing liquids during flu attacks.
- Special K, a breakfast cereal, was advertised for afternoon or late-night snacking.

Influencing

Effective advertising influences prospective customers to try advertised products and services. Sometimes advertising influences *primary demand*—that is, creating demand for an entire product category. More frequently, advertising attempts to build *secondary demand,* the demand for a company's brand. Advertising by both B2C and B2B companies provides consumers and customers with reasoned

IMC >> i.m.c. focus

A National Advertising Effort for Starbucks

Starbucks, the famous chain of specialty coffee stores, was founded in Seattle in 1971, although it wasn't until 1987 that any expansion beyond Seattle occurred. In less than 40 years, the chain grew from a single store to now more than 10,000 U.S. locations and thousands more in other countries. Starbucks' store growth in the United States is ambitious, to say the least, with new-store additions exceeding 1,500 each year. Some analysts contend that Starbucks has reached a saturation point and cannot sustain the continual addition of large numbers of new stores, but executives at Starbucks counter that demand for specialty coffees remains largely untapped and that there is considerable potential for additional growth. (You may recall back in Chapter 5 the discussion of McDonald's entry into the specialty coffee business, which seemingly supports the view that much latent demand remains to be fulfilled.)

It is questionable whether Starbucks will be able to achieve its ambitious growth plans and maintain sales levels in existing stores. That is, although the addition of new Starbucks outlets likely will add to the overall level of Starbucks' corporate revenue and profit, existing stores may experience lost volume from customers shifting their purchases to new Starbucks outlets—the net effect being that incremental revenues and profits may not be proportionate to the number of new stores being added. What can Starbucks do to achieve its ambitious growth plans while maintaining proportionate sales volume at all of its stores?

Historically, Starbucks'growth was achieved with low levels of advertising and mostly via the power of word of mouth—satisfied customers telling other people, who in turn further spread the word, and so on. But by late 2007 Starbucks executives determined that they would have to increase the level of advertising effort. The company launched its first national television advertising campaign in November 2007. Starbucks' CEO explained that the company was getting into national TV advertising to sustain store growth and with the objective of reaching out to a broader audience that had not previously experienced Starbucks. This move into TV advertising reflects a significant development for a company that heretofore was able to grow at a double-digit rate without advertising at the level undertaken by most businesses that compete in the retail food and beverage business. It is unknown at the time of this writing whether this advertising initiative will be successful.

SOURCE: Janet Adamy, "At Starbucks, Too Many, Too Quick?" *The Wall Street Journal,* November 15, 2007, B1; Janet Adamy, "Starbucks Turns to TV in Bid to Boost Results," *The Wall Street Journal,* November 16, 2007, A14; Starbucks Timeline and History, http://www.starbucks.com/aboutus/timeline.asp (accessed December 30, 2007).

arguments and emotional appeals for trying one brand versus another. The *IMC Focus* insert describes the inaugural national TV advertising campaign the Starbucks specialty coffee chain undertook in an attempt to influence consumers to purchase specialty coffees at that chain's stores rather than elsewhere.

Reminding and Increasing Salience

Advertising keeps a company's brand fresh in the consumer's memory. When a need arises that is related to the advertised product, the influence of past advertising makes it possible for the advertiser's brand to come to the consumer's mind as a purchase candidate. This has been referred to as making a brand more *salient;* that is, enriching the memory trace for a brand such that the brand comes to mind in relevant choice situations.[19] Effective advertising also increases the consumer's interest in mature brands and thus the likelihood of purchasing brands that otherwise might not be chosen.[20] Advertising has been demonstrated, furthermore, to influence brand switching by reminding consumers who have not recently purchased a brand that the brand is available and that it possesses favorable attributes.[21]

Adding Value

There are three basic ways by which companies can add value to their offerings: innovating, improving quality, and altering consumer perceptions. These three value-added components are completely interdependent as astutely captured in the following quote:

> *Innovation without quality is mere novelty. Consumer perception without quality and/or innovation is mere puffery. And both innovation and quality, if not translated into consumer perceptions, are like the sound of the proverbial tree falling in the empty forest.*[22]

Advertising adds value to brands by influencing perceptions. Effective advertising causes brands to be viewed as more elegant, more stylish, more prestigious, of higher quality, and so on. Indeed, research involving over 100 brands drawn from five nondurable products (e.g., paper towels and shampoo) and five durable products (e.g., televisions and cameras) has demonstrated that greater ad spending influences consumers to perceive advertised brands as higher in quality.[23] Effective advertising, then, by influencing perceived quality and other perceptions, can lead to increased market share and greater profitability.[24]

By adding value, advertising can generate for brands more sales volume, revenue, and profit and reduce the risk of unpredictable future cash flows. In finance parlance, all of this can be captured in the concept of discounted cash flow (DCF). By making a brand more valuable, advertising generates incremental DCF. One advertising practitioner eloquently captured advertising's value-adding role with this claim: "Advertising builds brands. Brands build the business. Let the discounted cash flow!"[25] And, in a world of accountability, it is absolutely imperative that advertising deliver positive financial results. It has even been demonstrated that firms that invest greater percentages of their sales revenues in advertising can reduce the risk that their stock values will fall during a period of general declines in stock market valuations.[26]

Assisting Other Company Efforts

Advertising is just one member of the marcom team. Advertising's primary role is at times to facilitate other marcom efforts. For example, advertising may be used as a vehicle for delivering coupons and sweepstakes and attracting attention to these and other promotional tools. Another crucial role is to assist sales representatives. Advertising pre-sells a company's products and provides salespeople with valuable introductions prior to their personal contact with prospective customers. Sales effort, time, and costs are reduced because less time is required to inform prospects about product features and benefits. Moreover, advertising legitimizes or makes more credible the sales representative's claims.[27]

Advertising also enhances the effectiveness of other marcom tools. For example, consumers can identify product packages in the store and more readily recognize a brand's value following exposure to advertisements for it on television or in a magazine. Advertising also can augment the effectiveness of price deals. Customers are known to be more responsive to retailers' price deals when retailers advertised that fact compared to when retailers offer a deal absent any advertising support.[28]

The Advertising Management Process

As intimated in the *Marcom Insight* at the beginning of the chapter, people sometimes suggest that creating advertisements is a simple act and that anyone can do it. That viewpoint is, in a sense, not entirely incorrect. Any literate person can construct an advertisement. Of course, any literate person also can write a story or craft a poem. But not all storytellers or poets are particularly good, and the outcome of their efforts often is ineffective. So it is with advertising: The issue is not just doing it, but doing it well, so well that the advertising gains attention and ultimately influences purchase choices. The challenge of advertising goes beyond the act of creating messages and involves also the task of placing ads in the right advertising media and selecting appropriate measures to assess whether an advertising campaign has achieved its goals.

Advertising management can thus be thought of as the process of creating ad messages, selecting media in which to place the ads, and measuring the effects of the advertising efforts: messages, media, and measures. This process generally involves at least two parties, the organization that has a product or service to advertise, the *client,* and the independent organization that is responsible for creating ads, making media choices, and measuring results, the *agency.* The following sections first examine advertising management from the client's perspective and then the agent's. Because most advertising is undertaken for specific brands, the client typically is represented by an individual who works in a brand- or product-management position. This individual and his or her team are responsible for marcom decisions that affect the brand's welfare.

Managing the Advertising Process: The Client Perspective

Figure 7.2 graphically illustrates the advertising management process, which consists of three sets of interrelated activities: advertising strategy, strategy implementation, and assessing ad effectiveness.

Formulating and Implementing Advertising Strategy

Advertising strategy formulation involves four major activities (see the top box in Figure 7.2). The first two, setting objectives and devising budgets, were described in Chapter 6 when discussing these activities in the context of all marcom elements. Message creation, the third aspect of formulating advertising strategy, is the subject of chapters 8 and 9. The fourth element, media strategy, the topic of chapters 11 through 14, involves the selection of media categories and specific vehicles to deliver advertising messages. (The term *vehicle* is used in reference to, say, the specific TV program in which an advertisement is to be placed—TV is the medium, the program is the vehicle.)

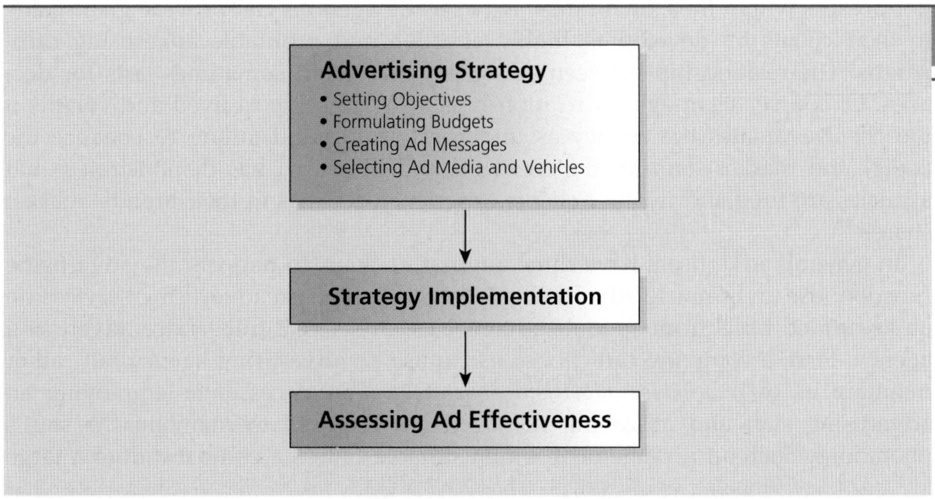

figure 7.2

The Advertising Management Process

Implementing Advertising Strategy

Strategy implementation deals with the tactical, day-to-day activities that must be performed to carry out an advertising campaign. For example, whereas the decision to emphasize television over other media is a strategic choice, the selection of specific types of programs and times at which to air a commercial is a tactical implementation matter. Likewise, the decision to emphasize a particular brand benefit is a strategic message consideration, but the actual way the message is delivered is a matter of creative implementation. This text focuses more on strategic than tactical issues.

Measuring Advertising Effectiveness

Assessing effectiveness is a critical aspect of advertising management—only by evaluating results is it possible to determine whether objectives are being accomplished. This often requires that baseline measures be taken before an advertising campaign begins (to determine, for example, what percentage of the target audience is aware of the brand name) and then afterward to determine whether the objective was achieved. Because research is fundamental to advertising control, Chapter 10 explores a variety of measurement techniques that are used for evaluating advertising effectiveness.

The Role of Advertising Agencies

Message strategies and decisions most often are the joint enterprise of the companies that advertise (the clients) and their advertising agencies. This section examines the role of advertising agencies and describes how agencies are organized. Table 7.3 lists the top-25 advertising agencies in the United States according to revenue. Two observations are pertinent. First, all of these agencies were at one time independent businesses; now, due to mergers and acquisitions, most are owned by large marketing organizations such as Omnicom Group (New York), WPP Group (London), Interpublic Group (New York), Publicis Groupe (Paris), and Havas (Suresnes, France). Second, it is apparent that most of the major U.S. ad agencies are located in New York City, which for many years has been the world's major advertising center. Needless to say, there literally are thousands of ad agencies throughout the United States and worldwide, although most generate revenues only a small fraction of those shown in Table 7.3.

To appreciate why a company would use an ad agency, it is important to recognize that businesses routinely employ outside specialists: lawyers, financial advisors, management consultants, tax specialists, and so on. By their very nature, these "outsiders" bring knowledge, expertise, and efficiencies that companies do not possess within their own ranks. Advertising agencies can provide great value to their clients by developing highly effective and profitable advertising campaigns. The relationship between ad agency and client sometimes lasts for decades. Of course, client-agency relationships also can be short lived and volatile if the client evaluates the agency as underperforming and failing to enhance the equity and market share of the client's brand. Research has demonstrated that agencies are fired shortly after clients experience declines in their brands' market shares.[29]

In general, advertisers have three alternative ways to perform the advertising function: use an in-house advertising operation, purchase advertising services on an as-needed basis from specialized agencies, or select a full-service advertising agency. First, a company can choose *not* to use an advertising agency but rather maintain its own *in-house advertising operation*. This necessitates employing an advertising staff and absorbing the overhead required to maintain the staff's operations. Such an arrangement is unjustifiable unless a company does a large

table 7.3

Top-25 U.S. Advertising Agencies in Ad Revenue, 2006

Rank	Agency	Headquarters	Ad Revenue (in millions)
1	JWT [WPP]	New York	$445.40
2	BBDO Worldwide [Omnicom]	New York	444.2
3	McCann Erickson Worldwide [Interpublic]	New York	443.4
4	Leo Burnett Worldwide [Publicis]	Chicago	312
5	Ogilvy & Mather Worldwide [WPP]	New York	290
6	DDB Worldwide Communications Group [Omnicom]	New York	277.9
7	Y&R [WPP]	New York	250
8	Grey Worldwide [WPP]	New York	235.7
9	Saatchi & Saatchi [Publicis]	New York	212.6
10	DraftFCB [Interpublic]	Chicago/New York	210.8
11	Publicis [Publicis]	New York	208
12	TBWA Worldwide [Omnicom]	New York	199
13	Euro RSCG Worldwide [Havas]	New York	182.1
14	Doner	Southfield, Mich.	162.5
15	Richards Group	Dallas	160
16	Deutsch [Interpublic]	New York	159.9
17	Campbell-Ewald [Interpublic]	Warren, Mich.	145
18	Bernard Hodes Group [Omnicom]	New York	123.8
19	GSD&M [Omnicom]	Austin, Texas	120
20	Hill Holliday [Interpublic]	Boston	120
21	Cramer-Krasselt	Chicago	117.9
22	Mullen [Interpublic]	Wenham, Mass.	112
23	RPA	Santa Monica, Calif.	105.2
24	Goodby, Silverstein & Partners [Omnicom]	San Francisco	102
25	Ambrosi	Chicago	94.1

Source: "Top 25 Agency Brands by Advertising Revenue," *Advertising Age*, April 25, 2007 (no page listed). Most revenue amounts have been estimated. Where appropriate, each agency's parent company is shown in brackets.

amount of continual advertising. Even under these conditions, most businesses instead choose to use the services of advertising agencies.

A second way for a client to accomplish the advertising function is to *purchase advertising services à la carte*. That is, rather than depending on a single full-service agency to perform all advertising and related functions, an advertiser may recruit the services of a variety of firms with particular specialties in distinct aspects of advertising, including creative work, media selection, advertising research, and so on. This arrangement's advantages include the ability to contract for services only when they are needed, thus yielding potential cost efficiencies. On the downside, specialists (so-called *boutiques*) sometimes lack financial stability and may be poor in terms of cost accountability.

Third, *full-service advertising agencies* perform at least four basic functions for the clients they represent: (1) creative services, (2) media services, (3) research services, and (4) account management. They also may be involved in the advertiser's total marketing process and, for a fee, perform other marcom functions, including sales promotion, publicity, package design, strategic marketing planning, and sales forecasting. Why would an advertiser want to employ the services of a full-service agency? The primary advantages include acquiring the services of specialists with in-depth knowledge of advertising and obtaining negotiating leverage with the media. The major disadvantage is that some control over the advertising function is lost when it is performed by an agency rather than in house. Nonetheless, brand managers frequently utilize the services of full-service ad agencies because these agencies understand their clients' businesses and are capable of producing equity-enhancing advertising campaigns. Understanding the client's business and "good chemistry" between client and agency are the two primary reasons cited by managers for choosing a particular ad agency partner.[30]

Creative Services

Advertising agencies have staffs of copywriters, graphic artists, and creative directors who create advertising copy and visualizations. Advertising agencies on occasion create brilliant advertising campaigns that enhance brand equity and increase a brand's sales volume, market share, and profitability. Often, however, advertisements are not sufficiently clever or novel to break through the clutter of surrounding advertising.

Media Services

This unit of an advertising agency is charged with selecting the best advertising media for reaching the client's target market, achieving ad objectives, and meeting the budget. *Media planners* are responsible for developing overall media strategy (where to advertise, how often, when, etc.), and media buyers then procure specific vehicles within particular media that media planners have selected and clients have approved. The complexity of media buying requires the use of sophisticated analysis and continual research of changing media costs and availability. Experts in media and vehicle selection are able to make more effective decisions than are brand managers on the client side who have no particular expertise in media and vehicle selection.

Research Services

Full-service advertising agencies employ research specialists who study their clients' customers' buying habits, purchase preferences, and responsiveness to advertising concepts and finished ads. Focus groups, mall intercepts, ethnographic studies by trained anthropologists, and acquisition of syndicated research data are just some of the services agencies' research specialists perform.

Account Management

This facet of a full-service advertising agency provides the mechanism to link the agency with the client. Account managers act as liaisons so that the client does not need to interact directly with several different service departments and specialists. In most major advertising agencies, the account management department includes account executives and management supervisors. *Account executives* are involved in tactical decision making and frequent contact with brand managers and other client personnel. Account executives are responsible for seeing that the client's interests, concerns, and preferences have a voice in the advertising agency and that the work is being accomplished on schedule. Account executives report to *management supervisors,* who are more involved in actually getting new business for the agency and working with clients at a more strategic level. Account executives are groomed for positions as management supervisors.

Agency Compensation

There are three basic methods by which clients compensate agencies for services rendered: (1) receiving commissions from media, (2) being compensated based on a fee system, and (3) earning compensation based on outcomes.

1. *Commissions from media* for advertisements aired or printed on behalf of the agency's clients provided the primary form of ad agency compensation in the

past. Historically, U.S. advertising agencies charged a standard commission of 15 percent of the gross amount of billings.[31] To illustrate, suppose the Creative Advertising Agency buys $200,000 of space in a certain magazine for its client, ABC Company. When the invoice for this space comes due, Creative would remit payment of $170,000 to the magazine ($200,000 less Creative's 15 percent commission); bill ABC for the full $200,000; and retain the remainder, $30,000, as revenue for services rendered. The $30,000 revenue realized by Creative was, in the past, regarded as fair compensation to the agency for its creative expertise, media-buying insight, and ancillary functions performed in behalf of its client, ABC Company.

The 15 percent compensation system has, as one may suppose, been a matter of some controversy between client marketing executives and managers of advertising agencies. The primary area of disagreement is whether 15 percent compensation is too much (the marketing executives' perspective) or too little (the ad agencies' perspective). The disagreement has spurred the growth of alternative compensation systems. Indeed, today just a fraction of advertisers still pay a 15 percent commission. Although there are alternatives to the commission system, it probably will not vanish entirely. Rather, a reduced commission system, by which the ad agency is compensated with a flat fee that is less than 15 percent, has experienced increased usage.

2. The most common compensation method today is a *labor-based fee system,* by which advertising agencies are compensated much like lawyers, tax advisors, and management consultants. That is, agencies carefully monitor their time and bill clients an hourly fee based on time commitment. This system involves price negotiations between advertisers and agencies such that the actual rate of compensation is based on mutual agreement concerning the worth of the services rendered by the advertising agency.
3. *Outcome- or performance-based programs* represent the newest approach to agency compensation. Ford Motor Company, for example, uses a compensation system whereby it negotiates a base fee with its agencies to cover the cost of services provided and additionally offers incentive payments that are tied to brand performance goals such as targeted revenue levels. Procter & Gamble (P&G) employs a sales-based model whereby ad agencies are compensated based on a percentage of sales that a P&G brand obtains. The agency's compensation rises with sales gains and falls with declines. Needless to say, this incentive-based system encourages, indeed demands, agencies to use whatever IMC programs are needed to build brand sales. P&G's best interest (growth in brand sales and market share) and the agency's best interest (increased compensation) are joined by this compensation system in a hand-in-glove fashion. In addition to these companies, many others are turning away from the historical commission-based system and toward some form of outcome-based compensation program. The success of outcome-based programs will depend on demonstrating that advertising and other marcom efforts agencies initiate do indeed translate into enhanced brand performance.[32]

Ad-Investment Considerations

Thus far we have introduced the topic of advertising, presented facts illustrating its magnitude, discussed its functions, provided an overview of the advertising management process from the client's perspective, and described the functioning and compensation of advertising agencies. It is pertinent to ask now whether the billions of dollars invested in advertising are warranted. More precisely, when is it justifiable to invest in advertising, and when is it appropriate to disinvest?

We can better appreciate the issues surrounding this complex question by examining a few equations that will put things into crisper perspective. These equations deal with the relations among sales volume (or simply volume), sales revenue (or simply revenue), and profit.

(7.1) **Profit = Revenue − Expenses**

(7.2) **Revenue = Price × Volume**

(7.3) **Volume = Trial + Repeat**

We see first with Equation 7.1 that a brand's profit during any accounting period—such as a business quarter or an entire year—is a function of its revenue minus expenses. Because advertising is an expense, total profit during an accounting period can be increased by reducing advertising expenses. At the same time, an undesirable effect of reducing advertising is that revenue may decline because fewer units can be sold or the price per unit has to be reduced in the absence of adequate advertising support (see Equation 7.2). We can further note from Equation 7.3 that sales volume (i.e., number of units sold) is obtained by a combination of recruiting more *trial,* or first-time, users to a brand and encouraging users to continue purchasing the brand—that is, to remain *repeat* purchasers.

Whether one chooses to invest or disinvest in advertising depends largely on expectations about how advertising will influence a brand's sales volume (Equation 7.3) and revenue (Equation 7.2). Let us look at arguments first for investing and then for disinvesting.

The Case for Investing in Advertising

In terms of profitability, investing in advertising is justified only if the incremental revenue generated from the advertising exceeds the advertising expense. In other words, if the advertising expense is $X, then over the long term (i.e., not necessarily immediately) revenue attributable to the advertising must be more than $X to justify the investment. On what grounds might one expect that the revenue will exceed the advertising expense? In terms of Equation 7.3, it might be expected that effective advertising will attract new triers to a brand and encourage repeat purchasing. (Obviously, advertising is not the only marcom tool able to generate trial and repeat purchasing; indeed, sales promotions perform both roles in conjunction with advertising.) Hence, effective advertising should build sales volume by enhancing brand equity—both by increasing brand awareness and by enhancing brand image (recall the discussion in Chapter 2).

Equation 7.2 shows that the other determinant of revenue besides sales volume is the unit price at which a brand is sold. Advertising has the power to enhance a brand's perceived quality and thus the ability of brand managers to charge higher prices; that is, consumers are willing to pay more for brands they perceive as higher quality. Taken together, then, the case for investing in advertising is based on the belief that it can increase profitability by increasing sales volume, enabling higher selling prices, and thus increasing revenue beyond the incremental advertising expense.

The Case for Disinvesting

As previously noted, firms often choose to reduce advertising expenditures either when a brand is performing well or during periods of economic recession. This is a seductive strategy because a reduction in expenses, everything else held constant, leads to increased profits (Equation 7.1). But is "everything else held constant" when advertising budgets are cut or, worse yet, severely slashed? The implicit assumption is that revenue (and revenue's constituent elements, volume and price) will *not* be affected adversely when ad budgets are diminished. However, such an assumption is based on Pollyanna-like thinking that past advertising will continue to affect sales volume positively, even when advertising in the current period is curtailed or reduced. The assumption also is somewhat illogical. On the one hand, it presumes that past advertising will carry over into the future to maintain revenue; on the other hand, it neglects to acknowledge that the absence of advertising in the present period will have an adverse effect on revenues in subsequent periods!

Which Position Is More Acceptable?

The profit effect of reducing advertising expenses is relatively certain: For every dollar not invested in advertising, there is a dollar increase in short-term profit—assuming, of course, that the reduction in advertising does not adversely affect revenue. It is far less certain, however, that maintaining or increasing advertising expenditures will increase profits. This is because it is difficult to know with certainty whether advertising will build brand volume or enable higher prices; either outcome or both will lead to increased revenues. Yet, and it is a *big* yet, most sophisticated companies are willing to place their bets on advertising's ability to boost revenues and thus enhance profits from the *revenue-increase side* rather than from the *expense-reduction side.*

A Deposit in the Brand Equity Bank

The reason many marketing executives continue to invest in advertising, even during economic downturns, is because they believe advertising will enhance a brand's equity and increase sales. You will recall from the discussion in Chapter 2 that marcom efforts enhance a brand's equity by creating brand awareness and forging favorable, strong, and perhaps unique associations in the consumer's memory between the brand and its features and benefits. When advertising and other forms of marketing communications create unique and positive messages, a brand becomes differentiated from competitive offerings and is relatively insulated from future price competition.

Advertising's long-term role has been described in these terms: "Strong advertising represents a deposit in the brand equity bank."[33] This clever expression nicely captures the advertising challenge. It also correctly notes that not all advertising represents a deposit in the brand equity bank, only advertising that is *strong*—that is, different, unique, clever, and memorable.

Advertising versus Pricing Elasticity

Returning more directly to the issue of investing or disinvesting in advertising, we have to grapple with the following challenge: What are the alternative ways by which brand managers can grow their brands' sales volume, revenue, and profits? Increasing advertising is one option; reducing price—via outright price cuts or through promotional dealing—is another. Which option is more promising? The answer requires we have a common measure, or metric, for comparing the effects of increasing advertising versus decreasing prices. The concept of *elasticity* provides just such a metric.

Elasticity, as you will recall from a basic economics or marketing course, is a measure of how responsive the demand for a brand is to changes in marketing variables such as price and advertising. We can calculate elasticity coefficients for price (E_P) and advertising (E_A), respectively, based on the following equations:

$$E_P = \text{Percentage change in quantity demanded} \div \text{Percentage change in price} \tag{7.4}$$

$$E_A = \text{Percentage change in quantity demanded} \div \text{Percentage change in advertising} \tag{7.5}$$

To illustrate these concepts, consider the situation faced by a recent college graduate, Aubrey, who sells T-shirts imprinted with thematic messages. (Students well familiar with the concept of elasticity are encouraged to skip this basic treatment and resume reading three paragraphs from now in the subsection titled Average Price and Advertising Elasticities.)

Aubrey has being doing a pretty good business but thinks he can increase revenues and profits by lowering the price at which he sells imprinted T-shirts. (The *law of inverse demand* says that sales volume, or quantity, typically increases when prices are reduced, and vice versa.) Last week (let's refer to this as week 1) Aubrey priced his product at $10 each and sold 1,500 shirts (P1 = $10; Q1 = 1,500). He decided the following week, week 2, to reduce the price to $9, and then sold 1,800 shirts (P2 = $9; Q2 = 1,800). Applying Equation 7.4, we quickly see that the percentage change in quantity demanded is 20 percent. That is, (1,800 − 1,500) ÷ 1,500 = 20 percent. Thus, with an 11 percent decrease in price—that is, (10 − 9) ÷ 9—he realized a 20 percent increase in quantity sold. The price elasticity (E_P) expressed as an absolute value is 1.82 (i.e., 20 ÷ 11). (Refer to Equation 7.4 to see how the elasticity coefficient for price, E_P, is calculated.) Aubrey was pleased with this result because total revenue in week 2 was $16,200 (P2 × Q2 = $9 × 1,800 = $16,200) compared with the $15,000 revenue obtained in week 1 ($10 × 1,500). Thus, although he reduced the price of T-shirts, he enjoyed an 8 percent increase in revenue—that is, ($16,200 − $15,000) ÷ $15,000.

Let us now consider the possibility that, rather than reducing price, Aubrey decided to increase the amount of advertising from week 1 to week 2. Suppose that in week 1 he had spent $1,000 advertising in the local newspaper. As before, he obtained $15,000 revenue in week 1 from selling 1,500 T-shirts at a price of $10 each. Suppose in week 2 he increased the level of advertising to $1,500 (a 50 percent increase over week 1) and sold 1,600 shirts at $10 each. In this case, the percentage change in quantity demanded is 6.67 percent. That is, (1,600 − 1,500) ÷ 1,500 = 6.67 percent. This increase in quantity sold was enjoyed with a 50 percent increase in ad expenditures. Thus, applying Equation 7.5, the advertising elasticity (E_A) is 6.67 ÷ 50 = 0.133. Whereas Aubrey received $15,000 in week 1 revenue (P1 = $10; Q1 = 1,500), revenue increased in week 2 by $1,000 (P2 = $10; Q2 = 1,600). This increased revenue ($1,000) was obtained with a $500 increase in advertising, so Aubrey enjoyed a $500 increase in profit—not a bad week's work for a young entrepreneur!

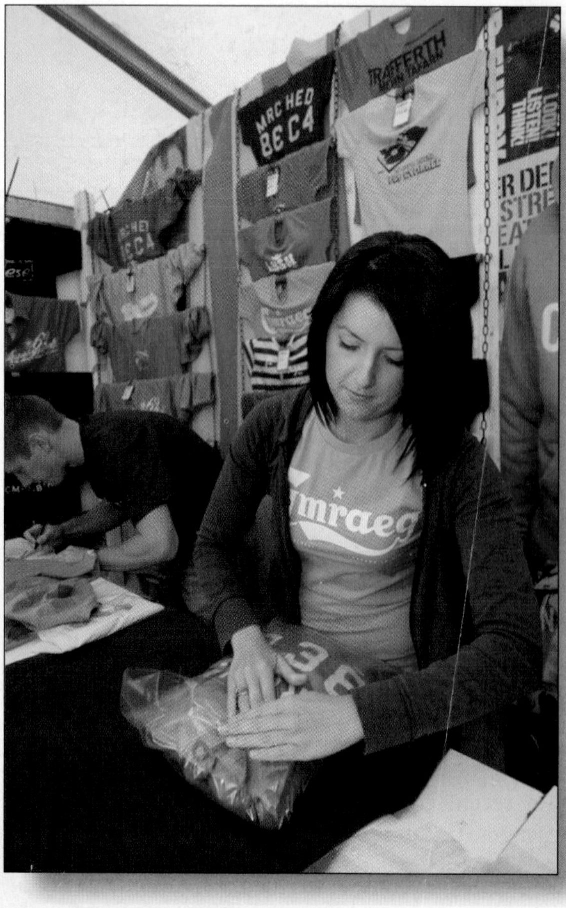

© Keith Morris / Alamy

Average Price and Advertising Elasticities Let us relate this simple example to a more general point that tells us something about how advertising works and whether increases in advertising can be justified, especially when juxtaposed with the alternative possibility of merely reducing prices. We know a lot about advertising and price elasticities. An important study determined that the average price and advertising elasticities for 130 brands of durable and nondurable products were 1.61 and 0.11, respectively.[34] (The price elasticity is presented here as an absolute value, although technically it should have a negative sign insofar as price increases typically result in volume decreases and price decreases result in volume increases.) A price elasticity of 1.61 is to be interpreted as meaning that a 1 percent reduction in price leads to a 1.61 percent increase in sales volume; similarly, the ad elasticity coefficient of 0.11 indicates that a 1 percent increase in ad expenditures increases volume by just 0.11 percent.

Hence, sales volume is about 14.6 times (1.61 ÷ 0.11) more responsive, on average, to changes in price than to changes in advertising. For just durable goods, the average price and advertising elasticities are 2.01 and 0.23, which indicates that sales volume for these goods is, on average, 8.7 times more responsive to price discounts than advertising increases. Comparatively, for nondurable goods, the average price and advertising elasticities are 1.54 and 0.09, respectively, indicating that, on average, sales volume is 17 times more responsive to price cuts than advertising increases.

What's a Manager to Do? Do these results indicate that brand managers should always discount prices and never increase advertising? Absolutely not! As you have learned from this text and elsewhere, every situation is unique. Pat answers ("This is how you should do it.") are flat out wrong and misleading! Every brand does not experience the same price and advertising elasticities as presented here. "On average," as used in our discussion, means that some brands are at the average, whereas others are above or below the average; there is, in other words, a distribution of elasticity coefficients around the average. In general, we can consider four combinations of advertising and price elasticities. For each situation we will identify the appropriate strategy for increasing profit, whether to increase advertising or to reduce price:[35]

- *Situation 1: Maintain the status quo.* Consider a situation where consumers have well-established brand preferences such as during the decline stage of a product's life cycle or in established niche markets. In a market such as this, demand would not be very price elastic or advertising elastic; consequently, profits would be maximized by basically adhering to the status quo and maintaining the present price and advertising levels. In short, facing a situation such as this, brand managers should neither discount prices nor increase levels of advertising.
- *Situation 2: Build image via increased advertising.* In a situation where demand is more advertising elastic than price elastic, it is advisable to spend relatively more on advertising increases than price discounts. This situation is likely for new products, luxury goods, and products characterized by symbolism and imagery (cosmetics, designer labels in apparel and home furnishings, expensive brands of distilled spirits, etc.). The profit-increasing strategy in a situation such as this is to build a brand's image by increasing advertising.
- *Situation 3: Grow volume via price discounting.* This third situation is characterized by mature consumer goods markets where consumers have complete information about most brands in the category and brand switching is frequent. Because brands are little differentiated, the market is more price than advertising elastic. Profit increases are obtained more from price discounts than advertising investments.
- *Situation 4: Increase advertising and/or discount prices.* This is a situation where the market is both price elastic and advertising elastic. This would be expected when brands in the product category are inherently differentiable (cereals, automobiles, appliances, etc.) and for products that are seasonal (e.g., lawn products, seasonal clothing, and special holiday gift items). In situations such as these, informative advertising can influence consumers' beliefs about product attributes (e.g., Scotts fertilizer is longer-lasting than competitive brands), but because brands are similar, consumers also are eager to compare prices.

Given knowledge of the price and advertising elasticities that exist in a particular situation, it is possible to determine mathematically whether it is more profitable to increase advertising or discount price. The mathematics is beyond the scope of this text, but the interested reader is referred to additional sources.[36] It is hoped that this section conveyed the point that the choice to invest (increase) or disinvest (decrease) in advertising can be made only after determining the relative advertising and price elasticities that confront a brand in a particular market situation. We have provided some general guidelines in the previously mentioned situations as to when it might be advisable to increase advertising expenditures or discount prices. It is critical to appreciate that every situation is unique.

It is important to understand that "on average" applies to all brands in a product category but that particular brands may distinguish themselves by developing really clever advertising that serves to create an appealing advertising image or presents functional information in an especially compelling manner.

Your job as a brand manager is to work with your advertising agency to develop campaigns that distinguish your brand from the crowd of competitors. Please note, by comparison, that the average professional basketball player scores only around, say, 5 to 10 points per game. But players such as Kobe Bryant, Allen Iverson, Dirk Nowitzki, Kevin Garnett, and Lebron James average more than 20 points per game. Perhaps your brand can also perform above the average with effective advertising. If it cannot, and the average advertising elasticity in your product category is low, then the appropriate strategy is probably not to invest in additional advertising but to maintain or even lower prices. In other words, it is inadvisable to waste money on advertising if the circumstances (such as situations 1 and 3) dictate against further advertising investment. However, if the market is responsive to advertising (such as situations 2 or 4), then be prepared to invest in developing creative and effective (i.e., "strong") advertising campaigns so that your advertising represents a deposit in the brand equity bank.

Ad Spending, Advertising Elasticity, and Share of Market

The effect of advertising for a brand on its sales volume, revenue, and market share—that is, its proportional representation of total product category revenue—is determined both by how much it spends relative to other brands in the category (its share of voice, or SOV) and how effective its advertising is. It was mentioned earlier that *strong* advertising is a deposit in the brand equity bank. Full appreciation of this statement requires that we explore the concept of advertising "strength." We have, in fact, a measure of advertising strength, and that measure is the familiar concept we've been discussing, namely, *advertising elasticity*. Table 7.4 presents real data for the top-10 U.S. beer brands from a recent year as a basis for illustrating advertising elasticity and the concept of strength. However, before proceeding, it is necessary to introduce a final equation, Equation 7.6.

$$(7.6) \quad \mathrm{SOM}_i = \mathrm{A}_i^e / \sum_{j=1}^{n} \mathrm{A}_j^e$$

Table 7.4

The Effect of Advertising Elasticity on Brands Share of Market

Beer Brand	Ad Spend ($ million) (A)	Hypothetical elasticity coefficients (B)	(A) ^ (B)* (C)	Predicted SOM (1) (D)	(A) ^ (B)† (E)	Predicted SOM (2) (F)
Budweiser	$338.60	.11	1.90	12.83%	1.90	12.46%
Miller	227.50	.11	1.82	12.28	2.26	14.82
Coors	160.30	.11 OR .15	1.75	11.82	1.75	11.48
Busch	22.50	.11	1.41	9.52	1.41	9.25
Natural	0.10	.11	0.78	5.25	0.78	5.10
Corona	52.80	.11	1.55	10.46	1.55	10.16
Michelob	40.10	.11	1.50	10.15	1.50	9.85
Heineken	111.50	.11	1.68	11.36	1.68	11.03
Milwaukee's Best	5.20	.11	1.20	8.11	1.20	7.87
Keystone	6.00	.11	1.22	8.23	1.22	8.00
Column Sums	$964.60	NA	14.79	100%	15.23	100%

*Assumes elasticity coefficients for all 10 beer brands are equal at 0.11.
†Assumes that Miller's elasticity coefficient is 0.15, whereas all other brands' elasticities remain at 0.11.

Source: "Top 10 Beer Brands," *Advertising Age*, June 25, 2007, S–10.

Equation 7.6 indicates that a brand's predicted market share (i.e., the SOM for the *i*th brand in a product category) depends on its level of advertising (A_i) raised to the power of its advertising elasticity (e) in comparison to the total level of advertising for all brands in the category (brands $j = 1$ to n, where n is the total number of brands in the category) raised to the power of their elasticity coefficients.[37] This may seem a little abstract, but Table 7.4 brings this formulation to life with a straightforward example drawn from the U.S. beer industry.

The first column of data, column A, indicates the advertising expenditures in a recent year for each of the top-10 U.S. beer brands. For example, Anheuser-Busch spent a total of $338.60 million to advertise its flagship brand, Budweiser. Total ad expenditures among these 10 brands approached $1 billion ($964.60 million). Column B makes the simplifying assumption that advertising for every brand of beer is equally strong (or equally weak), as indicated by identical elasticity coefficients of 0.11, which, as pointed out previously, is the average advertising elasticity across many consumer products. Note that two coefficients are presented for Miller beer, either 0.11 or 0.15. We'll subsequently explain why two coefficients are shown for this particular brand.

In column C the ad spend is raised to the power of the elasticity coefficient, with the symbol ^ indicating a power function. Thus, Budweiser's ad spend of $338.60 million raised to the power of 0.11 equals 1.90, and Miller's spend raised to the same power equals 1.82. (Of course, the remaining entries in column C were calculated in similar fashion.) Each value in Column C, one for each of the 10 beer brands, is the numeric equivalent to the A_i^e term in Equation 7.6. The summation of all of the values in column C is 14.79, which represents the numerical counterpart to the summation term in Equation 7.6, namely ΣA_j^e.

Thus, following Equation 7.6, each value in column C is divided by the summation of all values to yield, in column D, predicted market shares for each of the 10 beer brands. Of course, Equation 7.6 makes the simplifying assumption that advertising is the sole determinant of market share. If that were the case, then the market shares in column D should correlate strongly with actual market shares. In fact, although not shown in Table 7.4, the correlation between actual and predicted market shares equals 0.55, which indicates that advertising is an important determinant of market shares in the beer industry.

Column E provides a new set of values that have been derived by assuming that all elasticity coefficients remain equal at 0.11 with the exception of Miller's, which now is assumed to be 0.15. The assumption, in other words, is that Miller's advertising is "stronger" than its competitors', due perhaps to more creative advertising content or a novel and compelling ad message. If this in fact were the case, then predicted market shares would look like those in column F. Note carefully that Miller's predicted market share has increased by about 2.5 share points (from 12.28 in column D to 14.82 in column F), whereas the shares for all other beers have declined. Miller's gain (due to hypothetically superior advertising) has come at the expense of its competitors.

In sum, this exercise has shown how it is possible to translate the idea of advertising "strength" into numerical values by capitalizing on the concept of advertising elasticity. Equation 7.6 is based on the simplifying assumption that advertising alone influences market share, but, simplification aside, it enables us to see the effect of creating better, more creative, and stronger advertising: Namely, stronger advertising vis-à-vis competitors' efforts can lead to increased market shares. The following two chapters will go into much greater detail in developing the concept of advertising creativity and ad message strategies.

Summary

This chapter offered an introduction to advertising. First, advertising was defined as a paid, mediated form of communication from an identifiable source that is designed to persuade the receiver to take some action, either now or in the future. We then looked at the magnitude of advertising in the United States and elsewhere. For example, ad expenditures in the United States totaled approximately $294 billion in 2008, and global ad spending outside the United States in 2008 was estimated to total approximately $360 billion. Also discussed in this context were advertising-to-sales ratios for several illustrative product categories.

Next explored were the functions advertising performs, which include informing, influencing, reminding and increasing salience, adding value, and assisting other company efforts. Following this, the advertising management process was examined from the perspectives of clients. The role of advertising agencies then was discussed, and methods of compensation were reviewed.

A concluding section provided a detailed discussion of the arguments favoring investment in advertising and counterarguments regarding circumstances when it is advisable to disinvest. In the context of this discussion, considerable attention was devoted to the issue of advertising versus pricing elasticities. We pointed out that sales volume is about 14.6 times more responsive, on average, to changes in price than to changes in advertising. Although this would seem to suggest that revenue is best grown by reducing prices rather than increasing ad spending, the point was made that not all advertisers are "average" and not all advertising situations are the same. Thus, whether increasing advertising or reducing price is a better strategy depends entirely on the situation facing each particular product category and competitor in that category. In conclusion we examined the role of advertising expenditures and elasticity coefficients in determining market shares.

Discussion Questions

1. Describe circumstances when each of the five advertising functions described in the chapter might be more important than the others.
2. Advertising is said to be "a deposit in the brand equity bank," but only if the advertising is "strong." Explain.
3. Provide an example of usage expansion advertising other than those illustrated in the chapter.
4. Present arguments for and against using advertising agencies.
5. Ad agency compensation is increasingly turning to performance- or outcome-based compensation. Explain how this form of ad agency compensation works and why it potentially is superior to alternative methods of compensating ad agencies.
6. Using Equations 7.1 through 7.3, explain the various means by which advertising is capable of influencing a brand's profitability.
7. In the context of the discussion of price and advertising elasticities, four situations were presented by comparing whether price or advertising elasticity is stronger. Situation 2 was characterized as "build image via increased advertising." In your own terms, explain why in this situation it is more profitable to spend relatively more on advertising rather than reduce a brand's price.
8. Research results were presented showing that sales volume is about 14.6 times more responsive, on average, to changes in price than to changes in advertising. Explain exactly what this means for the manager of a brand who is considering whether to grow sales by increasing advertising expenditures or lowering the price.
9. Data in this same section indicated that nondurable goods (versus durables) are relatively more responsive to price cuts than advertising increases. Offer an explanation for this differential.
10. Show your understanding of Equation 7.4 and the data presented in Table 7.4 by constructing a spreadsheet (using, for example, Microsoft Excel) and altering the elasticity coefficients for different beers. For example, just as Miller's elasticity coefficient was changed from 0.11 to 0.15 while holding all the others constant at 0.11, you may want to vary the coefficient for, say, Heineken.

End Notes

1. Sam Hill, "Advertising Is Rocket Science," *Advertising Age,* January 26, 2004, 18.
2. Ibid.
3. Ibid.
4. Jef I. Richards and Catharine M. Curran, "Oracles on 'Advertising': Searching for a Definition," *Journal of Advertising* 31 (summer 2002), 63–77.
5. Timothy Aeppel, "For Parker Hannifin, Cable TV Is the Best," *Wall Street Journal Online,* August 7, 2003, http://online.wsj.com.
6. Based on an estimate by advertising authority Robert Cohen. Reported in Stuart Elliott, "Advertising: Forecasters Say Madison Avenue Will Escape a Recession, Just Barely," *The New York Times* (http://www.nytimes.com), December 4, 2007 (accessed December 19, 2007).
7. Bradley Johnson, "Consumers Cite Past Experience as the No. 1 Influencer When Buying," *American Demographics,* November 20, 2006, 21.
8. The global advertising estimate is from Ibid.
9. Steve King, "Ad Spending in Developing Nations Outpaces Average," *Advertising Age,* June 18, 2007, 23.
10. "100 Leading National Advertisers," *Advertising Age,* June 25, 2007, S-4.
11. This oft-repeated quote is attributed to Revlon's founder, Charles Revson, although the source is unknown to this author.
12. Laurel Wentz and Mercedes M. Cardona, "Ad Fall May Be Worst Since Depression," *Advertising Age,* September 3, 2001, 1, 24.
13. Jennifer Lawrence, "P&G's Artzt on Ads: Crucial Investment," *Advertising Age,* October 28, 1991, 1, 53.
14. Bernard Ryan, Jr., *It Works! How Investment Spending in Advertising Pays Off* (New York: American Association of Advertising Agencies, 1991), 11.
15. These functions are similar to those identified by the noted advertising pioneer James Webb Young. For example, "What Is Advertising, What Does It Do," *Advertising Age,* November 21, 1973, 12.
16. The idea of publicizing brands is based on the ideas of Andrew Ehrenberg and colleagues who regard advertising as a form of creative publicity. See Andrew Ehrenberg, Neil Barnard, Rachel Kennedy, and Helen Bloom, "Brand Advertising as Creative Publicity," *Journal of Advertising Research* 42 (August 2002), 7–18.
17. Giles D'Souza and Ram C. Rao, "Can Repeating an Advertisement More Frequently than the Competition Affect Brand Preference in a Mature Market?" *Journal of Marketing* 59 (April 1995), 32–42. See also A. S. C. Ehrenberg, "Repetitive Advertising and the Consumer," *Journal of Advertising Research* (April 1974), 24–34; Stephen Miller and Lisette Berry, "Brand Salience versus Brand Image: Two Theories of Advertising Effectiveness," *Journal of Advertising Research* 28 (September/October 1998), 77–82.
18. The term usage expansion advertising and the examples are from Brian Wansink and Michael L. Ray, "Advertising Strategies to Increase Usage Frequency," *Journal of Marketing* 60 (January 1996), 31–46.
19. Ehrenberg et al., "Brand Advertising as Creative Publicity," 8.
20. Karen A. Machleit, Chris T. Allen, and Thomas J. Madden, "The Mature Brand and Brand Interest: An Alternative Consequence of Ad-Evoked Affect," *Journal of Marketing* 57 (October 1993), 72–82.
21. John Deighton, Caroline M. Henderson, and Scott A. Neslin, "The Effects of Advertising on Brand Switching and Repeat Purchasing," *Journal of Marketing Research* 31 (February 1994), 28–43.
22. *The Value Side of Productivity: A Key to Competitive Survival in the 1990s* (New York: American Association of Advertising Agencies, 1989), 12.
23. Sridhar Moorthy and Hao Zhao, "Advertising Spending and Perceived Quality," *Marketing Letters* 11 (August 2000), 221–234.
24. *The Value Side of Productivity,* 13–15. See also, Larry Light and Richard Morgan, *The Fourth Wave: Brand Loyalty Marketing* (New York: Coalition for Brand Equity, American Association of Advertising Agencies, 1994), 25.
25. Jim Spaeth, "Lost Lessons of Brand Power," *Advertising Age,* July 14, 2003, 16.
26. Leigh McAlister, Raji Srinivasan, and MinChung Kim, "Advertising, Research and Development, and Systematic Risk of the Firm," *Journal of Marketing* 71 (January 2007), 35–48.
27. The synergism between advertising and personal selling does not always equate to a one-way flow from advertising to personal selling. In fact, one study has demonstrated a reverse situation, in which personal sales calls sometimes pave the way for advertising. See William R. Swinyard and Michael L. Ray, "Advertising-Selling Interactions: An Attribution Theory Experiment," *Journal of Marketing Research* 14 (November 1977), 509–516.
28. Albert C. Bemmaor and Dominique Mouchoux, "Measuring the Short-Term Effect of In-Store Promotion and Retail Advertising on Brand Sales: A Factorial Experiment," *Journal of Marketing Research* 28 (May 1991), 202–214.
29. Mukund S. Kulkarni, Premal P. Vora, and Terence A. Brown, "Firing Advertising Agencies," *Journal of Advertising* 32 (Fall 2003), 77–86.
30. Kate Maddox, "It's So Good To Be Understood," *BtoB,* January 15, 2007, 25.
31. The 15 percent rate was for advertisements placed in newspapers and magazines, and on television and radio. The discount paid to advertising agencies for outdoor advertising has historically been slightly higher at 16.67 percent.
32. A theoretical treatment of outcome-based compensation programs is provided by Deborah F. Spake, Giles D'Souza, Tammy Neal Crutchfield, and Robert M. Morgan, "Advertising Agency Compensation: An

Agency Theory Explanation," *Journal of Advertising* 28 (Fall 1999), 53–72.

33. John Sinisi, "Love: EDLP Equals Ad Investment," *Brandweek*, November 16, 1992, 2.
34. Raj Sethuraman and Gerard J. Tellis, "An Analysis of the Tradeoff between Advertising and Price Discounting," *Journal of Marketing Research* 28 (May 1991), 160–174. A recent study reveals that the average price elasticity based on an analysis of over 1,800 elasticity coefficients is even larger than previously thought. In fact, compared to Sethuraman and Tellis's estimated price elasticity of –1.61, this more complete and recent study yielded a mean price elasticity coefficient of –2.62. See Tammo H. A. Bijmolt, Harald J. van Heerde, and Rik G. M. Pieters, "New Empirical Generalizations on the Determinants of Price Elasticity," *Journal of Marketing Research* 42 (May 2005), 141–156.
35. Adapted from Sethuraman and Tellis ibid., especially Figure 1, p. 163, and the surrounding discussion.
36. See ibid., p. 164.
37. This formulation is based on an Internet posting by Gerard Tellis on ELMAR-AMA, June 4, 2003, http://elmar.ama.org.

8

Effective and Creative Advertising Messages

Most people would agree that TV commercials are generally of average quality, not especially bad or good. Some commercials, although relatively few, are so dreadful that we are immediately repulsed. At the opposite end of the ad-quality distribution, are a small number of exceptionally good commercials. One such commercial, for Apple's Macintosh computer, aired on a single occasion 25 years ago. Many advertising pundits consider it to be the best advertising execution of all time.

Apple Computers had just developed the world's most user-friendly computer and needed breakthrough advertising to introduce its new Macintosh brand, which was a revolution in computing technology. Steve Jobs, the co-founder of Apple, who was only 29 at the time of the Macintosh introduction, instructed his advertising agency, Chiat/Day, to create an explosive television commercial that would portray the Macintosh as a truly revolutionary machine. The creative people at Chiat/Day faced a challenging task, especially since Macintosh's main competitor was the powerful and much larger "Big Blue" (IBM). (In 1984, Dell, Hewlett-Packard, and other personal computer brands were nonexistent. It was only Apple versus IBM in the personal computer business, and IBM was the well-established leader known for its corporate computers.) However, Chiat/Day produced a commercial in which IBM was obliquely caricatured as the much-despised and feared institution reminiscent of the Big Brother theme in George Orwell's book *1984.* (In the book, political power is controlled by Big Brother, and individual dignity and freedom are superseded by political conformity.) The one-minute commercial created in this context, dubbed "1984," was run during the Super Bowl XVIII on January 22, 1984, and was never repeated on commercial television. This was not because it was ineffective; to the contrary, its incredible word-of-mouth-producing impact negated the need for repeat showings.

> *The commercial . . . opens on a room of zombie-like citizens staring at a huge screen where Big Brother is spewing a relentless cant about "information purification . . . unprincipled dissemination of facts" and "unification of thought."*
>
> *Against this ominous backdrop, a woman in athletic wear [a white jersey top and bright red running shorts, which was the only primary color in the commercial] runs in and hurls a sledgehammer into the screen, causing a cataclysmic explosion that shatters Big Brother. Then the message flashes on the TV screen: "On January 24th, Apple Computer will introduce Macintosh. And you'll see why 1984 won't be like '1984.'"*[1]

This remarkable advertising is considered by some to be the greatest TV commercial ever made.[2] It grabbed attention; it broke through the clutter of the many commercials aired during the Super Bowl; it was memorable;

it was discussed by millions of people; and, ultimately, it played an instrumental role in selling truckloads of Macintosh computers. Moreover, it created a unique image for the Mac (short for Macintosh) as described adroitly by one observer.

> *The Mac is female. Conversely, IBM must be male. IBM is not just male, it is Big Brother male. And Apple is not just female, but New Female. She is strong, athletic, independent, and, most important, liberated. After all, that's what the young athlete is all about. She is, in terms of the 1980s, empowerment and freedom.*[3]

Chapter Objectives

After reading this chapter you should be able to:

1. Appreciate the factors that promote effective, creative, and "sticky" advertising.
2. Describe the features of a creative brief.
3. Explain alternative creative styles of advertising messages.
4. Understand the concept of means-end chains and their role in advertising strategy.
5. Appreciate the MECCAS model and its role in guiding message formulation.
6. Recognize the role of corporate image and issue advertising.

>>Marcom Insight:

Perhaps the Greatest TV Commercial of All Time

Introduction

Advertisers in most product categories, including B2B as well as B2C, generally confront an advertising context where audiences are continually bombarded by advertisements. This state of affairs, referred to as advertising *clutter,* means that ad messages must be sufficiently creative to gain the receiver's attention and accomplish even more ambitious goals such as enhancing brand images and motivating prospects to purchase advertised products. The present chapter, which is the first of two to examine the message aspect of advertising, surveys questions such as these: What is advertising creativity? What makes a good advertising message? What is required for an advertisement to have lasting impact? What are the different types of creative styles, and when and why is each used? How can understanding consumer values lead to the production of effective advertisements?

This chapter first addresses the matter of what makes advertising effective and the related subject of creative advertising. A second section describes various forms of creative approaches that are widely used by advertising practitioners. A following topic is the concept of means-end chains as a mechanism for bridging the advertiser's creative process with the values that drive consumers' product and brand choices. Finally, the discussion moves away from brand-oriented advertising and examines corporate image and issue advertising.

Creating Effective Advertising

Having in the previous chapter provided an overview of advertising agencies, the creators of advertisements, we turn now to the issue of how the advertising agency and client work together to develop effective advertising campaigns. No simple answer is possible, but toward this end we first must attempt to understand the meaning of *effective advertising.* It is easy, in one sense, to define effective advertising: Advertising is effective if it accomplishes the advertiser's objectives. This perspective defines effectiveness from the *output side,* or in terms of what it accomplishes. It is much more difficult to define effective advertising from an *input perspective,* or in terms of the composition of the advertisement itself. There are many viewpoints on this issue. For example, a practitioner of direct-mail advertising probably has a different opinion about what constitutes effective advertising than would Steve Hayden, the inspirational source behind the "1984" Macintosh commercial that was described in the chapter-opening *Marcom Insight* vignette.

Although it is impractical to provide a singular, all-purpose definition of what constitutes effective advertising, it is possible to talk about general characteristics.[4] At a minimum, effective advertising satisfies the following considerations:

1. *It extends from sound marketing strategy.* Advertising can be effective only if it is compatible with other elements of an integrated and well-orchestrated marcom strategy. As established in Chapter 1, all marcom tools must be integrated and "speak" with a single voice.
2. *Effective advertising takes the consumer's view.* Advertising must be stated in a way that relates to the consumer's—rather than the marketer's—needs, wants, and values. In short, effective advertising *connects* with the target audience by reflecting keen insight into what consumers are looking for when making brand-selection decisions in specific product categories. An advertising practitioner who specializes in creative thinking has stated the issue in these terms: "Consumers don't want to be bombarded with ads—they want to be inspired by ideas that will change their lives. Ads create

transactions. Ideas create transformations. Ads reflect our culture, ideas imagine our future."[5]

3. *It finds a unique way to break through the clutter.* Advertisers continually compete for the consumer's attention. Gaining attention is no small task considering the massive number of print advertisements, broadcast commercials, Internet ads, and other sources of information consumers see daily. Indeed, the situation in television advertising has been characterized as "audiovisual wallpaper"—a sarcastic implication that consumers pay about as much attention to commercials as they do to the detail in their wallpaper after seeing it for years.[6]
4. *Effective advertising never promises more than it can deliver.* This point speaks for itself, both with respect to ethics and in terms of smart business sense. Consumers learn when they have been deceived and will resent the advertiser. Effective advertising promises no more than the advertised product is capable of delivering.
5. *It prevents the creative idea from overwhelming the strategy.* The purpose of advertising is to inform, inspire, and ultimately sell products; the purpose is not to be creative merely for the sake of being clever. It is claimed, although perhaps unfairly, that advertising agencies place excessive emphasis on winning awards at the various annual ceremonies the ad industry conducts—for example, the Cannes Lions International Advertising Festival in France, the London International Advertising Awards, and the Clio Awards in the United States.

   Effective advertising is creative with a purpose. That is, upon determining the specific tasks, or objectives (see previous chapter), that an advertising campaign must accomplish, it is the challenge of the advertising team—the advertising agency along with the client's brand management group—to develop advertising executions that connect with the target audience, cut through the clutter, and position the brand optimally in view of the brand's strengths relative to competitive brands. The following section discusses what it means to be creative.

Creativity: The CAN Elements

Effective advertising is usually *creative.* But what is creativity? Unfortunately, there is no simple answer to this elusive aspect of advertising.[7] There is some agreement, however, that creative ads share three common features: connectedness, appropriateness, and novelty (CAN).[8]

Connectedness

Connectedness addresses whether an advertisement reflects *empathy* with the target audience's basic needs and wants as they relate to making a brand-choice decision in a product category. An advertisement is said to be connected if it reflects an understanding of target audience members' motivations. For example, if most members of a target audience are concerned about social status when buying a new automobile, then an advertisement that fails to reflect the role of social status is unconnected with consumers. In contrast, if competitive price and speed of delivery are paramount to corporate purchasing agents, then ads that reflect these motivations *are* connected.

Connected ads are, in short, *relevant* to the brand's target audience—they contain information and reflect emotions that are congenial with the type of information consumers are seeking or the emotions they are experiencing when forming impressions of brands and making brand-selection decisions. To be considered creative, an advertisement must first and foremost create a bond, a connection with the target audience.

Appropriateness

Whereas connectedness requires that an advertisement provide information or create feelings that resonate with the target audience's motivations, the element of appropriateness evaluates creativity from the standpoint of the advertising message. In this sense, **appropriateness** means that an advertisement must provide information that is pertinent to the advertised brand relative to other brands in the product category. In terms of the detailed discussion of positioning (Chapter 5), an advertisement is appropriate to the extent that the message is on target for delivering the brand's positioning strategy and capturing the brand's relative strengths and weaknesses vis-à-vis competitive brands. Appropriate ads also are coherent in the sense that all message elements work in concert to deliver a singular, unambiguous message.

Novelty

Novel ads are unique, fresh, and unexpected. They differ from consumers' expectations of a typical ad for a brand in a particular product category. Novelty draws consumers' attention to an ad so that they engage in more effortful information processing, such as attempting to comprehend the meaning of the advertised brand. Unoriginal advertising is unable to break through the competitive clutter and grab the consumer's attention.

Novelty is the element most often associated with advertising creativity, but it is important to understand that novelty is merely one component of advertising creativity. In an entirely different context but nonetheless applicable to advertising, jazz musician Charlie Mingus captured this same idea when stating, "Creativity is more than just being different. Anybody can play weird, that's easy. What's hard is to be as simple as Bach. Making the simple complicated is commonplace, making the complicated simple, awesomely simple, that's creativity."[9]

Advertising agencies sometimes develop ads that are unique, different, unexpected, and weird. However, such ads are not creative simply by being unusual, odd, or bizarre. To be considered truly creative, ads must also resonate positively with the target audience (the element of connectedness) and present information or reflect feelings that echo the brand's positioning strategy (the element of appropriateness). Novel advertisements can be considered creative only if they also are connected and appropriate. Such ads CAN be effective!

Getting Messages to "Stick"

Beyond being creative, advertisers want their advertising to "stick." **Sticky ads** are ads for which the audience comprehends the advertiser's intended message; they are remembered, and they change the target audience's brand-related opinions or behavior.[10] Such ads have *lasting impact:* they stick.

Consider the following illustration of a sticky message. This message is an urban legend (more on this in Chapter 18), and although it is patently *false* it nonetheless has been widely circulated and accepted as true by many people. The short version of this urban legend is that thieves at shopping malls rob women in restrooms and leave them naked so the thieves can beat a hasty retreat without being apprehended. A more complete version of the legend is that a male thief enters a women's restroom and remains concealed in a stall until only one woman is in the room. At that point he stands on a toilet; points a handgun into the next stall; demands the woman's valuables; orders the woman to remove her clothes, place them in a bag, and slip them into his stall. He then departs the scene, places an out-of-order sign on the restroom door, and makes his retreat. The thief has plenty of time to get away, according to the legend, because naked women are too embarrassed to leave the restroom and expose themselves to others.[11]

I think most readers would agree that this is a "sticky" message. It is highly memorable, very concrete, frightening, somewhat believable, and worthy of passing along to others so as to caution them to be careful when using shopping mall restrooms. But beyond this one illustration, what are the features of sticky messages in general? We now describe six common features of messages that tend to stick—that is, have relatively lasting impact. Although the naked-woman illustration applies to a unique form of message, namely an urban legend, the following six features are applicable to any type of message, including advertisements.[12]

Simplicity

Sticky advertisements are both *simple* and *profound.* Just as the naked-woman legend is simple and profound, an advertisement can be said to be simple when it represents the brand's core idea or key positioning statement, i.e., the advertising execution is stripped to its critical essence and captures the key element that needs to be communicated. Simple advertisements are *appropriate* in the sense of the term's CAN elements of creativity usage. Advertisements that violate the simplicity feature fail to capture the brand's essence—its positioning strategy—or present excessive information that dilutes the message of what precisely is the brand's essence.

Unexpectedness

Sticky advertisements generate interest and curiosity when they deviate from audience members' expectations. In Chapter 5 we pointed out that it is difficult for marketing communicators to capture consumers' attention because the marketplace is cluttered with commercial messages and communicators must overcome consumers' natural tendency to attend selectively only those messages that are relevant to their goals. Note the similarity of unexpectedness to the *novelty* element in the list of creative CAN features. Sticky messages also are creative.

The naked-woman legend satisfies the unexpected criterion insofar as we typically think of mall restrooms as safe and free of thugs who force women to disrobe. This unexpectedness, or novelty of the message, captures attention, is easily comprehended, and virtually demands that the recipient pass along the message to others—this is why myths become urban legends. Advertisements, too, must show evidence of unexpectedness if they are to stand much chance of sticking with audience members. Advertisers often use wacky techniques to capture the audience's attention, such as, for example, advertisements for Wendy's restaurants showing men with bright red pigtails, which, of course, is the hairstyle worn by little Wendy (the daughter of Wendy's founder and the namesake for the fast-food chain).

Concreteness

Sticky ideas possess concrete images as compared to abstract representations. For example, the image of a thief forcing a woman to disrobe and hand over her valuables is highly concrete, and thus sticky. As will be discussed in further detail in Chapter 9, advertisers "concretize" their messages to facilitate both consumer learning and retrieval of brand information. *Concretizing* is based on the straightforward idea that it is easier for people to remember and retrieve tangible rather than abstract information. Claims about a brand are more concrete (versus abstract) when they are made perceptible and vivid. Concretizing is accomplished by using tangible, substantive (i.e., concrete) words and demonstrations. For example, a marketer of pickup trucks demonstrates concreteness when showing the truck lugging a huge load. Comparatively, a claim that the truck is "tough" would be abstract without the support of a demonstration.

Let's consider one additional illustration of concreteness. As many readers know, there is a serious, drug-resistant infection that results when scratches and wounds come into contact with staphylococcus (staph) bacteria. This is a matter of considerable concern to college students and their parents, especially given that students are exposed to environments—gyms, locker rooms, dorm restrooms, etc.—where staph bacteria are widespread. This infection is called Methicillin-resistant Staphylococcus aureus (MRSA). This mention of the name makes MRSA seem more familiar than it may have been prior to your reading this paragraph, but the fact is that most people have great difficulty remembering the initials let alone the full name. Alternatively, this serious infection sometimes is referred to as the "Superbug"—i.e., a drug-resistant organism. Ask yourself, which image is more concrete: MRSA or Superbug? Because your likely response is the latter, you now have an enhanced appreciation of why concrete ideas (Superbug) are stickier than abstract ones (MRSA).

Credibility

Sticky advertisements are *believable*. They have a sense of authority and provide reasons why they should be accepted as fact. For example, the naked-woman urban legend was disseminated on the Internet by attributing it to an AP (Associated Press) News Wire story. Although entirely untrue, this respected news source possesses credibility and thus made the message stickier than if, say, the message had been attributed to an unknown, small-town newspaper. Chapter 9 will discuss in greater detail the nature and importance of credibility when describing the role of celebrity endorsers. It suffices for now to say that credible messages stick with us because we accept them as fact rather than discount them as bogus.

Emotionality

People care about ideas that generate emotions and tap into feelings. For example, the urban legend about shopping mall thievery is sticky because it taps into the emotion of *fear*—the fear emotion is common to many urban legends because it is a particularly profound emotion. In a similar vein, advertisers can get people to care about their brands by appealing to emotions that are relevant to the product category in which the advertised brand competes. The idea of appealing to emotions is fleshed out in a subsequent section of this chapter when the emotional creative strategy is discussed and illustrated.

Storytelling

The sixth element of sticky messages is telling stories. By definition, stories have plots, characters, and settings—all features of which are contained in the naked-woman-in-a-restroom urban legend story. Advertisers also occasionally tell stories in order to capture the key elements of their brands. An especially good example of this is the long-running ad campaign for Subway restaurants based on the real-life character named Jared.[13] Subway's advertising agency has used Jared's story as the basis for its campaign touting that Subway sandwiches can promote weight loss. At one point in his life, Jared weighed in excess of 400 pounds and had a 60-inch waist. Following a hospital visit after experiencing chest pains, his physician father warned him that he might not live past 35 unless he undertook a dramatic weight loss regimen. This got Jared's attention, and he proceeded to develop his own, all-Subway diet consisting of eating a foot-long veggie sub for lunch and a six-inch turkey sub for dinner. This diet along with increased exercise resulted in Jared's losing nearly 250 pounds. To make a long story short, the Subway chain eventually learned of Jared's personal diet and built an advertising campaign around his story. This story is inspiring, and it obviously has stuck with thousands of consumers who now believe that Subway sandwiches are healthier than the fare at other fast-food restaurants.

Stories embody most of the stickiness elements previously discussed: They often are simple and profound, generally are concrete, include unexpected and emotional elements, and often come across as highly credible. Jared's story reflects all of these characteristics.

To sum up, sticky messages are those that have lasting impact. The elements of sticky messages are Simplicity, Unexpectedness, Concreteness, Credibility, Emotionality, and Storytelling, or SUCCESs.[14] (Think of this last, unrelated, lower case "s" as standing for *stickiness;* of course, the first six capitalized letters stand for the message characteristics responsible for sticky advertisements.) The SUCCESs acronym is an apt mnemonic for capturing the elements that are required for creating advertising messages that stick with consumers.

In closing this section, note that sticky advertisements need not necessarily satisfy all six SUCCESs elements. Most advertisements do not, in fact. The use of stories, for example, is relatively rare in advertising, and most advertisements make no special effort to establish credibility other than relying on the reputation of the advertiser. However, everything else held constant, it generally can be assumed that the more SUCCESs elements contained in an advertisement, the greater the likelihood that the message will stick with consumers.

Illustrations of Creative and Sticky Advertising Executions

In addition to the highly creative (and effective!) advertisement presented in the chapter opening *Marcom Insight* insert, the following examples illustrate individual advertisements and advertising campaigns that, in the author's opinion, register high marks on the CAN facets of creativity and the SUCCESs elements of stickiness.

Miss Clairol: "Does She . . . or Doesn't She?"

Imagine yourself employed as a copywriter in a New York advertising agency in 1955. You have just been assigned creative responsibility for a product that heretofore (as of 1955) had not been nationally marketed or advertised. The product: hair coloring. The brand: Miss Clairol. Your task: devise a creative strategy that will convince millions of American women to purchase Miss Clairol hair coloring—at the time called Hair Color Bath. This challenge occurred, by the way, in a cultural context where it was considered patently inappropriate for respectable women to smoke in public, wear long pants, or color their hair.

The person actually assigned this task was Shirley Polykoff, a copywriter for the Foote, Cone & Belding agency. At the time of the Miss Clairol campaign, there was no hair-coloring business. Women were even ashamed to color their own hair due to social disapproval and because at-home hair color often turned out looking unnatural. A product that provided a natural look stood a strong chance of being accepted, but women would have to be convinced that an advertised hair-coloring product would, in fact, give them that highly desired natural look.

Shirley Polykoff explains the background of the famous advertising line that convinced women Miss Clairol would produce a natural look.

> *In 1933, just before I was married, my husband had taken me to meet the woman who would become my mother-in-law. When we got in the car after dinner, I asked him, "How'd I do? Did your mother like me?" and he told me his mother had said, "She paints her hair, doesn't she?" He asked me, "Well, do you?" It became a joke between my husband and me; anytime we saw someone who was stunning or attractive we'd say, "Does she, or doesn't she?" Twenty years later [at the time she was working on the Miss Clairol account], I was walking down*

Park Avenue talking out loud to myself, because I have to hear what I write. The phrase came into my mind again. Suddenly, I realized, "That's it. That's the campaign." I knew that [a competitive advertising agency] couldn't find anything better. I knew that immediately. When you're young, you're very sure about everything.[15]

The advertising line "Does she . . . or doesn't she?" actually was followed with the tagline "Hair color so natural only her hairdresser knows for sure!" The headline grabbed the reader's attention, whereas the tagline promised a conclusive benefit: The product works so well that only an expert would recognize that her hair color was not her actual color. This brilliant advertising persuaded millions of American women to become product users and led to dramatically increased sales of Miss Clairol.[16]

In terms of the six stickiness elements, this campaign performs extremely well with respect to at least five of these features: simplicity, concreteness, credibility, emotionality, and storytelling.

Absolut Vodka

Imported brands of vodka were virtually nonexistent in the United States until the early 1980s. Three brands (Stolichnaya from Russia, Finlandia from Finland, and Wybrowa from Poland) made up less than 1 percent of the total U.S. vodka market. Absolut vodka from Sweden—a country previously not associated with vodka—was introduced to the United States in 1980. In addition to having a great name (suggesting the unequivocally best, or *absolute,* vodka), the brand's most distinguishing feature was a unique bottle—crystal clear with an interesting shape.

With a small budget and the capability of advertising only in print media (broadcast advertising of beer, wine, and distilled spirits was not permitted), the brand's advertising agency, TBWA, set about the task of rapidly building brand awareness. The agency's brilliant idea was simply to feature a full-page shot of the bottle with a two-word headline: The first word would always be the brand name, Absolut, used as an adjective to modify a second word that (1) described the brand (e.g., Absolut Perfection); (2) characterized its consumer (e.g., Absolut Sophisticate); or (3) associated the brand with positive places, people, or events (e.g., Absolut Barcelona). Literally hundreds of print ads were executed over the next quarter century, and Absolut rose to the top in the vodka industry, only to be knocked off its perch by the early 2000s when luxury brands such as Grey Goose, Ketel One, and many others were introduced. (A Web site with illustrations of Absolut's print ads is available at http://www.absolutad.com.) The campaign was discontinued in 2007 and replaced with another campaign titled "In an Absolut World." The rationale for discontinuing the earlier, famous campaign is presented in the *Global Focus* insert.

This campaign performs especially well on the simplicity aspect of the SUCCESs model.

The Aflac Duck

Until the early 2000s, a supplementary insurance company named the American Family Life Assurance Company (Aflac) was anything but a household name. In fact, that was the problem: Despite having invested heavily in advertising for a number of years, most consumers had never heard the name Aflac or little remembered it. Aflac's chief executive officer and chairperson knew that a creative advertising campaign was needed to generate the necessary level of *brand awareness.* Hired for this purpose was, at the time, a little known ad agency—the Kaplan Thaler Group. The creative team assigned to the project generated many

global focus

Why Dump an Extraordinarily Successful Ad Campaign?

Absolut's bottle-oriented print advertising campaign included some 1,500 print executions and extended over 25 years, with one brilliant ad followed by another. The campaign was extremely effective for a number of years, but the vodka industry changed, and by the 1990s there were literally dozens of premium vodka brands that competed with Absolut. Absolut no longer was *the* superpremium brand, and the advertising simply wore out—or perhaps, alternatively, the people in charge of the advertising grew tired of creating one "Absolut This" ad followed by the next "Absolut That" ad. Also, research conducted in nine countries indicated that consumers had become less involved with the bottle campaign and were no longer inspired by it.

A new campaign titled "In an Absolut World" was introduced in 2007 to replace the famous bottle campaign. The new campaign presents images of what it would be like to live in an ideal, Absolut world. In one execution, for example, pregnant men are portrayed alongside their elated wives. In another execution, police and protesters are shown "fighting"—not with guns and clubs, but with pillows! The message conveyed is that Absolut is the ideal brand of vodka for this ideal world. Whereas the original bottle campaign was restricted to print advertising, this new campaign is appropriate for various media, including television and the Internet.

SOURCES: Adapted from Jeremy Mullman, "Why Absolut Said Bye-Bye to the Bottle," *Advertising Age,* May 28, 2007, 3, 28; Keith McArthur, "Absolut Vodka Maker Replaces Iconic Ad Campaign," http://great-ads.blogspot.com/2007/04/absolut-vodka-maker-replaces-iconic-ad.html (accessed January 2, 2008).

ideas for a campaign, but after weeks of creative effort none passed the key test of whether consumers would remember the company for whom the advertising was undertaken.

Just days before the deadline, a member of the creative team took a long walk during his lunch break and started voicing out loud the name "Aflac." After repeating the name over and over, it dawned on him that he sounded like a quacking duck. With great excitement he returned to his office and, along with his creative teammate, quickly wrote the first spot for an Aflac commercial featuring the now-famous "spokesduck." This creative insight initiated one of advertising's most heralded ad campaigns debuting on December 31, 1999 in CNN's Millenium Special and subsequently running on every major college football game. Incorporated seamlessly into dialogue about supplemental insurance in each ad execution, the unnoticed duck exclaimed, "Aflac!!" in response to questions such as "What is supplemental insurance? What is it called?" The ad campaign registered incredible results from its inception and increased Aflac's brand identity from 10 percent to more than 90 percent![17] In 2006, Aflac kicked off a successful campaign geared at small businesses, and in 2008, the company unveiled new business-to-business ads designed to reach companies of all sizes and complement the ongoing consumer commercials. Like before, the iconic duck is found in new situations, each time showing a business how it can benefit with Aflac.

Today, the Aflac Duck continues to score with consumers and businesses. With research showing that as long as the duck continues to find himself in the most unlikely scenarios, he will continue to resonate with consumers and enhance Aflacs image.[18] This campaign performs extremely well with respect to creativity, and with at least two of the stickiness elements: simplicity and concreteness.

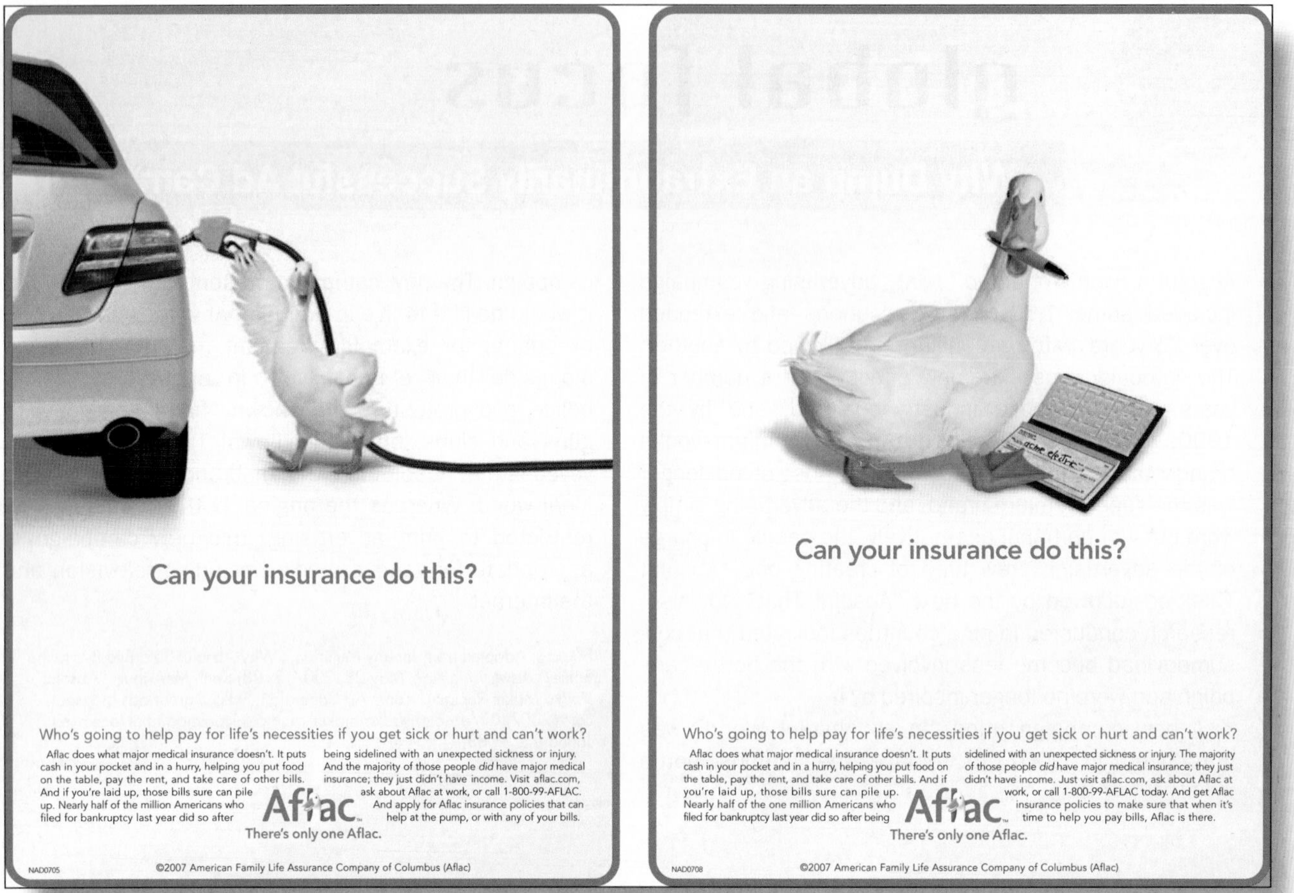

© Courtesy of Aflac

Figure 8.1

Illustrations of the Aflac Advertising Campaign with the "Spokesduck."

Nike Shoes

Sports shoe and apparel company, Nike, and its advertising agency, Wieden + Kennedy, are known for their original and often captivating advertising. This was typified in 2004 when Wieden + Kennedy created an absorbing campaign for Nike. Professional athletes were shown in various executions playing hockey, volleyball, baseball, bowling, boxing, and so on. You might be wondering, What's the big deal? Hundreds of commercials for sporting goods have done the same thing. The brilliance in these ads was the nifty juxtaposition of famous athletes with sports other than those for which they are known. For example, tennis player Andre Agassi was portrayed playing baseball; now-disgraced quarterback Michael Vick (of pit-bull fighting shame) was shown as a hockey player par excellence; seven-time Tour de France winner Lance Armstrong was portrayed as an accomplished boxer; tennis player Serena Williams was shown making a vicious serve in volleyball; and baseball pitcher Randy Johnson looked like a professional bowler. As with other Nike commercials, this campaign made the nuanced point that Nike, like the famous athletes who endorse its products, is somehow special and out of the ordinary.[19]

These advertisements score well on several SUCCESs elements: simplicity, unexpectedness, concreteness, and emotionality.

Honda U.K.

A two-minute TV commercial introduced in the United Kingdom celebrated the remarkable engineering that goes into an automobile, the Honda Accord in particular. The commercial, titled "Cog," itself represented a mechanical wonder and supposedly required over 600 takes before it was perfected. Later downloaded to the Internet, the commercial illustrated through a painstaking sequence of events various automobile parts being synchronized in a chain of events reminiscent of watching a kinetic sculpture where a ball rolls down a slide, drops in a tube, spins onto a shelf, flips into a basket, and eventually arrives at the bottom. The advertisement was intended to demonstrate to consumers all the parts and technological marvels that go into making a Honda Accord. Garrison Keillor, the emcee of the American radio program *Prairie Home Companion,* provided the off-screen voice that served to make sense of the intricate visual action in the commercial when simply intoning, "Isn't it nice when things just work?" The "Cog" commercial is clearly the stuff of advertising legend. (To view the commercial, google Cog and Honda and you'll be able to locate the commercial online.)

Simplicity, unexpectedness, and concreteness are the three SUCCESs elements that best represent this advertisement.

The Apple iPod and Silhouetted Images

With iPod's ability to hold thousands of songs and images, iPod owners can listen to their favorite tunes or view images whenever and wherever they choose. Although the product is technologically advanced, TV commercials for the iPod were simple in design yet highly creative. Every execution in the iPod campaign featured silhouetted figures against neon backgrounds holding iPods, listening and gyrating to music. The ad creativity is primarily in simplicity of design and differentiation from typical commercials where identifiable individuals (not silhouetted figures) are shown using products and conversing.

The iPod commercials score very favorably on the simplicity and unexpectedness elements.

Guinness Beer in Africa

Guinness beer, the famous brand from Ireland, is known throughout much of the world and has long been the preferred beverage among Irish consumers. But things have changed in recent years. Many younger Irish are not especially fond of Guinness, and sales volume in Ireland has declined due in large part to competitors' efforts to steal share through price discounting, and also to a swing in preference toward increased wine consumption. Confronted with this disturbing situation, the makers of Guinness increased advertising activity in other countries in order to grow the brand and offset declining sales at home. One growth area is Africa, where substantially more Guinness is now consumed than in Ireland!

One reason for the growing consumption of Guinness in Africa is the success of an advertising campaign built around a fictional international journalist named Michael Power. Ad agency Saatchi & Saatchi introduced the Power character in five-minute action-adventure ads. In advertisements running from 1999 to 2006, Power was portrayed in these ads as an action hero, overcoming obstacles through his inner strength, quick thinking, and perseverance rather than by brute force. In addition to his intellect, Power was stylish, physically fit, athletic, and friendly. He was often shown in advertisements enjoying a Guinness with his friends. In Africa, Michael Power and Guinness have images that are inextricably linked.[20]

These commercials score impressively on the concreteness, credibility, emotionality, and storytelling aspects of the SUCCESs framework.

Advertising Successes and Mistakes

The foregoing discussion has described general features of creative and "sticky" advertising and presented several illustrative campaigns. It will be useful at this point to provide a conceptual framework that identifies the conditions under

figure 8.2

Combination of Message Convincingness and Execution Quality

MESSAGE (VALUE PROPOSITION)	EXECUTION: Effective	EXECUTION: Ineffective
Convincing	SUCCESSFUL CAMPAIGNS	AGENCY MISTAKES
Unconvincing	MARKETING MISTAKES	COMPLETE DISASTERS

which advertising campaigns are likely to succeed or fail. Figure 8.2 offers such a framework by conceptualizing advertising's impact as extending from a combination of message convincingness and execution quality.[21]

An advertising message can be thought of as providing the reader, viewer, or listener with a *value proposition.* A **value proposition** is the essence of a message and the reward to the consumer for investing his or her time attending to an advertisement. The reward may come in the form of needed information about a brand or may simply represent an enjoyable experience, such as tens of thousands of people obtained when viewing the "Cog" commercial. Research indicates that starting with a strong selling proposition substantially increases the odds of creating effective advertisements.[22]

Although having a convincing message is a necessary condition for creating an effective advertisement, it is insufficient. As shown in Figure 8.2, the ad also must be executed effectively. Hence, advertising messages can be conceptualized in terms of a fourfold classification—(1) successful campaigns, (2) marketing mistakes, (3) agency mistakes, and (4) complete disasters—based on whether value propositions are convincing or unconvincing and whether agency executions of these propositions are effective or ineffective.

Successful Campaigns

Successful campaigns arise from a combination of having a message founded on a convincing value proposition and an effective (i.e., creative, sticky) execution. In short, successful campaigns communicate meaningful value propositions effectively. Both the brand management team (client side) and the creative team (agency side) have done their work well in this situation.

Marketing Mistakes

The advertising agency may come up with a creative execution, but this cannot make up for the absence of a convincing value proposition. *Marketing mistakes* result from brand management's failure to identify a meaningful value proposition that distinguishes the brand from competitive offerings. *A bad idea well executed is nonetheless a mistake.* An ad agency may be fired when a campaign does not meet expectations, but the fault in this case resides with brand management for failing to provide the ad agency with good raw material to work with. As the saying goes, you can't make a silk purse out of a sow's ear.

Agency Mistakes

This form of failed ad campaign is unsuccessful due to the ad agency's inability to design an effective execution, even though its brand management client has presented it with a value proposition that should have represented a convincing message. This situation, in short, represents a good idea that has been blown, defeat stolen from the jaws of victory.

Complete Disasters

Poor value propositions and mediocre executions are the stuff of advertising *disasters*. Responsibility for failure is evenly distributed between the brand management and creative teams. Disasters can be avoided by conducting research that pretests both the proposition and the creative strategy prior to printing or airing a final advertisement.

How can an agency or its client know in advance—that is, prior to printing or airing—whether an advertisement is likely to be successful? First, research that examines consumers' product-related needs, expectations, and past experiences should provide the brand manager with a good idea about the likely effectiveness of a particular value proposition. Many advertising agencies in the United Kingdom, the United States, and elsewhere include a position in their organizations called *account planning*. Although the job specifics vary somewhat from agency to agency, *account planners* represent the voice of the customer. Account planners interpret customer research, often of a qualitative nature, which becomes key input into creative advertising development.[23] Second, execution effectiveness can be judged by pretesting advertisements before actually initiating an advertising campaign. Chapter 10 will discuss in detail methods to assess message and execution effectiveness.

Constructing a Creative Brief

The work of copywriters and other creative advertising practitioners is directed by a framework known as a creative brief, which is a document designed to channel copywriters' and other creatives' efforts toward a solution that will serve the interests of the client. The term *brief* is used to mean that a client for an advertising project (such as a brand management team) is informing, or briefing, an advertising agency of the client's expectations for a proposed advertising campaign. A **creative brief** is an informal pact between client and agency that represents agreement on what an advertising campaign is intended to accomplish.

Although creative briefs vary in terms of their degree of specificity, most briefs would minimally include answers to the following questions:

Background

The initial question that must be addressed is: *What is the background to this job?* The answer requires a brief explanation regarding why the advertising agency is being asked to perform a certain advertising job. What is it that the client wishes to achieve with the campaign? For example, the purpose may be to launch a new brand, gain back lost sales from a competitor, or introduce a new version of an established product. Part of the background explanation would include analyses of the competitive environment and cultural dynamics related to the product category that could influence the brand's success potential.

Target Audience

Whom do we need to reach with the ad campaign? This is a precise description of the exemplary target market. With knowledge of the behaviorgraphic, psychographic, demographic, or geodemographic characteristics of the intended customer (see Chapter 4), creatives have a specific target at which to direct their efforts. This is as essential in advertising as it is in certain athletic events. For example, the late golf sage Harvey Penick offered the following advice to pupils trying to improve their golf games: "Once you address the golf ball, hitting it has got to be the most important thing in your life at that moment. Shut out all thoughts other than picking out a target and taking dead aim at it."[24] His point to golfers about taking "dead aim" is also applicable to advertising creatives: You can't hit a target unless you know where to aim!

Thoughts and Feelings

What do members of the target audience currently think and feel about our brand? Here is where research and account planning are needed as the foundation for the advertising job. The advice here is to perform research *prior* to developing creative advertisements. With the assistance of account planners in interpreting research results, ad creatives are then prepared to design research-based advertising that speaks to the target audience in terms of their known thoughts and feelings about the brand rather than relying on mere suppositions. Sure, effective ads can be created absent any formal research (recall the Aflac ad and how it came about); however, the odds of success are much improved if formal research precedes creative activity.

The people who write advertising copy and create visual imagery must summon their full talents to develop effective advertising. Creatives often complain that marketing research reports and other such directives excessively constrain their opportunities for full creative expression. Although creatives deserve empathy for their desire for unconstrained artistic expression, one cannot forget that advertising is a business with an obligation to sell products. Their ultimate purpose is to write advertising copy that affects consumers' expectations, attitudes, and eventually purchase behavior (sooner rather than later, it is hoped). Advertising creatives do not have the luxury to create for the mere sake of engaging in a creative pursuit.[25]

Objectives and Measures

What do we want the target audience to think or feel about the brand, and what measurable effects is the advertising designed to accomplish? This guideline simply reminds everyone what the client wants the advertising to accomplish. It calls for a short statement about the crucial feelings or thoughts that the advertisement should evoke in its intended audience. For example, the ad might be designed to move the audience emotionally, to make them feel deserving of a better lifestyle, or to get them to feel anxious about a currently unsafe course of behavior. Is there a current perception that needs to be changed? For example, if a large number of consumers in the target market consider the brand overpriced, how can we change that perception and convince them that the brand actually is a good value due to its superior quality? Knowing this, creatives can then design appropriate advertisements to achieve that objective. Given multiple objectives, it is desirable to prioritize them from most to least important and to focus on the most important objective.

Also, although not a typical practice in the ad industry when constructing creative briefs, it is helpful to indicate not only what objectives are to be accomplished but also how achievement of these objectives will be measured. By specifying measures in advance, client and agency are on the proverbial same page when follow-up research is performed to assess whether the advertising campaign has actually accomplished what it was designed to do.[26]

Behavioral Outcome

What do we want the target audience to do? Beyond thoughts and feelings, this guideline focuses on the specific *action* that the advertising campaign is designed to motivate in the target audience. The advertising might be intended to get prospects to request further information, to go online to participate in a sweepstake or contest, to contact a salesperson, or to go to a retail outlet within the next week to take advantage of a limited-time sales opportunity.

Positioning

What is the brand positioning? Copywriters are reminded that their creative work must reflect the brand's positioning statement. The brand management team must clearly articulate the brand's meaning, or what it is to stand for in the audience's collective mind. In this context, the creative brief might suggest to the advertising agency a slogan the client wants to use for the brand or request ideas from the agency for alternative slogans that might be used. The *IMC Focus* presents a number of well-known ad slogans and also provides information about consumers' ability to identify brand slogans correctly.

Message and Medium

What general message is to be created, and what medium is most appropriate for reaching the target audience? This guideline identifies the most differentiating and motivating message about the brand that can be delivered to the target audience. It should focus on brand benefits rather than product features. Because credibility and believability are key to getting the audience to accept the message proposition, this section of the creative brief supports the proposition with evidence about product features that back up the claimed benefits. Copywriters are required to work within this context but still have the freedom to be creative. With respect to the appropriate medium, it is the client's job in concert with the ad agency to identify what medium (or media) is (are) best for reaching the target audience. Creatives are told exactly what they are being asked to produce—perhaps a series of TV commercials along with supporting magazine ads.

Strategy

What is the strategy? The response to this question articulates a specific advertising strategy to accomplish the job. This strategy statement gives copywriters an understanding of how their creative work must fit into an overall marcom strategy that includes elements other than advertising. For example, the strategy statement may indicate that in addition to advertising, a new brand will be launched with a series of major events, an aggressive buzz-building campaign, and online promotions to encourage consumer trial.

Nitty-Gritty Details

When and how much? This section of a creative brief identifies the *deadline* for when the advertising job is to be presented to the client for approval and specifies the *budget* for production of creative deliverables such as finished TV commercials.

In sum, the creative brief is a document prepared by a brand management team (the client) perhaps working with an advertising agency's account executive and is intended to inspire creatives and channel their efforts. A truly valuable creative brief requires that the document be developed with a full understanding of the client's advertising needs. It also necessitates the acquisition of market research data that inform the agency about the competitive environment and about consumers' current perceptions of the to-be-advertised brand and its competition.

IMC >> i.m.c. focus

How Well Do You Know Advertising Slogans?

Slogans, or taglines, have always played an important role in advertising. Effective slogans encapsulate a brand's key positioning and value proposition and provide consumers with a memory tag for distinguishing one brand from another. Some slogans have been used with success for decades, as evidenced in the following list **(A)** of what some would regard as the top slogans of modern marketing. See if you can match the slogan with its company. (Answers are provided at the bottom.)

These famous slogans aside, it appears that current advertising slogans may be less effective, certainly less memorable, than are these famous slogans. A recent survey of 500 people determined that only 5 percent could correctly identify even half of the slogans in use by 29 advertisers. Only 3 of 29 slogans were correctly identified by more than 50 percent of the surveyed respondents. The following table **(B)** presents the slogans, the companies or brands using the slogans, and the percentages of correct identification.

(A)

Slogan		Company	
1. "A diamond is forever."	1. "Good to the last drop."	A. Maxwell House (1915)*	F. Morton Salt (1911)
2. "Just do it."	2. "Breakfast of Champions."	B. Wheaties (1935)	G. Clairol (1964)
3. "The pause that refreshes."	3. "Does she . . . or doesn't she?"	C. Wendy's (1984)	H. Coca-Cola (1929)
4. "Tastes great, less filling."	4. "When it rains it pours."	D. De Beers (1950)	I. Avis (1962)
5. "We try harder."	5. "Where's the beef?"	E. Miller Lite (1974)	J. Nike (1988)

*Slogan's date of inception

(B)

Company or Brand	Slogan	Percentage Correct Identification	Company or Brand	Slogan	Percentage Correct Identification
Allstate	"You're in good hands."	87%	Coca-Cola	"Real."	5
State Farm	"Like a good neighbor."	70	Dr Pepper	"Be you."	5
Wal-Mart	"Always low price. Always."	67	General Electric	"Imagination at work."	5
General Electric	"We bring good things to life."	39	Heineken	"it's all about the beer."	4
Sprite	"Obey your thirst."	35	Michelob Ultra	"Lose the carbs. Not the taste."	4
Taco Bell	"Think outside the bun."	34	Sears	"Good life. Great price."	4
McDonald's	"I'm loving it."	33	Chrysler	"Inspiration comes standard."	3
Capital One	"What's in your wallet?"	27	Corona	"Miles away from ordinary."	3
Gatorade	"Is it in you?"	19	Arby's	"What are you eating today?"	2
Chevrolet	"An American revolution."	17	Miller	"Good call."	1
J.C. Penney	"It's all inside."	15	Buick	"The sprit of American style."	1
Nissan	"Shift."	12	Kmart	"Right here, right now."	1
Toyota	"Get the feeling."	11	Staples	"That was easy."	0
Budweiser	"True."	10	Wendy's	"It's better here."	0
Sierra Mist	"Yeah, it's kinda like that."	6			

SOURCES: The table of matching slogans is from Deborah L. Vence, "The Test of Time," *Marketing News,* December 15, 2004, 8–9. The table with 29 brand slogans is from Becky Ebenkamp, "Slogans' Heroes, Zeroes," *Brandweek,* October 25, 2004, 17.

(A) Answers: 1, D; 2, J; 3, H; 4, E; 5, I; 6, A; 7, B; 8, G; 9, F; 10, C.

Alternative Styles of Creative Advertising

By the very nature of advertising and the process that goes into message development, there are innumerable ways to devise creative advertisements.[27] Several relatively distinct creative styles have evolved over the years and represent the bulk of contemporary advertising.[28] Table 8.1 summarizes six styles and groups them into three categories: functionally oriented, symbolically or experientially oriented, and product category dominance.

You may recall the discussion of positioning in Chapter 5 in which distinctions were made among functional, symbolic, and experiential needs or benefits. These same distinctions are maintained in the present explanation of different styles of creative advertising. *Functionally oriented* advertising appeals to consumers' needs for tangible, physical, and concrete benefits. *Symbolically or experientially oriented* advertising strategies are directed at psychosocial needs. The *category-dominance* strategies (generic and preemptive in Table 8.1) do not necessarily use any particular type of appeal to consumers but are designed to achieve an advantage over competitors in the same product category. Finally, it is important to note that, as is the case with most categorization schemes, the alternative styles covered in the following sections sometimes have fuzzy borders when applied to specific advertising executions. In other words, distinctions are sometimes very subtle rather than perfectly obvious, and a particular advertising execution may simultaneously use multiple creative approaches.

Unique Selling Proposition Creative Style

With the **unique selling proposition (USP) style,** an advertiser makes a superiority claim based on a unique product attribute that represents a *meaningful, distinctive consumer benefit.* The main feature of USP advertising is identifying an important difference that makes a brand unique and then developing an advertising claim that competitors either cannot make or have chosen not to make. The translation of the unique product feature into a relevant consumer benefit provides the USP. The USP approach is best suited for a company with a brand that possesses a relatively lasting competitive advantage, such as a maker of a technically complex item or a provider of a sophisticated service.

The Gillette Sensor razor used a USP when claiming that it is "the only razor that senses and adjusts to the individual needs of your face." NicoDerm CQ's USP was contained in the claim that this product is the only nicotine patch "you can wear for 24 hours." An Allegra advertisement included a USP in its claim that "only Allegra has fexofenadine for effective nondrowsy relief of seasonal allergy symptoms." Prescription drug Flonase used a comparative advertising method (more of which will be discussed in Chapter 9) in claiming that only it—but not Zyrtec, Clarinex, Claritin, or Allegra—is "approved [by the Food and Drug Administration] to relieve nasal symptoms caused by indoor allergies, outdoor allergies and nonallergic irritants." Dyson vacuum cleaners were promoted as the

table 8.1

Styles of Creative Advertising

Functional Orientation	Symbolic or Experiential Orientation	Category-Dominance Orientation
• Unique selling proposition	• Brand image • Resonance • Emotional	• Generic • Preemptive

only brand "not to lose suction." Wet Ones hands and face wipes promoted their brand as the only wipe that is alcohol and fragrance free.

In many respects the USP style is *the* optimum creative technique, because it gives the consumer a clearly differentiated reason for selecting the advertiser's brand over competitive offerings. If a brand has a truly meaningful advantage over competitive offerings, then advertising should exploit that advantage. The only reason USP advertising is not used more often is that brands in many product categories are pretty much at parity with one another. They have no unique physical advantages to advertise and therefore are forced to use strategies favoring the more symbolic, psychological end of the strategy continuum.

Brand Image Creative Style

Whereas the USP strategy is based on promoting physical and functional differences between the advertiser's brand and competitive offerings, the **brand image style** involves *psychosocial* rather than physical differentiation. Advertising attempts to develop an image or identity for a brand by associating the brand with *symbols.* In imbuing a brand with an image, advertisers draw meaning from the culturally constituted world (that is, the world of artifacts and symbols) and transfer that meaning to their brands. In effect, the well-known properties of the everyday world come to reside in the unknown properties of the advertised brand.[29]

Developing an image through advertising amounts to creating a *distinct identity* or *personality* for a brand. This is especially important for brands that compete in product categories in which there is little physical differentiation and all brands are relatively similar (bottled water, soft drinks, cigarettes, blue jeans, etc.). Thus, Pepsi at one time was referred to as the soft drink for the "new generation." Mountain Dew has consistently presented itself as a "with it" brand for teens who favor a somewhat alternative lifestyle. Absolut vodka, as previously discussed, has regularly associated itself with positive images that serve to enhance the brand's reputation for hipness. Perhaps the quintessential case of brand image advertising is the Marlboro cigarette campaign that is replete with images of cowboys. The cowboy—iconic of freedom and individuality—has by virtue of the advertising campaign become attached to the Marlboro brand; some of the meaning the cowboy image represents has now transferred to Marlboro. Cowboys are equated with freedom and individuality; Marlboro is equated with cowboys; hence, by association, Marlboro itself has come to represent the qualities of the cowboy life.

Brand image advertising is *transformational* (versus informational) in character. That is, **transformational advertising** associates the experience of using an advertised brand with a unique set of psychological characteristics that typically would *not* be associated with the brand experience to the same degree without exposure to the advertisement. Such advertising is transforming (versus informing) by virtue of endowing brand usage with a particular experience that is different from using any similar brand. As the result of repeated advertising, the brand becomes associated with its advertising and the people, scenes, or events in those advertisements.[30]

Transformational advertisements contain two notable characteristics: (1) they make the experience of using the brand richer, warmer, more exciting, or more enjoyable than what would be the case based solely on an objective description of the brand and (2) they connect the experience of using the brand so tightly with the experience of the advertisement that consumers cannot remember the brand without recalling the advertising experience. Marlboro cigarettes and cowboys, for example, are inextricably woven together in many consumers' cognitive structures.[31] Guinness beer and the fictional character Michael Power also are, as previously mentioned, inseparable in most African consumers' minds.

Resonance Creative Style

When used in an advertising context, the term *resonance* is analogous to the physical notion of noise resounding off an object. In a similar fashion, an advertisement resonates (*patterns*) the audience's life experiences. A resonant advertising strategy extends from psychographic research and structures an advertising campaign to pattern the prevailing lifestyle orientation of the intended market segment.

Resonant advertising does *not* focus on product claims or brand images but rather seeks to present circumstances or situations that find counterparts in the real or imagined experiences of the target audience. Advertising based on this strategy attempts to match "patterns" in an advertisement with the target audience's stored experiences. For example, Unilever's Dove brand of soap introduced a campaign that associated the brand with "real" women (e.g., Figure 8.3)—that is, actual women who are gray, freckled, wrinkled, plump, and imperfect, but nonetheless beautiful—rather than highly attractive models who are depicted in ads without imperfections and whose beauty is typically unachievable. The imperfections of real women resonate with the target audience, which better identifies with flawed than flawless beauty because the former is real but the latter is manufactured.

© Image courtesy of The Advertising Archives

Figure 8.3

Illustration of Resonance Creative Strategy

Emotional Creative Style

Emotional advertising is the third form of symbolically or experientially oriented advertising. Much contemporary advertising aims to reach the consumer at a visceral level through the use of emotional strategy. Many advertising practitioners and scholars recognize that products often are bought on the basis of emotional factors and that appeals to emotion can be very successful if used appropriately and with the right brands. The use of emotion in advertising runs the gamut of positive and negative emotions, including appeals to romance, nostalgia, compassion, excitement, joy, fear, guilt, disgust, and regret. Chapter 9 will treat several of these emotionally charged appeals in some detail.

Although the emotional strategy can be used when advertising virtually any brand, emotional advertising seems to work especially well for product categories that naturally are associated with emotions (foods, jewelry, cosmetics, fragrances, fashion apparel, etc.). For example, the advertisement for DKNY fragrance (Figure 8.4) is an obvious appeal to romance.

Generic Creative Style

An advertiser employs a **generic style** when making a claim that any company that markets a brand in that product category could make. The advertiser makes *no* attempt to differentiate its brand from competitive offerings or to claim superiority. This strategy is most appropriate for a brand that *dominates a product category.* In such instances, the firm making a generic claim will enjoy a large share of any primary demand stimulated by advertising.

For example, Campbell's dominates the prepared-soup market in the United States, selling nearly two thirds of all soup. Any advertising that increases overall

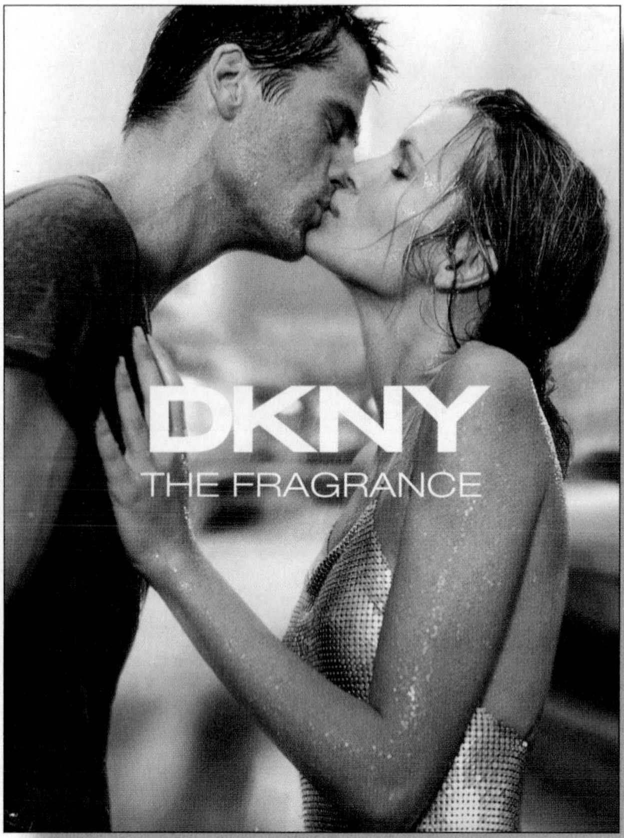

© Image courtesy of The Advertising Archives

Figure 8.4

Illustration of Emotional Creative Strategy

soup sales naturally benefits Campbell's. This explains the "Soup is good food" campaign used by Campbell's in years past. This advertising extolled the virtues of eating soup without arguing why people should buy Campbell's soup. Campbell's followed this campaign with another one that simply declared, "Never underestimate the power of soup." Along similar lines, AT&T's "Reach out and touch someone" campaign, which encouraged more long-distance calling, was a wise strategy in light of this company's one-time grip on the long-distance telephoning market (intense competition has since weakened that grip).

Preemptive Creative Style

The **preemptive style,** a second category-dominance technique, is employed when an advertiser makes a generic-type claim but does so with an *assertion of superiority.* This approach is most often used by advertisers in product or service categories where there are few, if any, functional differences among competitive brands. Preemptive advertising is a clever strategy when a meaningful superiority claim is made because it effectively precludes competitors from saying the same thing. Any branch of the military service could claim that they enable recruits to "be all you can be," but no other branch could possibly make such a claim after the Army adopted this as its unique statement. The huge JP Morgan Chase, which resulted from the merger of Chase Manhattan and Chemical banks, undertook a $45 million advertising campaign shortly after the merger that referred to Chase as "the Relationship Company." In clear recognition of the value of preemption, the chief marketing officer for Chase justified the campaign by stating, "the idea is to stamp that word [*relationship*] on our brand enough to preempt the use of it by anyone else in the category."[32]

The maker of Visine eyedrops advertised that this brand "gets the red out." All eyedrops are designed to get the red out, but by making this claim first, Visine made a dramatic statement that the consumer will associate only with Visine. No other company could subsequently make this claim for fear of being labeled a mimic. An advertisement for Hanes Smooth Illusions panty hose used a smart preemptive claim in comparing the brand to "liposuction without surgery." Another clever preemptive campaign was introduced by Nissan Motor some years ago with its advertising of the Maxima. Preceding the campaign, the Maxima competed against models such as the Ford Taurus and the Toyota Cressida in the upper-middle segment of the industry. To avoid stiff price competition and price rebates, Nissan wanted a more upscale and high-performance image for the Maxima. Based on extensive research, Maxima's advertising agency devised a clever preemptive claim touting the Maxima as the "four-door sports car." Of course, all sedans have four doors, but Maxima preempted sports car status with this one clever claim. Its sales immediately increased by 43 percent over the previous year despite a price increase.[33]

A final illustration of the preemptive strategy is Citibank's advertising campaign to create awareness for identity theft. In a series of television executions, identity thieves were shown "occupying" the personas of their victims. For example, out of the mouth of an elderly woman comes the voice of a male thief who stole her credit card and made purchases under her assumed identity. Although any financial institution could have taken the lead in promoting the importance of protecting against identity theft, none could follow after Citibank preempted that advertising landscape.

Section Summary

We have discussed six general creative styles and categorized them as functional, symbolic/experiential, or category-dominance oriented. These alternatives help to understand the different approaches available to advertisers and the factors influencing the choice of creative style. It would be incorrect to think of these approaches as pure and mutually exclusive. Because there is some unavoidable overlap, it is possible that an advertiser may consciously or unconsciously use two or more styles simultaneously.

In fact, some advertising experts contend that advertising is most effective when it reflects both ends of the creative advertising continuum—that is, by addressing both functional product benefits and symbolic or psychosocial benefits. A New York advertising agency provided evidence in partial support of the superiority of combined benefits over using only functional appeals. The agency tested 168 television commercials, 47 of which contained both functional and psychosocial appeals and 121 of which contained functional appeals only. Using recall and persuasion measures, the agency found that the ads containing a combination of functional and psychosocial appeals outperformed the functional-only ads by a substantial margin.[34]

Finally, it is important to recognize that whatever creative style is chosen, it must be clearly positioned in the customer's mind. That is, effective advertising must establish a *clear meaning of what the brand is and how it compares with competitive offerings.* Effective positioning requires that a company be fully aware of its competition and exploit competitive weaknesses. A brand is positioned in the consumer's mind relative to competition. The originators of the positioning concept contend that successful companies must be "competitors oriented," look for weak points in their competitors' positions, and then launch marketing attacks against those weak points.[35] These same management consultants claim that many marketing people and advertisers are in error when operating under the assumption that marketing and advertising are a battle of products. Their contrary position is this:

> *There are no best products. All that exists in the world of marketing are perceptions in the minds of the customer or prospect. The perception is the reality. Everything else is an illusion.*[36]

This perhaps is a bit overstated, but the point is that how good (or prestigious, dependable, sexy, etc.) a brand is depends more on what people think than on objective reality. And what people think is largely a function of effective advertising that creates a USP, builds an attractive image, or otherwise differentiates the brand from competitive offerings and lodges the intended meaning securely in the customer's mind.

The important takeaway here is that the choice of creative strategy for advertising a particular brand is determined by three key considerations. (1) What are the target audience's needs and motivations related to the product category? (2) What are the brand's strengths and weaknesses relative to competitive brands in the category? (3) How are competitors advertising their brands? Armed with answers to all three questions, the brand management team along with its advertising agency is prepared to develop an advertising campaign employing a creative strategy that will simultaneously appeal to the target audience and provide maximal advantage vis-à-vis the creative strategies competitive brands are using.

Means-End Chaining and the Method of Laddering as Guides to Creative Advertising Formulation

The preceding discussion emphasized, if only implicitly, that the consumer (or customer in the case of B2B marketing) should be the foremost determinant of advertising messages. The notion of a means-end chain provides a useful framework for understanding the relationship between consumers or customers and advertising messages. A means-end chain represents the linkages among brand *attributes,* the *consequences* obtained from using the brand and "consuming" the attributes, and the *personal values* that the consequences reinforce.[37] These linkages represent a means-end chain because the consumer sees the brand and its attributes, the consumption of which has consequences, as the *means* for achieving a valued end state resulting from these consequences. Schematically, the means-end chain is as follows:

[Attributes → Consequences] → {Values}

[Means] → {End}

Attributes are features or aspects of advertised brands. In the case of automobiles, for example, attributes include size, storage capacity, engine performance, aesthetic features, and so on. **Consequences** are what consumers hope to receive (*benefits*) or avoid (*detriments*) when consuming brands. Increased status, convenience, performance, safety, and resale value are positive consequences associated with automobiles (benefits), whereas breakdowns, mishandling, and poor resale value are negative consequences that consumers wish to avoid (detriments). In the case of large-screen plasma TVs, screen size and resolution are product attributes leading to consequences such as remarkably clear images vis-à-vis old-fashioned TVs (benefit) but also high energy consumption (detriment) versus TVs based on LED technology (light-emitting diodes).

In sum, the important thing to appreciate is that attributes reside in brands, whereas consumers experience consequences as a result of brand acquisition and usage. Together, brand attributes and the consequences of consuming these attributes are the *means* whereby people achieve valued *ends.*

Values represent those enduring beliefs people hold regarding what is important in life.[38] They pertain to end states that people desire in their lives, they transcend specific situations, and they guide selection or evaluation of behavior.[39] In general, values determine the relative desirability of consequences and serve to organize the meanings for products and brands in consumers' cognitive structures.[40]

Values represent the starting point, the catalyst, and the source of motivation for many aspects of human behavior. Consumer behavior, like other facets of behavior, involves the pursuit of valued states, or outcomes. Brand attributes and their consequences are not sought per se, but rather are desired as means to achieving valued end states. From the consumer's perspective, the *ends* (values) drive the *means* (attributes and their consequences). Let us now examine more fully the values that energize human behavior.

The Nature of Values

Psychologists have conducted extensive research on values and constructed numerous value typologies. This chapter takes the view that 10 basic values

table 8.2

Ten Universal Values

1. Self-direction	6. Security
2. Stimulation	7. Conformity
3. Hedonism	8. Tradition
4. Achievement	9. Benevolence
5. Power	10. Universalism

Source: Reprinted from *Advances in Experimental Social Psychology*, Vol. 25, Shalom H. Schwartz, "Universals in the Content and Structure of Values: Theoretical Advances and Empirical Tests in 20 Countries," pp. 1–65, 1992, with permission from Elsevier.

adequately represent the important human values people in a wide variety of culturally diverse countries share. Table 8.2 lists these 10 values.[41] Research identified these values based on studies conducted in 20 culturally diverse countries: Australia, Brazil, Estonia, Finland, Germany, Greece, Holland, Hong Kong, Israel, Italy, Japan, New Zealand, the People's Republic of China, Poland, Portugal, Spain, Taiwan, the United States, Venezuela, and Zimbabwe. People in these countries shared the same values, each of which is now briefly described:[42]

1. *Self-direction.* Independent thought and action is the defining goal of this value type. It includes the desire for freedom, independence, choosing one's own goals, and creativity.
2. *Stimulation.* This value derives from the need for variety and achieving an exciting life.
3. *Hedonism.* Enjoying life and receiving pleasure are fundamental to this value type.
4. *Achievement.* Enjoying personal success through demonstrating competence according to social standards is the defining goal of this value type. Being regarded as capable, ambitious, intelligent, and influential are different aspects of the achievement value.
5. *Power.* The power value entails the attainment of social status and prestige along with control or dominance over people and resources (wealth, authority, social power, and recognition).
6. *Security.* The essence of this value type is the longing for safety, harmony, and the stability of society. This value includes concern for personal and family safety and even national security.
7. *Conformity.* Self-discipline, obedience, politeness, and, in general, restraint from actions and impulses that are likely to upset or harm others and violate social norms are at the root of this value type.
8. *Tradition.* This value encompasses respect, commitment, and acceptance of the customs that one's culture and religion impose.
9. *Benevolence.* The motivational goal of benevolence is the preservation and enhancement of the welfare of one's family and friends. It includes being honest, loyal, helpful, a true friend, and loving in a mature manner.
10. *Universalism.* Universalism represents individuals' motivation to understand, appreciate, tolerate, and protect the welfare of all people and of nature. It incorporates notions of world peace, social justice, equality, unity with nature, environmental protection, and wisdom.

Which Values Are Most Relevant to Advertising?

The 10 values just presented are apt descriptions of human psychology around the world. It is important to note, however, that they apply to *all* aspects of life and not to consumer behavior per se. Consequently, all 10 values are *not* equally important to consumers and thus not equally applicable to advertisers in their campaign-development efforts. Before reading on, take a few moments to review the 10 values and identify those that you consider most applicable to products and brands that are most frequently advertised in the mass media.

If you are like me, you will have concluded that the first six values—self-direction through security—apply to many advertising and consumption situations, whereas the last four are less typical drivers of much consumer behavior. These latter four values certainly are applicable under select advertising situations (e.g., advertising efforts by nonprofit organizations such as churches and charitable organizations) and perhaps even more so in the East than in the West, but they do not typify usual consumer behavior for most products and services. Hence, you should realize that self-direction, stimulation, hedonism, achievement, power, and security are the valued end states that drive the bulk of consumer behavior and thus are the goals to which advertisers must appeal.

Advertising Applications of Means-End Chains: The MECCAS Model

The creation of effective advertisements demands that brand managers possess a clear understanding of what people value from product categories and specific brands. Because consumers differ in what they value from a particular brand, it is meaningful to discuss values only at the *market segment* level. A brand advertiser, armed with knowledge of segment-level values, is in a position to know what brand attributes and consequences to emphasize to a particular market segment as the means by which that brand can help consumers achieve a valued end state. A formal model, called MECCAS—standing for *m*eans-*e*nd *c*onceptualization of *c*omponents for *a*dvertising *s*trategy—provides a procedure for applying the concept of means-end chains to the creation of advertising messages.[43]

Table 8.3 presents and defines the various levels of the MECCAS model. Note that the components include a *value orientation, brand consequences* and *brand attributes*, and a *creative strategy and leverage point* that provide the structure for presenting the advertising message and the means for tapping into or activating the value orientation.[44] The *value orientation* represents the consumer value or end level on which the advertising strategy focuses and can be thought of as the *driving force* behind the advertising execution. Every other component is geared toward achieving the end level. Please study the remaining definitions carefully

table 8.3

A MECCAS Model Conceptualization of Advertising Strategy

Component	Definition
Value orientation ↑	The end level (value) to be focused on in the advertising; it serves as the driving force for the advertising execution.
Brand consequences ↑	The major positive consequences, or benefits of using the brand, that the advertisement verbally or visually communicates to consumers.
Brand attributes ↑	The brand's specific attributes or features that are communicated as a means of supporting the consequence(s) of using the brand.
Creative strategy and leverage point	The overall scenario for communicating the value orientation and the manner (leverage point) by which the advertisement will tap into, reach, or activate the key value that serves as the ad's driving force.

Source: Adapted from Thomas J. Reynolds and Jonathan Gutman, "Advertising Is Image Management," *Journal of Advertising Research* 24 (February/March 1984), 27–36. Reprinted with permission from *Journal of Advertising Research*, © Copyright 1984, by the Advertising Research Foundation.

in Table 8.3 before moving on to the illustrative applications of the MECCAS approach that are described next.

The following sections apply the MECCAS framework in analyzing six advertisements, one for each of the first six values shown in Table 8.2 . It is important to note that these applications are the author's post hoc interpretations. It is unknown whether the advertisers in these cases actually performed formal means-end analyses in developing their ads. Nonetheless, these analyses will provide an enhanced understanding of how the means-end logic (attributes → consequences → values) can be translated into the design of actual advertisements.

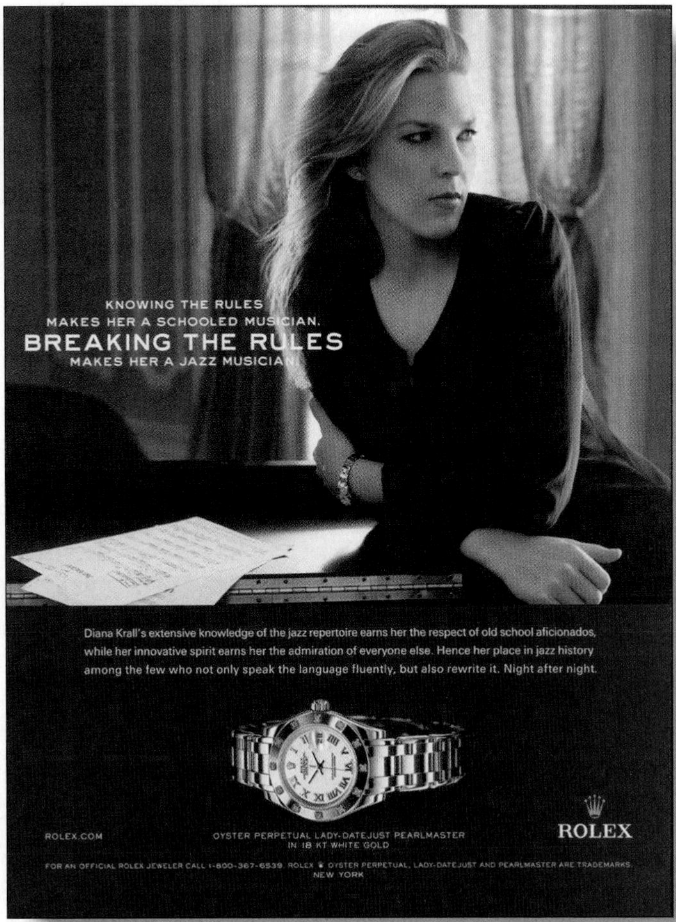

© Image courtesy of The Advertising Archives

Figure 8.5

MECCAS Illustration for Self-Direction Value

Self-Direction and Rolex Watches

Self-direction includes the desire for freedom, independence, and choosing one's own goals. The value orientation serving as the driving force in the Rolex advertisement (Figure 8.5) is an unadorned appeal to consumers' need to reject conformity (see the ad's headline "Breaking the Rules"), which represents an appeal to those consumers who desire to choose freely and be unconstrained by the dictates of social pressures.

Hedonism and a Steak

Fundamental to the hedonism value is enjoying life and receiving pleasure. The ad in Figure 8.6 shows a mouth-watering photo of steak, a product much enjoyed by most nonvegetarians. The catchy headline—"There's no such thing as a chicken knife"—intimates that only steak, unlike chicken, is worthy of having a utensil named for it. The advertiser, The Beef Checkoff Program, is clearly appealing to people's desire to enjoy one of life's little pleasures.

Achievement and Home Depot

In an appeal to competence and accomplishment—the elements of achievement—the advertisement in Figure 8.7 tells a little story (recall the storytelling component of the SUCCESs framework) based on a typical customer's triumph in remodeling her home. Amy, with the implied assistance of Home Depot's personnel, proved "just how much she really can handle" and overcame others' doubts that remodeling her home "would be too much for a single mom to handle." This Home Depot ad represents an unmistakable appeal to the value consumers' place on achieving home-improvement goals.

Power and the Hummer Alpha

As a valued end state, power entails the attainment of social status and prestige along with control or dominance over people and resources (e.g., authority, social power, and recognition). The ad in Figure 8.8 for the Hummer Alpha refers to this vehicle as "the powerful H3 Alpha." The body copy, which provides the ad's leverage point, suggests that prospective purchasers—alpha males, no doubt—have to pass an extraordinarily rigorous "physical exam" in order to be able to purchase an Alpha. The insinuation is that it takes a tough individual to own a Hummer Alpha: The vehicle is powerful and so is its owner. This ad subtly

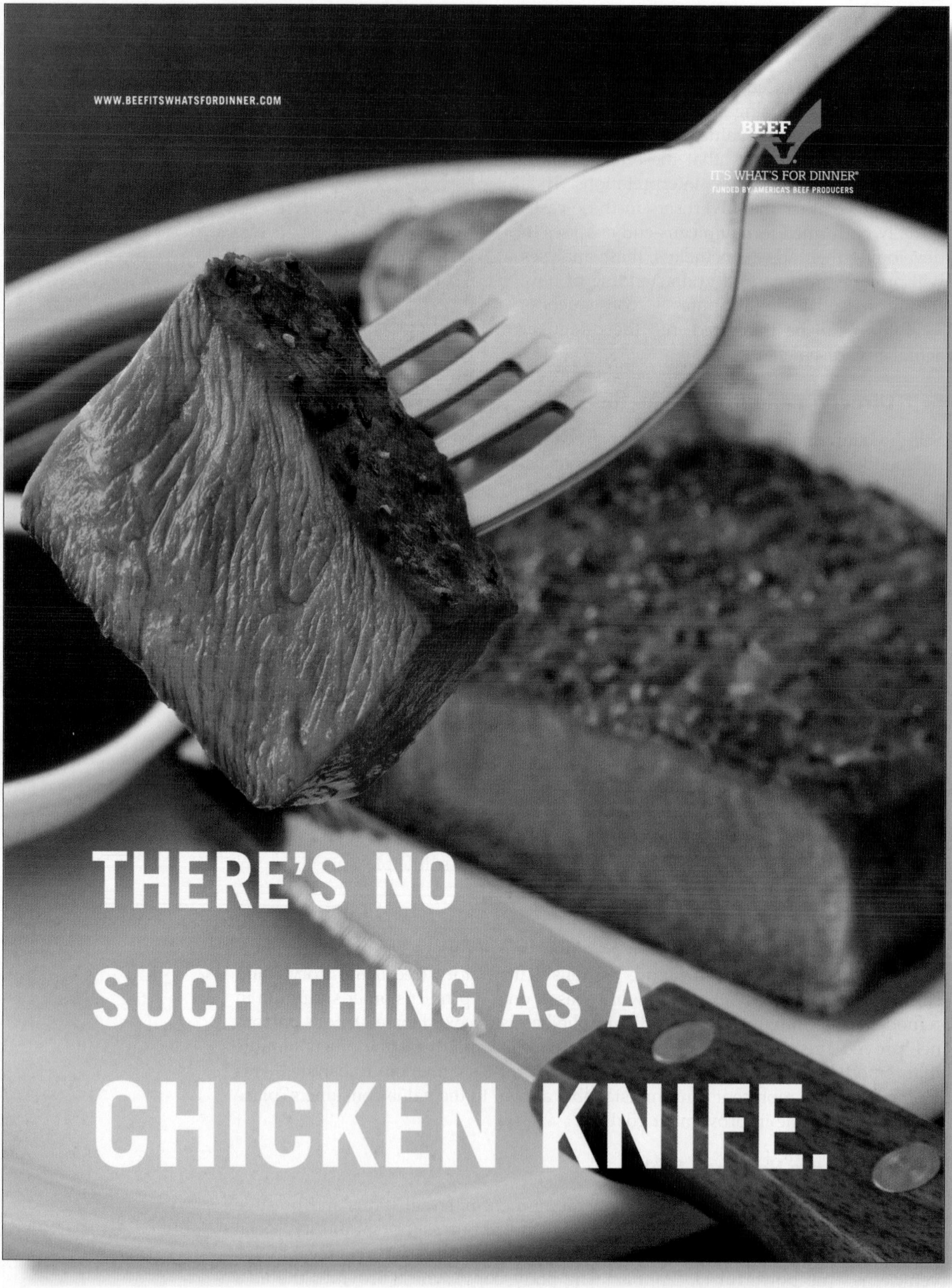

Figure 8.6

MECCAS Illustration for Hedonism Value

conveys to potential purchasers of Hummer Alphas that they will be perceived as tough, rigorous, powerful individuals and will attain status and prestige from their acquisition of this vehicle.

Security and Neosporin

Personal and family safety are aspects of the security value pertinent to the ownership and consumption of many products. An advertisement for Neosporin antibiotic ointment uses the storytelling method in its implicit suggestion that even very small cuts and scrapes might lead to serious infection. The story describes Neosporin's attributes and states that it provides better protection against serious infection (MRSA?) than other brands. The leverage point for the valued end state of security is apparent in the visual of a healthy child embracing her mother, who declares "I will never leave another cut untreated."

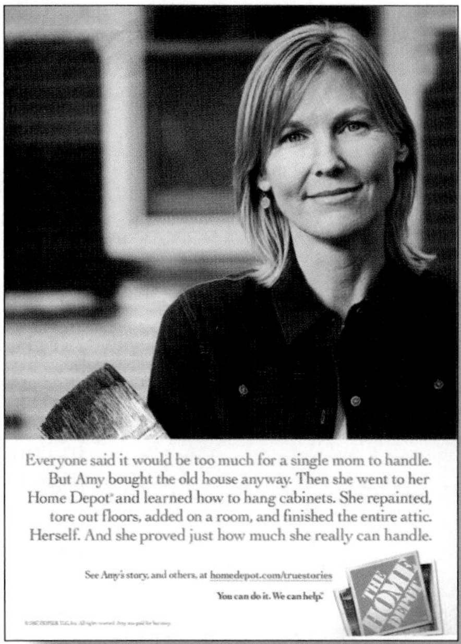

Identifying Means-End Chains: The Method of Laddering

Laddering is a research technique that has been developed to identify linkages between attributes (A), consequences (C), and values (V). The method is termed *laddering* because it leads to the construction of a hierarchy, or ladder, of relations between a brand's attributes and consequences (the means) and consumer values (the end). **Laddering** involves in-depth, one-on-one interviews that typically last 30 minutes to more than one hour. In contrast to surveys, laddering attempts to get at the root or deep reasons why individual consumers buy certain products and brands.[45]

An interviewer first determines which attributes the interviewee feels are most important in the product category and, from there, attempts to identify the linkages in the interviewee's mind from attributes to consequences and from consequences to abstract values. In conducting a laddering interview, the interviewer refers the interviewee to a specific attribute and then, through directed probes, attempts to detect how the interviewee links that attribute with more abstract consequences and how the consequences are linked with even more abstract values. After linkages for the first attribute are exhausted, the interviewer moves on to the next salient attribute, and then the next, until all important attributes have been explored; this typically ranges from three to seven attributes. Probing is accomplished with questions such as the following:[46]

- Why is that particular attribute important to you?
- How does that help you out?
- What do you get from that?
- Why do you want that?
- What happens to you as a result of that?

Let us illustrate the method of laddering with the advertisement for the Home Depot in Figure 8.7. Imagine that an interviewer asks a consumer why it is important to her to perform do-it-yourself household improvements. Her response is, "I don't want to have to depend on anyone." A follow-up probe by the interviewer ("How does that help you out?") results in this consumer claiming that "it is important that I have a nice home, and I can't afford to pay for someone else to repair it." In response to a prompt of "Why is that important to you?" she comments, "I want my parents to be proud of me. I want them to

Everyone said it would be too much for a single mom to handle. But Amy bought the old house anyway. Then she went to her Home Depot and learned how to hang cabinets. She repainted, tore out floors, added on a room, and finished the entire attic. Herself. And she proved just how much she really can handle.

See Amy's story, and others, at homedepot.com/truestories
You can do it. We can help.

Figure 8.7

MECCAS Illustration for Achievement Value

Figure 8.8

MECCAS Illustration for Power Value

The physical required to purchase an Alpha consists of a pentadecathlon followed by a marathon followed by 500 squat thrusts. Then you have to wrestle a tiger with your bare hands.

HUMMER.COM

THE POWERFUL H3 **ALPHA** V8 IS HERE.

HUMMER LIKE NOTHING ELSE

know that I can raise their grandchildren by myself and that I will provide a nice home for them."

We see in this hypothetical description that doing her home improvements is ultimately linked to the achievement value and the resulting satisfaction from having proud parents. The advertisement in Figure 8.7 apparently is based on the view that there is a market segment of consumers like Amy who want to improve their homes and thus realize their ambitions, achieve recognition, and perhaps make others—as well as themselves—proud of their accomplishments.

Practical Issues in Identifying Means-End Chains

In conclusion, the important point to remember about the MECCAS approach is that it provides a systematic procedure for linking the advertiser's perspective (i.e., a brand with attributes that have desirable and undesirable consequences) with the consumer's perspective (the pursuit of products and brands to achieve desired end states, or values). Effective advertising does not focus on product attributes and consequences per se; rather, it is directed at showing how the advertised brand will benefit the consumer and enable him or her to achieve what he or she most desires in life—self-determination, stimulation, hedonism, and the other values listed in Table 8.2. Products and brands vary in terms of which values they are capable of satisfying; nonetheless, all are capable of fulfilling some value(s), and it is the role of sophisticated advertising and the marketing research on which it is based to identify and access those values. Advertising and other forms of marketing communications are most relevant to the consumer and thus most effective for the advertised brand when they are based on strong linkages between the right set of attributes, consequences, and values.[47]

All said, it is pertinent to note that the means-end approach and the method of laddering are not without critics. The primary criticisms are several: First, some claim that the laddering method "forces" interviewees to identify hierarchies among attributes, consequences, and values that may actually not have existed before the interview and absent the interviewer's directive probes. Second, some suggest that consumers may possess clear-cut linkages between attributes and consequences but not necessarily between consequences and values. Finally, some criticize laddering on grounds that the ultimate hierarchy constructed is a crude aggregation of A → C → V chains from multiple individuals into a single chain that is assumed to represent all consumers in the target audience.[48]

These criticisms are not unfounded, but the reality is that all methods for creative strategy development in advertising have their imperfections. The value of laddering is that it forces advertisers to identify how consumers relate product attributes to more abstract states such as benefits and values. This systematic approach thereby ensures that advertising emphasis will be placed on communicating benefits and implying valued end states rather than focusing on attributes per se. It is likely for some product categories and particular brands that consumers do not possess clear linkages between brand consequences and values. So, although the means-end chain may entail only A → C links rather than the full set of A → C → V links, the systematic laddering procedure serves its purpose by encouraging creative personnel to focus on product benefits rather than attributes.

Corporate Image and Issue Advertising

The type of advertising discussed to this point is commonly referred to as *brand-oriented advertising*. Such advertising focuses on a specific brand and attempts ultimately to influence consumers to purchase the advertiser's brand.

Another form of advertising, termed *corporate advertising,* focuses not on specific brands but on a corporation's overall image or on economic or social issues relevant to the corporation's interests. This form of advertising is prevalent.[49] Consistent spending on corporate advertising can serve to boost a corporation's equity, much in the same fashion that brand-oriented advertising represents a deposit in the brand equity bank. Two somewhat distinct forms of corporate advertising are discussed in the following sections: (1) image advertising and (2) issue, or advocacy, advertising.[50]

Corporate Image Advertising

Corporate image advertising attempts to increase a firm's name recognition, establish goodwill for the company and its products, or identify itself with some meaningful and socially acceptable activity. This type of corporate advertising is concerned with creating favorable images among audiences such as consumers, stockholders, employees, suppliers, and potential investors. Such advertising asks for no specific action from the target audience(s) other than a favorable attitude toward the corporation and passive approval for the company's activities.[51] For example, a General Motors advertisement for hybrid-powered buses did not promote any specific General Motors vehicle but rather, like other corporate image advertisements, attempted to enhance the company's image by associating it with fuel efficiency and conservation. The ad in Figure 8.9 reflects another illustration of corporate social responsibility advertising. In this example, the Goldfish® brand has developed a program called Fishful Thinking™ to help Moms inspire optimism and positive thinking in children. By aligning with a higher order purpose, the Goldfish® brand is positioning itself well to deepen its relationship with consumers.

In general, research has found that executives regard name identity and image building to be the two most important functions of corporate advertising.[52] Corporate image advertising is directed at more than merely trying to make consumers feel good about a company. Companies are increasingly using the image of their firms to enhance sales and financial performance.[53] Research has shown that a positive corporate image can favorably affect consumers' product evaluations, especially when the purchase decision is risky.[54] Corporate advertising that does not contribute to increased sales and profits is difficult to justify in today's climate of accountability.

Figure 8.9

Illustration of Corporate Image Advertisement

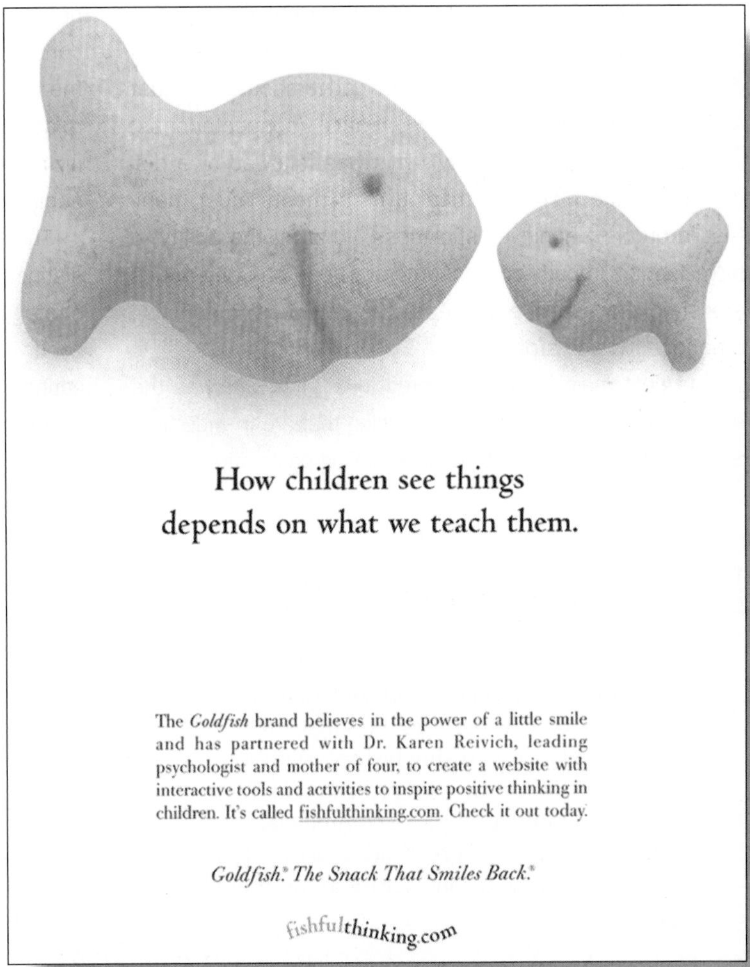

How children see things depends on what we teach them.
The *Goldfish* brand believes in the power of a little smile and has partnered with Dr. Karen Reivich, leading psychologist and mother of four, to create a website with interactive tools and activities to inspire positive thinking in children. It's called fishfulthinking.com. Check it out today.
Goldfish® The Snack That Smiles Back®
fishfulthinking.com

Pepperidge Farms® GoldFish®

Corporate Issue (Advocacy) Advertising

The other form of corporate advertising is issue, or advocacy, advertising. When using **issue advertising,** a company takes a position on a controversial social issue of public importance with the intention of swaying public opinion.[55] It does so in a manner that supports the company's position and best interests while expressly or implicitly challenging the opponent's position and denying the accuracy of their facts.[56] Imagine, for example, a major petroleum company undertaking an advertising campaign that challenges the economic prudence and energy efficiency of the fledgling corn-based ethanol industry. Such advocacy would serve the corporation's purposes if it convinced the voting populace and their representatives that special funding to prop up the ethanol industry is unjustified.

Issue advertising is a topic of considerable controversy.[57] Business executives are divided on whether this form of advertising represents an effective allocation of corporate resources. Critics question the legitimacy of issue advertising and challenge its status as a tax-deductible expenditure. Since further discussion of these points is beyond the scope of this chapter, the interested reader is encouraged to review the sources contained in the last endnote.[58]

Summary

The chapter examined creative advertising and presented a number of illustrations of creative advertising campaigns. An important initial question asked, what are the general characteristics of effective advertising? Discussion pointed out that effective advertising must (1) extend from sound marketing strategy, (2) take the consumer's view, (3) break through the competitive clutter, (4) never promise more than can be delivered, and (5) prevent the creative idea from overwhelming the strategy. A following section described three characteristics that advertisements must satisfy to be considered truly creative (connectedness, appropriateness, and novelty). This was followed by a discussion of the elements that advertisements must manifest in order to achieve "stickiness," that is, the ability to have lasting impact on consumers. These characteristics are simplicity, unexpectedness, concreteness, credibility, emotionality, and storytelling.

The next major subject covered in this chapter was the alternative forms of creative advertising that are in wide use. Six specific creative styles—unique selling proposition, brand image, resonance, emotional, generic, and preemptive—were described and examples given.

The chapter then turned to the concept of means-end chains and the MECCAS framework (means-end conceptualization of components for advertising strategy) that is used in designing actual advertisements and campaigns. Means-end chains and MECCAS models provide bridges between product attributes and the consequences to the consumer of realizing product attributes (the means) and the ability of these consequences to satisfy consumption-related values (the end). MECCAS models provide an organizing framework for developing creative ads that simultaneously consider attributes, consequences, and values.

The final subject discussed was corporate advertising. A distinction was made between conventional brand-oriented strategy and advertising that focuses on facilitating corporate goodwill, enhancing a corporation's overall image, and advocating matters of economic or social significance that are relevant to a corporation. Two forms of corporate advertising, image and issue (advocacy) advertising, were described.

Discussion Questions

1. The *Marcom Insight* described the famous MacIntosh Computer advertisement and characterized it as perhaps the single greatest commercial in advertising history. Without using any of the examples presented in this chapter, identify a couple of commercials that you regard as truly "great" advertising. Be sure to explain why you consider these commercials great.
2. Early in the chapter when discussing how effective advertising must take the consumer's view, the following quotation was presented: "Consumers don't want to be bombarded with ads—they want to be inspired by ideas that will change their lives. Ads create transactions. Ideas create transformations. Ads reflect our culture, ideas imagine our future." What, in your opinion, does this quote mean?

3. When discussing the concept of advertising novelty, the chapter stated that novelty is a necessary but insufficient condition for advertising creativity. Explain what this means.
4. In context of the section on "sticky" advertisements, provide three examples of advertisers' efforts to concretize their advertisements. Television commercials would be a good source of ideas. Explain the specific elements in your chosen commercials that illustrate concreteness.
5. Analyze three magazine advertisements in terms of which of the SUCCESs elements each ad satisfies.
6. In your view, which of the SUCCESs elements are most important? Offer an explanation and then rank the six elements from most to least important in terms of their ability to achieve message stickiness.
7. When discussing the creative advertising style known as unique selling proposition, or USP, it was claimed that in many respects the USP style is *the* optimum creative technique. Explain whether you agree or disagree with this assertion.
8. Several examples of brand image advertisements were offered in the chapter. Identify two additional examples of advertisements that appear to be using the brand image, or transformational, creative style.
9. One requirement for effective advertising is the ability to break through competitive clutter. Explain what this means, and provide several examples of advertising methods that successfully accomplish this.
10. Select a magazine or newspaper advertisement and apply the MECCAS model to interpret the ad. Describe what you consider to be the ad's value orientation, its leverage point, and so on.
11. Explain the differences between the USP and brand image creative styles, and indicate the specific conditions under which each is more likely to be used. Provide one illustration of each creative style, using examples other than those used in the text.
12. Using the laddering procedure that was described in the chapter, select a product category of your choice, interview one individual (preferably not a close friend), and construct that person's hierarchical map, or ladder, for *two* product attributes that are important to that person. In other words, after first determining the two product attributes (or features) that this person considers most important in making a choice among brands in the product category you have selected, use the types of probing questions listed in the chapter to see how this individual mentally connects product attributes with consequences, and how, in turn, these consequences extend into valued end states. Be persistent!
13. Some critics contend that advocacy, or issue, advertising should not be treated as a legitimate tax-deductible expenditure. Present and justify your opinion on this matter.
14. Select two advertising campaigns that have been on television for some time. Describe in detail what you think their creative message styles are.

End Notes

1. Based on Bradley Johnson, "The Commercial, and the Product, That Changed Advertising," *Advertising Age,* January 10, 1994, 1, 12–14.
2. Bob Garfield, "Breakthrough Product Gets Greatest TV Spot," *Advertising Age,* January 10, 1994, 14; "The Most Famous One-Shot Commercial Tested Orwell, and Made History for Apple Computer," *Advertising Age,* November 11, 1996, A22.
3. James B. Twitchell, *20 Ads That Shook the World: The Century's Most Groundbreaking Advertising and How It Changed Us All* (New York: Crown Publishers, 2000), 190.
4. The following points are a mixture of the author's views and perspectives presented by A. Jerome Jewler, *Creative Strategy in Advertising* (Belmont, Calif.: Wadsworth, 1985), 7–8; and Don E. Schultz and Stanley I. Tannenbaum, *Essentials of Advertising Strategy* (Lincolnwood, Ill.: NTC Business Books, 1988), 9–10.
5. Joey Reiman, "Selling an Idea for $1 Million," *Advertising Age,* July 5, 2004, 15.
6. Stan Freberg, "Irtnog Revisited," *Advertising Age,* August 1, 1988, 32.
7. For interesting discussion on creativity and the creative process in advertising, review the following sources: Jaafar El-Murad and Douglas C. West, "The Definition and Measurement of Creativity: What Do We Know?" *Journal of Advertising Research* 44 (June 2004), 188–201; Vincent J. Blasko and Michael P. Mokwa, "Paradox, Advertising and the Creative Process," in *Current Issues and Research in Advertising,* ed. J. H. Leigh and C. R. Martin, Jr. (Ann Arbor: Graduate School of Business Administration, University of Michigan, 1989), 351–366; and Jacob Goldenberg, David Mazursky, and Sorin Solomon, "Creative Sparks," *Science* 285 (September 1999), 1495–1496.

8. These three elements represent the author's perspective along with a blending of research evidence from these sources: Scott Koslow, Sheila L. Sasser, and Edward A. Riordan, "What Is Creative to Whom and Why? Perceptions in Advertising Agencies," *Journal of Advertising Research* 43 (March 2003), 96–110; Swee Hoon Ang, Yih Hwai Lee, and Siew Meng Leong, *Journal of the Academy of Marketing Science* 35 (June 2007), 220–232.
9. Lou Centlivre, "A Peek at the Creative of the '90s," *Advertising Age,* January 18, 1988, 62.
10. Chip Heath and Dan Heath, *Made to Stick* (New York: Random House, 2007).
11. http://www.snopes.com/crime/warnings/restroom.asp (accessed January 8, 2008).
12. The following discussion of all six features is adapted from Heath and Heath, *Made to Stick.*
13. This description is based on ibid., p. 218 ff.
14. This acronym is not original to this text but rather is attributable to ibid.
15. Based on an interview by Paula Champa in "The Moment of Creation," *Agency,* May/June 1991, 32.
16. For additional reading on this famous advertisement, see Twitchell, *20 Ads That Shook the World,* 118–125.
17. Linda Kaplan Thaler and Robin Koval, *Bang! Getting Your Message Heard in a Noisy World* (New York: Currency Doubleday , 2003), 24.
18. Lisa Sanders, "AFLAC CMO Says: Shut the Duck Up," *Advertising Age,* February 19, 2007, 1, 63.
19. Some of the ideas for this description are inspired by the eloquent comments of Bob Garfield in his review of the Nike commercials, *Advertising Age,* April 5, 2004, 37.
20. Susanna Howard, "Guinness Pours Hopes on Africa," *Wall Street Journal Online,* October 27, 2003, http://online.wsj.com; Bill Britt, "Guinness Unspools Feature Film," *Madison+Vine Online,* February 26, 2003, http://adage.com/madisonandvine. See also http://en.wikipedia.org/wiki/Michael_Power_(Guinness_character).
21. This framework is from the world-famous management consulting firm, McKinsey & Company, in an undated document supplied to me by a company that had secured McKinsey's services.
22. Research by ARS Group, a company that specializes in advertising research, reports that starting with a strong selling proposition leads to effective advertising about 70 percent of the time. This was reported in the company's newsletter, "Better Practices in Advertising," Issue 1, July 2002, 1.
23. An interesting article on account planning, and the difference in its application in the United Kingdom and the United States, is Christopher E. Hackley, "Account Planning: Current Agency Perspectives on an Advertising Enigma," *Journal of Advertising Research* 43 (June 2003), 235–245.
24. Harvey Penick with Bud Shrake, *Harvey Penick's Little Red Book* (New York: Simon & Schuster, 1992), 45.
25. Interestingly, research has shown that advertising copy tends to be based on copywriters' own implicit theories of how advertising works on consumers. See Arthur J. Kover, "Copywriters' Implicit Theories of Communication: An Exploration," *Journal of Consumer Research* 21 (March 1995), 596–611.
26. Don E. Schultz brought this idea to the author's attention in "Determine Outcomes First to Measure Efforts," *Marketing News,* September 1, 2003, 7.
27. A good review of the literature along with the presentation of an insightful message strategy model are provided by Ronald E. Taylor, "A Six-Segment Message Strategy Wheel," *Journal of Advertising Research* 39 (November/December 1999), 7–17.
28. The following discussion represents an adaptation of Charles F. Frazer, "Creative Strategy: A Management Perspective," *Journal of Advertising* 12, no. 4 (1983), 36–41. For other perspectives on creative strategies, see Henry A. Laskey, Ellen Day, and Melvin R. Crask, "Typology of Main Message Strategies for Television Commercials," *Journal of Advertising* 18, no. 1 (1989), 36–41; and Taylor, "A Six-Segment Message Strategy Wheel."
29. Grant McCracken, "Culture and Consumption: A Theoretical Account of the Structure and Movement of the Cultural Meaning of Consumer Goods," *Journal of Consumer Research* 13 (June 1986), 74.
30. Christopher P. Puto and William D. Wells, "Informational and Transformational Advertising: The Differential Effects of Time," in *Advances in Consumer Research,* vol. 11, ed. Thomas C. Kinnear (Provo, Utah: Association for Consumer Research, 1984), 638–643. See also David A. Aaker and Douglas M. Stayman, "Implementing the Concept of Transformational Advertising," *Psychology & Marketing* 9 (May/June 1992), 237–253.
31. Puto and Wells, "Informational and Transformational Advertising," 638.
32. Terry Lefton, "Cutting to the Chase," *Brandweek,* April 7, 1997, 47.
33. This description is based on "Four-Door Sports Car," *1990 Winners of the Effie Gold Awards: Case Studies in Advertising Effectiveness* (New York: American Marketing Association of New York and the American Association of Advertising Agencies, 1991), 124–131.
34. Kim Foltz, "Psychological Appeal in TV Ads Found Effective," *Adweek,* August 31, 1987, 38. Note that this research referred to rational rather than functional appeals, but rational is essentially equivalent to functional.
35. Jack Trout and Al Ries, "The Positioning Era: A View Ten Years Later," *Advertising Age,* July 16, 1979, 39–42.
36. Al Ries and Jack Trout, *The 22 Immutable Laws of Marketing* (New York: Harper Business, 1993), 19.
37. See Thomas J. Reynolds and Jerry C. Olson, *Understanding Decision Making: The Means-End Approach to Marketing and Advertising Strategy* (Mahwah, NJ: Erlbaum, 2001). See also Jonathan Gutman, "A Means-End Chain Model Based on Consumer Categorization Processes," *Journal of Marketing* 46 (spring 1982), 60–72; Thomas J. Reynolds and Jonathan Gutman, "Advertising Is Image Management," *Journal of Advertising Research* 24 (February/March 1984), 27–36; Thomas J. Reynolds and Jonathan Gutman, "Laddering Theory, Method, Analysis, and Interpretation," *Journal of Advertising Research* 28 (February/March 1988), 11–31; and Thomas J. Reynolds and Alyce Byrd Craddock, "The Application of MECCAS Model to the Development

and Assessment of Advertising Strategy: A Case Study," *Journal of Advertising Research* 28 (April/May 1988), 43–59.

38. For further discussion of cultural values, see Lynn R. Kahle, Basil Poulos, and Ajay Sukhdial, "Changes in Social Values in the United States during the Past Decade," *Journal of Advertising Research* 28 (February/March 1988), 35–41; Sharon E. Beatty, Lynn R. Kahle, Pamela Homer, and Shekhar Misra, "Alternative Measurement Approaches to Consumer Values: The List of Values and the Rokeach Value Survey," *Psychology and Marketing* 2, no. 3 (1985), 181–200; Wagner A. Kamakura and Jose Afonso Mazzon, "Value Segmentation: A Model for the Measurement of Values and Value Systems," Journal of Consumer Research 18 (September 1991), 208–218; and Wagner A. Kamakura and Thomas P. Novak, "Value-System Segmentation: Exploring the Meaning of LOV," *Journal of Consumer Research* 19 (June 1992), 119–132.
39. Shalom H. Schwartz, "Universals in the Content and Structure of Values: Theoretical Advances and Empirical Tests in 20 Countries," *Advances in Experimental Social Psychology* 25 (1992), 4.
40. J. Paul Peter and Jerry C. Olson, *Consumer Behavior: Marketing Strategy Perspectives* (Homewood, Ill.: Irwin, 1990).
41. Schwartz, "Universals in the Content and Structure of Values." Another value typology that has been validated across 30 countries is available in Simeon Chow and Sarit Amir, "The Universality of Values: Implications for Global Advertising Strategy," *Journal of Advertising Research* 46 (September 2006), 301–314.
42. These descriptions are based on ibid., 5–12.
43. Jerry Olson and Thomas J. Reynolds, "Understanding Consumers' Cognitive Structures: Implications for Advertising Strategy," in *Advertising and Consumer Psychology*, ed. L. Percy and A. Woodside (Lexington, Mass.: Lexington Books, 1983), 77–90.
44. The language used in Table 8.3 is adapted from that employed in the various writings of Gutman, Reynolds, and Olson such as those cited in endnote 37. It is the author's opinion that the present terminology is more user friendly without doing a disservice to the original MECCAS conceptualization.
45. Brain Wansink, "Using Laddering to Understand and Leverage a Brand's Equity," *Qualitative Market Research: An International Journal* 6 no. 2, 111–118.
46. Thomas J. Reynolds, Clay Dethloff, and Steven J. Westberg, "Advancements in Laddering," in Thomas J. Reynolds and Jerry C. Olson, *Understanding Decision Making*, 91–118.
47. Thomas J. Reynolds and David B. Whitlark, "Applying Laddering Data to Communications Strategy and Advertising Practice," *Journal of Advertising Research* 35 (July/August 1995), 9.
48. See John R. Rossiter and Larry Percy, "The a-b-e Model of Benefit Focus in Advertising," in Thomas J. Reynolds and Jerry C. Olson, *Understanding Decision Making*, 183–213; and Joel B. Cohen and Luk Warlop, "A Motivational Perspective on Means-End Chains," in Thomas J. Reynolds and Jerry C. Olson, *Understanding Decision Making*, 389–412.
49. David W. Schumann, Jan M. Hathcote, and Susan West, "Corporate Advertising in America: A Review of Published Studies on Use, Measurement, and Effectiveness," *Journal of Advertising* 20 (September 1991), 35–56. This article provides a thorough review of corporate advertising and is must reading for anyone interested in the topic. For evidence of the increase in corporate advertising, see Mercedes M. Cardona, "Corporate-Ad Budgets at Record High: ANA Survey," *Advertising Age*, April 27, 1998, 36.
50. This distinction is based on a classification by S. Prakash Sethi, "Institutional/Image Advertising and Idea/Issue Advertising as Marketing Tools: Some Public Policy Issues," *Journal of Marketing* 43 (January 1979), 68–78. Sethi actually labels the two subsets of corporate advertising as "institutional/image" and "idea/issue." For reading ease, they are shortened here to image versus issue advertising.
51. Ibid.
52. Charles H. Patti and John P. McDonald, "Corporate Advertising: Process, Practices, and Perspectives (1970–1989)," *Journal of Advertising* 14, no. 1 (1985), 42–49.
53. Lewis C. Winters, "Does It Pay to Advertise to Hostile Audiences with Corporate Advertising?" *Journal of Advertising Research* 28 (June/July 1988), 11–18.
54. Zeynep Gürhan-Canli and Rajeev Batra, "When Corporate Image Affects Product Evaluations: The Moderation Role of Perceived Risk," *Journal of Marketing Research* 41 (May 2004), 197–205.
55. Bob D. Cutler and Darrel D. Muehling, "Advocacy Advertising and the Boundaries of Commercial Speech," Journal of Advertising 18, no. 3 (1989), 40.
56. Sethi, "Institutional/Image Advertising," 70.
57. For discussion of the First Amendment issues surrounding the use of advocacy advertising, see Cutler and Muehling, "Advocacy Advertising and the Boundaries of Commercial Speech"; and Kent R. Middleton, "Advocacy Advertising, The First Amendment and Competitive Advantage: A Comment on Cutler & Muehling," *Journal of Advertising* 20 (June 1991), 77–81.
58. Louis Banks, "Taking on the Hostile Media," *Harvard Business Review* (March/April 1978), 123–130; Barbara J. Coe, "The Effectiveness Challenge in Issue Advertising Campaigns," *Journal of Advertising* 12, no. 4 (1983), 27–35; David Kelley, "Critical Issues for Issue Ads," *Harvard Business Review* (July/August 1982), 80–87; Ward Welty, "Is Issue Advertising Working?" *Public Relations Journal* (November 1981), 29. For an especially thorough and insightful treatment of issue advertising, particularly with regard to the measurement of effectiveness, see Karen F. A. Fox, "The Measurement of Issue/Advocacy Advertising," in *Current Issues and Research in Advertising*, vol. 9, ed. James H. Leigh and Claude R. Martin, Jr. (Ann Arbor: Division of Research, Graduate School of Business Administration, University of Michigan, 1986), 61–92.

9

Message Appeals and Endorsers

You might recall viewing television advertisements in which Apple's Mac computer was compared with non-Macs, those simply referred to as PCs. In a series of executions, a relatively hip guy (actor Justin Long, who starred in the movie *Accepted*), shown wearing clothing that could be described as cool office casual, personified the Mac. Comparatively, a nerdish, bumbling character (actor John Hodgman from the *Daily Show*) dressed in more formal business clothing embodied the generic PC. In every execution of the campaign, the hip Mac character put down the nerdish PC person and implied superiority of the Mac computer.

We have every reason to believe that this campaign was successful in the United States based on the number of different advertising executions that were run over an extended period. Interestingly, however, Apple had to alter the campaign substantially when introducing it to the Japanese market. First, whereas direct comparisons are commonplace in U.S. advertising, Japanese consumers are put off by the use of a confrontational style of advertising, which is considered to be rude, immodest, and lacking class. Second, in an interesting cultural reversal, the formal clothing style worn by the PC character in the American version of this advertising campaign is evaluated more positively in Japan in comparison to the office-casual clothing worn by the person who personified the Mac computer.

Given these cultural differences between the United States and Japan, advertising for Apple's Mac computer required change before introduction to the Japanese market. For the Japanese versions, friendly banter between the Mac and PC characters replaced the more confrontational form of U.S. advertising. Instead of having the actors wear clothes that cast the PC character as nerdish and the Mac person as hip, the Japanese version made a more subtle distinction between the two characters by having the PC personality wear office attire and the Mac individual wear weekend clothing. Mac also gave PC a nickname, *waaku,* which is a good-natured Japanese version of the word "work."[1]

Two of the issues touched on here—the use of humor and the application of comparative advertising—are among the many topics covered in this chapter. Also, the initial section dealing with enhancing consumers' motivation, opportunity, and ability to process advertising messages is related to this vignette because the use of humor and comparative advertising are tactics for increasing the audience's motivation to attend to and process advertisements.

© AP Images/Chiaki Tsukumo

Chapter Objectives

After reading this chapter you should be able to:

1. Appreciate the efforts advertisers undertake to enhance the consumer's motivation, opportunity, and ability to process ad messages.
2. Describe the role of endorsers in advertising.
3. Explain the requirements for an effective endorser.
4. Appreciate the factors that enter into the endorser-selection decision.
5. Discuss the role of Q Scores in selecting celebrity endorsers.
6. Describe the role of humor in advertising.
7. Explain the logic underlying the use of appeals to fear in advertising.
8. Understand the nature of appeals to guilt in advertising.
9. Discuss the role of sex appeals, including the downside of such usage.
10. Explain the meaning of subliminal messages and symbolic embeds.
11. Appreciate the role of music in advertising.
12. Understand the function of comparative advertising and the considerations that influence the use of this form of advertising.

>>Marcom Insight:

The Use of Humor and Comparisons in Advertising

Introduction

As pointed out repeatedly in Chapter 8, advertisers continually face the challenges of dealing with ad clutter and with audiences that often are disengaged and uninterested in the advertiser's message. To be effective, advertising must break through the clutter and sufficiently motivate the audience to pay attention and engage in higher-order processing of ad messages. Effective advertising, as Chapter 8 notes, is usually creative, and creative ads tend to be connected, appropriate, and novel (the CAN elements).

This chapter surveys some of the common approaches that are used in creating advertising messages. First examined is how advertisers increase consumers' motivation, opportunity, and ability to process advertising messages. The next major section examines the widespread use of endorsers in advertising. Following sections are devoted to five types of messages that are prevalent in advertising: (1) humor, (2) appeals to fear, (3) appeals to guilt, (4) sex appeals, and (5) subliminal messages. The chapter concludes with reviews of music's role in advertising and the pros and cons of using comparative advertisements.

Where possible, an attempt is made to identify *generalizations* about the creation of effective advertising messages. Generalizations, however, are not the same as scientific laws or principles. These higher forms of scientific truth (such as Einstein's general theory of relativity and Newton's law of gravity) have not been established in the realm of advertising for several reasons: First, the buyer behavior that advertising is designed to influence is complex, dynamic, and variable across situations, which consequently makes it difficult to arrive at straightforward explanations of how advertising elements operate in all situations and across all types of market segments. (Recall in this context the *Marcom Insight* in Chapter 7 that posed the question, "Is advertising rocket science?") Second, advertisements are themselves highly varied entities that differ in many ways in addition to their use of humor, or sex, or appeals to fear, or any other single dimension. This complexity makes it difficult to draw universal conclusions about any particular feature of advertising. Third, because products differ in terms of technological sophistication and ability to involve consumers, among other things, it is virtually impossible to identify advertising approaches that are effective across all products, services, and situations.

Thus, the findings presented and the conclusions drawn should be considered tentative rather than definitive. In accordance with the philosopher's advice, "seek simplicity and distrust it,"[2] it would be naive and misleading to suggest that any particular advertising technique will be successful under all circumstances. Rather, the effectiveness of any message format depends on conditions such as the nature of the competition, the character of the product, the degree of brand equity and market leadership, the advertising environment, and the extent of consumer involvement. Throughout the text we have emphasized the importance of an "it depends" mind-set, and it is important that you bring this orientation to your reading of the following sections.

Enhancing Consumers' Motivation, Opportunity, and Ability to Process Advertisements

There is no single way to influence people to form favorable attitudes toward brands or to act in ways marketing communicators desire. Rather, the appropriate influence strategy depends both on *consumer characteristics* (their motivation, opportunity, and ability to process marcom messages) and on *brand strengths.* If consumers are interested in learning about a product, and a company's brand has clear advantages over competitive brands, then the appropriate persuasion tactic is obvious: *design a message telling people explicitly why your brand is superior.* The result should be equally clear: Consumers likely will be swayed by your arguments, which will lead to a relatively enduring attitude change and a strong chance they will select your brand over competitive offerings.[3]

The reality, however, is that brands in most product categories are similar, so consumers generally are not anxious to devote mental effort toward processing messages that provide little new information. Thus, the marketing communicator, faced with this double whammy (only slightly involved consumers and a me-too brand), has to find ways to enthuse consumers sufficiently such that they will listen to or read the communicator's message. Hence, anything marketing communicators can do to enhance the *MOA factors* (motivation, opportunity, and ability) likely will increase communication effectiveness.

Figure 9.1 provides a framework for the following discussion of how marketing communicators can enhance the MOA factors.[4] Each of six strategies will be discussed and illustrated with examples. At the risk of redundancy, it is important to emphasize that it cannot be assumed that consumers will attend to marcom messages and process them just because they are printed, broadcast, or disseminated

figure 9.1

Enhancing Consumers' Motivation, Opportunity, and Ability to Process Brand Information

I. Enhance Consumers' MOTIVATION to . . .

A. Attend to the message by . . .

- Appealing to hedonic needs (appetite appeals, sex appeals)
- Using novel stimuli (unusual pictures, different ad formats, large number of scenes)
- Using intense or prominent cues (action, loud music, colorful ads, celebrities, large pictures)
- Using motion (complex pictures; edits and cuts)

B. Process brand information by . . .

- Increasing relevance of brand to self (asking rhetorical questions, using fear appeals, using dramatic presentations)
- Increasing curiosity about the brand (opening with suspense or surprise, using humor, presenting little information in the message)

II. Enhance Consumers' OPPORTUNITY to . . .

A. Encode information by . . .

- Repeating brand information
- Repeating key scenes
- Repeating the ad on multiple occasions

B. Reduce processing time by . . .

- Creating Gestalt processing (using pictures and imagery)

III. Enhance Consumers' ABILITY to . . .

A. Access knowledge structures by . . .

- Providing a context (employing verbal framing)

B. Create knowledge structures by . . .

- Facilitating exemplar-based learning (using concretizations, demonstrations, and analogies)

SOURCE: Adapted from Deborah J. MacInnis, Christine Moorman, and Bernard J. Jaworski, "Enhancing and Measuring Consumers' Motivation, Opportunity, and Ability to Process Brand Information from Ads," *Journal of Marketing* 55 (October 1991), 36. Reprinted with permission from *Journal of Marketing*, published by the American Marketing Association.

through some other medium. Rather, it is essential that special efforts be made to increase consumers' motivation, opportunity, and ability to process messages. Please carefully examine Figure 9.1 before proceeding so that you have a general appreciation of the topics that will be discussed next.

Motivation to Attend to Messages

Figure 9.1 shows that one of the communicator's objectives is to increase the consumer's motivation to attend to the message and to process brand information. This section discusses just the attention component; the following section will consider the processing element.

There are two forms of attention: voluntary and involuntary.[5] **Voluntary attention** is engaged when consumers devote attention to an advertisement or other marcom message that is perceived as *relevant* to their current purchase-related goals. In other words, messages are voluntarily attended to if they are perceived as pertinent to our needs. Marketing communicators attract voluntary attention by appealing to consumers' informational or hedonic needs. **Involuntary attention,** conversely, occurs when attention is captured by the use of attention-gaining techniques rather than by the consumer's inherent interest in the topic at hand. Novel stimuli, intense or prominent cues, complex pictures, and, in the case of broadcast ads, edits and cuts of the sort seen with MTV-like videos are some of the techniques used to attract attention that otherwise would not be given.

Appeals to Informational and Hedonic Needs

Figure 9.2

An Appeal to Informational Needs

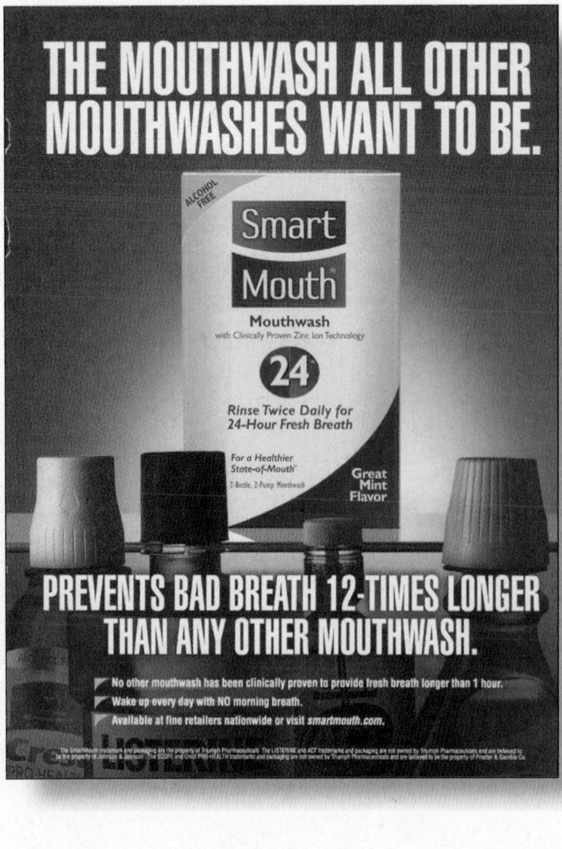

THE MOUTHWASH ALL OTHER MOUTHWASHES WANT TO BE.
ALCOHOL FREE
Smart
Mouth
Mouthwash
with Clinically Proven Zinc Ion Technology
24
Rinse Twice Daily for 24-Hour Fresh Breath
For a Healthier State-of-Mouth
Great Mint Flavor
PREVENTS BAD BREATH 12-TIMES LONGER THAN ANY OTHER MOUTHWASH.
No other mouthwash has been clinically proven to provide fresh breath longer than 1 hour.
Wake up every day with NO morning breath.
Available at fine retailers nationwide or visit smartmouth.com.

© Courtesy of Triumph Pharmaceuticals Inc.

Consumers are most likely to attend to those messages that serve their informational needs and those that make them feel good and bring pleasure (that is, those that serve their hedonic needs). Regarding *informational needs,* consumers are attracted to those stimuli that supply relevant facts and figures. A student who wants to move out of a dormitory and into an apartment, for example, will be on the lookout for information pertaining to apartments. An apartment seeker will attend to classified ads and overheard conversations about apartments, even when he or she is not actively looking for information. As another illustration, consider the advertisement in Figure 9.2 for Smart Mouth mouthwash. The ad informatively points out that this brand "prevents bad breath 12-times longer than any other mouthwash" and also supplies other pertinent details that provide reasons for consumers to consider purchasing this brand. (This advertisement uses a technique described later in the chapter as an *indirect comparison.*)

Hedonic needs are satisfied when consumers attend to messages that make them feel good and serve their pleasure needs. People are most likely to attend to those messages that have become associated with good times, enjoyment, and things we value in life. For example, the use of children, warm family scenes, and sex or romance appeals are just some of the commonly used attention-gaining techniques widely used in advertisements. Similarly, advertisements for appetizing food products are especially likely to be noticed when people are hungry. For this reason, many restaurants and fast-food marketers advertise on the radio during the after-work rush hour. Fast-food advertisers also promote their products on late-night television for the same reason. Needless to say, the best time to reach consumers with a message is just at the time they are experiencing a need for the product category in which the brand resides.

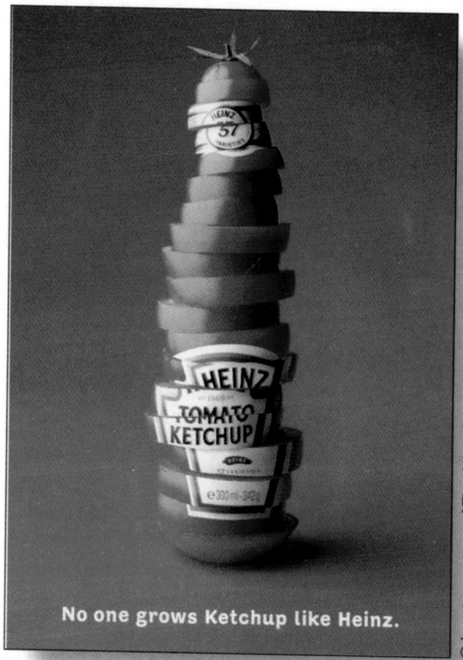

© Image courtesy of The Advertising Archives

Figure 9.3

Using Novelty to Attract Attention

Use of Novel Stimuli

There are innumerable ways marketing communicators use novelty to attract involuntary attention. In general, **novel messages** are, as discussed in Chapter 8, *unusual, distinctive, unpredictable, and somewhat unexpected.* Such stimuli tend to produce greater attention than those that are familiar and routine. This can be explained by the behavioral concept of *human adaptation.* People adapt to the conditions around them: As a stimulus becomes more familiar, people become desensitized to it. Psychologists refer to this as *habituation.* For example, if you drive past a billboard daily, you likely notice it less on each occasion. If the billboard were removed, you probably would notice it was no longer there. In other words, *we notice by exception.*

Examples of novelty abound. For example, Figure 9.3 is an advertisement for Heinz ketchup that employs an eye-catching graphic with corresponding copy to make the compelling point that Heinz ketchup is unique. The traditional Heinz bottle is displayed as a layer of tomato slices and is capped off with a stem-attached section of tomato. The copy at the ad's bottom brings clarity to the bottle graphic when claiming that "No one grows Ketchup like Heinz." This novel advertisement both attracts attention while conveying subtly the point that the Heinz brand of ketchup is unique.

Figure 9.4

Using Intensity to Attract Attention

WM. WRIGLEY JR. COMPANY

Use of Intense or Prominent Cues

Intense and prominent cues (those that are louder, more colorful, bigger, brighter, etc.) increase the probability of attracting attention. This is because it is difficult for consumers to avoid such stimuli, which leads to *involuntary attention.* One need only walk through a shopping mall, department store, or supermarket and observe the various packages, displays, sights, sounds, and smells to appreciate the special efforts marketing communicators take to attract attention.

Advertisements, too, utilize intensity and prominence to attract attention. For example, the advertisement in Figure 9.4 for Orbit White Melon Breeze, a gum product for removing stains and whitening teeth, effectively uses brightness and vivid color and contrast (along with novelty) to attract attention to a shot of the product package with the brand name prominently displayed. Figure 9.5 (for Kettle Chips) creatively uses a cow to draw attention to the brand and to convey the point that Kettle Chips are made with real cheese.

Using Motion

Advertisers sometimes employ motion to both attract and direct consumer attention to the brand name and to pertinent ad copy. (Motion obviously is used in TV commercials, which is an inherently dynamic medium. However, the issue is

Figure 9.5

Using Prominence to Attract Attention

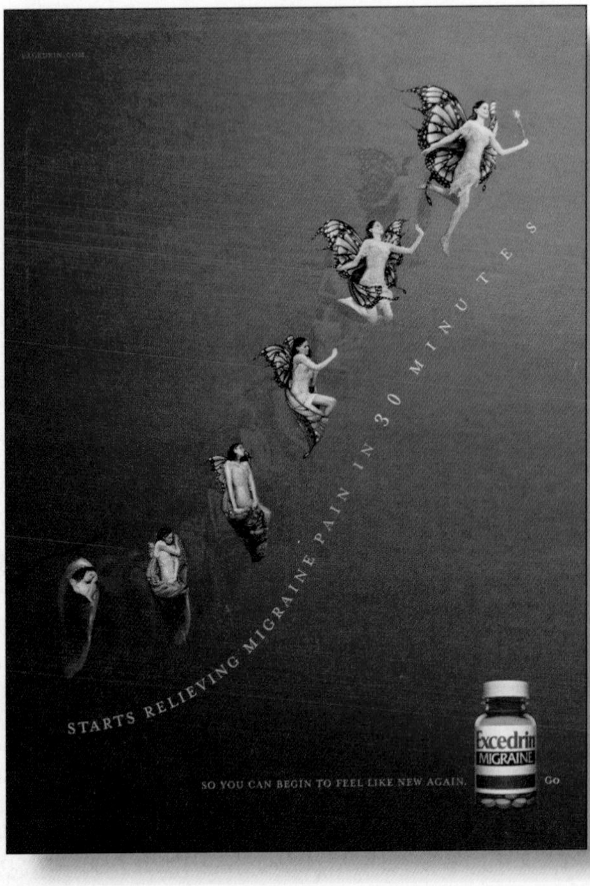

Figure 9.6

Using Motion to Attract Attention

more germane with print advertising—magazines and newspapers—which is a static form of advertising display. Hence, artistic and photographic techniques are employed that produce a semblance of movement, although nothing is of course actually moving.) Falling objects (e.g., a flipping coin), people appearing to be running, and automobiles in motion are some of the techniques used in print ads to attract attention. The advertisement for Excedrin Migraine pills (Figure 9.6) portrays a sense of movement and also conveys that Excedrin users will start receiving relief in just 30 minutes—an active butterfly (post-usage) released from a state of cocoon-like dormancy (pre-usage).

Motivation to Process Messages

Enhanced processing motivation means that the ad receiver has increased interest in reading or listening to the ad message to determine what it has to say that might be of relevance. Among other desirable outcomes, increased processing motivation has been shown to strengthen the impact of brand attitudes on purchase intentions.[6] To enhance consumers' motivation to process brand information, marketing communicators do two things: (1) enhance the *relevance* of the brand to the consumer and (2) enhance *curiosity* about the brand. Methods for enhancing brand relevance include using *fear appeals* (discussed later in the chapter), employing *dramatic presentations* to increase the significance of the brand to consumers' self-interests, and raising *rhetorical questions* that activate consumer interest in the advertised brand.[7] (Rhetorical questions are not questions in the strict sense that an answer is being requested, rather they are figurative questions that encourage people to reflect on what the implied answer to the question must be.).

Using *humor*, presenting *little information* in the message (and thereby encouraging the consumer to think about the brand), or opening a message with *suspense or surprise* can enhance curiosity about a brand. The ad for Viva paper towels (Figure 9.7) uses an element of *suspense* (a spaghetti and meatball plate precariously perched on the edge of a cabinet) to attract the reader's attention and give him or her reason to further examine this advertisement. Attention is immediately drawn to the colorful plate (in vivid contrast to the grey wall), and then the vertical indentations in the wall naturally direct attention down to the all-important product shot and the information about this brand.

Opportunity to Encode Information

Marketing messages have no chance of effectiveness unless consumers comprehend information about the brand and incorporate it with information related to the product category in their existing memory structure. Hence, the communicator's goal is to get consumers to *encode* information and, toward this end, to make it as simple and quick as possible for them to do so. The secret to facilitating encoding is *repetition:* The marketing communicator should repeat brand information, repeat key scenes, and repeat the advertisement on multiple occasions.[8] Through repetition consumers have an increased opportunity to encode the important information the communicator wishes to convey. This is why we see advertisements repeated night after night on TV, sometimes to excess. But advertisers know that repetition is required to get their point across.

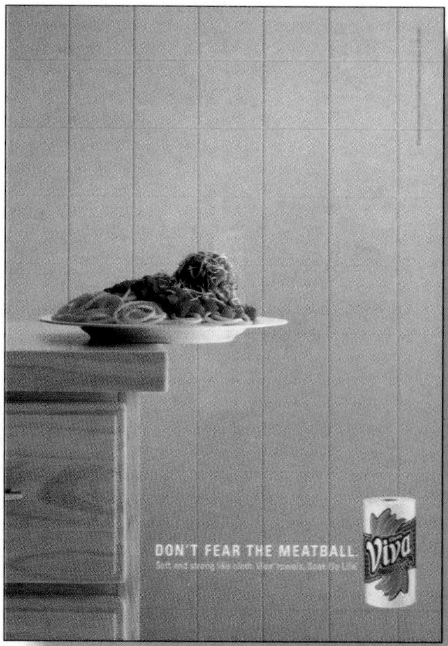

Courtesy of Kimberly-Clark Corporation

Figure 9.7

Using Suspense to Enhance Processing Motivation

Opportunity to Reduce Processing Time

Opportunity to process is further enhanced if the communicator takes extra measures to *reduce the time* required of the consumer to read, listen to, and ultimately discern the meaning of a marcom message. The use of pictures and imagery create a form of total-message processing (or *gestalt*) whereby the consumer can readily encode the totality of the message rather than having to process information bit by bit or to think much about what the advertiser is claiming. This is in line with the old adage that a picture is worth a thousand words. Consider the advertisement in Figure 9.8 for NyQuil Cold & Flu medicine. The image of a comfortable bed placed in a teaspoon conveys the impression that a teaspoon of NyQuil promotes a "great night's sleep." The attention-capturing pictorial combined with the minimal verbal content in this ad succeed in creating the gestalt impression that this brand will deliver something (sleep!) that the cold or flu sufferer much desires.

Ability to Access Knowledge Structures

A brand-based *knowledge structure* represents the associative links in the consumer's long-term memory between the brand and thoughts, feelings, and beliefs about that brand. In general, people are most able to process new information that relates to something they already know or understand. For example, if one knows a lot about computers, then information presented in computer language is readily comprehended. In general, the marketing communicator's task is to enable consumers either to *access* existing knowledge structures or to *create* new knowledge structures.

To facilitate consumer accessing of knowledge structures, marketing communicators need to provide a context for the text or pictures. *Verbal framing* is one way of providing a context. This means that pictures in an ad are placed in the context of, or framed with, appropriate words or phrases so ad receivers can better understand brand information and the key selling point of the marcom message. In an advertisement for DuPont's Teflon brand of scratch-resistant coatings, attention is drawn to the incongruous image of a skillet filled with copper wiring, tacks, and shards of glass. Most consumers believe that nonstick skillets can be easily damaged when scratched with sharp objects. Against this prevailing knowledge structure and in view of the incongruous visual, ad copy must clarify this image. The limited copy simply points out that DuPont Teflon coatings are scratch resistant and encourages readers to visit their Web site (http://teflon.com) for further information.

Figure 9.8

Using a Gestalt to Reduce Processing Time

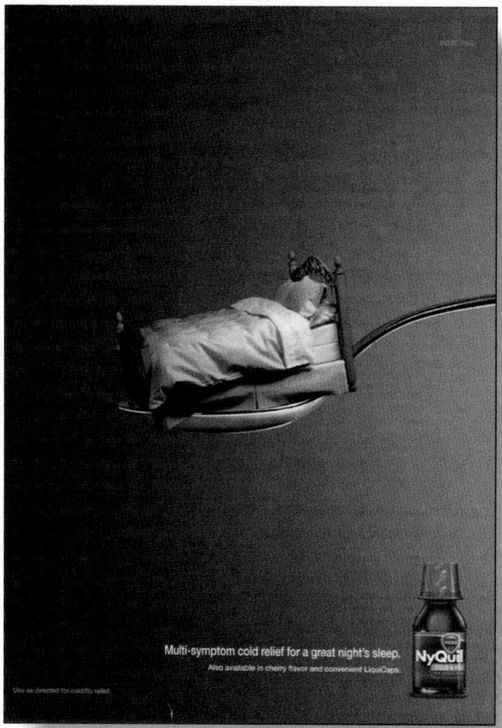

© Courtesy of the Procter & Gamble Company

Ability to Create Knowledge Structures

Sometimes marketing communicators need to *create* knowledge structures for information they want consumers to have about their brands. This is accomplished by facilitating *exemplar-based learning*. An *exemplar* is a specimen or model of a particular concept or idea. By using concretizations, demonstrations, or analogies, the marketing communicator can facilitate learning by appealing to exemplars. Consider, for example, the concept of freshness. We all know what freshness means, but it is a rather abstract concept that is difficult to verbalize. That is, it is difficult to explain what freshness means without resorting to an example. Diet Pepsi's brand managers faced this situation when introducing the practice of "freshness dating"—that is, printing on the soft-drink container the final date up to which the beverage remained fresh. If you were Diet Pepsi's brand manager, what grocery products might you use to exemplify freshness? Their choice was to use exemplars in the form of pictures of products that people routinely inspect for freshness (squeeze an orange, pinch a loaf of bread) and, by analogy, communicate the idea that consumers should check Diet Pepsi cans to ensure that the contents are not outdated. The advertisement (Figure 9.9) for Hidden Valley Ranch dressing uses the analogy that this brand is like the proverbial "icing on the cake" that enhances the taste of vegetables—just like cake icing improves the taste of cake.

Concretizations

Concretizing, which was briefly discussed in the prior chapter, is used extensively in advertising to facilitate both consumer learning and retrieval of brand information. **Concretizing** is based on the straightforward idea that it is easier for people to remember and retrieve *tangible* rather than abstract information. Claims about a brand are more concrete (versus abstract) when they are made perceptible, palpable, real, evident, and vivid. Concretizing is accomplished by using concrete words and examples. Here are some illustrations:

1. An advertisement for Johnson's baby powder positioned the brand as capable of making the user's body feel "as soft as the day you were born." To concretize this claim, a series of age-regression scenes revealed, first, a shot of a woman in her 30s, then a shot as she looked in her 20s, next as an early teenager, and finally as a baby. Accompanying music was played throughout to the lyrics "Make me, make me your baby." This beautiful and somewhat touching ad made concrete Johnson's claim that its baby powder will make users feel as soft as the day they were born.
2. The makers of Anacin tablets needed a concrete way to present their brand as "strong pain relief for splitting headaches." The idea of a splitting headache was concretized by showing a hardboiled egg splitting with accompanying sound effects.
3. Tinactin, a treatment for athlete's foot, concretized its relief properties by showing a person's feet literally appearing to be on fire (representing the fiery sensation of athlete's foot), which is "extinguished" by an application of Tinactin.
4. To convey the notion that Purina brand Hi Pro dog food will recharge an active dog and keep it running, a magazine ad portrayed the brand in the form of a battery, which is a widely recognized apparatus for charging electrical objects. In effect, the battery in this symbolic concretization conveyed pictorially the more abstract claim contained in the ad's body copy.
5. To establish in consumers' minds that Tums EX is "twice as strong as Rolaids," the commercial showed a sledgehammer behind Tums and a regular-sized hammer behind Rolaids. The commercial then showed the sledgehammer driving in a nail twice as quickly as the regular hammer, thus concretizing Tums' claim.
6. Another Tums advertisement claimed in its headline that "scientific studies find Tums to be the purest form of calcium available." This claim was concretized with the visual display of a package of Tums inside an empty milk bottle,

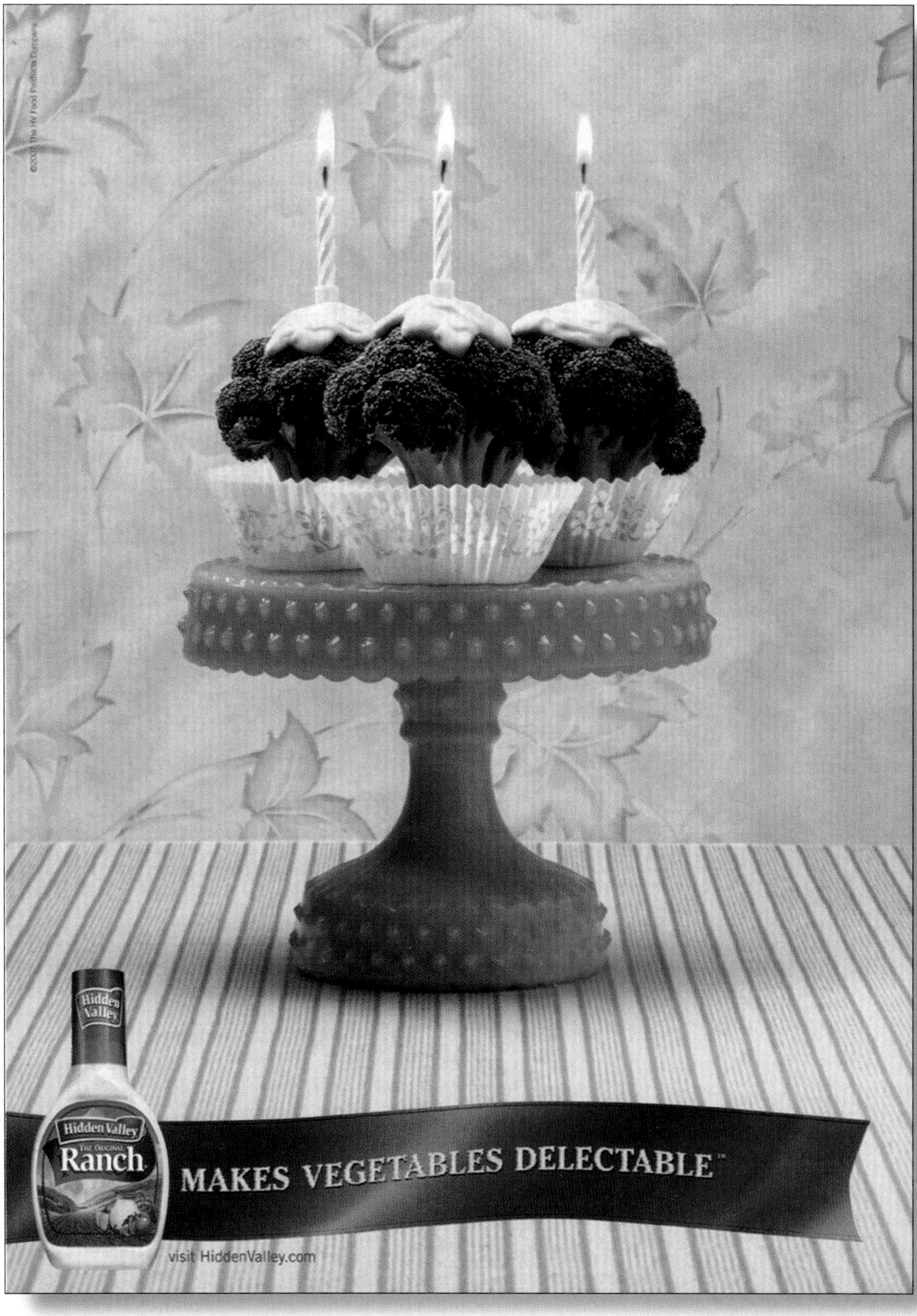

Figure 9.9

The Use of Analogy to Create a Knowledge Structure

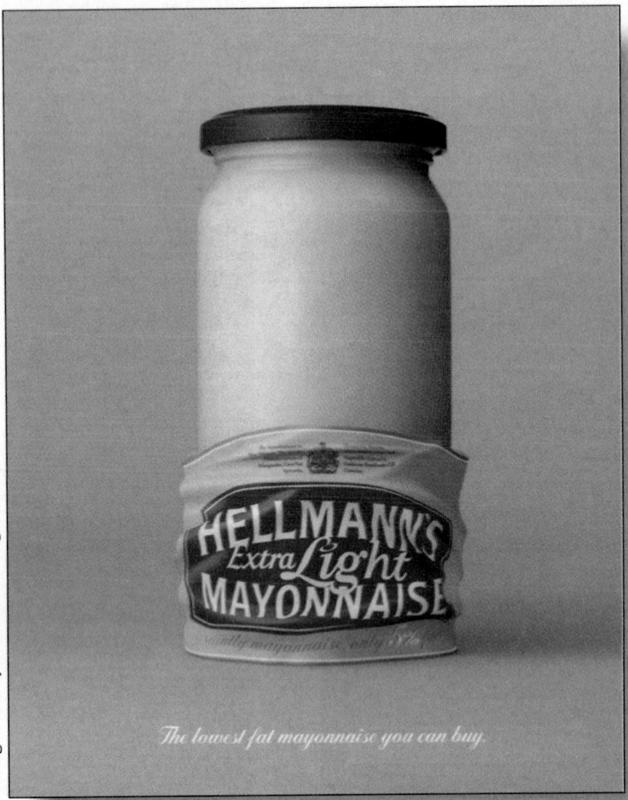

© Image courtesy of The Advertising Archives

Figure 9.10

Exemplar-Based Learning with Concretization

an exemplar of calcium, and with the juxtaposed words calcium and Tums forming the new word Calciums.

7. Finally, the advertisement for Hellmann's (Figure 9.10) shows a jar of Hellmann's Extra Light mayonnaise that has become so thin its label is falling down, thereby concretizing the tacit claim that this brand is a good choice for managing weight.

Section Summary

The foregoing discussion has emphasized that advertisers, along with other marketing communicators, benefit from enhancing consumers' motivation, opportunity, and ability to process marketing messages. A variety of communication devices enables advertisers to achieve their goals in the hopes of influencing consumers' brand-related attitudes, purchase intentions, and, ultimately, their behavior. Anything the advertiser can do to enhance consumers' MOA factors—motivation, opportunity, and ability to attend to and process ad messages—will benefit a brand's equity and increase the odds that consumers will purchase that brand rather than a competitive offering. One way to increase consumers' motivation to attend and process ad messages is by using celebrity endorsers.

The Role of Celebrity Endorsers in Advertising

Advertised brands frequently receive endorsements from a variety of popular public figures. It has been estimated that approximately one sixth of ads worldwide feature celebrities.[9] In addition to celebrity endorsements, products receive the explicit or tacit support of noncelebrities, also known as typical-person endorsers. The following discussion is limited to celebrity endorsers.

Television stars, movie actors, famous athletes, and even dead personalities are widely used to endorse brands. Advertisers and their agencies are willing to pay huge salaries to celebrities who are liked and respected by target audiences and who will, it is hoped, favorably influence consumers' attitudes and behavior toward the endorsed brands. For the most part, such investments are justified. For example, stock prices have been shown to rise when companies announce celebrity endorsement contracts[10] and to fall when negative publicity reaches the media about a celebrity who endorses one of the company's brands.[11]

Top celebrities receive enormous payments for their endorsement services. For example, in a recent year golfer Tiger Woods earned $100 million from endorsement deals with multiple companies. To put this amount of money in perspective, a person earning a not-so-paltry annual income of $250,000 would have to work 400 years at that salary to earn as much as Tiger Woods received in a single year from his endorsement activities! Table 9.1 lists the endorsement incomes of America's top endorsing-earning athletes.

table 9.1

Top Endorsement Incomes of American Athletes, 2007

Rank	Athlete	Sport	Endorsement Earnings
1	Tiger Woods	Pro golf	$100,000,000
2	Phil Mickelson	Pro golf	$ 47,000,000
3	LeBron James	NBA basketball	$ 25,000,000
4	Dale Earnhardt Jr.	NASCAR	$ 20,000,000
5	Michelle Wie	Pro golf	$ 19,500,000
6	Kobe Bryant	NBA basketball	$ 16,000,000
7 (tie)	Shaquille O'Neal	NBA basketball	$ 15,000,000
7 (tie)	Jeff Gordon	NASCAR	$ 15,000,000
9	Peyton Manning	NFL football	$ 13,000,000
10	Dwyane Wade	NBA basketball	$ 12,000,000
11	Tom Brady	NFL football	$ 9,000,000
12	Kevin Garnett	NBA basketball	$ 8,000,000
13 (tie)	Brett Favre	NFL football	$ 7,000,000
13 (tie)	Allen Iverson	NBA basketball	$ 7,000,000
13 (tie)	Derek Jeter	Major league baseball	$ 7,000,000
13 (tie)	Michael Vick	NFL football	$ 7,000,000
17 (tie)	Tracy McGrady	NBA basketball	$ 6,000,000
17 (tie)	Alex Rodriguez	Major league baseball	$ 6,000,000
19	Vince Carter	NBA basketball	$ 5,000,000
20 (tie)	Roger Clemens	Major league baseball	$ 3,500,000
20 (tie)	Tim Duncan	NBA basketball	$ 3,500,000

Source: Adapted from Jonah Freedman, "The Fortunate 50," *SI.com*, http://sportsillustrated.cnn.com/more/specials/fortunate50/2007/index.html (accessed January 14, 2008).

Endorser Attributes: The TEARS Model

Extensive research has demonstrated that two general attributes, *credibility* and *attractiveness*, contribute to an endorser's effectiveness, and that each consists of more distinct subattributes.[12] To facilitate the student's memory with respect to endorser characteristics, we use the acronym TEARS to represent five discrete attributes: trustworthiness and expertise are two dimensions of credibility, whereas physical attractiveness, respect, and similarity (to the target audience) are components of the general concept of attractiveness. Table 9.2 lists and defines all five attributes.

table 9.2

The Five Components in the TEARS Model of Endorser Attributes

T = Trustworthiness	The property of being perceived as believable, dependable—as someone who can be trusted.
E = Expertise	The characteristic of having specific skills, knowledge, or abilities with respect to the endorsed brand.
A = Physical attractiveness	The trait of being regarded as pleasant to look at in terms of a particular group's concept of attractiveness.
R = Respect	The quality of being admired or even esteemed due to one's personal qualities and accomplishments.
S = Similarity (to the target audience)	The extent to which an endorser matches an audience in terms of characteristics pertinent to the endorsement relationship (age, gender, ethnicity, etc.).

Credibility: The Process of Internalization

In its most basic sense, *credibility* refers to the tendency to believe or trust someone. When an information source, such as an endorser, is perceived as credible, audience attitudes are changed through a psychological process called *internalization*. **Internalization** occurs when the receiver accepts the endorser's position on an issue as his or her own. An internalized attitude tends to be maintained even if the source of the message is forgotten or if the source switches to a different position.[13]

Two important subattributes of endorser credibility are trustworthiness and expertise. **Trustworthiness,** the *T* in the TEARS model, refers to the honesty, integrity, and believability of a source. Although expertise and trustworthiness are not mutually exclusive, often a particular endorser is perceived as highly trustworthy but not especially expert. An endorser's trustworthiness rests on the audience's perception of his or her endorsement motivations. If consumers believe that an endorser is motivated purely by self-interest, that endorser will be less persuasive than someone regarded as having nothing to gain by endorsing the brand.

A celebrity earns the audience's trust through the life he or she lives professionally (on the screen, on the sports field, in public office, etc.) and personally, as revealed to the general public via the mass media. Advertisers capitalize on the value of trustworthiness by selecting endorsers who are widely regarded as being honest, believable, and dependable people.[14] It is little surprise that Tiger Woods tops the list of American athletes in terms of endorsement income (see Table 9.1). Woods is widely regarded as above reproach both in his personal and professional lives.

In general, endorsers must establish that they are not attempting to manipulate the audience and that they are objective in their presentations. By doing so, they establish themselves as trustworthy and, therefore, credible. Also, an endorser has a greater likelihood of being perceived as trustworthy the more he or she matches the audience in terms of distinct characteristics such as gender and ethnicity. When a spokesperson matches the audience's ethnicity, for example, spokesperson trustworthiness is enhanced, which, in turn, promotes more favorable attitudes toward the advertised brand.[15]

The second aspect of endorser credibility is expertise, the *E* component of the TEARS model. **Expertise** refers to the knowledge, experience, or skills possessed by an endorser as they relate to the endorsed brand. Hence, athletes are considered to be experts when it comes to the endorsement of sports-related products. Models are similarly perceived as possessing expertise with regard to beauty-enhancing products and fashion items. Successful businesspeople are regarded as experts in matters of managerial practices. For example, Donald Trump, due to his extensive business background in commercial real estate transactions and otherwise, would be regarded as high in expertise in business matters and thus was a logical choice of star for the creators of *The Apprentice* TV program. Expertise is a perceived rather than an absolute phenomenon. Whether an endorser is indeed an expert is unimportant; all that matters is how the target audience perceives the endorser. An endorser who is perceived as an expert on a given subject is more persuasive in changing audience opinions pertaining to his or her area of expertise than an endorser who is not perceived as an expert.

Attractiveness: The Process of Identification

The second general attribute that contributes to endorser effectiveness, **attractiveness,** means more than simply physical attractiveness—although that can be a very important attribute—and includes any number of virtuous characteristics that consumers may perceive in an endorser: intellectual skills, personality properties, lifestyle characteristics, athletic prowess, and so on. When consumers find something in an endorser that they consider attractive, persuasion occurs through **identification.** That is, when consumers perceive a celebrity endorser to be attractive, they identify with the endorser and are likely to adopt the endorser's attitudes, behaviors, interests, or preferences.

The TEARS model identifies three subcomponents of the general concept of attractiveness: *physical attractiveness, respect,* and *similarity.* That is, an endorser is regarded as attractive—in the general sense of this concept—to the extent that he or she is considered physically attractive, respected for reasons other than physical attractiveness, or regarded as similar to the target audience in terms of any characteristic that is pertinent to a particular endorsement relationship. Perceived attractiveness can be achieved via any one of these attributes and does not require that a celebrity encompass all simultaneously; however, it goes without saying that a celebrity who possesses the entire "package" of attractiveness attributes would represent awesome endorsement potential—again, does Tiger Woods come to mind?

First, **physical attractiveness**—the *A* component in the TEARS model—is a key consideration in many endorsement relationships.[16] Perhaps no better illustration of this is possible than professional golfer's Michelle Wie's success as an endorser. Wie earned nearly $20 million in endorsement deals in a recent year (see Table 9.1), which is an incredible feat considering she has never won a professional golfing event. There is a good reason why advertising agents and their brand management clients often select highly attractive celebrities to endorse products: Research has supported the intuitive expectation that physically attractive endorsers produce more favorable evaluations of ads and advertised brands than do less attractive communicators.[17]

Respect, the *R* in the TEARS model, is the second component of the overall attractiveness attribute. **Respect** represents the quality of being admired or even esteemed due to one's personal qualities and accomplishments. Whereas a celebrity's physical attractiveness may be considered the "form" aspect of the overall attractiveness attribute, respect is the "function" or substantive element. Sometimes function (respect) trumps form (physical attractiveness), even in brand-endorser relations.

Celebrities are respected for their acting ability, athletic prowess, appealing personalities, their stands on important societal issues (the environment, political issues, war and peace, etc.), and any number of other qualities. Perhaps ex-boxer Muhammad Ali personifies the respect dimension more than any other athlete in the world—both for the incredible skills he displayed in the ring and his stand on issues outside the ring. Individuals who are respected also generally are liked, and it is this likeability factor that can serve to enhance a brand's equity when a celebrity endorser enters into an endorsement relationship with the brand. In turn, the brand acquires some semblance of the characteristics that are admired in the celebrity who endorses the brand. In sum, when a respected or liked celebrity enters into an extended endorser relationship with a brand, the respect for and liking of the celebrity may extend to the brand with which he or she is linked, thus enhancing a brand's equity via the positive effect on consumers' brand-related beliefs and attitudes.

Similarity, the third attractiveness component and the *S* in the TEARS model, represents the degree to which an endorser matches an audience in terms of characteristics pertinent to the endorsement relationship—age, gender, ethnicity, and so on. Similarity is an important attribute because people tend to prefer individuals who share with them common features or traits. This, of course, is reminiscent of the cliché that "birds of a feather flock together."

As it applies to the domain of brand-celebrity relationships, the importance of similarity implies that it typically is desirable for a celebrity to match his or her endorsed brand's target audience in terms of pertinent demographic and psychographic characteristics. There is some evidence that a matchup between endorser and audience similarity is especially important when the product or service in question is one where audience members are *heterogeneous* in terms of their taste and attribute preferences. For example, because people differ greatly in terms of what they like in restaurants, plays, and movies, a spokesperson perceived to be similar to the audience is expected to have the greatest effect in influencing their attitudes and choices. In contrast, when preferences among audience members are relatively *homogeneous* (such as might be expected with services such as plumbing, dry cleaning, and auto repair), the matchup between spokesperson and audience similarity is *not* that important. Rather, it is the spokesperson's experience or expertise with the product or service that appears to have the greatest influence in shaping the audience's attitudes and subsequent behavior.[18]

Endorser Selection Considerations: The "No Tears" Approach

The preceding section described the celebrity attributes that are important in determining celebrities' effectiveness as endorsers. The TEARS model identified five attributes that were grouped under the two general components of credibility and attractiveness. Now let us turn to how brand managers and their advertising agencies actually select particular endorsers to align with their brands. In a takeoff on the TEARS acronym, endorser selection is described here as the "no-tears" approach. Compared with the prior usage of TEARS, the current lowercase usage is applied in the real sense of the word tears. In other words, the current discussion is directed at identifying how brand managers and their agencies actually go about selecting celebrities so as to avoid the grief (metaphorically, the tears) of making an unwise decision.

Advertising executives use a variety of factors in selecting celebrity endorsers. The following appear to be the most important: (1) celebrity and audience matchup, (2) celebrity and brand matchup, (3) celebrity credibility, (4) celebrity attractiveness, (5) cost considerations, (6) a working ease or difficulty factor, (7) an endorsement saturation factor, and (8) a likelihood-of-getting-into-trouble factor.[19]

1. Celebrity and Audience Matchup

The first question a brand manager must pose when selecting an endorser is, "Will the target market positively relate to this endorser?" Shaquille O'Neal, LeBron James, Allen Iverson, and other National Basketball Association (NBA) superstars who endorse basketball shoes match up well with the predominantly teenage audience who aspire to slam dunk basketballs, block shots, intercept passes, and sink 25-foot jump shots. Yao Ming (NBA basketball player) matches well with the growing number of Chinese youth who also aspire to basketball stardom. And Serena Williams (tennis star and fashion devotee) matches well with young women of all races who admire an athlete who is both highly competent and attractive physically and otherwise.

2. Celebrity and Brand Matchup

Advertising executives require that the celebrity's behavior, values, appearance, and decorum be compatible with the image desired for the advertised brand. For example, the chief marketing officer at cosmetics firm Elizabeth Arden explained the choice of supermodel and actress Catherine Zeta-Jones in these terms: "Catherine has [a] great career and family, she's a mom, and she has a timeless beauty, which is exactly the image we want to project."[20]

If a brand has a wholesome image or wants to project this particular attribute, then the celebrity endorser should personify wholesomeness. For example, German athletic shoemaker Adidas signed NBA players Tim Duncan, Kevin

Garnett, and Tracy McGrady to endorse that brand because they all are modest individuals with wholesome images. Comparatively, a brand intentionally casting itself with a "bad boy" image would select entirely different endorsers. Again using the NBA, Allen Iverson or Vince Carter fit well with this latter image. Suppose a brand manager wished to enhance a brand's equity by portraying the brand as incomparable in terms of durability, dependability, and consistency. Who better to personify these characteristics than, say, Cal Ripken, the Baltimore Orioles baseball player who played in 2,632 consecutive baseball games prior to retiring. See the *Global Focus* insert for discussion of why China's Li Ning Co., the leading Chinese athletic-shoe brand, chose the relatively unknown NBA player, Damon Jones, to endorse Li Ning shoes.

3. Celebrity Credibility

A celebrity's credibility is a primary reason for selecting a celebrity endorser. People who are trustworthy and perceived as knowledgeable about the product category are best able to convince others to undertake a particular course of action. This partially explains why most any product recommended by Oprah Winfrey obtains success virtually overnight. We previously described the two components

global focus

Two Unknowns (to Americans) Connect in China

You possibly have never heard of Li Ning, which is the largest supplier of sports shoes in the People's Republic of China. (Readers who are familiar with Li Ning likely gained this familiarity from the company's presence as a sponsor of the 2008 Summer Olympics held in China.) Unless you are a big fan of the National Basketball Association, you probably also are unaware of a basketball player named Damon Jones—who, at the time of this writing, was a guard for the Cleveland Cavaliers, but who since 1998 also has played for nine other NBA teams.

Li Ning produces shoes and sportswear mostly for the Chinese market. Its major shoe lines are the Flying Armor series of basketball shoes and Flying Feather running shoes. With sales less than $1 billion, but growing rapidly, Li Ning executives desired to further grow the brand and to offset the rapid gains in China from global brands Nike and Adidas. The company selected an obvious tactic for achieving this goal, namely, using an NBA player—Damon Jones—to endorse the brand. NBA basketball is very popular in China, due in large part to the success of Yao Ming and upstart Chinese players such as Yi Jianlian. In fact, the NBA considers China to be its second-largest market.

Why choose Damon Jones to endorse the Li Ning brand in China? The Li Ning advertising slogan is *yiqie jie you keneng*, which translates as "anything is possible." Damon Jones's career as an NBA player matches well with Li Ning's slogan. Jones was an undrafted player who worked extremely hard first to get into the league and then to stay there. His career demonstrates to young basketball fans that hard work enables unexpected achievement—anything is possible! However, there were other factors in play in the choice of Damon Jones to endorse the Li Ning brand. Perhaps most important, as a relatively small company, Li Ning could not afford that huge cost it would have incurred to pay for an NBA superstar's endorsement. Moreover, Li Ning wanted an endorser who was "hungry" for a shoe contract, who would willingly travel to China with some regularity, would happily meet with Chinese youth and demonstrate his skills while wearing Li Ning shoes and apparel items, would reflect a positive image, and would otherwise interact with the brand without being a "hassle factor." Damon Jones satisfied all criteria, and the relationship between Li Ning and Jones is off to a good start.

SOURCES: Stephanie Kang and Geoffrey A. Fowler, "Li Ning Wanted an NBA Endorser, And Damon Jones Needed a Deal," *The Wall Street Journal*, June 24, 2006, A1; "Li Ning Company Limited," http://en.wikipedia.org/wiki/Li-Ning_Company_Limited(accessed January 16, 2008).

of credibility, trustworthiness and expertise, in the context of the TEARS model, so further discussion is unnecessary.

4. Celebrity Attractiveness

In selecting celebrity spokespeople, advertising executives evaluate different aspects that can be lumped together under the general label *attractiveness.* As discussed earlier in the context of the TEARS model, attractiveness is multifaceted and includes more than physical attractiveness. It also is important to note that advertising executives generally regard attractiveness as less important than credibility and endorser matchup with the audience and the brand.

5. Cost Considerations

How much it will cost to acquire a celebrity's services is an important consideration but one that should not dictate the final choice. Everything else held constant, a less costly celebrity will be selected over a more costly alternative. But, of course, everything else is not held constant. Hence, as with any managerial decision involving choices among alternatives, brand managers must perform a cost-benefit analysis to determine whether a more expensive celebrity can be justified in terms of a proportionately greater return on investment. This, unfortunately, is not a simple calculation because it is difficult to project the revenue stream that will be obtained from using a particular celebrity endorser. Difficulty aside, management must attempt to calculate the alternative returns on investment given multiple options of celebrities who would appropriately fit with a brand's desired image and its target market.

6. Working Ease or Difficulty Factor

Some celebrities are relatively easy to work with, whereas others are difficult—stubborn, noncompliant, arrogant, temperamental, inaccessible, or otherwise unmanageable. Brand managers and their advertising agencies would prefer to avoid the "hassle factor" of dealing with individuals who are unwilling to flex their schedules, hesitant to participate with a brand outside of celebrity-restricted bounds, or otherwise difficult. For example, jeanswear maker Tarrant Apparel Group filed a civil suit against pop singer Jessica Simpson on grounds that she "would not pose for photos nor provide photographs to promote" the line of apparel that carried her name.[21] Although Simpson matched well with the brand and with the brand's target market, it appears that the endorsement relationship failed because she was difficult to work with.

7. Saturation Factor

Another key consideration, certainly not as important as the previous factors but one that nonetheless has to be evaluated, is the number of other brands the celebrity is endorsing. If a celebrity is overexposed—that is, endorsing too many products—his or her perceived credibility may suffer.[22] Tiger Woods, who may be the most impactful endorser in the history of advertising endorsements, intentionally limits the number of brands he endorses (e.g, Nike, Buick, and EA Sports), although he could endorse dozens of other brands if he were so inclined.[23]

8. The Trouble Factor

This final factor evaluates the likelihood that a celebrity will get into trouble after an endorsement relation is established. The potential that a celebrity may get into trouble is a matter of considerable concern to brand managers and ad agencies. Suppose a celebrity is convicted of a crime or has his or her image blemished in some way during the course of an advertising campaign. What are the potential negative implications for the endorsed brand? Frankly, there are no simple answers to this provocative question, although researchers are beginning to explore the issue in a sophisticated fashion.[24]

Many advertisers and advertising agencies are reluctant to use celebrity endorsers. Their concern is not without justification. Consider some of the celebrity-related incidents making news in recent years and during past decades: (1) Basketball player Kobe Bryant was convicted, although subsequently acquitted, of a rape charge in Colorado. Shortly thereafter, McDonald's Corporation refused to renew Bryant as a spokesperson, as did a much smaller Italian company that makes Nutella chocolate-hazelnut spread. Bryant nonetheless has made a relatively swift comeback from his damaged-goods image; Table 9.1 shows that Bryant is the sixth top endorser among American athletes with endorsement income in 2007—barely four years after his rape charge—of $16,000,000. (2) Swimmer and Olympic gold-medalist Michael Phelps was arrested on a DUI (driving under the influence) charge after returning from the Olympics in Athens. (3) Track star Marion Jones's reputation was tarnished by an investigation and subsequent conviction that she had used performance-enhancing drugs. (4) Record-setting homerun hitter Barry Bonds was accused of using performance-enhancing drugs (as were a number of other Major League Baseball players). (5) Boxer Mike Tyson—an active endorser before a series of mishaps—was convicted on a rape charge and served a prison sentence (not to mention the fact that he bit a chunk out of opponent Evander Holyfield's ear during a match following his prison sentence). (6) Actress Cybill Shepherd had a lucrative endorsement deal with the beef industry but embarrassed the industry by revealing to the press that she avoided eating beef. (7) Entertainer Michael Jackson was arraigned on child-molestation charges, although subsequently exonerated. (8) Tennis player Jennifer Capriati's promising career was sidetracked at an early age with emotional problems and allegations of drug abuse. She later mounted a successful comeback, but her endorsement earnings never came anywhere close to the levels tennis stars such as the Williams sisters, Serena and Venus, Anna Kournikova, and Maria Sharapova achieved. (9) Ex–football player and actor O. J. Simpson was indicted for, but not convicted of, murder. (10) Britney Spears, Lindsey Lohan, and Paris Hilton have frequently been in the news on charges of alcohol and drug abuse. (11) Professional quarterback Michael Vick was arrested, convicted, and imprisoned for participating in a dog-fighting ring. His $7,000,000 in celebrity earnings in 2007 (see Table 9.1) likely will be $0 in 2008 and thereafter, although perhaps he may later redeem himself and be accepted again as a product endorser.

Due to the risks of such incidents after the consummation of multimillion-dollar celebrity endorsement contracts, there has been increased scrutiny in selecting celebrity endorsers.[25] No selection procedure is failsafe, however, and it is for this reason that some advertisers and their agencies avoid celebrity endorsements altogether. An alternative is to use the "endorsements" of celebrities who are no longer living. Dead celebrities are well known and respected by consumers in the target audiences to whom they appeal, and, best of all, their use in advertising is virtually risk free because they cannot engage in behaviors that will sully their reputations and resonate adversely to the brands they posthumously endorse. Another risk-free option is the use of *spokescharacters* (the Aflac duck, the Pillsbury Doughboy, Geico's gecko, Kmart's Mr. Bluelight, etc.) in lieu of human endorsers who are susceptible to pratfalls that tarnish images of the brands with which endorsers are associated.[26]

The Role of Q Scores

Needless to say, the selection of high-priced celebrity endorsers is typically undertaken with considerable thought on the part of brand managers and their advertising agencies. Their selection process is facilitated with Performer Q Scores that are commercially available from a New York–based firm called Marketing

Evaluations (http://www.qscores.com/pages/Template1/site11/30/default.aspx). For reasons that will shortly become apparent, the *Q* in Q Score signifies quotient.

Marketing Evaluations obtains Q Scores for over 1,700 public figures (entertainers, athletes, and other famous people) by mailing questionnaires to a representative national panel of 1,800 individuals. Participants are asked two straightforward questions for each public figure: (1) Have you heard of this person? (a measure of *familiarity*); and (2) If so, do you rate him or her poor, fair, good, very good, or one of your favorites? (a measure of *popularity*). The calculation of each performer's Q score, or *quotient,* is accomplished by determining the percentage of panel members who respond that a particular performer is "one of my favorites" and then dividing that number by the percentage who indicate that they have heard of that person. In other words, *the popularity percentage is divided by the familiarity percentage, and the quotient is that person's Q Score.* This rating simply reveals the proportion of a group that is familiar with a person and who regard that person as one of their favorites.

For example, assume that a study by Marketing Evaluations determines that 90 percent of panel participants indicate that they are familiar with Britney Spears and that 15 percent consider her a favorite. Hence, Britney's Q Score (which is expressed without a decimal point) is reported as 17 (i.e., 15 divided by 90 is roughly 17). Comparatively, assume in this same survey that Brad Pitt had an extremely high Q Score of 58, which was obtained by dividing the 55 percent of respondents who considered him one of their favorites by the 95 percent who were familiar with him. It comes as little surprise that advertisers have not flocked to Britney to sign her up to endorse their products, whereas many advertisers would select Brad as their brand endorser if he were so inclined.

Q Scores provide useful information to brand managers and advertising agencies, but there is more to selecting a celebrity to endorse a brand than simply scouring through the pages of Q Scores. Subjective judgment ultimately comes into play in determining whether a prospective celebrity endorser matches well with the brand image and its intended target market.

The Role of Humor in Advertising

Politicians, actors and actresses, public speakers, professors, and indeed all of us at one time or another use humor to create a desired reaction. Advertisers also turn to humor in the hopes of achieving various communication objectives—gaining attention, guiding consumer comprehension of product claims, influencing attitudes, enhancing recall, and, ultimately, creating customer action. The use of humor in advertising is extensive, representing approximately 25 percent of all television advertising in the United States and more than 35 percent in the United Kingdom.[27]

A study based on a sampling of television advertisements from four countries (Germany, Korea, Thailand, and the United States) determined that humorous advertisements in all of these countries generally involve the use of *incongruity resolution.*[28] Humor in U.S. magazine and radio advertising also typically employs incongruity resolution.[29] Incongruity exists when the meaning of an ad is not immediately clear. Baffled by the incongruity, the consumer is provoked to understand the ad's meaning and resolve the incongruity. When the meaning is eventually determined—as, for example, when the humor in an ad is detected—a feeling of surprise is experienced, and it is this sensation of surprise that generates a humorous response.[30] In turn, this humorous response can elicit a favorable attitude toward the advertisement and perhaps toward the advertised brand itself.[31]

The Fresh Step advertisement in Figure 9.11 illustrates the use of humor in magazine advertising. The prominent visual depicts a cat that apparently is trying hard not to have a bathroom mistake. The incongruity resolution in this ad occurs when the magazine reader examines the copy at the bottom declaring "It's hard to find your litter box if you can't smell it." The point of the ad, made with subtle humor, is that Fresh Step contains odor-eliminating carbon that "prevents" cats from finding their litter boxes. In general, humor is used relatively infrequently in magazine advertising compared with its use in broadcast media, TV and radio.[32]

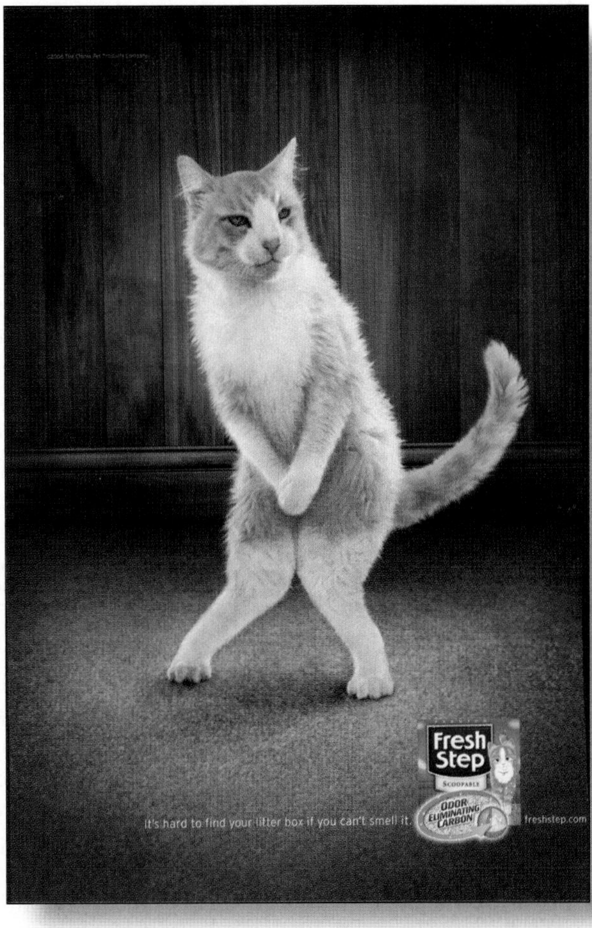

Courtesy of the Clorox Pet Products Company

Figure 9.11

The Use of Humor in Magazine Advertising

Whether humor is generally effective and what kinds of humor are most successful are matters of some debate among advertising practitioners and scholars.[33] Advertising agency executives consider humor to be especially effective for purposes of *attracting attention* to an advertisement and *creating brand awareness.*[34] There is some evidence that humor serves to influence consumers' attitudes toward advertisements positively, which, in turn, affects their attitudes favorably toward the advertised brands; however, this chain of influence (humor → attitude toward the advertisement → attitude toward the advertised brand) is most likely to occur only when consumers are weakly motivated to process the more substantive message points in the advertisement.[35] Research on the effects of humor leads to the following tentative generalizations:[36]

- Humor is an effective method for attracting attention to advertisements.
- Humor can elevate consumers' recall of message points in advertisements.[37]
- Humor enhances liking of both the advertisement and the advertised brand.
- Humor does not necessarily harm comprehension and may in fact increase memory for advertising claims if the humor is relevant to the advertised brand.[38]
- Humor does not offer an advantage over nonhumor at increasing persuasion.
- Humor does not enhance source credibility.
- The nature of the product affects the appropriateness of using humor. Specifically, humor is used more successfully with established rather than new products. Humor also is more appropriate for products that are more feeling oriented, or experiential, and those that are not very involving (such as inexpensive consumer packaged goods).

When used correctly and in the right circumstances, humor can be an extremely effective advertising technique. A complication of using humor in advertising is that humorous appeals vary in their effectiveness across demographic groups and even among individuals. For example, men and women are not equally attentive to humorous ads.[39] In addition to demographic differences in responsiveness to humor, research evidence also shows that humorous ads are more effective than nonhumorous ads *only when consumers' evaluations of the advertised brand are already positive.* When prior evaluations are negative toward the advertised brand, humorous ads have been shown to be less effective than nonhumorous ads.[40] This finding has a counterpart in interpersonal relations: When you like someone, you are more likely to consider his or her attempt at humor to be funny than if you do not like that person. Finally, research shows that individuals who have a higher *need for humor* (i.e., the tendency to seek out amusement, wit, and nonsense) are more responsive to humorous ads than are those with a lower need on this personality trait.[41]

In sum, humor in advertising can be an extremely effective device for accomplishing a variety of marketing communications objectives. Nonetheless, advertisers should *proceed cautiously* when contemplating the use of humor. First, the effects of humor can differ due to differences in audience characteristics—what strikes some people as humorous is not at all funny to others.[42] Second, the definition of what is funny in one country or region of a country is not necessarily the same in another. Finally, a humorous message may be so distracting to an audience that receivers ignore the message content. There is indeed a fine line in advertising between entertaining (via humor) and providing information sufficient to influence attitudes and behavior. Thus, advertisers should carefully research their intended market segments before venturing into humorous advertising.

Appeals to Consumer Fears

As discussed in an earlier section of this chapter, marketing communicators employ a variety of techniques to enhance consumers' information-processing motivation, opportunity, and ability. As would be expected, the appeal to fear is especially effective as a means of enhancing motivation. The unfortunate fact is that consumers live in a world where the threat of terrorism is ever present, natural disasters occur occasionally such as the horrific tsunami in countries surrounding the Indian Ocean, and crime and health-related problems abound. It is estimated that nearly 15 million Americans suffer from irrational fears and that anxiety disorders afflict approximately 13 percent of adults.[43]

Advertisers, realizing that people have fears, rational as well as irrational, attempt to motivate consumers to process information and to take action by appealing to their fears. Appeals to fears in advertising identify the negative consequences of either: (1) *not using the advertised brand* or (2) *engaging in unsafe behavior* (such as drinking and driving, smoking, using drugs, eating unhealthy foods, driving without seat belts, text messaging while driving, and engaging in unprotected sex).[44]

Fear Appeal Logic

The underlying logic is that appeals to consumer fears will stimulate audience involvement with a message and thereby promote acceptance of message arguments. The appeal to consumer fears may take the form of *social disapproval* or *physical danger*. For example, mouthwashes, deodorants, toothpastes, and other products appeal to fears when emphasizing the social disapproval we may suffer if our breath is not fresh, our underarms are not dry, our teeth are not perfectly white, and so on. Smoke detectors, automobile tires, unsafe sex, driving under the influence of alcohol and other drugs, and being uninsured are a sampling of products and themes used by advertisers to induce fear of physical danger or impending problems. Healthcare ads frequently appeal to fears, and advertising agencies justify the use of these appeals with logic such as, "Sometimes you have to scare people to save their lives."[45]

Appropriate Intensity

Aside from the basic ethical issue of whether fear should be used at all, the fundamental issue for advertisers is determining *how intense* the threat should be. Should the advertiser employ a slight threat merely to get the consumer's attention, or should a heavy threat be used so the consumer cannot possibly miss the point the advertiser wishes to make? Although numerous studies have been performed, there is no consensus on what threat intensity is optimal. There is, however, some consistency in the demonstration that the more an audience experiences fear from an advertised threat, the more likely they will be persuaded to take the recommended action.[46]

In general, it appears that the degree of threat intensity that is effective in evoking fear in an audience depends in large part on *how much relevance* a topic has for an audience—the greater the relevance, the lower the threat intensity that is needed to activate a response. In other words, people who are highly involved in a topic can be motivated by a relatively "light" appeal to fear, whereas a more intense level of threat is required to motivate uninvolved people.[47]

To illustrate the relation between threat intensity and issue relevance, let us compare a low-threat advertising campaign for Michelin tires with the much more intense appeal of advertisements designed to discourage drinking and driving. A long-standing Michelin advertising campaign contained a series of television commercials that showed adorable babies sitting on or surrounded by tires. These commercials were subtle reminders (low levels of threat) for parents to consider buying Michelin tires to ensure their children's safety. A low level of threat to evoke fear is all that is needed in this situation, because safety for their children is the most relevant concern for most parents.

Consider, by comparison, the level of threat needed to reach high school students and other young people who are the target of public service announcements that attempt to discourage both drinking and driving and engaging in text messaging while driving. The last thing many young people want to hear is what they should or should not be doing. Hence, although safety is relevant to most everyone, it is less relevant to young people who consider themselves invulnerable. Consequently, very intense appeals to fear are needed to impress on high schoolers the risk in which they place themselves and their friends when drinking/text messaging and driving.[48]

The Related Case of Appeals to Scarcity

Advertisers and other persuasion agents appeal to scarcity when emphasizing in their messages that things become more desirable when they are in great demand but short supply.[49] Simply put, an item that is rare or becoming rare is more valued. Salespeople and advertisers use this tactic when encouraging people to buy immediately with appeals such as "Only a few are left," "We won't have any more in stock by the end of the day," and "They're really selling fast."

The theory of **psychological reactance** helps explain why scarcity works.[50] This theory suggests that people react against any efforts to reduce their freedom or choices. Removed or threatened choices are perceived as even more desirable than previously. Thus, when products are made to seem less available, they become more valuable in the consumer's mind. Of course, appeals to scarcity are not always effective. But if the persuader is credible and legitimate, then an appeal may be effective if it activates a response such as "Not many of this product remain, so I'd better buy now and pay whatever it takes to acquire it."

Perhaps nowhere in the world is scarcity more used as an influence tactic than in Singapore. In the Hokkien dialect of Chinese, the word *kiasu* means the "fear of losing out." Singaporeans, according to a lecturer in the philosophy department at National University, will take whatever they can secure, even if they are not sure they really want it.[51] Many Singaporeans apparently share a herd mentality—no one wants to be different. Marketers, needless to say, have exploited this cultural characteristic to sell all types of products. For example, a Singapore automobile dealership announced that it was moving its location and offered for sale 250 limited-edition BMW 316i models, priced at $78,125 for a manual transmission and

$83,125 for an automatic. All 250 models were sold within four days, and the dealer was forced to order another 100, which were quickly sold even though delivery was unavailable for months.

The kiasu mentality makes Singaporeans virtually "sitting ducks" for users of the scarcity tactic. However, Singaporean consumers, like consumers everywhere, are only susceptible to such a persuasion tactic in those situations in which there is in fact scarcity. Consumers otherwise would become skeptical of such transparent attempts to mislead them and reject such blatant efforts to sell products by using deceit.

Appeals to Consumer Guilt

Like appeals to fear, appeals to guilt attempt to trigger negative emotions. People feel guilty when they break rules, violate their own standards or beliefs, or behave irresponsibly.[52] Appeals to guilt are powerful because they motivate emotionally mature individuals to undertake responsible action leading to a reduction in the level of guilt. Advertisers and other marketing communicators appeal to guilt and attempt to persuade prospective customers by asserting or implying that feelings of guilt can be relieved by using the promoted product.[53] An analysis of a broad spectrum of magazines revealed that about 1 of 20 ads contains an appeal to guilt.[54] Consider, for example, a magazine advertisement for Veterinary Pet Insurance, a company that markets insurance for the coverage of unexpected pet accidents or illness. The headline surrounding the photo of a sad-looking dog puts the pet owner on a guilt trip when stating, "[Your pet] will never know you can't afford the treatment. But you will." This advertisement represents an appeal to anticipatory guilt. That is, the ad attempts to induce a sense of guilt in readers by suggesting that people fail to take proper care of their pets if they are unable to pay for veterinary treatment. If the ad works as designed, consumers will purchase pet insurance as a way of allaying guilt feelings.

Evidence, albeit limited, suggests that appeals to guilt are *ineffective* if advertisements containing guilt appeals *lack credibility* or advertisers are perceived as having *manipulative intentions.* When ads are perceived as lacking credibility or attempting to manipulate the receiver, feelings of guilt are mitigated rather than increased.[55] Thus, appeals to guilt have little opportunity to influence beliefs, attitudes, or message-relevant behaviors positively if the advertising is perceived as lacking in credibility or as being manipulative. It is important to emphasize again the "it depends" nature of advertising. In this case, whether ads appealing to guilt are effective depends in large part on perceived ad credibility and manipulative intent.

The Use of Sex in Advertising

Whereas the previous two sets of advertising appeals—to fear and guilt—are fundamentally negative (i.e., people generally avoid these two emotions), the use of sex in advertising appeals to something that people generally approach rather than avoid. Sex appeals in advertising are used frequently and with increasing explicitness. Whereas the use of such explicit sex was unthinkable not many years ago, it now represents part of the advertising landscape.[56] The trend is not restricted to the United States; indeed, sexual explicitness is more prevalent and more overt elsewhere—for example, in Brazil and certain European countries.

What Role Does Sex Play in Advertising?

Actually, it has several potential roles.[57] First, sexual material in advertising acts to attract and hold attention for a longer period, often by featuring attractive models in provocative poses.[58] This is called the *stopping-power role* of sex. An advertising campaign for Three Olives vodka typifies this role. Each execution in this campaign portrays an attractive, seductively posed female model in a huge martini glass. Placed conspicuously beside the model-filled martini glass is a rhetorical question (recall the earlier discussion of rhetorical questions in the context of MOA factors): "What's in your martini?" There is a clear double entendre in this question, on the one hand suggesting that Three Olives should be the vodka in your glass, and, on the other, intimating that by drinking Three Olives one is likely to attract beautiful women.

A second potential role is to *enhance recall* of message points. Research suggests, however, that sexual content or symbolism will enhance recall only if it is appropriate to the product category and the creative advertising execution.[59] Sexual appeals produce significantly better recall when the advertising execution has an appropriate relationship with the advertised product.[60]

A third role performed by sexual content in advertising is to *evoke emotional responses,* such as feelings of arousal and even lust.[61] These reactions can increase an ad's persuasive impact, with the opposite occurring if the ad elicits negative feelings such as disgust, embarrassment, or uneasiness.[62] The advertisement for the Three Olives brand of vodka described previously probably was designed to arouse feelings in the target audience of predominantly young and middle-aged men. The appeal to lust is typified by a Diet Coke television commercial that was aired in the 1990s in which a group of voyeuristic women is shown watching with palpable pleasure from their office building a sexy worker at a nearby construction site taking off his shirt and then opening a Diet Coke.

Whether sexual content elicits positive or negative reactions depends on the *relevance* of the sexual content to the advertised subject matter. An interesting marketing experiment tested this by varying magazine ads for two products, a ratchet wrench set (a product for which sexual appeal is irrelevant) and a body oil (a relevant sex-appeal product). The study also manipulated three versions of dress for the female model who appeared in the ads: In the *demure* version, the model was shown fully clothed in a blouse and slacks; in the *seductive* version, she wore the same clothing as in the demure version, but the blouse was completely unbuttoned and knotted at the bottom, exposing some midriff and cleavage; and in the *nude* version, the model was completely undressed. Study findings revealed that the seductive model and body oil combination was perceived most favorably by all respondents. Women regarded the nude model and ratchet set as least appealing.[63] This study was conducted over three decades ago, and it is uncertain whether the same findings would be obtained in the sexually more explicit society in which we now live.

Sexual content stands little chance of being effective unless it is directly relevant to an advertisement's primary selling point. When used appropriately, however, sexual content is capable of eliciting attention, enhancing recall, and creating a favorable association with the advertised product.

The Potential Downside of Sex Appeals in Advertising

The presentation to this point has indicated that when used appropriately, sex appeals in advertising can be effective. The discussion would be incomplete without mentioning the potential hazards of using sex appeals. Evidence suggests that the use of explicit sexual illustrations in advertisements may interfere with consumers'

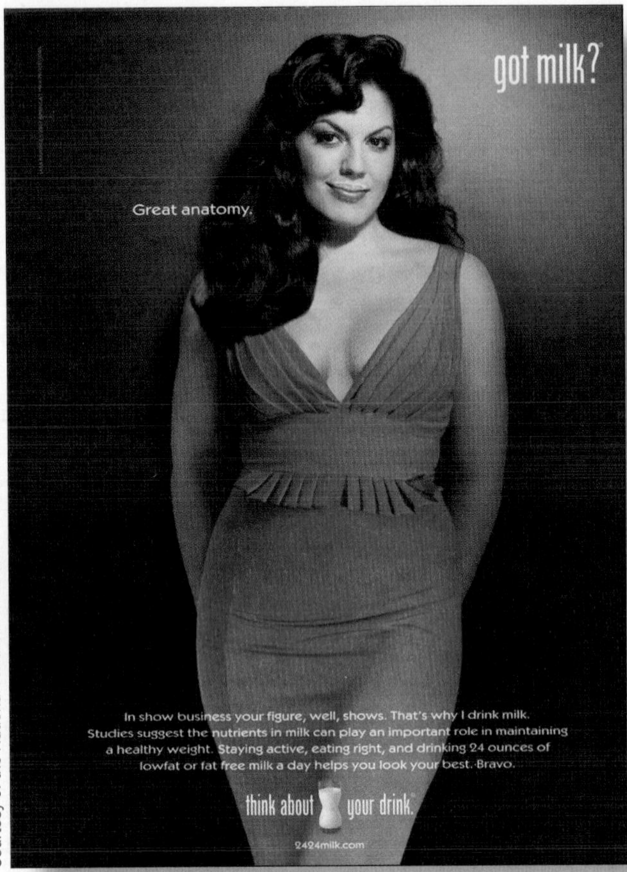
got milk?
Great anatomy.
In show business your figure, well, shows. That's why I drink milk. Studies suggest the nutrients in milk can play an important role in maintaining a healthy weight. Staying active, eating right, and drinking 24 ounces of lowfat or fat free milk a day helps you look your best. Bravo.
think about your drink.
2424milk.com

Courtesy of the National Fluid Milk Processor Promotion Board

Figure 9.12

An Appropriate Use of Sex in Advertising

processing of message arguments and reduce message comprehension.[64] Moreover, many people are offended by advertisements that portray women (and men) as brainless sex objects. For example, an outcry ensued in response to an advertisement for Old Milwaukee beer featuring a boat full of beautiful Scandinavian-looking women wearing blue bikinis who appeared out of nowhere in front of a group of fishermen. Female employees of Stroh Brewery Company, the makers of Old Milwaukee, sued their employer, claiming that the advertisement created an atmosphere conducive to sexual harassment in the workplace.[65] Regardless of the merits of this particular case, the general point is that sex in advertising can be demeaning to females (and males) and, for this reason, should be used cautiously.

A TV advertisement for Miller Lite beer (dubbed "Catfight") perhaps typifies the questionable use of sexual content in advertising. (This ad was previously discussed in the *IMC Focus* Chapter 6.) The ad aired on many occasions during NFL games in the 2002–2003 football season. You may recall seeing the ad, which portrayed two sexy women literally ripping each other's clothes off in a swimming pool and later in wet cement as they supposedly fought over whether Miller Lite beer was the beer of choice because it was "better tasting" or because it was "less filling." This ad doubtlessly caught the attention of millions of people who view NFL football, and perhaps aroused emotions and aided brand name recall. At the same time, this ad raises distinct ethical issues about advertising propriety. The fact remains that many people—men as well as women—are offended by advertisements that portray individuals as brainless sex objects. The use of sex in advertising is a matter of concern to people and advertising regulators throughout the world.[66] Sex in advertising can be demeaning and, for this reason, should be used cautiously.

In concluding this section, it should be noted that "showing skin" in advertisements does not necessarily equate with being sexist or sexually objectifying men or women. For example, the "Got Milk?" ad (Figure 9.12) represents an attention-getting portrayal of an actress that ties in with the ad's body copy regarding the nutrients in milk playing an important role in "maintaining a healthy weight" and helping consumers to "look your best."

Subliminal Messages and Symbolic Embeds

The word *subliminal* refers to the presentation of stimuli at a speed or visual level that is *below the conscious threshold of awareness.* One example is self-help audiotapes (such as tapes to help one quit smoking) that play messages at a decibel level indecipherable to the naked ear. Stimuli that are imperceptible by the conscious senses may nonetheless be perceived subconsciously. This possibility has generated considerable concern from advertising critics and has fostered much speculation from researchers. Although it is highly unlikely that advertisers use subliminal methods, surveys have shown that a large percentage of Americans believe advertisers do use them.[67] Representatives of the advertising community strongly disavow using subliminal advertising.[68]

The original outcry concerning subliminal advertising occurred over 50 years ago in response to a researcher who claimed to have increased the sales of Coca-Cola and popcorn in a New Jersey movie theater by using subliminal messages. At five-second intervals during the movie *Picnic,* subliminal messages saying "Drink Coca-Cola" and "Eat Popcorn" appeared on the screen for a mere 1/3,000 second. Although the naked eye could not possibly have seen these messages, the researcher, James Vicary, claimed that sales of Coca-Cola and popcorn increased 58 percent and 18 percent, respectively.[69] Although Vicary's research is scientifically meaningless because he failed to use proper experimental procedures, the study nonetheless raised public concerns about subliminal advertising and led to congressional hearings.[70] Federal legislation in the United States was never enacted, but since then subliminal advertising has been the subject of concern by advertising critics, a matter of embarrassment for advertising practitioners, and an issue of curiosity to advertising scholars.[71]

The fires of controversy were fueled again in the 1970s and 1980s with the publication of three provocatively titled books: *Subliminal Seduction, Media Sexploitation,* and *The Clam Plate Orgy.*[72] The author of these books, Wilson Key, claimed subliminal advertising techniques are used extensively and have the power to influence consumers' choice behaviors.

Why It Is Unlikely That Subliminal Advertising Works

Many advertising practitioners and marcom scholars discount Key's arguments and vehemently disagree with his conclusions. Part of the difficulty in arriving at clear answers as to who's right and who's wrong stems from the fact that commentators differ in what they mean by subliminal advertising. In fact, there are three distinct forms of subliminal stimulation. A first form presents *visual stimuli* at a very rapid rate by means of a device called a *tachistoscope* (say, at 1/3,000 second as in Vicary's research). A second form uses *accelerated speech in auditory messages.* The third form involves the *embedding of hidden symbols* (such as sexual images or words) in print advertisements.[73]

This last form, embedding, is what Key has written about and is the form that advertising researchers have studied. To better appreciate embedding, consider an advertisement for Edge shaving gel that ran in magazines a number of years ago. This ad featured a picture of a lathered-up man with a look of near ecstasy on his face and a prominent shot of the Edge shaving gel can grasped in his fingertips. In addition to including clearly visible evocative scenes (e.g., a scene of a sexy male on a surfboard surfing in symbolic Freudian fashion through a water tunnel), the ad also included *three vague nude figures* that were airbrushed into the shaving lather above the man's lip.

The key issue is this: Would the inclusion of nude figures in this advertisement influence consumers to actually purchase Edge gel? To answer this we need to examine the process that would have to operate for embedding to influence consumer choice behavior. The first step in the process requires that consumers consciously or subconsciously process the embedded symbol (the nude figures) in the Edge magazine ad. Second, as the result of processing the cue, consumers would have to develop a greater desire for Edge shaving gel than they had before seeing the ad. Third, because advertising is done at the brand level and because advertisers are interested in selling their brands and not just any brand in the product category, effective symbolic embedding would require that consumers develop a desire for the specific brand, Edge in this case, rather than just any brand in the category. Finally, consumers would need to transfer the desire for the advertised brand into actual purchase behavior.

Is there evidence to support this chain of events? Despite a few limited studies on the issue, there are a variety of practical problems that probably prevent embedding from being effective in a realistic marketing context.[74] Perhaps the major reason why embedding in advertising has little effect is because the images have to be concealed to preclude consumers' detection. Many consumers would resent such tricky advertising efforts if they knew they existed. Thus, precluding detection from consumers means that embedding is a relatively weak technique compared with more vivid advertising representations. Because the majority of consumers devote little time and effort in processing advertisements, a weak stimulus means that most consumers would not be influenced much.[75]

Even if consumers do attend to and encode sexual embeds under natural advertising conditions, there remains serious doubt that this information would have sufficient impact to affect brand choice behavior. Standard (supraliminal) advertising information itself has difficulty influencing consumers. How possibly could subliminal information be any more effective? For example, would men choose Edge shaving gel just because they consciously or subconsciously spotted nude women in the advertisement for that product?

Subliminal advertising of the embedded-symbol variety likely is ineffective due to the use of weak stimuli. The following quote sums up this viewpoint. Please note that the quote acknowledges that *subliminal perception* is a bona fide phenomenon (i.e., extensive research has demonstrated that people *are* capable of perceiving stimuli in the absence of conscious awareness of those stimuli), but the weak effects of subliminal stimuli are nullified under actual market circumstances where, for example, many brands compete for the consumer's attention at the point of purchase.

> *A century of psychological research substantiates the general principle that more intense stimuli have a greater influence on people's behavior than weaker ones. While subliminal perception is a bona fide phenomenon, the effects obtained are subtle and obtaining them typically requires a carefully structured context. Subliminal stimuli are usually so weak that the recipient is not just unaware of the stimulus but is also oblivious to the fact that he/she is being stimulated. As a result, the potential effects of subliminal stimuli are easily nullified by other ongoing stimulation in the same sensory channel or by attention being focused on another modality. These factors pose serious difficulties for any possible marketing application.*[76]

We thus conclude that the symbolic embed form of subliminal advertising likely is ineffective and unable to influence consumer choice behavior. Discussion turns now to a different technique, *subliminal primes,* that may be capable of influencing consumer choice behavior.

A Unique Situation Where Subliminal Stimuli May Influence Brand Choice

Much human behavior is *not* under conscious control but rather occurs virtually *automatically* (i.e., without cognitive intervention). Capitalizing on this aspect of human psychology, communicators may be able to employ a technique called *subliminal priming* to affect consumers' brand choices. In brief, subliminal priming involves presenting people with single words or images at a speed that is below the conscious threshold. These words/images can activate, or prime, people's knowledge, beliefs, stereotypes, or other cognitions.

These cognitions, in turn, are capable of influencing individuals' behavior under the right conditions. In particular, for subliminal priming to be effective, the primed topic must be compatible with the individual's current need states, motivations, or goals. In other words, one cannot be subliminally induced to act in a certain way unless he or she has a need to act in that way.[77] For example, individuals who are primed with words such as "generous," "help," and "give"—all relating to generosity—will not automatically contribute money to a charitable cause unless they have an inherent desire to help others. Moreover, a primed need does not remain an active driver of judgments and behavior over the long run, but is limited in its length of influence.

Hence, an advertiser may subliminally activate a certain thought or feeling relating to a brand, but the consumer would not act on that thought or feeling if he or she is not presently in the market to purchase a product that relates to it. In general, it would be expected that mass-media advertising would have little effectiveness in this regard given that exposure to ads and purchase decisions typically are separated in time. However, point-of-purchase advertising (e.g., in-store radio programming) may provide an opportune (albeit unethical) medium for subliminally priming consumers into purchasing particular brands.

The foregoing discussion may have presented the reader with mixed signals: On the one hand, it was claimed that embeds in advertising likely are unable to influence consumer choice behavior. Then, on the other hand, the last two paragraphs have suggested that the use of subliminal primes might work. As pointed out early in the chapter as well as elsewhere in the text, marcom techniques generally are not effective under all circumstances. Rather, in adherence to an "it-depends" principle, the only proper conclusion is that subliminal advertising probably is ineffective under most circumstances, although the possibility remains that it is capable of influencing consumer choice behavior under limited conditions. The *IMC Focus* describes a study that used subliminal priming and demonstrated that this form of subliminal "advertising" is capable of influencing brand choice. Please carefully read this insert so that you can appreciate this unique situation where subliminal priming was shown to affect consumers' brand choices.

The Functions of Music in Advertising

Music has been an important component of the advertising landscape virtually since the beginning of recorded sound. Jingles, background music, popular tunes, and classical arrangements are used to attract attention, convey selling points, set an emotional tone for an advertisement, and influence listeners' moods. Well-known entertainers, nonvocal musical accompaniment, and unknown vocalists are used extensively in promoting everything from fabric softeners to automobiles. A Celine Dion song, "I Drove All Night," was featured in a series of Chrysler commercials. Famous rocker Bob Dylan's "Love Sick" was introduced in commercials for Victoria's Secret. Chevrolet launched a major advertising campaign around songs that cited Chevy or Chevy products, including tunes from the Beach Boys ("409"), Don McLean ("American Pie"), Elton John ("Crocodile Rock"), and Prince ("Little Red Corvette").[78] Songs featured on Wilco's "Sky Blue Sky" appeared in a series of Volkswagen commercials. The Album Leaf's "Always for You" appeared in a Cadillac Escalade commercial.[79]

Many advertising practitioners and scholars regard music as capable of performing a variety of useful communications functions. These include *attracting attention* to commercial messages, *putting consumers in a positive mood* while hearing or viewing these messages, making them *more receptive to message arguments,* and even *communicating meanings about advertised brands.*[80] Consider, for example, the use of music in a famous Pepsi advertisement. In this commercial a security camera captures the antics of a Coke delivery man in a supermarket. While the famous Hank Williams song, "Your Cheatin' Heart," plays in the background, the deliveryman is seen approaching a Pepsi cooler that is adjacent to his own Coca-Cola cooler. The delivery man is shown sneaking a look at the Pepsi cooler, opening it, and then removing a can of Pepsi—at which time dozens of Pepsi cans cascade to the floor

IMC >> i.m.c. focus

Subliminal Priming and Brand Choice

Imagine that you have been asked to participate in a study at your university. Upon arriving at the study location, the experimenter informs you and fellow participants that the study entails a *visual detection task.* She explains that you will be presented with 25 separate images on a computer screen and that each image consists of a string of capital B's (BBBBBBBBB). She further notes that on occasion the string of B's will contain a single lower-case b such as BBBBbBBBB. Your task is to be vigilant and to identify how many of the 25 strings of capital B's contain a small b.

Researchers in the Netherlands used this research procedure to disguise the purpose of a study that actually involved a form of subliminal advertising. Research participants saw not only 25 strings of capital B's intermingled occasionally with small b's, but also, unbeknownst to them, separate images of *subliminally primed words* that appeared on the screen prior to the images containing strings of B's. The primed words were on the computer screen for the extremely short duration of only 23 milliseconds (i.e., 23/1000 second). The researchers wondered whether subliminally priming participants with an actual brand name would subsequently influence them to choose that brand at the end of the experimental session.

As typical in an experiment, approximately half of the participants were assigned to a "treatment" group and the other half were assigned to a "control" group. All participants participated in the identical visual detection task. However, "treatment group" participants were primed on multiple occasions with the brand name "Lipton Ice," whereas "control group" participants were primed an equal number of times with "Npeic Tol," which is a nonword that contains the same letters as in Lipton Ice.

The experiment involved an additional study feature: Prior to participating in the visual detection task and before being exposed to primed words, half of the participants ate a salty food item that made them extremely thirsty (the "thirsty condition"), whereas the other half did not consume this salty item ("non-thirsty condition").

Following the visual detection task, participants were asked to indicate which of two beverages they would prefer to drink—either Lipton Ice tea or Spa Rood, a Dutch brand of mineral water. The researchers predicted that participants who were primed with the word "Lipton Ice" would be much more likely to choose that brand, but only if they were in the "thirsty condition." In other words, because participants in the "thirsty condition" would have had a need that was congruent with the word they had been primed with, the subliminal prime was expected to influence them to select Lipton Ice when given a choice between it and the other beverage. However, even though participants in the "non-thirsty condition" also had been repeatedly subliminally primed with the word "Lipton Ice," they were not expected to select the Lipton Ice brand (versus Spa Rood water) overwhelmingly when given that option, because they, unlike those in the "thirsty condition," did not have a need that was compatible with the subliminal prime.

The research results bore out the researchers' prediction. Specifically, about 85 percent of participants in the "thirsty condition" who received the Lipton Ice prime selected the Lipton Ice brand when given the choice between it and Spa Rood. Comparatively, only 20 percent of participants in the "thirsty condition" who received the Npeic Tol prime selected Lipton Ice. Considering participants in the "non-thirsty condition," those who received the Lipton Ice prime were more likely to select Lipton Ice than were those participants who received the Npeic Tol prime, but the differential in choosing Lipton Ice (about 54 percent versus 32 percent) was far less than the differential for those participants in the "thirsty condition" (80 percent versus 20 percent).

Findings from this study make it clear that subliminal advertising—in the form of subliminally primed words—is capable of influencing consumer choice behavior under *ideal conditions,* namely, when brand choice closely follows exposure to subliminally primed words. Additional research is needed to determine whether this effect will occur under more realistic marketplace conditions, such as when exposure to brand-name primes and brand choice are *not* close in time and when priming occurs in an actual shopping environment where consumers are exposed to numerous brands and make multiple brand-selection decisions. The present research can thus be considered intriguing but not definitive with respect to the question of whether subliminal advertising "works" under natural marketplace conditions.

SOURCE: Adapted from Johan C. Karremans, Wolfgang Stroebe, and Jasper Claus, "Beyond Vicary's Fantasies: The Impact of Subliminal Priming and Brand Choice," *Journal of Experimental Social Psychology* 42 (November 2006), 792–798.

NOTE: This description is a simplification of this research and only describes one of the two studies performed by the researchers.

with a huge noise, much to the deliveryman's embarrassment. This classic advertisement is an outstanding attention getter that subtly conveys the message that perhaps Pepsi *is* better than Coke. The ad would not have been nearly as effective without the background music, "Your Cheatin' Heart," which served to elevate interest in the commercial as well as to coordinate the advertising scene (a deliveryman engaging in "cheating" behavior) perfectly with the commercial's key point: Pepsi is so good that even a Coke employee will switch loyalty.

Brief review of a classic study demonstrates the potential influence that music can have when placed in an advertising context.[81] This study used classical conditioning in an effort to influence study participants' preferences for a ballpoint pen.[82] As you may recall from a course in psychology or consumer behavior, an *unconditioned stimulus (US)* is something in the environment that naturally evokes pleasant feelings or thoughts in people. For example, babies, puppies, spring flowers, and the first snowfall of the season engender positive feelings in most people. A *conditioned stimulus (CS)* is one that is emotionally or cognitively neutral prior to the onset of a conditioning experiment. In simple terms, classical conditioning is achieved when the pairing of US and CS results in a transfer of feeling from the US (music in the present case) to the CS (the ballpoint pen).

Experimental participants in this study were informed that an advertising agency was trying to select music for use in a commercial for a ballpoint pen. Participants then listened to music while they viewed slides of the pen. The positive US for half the participants was music from the movie *Grease,* and the negative US for the remaining participants was classical Asian Indian music. This research demonstrated that the simple association between the music and the pen influenced product preference: Nearly 80 percent of the participants exposed to the *Grease* music chose the advertised pen, whereas only 30 percent of the participants exposed to the Asian Indian music chose the advertised pen.[83]

It is noteworthy that consumers are sometimes highly critical of advertisers that appropriate well-known songs for inclusion in commercials. Because people often associate particular musicians and songs with specific times in their lives and with personal happenings, they resent it when advertisers irreverently use beloved music for commercial purposes. For example, many baby boomers would find it disquieting to hear the music of artists such as Bob Dylan, Neil Young, and Van Morrison being used to sell products. Beatles' fans were upset upon hearing that group's 1967 anthem "All You Need Is Love" in a commercial for Procter & Gamble's Luvs brand of disposable diapers.

The Role of Comparative Advertising

The practice in which advertisers directly or indirectly compare their products against competitive offerings and claim superiority is called **comparative advertising.** Comparative ads vary both with regard to the explicitness of the comparisons and with respect to whether the target of the comparison is named or referred to in general terms.[84] In some countries (e.g., Belgium, Hong Kong, and Korea) it is illegal to use comparative advertising; and with the exception of the United States and Great Britain, advertising comparisons are used infrequently in those countries where they are legal.[85]

To better appreciate comparative advertising, it will be useful to examine a couple of examples. The ad in Figure 9.13 for Vicks NyQuil compares itself *directly* against competitor Tylenol Cold Multi-Symptom Nighttime Liquid. The ad indicates that Vicks NyQuil offers up to eight hours of cough relief in comparison to Tylenol's providing only four hours of relief.

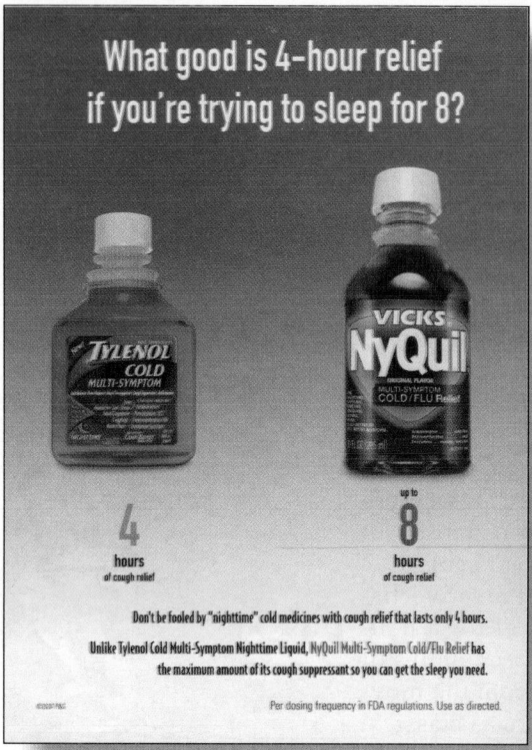

© Courtesy of the Procter & Gamble Company

Figure 9.13

Illustration of a Direct Comparison Advertisement

Figure 9.14

Illustration of an Indirect Comparison Advertisement

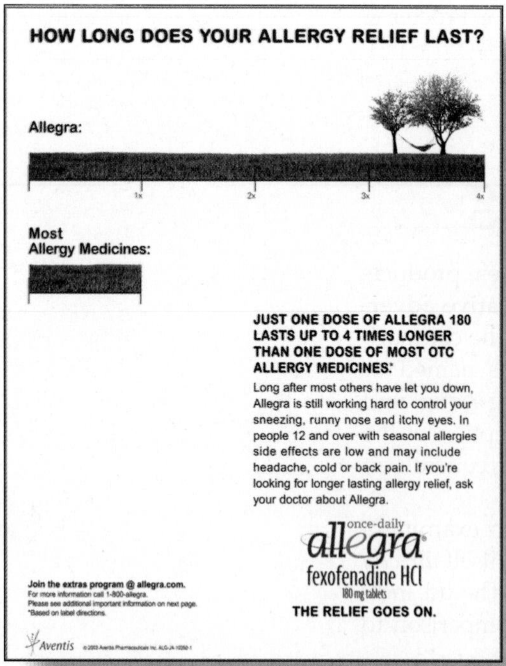

© Courtesy of Allegra

Consider now the indirect comparison advertisement for Allegra in Figure 9.14. Without mentioning any competitive brands, this ad shows graphically and in its copy that a dose of Allegra "lasts up to 4 times longer than one dose of most OTC [over-the-counter] allergy medicines."

Is Comparative Advertising More Effective?

In deciding whether to use a comparative advertisement or a more conventional noncomparative format, an advertiser must confront questions such as the following:[86]

- How do comparative and noncomparative advertisements match up in terms of impact on brand awareness, consumer comprehension of ad claims, and credibility?
- Do comparative and noncomparative ads differ with regard to effects on brand preferences, buying intentions, and purchase behavior?
- How do factors such as consumer brand preference and the advertiser's market share influence the effectiveness of comparative advertising?
- Under what specific circumstances should an advertiser use comparative advertising?

Researchers have performed numerous studies that have examined the processes by which comparative advertising operates, the results it produces, and how its effects contrast with those from noncomparative ads.[87] Findings are at times inconclusive and even contradictory. Lack of definitive results is to be expected, however, because advertising is a complex phenomenon that varies from situation to situation in terms of executional elements, audience demographics, media characteristics, and other factors. However, a major review of research that has tested comparative versus noncomparative advertising suggests the following tentative conclusions:[88]

- Comparative advertising is better at enhancing brand name recall.
- Comparative advertising promotes better recall of message arguments.
- Comparative advertising is considered somewhat less believable than noncomparative advertising.
- Comparative advertising is responsible for generating more favorable attitudes toward the sponsoring brand, especially when the brand is a new (versus established) brand.
- Comparative advertising generates stronger intentions to purchase the sponsored brand.
- Comparative advertising generates more purchases.

It is obvious from this list that a variety of advantages accrue to the use of comparative versus noncomparative advertising. However, as is always the case, one form of advertising is not universally superior to another under all circumstances. The following section identifies some specific issues that should be considered when deciding whether to use a comparative advertisement.

Considerations Dictating the Use of Comparative Advertising

Situational Factors

Characteristics of the audience, media, message, company, and product all play important roles in determining whether comparative advertising will be more effective than noncomparative advertising. For example, comparative advertisements seem to be evaluated less favorably by people holding a prior preference for the comparison brand (the brand that the advertised brand is compared against) than by those without a prior preference for that brand.

Distinct Advantages

Comparative advertising is particularly effective for promoting brands that possess distinct advantages relative to competitive brands.[89] When a brand has a distinct advantage over competitive brands, comparative advertising provides a powerful method to convey this advantage. The advertisement for Vicks NyQuil (Figure 9.14) typifies this situation. Relative to noncomparative advertising, comparative advertising has also been shown to increase the perceived similarity between a challenger brand in a product category and the category leader.[90] However, research also has demonstrated that indirect comparative advertisements can be more effective than direct comparative ads in certain circumstances. One study found that direct comparison ads are more effective than indirect comparative ads in positioning a brand as superior to a *specific* competitive brand, but indirect comparative ads were better at positioning a brand as superior to *all brands in the category*.[91]

The Credibility Issue

The effectiveness of comparative advertising increases when comparative claims are made to appear more credible. There are three ways to accomplish this: (1) have an independent research organization support the superiority claims, (2) present impressive test results to back up the claims, and (3) use a trusted endorser as the spokesperson.

Assessing Effectiveness

Because comparative advertisements make claims for an advertised brand relative to another brand and because consumers encode this comparative information in a relative fashion, measurement techniques in assessing the effectiveness of comparative advertising are most sensitive when questions are *worded in a relative fashion.* That is, for maximal sensitivity, the question context, or wording, should match the consumer's encoding mind-set. For example, with reference to the Vicks NyQuil advertisement (Figure 9.14), there are two *alternative* questions that could be framed to ascertain whether consumers perceive Vicks NyQuil as an effective brand in providing cough relief: (1) How likely is it that the cough-relief effects of Vicks NyQuil are long lasting? (*nonrelative* framing) or (2) How likely is it that Vicks NyQuil provides longer lasting cough relief than Tylenol Cold Multi-Symptom? (*relative* framing). Research has shown that relative framing does a better job of assessing consumers' beliefs after their exposure to comparative advertisements.[92]

Summary

This chapter discussed three general topics. The first major section focused on methods advertisers use to enhance an audience's motivation, opportunity, and ability to process ad messages. This section included descriptions and illustrations of advertising efforts to heighten consumers' motivation to attend to and process messages, measures to augment consumers' opportunity to encode information and reduce processing time, and techniques used to increase consumers' ability to access knowledge structures and create new structures.

The second major section dealt with the role of endorsers in advertising. The TEARS model (trustworthiness, expertise, physical attractiveness, respect, and similarity) provided a convenient acronym for thinking about the endorser attributes that play major roles in determining their effectiveness. The following factors appear to be the most important ones brand managers use in actually selecting celebrity endorsers: (1) celebrity and audience matchup, (2) celebrity and brand matchup, (3) celebrity credibility, (4) celebrity attractiveness, (5) cost considerations, (6) a working ease or difficulty factor, (7) an endorsement saturation factor, and (8) a likelihood-of-getting-into-trouble factor. Discussion of celebrity endorsers indicates that endorsers have an influence on consumers via the attributes of credibility and attractiveness. Credibility functions via the process of internalization, whereas attractiveness operates through an identification mechanism.

Finally several sections were devoted to a variety of message appeals in advertising. Widely used advertising techniques discussed in this chapter include humor, appeals to fear, appeals to guilt, sex appeals, subliminal messages, the use of music, and comparative advertisements. Discussion covered empirical research and indicated the factors involved in selecting each of these message elements.

Discussion Questions

1. Using the concepts of attractiveness, expertise, and trustworthiness, explain what makes Tiger Woods an effective (and extremely well paid!) endorser. Do the same for Maria Sharapova.
2. Presented early in the chapter was a quote from philosopher Alfred North Whitehead stating, "Seek simplicity and distrust it." What does this quote mean in terms of the effectiveness of particular advertising appeals, such as the use of humor?
3. Locate examples of magazine advertisements that illustrate each of the following: (a) an effort to increase consumers' motivation to process brand information, and (b) an attempt to enhance consumers' opportunity to encode information. Justify why your chosen examples are good illustrations.
4. Locate two advertisements that illustrate exemplar-based learning, and provide explanations as to how the chosen advertisements facilitate exemplar-based learning.
5. Attractiveness as an attribute of endorsers includes but is not restricted to physical attractiveness. Many would regard British soccer star David Beckham (of *Bend It Like Beckham* fame) as attractive. In what ways other than physical attractiveness might he be considered attractive?
6. Considering the likelihood-of-getting-into-trouble factor, identify three entertainment or sports celebrities that you, as a brand manager, would be reluctant to have endorse your brand for fear they would get into some sort of trouble.
7. Comedian and TV actor Bill Cosby for many years endorsed JELL-O pudding. Suppose you were brand manager for JELL-O and tasked with coming up with a replacement for Mr. Cosby. Who would you select? Justify the rationale behind your choice.
8. Infomercials are long commercials that generally last from 30 to 60 minutes. These commercials typically air during fringe times and frequently promote products such as diet aids, balding cures, and exercise products. These infomercials often use endorsements from physicians and other health professionals to buttress claims about the promoted brand's efficacy. Using concepts from this chapter, explain why health professionals are used in this form of advertising.

9. You have probably seen a number of public service announcements along the lines of those described in the fear appeals section to discourage drinking and driving. In your opinion, is this form of advertising effective in altering the behavior of people your age? Be specific in justifying your answer.
10. The fear of getting AIDS should be relevant to many college students. Accordingly, would you agree that a relatively weak fear appeal should suffice in influencing students to either abstain from sexual relations or practice safe sex? If you disagree, then how can you reconcile your disagreement with the degree-of-relevance explanation?
11. Identify three or four products for which you feel appeals to guilt might be a viable approach to persuading consumer acceptance of a brand. What kinds of products do not lend themselves to such appeals? Explain why you feel these products would be inappropriate.
12. Consumers occasionally find television commercials humorous and enjoyable. Some advertising pundits claim that such commercials may capture attention but are frequently ineffective in selling products. What is your viewpoint on this issue? Justify your position.
13. Identify two or three television commercials that you consider humorous. Is the use of humor appropriate for the brands advertised in these commercials and given their likely target audiences? Justify your responses.
14. Identify several TV commercials or magazine ads that use sex appeals. Describe each advertisement and then explain whether an appeal to sex is appropriate or inappropriate for the brand.
15. Comment on the following allegation: "There is too much use of sex in advertising."
16. The article titled "Understanding Jingles and Needledrop: A Rhetorical Approach to Music in Advertising" (see endnote 80) suggests that music in commercials communicates specific meanings to listeners and viewers. In other words, music "speaks" to people by conveying a sense of speed, excitement, sadness, nostalgia, and so on. Identify two commercials in which music communicates a specific emotion or other state or action to consumers, and identify this emotion, state, or action.
17. Photocopy one or two examples of comparative advertisements from magazines. Analyze each ad in terms of why you think the advertiser used a comparative-advertising format and whether you think the advertisement is effective. Justify your position.

End Notes

1. Based on Geoffrey A. Fowler, Brian Steinberg, and Aaron O. Patrick, *The Wall Street Journal,* March 1, 2007, B1.
2. This quote is attributable to British mathematician and philosopher Alfred North Whitehead. The original source is unknown to this author.
3. Richard E. Petty and John T. Cacioppo, *Attitudes and Persuasion: Classic and Contemporary Approaches* (Dubuque, Iowa: Wm. C. Brown Company, 1981). See also Richard E. Petty, Rao H. Unnava, and Alan J. Strathman, "Theories of Attitude Change," in *Handbook of Consumer Behavior,* ed. T. S. Robertson and H. H. Kassarjian (Englewood Cliffs, N.J.: Prentice Hall, 1991), 241–280.
4. The ensuing discussion is based on the work of Deborah J. MacInnis, Christine Moorman, and Bernard J. Jaworski, "Enhancing and Measuring Consumers' Motivation, Opportunity, and Ability to Process Brand Information from Ads," *Journal of Marketing* 55 (October 1991), 32–53.
5. James R. Bettman, Mary Frances Luce, and John W. Payne, "Constructive Consumer Choice Processes," *Journal of Consumer Research* 25 (December 1998), 193; Daniel Kahneman, *Attention and Effort* (Englewood Cliffs, N.J.: Prentice Hall, 1973).
6. Scott B. MacKenzie and Richard A. Spreng, "How Does Motivation Moderate the Impact of Central and Peripheral Processing on Brand Attitudes and Intentions?" *Journal of Consumer Research* 18 (March 1992), 519–529.
7. For reading on the role and effectiveness of rhetorical questions in advertising, see a series of articles by Edward F. McQuarrie and David Glen Mick: "Figures of Rhetoric in Advertising Language," *Journal of Consumer Research* 22 (March 1996), 424–438; "Visual Rhetoric in Advertising: Text Interpretive, Experimental and Reader Response Analyses," *Journal of Consumer Research* 26 (June 1999), 37–54; and "Visual and Verbal Rhetorical Figures under Directed Processing versus Incidental Exposure to Advertising," *Journal of Consumer Research* 29 (March 2003), 579–587. See also Rohini Ahluwalia and Robert E. Burnkrant, "Answering Questions about Questions: A Persuasion Knowledge Perspective for Understanding the Effects of Rhetorical Questions," *Journal of Consumer Research* 31 (June 2004), 26–42.

8. For a fascinating article on the role of advertising repetition, see Prashant Malaviya, "The Moderating Influence of Advertising Context on Ad Repetition Effects: The Role of Amount and Type of Elaboration," *Journal of Consumer Research* 34 (June 2007), 32–40.
9. Erin White, "Found in Translation?" *Wall Street Journal Online,* September 20, 2004, http://online.wsj.com.
10. Jagdish Agrawal and Wagner A. Kamakura, "The Economic Worth of Celebrity Endorsers: An Event Study Analysis," *Journal of Marketing* 59 (July 1995), 56–62.
11. Therese A. Louie, Robert L. Kulik, and Robert Johnson, "When Bad Things Happen to the Endorsers of Good Products," *Marketing Letters* 12 (February 2001), 13–24.
12. It is important to note that although the present discussion is framed in terms of endorser characteristics, more general treatment of the topic refers to source characteristics. For a classic treatment of the subject, see Herbert C. Kelman, "Processes of Opinion Change," *Public Opinion Quarterly* 25 (spring 1961), 57–78. For a more current treatment, see Daniel J. O'Keefe, *Persuasion Theory and Research* (Newbury Park, Calif: Sage, 1990), chap. 8. For a recent discussion of the various processes by which a message source, such as a celebrity, influences consumers, see Yong-Soon Kang and Paul M. Herr, "Beauty and the Beholder: Toward an Integrative Model of Communication Source Effects," *Journal of Consumer Research* 33 (June 2006), 123–130.
13. Richard E. Petty, Thomas M. Ostrom, and Timothy C. Brock, eds., *Cognitive Responses in Persuasion* (Hillsdale, N.J.: Lawrence Erlbaum Associates, 1981), 143.
14. It has been demonstrated, however, that under select conditions, a less trustworthy, although expert, source may be more effective than an equally expert but more trustworthy source. This is because people tend to elaborate more on persuasive arguments presented by less (versus more) trustworthy sources and form attitudes that both are held more strongly and are relatively more resistant to change. See Joseph R. Priester and Richard E. Petty, "The Influence of Spokesperson Trustworthiness on Message Elaboration, Attitude Strength, and Advertising Effectiveness," *Journal of Consumer Psychology* 13, no. 4 (2003), 408–421.
15. Rohit Deshpande and Douglas Stayman, "A Tale of Two Cities: Distinctiveness Theory and Advertising Effectiveness," *Journal of Marketing Research* 31 (February 1994), 57–64.
16. For information about how to measure attractiveness, see Roobina Ohanian, "Construction and Validation of a Scale to Measure Celebrity Endorsers' Perceived Expertise, Trustworthiness, and Attractiveness," *Journal of Advertising* 19, no. 3 (1990), 39–52.
17. W. Benoy Joseph, "The Credibility of Physically Attractive Communicators: A Review," *Journal of Advertising* 11, no. 3 (1982), 15–24; Lynn R. Kahle and Pamela M. Homer, "Physical Attractiveness of the Celebrity Endorser: A Social Adaptation Perspective," *Journal of Consumer Research* 11 (March 1985), 954–961. However, empirical evidence is mixed as to whether an attractive endorser benefits a brand only when there is a good matchup between the endorser and the brand or whether, alternatively, attractive endorsers are more beneficial for a brand regardless of how well the endorser matches with the brand. For discussion, review the following two articles: Brian D. Till and Michael Busler, "The MatchUp Hypothesis: Physical Attractiveness, Expertise, and the Role of Fit on Brand Attitude, Purchase Intent and Brand Beliefs," *Journal of Advertising* 29 (fall 2000), 1–14; Michael A. Kamins, "An Investigation into the 'MatchUp' Hypothesis in Celebrity Advertising: When Beauty May Be Only Skin Deep," *Journal of Advertising* 19, no. 1 (1990), 4–13. See also John D. Mittelstaedt, Peter C. Riesz, and William J. Burns, "Why Are Endorsements Effective? Sorting among Theories of Product and Endorser Effects," *Journal of Current Issues and Research in Advertising* 22 (spring 2000), 55–66.
18. Lawrence Feick and Robin A. Higie, "The Effects of Preference Heterogeneity and Source Characteristics on Ad Processing and Judgments about Endorsers," *Journal of Advertising* 21 (June 1992), 9–24.
19. Two studies have addressed this issue: B. Zafer Erdogan, Michael J. Baker, and Stephen Tagg, "Selecting Celebrity Endorsers: The Practitioner's Perspective," *Journal of Advertising Research* 41 (May/June 2001), 39–48; Alan R. Miciak and William L. Shanklin, "Choosing Celebrity Endorsers," *Marketing Management* 3 (winter 1994), 51–59.
20. Christine Bittar, "Cosmetic Changes Beyond Skin Deep," *Brandweek,* May 17, 2004, 20.
21. Teri Agins, "Jeans Maker Tarrant Sues Singer Jessica Simpson," *The Wall Street Journal,* April 12, 2006, B3.
22. Carolyn Tripp, Thomas D. Jensen, and Les Carlson, "The Effects of Multiple Product Endorsements by Celebrities on Consumers' Attitudes and Intentions," *Journal of Consumer Research* 20 (March 1994), 535–547.
23. Rich Thomaselli, "Dream Endorser," *Advertising Age,* September 25, 2006, 1, 37.
24. For example, see Therese A. Louie and Carl Obermiller, "Consumer Response to a Firm's Endorser (Dis) Association Decisions," *Journal of Advertising* 31 (winter 2002), 41–52; Louie, Kulik, and Johnson, "When Bad Things Happen"; Brian D. Till and Terence A. Shimp, "Endorsers in Advertising: The Case of Negative Celebrity Information," *Journal of Advertising* 27 (spring 1998), 67–82; and R. Bruce Money, Terence A. Shimp, and Tomoaki Sakano, "Celebrity Endorsements in Japan and the United States: Is Negative Information All That Harmful?" *Journal of Advertising Research* 46 (March 2006), 113–123.
25. Richard Tedesco, "Sacked," *Promo,* September 2007, 22–31.
26. Judith A. Garretson and Scot Burton, "The Role of Spokescharacters as Advertisement and Package Cues in Integrated Marketing Communications," *Journal of Marketing* 69 (October 2005), 118–132.
27. Marc Weinberger and Harlan Spotts, "Humor in U.S. versus U.K. TV Advertising," *Journal of Advertising* 18, no. 2 (1989), 39–44. For further discussion of differences between American and British advertising, see Terence Nevett, "Differences between American and British Television Advertising: Explanations and

Implications," *Journal of Advertising* 21 (December 1992), 61–71.
28. Dana L. Alden, Wayne D. Hoyer, and Chol Lee, "Identifying Global and Culture-Specific Dimensions of Humor in Advertising: A Multinational Analysis," *Journal of Marketing* 57 (April 1993), 64–75.
29. Harlan E. Spotts, Marc G. Weinberger, and Amy L. Parsons, "Assessing the Use and Impact of Humor on Advertising Effectiveness: A Contingency Approach," *Journal of Advertising* 26 (fall 1997), 17–32; Karen Flaherty, Marc G. Weinberger, and Charles S. Gulas, "The Impact of Perceived Humor, Product Type, and Humor Style in Radio Advertising," *Journal of Current Issues and Research in Advertising* 26 (spring 2004), 25–36.
30. Josephine L. C. M. Woltman Elpers, Ashesh Mukherjee, and Wayne D. Hoyer, "Humor in Television Advertising: A Moment-to-Moment Analysis," *Journal of Consumer Research* 31 (December 2004), 592–598.
31. For a formal theoretical account, see Dana L. Alden, Ashesh Mukherjee, and Wayne D. Hoyer, "The Effects of Incongruity, Surprise and Positive Moderators on Perceived Humor in Television Advertising," *Journal of Advertising* 29 (summer 2000), 1–16.
32. Differences in the use of humor across advertising media are demonstrated in Marc G. Weinberger, Harlan Spotts, Leland Campbell, and Amy L. Parsons, "The Use and Effect of Humor in Different Advertising Media," *Journal of Advertising Research* 35 (May/June 1995), 44–56.
33. A thorough review of the issues is provided in two valuable reviews: Paul Surgi Speck, "The Humorous Message Taxonomy: A Framework for the Study of Humorous Ads," *Current Issues and Research in Advertising,* vol. 3, ed. J. H. Leigh and C. R. Martin Jr., (Ann Arbor: Graduate School of Business Administration, University of Michigan, 1991), 1–44; Marc G. Weinberger and Charles S. Gulas, "The Impact of Humor in Advertising: A Review," *Journal of Advertising* 21 (December 1992), 35–59.
34. Thomas J. Madden and Marc G. Weinberger, "Humor in Advertising: A Practitioner View," *Journal of Advertising Research* 24, no. 4 (1984), 23–29.
35. Yong Zhang and George M. Zinkhan, "Responses to Humorous Ads," *Journal of Advertising* 35 (winter 2006), 113–128.
36. Based, in part, on Weinberger and Gulas, "The Impact of Humor in Advertising: A Review," 56–57, as well as on more recent research.
37. Thomas W. Cline and James J. Kellaris, "The Influence of Humor Strength and Humor-Message Relatedness on Ad Memorability," *Journal of Advertising* 36 (spring 2007), 55–68.
38. For discussion on this point, see H. Shanker Krishnan and Dipankar Chakravarti, "A Process Analysis of the Effects of Humorous Advertising Executions on Brand Claims Memory," *Journal of Consumer Psychology* 13, no. 3 (2003), 230–245.
39. Thomas J. Madden and Marc G. Weinberger, "The Effects of Humor on Attention in Magazine Advertising," *Journal of Advertising* 11, no. 3 (1982), 4–14.
40. Amitava Chattopadhyay and Kunal Basu, "Humor in Advertising: The Moderating Role of Prior Brand Evaluation," *Journal of Consumer Research* 27 (November 1990), 466–476.
41. Thomas W. Cline, Moses B. Altsech, and James J. Kellaris, "When Does Humor Enhance or Inhibit Ad Responses? The Moderating Role of the Need for Humor," *Journal of Advertising* 32 (fall 2003), 31–46; Cline and Kellaris, "The Influence of Humor Strength and Humor-Message Relatedness on Ad Memorability."
42. See Yong Zhang, "Responses to Humorous Advertising: The Moderating Effect of Need for Cognition," *Journal of Advertising* 25 (spring 1996), 15–32; also, Flaherty, Weinberger, and Gulas, "The Impact of Perceived Humor, Product Type, and Humor Style in Radio Advertising."
43. Marianne Szegedy-Maszak, "Conquering Our Phobias: The Biological Underpinnings of Paralyzing Fears," *U.S. News & World Report,* December 6, 2004, 67–74.
44. Please note that there is a related advertising form referred to as "shock advertising" that does not appeal to fear per se but that deliberately intends to startle and even offend its audience. Tentative research on this topic has demonstrated that shock advertising is perhaps even better than appeals to fear in activating attention and encouraging the audience to engage in message-relevant behaviors. See Darren W. Dahl, Kristina D. Frankenberger, and Rajesh V. Manchanda, "Does It Pay to Shock? Reactions to Shocking and Nonshocking Advertising Content among University Students," *Journal of Advertising Research* 43 (September 2003), 268–280.
45. This is a quote from Jerry Della Femina, a well-known advertising agency executive and former copywriter. Cited in Emily DeNitto, "Healthcare Ads Employ Scare Tactics," *Advertising Age,* November 7, 1994, 12.
46. Herbert J. Rotfeld, "Fear Appeals and Persuasion: Assumptions and Errors in Advertising Research," *Current Issues and Research in Advertising,* vol. 11, ed. J. H. Leigh and C. R. Martin, Jr. (Ann Arbor: Graduate School of Business Administration, University of Michigan, 1988), 21–40.
47. Peter Wright, "Concrete Action Plans in TV Messages to Increase Reading of Drug Warnings," *Journal of Consumer Research* 6 (December 1979), 256–269. For an explanation of the psychological mechanism by which fear-intensity operates, see Punam Anand Keller and Lauren Goldberg Block, "Increasing the Persuasiveness of Fear Appeals: The Effect of Arousal and Elaboration," *Journal of Consumer Research* 22 (March 1996), 448–459.
48. For further reading on the use of appeals to fear in anti-drinking-and-driving campaigns, see Karen Whitehill King and Leonard N. Reid, "Fear Arousing Anti-Drinking and Driving PSAs: Do Physical Injury Threats Influence Young Adults?" *Current Issues and Research in Advertising,* vol. 12, ed. J. H. Leigh and C. R. Martin, Jr. (Ann Arbor: Graduate School of Business Administration, University of Michigan, 1990), 155–175. Other relevant articles on fear appeals include John F. Tanner, James B. Hunt, and David R. Eppright, "The Protection Motivation Model: Normative Model of Fear Appeals," *Journal of Marketing* 55 (July 1991), 36–45;

Tony L. Henthorne, Michael S. LaTour, and Rajan Natarajan, "Fear Appeals in Print Advertising: An Analysis of Arousal and Ad Response," *Journal of Advertising* 22 (June 1993), 59–70; and James T. Strong and Khalid M. Dubas, "The Optimal Level of Fear-Arousal in Advertising: An Empirical Study," *Journal of Current Issues and Research in Advertising* 15 (fall 1993), 93–99.

49. Robert B. Cialdini, *Influence: Science and Practice*, 4th ed. (Boston: Allyn & Bacon, 2001).
50. Jack W. Brehm, *A Theory of Psychological Reactance* (New York: Academic Press, 1966). See also Mona Clee and Robert Wicklund, "Consumer Behavior and Psychological Reactance," *Journal of Consumer Research* 6 (March 1980), 389–405.
51. Ian Stewart, "Public Fear Sells in Singapore," *Advertising Age*, October 11, 1993, I8. Singaporeans even make fun of themselves regarding their kiasu behavior. "Mr. Kiasu" is a popular comic book character, and a small cottage industry has sprung up around the character.
52. Carroll E. Izard, *Human Emotions* (New York: Plenum, 1977).
53. Robin Higie Coulter and Mary Beth Pinto, "Guilt Appeals in Advertising: What Are Their Effects?" *Journal of Applied Psychology* 80 (December 1995), 697–705; Bruce A. Huhmann and Timothy P. Brotherton, "A Content Analysis of Guilt Appeals in Popular Magazine Advertisements," *Journal of Advertising* 26 (summer 1997), 35–46.
54. Huhmann and Brotherton, "A Content Analysis of Guilt Appeals in Popular Magazine Advertisements," 36.
55. June Cotte, Robin A. Coulter, and Melissa Moore, "Enhancing or Disrupting Guilt: The Role of Ad Credibility and Perceived Manipulative Intent," *Journal of Business Research* 58 (March 2005), 361–368.
56. A content analysis of magazine advertising indicates that the percentage of ads with sexual content had not changed over a two-decade period. What changed, however, was that sexual illustrations had become more overt. Female models were more likely than male models to be portrayed in nude, partially nude, or suggestive poses. See Lawrence Soley and Gary Kurzbard, "Sex in Advertising: A Comparison of 1964 and 1984 Magazine Advertisements," *Journal of Advertising* 15, no. 3 (1986), 46–54.
57. For a variety of perspectives on the role of sex in advertising, see Tome Reichert and Jacqueline Lambiase, eds., *Sex in Advertising: Perspectives on the Erotic Appeal* (Mahwah, N.J.: Lawrence Erlbaum, 2003).
58. Robert S. Baron, "Sexual Content and Advertising Effectiveness: Comments on Belch et al. (1981) and Caccavale et al. (1981)," in *Advances in Consumer Research*, vol. 9, ed. Andrew Mitchell (Ann Arbor, Mich.: Association for Consumer Research, 1982), 428.
59. Larry Percy, "A Review of the Effect of Specific Advertising Elements upon Overall Communication Response," in *Current Issues and Research in Advertising*, vol. 2, ed. J. H. Leigh and C. R. Martin,Jr. (Ann Arbor: Graduate School of Business Administration, University of Michigan, 1983), 95.
60. David Richmond and Timothy P. Hartman, "Sex Appeal in Advertising," *Journal of Advertising Research* 22 (October/November 1982), 53–61.
61. Michael S. LaTour, Robert E. Pitts, and David C. Snook-Luther, "Female Nudity, Arousal, and Ad Response: An Experimental Investigation," *Journal of Advertising* 19, no. 4 (1990), 51–62.
62. Baron, "Sexual Content and Advertising Effectiveness," 428.
63. Robert A. Peterson and Roger A. Kerin, "The Female Role in Advertisements: Some Experimental Evidence," *Journal of Marketing* 41 (October 1977), 59–63.
64. Jessica Severn, George E. Belch, and Michael A. Belch, "The Effects of Sexual and Nonsexual Advertising Appeals and Information Level on Cognitive Processing and Communication Effectiveness," *Journal of Advertising* 19, no. 1 (1990), 14–22.
65. Ira Teinowitz and Bob Geiger, "Suits Try to Link Sex Harassment Ads," *Advertising Age*, November 18, 1991, 48.
66. A study of consumers in Denmark, Greece, New Zealand, and the United States revealed consistent criticism of sexist role portrayals. See Richard W. Pollay and Steven Lysonski, "In the Eye of the Beholder: International Differences in Ad Sexism Perceptions and Reactions," *Journal of International Consumer Marketing* 6, vol. 2 (1993), 25–43.
67. Three surveys have demonstrated this fact. For the most recent review of these surveys, see Martha Rogers and Kirk H. Smith, "Public Perceptions of Subliminal Advertising: Why Practitioners Shouldn't Ignore This Issue," *Journal of Advertising Research* 33 (March/April 1993), 10–18.
68. Martha Rogers and Christine A. Seiler, "The Answer Is No: A National Survey of Advertising Industry Practitioners and Their Clients about Whether They Use Subliminal Advertising," *Journal of Advertising Research* 34 (March/April 1994), 36–45.
69. This description is adapted from Martin P. Block and Bruce G. Vanden Bergh, "Can You Sell Subliminal Messages to Consumers?" *Journal of Advertising* 14, no. 3 (1985), 59.
70. Vicary himself acknowledged that the study that initiated the original furor over subliminal advertising was based on too small an amount of data to be meaningful. See Fred Danzig, "Subliminal Advertising—Today It's Just Historic Flashback for Researcher Vicary," *Advertising Age*, September 17, 1962, 42, 74.
71. For example, see Sharon E. Beatty and Del I. Hawkins, "Subliminal Stimulation: Some New Data and Interpretation," *Journal of Advertising* 18, no. 3 (1989), 4–8.
72. Wilson B. Key, *Subliminal Seduction: Ad Media's Manipulation of a Not So Innocent America* (New York: Signet, 1972); *Media Sexploitation* (New York: Signet, 1976); The *Clam Plate Orgy: And Other Subliminal Techniques for Manipulating Your Behavior* (New York: Signet, 1980). Key has since written *The Age of Manipulation: The Con in Confidence, the Sin in Sincere* (New York: Holt, 1989).
73. For a sophisticated treatment of visual imagery and symbolism in advertising (although not dealing with

subliminal advertising per se), see Linda M. Scott, "Images in Advertising: The Need for a Theory of Visual Rhetoric," *Journal of Consumer Research* 21 (September 1994), 252–273.

74. Ronnie Cuperfain and T. K. Clarke, "A New Perspective of Subliminal Perception," *Journal of Advertising* 14, no. 1 (1985), 36–41; Myron Gable, Henry T. Wilkens, Lynn Harris, and Richard Feinberg, "An Evaluation of Subliminally Embedded Sexual Stimuli in Graphics," *Journal of Advertising* 16, no. 1 (1987), 26–31; William E. Kilbourne, Scott Painton, and Danny Ridley, "The Effect of Sexual Embedding on Responses to Magazine Advertisements," *Journal of Advertising* 14, no. 2 (1985), 48–56.
75. For discussion of the practical difficulties with implementing subliminal advertising and the questionable effectiveness of this advertising technique, see Timothy E. Moore, "Subliminal Advertising: What You See Is What You Get," *Journal of Marketing* 46 (spring 1982), 41; and Joel Saegert, "Why Marketing Should Quit Giving Subliminal Advertising the Benefit of the Doubt," *Psychology & Marketing* 4 (summer 1987), 107–120.
76. Moore, "Subliminal Advertising: What You See Is What You Get," 46.
77. For an accessible treatment on the issue of automatic, or noncontrolled motivation and behavior, see John A. Bargh, "Losing Consciousness: Automatic Influences on Consumer Judgment, Behavior, and Motivation," *Journal of Consumer Research* 29 (September 2002), 280–285. See also John A. Bargh and Tanya L. Chartrand, "The Unbearable Automaticity of Being," *American Psychologist* 54 (July 1999), 462–479.
78. Vanessa O'Connell, "GM Sings Tunes Inspired by Its Chevrolet Brand," *Wall Street Journal Online,* October 1, 2002, http://online.wsj.com.
79. Music from Wilco and The Album Leaf was identified in a blog that reports on music in commercials: http://trendymusicincommercials.blogspot.com.
80. Very good reviews of music's various advertising functions are available in Gordon C. BrunerII, "Music, Mood, and Marketing," *Journal of Marketing* 54 (October 1990), 94–104; Linda M. Scott, "Understanding Jingles and Needledrop: A Rhetorical Approach to Music in Advertising," *Journal of Consumer Research* 17 (September 1990), 223–236; Deborah J. MacInnis and C. Whan Park, "The Differential Role of Characteristics of Music on High and Low-Involvement Consumers' Processing of Ads," *Journal of Consumer Research* 18 (September 1991), 161–173; James J. Kellaris and Robert J. Kent, "The Influence of Music on Consumers' Temporal Perceptions: Does Time Fly When You're Having Fun?" *Journal of Consumer Psychology* 1, no. 4 (1992), 365–376; James J. Kellaris, Anthony D. Cox, and Dena Cox, "The Effect of Background Music on Ad Processing: A Contingency Explanation," *Journal of Marketing* 57 (October 1993), 114–125; James J. Kellaris and Robert J. Kent, "An Exploratory Investigation of Responses Elicited by Music Varying in Tempo, Tonality, and Texture," *Journal of Consumer Psychology* 2, no. 4 (1993), 381–402; Kineta Hung, "Framing Meaning Perceptions with Music: The Case of Teaser Ads," *Journal of Advertising* 30 (fall 2001), 39–50; Michelle L. Roehm, "Instrumental vs. Vocal Versions of Popular Music in Advertising," *Journal of Advertising Research* 41 (May/June 2001), 49–58; Rui (Juliet) Zhu and Joan Meyers-Levy, "Distinguishing between the Meanings of Music: When Background Music Affects Product Perceptions," *Journal of Marketing Research* 42 (August 2005), 333–345; and Steve Oakes, "Evaluating Empirical Research into Music in Advertising: A Congruity Perspective," *Journal of Advertising Research* 47 (March 2007), 38–50.
81. Gerald J. Gorn, "The Effects of Music in Advertising on Choice Behavior: A Classical Conditioning Approach," *Journal of Marketing* 46 (winter 1982), 94–101.
82. Tecnically, this study is better characterized as an evaluative conditioning study rather than an application of classical (Pavlovian) conditioning. For review of evaluative conditioning, see Bryan Gibson, "Can Evaluative Conditioning Change Attitudes toward Mature Brands? New Evidence from the Implicit Association Test," *Journal of Consumer Research* 35 (June 2008), 178–188.
83. A replication of this study failed to obtain supporting evidence, thereby calling into question the ability to generalize from Gorn's prior research. See James J. Kellaris and Anthony D. Cox, "The Effects of Background Music in Advertising," *Journal of Consumer Research* 16 (June 1989), 113–118.
84. See Darrell D. Muehling, Donald E. Stem, Jr., and Peter Raven, "Comparative Advertising: Views from Advertisers, Agencies, Media, and Policy Makers," *Journal of Advertising Research* 29 (October/November 1989), 38–48.
85. Naveen Donthu, "A Cross-Country Investigation of Recall of and Attitude toward Comparative Advertising," *Journal of Advertising* 27 (summer 1998), 111–122.
86. These questions are adapted from Stephen B. Ash and ChowHou Wee, "Comparative Advertising: A Review with Implications for Further Research," in *Advances in Consumer Research,* vol. 10, ed. R. P. Bagozzi and A. M. Tybout (Ann Arbor, Mich.: Association for Consumer Research, 1983), 374.
87. A sampling of significant comparative advertising research includes the following: Cornelia Droge and Rene Y. Darmon, "Associative Positioning Strategies through Comparative Advertising: Attribute versus Overall Similarity Approaches," *Journal of Marketing Research* 24 (November 1987), 377–388; Cornelia Pechmann and David W. Stewart, "The Effects of Comparative Advertising on Attention, Memory, and Purchase Intentions," *Journal of Consumer Research* 17 (September 1990), 180–191; Cornelia Pechmann and S. Ratneshwar, "The Use of Comparative Advertising for Brand Positioning: Association versus Differentiation," *Journal of Consumer Research* 18 (September 1991), 145–160; Cornelia Pechmann and Gabriel Esteban, "Persuasion Processes Associated with Direct Comparative and Noncomparative Advertising and Implications for Advertising Effectiveness," *Journal of Consumer Psychology* 2, no. 4 (1993), 403–432; Randall L. Rose, Paul W. Miniard, Michael J. Barone, Kenneth C. Manning, and

Brian D. Till, "When Persuasion Goes Undetected: The Case of Comparative Advertising," *Journal of Marketing Research* 30 (August 1993), 315–330; Shailendra Pratap Jain, Bruce Buchanan, and Durairaj Maheswaran, "Comparative versus Noncomparative Advertising: The Moderating Impact of Prepurchase Attribute Verifiability," *Journal of Consumer Psychology* 9, no. 4 (2000), 201–212; Shi Zhang, Frank R. Kardes, and Maria L. Cronley, "Comparative Advertising: Effects of Structural Alignability on Target Brand Evaluations," *Journal of Consumer Psychology* 12, no. 4 (2002), 303–312; Michael J. Barone, Kay M. Palan, and Paul W. Miniard, "Brand Usage and Gender as Moderators of the Potential Deception Associated with Partial Comparative Advertising," *Journal of Advertising* 33 (spring 2004), 19–28.

88. Dhruv Grewal, Sukuman Kavanoor, Edward F. Fern, Carolyn Costley, and James Barnes, "Comparative versus Noncomparative Advertising: A Meta-Analysis," *Journal of Marketing* 61 (October 1997), 1–15.
89. Terence A. Shimp and David C. Dyer, "The Effects of Comparative Advertising Mediated by Market Position of Sponsoring Brand," *Journal of Advertising* 7, no. 3 (1978), 13–19.
90. Gerald J. Gorn and Charles B. Weinberg, "The Impact of Comparative Advertising on Perception and Attitude: Some Positive Findings," *Journal of Consumer Research* 11 (September 1984), 719–727.
91. Paul W. Miniard, Michael J. Barone, Randall L. Rose, and Kenneth C. Manning, "A Further Assessment of Indirect Comparative Advertising Claims of Superiority Over All Competitors," *Journal of Advertising* 35 (winter 2006), 53–64.
92. Rose, Miniard, Barone, Manning, and Till, "When Persuasion Goes Undetected: The Case of Comparative Advertising"; Paul W. Miniard, Randall L. Rose, Michael J. Barone, and Kenneth C. Manning, "On the Need for Relative Measures When Assessing Comparative Advertising Effects," *Journal of Advertising* 22 (September 1993), 41–57. For an alternative explanation of why relative framed messages are more effective, see Zhang, Kardes, and Cronley, "Comparative Advertising: Effects of Structural Alignability on Target Brand Evaluations."

10

Measuring Advertising Message Effectiveness

In their studies of thousands of TV commercials that have been aired in the United States, Europe, and elsewhere, Millward Brown, a global advertising research company, has determined that "watchable" commercials—those which involve the viewer and are enjoyable to watch—are much more likely than ordinary commercials to be remembered and are substantially more likely to drive sales.[1] But what makes one commercial more watchable than another? Based on Millward Brown's research, here are some of the characteristics that distinguish watchable from less-watchable commercials:

Humor. Humor in advertising, when done effectively, is a key determinant of commercial watchability. Humor increases viewer involvement and enjoyment.

Music. Music is featured prominently in slightly over 50 percent of commercials that are classified as watchable; comparatively, ordinary commercials emphasize music only about 20 percent of the time.

Voice-Overs. Watchable ads rarely include continuous voice-overs (only about 10 percent of the time), whereas ordinary ads often use this technique (about 50 percent of the time). Watchable ads tend to use voice-overs only at the end of commercials.

Pace. Watchable ads are more likely to be fast-paced compared to ordinary ads.

Celebrities. Watchable ads use celebrities considerably more often than ordinary ads. Celebrities are excellent attention-getters and can be chosen to attract a specific age group, people who share a particular passion, and so on.

Cute Things. Commercials that include children or animals—babies sleeping, playing, learning to walk; puppies romping, nipping, and napping—tend to be more watchable, primarily because these "cute things" increase viewing enjoyment if not necessarily involvement.

For TV commercials to be successful, it is critical that the viewer's attention be captured and maintained. Many commercials initiate involuntary attention by using loud sounds or flashing lights, but these do not necessarily increase viewer involvement or enjoyment. Moreover, other commercials may be enjoyable to view, but may not be particularly involving or link the message well with the advertised brand. The concept of watchability is relatively new in advertising. Its point of emphasis is that an effective, impactful commercial must be involving and enjoyable.

This then takes us to the subject of the present chapter: Advertising research is needed to test commercials both before they are printed or aired (pretesting research) and after they appear in magazines

© AP Images/PRNewsFoto/Serta

and newspapers or on television and radio (posttesting research). Advertisers cannot assume that creative executions will be effective; rather, they must test ads for effectiveness. Watchability is just one of various indicators of advertising effectiveness.

Chapter Objectives

After reading this chapter you should be able to:

1. Explain the rationale and importance of message research.
2. Describe the various research techniques used to measure consumers' recognition and recall of advertising messages.
3. Illustrate measures of emotional reactions to advertisements.
4. Explicate the role of persuasion measurement, including pre- and posttesting of consumer preference.
5. Explain the meaning and operation of single-source measures of advertising effectiveness.
6. Examine some key conclusions regarding television advertising effectiveness.

>>Marcom Insight:

What Makes a Commercial Watchable?

Introduction to Advertising Research

The two preceding chapters examined the role of advertising creativity (Chapter 8) and explored the role of endorsers and forms of advertising executions—humor, sex appeals, appeals to guilt, and so on (Chapter 9). A well-defined value proposition is the key to advertising effectiveness, but there are "different ways to skin the cat"; that is, different types of creative advertising strategies (e.g., USP, brand image, and generic) and different message strategies can accomplish the all-important marcom objectives that were described back in Chapter 6. In short, brand managers and their advertising agencies have many options when creating advertising messages.

At the same time, the brand management team is responsible for researching whether proposed advertisements stand a good chance of being successful *prior* to investing money in printing or airing ads. It would, in other words, be presumptuous at best or even foolhardy to assume that a proposed advertisement will be successful absent any research-based evidence. The demand for *accountability* that is prevalent throughout business (recall the discussion back in Chapter 2) necessitates that ads be tested before they are placed in media and then again during or after the period in which they have been printed or broadcast.

Sound business practice requires that efforts be made to determine whether advertising expenditures are justified, especially considering the amount of money that is invested in advertising both in the United States and worldwide. Accordingly, a significant amount of time and money are spent on testing message effectiveness. This chapter surveys some of the most important techniques used in the advertising research business.

It's Not Easy or Inexpensive

Measuring message effectiveness is a difficult and expensive task. Nonetheless, the value gained from undertaking the effort typically outweighs the drawbacks. In the absence of formal research, most advertisers would not know whether proposed ad messages are going to be effective or whether ongoing advertising is doing a good job, nor could they know what to change to improve future advertising efforts. Advertising research enables management to increase advertising's contribution toward achieving marketing goals and yielding a reasonable return on investment.

Contemporary message research traces its roots to the 19th century, when measures of recall and memory were obtained as indicators of print advertising effectiveness.[2] Today, most national advertisers would not even consider airing a television commercial or placing a magazine advertisement without testing it first. A survey of the largest advertisers and advertising agencies in the United States determined that more than 80 percent of the respondents from each group pretest television commercials before airing them on a national basis.[3] Interestingly, these commercials typically are tested in a preliminary form rather than as finished versions. The purpose of testing commercials in rough form is to enable an economic means of screening out bad ideas at significantly lower expense than is necessitated in developing finished commercials.[4] Research has shown that results from testing prefinished commercials closely parallel those from tests performed on finalized commercials.[5] The *IMC Focus* describes the various prefinished forms in which TV commercials typically are tested. It is important to read this insert, because at different points throughout the chapter reference will be made to these various prefinished forms.

What Does Advertising Research Involve?

Advertising research encompasses a variety of purposes, methods, measures, and techniques. Broadly speaking, we can distinguish two general forms of ad research:

IMC >> i.m.c. focus

Testing TV Commercials in Prefinished Form

An advertising agency works from a creative brief that has been developed in conjunction with the client-side brand management team. As described in Chapter 8, the creative brief is a document designed to inspire copywriters by channeling their creative efforts toward a solution that will serve the interests of the client. The creative brief represents an informal pact between client and advertising agency that secures agreement on what an advertising campaign is intended to accomplish. Among other features, the creative brief identifies the brand positioning, the overall marketing strategy for the brand, and a statement of the brand's key value proposition. Working from this brief, copywriters and other agency personnel develop two or more creative executions that are considered suitable for accomplishing agreed-on objectives. However, rather than immediately producing a finished commercial, which can easily cost $500,000 or more, it is practical and cost-efficient to test the advertising concept in a prefinished form. There are five prefinished forms that are tested in television commercial research. The form furthest removed from a finished commercial is the storyboard, whereas the other forms become more like a produced commercial as we progress from the animatics form to the liveamatics version. Each is briefly described here.

1. *Storyboards:* This prefinished version presents a series of key visual frames and the corresponding script of the audio. The sequence of visual frames is literally pasted on a poster-type board, hence the storyboard name. The storyboard version, unlike a dynamic commercial, is completely static. Drawings of people replace the actual actors or celebrities who ultimately will appear in the finished commercial. Testing of storyboards often is done in focus group settings with small groups of consumers.
2. *Animatics:* This is a film or videotape of a sequence of drawings with simultaneous playing of audio to represent a proposed commercial. The animatic version maintains the primitive nature of the storyboard but incorporates an element of dynamism by videotaping the sequence of drawings.
3. *Photomatics:* A sequence of photographs is filmed or videotaped and accompanied by audio to represent a proposed commercial. This version is increasingly realistic because photographs of real people are displayed rather than, as in the case of storyboards or animatics, merely shown as drawn renderings of real people.
4. *Ripomatics* (also called steal-o-matics): Footage is taken from existing commercials and spliced together to represent the proposed commercial. Hence, the ripomatics version captures the realism of an actual commercial but does not entail the huge expense associated with filming an original commercial.
5. *Liveamatics:* This prefinished version entails filming or videotaping live talent to represent the proposed commercial. This version is the closest to a finished commercial, but it does not fully represent the actual settings or talent that will be used in the finished commercial.

SOURCES: Adapted from David Olson, "Principles of Measuring Advertising Effectiveness," American Marketing Association, http://www.marketingpower.com (accessed October 14, 2004); and Karen Whitehill King, John D. Pehrson, and Leonard N. Reid, "Pretesting TV Commercials: Methods, Measures, and Changing Agency Roles," *Journal of Advertising* 22 (September 1993), 85–97.

measures of *media effectiveness* and those of *message effectiveness.* Subsequent chapters will address the matter of media effectiveness; the present chapter focuses exclusively on measuring *message effectiveness.*

Achieving brand awareness, conveying copy points, influencing attitudes, creating emotional responses, and affecting purchase choices are the various foci of message research. In short, **message research** is undertaken to test the effectiveness of advertising messages. (Message research also is called *copy research,* or *copy testing,* but these terms are too limiting inasmuch as message research involves testing all aspects of advertisements, not just the verbal copy material.)

There are four stages at which ad message research might be conducted: (1) at the copy development stage; (2) at the "rough" stage (i.e., in prefinished form such as animatics and photomatics; see *IMC Focus*); (3) at the final production stage, but prior to placing the ad in magazines, on TV, or in other media; and (4) after the ad has been run in media.[6] In other words, advertising research involves both *pretesting* messages during developmental stages (prior to actual placement in advertising media) and *posttesting* messages for effectiveness after they have been aired or printed. Pretesting is performed to eliminate ineffective ads before they are ever run, while posttesting is conducted to determine whether messages have achieved established objectives.

Sometimes research is done under natural advertising conditions and other times in simulated or laboratory situations. Measures of effectiveness range from paper-and-pencil instruments (such as attitude scales) to physiological devices (e.g., pupillometers that measure eye movement). It should be clear that there is no single encompassing form of message research. Rather, measures of advertising effectiveness are as varied as the questions that advertisers and their agencies want answered.

Industry Standards for Message Research

Although message-based research is prevalent, much of it is not of the highest caliber. Sometimes it is unclear exactly what the research is attempting to measure, measures often fail to satisfy the basic requirements of sound research, and results occasionally have little to say about whether tested ads stand a good chance of being effective.

Members of the advertising research community have been mindful of these problems and have sought a higher standard of performance from advertising researchers. U.S. advertising agencies formulated a major document, called **Positioning Advertising Copy Testing (PACT),** to remedy the problem of mediocre or flawed advertising research. The document is directed primarily at television advertising but is relevant to the testing of advertising in all media.

The PACT document consists of nine message-testing principles.[7] More than mere pronouncements, these principles represent useful guides to how advertising research should be conducted. It is unnecessary to memorize these principles; rather, your objective in reading the following principles should be simply to appreciate what constitutes good message research practice. (Note that the developers of the PACT principles referred to copy testing rather than message research. The following descriptions retain the use of copy testing, although as noted previously, message research is a more apt label.)

Principle 1

A good copy testing system needs to provide measurements that are *relevant to the advertising objectives.* The specific objective(s) that an advertising campaign is intended to accomplish (such as creating brand awareness, influencing brand image, or creating warmth) should be the first consideration in determining the methods to assess advertising effectiveness. For example, if the objective for a particular advertising campaign is to evoke strong emotional reactions from viewers, a measure of brand awareness would likely be insufficient for determining if the message succeeded in accomplishing its objective.

Principle 2

A good copy testing system *requires agreement about how the results will be used in advance of each specific test.* Specifying the use of research results before data collection ensures that all parties involved (advertiser, agency, and research firm) agree on the research goals and reduces the chance of conflicting interpretations of test results. This principle's intent is to encourage the use of decision rules or action standards that, before actual testing, establish the test results that must be achieved for the test advertisement to receive full media distribution.

Principle 3

A good copy testing system provides *multiple measurements* because single measurements are generally inadequate to assess the totality of an ad's performance. The process by which advertisements influence customers is complex, so multiple measures are more likely than single measures to capture the various advertising effects.

Principle 4

A good copy testing system is based on *a model of human response to communications*—the reception of a stimulus, the comprehension of the stimulus, and the response to the stimulus. Because advertisements vary in the impact they are intended to achieve, a good copy testing system is capable of answering questions that are patterned to the underlying model of behavior. For example, if consumers purchase a particular product for primarily emotional reasons, then message research should use a suitable measure of emotional response rather than simply measuring recall of copy points. It is interesting to note that message research has historically focused excessively on the rational, cognitive aspect of human behavior and devoted insufficient attention to emotions and feelings—factors that are increasingly being recognized by scholars and practitioners as just as important, if not more influential, than cognition in driving consumer behavior.[8] A later discussion will discuss the role of emotionality in advertising and in message-based advertising research.

Principle 5

A good copy testing system allows for consideration of *whether the advertising stimulus should be exposed more than once.* This principle addresses the issue of whether a single test exposure (showing an ad or commercial to consumers only once) provides a sufficient test of potential impact. Because multiple exposures are often required for advertisements to accomplish their full effect, message research should expose a test ad to respondents on two or more occasions when the communications situation calls for such a procedure.[9] For example, a single-exposure test is probably insufficient to determine whether an advertisement successfully conveys a complex benefit. Conversely, a single exposure may be adequate if an advertisement is designed solely to create name awareness for a new brand.

Principle 6

A good copy testing system recognizes that a more finished piece of copy can be evaluated more soundly; therefore, a good system requires, at minimum, that *alternative executions be tested in the same degree of finish.* Test results typically vary depending on the degree of finish, as, for example, when testing a photomatic or ripomatic version of a television commercial (see the *IMC Focus*). Sometimes the amount of information lost from testing a less-than-finished ad is inconsequential; sometimes it is critical.

Principle 7

A good copy testing system *provides controls to avoid the bias normally found in the exposure context.* The context in which an advertisement is contained (e.g., the clutter or lack of clutter in a magazine) will have a substantial impact on how the ad is received, processed, and accepted. For this reason, copy testing procedures should attempt to duplicate the eventual context of an advertisement or commercial.

Principle 8

A good copy testing system takes into account *basic considerations of sample definition.* This typically requires that the sample be representative of the target audience to which test results are to be generalized and that the sample size be sufficiently large to permit reliable statistical conclusions.

Principle 9

Finally, a good copy testing system can *demonstrate reliability and validity.* Reliability and validity are basic requirements of any research endeavor. As applied to message research, a reliable test yields consistent results each time an advertisement is tested, and a valid test is predictive of marketplace performance.

The foregoing principles establish a high set of standards for the advertising research community and should be viewed as mandatory if advertising effectiveness is to be tested in a meaningful way.

What Do Brand Managers and Ad Agencies Want to Learn from Message Research?

As established back in Chapter 2, marcom efforts are directed at enhancing brand equity with the expectation that enhanced equity will lead ultimately to increases in brand sales and market share. You will recall from the discussion in Chapter 2 that brand equity from the consumer's perspective consists of two elements: *brand awareness* and *brand image.* Advertising's role is thus to augment brand awareness, alter the brand-based attribute and benefit associations that constitute a brand's image, and ultimately effect increases in a brand's sales and market share. Hence, message research is needed to provide diagnostic information about an advertisement's prospective equity-enhancing and sales-expanding potential (pretesting research) and to determine whether finalized advertisements actually accomplished these goals (posttesting research).

Before proceeding, it is important to note that members of the advertising community have attempted for many years to ascertain which measures of advertising best predict advertising effectiveness. Particularly notable is a major study funded by the influential Advertising Research Foundation (ARF) that assessed which of 35 different measures best predict the sales effectiveness of television commercials.[10] Although representing a heroic effort, results from ARF's Copy Research Validity Project are both inconclusive and controversial.[11] Probably the only definitive conclusion that can be made is that *no one measure is always most appropriate or universally best.* Each brand-advertising situation requires a careful assessment of the objectives that advertising is intended to accomplish and then the use of research methods that are appropriate for determining whether these objectives have been accomplished.

Given the scope of advertising research techniques in use, it would be impossible in this chapter to provide an exhaustive treatment. Literally dozens of methods for measuring message effectiveness have appeared over the years, and many companies specialize in measuring advertising effectiveness—firms such as the Starch Readership Service, the Bruzzone Research Company, Millward Brown, Ameritest, Gallup & Robinson, Mapes and Ross, Ipsos-ASI, the ARSgroup, and so on.

Two General Forms of Message Research

Broadly speaking, message research comes in two general forms: qualitative and quantitative. We first will describe qualitative research somewhat briefly and then devote primary attention to quantitative methods. This is not because the latter is more important; rather, the simple fact is that quantitative research has dominated in the ad industry and has a more established history of use in comparison to qualitative procedures.

Qualitative Message Research

This form of research is called *qualitative* because it is not based on producing numerical results and statistical analyses related to advertising copy and people's responses to that copy. Rather, qualitative research is concerned with generating insights into and interpretations of those advertising elements that influence people's responses to advertisements. Focus groups represent one form of qualitative ad research. For example, panels of focus group participants are presented with a storyboard version of a proposed new commercial, and then with the probing of a moderator are urged to share their thoughts and feelings about the commercial.

There are more sophisticated forms of qualitative advertising research that seek to better understand the meaning consumers derive from advertisements and the mental models that drive their thinking and behavior. One such method is *ethnographic research.* This form of research requires that advertising researchers fully immerse themselves into the study of the role that products and brands play in peoples' lives. Ethnography relies less on asking large samples of people questions about their opinions and beliefs and more on in-depth *observations* of the behavior of a small number of consumers. Ethnographers observe people's behavior in their homes or in other natural habitats where consumption and sometimes production of goods and services takes place. In addition to observing natural consumer behavior, ethnographic researchers also perform in-depth interviews with consumers to learn about their consumption behavior and the forces, such as advertising, that influence that behavior.[12]

The Zaltman Metaphor Elicitation Technique (ZMET)

A specific form of ethnographic research is the Zaltman Metaphor Elicitation Technique (ZMET).[13] This technique is based on several underlying premises, such as the fact that most human communication involves *nonverbal elements* (pictures, scenes, and music), that people's thoughts and feelings occur nonverbally as images, and that metaphors are the key mechanism for tapping into people's thoughts and feelings.[14] (A **metaphor** is based on the idea that people understand and experience things in terms of other things. For example, we refer to someone as having "eagle eyes" to mean he or she has keen sight; we sometimes characterize products as "lemons" to suggest they are fatally flawed. Hence, "eagle eyes" and "lemons" are metaphors that stand for something else.) Metaphors serve to reveal people's thoughts and shape them as well. By understanding the metaphors people use when thinking about brands, it is possible to apply this insight in developing advertising copy that resonates with people's brand-relevant thoughts and feelings.

The details about how a ZMET is implemented are beyond the scope of this text. (Refer to the articles cited in endnote 13 for specifics.) Many readers will have been exposed to ZMET in a prior course in marketing research. In any event, the important takeaway from this brief discussion is that qualitative research such as the Zaltman Metaphor Elicitation Technique can be invaluable as input into developing advertising copy. Hence, unlike the quantitative techniques that follow, ZMET is used as a basis for developing advertising copy rather than for testing that copy.

Quantitative Message Research

Quantitative message research is concerned with measuring the effects an advertisement may have (pretest research) or has had (posttest research). The following sections discuss some of the more popular methods national advertisers use. Two key points are needed before proceeding. It first is important to realize that many advertisers—especially smaller companies and organizations—do *not* conduct any advertising research, in either testing proposed advertising copy or testing ads that have been printed or aired in the form of, say, finished newspaper ads or TV commercials. The excuse given is that there is not sufficient time or funding to perform the research. Frankly, this is a bit lame given that the cost of making a mistake (for example, airing bad commercials) is far greater than the cost in terms of both time and money of testing ad copy. I would go so far as to say that no ad should ever be placed in media prior to conducting at least "quick and dirty" research, although more formal research is preferable.

A second preliminary point that will set the stage for the detailed presentation of quantitative message research methods is contained in this quote:

> *Measurement is the first step that leads to control and eventually to improvement. If you can't measure something, you can't understand it. If you can't understand it, you can't control it. If you can't control it, you can't improve it.*[15]

The point is that advertising research is crucial in order to measure the effects that advertisements have so that improvements can be made on a continual basis.

What exactly does quantitative message research measure? To address this question, it will be helpful to return to one of the previously discussed copy testing principles. PACT principle 4 stated that a good copy testing measurement system is based on a model of human response to communications. In other words, before determining precisely what to measure, it is essential to know which types of responses advertising is capable of eliciting. Think about it for a while. What effects might advertising have? *Have you thought about it?* Well, advertisements can have a variety of effects, including the following: (1) creating brand awareness; (2) teaching prospective customers about brand features and benefits; (3) forging emotional connections with people; (4) influencing purchase-relevant beliefs and positively (or negatively!) affecting attitudes toward advertised brands; (5) shifting people's preferences from one brand to another; and, ultimately, (6) encouraging trial and repeat purchase behavior.

Advertising has the ability to influence people in a variety of ways. Brand managers, their ad agencies, and research vendors can effectively measure the impact of advertising only by first determining what effect an advertising campaign is designed to accomplish. That determined, it then is a matter of conducting research to measure whether the campaign has accomplished the outcomes for which it was created. As the previous quote stated, if you can't measure, you can't control. And if you can't control, you can't influence.

As a matter of convenience (and some necessary simplification), we will categorize message research into four groups of measures: (1) recognition and recall, (2) emotional reactions, (3) persuasion, and (4) sales response. The intent is to provide a representative sampling of the primary measurement techniques that brand managers and their ad agencies use for measuring advertising effectiveness. These general categories and the specific measures contained within each category are summarized in Table 10.1.

In brief, measures of *recognition and recall* assess whether advertising has successfully influenced brand awareness and influenced brand-related thoughts and feelings. Measures of *emotional reaction* provide indicators of whether advertisements have emotionally aroused consumers. Measures of *persuasive impact* represent prebehavioral indicators of whether an advertisement is likely to influence purchase intentions and behavior. Finally, measures of *sales response* determine whether an advertising campaign has affected consumers' purchases of an advertised brand.

table 10.1

Illustrative Message Research Methods

Measures of Recognition and Recall
- Starch Readership Service (magazines)
- Bruzzone tests (TV)
- Burke day-after recall testing (TV)

Measures of Emotional Reactions
- Brain imaging
- Self-reports
- Physiological tests

Measures of Persuasion
- Ipsos-ASI Next*TV method
- ARS Persuasion method

Measures of Sales Response (single-source systems)
- IRI's BehaviorScan
- Nielsen's ScanTrack

Measures of Recognition and Recall

After exposure to an advertisement, consumers may experience varying degrees of awareness, the most basic of which is simply noticing an ad without processing specific elements. Advertisers intend, however, for consumers to heed specific parts, elements, or features of an ad and associate those with the advertised brand. Recognition and recall both represent elements of consumers' memories for advertising information, but *recognition measures,* which can be equated with multiple-choice test questions, tap a more superficial level of memory compared with *recall measures,* which are similar to essay questions.[16] It also will be noted from the discussion of brand equity in Chapter 2 that recognition is a lower level of brand awareness than recall. In other words, brand managers want consumers not only to recognize a brand name and its attributes or benefits but also to recall this information freely from memory without cues or reminders.

Several commercial research firms provide advertisers with information on how well their ads perform in terms of generating awareness, which typically is assessed with recognition or recall measures. Three services are described in the following sections: Starch Readership Service (magazine recognition), Bruzzone tests (television recognition primarily), and day-after recall tests (television recall).[17]

Starch Readership Service

Starch Readership Service, a testing service of a company named GfK Custom Research North America, measures the primary objective of a *magazine ad*—namely, to be seen and read. Starch examines reader awareness of advertisements in consumer magazines and business publications. Over 75,000 advertisements are studied annually based on interviews with more than 100,000 people involving more than 140 publications. Sample sizes range from 100 to 150 individuals per issue, with most interviews conducted in respondents' homes or, in the case of business publications, in offices or places of business. Interviews are conducted during the early life of a publication. Following a suitable waiting period after the appearance of a publication to give readers an opportunity to read or look through their issue, interviewing commences and continues for a full week (for a weekly publication), two weeks (for a biweekly), or three weeks (for a monthly publication).

Starch interviewers locate eligible readers of each magazine issue studied. An *eligible reader* is one who has glanced through or read some part of the issue prior to the interviewer's visit and who meets the age, sex, and occupation requirements set for the particular magazine. Once eligibility is established, interviewers turn the pages of the magazine, inquiring about each advertisement being studied. Respondents are first asked, "Did you see or read any part of this advertisement?" If a respondent answers "Yes," a prescribed questioning procedure is followed to determine the respondent's awareness of various parts of the ad (illustrations, headline, etc.). Respondents are then classified as *noted, associated, read-some,* or *read-most* readers according to these specific definitions:[18]

- *Noted* is the percentage of people interviewed who remembered having previously seen the advertisement in the issue being studied.
- *Associated* is the percentage of people interviewed who not only noted the ad but also saw or read some part of it that clearly indicated the name of the brand or advertiser.
- *Read some* is the percentage of people interviewed who read any part of the ad's copy.
- *Read most* is the percentage of people interviewed who read half or more of the written material in the ad.

For each magazine advertisement that has undergone a Starch analysis, indices are developed for that ad's noted, associated, read-some, and read-most scores. Two sets of indices are established: One index compares an advertisement's scores against the average scores for *all ads* in the magazine issue, and the second (called the Adnorm index) compares an advertisement's scores against other ads in the *same product category* as well as with the same size (e.g., full-page) and color classifications (e.g., four-color). Hence, an advertisement that achieves an average value receives an index of 100. By comparison, a score of 130, for example, would mean that a particular ad scored 30 percent above comparable ads, whereas a score of 75 would indicate it scored 25 percent below comparable ads.

Figure 10.1 illustrates a Starch-rated advertisement from an issue of *Sports Illustrated* magazine. This Kia Sorento ad contains a large amount of body copy. The Starch Readership scores for this ad reflect that 39 percent of the respondents remembered having previously seen (or *noted*) the ad, 37 percent *associated* it, 27 percent *read some* of it, and 10 percent *read most* of the body copy contained in this ad. (For readers who are experienced with the Starch procedure, note that Starch used to attach little yellow labels on advertisements to indicate these percentages, but it no longer affixes these labels; rather, scores are provided in a separate report.)

A Jose Cuervo Especial tequila ad with obvious sex-oriented appeal shows a man and a woman in wet bathing suits, with the woman's legs wrapped around the man's chest. It attracts attention and perhaps creates an emotional bond with the brand, even though only a small bottle of the tequila is shown in one corner of the ad. Containing virtually no body copy other than a three-word headline, "PURSUE YOUR DAYDREAMS," this ad's noted, associated, read-some, and read-most scores were substantially higher than the corresponding scores for the Kia Sorento, at 58, 54, 39, and 39 percent, respectively. (See the *Global Focus* insert for interesting commentary about developments in tequila marketing.)

A basic assumption of the Starch procedure is that respondents in fact do remember whether they saw a particular ad in a specific magazine issue. The Starch technique has sometimes been criticized because in so-called *bogus ad studies* (i.e., studies that use prepublication or altered issues), respondents report having seen ads that actually never ran. The company that conducts Starch studies does

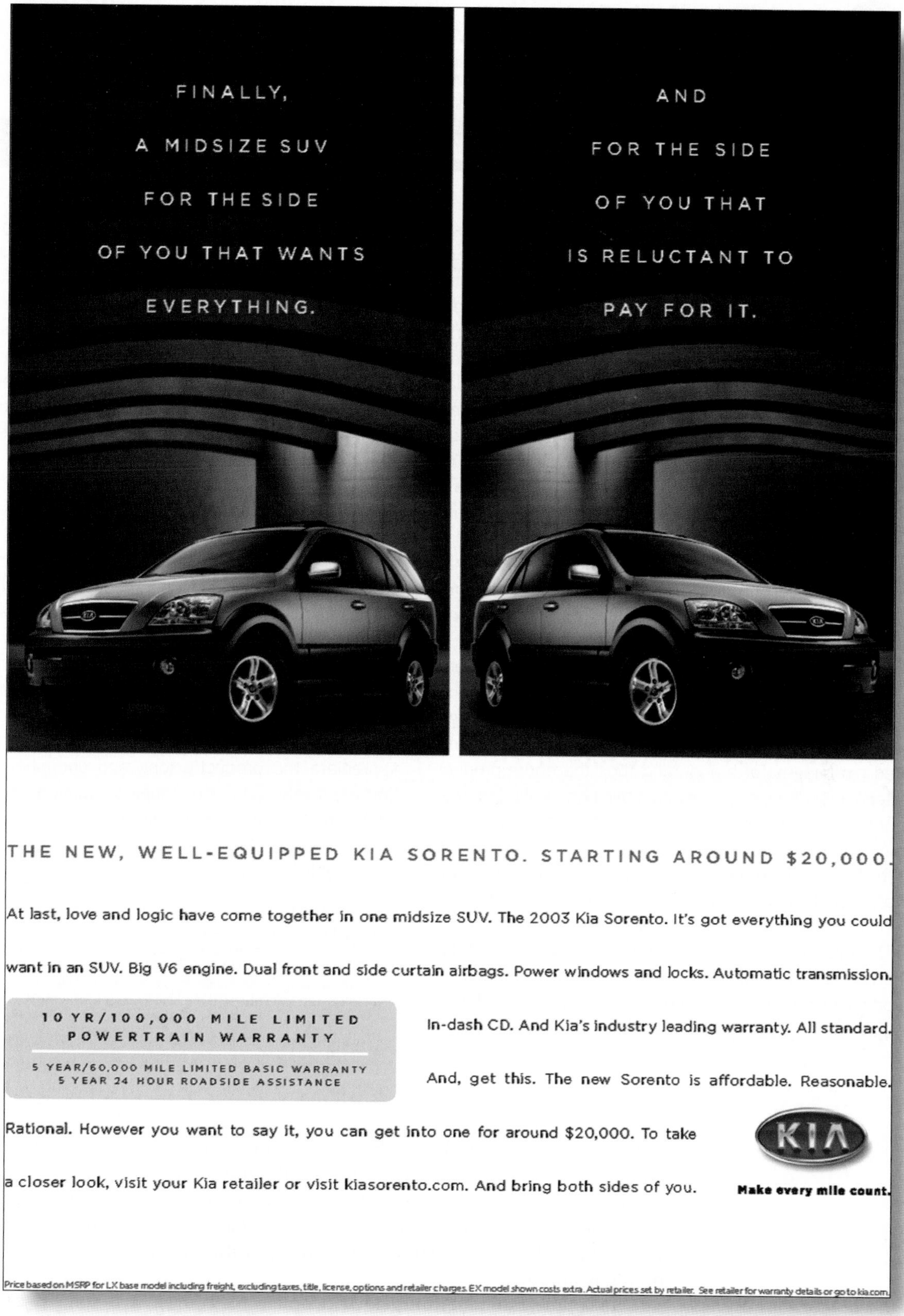

Courtesy of KIA Motors America, Inc.

Figure 10.1

Starch-Rated Advertisement for the Kia Sorento

global focus

Is What's Good for Vodka Good for Tequila?

The distilled spirits industry is more dynamic than most, probably because the age group composed of the most trendsetters, perhaps ages 25–39, is constantly losing members and gaining others as people age, and new generations typically differ from their predecessors. Trends in liquor consumption seem to shift every generation or so in lockstep with cultural developments that influence what's hot and what's not, what's hip and what's mundane. For example, consumption of Scotch whiskey increased for a while during the go-go days of the Internet boom in the 1990s with young professionals finding this drink compatible with cigar smoking, male bonding, and activities of this nature that were popular at the time. Consumption of "white" liquors (e.g., vodka) increased when more traditional "brown" liquors (Scotch, bourbon, etc.) were perceived as "dad's drink," excessively masculine, and passé.

Vodka is perhaps the one liquor that has for the past several decades been the steadiest performer among distilled spirits products. This, no doubt, is due in large part to advertising campaigns such as Absolut's that created hip images for brands and thus the entire product category. Vodka marketers also have been willing to augment the product by adding flavorful tastes (citron, lemon, vanilla, etc.) to a product that has little taste of its own. These added flavors have made vodka a more palatable drink and broadened the market by catering to consumers with multiple taste preferences.

Tequila marketers are now taking a page from vodka marketers' playbook and adding flavors to tequila, a product historically consumed in its "raw" form. A Las Vegas company named Tukys pioneered the trend. Tukys imports tequila in bulk from Mexico and then mixes it with flavors in the United States. Tukys's line of tequila includes flavors such as watermelon, lime, coffee, strawberry, and orange/mandarin. Tukys's pioneering effort created a market for flavored tequila, and heavyweight competitor Jose Cuervo, which owns about half of the U.S. tequila market, followed in 2006 with its own line of flavored tequila products. Sales of flavored tequila grew by nearly 50 percent during 2007, which attests to the power of Jose Cuervo's marketing.

Ethicists have good reason to be concerned that such marketing gimmicks serve to recruit younger people to a product category they otherwise might avoid due to a taste perceived as too harsh. Beyond this, and strictly from a strategic marketing perspective, a possible downside to flavoring tequila is that this could fundamentally change consumer perceptions of tequila—from a traditional drink with a strong Mexican heritage and a distinct taste created by fermenting blue agave plants, a spiky-leafed member of the lily family, to a faddish beverage consumed by nontraditionalists and those who do not appreciate the product's long and cherished heritage. Comparatively, can you imagine distillers in Scotland adding flavors to Scotch whiskey—say, vanilla Scotch, lemon Scotch, cherry Scotch, or others? It is virtually unthinkable, is it not?

SOURCES: Adapted from James Arndofer, "Tequila Tries a Flavor Shot to Maintain Sales," *Advertising Age*, January 10, 2005, 4, 36; "Tequila + Flavor," April 14, 2006, http://www.beverage-news.com/4-14flavoredtequila.html (accessed January 30, 2008); "Wholesa lers vs. Retailers: He Said, She Said," January 7, 2008, http://www.winespiritsdaily.com/2008/01/wholesalers-vs-retailers-he-said-she.html (accessed January 30, 2008).

not consider such studies valid and claims that the bogus studies have not adhered to proper procedures for qualifying issue readers and questioning respondents. Research demonstrates that when properly interviewed, most respondents are able to identify the ads they have seen or read in a specific issue with a high degree of accuracy; according to this research, false reporting of ad noting is minimal.[19]

Due to the inherent frailties of people's memories, it is almost certain that Starch scores do *not* provide exact percentages but rather are biased to some degree by people reporting they have seen or read an ad when in fact they have not. Another potential source of bias is people reporting they have *not* seen an ad when, in fact, they have. Nonetheless, it is not exact scores that are critical but rather comparisons between scores for the same ad placed in different magazines or comparative scores among different ads placed in the same magazine issue. For example, the Kia Sorento ad in Figure 10.1 obtained index scores (called Adnorm index scores) of 72 (noted), 74 (associated), 73 (read some), and 59 (read most). These indices mean that this ad performed 28 percent worse than the average noted score (an index of 100 indicates an average-performing ad; hence 100 – 72 = 28 percent worse) for all of the advertisements of similar size and color in this particular issue of *Sports Illustrated,* 26 percent worse than the median associated score, 27 percent worse than the median read-some score, and 41 percent worse than the median read-most score. It is obvious that this ad was a below-average performer. Comparatively, the Adnorm indices for the Jose Cuervo Especial tequila ad discussed earlier are 107 (noted), 108 (associated), 105 (read some), and 229 (read most). Compared to similarly sized advertisements, the evocative Jose Cuervo ad performed slightly above average in terms of noted, associated, and read-some scores but dramatically above average with respect to its read-most score. Because Starch has been performing these studies since the 1920s and has compiled a wealth of baseline data, or norms, advertisers and media planners can make informed decisions concerning the relative merits of different magazines and informed judgments regarding the effectiveness of particular advertisements.

Bruzzone Tests

The Bruzzone Research Company (BRC) provides advertisers with a test of consumer *recognition* of television commercials along with their evaluations of these commercials. (BRC also tests magazine advertisements, but the discussion here is limited to TV commercials.) Historically, BRC mailed a set of photoboard commercials to a random sample of households and encouraged responses by providing a nominal monetary incentive. Starting in the late 1990s, BRC's data collection turned to the Internet and away from mailed distribution, as testing commercials online proved more efficient, less costly, and equally valid to the mailing procedure.[20]

In its standard testing procedure, BRC emails 15 commercials to a sample of online users. For each tested commercial, respondents first see this question: "Do you remember seeing this commercial on TV?" This question is followed by a series of six key scenes from the commercial and corresponding script. Immediately below the six-scene presentation are three response options: "Yes," "No," and "Not Sure." Respondents who respond "Yes" (that they do remember seeing this commercial) continue answering a series of questions about the commercial. (Those who answer "No" or "Not Sure" skip to the next tested commercial.) Importantly, anything that identifies the advertiser (such as mentioning the brand name in the script) is removed, so that those who noticed the commercial can indicate whether they remember the name of the advertised brand. (For a demonstration of BRC's online testing procedure, go to http://www.bruzzone-research.com/ONLINE_DEMOq.HTM. It will be worthwhile to review this Web site, which will enhance your understanding of the following discussion.)

The script from an illustrative Bruzzone test is shown in Figure 10.2.[21] This 30-second commercial—titled "Carne Asada Taquitos" and sponsored by Taco Bell—aired first during the 2007 Super Bowl and was tested by BRC shortly after the airing. Review of the script indicates that the commercial focuses on two lions chitchatting about Taco Bell's new (at the time) grilled steak taco, or, in Spanish, *carne asada taquitos.* The commercial is humorous in a low-key fashion, is somewhat engaging, and is watchable (in reference to the discussion of commercial watchability that was discussed in the *Marcom Insight* section that opened the chapter).

The Bruzzone testing procedure first requests respondents to indicate whether they recall having seen this commercial. Respondents subsequently are asked to indicate how interested they are in the commercial and how it makes them feel about the advertised brand (Taco Bell's grilled steak taco). Respondents also are requested to describe their feelings by checking any of 27 adjectives that, in their

figure 10.2

Script for Taco Bell's "Carne Asada Taquitos" Commercial

1st Lion:	Do you smell that?
2nd Lion:	Yeah, campers. I like the guy on the right.
1st Lion:	No, no, no, the steak grilled Taquitos. The Carne (rolls "r") Asada steak.
2nd Lion:	Carne Asada.
1st Lion:	Yeah, I know. It's fun to say. It's like Carne (emphasis on rolling the "r") Asada.
2nd Lion:	Carne Asada.
1st Lion:	No, you say it sexy like this, Carne (rolling the "r") Asada.
2nd Lion:	Carne Asada.
1st Lion:	No, no, sexy like Ricardo Montalban. You know, Carne (rolling the "r') Asada.
2nd Lion:	Carne Asada. Ricardo Montalban?
Announcer:	(Company) New Steak Grilled Taquito with Carne (rolling the "r") Asada steak. For a vente Carne Asada.
2nd Lion:	Oh, ok, Carne Asada.
1st Lion:	No, still no.
Announcer:	Think outside the bun.

opinion, characterize the commercial—items such as amusing, appealing, believable, clever, and so on. Following these ratings, respondents indicate whether it is appropriate for the advertiser (Taco Bell, in this case) to air this commercial. They then make known how much they liked the commercial (from "Liked it a lot" to "Disliked it a lot") and whether they remember which brand was being advertised.

Because BRC has performed hundreds of such tests (BRC tested nearly 800 ads aired during the 16 Super Bowls played between 1992 and 2007), it has established norms for average commercial performance against which a newly tested commercial can be compared. BRC's Advertising Response Model (ARM) links responses to the 27 descriptive adjectives to consumers' attitudes toward both the advertisement (attitude toward the ad) and the advertised product (attitude toward the product), and ultimately to the overall impact of the ad (overall impact). Figure 10.3 presents the ARM analysis for Taco Bell's "Carne Asada Taquitos" commercial.

Notice first in the upper-right corner the color coding for this analysis. Specifically, adjectives coded in *yellow* indicate that the commercial performed better than average (compared to BRC norms), words coded in *light blue* reveal average performance, and those adjectives coded in *red* indicate below-average performance. A review of Figure 10.3 shows that the Taco Bell commercial scored above average on indicators of humor, uniqueness, warmth, importance, and clarity. At the same time, the ad performed below average on energy (it was an intentionally subdued ad). Moving from left to right on Figure 10.3, it further can be seen that the ad performed at just an average level in terms of entertainment value, empathy, and relevance. As a result, the ad scored at just an average level (based on Bruzzone norms) in terms of both attitude toward the ad and attitude toward the product. The result was a Super Bowl commercial whose overall impact was in the average range for the dozens of Super Bowl commercials that Bruzzone tested in 2007.

By comparison, consider another commercial sponsored by Anheuser-Busch titled "Thanking the Troops." Perusal of the six key scenes in Figure 10.4 reveals that this commercial involves an airport setting in which passengers awaiting

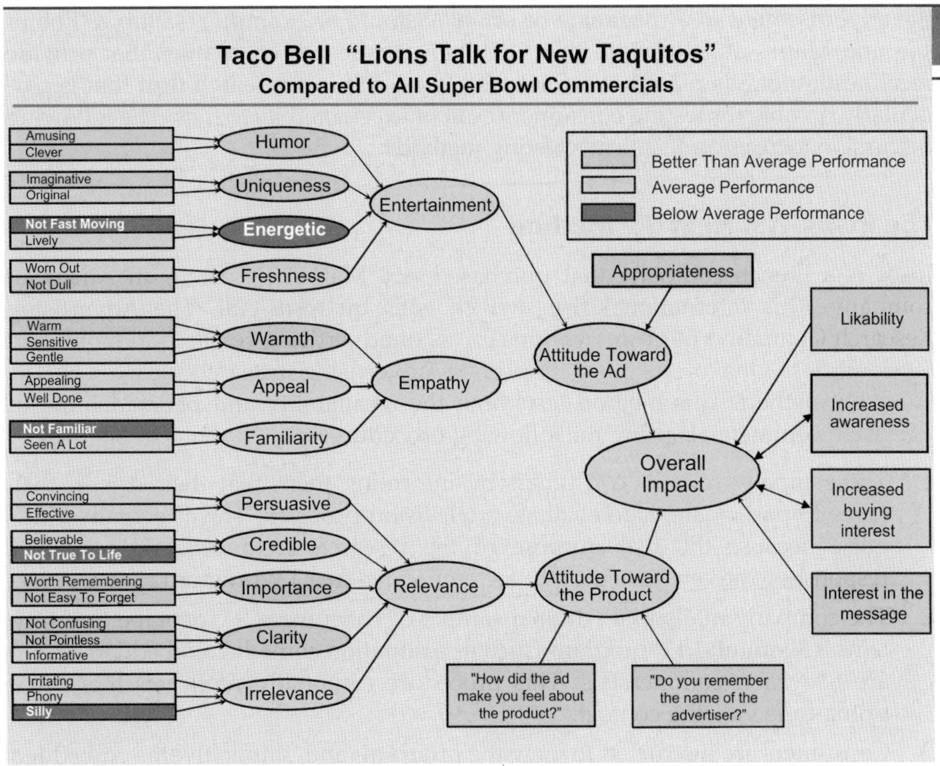

figure 10.3

Advertising Response Model (ARM) for the "Carne Asada Taquitos" Commercial

flights give a standing ovation to U.S. troops who are in route to their plane. Figure 10.5 presents the ARM analysis for this commercial. The "Thanking the Troops" commercial scored above average on indicators of uniqueness, freshness, warmth, persuasiveness, credibility, importance, and clarity. At the same time, the ad performed below average on energy and humor (it obviously was not intended to be energetic or humorous). Moving from left to right in Figure 10.5, it further can be seen that the ad performed at just an average level in terms of entertainment value but, as expected, above average in terms of empathy and relevance. As a result, the ad scored above average in terms of both attitude toward the ad and attitude toward the product, and the commercial's overall impact was above average. This was a highly effective commercial by Bruzzone standards, and in view of the emotional impact also a highly watchable ad (based on Millward Brown's conceptualization of watchability as described in the chapter opening *Marcom Insight* insert).

In sum, BRC testing provides a valid prediction of actual marketplace performance along with being relatively inexpensive compared with other copy testing methods. Because a Bruzzone test cannot be implemented until after a finished TV commercial has actually been aired, it does not provide a before-the-fact indication of whether a commercial should be aired in the first place. Nevertheless, BRC's testing offers important information for evaluating a commercial's effectiveness and whether it should continue to run.

Day-After Recall Testing

Various companies test advertisements to determine whether viewers have been sufficiently influenced to recall having seen

Figure 10.4

Key Scenes and Questions from BRC's Test of the "Thanking the Troops" Commercial

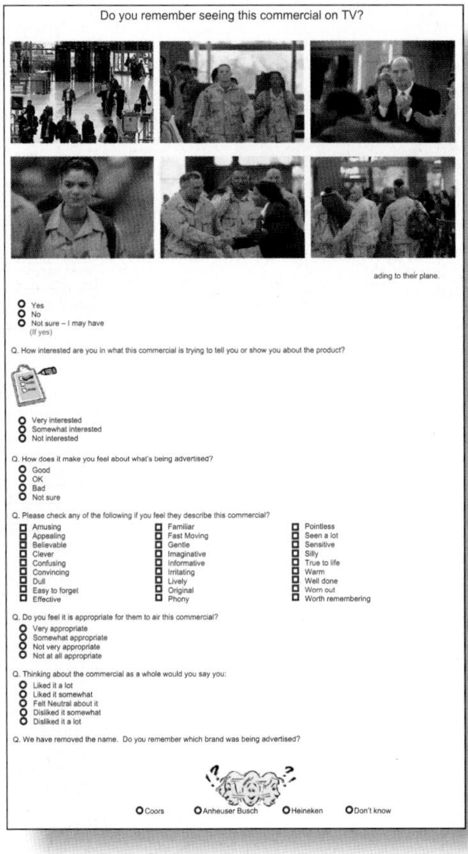

the advertisement in a magazine or on television. For example, Gallup & Robinson and Mapes and Ross are two well-known research companies that provide recall testing of ads placed in *print media.* Ipsos-ASI is a research firm that is particularly notable for testing consumer recall of *television commercials.* The following discussion focuses on this firm's testing method.

The Ipsos-ASI Next*TV Method

Ipsos is a French company that purchased ASI Market Research, an American company. This international firm (which goes by Ipsos-ASI, The Advertising Research Company) performs various forms of advertising research in more than 50 countries. One of its most important advertising research services is the Next*TV method. This method tests both the recallability and persuadability of television commercials using the following procedure:

1. The company recruits consumers by informing them that their task, if they agree to participate, is to evaluate a television program. This is actually a disguise because the real purpose of the research is to evaluate consumer responses to advertisements that are embedded in a TV program.
2. The company mails to a national sample of consumers a videotape that contains a 30-minute TV program (such as a situation comedy); embedded within are television commercials. This procedure essentially replicates the actual prime-time viewing context.
3. Consumers are instructed to view the program (and, implicitly, the embedded advertising) from the videotape. The viewing context is thus actual, in-home viewing, the same as when consumers view any television advertisement under natural viewing conditions.
4. One day after viewing the videotaped TV program (and advertisements), Ipsos-ASI personnel contact sampled consumers and measure their reactions to the TV program (in concert with the original disguise) and to the advertisements, which, of course, is the primary objective.
5. Ipsos-ASI then measures message recall.

figure 10.5

Advertising Response Model (ARM) for the "Thanking the Troops" Commercial

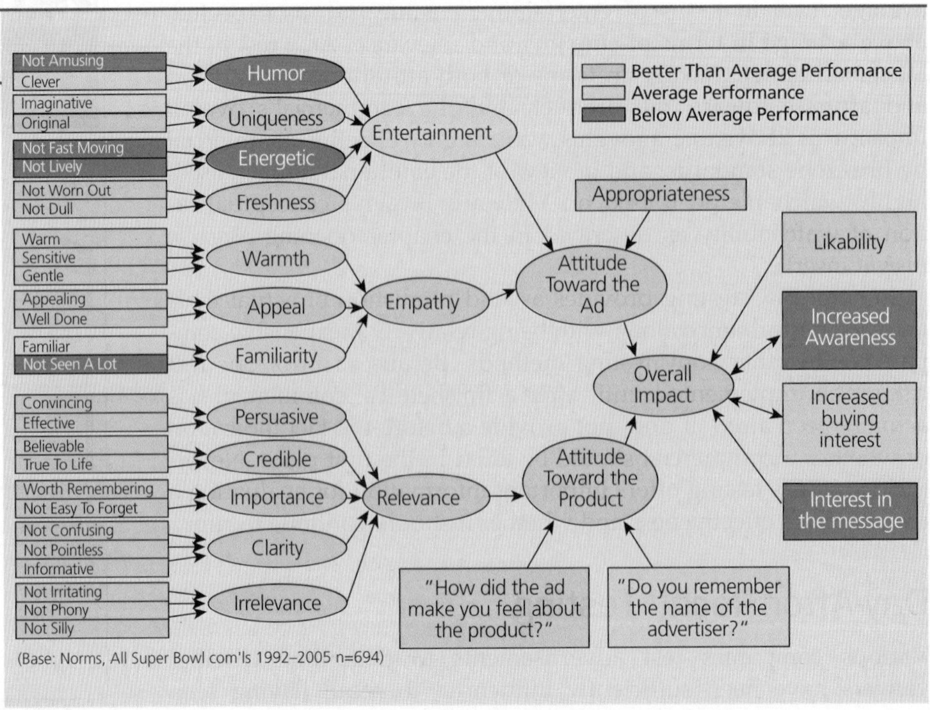

Used with permission from the ARS Group

Ipsos-ASI Next*TV employs the same basic methodology around the world. The in-home videotape methodology provides a number of advantages. First, the in-home exposure makes it possible to measure advertising effectiveness in a natural environment. Second, by embedding test advertisements in actual programming content, it is possible to assess the ability of TV commercials to break through the clutter, gain the viewer's attention, and influence message recallability and persuadability. Third, by measuring recall one day after exposure, Ipsos-ASI can determine how well tested commercials are remembered after this delay period. Fourth, the videotape technology allows the use of representative national sampling. Finally, by providing several alternative measures of persuasion, the Next*TV method allows brand managers and their ad agencies to select the measures that best meet their specific needs.

The Recall Controversy

Considerable controversy has surrounded the use of recall as an indicator of advertising effectiveness.[22] For example, Coca-Cola executives reject recall as a valid measure of advertising effectiveness because, in their opinion, recall simply measures whether an ad is received but not whether the message is accepted.[23] It also is known that measures of recall are biased in favor of younger consumers. This is to say that recall scores deteriorate with age progression.[24] Third, there is mounting evidence that the recall scores generated by advertisements are not predictive of sales performance; that is, regardless of which measure of recall is used, the evidence suggests that sales levels do not increase with increasing levels of recallability.[25] Finally, there is some evidence that recall testing significantly *understates the memorability* of commercials that employ *emotional or feeling-oriented themes* and is biased in favor of rational or thought-oriented commercials.[26] Research has even demonstrated a negative correlation between how well consumers recall ads and how much they like them.[27]

In closing this section, it is important to appreciate that no single measure of advertising effectiveness is perfect for every situation. Recall measurement certainly has limitations, but this does not mean that it is inappropriate or inadvisable to measure recall. Rather, measures in addition to recall (and recognition) should also be obtained. Subsequent sections describe these other measures, including measurement of emotional reactions, persuasion effects, and sales impact.

Measurement of Emotional Reactions

Researchers have increasingly recognized that advertisements that positively influence receivers' feelings and emotions can be extremely successful. This is because consumer behavior is governed not by reason alone—or even primarily by reason—but also by gut feelings and emotions. Indeed, some brands are virtually loved because they connect with consumers by creating a strong emotional bond. Such brands have been referred to as "lovemarks," which are brands that are embraced with a passion.[28] Needless to say, brand managers cherish lovemark status for their brands, which necessitates that they appeal to consumers' emotions as well as to their minds.

Given the importance of emotions in consumer behavior and the trend toward more advertising directed at emotions, there has been a corresponding increase in efforts to measure consumers' emotional reactions to advertisements.[29] This is fully justified considering research has shown that ads that are better liked—often because they elicit positive emotions—are more likely to be remembered and to persuade.[30]

Advertising researchers use three general ways to measure consumers' emotional responses to advertisements: (1) brain imaging, (2) self-report measures, and (3) physiological measures. Most of the following discussion is based on this last set of physiological measures, but brief discussion is devoted to the first two.

Neuroscience and Brain Imaging

The first method, brain imaging, is the newest rage in advertising research. Brain imaging applies knowledge from the field of *neuroscience* and uses a functional Magnetic Resonance Imaging device (fMRI). Brain imaging using fMRI equipment detects changes in blood oxygenation and flow that occur in response to neural activity. When a brain area is more active, it consumes more oxygen to meet this increased demand, which increases blood flow to the active area. Greater blood flow into emotional centers of the brain indicates increased amounts of emotional response to advertisements. (As a reminder, you may recall reading the *IMC Focus* in Chapter 2 that described a neuroscience test of why consumers prefer Coca-Cola over Pepsi.)

Although it is important to introduce students to this new method for measuring consumers' emotional reactions to advertisements, this form of measurement is not without limitations and is in its infancy as it relates to understanding emotional reactions to advertisements. Much work remains before advertising researchers can be confident that the results from fMRI provide reliable and valid tests of consumers' emotional reactions to advertisements. Neuroscientists are investing considerable research in this area, and advertising research firms will increasingly capitalize on the knowledge that is generated and the improvements in measurement technology that will be forthcoming.

Self-Report Measurement

A second method widely used to determine consumers' emotional responses to advertisements is **self-report measurement.** Consumers' emotional reactions in response to advertisements are measured by asking them to self-report their feelings. Both verbal and visual self-reports are used for this purpose.[31] With *verbal self-reports,* researchers ask consumers to rate their emotional reactions to a particular advertisement on conventional rating scales. For example, respondents might be asked to indicate their degree of agreement or disagreement with a statement such as: "This ad gave me a warm feeling." *Visual self-reports,* in contrast, use cartoon-like characters to represent different emotions and emotional states. For each emotion that an advertisement might elicit, consumers select one of several cartoon characters to reflect their emotional reaction to the advertisement. Imagine, for example, that a researcher might use "smiling faces" varying in their degree of smiling to assess the strength of consumers' emotional reactions to a particular advertisement.

Physiological Testing

The third general method for measuring consumers' emotional responses to advertisements is **physiological testing devices** that measure any of several autonomic responses to advertisements. *Autonomic responses* occur in the autonomic nervous system, which consists of the nerves and ganglia that furnish blood vessels, the heart, smooth muscles, and glands. Because individuals have little voluntary control over the autonomic nervous system, researchers use changes in physiological functions to indicate the actual, unbiased amount of arousal resulting from advertisements. Such responses include facial expressions, sweating, and heart rate.[32] Psychologists have concluded that these physiological functions are indeed sensitive to psychological processes of concern in advertising.[33]

To appreciate the potential value of such physiological measurement, consider the case of the previously described Jose Cuervo Especial advertisement that promotes the advertised brand by placing it in the context of a young couple in a provocative embrace along with the suggestive headline, "Pursue your daydreams." During pretesting of this ad, some people may respond that they really find it appealing. Others, when asked what they think of it, may indicate that they dislike the ad because they consider it too sexually suggestive and gratuitous. Still others may even feign aggravation to make (what they perceive to be) a favorable impression on the interviewer. That is, the latter group may actually enjoy the ad but say otherwise in response to an interviewer's query, thereby disguising their true evaluation. Here is where measures of physiological arousal have a potential role to play in advertising research—namely, to prevent self-monitoring of feelings and biased responses to standard paper-and-pencil measures.

The Galvanometer

The **galvanometer** (also referred to as the psychogalvanometer) is a device for measuring *galvanic skin response,* or *GSR.* (*Galvanic* refers to electricity produced by a chemical reaction.) When some element in an advertisement activates the consumer's autonomic nervous system, a physical response occurs in the sweat glands located in the palms and fingers. These glands open to varying degrees depending on the intensity of the arousal, and skin resistance drops when the sweat glands open. By sending a very fine electric current through one finger and out the other and completing the circuit through an instrument called a *galvanometer,* testers are able to measure both the degree and the frequency with which an advertisement activates emotional responses. Simply, the galvanometer indirectly assesses the degree of emotional response to an advertisement by measuring minute amounts of perspiration.

There is evidence that GSR is a valid indicator of the amount of warmth an advertisement generates.[34] Many companies have found the galvanometer to be a useful tool for assessing the potential effectiveness of advertisements, direct-mail messages, package copy, and other marcom messages. Advertising research practitioners who use the galvanometer claim that it is a *valid* predictor (see PACT principle 9) of an advertisement's ability to *motivate* consumer purchase behavior.[35] Indeed, in recognition of the galvanometer's ability to reveal an advertisement's motivational properties, practitioners also refer to GSR research as the Motivational Response Method, or MRM.

The Pupillometer

Using a device called a **pupillometer,** pupillometric tests in advertising are conducted by measuring respondents' pupil dilation as they view a television commercial or focus on a printed advertisement. Respondents' heads are in a fixed position to permit continuous electronic measurement of changes in pupillary responses. Responses to specific elements in an advertisement are used to indicate positive reaction (greater dilation) or negative reaction (smaller relative dilation). Although not unchallenged, some scientific evidence since the late 1960s suggests that pupillary responses are correlated with people's arousal to stimuli and perhaps even with their likes and dislikes.[36]

Measures of Persuasion

Measures of persuasion are used when an advertiser's objective is to influence consumers' attitudes toward and preference for the advertised brand. Firms that perform this type of research include, among others, Ipsos-ASI and ARSgroup.

The following sections describe the Ipsos-ASI Next*TV method and the ARSgroup's persuasion method. More discussion is devoted to the latter advertising research procedure because the ARSgroup has done a particularly outstanding job in documenting its commercial service. (Parenthetically, it may have occurred to you that companies in the advertising research business have strange names. Actually, these names are no stranger than are the names of well-known companies such as IBM or AT&T. The research companies' names just seem strange because you probably were unfamiliar with them prior to reading this chapter.)

The Ipsos-ASI Next*TV method

This method was described in detail when previously discussing measures of advertising recall. (It will be worth your time to return to the prior description for review.) In brief, the Next*TV method involves having a sample of consumers view videotapes of TV programs in their homes, and embedded in these programs are TV commercials. The day after consumers have viewed the program and commercials, researchers call them back and measure both their ability to recall the commercials and whether they have been persuaded. Persuasion is measured by assessing consumers' attitudes toward advertised brands, their shift in brand preferences, and their brand-related buying intentions.

The ARS Persuasion Method

The ARSgroup is one of the most active message-testing research suppliers in the world. This company tests individual selling propositions, completed television commercials, and other marcom messages. Commercials are tested at varying stages of completion ranging from rough-cut (e.g., animatics or photomatics) to finished form. The testing procedure is called the ARS Persuasion method, where ARS stands for Advertising Research System. The ARS testing procedure is as follows:

> *Commercials are exposed in regular ARS test sessions to [800 to 1,000] men and women (aged 16+) drawn randomly from [eight] metropolitan areas and invited to preview typical television material. Each test commercial and other unrelated commercials are inserted into the television programs. While at the central location, a measurement of ARS Persuasion is made by obtaining brand preferences before and after exposure to the programs. The ARS Persuasion measure is the percent of respondents choosing the test product over competition after exposure to the TV material minus the percent choosing the test product before exposure.*[37]

In other words, the ARS Persuasion method first has respondents indicate which brands they would prefer to receive from various product categories if their names were selected in a drawing to win a "basket" of free items (the *premeasure*). Among the list of products and brands is a "target brand" for which, unbeknown to respondents, they subsequently will be exposed to a commercial that is being tested. After exposure to a television program, within which is embedded the test commercial, respondents again indicate which brands they would prefer to receive if their names were selected in a drawing (the *postmeasure*). The ARS Persuasion score simply represents the postmeasure percentage of respondents preferring the target brand minus the premeasure percentage who prefer that brand (see the following equation). A positive score indicates that the test commercial has shifted preference *toward* the target brand and reinforced brand preference among pre-choosers.

$$\text{ARS Persuasion Score} = \text{Post \% for target brand} - \text{Pre \% for target brand} \quad (10.1)$$

The ARS group has tested over 40,000 commercials, and from these tests it has established—albeit not without challenge[38]—that its ARS Persuasion scores predict the magnitude of actual sales performance when commercials are aired. That is, higher-scoring commercials generate greater sales volume and larger market share gains.

Predictive Validity of ARS Persuasion Scores

Based on the results of 332 commercials that were tested in seven countries—including Belgium, Germany, Mexico, and the United States—principals at the ARSgroup have demonstrated how ARS Persuasion scores relate to changes in market share.[39] A total of 148 brands (some with multiple commercials tested) representing 76 product categories were involved in the analysis. All 332 commercials were tested under the procedures described previously, and then market-share levels under actual in-market circumstances were compared during a period after advertising commenced for the brands versus a period prior to any advertising. Hence, the key issue is whether ARS Persuasion scores accurately predict the magnitude of market-share gain (or loss) following advertising. In other words, are the scores generated from the ARSgroup's laboratory testing predictive of actual marketplace performance? This obviously is a validity issue as described previously under PACT principle 9. Results from these 332 tests are presented in Table 10.2. This global validation revealed that ARS Persuasion scores are predictive of market-share changes, yielding, in fact, a high correlation coefficient ($r = 0.71$) and an impressive coefficient of determination ($r^2 = 0.51$).

To understand fully what these results reveal, let us carefully examine the first row in Table 10.2. This row includes all commercials that received very low (less than 2.0) ARS Persuasion scores, and implies that commercials scoring less than 2.0 are probably incapable of driving market-share gains. In fact, as shown under the "Average Share Change" column, commercials scoring less than 2.0 on the ARS Persuasion measure experienced, on average, *losses* of 0.2 market-share points. Looking at the next four columns reveals that for those commercials yielding ARS Persuasion scores of less than 2.0, only 47 percent were able to maintain market share or yield some small incremental growth. Comparatively, 53 percent (i.e., 100 − 47) of these low-scoring commercials actually suffered market-share losses! Moreover, only 2 percent of these low-scoring commercials generated gains of one full market-share point or more, and none experienced gains of two or more share points.

At the other extreme, 100 percent of the highly effective commercials (i.e., those with ARS Persuasion scores of 12.0 or higher) yielded positive share gains. Indeed, all 100 percent of these high-performance commercials produced gains of 0.5 share points or better, with 94 percent yielding gains of at least 1.0 share point, and 83 percent providing gains of at least 2.0 share points. The average gain in

table 10.2

ARS Persuasion Scores and In-Market Results

ARS Persuasion Score Range	Average Share Change	Percentage of Ads Achieving Share-Point Difference of:			
		0.0+	0.5+	1.0+	2.0+
<2.0	−0.2	47%	12%	2%	0%
2.0 – 2.9	0.0	53	19	6	0
3.0 – 3.9	0.5	80	46	26	6
4.0 – 6.9	0.8	80	58	33	9
7.0 – 8.9	1.6	100	87	56	36
9.0 – 11.9	2.2	100	97	72	49
12.0+	5.4	100	100	94	83

Source: "Summary of the ARS Group's Global Validation and Business Implications 2004 Update," June 2004, 17.

market-share points for commercials receiving ARS Persuasion scores of 12.0+ was an impressive 5.4.

Let us examine one additional row of data, specifically, that for commercials receiving ARS Persuasion scores in the middle range of 4.0 to 6.9. Commercials in this range yielded an average gain of 0.8 market-share points. Eighty percent of the commercials in this range either maintained or increased their brands' market shares, with 58 percent of the commercials yielding share gains of 0.5 share points or greater, 33 percent producing gains of 1.0 full share point or more, and 9 percent generating gains of 2.0 or more share points. Entries for the other ranges can be interpreted in a similar fashion.

It is apparent from these 332 test cases that ARS Persuasion scores are valid predictors of in-market performance. In sum, the higher the ARS Persuasion score, the greater the likelihood that a tested commercial will produce positive sales gains when the focal brand is advertised under real-world, in-market conditions. This global study thus informs advertisers that they should not place advertising weight behind commercials that have tested poorly. Table 10.2 reveals, in fact, that commercials with a 2.0 or lower ARS Persuasion score most likely will *not* produce a positive share gain, and that a large percentage (i.e., 100 − 53 = 47 percent) of those scoring in the 2.0 to 2.9 range also are likely to suffer share losses. It is only when commercials test in the 3.0 to 3.9 range or higher that meaningful share gains can be anticipated.

The ARSgroup has, of course, a vested interest in reporting that its testing system provides accurate predictions of marketplace performance; nonetheless, the fact that articles authored by the ARSgroup's principals have been published in peer-reviewed journals (e.g., the *Journal of Advertising Research*) authenticates their conclusions. Moreover, advertising scholars have provided independent endorsement of the ARS Persuasion technique.[40]

Measures of Sales Response (Single-Source Systems)

Determining the sales impact of advertising is—as discussed in Chapters 2, 6, and 7—a most difficult task. However, research procedures now are capable of assessing the effects an advertising campaign has on a brand's sales—especially in the case of consumer packaged goods (CPG). (Please note that discussion will be limited to advertising, but the major providers of single-source systems discussed in this section also offer procedures for testing the sales-generating effects of other marcom variables such as sales promotions and point-of-purchase materials.)

So-called single-source systems (SSSs) have evolved to measure the effects of advertising on sales. SSSs became possible with the advent of three technological developments: (1) *electronic television meters,* (2) *optical laser scanning* of universal product codes (UPC symbols), and (3) *split-cable* technology. *Single-source systems* gather purchase data from panels of households using optical scanning equipment and merge them with household demographic characteristics and, most important, with information about causal marketing variables, such as advertisements, that influence household purchases. The following sections describe two major single-source systems: ACNielsen's ScanTrack and IRI's BehaviorScan.

ACNielsen's ScanTrack

There are two very interesting characteristics of ScanTrack's data-collection procedure. First, and most important, ScanTrack collects purchase data by having its hundreds of panel households (the Homescan Consumer Panel) use *handheld scanners.* These scanners are located in panel members' homes, usually mounted to a kitchen or pantry wall. Upon returning from a shopping trip, ScanTrack panelists are directed to record purchases of *every bar-coded product purchased,* regardless of the store where purchased—a major grocery chain, independent supermarket, mass merchandiser, or wholesale club.[41]

A second distinguishing characteristic of ScanTrack is that panel members also use their handheld scanners to enter any coupons used and to record all store deals and in-store features that influenced their purchasing decisions. Each panel member transmits purchases and other data to Nielsen every week by calling a toll-free number and holding up the scanner to a phone, which records the data via a series of electronic beeps. ACNielsen's ScanTrack has provided advertisers and their agencies with invaluable information about the short- and long-term effects of advertising.

IRI's BehaviorScan

Information Resources Inc. (IRI) pioneered single-source data collection when it introduced its BehaviorScan service a generation ago. IRI operates BehaviorScan panel households in five markets around the United States: Pittsfield, Massachusetts; Eau Claire, Wisconsin; Cedar Rapids, Iowa; Midland, Texas; and Grand Junction, Colorado. (IRI also has BehaviorScan panels in many other countries.) These small cities were chosen because they are located far enough from television stations that residents must depend on *cable TV* to receive good reception. Moreover, grocery stores and drugstores in these cities are equipped with optical scanning devices that read UPC symbols from packages and thereby record exactly which product categories and brands panel household members purchase.

In each market, approximately 3,000 households are recruited to participate in a BehaviorScan panel, and about one third of these households are equipped with electronic meters attached to TV sets. Panel members are eligible for prize drawings as remuneration for their participation. Because each BehaviorScan household has an identification card that is presented at the grocery store checkout on every shopping occasion, IRI knows precisely which items each household purchases by merely linking up optically scanned purchases with ID numbers. (Starting in 2002, IRI also began supplying panel members with handheld scanners to record purchases in stores other than traditional grocery stores, such as mass merchandise outlets and supercenters. This enabled IRI's BehaviorScan procedure to provide coverage of all retail outlets, as does ACNielsen's ScanTrack method.)

Panel members also provide IRI with detailed demographic information, including family size, income level, number of televisions owned, the types of newspapers and magazines read, and who in the household does most of the shopping. (Please note that ACNielsen's ScanTrack procedure also collects this type of information.) IRI then combines all these data into a *single source* and thereby determines which households purchase which products and brands and how responsive they are to advertising and other purchase-causing variables. Thus, **single-source data** consist of (1) household demographic information; (2) household purchase behavior; and (3) household exposure to (or, more technically, the opportunity to see) new television commercials that are tested under real-world, *in-market* test conditions.

The availability of cable TV enables IRI (with the cooperation of cable companies and advertisers) to intercept a cable signal before it reaches households, *split the signal,* and send different advertisements to two panels of households (test versus control). Hence, the split-cable feature and optically scanned purchase data enable IRI to know which commercial each household had an opportunity to see and how much of the advertised brand the household purchases.

Weight versus Copy Tests

IRI's BehaviorScan procedure enables testing of television commercial effectiveness. Two types of tests are offered: weight tests and copy tests. In both types, a test commercial is aired in, say, two BehaviorScan markets for up to a full year. With *weight tests*, panel households are divided into test and control groups. The identical commercial is transmitted to both groups, but the number of times the commercial is aired (its so-called "weight") is varied between the groups during the course of the test period. Any difference between the groups' aggregate purchase behavior for the tested brand is obviously attributable to the advertising weight differential between the two groups.

The second form of testing, *copy tests*, holds the amount of weight constant but varies commercial content. That is, a test group is exposed during the course of the testing period to a new commercial, whereas a control group has an opportunity to see either a public service announcement (PSA) or an old commercial for the same brand inserted in place of the new commercial. Regardless of the type of test, aggregating purchase data across all households in each of the two groups simplifies determining whether differences in advertising copy or weight generate differences in purchase behavior.

The Testing Procedure

To better understand how BehaviorScan's single-source data can be used to show the relationship between advertising and sales activity, consider a situation in which a manufacturer of a new snack food is interested in testing the effectiveness of a television commercial promoting this brand. BehaviorScan would do the following: (1) select, say, two markets in which to conduct the test (perhaps Midland, Texas and Grand Junction, Colorado); (2) stock the manufacturer's brand in all grocery stores and perhaps drugstores located in these markets; (3) selectively broadcast a new commercial for the brand using special split-cable television so approximately one half of the panel members in each market are exposed either to the new commercial or to PSAs; (4) record electronically (via optical scanners) grocery purchases all panel members made; and (5) compare the purchase behavior of the two groups of panel members who were exposed either to the new commercial or to PSAs.

If the advertising is effective, a greater proportion of the panel members exposed to the test commercial should buy the promoted item than those only exposed to the PSAs. The percentage of panel members who make a trial purchase of the advertised brand would thereby indicate the effectiveness of the new television commercial, and the percentage that make a repeat purchase would indicate how much the brand is liked.

In sum, single-source systems of advertising measurement (ACNielsen's ScanTrack and IRI's BehaviorScan) enable brand managers and their advertising agents to determine whether advertisements do more than just increase brand awareness, facilitate message recall, influence consumers' brand-related attitudes, or achieve other pre-behavioral goals. Beyond this, single-source systems address the critical issue of whether an advertising campaign has actually driven increases in brand sales and augmented the brand's market share.

Some Major Conclusions about Television Advertising

Extensive testing the ARSgroup has performed has played a significant role in enhancing our understanding of the strengths and limitations of television advertising. Four major conclusions can be drawn with respect to what it takes for television advertising to enhance a brand's sales performance and market share growth successfully: (1) ad copy must be distinctive, (2) ad weight without persuasiveness is insufficient, (3) the selling power of advertising wears out over time, and (4) advertising works quickly if it works.[42]

Conclusion 1—All Commercials Are Not Created Equal: Ad Copy Must Be Distinctive

Research by the ARSgroup has shown that commercials having *strong selling propositions* are distinctive and thereby tend to achieve higher ARS Persuasion scores. What determines whether a commercial has a strong selling proposition? Research indicates that any differentiating information concerning a new brand or a new feature of an existing brand gives a selling proposition a significantly higher chance of a superior score.[43] Although commercials for new brands and those with new features are more persuasive on average, advertising for established brands also can be very persuasive via *brand differentiation*—that is, by distinguishing the advertised brand from competitive offerings and providing consumers with a distinctive reason to buy it.[44] The photoboard version of a Mentadent ProCare toothbrush television commercial (Figure 10.6) illustrates an advertisement that obtained a high ARS Persuasion score of 11.2 because the ad contained the strong selling proposition that this toothbrush has a flexible handle that allows gentle brushing.

The foregoing discussion has illustrated a key advertising principle: Effective advertising must be persuasive and distinctive; it must possess a strong selling proposition. Appreciation of this point necessitates rigorous testing of proposed advertisements prior to committing any media dollars to their airing or printing. Reminiscent of the classic parental admonition to children to "look before you cross the street," a similar exhortation can be made to advertisers when formulating advertising messages: "Test before you air or print!" To put it bluntly, it is foolhardy to invest money in a media campaign without first having ensured that the advertising message is fully capable of shifting brand preference toward the advertised brand. It is for this reason that sophisticated advertisers should always pretest proposed advertisements prior to printing or airing them.

Figure 10.6

Illustration of a Commercial with a Strong Selling Proposition

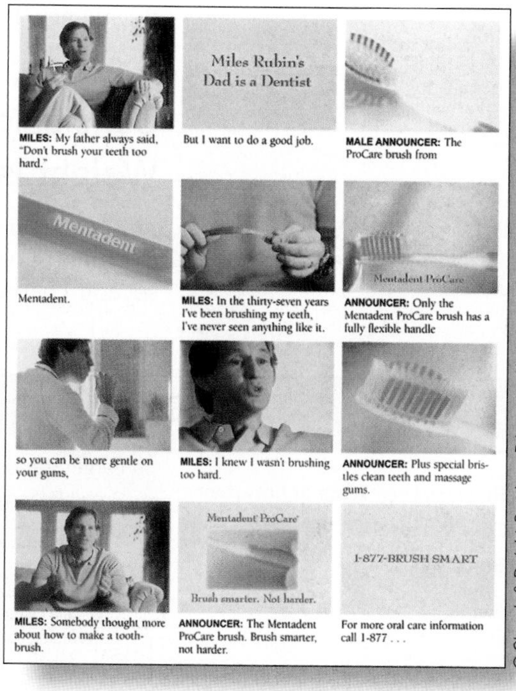

Evidence from Frito-Lay's Copy Tests

To test the effectiveness of television commercials for its various salted snack and cookie brands, marketing researchers and brand managers at Frito-Lay commissioned IRI to perform 23 split-panel experiments in BehaviorScan markets over a four-year period.[45] All 23 experiments were copy (versus weight) tests that involved comparing one group of households who were exposed to advertising for a Frito-Lay brand (advertising households) against another group that had no opportunity to see the advertising (control households). Each of the 23 tests was conducted in at least two BehaviorScan markets and lasted a full year. In addition to the advertising versus no-advertising condition, Frito-Lay's BehaviorScan tests also were classified in terms of (1) whether the tested brand was a new brand (e.g., SunChips was new at the time of the test) or an established brand (e.g., Ruffles); and (2) whether sales for the brand were relatively large (e.g., Doritos) or small (e.g., Rold Gold).

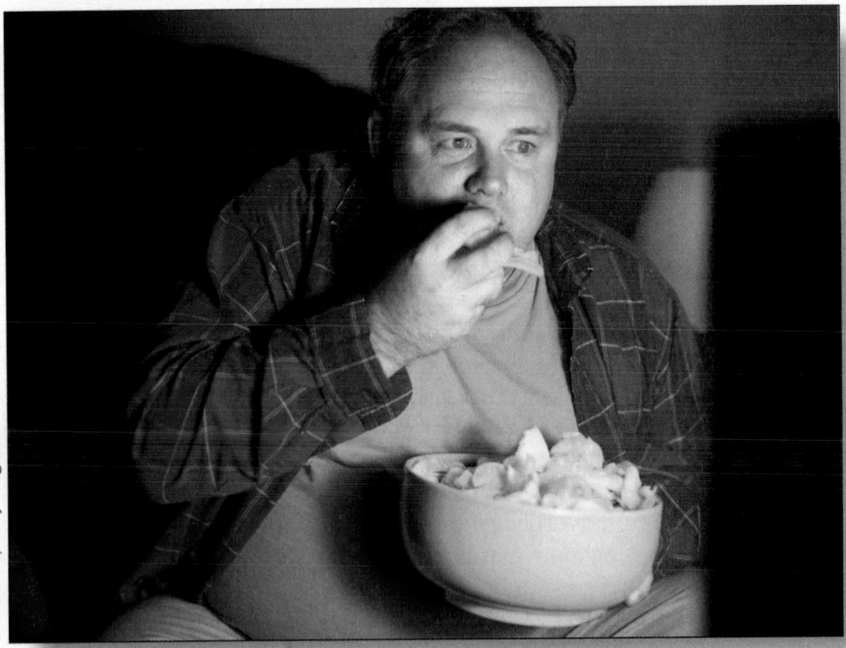
© Photodisc/Getty Images

The objective in conducting these tests was to determine whether sales volume would be greater in households exposed to advertisements for Frito-Lay brands versus those households that had no opportunity to be exposed to these television commercials. Results from the 23 Frito-Lay BehaviorScan tests are summarized in Table 10.3.

The first notable observation from Table 10.3 is that advertising for 57 percent of the 23 tested brands generated significant increases in sales volume during the one-year test duration. (Although not shown in Table 10.3, the average gain in sales volume between the advertising versus no-advertising household panels was 15 percent across the 12 advertisements that yielded significant sales increases.) A second key finding shown in Table 10.3 is that advertising for the small sales-volume brands was much more effective in driving sales gains than was advertising for the large brands. In fact, of the 12 small brands tested, 83 percent, or 10 brands, experienced significant increases in sales as a result of their one-year advertising efforts. A third important finding is that advertising for 88 percent of the new brands generated significant sales gains, whereas only 40 percent of the established brands resulted in sales gains from advertising.

The 23 BehaviorScan tests of Frito-Lay brands reveal that advertising is not always effective; indeed, it was effective in only slightly more than one half of the tests. Importantly, this research supports the finding that advertising is effective only when it provides distinctive, newsworthy information, such as when introducing new brands or line extensions.

Conclusion 2—More Is Not Necessarily Better: Weight Is Not Enough

Fully appreciating this second major conclusion requires that we first understand the concept of advertising "weight." This concept will be covered more in the next several chapters, but for now, ad *weight* should be understood as meaning the

table 10.3

BehaviorScan Tests of Advertising Effectiveness for 23 Frito-Lay Brands

	Established Brands	New Brands	Total
Large Brands	13% (n = 8)*	67% (n = 3)	27% (n = 11)
Small Brands	71 (n = 7)	100 (n = 5)	83 (n = 12)
Total	40 (n = 15)	88 (n = 8)	57 (n = 23)

*Table entries are to be interpreted as follows: A total of 8 (out of 23) tests involved large, established brands. Of the 8 tests conducted with this particular combination of brands, only one test, or 13 percent, detected a statistically significant increase in sales volume in those households exposed to advertising compared to the no-advertising control households.

frequency with which an advertisement is repeated to the same group of panel members in an IRI BehaviorScan test. (The following chapter will provide a more sophisticated explanation of weight when discussing the media planning concept of *gross rating points,* or *GRPs.*) More frequent airing of a TV commercial implies greater advertising weight, or more GRPs. Obviously, advertising weight and spending also correlate—the more weight, the higher the cost.

Given this background, we now consider a second important conclusion about advertising effectiveness—that the amount of advertising weight invested in a brand does *not* by itself provide a good predictor of sales performance. In other words, merely increasing advertising weight does not directly translate into better performance for a brand. Advertising copy *must also be distinctive and persuasive* (as previously established) for advertising to have a positive impact on a brand's sales and market share. An advertising practitioner perhaps said it best when stating that "airing ineffective advertising is like being off-air; it just costs more."[46] It cannot be overemphasized that unpersuasive, nondistinctive advertising is not worth airing or printing.

This conclusion receives support from a landmark study that analyzed numerous tests based on BehaviorScan single-source data. A well-known advertising scholar and his colleagues determined that when advertisements are unpersuasive, there is no more likelihood of achieving sales volume increases even when doubling and tripling TV advertising weight.[47]

The virtual independence between advertising weight and sales is clearly demonstrated in Table 10.4. The results presented in this table are based on studies using single-source data for various brands of CPGs. The data in Table 10.4 are derived from *weight tests* whereby two panels of households had an opportunity to see the identical commercial for a particular brand, but the amount of

table 10.4

Relations among Advertising Weight, Persuasion Scores, and Sales

Test Number	Weight Difference	ARS Persuasion Score	Sales Difference
1	334 GRPs	−1.3	NSD*
2	4,200	0.6	NSD
3	406	1.8	NSD
4	1,400	2.6	NSD
5	695	2.7	NSD
6	800	2.8	NSD
7	2,231	3.5	NSD
8	1,000	3.6	NSD
9	900	3.7	NSD
10	1,800	4.0	NSD
11	947	4.2	NSD
12	820	4.3	NSD
13	1,364	4.4	NSD
14	1,198	4.4	NSD
15	583	5.9	SD†
16	1,949	6.7	SD
17	580	7.0	SD
18	778	7.7	SD
19	1,400	9.0	SD
20	860	9.3	SD

*NSD: Purchases of the advertised brand were *not* significantly different between the two split-cable panels at a 90 percent confidence level.

†SD: Purchases of the advertised brand were significantly different between the two split-cable panels at a 90 percent confidence level.

Source: Margaret Henderson Blair, "An Empirical Investigation of Advertising, Wearin, and Wearout," *Journal of Advertising Research* 27 (December 1987/January 1988), 45–50. Reprinted with permission from the *Journal of Advertising Research*, © 1987, by the Advertising Research Foundation.

spending, or weight, was varied between the two panels. These households' subsequent purchases of the advertised brand are later compared based on purchase data acquired via optical scanning devices in grocery stores.

Table 10.4 presents data from 20 weight tests, each involving an actual marketplace examination of advertising's influence on the sales of a branded grocery product. In each test, there are two key features of the advertising effort. First is the number of GRPs, or weight, used to advertise the brand. This is expressed in Table 10.4 as the *weight difference* between the two panels of households. A difference of zero would mean that an identical amount of advertising weight (in terms of GRPs) was aired during the test period to both groups of households, whereas a positive weight difference indicates that one group was exposed to more commercials for the brand than was the other group. The second key advertising feature is the ARS Persuasion score that the test commercial obtained in each test. These scores range from a low of –1.3 (test 1) to a high of 9.3 (test 20). Finally, for each reported test, the last column indicates whether a statistically significant sales difference occurred between the two panels.

Thus, test 8, for example, shows a weight difference of 1,000 GRPs between the two panels. However, the tested commercial in this case received a below-average ARS Persuasion score of 3.6. Given this combination of a heavy weight difference between the two panels and a relatively unpersuasive commercial, the result was no significant difference (NSD) in sales between the two panels of households at the end of the full-year testing period. In other words, heavy advertising weight was unable to compensate for an unpersuasive commercial.

Now let us examine test 15. The weight difference between the two panels of households amounted to 583 GRPs, but the new commercial in this test received an ARS Persuasion score of 5.9. The result: A significant difference (SD) in sales was recorded when the tested brand was advertised with a moderately persuasive commercial.

Table 10.4 also demonstrates that no significant sales differences are obtained even in instances of huge weight differences such as in tests 2 (a 4,200 GRP difference) and 7 (a 2,231 GRP difference). These two tests corresponded (at the time of the research) with annual ad expenditures of $21 million and $11 million, yet no differential sales response materialized after a full year. Comparatively, notice in tests 15 through 20 that significant sales differences *are* observed even when the weight differences are relatively small compared with the weight differences in tests 2 and 7. Hence, it can be concluded that the primary determinant of sales differences in these tests was the *persuasiveness* of the tested commercials. Whenever the ARS Persuasion score was 5.9 or greater, significant sales differences were detected at the end of the test; in all instances in which the ARS Persuasion score was below 5.9, no significant sales differences were obtained.

Provided these results generalize beyond the tested commercials, the implication is that a commercial's persuasiveness is absolutely critical: Persuasiveness, and not mere advertising weight, is the prime determinant of whether an advertising campaign will translate into improved sales performance. Investing advertising in unpersuasive commercials is akin to throwing money away. Advertising weight is important, but only if a commercial presents a persuasive story![48]

Campbell Soup Company Findings

Research the ARSgroup conducted for the Campbell Soup Company provides additional evidence regarding the importance of commercial persuasiveness.[49] Figure 10.7 presents the results of ARSgroup's testing of various commercials for an undisclosed Campbell Soup Company brand, which we will assume to be Prego spaghetti sauce. Note that the horizontal axis is broken into 18 four-week periods, and that the vertical axis of the graph depicts this brand's market shares. The graph shows that Prego's market share during the first four-week period was 19.6.

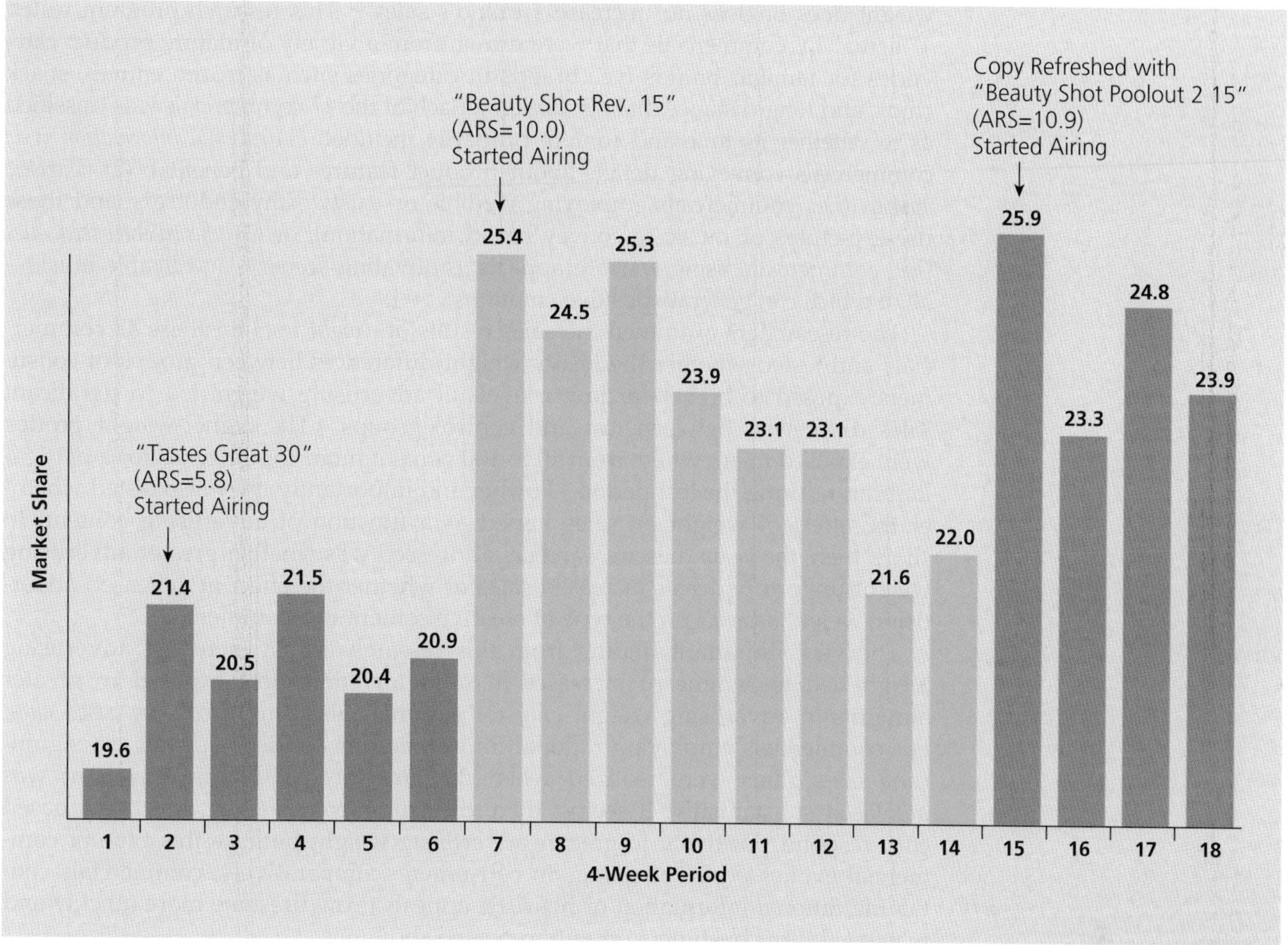

Used with permission from the ARS Group

Figure 10.7

The Role of Sales-Effective Advertising for an Undisclosed Campbell Soup Brand

Notice next that a new commercial (titled "Tastes Great 30," with the *30* signifying a 30-second commercial) was aired during the second four-week period. This commercial, when the ARSgroup tested it, received an ARS Persuasion score of 5.8. Shortly after airing this new commercial, Prego's market share jumped from 19.6 to 21.4—an increase of nearly 2 share points. Thereafter, Prego's market share varied from a low of 20.4 (period 5) to a high of 21.5 (period 4). Then in period 7, when a new commercial started airing ("Beauty Shot Revised 15"), Prego's market share jumped by an incredible 4.5 share points to 25.4.

Notice how this result correlates to the strength of the new commercial, which obtained an ARS Persuasion score of 10.0. Over the next several months, the market share for Prego fell to 22.0 (period 14). Then in period 15 another new commercial began airing ("Beauty Shot Poolout 2 15"). This commercial, which obtained an ARS Persuasion score of 10.9, immediately increased Prego's sales to a 25.9 market share. By period 18 the share had declined to a 23.9, but compared with the initial share of 19.6 in period 1, this still represented a gain of 4.3 share points in slightly more than a year—a substantial market-share gain by any standard in an established product category. These results indicate that persuasive commercials can have a rather dramatic effect in increasing market share.

The Relationship between Media Weight and Creative Content

Beyond results from the ARSgroup, important research from the academic front has provided further insight into the conditions under which additional advertising weight does or does not increase a brand's sales.[50] This research program tested 47 actual TV commercials that were drawn from a variety of mature product categories for familiar brands (i.e., brands in categories such as frozen entrees, snack chips, and long-distance dialing services). Each of the 47 commercials was classified as to whether its tone and content primarily included (1) *rational information* (i.e., commercials conveying details about product features and benefits); (2) *heuristic appeals* (i.e., commercials employing credible or trustworthy endorsers, and those using pictures or music to convey brand information); or (3) *affectively based cues* (i.e., commercials using warmth appeals, captivating scenery, and likable music—all of which can generate positive emotions).

The researchers examined the sales results of *weight tests* for these 47 commercials and tested whether the heavy weight differences between groups of consumers exposed to higher- or lower-levels of advertising weight led to significant sales differences between test and control groups. (The higher-weight groups were exposed to anywhere from 50 to 100 percent more commercials for a particular brand during the test period.) Further and importantly, they also tested whether the effect of weight on sales varied as a function of advertising content. In short, then, the issue these researchers addressed was whether greater advertising weight uniformly drives increased sales or whether the effect of increased advertising weight *depends* on the type of creative content in a commercial.

The very important finding from this research is that increased advertising weight led to significant increases in sales for consumers exposed to greater amounts of advertising weight *only* for commercials using *affectively based cues.* For commercials employing rational information or heuristic appeals, no significant sales gains were realized when the amount of advertising weight was increased substantially. It seems, then, that commercials using affectively based cues respond positively to greater advertising weight because this type of commercial evokes positive feelings in consumers; comparatively, commercials containing rational information or heuristic appeals grow tiresome more quickly and may even turn consumers off with repeated showings.

It is important to realize that this research included only commercials drawn from mature product categories and included only familiar brands. The results possibly do not generalize to commercials for new product categories or new brands in mature categories. In either event, heavy advertising weight thrown behind informative advertisements (i.e., those supplying rational information or using heuristic appeals) may *not* serve very well to drive sales. Conversely, putting more weight behind ads using affectively based cues (i.e., emotional ads) may well increase sales rather substantially.

Conclusion 3—All Good Things Must End: Advertising Eventually Wears Out

Another important lesson learned from the previous presentation of the Campbell's Prego case, and supported by abundant other evidence, is that advertising ultimately *wears out* and hence must be periodically refreshed to maintain or increase a brand's sales.[51] Academic and practitioners' research has convincingly demonstrated that with the accumulation of GRPs for a brand, the persuasive power of that brand's advertising declines over time.[52] This is referred to as **wearout,** the result of which is diminished effectiveness of advertising as GRPs accumulate over time. Interestingly, *familiar brands* (i.e., those for which consumers have direct usage experience or have learned about the brand via information from marcom messages) have been shown to wear out more slowly than unfamiliar brands.[53] This suggests that stronger brands—that is, those with greater equity (recall discussion in Chapter 2)—can continue to use creative executions for a longer period of time, need to refresh advertising less frequently, and thus obtain a bigger bang for the advertising buck. The old saying that "knowledge begets knowledge" has a counterpart in this context: "success begets more success." Familiar brands that possess greater brand equity enjoy increased marcom effectiveness by postponing the onset of advertising wearout.

The moral from conclusion 3 is that it is important to retest commercials periodically (using, for example, the ARS Persuasion measurement) to determine how much persuasive power remains in a commercial. When the persuasive power falls into the 3.0 to 3.9 range or even below (see Table 10.2), it probably is time to replace the commercial with a new or revised execution.

Conclusion 4—Do Not Be Stubborn: Advertising Works Quickly or Not at All

Due to the difficulty of precisely determining what effect advertising has on sales, in many instances advertisers initiate an advertising campaign and then stick with it for an extended period. Even though there may be no initial evidence that advertising is moving the sales dial, there is a tendency among some advertisers to "hang in there," hoping that with repeated exposures (increased weight) the advertising will eventually achieve positive results. Thoughts such as "Let's not drop the campaign too quickly" or "We just have to be patient" often are applied to sustain a questionable advertising campaign.

Insight into the issue of how long advertisers should stick with an ad campaign is available from the previously discussed findings from Frito-Lay's series of 23 BehaviorScan copy tests. Although not apparent in Table 10.3, a fourth notable result from the Frito-Lay BehaviorScan testing is that in all 12 (of 23) cases where advertisements for Frito-Lay brands drove significant sales increases, the effects occurred within the first six months. More dramatically, in 11 of the 12 tests with significant sales gains, the increased sales occurred within *the first three months*! When advertising works, it works relatively quickly or not at all.

Note that although there is some virtue to being patient, there is a difference between being patient and stubborn. Sometimes advertisers have to accept the fact that an advertising campaign simply is not driving sales increases. The economic concept of *sunk costs* is relevant in this context. That concept, in particular, informs us that decisions should not be made with respect to past expenditures but in terms of future prospects. Costs sunk in the past cannot justify continuing with something that is not producing sales gains. Wise decision makers must be prepared to walk away from past mistakes (such as ill-advised advertising campaigns), accept the fact that past expenditures are sunk, endeavor not to repeat the same mistake, and, in the vernacular, strive not to throw good money after bad.

Summary

Although difficult and often expensive, measuring message effectiveness is essential for advertisers to better understand how well their ads are performing and which changes they need to make to improve performance. Message-based research evaluates the effectiveness of advertising messages. Dozens of techniques for measuring advertising effectiveness have evolved over the years. The reason for this diversity is that advertisements perform various functions and multiple methods are needed to test different indicators of advertising effectiveness.

Starch Readership Service, Bruzzone tests, and day-after recall tests are techniques for measuring recognition and recall. Physiological measures such as galvanic skin response and pupil dilation are used to assess emotional arousal advertisements activate. The Ipsos-ASI Next*TV method is a videotape, in-home system for measuring consumer reactions to television commercials. ARSgroup's Persuasion testing is used to measure preference shifts employing a pre- and post-measurement of consumer preference for a brand before and after they have seen the brand's advertisement. The impact of advertising on actual purchase behavior is assessed with single-source data collection systems (IRI's BehaviorScan and Nielsen's ScanTrack) that obtain optical-scanned purchase data from household panels and then integrate them with television-viewing behavior and other marketing variables.

No single technique for measuring advertising effectiveness is ideal, nor is any particular technique appropriate for all occasions. The choice of technique depends on the specific objective an advertising campaign is intended to accomplish. Moreover, multiple measurement methods are usually preferable to single techniques to answer the many questions involved in attempts to assess advertising effectiveness.

The final major section presented conclusions about TV commercial effectiveness based on research that has measured advertising persuasiveness, explored the role of increasing advertising weight, examined the impact of creative copy, and determined whether these advertising factors generate meaningful sales gains. Four major conclusions are drawn: (1) ad copy must be distinctive in order to drive sales gains; (2) more advertising weight does not necessarily equate to increased sales; (3) advertising eventually wears out; and (4) if advertising is going to work, it will achieve its positive effect relatively quickly.

Discussion Questions

1. It is desirable that measurements of advertising effectiveness focus on sales response rather than on some precursor to sales, yet measuring sales response to advertising is typically difficult. What complicates the measurement of sales response to advertising? To answer this question, please return to Chapter 6 and the section on using sales as an objective for marcom programs.
2. PACT principle 2 states that a good copy testing system should establish how results will be used in advance of each copy test. Explain the specific meaning and importance of this copy testing principle. Construct an illustration of an anticipated result lacking a sufficient action standard and one with a suitable standard.
3. What's the distinction between the pre- and post-testing forms of advertising research? Which in your opinion is more important? Be sure to justify your response.
4. The Bruzzone test is based on a measure of recognition in comparison to day-after recall testing, which, of course, is based on a recall measure. Present an argument as to why the Bruzzone recognition measurement might be more appropriate than the recall measurement in attempting to determine the effectiveness of television commercials. To facilitate your discussion, consider the difference between multiple-choice testing (a form of recognition measurement) and essay testing (a form of recall measurement).
5. Offer your interpretation of the following quote presented earlier in the chapter: "If you can't measure something, you can't understand it. If you can't understand it, you can't control it. If you can't control it, you can't improve it."
6. If you were an account executive in an advertising agency, what would you tell clients to convince them to use (or not to use) the Starch Readership Service?
7. A test of television advertising effectiveness BehaviorScan performs will cost you, as brand manager of a new brand of cereal, over $250,000. Why might this be a prudent investment in comparison to spending $50,000 to perform an awareness study?
8. Assume that several years from now, after you have graduated college and begun a career, you open your mail one day and find a letter from Information Resources Inc. (IRI) requesting you to become a BehaviorScan panel member. Would you have any reservations about agreeing to do this? Assume that the letter is from ACNielsen, instead of IRI, requesting your participation in ScanTrack. What would be your reservations, if any, in this case?
9. Select three recent television commercials for well-known brands, identify the objective(s) each appears to be attempting to accomplish, and then propose a procedure for how you would go about testing the effectiveness of each commercial. Be specific.

10. Television commercials are tested in various stages of completion, including storyboards, animatics, photomatics, ripomatics, liveamatics, and finished commercials (see *IMC Focus*). What reservations might you have concerning the ability to project results from testing prefinished commercials to actual marketplace results with real commercials? Be specific and refer to the PACT principles where appropriate.
11. What are your thoughts about the value (or lack of value) of using measures of physiological response such as the galvanometer?
12. Turn to Table 10.2 and inspect the row in that table having an ARS Persuasion score range of 7.0 to 8.9. With that particular row in mind, interpret the entries under each of the four columns of share-point differences. For example, what is the specific interpretation of 56 percent under the column heading *1.0+*?
13. Compare and contrast the Ipsos-ASI Next*TV measure with the ARSgroup's Persuasion method.
14. In the context of the discussion of single-source data, explain the difference between weight tests and copy tests. Illustrate your understanding of the difference between these two types of tests by designing a hypothetical weight test and then a copy test for the same brand.
15. With reference to Frito-Lay's copy tests in Table 10.3, the results reveal that of the 23 commercials tested, only 57 percent of the tests generated significant differences in sales between the split panels tested. Assume that Frito-Lay's results are applicable to television advertising in general. What is your general conclusion from this key finding?
16. Offer an explanation as to why, in general, increasing advertising weight is an insufficient means of increasing brand sales.
17. Explain your understanding of why in the case of mature products with familiar brands greater advertising weight is effective in increasing sales only when affective cues are used in advertising the brand.
18. In your opinion, why do commercials for familiar brands with strong equities wear out less rapidly than is the case for unfamiliar brands?

End Notes

1. These facts and the remaining comments are adapted from Nigel Hollis, "Understanding the Power of Watchability Can Strengthen Advertising Effectiveness," *Marketing Research* (spring 2004), 22–26.
2. Karen Whitehill King, John D. Pehrson, and Leonard N. Reid, "Pretesting TV Commercials: Methods, Measures, and Changing Agency Roles," *Journal of Advertising* 22 (September 1993), 85–97.
3. Ibid.
4. John Kastenholz, Charles Young, and Tony Dubitsky, "Rehearse Your Creative Ideas in Rough Production to Optimize Ad Effectiveness." Paper presented at the Advertising Research Foundation Convention, New York City, April 26–28, 2004.
5. Ibid.
6. This description is based on Allan L. Baldinger in the *Handbook of Marketing Research: Uses, Misuses, and Future Advances,* Rajiv Grover and Marco Vriens, eds. (Thousand Oaks: Calif.:Sage, 2006).
7. Material for this section is extracted from the PACT document, which is published in its entirety in the *Journal of Advertising* 11, no. 4 (1982), 4–29.
8. See, for example, Bruce F. Hall, "A New Model for Measuring Advertising Effectiveness," *Journal of Advertising Research* 42 (April 2002), 23–31.
9. Herbert E. Krugman, "Why Three Exposures May Be Enough," *Journal of Advertising Research* 12 (December 1972), 11–14.
10. Russell I. Haley and Allan L. Baldinger, "The ARF Copy Research Validity Project," *Journal of Advertising Research* 31 (March/April 1991), 11–32.
11. John R. Rossiter and Geoff Eagleson, "Conclusions from the ARF's Copy Research Validity Project," *Journal of Advertising Research* 34 (May/June 1994), 19–32.
12. Various articles devoted to ethnographic advertising research are covered in an issue of the *Journal of Advertising Research* 46 (September 2006). See in this issue Jane Fulton Suri and Suzanne Gibbs Howard, "Going Deeper, Seeing Further: Enhancing Ethnographic Interpretations to Reveal More Meaningful Opportunities for Design," 246–250; Eric J. Arnould and Linda L. Price, "Market-Oriented Ethnography Revisited," 251–262; Gwen S. Ishmael and Jerry W. Thomas, "Worth a Thousand Words," 274–278.
13. Gerald Zaltman and Robin Higie Coulter, "Seeing the Voice of the Customer: Metaphor-Based Advertising Research," *Journal of Advertising Research* 35 (July/August 1995), 35–51; Robin A. Coulter, Gerald Zaltman, and Keith S. Coulter, "Interpreting Consumer Perceptions of Advertising: An Application of the

Zaltman Metaphor Elicitation Technique," *Journal of Advertising* 30 (winter 2001), 1–21.

14. Zaltman and Coulter, "Seeing the Voice of the Customer: Metaphor-Based Advertising Research."
15. A quote attributable to H. James Harrington, chairman of the board of Emergence Technology Ltd., as presented in Amy Miller and Jennifer Cioffi, "Measuring Marketing Effectiveness and Value: The Unisys Marketing Dashboard," *Journal of Advertising Research* 44 (September 2004), 238.
16. For an in-depth discussion of the differences between recognition and recall measures, see Erik du Plessis, "Recognition versus Recall," *Journal of Advertising Research* 34 (May/June 1994), 75–91. For additional reading on advertising recognition and its relation to advertising factors (such as ad likeability), see Jens Nördfalt, "Track to the Future? A Study of Individual Selection Mechanisms Preceding Ad Recognition and Their Consequences," *Journal of Current Issues and Research in Advertising* 27 (spring 2005), 19–30. For further discussion of the distinction between recognition and recall as separate aspects of memory, see James H. Leigh, George M. Zinkhan, and Vanitha Swaminathan, "Dimensional Relationships of Recall and Recognition Measures with Selected Cognitive and Affective Aspect of Print Ads," *Journal of Advertising* 35 (spring 2006), 105–122.
17. For further details on other services, see David W. Stewart, David H. Furse, and Randall P. Kozak, "A Guide to Commercial Copytesting Services," in *Current Issues and Research in Advertising*, ed. James H. Leigh and Claude R. Martin, Jr. (Ann Arbor: Division of Research, Graduate School of Business, University of Michigan, 1983), 1–44; and Surendra N. Singh and Catherine A. Cole, "Advertising Copy Testing in Print Media," in *Current Issues and Research in Advertising*, ed. James H. Leigh and Claude R. Martin, Jr. (Ann Arbor: Division of Research, Graduate School of Business, University of Michigan, 1988), 215–284.
18. These definitions are available in any Starch Readership Report.
19. D. M. Neu, "Measuring Advertising Recognition," *Journal of Advertising Research* 1 (1961), 17–22. For an alternative view, see George M. Zinkhan and Betsy D. Gelb, "What Starch Scores Predict," *Journal of Advertising Research* 26 (August/September 1986), 45–50.
20. Donald E. Bruzzone, "Tracking Super Bowl Commercials Online," *ARF Workshop Proceedings*, October 2001, 35–47.
21. Appreciation for this illustration is extended to Mr. R. Paul Shellenberg, director of sales, and Mr. Donald E. Bruzzone, president, of Bruzzone Research Company, Alameda, California.
22. The value of commercial recall testing has been questioned by Joel S. Dubow, "Point of View: Recall Revisited: Recall Redux," *Journal of Advertising Research* 34 (May/June 1994), 92–106.
23. "Recall Not Communication: Coke," *Advertising Age*, December 26, 1983, 6.
24. Joel S. Dubow, "Advertising Recognition and Recall by Age—Including Teens," *Journal of Advertising Research* 35 (September/October 1995), 55–60.
25. Leonard M. Lodish et al., "How T.V. Advertising Works: A Meta-Analysis of 389 Real World Split Cable T.V. Advertising Experiments," *Journal of Marketing Research* 32 (May 1995), 135. See also John Philip Jones and Margaret H. Blair, "Examining 'Conventional Wisdoms' about Advertising Effects with Evidence from Independent Sources," *Journal of Advertising Research* 36 (November/December 1996), 42.
26. John J. Kastenholz and Chuck E. Young, "The Danger in Ad Recall Tests," *Advertising Age,* June 9, 2003, 24; Jack Honomichl, "FCB: Day-After-Recall Cheats Emotion," *Advertising Age,* May 11, 1981, 2; David Berger, "A Retrospective: FCB Recall Study," *Advertising Age,* October 26, 1981, S36, S38.
27. John Kastenholz, Chuck Young, and Graham Kerr, "Does Day-After Recall Testing Produce Vanilla Advertising?" *Admap,* June 2004, 34–36; Lisa Sanders and Jack Neff, "Copy Tests Under Fire from New Set of Critics," *Advertising Age,* June 9, 2003, 6.
28. John Pawle and Peter Cooper, "Measuring Emotion—Lovemarks, The Future Beyond Brands," *Journal of Advertising Research* 46 *(March 2006), 39.*
29. Judie Lannon, "New Techniques for Understanding Consumer Reactions to Advertising," *Journal of Advertising Research* 26 (August/September 1986), RC6–RC9; Judith A. Wiles and T. Bettina Cornwell, "A Review of Methods Utilized in Measuring Affect, Feelings, and Emotion in Advertising," in *Current Issues and Research in Advertising,* ed. James H. Leigh and Claude R. Martin, Jr. (Ann Arbor: Division of Research, Graduate School of Business, University of Michigan, 1991), 241–275.
30. Steven P. Brown and Douglas M. Stayman, "Antecedents and Consequences of Attitude toward the Ad: A Meta-Analysis," *Journal of Consumer Research* 19 (June 1992), 34–51; Haley and Baldinger, "The ARF Copy Research Validity Project"; David Walker and Tony M. Dubitsky, "Why Liking Matters," *Journal of Advertising Research* 34 (May/June 1994), 9–18.
31. For in-depth discussion of self-report measures of emotions, see Karolien Poels and Siegfried Dewitte, "How to Capture the Heart? Reviewing 20 Years of Emotion Measurement in Advertising," *Journal of Advertising Research* 46 (March 2006), 18–37.
32. See ibid. for in-depth treatment.
33. Paul J. Watson and Robert J. Gatchel, "Autonomic Measures of Advertising," *Journal of Advertising Research* 19 (June 1979), 15–26.
34. For an especially thorough and insightful report on the galvanometer, see Priscilla A. LaBarbera and Joel D. Tucciarone, "GSR Reconsidered: A Behavior-Based Approach to Evaluating and Improving the Sales Potency of Advertising," *Journal of Advertising Research* 35 (September/October 1995), 33–53.
35. Ibid.
36. For a detailed discussion of pupil dilation and other physiological measures, see Joanne M. Klebba, "Physiological Measures of Research: A Review of Brain Activity, Electrodermal Response, Pupil Dilation, and Voice Analysis Methods and Studies," in *Current Issues and Research in Advertising,* ed. James H. Leigh and Claude

R. Martin, Jr. (Ann Arbor: Division of Research, Graduate School of Business, University of Michigan, 1985), 53–76. See also John T. Cacioppo and Richard E. Petty, *Social Psychophysiology* (New York: The Guilford Press, 1983).

37. Anthony J. Adams and Margaret Henderson Blair, "Persuasive Advertising and Sales Accountability: Past Experience and Forward Validation," *Journal of Advertising Research* 32 (March/April 1992), 25. Note: This quotation actually indicated that 1,000 respondents are drawn from four metropolitan areas. However, subsequent company newsletters and reports indicate that 800 to 1,000 respondents are randomly selected from eight metropolitan areas.
38. Leonard M. Lodish, "J. P. Jones and M. H. Blair on Measuring Advertising Effects—Another Point of View," *Journal of Advertising Research* 37 (September/October 1997), 75–79.
39. The ARS Group, Evansville, IN, "Summary of the ARS Group's Global Validation and Business Implications 2004 Update," June 2004. Note that an earlier validation study the ARS Group undertook was published in the following source: Margaret Henderson Blair and Michael J. Rabuck, "Advertising Wearin and Wearout: Ten Years Later: More Empirical Evidence and Successful Practice," *Journal of Advertising Research* 38 (September/October 1998), 1–13.
40. For example, John Philip Jones, "Quantitative Pretesting for Television Advertising," in *How Advertising Works: The Role of Research,* ed. John Philip Jones (Newbury Park, Calif: Sage Publications 1998), 160–169.
41. Information for this description is from Andrew M. Tarshis, "The Single Source Household: Delivering on the Dream," *AIM* (a Nielsen publication) 1, no. 1 (1989).
42. These conclusions are based on Margaret Henderson Blair and Karl E. Rosenberg, "Convergent Findings Increase Our Understanding of How Advertising Works," *Journal of Advertising Research* 34 (May/June 1994), 35–45. Of course, other research by practitioners and academics converge on these general conclusions.
43. Scott Hume, "Selling Proposition Proves Power Again," *Advertising Age,* March 8, 1993, 31.
44. Lee Byers and Mark Gleason, "Using Measurement for More Effective Advertising," *Admap,* May 1993, 31–35.
45. Dwight R. Riskey, "How T.V. Advertising Works: An Industry Response," *Journal of Marketing Research* 34 (May 1997), 292–293. For more complete reporting on the effectiveness of TV advertising, see Lodish et al., "How T.V. Advertising Works: A Meta-Analysis of 389 Real World Split Cable T.V. Advertising Experiments," *Journal of Marketing Research* 32 (May, 1995), 125–139; and Leonard M. Lodish et al., "A Summary of Fifty-Five In-Market Experimental Estimates of the Long-Term Effect of TV Advertising," *Marketing Science* 14, no. 3 (1995), G133–G140.
46. The quote is from Jim Donius as cited in Don Bruzzone, "The Top 10 Insights about Measuring the Effect of Advertising," *Bruzzone Research Company Newsletter,* October 28, 1998, principle 8.
47. Lodish et al., "How T.V. Advertising Works," 128.
48. Compared with the results presented in Table 10.4, research by Lodish et al. does not demonstrate a strong relationship between commercial persuasiveness and sales. See Table 11 in "How T.V. Advertising Works," 137.
49. Adams and Blair, "Persuasive Advertising and Sales Accountability."
50. Deborah J. MacInnis, Ambar G. Rao, and Allen M. Weiss, "Assessing When Increased Media Weight of Real-World Advertisements Helps Sales," *Journal of Marketing Research* 39 (November 2002), 391–407.
51. Lodish et al.'s findings also support this conclusion. See "How T.V. Advertising Works."
52. For review, see Connie Pechmann and David W. Stewart, "Advertising Repetition: A Critical Review of Wearin and Wearout," *Current Issues and Research in Advertising* 11 (1988), 285–330; David W. Stewart, "Advertising Wearout: What and How You Measure Matters," *Journal of Advertising Research* 39 (September/October 1999), 39–42; Blair and Rabuck, "Advertising Wearin and Wearout"; and MacInnis, Rao, and Weiss, "Assessing When Increased Media Weight of Real-World Advertisements Helps Sales."
53. Margaret C. Campbell and Kevin Lane Keller, "Brand Familiarity and Advertising Repetition Effects," *Journal of Consumer Research* 30 (September 2003), 292–304.

11

Advertising Media: Planning and Analysis

The cost of placing a 30-second commercial on the National Football League Super Bowl increased from $400,000 in 1984 to $2.7 million in 2008, which equates to $90,000 per second.[1] However, because the audience for the Super Bowl is huge, totaling over 90 million American households, advertisers during the Super Bowl extravaganza justify the expense on grounds that the cost of reaching potential customers is reasonable.[2] In fact, nearly one third of American consumers watch the Super Bowl. A recent Super Bowl drew 17 percent of children age 2-11, 26.5 percent of those age 12-17, 34.4 percent of the 18-49 age group, 37.5 percent of 25-54, and 36.9 percent of people 55 and older.[3] Super Bowl advertisers further justify their decision to advertise during the Super Bowl on the basis that consumers are much more engaged when viewing this program than they typically are when watching other TV programs.

Nevertheless, one may question whether the sizable investment in this television extravaganza can be justified, especially considering that 30-second spots on the top-rated prime-time television programs sell for a fraction of that cost, typically in the range of $100,000–$350,000 (as of 2008). Media planners at a company that specializes in media selection questioned whether the Super Bowl represented a prudent buy and proposed another way to spend the amount of money equivalent to purchasing a 30-second Super Bowl spot.[4] They developed an alternative media plan that consisted of (1) buying advertising time on all network programs aired at the same time on Tuesday evening; (2) securing advertising time on all network programs aired at the same time on Sunday evening (e.g., Sunday night movies); and (3) purchasing a final single spot from the Fox network's Saturday night programming. (The Tuesday and Sunday night buys are called roadblocks because advertising purchased on all network programs aired simultaneously acts, metaphorically, as a roadblock to ensure that all consumers viewing TV at this time will be exposed to the brand's advertising.) This alternative media plan was able to secure 13 prime-time advertising spots, or a total time of 6.5 minutes, compared with purchasing a single 30-second ad on the Super Bowl. Comparative GRPs (gross rating points, a concept described in detail later in the chapter) for the Super Bowl media buy and the alternative plan are as follows.

Whereas a single 30-second ad on the Super Bowl provided 40 GRPs based on the 18-to-49 age group, 42 GRPs based on the 25-to-54 group, and so on, the equivalently priced 13 spots yielded considerably more GRPs. For example, for all adults ages 25 to 54, the 78 GRPs from the 13 prime-time spots were 86 percent greater than the 42 GRPs generated by the Super Bowl advertisement.

Hence, one can conclude that advertisers should not advertise on the Super Bowl but rather would be better served by investing their advertising money

© AP Images/PRNewsFoto/CareerBuilder.com

elsewhere. Correct? Not necessarily! One also needs to factor in the all-important issue of advertising impact. People react with a relatively unenthusiastic response to advertisements placed during the programs contained in the alternative (13-spot) media buy. Comparatively, advertisements placed during the Super Bowl are, like the program itself, a special event. Consumers look forward to new, dramatic advertisements and often talk about the ads well after the Super Bowl is over. In fact, evidence indicates that people enjoy watching TV commercials during the Super Bowl. One survey determined that a sample of women indicated that they prefer viewing the ads to watching the game.[5] Because journalists comment about Super Bowl advertisements in magazines and newspapers, and on the Internet, advertisers receive a secondary form of brand contact. In short, all advertising does not have equivalent impact. When planners are buying advertising media, considerations, often subjective, other than mere comparisons of cost and rating points have to be factored into the decision.

Chapter Objectives

After reading this chapter you should be able to:

1. Describe the major factors used in segmenting target audiences for media planning purposes.
2. Explain the meaning of reach, frequency, gross rating points, target rating points, effective reach, and other media concepts.
3. Discuss the logic of the three-exposure hypothesis and its role in media and vehicle selection.
4. Describe the use of the efficiency index procedure for media selection.
5. Distinguish the differences among three forms of advertising allocation: continuous, pulsed, and flighted schedules.
6. Explain the principle of recency and its implications for allocating advertising expenditures over time.
7. Perform cost-per-thousand calculations.
8. Review actual media plans.

>>Marcom Insight:

Is Super Bowl Advertising Worth the Expense?

Introduction

The previous three chapters have examined the message component of advertising strategy. Although effective messages are essential for successful advertising, these messages are of little use unless advertising media are selected that will effectively reach the intended target audience. This chapter and the following three are devoted to media considerations. The present chapter explores the media planning process and the various factors that go into selecting media. Chapter 12 examines the traditional print and broadcast media—magazines, newspapers, television, and radio. Chapter 13 focuses on online media, while Chapter 14 examines alternative advertising media (e.g., product placements in movies and cinema advertising).

Some Useful Terminology: Media versus Vehicles

Advertising practitioners distinguish between advertising *media* and *vehicles.* **Media** are the general communication methods that carry advertising messages—that is, television, magazines, newspapers, and so on. **Vehicles** are the specific broadcast programs or print choices in which advertisements are placed. For example, television is a specific medium, and *American Idol, CBS Evening News,* and *Monday Night Football* are vehicles for carrying television advertisements. Magazines are another medium, and *Time, Business Week, Ebony,* and *Cosmopolitan* are vehicles in which magazine ads are placed. Each medium and each vehicle has a set of unique characteristics and virtues. Advertisers attempt to select those media and vehicles that are most compatible with the advertised brand in reaching its target audience affordably and conveying the intended message. The *Global Focus* insert provides a source on the Internet for obtaining useful information about media vehicles in countries around the world. Be sure to visit this Web site to see the wealth of available information.

Messages and Media: A Hand-in-Glove Relation

Advertising message and media considerations are inextricably related. Media and messages represent a hand-in-glove relationship, where each must be

global focus

Searching for Media Options around the Globe

Suppose you are interested in learning about news media in any city and state in the United States. Perhaps your interest goes beyond the United States and you wish to know what news media and advertising outlets may be available in most any city in the world. How would you learn, for example, what newspapers are available in Moscow, or what TV stations exist in Barcelona? Fortunately, there is an independent site on the Internet named the Kidon Media-Link (http://www.kidon.com/media-link) that makes this information available. Kidon's Web site provides direct links to various news sources, which represent potential advertising outlets. Go to the Kidon Media-Link homepage, select the continent where a city of interest is located, identify the country, navigate to the desired city, and then inspect available media. Up to date news is provided at the media outlets available in that city. It is worth your time to access http://www.kidon.com and learn more about this interesting resource that provides direct links to global media.

compatible with the other. It has been said that advertising creatives "can't move until they deal with a media strategist."[6] Creatives and media specialists must team up to design advertisements that effectively and efficiently deliver the right brand concept to the intended target audience. Advertising practitioners agree that reaching a specific audience effectively is the most important consideration in selecting advertising media.[7] Advertisers are placing more emphasis than ever on media planning, and media planners have achieved a level of unparalleled stature.[8] This is because an advertising message can be effective only when placed in the media and vehicles that best reach the target audience at a justifiable expense.

The choice of media and vehicles is, in many respects, the most complicated of all marketing communications decisions due to the variety of decisions that must be made. In addition to determining which general media categories to use (television, radio, magazines, newspapers, outdoor, Internet, or alternative media), the media planner must also pick specific vehicles within each medium and decide how to allocate the available budget among the various media and vehicle alternatives. Additional decisions involve choosing geographical advertising locations and determining how to distribute the budget over time. The complexity of media selection is made clear in the following commentary:

> *An advertiser considering a simple monthly magazine schedule, out of a pool of 30 feasible publications meeting editorial environment and targeting requirements, must essentially consider over one billion schedules when narrowing the possibilities down to the few feasible alternatives that maximize campaign goals within budget constraints. Why over one billion possible schedules? There are two outcomes for each monthly schedule, either to use a particular publication or not to do so. Therefore, the total number of possible schedules equals two raised to the 30th power (i.e., $2^{30} = 1{,}073{,}741{,}800$).... Now imagine how the options explode when one is also considering 60 prime time and 25 daytime broadcast television network programs, 12 cable television networks, 16 radio networks, 4 national newspapers, and 3 newspaper supplements, with each vehicle having between 4.3 [i.e., the average number of weeks in a month] and perhaps as many as 20 or more possible insertions per month.*[9]

Selecting and Buying Media and Vehicles

It will be useful to examine how the advertising industry makes buying decisions related to media and vehicles. As discussed in Chapter 7, traditional full-service advertising agencies have historically been responsible for both creating advertising messages for their clients' brands and planning and buying media time and space in which to place those messages. However, a recent and dramatic change has occurred in the manner in which media planning is performed. An event that rocked the advertising industry was General Motors' (GM) decision to consolidate in a single company its media planning and buying for its many automobile brands. Whereas in the past media planning and buying took place in each advertising agency that represented each GM brand, now *all* media planning is done in a single company under an organization referred to as GM Planworks. This unit handles media planning amounting annually to approximately $3 billion. By consolidating media planning and buying, GM achieves significant cost savings for its various brands.[10]

Other major corporations have followed GM's lead in "unbundling" media planning from creative services. Unilever moved its $700 million U.S. media buying clout from its various ad agencies to a single media buyer. Likewise, Kraft Foods consolidated its $800 million North American media planning and buying account into a single media planner and buyer.

Traditional full-service advertising agencies have criticized these moves. They claim that creative services and media planning go hand in hand, and that the symbiotic relationship between these services is damaged when ad agencies are relegated to just creating ad messages while independent firms are fully responsible for planning media selection. A top official of a major ad agency had this to say:

You can't keep compartmentalizing each aspect of an account. Many of the insights we get come from the media side, and that informs the creative side and vice versa. I have a hard time believing that [ad agencies] can be as effective without that kind of close relationship.[11]

The chief executive officer of a media planning company presented a counterperspective.

Separating media buying and planning [from creative] can be beneficial to clients who work in a multi-brand environment. Even though GM has different car lines, with different goals and strategies, there's something to be said for bringing all the planning operations together into one centralized location. It gives them an opportunity to apply learning and strategic thinking across the portfolio in a way that's faster and more efficient.[12]

There obviously are arguments on both sides of the issue, yet the proverbial genie is now out of the bottle. The historical role of the all-powerful full-service advertising agency has diminished. Perhaps of greatest significance is that this development accentuates the importance of the media planning aspect of the advertising process. Creating effective advertising messages is critical, but it is essential also that these messages be placed in the right media and vehicles.

The Media-Planning Process

Media planning is the design of a strategy that shows how investments in advertising time and space will contribute to the achievement of marketing objectives. The challenge in media planning is determining how best to *allocate* the fixed advertising budget for a particular planning period among ad media, across vehicles within media, and over time. As shown in Figure 11.1, media planning involves coordinating three levels of strategy: marketing, advertising, and media strategy. The overall *marketing strategy* (consisting of target market identification and marketing mix selection) provides the impetus and direction for the choice of both advertising and media strategies. The *advertising strategy*—involving advertising objectives, budget, and message and media strategies—thus extends naturally from the overall marketing strategy.

For illustration purposes, let us consider an advertising campaign for the Smart Fortwo vehicle. As background, the Smart Fortwo entered the U.S. market in early 2008. It is the cousin of the European Smart car that has been available since the late 1990s and has already sold more than 770,000 in 36 countries.[13] The Smart Fortwo is a car with two seats that also has reasonable luggage space contained in a body that is 8 feet and 10 inches long.[14] Prices for different Fortwo models range from less than $12,000 to over $17,000 for the Fortwo Passion convertible.[15]

Although it is too early (at the time of this writing) to know which American consumers will purchase the Fortwo, in other countries the Smart car has appealed to urban dwellers who need a small car for parking in the tight spaces that are common in large European cities and also those who desire a relatively inexpensive and gas-efficient vehicle. Let us assume that the Fortwo will be marketed in the United States mostly to single urban dwellers, although the media campaign will be more far reaching and include appeals to suburbanites as well. Assume further that prospective customers are cosmopolitan, environmentally

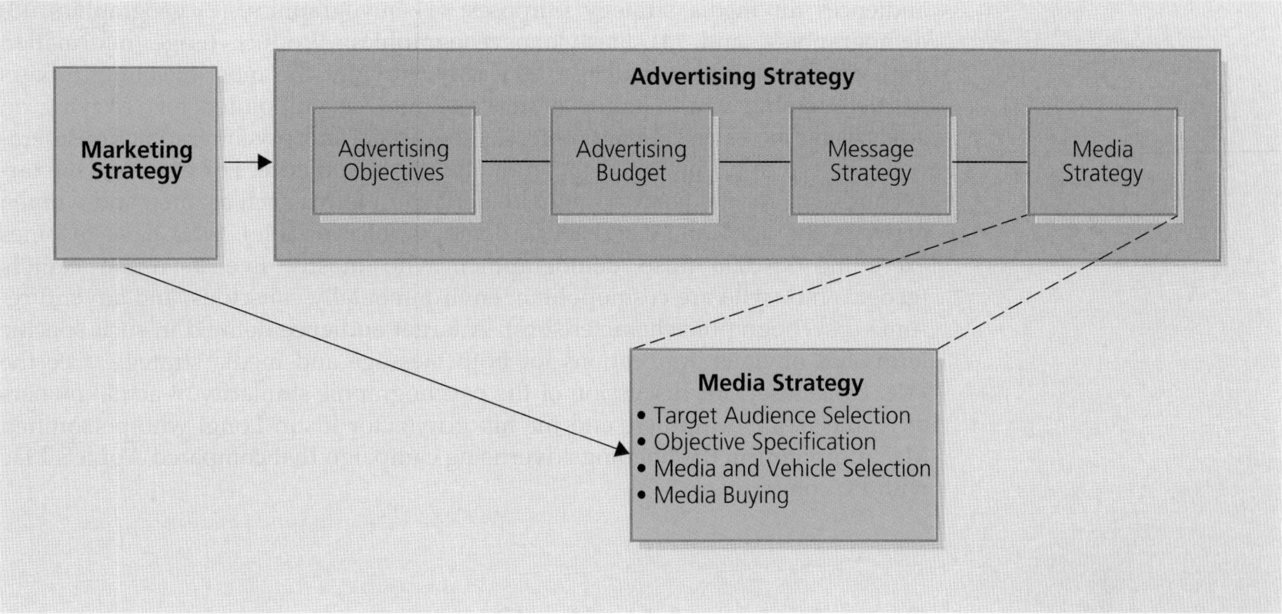

Figure 11.1

Model of the Media-Planning Process

conscious, and adventuresome. The media strategy for the Fortwo naturally must extend from Smart USA's (a division of Daimler AG's Mercedes-Benz brand) strategy to sell approximately 30,000 Fortwos at retail in 2009.

Media strategy is inextricably related to the other aspects of advertising strategy (see Figure 11.1). Let us assume that the Fortwo has a $15 million advertising budget for 2009, which equates to $500 advertising per each of the 30,000 cars expected to be sold in 2009. Suppose further that the objective is to create brand awareness for the Fortwo among targeted consumers and to convey the image of a convenient, fuel-efficient, and adventurous car. Advertising strategy decisions simultaneously impose constraints on media strategy ($15 million is the maximum amount that could be spent on the 2009 Fortwo campaign) and provide direction for media selection.

The media strategy itself consists of four sets of interrelated activities (see Figure 11.1).

1. Selecting the target audience
2. Specifying media objectives
3. Selecting media categories and vehicles
4. Buying media

The following sections discuss the first three activities in detail. Media buying is discussed only in passing because it is a specialized topic better suited for an elective course one might take as part of a communications or journalism major.

Selecting the Target Audience

Effective media strategy requires, first, that the target audience be pinpointed. Failure to define the audience precisely results in wasted exposures; that is, some nonpurchase candidates are exposed to advertisements, whereas prime candidates are missed. Four major types of information are used in segmenting target audiences for media strategy purposes: (1) buyographics, (2) geographics, (3) demographics, and (4) lifestyle/psychographics. Product usage information (buyographics), when available, generally provides the most meaningful basis for determining which target audience should be pinpointed for receiving an advertising message.[16] Geographic, demographic, and psychographic considerations are typically combined to define the target audience. For example, the target audience for the Fortwo might be defined in terms such as: men and women between the ages of 18 and 49 (a demographic variable), who have incomes exceeding $50,000 (also demographic), who mostly live in urban centers (geographic), who are cosmopolitan, environmentally conscious, and adventuresome (psychographic characteristics). A target audience defined in such specific terms has obvious implications for both message and media strategy. (See the *IMC Focus* insert for discussion of the psychographic similarity of actual owners of Apple's Mac computers and the hip guy (actor Justin Long) who personified Mac computers in the ongoing advertising campaign that compared Apple's Mac with PC computers.)

Specifying Media Objectives

Having pinpointed the audience to whom advertising messages will be directed, the next media-planning consideration involves specifying the *objectives* that an advertising schedule is designed to accomplish during the planned advertising period. Media planners, in setting objectives, confront issues such as: (1) what proportion of a target audience do we want to reach with our advertising message during a specified period, (2) with what frequency do we need to expose the audience to our message during this period, (3) how much total advertising is necessary to accomplish the first two objectives, (4) how should we allocate the advertising budget over time, (5) how close to the time of purchase should the target audience be exposed to our advertising message, and (6) what is the most economically justifiable way to accomplish the other objectives?

Practitioners have technical terms they associate with each of these six objectives: (1) *reach*, (2) *frequency*, (3) *weight*, (4) *continuity*, (5) *recency*, and (6) *cost*. The following sections treat each objective as a separate matter. A later section addresses their interdependence

© BERND WEISSBROD/dpa/Landov

Reach

Advertising managers and media specialists generally regard reaching specific audiences efficiently as the most important consideration when selecting media and vehicles.[17] The issue of reach deals with getting an advertising message heard or seen by the targeted audience.

More precisely, **reach** represents the *percentage of the target audience* that is exposed, *at least once*, during a specified time frame to the *vehicles* in which our advertising message is inserted. The time frame the majority of media planners use is a *four-week period*. (Thus, there are 13 four-week media-planning periods during a full year.) Some media specialists also use the single week as the planning period.

Regardless of the length of the planning period—whether one week, four weeks, a full year, or some other length of time—reach represents the percentage of all target customers who have an *opportunity to see or hear* the advertiser's message one or more times during this time period. (Advertising people use the expression *opportunity to see,* or *OTS,* to refer to all advertising media, whether visual or auditory.) Advertisers never know for sure whether members of their target audiences actually see or hear an advertising message, of course. Advertisers only know to which media vehicles the target audience is exposed. From the... it then can be inferred that people have had an

op ... d in the vehicles.

... reach are *1+* (read "one-plus"),

ne ... ll become clear why these terms

are

D

Se ... hieved with a particular media

scl ... hicles within each medium, and

(3) ... advertising.

focus

' Personalities Match the Mac
sonality?

back in
paign by
inst PCs.
the Mac
er embo-
ompared

anything
mercials?
hat many
guy in the
lia scored
ners—on

20 personality elements. Here are some of the key findings regarding Mac owners' psychographic profiles:

- **Superiority**–Mac owners in general have a strong sense of self-importance and are more likely than PC owners to regard themselves as "extraordinary." Mac owners are less modest than PC owners and have a strong need for recognition.
- **Openness**–As a group, Mac owners are more intellectually curious and comfortable with emotions than the population at large. They also are disproportionately more likely to drink coffee at coffeehouses such as Starbucks regularly, to buy organic foods, and to drive hybrid cars.
- **Music Enthusiasts**–Mac owners are more likely to buy music CDs, to listen to music on their computers, and to download and pay for more music than PC owners.
- **Dogmatism**–Compared with PC owners, Mac users are *less* dogmatic and more liberal both politically and socially.
- **Ecology Consciousness**–Mac owners tend to be more environmentally conscious than the general population and are willing to pay more for electronic products that are "greener."

About 40 executions of the "Mac versus PC" advertising campaign aired between 2006 and 2008. And during this period, the market share for Mac computers jumped from approximately 2.5 percent to somewhere around 7 percent. Although factors other than advertising undoubtedly played a significant role in Mac's rise, the advertising campaign also has played a significant role in catapulting the Mac computer to a third rank among sellers of computers in the United States.

SOURCE: Adapted from Beth Snyder Bulik, "Mac Owners Just Like, Well, the Mac Guy," *Advertising Age,* January 28, 2008, 6.

Generally speaking, more prospective customers are reached when a media schedule allocates the advertising budget among *multiple media* rather than to a single medium. For example, if the Fortwo were advertised only on network television, its advertisements would reach fewer people than if it also were advertised on cable TV, in magazines, on the radio, and in national newspapers. If an advertiser were to advertise a brand only in, say, newspapers, it would miss 40 percent of the adult population in the United States which does not regularly read a daily newspaper. Likewise, advertising only on select TV programs would miss people who do not view those particular programs. Hence, using multiple media increases the odds of reaching a greater proportion of the target audience. In general, the more media options used, the greater the chances that an advertising message will come into contact with people whose media habits differ.

A second factor influencing reach is the *number and diversity of media vehicles used.* For example, if Fortwo's media planners were to choose to advertise this automobile in, say, just a single magazine (e.g., *Cosmopolitan*) rather than in a variety of magazines, the advertising effort would reach far fewer consumers. Having just read this paragraph, it should be obvious—at least in hindsight—that an ad campaign that uses different vehicles within each medium will better cover the intended audience than focusing exclusively on a single or limited number of vehicles. Again using *Cosmopolitan* for an example, if Fortwo were advertised only in that particular magazine, the ad campaign would fail to reach all people in the target audience who do *not* read that magazine.

Third, *diversifying the dayparts* used to advertise a brand can increase reach. For example, network television advertising during prime time and cable television advertising during fringe times would reach more potential automobile purchasers than advertising exclusively during prime time.

In sum, reach is an important consideration when developing a brand's media schedule. Advertisers wish to reach the highest possible proportion of the target audience that the budget permits. However, reach by itself is an inadequate objective for media planning because it tells nothing about *how often* target customers need to be exposed to the brand's advertising message for it to accomplish its goals. Therefore, frequency of advertising exposures must also be considered.

Frequency

Frequency signifies the number of times, on average, during the media-planning period that members of the target audience are exposed to the media *vehicles* that carry a brand's advertising message. Frequency actually represents a media schedule's *average frequency,* but media people use the term *frequency* as a shorthand way of referring to average frequency.

To better understand the concept of frequency and how it relates to reach, consider the simplified example in Table 11.1. This example provides information about 10 hypothetical members of the target audience for the Fortwo and their exposure to *Cosmopolitan* magazine over four consecutive weeks. (We are assuming for purposes of this simplified example that *Cosmopolitan* is the sole vehicle used for advertising the Fortwo.) Audience member A, for example, is exposed to *Cosmopolitan* on two occasions, weeks two and three. Member B is exposed to *Cosmopolitan* all four weeks. Member C is never exposed to this magazine during the four-week period. Member D is exposed three times, in weeks one, three, and four, and so on for the remaining six members of Fortwo's mini audience. Notice in the last column of Table 11.1 that for each week, only 5 of 10 households (50 percent) are exposed to *Cosmopolitan* and thus have an opportunity to see an advertisement for the Smart Fortwo placed in this advertising vehicle. This reflects the fact that a single vehicle (in this case, *Cosmopolitan*) rarely reaches the full target audience.

table 11.1

Hypothetical Frequency Distribution for the Fortwo Advertised in *Cosmopolitan* Magazine

	Target Audience Member										
Week	A	B	C	D	E	F	G	H	I	J	Total Exposures
1		X		X	X		X		X		5
2	X	X			X		X		X		5
3	X	X		X				X		X	5
4		X		X		X	X			X	5
Total Exposure	2	4	0	3	2	1	3	1	2	2	

Summary Statistics			
Frequency Distribution (*f*)	Percentage *f*	Percentage *f*+	Audience Members
0	10%	100%	C
1	20	90	F, H
2	40	70	A, E, I, J
3	20	30	D, G
4	10	10	B

Reach (1+ exposures) = 90
Frequency = 2.2
GRPs = 200

The Concept of Frequency Distribution

Presented at the bottom of Table 11.1 are the frequency distribution and summary reach and frequency statistics for the Fortwo's media schedule. A *frequency distribution* represents the percentage of audience members (labeled "Percentage *f*" in Table 11.1) who are exposed *f* times (where $f = 0, 1, 2, 3$, or 4) to the *Cosmopolitan* magazine and thus have an opportunity to see ads for the Fortwo carried in that magazine. The cumulative frequency column (labeled "Percentage *f*+") indicates the percentage of the 10-member audience that has been exposed *f* or more times to *Cosmopolitan* magazine during this four-week period (again, $f = 0$, 1, 2, 3, or 4).

For example, the percentage exposed at least two times is 70 percent. Note carefully that for any value of *f*, the percentage in the Percentage *f*+ column simply represents the summation from the Percentage *f* column of that value plus all greater values. Reading from the Percentage *f* column in Table 11.1, you will see that the percentage of target audience members exposed exactly two times is 40 percent (namely, audience members A, E, I, and J). The percentage exposed exactly three times is 20 percent (members D and G). And the percentage exposed four times is 10 percent (member B). Hence, the cumulative percentage of audience members exposed two or more times (i.e., the percentage *f*+ when $f = 2$) is 70 percent ($40 + 20 + 10 = 70$).

With this background, we now are in a position to illustrate how both reach and frequency are calculated. It can be seen in Table 11.1 that 90 percent of the 10 audience members for the Fortwo advertisement have been exposed to one or more ads during the four-week advertising period. (Reading from the Percentage *f*+ column, with $f = 1$, it can be seen that the 1+ cumulative percentage is 90.) This figure, 90 percent, represents the *reach* for this advertising effort. Note that advertising practitioners drop the percent sign when referring to reach and simply refer to the number. In this case, reach equals 90.

Frequency is the average of the frequency distribution. In this situation, frequency equals 2.22. That is, 20 percent are reached one time, 40 percent are reached two times, 20 percent are reached three times, and 10 percent four times. Or, arithmetically, average frequency (or simply, frequency) equals

$$(11.1) \quad \frac{(1 \times 20) + (2 \times 40) + (3 \times 20) + (4 \times 10)}{90} = \frac{200}{90} = 2.22$$

This hypothetical situation thus indicates that 90 percent of the Fortwo's target audience is reached by the advertising schedule and that they are exposed an average of 2.2 times during the four-week advertising schedule in *Cosmopolitan.* This value, 2.2, represents this simplified media schedule's frequency. (The exact frequency is 2.22; however, media practitioners conventionally round frequency figures to a single decimal place.) Note carefully that the sum of all frequencies (the numerator in the previous calculation) is divided by the reach figure to obtain frequency (reach = 90).

Weight

A third objective involved in formulating media plans is determining how much advertising volume (termed *weight* by practitioners) is required to accomplish advertising objectives. Different metrics are used in determining an advertising schedule's weight during a specific advertising period. This section describes three weight metrics: gross ratings, target ratings, and effective ratings. First, however, it will be useful to explain the meaning of ratings.

What Are Ratings?

The concept of ratings has a unique meaning in the advertising industry unlike its everyday meaning. When people typically use the word *rating,* they are referring to a judgment about something. For example, a movie (or a restaurant, CD, etc.) might be rated on a five-star scale from terrible (= 1 star) to wonderful (= 5 stars). However, in the context of advertising, the term "ratings" refers to the percentage of an audience that has an *opportunity to see* an advertisement placed in that vehicle.

Let us illustrate the meaning of ratings using television as an example. As of 2009, there were approximately 114.5 million households in the United States who had television sets.[18] Therefore, a single **rating point** during this period represents 1 percent of all television households, or 1,145,000 households.

Suppose, for example, that during one week in 2009 a TV program named *House* had roughly 10 million households tuned in. *House*'s rating during that week would thus be 8.7 (i.e., 10 ÷ 114.5), which would indicate in a straightforward fashion that about 9 percent of all TV households viewed *House* during this one weekly episode in 2009. This, quite simply, is the meaning of ratings. It is important to recognize that the concept of ratings applies to all media and vehicles, not just to television and TV programs.

Gross Rating Points (GRPs)

Notice at the bottom of Table 11.1 that Fortwo's ad schedule in *Cosmopolitan* yields 200 GRPs. **Gross rating points,** or **GRPs,** reflect the weight that a particular advertising schedule has delivered. The term *gross* is the key. GRPs indicate the total coverage, or *duplicated audience,* exposed to a particular advertising schedule. Compare these terms with the alternative terms given earlier for *reach*—that is, *net coverage* and *unduplicated audience.*

Returning to our hypothetical example of an advertisement for the Fortwo in *Cosmopolitan,* the reach was 90, meaning that 9 of the 10 households in our mini audience were exposed to at least a single issue of *Cosmo* magazine. The gross rating points in this example amount to 200 GRPs because audience members were exposed multiple times (2.22 times on average) to the vehicles that carried the Fortwo advertisement during the four-week ad schedule.

It should be apparent from this discussion that GRPs represent the arithmetic product of reach times frequency.

$$\begin{aligned} \text{GRPs} &= \text{Reach(R)} \times \text{Frequency(F)} \\ &= 90 \times 2.22 \\ &= 200 \end{aligned}$$

© AP Images/Seth Wenig

By simple algebraic manipulation the following additional relations are obtained:

$$\text{R} = \text{GRPs} \div \text{F}$$
$$\text{F} = \text{GRPs} \div \text{R}$$

In other words, with knowledge of any two pieces of information from among R, F, and GRPs, it is easy to calculate the third by simple mathematical derivation.

Determining GRPs in Practice

In advertising practice, media planners make media purchases by deciding how many GRPs are needed to accomplish established objectives. However, because the frequency distribution and reach and frequency statistics are unknown before the fact (i.e., at the time when the media schedule is determined), media planners need some other way to determine how many GRPs will result from a particular schedule.

There is, in fact, a simple way to make this determination. GRPs are ascertained by simply summing the ratings obtained from the individual vehicles included in a prospective media schedule. Remember, gross rating points are nothing more than *the sum of all vehicle ratings in a media schedule.* For example, during the week of January 21 to January 27, 2008, the 10 most highly rated TV programs were as follows:

Program	Network	Household Rating
American Idol—Tuesday	Fox	16.2
American Idol—Wednesday	Fox	15.1
Moment of Truth	Fox	12.9
60 Minutes	CBS	9.5
CSI	CBS	8.6
Hallmark Hall of Fame	CBS	8.6
Deal or No Deal—Monday	NBC	8.5
Deal or No Deal—Wednesday	NBC	8.5
House	Fox	8.5
Law and Order: SVU	NBC	8.4

SOURCE: Nielsen Top 10 TV Ratings: Broadcast TV Programs @ Nielsen Media Research, http://www.nielsenmedia.com (accessed February 4, 2008).

Suppose by chance that an advertiser had placed a single ad on each of these TV programs during the week of January 21–27, 2008. This being the case, the advertiser would have accumulated 104.8 GRPs when advertising in these particular programs ($16.2 + 15.1 + \cdots + 8.4 = 104.8$). In short, the gross ratings generated by a particular media schedule simply equals the *sum of the individual ratings* obtained across all vehicles included in that schedule.

Target Rating Points (TRPs)

A slight but important variant of GRPs is the notion of target rating points. **Target rating points**, or **TRPs,** adjust vehicle ratings to reflect just those individuals *who match the advertiser's target audience.* Returning to the Fortwo example, let us assume that the advertising target for this model is primarily people between the ages of 18 and 49 who have incomes of $50,000 or more and generally reside in urban areas. Considering the 10 TV programs listed previously, assume that, for simplicity, only 30 percent of the total audience exposed to each of these programs actually match Fortwo's target market. Hence, although placing a single ad in each of these programs yields 104.8 *gross* rating points, this same schedule produces only 31.4 *target* rating points (i.e., $104.8 \times 0.3 = 31.4$).

It should be obvious from this simple illustration that GRPs represent some degree of wasted coverage because some audience members fall outside the target audience the advertiser wishes to reach. Comparatively, target rating points, TRPs, represent a better indicator of a media schedule's *non-wasted weight.* GRPs equal *gross* weight, some of which is wasted; TRPs equal *net* weight, none of which is wasted.

The Concept of Effective Reach

Alternative media schedules are usually compared in terms of the number of GRPs (or TRPs) that each generates. A greater number of GRPs (or TRPs) does not necessarily indicate superiority, however. Consider, for example, two alternative media plans that require the exact same budget. We will refer to these plans as plan X and plan Z. Plan X generates 95 percent reach and an average frequency of 2.0, thereby yielding 190 GRPs. (Note again that reach is defined as the proportion of the audience exposed one or more times to advertising vehicles during the course of a typical four-week campaign.) Plan Z provides for 166 GRPs from a reach of 52 percent and a frequency of 3.2.

Which plan is better? Plan X is clearly superior in terms of total GRPs and reach, but Plan Z has a higher frequency level. If the brand in question requires a greater number of exposures for the advertising to achieve effectiveness, then Plan Z may be superior even though it yields fewer GRPs. By the way, the same comparison would apply as well if this example were in terms of TRPs rather than GRPs.

It is for the reason suggested in the preceding comparison that many advertisers and media planners have become critical of the GRP and TRP concepts, contending that "[these concepts] rest on the very dubious assumption that every exposure is of equal value, that the 50th exposure is the same as the tenth or the first."[19] Although the GRP and the TRP metrics remain very much a part of media planning, the advertising industry has turned away from the exclusive use of "raw" advertising weight toward a concept of media *effectiveness.*[20] The determination of media effectiveness takes into consideration *how often* members of the target audience have an opportunity to be exposed to advertising messages for the focal brand. Media practitioners often use the terms *effective reach* and *effective frequency* interchangeably to capture the idea that an effective media schedule delivers a sufficient but not excessive number of ads to the target audience. Although either term is acceptable, hereafter we will simply refer to *effective reach.*

Effective reach is based on the idea that an advertising schedule is effective only if it does not reach members of the target audience *too few* or *too many* times during the media scheduling period, which, as noted previously, is typically a four-week period. In other words, there is a theoretical optimum range of exposures to an advertisement with minimum and maximum limits. But what constitutes too few or too many exposures? This, unfortunately, is one of the most complicated issues in all of advertising. The only statement that can be made with certainty is, "It depends!"

It depends, in particular, on considerations such as the level of consumer awareness of the advertised brand, its market share, the audience's degree of loyalty to the brand, message creativity and novelty, and the objectives that advertising is intended to accomplish for the brand. In fact, high levels of weekly exposure to a brand's advertising may be unproductive for loyal consumers because of a leveling off of ad effectiveness.[21] Specifically, brands with higher market shares and greater customer loyalty typically require *fewer* advertising exposures to achieve minimal levels of effectiveness. Likewise, it would be expected that distinctive advertising campaigns require *fewer* exposures to accomplish their objectives. The higher up the hierarchy of effects the advertising is attempting to move the consumer, the *greater* the number of exposures needed to achieve minimal effectiveness. For example, fewer exposures probably would be needed merely to make consumers aware that there is a brand named Fortwo than would be required to convince them that although Fortwo is small it is relatively safe.

How Many Exposures Are Needed?

It follows from the foregoing discussion that the minimum and maximum numbers of effective exposures can be determined only by conducting sophisticated research. Because research of this nature is time-consuming and expensive, advertisers and media planners generally have used rules of thumb in place of research in determining exposure effectiveness. Advertising industry thinking on this matter has been heavily influenced by the so-called **three-exposure hypothesis**, which addresses the *minimum* number of exposures needed for advertising to be effective. Its originator, an advertising practitioner named Herbert Krugman, argued that a consumer's initial exposure to a brand's advertising initiates a response of "what is it?" The second exposure triggers a response of "what of it?" And the third exposure and those thereafter are merely reminders of the information that the consumer already has learned from the first two exposures.[22]

This hypothesis, which was based on little empirical data and a lot of intuition, has virtually become gospel in the advertising industry. Many advertising practitioners have interpreted the three-exposure hypothesis to mean that media schedules are *ineffective* when they deliver average frequencies of *fewer than three exposures* to the advertising vehicle in which a brand's advertisement is placed.

Although there is some intuitive appeal to the notion that frequencies of fewer than three are insufficient, this interpretation of the three-exposure hypothesis is too literal and also fails to recognize that Krugman's hypothesis had in mind three exposures to an advertising *message* and not three exposures to vehicles carrying the message.[23] The difference is that vehicle exposure, or what we previously referred to as *opportunity to see* an ad *(OTS)*, is *not* tantamount to advertising exposure. A reader of a magazine issue certainly will be exposed to some advertisements in that issue, but the odds are that he or she will not be exposed to all, or even most, of the dozens of advertisements placed in that issue. Likewise, a viewer of a TV program will probably miss some of the commercials placed during a

30- or 60-minute program or will be inattentive to some of those that are aired. Hence, the number of consumers who actually are exposed to any particular advertising message carried in a vehicle—what Krugman had in mind—is less than the number of people who are exposed to the vehicle that carries the message. (Before reading on, make sure that you fully understand this distinction between vehicle exposure and actual exposure to an advertisement.)

Aside from this general misunderstanding of the three-exposure hypothesis, it must also be recognized that no specific number of minimum exposures—whether 3, 7, 17, or any other number—is absolutely correct for all advertising situations. It cannot be overemphasized that what is effective (or ineffective) for one product or brand may not necessarily be so for another. "There is no magic number, no comfortable '3+' level of advertising exposures that works, even if we refer to advertising exposure rather than OTS."[24]

Effective Reach Planning in Advertising Practice

The mostly widely accepted view among media planners is that *fewer than 3 exposures* during a four-week media schedule is generally considered ineffective, while *more than 10 exposures* during this period is considered excessive. The range of effective reach, then, can be thought of as *3 to 10 exposures* during a designated media-planning period.

The use of effective reach rather than gross rating points as the basis for media planning can have a major effect on overall media strategies. In particular, effective reach planning generally leads to using *multiple media* rather than depending exclusively on television, which is often the strategy when using the GRP metric. Prime-time television is especially effective in terms of generating high levels of reach (1+ exposures) but may be deficient in terms of achieving effective reach (3+ exposures). Thus, the use of effective reach as the decision criterion often involves giving up some of prime-time television's reach to obtain greater frequency (at the same total cost) from other media.

This is illustrated in Table 11.2, which compares four media plans involving different combinations of media expenditures from an annual advertising budget of $25 million.[25] Plan A allocates 100 percent of the $25 million budget to network television advertising, plan B allocates 67 percent to television and 33 percent to network radio, plan C splits the budget between network television and magazines, and plan D allocates 67 percent to television and 33 percent to outdoor advertising.

Notice first that plan A (the use of 100 percent TV) leads to the lowest levels of reach, effective reach, frequency, and GRPs. An even (50/50) split of TV and magazines (plan C) generates an especially high level of reach (91 percent), while combinations of TV with radio (plan B) and TV with outdoor advertising (plan D) are especially impressive in terms of frequency, GRPs, and the percentage of consumers exposed three or more times.

More to the point, notice that the TV-only plan compared with the remaining plans yields far fewer GRPs and considerably fewer **effective rating points (ERPs)**. (Note that in Table 11.2 ERPs equal the product of effective reach, or 3+ exposures, times frequency; plan A, for example, yields 81 ERPs, i.e., $29 \times 2.8 = 81$.) Plan D, which combines 67 percent TV with 33 percent outdoor advertising, is especially outstanding in terms of the numbers of GRPs and ERPs generated. This is because outdoor advertising is seen frequently as people travel to and from work and participate in other activities.

Should we conclude from this discussion that plan D is the best and that plan A is the worst? Not necessarily. Clearly, the impact from seeing one billboard advertisement is generally far less than being exposed to a captivating television commercial. This illustration points out a fundamental aspect of media planning: *subjective factors* also must be considered when allocating advertising dollars.

	Plan A: TV (100%)	Plan B: TV (67%), Radio (33%)	Plan C: TV (50%), Magazines (50%)	Plan D: TV (67%), Outdoor (33%)
Reach (1+ exposures)	69%	79%	91%	87%
Effective reach (3+ exposures)	29%	48%	53%	61%
Frequency	2.8	5.5	3.2	6.7
GRPs	193	435	291	583
ERPs	81	264	170	409
Cost per GRP	$129,534	$57,471	$85,911	$42,882
Cost per ERP	$308,642	$94,697	$147,059	$61,125

Table 11.2

Alternative Media Plans Based on a $25 Million Annual Budget and Four-Week Media Analysis

Superficially, the numbers do favor plan D. However, judgment and past experience may favor plan A on the grounds that the only way to advertise this particular product effectively is by presenting dynamic action shots of people consuming and enjoying the product. Only television could satisfy this requirement. Other media (radio, magazines, and outdoor advertising) may be used to complement the key message TV ads drive home. (The strengths and limitations of each of these ad media are discussed in the following chapter.)

It is useful to return again to a point established in Chapter 6: *It is better to be vaguely right than precisely wrong.* Reach, frequency, effective reach, GRPs, TRPs, and ERPs are precise in their appearance but, in application, if used blindly, may be precisely wrong. Discerning decision makers never rely on numbers to make decisions for them. Rather, the numbers should be used solely as additional inputs into a decision that ultimately involves insight, wisdom, and judgment.

An Alternative Approach: Frequency Value Planning

Advertising scholars have proposed an alternative approach to the three-exposure doctrine.[26] The objective of *frequency value planning* is to select that media schedule (from a set of alternative schedules) that generates the most exposure value per GRP—or, stated differently, the objective is to select that media schedule that provides a "bigger bang for the buck." Frequency value planning is an approach that attempts to get the most out of an advertising investment in the sense of selecting the most *efficient* advertising schedule. The following implementation steps are involved:

Step 1. Estimate the *exposure utility* for each level of vehicle exposure, or OTS, that a schedule produces.[27] Exposure utility represents the worth, or value, of each additional opportunity for audience members to see an ad for a brand during the period of an advertising schedule. Table 11.3 lists OTSs from 0 to 10+ and their corresponding exposure utilities. (Note that these utilities are not invariant across all situations but have to be determined uniquely for each brand-advertising situation.) It can be seen that 0 vehicle exposures has, of course, an exposure utility of 0. One exposure adds the greatest amount of utility, assumed here to be 0.50 units; a second OTS contributes 0.13 additional units of utility (for an overall utility of 0.63); a third exposure contributes 0.09 more units to the second exposure (for an overall utility of 0.72 units); a fourth exposure adds 0.07 units of utility to the third exposure; and so on. One can readily see that this utility function reflects decreasing marginal utility with each additional OTS. At an OTS of 10, the maximum utility of 1.00 is achieved. Hence, this illustration proposes that OTSs in excess of 10 offer no additional utility. By graphing the utilities in Table 11.3, one can readily see that the function is nonlinear and concave to the origin. In other words, each additional exposure contributes decreasing utility.

table 11.3

Exposure Utilities for Different OTS Levels

OTS	Exposure Utility
0	0.00
1	0.50
2	0.63
3	0.72
4	0.79
5	0.85
6	0.90
7	0.94
8	0.97
9	0.99
10+	1.00

Step 2. Estimate the *frequency distribution* of the various media schedules that are under consideration. Computer programs, such as the program discussed later in the chapter, are available for this purpose. Table 11.4 shows the distributions for two alternative media schedules. Reading in Table 11.4 from column B (Schedule 1) and column D (Schedule 2), it can be seen that 15 percent of the target audience is estimated to be exposed zero times to Schedule 1 (8 percent exposed zero times to Schedule 2), 11.1 percent of the target audience is estimated to be exposed exactly one time to Schedule 1 (21.0 percent are exposed one time to Schedule 2), 12.5 percent of the audience exposed exactly two times to Schedule 1 (17.6 percent to Schedule 2), 13.2 percent three times to Schedule 1 (13.6 percent to Schedule 2), and so on.

Step 3. Estimate the *OTS value at each OTS level.*[28] Entries in the *OTS value* columns in Table 11.4 (column C for Schedule 1, column E for Schedule 2) are

Table 11.4

Frequency Distributions and Valuations of Two Media Schedules

		Schedule 1		Schedule 2	
OTS	(A) Exposure Utility	(B) Percentage of Target	(C) OTS Value (A × B)	(D) Percentage of Target	(E) OTS Value (A × D)
0	0.00	15.0%	0.000	8.0%	0.000
1	0.50	11.1	5.550	21.0	10.500
2	0.63	12.5	7.875	17.6	11.088
3	0.72	13.2	9.504	13.6	9.792
4	0.79	11.0	8.690	10.9	8.611
5	0.85	8.4	7.140	8.6	7.310
6	0.90	6.3	5.670	6.6	5.940
7	0.94	5.0	4.700	5.2	4.888
8	0.97	3.9	3.783	3.9	3.783
9	0.99	3.1	3.069	3.0	2.970
10+	1.00	10.5	10.500	1.6	1.600
Total Value:			66.481		66.482
GRPs:			398.6		333.8
Index of Exposure Efficiency (Value/GRPs):			0.167		0.199

calculated at each OTS level (OTS = 1, 2, 3,..., 10+) by simply taking the arithmetic product of the Exposure Utility at each OTS level times the Percentage of Target column. Hence, at an OTS of one exposure, the exposure value is 0.5 × 11.1 = 5.55 for Schedule 1 and 0.5 × 21.0 = 10.5 for Schedule 2. At an OTS of two exposures, the exposure value is 0.63 × 12.5 = 7.875 (Schedule 1) and 0.63 × 17.6 = 11.088 (Schedule 2), and so on.

Step 4. Determine the *total value across all OTS levels.* After calculating the value at each OTS level, the *total value* is obtained by simply summing the individual exposure values (5.55 + 7.875 + 9.504 + ··· + 10.5 = 66.481 for Schedule 1; 10.5 + 11.088 + 9.792 + ··· + 1.6 = 66.482 for Schedule 2, which is virtually identical to that for Schedule 1).

Step 5. Develop an *index of exposure efficiency.* This index is calculated by dividing each schedule's *total value* by the number of *GRPs* produced by that schedule. Total GRPs are determined from the data in Table 11.4 in the same way they were identified earlier from the data in Table 11.1. Specifically, Schedule 1's total of 398.6 GRPs (see bottom of Table 11.4) is calculated as (1 × 11.1) + (2 × 12.5) + (3 × 13.2) + ··· + (10 × 10.5). (You should ensure that you understand this by calculating the GRPs for Schedule 2.) The index of exposure efficiency for Schedule 1 is 0.167 (i.e., 66.481 ÷ 398.6), whereas the index value for Schedule 2 is 0.199 (i.e., 66.482 ÷ 333.8).

What can be concluded from these calculations? With higher index values representing greater *efficiency,* it should be clear that Schedule 2 in Table 11.4 is the more efficient media schedule. That is, Schedule 2 has a higher efficiency index than Schedule 1 because Schedule 2 accomplishes an equivalent exposure value (66.482 versus 66.481) but with fewer GRPs and hence less expense. Moreover, whereas Schedule 1 reaches a high percentage of the target audience 10 or more times (i.e., 10+ OTS = 10.5 percent), Schedule 2 focuses more on reaching the audience at least one time rather than wasting expenditures on reaching the audience 10 or more times. The 1+ OTS for Schedule 2 equals 92 percent, compared with Schedule 1's 1+ OTS of 85 percent.

Although this method of frequency value planning is theoretically sounder than the three-exposure heuristic, the latter is embedded in advertising practice whereas the former was introduced more recently. The implication is not that this newer procedure should be dismissed out of hand; the point, instead, is that advertising practice has not as yet widely adopted the approach. It is only fair to note that the difficulty with implementing frequency value planning is in estimating exposure utilities, such as those presented in Table 11.3. There simply is no easy way to estimate exposure utilities, which is why many media planners prefer to employ rules of thumb.

Continuity

Continuity involves the matter of how advertising is allocated during the course of an advertising campaign. The fundamental issue is this: Should the media budget be distributed uniformly throughout the period of the advertising campaign, should it be spent in a concentrated period to achieve the most impact, or should some other schedule between these two extremes be used? As always, the determination of what is best depends on the specifics of the situation. In general, however, a uniform advertising schedule may suffer from too little advertising weight at any one time. A heavily concentrated schedule, in contrast, can suffer from excessive exposures during the advertising period and a complete absence of advertising at all other times.

Advertisers have three general alternatives related to allocating the budget over the course of the campaign: *continuous, pulsing,* and *flighting* schedules. To understand the differences among these three scheduling options, consider the

© Herman Agopian/Taxi/Getty Images

advertising decision a local company that markets various dairy-based products faces. Figure 11.2 shows how advertising allocations might differ from month to month depending on the use of continuous, pulsing, or flighting schedules. Assume the annual advertising budget available to this marketer is $3 million.

Continuous Schedule

In a **continuous advertising schedule**, an equal or relatively equal number of ad dollars are invested throughout the campaign. The illustration in panel A of Figure 11.2 shows an extreme case of continuous advertising in which the advertiser allocates the $3 million advertising budget in equal amounts of exactly $250,000 for all 12 months.

Such an advertising allocation would make sense only if dairy products were consumed in essentially equal quantities throughout the year. However, although dairy products are consumed year-round, consumption is particularly high during May, June, July, and August when people increasingly eat ice cream, which is an especially important product in this company's product line and one for which sales are especially sensitive to advertising support. This calls for a *discontinuous* allocation of advertising dollars throughout the year.

Pulsing

In a **pulsing advertising schedule**, some advertising is used during every period of the campaign, but the amount of advertising varies from period to period. In panel B of Figure 11.2, a pulsing schedule for this dairy company shows that its advertising is especially heavy during the high ice cream–consumption months of May through August (spending $500,000 each month) but the company nonetheless advertises in every month throughout the year. The minimum advertising expenditure is $50,000 even in the relatively low ice cream–sales months of January, February, November, and December.

Flighting

In a **flighting schedule**, the advertiser varies expenditures throughout the campaign and allocates *zero* expenditures in some months. As demonstrated in panel C of Figure 11.2, the dairy company allocates $600,000 to each of the four high ice cream–consumption months (May through August), $200,000 each to moderate ice cream–consumption months (April, September, and October), but $0 to the five low-consumption months (January, February, March, November, and December).

Thus, pulsing and flighting are similar in that they both involve *differential levels of advertising expenditures* throughout the year, but the schedules differ in that some advertising takes place during every period with pulsing but not with flighting. The following analogies may help to eliminate any confusion between pulsing and flighting. *Pulsing* in advertising is similar to an individual's heartbeat or pulse. One's pulse changes continuously between some lower and upper bounds but is always present in a living person. Comparatively, a *flighting* schedule is like an airplane, which at times is on the ground but at different altitudes when in flight. Thus, a pulsed advertising schedule is always beating (some

figure 11.2

Continuous, Pulsing, and Flighting Advertising Schedules for a Brand of Ice Cream

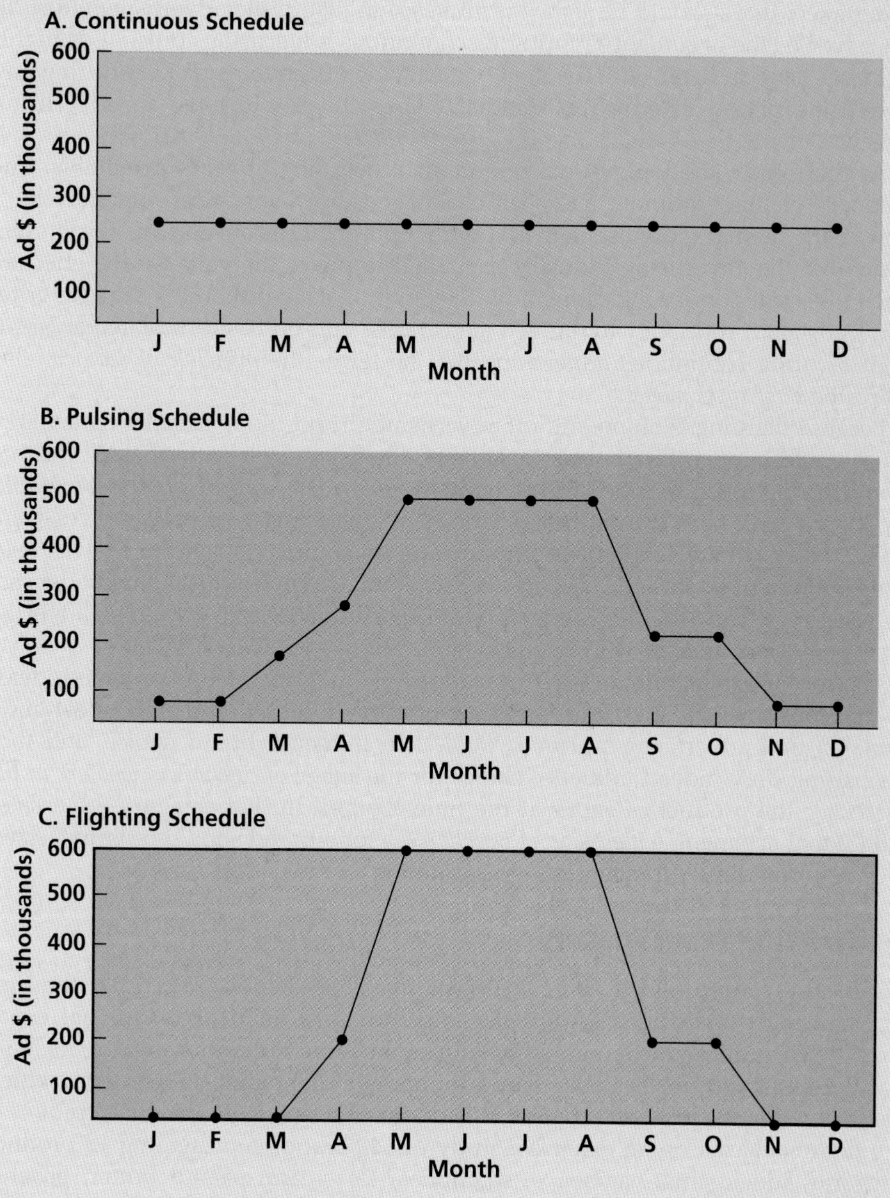

advertising is placed in every ad period), whereas a flighted schedule soars at times to very high levels but is nonexistent on other occasions.

Recency Planning (a.k.a. The Shelf-Space Model)

Some advertising practitioners argue that flighted and pulsed advertising schedules are necessitated by the tremendous increases in media costs, especially the expense of network television advertising. Few advertisers, according to the logic of discontinuous ad scheduling (i.e., flighted or pulsed schedules), can afford to advertise consistently heavily throughout the year. According to this argument, advertisers are forced to advertise only at select times—namely, during periods when there is the greatest chance of accomplishing communication and sales objectives. This argument further holds that during periods when advertising is undertaken, there should be *sufficient frequency* to justify the advertising effort. In other words, the argument favoring discontinuous advertising (pulsing or flighting) goes hand in hand with the goal of achieving effective reach (3+) during any advertising period in which a brand manager chooses to have an advertising presence.

At first blush, the logic of discontinuous scheduling appears irrefutable. The prudence of this argument has been challenged, however, most forcefully by a New York media specialist named Erwin Ephron. Ephron and his supporters assert that the advertising industry has failed to prove the value of the effective reach (3+) criterion for allocating advertising budgets and that this dubious criterion leads inappropriately to flighted allocations. Ephron has formulated an argument favoring continuous advertising that he terms the *principle of recency,* also called the *shelf-space model.*[29]

Because flighting is an on-and-off advertising proposition, consider by analogy what would happen to a brand's sales if retail shelves were out of stock for that brand during various times throughout the year. The brand obviously would experience zero sales during those periods of stock-outs when the shelves were empty. Sales would be obtained only during those times when the shelves held some amount of the brand. This, in a sense, is the way it is with flighted advertising schedules: The "shelves" are empty during certain periods (when no advertising is being run) and full during others.

The **recency principle**, or *shelf-space model,* is built on three interrelated ideas: (1) that consumers' *first exposure* to an advertisement for a brand is the most powerful; (2) that advertising's primary role is to influence brand choice, and that advertising does indeed influence choice for the *subset of consumers who are in the market* for the product category at the time a brand in that category advertises; and (3) that achieving a *high level of weekly reach* for a brand should be emphasized over acquiring heavy frequency. Let us examine all three ideas.

The Powerful First Exposure

Empirical evidence (albeit somewhat tentative) has demonstrated that the first exposure to advertising has a greater effect on sales than do additional exposures.[30] (The utility function given previously in Table 11.3 was based on the logic that the first exposure has the greatest impact.) Using single-source data, which was covered in the previous chapter, an advertising researcher produced provocative findings based on an extensive study of 142 brands representing 12 product categories (detergents, bar soaps, shampoos, ice cream, peanut butter, ground coffee, etc.). The researcher demonstrated that the first advertising exposure for these brands generated the highest proportion of sales and that additional exposures added very little to the first.[31]

Influencing Brand Choice

The concept of recency planning is based on the idea that consumer needs determine advertising effects. Advertising is especially effective when it occurs *close to the time when consumers are in the market for a particular product.* There is, in other words, a window of advertising opportunity for capturing the consumer's selection of the advertised brand versus other brands in the product category. "Advertising's job is to influence the purchase. Recency planning's job is to place the message in that window."[32]

Although recency planning is based on the idea that the first advertising exposure is the most powerful, this does not mean that a single exposure is sufficient. The point instead is that in the short-term additional exposures are likely to be wasted on consumers who are not in the market for the product. The logic, in other words, is that a brand can achieve greater sales volume by reaching more consumers a single time during an advertising period (a reach objective) rather than reaching fewer consumers more often (a frequency objective).

The advertising budget is not necessarily lower with recency planning; rather, the budget is allocated differently than is a flighted advertising budget. In particular, recency planning allocates the budget over more weeks throughout the year and invests less weight (fewer GRPs or TRPs) during the weeks in which advertising is undertaken. Recency planning uses *one week,* rather than four weeks, as the planning period and attempts to reach as many target consumers as possible in as many weeks as the budget will permit.

Optimizing Weekly Reach

Accordingly, it can be argued that media planners should devise schedules that are geared toward providing a continuous (or near continuous) presence for a brand with the objective of optimizing *weekly reach* rather than effective reach as embodied in the three-exposure hypothesis.

The logic of recency planning can be summarized as follows:

1. Contrary to the three-exposure hypothesis, which has been interpreted to mean that advertising must *teach* consumers about brands (therefore requiring multiple exposures), the recency principle, or shelf-space model, assumes that the role of advertising is *not* to teach but to influence consumers' *brand selection.* "Unless it's a new brand, a new benefit, or a new use, there is not much learning involved."[33] Hence, the purpose of most advertising is to remind us of, reinforce, or evoke earlier messages rather than to teach consumers about product benefits or uses.
2. With the objective of influencing brand selection, advertising must therefore reach consumers when they are ready to buy a brand. The purpose of advertising by this logic is to "rent the shelf" so as to ensure a brand presence close to the time when consumers make purchase decisions. *Out of sight, out of mind* is a key advertising principle.
3. Advertising messages are most effective when they are *close to the time of purchase,* and a single advertising exposure is effective if it reaches consumers close to the time when they are making brand-selection decisions.
4. The cost effectiveness of a single exposure is approximately *three times greater* than the value of subsequent exposures.[34]
5. Hence rather than concentrating the advertising budget to achieve multiple exposures only at select times throughout the year, planners should allocate the budget to *reach more consumers more often.*
6. In a world without budget constraints, the ideal advertising approach would be to achieve a weekly reach of 100 (i.e., to reach 100 percent of the target audience at least one time) and to sustain this level of reach for all 52 weeks of the year. Such a schedule would yield 5,200 weekly reach points. Because most advertisers cannot afford to sustain such a constant level of advertising, the next best approach is to *reach as high a percentage of the target audience as possible for as many weeks as possible.* This goal can be accomplished by (1) using 15-second TV commercials as well as more expensive 30-second spots; (2) spreading the budget among cheaper media (e.g., radio) rather than spending exclusively on television advertising; and (3) buying cheaper TV programs (cable, syndicated) rather than exclusively prime-time network programs. All of these strategies free up advertising dollars and permit an advertising schedule that will reach a high percentage of the target audience continuously rather than sporadically.

Toward Reconciliation: It Depends!

The concept of scheduling media to achieve a continuous rather than sporadic presence has considerable appeal. However, no single approach is equally effective for all brands. The logic of recency planning recognizes this when suggesting (in the first point previously) that for new brands, new benefits, or different ways of using a brand, the advertising objective indeed may be to teach rather than merely remind. Another advertising executive summarized the issue well.

> *We've always believed that the first exposure is the most powerful, yet we don't want to have hard and fast rules. Every brand is a different situation. The leader in a category has different frequency needs than a competitor with less market share. It's not fair to say every brand has the same need for frequency.*[35]

As a student it may be somewhat disconcerting to receive "mixed signals" such as these. Assuredly, it would be easier if there were hard-and-fast rules or straightforward principles that said, "Here is how you should do it." Advertising practice, unfortunately, is not as simple as this. We repeat a theme that has been emphasized throughout the text: What works best depends on the specific circumstances facing a brand. If the brand is *mature* and well established, then effective weekly reach (the shelf-space model) is probably an appropriate way to allocate the advertising budget. Conversely, if the brand is *new,* or if *new benefits or uses* for the brand have been developed, or if the advertising *message is complex,* then the budget should be allocated in a manner that achieves the frequency necessary to teach consumers about brand benefits and uses. In other words, when any of these latter conditions prevail, a flighted ad schedule is more appropriate than a weekly reach schedule.

These opposing viewpoints about how advertising works can be distinguished as the "strong" and "weak" models of advertising.[36] The *strong model* takes the position that advertising is important because it teaches consumers about brands and encourages trial purchases leading to the prospect of repeat buying. The *weak model* contends that most advertising messages are not important to consumers and that consumers do not learn much from advertising. This is because advertising usually is for brands that consumers already know about. In this case, advertising merely serves to *remind* consumers about brands they already know.

Reconciliation between these opposing viewpoints comes from appreciating the fact that advertising at any time *does* have influence on a relatively small percentage of consumers, and these are the consumers who happen to be in the market for the product at the time of the advertising. For example, a newspaper advertisement announcing a retailer's special sale for a particular brand of television may encourage store traffic and purchases from the relatively small subset of consumers who, at this time, need a new television set. Most consumers, however, do not need a new television set at this particular time. It thus may be said that advertising achieves its effectiveness "through a chance encounter with a ready consumer."[37]

Should it be concluded from this discussion that a single advertising exposure is all that is necessary and that advertising time and space should be scheduled so that recency is optimized and frequency is neglected? Absolutely not. Rather, what you should understand is that the specific advertising situation dictates whether emphasis on reach or frequency is more important. Brands familiar to consumers require less frequency, whereas new or relatively unfamiliar brands require higher levels of frequency. Brands that employ complex messages (e.g., containing technical details or subtle claims) also generally require more frequency.[38] Brands offering special deals for a short period also require greater frequency. For example, when a fast-food chain is offering, say, a special sandwich for a limited period, frequent advertising is required to "teach" consumers about the deal and to encourage increased store traffic.

Cost Considerations

Media planners attempt to allocate the advertising budget in a cost-efficient manner subject to satisfying other objectives. One of the most important and universally used indicators of media efficiency is the cost-per-thousand criterion. **Cost per thousand** (abbreviated **CPM**, with the *M* representing the Roman numeral for 1,000) is the cost of reaching 1,000 people. The measure can be refined to mean the cost of reaching 1,000 members of the target audience, excluding those people who fall outside the target market. This refined measure is designated **CPM-TM**.

CPM and CPM-TM are calculated by dividing the cost of an advertisement placed in a particular advertising vehicle by the vehicle's total-market reach (CPM) or by its target-market reach (CPM-TM):

CPM = Cost of ad ÷ Number of *total* contacts reached (expessed in thousands)

CPM-TM = Cost of ad ÷ Number of *target market* contacts reached (expressed in thousands)

The term *contacts* is used here to represent any type of advertising audience (television viewers, magazine readers, radio listeners, etc.) that is reached by a single advertising placement in a particular vehicle.

Illustrative Calculations

To illustrate how CPM and CPM-TM are calculated, consider the following unconventional advertising situation. During Saturday football games at a major university, a local airplane advertising service flies messages on a trailing device that extends behind the plane. The cost is $500 per message. The football stadium holds 80,000 fans and is filled to capacity every Saturday. Hence, the CPM in this situation is $6.25, which is the cost per message ($500) divided by the number of thousands of people (80) who potentially are exposed to (i.e., have an opportunity to see, or OTS) an advertising message trailing from the plane.

Now assume that a new student bookstore uses the airplane advertising service to announce its opening to the approximately 20,000 students who are typically in attendance at each game. Because the target market in this instance is only a fraction of the total audience, CPM-TM is a more appropriate cost-per-thousand statistic. CPM-TM in this instance is $25 ($500 ÷ 20)—which of course is four times higher than the CPM statistic because the target audience is one fourth the size of the total audience.

To further illustrate how CPM and CPM-TM are calculated, consider a more conventional advertising situation. Suppose an advertiser promoted its brand on the reality program *American Idol,* and that during a particular week *American Idol*'s Nielsen rating is 16.2, meaning that viewers in approximately 18.3 million households had an OTS for any commercial aired on that program. At a cost of $780,000 for a 30-second commercial on Tuesday evening airings of *American Idol* during the 2008 season, the CPM is as follows:

Total viewership = 18,273,600 Households

Cost of 30-second commercial = $780,000

CPM = $780,000 ÷ 18,273.6

= $42.68

If we assume that the advertised brand's target market consists only of girls and women between the ages of 13 and 34 and that this submarket represents

60 percent of the total audience—or 10,964,160 girls and women who view *American Idol*—then the CPM-TM is

$$\begin{aligned}\textbf{CPM-TM} &= \$780,000 \div 10,964.16\\ &= \$71.14\end{aligned}$$

Use with Caution!

The CPM and CPM-TM statistics are useful for comparing the *cost-efficiency* of different advertising vehicles. They must be used cautiously, however, for several reasons. First, these are measures of cost-efficiency—not of effectiveness. A particular vehicle may be extremely efficient but totally ineffective because it (1) reaches the wrong audience (if CPM is used rather than CPM-TM) or (2) is inappropriate for the product category and the brand advertised. By analogy, a Smart Fortwo car is undoubtedly more efficient in terms of miles-per-gallon than a large SUV but may be less effective for one's purposes.[39]

A second limitation of CPM and CPM-TM measures is their lack of comparability across media. As is emphasized in the following chapter, the various media perform unique roles and are therefore priced differently. A lower CPM for radio does not mean that buying radio time is better than buying a more expensive (CPM-wise) television schedule.

Finally, CPM statistics can be misused unless vehicles within a particular medium are compared on the same basis. For example, the CPM for an advertisement placed on daytime television is lower than that for a prime-time program, but this represents a case of comparing apples with oranges. The proper comparison would be between two daytime programs or between two prime-time programs rather than across dayparts. Similarly, it would be inappropriate to compare the CPM for a black-and-white magazine ad with a four-color magazine ad unless the two ads are considered equal in terms of their ability to present the brand effectively.

The Necessity of Making Tradeoffs

We have now discussed various media-planning objectives—reach, frequency, weight, continuity, recency, and cost—in some detail. Each was introduced without direct reference to the other objectives. It is important to recognize, however, that these objectives are actually somewhat at odds with one another. That is, given a fixed advertising budget (e.g., $15 million for the Fortwo), the media planner cannot simultaneously optimize reach, frequency, and continuity objectives. Tradeoffs must be made because media planners operate under the constraint of fixed advertising budgets. Hence, optimizing one objective (e.g., minimizing CPM or maximizing GRPs) requires the sacrifice of other objectives. This simply is due to the mathematics of constrained optimization: Multiple objectives cannot simultaneously be optimized when constraints (like limited budgets) exist.

With a fixed advertising budget, the media planner can choose to maximize reach or frequency but not both. With increases in reach, frequency is sacrificed and vice versa: if you want to reach more people, you cannot reach them as often with a *fixed* advertising budget; if you want to reach them more often, you cannot reach as many. (Parenthetically, this discussion may remind you of a lesson you learned in basic statistics about the tradeoff between committing Type I (alpha) and Type II (beta) errors while holding sample size constant. That is, with a fixed sample size, decisions to decrease a Type I error (say, from .05 to .01) must inevitably result in an increase in the Type II error and vice versa.)

As an advertising practitioner, "you can't have your cake and eat it too." The brand manager faced with an advertising budget constraint, which always is the case, must decide whether frequency is more important (the three-exposure hypothesis) or reach is more imperative (the recency principle).

Thus, each media planner must decide what is best given the particular circumstances surrounding the advertising decision facing his or her brand. As previously discussed, achieving *effective reach* (3+ exposures) is particularly important when brands are new or when established brands have new benefits or uses. In these circumstances, the task of advertising is to *teach* consumers, and part of teaching is *repetition*. The more complex the message, the greater the need for repetition to convey the message effectively. However, for established brands that already are well known by consumers, the advertising task is more one of *reminding* consumers about the brand. The ad budget in this situation is best allocated to achieve the maximum level of *reach*.

Media-Scheduling Software

On top of the difficult task of making intelligent tradeoffs among sometimes opposing objectives (reach, frequency, etc.), there literally are thousands, if not millions, of possible advertising schedules that could be selected depending on how the various media and media vehicles are combined. Fortunately, this daunting task is facilitated by the availability of computerized models to assist media planners in selecting media and vehicles. These models essentially attempt to optimize an objective function (e.g., selecting a schedule that yields the greatest level of reach or the highest frequency), subject to satisfying constraints such as not exceeding the upper limit on the advertising budget. A computer algorithm (a problem-solving computer program) searches through the possible solutions and selects the specific media schedule that optimizes the objective function and satisfies all specified constraints.

For illustration purposes, let us assume that a media planner has decided to invest $6 million in a one-month advertising campaign that will launch a hypothetical SUV that is relatively small, has a hybrid engine, is fuel-efficient, and is to be named Esuvee-H.[40] The budget will be allocated between television and magazine advertising, with $4.5 million to be invested on the former during the introductory month and another $1.5 million to be spent on the latter. (To simplify the discussion, only the magazine component of the media schedule is described.) Assume further that the target market for the Esuvee-H consists of men between the ages of 18-49 who have incomes exceeding $45,000 and who are outdoor oriented.

Using a computerized media-scheduling program to select the "best" magazine vehicles from a large set of magazine options would entail the following steps:

Step 1. Develop a *media database*. This initial aspect of media planning involves three activities: (1) identify prospective advertising vehicles, (2) specify their ratings, and (3) determine individual vehicle cost. Table 11.5 illustrates the essential information contained in the media database for the Esuvee-H.

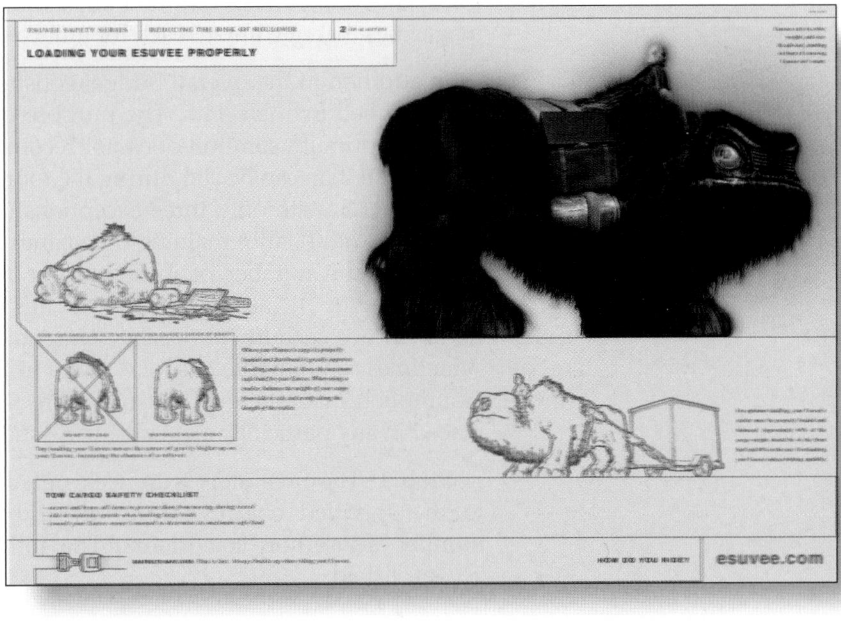

Source: "How Do You Ride? What Everyone Needs to Know about SUV Safety." Used with permission from Peppercom Strategic Communications.

table 11.5

Media Database for the Esuvee-H

Magazine	Rating	4C/Open Cost*	Maximum Insertions†
American Hunter	7.0	$ 29,830	1
American Rifleman	8.7	44,470	1
Bassmaster	8.8	34,855	1
Car & Driver	10.8	149,350	1
Ducks Unlimited	2.9	24,925	1
ESPN Magazine	15.6	148,750	2
Field & Stream	18.7	101,600	1
Game & Fish	5.8	20,540	1
Guns & Ammo	13.5	30,780	1
Hot Rod	18.5	72,790	1
Maxim	24.6	179,000	1
Men's Fitness	9.5	49,425	1
Men's Health	18.3	121,425	1
Motor Trend	14.5	127,155	1
North American Hunter	10.5	27,210	1
Outdoor Life	15.7	55,700	1
The Sporting News	10.7	49,518	4
Sports Illustrated	44.3	226,000	4

*4C/open stands for a full-page, four-color ad purchased without a quantity discount. Cost information is from *Marketer's Guide to Media*, 27 (New York: VNU Business Publications USA, 2004), 149–152.

†Maximum insertions are based on how frequently a magazine is published. *The Sporting News* and *Sports Illustrated* are published weekly, which thus would enable one ad in each of the weeks during the four-week scheduling period. With the exception of *ESPN Magazine*, which is published every other week, all other magazines under consideration are published monthly.

Step 2. Select the *criterion for optimizing the media schedule.* Media-schedule optimization alternatives include maximizing reach (1+), effective reach (3+), frequency, and GRPs. In the illustration to follow, *maximizing reach* has been selected as the optimizing criterion for the Esuvee-H's one-month introductory magazine campaign.

Step 3. Specify *constraints.* These include (1) determining a *budget constraint* for the media planning period, and (2) identifying *the maximum number of ad insertions for each vehicle.* The introductory one-month magazine budget constraint has been set at $1.5 million. The computer algorithm is being "told," in other words, to select magazines that maximize reach for an expenditure not to exceed $1.5 million.

In addition to the overall budget constraint, magazine-insertion constraints also are identified in Table 11.5. The purpose of these insertion constraints is to assure that the optimum solution does not recommend inserting more ads in a particular publication than can be run during the four-week scheduling period. As can be seen in Table 11.5, with only three exceptions (*ESPN Magazine, The Sporting News,* and *Sports Illustrated*), all remaining magazines are issued only once per month. Hence, the maximum number of insertions for most of the magazines in Table 11.5 is constrained to "1," although up to "2" ads will be permitted in *ESPN Magazine* and up to "4" ads each in *The Sporting News* and *Sports Illustrated.* Although advertisers sometimes run multiple ads for a brand in the same magazine issue, the simplifying assumption made here is that not more than one ad for the Esuvee-H should be placed in any particular magazine per issue.

Step 1. The final step is to seek out the optimum media schedule according to the specified objective function and subject to satisfying the budget and number-of-insertion constraints. The following illustration reveals how this is accomplished.

Hypothetical Illustration: A One-Month Magazine Schedule for the Esuvee-H

Let us assume that a media planner for the Esuvee-H is in the process of choosing the optimal four-week schedule from among magazines considered appropriate for reaching men ages 18 to 49 who have household incomes of $45,000 or greater, and who are outdoor oriented (i.e., they like to hunt, fish, cycle, camp, etc.). Let us assume that there are approximately 67 million male Americans ages 18 to 49. On the assumption that only 40 percent of this group satisfies the Esuvee-H's income target of $45,000 or greater, the target market is reduced to 26.8 million prospective customers for the Esuvee-H (i.e., 0.4 × 67 million). All subsequent planning is based on this estimate.

The Esuvee-H Database

The media planner has prepared a database consisting of 18 magazines considered suitable for reaching the target audience (Table 11.5). These magazines were selected because they are read predominantly by male readers who engage in outdoor activities such as hunting, fishing, and cycling and who have household incomes of $45,000 or greater.

The second key input was magazine ratings. Ratings (see the second column in Table 11.5) were determined by dividing each magazine's audience size by the size of Esuvee-H's target market, which, as indicated, is estimated as 26.8 million potential customers.[41] Next, costs (the third column) were designated according to the price each magazine charged for a one-time placement of a full-page, four-color advertisement. Finally, maximum insertions (the last column) were based on each magazine's publication cycle. As noted previously, 15 of the 18 magazines are published once per month, whereas *ESPN Magazine* is published bimonthly and *Sporting News* and *Sports Illustrated* are published weekly. Hence, only one ad each can be placed during the four-week period in 15 of the magazines, whereas it is possible to place up to two ads in *ESPN Magazine* and up to four ads each in *Sporting News* and *Sports Illustrated.*

The Objective Function and Constraints

The information in Table 11.5 was input into a computerized media scheduling program.[42] With this information, the program was instructed to maximize reach (1+) without exceeding a budget of $1.5 million for this four-week introductory magazine advertising campaign.

The Optimal Schedule

Had advertisements been placed in all 18 magazines listed in Table 11.5 (including multiple insertions in the three magazines where multiple insertions were permissible—*ESPN Magazine, The Sporting News,* and *Sports Illustrated*), the total advertising cost would have amounted to nearly $2.5 million. This amount would have been unacceptable, because a $1.5 million budget constraint was imposed on magazine advertising. It thus was necessary to select from these magazines such that the budget constraint was met and the goal to maximize reach was satisfied. This is precisely what media-scheduling algorithms accomplish.

Given 18 magazines with different numbers of maximum insertions in each, there are numerous combinations of magazines that could be selected. However, in a matter of seconds, the scheduling algorithm identified the single combination of magazines that would maximize reach for an expenditure of $1.5 million or less. The solution is displayed in Table 11.6.

table 11.6

ADplus Magazine Schedule for the Esuvee-H

	Frequency (f) Distribution		
	f	%f	%f+
XYZ Ad Agency	0	27.8	100.0
Esuvee-H	1	5.1	72.2
Target: 26,800,000	2	10.3	67.1
Males/18–49/$45K HHI/Outdoor	3	14.7	56.8
	4	15.2	42.1
	5	11.7	26.9
	6	7.3	15.1
	7	4.1	7.8
	8	2.2	3.7
	9	1.0	1.5
	10+	0.5	0.5

Summary Evaluation	
Reach (1+)	72.2
Effective reach (3+)	56.8
Gross rating points (GRPs)	293.9
Average frequency (F)	4.1
Gross impressions (000s)	78,765.2
Cost-per-thousand (CPM)	$18.32
Cost-per-rating point (CPP)	$4,909

Vehicle List	Rating	Ad Cost	CPM-MSG	Ads	Total Cost	Mix
Guns & Ammo	13.5	$ 30,780	$16.20	1	$ 30,780	2.1%
North American Hunter	10.5	27,210	18.42	1	27,210	1.9
Game & Fish	5.8	20,540	25.17	1	20,540	1.4
Outdoor Life	15.7	55,700	25.22	1	55,700	3.9
Hot Rod	18.5	72,790	27.96	1	72,790	5.0
Bassmaster	8.8	34,855	28.15	1	34,855	2.4
American Hunter	7.0	29,830	30.29	1	29,830	2.1
The Sporting News	10.7	49,518	32.89	4	198,072	13.7
Sports Illustrated	44.3	226,000	36.26	2	452,000	31.3
American Rifleman	8.7	44,470	36.33	1	44,470	3.1
Men's Fitness	9.5	49,425	36.98	1	49,425	3.4
Field & Stream	18.7	101,600	38.62	1	101,600	7.0
Men's Health	18.3	121,425	47.16	1	121,425	8.4
Maxim	24.6	179,000	51.72	1	179,000	12.4
Ducks Unlimited	2.9	24,925	61.09	1	24,925	1.7
		Totals:	$27.78	19	$1,442,622	100.0%

Table 11.6 shows that the optimal schedule consists of four ads in *The Sporting News*, two ads in *Sports illustrated*, and one ad each in 13 other magazines. (Three magazines—*Car & Driver, ESPN Magazine*, and *Motor Trend*—were not included in the final solution. Perusal of Table 11.5 reveals that these magazines are relatively expensive in view of the ratings delivered.) The total cost of this schedule is $1,422,622, which is under the specified upper limit of $1.5 million by $77,378. Note that the inclusion of any single additional advertisement would have exceeded the imposed budget limit. The least expensive magazine of the three that are not included is *Motor Trend* at a cost of $127,155. Had an advertisement been placed in

this magazine (or in *Car & Driver* or *ESPN Magazine*), the total cost would have exceeded the budget constraint of $1,500,000. The solution in Table 11.6 is *the* optimum solution for maximizing reach subject to satisfying the budget constraint.

Interpreting the Solution

Let us carefully examine the data in Table 11.6. Notice first that the information in the upper-left corner provides details about the media schedule (ad agency, client name, target size, and target description).

The next pertinent information to observe in Table 11.6 is the *frequency distribution*. To interpret this frequency distribution, recall the earlier discussion (Table 11.1) of the 10-household market for the Smart Fortwo advertised in *Cosmopolitan* magazine. It will be helpful to review the concepts of (1) exposure level (*f*); (2) frequency distribution, or percentage of audience exposed at each level of *f* (Percentage *f*); and (3) cumulative frequency distribution (Percentage *f*+). When *f* equals zero, the Percentage *f* and Percentage *f*+ values in Table 11.6 are 27.8 and 100, respectively. This is to say that the 27.8 percent of the 26.8 million target audience members for the Esuvee-H will *not* be exposed to any of the 15 magazines that made it into the optimal solution and that are listed at the bottom of Table 11.6. The cumulative frequency when *f* equals zero is of course 100—that is, 100 percent of the audience members will be exposed zero or more times to magazine vehicles in Esuvee-H's four-week advertising schedule.

Note further that Percentage *f* and Percentage *f*+ are 5.1 and 72.2 when *f* equals 1. That is, the computer program estimates that 5.1 percent of the target audience will be exposed to *exactly* one of the 15 magazines, and 72.2 percent of the audience will be exposed to one or more of the magazines during this four-week period. Note carefully under the summary evaluation in the middle of Table 11.6 that *reach* equals 72.2 percent. With reach defined as the percentage of the target audience exposed one or more times (i.e., 1+), the level of reach is determined merely by identifying the corresponding value in the Percentage *f*+ column, which, when *f* equals 1, is 72.2 percent. It should also be clear that because 27.8 percent of the audience is exposed zero times, the complement of this value (100 – 27.8 = 72.2 percent) is the percentage of the audience exposed one or more times—that is, the percentage of the audience reached.

Hence, this optimum schedule yields a reach of 72.2, which is the maximum level of reach that any combination of the 18 magazines included in the database (Table 11.5) could achieve within a budget constraint of $1.5 million.

This optimal schedule produces 293.9 *GRPs*. These GRPs, by the way, are calculated by multiplying the ratings for each magazine by the number of ads placed in that magazine [(*Guns & Ammo* = 13.5 × 1) + (*North American Hunter* = 10.5 × 1) + . . . (*Ducks Unlimited* = 2.9 × 1) = 293.9 GRPs].

Further, this magazine schedule is estimated to reach the audience an average of 4.1 times (see *average frequency* under the summary evaluation in Table 11.6). Having defined earlier that frequency equals GRPs ÷ reach, you can readily calculate that the level of frequency equals 293.9 ÷ 72.2 = 4.0706, which is rounded in Table 11.6 to 4.1.

Effective reach (i.e., 3+) is 56.8 percent. That is, nearly 57 percent of the total audience are exposed to three or more vehicles. This value is obtained from the frequency distribution at the top of Table 11.6 by reading across from *f* = 3 to the corresponding *percentage f*+ column.

The *cost per thousand (CPM)* is $18.32. This value is calculated as follows: (1) audience size is 26,800,000; (2) 72.2 percent—or 19,349,600 of the audience members—are reached by the schedule of magazines shown in Table 11.6; (3) each person reached is done so on average 4.0706 times (in Table 11.6, frequency is presented only to a single decimal point and is rounded up to 4.1); (4) the number of gross impressions, which is the number of people reached multiplied by the average number of times they are reached, is thus 78,765,200 (see summary evaluation in Table 11.6); (5) the *total cost* of this media schedule is $1,422,622 (see the bottom of the Total Cost column in Table 11.6); and (6) hence, the CPM is $1,442,622 ÷ 78,765.2 = $18.32.

Finally, the *cost per rating point (CPP)* is $4,909. This is calculated simply by dividing the total cost by the number of GRPs produced (i.e., $1,442,622 ÷ 293.9 GRPs).

Does Table 11.6 present a good media schedule? In terms of reach, the schedule is the best possible one that could have been produced from the combinations of 18 magazines that were input into the media scheduling algorithm and subject to a $1.5 million budget constraint. No other combination from among these magazines could have exceeded this schedule's reach of 72.2 percent. Note carefully, however, that this *opportunity to see* (OTS) the advertisement for the Esuvee-H is not tantamount to having actually seen the advertisement. As earlier noted, television advertising is to be run simultaneously with the magazine schedule. The combination of these media can be expected to produce much more impressive numbers and to achieve Esuvee-H's introductory advertising objectives.a

There's No Substitute for Judgment and Experience

It is critical to emphasize that media models such as what has just been illustrated do not make the ultimate scheduling decision. All they can do is efficiently perform the calculations needed to determine which single media schedule will optimize some objective function such as maximizing reach or GRPs. Armed with the answer, it is up to the media planner to determine whether the media schedule satisfies other, nonquantitative objectives such as those described in the following chapter.

Review of Media Plans

Now that fundamental issues in media scheduling have been identified, it will be useful to consider several actual media plans for general appreciation. First discussed is a plan for Diet Dr Pepper, followed by the plan used to introduce the Saab 9–5 luxury automobile. The final plan is for two brands of Olympus cameras. The objective in presenting these plans is for students to gain deeper understanding of the considerations that go into developing media plans and the specific architecture of such plans. It certainly is not the intent that students attempt to commit this material to memory.

© Alpha/Landov

The Diet Dr Pepper Plan

An award-winning advertising campaign for Diet Dr Pepper the Young & Rubicam advertising agency developed illustrates a media schedule for a consumer packaged good.[43] Although this is not a current schedule, which explains why the following description is framed in past tense, the fundamentals are as applicable now as when the schedule was implemented.

Campaign Target and Objectives

The target audience for Diet Dr Pepper consisted primarily of adults ages 18 to 49 who were present or prospective diet soft-drink consumers. The objectives for the Diet Dr

Pepper advertising campaign (titled "The Taste You've Been Looking For") were as follows:

1. To increase Diet Dr Pepper sales by 4 percent and improve its growth rate to at least 1.5 times that of the diet soft-drink category.
2. To heighten consumers' evaluations of the key product benefit and image factors that influence brand choice in this category: it is refreshing, tastes as good as regular Dr Pepper, is a good product to drink at any time, and is a fun brand to drink.
3. To enhance those key brand-personality dimensions that differentiate Diet Dr Pepper from other diet drinks—particularly that Diet Dr Pepper is a unique, clever, fun, entertaining, and interesting brand to drink.

Creative Strategy

The creative strategy for Diet Dr Pepper positioned the brand as "tasting more like regular Dr Pepper." This was a key claim based on research revealing that nearly 60 percent of initial trial users of Diet Dr Pepper were motivated by the desire to have a diet soft drink that tasted like regular Dr Pepper. The cornerstone of the campaign entailed the heavy use of 15-second commercials, which historically had not been used by major soft-drink brands, Coca-Cola and Pepsi-Cola; they preferred the entertainment value of longer commercials. The aggressive use of 15-second commercials enabled Diet Dr Pepper to convey its key taste claim ("Tastes more like regular Dr Pepper") and differentiate the brand from competitive diet drinks. Moreover, by employing cheaper 15-second commercials, it was possible to buy considerably more commercial spots and hence achieve greater weekly reach (recall the prior discussion of the shelf-space model), to obtain greater frequency, and to generate more weight (GRPs) for the same advertising budget. Diet Dr Pepper's advertising expenditures for the year totaled $20.3 million.

Media Strategy

The advertising schedule for Diet Dr Pepper generated a total of 1,858 GRPs, with a cumulative *annual* reach of 95 and frequency of 19.6. These media-weight values were accomplished with the national media plan summarized as a flowchart in Table 11.7.

Each of the 12 months and the week-beginning dates (Mondays) are listed across the top of the chart. Table entries reflect the GRPs each TV vehicle achieved for each weekly period based on targeted adults in the age category 18 to 49. The first entry, a 41 for the *NFL Championship Games,* indicates that placing advertisements for Diet Dr Pepper during the football games televised the week beginning January 17 produced 41 gross rating points. Ten additional GRPs were garnered by placing an ad on the *Road to the Super Bowl* program that aired during the week of January 24.

Note that the Diet Dr Pepper media plan consisted of (1) placing advertisements during professional and college football games (SEC stands for Southeastern Conference); (2) sponsoring various special events (e.g., the *Country Music Awards* and golfing events); and (3) continuously advertising during prime time, on late-night television (e.g., *David Letterman*), on syndicated programs, and on cable stations.

At the bottom of Table 11.7 is a summary of GRPs broken down by week (e.g., 86 GRPs during the week beginning January 10), by month (e.g., 227 GRPs during January), and by quarter (e.g., 632 GRPs produced during the first quarter, January through March). It can be seen that the media schedule was *flighted* insofar as advertisements were placed during approximately two thirds of the 52 weeks with no advertising during the remaining weeks. In sum, the media schedule was designed to highlight Diet Dr Pepper during a variety of special events and to maintain continuity throughout the year with prime-time network advertising and less expensive support on syndicated and cable programming.

table 11.7

Media Plan for Diet Dr Pepper

ADULTS 18–49 GRPs	JAN					FEB				MAR				APR				MAY					JUN			
	27	3	10	17	24	31	7	14	21	28	7	14	21	28	4	11	18	25	2	9	16	23	30	6	13	20
SPORTS																										
NFL Championship Games				41																						
Road to the Superbowl					10																					
FOX "Game of the Week"																										
NBC "Game of the Week"																										
NBC Thanksgiving Game																										
ABC *Monday Night Football*																										
4Q Sports Total				41	10																					
SEC Championship Game																										
SEC-CFA Regular Game																										
SEC Thanksgiving Game																										
SEC Local/Conference Fee																										
SEC Sponsorship Total																										
TOTAL SPORTS				41	10																					
EVENTS																										
McDonald's Golf Classic																				1						
Daytime Emmy Awards																						23				
Country Music Awards																			32							
Garth Brooks Special																			12							
Michael Bolton Sponsorship																										
May Event Print																			17			18				
JC Penney LPGA Golf																										
Harvey Penick Special																							1			
Diners Club Golf																										
TOTAL EVENTS																			61	18	17	41	1			
CONTINUITY																										
Prime			53			53				53		54		34	35		35				35					35
May Event Prime Scatter																			29		28					
Late Night			6	5						5				3					3		4					
Syndication			14			14				13				8			8				8					8
Cable			13			14				14				11			11				11					
TOTAL CONTINUITY			86	126	15	86	81			85		68		56	57		54		86	28	86		58			43
Integration-to-date																										
Total Diet Plan			86	126	15	86	81			85		68		56	57		54		147	46	103	127	59			43
A18-49 GRPs/Week																										
Amount Over Budget																										
A18-49 GRPs/Month	227					167				238				167				477					102			
A18-49 GRPs/Quarter	632													746												

Saab 9–5's Media Plan

The 9–5 model represented Saab's entry in the luxury category and was designed to compete against well-known high-equity brands, including Mercedes, BMW, Volvo, Lexus, and Infiniti.[44] Despite being a unique automobile company—with a

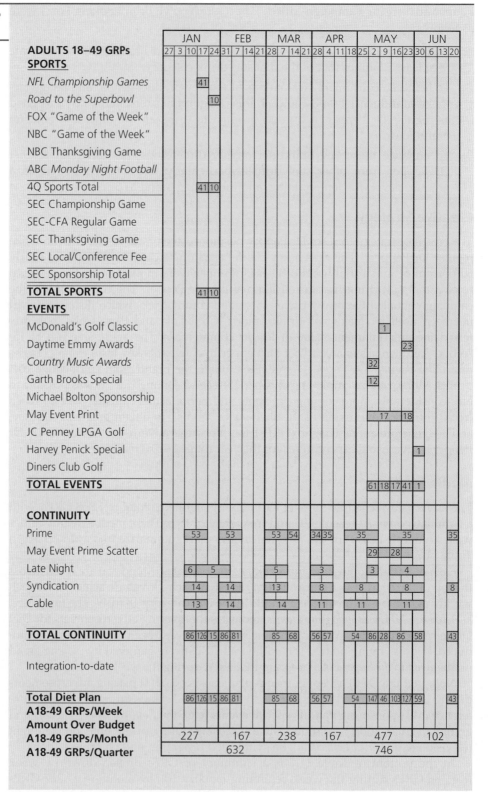

table 11.7

Media Plan for Diet Dr Pepper (*Continued*)

	JUL					AUG				SEP				OCT					NOV				DEC			
ADULTS 18–49 GRPs	27	4	11	18	25	1	8	15	22	29	5	12	19	26	3	10	17	24	31	7	14	21	28	5	12	19
SPORTS																										
NFL Championship Games																										
Road to the Superbowl																										
FOX "Game of the Week"														28							24			25		
NBC "Game of the Week"																13				22				20		
NBC Thanksgiving Game																						22				
ABC *Monday Night Football*																22		20	10	24						25
4Q Sports Total														28		35		20	10	46	24	22		45		25
SEC Championship Game																								33		
SEC-CFA Regular Game															8											
SEC Thanksgiving Game																						6				
SEC Local/Conference Fee																										
SEC Sponsorship Total															8							6		33		
TOTAL SPORTS														28	8	35		20	10	46	24	28		78		25
EVENTS																										
McDonald's Golf Classic																										
Daytime Emmy Awards																										
Country Music Awards																										
Garth Brooks Special																										
Michael Bolton Sponsorship																										
May Event Print																										
JC Penney LPGA Golf																										
Harvey Penick Special																										
Diners Club Golf																										
TOTAL EVENTS																										
CONTINUITY																										
Prime	25				25				26																	
May Event Prime Scatter																										
Late Night																										
Syndication																										
Cable																										
TOTAL CONTINUITY	25				25				26																	
Integration-to-date																										
Total Diet Plan	25				25				26					28	8	35		20	10	46	24	28		78		15
A18-49 GRPs/Week																										
Amount Over Budget																										
A18-49 GRPs/Month	75					51				52				91					108				103			
A18-49 GRPs/Quarter	**178**													**302**												

respected background in airplane manufacturing—Saab had done relatively little to enhance its brand image in the United States. Saab suffered from a low level of consumer awareness and a poorly defined brand image.

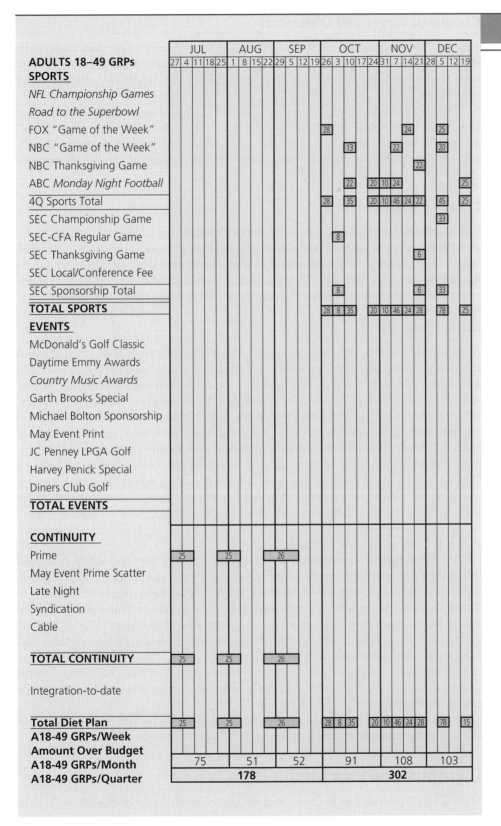

Campaign Target and Objectives

Prior to the introduction of the 9–5 model, Saab's product mix had historically attracted younger consumers. Achieving success for its new luxury sedan required that the advertising appeal to upscale families and relatively affluent older consumers.

The introductory advertising campaign was designed to achieve the following objectives: (1) generate excitement for the new 9–5 model line; (2) increase overall awareness for the Saab name; (3) encourage consumers to visit dealers and test-drive the 9–5; and (4) produce retail sales of 11,000 units of the 9–5 during the introductory year.

Creative Strategy

The Saab 9–5 was positioned as a luxury automobile capable of delivering an ideal synthesis of performance and safety. Creative advertising executions portrayed Saab as a premium European luxury manufacturer and were designed to have a hint of mystery and wit. An intensive media campaign was needed to deliver the creative executions and achieve the company's three advertising objectives.

Media Strategy

An integrated media campaign was designed to generate high levels of reach and frequency among the target group of older and financially well-off consumers and ultimately to sell at retail 11,000 Saab 9–5 vehicles. The media schedule is presented in Table 11.8. It first will be noted that TV advertising started in January, which was before the 9–5's introduction in April. Network and cable TV advertising ran from mid-January through early February and then again throughout May following the 9–5's introduction. Notice that the initial network TV campaign accumulated 74 GRPs for each of three weeks (the weeks beginning January 19, January 26, and February 2) and that accompanying advertising on cable TV amassed 40 GRPs for each of these same three weeks. Following the 9–5's introduction, the May television schedule accumulated 95 and 60 GRPs, respectively, on network and cable TV. Or, in other words, a total of 620 television GRPs $[(95 \times 4) + (60 \times 4)]$ were purchased in May.

Table 11.8 further reveals that magazine advertising for the Saab 9–5 started in late January and continued for the remainder of the year without interruption. Various magazines were used to reach Saab's designated market for the 9–5. These included automotive magazines (e.g., *Car & Driver* and *Road & Track*), sports publications (e.g., *Ski* and *Tennis*), home magazines (e.g., *Martha Stewart Living* and *Architectural Digest*), business magazines (e.g., *Money, Forbes,* and *Working Women*), and general interest publications (e.g., *Time* and *New York Magazine*). National newspaper advertising in *USA Today* and the *Wall Street Journal* also ran throughout the year. And finally, Internet banner advertising ran continuously throughout the introductory year.

In sum, this was a highly successful media plan that achieved its objectives and led to a successful introduction of the Saab 9-5 luxury automobile.

Olympus Camera Media Plan

The camera business has become increasingly competitive and diverse with new players entering the industry on a regular basis.[45] Where at one time it was primarily Kodak, Canon, Olympus, and Nikon that dominated the industry, now firms such as Sony and Hewlett-Packard also compete for the buying public's camera purchases. The modern camera industry is now one of sophisticated consumer electronics rather than simply point-and-click devices. To transition the company's camera business into the broader world of consumer electronics successfully,

table 11.8

Media Plan for the Saab 9–5

<table>
<tr><th></th><th colspan="4">JAN</th><th colspan="4">FEB</th><th colspan="5">MAR</th><th colspan="4">APR</th><th colspan="5">MAY</th><th colspan="4">JUN</th></tr>
<tr><th></th><th>29</th><th>5</th><th>12</th><th>19</th><th>26</th><th>2</th><th>9</th><th>16</th><th>23</th><th>2</th><th>9</th><th>16</th><th>23</th><th>30</th><th>6</th><th>13</th><th>20</th><th>27</th><th>4</th><th>11</th><th>18</th><th>25</th><th>1</th><th>8</th><th>15</th><th>22</th></tr>
<tr><td>Network TV</td><td></td><td></td><td></td><td colspan="3">74 wk</td><td></td><td></td><td></td><td></td><td></td><td></td><td></td><td></td><td></td><td></td><td></td><td colspan="4">95 wk</td><td></td><td></td><td></td><td></td><td></td></tr>
<tr><td>Network Cable</td><td></td><td></td><td></td><td colspan="3">40 wk</td><td></td><td></td><td></td><td></td><td></td><td></td><td></td><td></td><td></td><td></td><td></td><td colspan="4">60 wk</td><td></td><td></td><td></td><td></td><td></td></tr>
<tr><td>Magazines</td><td></td><td></td><td></td><td></td><td colspan="22"></td></tr>
<tr><td>Newspapers</td><td colspan="26"></td></tr>
<tr><td>USA Today</td><td colspan="26"></td></tr>
<tr><td>3 PBW (2X)</td><td></td><td></td><td></td><td></td><td></td><td></td><td></td><td></td><td></td><td></td><td></td><td></td><td></td><td>1X</td><td></td><td>1X</td><td></td><td></td><td></td><td></td><td></td><td></td><td></td><td></td><td></td><td></td></tr>
<tr><td>SPBW (1X)</td><td></td><td></td><td></td><td></td><td></td><td></td><td></td><td></td><td></td><td></td><td></td><td></td><td></td><td></td><td>1X</td><td></td><td></td><td></td><td></td><td></td><td></td><td></td><td></td><td></td><td></td><td></td></tr>
<tr><td>PBW (12X)</td><td></td><td></td><td></td><td></td><td></td><td></td><td></td><td></td><td></td><td></td><td></td><td></td><td></td><td></td><td></td><td></td><td></td><td></td><td></td><td></td><td></td><td></td><td></td><td></td><td></td><td></td></tr>
<tr><td>T Page (58X)</td><td></td><td>1X</td><td></td><td>1X</td><td>1X</td><td>1X</td><td></td><td>1X</td><td></td><td>2X</td><td>2X</td><td>2X</td><td>2X</td><td>2X</td><td>2X</td><td>2X</td><td>2X</td><td>2X</td><td>1X</td><td>1X</td><td></td><td>1X</td><td></td><td>1X</td><td></td><td>1X</td></tr>
<tr><td>1/4 PBW (8X)</td><td></td><td></td><td></td><td></td><td></td><td></td><td></td><td></td><td></td><td></td><td></td><td>4X</td><td>2X</td><td>2X</td><td></td><td></td><td></td><td></td><td></td><td></td><td></td><td></td><td></td><td></td><td></td><td></td></tr>
<tr><td>Wall Street Jrnl</td><td colspan="26"></td></tr>
<tr><td>3 PBW (2X)</td><td></td><td></td><td></td><td></td><td></td><td></td><td></td><td></td><td></td><td></td><td></td><td></td><td></td><td>1X</td><td></td><td>1X</td><td></td><td></td><td></td><td></td><td></td><td></td><td></td><td></td><td></td><td></td></tr>
<tr><td>SPBW (1X)</td><td></td><td></td><td></td><td></td><td></td><td></td><td></td><td></td><td></td><td></td><td></td><td></td><td></td><td></td><td>1X</td><td></td><td></td><td></td><td></td><td></td><td></td><td></td><td></td><td></td><td></td><td></td></tr>
<tr><td>PBW (12X)</td><td></td><td></td><td></td><td></td><td></td><td></td><td></td><td></td><td></td><td></td><td></td><td></td><td></td><td></td><td></td><td></td><td></td><td></td><td></td><td></td><td></td><td></td><td></td><td></td><td></td><td></td></tr>
<tr><td>4 col x 14" (63X)</td><td></td><td>1X</td><td>1X</td><td></td><td>1X</td><td>1X</td><td>1X</td><td></td><td>1X</td><td>2X</td><td>2X</td><td>2X</td><td>2X</td><td>2X</td><td>2X</td><td>2X</td><td>2X</td><td>2X</td><td>1X</td><td>1X</td><td>1X</td><td>1X</td><td>1X</td><td>1X</td><td>1X</td><td>1X</td></tr>
<tr><td>4 col x 8" (8X)</td><td></td><td></td><td></td><td></td><td></td><td></td><td></td><td></td><td></td><td></td><td></td><td>2X</td><td>4X</td><td>2X</td><td></td><td></td><td></td><td></td><td></td><td></td><td></td><td></td><td></td><td></td><td></td><td></td></tr>
<tr><td>Interactive</td><td colspan="26"></td></tr>
</table>

<table>
<tr><th></th><th colspan="4">JUL</th><th colspan="5">AUG</th><th colspan="4">SEP</th><th colspan="4">OCT</th><th colspan="5">NOV</th><th colspan="4">DEC</th></tr>
<tr><th></th><th>29</th><th>6</th><th>13</th><th>20</th><th>27</th><th>3</th><th>10</th><th>17</th><th>24</th><th>31</th><th>7</th><th>14</th><th>21</th><th>28</th><th>5</th><th>12</th><th>19</th><th>26</th><th>2</th><th>9</th><th>16</th><th>23</th><th>30</th><th>7</th><th>14</th><th>21</th></tr>
<tr><td>Network TV</td><td colspan="26"></td></tr>
<tr><td>Network Cable</td><td colspan="26"></td></tr>
<tr><td>Magazines</td><td colspan="26"></td></tr>
<tr><td>Newspapers</td><td colspan="26"></td></tr>
<tr><td>USA Today</td><td colspan="26"></td></tr>
<tr><td>3 PBW (2X)</td><td colspan="26"></td></tr>
<tr><td>SPBW (1X)</td><td colspan="26"></td></tr>
<tr><td>PBW (12X)</td><td></td><td></td><td></td><td></td><td></td><td></td><td></td><td></td><td></td><td></td><td></td><td></td><td></td><td>1X</td><td>3X</td><td>2X</td><td></td><td></td><td></td><td></td><td>3X</td><td>1X</td><td>2X</td><td></td><td></td><td></td></tr>
<tr><td>T Page (58X)</td><td></td><td>1X</td><td>1X</td><td>1X</td><td>1X</td><td>1X</td><td>1X</td><td>1X</td><td>1X</td><td>1X</td><td>1X</td><td>1X</td><td>2X</td><td>1X</td><td></td><td>1X</td><td>2X</td><td>2X</td><td>2X</td><td>2X</td><td></td><td>1X</td><td>1X</td><td>2X</td><td>2X</td><td>1X</td></tr>
<tr><td>1/4 PBW (8X)</td><td colspan="26"></td></tr>
<tr><td>Wall Street Jrnl</td><td colspan="26"></td></tr>
<tr><td>3 PBW (2X)</td><td colspan="26"></td></tr>
<tr><td>SPBW (1X)</td><td colspan="26"></td></tr>
<tr><td>PBW (12X)</td><td></td><td></td><td></td><td></td><td></td><td></td><td></td><td></td><td></td><td></td><td></td><td></td><td></td><td>1X</td><td>2X</td><td>2X</td><td>1X</td><td></td><td></td><td></td><td>2X</td><td>1X</td><td>2X</td><td>1X</td><td></td><td></td></tr>
<tr><td>4 col x 14" (63X)</td><td>1X</td><td>2X</td><td>1X</td><td>1X</td><td>1X</td><td>1X</td><td>1X</td><td>1X</td><td>1X</td><td>1X</td><td></td><td>1X</td><td>2X</td><td>1X</td><td>1X</td><td>1X</td><td>1X</td><td>2X</td><td>2X</td><td>2X</td><td>1X</td><td>1X</td><td>1X</td><td>1X</td><td>2X</td><td>1X</td></tr>
<tr><td>4 col x 8" (8X)</td><td colspan="26"></td></tr>
<tr><td>Interactive</td><td colspan="26"></td></tr>
</table>

Legend:

1X, 2X, etc. = Number of insertions per week placed in *USA Today* or WSJ (1X = one insertion, 2X - two insertions, etc.)
3 PBW = 3 pages black & white magazine ad
SPBW = Spread page B&W (ad runs across 2 pages like a centerfold)

PBW = 1-page black & white
T Page = An odd shaped add placement
1/4 PBW = 1/4 page B&W
Interactive = Internet banner ad placed on *The Wall Street Journal Interactive Edition*

executives at Olympus realized the company would need to implement a marcom program that would change both consumer and retailer perceptions of Olympus—a change from the belief that Olympus is merely a point-and-click camera maker to the perception that it is a major player in designer electronics. The shift began in earnest when Olympus asked The Martin Agency to develop a media campaign for introducing two new brands, the Stylus Verve and the m:robe.

Campaign Objectives

The first product, Stylus Verve, had all of the features of Olympus' flagship Stylus Digital line, but was uniquely designed and available in six colors. To make the jump even more substantial, Olympus introduced a wholly new product to the market in early 2005, the m:robe—a combination MP3 player and camera. The Martin Agency's job was to create a media plan that would serve to introduce the Stylus Verve and the m:robe successfully and simultaneously to facilitate the shift in marketplace perceptions that Olympus was a maker of designer electronics items and not merely cameras.

The Strategy

A high-impact, event-driven media strategy was developed to meet these objectives. Overall, the idea was to place the Olympus message in media that people talk about, that generate buzz, that yield free media coverage, that have longevity, and that are influential. Moreover, it was important that the selected media reach both men and women and be suitable for Olympus' key, fourth-quarter selling season running from October through December.

Media and Vehicles

TV programs were selected to deliver high viewership and to satisfy the criteria previously mentioned. Considered especially suitable were high-impact and widely viewed programs that aired only once a year. Ads for the Stylus Verve were placed in programs such as the *World Series,* the *American Music Awards, Macy's Thanksgiving Day Parade,* and *Dick Clark's Rockin' New Years Eve.* The m:robe was launched in the ultimate high-profile program, the *Super Bowl,* followed by *The Grammys.* Network cable added frequency and continuity to the network TV schedule. Ad placements on cable channels E! and ESPN complimented and extended the entertainment and sporting events. The addition of programs such as *Sex and the City* and *Friends* rounded out the TV schedule and further served to generate buzz for the Verve and m:robe.

In addition to TV spots, magazine issues such as *People*'s "Sexiest Man Alive," *Sports Illustrated*'s "Sportsman of the Year," and *Time*'s "Person of the Year" carried four-page gatefold ads for the Stylus Verve. These special magazine issues reach millions of consumers who were exposed to ad messages in a positive context. Moreover, these special issues have a "life of their own" when people talk, for example, about whether they agree with *People*'s choice of the sexiest man alive. As part of the m:robe launch, the biggest magazine issue of the year, *Sports Illustrated*'s "Swimsuit" edition, was utilized, along with *Rolling Stone*'s "Richest Rock Stars" issue, a perfect tie in with the music aspect of the product.

Out of home (OOH) also played a role using a combination of impact units purchased within four key Olympus markets and in-theater advertising in the top-25 markets. Impactful OOH units were selected based on high-traffic areas, as well as proximity to key Olympus retailers. A five-week flight of in-theater advertising starting Thanksgiving weekend capitalized on the heavy holiday movie traffic. Additionally, an online element of highly visible brand placements and sponsorships was developed for both the Stylus Verve and the m:robe. The chosen sites had to be contextually relevant for the target and included high-traffic areas on the Web featuring entertainment and sporting events—for example, E! Online for entertainment and Fox Sports for its coverage of World Series baseball and the National Football League.

The online advertising element for the m:robe brand went beyond just Web site advertising and entered a whole new dimension. With the m:robe propelling Olympus into the consumer electronics category, the online element needed to express the m:robe experience and help define its points of differentiation from competitive brands while helping support ad placements during the Super Bowl. To achieve these objectives, a nonbranded interactive Web site was developed featuring the pop-locking dance moves that would later be viewed as the focus of the Olympus Super Bowl spots. (Pop locking is a stylized form of dancing in which people or animated characters tense up, or pop their muscles quickly, and lock out their joints. The "robot" dance is one form of pop locking.) The interactive Web site allowed users to make the Web site characters pop lock or see themselves pop lock by uploading a picture of their head to the site. This Web site was

Table 11.9

Media Plan for Olympus' Stylus Verve and m:robe Brands

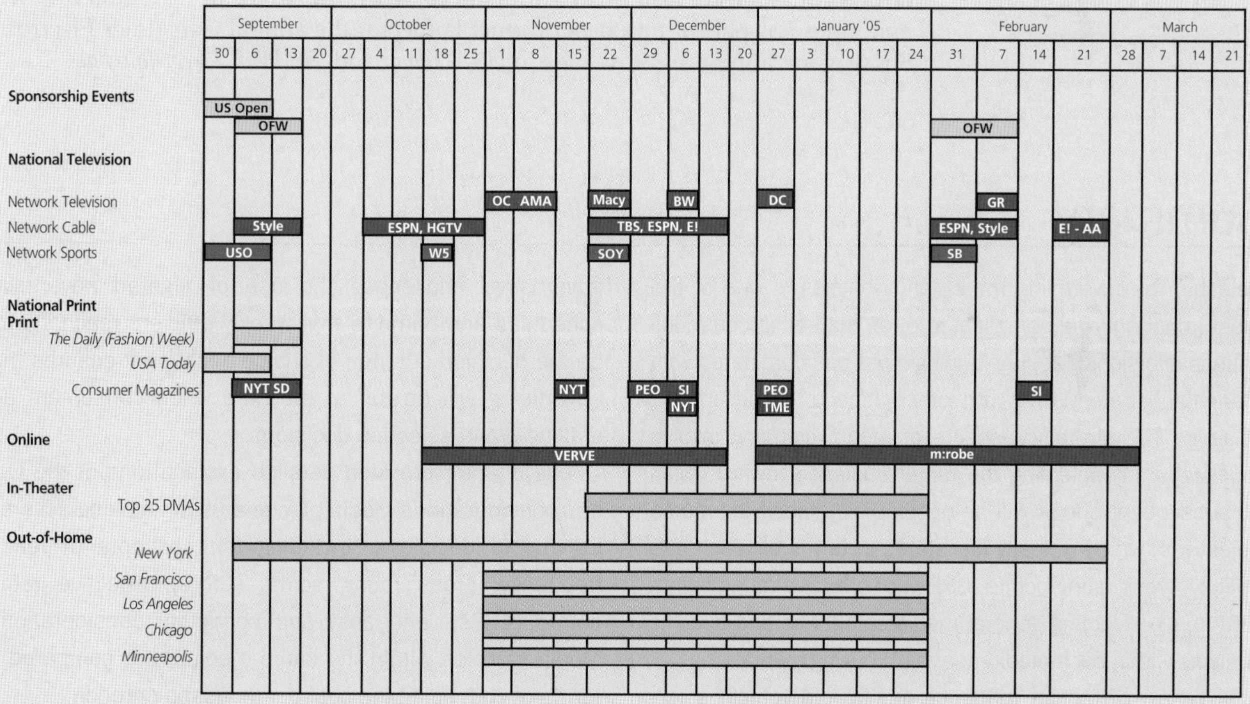

Television Event Programs

US Open on CBS
Style Network - Fashion Week Coverage (Sept and Feb)
ESPN: NFL and high-profile programming
HGTV: High-profile prime and weekend day
World Series Game #3
The OC Premiere
American Music Awards
Macy's Parade
Sports Illustrated Sportsman of the Year on FOX
Barbara Walter's 25 Most Intruiging People
Dick Clark's Rockin New Year's Eve
Super Bowl coverage on ESPN
Super Bowl
Grammy Awards
Academy Awards on E!
TBS: *Seinfeld, Friends, Everybody Loves Raymond, Sex and the City*
ESPN: NFL and high-profile programming
E! / Style bonus: Entertainment/high-profile programming

Newspapers and Consumer Magazines

NYT = *New York Times*
SD = *Time Style & Design*
PEO = *People Magazine*
SI = *Sports Illustrated*
TME = *Time Magazine*

passed along to friends and family, getting picked up on blogs and other Web sites in the process.

Table 11.9 presents a flowchart of the integrated media plan for Olympus' Stylus Verve and m:robe brands. Because the plan was not bought specifically in terms of generating designated levels of gross ratings, no point totals are presented. Note the diversity of media used (sponsored events, national TV, print, online, in-theater, and OOH) and the various vehicles used in each medium.

Results

The Stylus Verve advertising campaign launched during the US Tennis Open in August and concluded with New Years. During this period, unaided awareness of Olympus increased by 23 percent. The advertising also contributed to an increase in consumers believing that Olympus was trendy and innovative. The m:robe launch raised awareness of Olympus as a player in the digital music category from 0 percent to 5 percent, which was on par with the more established iRiver brand; moreover, 20 percent of the respondents to an advertising tracking study indicated that they believe Olympus offers good quality features. This compares favorably with Apple's iPod score of 17 percent on this same feature. Retailer perceptions were also greatly influenced when the Super Bowl media buy was announced as part of m:robe's product launch at the annual Consumer Electronic Show, generating press coverage in *USA Today* and *The Wall Street Journal.*

Summary

Selection of advertising media and vehicles is one of the most important and complicated of all marketing communications decisions. Media planning must be coordinated with marketing strategy and with other aspects of advertising strategy. The strategic aspects of media planning involve four steps: (1) selecting the target audience toward which all subsequent efforts will be directed; (2) specifying media objectives, which typically are stated in terms of reach, frequency, gross rating points (GRPs), or effective rating points (ERPs); (3) selecting general media categories and specific vehicles within each medium; and (4) buying media.

A variety of factors influence media and vehicle selection; most important are target audience, cost, and creative considerations. Media planners select media vehicles by identifying those that will reach the designated target audience, satisfy budgetary constraints, and be compatible with and enhance the advertiser's creative message. There are numerous ways to schedule media insertions over time, but media planners have typically used some form of pulsed or flighted schedule whereby advertising is on at times, off at others, but never continuous. The principle of recency, also referred to as the shelf-space model of advertising, challenges the use of flighted advertising schedules and purports that weekly efficient reach should be the decision criterion of choice because it ensures that advertising will be run at the time when consumers are making brand selection decisions.

The chapter provided detailed explanations of the various considerations media planners use in making advertising media decisions, including the concepts of reach, frequency, gross rating points (GRPs), effective rating points (ERPs), and cost and continuity considerations. Media vehicles within the same medium are compared in terms of cost using the cost-per-thousand criterion.

The chapter included a detailed discussion of a computerized media-selection model. This model requires information about vehicle cost, ratings, maximum number of insertions, and a budget constraint and then maximizes an objective function subject to that budget. Optimization criteria include maximizing reach (1+), effective reach (3+), frequency, or GRPs.

The chapter concluded with descriptions of media plans for Diet Dr Pepper, the Saab 9–5, and the Stylus Verve and m:robe brands of Olympus cameras.

Discussion Questions

1. Why is target audience selection the critical first step in formulating a media strategy?
2. Compare and contrast TRPs and GRPs as media selection criteria.
3. Why is reach also called net coverage or unduplicated audience?
4. A television advertising schedule produced the following vehicle frequency distribution:

f	Percentage *f*	Percentage *f*+
0	31.5	100.0
1	9.3	68.5
2	7.1	59.2
3	6.0	52.1
4	5.2	46.1
5	4.6	40.9
6	4.1	36.3
7	3.7	32.2
8	3.4	28.5
9	3.1	25.1
10+	22.0	22.0

   a. What is the reach for this advertising schedule?
   b. What is the effective reach?
   c. How many GRPs does this schedule generate?
   d. What is the frequency for this schedule?
5. Assume that the TV advertising schedule in Question 4 cost $2 million and generated 240 million gross impressions. What are the CPM and CPP?
6. A publication called the *LNA Ad $ Summary* (*LNA* standing for *Leading National Advertisers*) is an invaluable source for determining how much money brands invest in advertising. Go to your library and find the most recent version of *LNA*. Identify the advertising expenditures and the media used in advertising the following brands: Mountain Dew, Pantene shampoo, and Nike footwear.
7. With reference to the three-exposure hypothesis, explain the difference between three exposures to an advertising message versus three exposures to an advertising vehicle.
8. When an advertiser uses the latter, what implicit assumption is that advertiser making?
9. Describe in your own words the fundamental logic underlying the principle of recency (or what also is referred to as the shelf-space model of advertising). Is this model always the best model to apply in setting media allocations over time?
10. A TV program has a rating of 17.6. With approximately 112.8 million television households in the United States as of 2008, what is that program's CPM if a 30-second commercial costs $600,000? Now assume that an advertiser's target audience consists only of people ages 25 to 54, which constitutes 62 percent of the program's total audience. What is the CPM-TM in this case?
11. Which is more important for an advertiser: maximizing reach or maximizing frequency? Explain in detail.
12. Reach will be lower for an advertised brand if the entire advertising budget during a four-week period is devoted to advertising exclusively on a single program than if the same budget is allocated among a variety of TV programs. Why?
13. Following are the ratings and number of ad insertions on five cable TV programs designated as C1 through C5: C1 (rating = 7, insertions = 6); C2 (rating = 4, insertions = 12); C3 (rating = 3, insertions = 20); C4 (rating = 5, insertions = 10); C5 (rating = 6, insertions = 15). How many GRPs would be obtained from this cable TV advertising schedule?
14. Assume that in Canada there are 30 million TV households. A particular prime-time TV program aired at 9 PM and had a *rating* of 18.5 and a 32 *share.* At the 9 PM airtime, how many TV sets were tuned into this or another program? (Hint: Ratings are based on total households, whereas share is based on just the households that have their TV sets on at a particular time, in this case at 9 PM. Because the numerator value remains constant in both the calculation of ratings and share values, by simple algebraic manipulation you can determine from the rating information the number of households with their sets on.)

End Notes

1. "Bet on Advertisers, Instead," *The Wall Street Journal*, February 1, 2008, C12.
2. Super Bowl XLII, which resulted in underdog New York Giants beating the undefeated (at the time) New England Patriots drew a record audience with more than 97 million viewers. With a cost of $270,000 per 30-second commercial, this equates to a cost-per-thousand (CPM) of $27.84. Information on audience size is from Rebecca Dana, "Fox Scores on Record-Breaking Night," *The Wall Street Journal*, February 5, 2008, B3.
3. Bradley Johnson, "CFOs Cringe At Price, But Bowl Delivers the Masses," *Advertising Age*, January 29, 2007, 8.
4. Rob Frydlewicz, "Missed Super Bowl? Put Your Bucks Here," *Advertising Age*, January 30, 1995, 18.
5. Joe Mantese, "Majority Prefer Super Bowl Ads, Socializing vs. the Game Itself," *MediaDailyNews*, February 7, 2005.
6. Thom Forbes, "Consumer Central: The Media Focus Is Changing—And So Is the Process," *Agency*, winter 1998, 38.
7. Karen Whitehill King and Leonard N. Reid, "Selecting Media for National Accounts: Factors of Importance to Agency Media Specialists," *Journal of Current Issues and Research in Advertising* 19 (fall 1997), 55–64.
8. Kate Maddox, "Media Planners in High Demand," *BtoB*, November 8, 2004, 24; Ave Butensky, "Hitting the Spot," *Agency*, winter 1998, 26.
9. Kent M. Lancaster, "Optimizing Advertising Media Plans Using ADOPT on the Microcomputer," working paper, University of Illinois, December 1987, 2–3. (Note that in the last line of this quote Lancaster actually used 30 rather than 20 possible insertions. I have changed it to 20 so as not to create confusion with the earlier reference to "30 feasible publications.")
10. Laura Freeman, "Taking Apart Media," *Agency*, winter 2001, 20–25.
11. Ibid., 22.
12. Ibid., 23.
13. Roland Jones, "Smart's Fortwo Aiming for Big U.S. Sales," November 21, 2007, http://www.msnbc.msn.com/id/21882844 (accessed February 4, 2008).
14. Jared Gail, "First Drive: 2008 Smart Fortwo, Previews," http://www.caranddriver.com/previews/14310/first-drive-2008-smart-fortwo.html (accessed February 4, 2008).
15. Jones, "Smart's Fortwo Aiming for Big U.S. Sales."
16. Henry Assael and Hugh Cannon, "Do Demographics Help in Media Selection?" *Journal of Advertising Research* 19 (December 1979), 7–11; Hugh M. Cannon and G. Russell Merz, "A New Role for Psychographics in Media Selection," *Journal of Advertising* 9, no. 2 (1980), 33–36, 44.
17. Karen Whitehill KingLeonard N. Reid, and Wendy Macias, "Selecting Media for National Advertising Revisited: Criteria of Importance to Large-Company Advertising Managers," *Journal of Current Issues and Research in Advertising* 26 (spring 2004), 59–68.
18. This figure is based on extrapolating by 1.3 percent the number of TV households estimated by the Nielsen Company for 2008. Nielsen estimated 112.8 million TV households in the United States for 2008 and indicated that this number represented a 1.3 percent increase over 2007. We arrive at 114.5 million by assuming an additional increase of 1.3 percent in 2009. See "Nielsen Reports 1.3% Increase in U.S. Television Households for the 2007-2008 Season," http://www.nielsen.com/media/pr_070823.html (accessed February 4, 2008).
19. A quote from advertising consultant Alvin Achenbaum cited in B. G. Yovovich, "Media's New Exposures," *Advertising Age*, April 13, 1981, S7.
20. One study found that more than 80 percent of advertising agencies use effective reach as a criterion in media planning. See Peggy J. KreshelKent M. Lancaster, and Margaret A. Toomey, "How Leading Advertising Agencies Perceive Effective Reach and Frequency," *Journal of Advertising* 14, no. 3 (1985), 32–38.
21. Gerard J. Tellis, "Advertising Exposure, Loyalty, and Brand Purchase: A Two-Stage Model of Choice," *Journal of Marketing Research* 25 (May 1988), 134–144.
22. Herbert E. Krugman, "Why Three Exposures May Be Enough," *Journal of Advertising Research* 12, no. 6 (1972), 11–14.
23. This point is made especially forcefully by Hugh M. Cannon and Edward A. Riordan, "Effective Reach and Frequency: Does It Really Make Sense?" *Journal of Advertising Research* 34 (March/April 1994), 19–28.
24. Ibid., 24.
25. Adapted from "The Muscle in Multiple Media," *Marketing Communications*, December 1983, 25.
26. Cannon and Riordan, "Effective Reach and Frequency," 25–26. The following illustration is adapted from this source.
27. The original authors of this procedure referred to it as exposure value rather than exposure utility, but this use of *value* gets confused with a later use of *value*.
28. A procedure for estimating these values is available in Hugh M. CannonJohn D. Leckenby, and Avery Abernethy, "Beyond Effective Frequency: Evaluating Media Schedules Using Frequency Value Planning," *Journal of Advertising Research* 42 (November/December 2002), 33–47.
29. Erwin Ephron, "More Weeks, Less Weight: The Shelf-Space Model of Advertising," *Journal of Advertising Research* 35 (May/June 1995), 18–23. See also Ephron's various writings archived at his Web site, Ephron on Media (http://www.ephrononmedia.com).
30. Ibid., 5–18. See also John Philip Jones, "Single-Source Research Begins to Fulfill Its Promise," *Journal of Advertising Research* 35 (May/June 1995), 9–16; Lawrence D. Gibson, "What Can One TV Exposure Do?" *Journal of Advertising Research* 36 (March/April 1996), 9–18; and Kenneth A. Longman, "If Not Effective Frequency, Then What?" *Journal of Advertising Research* 37 (July/August 1997), 44–50.

31. Jones, "Single-Source Research Begins to Fulfill Its Promise." Despite these findings, which have had considerable impact on the advertising community, there is some counterevidence suggesting that Jones's research results are not solely the result of advertising exposure but in fact are correlated with sales promotion activity. In other words, what may appear to be the exclusive impact of successful advertising may actually be due at least in part to a brand's sales promotion activity (such as couponing or cents-off dealing) that takes place at the same time that advertising for the brand is running on television. Until research evidence is more definitive on this matter, a reasonable conclusion is that Jones's measure of advertising effectiveness is interesting but perhaps simplistic in the absence of proper experimental or statistical controls for sales promotions, price changes, and other potential determinants of a brand's sales volume. For counterperspectives to Jones's claims, see Gary SchroederBruce C. Richardson, and Avu Sankaralingam, "Validating STAS Using BehaviorScan," *Journal of Advertising Research* 37 (July/August 1997), 33–43. For another challenge, see Gerard J. Tellis and Doyle L. Weiss, "Does TV Advertising Really Affect Sales? The Role of Measures, Models, and Data Aggregation," *Journal of Advertising* 24 (fall 1995), 1–12.
32. Erwin Ephron, "What Is Recency?" Ephron on Media, http://www.ephrononmedia.com.
33. Ephron, "More Weeks, Less Weight: The Shelf-Space Model of Advertising," 19.
34. Ibid., 20.
35. A quote from Joanne Burke, senior vice president worldwide media research director, TN Media, New York, in Laurie Freeman, "Effective Weekly Planning Gets a Boost," *Advertising Age,* July 24, 1995, S8, S9.
36. Erwin Ephron, "Recency Planning," *Journal of Advertising Research* 37 (July/August 1997), 61–65.
37. Ibid., 61.
38. For elaboration on these points, see Gerard J. Tellis, "Effective Frequency: One Exposure or Three Factors?" *Journal of Advertising Research* 37 (July/August 1997), 75–80.
39. This analogy is adapted from Charles H. Patti and Charles F. Frazer, *Advertising: A Decision-Making Approach* (Hinsdale, Ill.: Dryden Press, 1988), 369.
40. This name, although hypothetical, was actually borrowed from a safety campaign launched a few years ago that was aimed at young drivers to educate them about SUV driving safety. For example, because SUVs have a higher center of gravity than passenger cars, there is a greater risk of rollover resulting from speeding, abrupt maneuvers, aggressiveness, and so on. An "H" has been added to the Esuvee name to signify a hybrid SUV.
41. To construct Table 11.5, magazine audience sizes were based on the larger of the estimated audience sizes provided by Simmons and MRI. Figures were obtained from *Marketer's Guide to Media: 2004,* vol. 27 (New York: VNU Business Publications USA, 2004), 164–168. Because many of the readers of these magazines do not satisfy the income requirement of $45,000 or are not within the 18–49 age category targeted for the Esuvee-H, each magazine's total audience size was arbitrarily reduced by 50 percent prior to being divided by the target audience size of 26.8 million.
42. The program is ADplus, which was developed by Kent Lancaster and is distributed by Telmar Information Services Corp., 470 Park Ave. South, 15th Floor, New York, NY 10016 (phone: 212-725-3000). It is noteworthy that a newer version of ADplus is available from Telmar under the name InterMix. However, when I ran the program using the database provided in Table 11.5, it generated a perverse solution (i.e., a solution I know to be wrong). Requests were made of the program developer, Kent Lancaster, to aid me in determining why the program generated an inappropriate solution. Unfortunately, he was unable to be of assistance. Accordingly, my faith in InterMix is diminished and I have chosen to use its predecessor, ADplus. Newer versions of ADplus, or of InterMix, may generate somewhat different solutions than are presented here (see Table 11.6). Professor Lancaster informed me that the InterMix uses "heuristic procedures," and apparently the "heuristics" have changed over time. In any event, the results presented in Table 11.6 are for illustration purposes only and are intended simply to explain how the various media diagnostics (reach, frequency, etc.) are generated.
43. The following descriptions are based on a summary of a Diet Dr Pepper's advertising campaign prepared by Young & Rubicam. Appreciation for these materials is extended to Chris Wright-Isak and John T. O'Brien.
44. Appreciation is extended to Dr. Jack Lindgren of the University of Virginia for facilitating my access to this media plan and to the Martin Agency (Richmond, VA) for making this plan available. The description provided herein is an adaptation of the Martin Agency's media plan for the Saab 9-5.
45. Appreciation is extended to Dr. Lauren Tucker of the Martin Agency (Richmond, VA) for facilitating my access to this media plan. I also greatly appreciate the assistance of Ms. Lori Baker of the Martin Agency in providing me with the plan discussed in this section. The description provided herein is an adaptation of the plan provided by Ms. Baker in April 2005.

12

Traditional Advertising Media

Television as an advertising medium has undergone rather dramatic changes in the past decade or so. The average television household now has upward of 90 or more TV channels from which to choose, which means that advertisements simply do not reach the large numbers of consumers they once did. Beyond this audience fractionalization, people have many more entertainment options to distract them from watching TV. Then to complicate matters for advertisers further, the number of households owning digital video recorders (DVRs) is continually increasing, and the owners of these devices often use them to skip completely or fast-forward through commercials. Finally, the cost of TV advertising remains high, which means that ads placed on television must be effective in order to yield a positive return on investment (ROI).

Recent studies have concluded, however, that TV advertising is declining in effectiveness. Research conducted by the Association of National Advertisers in conjunction with Forrester Research surveyed over 100 national advertisers who invest heavily in TV advertising. Over three quarters of the surveyed executives are of the opinion that traditional TV advertising has declined in effectiveness, and many intend to reduce their TV advertising budgets in the near future.[1]

A study conducted by McKinsey & Company, the famous global consulting firm, concludes that traditional TV advertising will be only one third as effective in 2010 as it was in 1990.[2] The study reports that ad spending on prime-time TV over the past decade increased by nearly 40 percent while the number of viewers decreased by about 50 percent, the result being a much higher cost per viewer reached.

A final important study—referred to as the Deutsche Bank report—presented data showing that a high percentage of the TV advertisements for mature brands in the consumer packaged goods (CPG) category do not yield positive ROIs.[3] The study used marketing-mix modeling, which was briefly described in Chapter 2, to assess TV advertising's short- and long-term effectiveness for 23 well-known CPG brands—e.g., Coca-Cola Classic, Campbell's soup, Heinz ketchup, Swiffer, Mach3 razors and blades, and Crest Whitestrips. Results indicated that only 5 of the 23 brands examined (22 percent) enjoyed positive ROI from TV advertising in the short term (i.e., less than one year), whereas 12 of the 23 brands (52 percent) yielded positive ROIs in the long term. Newer brands and those representing meaningful new products were substantially more likely to yield positive returns than were

© AP Images

mature brands. That new brands perform better than mature brands should come as no surprise in view of the previous discussion in Chapter 10, where it was emphasized that TV advertising generally is effective only when the advertising is persuasive and provides distinctive, newsworthy information, such as when introducing new brands.

The takeaway from these research reports should not be that television advertising is necessarily a wasted investment. The message, instead, is that advertisers must have something important to say about their brands and that commercials must be presented in an attention-getting, creative fashion if there is to be a reasonable likelihood that investments in TV commercials will deliver positive ROIs.

Chapter Objectives

After reading this chapter you should be able to:

1. Describe the four major traditional advertising media (newspapers, magazines, radio, and television).
2. Discuss newspaper advertising and its strengths and limitations.
3. Evaluate magazine advertising and its strengths and limitations.
4. Describe radio advertising and its strengths and limitations.
5. Discuss television advertising and its strengths and limitations.
6. Appreciate the research methods that are used for each ad medium to determine the size of the audience exposed to advertising vehicles.

>>Marcom Insight:

Is TV Advertising Declining in Effectiveness?

Introduction

This chapter focuses on the four major mass advertising media: newspapers, magazines, radio, and television. Separate sections focus on each of these four major media, with primary emphasis devoted to exploring each medium's strengths and limitations and to explaining the research methods that are used for measuring the number of people who are exposed to advertising vehicles within each medium.

Advertising in the United States in these four media totaled approximately $190 billion in a recent year. Television commanded nearly 42 percent of these total expenditures, newspapers approximately 31 percent, magazines (including business-to-business magazines) about 16 percent, and radio slightly over 11 percent.[4]

Some Preliminary Comments

It is important to recognize that no advertising medium is always best. The value or worth of a medium depends on the circumstances confronting a brand at a particular time: its advertising objective, the target market toward which this objective is aimed, and the available budget. An analogy will clarify this point. Suppose someone asked you, "What type of restaurant is best?" You likely would have difficulty offering a single answer because you would recognize that what is best depends on your particular needs on a specific occasion. In some circumstances price and speed of service are of the essence, and fast-food restaurants like McDonald's would win out. On other occasions ambiance is the most important consideration, and a classy French restaurant might be considered ideal. In yet another situation you may be looking for a balance between dining elegance and a reasonable price and favor a middle-of-the-road eating establishment. In sum, there is no such thing as a universally "best" restaurant.

The same is true of advertising media. Which medium is "best" depends entirely on the advertiser's objectives, the creative needs, the competitive challenge, and the budget available. The best medium, or combination of media, is determined by conducting a careful examination of the advertised brand's needs and resources.

The following presentation of ad media progresses in the following order: first covered are the two print media, newspapers and magazines. Then examined are the broadcast media, radio and television. TV receives the most in-depth treatment because it commands the greatest amount of advertising dollars and because ongoing developments in this medium are the most dynamic.

Newspapers

Newspapers reach approximately 53 million U.S. households during the week and about 55 million on Sundays.[5] Fifty percent of all adults in the United States read a daily newspaper, and about 57 percent read a Sunday newspaper.[6] Newspapers historically were the leading advertising medium, but television surpassed newspapers as the medium that receives the greatest amount of advertising expenditures. This is partially attributable to the fact that newspaper readership has been on a constant decline for years.

Local advertising is clearly the mainspring of newspapers. However, newspapers have become more active in their efforts to increase national advertising. The Newspaper Advertising Bureau (NAB), a nonprofit sales and research organization, has facilitated these efforts. The NAB offers a variety of services that assist both newspapers and national advertisers by simplifying the task of buying newspaper space and by offering discounts that make newspapers a more attractive medium.

Buying Newspaper Space

A major problem in the past when buying newspaper space, especially for advertisers that purchased space from newspapers in many cities, was that newspaper page size and column space varied, which prevented an advertiser from preparing a single advertisement to fit every newspaper. Analogously, imagine what it would be like to advertise on television if, rather than having fixed 15-, 30-, or 60-second commercials for all networks and local stations, some local stations ran only 28-second commercials, while others preferred 23-second, 16-second, or 11-second commercials. Buying time on television would be nightmarish for advertisers. So it was in buying newspaper space until the advertising industry adopted a standardized system known as the **Standardized Advertising Unit (SAU) system,** which enables advertisers to purchase any one of *56 standard ad sizes* to fit the advertising publishing parameters of all U.S. newspapers.

Under this system, advertisers prepare advertisements and purchase space in terms of column widths and depth in inches. There are six column widths:

1 column:	$2\frac{1}{16}$ inches
2 columns:	$4\frac{1}{4}$ inches
3 columns:	$6\frac{7}{16}$ inches
4 columns:	$8\frac{5}{8}$ inches
5 columns:	$10\frac{13}{16}$ inches
6 columns:	13 inches

Space *depth* varies in size from 1 inch to 21 inches. Thus, an advertiser can purchase an ad as small as 1 inch by $2\frac{1}{16}$ inches or as large as 13 inches by 21 inches with numerous in-between combinations of widths and depths. A chosen size for a particular advertisement can then be run in newspapers throughout the country. Space rates can be compared from newspaper to newspaper and adjusted for circulation differences. For example, in a recent year the daily SAU column-inch rate for the *Chicago Tribune* (circulation: 576,100) was $731, whereas the same rate in the competitive *Chicago Sun-Times* (circulation: 382,800) was $499.[7] On the surface, the *Sun-Times* is cheaper than the *Tribune,* but when adjusted to a per-thousand-readers basis, the cost per thousand (CPM) of procuring a column inch in the *Tribune* is approximately $1.27 (i.e., $731 ÷ 576.1) compared with a CPM of about $1.30 (i.e., $499 ÷ 382.8) for the *Sun-Times.* Hence, it is actually slightly cheaper, on a CPM basis, to advertise in the *Tribune.* Of course, the advertiser must observe audience characteristics, newspaper image, and other factors when making an advertising decision rather than considering only cost.

The choice of an advertisement's position must also be considered when buying newspaper space. Space rates apply only to advertisements placed ROP (*run of press*), which means that the ad appears in any location, on any page, at the discretion of the newspaper. Premium charges may be assessed if an advertiser has a preferred space positioning, such as at the top of the page in the financial section. Premium charges, if assessed, are negotiated between the advertiser and the newspaper.

© Hugh Sitton/Stone/Getty Images

table 12.1

Newspaper Advertising's Strengths and Limitations

Strengths	Limitations
Audience in appropriate mental frame to process messages	Clutter
Mass audience coverage	Not a highly selective medium
Flexibility	Higher rates for occasional advertisers
Ability to use detailed copy	Mediocre reproduction quality
Timeliness	Complicated buying for national advertisers
	Changing composition of readers

Newspaper Advertising's Strengths and Limitations

As with all advertising media, newspaper advertising has various strengths and limitations (see Table 12.1).

Newspaper Advertising's Strengths

Because people read newspapers for news, they are in the *right mental frame to process advertisements* that present news of store openings, new products, sales, and so forth.

Mass audience coverage, or broad reach, is a second strength of newspaper advertising. Coverage is not restricted to specific socioeconomic or demographic groups but rather extends across all strata. However, newspaper readers on average are more economically upscale than television viewers. College graduates are more likely to read a newspaper than the population at large. Because economically advantaged consumers are comparatively light TV viewers, newspaper advertising provides a relatively inexpensive medium for reaching these consumers. Special-interest newspapers also reach large numbers of potential consumers. For example, the vast majority of college students read a campus newspaper. A recent survey revealed that 71 percent of college students had read at least one of the last five issues of their college newspaper.[8]

Flexibility is perhaps the greatest strength of newspapers. National advertisers can adjust copy to match the specific buying preferences and peculiarities of localized markets. Local advertisers can vary copy through in-paper inserts targeted to specific ZIP Codes. In addition, advertising copy can be placed in a newspaper section that is compatible with the advertised product. Retailers of wedding accessories advertise in the bridal section, providers of financial services advertise in the business section, sporting goods stores advertise in the sports section, and so forth. A second facet of newspaper flexibility is that this medium enables advertisers to design ads of many different sizes (56 in total); few size or length options are possible in other mass media.

The *ability to use detailed copy* is another of newspaper advertising's strengths. Detailed product information and extensive editorial passages are used in newspaper advertising to an extent unparalleled by any other medium.

Timeliness is the final significant strength of newspaper advertising. Short lead times (the time between placing an ad and having it run) permit advertisers to tie in advertising copy with local market developments or newsworthy events. Advertisers can develop copy or make copy changes quickly and thereby take advantage of dynamic marketplace developments.

Newspaper Advertising's Limitations

Clutter is a problem in newspapers, as it is in all of the other major media. A reader perusing a newspaper is confronted with many ads, all of which compete for the reader's limited time and only a subset of which receive the reader's attention. It is noteworthy, however, that a national survey of consumers revealed that they perceived newspapers as being significantly less cluttered with advertisements than television, radio, and magazines.[9]

A second limitation of newspaper advertising is that newspapers are *not a highly selective medium.* Newspapers are able to reach broad cross sections of people but, with few exceptions (such as campus newspapers), are unable to reach specific groups of consumers effectively. Media specialists consider newspapers to fare poorly in comparison to network television in efficiently targeting specific audiences.[10]

Occasional users of newspaper space (such as national advertisers who infrequently advertise in newspapers) pay higher rates than do heavy users (such as local advertisers) and have difficulty in securing preferred, non-ROP positions. In fact, newspapers' price lists (called *rate cards*) show higher rates for national than local advertisers.

Newspapers generally offer a *mediocre reproduction quality.* For this and other reasons, newspapers are not generally known to enhance a product's perceived quality, elegance, or snob appeal, as can magazines and television.

Buying difficulty is a particularly acute problem in the case of the national advertiser who wishes to secure newspaper space in multiple markets. On top of the high rates charged to national advertisers, each newspaper must be contacted individually. Fortunately, as mentioned previously, the NAB has made great strides toward facilitating the purchase of newspaper space by national advertisers.

A final significant problem with newspaper advertising involves the *changing composition of newspaper readers.* Although most everyone used to read a daily newspaper, readership has declined progressively during the past generation. The most faithful newspaper readers are individuals aged 45 and older, but the large and attractive group of consumers aged 30 to 44 are reading daily newspapers less frequently than ever.

Readership of the printed newspapers has declined, however it is noteworthy that all major newspapers have created Web sites that attract readers who do not pay for printed newspapers. Hence, actual readership of newspapers—the combination of electronic and print readership—is considerably higher than reported circulation levels for printed newspapers. Newspaper companies are increasing their advertising revenues by including search engines on their Web sites and then charging for advertisements that pop up alongside search results.[11]

Magazines

Although considered a mass medium, there are literally thousands of special-interest magazines, both consumer- and business-oriented, that appeal to audiences that manifest specific interests and lifestyles. In fact, Standard Rate and Data Service (now known simply as SRDS Media Solutions), a company that tracks information for the magazine industry (as well as for most other media), identifies well over 3,000 consumer magazines in dozens of specific categories, such as automotive (e.g., *Motor Trend*); general editorial (e.g., the *New Yorker*); sports (e.g., *Sports Illustrated*); and women's fashions, beauty, and grooming (e.g., *Glamour*). In addition to consumer magazines, thousands of other publications are classified as business magazines. Advertisers obviously have numerous options when selecting magazines to promote their products either to consumers or to businesspeople. Advertisers and media planners turn to SRDS (http://www.srds.com) to obtain information on standardized ad rates, contact information, reader profiles, and other information, which facilitates media planning and buying.

Buying Magazine Space

A number of factors influence the choice of magazine vehicles in which to advertise. Most important is selecting magazines that reach the type of people who constitute the advertiser's target market. However, because the advertiser typically can choose from several alternative vehicles to satisfy the target market objective, cost considerations also play an extremely important role.

Advertisers interested in using the magazine medium can acquire a wealth of demographic data about the composition of a magazine's readership. This information is provided in each magazine's *media kit* that is made available to ad agencies and prospective advertisers. Media kits can be found online for many magazines. For example, Figure 12.1 presents the demographic profile for *Golf Digest* magazine based on data presented by Condé Nast, which is the owner of this magazine and many others. The median age of *Golf Digest's* readership is 50.2 with a median household income of $131,445. It is apparent that this magazine has its greatest appeal among older, economically prosperous consumers.

Also presented in Figure 12.1 are specific breakdowns by age, education, occupation, and household income. For each demographic grouping, the first column contains audience size expressed in thousands, the second column presents percentage breakdowns for each demographic subgroup that represent that subgroup's composition of *Golf Digest's* total audience, and the last column indexes each percentage against that group's proportionate population representation. For example, 24 percent of *Golf Digest's* readers fall in the age group of 35–44, 60 percent graduated college, 53 percent are employed in professional and managerial positions, and 37 percent have household incomes of $150,000 or more. As mentioned, the last column in Figure 12.1 indexes each subgroup's composition of *Golf Digest's* readership against that group's proportionate population representation. For example, the 18–34 age group composes only 10 percent of *Golf Digest's* total

figure 12.1

***Golf Digest's* Demographic Profile**

	Audience (in thousands)	Composition (%)	Index
Total Aud.	2,651	100%	100
Age			
18–34	269	10%	69
35–44	631	24	85
45–54	793	30	94
55–64	603	23	125
65+	354	13	181
Median Age	50.2		
Education			
Graduated College	1,602	60%	107
Attended College	2,215	84	107
Occupation			
Top Management	591	22%	133
Professional/ Managerial	1,412	53	98
Household Income (HHI)			
$100,000+	2,088	79%	106
$150,000+	967	37	130
$250,000+	323	12	162
Median HHI	$131,445		

Source: Condé Nast, September 2006, http://www.condenastmediakit.com/gd/circulation.cfm (accessed March 3, 2008).

figure 12.2

Partial Rate Card for *Sports Illustrated* (Rate base = 3,150,000)

	4-Color	B&W
Full Page	$320,000	$194,350
2/3 Page	$262,315	$159,965
1/2 Page	$218,500	$133,170
1/3 Page	$145,820	$ 89,585
Second Cover Spread	$735,885	N/A
Third Cover	$352,015	N/A
Back Cover	$415,955	N/A

Source: *Sports Illustrated* Rate Card #66, effective January 14, 2008, http://sportsillustrated.cnn.com/adinfo/si/ratecard2008.pdf (accessed March 3, 2008).

audience, which is substantially below that group's proportionate representation in the total population. This underrepresentation is reflected in the 18–34 age group having an index of only 69. Comparatively, the 65+ age group (i.e., retirees who have a lot of time to play golf and read golf magazines) constitutes 13 percent of *Golf Digest's* total audience, but the high index of 181 reflects that this age group reads this particular magazine disproportionately more than its population representation.

Media kits also provide prospective advertisers with pertinent cost information in the form of *rate cards.* A partial rate card for *Sports Illustrated* magazine is presented in Figure 12.2. This card includes advertising rates for different page sizes (full page, two-thirds page, half page, one-third page, etc.), and for four-color and black-and-white (B&W) ads. For example, an advertiser would pay $320,000 to place a full-page, four-color ad in *Sports Illustrated* on a one-time (open) rate basis. However, as is typical in magazines' price policies, cumulative discounts are available based on the number of pages advertised in *Sports Illustrated* during 12 consecutive months. Cumulative quantity discounts provide clear incentives for advertisers to remain with a particular magazine.

Although every magazine has its own media kit, advertisers and their agencies do not have to contact each magazine to obtain them. SRDS compiles media kits and then makes them available (of course, for a fee) to advertisers and their agencies. Also, rate cards can be obtained online by simply conducting a search such as inputting "Sports Illustrated rate card" into Google. Information for each magazine (or *book* as they are referred to in the advertising industry) includes editorial features, rates, readership profiles, circulation, and contact information.

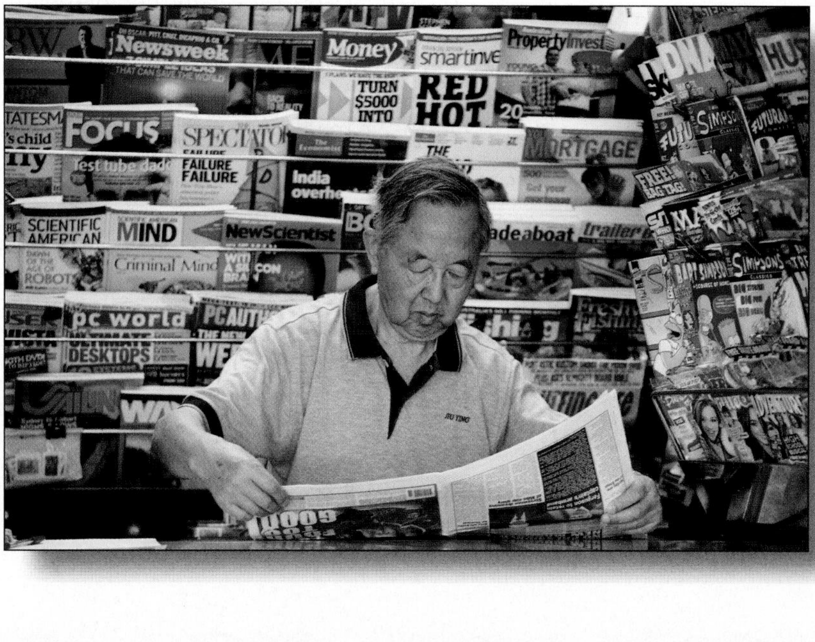

Advertisers use the CPM measure introduced in Chapter 11 and discussed earlier in the context of the newspaper medium to compare different magazine buys. CPM information for each magazine is available from two syndicated magazine services: Mediamark Research Inc. (MRI) and Simmons Market Research Bureau (SMRB). These services provide CPM figures for general reader categories (e.g., total men) and also break out CPMs for subgroups (e.g., men ages 18 to 49, male homeowners). These more specific subgroupings enable the advertiser to compare different magazine vehicles in terms of cost per thousand for reaching the target market (CPM-TM) rather than only in terms of gross CPMs. Cost-per-thousand data are useful in making magazine vehicle selection decisions, but many other factors must be taken into account.

Magazine Advertising's Strengths and Limitations

Magazine advertising too has both strengths and limitations, depending on the advertisers' needs and resources (see Table 12.2).

Magazine Advertising's Strengths

Some magazines reach *very large audiences.* For example, magazines like *Better Homes & Gardens, Reader's Digest, Sports Illustrated,* and *Time* have total audiences that exceed 25 million readers.

However, the ability to pinpoint specific audiences (termed *selectivity*) most distinguishes magazine advertising from other media. If a potential market exists for a product, there most likely is at least one periodical that reaches that market. Selectivity enables an advertiser to achieve effective, rather than wasted, exposure. This translates into more efficient advertising and lower costs per 1,000 target customers.

Magazines are also noted for their *long life.* Unlike other media, magazines often are used for reference and kept for weeks around the home (and in barber shops, and beauty salons, and dentists' and doctors' offices, etc.). Magazine subscribers sometimes pass along their copies to other readers, further extending a magazine's life.

In terms of qualitative considerations, magazines as an advertising medium are exceptional with regard to elegance, quality, beauty, prestige, and snob appeal. These features result from the *high level of reproduction quality* and from the surrounding editorial content that often transfers to the advertised product. For example, food items advertised in *Bon Appétit* always look elegant, furniture items in *Better Homes & Gardens* look tasteful, and clothing items in *Cosmopolitan* and *Gentlemen's Quarterly* (GQ) appear especially fashionable.

Magazines are also a particularly good source for providing *detailed product information* and for conveying this information with a *sense of authority.* That is, because the editorial content of magazines often includes articles that themselves represent a sense of insight, expertise, and credibility, the advertisements carried in these magazines convey a similar sense of authority, or correctness.

A final and especially notable feature of magazine advertising is its creative ability to get consumers *involved in ads* or, in a sense, to attract readers' interest and to engage them to think about the advertised brands. This ability is due to the self-selection and reader-controlled nature of magazines compared with more intrusive media such as radio and television. A cute, albeit unintentional, portrayal

table 12.2 Magazine Advertising's Strengths and Limitations

Strengths	Limitations
Some magazines reach large audiences	Not intrusive
Selectivity	Long lead times
Long life	Clutter
High reproduction quality	Somewhat limited geographic options
Ability to present detailed information	Variability of circulation patterns by market
Ability to convey information authoritatively	
High involvement potential	

of this ability appeared in the *Family Circus* comic strip, which typically presents the thoughts of preschool-age children as they contemplate the world around them. This particular strip opens with Billy saying to his sister, Dolly, "I'll tell you the difference between TV, radio, and books.... TV puts stuff into your mind with pictures and sound. You don't even hafta think." In the next box he states, "Radio puts stuff into your mind with just sounds and words. You make up your own pictures." And in the final section, Billy proclaims, "Books are quiet friends! They let you make up your own pictures and sounds. They make you think."[12] Substitute the word magazines for books, and you have a pretty good characterization of the power of magazine advertising.

Magazine Advertising's Limitations

Several limitations are associated with magazine advertising (see Table 12.2). First, unlike TV and radio, which by their very nature infringe on the attention of the viewer and listener, magazine advertising is *not intrusive;* readers control their exposure to a magazine ad.

A second limitation is *long lead times.* In newspapers and the broadcast media, it is relatively easy to change ad copy on fairly short notice and in specific markets. Magazines, by comparison, have long closing dates that require advertising materials to be on hand for weeks in advance of the actual publication date. For example, for four-color ads the closing dates for the following sampling of magazines are shown in parentheses: *Better Homes & Gardens* (7 weeks), *Cosmopolitan* (10 weeks), *Sports Illustrated* (4 weeks), and *Time* (5 weeks).[13]

As with other advertising media, *clutter* is a problem with magazine advertising. In certain respects clutter is a worse problem with magazines than, say, television, because readers can become engrossed in editorial content and skip over advertisements.

Magazine advertising also provides *fewer geographic options* than do other media, although some large circulation magazines such as *Sports Illustrated* provide considerable selectivity. For example, *Sports Illustrated* offers advertising rates for seven key regions, all 50 states, and 33 metropolitan areas. An advertiser could choose to advertise in *Sports Illustrated* only in the Cleveland, Ohio, area, say, and in so doing pay $20,142 for a full-page, four-color ad. Comparatively, the same ad in a larger market such as Los Angeles would cost $34,145.[14]

A final limitation of magazine advertising is *variability in circulation patterns* from market to market. *Rolling Stone* magazine, for example, is read more in metropolitan than rural areas. Hence, advertisers who are interested, say, in reaching young men would not be very successful in reaching nonmetropolitan readers. This would necessitate placing ads in one or more magazines other than *Rolling Stone,* which would up the total cost of the media buy. Radio, TV, or both might better serve the advertiser's needs and provide more uniform market coverage.

Magazine Audience Measurement

When selecting magazine vehicles, it is critical for advertisers to know the audience size candidate magazines reach. Determining the size of a particular magazine's readership might seem a simple task that merely involves tallying the number of subscribers to a magazine. Unfortunately, it is more complicated than this because several factors make subscription counting an inadequate way of determining a magazine's readership: First, magazine subscriptions are collected through a variety of intermediaries, making it difficult to obtain accurate lists of who subscribes to which magazines. Second, magazines often are purchased from newsstands, supermarkets, and other retail outlets rather than through subscriptions, thus completely eliminating knowledge of who purchases which magazines. Third, magazines that are available in public locations such as doctors' offices, barber shops, and beauty salons are read by numerous people and not just the subscriber. Finally, individual magazine subscribers often share issues with other people.

For these reasons, the number of subscriptions to a magazine and the number of people who actually read the magazine are not equivalent. Fortunately, two previously mentioned services—MRI and Simmons—specialize in measuring magazine readership and determining audience size. These companies offer very similar, yet competitive, services.

In brief, both services take large, national probability samples and query respondents to identify their media consumption habits (e.g., which magazines they read) and determine their purchase behaviors for an extensive variety of products and brands. Statisticians then employ inference procedures to generalize sample results to the total population. Advertisers and media planners use the readership information along with detailed demographic and product and brand usage data to evaluate the absolute and relative value of different magazines.

Advantages aside, not all is perfect in the world of magazine audience measurement due to three notable problems: (1) respondents to readership surveys are asked to rate numerous magazines (as well as many vehicles in other media), which can lead to fatigue and hasty or faulty responses; (2) sample sizes often are small, especially for small-circulation magazines, which leads to high margins of sampling error when generalizing to the total population; and (3) sample composition may be unrepresentative of audience readership.[15] Also, because these two readership services use different research methods, their results often are discrepant. Consider, for example, Simmons' versus MRI's estimates for the following large-circulation magazines: *Better Homes & Gardens* (48.47 million readers estimated by Simmons versus 37.92 million readers estimated by MRI), *Cosmopolitan* (24.25 million versus 16.87 million), and *National Geographic* (45.38 million versus 31.62 million).[16] In percentage terms and using the smaller estimate as the base, these differences are 27.8, 43.7, and 43.5 percent, respectively. Media planners thus confront the challenge of determining which service is right or whether both are wrong in their estimates of audience size.[17]

Using Simmons and MRI Reports

Despite these problems, media planners must make the most of the audience estimates and readership profiles Simmons and MRI generate. Both companies produce annual reports of product and brand usage data and provide detailed media information. Using imported beer/ale as an illustration, Table 12.3 provides a pared-down report that will be useful for explaining the construction and interpretation of Simmons and MRI reports.[18] Your library may subscribe to an electronic version of either a Simmons or MRI data base. If so, you should access a recent report and inspect the vast amount of information that is provided in these reports.

MRI and Simmons reports are structurally equivalent to the data contained in Table 12.3. Each of the detailed tables in these reports present cross-tabulations of demographic segments by product or brand usage. Table 12.3 presents usage of imported beer/ale delineated by age groupings, educational status, geographic region, and Internet and TV quintiles (which will be explained subsequently). (For simplicity, all subsequent references to imported beer/ale will be shortened to imported beer.) The table is to be interpreted as follows:

1. The first row (*Total*) shows the occurrence of imported beer purchases in the total U.S. population. Thus, of the 218,289,000 adults living in the United States at the time of data collection, 42,264,000 (see column A), or 19.4 percent (see column B, *% Across*), drank imported beer at least once within the last six months.

table 12.3

Illustration of a MRI Report for Imported Beer/Ale (Based on all adults indicating whether they have drunk imported beer/ale within the last six months)

	Total '000	A '000	B % Across	C % Down	D Index
Total	218,289	42,264	19.4	100	100
Age 18–24	28,098	6,494	23.1	15.4	119
Age 25–34	39,485	10,247	26	24.2	134
Age 35–44	43,532	10,241	23.5	24.2	122
Age 45–54	42,127	8,028	19.1	19	98
Age 55–64	29,660	4,540	15.3	10.7	79
Age 65+	35,387	2,713	7.7	6.4	40
Educ: graduated college plus	54,849	15,545	28.3	36.8	146
Educ: attended college	59,432	11,454	19.3	27.1	100
Educ: graduated high school	69,653	10,061	14.4	23.8	75
Educ: did not graduate HS	34,355	5,204	15.1	12.3	78
Educ: post graduate	17,836	4,847	27.2	11.5	140
Census Region: Northeast	41,475	10,346	24.9	24.5	129
Census Region: South	79,054	12,893	16.3	30.5	84
Census Region: North Central	49,092	7,658	15.6	18.1	81
Census Region: West	48,668	11,366	23.4	26.9	121
Internet Quintile I (Heavy)	43,620	11,443	26.2	27.1	135
Internet Quintile II	43,677	10,170	23.3	24.1	120
Internet Quintile III	43,664	8,773	20.1	20.8	104
Internet Quintile IV	43,659	6,059	13.9	14.3	72
Internet Quintile V (Light)	43,668	5,819	13.3	13.8	69
TV (Total) Quintile I	43,655	6,230	14.3	14.7	74
TV (Total) Quintile II	43,642	7,802	17.9	18.5	92
TV (Total) Quintile III	43,675	8,943	20.5	21.2	106
TV (Total) Quintile IV	43,658	9,564	21.9	22.6	113
TV (Total) Quintile V	43,658	9,726	22.3	23	115

Source: MRI Reporter, Fall 2006.

2. Each set of detailed entries shows the estimate in four different ways (denoted as columns A, B, C, and D) for the product category (imported beer in this case) and the specified population grouping:

    a. *Column A* presents the estimate of *total product users* (expressed in thousands). Note carefully that Table 12.3 presents data in thousands, shown as '000, so the value of 42,264 in the top row stands for 42,260,000 drinkers of imported beer. Of the 42,264,000 total drinkers of imported beer, 6,494,000 are in the 18–24 age category, 10,247,000 in the 24–34 age group, and so on.

    b. *Column B (% Across)* reflects each subgroup's proportionate representation with respect to the total number of product users in the product category. For example, of the 28,098,000 people in the 18–24 age group (see the value under the Total column), MRI estimates that 6,494,000 in that subgroup are imported beer drinkers. Thus, the percent across values in Column B (23.1 percent in this case) simply represents the proportionate representation of each value under column A compared with its corresponding value under the Total column.

c. *Column C* (*% Down*) represents the percentage of product users in each demographic subgroup compared with the total number of product users. For example, 6,494,000 of the 42,264,000 total drinkers of imported beer are in the 18–24 age group. This age group thus represents 15.4 percent of the total number of imported beer drinkers. Note that each value in column C (% Down) is calculated by dividing the column A value for a particular row by the total value in column A (i.e., 42,264,000).

d. *Column D* (*Index*) is a measure of a particular demographic group's proportionate product consumption compared with the total population's proportionate product consumption. For example, 19.4 percent of all American adults are at least occasional imported beer drinkers. Comparatively, 23.1 percent of consumers in the 18–24 age group are imported beer drinkers (these two figures, 19.4 and 23.4 percent, respectively, are shown in Column B, % Across). The index values in Column D reflect this relationship. Hence, the index value for consumers aged 18–24 is calculated as follows: $(23.1 \div 19.4) \times 100 = 119$. This index indicates that people in the 18–24 age group are 19 percent *more likely* than the general population to drink imported beer. Comparatively, older consumers in the 55–64 age group with an index of 79 $[(15.3 \div 19.4) \times 100 = 79]$ are 21 percent *less likely* than the general population, with an index of 100, to drink imported beer. All in all, the index numbers for age groups indicate that imported beer consumption generally declines with increasing age. Similarly, the index numbers based on educational attainment (see Table 12.3) indicate that people who have graduated college and those with postgraduate degrees are disproportionately more likely to drink imported beer. Comparatively, individuals with high school degrees and those who did not graduate high school are disproportionately less likely to drink imported beer.

Does this mean that imported beer marketers should cater only to younger consumers and those with higher education and neglect the others? Probably not. For example, although people ages 45 to 54 (index = 98) are proportionately less likely than the younger age groups to consume imported beer, there are, nonetheless, a total of approximately eight million people in this age group who do consume imported beer. It thus would make little sense to disregard such a large number of consumers simply because the index number is slightly less than 100. Although prudent imported beer marketers would not neglect these older consumers, the index numbers in Table 12.3 suggest that less media emphasis, or weight, should be directed at older consumers than the weight targeted at the younger consumers.

Turning to the Internet and TV data in Table 12.3, notice under the Total column that the total number of American adults (218,289,000) has been divided into five basically equal-sized groups (quintiles) based on their Internet and TV usage. Hence, Quintile I represents the heaviest Internet users and the heaviest TV viewers, whereas Quintile V represents the lightest Internet users and lightest TV viewers. Column D in Table 12.3 reveals that heavier Internet users are disproportionately more likely to be drinkers of imported beer (index numbers of 135 and 120 for Quintiles I and II) and that imported beer consumption declines in the lighter Internet quintiles. Conversely, heavy TV viewers (Quintiles I and II) are disproportionately less likely than the lighter viewer quintiles to consume imported beer. How might an advertiser use these data?

In using media data supplied in MRI and Simmons reports, the advertiser must weigh various pieces of information to make intelligent use of these reports. There is evidence that media planners too often use MRI and Simmons data in a simplistic manner that fails to utilize fully all information provided by these reports.[19] The tendency is to focus excessively on the index numbers contained in Column D. Although the index numbers reflect a subgroup's proportionate product-usage representation compared with the total population's product usage, the index numbers fail to tell the whole story.

It is essential to go beyond the index numbers and consider each demographic subgroup's total size and potential for growth in using the product category. Thus, for example, although Americans who have only a high school education drink imported beer proportionately less than those who have graduated college (index numbers of 75 for high school grads versus 146 for college grads; see Table 12.3), the number of high-school-only grads (69,653,000) is considerably larger than the number of college grads (54,849,000). Hence, an imported beer advertiser should not neglect people who have not graduated college, but rather might cultivate this market by developing advertisements that appeal to their lifestyles and advertising in media vehicles that are particularly effective in reaching them.

Customized Magazines

Discussion to this point has focused on magazines that are published by companies whose primary business is creating and distributing magazines, i.e., magazine publishers. However, there has been a major development in recent years wherein marketers of specific brands are developing newsletters and magazines that focus on their brands and issues related to these brands and the interests of brand purchasers. These customized magazines are distributed free of charge to brand users either online in electronic form ("e-zines") or in printed form.

One of the primary purposes for brand marketers to create customized magazines is to reach out to existing brand users and to create a bond that will result in increased levels of *customer loyalty*. For example, *Lexus Magazine* is distributed to owners of Lexus automobiles. The magazine, both in printed and electronic forms, provides useful and entertaining information related to travel and other topics and achieves a high level of readership. This customized magazine is distributed throughout the world, with the North American version alone having a circulation of 800,000 per issue.[20] Bloomingdale's, the famous New York department store, sends its customized magazine, *The Little Brown Book,* to 180,000 of its best customers—shoppers who spend between $3,500 and $5,000 per year on the Bloomingdale's credit card.[21] This magazine provides Bloomingdale's prime customers with fashion updates; stories on art, culture, and entertainment; and promotional offers available only to magazine recipients.

Customized publishing is definitely on the rise and is capturing a growing percentage of many companies' marcom budgets. In fact, one survey revealed that customized publishing accounts for nearly one fourth of the total money that companies allocate for marketing, advertising, and communications.[22] Customized magazines thus represent a valuable marcom tool for reaching and maintaining the loyalty of a brand's existing customers. Customized magazines do not replace advertisements placed in traditional (i.e., noncustomized magazines) because advertisements placed in traditional magazines reach prospective customers as well as current brand users. Nonetheless, customized magazines have a unique role in a brand's overall marcom program, especially as a means of maintaining a continuous dialogue with current brand users.

Radio

Radio is a nearly ubiquitous medium: There are nearly 14,000 commercial radio stations in the United States; almost 100 percent of all homes have radios; most homes have several; virtually all cars have a radio; more than 50 million radios are purchased in the United States each year; and radio in the United States reaches about 93 percent of all people age 12 or older.[23] These impressive figures indicate radio's strong potential as an advertising medium. Although radio has always been a favorite of local advertisers, regional and national advertisers have increasingly recognized radio's advantages as an ad medium.

Buying Radio Time

Radio advertisers are interested in reaching target customers at a reasonable expense while ensuring that the station format is compatible with a brand's image and its creative message strategy. Several considerations influence the choice of radio vehicle. *Station format* (classical, progressive, country, top-40, talk, etc.) is a major consideration. Certain formats are obviously most appropriate for particular products and brands.

A second consideration is the *choice of geographic areas to cover.* National advertisers buy time from stations whose audience coverage matches the advertiser's geographic areas of interest. This typically means locating stations in preferred metropolitan statistical areas (MSAs) or in so-called areas of dominant influence (ADIs), which number approximately 200 in the United States and correspond to the major television markets.

A third consideration in buying radio time is the *choice of daypart.* Radio dayparts include the following:

Morning drive:	5 AM to 10 AM
Midday:	10 AM to 3 PM
Afternoon drive:	3 PM to 7 PM
Evening:	7 PM to Midnight
Late night:	Midnight to 7 AM

Rate structures vary depending on the attractiveness of the daypart; for example, morning and afternoon drive times are more expensive than midday and late night dayparts. Information about rates and station formats is available in Spot Radio Rates and Data, a source published by SRDS Media Solutions.

Radio Advertising's Strengths and Limitations

This section examines the advantages and also explores some of the problems with radio advertising (see the summary in Table 12.4).

Radio Advertising's Strengths

The first major strength of radio is that it is second only to magazines in its *ability to reach segmented audiences.* An extensive variety of radio programming enables advertisers to pick specific formats and stations to be optimally compatible with both the composition of their target audience and their creative message strategies. Radio can be used to pinpoint advertisements to specific groups of consumers: teens, Hispanics, sports fanatics, news addicts, jazz enthusiasts, political conservatives, and so on. As noted earlier, there are nearly 14,000 commercial radio stations in the United States, and these stations are formatted to cater to special listening interests.

A second major advantage of radio advertising is its *ability to reach prospective customers on a personal and intimate level.* Local store merchants and radio

table 12.4

Radio Advertising's Strengths and Limitations

Strengths	Limitations
Ability to reach segmented audiences	Clutter
Intimacy	No visuals
Economy	Audience fractionalization
Short lead times	Buying difficulties
Transfer of imagery from TV	
Use of local personalities	

announcers can be extremely personable and convincing. Their messages sometimes come across as if they are personally speaking to each audience member. A top-level advertising agency representative metaphorically described radio as a "universe of private worlds" and a "communication between two friends."[24] In other words, people select radio stations in much the same way that they select personal friends. People listen to those radio stations with which they closely identify. Because of this, radio advertising is likely to be received when the customer's mental frame is most conducive to persuasive influence. Radio advertising, then, is a personal and intimate form of friendly persuasion that has potential to increase consumers' engagement with advertisements placed in this medium.

Economy is a third advantage of radio advertising. In terms of target audience CPM, radio advertising is considerably cheaper than other mass media. Over the past several decades, radio's CPM has increased less than any other advertising medium.

Another relative advantage of radio advertising is *short lead times.* Because radio production costs are typically inexpensive and scheduling deadlines are short, copy changes can be made quickly to take advantage of important developments and changes in the marketplace. For example, a sudden weather change may suggest an opportunity to advertise weather-related products. A radio spot can be prepared quickly to accommodate the needs of the situation. Radio advertising copy can be changed swiftly in response to changing inventory levels and special events and holidays.

A very important advantage of radio advertising is its *ability to transfer images from television advertising.* A memorable television advertising campaign that has been aired frequently effects in consumers a mental association between the sight and sound elements in the commercial. This mental image can then be transferred to a radio commercial that uses the TV sound or some adaptation of it. The radio commercial thus evokes in listeners a mental picture of the TV ad—much in the fashion that Billy described in the *Family Circus* cartoon mentioned earlier.[25] The advertiser effectively gains the advantage of TV advertising at the lower cost of radio. By using a combination of TV and radio advertising, the advertiser is able to achieve higher levels of reach and frequency than would be achieved if the entire budget were invested exclusively in television advertising.

A final strength of radio advertising is its ability to avail itself of the reputations and the sometimes bigger-than-life persona of *local personalities.* Radio personalities in local markets are often highly respected and admired, and their endorsement of, say, a retail establishment can serve to enhance that establishment's image and drive purchases to the store.

Radio Advertising's Limitations

Radio's foremost limitation, one it shares with other ad media, is that it is *cluttered* with competitive commercials and other forms of noise, chatter, and interference. Radio listeners frequently switch stations, especially on their car radios, to avoid commercials.[26] The irritation of having to listen to one commercial after another partially explains why many people have turned to iPods and other brands of portable digital-audio players as an alternative to radio listening. The iPod's growing popularity has been shown, in fact, to correlate with reduced radio ratings. So-called AQH ratings, which measure the number of people tuned to radio during an average quarter hour (AQH) as a percentage of the population, fell by almost 6 percent during a recent five-year period, with the ratings decline among the college-aged demographic (18–24) even greater at 11 percent.[27]

A second limitation is that radio is the only major medium that is *unable to employ visualizations.* However, radio advertisers attempt to overcome the medium's visual limitation by using sound effects and choosing concrete words to conjure up mental images in the listener. It is important to note that many advertising campaigns use radio as a supplement to other media rather than as a stand-alone medium. This reduces radio's task from creating visual images to reactivating images that already have been created by ads placed in visual media—television, the Internet, and magazines. In contrast, information-based advertising campaigns do not necessarily require visualizations, and radio under such circumstances is fully capable of delivering brand-based information—for example, a mortgage company's interest rate, a special sale at a local department store, or the location of an automobile repair shop.

A third problem with radio advertising results from a high degree of *audience fractionalization.* Selectivity is a major advantage of radio advertising, but at the same time the advertiser is unable to reach a diverse audience because each radio station and program has its own unique set of audience demographics and interests.

A final limitation is the *difficulty of buying radio time.* This problem is particularly acute in the case of the national advertiser that wishes to place spots in different markets throughout the country. With nearly 14,000 commercial radio stations operating in the United States, buying time is complicated by unstandardized rate structures that include a number of combinations of fixed and discount rates. One prospect that may offset this problem is the growth of the fledgling satellite radio industry. Companies such as Sirius Satellite Radio and XM Satellite Radio can broadcast nationally (even internationally) and thus offer advertisers an opportunity to reach large audiences and pay a single rate for the purchased airtime. XM and Sirius announced plans to merge in 2007, but as of mid-2008 the merger has not yet received final approval from the Federal Communications Commission and the Department of Justice.

Radio Audience Measurement

Radio audiences are measured both nationally and locally. Arbitron is the major company at both the national and the local levels involved with measuring radio listenership and audience demographics. At the *national level,* Arbitron owns a service that goes by the acronym RADAR, which stands for Radio's All Dimension Audience Research. The RADAR service produces radio-listening estimates by recruiting 70,000 individuals age 12 and older, who, during a one-week period, make diary entries that identify their daily listening behavior, including the radio stations they listened to, the time of day they listened to each station, and their location when they listened (e.g., in the car, at home, or at work). RADAR's research provides ratings estimates for network radio programming and audience demographic characteristics. Advertisers use this information to select network programming that matches their intended target audiences.

At the *local level,* there used to be two major research services that measured radio audience sizes: Birch Scarborough Research and Arbitron. However, in the early 1990s Birch discontinued operations, leaving Arbitron the sole supplier of local radio ratings data. Arbitron measures listening patterns in over 250 markets located throughout the United States. Arbitron researchers obtain data in each market from 250 to 13,000 randomly selected individuals age 12 or older. Respondents are compensated for maintaining *diaries* of their listening behavior for a seven-day period. Subscribers to the Arbitron service (thousands of radio stations, advertisers, and agencies) receive reports that detail people's listening patterns, station preferences, and demographic breakdowns. This information is invaluable to advertisers and their agencies for purposes of selecting radio stations whose listener compositions match the advertiser's target market.

Arbitron is in the process of attempting to get away from the paper-diary method of data collection by having people carry pager-like meters throughout the day. This data-collection method, called the *Portable People Meter,* is in testing at the time of this writing. More will be said about people meters in the context of measuring TV viewing.

Television

Television is practically ubiquitous in the United States and throughout the rest of the industrialized world. Television sets are present in slightly more than 98 percent of all American households, which amounted to 112.8 million TV households in the United States as of September 2007.[28] As an advertising medium, television is uniquely personal and demonstrative, yet it is also expensive and subject to considerable competitive clutter. Consumers consider television the most cluttered of all ad media.[29]

Before elaborating on television's specific strengths and weaknesses, it first will be instructive to examine two specific aspects of television advertising: (1) the different programming segments, or so-called dayparts; and (2) the alternative outlets for television commercials (network, spot, syndicated, cable, and local).

Television Programming Dayparts

Advertising costs, audience characteristics, and programming appropriateness vary greatly at different times of the day. As with radio, these times are referred to as *dayparts*. There are seven TV dayparts, with the following shown for Eastern Standard Time:

Early morning:	5 AM to 9 AM
Daytime:	9 AM to 4 PM
Early fringe:	4 PM to 7 PM
Prime access:	7 PM to 8 PM
Prime time:	8 PM to 11 PM
Late fringe:	11 PM to 2 AM
Overnight:	2 AM to 5 AM

The three major dayparts are daytime, fringe time, and prime time, each of which has its own strengths and weaknesses.

Daytime

The period that begins with the early morning news shows and extends to 4:00 PM is known as *daytime*. Early daytime appeals first to adults with news programs and then to children with special programs designed for them. Afternoon programming—with its special emphasis on soap operas, talk shows, and financial news—appeals primarily to people working at home, retirees, and, contrary to the stereotype, even young men.[30]

Fringe Time

The period preceding and following prime time is known as *fringe time*. Early fringe starts with afternoon reruns and is devoted primarily to children but becomes more adult oriented as prime time approaches. Late fringe appeals chiefly to young adults.

Prime Time

The period between 8:00 PM and 11:00 PM (or between 7:00 PM and 10:00 PM in some parts of the United States) is known as *prime time*. The best and most expensive programs are scheduled during this period. Audiences are largest during prime time. Table 12.5 indicates the average prime-time audience size for the four major U.S. networks during one week in 2008. The audience sizes range from 13.76 million viewers on average for Fox down to 7.27 million average viewers for NBC. Interestingly, the total audience size these four major networks garnered during

table 12.5

Average Prime-Time Audience (in millions) for Four Major Networks

Network	Estimated Viewers (in millions)
Fox	13.76
CBS	8.15
ABC	7.98
NBC	7.27
Total	37.16

Source: Nielsen Media Research, reported in Bill Gorman, "Weekly Network Ratings," February 25-March 2, 2008, http://tvbythenumbers.com/2008/03/04/weekly-network-ratings-february-25-march-2/2826 (accessed March 7, 2008).

this one week is approximately 37 million; comparatively, the total audience size during 1994–1995 was just over 62 million. This decline of about 40 percent reflects the continuing trend wherein network TV is capturing smaller audiences while cable TV's audience base continues to grow.[31]

The networks naturally charge the highest rates for prime-time advertising. Popular prime-time programs sometimes reach as many as 20 million U.S. households. Advertisers pay dearly to reach the large numbers of households highly popular prime-time programs deliver. For example, the fabulously successful *American Idol* singing-competition program charges advertisers over $600,000 for a single 30-second commercial. With the exception of *American Idol,* the 10 highest-priced programs for the 2007–2008 television season are shown in Table 12.6, where it can be seen that the cost for a single 30-second commercial placed on these programs ranges from a low of $208,000 (*Private Practice* and *Survivor: China*) to a high of $419,000 (*Grey's Anatomy*). Note that these advertising prices are for just the 10 most expensive TV programs. Most 30-second commercials broadcast on prime-time TV during the 2007–2008 season were in the range of $50,000 to $200,000.

Network, Spot, Syndicated, Cable, and Local Advertising

Television messages are transmitted by local stations, which are either locally owned cable television systems or affiliated with the five commercial networks (ABC, CBS, NBC, Fox, and The CW) or with an independent cable network (such as TBS, the Turner Broadcasting System). This arrangement of local stations and networks allows for different ways of buying advertising time on television.

table 12.6

The 10 Highest Priced TV Programs, 2007–2008 (price per 30-second commercial)

Program	Network	Price
Grey's Anatomy	ABC	$419,000
Sunday Night Football	NBC	$358,000
The Simpsons	Fox	$315,000
Heroes	NBC	$296,000
House	Fox	$294,000
Desperate Housewives	ABC	$270,000
CSI: Crime Scene Investigation	CBS	$248,000
Two and a Half Men	CBS	$231,000
Private Practice	ABC	$208,000
Survivor: China	CBS	$208,000

Source: "2007–2008 TV Season: Network Pricing," *Advertising Age*, December 31, 2007, 45.

© F Micelotta/American Idol 2008/Getty Images for Fox

Network Television Advertising

Companies that market products nationally often use network television to reach potential customers throughout the country. The advertiser, typically working through an advertising agency, purchases desired time slots from one or more of the networks and advertises at these times on all local stations that are affiliated with the network. The cost of such advertising depends on the time of day when an ad is aired, the popularity of the television program in which the ad is placed, and the time of year. The average cost for all 30-second prime-time television commercials during each of the four quarters in one recent year were: first quarter (January–March), $134,800; second quarter (April–June), $147,900; third quarter (July–September), $106,300; and fourth quarter (October–December), $132,300.[32]

Network television advertising, although expensive in terms of per-unit cost, can be a cost-efficient means to reach mass audiences. Consider a 30-second commercial that costs $300,000 and reaches 15 percent of the 112.8 million American households with TV sets, or about 16.44 million households. Although $300,000 is a lot to pay for 30 seconds of commercial time, reaching 16.92 million households means that the advertiser would have paid approximately only $17.73 to reach every 1,000 households.

Network advertising is inefficient, and in fact unfeasible, if the national advertiser chooses to concentrate efforts only on select markets. For example, some brands, although marketed nationally, are directed primarily at consumers in certain geographic locales. In this case, it would be wasteful to invest in network advertising, which would reach many areas where target audiences are not located.

Spot Television Advertising

The national advertiser's alternative to network advertising is *spot advertising*. As the preceding discussion intimated and as the name suggests, this type of advertising is placed (spotted) only in selected markets.

Spot advertising is particularly desirable when a company rolls out a new brand market by market before it achieves national distribution, when a marketer needs to concentrate on particular markets due to poor performance in these markets or aggressive competitive efforts, or when a company's product distribution is limited to one or a few geographical regions. Also, spot advertising is useful even for those advertisers who use network advertising but need to supplement the national coverage with greater amounts of advertising in select markets that have particularly high brand potential.

Syndicated Advertising

Syndicated programming occurs when an independent company—such as Disney-ABC Domestic Television Company and Sony Pictures Television—markets a TV show to as many network-affiliated or cable television stations as possible. Because an independent firm markets syndicated programs to individual television stations, the same syndicated program will appear on, say, NBC stations in some markets and on ABC or CBS stations in other markets. Syndicated programs are either original productions or shows that first appeared on network television and are subsequently shown as reruns.

Cable Advertising

Unlike network television, which is free to all TV owners, cable television requires users to subscribe (pay a fee) to a cable service and have their sets specially wired to receive signals via satellite or other means. Although cable television has been available since the 1940s, only in recent decades have advertisers turned to cable as a valuable advertising medium. Growing numbers of major national companies now advertise on cable TV. Cable television's household penetration increased from less than 25 percent of all households in 1980 to a current level of about 85 percent of U.S. households with television sets.[33] Advertising spending on cable TV is climbing steadily.

Cable advertising is attractive to national advertisers for several reasons. First, because cable networks focus on narrow areas of viewing interest (so-called *narrowcasting*), advertisers are able to reach more finely targeted audiences (in terms of demographics and psychographics) than when using network, syndicated, or spot advertising. Indeed, cable stations are available to reach almost any imaginable viewing preference. A brand marketer can select cable stations that appeal to a variety of specific viewing interests such as cooking and eating (Food Network); golfing (Golf Channel); sports in general (ESPN, ESPN2, etc.); music entertainment (Country Music Television, MTV, and VH1); nature, science, and animal life (Animal Planet, Discovery Channel, and Outdoor Life Network); general education (the History Channel and Travel Channel); and so forth.

A second reason that cable advertising appeals to national advertisers is that high network advertising prices and declining audiences have compelled advertisers to experiment with media alternatives such as cable. A third factor behind cable advertising's growth is the demographic composition of cable audiences. Cable subscribers are more economically upscale and younger than the population as a whole. By comparison, the heaviest viewers of network television tend to be somewhat economically downscale. It is little wonder that the relatively upscale characteristics of cable viewers have great appeal to many national advertisers.

Local Television Advertising

National advertisers historically dominated television advertising, but local advertisers have turned to television in ever greater numbers. Local advertisers often find that the CPM advantages of television along with the ability to demonstrate products justify the TV medium. Many local advertisers are using cable stations to an unprecedented degree. In fact, the growth rate in local cable advertising is faster than other ad media.[34]

Television Advertising's Strengths and Limitations

Like the other forms of media, advertising on television has a number of strengths and limitations (see the summary in Table 12.7).

Television Advertising's Strengths

Beyond any other consideration, television possesses the unique capability to *demonstrate a product in use.* No other medium can reach consumers simultaneously through auditory and visual senses. Viewers can see and hear a product being used, identify with the product's users, and imagine using the product.

Television also has *intrusion value* unparalleled by other media. That is, television advertisements engage one's senses and attract attention even when one would prefer not to be exposed to an advertisement. In comparison, it is much easier to avoid a magazine or newspaper ad by merely flipping the page, or to avoid a radio ad by changing channels. But it is often easier to sit through a television commercial rather than attempting to avoid it either physically or mentally. Of course, as will be discussed shortly, remote controls and digital video recorders have made it easier for viewers to avoid television commercials via zipping and zapping.

A third relative advantage of television advertising is its combined *ability to provide entertainment and generate excitement.* Advertised products can be brought to life or made to appear even bigger than life. Products advertised on television can be presented dramatically and made to appear more exciting and less mundane than perhaps they actually are.

Television also has the unique ability to *reach consumers one on one,* as is the case when a spokesperson or endorser touts a particular product. Like a sales presentation, the interaction between spokesperson and consumer takes place on a personal level.

More than any other medium, television is able to *use humor* as an effective advertising strategy. As discussed in Chapter 9, many of the most memorable commercials are those using a humorous format.

In addition to its effectiveness in reaching ultimate consumers, television advertising also is *effective with a company's sales force and its retailers* (a.k.a., "the trade"). Salespeople find it easier to sell new or established brands to the trade when a major advertising campaign is planned. The trade has added incentive to increase merchandise support (e.g., through advertising features and special display space) for a brand that is advertised on television.

The greatest relative advantage of television advertising, however, is its *ability to achieve impact,* that is, to activate consumers' awareness of ads and enhance their receptiveness to sales messages.

table 12.7

Television Advertising's Strengths and Limitations

Strengths	Limitations
Demonstration ability	Rapidly expanding cost
Intrusion value	Erosion of viewing audiences
Ability to generate excitement	Audience fractionalization
One-on-one reach	Zipping and zapping
Ability to use humor	Clutter
Effective with sales force and trade	
Ability to achieve impact	

Television Advertising's Limitations

As an advertising medium, television suffers from several distinct problems. First, and perhaps most serious, is the *rapidly escalating advertising cost.* The cost of network television advertising has more than tripled over the past two decades. A dramatic illustration of this is the increasing cost of buying advertising time during the Super Bowl. In 1975 a 30-second commercial cost $110,000. By 2008, the average price for placing a 30-second ad on Super Bowl XLII was $2.7 million! (For more on Super Bowl advertising, see the *IMC Focus.*) In addition to the cost of buying airtime, it is costly to produce television commercials. The average cost of making a national 30-second commercial was $372,000 in a recent year.[35]

A second problem is the *erosion of television viewing audiences.* Syndicated programs, cable television, the Internet, and other leisure and recreational alternatives have diminished the number of people viewing network television. The five major networks' share of television audiences during prime time fell from over 90 percent around 1980 to just about 60 percent today. Program ratings have consistently fallen over the past 40 years. Whereas the most popular programs used to have ratings in the 50s (meaning that more than 50 percent of all television households were tuned in to these programs), the top-rated programs now rarely obtain a rating of 20.

Today it is uncommon for a show to have a rating above 15. For example, the 10 top-rated programs during the week of February 25, 2008, are shown in Table 12.8. The highest rated program, *American Idol* (Tuesday broadcast), had a rating of 16.0, and the tenth-ranked program (*Lost*) had a rating of only 7.7.[36] Ratings on network television continue to slide.

There also has been substantial *audience fractionalization.* Advertisers cannot expect to attract large homogeneous audiences when advertising during any particular program due to the great amount of program selection now available to television viewers.

Fourth, when watching TV programs, viewers spend much of their time *switching from station to station,* zapping or zipping commercials. **Zapping** occurs when viewers switch to another channel when commercials are aired, prompting one observer to comment (only partially with tongue in cheek) that the remote control "zapper" is the greatest threat to capitalism since Karl Marx.[37] Research reveals that perhaps as much as one third of the potential audience for a TV commercial may be lost to zapping.[38] Although zapping is extensive, one intriguing study presented evidence suggesting that commercials that are zapped are actively processed prior to being zapped and may have a more positive effect on brand purchase behavior than commercials that are not zapped.[39] This provocative prospect certainly requires further support before being accepted as fact.

In addition to zapping, television viewers also engage in zipping. **Zipping** takes place when ads that have been recorded along with program material using a *digital video recorder* (of the TiVo variety) are fast-forwarded (zipped through) when the viewer watches the prerecorded material. Research has shown that zipping is extensive.[40] DVRs from companies such as TiVo and ReplayTV allow viewers to fast-forward past commercials by simply pushing a skip button that fast-forwards in 30-second intervals, which, by no coincidence, is the standard length of a TV commercial.

It is estimated that current DVR penetration in U.S. households is nearly 25 percent, which means that over 28 million households had DVRs as of 2008.[41] Many DVR owners use the technology to fast-forward through commercials or skip them altogether. One study found that nearly 60 percent of male viewers skip commercials and an even greater percentage of female viewers, nearly 70 percent, do the same.[42] Fast-forwarding through commercials is particularly high (upward of 75 percent) when programs are prerecorded for later viewing; however, fast-forwarding of commercials drops considerably (to below 20 percent) when people

IMC >> i.m.c. focus

The Rising Cost of Super Bowl Advertising

The Super Bowl football game, which pits the winners of the National and American conferences of the National Football League, is for many Americans the most important sporting event of the year. Super Bowl Sunday, which occurs annually in late January or early February, has been described as the third or fourth largest "holiday" celebrated in America. People throw parties and consume large quantities of food and drink while watching the clash of professional football teams. This event is one of the few remaining television spectaculars that can be described as mass television. The sponsoring TV network is able to command huge prices for 30-second commercials because advertisers know they can reach nearly 90 million people with an advertisement placed during this single program. In fact, the 2008 Super Bowl (between the undefeated New England Patriots and the underdog New York Giants that won the game) attracted an average of 97.5 million viewers, which made this the highest viewed Super Bowl up to this time.

Advertising rates have basically doubled in slightly over a decade, from $1,130,577 in 1995 to $2,364,390 in 2008 (both cost figures have been adjusted for inflation to 2000 dollars). The following table provides detailed statistics for every Super Bowl from its inception in 1967 through 2008. Note that the prices for each year have been adjusted for inflation and are presented in constant 2000 dollars. For example, the actual price of a 30-second commercial during Super Bowl XLII in 2008 was $2,700,000, which, when adjusted for inflation, amounts to $2,364,390 in 2000 dollars. Interestingly, because the number of TV households grows annually, Super Bowl XLII in 2008 had the largest number of Super Bowl viewers of all time, but its rating of 43.3 is considerably lower than the record-high rating of 49.1 over a quarter century ago in 1982.

SOURCE: Brian Steinberg, "Super Bowl Busts Ratings Records on 'The Greatest Day Ever' for Fox," *Advertising Age*, February 11, 2008, 21; Claire Atkinson, "Super Bowl: It's a Big (Ad) Deal," *Advertising Age*, January 3, 2005, 10 (ratings for 2002–2004 are provided in this source; all other ratings are from the following sources); Richard Linnett and Wayne Friedman, "No Gain," *Advertising Age*, January 15, 2001, 43; Wayne Friedman, "Second Down," *Advertising Age*, September 3, 2001, 3, 22. The 2005 rating is from "Super Bowl Ratings Down from '04," CBSNews.com, February 7, 2005, http://www.cbsnews.com (accessed June 7, 2005).

Year	Price (adjusted for inflation to 2000 dollars)	Rating (% of U.S. households tuned to Super Bowl)	Year	Price (adjusted for inflation to 2000 dollars)	Rating (% of U.S. households tuned to Super Bowl)
1967	$216,665	23.0%	1988	873,880	41.9
1968	267,362	36.8	1989	937,923	43.5
1969	316,901	36.0	1990	922,800	39.0
1970	347,264	39.4	1991	1,012,041	41.9
1971	306,311	39.9	1992	982,466	40.3
1972	353,493	44.2	1993	1,013,529	45.1
1973	401,645	42.7	1994	1,046,356	45.5
1974	373,957	41.6	1995	1,130,577	41.3
1975	352,286	42.4	1996	1,207,967	46.0
1976	378,515	42.3	1997	1,288,224	43.3
1977	460,604	44.4	1998	1,374,172	44.5
1978	488,888	47.2	1999	1,654,742	40.2
1979	526,868	47.1	2000	2,100,000	43.3
1980	575,030	46.3	2001	2,050,000	41.1
1981	614,707	44.4	2002	1,824,380*	40.4
1982	615,995	49.1	2003	2,172,801	40.7
1983	691,968	48.6	2004	2,144,750	41.4
1984	746,246	46.4	2005	2,210,400	43.4
1985	800,651	46.4	2006	2,268,500	41.6
1986	864,644	48.3	2007	2,128,618	42.6
1987	872,117	45.8	2008	2,364,390	43.3

*The actual costs of Super Bowl advertising for every year from 2002 to 2008 were deflated to 2000 dollars using the Gross Domestic Product Deflator Inflation Calculator, http://cost.jsc.nasa.gov/inflateGDP.html. Values for the remaining years (from 1967 to 2001) were already calculated from the 2001 source materials presented in the source documentation.

Rank*	Program	Network	Rating**	Viewers (000)***
1	*American Idol–Tuesday*	FOX	16.0	28,592
2	*American Idol–Wednesday*	FOX	15.7	27,553
3	*American Idol–Thursday*	FOX	14.9	26,232
4	*Oprah's Big Give*	ABC	9.5	15,680
5	*Deal or No Deal–Monday*	NBC	9.2	15,425
6	*ABC Premiere Event–Special*	ABC	8.6	12,688
7	*Don't Forget the Lyrics*	FOX	8.4	14,395
7	*Extreme Makeover: Home Edition*	ABC	8.4	14,874
9	*60 Minutes*	CBS	8.1	12,336
10	*Law and Order*	NBC	7.7	11,437
10	*Lost*	ABC	7.7	12,893

*Based on household rating percentage from Nielsen Media Research's National People Meter sample for the week beginning February 25, 2008.
**As of September 20, 2007, there were an estimated 112.8 million TV households. A single rating point represents 1 percent, or 1,128,000 households.
***Total viewers includes all persons over the age of two.

Source: "Top 10 Broadcast TV Programs for the Week of February 25, 2008," Nielsen Media Research.

Table 12.8

Top-10 Prime-Time Broadcast TV Programs

watch live programs.[43] The implication is clear: Commercials are more likely to be watched during live programs, which perhaps explains why programs such as *American Idol* command such premium prices.

As the penetration of DVRs increases, many advertisers may switch to media other than television for concern that TV simply isn't delivering the eyeballs for which they are paying. However, noteworthy research Procter & Gamble conducted came to the conclusion that consumers fast-forwarding through ads with DVRs recall those ads at about the same level as do people who see the ad at normal speed in real time.[44] Nonetheless, other indicators of advertising effectiveness (feelings of warmth, likeability, overall persuasion) may be negatively affected when fast-forwarding, which thus makes it inappropriate to conclude that "TiVo-ing" does not diminish commercial effectiveness.

Given the reality of Tivo-ing—i.e., viewers fast-forwarding through commercials—advertisers are devising techniques to diminish this behavior. For example, during a broadcast of *Mythbusters*—a TV program that uses science in an attempt to dispel myths and urban legends—a brief ad for Guinness beer included a scene where one character in the ad asked another whether it is a myth that a bottle of Guinness contains only 125 calories. After being told that the calorie count is accurate, a voice-over declared: "*Mythbusters,* sponsored by Guinness."[45] KFC also attempted to circumvent consumers from fast-forwarding through recorded programs by including in its commercial a single frame that contained the code word "Buffalo." Only viewers who used their DVR to slow the ad and watch it frame by frame could see the code word. KFC announced details of when the ad would run to ensure that viewers would know when to pause their DVRs. Viewers who spotted the code word could go to KFC's Web site and claim a coupon for a free Buffalo Snackers sandwich. Over 100,000 people claimed coupons for the free sandwich after entering the hidden code on KFC's Web site. During the weeks the ad ran, KFC's Web site drew 40 percent more traffic that usual.[46]

Finally, whereas DVRs allow consumers to *time-shift* their TV viewing—i.e., people record programs and view them whenever convenient—there is another technology that provides consumers with further *control* over TV viewing. In particular, the *Slingbox* enables individuals to *place-shift* their viewing of live TV programs. This technology is described in the *Global Focus* insert.

Clutter is a fifth serious problem with television advertising. Clutter refers to the growing amount of nonprogram material, including public service messages

global focus

Place-Shifting TV Viewing

Suppose you, as an American citizen, are working in Europe (or Asia, or wherever) and that you miss watching live broadcasts of your favorite college or professional athletic team. These programs are not, of course, televised live in London, Paris, Amsterdam, Tokyo, or anywhere else you may be located. You could have a family member back in the States send you a recording, but watching a game several days after it has been played is not nearly as enjoyable as seeing it in real time. What's a person to do?

A solution is a device called the *Slingbox.* To explain how the *Slingbox* works, let us assume that you are a graduate of The Ohio State University with an MBA from the University of Pennsylvania's Wharton School. Having specialized in international business, your first job takes you to Barcelona, Spain, where you work for an American company that has offices located around the globe. You love your job and the excitement of living in Barcelona, but every Saturday in the fall you miss watching your beloved OSU Buckeyes play football. The solution is the *Slingbox,* a device that weighs two pounds and costs less than $200.

Here's how you could watch live broadcasts of Ohio State football games using the *Slingbox* technology. First, you could have your father back in Ohio connect a newly purchased *Slingbox* to his TV. He would then connect the *Slingbox* to his computer network/router. Dad would mail you the software for the *Slingbox* (called SlingPlayer), and you would load this software on your computer or even on a Windows-enabled mobile phone. That done, you are now prepared to watch live broadcasts of your Ohio State football team in Barcelona or anywhere else in the world where you have Internet connection.

It should be obvious that the *Slingbox* enables place-shifting anywhere, whether in another city in your home state or across the globe. Importantly, the *Slingbox* technology reflects another move in the direction of consumers' gaining increasing control over TV viewing. Whereas DVR devices enable time-shifting of TV viewing, the *Slingbox* facilitates place-shifting. And the fact that consumers are increasingly involved in developing their own TV commercials—often as part of contests sponsoring brands undertake—enables consumers to have even partial control over the content of some TV commercials. All in all, control continues to shift from marketers to consumers.

SOURCES: http://www.slingmedia.com (accessed March 9, 2008); Abbey Klaassen, "Why This Box Changes Everything," *Advertising Age,* June 5, 2006, 1, 49.

and promotional announcements for stations and programs, but especially commercials. In fact, out of every broadcast hour of prime-time television, nonprogram content ranges slightly over 15 minutes among the major TV networks, or more than 25 percent of the time.[47] As noted earlier, consumers perceive television to be the most cluttered of all major advertising media. Clutter has been created by the network's increased use of promotional announcements to stimulate audience viewing of heavily promoted programs and by advertisers' increased use of shorter commercials. Whereas 60-second commercials once were prevalent, the duration of the vast majority of commercials today is only 30 or 15 seconds.[48] The effectiveness of television advertising has suffered from the clutter problem, which creates a negative impression among consumers about advertising in general, turns viewers away from the television set, and perhaps reduces advertising recognition and recall.[49]

Infomercials

Discussion of television advertising would not be complete without at least a brief mention of the infomercial. Introduced to television in the early 1980s, the long commercial, or **infomercial,** is an alternative to the conventional, short form of television commercial. By comparison, infomercials are full-length commercial

© Robin Nelson/Photo Edit

segments that typically last 28 to 30 minutes and combine product news and entertainment. Infomercials account for nearly one fourth of the programming time for most cable stations. Marketers' increased use of infomercials extends from two primary factors: First, technologically complicated products and those that require detailed explanations benefit from the long commercial format. Second, the infomercial format is in lockstep with increasing demands for marketing accountability insofar as most orders obtained from infomercials occur within 24 hours or so after an infomercial is aired.[50] Due to the rapid response, it is very easy to determine whether infomercials are moving the sales dial; comparatively, such rapid sales response is rarely the case with most products advertised via traditional commercials.

In the early years, infomercials were restricted primarily to unknown companies selling skin-care products, balding treatments, exercise equipment, and other such products. However, the growing respectability of this form of advertising has encouraged a number of consumer goods companies to promote their brands via infomercials. Well-known infomercial users include Avon, Braun, Clairol, Chrysler, Estée Lauder, Hoover, Pioneer, Procter & Gamble, and Sears. Manufacturers of consumer durables are increasingly using infomercials, such as the following successful Kodak infomercial application.

Kodak introduced a 30-minute infomercial to promote its new DC210 zoom digital camera. Eastman Kodak previously had little sales and profit to show for the $500 million it had invested in digital imaging. The infomercial, which cost nearly $400,000 to produce, included a toll-free number that invited viewers to request a $175 coupon that was good toward the purchase of the camera and other Kodak products at retail locations. Follow-up research indicated that approximately 1 out of 12 callers who received the discount coupon ordered the camera at a retail outlet, an impressive statistic considering DC210's retail price was $899 at the time of the promotion. Retail sales in cities where the DC210 infomercials were aired exceeded by 80 percent sales of this brand in cities without infomercials. Moreover, retail selling time was substantially reduced because consumers were presold by the infomercial. Kodak officials concluded that the infomercial was a cost-effective way to introduce consumers to the advantages of digital imaging.[51]

Numerous advertisers have found infomercials on television to be an extremely effective tool for moving merchandise. This long-form commercial is apparently here to stay. Although consumers have complaints with infomercials (e.g., that some make false claims and are deceptive),[52] this form of long commercial appears to be especially effective for consumers who are brand and price conscious and who highly value shopping convenience.[53]

Brand Placements in Television Programs

Returning to our earlier discussion of advertising clutter and consumers' responses in the form of zipping and zapping behavior, many observers fear that television advertising is no longer as effective as it used to be. (Recall the discussion of the various studies presented in the chapter opening *Marcom Insight.*) Brand managers and network television executives have responded to consumers' zipping and zapping behavior by borrowing from the movie industry and finding a way to circumvent TV viewers' fondness for avoiding commercials. Have you noticed brands appearing more often in television programs? This is not by happenstance; rather, brand managers are paying to get prominent placements for their brands—precisely as they have done in placing their products in movies. The widely viewed *Survivor* program epitomizes the use of product placements, perhaps to the point where TV viewers now realize that the brands placed in *Survivor* episodes are little more than thinly disguised commercials. And the ever-present display of Coca-Cola on the set of *American Idol* is yet another instance of brand placement as commercial message.

Compared with movie placements, brand appearances in TV programs have the advantages of (1) much larger audiences; (2) more frequent exposure; and (3) global reach, especially when programs are rerun around the world under syndication.[54]

Brand placements on TV can be very effective provided the brand is displayed in a context that appropriately matches the brand's image. The downside with placements in TV programs is that brand managers relinquish the full control available to them by comparison when providing the final approval for TV commercials. Interestingly, the more people feel a sense of connection with a TV program—that is, they identify with a program's characters, issues, and images—the higher their recall of brands that are placed in that program.[55] This obviously implies that TV programs that create a heightened sense of connectedness among their audiences are more effective vehicles in which to place brands in comparison to programs that fail to achieve high levels of connectedness.

Television Audience Measurement

As noted earlier, a 30-second commercial on prime-time television for national airing can cost as much as $2,700,000 (for a Super Bowl spot in 2008) or less than $100,000. Of course, the cost of advertising on spot television (i.e., non-national) is considerably cheaper because the market covered is much smaller. Also, advertising on cable stations and syndicated programs typically is cheaper than on network TV, again due to smaller audience sizes. Whatever the case, the reason for the disparity in commercial costs is *ratings.* Generally speaking, higher-rated programs command higher prices. Because prices and ratings go hand in hand, the accurate measurement of program audience size—the basis on which ratings are determined—is a critically important, multimillion-dollar industry. Advertising researchers continually seek ways to measure more accurately the size of TV program audiences. The following discussion will distinguish network (national) and local audience measurement. Inherent in this distinction is whether audience-size data are collected via electronic technology (so-called people meters) or paper diaries.

National (Network) Audience Measurement: Nielsen's People Meter Technology

The people meter, by Nielsen Media Research, represents perhaps the most important and controversial research innovation since the advent of television audience measurement.[56] Nielsen uses the people meter technology by outfitting a national sample of households with TV set-top boxes that require consumers to punch a button to record their viewing. Ten thousand households (of 112.8 million TV households in the United States as of 2007) are currently included in Nielsen's sample. The box has eight buttons for family members and two additional buttons for visitors (see Figure 12.3). A family member (or visitor) is requested to push his or her designated numerical button each time he or she selects a particular program. The meter automatically records which programs are being watched, which family members are in attendance, and how many households are watching. These data are then statistically extrapolated to all households to arrive at estimates of each program's ratings on a given occasion, such as *American Idol* on a particular Tuesday. Information from each household's people meter

figure 12.3

Nielsen People Meter

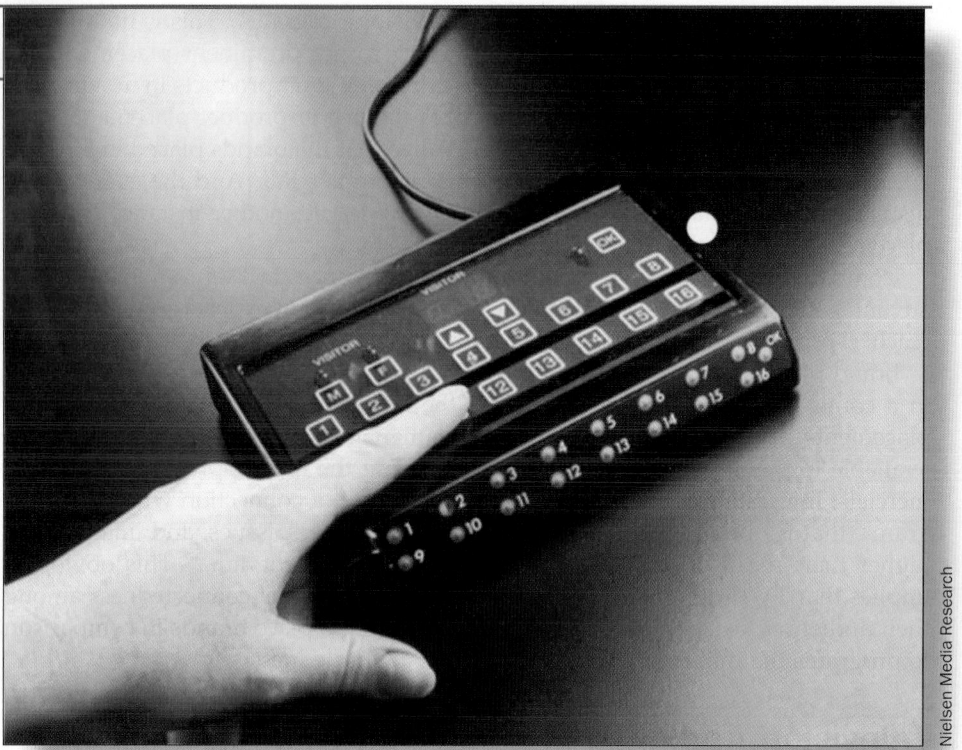

is fed daily into a central computer via telephone lines, although typically only about 80 percent of the 10,000 households actually transmit data to Nielsen.[57] This viewing information is then combined with each household's demographic profile to provide a single source of data about audience size and composition.

You might be wondering, why would anyone take the time to push a button on every occasion they sit down to watch TV? In actuality, some portion of the participating households and household members probably are *not* especially faithful in pushing their button(s) to identify they are viewing TV. However, because Nielsen compensates participating households—up to $600 for a two-year period—many participants feel obligated to perform the task.

People meters likely are here to stay in one form or another, and probably so is the controversy surrounding their use. The major networks, which pay Nielsen more than $10 million annually for its data, are growing increasingly critical of Nielsen's data. They claim that Nielsen undercounts major segments of the population, especially young people and viewers watching TV outside the home.

Local Audience Measurement: Nielsen's Diary Panels

The 10,000 households on which Nielsen's network audience measurement is based are scattered around the United States. For example, in the city where I am located (Columbia, South Carolina—a metropolitan area with over 500,000 residents and one of the top-100 TV markets in the United States), there may be only 50 or fewer households that are included in Nielsen's national sample. Obviously, there are many more households represented in much larger markets (New York City, Los Angeles, Chicago, etc.), but fewer in smaller markets. Considering just Columbia, South Carolina, for illustration, it should be obvious that the 50 or so households included as part of Nielsen's national people meter sample are far too few to draw statistically reliable estimates of TV viewing in the Columbia market.

Given this statistical fact, Nielsen has used an alternative data collection procedure for estimating TV program ratings in local markets. Nielsen has since the

1950s used *paper diaries* to collect information regarding audience viewing habits and the composition of households that view particular programs. **Paper diaries** of TV viewing behavior are filled out by a sample of 375,000 households from local markets throughout the United States. Each of these households completes a 20-page diary four times a year—February, May, July, and November, which are the months known in the TV industry as "sweep" periods. Randomly selected households in 210 markets throughout the United States fill out the diaries, which are delineated for each day of the week into 15-minute chunks. Participating households identify which household member(s) watch which TV programs during each 15-minute chunk.[58] You might be thinking, who would take the time to record their viewing behavior faithfully? Needless to say, this measurement system is imperfect because some participating households do not carefully record who watched what. Further, over 10 percent of households return diaries with substantial sections blank or containing illegible entries due to poor handwriting.

Local Audience Measurement: Nielsen's Local People Meters

It is for these reasons that the TV industry has insisted on a superior method of measuring viewing behavior in local markets. Enter the *local people meter technology.* Local people meters (LPMs) are the same devices Nielsen uses for its national audience measurement. Compared to paper diaries, which collect crucial viewing and demographic information only during the four sweep months, LPMs provide media buyers with daily feedback about audience size and composition for particular programs.

LPMs are currently available in 10 major markets that represent approximately 30 percent of all TV households in the United States—Boston, Chicago, Los Angeles, New York, San Francisco, Dallas–Fort Worth, Detroit, Philadelphia, Atlanta, and Washington, D.C. By 2011 the LPM service will be expanded to include the top 25 U.S. markets. In fact, Nielsen is expected to eliminate by 2011 the antiquated paper diary method, which was developed when there were just three major TV networks in the United States.[59] With multiple networks and numerous cable stations, the diary method of recording TV viewing has outlived its original purpose. In markets where people meters are available, it has been shown that more young adults (18-to-34 year-olds) view TV than the diary method indicates. This is because young adults are too busy to fill out paper diaries as conscientiously as older adults.[60]

Measuring Away-from-Home Viewers (and Listeners)

Needless to say, much radio listening and TV viewing occurs outside the home. For example, millions of college students listen to radios and watch TV in their dorms, but the traditional Arbitron and Nielsen measuring systems do not include this group in their samples. Likewise, people often consume radio and TV while at bars and restaurants; when they are exercising in gyms; while working in offices, stores, and factories; and so on. Yet the traditional Arbitron (radio) and Nielsen (TV) systems miss these out-of-home listening and viewing experiences. It is for this reason that Arbitron and Nielsen undertook a collaborative effort starting in 2005 to measure people's radio listening and television viewing when they are away from home.[61] Unfortunately, the collaborative effort was discontinued in 2008.

A New Challenger to Nielsen

Nielsen is often criticized for its monopoly powers because it has been the only major service involved with estimating national and local TV audiences. However, a company called TNS Media Research started competing with Nielsen in 2008.

TNS collects viewing data from 100,000 set-top boxes that are available from subscribers to DirecTV.[62] This much larger sample of households in comparison with Nielsen's sample size is expected to yield estimates of TV viewing that are more statistically reliable. Moreover, TNS's set-top box data will provide second-by-second information about TV viewing (compared with Nielsen's minute-by-minute data) and will include data pertaining to TV commercial viewing as well as program viewing. It is too soon to know (as of mid 2008) whether the TNS/DirecTV collaboration will indeed offer a viable alternative to Nielsen, but the prospect of a TV viewing alternative to Nielsen poses an exciting prospect for the many advertisers who have doubts about the accuracy of Nielsen's estimates of TV program and commercial viewing.

Summary

Excluding out-of-home advertising (covered in Chapter 20) and Internet advertising (covered in Chapter 13), there are four major media available to media planners: newspapers and magazines (print media), and radio and television (broadcast media). Each medium has unique qualities with strengths and weaknesses. This chapter provided a detailed analysis of each medium. Newspapers provide mass audience coverage and reach readers who are in the appropriate mental frame to process messages. But newspapers suffer from high clutter and limited selectivity, among other limitations. Magazines enable advertisers to reach selective audiences and to present detailed information in an involving manner. This medium lacks intrusiveness, however, and also experiences considerable clutter. Radio also has the ability to reach segmented audiences and is economical. Clutter and the lack of visuals are notable weaknesses. Finally, television is an intrusive medium that is able to generate excitement, demonstrate brands in use, and achieve impact. Television advertising suffers from clutter, audience fractionalization, and high cost.

In addition to examining each medium's strengths and limitations, the chapter also examined how media space and time are purchased. Another major focus was the measurement of audience size and composition for each medium. Specific coverage included Mediamark Research Inc. and the Simmons Market Research Bureau for magazine measurement, the Arbitron service for radio audience measurement, and Nielsen Media Research for TV audience measurement. Detailed discussion of Nielsen's people meter system—including local people meters (LPMs) and portable people meters (PPMs)—was provided along with mention of its historical paper diary method for measuring local audiences.

Discussion Questions

1. What are the advantages and disadvantages of cable television advertising? Why are more national advertisers turning to cable television as a viable advertising medium?
2. Assume you are brand manager for a new product line of book bags designed for college students. These bags come in each university's school colors and are imprinted with the school's mascot. Assume you have $5 million to invest in a two-month magazine advertising campaign (July and August). Which magazines would you choose for this campaign? Justify your choices.
3. Assume you are a manufacturer of various jewelry items. Graduation rings for high school students are among the most important items in your product line. You are in the process of developing a media strategy aimed specifically at high school students. With an annual budget of $10 million, what media and specific vehicles would you use? How would you schedule the advertising over time?
4. Examine a copy of the most recent Spot Radio Rates and Data available in your library and compare the advertising rates for three or four of the radio stations in your hometown or university community.
5. Pick your favorite clothing store in your university community (or hometown) and justify the

choice of one radio station that the clothing store should select for its radio advertising. Do not feel constrained by what the clothing store may be doing already; focus instead on what you think is most important. Be certain to make explicit all criteria used in making your choice and all radio stations considered.

6. Magazine A is read by 11,000,000 people and costs $52,000 for a full-page, four-color advertisement. Magazine B reaches 15,000,000 readers and costs $68,000 for a full-page, four-color advertisement. Holding all other factors constant, in which magazine would you choose to advertise and why?
7. Go online and see if you can locate a current (as of January of the present year) rate card for your favorite magazine. Carefully study this rate card and summarize your observations regarding price differentials for, say, black-and-white ads versus four-color ads of the same page size. (If you cannot locate a rate card for your favorite magazine, find one for your next favorite, and so on.)
8. Radio is the only major medium that is nonvisual. Is this a major disadvantage? Thoroughly justify your response.
9. In your opinion, will portable digital-audio players (e.g., Apple's iPod) eventually replace radio?
10. One marketer made the following assertion: "Infomercials are junk. I wouldn't waste my money advertising on this medium." What is your response to her contention?
11. Members of the advertising community often claim that people meters are flawed. What are some of the reasons why people meters may not yield precise information about the number of households tuned into a specific television program or provide accurate demographic information of the people who actually do view a particular program?
12. Locate a recent SMRB or MRI publication in your library and select a product large numbers of consumers use (soft drinks, cereal, candy bars, etc.). Pick out the index numbers for the 18–24, 25–34, 35–44, 45–54, 55–64, and 65 and older age categories. Show how the index numbers were calculated. Also, identify some magazines that would be especially suitable for advertising to the heavy users of your selected product category.
13. With the following data, fill in the empty blanks:

	Total '000	A '000	B % Across	C % Down	D Index
All Adults	218,289	35,144	16.1	100.0	100
Age 18–24	28,098	6,285	___	___	___
Age 25–34	39,485	10,509	___	___	___

14. Based exclusively on the data in question 13, if you were an advertiser deciding whether to advertise your brand just to people ages 18 to 24, just to the 25-to-34 age group, or to both age groups, what would be your decision? Provide a detailed rationale for your decision.
15. Why, in your opinion, is viewership of cable TV growing rather dramatically at the expense of network TV?
16. What effect, in your view, will digital video recorders (of the TiVo variety) have on television advertising effectiveness, say, 10 years from now?
17. What are your thoughts about brand placements in TV programs? Do you find these placements irritating or do you accept them as simply part of the programming landscape? Do you think they influence your attitudes toward advertised brands and purchase behavior?
18. Offer your thoughts about the likelihood that portable people meters (PPMs) will serve to track people's listening and viewing behaviors effectively when they are away from home.

End Notes

1. "TV Ads Losing Power, Survey Shows," *The Wall Street Journal*, March 23, 2006, B2.
2. Abbey Klaassen, "Major Turnoff: McKinsey Slams TV's Selling Power," *Advertising Age*, August 7, 2006, 1, 33.
3. Jack Neff, "TV Doesn't Sell Package Goods," *Advertising Age*, May 24, 2004, 1, 30.
4. These are estimated expenditures for 2008 published in "2007 Marketing Fact Book," *Marketing News*, July 15, 2007, 29.
5. *Marketer's Guide to Media*, 2007, vol. 30 (New York: Nielsen Business Media, Inc.), 184.
6. Ibid.

7. These circulation levels and rates are from ibid., 186.
8. Emily Steel, "Big Media on Campus," *The Wall Street Journal*, August 9, 2006, B1.
9. Michael T. Elliott and Paul Surgi Speck, "Consumer Perceptions of Advertising Clutter and Its Impact across Various Media," *Journal of Advertising Research* 38 (January/February 1998), 29–41.
10. Karen Whitehill King, Leonard N. Reid, and Margaret Morrison, "Large-Agency Media Specialists' Opinions on Newspaper Advertising for National Accounts," *Journal of Advertising* 26 (summer 1997), 1–18. This article indicates that ad agencies consider newspapers less effective as an advertising medium in most all respects compared with network television.
11. Julia Angwin and Joe Hagan, "As Market Shifts, Newspapers Try to Lure New, Young Readers," *The Wall Street Journal*, March 22, 2006, A1.
12. Bill Keane, *The Family Circus*, August, 9, 1992.
13. *Marketer's Guide to Media*, 151–154.
14. *Sports Illustrated* rate card #66, effective January 14, 2008.
15. Stephen M. Blacker, "Magazines Need Better Research," *Advertising Age*, June 10, 1996, 23; Erwin Ephron, "Magazines Stall at Research Crossroads," *Advertising Age*, October 19, 1998, 38.
16. *Marketer's Guide to Media*, 159–162.
17. For additional information on magazine audience measurement, see Thomas C. Kinnear, David A. Horne, and Theresa A. Zingery, "Valid Magazine Audience Measurement: Issues and Perspectives," in *Current Issues and Research in Advertising*, ed. James H. Leigh and Claude R. Martin, Jr. (Ann Arbor: Division of Research, Graduate School of Business, University of Michigan, 1986), 251–270.
18. The following information is based on *Mediamark Reporter* (Mediamark Research Inc., Fall 2006).
19. Kevin J. Clancy, Paul D. Berger, and Thomas L. Magliozzi, "The Ecological Fallacy: Some Fundamental Research Misconceptions Corrected," *Journal of Advertising Research* 43 (December 2003), 370–380, especially 377–379.
20. Sandy Blanchard, "Marketers on Custom Media," *Advertising Age*, January 29, 2007, C10.
21. Patricia Odell, "Back to Print," *Promo*, January 2007, 14.
22. "Custom Media 07," *Advertising Age*, January 29, 2007, C1.
23. *Marketer's Guide to Media*, 68.
24. Burt Manning, "Friendly Persuasion," *Advertising Age*, September 13, 1982, M8.
25. For further reading on the nature and value of imagery in advertising, see Paula Fitzgerald Bone and Pam Scholder Ellen, "The Generation and Consequences of Communication-Evoked Imagery," *Journal of Consumer Research* 19 (June 1992), 93–104; and Darryl W. Miller and Lawrence J. Marks, "Mental Imagery and Sound Effects in Radio Commercials," *Journal of Advertising* 21 (December 1992), 83–93.
26. A thorough study of this behavior was conducted by Avery M. Abernethy, "The Accuracy of Diary Measures of Car Radio Audiences: An Initial Assessment," *Journal of Advertising* 18, no. 3 (1989), 33–49.
27. Abbey Klaassen, "iPod Threatens $20B Radio-ad Biz," *Advertising Age*, January 24, 2005, 1, 57.
28. "Top Ten Broadcast TV Programs," Nielsen's Top 10 TV Ratings: Broadcast Programs, http://www.nielsenmedia.com (accessed March 5, 2008).
29. Elliott and Speck, "Consumer Perceptions of Advertising Clutter and Its Impact across Various Media."
30. Cynthia M. Frisby, "Reaching the Male Consumer by Way of Daytime TV Soap Operas," *Journal of Advertising Research* 42 (March/April 2002), 56–64.
31. Statistics in this paragraph are from two sources: Bill Gorman, "Weekly Network Ratings," February 25-March 2, 2008, http://tvbythenumbers.com/2008/03/04/weekly-network-ratings-february-25-march-2/2826 (accessed March 5, 2008); and Nielsen Media Research as reported in "Stiff Competition: TV Has Seen Better Days," *Marketing News*, December 15, 2004, 8.
32. *Marketer's Guide to Media*, 25.
33. *Marketer's Guide to Media*, 48.
34. Ellen Sheng, "Local Cable Advertising Heats Up as Viewership Further Fragments," *Wall Street Journal Online*, December 15, 2004, http://online.wsj.com.
35. Joe Mandese, "Amid Media Price Inflation, TV Production Costs Also Soar, Pose Threat to Addressability," *MediaPost's MediaDailyNews*, October 13, 2004, http://www.mediapost.com/news_main.cfm.
36. "Top Ten Broadcast TV Programs for the Week of February 25, 2008," Nielsen Media Research.
37. "The Toughest Job in TV," *Newsweek*, October 3, 1988, 72; Dennis Kneale, "'Zapping' of TV Ads Appears Pervasive," *The Wall Street Journal*, April 25, 1988, 21.
38. John J. Cronin, "In-Home Observations of Commercial Zapping Behavior," *Journal of Current Issues and Research in Advertising* 17 (fall 1995), 69–76.
39. Fred S. Zufryden, James H. Pedrick, and Avu Sankaralingam, "Zapping and Its Impact on Brand Purchase Behavior," *Journal of Advertising Research* 33 (January/February 1993), 58–66.
40. John J. Cronin and Nancy E. Menelly, "Discrimination vs. 'Zipping' of Television Commercials," *Journal of Advertising* 21 (June 1992), 1–7.
41. Steve McClellan, "TV Ads Are Less Effective, Survey Says," *Adweek.com*, February 20, 2008 (accessed March 8, 2008).
42. "Study: DVR Users Skip Live Ads, Too," *Brandweek*, October 18, 2004, 7.
43. Erwin Ephron, "Live TV Is Ready for Its Closeup," *Advertising Age*, March 22, 2004, 19.
44. Jack Neff, "P&G Study: PVR Ad Recall Similar to TV," *Advertising Age*, March 17, 2003, 4.
45. Suzanne Vranica, "New Ads Take on TiVo," *The Wall Street Journal*, October 5, 2007, B4.
46. Suzanne Vranica, "KFC Seems to Win Game of Chicken," *The Wall Street Journal*, March 20, 2006, B8.
47. Andrew Green, "Clutter Crisis Countdown," *Advertising Age*, April 21, 2003, 22.
48. For an interesting article that compares the effectiveness of 15- and 30-second commercials, see Surendra N. Singh and Catherine A. Cole, "The Effects of Length, Content, and Repetition on Television Commercial

Effectiveness," *Journal of Marketing Research* 30 (February 1993), 91–104.

49. Whether advertising clutter has adverse effects on brand name recall and message memorability is a matter of some dispute. For somewhat different accounts, see Tom J. Brown and Michael L. Rothschild, "Reassessing the Impact of Television Advertising Clutter," *Journal of Consumer Research* 20 (June 1993), 138–146; Robert J. Kent and Chris T. Allen, "Does Competitive Clutter in Television Advertising 'Interfere' with the Recall and Recognition of Brand Names and Ad Claims?" *Marketing Letters* 4, no. 2 (1993), 175–184; Robert J. Kent and Chris T. Allen, "Competitive Interference in Consumer Memory for Advertising: The Role of Brand Familiarity," *Journal of Marketing* 58 (July 1994), 97–105; and Robert J. Kent, "Competitive Clutter in Network Television Advertising: Current Levels and Advertiser Response," *Journal of Advertising Research* 35 (January/February 1995), 49–57.
50. Jim Edwards, "The Art of the Infomercial," *Brandweek,* September 3, 2001, 14–18.
51. "Digital Profits: A Case Study of Kodak's Infomercial," *Infomercial and Direct Response Television Sourcebook '98*, a supplement to *Adweek Magazines,* 20–21.
52. Paul Surgi Speck, Michael T. Elliott, and Frank H. Alpert, "The Relationship of Beliefs and Exposure to General Perceptions of Infomercials," *Journal of Current Issues and Research in Advertising* 14 (spring 1997), 51–66.
53. Research has indicated that infomercial shoppers are impulsive; see Naveen Donthu and David Gilliland, "Observations: The Infomercial Shopper," *Journal of Advertising Research* 36 (March/April 1996), 69–76. There is countervailing evidence that challenges the claim that infomercial shoppers are particularly impulsive; see Tom Agee and Brett A. S. Martin, "Planned or Impulse Purchases? How To Create Effective Infomercials," *Journal of Advertising Research* 41 (November/December 2001), 35–42.
54. Rosellina Ferraro and Rosemary J. Avery, "Brand Appearance on Prime-Time Television," *Journal of Current Issues and Research in Advertising,* 22 (fall 2000), 1–16.
55. Cristel Antonia Russell, Andrew T. Norman, and Susan E. Heckler, "The Consumption of Television Programming: Development and Validation of the Connectedness Scale," *Journal of Consumer Research* 31 (June 2004), 150–161.
56. For a technical analysis of the reliability of people-meter measurement, see Roland Soong, "The Statistical Reliability of People Meter Ratings," *Journal of Advertising Research* 28 (February/March 1988), 50–56.
57. Emily Nelson and Sarah Ellison, "Nielsen's Feud with TV Networks Shows Scarcity of Marketing Data," *Wall Street Journal Online,* October 29, 2003, http://online.wsj.com.
58. These details are from Brooks Barnes, "For Nielsen, Fixing Old Ratings System Causes New Static," *Wall Street Journal Online,* September 16, 2004, http://online.wsj.com.
59. Abbey Klaassen, "Down with Diaries: Nielsen Modernizes," *Advertising Age,* June 19, 2006, 8.
60. Monica M. Clark, "Nielsen's 'People Meters' Go Top 10," *The Wall Street Journal,* June 30, 2006, B2.
61. Joan Fitzgerald, "Evaluating Return on Investment of Multimedia Advertising with a Single-Source Panel: A Retail Case Study," *Journal of Advertising Research* 44 (September/October 2004), 262–270.
62. Stephanie Kang, "TNS Aims to Take Bite Out of Nielsen," *The Wall Street Journal,* January 31, 2008, B8.

13

Internet Advertising

The traditional advertising media, which were discussed in the previous chapter, commanded the bulk of marketing communicators' advertising budgets throughout most of the 20th century. Magazines and newspapers dominated during most of the first half of the past century, but with radio's advent as a broadcast medium in the early 1920s and television's ascendancy by the 1950s, a major change in the advertising landscape had occurred. Although newspaper advertising remained a dominant advertising medium into the 1980s, television captured an ever-growing portion of media expenditures. One could argue that television's heyday as an advertising medium has now passed with marketers' unceasing endeavors to identify advertising outlets that are less cluttered, more precise in targeting prospective customers, and more economical. Television's loss (along with the ad revenue losses other major media experienced) is largely due to the Internet's arrival as a viable advertising medium. In short, the purveyors of advertising media live in a zero sum world.

The concept of *zero sum* captures the idea that any gain for one constituent in a competitive environment represents a loss for another. The media environment is generally of this nature: Marketers' increased advertising expenditures on, say, television generally result in their decreased spending in other media such as magazines and radio. Today, the "800-pound gorilla" in the media world is online advertising. Forrester Research, an independent technology research company, reports that in one recent year nearly half of all marketers increased funding for online advertising while decreasing spending in traditional media such as magazines, newspapers, and postal mail. Moreover, Forrester Research forecasts that by 2010 online advertising and promotional spending will rival the combined spending allocated to cable and satellite TV and radio.[1] Indeed, online ad spending in the United States amounted to approximately $28 billion in 2008 and is expected to total $42 billion by 2011.[2]

According to another survey of over 2,000 Web users, consumers' Internet usage continues to grow at the expense of the traditional media. Sixty-one percent of the respondents to the survey indicated they now spend more time on the Internet than they did the previous year. Given the zero-sum character of time available for media consumption, 36 percent of the respondents indicated reduced television viewing, 34 percent expend less time reading magazines, 30 percent have decreased their newspaper reading, and 27 percent have cut their radio listening.[3]

It is virtually axiomatic that marketers chase eyeballs and ears wherever they happen to be located and place their advertising expenditures in those media where consumers allocate their time. The statistics thus indicate that the eyeballs and ears are increasingly being devoted to consumption of online media, and marketers, accordingly, are allocating greater portions of their marcom budgets to online media while reducing spending in the traditional media.

© Scott Barbour/Getty Images

Chapter Objectives

After reading this chapter you should be able to:

1. Appreciate the magnitude, nature, and potential for Internet advertising.
2. Be familiar with the two key features of Internet advertising: individualization and interactivity.
3. Understand how Internet advertising differs from advertising in conventional mass-oriented advertising media, as well as how the same fundamentals apply to both general categories of ad media.
4. Understand the various forms of Internet advertising: display ads, rich media, e-mail advertising, Web logs, search engine advertising, and advertising via behavioral targeting.
5. Appreciate the importance of measuring Internet advertising effectiveness and the various metrics used for this purpose.

>>Marcom Insight:

Gains for Online Advertising Are Losses for Traditional Media

Introduction

The Internet performs a multifaceted marketing function, serving as a mechanism for building demand, conducting transactions, filling orders, providing customer service, and serving as a versatile advertising medium. However, this chapter is *not* about e-commerce in general but rather is restricted to looking at the Internet as a rapidly growing *advertising medium*. It is important to recognize that the Internet's exact role as an advertising medium is in a state of flux: New technologies are continually emerging, and marketers are experimenting with varied uses of online communications. This chapter's objective is to overview most aspects of Internet advertising, hoping that students will fully appreciate both the changes occurring and the uncertainties of what exactly the future might bring. Nonetheless, upon completing this chapter, you will have developed an appreciation of the scope and potential of the Internet as a viable advertising medium—a medium that undoubtedly will, as described in the *Marcom Insight*, continue to steal advertising dollars from the traditional ad media.

Traditional advertising media, those covered in the previous chapter (television, radio, magazines, and newspaper), have served advertisers' needs for generations. In recent years, however, there have been increased efforts on the part of advertisers and their agencies to locate new media that are less costly, less cluttered, and potentially more effective than the established media. Some observers have gone so far as to claim that traditional advertising is on its deathbed.[4] The contention is that online advertising is superior to traditional media because it provides consumers with virtually full control over the commercial information they choose to receive or avoid. The Internet is claimed to be a better communications medium due to its versatility and superiority at targeting customers.[5] Most agree, however, that the Internet is nothing more than a potentially key element of IMC programs; it is not a replacement for conventional media.[6]

Dating back just to 1994, the World Wide Web has become an important advertising medium. Although at the time of this writing the Internet commands less than 10 percent of U.S. advertising revenue, total online advertising spending in the United States is expected to reach $42 billion by 2011.[7] Perhaps the most dramatic indicator of the Internet's growth as an advertising medium is the fact that advertising revenue Google and Yahoo! (search engine companies) generated in a recent year virtually equaled the combined prime-time ad revenues the major U.S. television networks garnered.[8] Many firms, both business-to-consumer (B2C) and business-to-business (B2B), are shifting larger percentages of their total marcom budgets to online advertising.

The Two i's of the Internet: Individualization and Interactivity

Individualization and interactivity (the Internet's two i's) are key features of the Internet and of advertising in that medium.[9] *Individualization* refers to the fact that the Internet user has control over the flow of information. This feature leads, in turn, to the ability to target advertisements and promotions that are relevant to the consumer. *Interactivity*, which is intertwined with individualization, allows for users to select the information they perceive as relevant and for brand managers to build relationships with customers via two-way communications. We now elaborate on the importance of the Internet's interactivity feature.

Traditional advertising media vary in the degree to which they are able to *engage* consumers, or, in other words, to generate mental activity. Traditional media engage the consumer in a relatively passive fashion: The consumer listens to or sees information about the advertised brand, but he or she has limited control over the amount or rate of information received. What you see (or hear) is what you get. There is action but no interaction. Whereas action involves a flow in one direction (from advertiser to consumer), interaction entails reciprocal behavior. This idea of *reciprocity* generally defines the nature of interactive media.

Interactive advertising enables the user (who no longer is a "receiver" in the traditional, passive model of communications) to control the amount or rate of information that he or she wishes to acquire from a commercial message. The user can choose to devote one second or 15 minutes to a message. He or she is, for all intents and purposes, involved in a "conversation" with the commercial message at a subvocal level. A request for additional information occurs with the push of a button, the touch of a screen, or the click of a mouse. In all instances, the user and source of commercial information are engaged in a give-and-take exchange of information—communications intercourse rather than mere transmission and reception. By analogy, a North American football quarterback and receivers are somewhat equivalent to the traditional media: The quarterback throws the ball, and the receivers attempt to catch it. Comparatively, in British rugby, players toss the ball back and forth as they advance downfield—each player both passes and receives; their relation is analogous to the give-and-take reciprocity that defines interactive advertising.[10]

The Internet is undeniably a more interactive advertising medium than most. Nonetheless, it is noteworthy that the Internet as a medium for advertising is *not* homogeneous; rather, there are a variety of different forms of online advertising. These range from e-mail and banner advertisements, which typically offer relatively little opportunity or desire for interaction, to ads encountered when one actively searches a product category or topic (referred to as search engine ads that appear as sponsored links when one conducts, say, a Google search), which generate more interaction.

The Internet Compared with Other Ad Media

In the early days of the World Wide Web (roughly from 1994 to 1999), many businesspeople thought the Internet would be an advertising panacea—a means of reaching millions of customers worldwide with ad messages in a way that would allow for greater accountability than traditional media enabled. The assumption was that people would be interested in receiving Internet ads and that the advertising would be effective in creating brand awareness, influencing attitudes and purchase intentions, and driving sales. The notion that the Internet was dramatically different from conventional ad media was as simplistic as the corresponding idea of a "new economy" that assumed that dot-com companies played under rules different from the conventional microeconomic principles that for generations have explained the requirements for success in the "old economy."

As covered in Chapter 12, each of the major advertising media has its unique set of advantages and disadvantages. Each ad medium is capable of achieving particular advertising objectives at a cost to the advertiser. In planning for and selecting a single advertising medium or, more likely, a portfolio of integrated media, the advertiser's objective is to achieve marketing objectives for the brand as inexpensively as possible. (Recall our mantra presented initially in Chapter 1: All marketing communications should be (1) directed to a particular *target market,* (2) clearly *positioned,* (3) created to achieve a *specific objective,* and (4) undertaken to accomplish the objective *within budget constraint.*)

From the discussion in the previous chapter, it should be obvious that no advertising medium is perfect for all purposes. The Internet is no exception, contrary to the early hype. One could argue, in fact, that the Internet's interactivity feature may sometimes represent a disadvantage rather than an advantage. According to this argument, the Internet user is in a "leaning forward" mind-set compared with, say, the TV viewer, who is "leaning back." Whereas the TV viewer is casually watching TV programs and advertisements in a relaxed mood (leaning back, so to speak), the Internet user is goal driven and on a mission to obtain information (leaning forward). In this mind-set, banner ads, pop-ups, and unsolicited e-mail messages simply represent an interruption, an obstacle to the user's primary mission for connecting to the Internet.[11]

Unsolicited advertisements viewed while in a leaning-forward mind-set are actively avoided and thus can have little possible effect, beyond perhaps achieving mere brand identification. Of course, Internet advertising is varied; generalizations such as these are not necessarily universal. In fact, current usage of Internet advertising—what some refer to as *Web 2.0* in contrast to the early version of online advertising, or Web 1.0—is much more mindful of users' needs, purposes, and gratifications obtained from online interactions with advertisements and other messages. Current online advertising has grown up, so to speak, and online advertisers are using the Internet with increased sophistication. There are various forms of Internet ads, each with unique characteristics.

Internet Advertising Formats

Internet advertisers use a variety of advertising formats. Table 13.1 lists the various forms of Internet advertising that are described in this chapter. Of course, all forms of Internet advertising are not equal in terms of ad expenditures, nor are all forms equally effective.[12] The two largest forms of online advertising—e-mail and search engine advertising—command perhaps 70 percent or more of all Internet advertising. Other forms of online advertising generate much smaller revenues.

The following sections examine the major forms of online advertising. It is important to appreciate that any sweeping and definitive claims would be misleading, because Internet advertising is so new, dating back less than two decades. Imagine, by comparison, the futility in the mid-1960s of providing a

table 13.1

Internet Advertising Formats

- Web Sites
- Display or Banner Ads
- Rich Media Formats
  - Pop-Ups
  - Interstitials
  - Superstitials
  - Video Ads
- Blogs, Podcasts, and Social Networks
  - Blogs
  - Podcasts
  - Social Networks
- E-mail
  - Opt-in Versus Spam
  - E-zines
  - Wireless E-mail Advertising
  - Mobile Phone Advertising
- Search Engine Advertising
  - Keyword-Matching Advertising
  - Content-Targeted Advertising
- Advertising via Behavioral Targeting

definitive treatment about the nature and effectiveness of TV advertising. Only with time have we learned how TV advertising performs, its strengths and limitations. Similarly, more time is needed before conclusive statements are possible about online advertising in its various forms.

Web Sites

A company's Web site is itself an advertisement for the company. However, beyond being a form of advertising, Web sites represent a venue for generating and transacting exchanges between organizations and their customers. Web sites can be considered the centerpiece of companies' online advertising efforts, with other advertising formats (e.g., banners, e-mail, and paid searches) simply serving to drive traffic to their Web sites. Hence, Web sites are key to successfully integrated online advertising programs. It is useless to drive prospects to a bad Web site—that is, one that is difficult to navigate, provides little useful information, is unattractive, fails to offer entertainment value, or is perceived as untrustworthy in the sense that it lacks privacy and security.[13]

A brand's Web site is an invaluable advertising medium for conveying information about the brand, its character, and its promotional offerings. Perhaps the major difference between Web sites and other online ad formats is that users seek out Web sites in a *goal-oriented fashion* (e.g., to learn more about a company or brand, to play a game, or to register for a contest), whereas other online formats typically are "stumbled upon accidentally."[14] Research has shown, for example, that half of all new-vehicle buyers visit Web sites prior to going to automobile dealerships; moreover, people who visit these Web sites spend, on average, about five hours online shopping for new vehicles.[15] Another study demonstrated that site visitations for newly released movies play a prominent role in predicting box office performance. Specifically, the greater the number of unique (not repeat) visits to a new movie's Web site, the more people actually see the movie in a cinema.[16]

A small-town retailer was fond of saying that "merchandise well displayed is half sold," implying, of course, that attractively displayed items capture the shopper's attention and invite purchase.[17] The same advice applies to Web-site construction: Attractive and user-friendly sites invite usage and revisits. Forrester Research, an organization well known in the area of Internet research, examined the Web sites of 259 B2C companies and 60 B2B firms. Forrester's research determined that text legibility is a major problem with the Web sites of both B2C and B2B companies. In fact, only 17 percent of the B2B sites and 20 percent of the B2C sites provided legible text.[18]

There is some tentative evidence that Web pages designed with relatively simple backgrounds (i.e., with minimal color and animation) might be preferred to more complex pages. A study using a state lottery as the focal Web site learned that the most complex background produced the least favorable attitudes toward the advertised service and the weakest purchase intentions.[19] It would be foolhardy to generalize this finding to other products, but it does suggest that too many bells and whistles in a Web site may distract attention away from the key message arguments on which involved consumers form their attitudes toward advertised products and services.

Because consumers visit Web sites with the objective of acquiring useful information or being entertained, it follows that Web sites are of most value when they fulfill consumers' goal-seeking needs by providing useful information rather than attempting to dazzle with excessive graphic cleverness. The architect's advice that "form follows function" certainly applies to the Web site as an online advertising tool. It has been demonstrated, for example, that the background color of a Web page affects the perceived speed of a download. That is, more relaxing colors (such as blue and green) are perceived to download more quickly than exciting colors (such as red and yellow).[20]

Display or Banner Ads

The most popular advertising format in the Internet's short advertising history has been the static advertisement known as a display, or banner ad. Banner ads, a staple of Internet advertising, are static ads—somewhat analogous to print ads placed in magazines and newspapers—that appear on frequently visited Web sites.

Click-through Rates

Click-through rates (CTRs) to banner ads are very low, averaging less than 0.3 percent. (Note: Click-through means that an Internet user, upon clicking a banner ad, is directed to the advertiser's Web site.) Banner ads for B2B companies receive somewhat higher CTRs than do those for B2C companies.[21] In other words, online users pay attention and solicit information from only a small percentage of all the Internet banner ads to which they are exposed. (Remember, exposure is necessary for but not equivalent to attention. Exposure merely indicates that the consumer has had a chance to see an advertisement.) Although the mere exposure to a banner ad can have some value in enhancing brand awareness, low CTRs reduce the effectiveness of banner ads.

Research has found that CTRs are a function of *brand familiarity*, with brands that consumers know best receiving substantially higher CTRs than unfamiliar brands.[22] Importantly, but not particularly surprisingly, this same research revealed that CTRs decrease with multiple exposures to banner ads for familiar brands, whereas the rates increase with more exposures to ads for unfamiliar brands. New and relatively unknown brands thus need to produce a banner-ad media schedule that allows for multiple exposures. Established brands, conversely, may not experience increased CTRs with multiple exposures.

This, however, does not necessarily imply that established brands do not benefit from banner advertising. On the contrary, such brands may achieve increasing levels of *brand awareness*—culminating in top-of-mind awareness, or TOMA, even though consumers choose not to click through to the brand's Web site. (Recall the discussion of brand awareness in Chapter 2, where a brand awareness pyramid portrayed a progression from brand unawareness, to brand recognition, to brand recall, and, ideally, ultimately to TOMA.) Banner advertising, along with other communications elements in an IMC program, can serve to facilitate increasing levels of brand awareness and thus enhance brand equity. Moreover, beyond merely enhancing brand equity, research evidence indicates—contrary to popular belief—that exposure to banner ads has a significant effect on actual purchase behavior.[23] That is, more exposure to banner ads leads to increased probability of purchasing Internet advertisers' products and services.

table 13.2

Types and Sizes of Internet Marketing Units (IMUs)

Type and Size of IMU (pixel size)	Square Pixels	Size Differential Versus Full Banner
Full Banner (468 × 60)	28,800	—
Skyscraper (120 × 600)	72,000	156%
Wide Skyscraper (160 × 600)	96,000	242
Rectangle (180 × 150)	27,000	−4
Medium Rectangle (300 × 250)	75,000	167
Large Rectangle (336 × 280)	94,080	235
Vertical Rectangle (240 × 400)	96,000	242
Square Pop-Up (250 × 250)	62,500	123

Standardization of Banner-Ad Sizes

The Internet Advertising Bureau (IAB), a leading trade association in the Internet advertising industry, facilitated standardization of banner sizes. The IAB endorsed seven Internet ad formats, labeled Internet marketing units (IMUs). These seven new IMUs compare with the earlier full banner, which was 468 × 60 pixels (28,080 square pixels).

Table 13.2 contrasts the new IMUs against this original full banner. This table makes it clear that the new IMUs are generally *considerably larger* than the original full banner ad. It is likely that the larger ad sizes increase attention and thus CTRs. A study conducted by a research firm for the IAB determined that the skyscraper and large rectangle IMUs were more than three to six times as effective in increasing brand awareness and favorable message associations as the 468 × 60 standard banner IMU.[24]

Rich Media: Pop-Ups, Interstitials, Superstitials, and Video Ads

It was only a matter of time before Internet advertisers began using online formats that were more dynamic than banners in their use of motion, sights, and sounds. This newer form of online advertising is referred to as *rich media,* and includes pop-up ads, interstitials, superstitials, and video advertisements. In other words, the relatively dull and inanimate form of banner advertising has naturally progressed to the attention-gaining, albeit annoying, animated form of online advertising. These rich media formats might even be compared to the low-budget ads on cable TV that use fast-talking salespeople, elevated noise levels, and dynamic movements to gain viewers' attention.

© AP Images/PRNewsFoto/American Express

Let us briefly distinguish rich media formats. **Pop-up ads** appear in a separate window that materializes on the screen, seemingly out of nowhere, while a selected Web page is loading. Pop-ups remain until they are manually closed. **Interstitials**—based on the word *interstitial,* which describes the space that intervenes between things—are, by comparison, ads that appear between (rather than within, as is the case with pop-ups) two content Web pages. Both pop-up ads and interstitials are obtrusive, but in different ways. The difference between pop-ups and interstitials is more than trite, as described compellingly in this quote:

> *First, unlike pop-ups, interstitials do not interrupt the user's interactive experience because they tend to run while the user waits for a page to download. Users, however, have less control over interstitials because there is no "exit" option to stop or delete an interstitial, which is common among pop-ups. In other words, with interstitials, users have to wait until the entire ad has run.*[25]

Superstitials are short, animated ads that play over or on top of a Web page. Finally, **online video ads** are audiovisual ads that range in length from 15 seconds to several minutes. With more households having access to broadband connection to the Internet, video ads are now feasible—unlike with dial-up connection, which was much too slow in downloading audiovisual files.

The various forms of rich media, although often a source of irritation, are effective attention getters. Internet advertisers, like advertisers in all other media, have to fight through the clutter to find ways to attract and hold the online user's attention. Bigger ads, ads popping up, and ads that offer sounds, animation, and movement are just some of the ways that have been devised to accomplish these objectives. These formats are more eye-catching and memorable than are standard (i.e., static) banner ads and yield higher CTRs.

However, in their effort to gain attention, rich media advertising formats also greatly annoy Internet users. One study determined that whereas only about 10 percent of respondents indicate they are "very annoyed" with TV ads, over 80 percent of these respondents revealed considerable annoyance with pop-ups.[26] Advertisers have accordingly reduced their use of pop-up ads, although interstitials, superstitials, and video ads are widely used. The growing importance of video ads warrants a separate section.

Video Ads and Webisodes

One of the fastest growing forms of Internet advertising is video ads, including so-called Webisodes, which are video ads that run as a series of episodes on Web sites. As noted earlier, video ads are audiovisual ads that are compressed into manageable file sizes and range in length from 15 seconds to several minutes. Research firm eMarketer predicts that online video advertising will grow to nearly $3 billion by 2010.[27]

Consider, for example, video advertising by well-known mayonnaise brand Hellmann's. Video ads for Hellmann's were placed on Yahoo's food section as part of a series titled "In Search of Real Food" starring the chef of a popular Food Network cable TV show. By linking with the popular Yahoo portal, Hellmann's had access to several million people who visit the Yahoo Food site. For another example of video advertising, see the *IMC Focus*, which describes Johnson & Johnson's use of animated Webisodes to promote its brand of baby lotion.

Blogs, Podcasts, and Social Networks

This section describes three interrelated forms of communication—blogs, podcasts, and social networks—that may someday play a prominent role in marcom programs for brands both B2B and B2C companies market.

IMC >> i.m.c. focus

Web Videos for Johnson's Baby Lotion

Johnson's Baby Lotion is an old brand that has been on the market since 1942. Referred to as the "Pink brand" in reference to the package color, Johnson's Baby Lotion competes in a product category that amasses nearly $1 billion annual sales, with Johnson's capturing about half of the market. Interestingly, Johnson's has not invested much in advertising the brand for a number of years. The last TV commercial for the Pink brand was in 1990, and the last print advertising was in 1991. The company's rationale for not advertising the brand is that sales have grown steadily without advertising. In recent years, however, competition has intensified in the baby-care market with the addition of several new competitors. A new advertising push to protect the Pink brand's market share was thus justified.

Although television advertising has been a mainstay for many of Johnson's brands, for the Pink brand the company chose not to advertise extensively on TV but turned instead to online advertising using a series of animated Webisodes. This choice was based on Johnson's belief that the Internet is a main source of information for young parents seeking baby-care advice. Based on research it has done on mothers and their babies, Johnson's is promoting its baby lotion brand as a means for parents to develop deeper bonds with their babies. The animated Webisodes (available at http://www.touchingbond.com) feature images of mothers touching and massaging their babies. The message conveyed to viewers is that Johnson's Baby Lotion plays a meaningful role in enhancing the emotional bond between mother and child. To drive traffic to the Web site that carries the Webisodes, Johnson's placed a series of ads on parent-focused Web sites.

SOURCE: Adapted from Emily Steel, "J&J's Web Ads Depart from TV Formula," *The Wall Street Journal*, February 12, 2008, B3.

Blogs

Web logs, or blogs for short, are, in a manner of speaking, "everyman's" way of communicating with others and establishing digital communities wherein individuals, mostly of like mind, can exchange their views on issues of personal relevance. It is in this context that products and brands are sometimes discussed. It is here where companies can endeavor to further enhance the equity of their brands by building brand awareness and enhancing (or protecting) their brand images. The importance of blogs to businesses has been stated in a direct and convincing fashion in the pages of *BusinessWeek* magazine:

> *Go ahead and bellyache about blogs. But you cannot afford to close your eyes to them, because they're simply the most explosive outbreak in the information world since the Internet itself. And they're going to shake up just about every business—including yours. It doesn't matter whether you're shipping paper clips, pork bellies, or videos of Britney in a bikini, blogs are a phenomenon that you cannot ignore, postpone, or delegate. Given the changes barreling down upon us, blogs are not a business elective. They're a prerequisite.*[28]

Much of the appeal of blogs is that a company can communicate directly with prospective customers, who in turn can become active communicators through their own posted comments. The interactive feature of the Internet that was described at the beginning of the chapter is perhaps realized better by blogs than any other form of online advertising.

In addition to brand marketers setting up their own blogs and communicating directly with prospective or existing customers, the reality is that thousands of blogs individuals create often discuss companies and their brands—sometimes positively, but perhaps more often negatively. It is for this reason that companies can learn a great amount about what is being said about their brands by monitoring and analyzing conversations that take place on blogs. Nielsen BuzzMetrics is one of a number of research companies that, for a fee, track and analyze what is being said in the blogosphere about a company or about its brands and competitive brands.[29] Another company, VML, developed a program named Seer to track influential bloggers and to monitor comments about companies and their brands. For example, shortly after Adidas introduced its Predator brand of soccer shoes in Europe, customers began noticing the colors of the shoe leather were quickly fading. Based on feedback from the Seer program, VML informed the German maker of Adidas that people were complaining about the leather, which prompted Adidas' marketing team to notify customers that the shoes' leather should be treated before wearing them.[30] This rapid feedback from the Seer program averted what could have become a virtual epidemic of negative word of mouth.

Blogs as an Advertising Format

Brand marketers can develop their own blogs or simply place advertisements on blogs that are appropriate for the advertiser's brand. For example, Google offers a service that enables small ads to be placed on blog sites. Only after a blog visitor clicks on the ad is revenue generated. Advertisers can turn to vendors such as Blogads (http://www.blogads.com), which is a network of blogs that accept advertising; the network matches advertisers with appropriate blogs at which to place their advertisements. Advertisers purchase ads through Blogads on a weekly or monthly basis, with costs varying based on the popularity of the blog.

Although the numbers indicate that blogging is growing exponentially, this does *not* necessarily mean that blogs represent a viable advertising medium. The value of blogs to their producers and consumers is the community created and the opportunity for a free and honest exchange of ideas. Because advertising is often perceived as less than fully objective and an intrusion, the purpose for producing and consuming blogs—that is, as a form of "citizen journalism"—may be antithetical with using blogs as an advertising vehicle. At the present time it is questionable whether blogs will represent a major advertising opportunity. The CEO of an organization that is dedicated to online advertising, the Interactive Advertising Bureau, cautions that "it's too soon to gauge blog's relevance as a stand-alone ad medium."[31]

Podcasts

Whereas traditional blogs are written documents, podcasting is an audio version of blogging. Podcasts are MP3 audio files that are available for free online and are accompanied by written blogs. Search engine PodNova (http://www.podnova.com) lists more than 90,000 podcast programs that are arranged alphabetically under virtually any topic one might contemplate.[32]

Podcasting is a way of publishing sound files to the Internet, allowing users to subscribe to a feed and receive new audio files automatically. In effect, podcasters self-produce radio-type programs. Consumers subscribe to podcasts using a special form of so-called aggregator software that periodically checks for and downloads new content, which then is playable on computers and digital audio players. Podcasting enables advertisers to target messages to consumers who share similar lifestyle characteristics as revealed by their self-selection to particular podcasts.[33] Numerous companies have created podcasts for communicating with present and prospective customers about their brands. For example, General Motors' podcasts feature interviews with company executives who discuss the company's newest cars. Nestle's Purina brand of pet foods offers podcasts called

"Animal Advice" that provide useful information to pet owners. Johnson & Johnson created a podcast for its Acuvue brand of contact lenses involving a series of episodes about teenage life called "Download with Heather & Jonelle."[34]

Social Networks

Social networking sites such as MySpace, Facebook, and Second Life have signed up millions of people around the globe who interact with "friends," share opinions and information, and create online communities of people who have similar interests and wish to share their experiences with others. It comes as little surprise that marketers have tapped into the celebrated social networking sites or have created their own social networks as a mechanism for communicating with consumers about their brands. Two illustrations of "independent" social networking initiatives are now described.

In an effort to learn more about its consumers and their needs and habits, Procter & Gamble (P&G) created two social networking sites that enable consumers to learn from one another and to share their experiences. P&G's "The People's Choice" site focuses on entertainment and allows consumers to share their views on matters such as reality TV programs, entertainers, musicians, and so on. P&G's second social networking site, "Capessa," targets women who wish to interact on matters such as health, weight loss, and pregnancy. In spirit with the nature of social networks and participants' strong desire not to be inundated with marketing messages, P&G does not commercialize either site with ad messages, although occasional pop-up ads may appear from P&G ads already run on Yahoo![35]

In appeals to reach 8-to 12-year-old girls, both Mattel Inc.'s Barbie and MGA Entertainment Inc.'s Bratz have created separate social networking sites—Barbiegirls.com and Be-Bratz.com. The Be-Bratz.com site, for example, is accessible only after purchasing a special Bratz doll that is equipped with a USB key. Users choose a screen name and their own online dolls (known as "avatars") that can be tailored to their tastes, including "buying" clothing for their avatars in an online store with virtual currency that is earned by playing games online. Participants can also customize their own online rooms and chat with other users.[36]

The use of social networks as a marcom tool is in its infancy. It therefore is premature at this time to describe the potential effectiveness of this form of marketing communications. It is certain, however, that social networking is a fact of online life. Wise marketing communicators will undoubtedly find ways to utilize universal networks of the MySpace variety or their own specially designed networks as a means to communicate with present and prospective customers.

E-mail Advertising

With millions of people online and the numbers increasing each year, it is little wonder that marketing communicators have turned to e-mail as a viable advertising medium. However, as with any other advertising medium, there is no such thing as a single type of e-mail message; they appear in many forms, ranging from pure-text documents to more sophisticated versions that use all the audiovisual powers of the Internet. Often firms send e-mail messages and encourage recipients to pass along the messages to their personal distribution list of other people. See the *Global Focus* insert for an application of e-mail advertising designed to build buzz.

E-mail can be a highly effective marcom tool for delivering advertising messages and providing sales incentives to mass audiences or to smaller targeted groups. However, this form of online communications has been spoiled somewhat by marketers sending junk mail in a practice known as "spamming." It is estimated that approximately two thirds of all commercial e-mail messages

global focus

Nescafé's Viral E-mail Effort in Argentina

Café con Leche, which is a mixture of coffee with milk, is marketed by Nescafé in Argentina and some other countries. Given a very small budget for marketing the brand in Argentina, it was necessary for Nescafé to come up with a clever marcom strategy. The plan devised involved the use of e-mails to create brand buzz. Users of Café con Leche who were known to be technology savvy and frequent forwarders of e-mail messages were recruited. The request made of these men and women, all in the 25-to-45 age group, was to pass along a commercial message for Café con Leche to at least 15 other people. The spot focused on two young women who were preparing an iced coffee with Café con Leche. Also included was a link to a Web site containing a virtual kitchen. Visitors to the site could click on ingredients located in cupboards and a refrigerator while following recipes to create coffee shakes with ice cream and to mix Café con Leche with rum or other ingredients. The intent, of course, was to increase user involvement with the brand and to demonstrate its variety of uses.

Within only a month of the launch of the campaign, the e-mail message was forwarded 100,000 times. Moreover, upward of 20 percent of visitors to the Web site responded to a survey by providing information about the brand and its uses. Beyond this specific application, which was unique at the time for Argentina, one may question why anyone would be willing to forward e-mail messages to other people. The fact is that all Internet users receive e-mails that encourage us to pass them along to others. Why are people willing to pass messages along? Research has determined that the major motives for passing e-mail messages along are because people enjoy doing so and find it entertaining and possibly of help to others.

SOURCE: Charles Newbery, "Nescafé Builds Buzz via Viral E-Mail Effort," *Advertising Age*, May 2, 2005, 24; Joseph E. Phelps, Regina Lewis, Lynne Mobilio, David Perry, and Niranjan Raman, "Viral Marketing or Electronic Word-of-Mouth Advertising: Examining Consumer Responses and Motivations to Pass Along E-mail," *Journal of Advertising Research* 44 (December 2004), 333–348.

represent spam.[37] Too many messages are sent, and too many represent spam rather than messages received from companies for whom the recipient has some interest. "Unspoiling" e-mail advertising is possible only by gaining recipients' permission to send them e-mail ads.

Opt-In E-mailing versus Spam

Imagine, for example, that a hypothetical consumer is interested in purchasing a digital camera and visits a Web site that appeared when she conducted a Google search for "digital cameras." While logged into this Web site, she received a query asking whether she would be interested in receiving more information about photographic equipment. She replied, "Yes," and provided her e-mail address as well as other information. The Web site electronically recorded her "permission granted" and, unknown to the unsuspecting shopper, sold her name and e-mail address to a broker that specializes in compiling lists. This list broker, in turn, sold her name and e-mail address to companies that market photographic equipment and supplies. Our hypothetical Internet user's name and e-mail address eventually appeared on a variety of lists, and she received numerous unsolicited e-mail messages for photographic equipment and supplies.

The solution to this problem is opt-in, or permission granted, e-mail. **Opt-in e-mailing** is the practice of marketers asking for and receiving consumers' permission to send them messages on particular topics. The consumer has agreed, or opted-in, to receive messages on topics of interest rather than receiving messages that are unsolicited. In theory, opt-in e-mailing serves both the marketer's and the consumer's interests. However, frequency and quantity of e-mail messages can become intrusive as more and more companies have access to your name and areas of interest. Consumers feel especially violated when the e-mail messages deal with topics that are irrelevant or only tangential to their primary interests. For example, when granting the original Web site permission to send photography-related messages, our unsuspecting consumer may have been interested only in information about digital cameras, when in fact she subsequently was bombarded with messages involving more aspects of photography and more photography products than she ever could have imagined. She knew not what she had opted for—some of the information received was relevant, most was not.

Although this example may appear to cast a negative evaluation of opt-in e-mail, the fact remains that advertisers who send messages to individuals whose interests are known, if only somewhat broadly, increase their odds of providing consumers with relevant information. Moreover, sophisticated marketers are using a more detailed opt-in procedure so they can better serve both their own needs for accurate targeting and consumers' needs for relevant information. For example, a consumer might say, "Send me information about men's clothes; but I don't have any kids, so don't send me anything about kids' clothiers. And I want to hear from you only once a month."[38]

Compare this with the practice of sending unsolicited e-mail messages, which, as noted previously, is a practice referred to as *spam.* Such messages offer little prospect that recipients will do much more than click on and then rapidly click off these unsolicited messages. One could argue that spam at least has a chance of influencing brand awareness, perhaps much like may happen when the consumer is perusing a magazine and unintentionally comes across an ad for a product in which he or she has little interest. However, whereas the consumer expects to see ads in magazines and realizes that this is part of the "cost of entry," the consumer does not wish to receive unsolicited e-mail messages. Hence, any brand awareness gain a marketer might obtain from e-mailing unsolicited messages is likely to be offset by the negative reaction consumers have to this form of advertising.

Anti-spam legislation under the rubric CAN-SPAM has been passed in the United States, and regulations against unsolicited e-mail are even more stringent in Europe. The spam problem represents a bothersome intrusion for consumers and also presents an economic cost to legitimate marketers that use commercial e-mail messages as an honest way of conducting business. In an effort to curtail spamming, the Federal Trade Commission has recommended to Congress a rewards program that pays anywhere from $100,000 to $250,000 as incentives for people to turn in spammers.[39]

Phishing

Perhaps even more troubling than spam is a related illegal e-mailing practice known as phishing. **Phishing** takes place when criminals send e-mail messages appearing to be from legitimate corporations and direct recipients to phony Web sites that are designed to look like companies' actual Web sites. These phony Web sites attempt to extract personal data from people such as their credit card and ATM numbers. Pronounced like fishing, the practice of phishing has the same intent—to cast line with hopes of hooking some suckers. Not only are consumers injured when their identities are stolen but also brand equity suffers when thieves masquerade as legitimate businesses.

E-mail Magazines (E-zines)

A growing form of e-mail advertising, briefly described in the prior chapter, known as *e-zines,* or sponsored e-mail, is the distribution of free magazine-like publications. These publications originally focused on trendy issues such as entertainment, fashion, and food and beverages, but e-zines have since broadened in their content and appeal. Most e-zines include a relatively small number of ads that link readers to the Web sites of stores and brands. In order to boost the credibility of their publications, e-zine editors clearly identify advertisements and avoid mentioning advertisers' products in editorial copy.[40] E-zines enable advertisers to reach highly targeted audiences and to deliver credible advertising messages that are clearly designated as such.

Wireless E-mail Advertising

Laptops with wireless modems, personal digital assistants, cellular phones, and pagers are invaluable tools for millions of businesspeople and consumers around the globe. These mobile appliances enable people to remain connected to the Web without being tethered to a wired laptop or desktop PC. Needless to say, advertisers would like to reach businesspeople and consumers on their wireless devices just as much as they covet contacting them when they are electronically wired into the Internet. This section discusses the nature and future of wireless advertising. Because wireless advertising is in its infancy, the following comments are necessarily somewhat speculative.

The growth of wireless advertising was made possible with the advent of wireless fidelity technology, commonly referred to as Wi-Fi. **Wi-Fi** is a technology that enables computers and other wireless devices such as cell phones to connect to the Internet via low-power radio signals instead of cables. Hence, users can have Internet access at base stations, or so-called *hotspots,* that are Wi-Fi equipped.

Companies that advertise via the Internet will have greater access to millions of consumers who, before wireless-enabled Internet access, could be reached only in their homes or offices, when consumers were not actually in the marketplace to make product and brand selections. Now consumers can be contacted at or close to the point of purchase where advertising can have greater impact in influencing brand choice. For example, it is one thing to receive an advertising message at home late at night several days prior to, say, going to the mall to shop casually. That advertising received in advance of the shopping trip may be forgotten prior to making product and brand choices. Comparatively, imagine sitting in a mall at a comfortable bench surfing the Web wirelessly and being exposed to an ad announcing a sale at a store located only 100 yards away. This advertising is likely to be substantially more effective than that received at a time and point separated from the buying decision. Wi-Fi has a huge future as an advertising medium for contacting business customers and everyday consumers.

Locating Hotspots

A challenge for Internet users is locating *hotspots* where wireless Internet connection is possible. Small and inexpensive Wi-Fi finders facilitate this goal. For example, a product called WiFi Seeker enables users simply to push a button and a light sweeping past four bars indicates when a Wi-Fi signal is detected. The WiFi Seeker also is useful for identifying the best place in a home or business for locating a base station.[41] Of course, numerous retailers are equipped with Wi-Fi technology, and a number of cities have installed citywide Wi-Fi technology, facilitating Internet access virtually anywhere. Companies have developed inexpensive portable devices that make it possible for users to set up temporary Wi-Fi networks at locations of their choice. These devices (e.g., Apple Computer's AirPort Express) require just access to a high-speed Internet connection such as a DSL line; then by plugging the device into the connecting line a hotspot is created.

Caution! It is important to be very cautious when computing at a hotspot, whether at a hotel, airport, or even at your local Starbucks. A spokesperson for the cybercrimes division of the Federal Bureau of Investigation points out that it should be assumed that "anything you are doing is being monitored."[42] Criminal hackers at hotspot locations can steal personal information, including credit card numbers, bank accounts, and other information. One is wise never to conduct financial transactions at a hotspot!

The Special Case of Mobile Phones

Cellular, or mobile, phones are nearly ubiquitous. It is estimated that there are more than three billion mobile phones around the world, which represents approximately one cell phone for every two people on Earth.[43] Most of these phones are equipped with Wi-Fi technology, which allows users virtually unlimited access to the Internet via their mobile phones.

Americans until recently have used their mobile phones primarily as talking devices, but Europeans and Asians have for years used these phones for transmitting text messages. Americans are following suit. Short Message System (SMS) allows users to send and receive text messages on their mobile phones of up to 160 characters in length. Multimedia Messaging Service (MMS) is a more advanced technology that permits transmitting messages along with graphics and sound. In a sense, the mobile phone is emerging into what amounts almost to a small laptop computer. Indeed, mobile phones are being dubbed the *third screen,* meaning that TV (the first screen), computers (the second screen), and now mobile phones are common audiovisual devices for receiving information, entertainment, and advertisements.

The growing numbers of mobile phone users indicate considerable potential for advertisers to reach people through these devices. (See the *Global Focus* insert about mobile phone ads in India.) Younger consumers are especially viable targets. It is estimated that about 75 percent of teens ages 15 to 19 and 90 percent of people in their early 20s use their cell phones for text messaging on a regular basis.[44]

Perhaps the more important issue, however, is whether people want to be contacted by advertisers. Because mobile phones are highly personal items (i.e., they go with us everywhere and often are in constant contact with our bodies), many critics of wireless advertising (as well as advertisers themselves) are concerned that unwanted messages represent an *invasion of privacy*. Feeling invaded, recipients of undesired advertisements may immediately delete the intruding item and harbor negative feelings toward the offending advertiser—"How dare you send me a message for a product or service about which I have absolutely no interest!"

In addition to privacy invasion, others are skeptical about wireless advertising's future on the grounds that advertising is antithetical to the reasons that people own mobile phones in the first place. The argument, in other words, is that people own mobile phones for reasons of enhancing time utilization and increasing work-related productivity while away from the workplace or home, and the last thing they want while using these devices is to receive unwanted, interrupting advertising messages. Another potential limit on the immediate future of effective wireless advertising is that the small screens on mobile phones limit the space for presenting creative advertising messages.

© Dennis MacDonald/PhotoEdit

global focus

Cell Phone Advertising in India

India is a huge country with over one billion citizens, many of whom live in villages and lack access to newspapers and television. However, cell phone usage is increasing at an incredible rate with millions of new subscribers every month. There probably is no place in the world that is riper for mobile phone advertising than India. This is attributable to two major factors: (1) many Indians, particularly those living in villages, lack access to major media, and (2) cellular call rates in India are extremely low with a one-minute call costing less than two cents.

Of course, most Indian citizens earn less than $3 a day, so even two cents per minute of cell phone usage is not a trivial charge. One prospect for further reducing the cost of cell phone usage is to subsidize calls through advertising. Although this may seem a dramatic move to people in other countries, this is precisely how television operates in countries such as the United States—advertising subsidizes the cost of TV viewing!

India's cellular network reaches 30,000 villages and is expected to increase threefold in several years. Because mobile phones reach millions of people who cannot be reached via mainstream media, the growth potential for mobile phone advertising in India is unparalleled. India's experience with mobile phone advertising may serve as a model for this form of advertising elsewhere around the world.

SOURCE: Adapted from Eric Bellman and Tariq Engineer, "India Appears Ripe for Cellphone Ads," *The Wall Street Journal*, March 10, 2008, B3.

It would seem, based on these downside arguments, that advertising on mobile phones has distinct limitations. Only the future will tell for sure. It is certain at the present, however, that many advertisers much desire the opportunity to reach prospective customers via their mobile phones. Another certainty is that successful text messaging from marketers must be based on an opt-in model, where message recipients have absolutely indicated their interest in receiving certain types of messages via mobile phones. Wireless ad recipients must have complete control over the advertising content they are willing to receive as well as when and where they receive ad messages. Advertisers must secure the wireless device user's permission to send him or her ad messages and make the user a *quid pro quo:* If you grant me (the advertiser) permission to send messages to you regularly, say once a week, I will provide you with useful information on topics of interest to you. Such an arrangement benefits the interests of both advertiser and consumer and thus provides an opportunity for the advertising community to profit from ads placed on mobile phones.

Many who are skeptical of a successful future for mobile phone advertising nonetheless believe this ad medium may have value for local retailers such as restaurants, entertainment complexes, and various service operations. Retail outlets can send promotional offers (e.g., coupons), price discounts, and other pertinent information to consumers in the local market. For example, a company named Mobile Campus sends text messages to college students who have signed up for the opt-in service. Students receive about two messages a day offering coupons and price discounts from local retailers. A student who has indicated that she likes Subway sandwiches, for example, might receive a text message from a local Subway outlet offering a half-price deal good for just that day. About 20 percent of the students at the University of Texas and at the University of Florida have signed up for Mobile Campus' opt-in service.[45]

Offering coupons via mobile phones is not restricted to college campuses. Major packaged goods companies such as Procter & Gamble, General Mills, and

Kimberly-Clark are themselves experimenting with coupon offers to mobile phone users. These companies have teamed up with the Kroger supermarket chain in a test of whether distributing coupons via mobile phones is effective and efficient. The consumers to be targeted via this test of mobile coupon effectiveness are young adults who are unlikely newspaper readers and thus do not receive coupons through this traditional medium. Here is how mobile couponing will work during this test: Consumers will download to their mobile phones a ring-tone-like application called Cellfire, which will allow them to check Cellfire's electronic "shopping mall" to see which brands are offering coupons. Consumers then identify which offers are of interest. These choices are automatically sent to computers at local Kroger stores, and consumers then automatically receive the discounts when purchasing the selected brands that offer the coupons. Only time will tell whether mobile couponing will work, but the prospects are exciting considering that coupon offers via cell phones are relatively inexpensive for marketers to offer and highly convenient for consumers—eliminating the need to clip coupons at home and to remember to take them to the store.[46]

Mobile phones offer a potentially attractive advertising medium as well as a method for distributing promotional offers. There remain, however, notable problems that may or may not be overcome. It is clear that spamming mobile phone users is totally ineffective and that successful advertisers must gain users' permission and allow them control over message content and how often, when, and where message receipt is acceptable. The next several years will provide us with a rearview-mirror perspective on whether wireless advertising is merely a passing fad or a viable, long-term advertising medium.

Search Engine Advertising

There are thousands of companies with Web sites on the Internet promoting their goods and services and encouraging prospective customers to place orders. The competition is intense because many other firms promote their own offerings. All of these competitors face the challenge of first getting prospective customers to visit their Web sites, and only subsequently can they hope to convert these Web surfers into actual purchasers. In view of the competitive intensity, how does a marketing organization attract prospective customers to its Web site? Well, of course, all of the previously discussed Internet advertising tools (display ads, rich media, e-mail, etc.) play a role in attracting people to Web sites. For the most part, however, these tools have limited ability to draw traffic, this due in large part to the fact that most Internet users do not click through to Web sites that are encountered via intrusive banner ads, pop-ups, e-mail messages, and so on.

There has to be a better way, and in fact there is. This better way is described with various terms such as search engine marketing, search engine advertising, keyword search, or simply search. *Search engine advertising* is the term preferred here because the text focuses on marcom and advertising rather than marketing in general. Further, the acronym for search engine advertising, *SEA,* nicely captures the idea that keywords are strategically placed in the Internet "sea" in hopes they will be found by cyberspace surfers.

The Fundamentals of Search Engine Advertising

So what does search engine advertising (SEA) entail? First, it is numerically the fastest growing form of Internet advertising and captures about 40 percent of the total expenditures that U.S. marketers spend on online advertising.[47] The Search Engine Marketing Professional Organization—a trade association for search marketing—has estimated that by 2011 North American companies will invest over $25 billion in this form of marketing communications.[48]

A second key to understanding SEA is realizing that Internet search engines include a variety of well-known services that people use when seeking information as they perform what can be referred to as *natural searches*—for example, one enters the expression "inexpensive book bags" when searching online for items of this sort. Google, MSN Search, and Yahoo! are the best known and most frequently used search engines. Google is far and away the dominant search engine.

A third critical element of SEA is that this form of advertising attempts to place messages in front of people precisely when their natural search efforts indicate they apparently are interested in buying a particular good or service. In this context, you might remember reading in Chapter 11 the following statement: Advertising achieves its effectiveness "through a chance encounter with a ready consumer."[49] Search engine advertising is, in many respects, the optimum form of advertising for purposes of increasing the chances of encountering ready consumers! That is, as described next in the context of "keywords," SEA places ads exactly where potential customers are searching.

A fourth key feature of SEA, and probably the most important, is the concept of keywords. **Keywords** are specific words and short phrases that describe the nature, attributes, and benefits of a marketer's offering. For example, suppose a consumer was performing an online search to locate a really specific product such as a navy blue sports coat. In performing a natural search for such an item, one consumer might input the expression "navy blue sports coat," another consumer may simply input "blue blazer," yet another may enter "dress jacket." In other words, there are many ways to search for the same item. When I entered "navy blue sports coat" into the Google search line, about 700 matches were returned. Of most relevance to the present discussion, the right side of the Google results page listed eight *sponsored links.* These links were for companies that paid Google to advertise their Web sites. For example, two of the links were for well-known retailers, Brooks Brothers (http://www.BrooksBrothers.com) and Nordstrom (http://www.nordstrom.com). Clicking through to the Web sites for these two companies revealed that both retailers offer multiple products for sale, of which navy blue sports coats are just one of many. Note that a future attempt to repeat this search would undoubtedly yield different results.

Now, from the perspective of a company that sells sports coats, it would be useful to have an ad for its product appear whenever consumers enter into a search engine any expression that might relate to navy blue sports coats. In other words, when natural search results are returned by Google, Yahoo!, MSN, or any other search engine, companies would like to have their Web sites listed as sponsored links. Why so? Well, as mentioned previously, when I entered "navy blue sports coat," nearly 700 items were returned. Because each Google page lists only 10 items and considering that most people will look into maybe only about five pages, this means that well over 600 potential items—including your company's listing—would never be seen unless it appeared somewhere on the first five pages of search results. Because advertising is all about increasing the odds that ready consumers will have a "chance encounter" with your ad (not just any ad), your task as an Internet advertiser is to increase these odds. Sponsored links to natural searches serve beautifully to accomplish this objective. The foregoing description can be summarized in the series of steps listed in Figure 13.1.

Purchasing Keywords and Selecting Content-Oriented Web Sites

There actually are two forms of search engine advertising available to online advertisers. One form, as described already, is *keyword search* (also called keyword

figure 13.1

The Role of Keywords in Increasing the Odds That Ready Consumers Encounter Your Ad

Step 1: Prospective purchasers of a specific good or service perform natural search using one or more search engines to locate that item.

Step 2: Matches to Internet shopper's search are generated by Google or another search engine.

Step 3: Alongside the matches are sponsored links that correspond to the keyword(s) entered by the shopper.

Step 4: These sponsored links appear because companies offering the searched item purchased corresponding keywords from the search engine company.

Step 5: Shoppers may click through to a sponsored Web site and purchase a desired item or, at least, consider this Web site for future purchases.

matching), and the other involves placing ads on content-oriented Web sites that provide appropriate contexts in which to advertise a particular type of product. Each form of SEA is described using Google's advertising services. Google is selected for illustration because it is by far the leading search engine and commands over 50 percent of all Internet searches.[50]

Keyword-Matching Advertising

To become a sponsored link to Internet shoppers' search results, interested advertisers must bid for and purchase keywords from search engine services such as Google. For example, the obvious keywords that a sports coat advertiser might employ to attract consumers to its Web site would include terms and phrases such as "sports coats," "blazers," "blue blazer," "blue sports coat," "blue sports jacket," "wool sports coat," "moderately priced blazers," and so forth. Google has a keyword advertising program called AdWords.

Interested students can learn more about AdWords by reviewing its demonstration at http://adwords.google.com. One will discover from the demonstration that prospective advertisers bid for keywords by indicating how much they are willing to pay each time an Internet shopper clicks on their Web site when it appears as a sponsored link. The cost per click (CPC) varies by country. In the United States, the cost ranges from one penny per click to as much as advertisers are willing to pay as a function of keyword quality. The higher an advertiser's bid, the more prominent the placement of the advertiser's sponsored link. That is, the highest bidder per keyword receives the top placement; the second highest bidder, the second placement; and so on. When purchasing keywords, advertisers also indicate the top amount they are willing to budget each day. So for example, if an advertiser is willing to pay only 20 cents per CPC for a particular keyword and specifies a daily budget limit of $300, then that advertiser could receive a maximum of 1,500 click throughs to its Web site on a given day for just that one keyword.

The keyword advertiser also can specify the country where ads are to be sponsored and particular local areas where ads are to be targeted. For example, advertisers of services provided in local communities are interested in reaching only people located in particular communities and surrounding areas. Google's AdWords program also provides advertisers with performance reports that indicate which keywords are generating the most click throughs and how much each keyword costs on average. Advertisers can then decide to drop usage of underperforming keywords or rebid how much they are willing to pay to use these words or phrases.

Content-Targeted Advertising

In addition to its AdWords service, Google has another program called AdSense. With this program, Google enables Internet advertisers to run ads on Web sites other than Google's own site. Advertisers specify the sites on which they want their ads to appear rather than picking keywords that are tied to Internet surfers' natural search behavior (as described previously for the AdWords program). Advertisers pay Google to run ads on selected Web sites, and then Google pays these Web sites about 80 percent of the revenue generated from advertisers.[51] In a sense, Google operates as an ad agency placing ads on other Web sites, taking as commission about 20 percent of the revenue and allowing the content-oriented Web sites to earn the bulk of the ad-placement cost.

This form of SEA is particularly attractive to marketers of products that people typically do *not* search for using keywords. For example, most people would not perform searches for staple products such as bread and milk; purchasing keywords for these products would likely yield few productive results. However, advertisers of these products could benefit greatly by placing ads on content-oriented Web sites that are devoted to matters of health and fitness. People who go to such Web sites might then encounter ads for bread or milk touting these products' health-related benefits. For example, several years ago a widely circulated report appeared in various media about the weight-loss benefits of drinking at least 24 ounces of milk daily along with undertaking a regular exercise regimen. The trade association responsible for promoting milk could have taken advantage of this publicity by placing ads on various health-oriented Web sites and linking the ads to media reports describing milk's weight-loss benefits.

In summary, SEA with programs such as Google's AdWords and AdSense provide Internet advertisers ways to place their ads in places where prospective customers are searching and thus to increase the odds of encountering ready consumers. The advantages are clear (cost efficiency, pinpointed targeting, and quick and easy assessment of ad effectiveness), yet SEA is not without problems.

SEA Is Not without Problems

The major problem with search engine advertising, especially the keyword-matching variety, is that of click fraud. **Click fraud** occurs when a competitor or other party clicks on a sponsored link repeatedly in order to foul up advertising effectiveness. Recall that advertisers pay for sponsored links on a cost-per-click basis, and that advertisers specify an upper limit on how much they are willing to budget daily. You may further recall that at 20 cents per click and with a daily limit of $300, the advertiser can achieve a total of only 1,500 click throughs on a given day. That being the case, a competitor could repeatedly click on a sponsored link until the 1,500 limit is reached, thus preventing any legitimate click throughs. As such, our hypothetical advertiser would receive zero benefit from its modest investment.

In addition to competitors engaging in click fraud, this practice also takes place when employees of content-oriented Web sites repeatedly click on advertised Web sites to increase the revenue a search engine such as Google pays to them. Again, advertisers suffering from fraudulent click throughs receive no benefit from their advertising. So-called *bot* software programs (short for robot) are used to click on ads automatically and repeatedly, thereby generating a lot of revenue for Web sites and wasting advertisers' honest investment that is intended to enhance their brand images and drive sales.

Estimates of click fraud's magnitude range from 5 percent to 20 percent.[52] The magnitude of the problem prompted a top executive at Google to describe click fraud as "the biggest threat to the Internet economy" and to encourage that something be done as quickly as possible to curtail the problem before it threatens the SEA business model.[53] The solution comes in the form of companies that specialize in click-fraud detection. The service these companies provide has been described as follows: "Click fraud detection technology identifies and alerts companies to suspicious activity while it is happening, allowing paid search managers to stall ads running on keywords where the abuse is happening, preventing further budget loss."[54]

Click fraud notwithstanding, it remains that SEA is generally a highly effective form of online advertising, and click fraud is simply a cost of doing business. Most authorities believe that the return on investment from SEA is unmatched by other forms of online marcom.

Advertising via Behavioral Targeting

The essence of online *behavioral targeting* is a matter of directing online advertisements to just those individuals who most likely are interested—as indicated by their online site-selection behavior—in making a purchase decision for a particular product category. Unlike content-oriented SEA where the advertiser must pay for every person who has an opportunity to see the advertiser's message, with behavioral targeting *only those consumers known to be interested in a particular product or service* would receive ads from a marketer that employs behavioral targeting. By being selective, advertisers are able to place ads on many more Web sites than they could afford when employing a relatively indiscriminate content-oriented campaign. Many argue that behavioral targeting takes Internet advertising to a level higher than SEA provides. In fact, one practitioner has dubbed behavioral targeting "search [engine advertising] on steroids."[55]

Internet advertisers, like the savvy conventional advertisers who preceded them, have turned increasingly to customer targeting as a means of increasing click-through rates and converting "clickers" into purchasers. With improved tracking technology, it has become possible to determine more about Internet surfers' consumer behavior and then to tailor the specific ads to which surfers are exposed. This is accomplished with electronic files (called *cookies*) that track users' online behavior. (For an accessible explanation of Internet cookies, see http://www.cookiecentral.com/c_concept.htm.) The following quote illustrates how cookies enable Internet advertisers to direct ads that are compatible with Internet users' product-usage interests:

> *If a golfer clicks on an ad for a golf magazine, that click is recorded. The next time our golf-loving Web surfer goes online, an ad server detects him or her, finds a golf banner and serves it up. By isolating that user, Internet ad companies can sell targeted golf-related advertising. The user doesn't have to go back to the same site to get the targeted ad, either. The ad-server companies [e.g., DoubleClick, 24/7 Media, Engage Technologies] sign up hundreds of client Web sites onto their ad networks, which enables the ad servers to follow users from Web site to Web site.*[56]

As always with any form of advertising, behavioral targeting is not without disadvantages. The most notable is that this form of

Courtesy of Golf Fitness Magazine, Inc.

targeting can be viewed as *an invasion of people's privacy*. Simply, many people feel violated knowing that their Web-search behavior is being closely tracked.[57] In an Internet advertising variation on the well-known physics principle that for every action there is an equally strong and opposing reaction, many consumers avoid Web ads by downloading ad-blocking software. Of course, nothing in life comes for free. Consumers receive free television programming because advertisers subsidize this freedom. Likewise, if ad-killing software becomes widely used, Internet users may have to pay for the Web content that we presently enjoy at no cost.

Measuring Internet Ad Effectiveness

A major concern for Internet advertisers is measuring the effectiveness of their advertising placements. This is, of course, exactly the same concern that brand managers have when advertising in conventional media, as was mentioned in the previous chapter when discussing audience measurement for each of the major media. Recall, for example, the services available for magazine audience measurement (Mediamark Research Inc. and Simmons Market Research Bureau), radio audience measurement (Arbitron's RADAR service), and television audience measurement (Nielsen's people meters). In every instance, these audience measurement services have been developed to determine as precisely as possible the numbers of readers, listeners, or viewers of particular advertising vehicles and to identify their demographic characteristics.

With the conventional media as a benchmark, the student can readily appreciate that Internet advertisers have precisely the same measurement concerns: How many people clicked through a particular Web ad? What are the demographic characteristics of these people? How many visited a particular Web site? What actions were taken following click throughs or site visits? Is this form of online advertising yielding a suitable return on investment?

Metrics for Measuring Internet Ad Performance

The word *metric* refers, in general, to a unit of measurement. As applied in the present context, the issue is one of which particular indicators are most appropriate for assessing the effectiveness of Web sites and ads placed on these sites. Thinking of Web sites as a type of advertising vehicle, as that term was used in the previous chapter when discussing traditional ad media, the measurement issue is one of assessing the worth or effectiveness of specific forms of online advertising. In actuality, a wide variety of metrics are used because advertisers have different measurement objectives and because formats for advertising online are highly varied in this new and dynamic arena of Web 2.0 applications. There are at least four general objectives, as follows, for assessing online advertising effectiveness and (in parentheses) a variety of metrics that can be used to indicate whether the objective has been accomplished.[58]

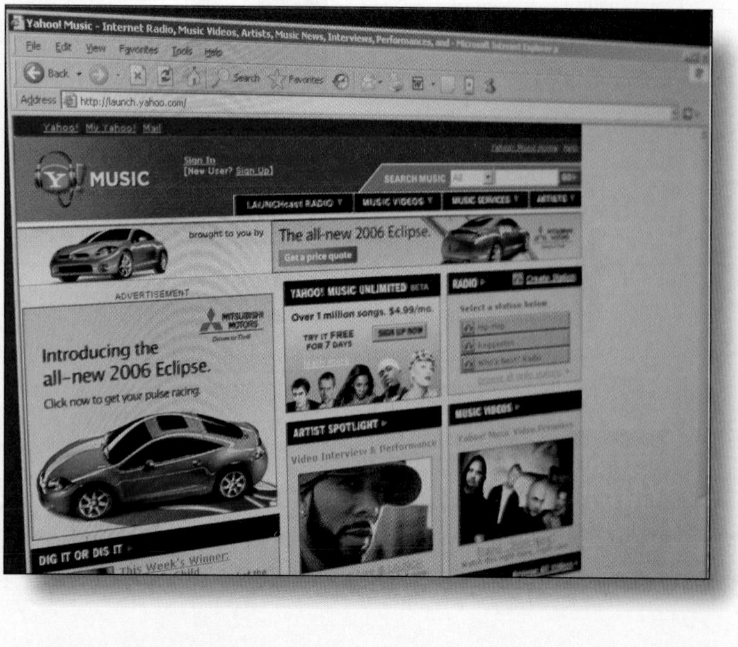

© ADAM BERRY/BLOOMBERG NEWS/Landov

1. The exposure value or popularity of a Web site or Internet ad (e.g., number of users exposed to an ad, number of unique visitors, and click-through rate)

2. The ability of a site to attract and hold users' attention and the quality of customer relationships (e.g., average time per visit, number of visits by unique visitors, and average interval between user visits)
3. The usefulness of Web sites (e.g., proportion of repeat visitors)
4. The ability to target users (e.g., profile of Web-site visitors and visitors' previous Web-site search behavior)

It should be apparent that many metrics are used to assess the effectiveness of Web sites and the ads placed on those sites. Because detailed discussion of these metrics is beyond the scope of this text, brief discussion is devoted to just three widely used metrics: click-through rates, cost per thousand impressions, and cost per action.

Click-through rates (CTR), as mentioned several times already, simply represent the percentage of people who are exposed to, say, an Internet-delivered ad and actually clicked their mouse on it. The click-through percentage has continued to decline, especially for banner ads, and many in the advertising community have become disenchanted with this metric—although some claim that banner ads can have a positive effect on brand awareness even if Internet users do not click through to learn more about the advertised brand.

Cost per thousand impressions (CPM) is a simple alternative to click-through rates that assesses how much (on a per-thousand-impressions basis) it costs to place an online ad. The only information the CPM metric reveals is what it costs (again, on a per-thousand-impressions basis) to have an ad come into potential contact with the eyeballs of Internet users. This measure captures Internet users' opportunity to see (OTS) an ad but provides no information about the actual effect of an advertisement.

Use of the CPM metric is beginning to give way to the *cost-per-action* (CPA) metric. The action in cost-per-action refers to determining the number of users who actually visit a brand's Web site, register their names on the brand's site, or purchase the advertised brand. Many advertisers prefer to pay for Internet advertising on a CPA rather than a CPM basis. The terms of purchasing Internet advertising on a CPA basis vary greatly, with higher prices paid for actions involving actual purchases or actions closer to purchase (such as registering for free samples of a brand) compared with merely clicking on, say, a banner ad. However, given that advertisers are interested in achieving specific results, especially increased sales of their brands, they are willing to pay more for metrics indicating that desired results have been achieved (i.e., CPA metrics) than for those, such as CTR, that merely promise the possibility of achieving desired results.

In summary, it should be apparent that there is no such thing as perfect measurability—for the Internet or for any other advertising medium. The difficulty of determining an ad medium's effectiveness is illustrated, in the extreme, by the following set of questions: "Consider the Nike logo on Tiger Woods's baseball cap: Does it make you more likely to buy a pair of the company's shoes? If so, would you admit it to a surveyor? Would you admit it to yourself? Would you even know it?"[59]

Summary

This chapter has covered a variety of online advertising media. Table 13.1 structured the discussion by identifying specific forms of Internet advertising. Online advertising spending is growing at an exponential rate in North America as well as elsewhere around the globe. In comparison to most other advertising media, the Internet possesses the two key features of *individualization* and *interactivity*. These features allow users to control the information they receive and the amount of time and effort devoted to processing advertising messages.

The bulk of the chapter discussed various forms of Internet advertising media. First, Web sites were considered the centerpiece of companies' online advertising efforts, with other advertising formats (e.g., banners, e-mail, and paid searches) serving to drive traffic to companies' sites. Display, or banner, ads are a popular form of Internet advertising, although click-through rates are notoriously low. Because CTRs to displays are trivially small, online advertisers have turned to new technology and larger ad sizes to grab the online surfer's attention. Rich-media formats such as pop-ups, interstitials, superstitials, and video ads have experienced increased usage due to their ability to attract attention. The downside of rich-media ads is that Internet users find them intrusive and annoying.

Web logs (blogs) were described as a potential advertising vehicle, but one with an uncertain future because users' reasons for blogging are antithetical to the role and purpose of advertising. The ubiquity of blogs, including the radio-type version known as podcasts, makes this an attractive prospect for advertisers, but only time will tell whether advertising on blogs and podcasts is an economically viable option. It simply is too early to know.

E-mail advertising is a widely used form of online advertising, although excessive spamming has somewhat compromised the effectiveness of this format. Permission-based, or opt-in, e-mail is an effort to legitimize the use of e-mail advertising, but many consumers simply do not like being advertised to on the Internet. E-mail magazines (e-zines) represent a more acceptable advertising medium because ads are clearly labeled for what they are, which explains why this form of sponsored e-mail is on the rise. Also, given the huge increase in wireless devices such as Wi-Fi-enabled laptops, personal digital assistants, and mobile phones, advertisers covet the opportunity to reach people when they are away from their homes and workplaces. Again, only time will tell whether, for example, mobile phones represent a viable advertising medium.

Search engine advertising (SEA) commands the largest Internet advertising investment at about 40 percent of all online ad expenditures. The fundamental concept underlying SEA is that advertisements can be located where consumers and B2B customers are searching. In other words, SEA increases the odds of encountering the ready consumer. Two forms of SEA are widely used: keyword matching and placing ads on content-oriented Web sites that match the advertiser's offering.

Behavioral targeting is a final form of Internet advertising discussed in this chapter. This form of advertising directs ads just to those individuals who most likely are interested in purchasing a particular good or service as indicated by their past online site-selection behavior. Behavioral targeting takes Internet advertising to a level higher than even SEA. In fact, one practitioner has dubbed behavioral targeting as search engine advertising on steroids.

The final topic discussed was measuring Internet ad effectiveness. The choice of metrics for measuring the effectiveness of Internet advertising is somewhat of a "moving target" due to the dynamic nature of online advertising and the many formats available to advertisers for reaching prospective customers online. Three specific metrics for measuring ad performance were described: click-through rates (CTR), cost per thousand impressions (CPM), and cost per action (CPA). This last metric is growing in usage because advertisers are interested in achieving particular results—e.g., influencing people to purchase products—and this is precisely what the CPA metric measures.

Discussion Questions

1. As noted in the text, some observers have gone so far as to claim that traditional advertising is on its deathbed and will eventually be supplanted by Internet advertising. What are your views on this?
2. Provide an interpretation of the meaning and importance for advertisers of the Internet's two i's, individualization and interactivity. Use your own words and ideas rather than merely feeding back what is described in the text.
3. The text described the Internet user as being in a "leaning-forward" mind-set compared with, say, the TV viewer who is "leaning back." Explain what this means and why the distinction is advantageous or problematic for Internet advertisers.
4. Describe your typical response behavior to Internet ads. That is, do you often click on banner ads? What's your reaction to pop-ups, interstitials, and superstitials?
5. Can banner ads be effective if less than 0.3 percent of all people click through them?
6. Do you believe that Internet companies' use of cookies invades your privacy? Would you

favor legislation that prevents the use of this technology? If such a law were passed, what would be the downside from the consumer's perspective?

7. Have you personally downloaded ad-blocking software onto your computer? What are the implications of this practice if millions of consumers had ad-blocking software loaded on their PCs and other Internet appliances?
8. The following set of questions was quoted in the chapter in reference to the Nike logo on Tiger Woods's baseball cap: Does it make you more likely to buy a pair of the company's shoes? If so, would you admit it to a surveyor? Would you admit it to yourself? Would you even know it? What implications do these questions (and their answers) hold for measuring Internet advertising effectiveness?
9. The Cookie Central Web site (http://www.cookiecentral.com) is dedicated to explaining exactly what cookies are and what they can do. Visit this site and present a discussion on how cookies can be and are used to compile lists for behavioral targeting purposes.
10. What has been your personal experience with e-mail advertising? Are you part of any opt-in lists whereby you receive regular (say weekly) e-mail messages? What proportion of the e-mail messages do you receive on a daily basis that you would consider spam?
11. One virtue of e-mail advertising is that different messages for the same product or service can be mailed to various customer groups that differ with respect to pertinent buyographic, demographic, or other characteristics. This ability to "mass customize" messages should increase marcom effectiveness, yet a cynic might look at this practice as a bit deceptive—somehow saying different things about your product to different audiences seems misleading. What is your view on this?
12. E-mail advertising is claimed to be very effective for viral marketing purposes—that is, buzz generation. This is accomplished by requesting an e-mail recipient to forward the message to a friend. Present your views on the effectiveness of the e-mail viral marketing practice. In other words, explain what makes e-mail buzz generation effective or not.
13. Behavioral targeting was characterized as search engine advertising on steroids. Explain what the practitioner who used this clever expression had in mind.
14. From the perspective of an advertiser for a low-involvement, packaged-goods product such as cereal, compare and contrast the strengths and weaknesses of the two forms of search engine advertising: keyword-matching versus content-targeted advertising.
15. What, in your view, is the potential of using blogs as an advertising medium?
16. What, in your view, is the potential of using mobile phones as an advertising medium?
17. What, in your view, is the potential of using social networking sites such as MySpace and Facebook as an advertising medium?

End Notes

1. US Online Marketing Forecast: 2005 to 2010, Forrester Research, Inc., May 2005, http://www.centerformediaresearch.com.
2. Kate Maddox, "Outlook Bright for Online Advertising," *BtoB*, January 14, 2008, 10.
3. Gavin O'Malley, "BURST! Internet Continues Snagging Eyeballs from TV," MediaPost Publications, http://www.publications.mediapost.com.
4. Roland T. Rust and Richard W. Oliver, "Notes and Comments: The Death of Advertising," *Journal of Advertising* 23 (December 1994), 71–77. See also Roland T. Rust and Sajeev Varki, "Rising from the Ashes of Advertising," *Journal of Business Research* 37 (November 1996), 173–181.
5. For example, Rafi A. MohammedRobert J. FisherBernard J. Jaworski, and Aileen M. Cahill, *Internet Marketing: Building Advantage in a Networked Economy* (New York: McGraw-Hill, 2002), 370.
6. Ibid., 375.
7. Maddox, "Outlook Bright for Online Advertising."
8. Kris Oser, "New Ad Kings: Yahoo, Google," *Advertising Age*, April 25, 2005, 1, 50.
9. Mohammed et al., *Internet Marketing: Building Advantage in a Networked Economy*, 371.
10. For more formal treatments of the concept of interactivity, see the following sources: Yuping Liu and L. J. Shrum, "What Is Interactivity and Is It Always Such a Good Thing? Implications of Definition, Person, and Situation for the Influence of Interactivity on Advertising Effectiveness," *Journal of Advertising* 31 (winter 2002), 53–64; Sally J. McMillan and Jang-Sun Hwang, "Measures of Perceived Interactivity: An Exploration of

the Role of Direction of Communication, User Control, and Time in Shaping Perceptions of Interactivity," *Journal of Advertising* 31 (fall 2002), 29–42; and Yuping Liu, "Developing a Scale to Measure the Interactivity of Websites," *Journal of Advertising Research* 43 (June 2003), 207–216. For an especially complete treatment of interactivity in Internet advertising, see Grace J. JohnsonGordon C. BrunerII, and Anand Kumar, "Interactivity and Its Facets Revisited: Theory and Empirical Test," *Journal of Advertising* 35 (winter 2006), 35–52.

11. The ideas in this paragraph are adapted from Terry Lefton, "The Great Flameout," *The Industry Standard,* March 19, 2001, 75–78.
12. Research has demonstrated that attitudes toward Internet ad formats are positively related to attitudes toward advertisements that are carried within these formats. See Kelli S. Burns and Richard J. Lutz, "The Function of Format," *Journal of Advertising* 35 (spring 2006), 53–63.
13. For in-depth treatment of the importance and role of privacy, security, and trust in Web sites, see the following sources: Ann E. Schlosser, Tiffany Barnett White, and Susan M. Lloyd, "Converting Web Site Visitors into Buyers: How Web Site Investment Increases Consumer Trusting Beliefs and Online Purchase Intentions," *Journal of Marketing* 70 (April 2006), 133–148; Jan-Benedict E. M. Steenkamp and Inge Geyskens, "How Country Characteristics Affect the Perceived Value of Web Sites," *Journal of Marketing* 70 (July 2006), 136–150.
14. Shelly Rodgers and Esther Thorson, "The Interactive Advertising Model: How Users Perceive and Process Online Ads," *Journal of Interactive Advertising* 1 (fall 2000), http://www.jiad.org/vol1/no1/Rodgers/index.html">.
15. Jean Halliday, "Half Hit Web before Showrooms," *Advertising Age,* October 4, 2004, 76.
16. Fred Zufryden, "New Film Website Promotion and Box-Office Performance," *Journal of Advertising* Research 40 (January/April 2000), 55–64.
17. I learned this advice from my dear late father, Aubrey Shimp, who worked in retailing for many years. I am not sure whether this was his own wisdom or whether it can be attributed to another source.
18. Mary Morrison, "Usability Problems Plague B-to-B Sites," *BtoB's Interactive Marketing Guide,* 2007, 10.
19. Julie S. StevensonGordon C. Bruner II, and Anand Kumar, "Webpage Background and Viewer Attitudes," *Journal of Advertising Research* 40 (January/April 2000), 29–34. See also Gordon C. Bruner II, and Anand Kumar, "Web Commercials and Advertising Hierarchy-of-Effects," *Journal of Advertising Research* 40 (January/April 2000), 35–42. The latter article involves research using a non-student sample and provides interesting refinement concerning the role of Web-page complexity.
20. Gerald J. GornAmitava ChattopadhyayJaideep Sengupta, and Shashank Tripathi, "Waiting for the Web: How Screen Color Affects Time Perception," *Journal of Marketing Research* 41 (May 2004), 215–225.
21. Ritu LohtiaNaveen Donthus, and Edmund K. Hershberger, "The Impact of Content and Design Elements on Banner Advertising Click-through Rates," *Journal of Advertising Research* 43 (December 2003), 410–418.
22. Micael Dahlen, "Banner Advertisements through a New Lens," *Journal of Advertising Research* 41 (July/August 2001), 23–30.
23. Puneet ManchandaJean-Pierre DubéKhim Yong Goh, and Pradeep K. Chintagunta, "The Effect of Banner Advertising on Internet Purchasing," *Journal of Marketing Research* 43 (February 2006), 98–108.
24. "Interactive Advertising Bureau/Dynamic Logic Ad Unit Effectiveness Study," Interactive Advertising Bureau, March/June 2001, http://www.iab.net.
25. Rodgers and Thorson, "The Interactive Advertising Model: How Users Perceive and Process Online Ads."
26. Jack Neff, "Spam Research Reveals Disgust with Pop-up Ads," *Advertising Age,* August 25, 2003, 1, 21.
27. Kate Maddox, "New Formats Drive User Engagement," *B2B's Interactive Marketing Guide,* 2007, 35.
28. Stephen Baker and Heather Green, "Blogs Will Change Your Business," *BusinessWeek,* May 2, 2005, 57.
29. Allison Enright, "Listen, Learn," *Marketing News,* April 1, 2007, 25–29.
30. Aaron O. Patrick, "Tapping into Customers' Online Chatter," *The Wall Street Journal,* May 18, 2007, B3.
31. Kate Fitzgerald, "Blogs Fascinate, Frighten Marketers Eager to Tap Loyalists," *Advertising Age,* March 5, 2007, S-4.
32. Paul Gillin, "Podcasting, Blogs Cause Major Boost," *B2B's Interactive Marketing Guide,* 2007, 30.
33. Albert Maruggi, "Podcasting Offers a Sound Technique," *Brandweek,* May 2, 2005, 21.
34. David Kesmodel, "Companies Tap Podcast Buzz to Sell Contact Lenses, Appliances," *The Wall Street Journal,* June 30, 2006, B1.
35. This description of P&G's social networking sites is based on Lisa Cornwell, "P&G Launches Two Social Networking Sites," *Marketing News,* February 1, 2007, 21.
36. This description is based on Nicholas Casey, "Online Popularity Contest Next in Barbie-Bratz Brawl," *The Wall Street Journal,* July 23, 2007, B1.
37. "DoubleClick's 2004 Consumer E-mail Study," DoubleClick, October 2004, http://www.doubleclick.com.
38. Jane E. Zarem, "Predicting the Next E-mail Business Model," *1 to 1 Magazine,* May/June 2001, 23.
39. "FTC Recommends Bounty to Nab Spammers," *Wall Street Journal Online,* September 16, 2004, http://online.wsj.com.
40. Elizabeth Weinstein, "Retailers Tap E-Zines to Reach Niche Audiences," *Wall Street Journal Online,* April 28, 2005, http://online.wsj.com.
41. David LaGesse, "Hunting for the Hottest Wi-Fi Spots," *U.S. News and World Report,* August 2, 2004, 84.
42. Joseph De Avila, "Wi-Fi Users, Beware: Hot Spots Are Weak Spots," *The Wall Street Journal,* January 16, 2008, D1.
43. Julie Liesse, "Mobile Moves Forward," *MobileMarketing,* November 19, 2007, 6.
44. Jyoti Thottam, "How Kids Set the (Ring) Tone," *Time,* April 4, 2005, 38–45.

45. Allison Enright, "(Third) Screen Tests," *Marketing News,* March 15, 2007, 17–18.
46. This description is based on Alice Z. Cuneo, "Package-goods Giants Roll Out Mobile Coupons," *Advertising Age,* March 10, 2008, 3, 26.
47. Carol Krol, "Search Draws Big Spending," *BtoB's Interactive Marketing Guide,* 2008, 19.
48. "Search Engine Marketing Shows Strength as Spending Continues on a Growth Track against Doom and Gloom Economic Background," http://www.sempo.org/news/releases/03-17-08 (accessed April 14, 2008).
49. Erwin Ephron, "Recency Planning," *Journal of Advertising Research* 37 (July/August 1997), 61.
50. *Advertising Age's Fact Pack* 2007, 10.
51. Kevin J. Delaney, "Google to Target Brands in Revenue Push," *Wall Street Journal Online,* April 25, 2005, http://online.wsj.com.
52. Ibid.
53. Ibid.
54. Lisa Wehr, "Click Fraud Detection Gives Instant Protection," *btobonline.com,* February 12, 2007, 17.
55. Richard Karpinski, "Behavioral Targeting," *i.Intelligence,* spring 2004, 16.
56. Alex Frangos, "How It Works: The Technology behind Web Ads," *Wall Street Journal Online,* April 23, 2001, http://online.wsj.com.
57. For reading on privacy and ethical issues in online marketing, see the special issue of the *Journal of Public Policy & Marketing* 19 (spring 2000), 1–73.
58. Subodh BhatMichael Bevans, and Sanjit Sengupta, "Measuring Users' Web Activity to Evaluate and Enhance Advertising Effectiveness," *Journal of Advertising* 31 (fall 2002), 97–106. This source identified a fifth objective that is not listed here (comarketing success).
59. Rob Walker, "The Holy Grail of Internet Advertising, the Ability to Measure Who Is Clicking on the Message, Is Under Assault," *New York Times,* August 27, 2001, C4.

14

Other Advertising Media

Clutter—A state or condition of confusion or disorderliness.

Direct—Proceeding to a target by the shortest route.

Precision—A state or quality of being exact.

Ingenuity—The quality of being clever or skillful in producing or designing something.

The preceding terms and their definitions are relevant for appreciating the various forms of "other" advertising media that are described in this chapter. So far, the text has reviewed the major forms of mass media (Chapter 12) and online advertising (Chapter 13). The present chapter explores a number of other media that can be used to supplement the media options covered in the two preceding chapters.

These other media—direct advertising through the postal service; brand placements in movies, on TV, in songs, and elsewhere; yellow-pages advertising; video-game advertising (a.k.a. advergaming); cinema advertising; and a wide variety of miscellaneous forms of advertising—are increasingly being used to avoid the clutter problem that characterizes the mass media.

Clutter, as defined previously, is a state of confusion or disorderliness. The traditional media and the Internet represent a disorderly state for individual advertisers as their attempts to capture the viewer's or listener's attention is offset by the efforts of hundreds of other advertisers attempting to accomplish the same goal. Any advertiser's message is easily lost amid the confusion caused by consumers being inundated by one advertisement after another.

Some of these other media, although not necessarily all, reach the target market via a *direct* route rather than through an intermediary such as a television network. For example, postal advertising, or what also is referred to as direct mail, provides advertisers with a means of directing messages to a well-defined target market that has been selected with *precision.* This is to say that postal advertising results in fewer wasted exposures and thus achieves more efficient delivery of advertising messages.

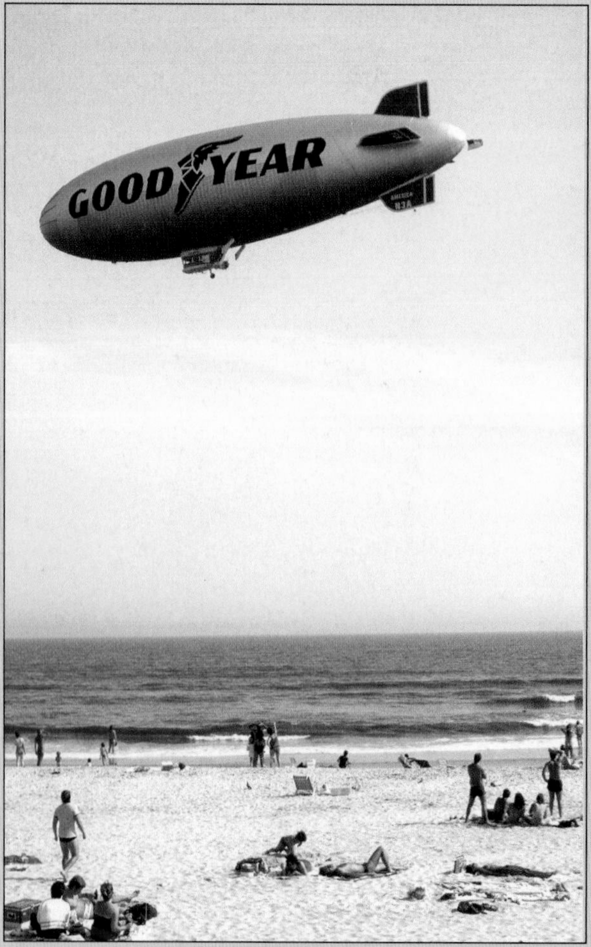

© Robert Brenner/Photo Edit

Also, brand placements inserted in movies, TV programs, music recordings, and elsewhere enable advertisers to reach desired target audiences with greater precision than is typically the case when placing ads in any of the various mass media. This is because the audiences for particular movies and TV programs tend to share many lifestyle and demographic characteristics.

Finally, the advertiser's choice of other ad media is limited only by the lack of *ingenuity.* With skill and cleverness, advertisers can use any of an endless number of ad media to reach target audiences efficiently and effectively. Virtually any blank surface can become a channel for delivering ad messages. For example, advertisements are placed on vehicles (buses and taxis), in restrooms, in the sky (skywriting), and even as temporary tattoos on peoples' body parts. The options are virtually limitless, bounded only by the lack of ingenuity.

Chapter Objectives

After reading this chapter you should be able to:

1. Explain why postal mail advertising is an efficient and effective ad medium.
2. Understand p-mail's five distinctive features compared to mass forms of advertising.
3. Appreciate the role of database marketing, data mining, and lifetime-value analysis.
4. Appreciate branded entertainment and brand placements in various venues (movies, TV, etc.).
5. Appreciate the value of yellow-pages advertising.
6. Recognize the growth and role of video-game advertising (advergaming).
7. Understand the role of cinema advertising.
8. Appreciate the potential value of various "alternative" ad media.

>>Marcom Insight:

Some Definitions Encapsulating This Chapter

Introduction

This chapter, as the title suggests, deals with the general topic of "other" advertising media. The vague term "other media" is used to include all forms of advertising that were not previously covered and will not be subsequently treated in this text. As such, mass-media advertising via traditional mass media such as television and magazines (the topic of Chapter 12) and Internet advertising (Chapter 13) are excluded. Word-of-mouth advertising and buzz generation are outside the scope of the present chapter but will be covered in Chapter 18. Also, out-of-home advertising, external store signage, and point-of-purchase advertising will be the subject of Chapter 20. Finally, advertising via sales promotion vehicles such as freestanding inserts (Chapter 16) and advertising that takes place at sponsored events and in support of worthy causes will be examined in Chapter 19.

Now that we know which topics are not covered in the present chapter, it will be useful to overview the topics that are examined. Table 14.1 facilitates this discussion. It can be seen that "other" forms of advertising include the following: direct advertising via postal mail, brand placements in movies and other outlets, yellow-pages advertising, advertising via video games (advergaming), cinema advertising, and a potpourri of alternative advertising.

These "other" advertising media generally are insufficient for performing the full marketing communications tasks that are necessary to build a brand's equity and to generate necessary sales volume to achieve a reasonable return on investment. However, these other advertising media can perform an invaluable role when used in a *supplementary capacity* to support a complete IMC program that places primary emphasis on advertising in the major advertising media and on the Internet. Finally, it should be noted that there are times when these "other" media—used separately or in conjunction with one another—may serve in a stand-alone capacity to achieve a brand's marcom objectives. For example, some brands—especially in the case of B2B marketing—may require only a direct mail campaign to achieve success, whereas other brands depend exclusively on these "other" ad media because their marcom budgets cannot afford to advertise in the traditional ad media.

Direct Advertising via Postal Mail

Chapter 13 discussed online advertising in its various forms, including e-mail advertising. This section of the chapter includes detailed coverage of *nonelectronic* mail advertising, or what we will refer to as "postal mail." Postal mail advertising, or, for short, *p-mail* (in parallel to e-mail) refers to any advertising matter the postal service delivers to the person whom the marketer wishes to influence. These advertisements take many forms, including letters, postcards, programs, calendars, folders, catalogs, videocassettes, blotters, order blanks, price lists, and menus.

table 14.1

Framework for Various Forms of "Other" Advertising

- Direct Advertising via Postal Mail
- Brand Placements in Movies, in TV Programs, and Elsewhere
- Yellow-Pages Advertising
- Video-Game Advertising (Advergaming)
- Cinema Advertising
- Potpourri of Alternative Ad Media

At least four factors account for the widespread use of p-mail by B2B as well as B2C marketers. First, the rising cost of television advertising and increasing audience fragmentation have led many advertisers to reduce investments in the television medium. Second, p-mailing enables unparalleled targeting of messages to desired prospects. Why? Because, according to one expert, it is "a lot better to talk to 20,000 prospects than 2 million suspects."[1] Third, increased emphasis on measurable advertising results has encouraged advertisers to use that medium—namely, p-mail—that most clearly identifies how many prospects purchased the advertised product. Fourth, many consumers have favorable attitudes toward mail advertisements and would be disappointed if they could not get direct mail offers and catalogs.

Illustrations of Successful P-mail Campaigns

Three examples of highly successful direct mail campaigns are described. One involves a B2B product, one a consumer packaged good, and the third a consumer durable. (For a fourth illustration, see the *Global Focus* insert.)

global focus

How a Major Production Mistake Turned into a Huge Direct Mailing Success

Scotland, the home of Scotch whisky, is understandably very proud of its ancient tradition of making high-quality Scotch whisky (or whisky for short). Distilleries in different regions of Scotland make their own unique versions of whisky, and millions of drinkers around the globe have strong preferences for those brands that best fit their palates. Many of the most famous brands of Scotch are referred to as "single malt" (in recognition that they are from a single distillery and use a single malted grain, barley), although some—generally less expensive—whiskies represent blends of two or more different versions and are referred to as blended whisky.

The "major production mistake" that the title above refers to involves the Glenmorangie Distillery, which is located in the Highlands of Scotland. One of Glenmorangie's brands is Ardbeg—a single malt whisky distilled in Islay, which is a small island west of the Scottish mainland. Due to a mistake committed by a production employee who pulled the wrong lever, two of Glenmorangie's brands—Ardbeg and Glen Moray—were accidentally blended together—resulting in an inferior blended Scotch whisky from the mixture of two single malt brands. The initial course of action facing Glenmorangie's executives was simply to suffer a huge economic loss and destroy the 15,000 bottles of what seemed to be a useless product. Could any thing else be done?

Rather than destroy 15,000 bottles, creative thinking led to the decision to market the "production mistake" as a unique new brand. The new brand of blended whisky, which actually was quite good, was named Serendipity—a name (based on well-known legend) that means "good luck in making unexpected and fortunate discoveries."[2]

A direct mail campaign (termed "Pity to Waste It") was developed to market Serendipity. A mailer was distributed to a list of 30,000 loyal Ardbeg drinkers. A booklet described Glenmorangie's production mistake and asked recipients to sign an "official pardon," which actually was an order form for Serendipity. The campaign was hugely successful. The mailing generated a 23 percent response rate and brought in sales of nearly $1 million at a cost of only $100,000. This was a one-time mistake that generated a handsome economic gain for the Glenmorangie Company rather than a huge loss, which attests to the power of creativity and the effective use of direct mail.

SOURCE: Adapted from Michael Raveane, "How the STORY Agency Turned a Major Mistake into a Marketing Masterpiece," *Deliver Magazine*, December 2007, 25–27.

The Caterpillar 414E Industrial Loader Campaign

Caterpillar manufacturers and markets an extensive line of heavy equipment products, including machinery for clearing land used for commercial building and residential house construction. However, Caterpillar was not faring well in the U.S. Southwest, which requires special equipment for leveling rough ground and preparing it for laying concrete slabs on which homes are built (unlike elsewhere in the United States where basements are more frequent). Caterpillar's dealers complained that they were losing business to competitors such as John Deere, which had machines that were better suited for ground leveling in the Southwest. Caterpillar responded by building the 414E industrial loader to enhance its competitiveness in this large region.

Caterpillar (or Cat for short) needed a marcom program that would make a strong impression on its dealers. The solution was to create a special event for the new 414E loader and then to promote that event via a direct mail campaign. The event designed was one that was timed to take place just prior to a NASCAR race. The objective was to have Cat dealers—the 414E's target market—construct a racecourse using the new 414E machine. This hands-on experience would allow dealers to learn firsthand the versatility of this new product. Then, upon construction, dealers were invited to race small vehicles (called dune buggies) on the newly constructed racecourse.

To create excitement about the product and to inform dealers of the upcoming event, a direct mail campaign (called "Eat My Dust") was devised. Direct mail pieces were distributed to 1,700 dealers, who were informed that they would have an opportunity to use the new 414E to build a racecourse and then to race dune buggies over it. Whereas the standard response rate to direct mail pieces is in the range of 1 to 3 percent, the 414E campaign drew a hugely successful 18 percent response. As a result, Caterpillar sold 28 of the 414E machines, some priced as high as $75,000; the Eat My Dust promotion cost less than $100,000. In other words, selling just two machines offset the total cost of the direct mail campaign and the racecourse event, with the remaining sales of 26 machines contributing to Caterpillar's bottom line. By any standard, this was a hugely successful campaign.[3]

The Stacy's Pita Chip Campaign

The Boston-based Stacy's Pita Chip Company was a successful operation, but its business was largely limited to the New England region. In an effort to expand its distribution nationwide, Stacy's needed a successful yet affordable marcom program. Budget limitations made it impossible for Stacy's to use mass media such as TV advertising, so a direct mail campaign was undertaken instead. The clever campaign they developed focused on the company's name, Stacy's. Accordingly, with the aid of outside companies that specialize in direct marketing, Stacy's was able to identify the names and addresses of 133,000 people named Stacy located throughout the United States.

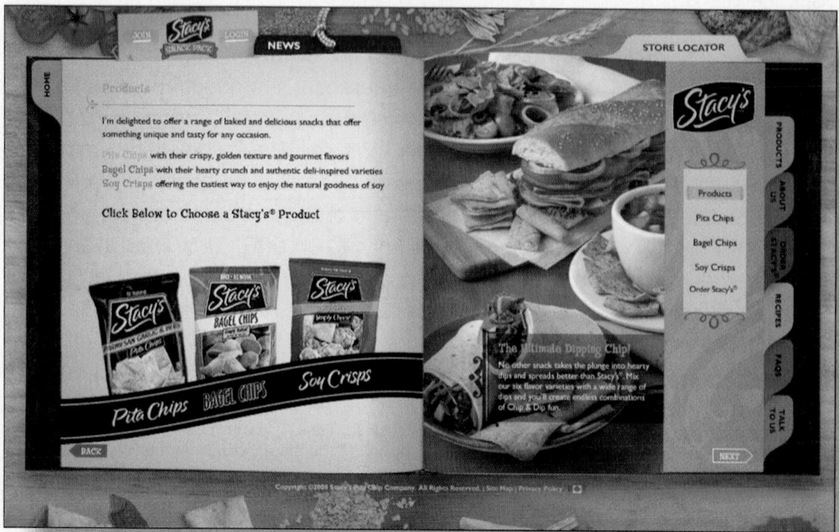

Each of the 133,000 Stacys was mailed a cardboard carton with gold lettering reading: "To Stacy, From Stacy." Product samples of five pita chip products were enclosed (e.g., Stacy's cinnamon sugar, Stacy's parmesan garlic) along with a $1 coupon and a postcard that enabled recipients to request free samples for a designated friend. The mailing also encouraged recipients to deliver a form letter to their local grocery store asking deli managers to stock Stacy's products.

It is too soon to know the campaign's financial success, but the Stacy's VP of marketing claims that a large amount of publicity was generated at a cost much less than what a single 30-second TV commercial would have cost the company.[4]

The Saab 9–5 Campaign

The Saab 9–5 represented Saab's first entry in the luxury category and was designed to compete against well-known high-equity brands, including Mercedes, BMW, Volvo, Lexus, and Infiniti. A total of 200,000 consumers, including 65,000 current Saab owners and 135,000 prospects, were targeted via multiple p-mailings with the objective of encouraging them to test-drive the 9–5. Mailings provided prospects with brand details and made an appealing offer for them to test-drive the 9–5. Names of the most qualified prospects were then fed to dealers for follow-up.

Saab's advertising agency designed four mailings: (1) an initial mailing announced the new Saab 9–5, provided a photo of the car, and requested recipients to complete a survey of their automobile purchase interests and needs; (2) a subsequent qualification mailing provided respondents to the first mailing with product information addressing their specific purchase interests (performance, safety, versatility, etc.) and offered a test-drive kit as an incentive for returning an additional survey; (3) a third mailing included a special issue from *Road & Track* magazine that was devoted to the Saab 9–5's product development process; and (4) a final test-drive kit mailing extended an offer for recipients to test-drive the 9–5 for three hours and also provided an opportunity for prospects to win an all-expenses-paid European driving adventure (through Germany, Italy, and Sweden) as incentive for test-driving the 9–5.

An outbound telemarketing campaign followed the p-mailings. Telephone calls were made to all people who responded to the initial mailings as well as to all prospects who had automobile leases or loans that were expiring. These callings reinforced the European test-drive offer and set up times for local dealers to call back to schedule test-drives. The direct marketing effort for the 9–5 was fabulously successful. Of the 200,000 initial prospects contacted by the introductory mailing, 16,000 indicated interest in test-driving the 9–5 (an 8 percent response rate), and more than 2,200 test-drives were scheduled.[5]

P-mail's Distinctive Features

P-mail expenditures are huge. In the United States alone, more than $60 billion is annually invested in p-mailing.[6] These expenditures include B2B as well as B2C direct mailings. P-mailing offers five distinctive features as compared to mass forms of advertising: targetability, measurability, accountability, flexibility, and efficiency:

- *Targetability.* P-mail is capable of targeting a precisely defined group of people. For example, Saab's advertising agency selected just 200,000 consumers to receive mailings for the Saab 9–5. These included 65,000 current Saab owners and 135,000 prospects, who satisfied income and car ownership requirements and passed other hurdles.
- *Measurability.* It is possible with p-mail to determine exactly how effective the advertising effort was because the marketer knows how many mailings were

sent and how many people responded. This enables ready calculations of cost per inquiry and cost per order. As previously noted, more than 2,200 consumers signed up for test-drives of the Saab 9–5. Proprietary dealer sales data reveal how many of the initial 200,000 mailings resulted in purchases.

- *Accountability.* As has been repeatedly pointed out in this text, marcom practitioners are increasingly being required to justify the results of their communications efforts. P-mailing simplifies this task because results can be readily demonstrated (as in the case of the Saab 9–5), and brand managers can justify budget allocations to p-mail.
- *Flexibility.* Effective p-mail can be produced relatively quickly (compared with, say, producing a TV commercial), so it is possible for a company to launch a p-mail campaign that meets changing circumstances. For example, if inventory levels are excessive, a quick postcard or letter may serve to reduce the inventory. P-mail also offers the advantage of permitting the marketer to test communications ideas on a small-scale basis quickly and out of the view of competitors. Comparatively, a mass-media effort cannot avoid the competition's eyes. P-mail also is flexible in the sense that it has no constraints in terms of form, color, or size (other than those imposed by cost and practical considerations). It also is relatively simple and inexpensive to change p-mail ads. Compare this with the cost of changing a television commercial.
- *Efficiency.* P-mail makes it possible to direct communications efforts just to a highly targeted group, such as the 200,000 consumers who received mailings for the Saab 9–5. The cost-efficiency resulting from such targeting is considerable compared with mass-advertising efforts.

An alleged disadvantage of p-mail is its expense. On a cost-per-thousand (CPM) basis, p-mail typically is more expensive than other media. For example, the CPM for a particular mailing may be as high as $200 to $300, whereas a magazine's CPM might be as low as $4. However, compared with other media, p-mail is much less wasteful and will usually produce the highest percentage of responses. Thus, on a *cost-per-order basis,* p-mail is often a better bargain.

Perhaps the major problem with p-mail is that many people consider it excessively intrusive and invasive of privacy. Consumers are accustomed to receiving massive quantities of mail and so have been "trained" to accept the voluminous amount of p-mail received. It is not the amount of mail that concerns most people but the fact that virtually any business or other organization can readily obtain their names and addresses.

Who Uses P-Mail and What Functions Does It Accomplish?

All types of marketers use p-mail as a strategically important advertising medium. Both B2B companies and marketers of consumer goods have turned increasingly to p-mailing as an advertising option. Packaged goods companies such as Ralston Purina, Kraft, Gerber Products, Sara Lee, Quaker Oats, and Procter & Gamble are some of the primary users of p-mailings. P-mailing by firms such as these is especially valuable for introducing new brands and distributing product samples.

Research and practical experience indicate that p-mail campaigns can achieve the following functions, all of which are straightforward and thus require no explanation:[7]

1. Increase sales and usage from current customers
2. Sell products and services to new customers
3. Build traffic at a specific retailer or Web site

4. Stimulate product trial with promotional offers and incentives
5. Generate leads for a sales force
6. Deliver product-relevant information and news
7. Gather customer information that can be used in building a database
8. Communicate with individuals in a relatively private manner and thereby minimize the likelihood of competitive detection; in other words, p-mail advertising, unlike mass advertising, reaches the customer and prospects under competitors' radar screens

The Special Case of Catalogs and Audiovisual Media

This section describes two rather unique forms of direct mail: catalogs and the audiovisual form of direct mail.

Catalogs

Cataloging is a huge enterprise, with more than 10 billion catalogs distributed annually in the United States alone. And cataloging is highly effective, as revealed by the findings from one study indicating that (1) more than two thirds of catalog recipients visit the catalog company's Web site, (2) sales to catalog recipients are over 150 percent greater on average compared to consumers not receiving a catalog, and (3) catalog recipients buy more items on average and spend more money than do non-recipients.[8]

From the marketer's perspective, catalog selling provides an efficient and effective way to reach prime prospects. From the consumer's perspective, shopping by catalog offers several advantages: (1) catalog shopping saves time because people do not have to find parking spaces and deal with in-store crowds; (2) catalog buying appeals to consumers who are fearful of shopping due to concerns about crime; (3) catalogs allow people the convenience of making purchase decisions at their leisure and away from the pressure of a retail store; (4) the availability of toll-free 800 numbers and online Web sites, credit-card purchasing, and liberal return policies make it easy for people to order from catalogs; (5) consumers are confident purchasing from catalogs because merchandise quality and prices often are comparable, or even superior, to what is available in stores; and (6) guarantees are attractive. Illustrative of this last point, consider the policy of L. L. Bean, the famous retailer from Maine:

> *All of our products are guaranteed to give 100 percent satisfaction in every way. Return anything purchased from us at any time if it proves otherwise. We will replace it, refund your purchase price or credit your credit card, as you wish. We do not want you to have anything from L.L. Bean that is not completely satisfactory.*

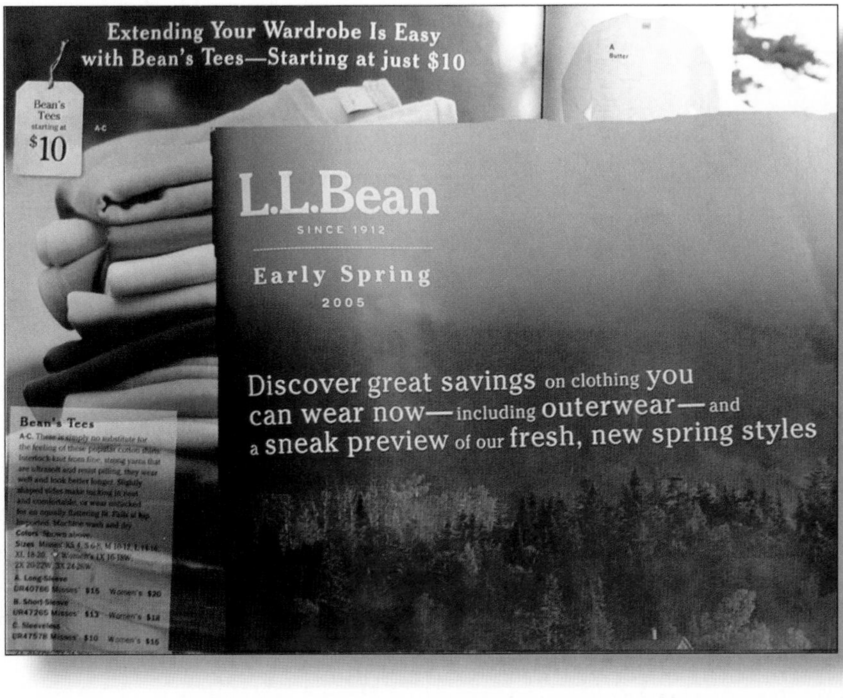

© Susan Van Etten

Although catalog marketing is pervasive, the growth rate has subsided for several reasons: First, industry observers note that the novelty of catalog scanning has worn off for many consumers. Second, as typically is the case when a product or service reaches maturity, the costs of catalog marketing have increased dramatically. A primary reason is that firms have incurred the expenses of developing more attractive catalogs and compiling better mailing lists in an effort to outperform their competitors. Costs have been further strained by third-class postal rate increases in recent years and sharp increases in paper prices.

Audiovisual Advertising

This form of direct advertising involves the use of electronic devices to present audiovisual advertising messages that have been captured in the form of videotapes, CD-ROMs, or DVDs. This form of advertising involves capturing key visual and audio information about a brand and distributing the information to business customers or to final consumers for projection on computer monitors or television screens.

Although there is limited research to verify the effectiveness of audiovisual advertising, firms in this industry maintain (albeit not without self-interest) that video advertising is both more effective and less expensive than print advertising delivered via direct mail. It is claimed that business customers and consumers are less likely to throw away an unsolicited audiovisual message than they are a brochure or other printed material and that videos are more persuasive. Although unverified in a scientific sense, it stands to reason that video advertising is potentially more entertaining than comparable print advertising and thus more effective in gaining attention and influencing memorability of an advertising message.

Companies are increasingly using the audiovisual medium to present consumers and B2B customers with detailed product information. Imagine, for example, how a tourist destination might effectively use audiovisual advertising. When a prospective tourist requests information, a disc could be mailed out that would contain the sights (video as well as still pictures) and sounds (music, wildlife and outdoor sounds, etc.) of the area and would present this information in a newsworthy and entertaining fashion. CD-ROMs and DVDs also have considerable potential in the area of B2B marketing. Audiovisual presentations of new products can be mailed to prospective customers, who are encouraged to call for additional information or to arrange a personal sales visit.

Of course, rather than direct mailing audiovisual materials, a marketer could simply direct prospective customers to a Web site that presents the images in a linked file. This would be less expensive for the marketer, but not all consumers have broadband access to the Web, which effectively eliminates the likelihood that prospective customers will view audiovisual files on their computers. Hence, direct mailing audiovisual materials in the form of CD-ROMS or DVDs is appropriate for certain target audiences but not all.

The Use of Databases

Successful direct mailing requires available computer databases and the *addressability* inherent in these databases. That is, databases enable contacts with present or prospective customers who can be accessed by companies whose databases contain p- and e-mail addresses along with other pertinent data such as demographic information. Direct advertising, in comparison to broadcast advertising, does not deal with customers en masse but rather creates individual relationships with each prospective customer. The following analogy aptly pits direct mail (also referred to as "addressable media") against broadcast media: "Broadcast media send communications; addressable media send and receive. Broadcasting targets its audience much as a battleship shells a distant island into submission; addressable media initiate conversations."[9]

An up-to-date database provides firms with a number of assets, including the ability (1) to direct advertising efforts to those individuals who represent the best prospects for a company's products or services, (2) to offer varied messages to different groups of customers, (3) to create long-term relationships with customers, (4) to enhance advertising productivity, and (5) to calculate the lifetime value of a customer or prospect. Due to the importance of customer lifetime value, the following section focuses on this fifth database asset.

Lifetime-Value Analysis

A key feature of database marketing is the need to consider each address contained in a database from a lifetime-value perspective. That is, each present or prospective customer is viewed as not just an address but also as a *long-term asset.* **Customer lifetime value** is the *net present value* (NPV) of the profit that a company stands to realize on the average new customer during a given number of years. This concept is best illustrated using the data in Table 14.2.

Assume, for illustration purposes, that a small specialty retailer has a database of 1,000 customers (see the intersection of row A and Year 1 column in Table 14.2). The following analysis illustrates how the average customer's NPV can be calculated over a time frame of five years.[10] First, the *retention rate* (see Row B) indicates the likelihood that people will remain customers of this particular retailer over the course of five years. It is assumed that 40 percent of 1,000 customers in Year 1 will continue to be customers in Year 2, or, in other words, 400 of the initial 1,000 customers will be remaining in Year 2 (see intersection of row A and the Year 2 column); 45 percent of these 400 customers, or 180 customers, will remain into Year 3; 50 percent will remain in Year 4; and 55 percent will remain in Year 5.

Row C indicates that the *average yearly sales* in years 1 through 5 are constant at $150. That is, customers on average spend $150 at this particular retail establishment. Thus, the *total revenue,* row D, in each of the five years is simply the product of rows A and C. For example, the 1,000 customers in Year 1 who spend on average $150 produce $150,000 of total revenue; the 400 customers in Year 2 generate $60,000 in total revenue; and so on.

Table 14.2

Customer Lifetime-Value Analysis

	Year 1	Year 2	Year 3	Year 4	Year 5
Revenue					
A Customers	1,000	400	180	90	50
B Retention rate	40%	45%	50%	55%	60%
C Average yearly sales	$150	$150	$150	$150	$150
D Total revenue	$150,000	$60,000	$27,000	$13,500	$7,500
Costs					
E Cost percentage	50%	50%	50%	50%	50%
F Total costs	$75,000	$30,000	$13,500	$6,750	$3,750
Profits					
G Gross profit	$75,000	$30,000	$13,500	$6,750	$3,750
H Discount rate	1	1.2	1.44	1.73	2.07
I NPV profit	$75,000	$25,000	$9,375	$3,902	$1,812
J Cumulative NPV profit	$75,000	$100,000	$109,375	$113,277	$115,088
K Lifetime value per customer	$75.00	$100.00	$109.38	$113.28	$115.09

Row E reflects the cost of selling merchandise to the store's customers. For simplification it is assumed that the cost is 50 percent of revenue. *Total costs* in each year, row F, are thus calculated by multiplying the values in rows D and E. *Gross profit,* row G, is calculated by subtracting total costs (row F) from total revenue (row D).

The *discount rate,* row H, is a critical component of NPV analysis and requires some discussion. As you may have learned in a basic finance class, the discount rate reflects the idea that money received in future years is not equivalent in value to money received today. This is because money received today, say $100, can be immediately invested and begin earning interest. Over time, the $100 grows more valuable as interest compounds and accumulates. Delaying the receipt of money thus means giving up the opportunity to earn interest. This being the case, $100 received in the future, say in three years, is worth less than the same amount received today. Some adjustment is needed to equate the value of money received at different times. This adjustment is called the discount rate and can be expressed as:

$$D = (1 + i)^n$$

where D is the discount rate, i is the interest rate, and n is the number of years before the money will be received. The discount rate given in row H of Table 14.2 assumes an interest rate of 20 percent. Thus, the discount rate in Year 3 is 1.44 because the retailer will have to wait two years (from Year 1) to receive the profit that will be earned in Year 3. That is:

$$(1 + 0.2)^2 = 1.44$$

The *NPV profit,* row I, is determined by taking the reciprocal of the discount rate (i.e., $1 \div D$) and multiplying the gross profit, row G, by that reciprocal. For example, in Year 3, the reciprocal of 1.44 is 0.694, which implies that the present value of $1 received two years later is only about $0.69 at an interest rate of 20 percent. Thus, the NPV of the $13,500 gross profit to be earned in Year 3 is $9,375. (You should perform the calculation for years 4 and 5 to ensure that you understand the derivation of NPV. Recall that the reciprocal of a particular value, such as 1.44, is calculated by dividing that value into 1.)

The *cumulative NPV* profit, row J, simply sums the NPV profits across the years. This summation reveals that the cumulative NPV profit to our hypothetical retailer, who had 1,000 customers in Year 1, of whom 50 remain after five years, is $115,088. Finally, row K, the *lifetime value per customer,* shows the average worth of each of the 1,000 people who were customers of our hypothetical retailer in Year 1. The average lifetime value of each of these customers, expressed as NPV over a five-year period, is thus $115.09.

Now that you understand the concept of lifetime-value analysis, we can turn to more strategic concerns. The key issue is this: What can a marketer do to enhance the average customer's lifetime value? There are five ways to augment lifetime value:[11]

1. Increase the *retention rate.* The more customers a firm has and the longer they are retained, the greater the lifetime value. It therefore behooves marketers and advertisers to focus on retention rather than just acquisition. Database marketing is ideally suited for this purpose because it enables regular communication with customers (through newsletters, frequency programs, e-mailing, and so on) and relationship building. Customer relationship management (CRM) is a widespread marketing practice—a practice justified by the ability to enhance the lifetime value of the average customer.
2. Increase the *referral rate.* Positive relations created with existing customers can influence others to become customers through the positive word of mouth a company's satisfied users express.

3. Enhance the *average purchase volume per customer.* Existing customers can be encouraged to purchase more of a brand by augmenting their brand loyalty. Product satisfaction and capable management of customer relations are means to building the base of loyal customers.
4. Cut *direct costs.* By altering the channel of distribution via direct marketing efforts, a firm may be able to cut costs and hence increase profit margins.
5. Reduce *marketing communications costs.* Effective database marketing can lead to meaningful reductions in marcom expenses because direct advertising often is more productive than mass-media advertising.

The Practice of Data Mining

Databases can be massive in size with millions of addresses and dozens of variables for each database entrant. The availability of high-speed computers and inexpensive computer software has made it possible for companies literally to mine their databases for the purpose of learning more about customers' buying behavior. The goal of **data mining** is to discover hidden facts contained in databases. Sophisticated data miners look for revealing relations among the variables contained in a database for purposes of using these relationships to better target prospective customers, develop cooperative marketing relations with other companies, and otherwise better understand who buys what, and when, how often, and along with what other products and brands they make their purchases.

Consider, for example, a credit card company that mines its huge database and learns that its most frequent and largest-purchase users are disproportionately more likely than the average credit card user to vacation in exotic locations. The company could use this information to design a promotional offering that has an exotic vacation site as the grand prize. A furniture chain mining its database learns that families with two or more children rarely make major furniture purchases within two years of buying a new automobile. Armed with this information, the chain could acquire automobile purchase lists and then direct advertisements to households that have not purchased a new automobile for two or more years. These examples are purely illustrative, but they provide a sense of how databases can be mined and used for making strategic advertising and promotional decisions.

Another use of databases is to segregate a company's customer list by the *recency* (R) of a customer's purchase, the *frequency* (F) of purchases, and the *monetary value* (M) of each purchase. Companies typically assign point values to accounts based on these classifications. Each company has its own customized procedure for point assignment (i.e., its own *R-F-M formula*), but in every case more points are assigned to more recent, more frequent, and more expensive purchases. The R-F-M system offers tremendous opportunities for database manipulation and mail targeting. For example, a company might choose to send out free catalogs only to accounts whose point totals exceed a certain amount.

Brand Placements in Movies and TV Programs

The practice of what typically is referred to as product placement—but is more appropriately dubbed *brand placement* because marketers promote specific brands, not products in general—has risen in recent years to unprecedented heights. It has been estimated that brand-placement spending in the United States amounted to around $3 billion in 2007, with TV placements accounting for approximately 70 percent of brand-placement expenditures.[12] Interestingly, there is relatively little scientific evidence regarding the effectiveness of brand placements, although the literature on this topic is growing.[13] Most of the evidence is anecdotal, and the discussion in this section will be in that vein.

In their efforts to present brand messages in a manner that does not appear blatant, marketers seek opportunities to have their brands mentioned in positive contexts—including movies, TV programs, books, songs, and so on. Brand placement activity is perfectly aligned with one of the five key features of IMC introduced in Chapter 1, namely that the customer represents the starting point for all marcom decisions. The essence of this principle, as it relates to media selection, is that marketing communicators must seek opportunities to present brand messages in positive contexts where potential customers naturally place themselves. People go to movies, watch TV programs, listen to music, and so on; hence, all of these venues are potentially attractive contexts in which to present brand messages. This then is the general rationale for so-called *branded entertainment,* that is, that brand messages placed in entertainment events are conveyed in a covert fashion compared to traditional advertising's overt approach and that brand placements do not come across as advertisements.

By way of comparison with traditional mass-media advertising, brand placements in movies, TV programs, and elsewhere have certain distinct advantages and disadvantages. First, in terms of advantages, brand placements generally are less intrusive than advertisements and thus less likely to be avoided. Second, because consumers, especially younger people, often dislike being marketed to, brand placements are less likely to be summarily rejected as just another persuasive attempt. Third, when a brand is appropriately connected with the plot of a movie (or TV program, song, etc.) and with the characters in that entertainment event, there is a strong potential for the placement to buttress or even augment a brand's image and to build an emotional connection with the target audience. Finally, a prominent placement can create a memorable association that serves to enhance consumers' memories (recognition and recall) of a brand and thus possibly their chances of selecting it from among competitive options.

On the downside, marcom practitioners lose some control of how their brands are positioned when movie and TV directors decide how exactly brands are placed in an entertainment event. An advertisement is a perfectly controlled context for a brand, but when a brand is placed in, say, a movie, the control of the positioning is to some degree lost to the movie's director. Another disadvantage of brand placements is the difficulty of measuring their effectiveness and their ROI. Finally, prices of brand placements are spiraling upward, and many brand managers consider the cost unreasonably high. For example, 79 percent of major marketers surveyed in a poll the Association of National Advertisers conducted believe branded-entertainment deals are overpriced.[14]

In sum, brand placements offer many potential advantages, but these do not come free of cost. We now discuss brand placements in movies and in TV programs.

Brand Placements in Movies

Brand placements in movies date back to the 1940s, yet the frequency is greater now than ever. It is virtually impossible to attend a movie without seeing various well-known brands (e.g., Apple, Coca-Cola, Ford, Nike, and Sony) appearing in these movies. For example, over 40 brands were placed in the 2008-released movie, *21* (a story about a group of M.I.T. students gambling in Las Vegas). Included among these brands were Beefeater Gin, Budweiser, Caesars Palace, Chrysler, Dunkin' Donuts, Grey Poupon, Gucci, Louis Vuitton, Pepsi, Pony, Samuel Adams, Sony PlayStation, and Twinkies. Interested readers can see the brands that are featured in favorite films by going to the following Web site: http://www.brandchannel.com/brandcameo_films.asp. This source has been tracking brand placements in movies since the early 2000s. It also identifies which brands are placed in the most films. For example, in 2007 Ford was the brand placed in the most films (20), followed by Apple (13), and Coca-Cola (11).

Do brand placements work? Public evidence of whether such "advertising" is effective is limited. There is evidence, however, that brand awareness and recall increase with more prominent placements.[15] It would seem that advertisers have little to lose and much to gain when using this form of supplemental marketing communications. The typical price for a brand placement ranges from as low as $25,000 to into the millions.[16] Several factors determine how much a brand placement is worth and thus how much it should cost a brand marketer to place a brand in a particular movie.[17] A first determinant is the amount of time the brand gets on screen. Placements in which a brand is in the foreground of a scene and in which the brand logo is clearly seen are more valuable to a brand and lead to higher prices than instances in which the brand is in the background and the logo is difficult to detect. Second, brand placements are more valuable (and thus are priced higher) when characters in the movie use the brand and perhaps mention it and exclaim its virtues. A third determinant of a placement's value is whether the brand appears during an important plot point in the movie (if it does, the placement is worth more). In short, the more time a brand placement receives, the more tightly it is woven into the movie's plot, and the more the brand and key movie characters are connected, the more valuable the placement is and the higher the price to be paid for garnering the placement.

Based on a large global study a major advertising media company conducted (over 11,000 interviews with consumers from 20 countries), younger consumers appear to be the most responsive to brand placements in movies.[18] Compared to older age groups, 16-to-24-year-olds were the most likely to notice brand placements in movies (57 percent) and to consider trying the brands seen in films (41 percent). The comparative notice and consider-trying statistics for 35-to-44-year-olds were 49 percent and 28 percent and, for 45-to-54-year-olds, 43 percent and 22 percent. Perhaps the most interesting finding was the difference across countries in the percentages of consumers saying they would try a brand if they saw it in a film. The percentages for a subset of countries were Mexico (53 percent), Singapore (49 percent), India (35 percent), Hong Kong (33 percent), the United States (26 percent), Finland (14 percent), Denmark (14 percent), the Netherlands (9 percent), and France (8 percent). Consumers from the latter four countries objected to brand placements because they felt they interfered with the film-making process.

Brand Placements in TV Programs

The topic of brand placements in TV programs was briefly mentioned in Chapter 12 when discussing television as a mass-advertising medium. A few additional comments are appropriate at this time. Brand placements in TV programs are prevalent. In fact, a study of prime-time TV programs determined that brands are placed in these programs an average of once every three minutes.[19] Brand-placement spending on television is even greater than in movies, accounting for perhaps as much as 70 percent of total brand-placement expenditures across all media outlets. The substantial increase in brand placements on TV has been concurrent with the growth of reality television programming. Programs such as *American Idol, Survivor,* and *The Apprentice* represent near-perfect contexts in which to place brands and provide brand managers with an alternative form of exposure to the traditional 30-second commercial. Of course, brand placements are not limited just to reality shows; they can be observed on most successful TV programs. Even reruns of TV sitcoms are being digitally remastered to include brands in scenes where they did not exist when initially produced.[20]

Brand marketers are attempting to get their brands integrated into TV programs in as seamless a fashion as possible. For example, Agent Jack Bauer, the daring Counter Terrorist Unit character on Fox network's *24*, always drives a Ford F-150 truck. Jack and the truck are inseparable. The truck appears in the program not as a prop, but as a natural element of the action-packed program. Likewise, Coca-Cola is ever present on the set of *American Idol*, with Randy, Paula, and Simon (the show's three panelists) regularly sipping from cups with the Coca-Cola logo vividly displayed.

Yellow-Pages Advertising

The yellow pages is an advertising medium that consumers turn to when they are seeking a product or service supplier and are prepared to make a purchase. In a typical week, an estimated 60 percent of all American adults use the yellow pages at least once. The heaviest yellow-pages users tend to fall most in the 25-to-49 age category, are college educated, and have relatively high household incomes ($60,000 and up).[21] Some of the major reasons people use yellow pages include saving time spent shopping around for information, saving energy and money, finding information quickly, and learning about products and services.

Advertising in the yellow pages is not a substitute for but a complement to other advertising media when used in an IMC program. This old advertising medium, with a past as a static form of communication in the pages of telephone directories, is seeing a new life with the creation of online yellow pages (e.g., http://www.yellowpages.com).

The online and print versions of the yellow pages together represent a huge advertising medium, with annual revenues exceeding $15 billion.[22] Over 7,000 localized yellow-pages directories are distributed annually to hundreds of millions of consumers. There are currently more than 4,000 headings for different product and service listings. Local businesses place the majority of yellow-pages ads, but national advertisers also are frequent users of the yellow pages. For example, in a recent year the following national companies all invested over $20 million advertising in the yellow pages: ServiceMaster ($51 million), U-Haul ($38 million), State Farm Insurance ($35 million), and Budget and Ryder ($20.5 million).[23]

Distinguishing Features of Yellow-Pages Advertising

The yellow pages differ from other ad media in several respects.[24] First, whereas consumers often avoid exposure to advertisements in other media, they actively seek out ads in the yellow pages. Second, the advertiser largely determines the quality of ad placement in the yellow pages by the actions it takes. For example, by placing a large ad, the advertiser receives prized placement (i.e., placement earlier in the sequence of ads under a particular category) than do purchasers of small ads; also, companies that are longtime yellow-pages advertisers receive the best ad placements.

A third distinguishing feature of yellow-pages advertising is that there are clear-cut limits on possible creative executions. That is, when advertising in the yellow pages, advertisers have fewer creative options available than when advertising in other media. It is noteworthy, however, that now advertisers in the yellow pages have greater color and graphic options available than solely using black print against a yellow background. Research indicates that the use of color and higher-quality graphics have positive effects in attracting attention, signaling product quality, and even increasing the likelihood that the advertised brand will be selected over competitive options.[25]

A fourth distinguishing characteristic of yellow-pages advertising is the method of purchase. Whereas advertising in mass media such as TV, radio, magazines, and newspapers allows for frequent adjustments in the creative execution and budget allocations, yellow-pages advertisements are purchased for a full year and thus cannot be changed in either purchase amount or creative execution.

Video-Game Advertising (a.k.a. Advergaming)

Brand managers and marcom practitioners are continually seeking ways to get their messages before difficult-to-reach consumers such as young men. Electronic games (video games) provide an excellent advertising medium for this purpose. These games typically are available on game consoles or online, and marketers either customize their own games or incorporate their brands into existing games. The producers of video games now actively pursue tie-ins with brand marketers, who pay for advertising space within the games. It is estimated that U.S. video-game advertising totaled about $400 million in 2008, and that worldwide spending on video-game advertising will reach nearly $2 billion by 2011.[26]

It is easy to understand why video games represent a potentially valuable ad medium considering that popular games sell millions of units, and users of these games play for an average of 40 hours before growing tired of them.[27] Moreover, JupiterResearch, a technology research firm, projects that there will be in excess of 60 million game players by 2009.[28] Although in the early years of this technology young men played video games most, today nearly 40 percent of game players are female.[29] (For further details about characteristics of game players, see the *IMC Focus* insert.)

Measuring Video-Game Audiences

Although growing at a reasonably rapid rate, expenditures on advergaming are minuscule in comparison to those on TV and other mass media. Nevertheless, in anticipation of continued growth, Nielsen (of TV ratings fame) has developed a

IMC >> i.m.c. focus

Profile of the Online Gaming Community

Research firm NPD has studied online gamers to better understand who plays games online and where and what games they play. Here are some of the key findings from NPD's research:

Gender–Women comprise slightly over 42 percent of the total online-game audience.

Income–The average household income for online gamers ranges between $35,000 and $75,000.

Age–The single largest age group of online gamers is kids ages 6 to 12, who account for 20 percent of all online gamers.

Console Ownership–Xbox 360 owners are disproportionately more likely to play games online than any other console owners, and, at an average of 7.1 hours per week, Xbox 360 owners spend more time playing games online than any other group of console owners.

Type of Games Played Online–Casual games (card, puzzle, and arcade games) are the favorite of 44 percent of online game players, followed by family entertainment games (25 percent) and multiplayer online games (19 percent). Approximately one sixth of all online gamers indicate that gambling and casino games are their favorites.

SOURCE: Adapted from Beth Snyder Bulik, "Who Is Today's Gamer? You Have No Idea," *Advertising Age*, May 14, 2007, 28.

© AP Images/PRNewsFoto/WildTangent

service called Nielsen GamePlay Metrics to measure video-game audiences. Nielsen tracks game usage through an audience panel of 12,000 U.S. homes. Employing a small monitor (somewhat akin to the set-top boxes used in TV measurement), Nielsen will be able to measure game-playing behavior and to capture key demographics of players.[30]

Cinema Advertising

In addition to placements of brands in movies, in recent years the movie theater has itself become a medium for placing advertising messages.[31] Expenditures on cinema advertising are trivial in comparison, say, to TV advertising, amounting to roughly $1 billion in a recent year.[32] Nonetheless, research has demonstrated that cinema advertisements that appear prior to a featured film do *not* antagonize consumers.[33]

Younger consumers, those in the 12–24 demographic, are more positively disposed toward cinema advertising than older individuals, making an attractive proposition for brand marketers given the difficulties of reaching the younger demographic group with traditional advertising media.[34] The prospect that cinema advertising has a bright future is perhaps best evidenced by Nielsen Media Research, which has introduced Nielsen Cinema, an in-theater audience measurement service that cinema companies and advertisers use for buying and selling cinema advertising.

Potpourri of Alternative Advertising Media

There is a medley of alternative media, all of which have minor but potentially useful roles to play *as part of* an integrated marcom program. Creative advertisers find many ways to reach customers using alternative media. For example, Figure 14.1 is an advertisement from the 3M Company that is directed at advertising agencies and their clients. On reading the advertisement you will see that 3M is suggesting that Post-it Notes can be used as a powerful advertising medium that will reach potential customers day after day, note after note. Figure 14.2 is a photo taken at a professional football stadium (the Carolina Panthers stadium in Charlotte, North Carolina), showing a cup holder emblazoned with an advertisement for Coca-Cola.[35]

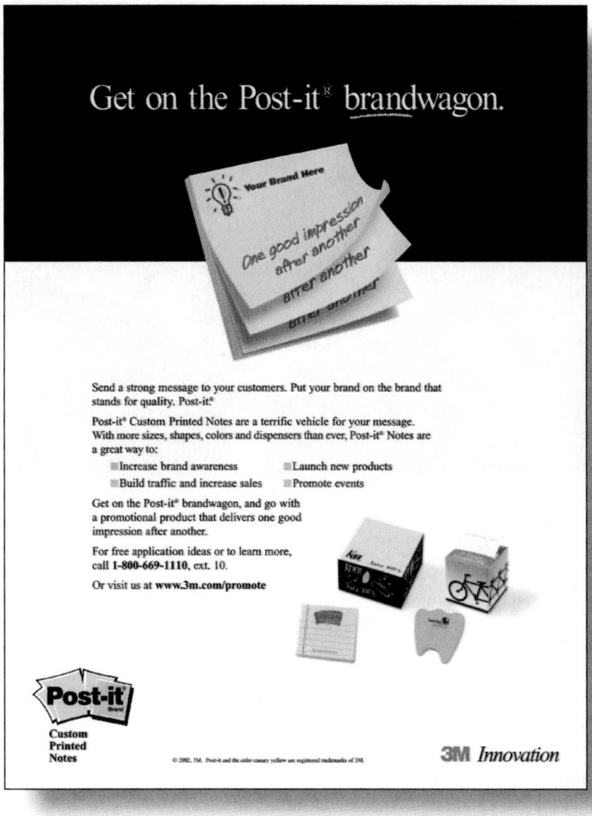

Courtesy of 3M

Figure 14.1

3M's Post-it Notes as an Advertising Medium

Why let space go to waste when it can be sold as an advertising outlet? Consider, for example, the space available on the sides of the many garbage trucks that daily navigate city streets. The maker of Glad trash bags put a message saying "New York City tough" on 2,000 New York City garbage trucks and 450 street sweepers. During a two-month advertising period, Glad's ad campaign generated about 17 million impressions (i.e., gross rating points) and boosted the brand's citywide market share by 2 percentage points.[36]

Advertisers have even turned to restroom space as a venue to convey their messages. For example, Axe deodorant from Unilever has been advertised in public restrooms in major U.S. markets. A company spokesman justified this choice by saying that Axe is a brand that "is about helping a guy attract women," and that guys are in the right mind-set to accept ad messages for a brand such as Axe during their restroom interludes when frequenting bars.[37]

An enterprising firm called The Fruit Label Company has used apples and other fruits and vegetables to carry mini-ads for movies and other products. Levi Strauss & Co. advertised Levi's 501 jeans on the back covers of *Marvel* and *DC* comics, an excellent medium because these two comic-book companies combined sell more than 10 million copies of their comic books every month. The comics provided Levi Strauss & Co. with an outlet for reaching the notoriously difficult-to-reach segment of boys ages 12 to 17.

Figure 14.2

A Football Stadium's Cup Holders as an Advertising Medium

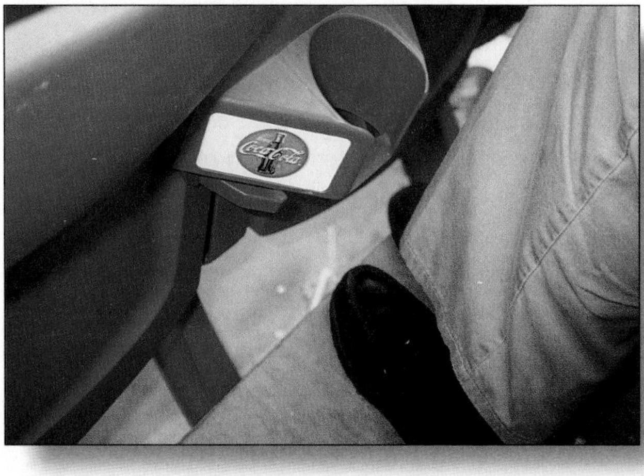

© Terence A. Shimp

Another interesting ad medium is skywriting. A company named Skytypers—with bases in California, Florida, and New York—"writes" sky messages in the form of white cloud formations. At a US Open tennis tournament in Flushing Meadows, New York, tennis patrons saw messages for brands such as Heineken, Dunkin' Donuts, Geico, and Song Airways. A message of 25 to 30 letters costs between $25,000 and $30,000 and can be seen by upwards of 2.5 million people in the 400-square-mile area surrounding the site of the US Open.[38] See the *IMC Focus* for a description of another fascinating advertising medium.

Finally, even the human body has been used as an advertising medium. A British company has paid students the equivalent of about $8 an hour to walk up and down busy streets with their foreheads temporarily imprinted with brand names. The company has a group of about 1,000 students who are willing to serve as walking billboards. Tattoo advertising also has appeared in the United States. Dunkin' Donuts ran a forehead tattoo promotion in conjunction with

© PRNewsFoto/Newscom

the National Collegiate Athletic Association (NCAA) March Madness basketball tourney. One hundred students from 10 universities in Massachusetts, Illinois, Georgia, and Florida earned between \$50 and \$100 per day to walk around their campuses with the Dunkin' Donuts logo temporarily tattooed on their foreheads.[39]

In conclusion, this brief discussion of alternative media was intended merely to demonstrate that imagination and good taste are the only limits to the choice of advertising media. These examples illustrate that virtually any blank surface can be converted into space for an advertisement. However, advertisers must be mindful of the advice about IMC presented in Chapter 1: Contact brand users wherever and whenever possible, use all appropriate touch points to convey messages that will increase brand awareness and augment images, and be sure to integrate messages across all touch points to assure they speak with a single voice. Multiple media are to little avail if their messages are inconsistent or possibly even conflicting.

Summary

This chapter has examined a variety of "other" advertising media. Table 14.1 structured the discussion by delineating the different forms of advertising covered in this chapter. Direct advertising via postal mail (p-mail) received the most extensive coverage in view of its widespread usage and huge investment in this medium.

Direct advertising is increasingly being viewed as a critical component of successful IMC programs. Indeed, for many firms direct advertising is the cornerstone of their communications efforts. The increased sophistication of database marketing has been largely responsible for the growing use and effectiveness of direct advertising. Major advances in computer technology have made it possible for companies to maintain huge databases containing millions of prospects and customers. An up-to-date database allows targeting of messages to prime prospects, provides for an ability to vary message content to different groups, enhances advertising productivity, enables the determination of a customer's lifetime value, and affords an opportunity to build long-term relations with customers. The availability of high-speed computers and inexpensive computer software has made it possible for companies literally to mine their databases to learn more about customers' buying behavior. Sophisticated data miners look for revealing relations that can be used to target prospective customers, develop cooperative marketing relations, and otherwise better understand who buys what, and when, how often, and along with what other products and brands they make their purchases.

Brand placements in movies and in TV programs is another rapidly growing ad medium. These placements provide advertisers with an opportunity to reach consumers in a rather covert fashion (in comparison to traditional advertising, which, in a manner of speaking, is "in your face") and to portray brands positively by connecting them with entertainment plots and characters.

Yellow-pages advertising and video-game advertising (also known as advergaming) also received prominent coverage in the chapter. The yellow pages (online as well as in print) are virtually a must for local advertisers in their quest to attract prospective customers and repeat purchases. Advergaming is a new but rapidly growing form of advertising that appeals mostly to young men but increasingly to girls and women who also are avid gamers.

Another interesting development in the search for alternative advertising media is the recent growth of cinema advertising. Most theaters now show commercials before presenting the featured movie. These ads often are the same ones shown on TV. The appeal of this medium is that it captures the attention of a young demographic group that is difficult to reach via traditional media. Moreover, shown prior to the commencement of the feature film, cinema advertising is not as disruptive as are TV commercials.

The final section reviewed a medley of alternative advertising media, namely, advertising options that generally are used to supplement mainstream media rather than to carry the full advertising load. The discussion included forms of advertising such as placing ads on garbage trucks, advertising in restrooms, and using airplanes to skywrite ads.

Discussion Questions

1. Virtually any space is a potential medium for a marketer's advertisement. Identify several novel forms of advertising media that go beyond the "other" media described in this chapter. Describe the target for each of these novel media, and offer an explanation as to why, in your opinion, each novel medium is effective or ineffective.
2. Can you recall any prominent brand placements in movies you have seen lately? What were these placements? Were the products "positioned" in positive or negative contexts? How successful, in your opinion, were these placements?
3. Have you ever viewed a CD-ROM or DVD advertisement? If so, what are your views on why this form of advertising was or was not effective?
4. Describe your use, if any, of yellow-pages advertising in recent weeks.
5. Assume you are the proprietor of a sports bar in a community of, say, 250,000 people. Can you offer any good reasons for not advertising your business in the yellow pages?
6. Provide two illustrative variables that a catalog marketer of men's or women's clothing (your choice) might include in its database.
7. Explain the meaning and importance of database "addressability."
8. The section describing database assets included the claim that an up-to-date database allows a marketing organization to create long-term relationships with customers. What does this mean?
9. Assume you are a direct marketer for a line of merchandise imprinted with the logos of major universities. These items are targeted to the fans and supporters of university athletic programs. Detail how you would compile an appropriate mailing list, one that would reach people who are most likely to purchase the logo merchandise. Use your college or university for illustration.
10. Following is a lifetime-value analysis framework similar to that presented in the chapter. Perform the calculations necessary to complete row K:

	Year 1	Year 2	Year 3	Year 4	Year 5
Revenue					
A Customers	2,000	___	___	___	___
B Retention rate	30%	40%	55%	65%	70%
C Average yearly sales	$250	$250	$250	$250	$250
D Total revenue	___	___	___	___	___
Costs					
E Cost percentage	50%	50%	50%	50%	50%
F Total costs	___	___	___	___	___
Profits					
G Gross profit	___	___	___	___	___
H Discount rate	1	1.15	___	___	___
I NPV profit	___	___	___	___	___
J Cumulative NPV profit	___	___	___	___	___
K Lifetime value per customer	___	___	___	___	___

11. Assume that, 10 years after graduating from your university or college, you are appointed to your school's Athletics Oversight Committee. The chair of the committee suggests that it would be useful to know the lifetime value of the average football season-ticket holder. Describe how you might go about estimating the average ticket holder's lifetime value over the first five years starting with the year that he or she first purchases season tickets. Refer to Table 14.2 to assist you with this analysis. Make whatever assumptions you deem necessary and then conduct the analysis. Using a spreadsheet program such as Microsoft Excel would obviously facilitate your analysis.
12. Your college or university no doubt has an organizational unit that is responsible for marketing merchandise to alumni and other customers—items emblazoned with your school's logo, such as sweatshirts, T-shirts, caps, coffee mugs, and so on. Assume that the merchandising unit in your school does not have an up-to-date computerized database. Explain how you would go about putting together such a database. What

specific information would you maintain in your computerized database for each customer? How would you use this information?

13. As a consumer who probably has spent considerable time perusing the pages of different catalogs, provide your perspective on the value of catalogs to you. Why would you (or why would you not) purchase from a catalog company?
14. What are your views on advergaming? Respond by commenting about this advertising practice both from the perspective of advertisers and from the viewpoint of game players.
15. Brand placements in movies and in TV programs represent a subtle, even covert, way to present a brand message. Traditional advertising, by comparison, is, in a manner of speaking, "in your face." One therefore could argue that traditional advertising is a more honest form of communications than the practice of branded entertainment. What are your views on this? Might one argue that brand placements are even a bit deceitful?
16. Visit http://www.brandchannel.com/brandcameo_films.asp and identify a movie that you either have seen or are at least familiar with. Examine the brands that have been placed in that movie and comment on why you think these brands chose to be placed in that particular movie.
17. What are your views on both the appropriateness and the effectiveness of placing advertisements in restrooms?
18. Given the chapter's discussion of "alternative" forms of ad media (on garbage trucks, in restrooms, in the sky, etc.) and the implication that any unused space is a potential advertising medium, identify two "spaces" advertisers are not currently using that could be used for placing ad messages. What kinds of brands would appropriately advertise on each of your suggested spaces, and what would be an appropriate target audience for messages placed on each space?
19. What is your reaction to advertisements in movie theaters that precede featured films? Does such advertising disturb you, or do you find it perfectly acceptable?

End Notes

1. Don Schultz as quoted in Gary Levin, "Going Direct Route," *Advertising Age*, November 18, 1991, 37.
2. http://wordnet.princeton.edu/perl/webwn?s=serendipity.
3. This description is adapted from Jeff Borden, "Eat My Dust," *Marketing News*, February 1, 2008, 20–22.
4. This description is adapted from Anne Stuart, "Do You Know Stacy?" *Deliver Magazine*, May 2007, 25–27.
5. Information for this description was provided by the marketing communication agency responsible for the campaign, The Martin Agency, Richmond, VA.
6. "Direct-mail Spending Expected to Soar This Year," http://delivermagazine.com (accessed April 21, 2008).
7. This list is slightly adapted from one provided by the U.S. Postal Service in a CD-ROM titled "How to Develop and Execute a Winning Direct Mail Campaign," circa 2001, http://www.usps.com.
8. "Direct Mail Perks Up Online Traffic, and Sales," December 14, 2007, http//delivermagazine.com (accessed April 17, 2008).
9. Robert C. Blattberg and John Deighton, "Interactive Marketing: Exploiting the Age of Addressability," *Sloan Management Review* (fall 1991), 5.
10. There are more sophisticated approaches to lifetime-value analysis, but this example contains all the elements essential to understanding the fundamentals of the approach.
11. Arthur M. Hughes, *Strategic Database Marketing* (Chicago: Probus, 1994), 17.
12. Patricia Odell, "Star Struck," *Promo*, April 2007, 16–21.
13. For exceptions, see Cristel Antonia Russell and Barbara B. Stern, "Consumers, Characters, and Products: A Balance Model of Sitcom Product Placement Effects," *Journal of Advertising* 35 (spring 2006), 7–22; Siva K. Balasubramanian, James A. Karrh, and Hemant Patwardhan, "Audience Response to Product Placements: An Integrative Framework and Future Research Agenda," *Journal of Advertising* 35 (fall 2006), 115–142; Cristel Antonia Russell and Michael Belch, "A Managerial Investigation into the Product Placement Industry," *Journal of Advertising Research* 45 (March 2005), 73–92; Cristel Antonia Russell, "Investigating the Effectiveness of Product Placements in Television Shows: The Role of Modality and Plot Connection Congruence on Brand Memory and Attitude," *Journal of Consumer Research* 29 (December 2002), 306–318. For coverage of practitioners' views on brand placement, see James A. Karrh, Kathy Brittain McKee, and Carol J. Pardun, "Practitioners' Evolving Views on Product Placement Effectiveness," *Journal of Advertising Research* 43 (June 2003), 138–149.
14. Abbey Klaasen, "Marketers Fear Being Fleeced at Corner of Madison and Vine," *Advertising Age*, March 28, 2005, 3, 124.
15. Ibid. See also, Emma Johnstone and Christopher A. Dodd, "Placements as Mediators of Brand Salience within a UK Cinema Audience," *Journal of Marketing Communications* 6 (September 2000), 141–158; and Alain

d'Astous and Francis Chartier, "A Study of Factors Affecting Consumer Evaluations and Memory of Product Placements in Movies," *Journal of Current Issues and Research in Advertising* 22 (fall 2000), 31–40.

16. Pola B. Gupta and Kenneth R. Lord, "Product Placement in Movies: The Effect of Prominence and Mode on Audience Recall," *Journal of Current Issues and Research in Advertising* 20 (spring 1998), 47–60.
17. Adapted from Brian Steinberg, "Product Placement Pricing Debated," *Wall Street Journal Online,* November 19, 2004, http://www.online.wsj.com.
18. Emma Hall, "Young Consumers Receptive to Movie Product Placements," *Advertising Age,* March 29, 2004, 8.
19. Carrie La Ferle and Steven M. Edwards, "Product Placement: How Brands Appear on Television," *Journal of Advertising* 35 (winter 2006), 65–86.
20. Patricia Odell, "Rewriting Placement History," *Promo,* March 2005, 8.
21. Joel J. Davis, "Section Five: Consumer Dynamics," *Understanding Yellow Pages,* http://www.ypa-academics.org/UYPII/section5.html.
22. Joel J. Davis, "Section One: Industry Overview," *Understanding Yellow Pages,* http://www.ypa-academics.org/UYPII/section1.html.
23. Ibid.
24. Avery M. Abernethy and David N. Laband, "The Customer Pulling Power of Different-sized Yellow Pages Advertisements," *Journal of Advertising Research* 42 (May/June 2002), 66–72.
25. For details see Karen V. Fernandez and Dennis L. Rosen, "The Effectiveness of Information and Color in Yellow Page Advertising," *Journal of Advertising* 29 (summer 2000), 61–73; Gerald L. Lohse and Dennis L. Rosen, "Signaling Quality and Credibility in Yellow Pages Advertising: The Influence of Color and Graphics on Choice," *Journal of Advertising* 30 (summer 2001), 73–85.
26. The U.S. estimate is reported in Abbey Klaassen, "Game-ad Boom Looms as Sony Opens Up PS3," *Advertising Age,* February 25, 2008, 1, 29; the worldwide estimate is cited in Laurie Sullivan, "Beyond In-game Ads: Nissan Takes Growing Market to Different Level," *Advertising Age,* June 17, 2007, 1, 37.
27. Kenneth Hein, "Getting in the Game," *Brandweek,* February 17, 2004, 26–28.
28. Suzanne Vranica, "Y&R Bets on Videogame Industry," *Wall Street Journal Online,* May 11, 2004, http://www.online.wsj.com.
29. Allison Enright, "In-game Advertising," *Marketing News,* September 15, 2007, 26–30.
30. Nick Wingfield, "Nielsen Tracker May Benefit Videogames as Ad Medium," *The Wall Street Journal,* July 26, 2007, B2.
31. For an interesting conceptual treatment of cinema advertising, see Joanna Phillips and Stephanie M. Noble, "Simply Captivating: Understanding Consumers' Attitudes toward the Cinema as an Advertising Medium," *Journal of Advertising* 36 (spring 2007), 81–94.
32. Diane Williams and Bill Rose, "The Arbitron Cinema Advertising Study 2007: Making Brands Shine in the Dark," http://www.arbitron.com/downloads/cinema_study_2007.pdf (accessed April 22, 2008).
33. Ibid.
34. Ibid.
35. I include this photo in honor of my late, great friend, John Kuhayda, and to his dear wife Patty and family. John was the embodiment of integrity and loyalty. Every moment we spent together was one of joy. His "dash" was too short but full of substance and character. He will always be my Padna, the Champ.
36. Jack Neff, "Trash Trucks: A New Hot Spot for Ads," *Advertising Age,* February 5, 2007, 8.
37. Lisa Sanders, "More Marketers Have to Go to the Bathroom," *Advertising Age,* September 20, 2004, 53.
38. Michael Applebaum, "Look, Up in the Sky: Brands!" *Brandweek,* September 13, 2004, 42.
39. Details about the British campaign and that for Dunkin' Donuts are from Arundhati Parmar, "Maximum Exposure," *Marketing News,* September 15, 2003, 6, 8.

CHAPTERS

15

Sales Promotion and the Role of Trade Promotions

16

Sampling and Couponing

17

Premiums and Other Promotions

Part 4

Sales Promotion Management

Part Four includes three chapters that cover trade- and consumer-oriented sales promotions. *Chapter 15* overviews sales promotions by explaining the targets of promotional efforts and the reasons underlying the rapid growth of promotions, and it outlines sales promotion's capabilities and limitations. The chapter also examines trade-oriented promotions, describing the most widely used forms of trade promotions and discussing forward buying, diverting, and the advent of manufacturer-oriented everyday low pricing. Account-specific marketing also receives prominent treatment. The chapter concludes with a discussion of nine empirical generalizations about trade and consumer promotions.

Two forms of consumer-oriented sales promotions, sampling and couponing, are the subjects of *Chapter 16.* The various forms of sampling programs and three major sampling initiatives are discussed (targeting, innovative distribution methods, and sampling's ROI). The second topic in Chapter 16, couponing, includes treatment of the various forms of coupons, the economic implications of couponing, and the process of coupon redemption and misredemption.

Chapter 17 continues coverage of consumer-oriented promotions by examining various promotions other than sampling and couponing. Each of the following promotional programs receives coverage: premiums, price-off promotions, bonus packs, promotional games, rebates/refunds, and sweepstakes/contests. The chapter concludes with a three-step procedure for evaluating sales promotion ideas and suggestions for how to conduct a postmortem analysis of promotions that have already "run."

15

Sales Promotion and the Role of Trade Promotions

A theme presented throughout this chapter is that the role of sales promotions, especially trade-oriented promotions, is largely a function of the relative *power* between manufacturers and retailers. Power, in a dictionary sense, describes the strength, might, or force that one entity has relative to another. In the marketplace, power involves the ability of one channel member to command or control another. Greater power relative to another is achieved with increased economic or noneconomic (e.g., informational) resources. Greater power means that one participant in a market relationship—such as a manufacturer or a retailer—has increased ability to influence the nature of the relationship and the terms of sale between the two parties. Weak trade partners have terms of sale imposed on them; more powerful partners can, at the extreme, dictate terms of sale. Wal-Mart, for example, is a mega-powerful retailer that is well known for commanding its suppliers to produce products that meet Wal-Mart's price and nonprice requirements.

An incident in the athletic footwear industry illustrates another application of power; a major power clash transpired between two industry giants—Nike, a manufacturer, and Foot Locker, a retailer. This collision occurred when the CEO of Foot Locker became infuriated at Nike's rigid terms of sale being imposed on Foot Locker (and other retail buyers) in both the selection of which of Nike's shoes Foot Locker would carry in its stores and how the shoes would be priced. Due to its industry dominance and power position, Nike requires retailers to buy all types of Nike shoes, not just the particular models that retailers deem most appropriate for their clientele. Also, Nike provides retailers lower markups on Nike shoes in comparison to the markups permitted by other athletic footwear makers.

Angered by Nike's rigid terms and power politics, Foot Locker's CEO announced it would cut Nike orders by 15 to 25 percent per year, or between $150 million and $250 million annually. How did Nike respond to Foot Locker's power play? On the one hand, Nike could relax its rigid terms so as to appease Foot Locker and prevent the huge loss of business. On the other hand, Nike could respond in kind by making its own power move. The latter is what happened: Nike slashed its planned shipments to Foot Locker by $400 million

© Susan Van Etten

(40 percent of the previous year's shipments) and withheld its most highly demanded shoes from being sold in Foot Locker stores. One power move trumped by another! A former Foot Locker executive opined that Foot Locker's CEO made the mistake of thinking that Nike is as dependent on his company as Foot Locker is reliant on Nike. "They've taught Foot Locker a lesson they'll never forget."[1]

Chapter Objectives

After reading this chapter you should be able to:

1 Understand the nature and purpose of sales promotions.

2 Know the factors that account for the increased investment in promotions, especially those that are trade oriented.

3 Recognize the tasks that promotions can and cannot accomplish.

4 Appreciate the objectives of trade-oriented promotions and the factors critical to building a successful trade promotion program.

5 Comprehend the various forms of trade allowances and the reasons for their use.

6 Be aware of forward buying and diverting and how these practices emerge from manufacturers' use of off-invoice allowances.

7 Appreciate the role of everyday low pricing (EDLP) and pay-for-performance programs as means of reducing forward buying and diverting.

8 Understand nine empirical generalizations about promotions.

>>Marcom Insight:

It's a Matter of Power—Nike versus Foot Locker

Introduction

The objective of this chapter and the two that follow is to provide a thorough introduction to sales promotion's role in the overall marcom function. This chapter introduces the topic of sales promotions and then examines the role of trade-oriented promotions. The following two chapters extend this introduction by analyzing promotion's job in influencing the actions of consumers.

The Nature of Sales Promotion

By definition, sales promotion (or simply **promotion**) refers to any *incentive* manufacturers, retailers, and even not-for-profit organizations use that serve to change a brand's perceived price or value *temporarily*. Manufacturers use promotions to induce the *trade* (wholesalers and retailers) or *consumers* to buy a brand and to encourage the manufacturer's *sales force* to sell it aggressively. Retailers use promotional incentives to encourage desired behaviors from their consumers—shop at this store rather than a competitor's, buy this brand rather than another, purchase larger quantities, etc. And not-for-profit organizations employ promotions to encourage desired behaviors such as getting people to increase their donations to worthy causes and to donate now rather than later.

The italicized features require comment. First, by definition, promotions involve incentives (i.e., price discounts or rewards) that are designed to encourage trade customers or end-user consumers to purchase a particular brand sooner, more frequently, in larger quantities, or to engage in some other behavior that will benefit the manufacturer or retailer that offers the promotion. Second, these incentives (allowances, rebates, sweepstakes, coupons, premiums, and so on) are additions to—not substitutes for—the basic benefits a purchaser typically acquires when buying a particular product or service. Third, the target of the incentive is the trade, consumers, the sales force, or all three parties. Finally, the incentive changes a brand's perceived price or value, but only temporarily. This is to say that a sales promotion incentive for a particular brand applies to a single purchase or perhaps several purchases during a period, but not to every purchase a trade customer or consumer would make over an extended time.

In contrast to advertising, which typically, although not always, is relatively long term in orientation and best suited to enhancing buyer attitudes and augmenting brand equity, promotion is more *short-term oriented* and capable of influencing *behavior* (rather than just attitudes or intentions). Indeed, the term *sales promotion* precisely captures this short-term, behavioral orientation as promotions are designed to promote purchases of the promoter's brand. Promotion has the character of urgency in its injunction to *act now* because tomorrow is too late.[2] Promotion has the power to influence behavior because it offers the buyer superior value in the short term and can make buyers feel better about the buying experience.[3]

Although consumer packaged goods (CPG) companies are the biggest users of promotions, all types of companies use promotional incentives. For example, restaurants offer coupons and other forms of price discounts and sometimes provide free desserts when a special entrée is purchased. Online companies offer free shipping for orders above a certain monetary amount. Furniture stores provide free gifts when selected items are purchased. Athletic teams use a variety of promotions to attract fans and to encourage their return. (See the *IMC Focus* for an interesting promotion the Los Angeles Dodgers baseball organization uses.) And automobile companies regularly offer rebates and cheap financing to attract purchasers.[4]

In an unconventional yet increasingly practiced form of promotion by not-for-profit organizations, a major state university wrote letters to hundreds of high

IMC >> i.m.c. focus

"Cheap Seats" and Free Eats

Have you ever attended a professional baseball game (or football game or soccer match) and sat in seats that were far from the playing field? It is not much fun is it, and what is the incentive to return to attend another game if you have to sit in the "cheap seats"? Well, the Los Angeles Dodgers baseball organization has come up with a novel incentive (a sales promotion) to encourage fans to sit in seats where the view is mediocre at best—and to pay relatively high prices for this "privilege."

In past years the 3,000 or so seats in Dodger stadium's right-field pavilion often sat empty, even when admission to these seats was priced at just $6 to $8. A creative way to lure fans to the right-field seats was needed, and Dodgers executives were up to the task. Their solution was to give fans seated in this section of the stadium the opportunity to eat as much food as desired at no cost. This all-you-can-eat incentive is not novel, as cruise ships and Las Vegas casinos have used this approach for years. However, it was a novel approach in the realm of baseball marketing.

So far it seems that the incentive is working, as more Dodger fans than ever are choosing seats in the right-field pavilion—and at an increased price of $20 or more per seat! The all-you-can-eat section opens 1.5 hours before game time and closes 2 hours after the start of the game. Fans in the right-field pavilion consume on average 2.5 hot dogs, 1 bag of peanuts or popcorn, and 1 plate of nachos per game. (Drink consumption is not recorded because drinks are self-serve.) It would seem that both Dodger executives and right-field fans are "fat and happy" as a result of this novel promotion. Other pro sports teams are considering starting their own all-you-can-eat programs. However, given the incidence of obesity in the United States, some people are critical of the all-you-can-eat program at Dodger Stadium; they perceive it as encouraging gluttony.

SOURCE: Adapted from Adam Thompson and Jon Weinbach, "Free Eats Sell Bad Ballpark Seats," *The Wall Street Journal,* May 16, 2007, B1.

school students who had been named National Merit Semifinalists and offered the following:

> *If you attain* ***finalist*** *status in the National Merit competition, we will offer you, upon admission to the university, a Presidential Scholarship that will pay the value of tuition for four years as well as on-campus housing during your freshman year. You will also receive a University National Merit Scholarship of at least $1,000 ... if, as a finalist, you do not receive another National Merit sponsored scholarship. In addition, you will receive $2,000 for use in summer research or study abroad. If you list [name of university] as your college of choice with the National Merit Scholarship Corporation, you also will receive a free laptop computer when you enroll.*

Although not your typical $1 coupon, free sample, or mail-in premium, this offer attempts to induce an action (enroll at this particular university) that is no different than efforts brand managers employ to encourage purchases of their brands. The point is clear: Promotions are used universally and can be extremely effective if used appropriately as part of an integrated marcom program.

Promotion Targets

Three groups—a manufacturer's sales force, retailers, and consumers—are targets of sales promotional efforts (see Figure 15.1). First, trade- and consumer-oriented

figure 15.1

Brand-Level Promotion Targets

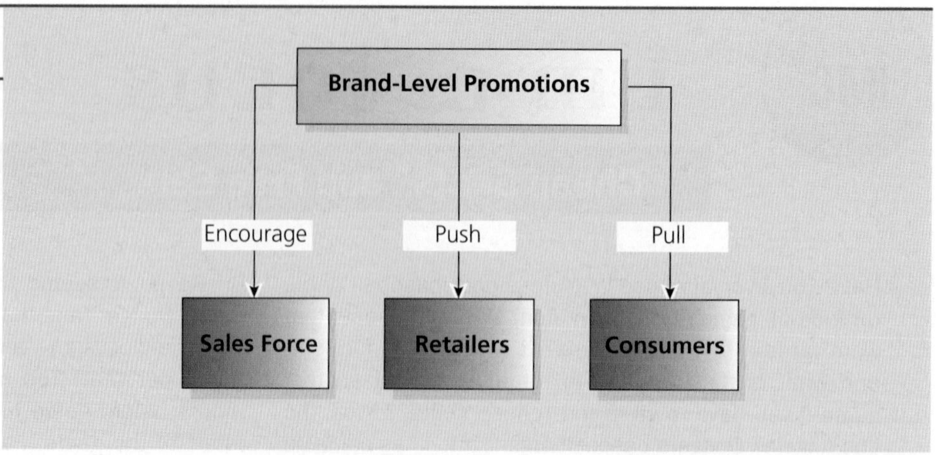

sales promotions provide the manufacturer's sales force with the necessary tools for aggressively and enthusiastically selling to wholesale and retail buyers. That is, salespeople have an incentive to put special selling emphasis behind promoted brands.

A second target of sales promotion efforts is the trade, including wholesalers but especially retailers. Various types of allowances, discounts, contests, and advertising support programs are used in a forward thrust from manufacturers to trade accounts (referred to as *push* efforts) that provide retailers with reasons for stocking, displaying, advertising, and perhaps placing the promoted brand on a price-discounted deal. Third, the use of consumer-oriented promotions (e.g., coupons, samples, premiums, cents-off deals, sweepstakes, and contests) serves to *pull* a brand through the channel by providing consumers with a special reason to purchase a promoted brand on a trial or repeat basis.

Increased Budgetary Allocations to Promotions

Advertising spending as a percentage of total marketing communications expenditures has declined in recent years, while promotion spending has steadily increased. Advertising expenditures as a proportion of companies' total marcom budgets used to average over 40 percent. However, beginning about a quarter century ago and continuing today, media advertising's portion of the average marcom budget has fallen to just about one quarter. In fact, an organization that tracks marcom spending estimates that trade promotions (including account-specific marketing, discussed later in the chapter) command 60 percent of total U.S. marcom expenditures, consumer advertising achieves 26 percent of the total, and consumer promotions capture the remaining 14 percent.[5] Why have firms shifted money from advertising and into promotions, especially trade-oriented promotions? The following section examines the major reasons underlying this shift.

Factors Accounting for the Shift

Several factors account for why brand managers have shifted budgetary allocations increasingly toward a greater proportion of trade promotions. However,

table 15.1

Push and Pull Strategies

	Company X (PUSH)	Company Y (PULL)
Personal Selling to Retailers	$13,500,000	$6,000,000
Sales Promotion to Retailers	12,000,000	150,000
Advertising to Retailers	2,400,000	300,000
Advertising to Consumers	1,800,000	20,550,000
Sales Promotion to Consumers	300,000	3,000,000
TOTAL	$30,000,000	$30,000,000

before we describe the reasons for this shift, it will be beneficial to review the concepts of push and pull marketing strategies briefly.

Push and *pull* are physical metaphors characterizing the promotional activities manufacturers undertake to encourage channel members (the trade) to handle and merchandise brands and to persuade consumers to purchase them. **Push** involves a forward thrust of effort, metaphorically speaking, whereby a manufacturer directs personal selling, advertising, and trade-oriented promotions to wholesalers and retailers. Through this combination of sales influence, advertising, and, perhaps especially, promotions in the form of allowances and other deals, manufacturers "push" channel members to increase their inventories of the manufacturer's brand versus competitive brands. **Pull,** in contrast, entails a backward tug, again speaking metaphorically, from consumers to retailers. This tug, or "pull," is the result of a manufacturer's successful advertising and consumer promotion efforts that encourage consumers to prefer, at least in the short term, the manufacturer's brand versus competitive offerings.

Table 15.1 illustrates the differences between push- and pull-oriented promotional strategies based on two companies' allocations of $30 million among different promotional activities. Company X emphasizes a *push strategy* by allocating most of its promotional budget to personal selling and trade promotions aimed at retail customers. Company Y uses a *pull strategy* by investing the vast majority of its budget in consumer advertising.

It is important to recognize that pushing and pulling are *not* mutually exclusive activities. Both efforts occur simultaneously. Manufacturers promote to consumers (creating pull) and to trade members (accomplishing push). The issue is not which strategy to use but rather which to emphasize. Effective marketing communications involves a combination of forces: exerting push to the trade and creating pull from consumers.

Historically, at least through the 1970s, the emphasis was on promotional pull (such as Company Y's budget in Table 15.1). Manufacturers advertised heavily, especially on network television, and literally forced retailers to handle their brands by creating consumer demand for those heavily advertised items. However, over the past generation, pull-oriented marketing has become less effective due in large part to the splintering of the mass media and audience fractionalization as discussed in Chapter 12. Along with this reduced effectiveness has come an increase in the use of push-oriented sales promotion practices (such as Company X's budget in Table 15.1).

Increased investment in sales promotion, especially trade-oriented promotions, has gone hand in hand with the growth in push marketing. Major developments that have given rise to sales promotion are summarized in Table 15.2 and discussed hereafter. It is important to emphasize that these developments are interdependent rather than separate and distinct. Hence, there is no particular order of importance implied by the listing in Table 15.2.

table 15.2

Developments Underlying the Growth in Promotions

- Shift in manufacturer versus retailer balance of power
- Increased brand parity and price sensitivity
- Reduced brand loyalty
- Splintered mass market and reduced media effectiveness
- Emphasis on short-term results in corporate reward structures
- Responsive consumers

Balance-of-Power Shift

Until roughly 1980, national manufacturers generally were more powerful and influential than the supermarkets, drugstores, mass merchandisers, and other retailers that carried manufacturers' brands. The reason was twofold. First, manufacturers were able to create consumer pull by virtue of heavy network television advertising, thus effectively requiring retailers to handle their brands whether retailers wanted to or not. Second, retailers did little research of their own and, accordingly, were dependent on manufacturers for information such as whether a new product would be successful. A manufacturer's sales representative could convince a buyer to carry a new product using test-market results suggesting a successful product introduction.

The balance of power began shifting when network television dipped in effectiveness as an advertising medium and, especially, with the advent of optical scanning equipment and other technologies that provided retailers with current information about product movement. Armed with a steady flow of data from optical scanners, retailers now know virtually on a real-time basis which brands are selling and which advertising and promotion programs are working. Retailers no longer need to depend on manufacturers for data. Instead, retailers use the facts they now possess to demand terms of sale rather than merely accepting manufacturers' terms.

The consequence for manufacturers is that for every promotional dollar used to support retailers' advertising or merchandising programs, one less dollar is available for the manufacturer's own advertising. Needless to say, retailers are not always more powerful than manufacturers, as indicated in the *Marcom Insight* where a manufacturer (Nike) was more powerful than its recalcitrant retailer (Foot Locker) and accordingly dictated the terms of sale.

Increased Brand Parity and Price Sensitivity

In earlier years when truly new products were being offered to the marketplace, manufacturers could effectively advertise unique advantages over competitive offerings. As product categories have matured, however, most new offerings represent only slight changes from those already on the market, thus resulting, more often than not, in greater similarities between competitive brands. With fewer distinct product differences, consumers have grown more reliant on price and price incentives (discounts, coupons, cents-off deals, refunds, etc.) as ways of differentiating parity brands. Because concrete advantages are often difficult to obtain, both manufacturers and retailers have turned increasingly to promotion to achieve temporary advantages over competitors.

Consumers are especially price sensitive during periods of economic downturns and the presence of recessionary or inflationary forces. It is then that we see all forms of discounts and price-reducing incentives being used, such as automobile manufacturers offering zero percent financing and home builders offering prospective homeowners the opportunity to purchase new homes without making down payments.

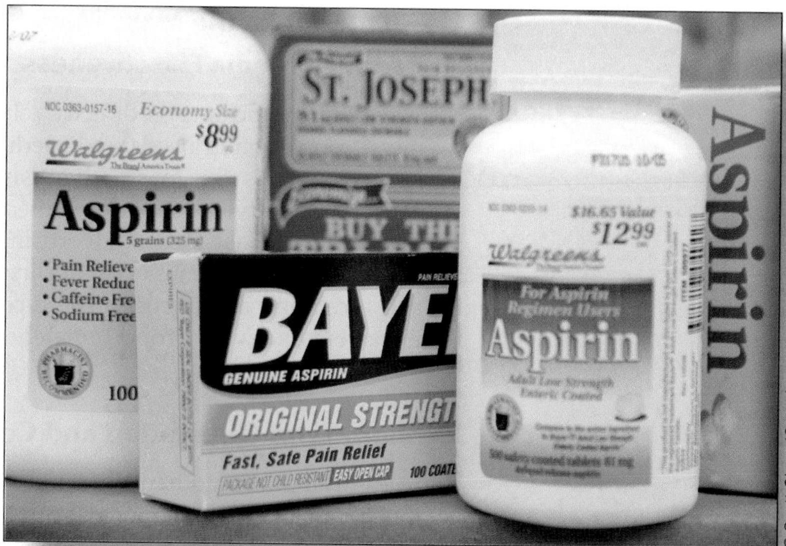

© Scott Olson/Getty Images

Reduced Brand Loyalty

Consumers probably are less loyal than they once were. This is partly because brands have grown increasingly similar, thereby making it easier for consumers to switch among brands. Also, marketers have effectively trained consumers to expect that at least one brand in a product category will always be on deal with a coupon, cents-off offer, or refund; hence, many consumers rarely purchase brands other than those on deal. (The term **deal** refers to any form of sales promotion that delivers a price reduction to consumers. Retailer discounts, manufacturer cents-off offers, and the ubiquitous coupon are the most common forms of deals.)

One team of researchers investigated the impact that deal promotions have on consumers' price sensitivity using eight years of data for a nonfood brand in the CPG category. These researchers determined that price promotions make consumers *more price sensitive in the long run.* Moreover, increased use of price promotions serves, for all intents and purposes, to "train" consumers to search for deals. Nonloyal consumers are especially likely to be conditioned by marketers' use of price deals.[6] Research also reveals that the use of coupons by brands in the mature liquid detergent category (brands such as Wisk, Era, and Bold) resulted in increased consumer price sensitivity and reduced brand loyalty.[7]

© David Young-Wolff/Photo Edit

The upshot of heightened dealing activity is that marketers have created a "monster" in the form of consumers' desire for deals. Reduced loyalty and increased brand switching have resulted, requiring more dealing activity to feed the monster's insatiable appetite. A major international study conducted in Germany, Japan, the United Kingdom, and the United States investigated the effects of price-related promotions (such as cents-off deals and coupons) on a brand's sales after a promotional period is over. The dramatic finding from this research, which examined dozens of brands in 25 CPG categories, is that these promotions have virtually *no impact* on a brand's long-term sales or on consumers' repeat buying loyalty. No strong aftereffects occurred because extra sales for the promoted brands came almost exclusively from a brand's long-term customer base. In other words, the people who normally buy a brand are the ones who are most responsive to the brand's price promotion. Hence, price promotions effectively serve to induce consumers to buy on deal what they would have bought at regular prices anyway. In sum, although price-related promotions typically result in immediate and huge sales spikes, these short-term gains generally do not positively influence long-term brand growth.[8]

Splintering of the Mass Market and Reduced Media Effectiveness

Advertising efficiency is directly related to the degree of homogeneity in consumers' consumption needs and media habits. The greater their homogeneity, the less costly it is for mass advertising to reach target audiences. However, as consumer lifestyles have diversified and advertising media have narrowed in their appeal, mass-media advertising's efficiency has weakened. On top of this, advertising effectiveness has declined with simultaneous increases in ad clutter and escalating media costs. These combined forces have influenced many brand managers to devote proportionately larger budgets to promotions at the expense of advertising.

Short-Term Orientation and Corporate Reward Structures

Sales promotions go hand in hand with the brand management system, which is the dominant organizational structure in CPG firms. The reward structure in firms organized along brand manager lines emphasizes *short-term sales response* rather than slow, long-term growth. In other words, brand managers' performances are assessed on an annual basis or even quarter-by-quarter. And sales promotion is incomparable when it comes to generating quick sales response. In fact, the majority of packaged-good brand sales are associated with some kind of promotional deal.[9]

Consumer Responsiveness

A final force that explains the shift toward sales promotion at the expense of advertising is that consumers respond favorably to money-saving opportunities and other value-adding promotions. Consumers would not be responsive to promotions unless there was something in it for them—and there is. All promotion techniques provide consumers with rewards (benefits, incentives, or inducements) that encourage certain forms of behavior brand managers desire. These rewards, or benefits, are both utilitarian and hedonic.[10] Consumers using sales promotions receive *utilitarian,* or functional, benefits of (1) monetary savings (e.g., when using coupons); (2) reduced search and decision costs (e.g., by simply availing themselves of a promotional offer and not thinking about other alternatives); and (3) improved product quality, because price reductions allow consumers to buy superior brands they might not otherwise purchase.

Consumers also obtain *hedonic* (i.e., nonfunctional) benefits when taking advantage of sales promotion offers, including (1) a sense of being a wise shopper when taking advantage of sales promotions;[11] (2) a need for stimulation and variety when, say, trying brands they otherwise might not purchase if it were not for attractive promotions; and (3) entertainment value when, for example, consumers compete in promotional contests or participate in sweepstakes.

A Consequence of the Increase: New Accounting Rules

In view of the major increase in sales promotions over the past quarter century, especially trade-oriented promotions, the organization responsible for establishing accounting standards in the United States—the Financial Accounting Standards Board (FASB)—reexamined how sales promotion expenditures should be handled on business organizations' income statements. Promotion expenditures historically were treated in exactly the same fashion as advertising expenditures, as *current expenses* that were deducted from top-line revenue. However, a unit of

FASB called the Emerging Issues Task Force proposed new accounting regulations (EITF 00-14 and 00-25) that went into effect in late 2001. EITF 00-14 and 00-25 require that those sales promotions used as a form of price discount—including promotions directed to retailers (e.g., off-invoice and slotting allowances, discussed later in this chapter) as well as to consumers (e.g., couponing expenditures and loyalty programs)—must now be treated as *reductions in sales revenue.*

Some companies (e.g., Procter & Gamble and Unilever) have long accounted for promotion expenditures in the way these new accounting regulations propose, but most firms did not, which thus created an apples and oranges situation when comparing top-line revenue figures. FASB's regulations were designed to create an apples-versus-apples environment by placing all firms on equal footing in how they account for price-oriented sales promotions. It was predicted that adherence to these new accounting rules would cut reported net sales for CPG companies by 8.5 percent on average, although the actual impact is unknown.[12]

Table 15.3 presents simplified income statements to illustrate the effect of this accounting change. For illustrative purposes, consider that a firm has $50 million in revenue, that its cost of goods sold equals $20 million, its general and administrative expenses total $10 million, its sales promotion expenditures amount to $8 million, and its advertising expenditures equal $5 million. Under the historical (pre-EITF 00-14 and 00-25) accounting procedures, top-line revenue would be recorded at the full amount of $50 million, and sales promotion expenditures along with the other expenses would be deducted from this amount to yield a bottom-line profit of $7 million (see entries under the "old" accounting procedure in Table 15.3). Under the "new" (post-EITF 00-14 and 00-15) accounting procedure and assuming identical expenditures, the bottom-line profit would remain at $7 million. Notice in Table 15.3, however, that the difference between the "old" and "new" procedures is in the amount recorded for the top-line revenue—specifically, $50 million under the "old" procedure compared to $42 million for the "new" procedure ($50 million sales minus $8 million promotion expenditures).

You might think that this is no big deal because the change in accounting procedures really has had no impact on the bottom-line figure. The significance of the change, however, is that it better reflects "true" levels of sales revenue, which was the intent of the FASB's regulations. When sales promotions represent little more than a price discount, the amount of discount should not be treated as revenue, which under the old accounting system served to inflate actual revenue and to mislead financial analysts, stockholders, and other parties regarding a firm's actual revenue generation. Moreover, sales forces compensated on the basis of top-line results were overcompensated because revenue itself was overstated. Hence, under the new accounting rules, price-discounting promotions are appropriately treated as direct reductions from sales revenue rather than as indirect expense reductions.

table 15.3

Illustration of "Old" and "New" Accounting Procedure

	"Old" Accounting Procedure	"New" Accounting Procedure
Revenue	$50,000,000	$42,000,000
Cost of Goods Sold	20,000,000	20,000,000
G&A Expenses	10,000,000	10,000,000
Sales Promotion	8,000,000	NA*
Advertising	5,000,000	5,000,000
Total Expenses	43,000,000	35,000,000
Pretax Profit	$ 7,000,000	$ 7,000,000

*The $8,000,000 spent on sales promotions has been deducted from the top line.

This change in accounting standards is not a trivial development in terms of managerial behavior with respect to allocating marcom budgets. Knowing that every dollar of price-discounting promotion is immediately deducted from the revenue line, brand managers might be motivated to allocate relatively more money into advertising or into other forms of sales promotions other than price discounts.

What Are Sales Promotion's Capabilities and Limitations?

Trade and consumer promotions are capable of accomplishing certain objectives and not others. Table 15.4 summarizes these "can" and "cannot" capabilities, each of which is then discussed.[13]

What Promotions Can Accomplish

Promotions cannot work wonders, but they are well-suited to accomplishing the following tasks.

Stimulate Sales Force Enthusiasm for a New, Improved, or Mature Product

There are many exciting and challenging aspects of personal selling; there also are times when the job can become dull, monotonous, and unrewarding. Imagine what it would be like to call on a customer repeatedly if you never had anything new or different to say about your brands or the marketing efforts that support them. Maintaining enthusiasm would be difficult, to say the least. Exciting sales promotions give salespeople persuasive ammunition when interacting with buyers; they revive enthusiasm and make the salesperson's job easier and more enjoyable.

table 15.4

Tasks That Promotions Can and Cannot Accomplish

Sales Promotions *Can*

- Stimulate sales force enthusiasm for a new, improved, or mature product
- Invigorate sales of a mature brand
- Facilitate the introduction of new products to the trade
- Increase on- and off-shelf merchandising space
- Neutralize competitive advertising and sales promotions
- Obtain trial purchases from consumers
- Hold current users by encouraging repeat purchases
- Increase product usage by loading consumers
- Preempt competition by loading consumers
- Reinforce advertising

Sales Promotions *Cannot*

- Compensate for a poorly trained sales force or for a lack of advertising
- Give the trade or consumers any compelling long-term reason to continue purchasing a brand
- Permanently stop an established brand's declining sales trend or change the basic nonacceptance of an undesired product

For example, Fiat Automobiles of Brazil had redesigned its Marea sedan and station wagon and was looking for an exciting promotion to motivate dealer salespeople and to encourage prospective customers to test-drive the Marea. The aspect of the promotional program aimed at salespeople involved "mystery shoppers" trained by Fiat who visited dealerships to test salespeople and managers on their technical knowledge of the Marea and their customer service skills. Salespeople and managers judged as having impeccable knowledge and sales skills received cash prizes. Additionally, each month, top-performing salespeople and managers earned additional cash prizes. At the campaign's end, top performers received paid vacations to Brazil's luxurious Comandatuba Island. The promotion was judged an incredible success.[14]

Invigorate Sales of a Mature Brand

Promotions can invigorate sales of a mature brand that requires a shot in the arm. Promotions cannot, however, reverse the sales decline for an undesirable product or brand.

Consider, for example, a promotion Bazooka bubble gum undertook in Latin America, where, as in the United States, Bazooka bubble gum is wrapped with a Bazooka Kid comic strip. The character in this comic strip is known to children in Argentina, Paraguay, and Uruguay as El Pibe Bazooka. Bazooka commanded over 40 percent of the gum market in these countries, but its share had fallen by more than 10 share points due to an onslaught of competitors. The maker of Bazooka gum, Cadbury, turned to its promotion agency for ideas to offset competitive inroads. The agency devised a promotion that temporarily replaced El Pibe Bazooka with Secret Clues that, when placed under a decoder screen, would reveal keys to "Bazooka Super Treasure." More than 150 million Secret Clues hit the market, and three million decoder screens were made available to kids through magazine and newspaper inserts and at candy stands and schools. After buying Bazooka and placing a Secret Clue under a decoder screen, kids learned immediately whether they would receive instant-win prizes such as T-shirts, soccer balls, and school bags. Kids could also enter a Super Treasure sweepstakes by mailing in 10 proofs of purchase. Top prizes included multimedia computers for winners and their schools along with stereo systems, TVs, bicycles, and other attractive items.

Consumer response was so overwhelming that Bazooka experienced distribution problems within several weeks of initiating the promotion. Bazooka sales increased by 28 percent and gained back about seven share points. This successful promotion demonstrates the power of sales incentives that catch the imagination of a receptive target market. Kids were encouraged to buy Bazooka gum to win instant prizes and to purchase the brand repeatedly to become eligible for very attractive sweepstakes awards.[15]

Facilitate the Introduction of New Products to the Trade

To achieve sales and profit objectives, marketers continually introduce new products and add new brands to existing categories. Promotions to wholesalers and retailers are typically necessary to encourage the trade to handle new offerings, which practitioners refer to as *stock-keeping units,* or SKUs. In fact, many retailers refuse to carry additional SKUs unless they receive extra compensation in the form of off-invoice allowances, display allowances, and slotting allowances. (Each of these forms of allowances is discussed later in the chapter.)

Increase On- and Off-Shelf Merchandising Space

Trade-oriented promotions, often in conjunction with consumer promotions, enable a manufacturer to obtain extra shelf space or more desirable space temporarily. This space may be in the form of extra facings on the shelf or off-shelf space in a gondola or an end-of-aisle display.[16]

Neutralize Competitive Advertising and Sales Promotions

Sales promotions can effectively offset competitors' advertising and promotion efforts. For example, one company's 50-cent coupon loses much of its appeal when a competitor simultaneously comes out with a $1 coupon. As previously described, Bazooka's promotion in Argentina, Paraguay, and Uruguay offset competitors' promotions and won back lost market share.

Obtain Trial Purchases from Consumers

Marketers depend on free samples, coupons, and other sales promotions to encourage trial purchases of new brands. Many consumers would never try new products or previously untried brands without these promotional inducements. Consider the following creative promotion that was extraordinarily successful in introducing a new line of lightbulbs in England.

Although consumers worldwide use massive quantities of lightbulbs, many people consider the brand name not all that important when selecting lightbulbs, because they assume that lightbulbs are essentially commodities—one bulb is as good (or bad) as the next. Against this perception, Philips Lighting attempted to create a differential advantage for its brand when introducing the Softone line of colored bulbs. But after more than a decade of marketing the brand, it had achieved a loyal following only among a small and predominantly older group of consumers. Philips attempted one more time to build demand for its Softone line—especially among younger families, who might become loyal product users for years.

This was quite a challenge considering that TV advertising was unable to convey the subtle colors of Softone bulbs adequately. It therefore was necessary to use some form of promotion to build brand awareness among the target segment and encourage trial purchase behavior—leading, hopefully, to repeat purchasing among loyal brand users. Philips hired a promotion agency to create a campaign that would achieve the dual awareness-building and trial-generating objectives. The available budget was just approximately $2 million.

The agency developed a program based on what it described as a "ludicrously simple idea." Certain households were selected to receive bags, each of which contained an information brochure, a coupon, and a brief questionnaire. The attractive brochure described the product's benefits and emphasized the mood-generating ability of colored lightbulbs. The coupon was worth 75 cents off the purchase of a bulb. Bags were distributed just to households targeted on their demographic and psychographic characteristics that made them prime prospects for purchasing the product. The distribution crews placed the bags in mailboxes. (Parenthetically, this would be illegal in the United States, which permits only the U.S. Postal Service to use mailboxes; such a restriction does not exist in England.)

You will note that the bags did not contain lightbulbs. Rather, a response sheet inside the bags asked recipients if they were interested in receiving a free bulb and, if so, which of seven colors they wanted. Interested households were instructed to hang the bag with the completed questionnaire on their outside doorknob. That same evening, distribution crews inspected each household's response sheet and slipped the preferred-color lightbulb into the bag.

A total of two million bags were distributed. Of these, 700,000 households requested a free bulb—for a response rate of 35 percent. Follow-up surveys revealed that over 50 percent of bulb recipients actually used the bulbs. A total of 160,000 coupons were redeemed, which at 8 percent is an incredibly high redemption level—as the previous chapter pointed out in the context of p-mailing. Sales in the six-month period following this special promotion doubled the prior average. Moreover, a subsequent bag distribution campaign was three times more efficient than the inaugural effort by focusing on neighborhoods near key retail accounts. This simple program illustrates how creative and strategically sound promotions can generate trial purchase behavior.[17]

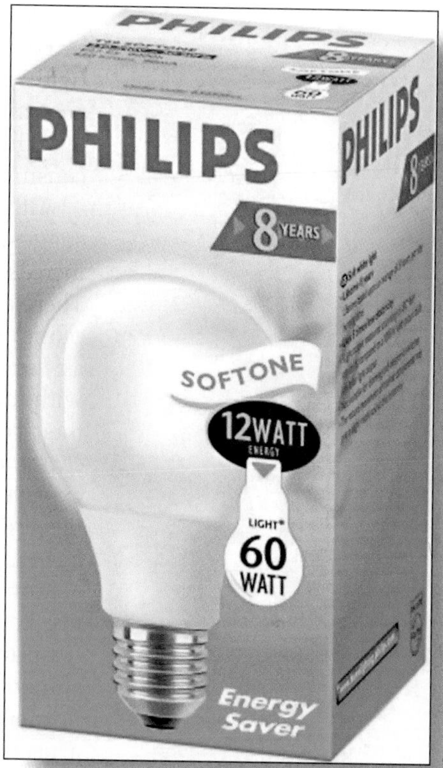

Courtesy of Philips

Hold Current Users by Encouraging Repeat Purchases

Brand switching is a fact of life all brand managers face. The strategic use of certain forms of promotion can encourage at least short-run repetitive purchasing. Premium programs, refunds, sweepstakes, and various continuity programs (all described in Chapter 17) are useful promotions for encouraging repeat purchasing.

Increase Product Usage by Loading Consumers

The effect of many deal-oriented promotions is to encourage consumer *stockpiling*—that is, to influence consumers to purchase more of a particular brand than they normally would to take advantage of the deal. Research has found that when readily stockpiled items (e.g., canned goods, paper products, and soap) are promoted with a deal, purchase quantity increases—or stated alternatively, the consumption rate accelerates—by a substantial magnitude in the short term.[18]

This practice prompts a critical question: Do these short-term increases from consumer stockpiling actually lead to *long-term* consumption increases of the promoted product category, or do they merely represent *borrowed future sales*? An important study found that price promotions do *not* increase category profitability but simply serve to shift short-term sales revenue from one brand to another. That is, sales gains in the short term induced by consumer stockpiling were offset by reduced demand in the long term.[19] This finding thus suggests that price-oriented promotions may encourage consumers to load up in the short term, but that this short-term loading simply steals purchases that otherwise would have been made during subsequent periods.

Please note that the foregoing finding is based on research involving a single product—a nonfood item (probably a brand from the household cleaning category) that the researchers could not disclose due to the manufacturer's proprietary concerns. Can this finding be generalized, or is the result idiosyncratic to this particular product category? No simple answer is possible, and, as usual, it depends on the circumstances surrounding a specific brand and the particular promotional event.

Other researchers, however, have provided tentative evidence that establishes the conditions when the practice of loading might have positive long-term effects. These researchers determined that loading does increase consumers' product usage, especially when *usage-related thoughts about a product are vivid in the consumer's memory*. For example, people will not necessarily consume more soup just because they have stockpiled above-average quantities. However, if soup is on their minds (due to an advertising campaign touting soup's versatility), consumption is likely to increase. Also, products that are regularly *visible* (such as perishable items placed in the front of the refrigerator) are likely to be used frequently if consumers have stockpiled them.[20]

This finding receives additional support from research that has examined the impact of consumer inventory levels on the amount of usage for two product categories, ketchup and yogurt. Researchers predicted that consumption of yogurt would be more sensitive to inventory level because unlike ketchup, yogurt can be consumed at different times of the day and under a variety of circumstances (with meals, as a snack, etc.). Their results supported this expectation as the amount of yogurt consumption, but not ketchup, was influenced by the quantity of yogurt available in consumers' refrigerators—more yogurt, more (than normal) consumption; more ketchup, no more (than normal) consumption.[21]

Although no simple conclusion is currently available, the empirical evidence suggests that marketer's price-oriented deals that encourage stockpiling promote increased long-term consumption for some product categories but not others. There are at least two conditions when increased consumption occurs from stockpiling: First, when stockpiled products are *physically visible* to consumers as well as *perishable,* the effect may be to encourage increased short-term consumption without stealing sales from future periods. Second, consumers seem to increase their consumption rate of stockpiled products when the product is *convenient to consume* compared with when it requires preparation. Hence, it would be expected that snack foods would be consumed more rapidly when larger quantities are available in the household than would, say, a product such as pasta that has to be prepared.[22]

Conversely, the use of price deals that lead consumers to stockpile products like ketchup and household cleaning products may simply serve to increase product purchasing in the short term without increasing long-term consumption. Consumers, in effect, stockpile these items when they go on deal but do not increase normal product usage. Thus, we would tentatively conclude that price dealing is a useful *offensive weapon* (that is, for purposes of increasing total consumption) only for items such as yogurt, cookies, and salty snacks, whereas products such as ketchup should be price promoted only for *defensive reasons* such as offsetting competitive efforts that attempt to steal market share.

Preempt Competition by Loading Consumers

When consumers are loaded with one company's brand, they are temporarily out of the marketplace for competitive brands. Hence, one brand's promotion serves to preempt sales of competitive brands.[23]

Reinforce Advertising

A final can-do capability of sales promotion is to reinforce advertising. A well-coordinated sales promotion effort can greatly strengthen an advertising campaign.

The relationship between advertising and promotion is two way. On the one hand, an exciting promotion can reinforce advertising's impact. On the other hand, advertising is increasingly being used as a communications mechanism for delivering promotional offerings. It is estimated, in fact, that upwards of one third of all media advertisements (TV, print, Internet, etc.) carry a promotional message.[24] The growing importance of promotion-oriented advertising is evidenced by the fact that promotion agencies are increasingly responsible for creating advertisements—a role historically of the traditional full-service advertising agency.

What Promotions Cannot Accomplish

As with other marketing communications elements, there are limits to what sales promotions are capable of accomplishing. Particularly notable are the following three limitations.

Inability to Compensate for a Poorly Trained Sales Force or for a Lack of Advertising

When suffering from poor sales performance or inadequate growth, some companies consider promotion to be the solution. However, promotions will provide at best a temporary fix if the underlying problem is due to a poor sales force, a lack of brand awareness, a weak brand image, or other maladies that only proper sales management and advertising efforts can overcome.

Inability to Give the Trade or Consumers Any Compelling Long-Term Reason to Continue Purchasing a Brand

The trade's decision to continue stocking a brand and consumers' repeat purchasing are based on continued satisfaction with the brand, which results from meeting profit objectives (for the trade) and providing benefits (for consumers). Promotions cannot compensate for a fundamentally flawed or mediocre brand unless the promotions offset the flaws by offering superior value to the trade and consumers.

Inability to Permanently Stop an Established Brand's Declining Sales Trend or Change the Basic Nonacceptance of an Undesired Product

Declining sales of a brand over an extended period indicate poor product performance or the availability of a superior alternative. Promotions cannot reverse the basic nonacceptance of an undesired brand. A declining sales trend can be reversed only through product improvements or perhaps an advertising campaign that breathes new life into an aging brand. Promotions used in combination with advertising efforts or product improvements may reverse the trend, but sales promotion by itself would be a waste of time and money when a brand is in a state of permanent decline.

The Role of Trade Promotions

With the shift in power from manufacturers to retailers, and with brands from competitive manufacturers becoming increasingly indistinct, retailers have pressured the manufacturers that supply them to provide attractive price discounts and other forms of promotional dollars as well.

Consider the case of Clorox. In the late 1990s, The Clorox Company acquired a firm named First Brands. One of First Brands' most important products was the line of plastic items (wraps and bags) under the Glad brand name. Clorox thought it could quickly boost sales of Glad products because First Brands had previously invested virtually nothing in media advertising behind the brand, relying instead almost exclusively on consumer promotions (primarily coupons) and heavy trade promotion spending. Clorox's strategy was to cut Glad's consumer and trade promotions and to invest heavily in mass-media advertising. Clorox cut trade promotion spending on Glad in 1999 and then again in 2000. Much to the disappointment of Clorox's marketing management, competitors did not follow. How did retailers react? They withdrew merchandise support, and Glad sales fell dramatically—as did Clorox's stock price, which dropped by about 20 percent in the two years after acquiring First Brands.[25]

With declining market share and a sagging stock price, Clorox responded in the only way it could: It returned to couponing and trade promotion spending.

Although Clorox's long-term strategy is to build Glad's brand equity via increased advertising spending and new product introductions, the fact remains that its effort to cut trade-promotion spending was rebuffed by large, powerful retailers. As previously discussed, the power of retailers continues to grow relative to that of manufacturers. As one observer noted, "Without unique products and strong advertising, package-goods brands have little choice but to pay up to maintain shelf space, especially as consolidation makes retailers more powerful."[26]

Trade Promotions' Scope and Objectives

As indicated earlier in the chapter, trade promotions represent over half of every manufacturer dollar invested in advertising and promoting new and existing products. Manufacturers' trade promotions are directed at wholesalers, retailers, and other marketing intermediaries (rather than at consumers). A manufacturer's consumer-oriented advertising and promotions are likely to fail unless trade promotions have succeeded in influencing channel intermediaries to stock adequate quantities. The special incentives manufacturers offer to their distribution channel members are expected to be passed through to consumers in the form of price discounts offered by retailers, often stimulated by advertising support and special displays. As we will see later, however, this does not always occur. (See the *Global Focus* insert for discussion of how Procter & Gamble has altered how it manages trade promotions globally to obtain a better return on investment.)

Even though trade promotions do not always work as intended, manufacturers have legitimate objectives for using trade-oriented promotions.[27] These objectives include the following:

1. Introducing new or revised products
2. Increasing distribution of new packages or sizes
3. Building retail inventories
4. Maintaining or increasing the manufacturer's share of shelf space
5. Obtaining displays outside normal shelf locations
6. Reducing excess inventories and increasing turnover
7. Achieving product features in retailers' advertisements
8. Countering competitive activity
9. Selling as much as possible to final consumers

Ingredients for a Successful Trade Promotion Program

To accomplish these myriad objectives, several ingredients are critical to building a successful trade promotion program.[28]

Financial Incentive

A manufacturer's trade promotion must offer retailers increased profit margins, increased sales volume, or both.

Correct Timing

Trade promotions are appropriately timed when they are (1) tied in with seasonal events during a time of growing sales (such as candy sales during Valentine's Day, Halloween, and Christmas); (2) paired with a consumer-oriented sales promotion; or (3) used strategically to offset competitive promotional activity.

global focus

An Altered Organization at Procter & Gamble to Better Manage Trade Promotion Spending

Procter & Gamble (P&G) is a huge global marketer with annual sales in excess of $70 billion. As indicated in Chapter 7, P&G spends mightily in advertising its brands, with annual expenditures in the United States amounting to nearly $5 billion in a recent year. P&G also invests heavily in trade promotions, estimated to exceed $2 billion annually in the United States alone. Like most other CPG manufacturers, P&G is concerned that some (perhaps much) of its trade promotion expenditures are ineffective. Part of the problem relates to the type of trade promotions that are used in marketing P&G brands, but perhaps an even bigger culprit is how the trade promotion budget is managed.

The management of trade promotions at P&G historically has been under the control of the *sales force.* By their very nature, sale force managers are motivated to use trade promotions as a means of building positive relations with retail customers and as a means of creating a sales climate that is maximally positive for the salespeople who call on these customers. It should come as little surprise to know that salespeople want to make retailers happy in order to reduce conflict, to make their jobs relatively stress free, and to generate high levels of sales volume. Sales managers and salespeople typically focus more on the top line (sales revenue) than on the bottom line (profit). These comments are not intended to suggest that sales departments are inherently wrong or misguided, but rather to indicate that the sales department is probably not the organizational unit that should control trade promotion spending if the corporate objective is elevate focus on the bottom line vis-à-vis the top.

Accordingly, P&G has moved control of trade promotion spending from the global groups that manage sales forces to the marketing directors who manage brand teams. Although this move may appear subtle (and even trivial), in actuality it is a significant change in how trade promotions are managed at P&G. With the shift of trade promotion spending to marketing directors who are responsible for managing brand teams, trade promotion now is accorded equal footing with the advertising and consumer promotion tools that marketing directors also manage. The managers who set brand strategy now can be expected to treat trade promotions as a critically important strategic tool that can work in conjunction with advertising and consumer promotions to enhance the equity of P&G's many brands marketed throughout the world and to assure that the focus of trade promotion spending concentrates on both bottom- and top-line performance.

SOURCE: Adapted from Jack Neff, "Trade Marketing Finally Gets Some Respect (Well, At P&G), *Advertising Age,* June 18, 2007, 3, 36.

Minimize the Retailer's Effort and Cost

The more effort and expense required, the less likely it is that retailers will cooperate in a program they see as benefiting the manufacturer but not themselves.

Quick Results

The most effective trade promotions are those that generate immediate sales or increases in store traffic. (As you will see in the next chapter, instant gratification is an important motivator of consumer responses to consumer-oriented promotions. This same motive applies to retailers as well.)

Improve Retailer Performance

Promotions are effective when they help the retailer do a better selling job or improve merchandising methods as, for example, by providing retailers with improved displays.

Trade Allowances

Manufacturers use this major type of trade-oriented promotions, **trade allowances,** to reward retailers for performing activities in support of the manufacturer's brand. These allowances, also called *trade deals,* encourage retailers to stock the manufacturer's brand, discount the brand's price to consumers, feature it in advertising, or provide special display or other point-of-purchase support.

By using trade allowances, manufacturers hope to accomplish two interrelated objectives: (1) increase retailers' purchases of the manufacturer's brand, and (2) augment consumers' purchases of the manufacturer's brand from retailers. The latter is based on the expectations that consumers are receptive to price reductions and that retailers will actually pass along to consumers the discounts they receive from manufacturers.

These expectations do not always become reality. Retailers often take advantage of allowances without performing the services for which they receive credit. In fact, a study of trade promotion spending by ACNielsen revealed that fewer than one third of surveyed manufacturers rated the value they received from trade promotion as "good" or "excellent."[29] Moreover, the vast majority of retailers think that trade promotions should serve to increase sales and profits of entire product categories without concern for whether a manufacturer's specific brand benefits from the trade promotion.[30]

There is, in short, a substantial rift between manufacturers and retailers over the matter of which party trade promotions are intended to benefit. Manufacturers use trade promotions to advance their brands' sales and profit performance. Retailers, in contrast, tend to regard trade dollars as an opportunity for increasing their profit margins and thus boosting bottom lines. This schism is easy to understand because parties to economic transactions often have conflicting objectives yet depend on each other for success.

Major Forms of Trade Allowances

There are three major forms of trade allowances: (1) off-invoice allowances, (2) bill-back allowances, and (3) slotting allowances.[31] As we will see in the following discussion, manufacturers use off-invoice and bill-back allowances by choice, but retailers impose slotting allowances.

Off-Invoice Allowances

The most frequently used form of trade allowance is an off-invoice allowance, which represents a manufacturer's temporary price reduction to the trade on a particular brand. **Off-invoice allowances** are, as the name suggests, deals offered periodically to the trade that permit retailers to *deduct a fixed amount from the invoice*—merely by placing an order during the period which the manufacturer is "dealing" a brand. In offering an off-invoice allowance, the manufacturer's sales force informs retail buyers that a discount of, say, 15 percent can be deducted from the invoice amount for all quantities purchased during the specified deal period. Many CPG manufacturers provide off-invoice allowances at regularly scheduled intervals, which for many brands is one 4-week period during every 13-week business quarter. This means that many brands are on off-invoice deals approximately 30 percent of the year.

A manufacturer in using an off-invoice allowance does so with the expectation that retailers will purchase more of the manufacturer's brand during the deal period than they normally would and, to sell off excess inventories rapidly, *will pass the deals on to consumers in the form of reduced prices*—which thus should spur consumers' purchasing of the manufacturer's price-reduced brand. However, as previously stated, retailers do not always comply with this expectation and, in fact, are typically not contractually bound to pass along discounted prices to consumers. Rather, retailers receive an off-invoice allowance (of, say, 15 percent) when purchasing the manufacturer's brand, but often they do not discount their selling prices to consumers or they reduce prices by substantially less than the full 15 percent.[32] Manufacturers estimate that retailers pass through to consumers only about one half of the trade funds they provide to retailers.

We will discuss two undesirable offshoots of off-invoice allowances later—forward buying and diverting—but first it will be useful to discuss the other two major forms of trade allowances, bill-back and slotting allowances.

Bill-Back Allowances

Retailers receive allowances for featuring the manufacturer's brand in advertisements (**bill-back ad allowances**) or for providing special displays (**bill-back display allowances**). As the expression indicates, retailers do *not* deduct bill-back allowances directly from the invoice by virtue of ordering products (as is the case with off-invoice allowances) but rather must earn the allowances *by performing designated advertising or display services* on behalf of the manufacturer's brand. The retailer effectively bills (i.e., charges) the manufacturer for the services rendered, and the manufacturer pays an allowance to the retailer for the services received.

To illustrate, assume that the sales force for the Campbell Soup Company informs retailers that during October they will receive a 5 percent discount on all cases of V8 juice purchased during this period provided they run newspaper advertisements in which V8 juice is prominently featured. With proof of having run feature ads in newspapers, retailers then would bill Campbell Soup for a 5 percent advertising allowance. Similarly, Campbell Soup's sales force could offer a 2 percent display allowance whereby retailers could receive an additional 2 percent discount on all purchases of V8 juice during the deal period for displaying V8 juice in prime locations.

Slotting Allowances

Slotting allowances are the fees manufacturers of both consumer packaged goods and durables pay retailers for access to the slot, or location, that the retailer must make available in its distribution center to accommodate the manufacturer's new brand. This form of trade allowance applies specifically to the situation where a manufacturer attempts to get one of its brands—typically a new brand—accepted by retailers.[33] Also called a *stocking allowance* or *street money,* a slotting allowance is not something manufactures of branded products choose to offer retailers. On the contrary, *retailers impose slotting allowances on manufacturers.* Retailers demand this fee of manufacturers supposedly to compensate them for added costs incurred when taking a new brand into distribution and placing it on the shelf. It should be obvious that manufacturers and retailers hold differing views regarding the appropriateness and value of the slotting-allowance practice.[34] The following discussion examines many of the key issues.[35]

When first used back in the 1960s, slotting allowances compensated retailers for the real costs of taking on a new stock-keeping unit, or SKU. The cost at that time averaged $50 per SKU per account. However, slotting allowances now can cost as much as $25,000 to $40,000 per item per store—although most slotting fees are much lower than this—and represent a healthy profit margin for retailers.[36] You probably are thinking, "This sounds like bribery." You also may be wondering, "Why do manufacturers tolerate slotting allowances?" Let's examine each issue.

First, slotting allowances are indeed a form of bribery. The retailer that demands slotting allowances denies the manufacturer shelf space unless the manufacturer is willing to pay the up-front fee—the slotting allowance—to acquire that space for its new brand. Second, manufacturers tolerate slotting allowances because they are confronted with a classic dilemma: Either they pay the fee and eventually recoup the cost through profitable sales volume, or they refuse to pay the fee and in so doing accept a fate of not being able to introduce new brands successfully. The expression "Between a rock and a hard place" appropriately describes the reality of slotting allowances from the manufacturer's perspective.

In certain respects, slotting allowances *are* a legitimate cost of doing business and, in fact, can serve to increase marketplace efficiency rather than being anticompetitive.[37] When, for example, a large multistore supermarket chain takes on a new brand, it incurs several added expenses. These expenses arise because the chain must make space for that new brand in its distribution center, create a new entry in its computerized inventory system, possibly redesign store shelves, and notify individual stores about the new SKU. In addition to these expenses, the chain takes the risk that the new brand will fail. This is a likely result in the grocery industry, where at least half of all new brands are failures. Hence, slotting allowances provide retailers with what effectively amounts to an insurance policy against the prospects that a brand will fail.

It is questionable, however, whether the actual expenses retailers incur are anywhere near the slotting allowances they charge. Large manufacturers can afford to pay slotting allowances because their volume is sufficient to recoup the expense. However, manufacturers of brands with small consumer franchises are frequently unable to afford these fees. Smaller manufacturers thus are placed at a competitive disadvantage when attempting to gain distribution for their new products.

How, you might be wondering, are retailers able to impose expensive slotting fees on manufacturers? The reason is straightforward: As noted earlier in the chapter, the balance of power has shifted away from manufacturers and toward retailers. Power means being able to call the shots, and increasing numbers of retailers are doing this. Also, CPG manufacturers have hurt their own cause by introducing thousands of new brands each year, most of which are trivial variants of existing products rather than distinct new offerings with meaningful profit opportunities for wholesalers and retailers. As such, every manufacturer competes against every other manufacturer for limited shelf space, and slotting allowances are simply a mechanism retailers use to exploit the competition among manufacturers. Furthermore, many grocery retailers find it easy to rationalize slotting allowances on the grounds that their net profit margins in selling groceries are minuscule (typically 1 percent to 1.5 percent) and that slotting allowances enable them to earn returns comparable to those manufacturers earn.

Further understanding of the rationale and dynamics underlying slotting allowances is possible by making a comparison with apartment prices in any college community. When units are abundant, different apartment complexes compete aggressively with one another and rental prices are forced downward to the benefit of students. But when apartments are scarce (which is typical in most college communities), prices often are inflated. The result: You may be forced to pay exorbitant rent to live in a second-rate, albeit conveniently located, apartment.

This is also the case in today's marketing environment. Each year retailers are confronted with requests to stock thousands of new brands (consider these new brands equivalent to potential tenants). The amount of shelf space (the number of apartments) is limited because relatively few new stores are being built. Hence, retailers can command slotting allowances (charge higher rent), and manufacturers are willing to pay the higher rent to "live" in desirable locations.

What can a manufacturer do to avoid paying slotting allowances? Sometimes nothing. But powerful manufacturers such as Procter & Gamble (P&G) and Kraft, for example, are less likely to pay slotting fees than are weaker national and particularly regional manufacturers. Retailers know that P&G's and Kraft's new brands probably will be successful because P&G and Kraft invest substantially in research to develop meaningful new products; spend heavily on advertising to create consumer demand for these products; and use extensive consumer promotions (e.g., sampling and couponing) to create strong consumer pull for their brands. Another way to avoid paying slotting allowances is simply to refuse to pay them and, if need be, to accept the consequence of being refused shelf space by some, if not most, retail chains.

© Susan Van Etten

In the final analysis, the issue of slotting allowances is extremely complicated. Manufacturers have legitimate reasons for not wanting to pay slotting allowances, but retailers have justification for charging them. Can both sides be right? Is the practice of slotting allowances a case of free-market competition working at its best, or at its worst? Simple answers are unavailable because the "correct" answer depends largely on which perspective—manufacturer's or retailer's—one takes on the matter.[38]

In the middle of this battle are government regulators, who have the responsibility of ensuring that the practice of slotting allowances does not reduce competition or harm consumers by forcing them to pay higher prices or limiting their options because smaller manufacturers are unable to gain shelf space for their new products. One regulatory agency, the Bureau of Alcohol, Tobacco, Firearms and Explosives, passed a ruling that prohibits the use of slotting fees in the marketing of alcohol products.[39] However, no prohibitions exist for the many other product categories where slotting allowances are charged. Although the Federal Trade Commission continues to investigate whether slotting allowances need to be regulated, it has not issued any regulation against retailers charging these fees.[40] In the meantime, slotting allowances remain for manufacturers an additional cost of introducing new products and an additional source of revenue for retailers. The power struggle goes on!

The Special Case of Exit Fees (Deslotting Allowances). Whereas slotting allowances represent a form of entry fee for getting a new brand into a grocery chain's distribution center, some retail chains charge manufacturers a fee for having unsuccessful brands removed from their distribution centers. These **exit fees** could just as well be called *deslotting allowances.* Here is how they operate: When introducing a new brand to a retail chain, the manufacturer and chain enter into a contractual arrangement. This arrangement stipulates the average volume of weekly product movement during a specified period that must be achieved for the manufacturer's brand to be permitted to remain in the chain's distribution center. If the brand has not met the stipulated average weekly movement, the chain will issue a deslotting charge. This charge, or exit fee, is intended to cover the handling costs for the chain to remove the item from its distribution center.

This practice may seem to be a marketplace application of the old saying about having salt rubbed into a wound. However, it really represents the fact that retailers, especially in the supermarket industry, no longer are willing to pay for manufacturers' new-product mistakes. There clearly is some economic logic to deslotting charges because these charges are another form of insurance policy to protect retail chains from slow-moving and unprofitable brands. To continue the apartment-rental analogy, a deslotting charge operates in much the same fashion as the stipulation between apartment owner and tenant regarding property damage. If the tenant damages an apartment, the apartment owner is fully justified in forfeiting all or part of the tenants' rental deposit. As such, the deposit provides the apartment owner with an insurance policy against potential negligence. This is precisely how an exit fee, or deslotting charge, operates.

Undesirable Consequences of Off-Invoice Allowances: Forward Buying and Diverting

Now that we have reviewed the three major forms of trade allowances—off-invoice, bill-back, and slotting allowances—we return to the first form of allowance and discuss the undesirable consequences that result from a manufacturer's use of off-invoice allowances.

Manufacturers' off-invoice allowances make considerable sense in theory, but in practice many retailers do not perform the services necessary to earn the allowances they receive from manufacturers. Large retail chains are particularly likely to take advantage of manufacturers' allowances without passing the savings along to consumers. A major reason is that large chains, unlike smaller chains, can merchandise their own *private brands* (or store brands). Because private brands can be sold at lower prices than manufacturers' comparable brands, large chains are able to use private brands to satisfy the needs of price-sensitive consumers while selling manufacturers' brands at their normal prices and pocketing the trade allowance as extra profit.

A second major problem with manufacturers' off-invoice allowances is that they often induce retailers to stockpile products to take advantage of the temporary price reductions. *Forward buying* and *diverting* are two interrelated practices retailers, especially those in the grocery trade, use to capitalize on manufacturers' trade allowances. Table 15.5 illustrates these practices.[41]

Forward Buying

As earlier noted, manufacturers' trade allowances are typically available for four weeks of each business quarter (which translates to about 30 percent of the year). During these deal periods, retailers buy larger quantities than needed for normal inventory and warehouse the excess volume, thereby avoiding purchasing the brand at its full price during the remaining 70 percent of the year when a deal is not offered. Retailers often purchase enough products on one deal to carry them over until the manufacturer's next regularly scheduled deal. This is the practice of **forward buying**, which, for obvious reasons, is also called *bridge buying*—the amount of inventory purchased during one deal period bridges all the way to the next deal period.

When a manufacturer marks down a product's price by, say, 15 percent, retail chains commonly stock up with a 10- to 12-week supply. A number of manufacturers sell 80 percent to 90 percent of their volume during the occasions (approximately 30 percent of the year) when they are on deal. It is estimated that forward buying costs manufacturers between 0.5 percent and 1.1 percent of retail prices, which translates into hundreds of millions of dollars annually.[42]

Retailers employ mathematical models that enable them to estimate the profit potential from a forward buy and the optimum number of weeks of inventory to purchase. The models take into consideration the amount of savings from a deal and then incorporate into their calculations the various added costs from forward buying. These added costs include warehouse storage expenses, shipping costs, and the cost of tying up money in inventory when that money could be used to

table 15.5

Illustration of Forward Buying and Diverting

1. In preparation for a huge promotional event in 2009 surrounding the Cinco de Mayo celebration of Mexican independence on May 5, Beauty Products Inc.—a hypothetical manufacturer of personal-care products—extends an *off-invoice offer* to grocery chains in the Los Angeles area. This promotion is a 15 percent off-invoice allowance on all orders placed for SynActive shampoo (a hypothetical brand) during the week beginning April 3, 2009, and extending through the week beginning April 24, 2009.
2. Assume that FB&D Supermarkets of Los Angeles (a hypothetical chain) orders 15,000 cases of SynActive—many more cases than it typically would sell in its own stores during any four-week period. Beauty Products Inc. has offered the 15 percent off-invoice allowance to FB&D Supermarkets with the expectation that FB&D will reduce SynActive's retail price to consumers by as much as 15 percent during the week of Cinco de Mayo festivities.
3. FB&D sells at the discounted price only 3,000 of the 15,000 cases purchased. (The remaining cases include some that are forward bought and some that will be diverted.)
4. FB&D resells 5,000 cases of SynActive at a small profit margin to Opportunistic Food Brokers—a company that services grocery retailers throughout the West. (This is the practice of *diverting.*)
5. FB&D later sells the remaining 7,000 cases of SynActive to shoppers in its own stores but at the regular, full price. (These 7,000 cases represent *forward buys.*)

earn a better return in some other manner. Retailers, when forward buying, balance savings from reduced purchasing costs against the added expenses of the kind just noted.

It may appear that forward buying benefits all parties to the marketing process, but this is not the case. First, as previously mentioned, a substantial portion of retailers' savings from forward buying often are not passed on to consumers. Second, forward buying leads to increased distribution costs because wholesalers and retailers pay greater carrying charges by holding inventories of large quantities of forward-bought items. In fact, the average grocery product takes up to 12 weeks from the time a manufacturer ships it until it reaches retail store shelves. This delay obviously is not due to transit time but rather reflects storage time in wholesalers' warehouses and retailers' distribution centers from stockpiling surplus quantities of forward-bought items. Third, manufacturers experience reduced margins due to the price discounts they offer and the increased costs they incur.

A notable case in point is the situation that confronted Campbell Soup Company with massive forward buying of its chicken noodle soup when that product was placed on trade deal. As much as 40 percent of its annual chicken noodle soup production was sold to wholesalers and retailers in just six weeks when this product was on deal. Because wholesalers and retailers forward-bought chicken noodle soup in large quantities, Campbell had to schedule extra work shifts and pay overtime to keep up with the accelerated production and shipping schedules. After years of falling prey to forward buying, Campbell implemented a *bill-and-hold program* whereby it invoices (bills) the retailer as soon as the retailer places a forward-bought order but delays shipping (holds) the order until the retailer requests desired quantities. This program smoothed out Campbell's production and shipping schedules by allowing retailers to purchase large amounts at deal prices while delaying shipments until inventory was needed. The bill-and-hold program has not eliminated forward buying, but the negative consequences for Campbell Soup Company have been reduced.

Diverting

Diverting occurs when a manufacturer restricts a deal to a *limited geographical area* rather than making it available nationally. As described in Table 15.5, a brand of shampoo named SynActive is available only in Los Angeles as part of the city's Cinco de Mayo festivities. The hypothetical manufacturer illustrated in Table 15.5 (Beauty Products Inc.) intends for only retailers in the Los Angeles area to benefit from the deal. However, retailers (such as FB&D Supermarkets in Table 15.5) engage in diverting by buying abnormally large quantities at the deal price and then selling off, at a small profit margin, the excess quantities through food brokers in *other geographical areas.* (Finance people would label diverting an application of *arbitrage* behavior.)

Retailers blame manufacturers for offering irresistible deals and argue that they must take advantage of the deals in any way legally possible to remain competitive with other retailers. Manufacturers could avoid the diverting problem by placing brands *on national deal only.* This solution is more ideal than practical, however, since regional marketing efforts are expanding, and local deals and regional marketing go hand in hand. Further complicating the problem is that products intended for foreign markets sometimes are diverted back into a domestic market.

There are other negative consequences of diverting. First, product quality potentially suffers due to delays in getting products from manufacturers to retail shelves. For example, Tropicana requires its chilled juices to be stored between 32 and 36 degrees. If unrefrigerated for a few hours because of careless diverting practices, the product can go bad, and consumers may form negative impressions of the brand. A second and potentially more serious problem could result from product tampering. In the event of product tampering, it would be difficult, if not impossible, to identify exactly where a diverted brand may have been shipped.

Don't Blame Retailers

The preceding discussion has perhaps made it seem that retailers are villains when engaging in the practices of forward buying and diverting. This would be an unfair representation of retail buyers, who are simply taking advantage of an opportunity that is provided by manufacturers offering attractive trade deals. One retail executive explains his company's forward buying and diverting in this fashion: "We are very aggressive when it comes to buying at the best price. We have to be. If we don't, somebody else will."[43] Retailers are simply exhibiting rational behavior when they forward buy and divert. The opportunity to increase profits is provided to retailers by manufacturers' indiscriminate off-invoice allowances, and smart retailers take advantage of these opportunities.

Efforts to Rectify Trade Allowance Problems

Because trade allowances spawn inefficiencies, create billions of added dollars in distribution costs, are often economically unprofitable for manufacturers, and perhaps inflate prices to consumers, a variety of efforts have been undertaken to alter fundamentally the way business is conducted, especially in the grocery industry.[44] The following sections are devoted to three practices some manufacturers undertake to minimize the negative effects of offering trade allowances: everyday low pricing, pay-for-performance programs, and account-specific marketing.

Everyday Low Pricing (EDLP)

Manufacturers lose billions of dollars every year to inefficient and ineffective trade deals stemming from the trade's practice of forward buying and diverting.

It is for this reason that the powerful P&G, under the leadership of then-chief executive officer Edwin Artzt, undertook a bold move in the 1990s to reduce the undesirable effects of retailers' forward buying and diverting. P&G introduced a new form of pricing called *everyday low pricing,* or EDLP, which the company also refers to as *value pricing*—signifying its desire to compete on the basis of providing product values and not mere price savings. Because some retailers also practice everyday low prices, we will distinguish between "back-door" EDLP manufacturers use from the "front-door" variety retailers practice.[45] Our interest is with the back-door variety of EDLP, which for clarity's sake we label EDLP(M) to stand for manufacturers' use of EDLP.

EDLP(M) is a form of pricing whereby a manufacturer charges the same price for a particular brand day in and day out. In other words, rather than charging high-low prices—that is, regular, or "high," prices for a period followed by off-invoice, or "low," prices for a shorter period—EDLP(M) involves charging the same price over an extended period. Because no off-invoice allowances are offered the trade under this pricing strategy, wholesalers and retailers have no reason to forward buy or divert. Hence, their profit is made from selling merchandise rather than from buying it.

How Has P&G Fared?

Researchers examined the effects of P&G's value pricing initiative over the first six years of its implementation.[46] The analysis encompassed a total of 24 product categories and 118 brands in these categories. From the year prior to P&G's implementation of EDLP through the first six years of the practice, P&G's advertising expenditures and net prices both increased by approximately 20 percent. During this same period, its expenditures on trade deals decreased by nearly 16 percent, and coupon spending was reduced by about 54 percent.

What was the effect of these changes? P&G lost about 18 percent market share on average across the 24 product categories analyzed. Value pricing clearly was a disaster for P&G, right? In actuality it was not. Although P&G suffered a significant decline in market share (due largely to competitors' retaliatory increases in promotional deals while P&G was cutting its own dealing activity), at the same time its overall profits increased by virtue of cutting trade deals and coupon activity and increasing net prices.[47] It could be argued that it is unwise ever to relinquish market share; however, in the final analysis, giving up market share can be justified if the share that remains generates greater profitability than what was obtained with a larger but less profitable share. Over the long haul, the bottom line (profits) is a more telling indicator of firm success than is the top line (sales).

What Have Other Manufacturers Done?

Manufacturers less powerful than P&G have found it difficult to convert to a pure system of everyday low pricing. Even P&G has experienced resistance and has deviated from pure EDLP pricing with some brands such as laundry detergents. Three major reasons account for why many retailers resist manufacturers' EDLP initiatives. First, those retailers that established distribution infrastructures necessary to practice forward buying have resisted EDLP(M).[48] Second, there is some evidence that EDLP(M) benefits the manufacturers that price their products in this fashion more than it does the retailers that pay EDLP(M) rather than high-low prices. Finally, it also has been argued that EDLP(M) takes some of the excitement out of retailing. With EDLP(M), the retailer charges the same price to consumers day after day. Comparatively, with high-low pricing, there are periods when retailers can advertise attractive price savings, which breaks the monotony of never varying the retail price. Although in the long term the consumer realizes no savings from high-low pricing, in the short term it may be exciting to receive an appealing discount.

Pay-for-Performance Programs

As noted earlier, many trade promotions, especially in the grocery industry, are unprofitable for manufacturers because they merely shift future buying to the present when the trade engages in forward buying and diverting. Manufacturers, accordingly, have a strong incentive to devise an alternative system to the traditional off-invoice allowance. One such system is so-called *pay-for-performance programs.*

Consider the case of Nestlé and why that company shifted trade spending in this direction. Marketing officials at Nestlé were fed up with blowing trade dollars that served little useful purpose. Accordingly, new contracts with retailers were drawn up and emphasized the minimum duties retailers' would have to perform to receive Nestlé's trade dollars, duties such as reducing retail prices for a specified period of time, featuring Nestlé's brands in retailers' circulars, and providing special displays. Retailers failing to meet Nestlé's contractual requirements became ineligible to receive promotional funds, or, at the extreme, Nestlé simply withdrew its brands from noncomplying retailers' stores.

Rewarding Selling Rather Than Buying

As the name suggests, **pay-for-performance** is a form of trade allowance that rewards retailers for performing the primary function that justifies a manufacturer's offering a trade allowance—namely, selling increased quantities of the manufacturer's brand to consumers. Pay-for-performance programs are designed to *reward retailers for selling the manufacturer's brand supported with a trade allowance rather than for merely buying the brand at an off-invoice price.*

One form of pay-for-performance programs is called *scanner-verified trade promotions* or *scan downs.* This name is based on the idea that retail sales volume for a trade-supported brand is recorded via optical scanning devices at the point of sale. Scan downs entail three key facets:[49]

1. A manufacturer agrees with a retailer on a period during which the retailer receives an allowance for all quantities of a promoted brand that are sold to consumers at the designated deal price (e.g., an item that regularly sells to consumers at $1.99 per unit is to be reduced to $1.79).
2. The retailer's own scanning data verify the exact amount of the promoted brand that has been sold during this period at the deal price (e.g., 5,680 units at $1.79 each).
3. The manufacturer pays the retailer quickly, say within five days, at the designated allowance for the quantity sold. The manufacturer then reimburses the retailer for the reduced margin in selling a certain number of units (e.g., 5,680 units at a reduced margin of $0.20, or $1,136) and compensates the retailer for the amount of the trade allowance (e.g., 5,680 units at $0.05 each, or $284.00; thus, the manufacturer would mail a check to the retailer totaling $1,420).

A Win-Win-Win Situation

Scanner-verified programs provide an incentive to the retailer only for the items sold at discount to consumers during the agreed-on time period. Thus, unlike off-invoice allowances, manufacturers using scan downs do not pay for allowances where no benefit is received. Rather, manufacturers compensate retailers only for those items that are sold to consumers at discounted prices. Hence, this form of pay-for-performance program benefits all parties: consumers, retailers, and manufacturers. Consumers win by receiving reduced prices; retailers win by obtaining allowances for moving increased quantities of manufacturers' promoted brands; and manufacturers win by increasing sales of their brands, if only temporarily. By comparison,

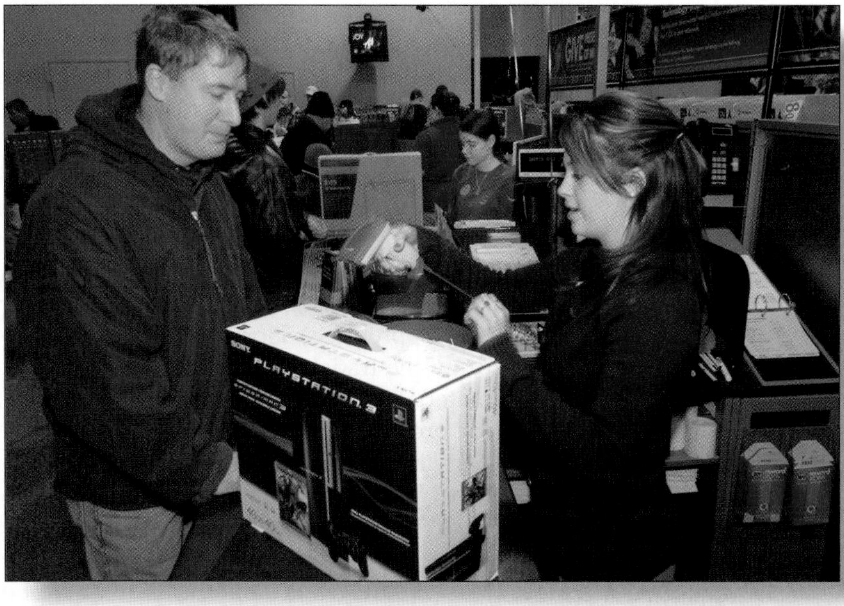

© Newscom

when using off-invoice allowances, manufacturers have no assurance that the off-invoice allowances given to retailers will be passed on to consumers.

In theory, then, with pay-for-performance programs, everyone wins. The rub, however, is that retailers do not win as much as they do with "gain without pain" off-invoice programs that offer rewards and require no effort other than placing an order. It is for this reason that manufacturers embrace pay-for-performance programs more heartily than retailers do. It also is for this reason that large, powerful manufacturers (e.g., Nestlé) sometimes need to take dramatic steps such as discontinuing selling their brands to retailers that fail to perform the duties that serve the manufacturer's promoted brand.

The technological infrastructure is available in the United States (as well in most other economically developed countries) to support this form of trade promotion, and well-known companies such as ACNielsen and Information Resources Inc. make it possible by serving, for a fee, as scanning agents. Scanning agents profit from performing the following functions: (1) collecting scanner data from retailers, (2) verifying the amount of product movement that meets the manufacturer's promotional requirements and warrants compensation, (3) paying the retailer, and (4) collecting funds from the manufacturer along with a commission for services rendered.

Customizing Promotions: Account-Specific Marketing

Account-specific marketing, also called *co-marketing,* is a descriptive term that characterizes promotional and advertising activity that a manufacturer *customizes* to specific retail accounts. To appreciate this practice fully, it is necessary to place it in the context of the off-invoice allowance promotion, which is a temporary price reduction that is offered to *all* customers. With off-invoice programs, a manufacturer's promotion dollars are anything but customized to the needs of specific retail accounts. In contrast, account-specific marketing directs promotion dollars to specific retail customers and develops in concert with the retailer advertising and promotion programs that simultaneously serve the manufacturer's brand, the retailer's volume and profit requirements, and the consumer's needs. Local radio tie-in advertising and loyalty programs using retailers' shopper databases are especially popular account-specific practices.

Some Examples

When introducing its expensive Photosmart photography system—a photo-scanning-and-printing system for home computers—Hewlett-Packard (HP) developed co-marketing arrangements with a small number of retailers. HP selected prime consumer prospects in each retailer's trade area and mailed invitations that appeared to be from the retailer, not HP. Prospective purchasers were invited to see an in-store demonstration and receive a chance to win a free Photosmart system.

An illustration from the CPG category is Hormel Foods' account-specific effort with the SPAM® Family of Products (the canned-meat product). To boost sales and to lure new consumers to the brand, Hormel Foods introduced the "SPAM Stuff" continuity program. Following in the footsteps of Marlboro, Kool-Aid, and Pepsi, all of which had previously launched "stuff" programs, Hormel Foods offered consumers points toward the acquisition of free items (such as beanbag characters, boxer shorts, mouse pads, mugs, and T-shirts) with each purchase of SPAM products. In addition to offering "freebies" to encourage consumers to try SPAM products, Hormel Foods developed some account-specific programs to draw the trade's attention to the brand. Retailers were given SPAM advertising materials for their advertising flyers. They also received local advertising support for promoting SPAM on the radio and in newspapers. To further excite retailer participation, Hormel Foods offered one supermarket per region with a "SPAM Day" promotion for the best in-store display. Winning stores received "SPAM-wear" for employees and customers, free SPAMBURGER hamburgers grilled in the store's parking lot, and personal appearances by SPAM Cans characters.

This surely was a lighthearted attempt on the part of Hormel Foods to increase interest in SPAM from both consumers and retailers. Silly as it may seem, programs like this often encourage retailers to devote greater attention to a brand (e.g., provide increased display space) and to entice consumers to purchase the brand more regularly.

What Does the Future Hold?

Account-specific marketing is a relatively recent innovation. First introduced by marketers in the packaged goods field, the practice eventually spread to companies that manufacture and market soft goods (e.g., apparel items) and durable items such as the HP Photosmart system. Because account-specific marketing requires a lot of effort in both development and implementation and is costly, interest among packaged goods companies already has peaked.[50] However, because powerful retailers benefit from well-designed account-specific programs, co-marketing is here to stay.

Generalizations about Promotions

The foregoing discussion has referred to research evidence regarding how promotions work and the objectives accomplished. Researchers—especially during the past two decades—have vigorously studied the functioning and effectiveness of sales promotions. These empirical efforts have enabled researchers to draw some tentative conclusions. These conclusions, more formally termed *empirical generalizations*, represent consistent evidence regarding different facets of promotion performance. Nine empirical generalizations are noteworthy (see Table 15.6).[51]

Generalization 1: Temporary retail price reductions substantially increase sales—but only in the short term

The evidence is clear that temporary retail price reductions generally result in substantial increases in short-term sales. These short-term sales increases are termed *sales spikes*. These spikes generally occur, however, at the expense of some reduction in consumer purchases of the promoted brand either preceding or following

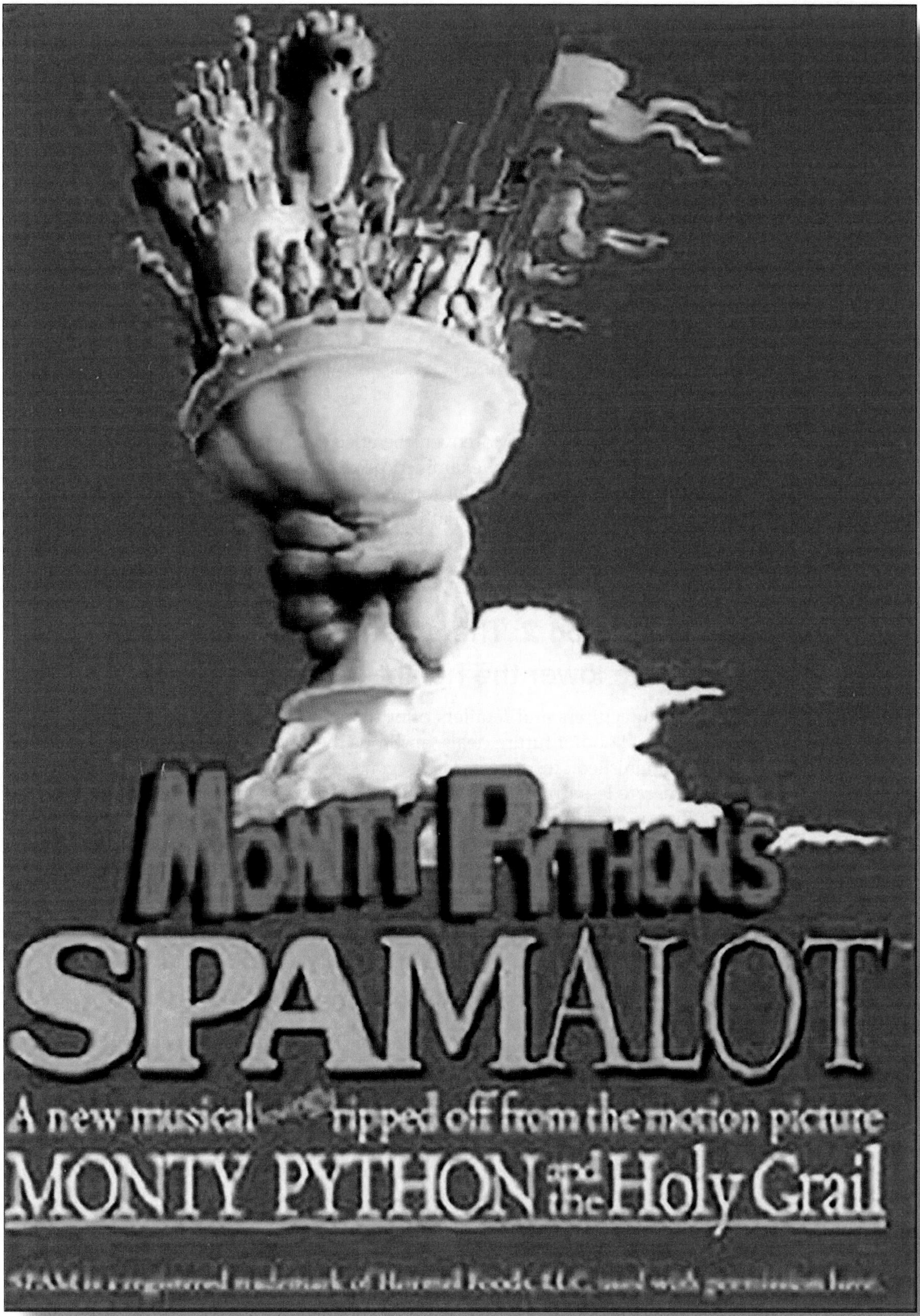
MONTY PYTHON'S
SPAMALOT
tripped off from the motion picture
MONTY PYTHON and the Holy Grail

table 15.6

Nine Empirical Generalizations about Promotions

1. Temporary retail price reductions substantially increase sales.
2. The greater the frequency of deals, the lower the height of the deal spike.
3. The frequency of deals changes the consumer's reference price.
4. Retailers pass through less than 100 percent of trade deals.
5. Higher-market-share brands are less deal elastic.
6. Advertised promotions can result in increased store traffic.
7. Feature advertising and displays operate synergistically to influence sales of discounted brands.
8. Promotions in one product category affect sales of brands in complementary and competitive categories.
9. The effects of promoting higher- and lower-quality brands are asymmetric.

Source: Adapted from Robert C. Blattberg, Richard Briesch, and Edward J. Fox, "How Promotions Work," *Marketing Science* 14, no. 3 (1995), G122–G132.

the promotional period.[52] Moreover, the effects of retail price promotions are *short lived*. For example, one study examined price promotions for various brands in the soup and yogurt categories—the former representing a storable product and the latter a perishable—and found that the effect these promotions had on consumers' purchase likelihood, brand choice, and purchase quantity lasted only a matter of several weeks and did not alter consumers' long-term purchase behavior.[53]

Generalization 2: The greater the frequency of deals, the lower the height of the deal spike

When manufacturers and retailers offer frequent deals, consumers learn to anticipate the likelihood of future deals, and thus their responsiveness to any particular deal is diminished. Infrequent deals generate greater spikes, whereas frequent deals generate less dramatic sales increases. The psychology underlying this generalization is straightforward: When deals are frequently offered, the consumer's *internal reference price* (i.e., the price the consumer expects to pay for a particular brand) is lowered, thus making the deal price less attractive and generating less responsiveness than would be the case if the deal were offered less frequently.

Generalization 3: The frequency of deals changes the consumer's reference price

A corollary to the preceding generalization is that frequent deals tend to reduce consumers' price expectation, or reference price, for the deal-offering brand. This lowering of a brand's reference price has the undesirable consequence of lowering the brand's equity and thus the seller's ability to charge premium prices. Taken together, Generalizations 2 and 3 indicate that excessive dealing has the undesirable effects of both reducing a brand's reference price and diminishing consumer responsiveness to any particular deal.

Generalization 4: Retailers pass through less than 100 percent of trade deals

As previously described, manufacturers' trade deals, which typically are offered to retailers in the form of off-invoice discounts, are not always passed on to consumers. Although a manufacturer offers, say, a 15 percent off-invoice allowance, perhaps only 60 percent of retailers will extend this allowance to consumers as lower retail prices. There is no legal obligation for retailers to pass through trade discounts. Retailers choose to pass along discounts only if their profit calculus leads them to the conclusion that greater profits can be earned from passing discounts to consumers rather than from directly "pocketing" the discounts. It is for this reason that manufacturers increasingly are implementing *pay-for-performance programs* that require retailers to perform specific services (e.g., provide special display space for a deal-offering brand) in order to receive discounts.

Generalization 5: Higher-market-share brands are less deal elastic

Suppose that a brand's price is reduced at retail by 20 percent and that sales volume increases by 30 percent. This would represent an *elasticity coefficient* of 1.5 (i.e., 30 ÷ 20), a value indicating that the increase in the quantity demanded is proportionately one and one-half times greater than the reduction in price. Generalization 5 suggests that for brands holding larger market shares, the deal elasticity coefficient generally is *smaller* than for smaller-share brands. The reason is straightforward: Smaller-share brands have proportionately more customers to gain when they are placed on deal, whereas larger-share brands have fewer remaining customers. As a result, larger-share brands when placed on deal gain "less bang for the promotional buck" compared with smaller-share brands.

Generalization 6: Advertised promotions can result in increased store traffic

Research suggests that store traffic generally benefits from brand-dealing activity. When exposed to a retailer's advertising featuring brands on deal, some consumers will switch stores, if only temporarily, to take advantage of attractive deals from stores other than those in which they most regularly shop.

Retailers refer to this temporary store-switching behavior as consumer "cherry picking," an apt metaphor. Interestingly, research has demonstrated that cherry-picking shopping behavior increases with increases in family size, when the head of household is a senior citizen, when a family does not have a working woman in the household, and with decreases in family income. All of these variables suggest that cherry-picking is greater when the *opportunity cost* of visiting multiple stores is reduced—for example, it is less costly in terms of time expenditure for a retired senior citizen to visit multiple stores to avail him- or herself of price discounts than it is for a younger, employed person.[54] This same research further revealed that cherry pickers save on average approximately 5 percent per item across all purchases. However, with gasoline prices increasing at a rapid rate (as of 2008), net savings from cherry picking will undoubtedly decline as cherry pickers must burn gasoline traveling from store to store to obtain deals.

Generalization 7: Feature advertising and displays operate synergistically to influence sales of discounted brands

When brands are placed on price deal, sales generally increase (see Generalization 1). When brands are placed on price deal and are advertised in the retailers' advertised features, sales increase even more (see Generalization 6). When brands are placed on price deal, are feature advertised, and receive special display attention, sales increase substantially more. In other words, the combined effects of advertising and display positively interact to boost a dealt brand's retail sales.

Generalization 8: Promotions in one product category affect sales of brands in complementary and competitive categories

An interesting thing often happens when a brand in a particular product category is promoted—namely, sales for brands in complementary and competitive categories are affected. For example, when Tostitos tortilla chips are promoted, sales of complementary salsa brands likely increase. Conversely, sales of brands in the competitive potato chip category could be expected to decrease as consumers' tortilla-chip purchases temporarily reduce their purchases of potato chips.

Generalization 9: The effects of promoting higher- and lower-quality brands are asymmetric

When a higher-quality brand is promoted, say, via a substantial price reduction, there is a tendency for that brand to attract switchers and thus steal sales from lower-quality brands.[55] However, a lower-quality brand on promotion is proportionately less likely to attract switchers from higher-quality brands. That is, switching behavior is *asymmetric*—the proportion of switchers drifting from low- to high-quality brands, when the latter is on deal, is higher than the proportion moving in the other direction when a low-quality brand is on deal.[56]

Summary

Sales promotion was introduced in this first of three chapters devoted to the topic. The precise nature of sales promotion was described. Promotion was explained as having three targets: the trade (wholesalers and retailers), consumers, and a company's own sales force. The chapter proceeded to discuss the reasons for a significant trend toward increased investment in promotions vis-à-vis advertising. This shift is part of the movement from pull- to push-oriented marketing, particularly in the case of CPGs. Underlying factors include a balance-of-power transfer from manufacturers to retailers, increased brand parity and growing price sensitivity, reduced brand loyalty, splintering of the mass market and reduced media effectiveness, a growing short-term orientation, and favorable consumer responsiveness to sales promotions.

The chapter also detailed the specific tasks that promotions can and cannot accomplish. For example, promotions cannot give the trade or consumers compelling long-term reasons to purchase. However, promotions are ideally suited for generating trial-purchase behavior, facilitating the introduction of new products, gaining shelf space for a brand, encouraging repeat purchasing, and performing a variety of other tasks.

Following this general introduction, the chapter presented the topic of trade-oriented sales promotions and described its various forms. Trade-oriented promotions represent on average over 50 percent of CPG companies' promotional budgets. These programs perform a variety of objectives. Trade allowances, or trade deals, are offered to retailers for performing activities that support the manufacturer's brand. Manufacturers find allowance promotions attractive for several reasons: they are easy to implement, can successfully stimulate initial distribution, are well accepted by the trade, and can increase trade purchases during the allowance period. However, two major disadvantages of trade allowances, especially of the off-invoice variety, are that retailers often do not pass them along to consumers and they may induce the trade to stockpile a product in order to take advantage of the temporary price reduction. This merely shifts business from the future to the present. Two prevalent practices in current business are forward buying and diverting. Another form of trade deal, called a slotting allowance, applies to new-product introductions. Manufacturers of grocery products typically are required to pay retailers a slotting fee for the right to have their product carried by the retailer. Exit fees, or deslotting charges, are assessed to manufacturers whose products do not achieve prearranged levels of sales volume.

To reduce forward buying and diverting, some manufacturers have revised their method of pricing products. P&G is most notable in this regard for introducing what it calls value pricing, or what others refer to as everyday low pricing by a manufacturer, or EDLP(M). This method of pricing eliminates the historical practice of periodically offering attractive trade deals and instead charges the same low price at all times. Another major development in the grocery industry that is aimed at curtailing forward buying and diverting is the implementation of pay-for-performance programs, which also are called scanner-verified systems, or scan downs. With this method of trade allowance, retailers are compensated for the amount of a manufacturer's brand that they sell to consumers, rather than according to how much they purchase from the manufacturer (as is the case with off-invoice allowances).

Discussion Questions

1. The term *promotional inducement* has been suggested as an alternative to sales promotion. Explain why this term is more descriptive than the established one.
2. Describe the factors that have accounted for sales promotion's rapid growth. Do you expect a continued increase in the use of promotion throughout the following decade?
3. Why, in your opinion, is the Internet a good medium for offering sales promotions to consumers?
4. Explain in your own words the meaning of push- versus pull-oriented promotional strategies. Using for illustration a well-known supermarket brand of your choice, explain which elements of this brand's marcom mix embody push and which embody pull.
5. Assume you are the vice president of marketing of a large, well-known CPG company (e.g., P&G, Unilever, or Johnson & Johnson). What steps might you take to restore a balance of power favoring your company in its relations with retailers?
6. Are promotions able to reverse a brand's temporary sales decline or a permanent sales decline? Be specific.
7. How can a manufacturer's use of trade- and consumer-oriented promotions generate enthusiasm and stimulate improved performance from the sales force?
8. Generalization 5 in the chapter claimed that higher-market-share brands are less deal elastic. Construct a realistic example to illustrate your understanding of this empirical generalization.
9. Generalization 8 asserted that promotions in one product category affect sales of brands in complementary and competitive categories. Tostitos tortilla chips exemplified this generalization. Provide examples of two additional brands and the complementary and competitive product categories that likely would be affected by promotions for your two illustrative brands.
10. Assume you are the marketing manager of a company that manufactures a line of paper products (tissues, napkins, etc.). Your current market share is 7 percent, and you are considering offering retailers an attractive bill-back allowance for giving your brand special display space. Comment on this promotion's chances for success.
11. In your own words, explain the practices of forward buying and diverting. Also, describe the advantages and disadvantages of bill-and-hold programs.
12. Assume you are a buyer for a large supermarket chain and that you have been asked to speak to a group of marketing students at a nearby university. During the question-and-answer session following your comments, a student makes the following statement: "My father works for a grocery product manufacturer, and he says that slotting allowances are nothing more than a form of larceny!" How would you defend your company's practice to this student?
13. Explain why selling private brands often enables large retail chains to pocket trade deals instead of passing their reduced costs along to consumers in the form of lower product prices.
14. In your own words, explain why EDLP(M) pricing diminishes forward buying and diverting.
15. In your own words, discuss how pay-for-performance programs, or scan downs, would, if widely implemented, virtually eliminate forward buying and diverting.

End Notes

1. Adapted from Maureen Tkacik, "In a Clash of the Sneaker Titans, Nike Gets Leg Up on Foot Locker," *Wall Street Journal Online,* May 13, 2003, http://www.online.wsj.com.
2. Jacques Chevron, "Branding and Promotion: Uneasy Cohabitation," *Brandweek,* September 14, 1998, 24.
3. Pierre Chandon, Brian Wansink, and Gilles Laurent, "A Benefit Congruency Framework of Sales Promotion Effectiveness," *Journal of Marketing* 64 (October 2000), 65–81. Robert M. Schindler, "Consequences of Perceiving Oneself as Responsible for Obtaining a Discount: Evidence for Smart-Shopper Feelings," *Journal of Consumer Psychology* 7, no. 4 (1998), 371–392.
4. A study of rebate programs concluded that automobile manufacturers' frequent use of rebates positively impacts revenue in the short run but has a negative effect on profits in the long run. See Koen Pauwels, Jorge Silva-Risso, Shuba Srinivasan, and Dominique M. Hanssens, "New Products, Sales Promotions, and Firm Value: The Case of the Automobile Industry," *Journal of Marketing* 68 (October 2004), 142–156.
5. These estimates are from Cannondale Associates Inc. as reported in Amy Johannes, "Trade Off," *Promo,* November 2007, 14.
6. Carl F. Mela, Sunil Gupta, and Donald R. Lehmann, "The Long-Term Impact of Promotion and Advertising on Consumer Brand Choice," *Journal of Marketing Research* 34 (May 1997), 248–261.
7. Purushottam Papatla and Lakshman Krishnamurthi, "Measuring the Dynamic Effects of Promotions on Brand Choice," *Journal of Marketing Research* 33 (February 1996), 20–35.
8. A. S. C. Ehrenberg, Kathy Hammond, and G. J. Goodhardt, "The After-Effects of Price-Related Consumer Promotions," *Journal of Advertising Research* 34 (July/August 1994), 11–21.
9. Robert C. Blattberg and Scott A. Neslin, "Sales Promotion: The Long and the Short of It," *Marketing Letters* 1, no. 1 (1989), 81–97.
10. Chandon, Wansink, and Laurent, "A Benefit Congruency Framework of Sales Promotion Effectiveness," 65–81. The following discussion of benefits is based on a typology these authors provided. See Table 1 on pages 68–69. Another insightful perspective along similar lines is provided in Figure 2 of Kusum L. Ailawadi, Scott A. Neslin, and Karen Gedenk, "Pursuing the Value-Conscious Consumer: Store Brands versus National Brand Promotions," *Journal of Marketing* (January 2001), 71–89.
11. Research indicates that consumers who take advantage of promotional deals feel good about themselves for being "smart shoppers" and that these feelings are particularly strong when consumers have a sense of being personally responsible for availing themselves of a deal. See Schindler, "Consequences of Perceiving Oneself as Responsible for Obtaining a Discount: Evidence of Smart-Shopper Feelings."
12. Jack Neff, "Accounting by New Rules," *Advertising Age,* July 15, 2002, 4.
13. This discussion is guided by Charles Fredericks, Jr., "What Ogilvy & Mather Has Learned about Sales Promotion," *The Tools of Promotion* (New York: Association of National Advertisers, 1975); and Don E. Schultz and William A. Robinson, *Sales Promotion Management* (Lincolnwood,Ill.: NTC Business Books, 1986), chap. 3.
14. "A Real Gasser," *Promo,* January 2002, 27.
15. Amie Smith and Al Urbanski, "Excellence x 16," *Promo,* December 1998, 136.
16. A *facing* is a row of shelf space. Brands typically are allocated facings proportionate to their profit potential to retailers. Manufacturers must pay for extra facings by offering display allowances or providing other inducements that increase the retailer's profit.
17. "Adventures in Light Bulbs," *Promo,* December 2000, 89.
18. Chakravarthi Narasimhan, Scott A. Neslin, and Subrata K. Sen, "Promotional Elasticities and Category Characteristics," *Journal of Marketing* 60 (April 1996), 17–30. See also Sandrine Macé and Scott A. Neslin, "The Determinants of Pre- and Postpromotion Dips in Sales of Frequently Purchased Goods," *Journal of Marketing Research* 41 (August 2004), 339–350.
19. Carl F. Mela, Kamel Jedidi, and Douglas Bowman, "The Long-Term Impact of Promotions on Consumer Stockpiling Behavior," *Journal of Marketing Research* 35 (May 1998), 250–262.
20. Brian Wansink and Rohit Deshpande, "'Out of Sight, Out of Mind': Pantry Stockpiling and Brand-Usage Frequency," *Marketing Letters* 5, no. 1 (1994), 91–100.
21. Kusum L. Ailawadi and Scott A. Neslin, "The Effect of Promotion on Consumption: Buying More and Consuming It Faster," *Journal of Marketing Research* 35 (August 1998), 390–398.
22. Pierre Chandon and Brian Wansink, "When Are Stockpiled Products Consumed Faster? A Convenience-Salience Framework of Postpurchase Consumption Incidence and Quantity," *Journal of Marketing Research* 39 (August 2002), 321–335.
23. For an empirical analysis of this effect, see Kusum L. Ailawadi, Karen Gedenk, Christian Lutzky, and Scott A. Neslin, "Decomposition of the Sales Impact of Promotion-Induced Stockpiling," *Journal of Marketing Research* 44 (August 2007), 450–467.
24. Betsy Spethmann, "Value Ads," *Promo,* March 2001, 74–79.
25. Jack Neff, "Clorox Gives in on Glad, Hikes Trade Promotion," *Advertising Age,* November 27, 2000, 22.
26. Ibid.
27. These objectives are adapted from a consumer promotion seminar conducted by Ennis Associates and sponsored by the Association of National Advertisers (New York, undated). See also Chakravarthi Narasimhan, "Managerial Perspectives on Trade and Consumer Promotions," *Marketing Letters* 1, no. 3 (1989), 239–251.
28. Don E. Schultz and William A. Robinson, *Sales Promotion Management* (Lincolnwood, Ill.: NTC Business Books, 1986), 265–266.

29. "ACNielsen Study Finds CPG Manufacturers and Retailers Increasing Their Use of Category Management Tools" May 3, 2004, http://us.nielsen.com/news/20040503.shtml (accessed July 28, 2008).
30. This study is by Cannondale Associates as reported in Christopher W. Hoyt, "You Cheated, You Lied," *Promo*, July 1997, 64.
31. For a slightly different classification, see Miguel I. Gómez, Vithala R. Rao, and Edward W. McLaughlin, "Empirical Analysis of Budget and Allocation of Trade Promotions in the U.S. Supermarket Industry," *Journal of Marketing Research* 44 (August 2007), 410–424.
32. For a technical treatment regarding the profit implications of a retailer's decision to pass through a manufacturer's allowance, see Rajeev K. Tyagi, "A Characterization of Retailer Response to Manufacturer Trade Deals," *Journal of Marketing Research* 36 (November 1999), 510–516.
33. The term slotting allowances was originally used only with reference to new products, but the term has over time become a catchall expression for all efforts by manufacturers to gain retailer support for its brands. The term is used here in its original sense.
34. These differences are placed in stark contrast in Table 3 of William L. Wilkie, Debra M. Desrochers, and Gregory T. Gundlach, "Marketing Research and Public Policy: The Case of Slotting Fees," *Journal of Public Policy & Marketing* 21 (fall 2002), 275–288.
35. For a more complete treatment of the issue, including the presentation of survey results from both manufacturers and retailers, see Paul N. Bloom, Gregory T. Gundlach, and Joseph P. Cannon, "Slotting Allowances and Fees: Schools of Thought and the Views of Practicing Managers," *Journal of Marketing* 64 (April 2000), 92–108.
36. Paula Fitzgerald Bone, Karen Russo France, and Richard Riley, "A Multifirm Analysis of Slotting Fees," *Journal of Public Policy & Marketing* 25 (fall 2006), 224–237.
37. For a thorough and sophisticated treatment of the economic issues surrounding slotting allowances, see K. Sudhir and Vithala R. Rao, "Do Slotting Allowances Enhance Efficiency or Hinder Competition," *Journal of Marketing Research* 43 (May 2006), 137–155.
38. See Wilkie, Desrochers, and Gundlach, "Marketing Research and Public Policy" for further discussion of the economic and, especially, public policy issues attendant to the practice of slotting allowances.
39. For an insightful discussion, see Gregory T. Gundlach and Paul N. Bloom, "Slotting Allowances and the Retail Sale of Alcohol Beverages," *Journal of Public Policy & Marketing* 17 (fall 1998), 173–184.
40. See David Balto, "Recent Legal and Regulatory Developments in Slotting Allowances and Category Management," *Journal of Public Policy & Marketing* 21 (fall 2002), 289–294.
41. This illustration is adapted from Zachary Schiller, "Not Everyone Loves a Supermarket Special," *Business Week*, February 17, 1992, 64.
42. Robert D. Buzzell, John A. Quelch, and Walter J. Salmon, "The Costly Bargain of Trade Promotion," *Harvard Business Review* 68 (March/April 1990), 145.
43. Jon Berry, "Diverting," *Adweek's Marketing Week*, May 18, 1992, 22.
44. An insightful demonstration of why trade allowances are unprofitable is provided in Magid M. Abraham and Leonard M. Lodish, "Getting the Most out of Advertising and Promotion," *Harvard Business Review* 68 (May/June 1990), 50–60.
45. For discussion of everyday low pricing by retailers, see Stephen J. Hoch, Xavier Dreze, and Mary E. Purk, "EDLP, Hi-Lo, and Margin Arithmetic," *Journal of Marketing* 58 (October 1994), 16–27.
46. Kusum L. Ailawadi, Donald R. Lehmann, and Scott A. Neslin, "Market Response to a Major Policy Change in the Marketing Mix: Learning from Procter & Gamble's Value Pricing Strategy," *Journal of Marketing* 65 (January 2001), 44–61.
47. This conclusion is based on profit estimations made in ibid., 57.
48. Kenneth Craig Manning, "Development of a Theory of Retailer Response to Manufacturers' Everyday Low Cost Programs" (Ph.D. dissertation, University of South Carolina, 1994).
49. Kerry E. Smith, "Scan Down, Pay Fast," *Promo*, January 1994, 58–59; "The Proof Is in the Scanning," *Promo*, February 1995, 15.
50. Betsy Spethmann, "Wake Up and Smell the Co-Marketing," *Promo*, August 1998, 43–47.
51. The following discussion is based on the outstanding synthesis of the literature provided by Robert C. Blattberg, Richard Briesch, and Edward J. Fox, "How Promotions Work," *Marketing Science* 14, no. 3 (1995), G122–G132. The order of generalizations presented here is adapted from Blattberg et al.'s presentation. Please refer to this article for coverage of the specific studies on which the generalizations are based.
52. Harald J. van Heerde, Peter S. H. Leeflang, and Dick R. Wittink, "The Estimation of Pre- and Postpromotion Dips with Store-Level Scanner Data," *Journal of Marketing Research* 37 (August 2000), 383–395.
53. Koen Pauwels, Dominique M. Hanssens, and S. Siddarth, "The Long-Term Effects of Price Promotions on Category Incidence, Brand Choice, and Purchase Quantity," *Journal of Marketing Research* 39 (November 2002), 421–439.
54. Edward J. Fox and Stephen J. Hoch, "Cherry-Picking," *Journal of Marketing* 69 (January 2005), 46–62.
55. What appears to be an asymmetric effect due to brand quality may actually be due to market share. In other words, smaller-market-share brands, which in many product categories are of lower quality, can attract more brand switchers compared to larger-market-share brands simply because small-share brands have proportionately greater numbers of consumers to attract from large-share brands than the latter have to recruit from small-share brands (see Generalization 5). For evidence relating to this issue, see Raj Sethuraman and V. Srinivasan, "The Asymmetric Share Effect: An Empirical Generalization on Cross-Price Effects," *Journal of Marketing Research* 39 (August 2002), 379–386.
56. For a review of interesting experimental research on this issue, see Stephen M. Nowlis and Itamar Simonson, "Sales Promotions and the Choice Context as Competing Influences on Decision Making," *Journal of Consumer Psychology* 9, no. 1 (2000), 1–16.

16

Sampling and Couponing

Try to recall your first few days on campus as a freshman. Life was great: You had money in your pocket. You felt absolutely no school-related pressure in that first week before the beginning of classes. It was exciting seeing all the new people, few of whom were from your high school, many from other states and different countries. However, one thing that may have surprised you this first week was that your campus probably looked like a shopping mall with people trying to get you to sign up for any of several credit cards, different cell phone programs, and perhaps other items. Also, you may have been surprised to receive a sampler pack of free items at the bookstore, and probably also coupons for discounts at local merchants. Your new campus was not much different than what you had always experienced: It was yet another venue for promoting products and hawking wares.

Marketers do indeed covet the opportunity to reach and influence college students. College campuses are an ideal venue for sampling and couponing products, largely because students' buying preferences are probably more open to influence than later in life. This is why companies such as Alloy Media + Marketing offer samples on campus through bookstores during the back-to-school period, when students are receptive to new ideas (and new products!), and also during the start of spring, when the change from cold to warm weather influences consumer behavior related to fashion items, leisure activities, and personal-care products.[1]

Marketers in a recent year spent almost $40 million on mobile tours to campuses where they gave away free samples and coupons. Commercial research indicates that nearly two thirds of students who receive a sample product subsequently purchase that item. It is little wonder that more than two million Campus Trial Paks are annually distributed in bookstores at over 1,100 campuses around the United States. For example, in one recent year SpongeBob SquarePants boxes included free samples of brands such as Clearasil, Vicks NyQuil, and Clairol Herbal Essences shampoo. Products also are sampled on days of hosted events such

as FHM Comedy Fest and the mtvU Campus Invasion Tour. Sampling of products builds excitement for the events as well as for the brands that are given to students.[2]

Chapter Objectives

After reading this chapter you should be able to:

1 Appreciate the objectives of consumer-oriented sales promotions.

2 Recognize that many forms of promotions perform different objectives for marketers.

3 Know the role of sampling, the forms of sampling, and the trends in sampling practice.

4 Be aware of the role of couponing, the types of coupons, and the developments in couponing practice.

5 Understand the coupon redemption process and misredemption.

6 Appreciate the role of promotion agencies.

>>Marcom Insight:

The Use of On-Campus Promotions to Influence Students' Purchase Behavior

Introduction

Building on the base developed in Chapter 15, which introduced the general topic of sales promotions and then focused on trade-oriented promotions, this chapter exclusively covers consumer-oriented promotions. The practices of sampling and couponing receive primary attention in this chapter; the subsequent chapter then explores additional forms of consumer-oriented promotions.

Before proceeding, it is appropriate to reiterate some advice that was provided in Chapter 1 and repeated elsewhere in the text. That guidance involved the relations among target markets, brand positioning, objectives, and budgets and was summarized in the form of the following mantra:

> *All marketing communications should be (1) directed to a particular* **target market,** *(2) clearly* **positioned,** *(3) created to achieve a* **specific objective,** *and (4) undertaken to accomplish the objective* **within budget constraint.**

This counsel, when considered in the context of consumer promotions, simply advises that target marketing and brand positioning are the starting points for all decisions. With precise target and clear positioning, brand managers are prepared to specify the objective a particular promotion program is designed to accomplish. Managers also must work diligently to ensure that promotion spending does not exceed their brands' budget limitations. This is the challenge that brand managers face when using consumer-oriented promotions to achieve strategic objectives.

Why Use Consumer Promotions?

In almost every product category, whether durable products or consumer packaged goods (CPGs), there are several brands available to wholesalers and retailers (the trade) to choose among and for consumers ultimately to select or reject for personal or family consumption. As a brand manager, your objective is to get your brand adequately placed in as many retail outlets as possible and to ensure that the brand moves off the shelves with frequency sufficient to keep retailers satisfied with its performance and to achieve your own profit objectives. This requires that you get consumers to try your brand and, hopefully, to become regular purchasers.

Your competitors have identical goals. They are attempting to garner the support of the same wholesalers and retailers that you desire and activate trial purchases and achieve purchase regularity from the consumers you also covet. Their gain is your loss. It is a vicious zero-sum game in the battle for trade customers and final consumers. You are unwilling to make it easy for your competitors, and they are not inclined to make your life a proverbial bed of roses.

Although the stakes pale in comparison, brand managers—like their military counterparts—are constantly attacking, counterattacking, and defending their turf against competitive inroads. Advertising plays a major role in this battle, flying above the day-to-day action, in a manner of speaking, and dropping "persuasive bombs." Sales promotion, in contrast, is analogous to an army's ground troops, who are engaged in the "dirty work" of fighting off the competition and engaging in hand-to-hand battle. Advertising alone is insufficient; promotion by itself is inadequate. Together they can make a formidable opponent.

Now, in answer to the question opening this section (Why use consumer promotions?), the short response is that promotions are used because they accomplish goals that advertising by itself cannot. Consumers often need to be induced to buy now rather than later, to buy your brand rather than a competitor's, to buy more rather than less, and to buy more frequently. Sales promotions are uniquely suited to achieving these imperatives. Whereas advertising can make consumers aware of your brand and shape a positive image, promotions serve to consummate the transaction.

Before proceeding, a final preliminary point is in order. This actually is a personal request regarding your study of this and the following chapter. In particular, as a consumer living in a market-oriented society who is exposed daily to the commonplace practice of marketers inundating us with many forms of promotions (coupons, samples, sweepstakes, games, rebates, etc.), you may think you already understand everything you need to know about these ordinary topics. Without a doubt, you do know a lot about promotions—at least at an experiential level. Yet, just as you are aware of Einstein's theory of relativity ($E = mc^2$), you probably do not actually understand the theory in a sophisticated fashion. Although promotions are trivial in comparison to Einstein's theory, the point is that you probably also do not understand sales promotions beyond a relatively superficial level. It is my wish that you study the material in these two chapters with the goal of *really understanding* why the various types of promotions are used and which unique objectives each is designed to accomplish. Sophisticated brand managers do not simply reach into a "bag" and pick out any promotional tool as if the multiple forms of promotions are completely interchangeable. Rather, each is chosen to accomplish strategic objectives to a degree better than alternative options, given the budget constraint.

Brand Management Objectives and Consumer Rewards

What objectives do brand managers hope to accomplish by using consumer-oriented promotions, and why are consumers receptive to samples, coupons, contests, sweepstakes, cents-off offers, and other promotional efforts? Answers to these interrelated questions will provide us with a useful framework for understanding why particular forms of promotions are useful in view of the goal(s) that must be accomplished for a brand at a given point in time.

Brand Management Objectives

The overarching objective of consumer-oriented promotions is to promote increased sales (*sales promotion = promoting sales*). Subsidiary to this overarching goal and in concert with trade-oriented promotions (the subject of the previous chapter), consumer promotions are capable of achieving various sales-influencing objectives for "our" brand:[3]

- Gaining trade support for inventorying increased quantities of our brand during a limited period and providing superior display space for our brand during this period
- Reducing brand inventory for a limited period when inventories have grown to an excessive level due to slow sales, economic conditions, or effective competitive actions caused
- Providing the sales force with increased motivation during a promotional period to gain greater distribution for our brand, better display space, or other preferential treatment vis-à-vis competitive brands
- Protecting our customer base against competitors' efforts to steal them away
- Introducing new brands to the trade and to consumers
- Entering new markets with established brands
- Promoting trial purchases among consumers who have never tried our brand or achieving retrial from those who have not purchased our brand recently
- Rewarding present customers for continuing to purchase our brand
- Encouraging repeat purchasing of our brand and reinforcing brand loyalty

- Enhancing our brand's image
- Increasing advertising readership
- Facilitating the process of continually expanding the list of names and addresses in our database

As can be seen, consumer promotions are used to accomplish a variety of objectives, with the ultimate goal of driving increased sales of our brand. Consumer promotions, when done effectively, can serve to gain the trade's support, inspire the sales force to improve performance, and, most important for present purposes, motivate consumers to commit a trial purchase of our brand and, ideally, to purchase it with greater frequency and perhaps even in larger quantities.

To simplify matters, the discussions of specific forms of consumer-oriented promotions in this and the following chapter focus primarily on objectives directed at *influencing consumer behavior* rather than initiating trade or sales-force action. We will focus on three general categories of objectives: (1) generating purchase trial and retrial, (2) encouraging repeat purchases, and (3) reinforcing brand images.

Some sales promotions (such as samples and coupons) are used primarily with the objective of influencing consumers to *try or retry a brand.* A brand manager employs these promotional tools to prompt nonusers to try a brand for the first time or to encourage retrial from prior users who have not purchased the brand for perhaps extended periods. At other times, managers use promotions to hold onto their current customer base by rewarding them for continuing to purchase the promoted brand or loading them with a stockpile of the manufacturer's brand so they have no need, at least in the short run, to switch to another brand. This is sales promotions' *repeat-purchase objective.* Sales promotions also can be used for *image reinforcement purposes.* For example, the careful selection of the right premium object or appropriate sweepstakes prize can serve to bolster a brand's image.

Consumer Rewards

Consumers would not be responsive to sales promotions unless there was something in it for them—and, in fact, there is. All promotion techniques provide consumers with rewards (benefits, incentives, or inducements) that *encourage certain forms of behavior* brand managers desire. These rewards, or benefits, are both utilitarian and hedonic.[4]

Consumers who respond to sales promotions receive various *utilitarian,* or functional, benefits: (1) obtaining monetary savings (e.g., when using coupons); (2) reducing search and decision costs (e.g., by simply availing themselves of a promotional offer and not having to think about other alternatives); and (3) obtaining improved product quality made possible by a price reduction that allows consumers to buy superior brands they might not otherwise purchase. Consumers also obtain *hedonic* benefits when taking advantage of sales promotion offers: (1) accomplishing a sense of being a wise shopper when taking advantage of sales promotions; (2) achieving a need for stimulation and variety when, say, trying a brand one otherwise might not purchase if it were not for an attractive promotion; and (3) obtaining entertainment value when, for example, the consumer competes in a promotional contest or participates in a sweepstakes. Consumer promotions also perform an informational function by influencing consumer beliefs about a brand—for example, by suggesting the brand is of higher quality than previously thought because it is co-promoted with another brand that is itself widely regarded as being high quality.[5]

The rewards consumers receive from sales promotions sometimes are immediate, while at other times they are delayed. An *immediate reward* is one that delivers monetary savings or some other form of benefit as soon as the consumer performs a marketer-specified behavior. For example, you potentially obtain immediate pleasure when you try a free food item or beverage that has been sampled in a supermarket or a club store such as Costco or Sam's Club. *Delayed rewards* are those that follow the behavior by a period of days, weeks, or even longer. For example, you may have to wait six or eight weeks before a mail-in premium item can be enjoyed.

Generally speaking, consumers are more responsive to immediate rewards than they are to delayed rewards. Of course, this is in line with the natural human preference for immediate gratification.

Classification of Promotion Methods

Table 16.1 presents a six-cell typology that was constructed by cross-classifying the two forms of consumer rewards (immediate versus delayed) with the three objectives for using promotions (generating trial purchases, encouraging repeat purchases, and reinforcing brand image).

Cell 1 in Table 16.1 includes three promotion techniques—samples, instant coupons, and shelf-delivered coupons—that encourage *trial or retrial purchase behavior* by providing consumers with an *immediate reward.* The reward is either monetary savings, in the case of instant coupons, or a free product, in the case of samples.

Optical scanner-delivered coupons, media- and mail-delivered coupons, and free-with-purchase premiums—all found in **cell 2**—are some of the techniques that generate consumer *trial/retrial* yet *delay the reward.* Coupons along with samples are the topics of the present chapter, while premiums and other forms of consumer-oriented promotions are covered in the following chapter.

Cells 3 and 4 contain promotional tools that are intended to encourage *repeat purchases* from consumers. Marketing communicators design these techniques to reward a brand's existing customers and to keep them from switching to competitive brands—in other words, to encourage repeat purchasing. *Immediate reward tools,* in **cell 3,** include price-offs; bonus packs; in-, on-, and near-pack premiums;

table 16.1

Major Consumer-Oriented Promotions

	Brand Management Objective		
Consumer Reward	**Generating Trial and Retrial**	**Encouraging Repeat Purchases**	**Reinforcing Brand Image**
Immediate	**Cell 1** • Samples 16* • Instant coupons 16 • Shelf-delivered coupons 16	**Cell 3** • Price-offs 17 • Bonus packs 17 • In-, on-, and near-pack premiums 17 • Games 17	**Cell 5** (No Promotions Match Cell 5's Conditions)
Delayed	**Cell 2** • Scanner-delivered coupons 16 • Media- and mail-delivered coupons 16 • Online coupons 16 • Mail-in premiums 17 • Free-with-purchase premiums 17	**Cell 4** • In- and on-pack coupons 16 • Rebates and refunds 17 • Phone cards 17 • Continuity programs 17	**Cell 6** • Self-liquidating premiums 17 • Sweepstakes and contests 17

*Indicates the chapter, either Chapter 16 or 17, in which this form of sales promotion is covered.

and games. *Delayed reward techniques,* listed in **cell 4,** include in- and on-pack coupons, refund and rebate offers, phone cards, and continuity programs.

Building a *brand's image* is primarily the task of advertising; however, sales promotion tools may support advertising efforts by reinforcing a brand's image. By nature, these techniques are *incapable of providing consumers with an immediate reward;* therefore, **cell 5** is vacant. **Cell 6** contains self-liquidating premiums and two promotional tools, contests and sweepstakes, that, if designed appropriately, can reinforce or even strengthen a brand's image in addition to performing other tasks.

It is important to reemphasize that the classification of promotional tools in Table 16.1 is necessarily simplified. First, the table classifies each technique with respect to the *primary objective* it is designed to accomplish. Note, however, that promotions are capable of accomplishing more than a single objective. For example, bonus packs (cell 3) are classified as encouraging repeat purchasing, but first-time triers also occasionally purchase brands that offer extra volume and represent a good value. The various forms of coupons located in cells 1 and 2 are designed primarily to encourage triers or retriers and to attract switchers from other brands. In actuality, however, current purchasers redeem most coupons, not new buyers. In other words, although intended to encourage trial purchasing and switching, coupons also invite repeat purchasing by rewarding present customers for continuing to purchase "our" brand.

Note also that two of the promotional tools in Table 16.1, *coupons* and *premiums,* are found in more than one cell. This is because these techniques achieve different objectives depending on the specific form of delivery vehicle. Coupons delivered through the media (newspapers, magazines, and online) or in the mail offer a form of delayed reward, whereas instant coupons that are peeled from a package at the point of purchase offer an immediate reward. Similarly, premium objects that are delivered in, on, or near a product's package provide an immediate reward, while those requiring mail delivery yield a reward only after some delay.

Sampling

Most practitioners agree that sampling is the premier sales promotion device for generating trial usage. Sample distribution is almost a necessity when introducing truly new products that can afford this form of promotion. Sampling is effective because it gives consumers an opportunity to experience a new brand personally. It allows an active, hands-on interaction rather than a passive encounter, as is the case with the receipt of promotional techniques such as coupons. A recent survey indicated that over 90 percent of consumers said they would buy a new brand if they liked a sample of the brand and considered its purchase price acceptable.[6]

By definition, **sampling** includes any method used to deliver an actual- or trial-sized product to consumers. The vast majority of manufacturers use sampling as part of their marcom programs to generate trials and leverage trade support. Companies use a variety of methods and media to deliver samples:

- *Direct mail:* Samples are mailed to households targeted by demographic characteristics or in terms of geodemographics (as discussed in Chapter 4).
- *Newspapers and magazines:* Samples often are included in magazines and newspapers, which represent cost-efficient forms of sampling for reaching a mass audience. For example, Viva is a brand that competes with Bounty, Brawny, and other brands in the paper towel category, where annual sales exceed $2 billion. Viva is premium priced due to its higher quality. To convince consumers that the higher price is justified, consumers needed to actually touch Viva towels. To get samples of Viva into the hands of consumers, sheets were stitched into issues of two magazines, *Reader's Digest* and *Every Day with*

i.m.c. focus

Sampling Food and Beverage Products with Taste Strips

Sampling food products or beverages in stores that handle these items is an effective way of encouraging consumers to try new products. This form of sampling is quite costly, however, because personnel must be employed to distribute food samples and items often have to be prepared before being served. Aside from the personnel and logistics expenses (and problems), the image of a brand may be tarnished if the person who hands out the sampled item has an attitude, is unkempt, slothful, or otherwise ill-suited for the job. Is there a better way to get food and beverage items into the hands and mouths of prospective purchasers without distributing actual samples. One company thinks there is.

A Pennsylvania company named First Flavor applies edible-film technology—i.e., thin plastic strips that dissolve in one's mouth (akin to Listerine breath strips)—as a means to enable consumers to sample the taste of new or mature products. These strips are embedded with flavors that mirror the taste of actual food and beverage products. Welch's (of grape juice fame) was one of the first companies that applied First Flavor's technology. In full-page ads placed in *People* magazine, readers saw an advertisement showing a bottle of Welch's grape juice on which was placed a peel-off strip with text reading "For a TASTY fact, remove & LICK." Personnel at Welch's conducted in-depth research to assure that the lickable strips tasted good and that they met the Food and Drug Administration's safety guidelines.

The ad in *People* magazine cost a couple hundred thousand dollars more to create compared to a typical full-page ad as a result of the added expenses of making the lickable strips and paying a bonus to *People* to compensate for its added production costs. Where in-store sampling of actual food and beverage items costs between \$600–\$800 per thousand people, the cost of First Flavor's strips is only about \$70–\$100 per thousand. Of course, only time will tell whether this cheaper form of sampling is anywhere near as effective in generating trial purchases as the "real thing," inviting people to eat actual food items during a shopping excursion.

Sources: Adapted from Mya Frazier, "A Marketing Tool That Melts in Your Mouth," *Advertising Age*, May 21, 2007, 18; Flora Lichtman, "Taste before You Buy," June 21, 2007, http://www.sciencefriday.com/news/062107/flavor0621071.html (accessed April 30, 2008); Suzanne Vranica, "Marketers Salivate over Lickable Ads," *The Wall Street Journal*, February 13, 2008, B3.

Rachel Ray.[7] (For another illustration of innovative magazine sampling, see the *IMC Focus* insert.)

- *Door-to-door sampling by distribution crews:* This form of sampling allows considerable targeting and possesses advantages such as lower cost and short lead times between when a brand manager requests sampling and when the sampling company ultimately delivers the samples. Companies that specialize in door-to-door sampling target household selection to fit the client's needs. Samples can be distributed just in blue-collar neighborhoods, in Hispanic areas, or in any other locale where residents match the sampled brand's target market.
- *On- or in-pack sampling:* This method uses the *package of another product* to serve as the sample carrier. A key requirement of this form of sampling is that the sampled brand and the carrier brand must be complementary with respect to their benefits, target audience characteristics, and image.
- *High-traffic locations and events:* Shopping centers, movie theaters, airports, and special events offer valuable forums for sample distribution. More will be said about this form of sampling in a later discussion of creative forms of sampling.
- *Sampling at unique venues:* Brand managers and their promotion agencies sometimes choose unique locations for sampling products that are especially appropriate for people at a certain stage of life, referred to as life's change points. Sampling to college students at the beginning of a new school year (see *Marcom Insight*) is one illustration of *change-point sampling.* Marriage offices are

another change-point for reaching newlyweds. Newlywed kits containing various products are sometimes presented to couples when they apply for marriage licenses. The rationale for this sampling location is that newlyweds in the United States spend in excess of $70 billion for their households in the first year after marriage.[8]

- *In-store sampling:* Demonstrators provide product samples in grocery stores and other retail outlets for trial while consumers are shopping. It is understandable that in-store sampling is the most frequent form of sampling as it offers samples to consumers where and when their purchase decisions can be influenced most immediately.[9] A toy store such as Toys "R" Us, for example, would be an appropriate outlet for reaching moms and kids; Blockbuster is an excellent venue for delivering samples to teens and young adults. And fast-food restaurants—such as KFC, McDonald's, Sonic, and Wendy's—have turned to sampling as a means for introducing new menu items.[10]
- *Internet sampling:* Brand managers are increasingly distributing samples online. They typically employ the services of companies that specialize in online sample delivery such as **startsampling.com** and **thefreesite.com**. These and other specialized companies serve as online sampling portals for the CPG companies they represent. Interested consumers enter these sampling sites and register to receive free samples for brands that interest them. Samples are then mailed in a timely fashion. Because mailing represents a major cost element, it is estimated that online sampling costs are perhaps three times greater than sampling in stores or at special events.[11] The justification for this added expense is that people who go online to request particular samples generally are really interested in those brands—and eventually may purchase them—in comparison, say, to people who receive a sample at an event. Hence, online sampling may be less wasteful than alternative forms of sampling. Although representing a useful way to distribute samples, it is doubtful that online sampling will displace alternative sampling methods.

Major Sampling Practices

Historically, many sampling efforts were unsophisticated and wasteful. In particular, there was a tendency to use mass-distribution outlets in getting sampled products in the hands of as many people as possible. Sophisticated sampling now insists on three prudent practices: (1) targeting rather than mass distributing samples, (2) using innovative distribution methods where appropriate, and (3) undertaking efforts to measure sampling's return on investment.

Targeting Sample Recipients

Sampling services that specialize in precision distribution (targeting) have emerged in recent years. For example, one sampling specialist aims for children under the age of 8 by distributing samples at zoos, museums, and other locations that appeal to young children and their parents. It also reaches children and teens (ages 9 to 17) at venues such as little league baseball fields, movie theaters, and skating centers. Suppose you wanted to reach pre-teens and pre-school-age children with free samples. This could be accomplished by distributing sample packs at stores such as Toys "R" Us, the advantage of which has been described in these terms:

> ***When you're giving your product to customers in Toys "R" Us, you can bet with 99 percent accuracy you're reaching families with children under 12 or grandparents with grandchildren that age. You don't have that kind of certainty of reach with other [forms of marketing communications].***[12]

Male high school students represent one of the most inaccessible markets because they are not particularly heavy television viewers or magazine readers.

© Spencer Grant/PhotoEdit

A company that specializes in targeted sample distribution developed a program that connected with teenage males by distributing gift packages of product samples (such as shaving cream, razors, mouthwash, and candy) at tuxedo rental shops. Recipients picked up their sample pack when they arranged to rent a prom tuxedo.

Samples are distributed to young adults (ages 18 to 24) at colleges and universities, malls, beaches, and concerts. Airports, shopping centers, and high-density retail districts are good sites for homing in on adults ages 25 to 54. Newlyweds, as mentioned previously, receive free samples when applying for marriage licenses.

How might you reach urban residents? A company that specializes in delivering samples to African-Americans and Latinos has established a network of several thousand African-American and Latino churches in which samples are distributed. Ministers in these churches often present sample bags to members of the congregation. This company also distributes samples to urban residents through a large network of beauty salons and barber shops.[13]

A final illustration of targeted sampling involves the distribution of Benadryl anti-itch cream conducted a few years ago by Warner-Lambert, then makers of Benadryl (since merged under the Pfizer name). Warner-Lambert wanted to develop a sampling program that would contact victims of itching caused by mosquito bites, heat rash, poison ivy, and so on. The objective was to approach prospective consumers at "point-of-itch" locations where they would be most receptive to learning about the virtues of Benadryl. The company considered sampling at retail lawn-and-garden departments but eliminated that prospect as not quite satisfying its point-of-itch objective. It eventually came up with the clever idea of sampling at KOA Kampground locations where people camp, enjoy the outdoors, and . . . itch. Twenty-five million people visit KOA Kampgrounds every year. During a two-summer period Warner-Lambert distributed six million Benadryl samples to 550 campgrounds, thereby achieving effective and cost-efficient sample distribution.[14]

All of these illustrations indicate that almost any group of consumers can be selectively sampled. The only limitation to targeted sampling is the absence of creativity!

Using Creative Distribution Methods

Companies are applying numerous creative ways to get sample merchandise into the hands of targeted consumers. To sample Cetaphil skin-care products, "pop-up shops" (temporary store-like facilities) were set up in three major cities: Atlanta, Chicago, and New York. Visitors to the "stores" received free hand massages with Cetaphil and also were invited to spin a wheel of fortune to take their chance at winning Cetaphil products such as skin cleanser and moisturizing lotion and cream. Over 250,000 samples of Cetaphil products were sampled during this promotional event, and to encourage subsequent purchasing visitors received a coupon worth $1 off any Cetaphil product.[15]

Progresso Soup, marketed by The Pillsbury Company (now owned by General Mills), employed a fleet of "Soupermen" to deliver cups of hot soup from backpack dispensers to consumers in cold-weather cities such as Cleveland, Chicago, Detroit, and Pittsburgh. From October through March, sampling teams visited consumers in these cities at sporting events, races, outdoor shows, and other locales—all of which represented ideal locations for getting consumers to try cups of hot Progresso soup.

Guinness Import Company sampled its unique beer using tractor trailers equipped with dozens of taps. These trailers traveled to Irish music festivals in cities such as New York, Chicago, and San Francisco. Guinness invested in the trailers because it regards hands-on sampling at special events as a good opportunity to create a unique brand usage experience and to avoid the clutter of mass-media advertising.

The famous Ben & Jerry's Homemade ice cream offers another illustration of creative sampling. After Ben & Jerry's was purchased by Unilever, the brand managers decided to sample the product to increase its market penetration and to convert new users from competitive brands. But how do you sample ice cream? It could be done in supermarkets, but that venue somehow does not quite fit with Ben & Jerry's image. Obviously, sampling through the mail also is out of the question. Given these product-sampling limitations, Ben & Jerry's marketing team decided to sample Ben & Jerry's ice cream at a special event titled "Urban Pasture," which was designed specifically for that purpose, and invited fans to "stop and taste the ice cream."

Requiring the event to match Ben & Jerry's upscale, pastoral image, the promotion planners created an "Urban Pasture" motif complete with cow mannequins, banners, lounge chairs, live bands, and, of course, free ice cream. The event toured 13 major U.S. cities, including Boston, Chicago, Los Angeles, and New York. The "Urban Pasture" set up in each city included a main stage, from which music was played, and sports and entertainment celebrities hosted ice-cream-scooping matches, with the winner at each tour stop receiving the opportunity to select a charity to receive an attractive donation—clearly in line with the brand's philanthropic image. Each "pasture" was up for a single day, but sampling crews remained in each city for at least an additional week during which time they sampled Ben & Jerry's ice cream from cow-bedecked buses.[16]

The promotion agency for Nivea for Men skin-care products devised a clever method to sample their product. Street teams distributed samples of Nivea products at almost 800 rail and subway stations across the United States. The brand enjoyed a 100 percent increase in sales in large part due to this creative sampling program.[17]

The marketers of EBoost, an immunity and energy booster, required a unique way to sample this brand so as to distinguish it from competitive offerings. The sampling solution was to distribute samples of EBoost to hotel guests—by placing samples on bedside tables and pillows or in bathrooms, or by handing out samples at check-in. Hotel sampling not only benefited EBoost but also the participating hotels that added value for their customers when giving away samples of a desirable product.[18] Managers of many brands other than EBoost have also enjoyed success in distributing samples in hotels.

Finally, if you were brand manager of a line of toilet tissue and thought sampling would benefit the brand, how would you provide consumers with free samples? Obviously, many of the traditional sampling methods would be inappropriate due to the high cost of sending out, say, millions of rolls of tissue. Brand managers of P&G's Charmin brand faced precisely this challenge. They had tried various sampling methods without success, but then someone hit upon the idea of sampling Charmin at outdoor events. The company manufactured a fleet of tractor-trailer mounted bathrooms (see Figure 16.1) and conducted the Charmin Potty Palooza tour at events such as state fairs and Oktoberfests. Each trailer was equipped with running water, wall-papered walls, faux-wood floors, Charmin toilet tissue, and various samples of P&G's other brands—Safeguard soap, Bounty paper towels, and Pampers diapers—along with changing tables. As described by Charmin's brand manager, "[Toilet tissue] is a category that consumers don't think much about. To break through that and understand the benefits of Charmin Ultra, you really need to try it." P&G's research indicated a 14 percent increase in Charmin sales among people who used P&G's Potty Palooza facilities.[19]

Figure 16.1

Sampling Charmin via a Fleet of Tractor Trailers

Estimating Return on Investment

As previously detailed in Chapter 2, marketing communicators are increasingly being held accountable for their decisions. Financial officers, senior marketing executives, and chief executives are demanding evidence that investments in advertising and promotions can be justified by the profits they return. Return on investment (ROI) is a tool that can be used to assess whether an investment in a sampling program is cost justified. Table 16.2 lays out the straightforward steps in applying an ROI analysis to a sampling investment.[20] Please read carefully the systematic procedure described in Table 16.2.

When Should Sampling Be Used?

Promotion managers use sampling to induce consumers to try either a brand that is new or one that is moving into a different market. While it is important to encourage trial usage for new brands, sampling is not appropriate for all new or improved products. Ideal circumstances include the following:[21]

table 16.2

Calculating the ROI for a Sampling Investment

- Step 1: *Determine the total cost of sampling,* which includes the cost of the sample goods plus the costs of distribution—mailing, door-to-door distribution, and so on. Assume, for example, that the cost of distributing a trial-sized unit is $0.60 and that 15,000,000 units are distributed; hence, the total cost is $9 million.
- Step 2: *Calculate the profit per unit* by determining the average number of annual uses of the product and multiplying this by the per-unit profit. Assume, for example, that on average six units of the sampled product are purchased per year and that the profit per unit is $1. Thus, each user promises the company a profit potential of $6 when they become users of the sampled brand.
- Step 3: *Calculate the number of converters* needed for the sampling program to break even. (Converters are individuals who after sampling a brand become users.) Given the cost of the sampling program ($9 million) and the profit potential per user ($6), the number of conversions needed in this case to break even is 1,500,000 (i.e., $9 million divided by $6). This number represents a 10 percent conversion rate just to break even (i.e., 1,500,000 divided by 15,000,000).
- Step 4: *Determine the effectiveness of the sampling.* For a sampling to be successful, the conversion rate must exceed the break-even rate with gains in the 10 to 16 percent range. In this case, this would mean a minimum of 1,650,000 people must become users after trying the sampled brand (i.e., 1,500,000 times 1.1) to justify the sampling cost and yield a reasonable profit from the sampling investment.

global focus

Introducing Oreos to China

Kraft Foods' Oreo cookies are one of the most popular dessert items in American grocery stores, with millions of packages sold weekly. Oreos are available in many other countries, but sales in China never achieved anywhere close to the volume enjoyed in the United States. As it turns out, Chinese consumers are not big cookie eaters, and Oreos are quintessentially an American cookie. After being on the Chinese market for a decade, Kraft's market research revealed that American-style Oreos were too sweet for the Chinese palate and that the price was too high. The options were obvious: either discontinue marketing Oreos in China or reformulate the product. Kraft chose the latter option and reformulated Oreos to be less sweet and less expensive. Interestingly, Kraft abandoned the circular sandwich version of Oreos, which did not resonate favorably with Chinese consumers, and replaced it with a chocolate-covered *wafer* filled with vanilla and chocolate cream.

Convincing Chinese consumers to try the new Oreo wafer was perhaps an even more challenging task than coming up with a suitable replacement for the American-style Oreo cookie. Although advertising was useful for making Chinese consumers aware of the new Oreo wafer, advertising alone would be insufficient to persuade Chinese consumers that Oreos taste good. Sampling clearly was required. The approach Kraft took for distributing product samples involved recruiting and training 300 college students to become Oreo brand ambassadors. These student ambassadors rode the streets of Beijing on bicycles and gave Oreo samples to more than 300,000 consumers. Oreo wafers quickly became the best-selling cookie in China, and Kraft doubled its Oreo revenue in that country.

SOURCE: Adapted from Julie Jargon, "Kraft Reformulates Oreo, Scores in China," *The Wall Street Journal*, May 1, 2008, B1.

1. Either when a new or improved brand is either *demonstrably superior* to other brands or when it has *distinct relative advantages* over brands that it is intended to replace. If a brand does not possess superiority or distinct advantages, it probably is not economically justifiable to give it away.
2. When the product concept is so innovative that it is *difficult to communicate by advertising alone.* For example, Procter & Gamble sampled its new line of olestra-made Fat Free Pringles to lunchtime crowds in 20 major cities. The brand management team knew that consumers had to experience for themselves that this fat-free version of Pringles tasted virtually the same as regular Pringles chips. The earlier examples of sampling Ben & Jerry's Homemade ice cream and Charmin toilet tissue further illustrate the need to sample products when advertising is insufficient for conveying the fundamental brand message. In general, sampling enables consumers to learn about product advantages that marketers would have difficulty convincing them of via advertising alone. (See the *Global Focus* insert for an application of this principle in China.)
3. When promotional budgets *can afford to generate consumer trial quickly.* If generating quick trial is not essential, then cheaper trial-impacting promotional tools such as coupons should be used.

Sampling Problems

There are several problems with sampling. First, it is expensive. Second, the postal service or other distributors can mishandle mass mailings of samples. Third, samples distributed door to door or in high-traffic locations may suffer from wasted distribution and not reach the hands of the best potential customers. Fourth, in- or on-package sampling excludes consumers who do not buy the carrying brand. Fifth, in-store sampling often fails to reach sufficient numbers of consumers to justify its expense.

A sixth problem with samples is that consumers may misuse them. Consider the case of Sun Light dishwashing liquid, a product of Lever Brothers. This product, which smells like lemons, was extensively sampled a number of years ago to more than 50 million households. Unfortunately, nearly 80 adults and children became ill after consuming the product, having mistaken the dishwashing liquid for lemon juice! According to a Lever Brothers' marketing research director at the time of the sampling, there is always a potential problem of misuse when a product is sent to homes rather than purchased with prior product knowledge at a supermarket.[22]

A final sampling problem, pilferage, can result when samples are distributed through the mail. This occurred in Poland shortly after the Iron Curtain separating Eastern from Western Europe was literally and symbolically demolished with the fall of Communist dominion in the East. P&G mailed 580,000 samples of Vidal Sassoon Wash & Go shampoo to consumers in Poland, the first ever mass mailing of free samples in that country. The mailing was a big hit—so big, in fact, that about 2,000 mailboxes were broken into. The shampoo samples, although labeled "Not for sale," turned up on open markets and were in high demand at a price of 60 cents each. P&G paid nearly $40,000 to the Polish Post, Poland's mail service, to deliver the samples. In addition to the cost of distribution, P&G paid thousands more to have mailboxes repaired.[23]

Due to its expense and because of waste and other problems, the use of sampling fell out of favor for a period of time as many marketers turned to less expensive promotions, especially couponing. However, with the development of creative solutions and innovations, brand managers and their promotion agencies have again become enthusiastic about sampling. Sampling has become more efficient in reaching specific target groups, its results are readily measurable, and the rising costs of media advertising have increased its relative attractiveness.

Couponing

A **coupon** is a promotional device that rewards consumers for purchasing the coupon-offering brand by providing cents-off savings, which typically range from a low of 30¢ to $1 or more, depending on the price of the couponed item. For example, Maxwell House coffee offered coupons for 45¢ and 90¢ for its filter packs and filter pack singles products (Figure 16.2).

Coupons are delivered through newspapers; magazines; freestanding inserts; direct mail; in or on packages; online; and at the point of purchase by package, shelf, and electronic delivery devices. Not all delivery methods have the same objective. *Instant coupons* (that is, those that can be peeled from packages at the point of purchase) provide immediate rewards to consumers and encourage trial purchases as well as repeat buying from loyal consumers (see Table 16.1). *Mail- and media-delivered coupons* delay the reward, although they also generate trial purchase behavior. Before discussing these specific coupon delivery modes in detail, it first will be instructive to examine pertinent developments in coupon use.

Couponing Background

Approximately 280 billion coupons are distributed annually in the United States,[24] and coupon promotions cost U.S. marketers about $7 billion annually.[25] Nearly all

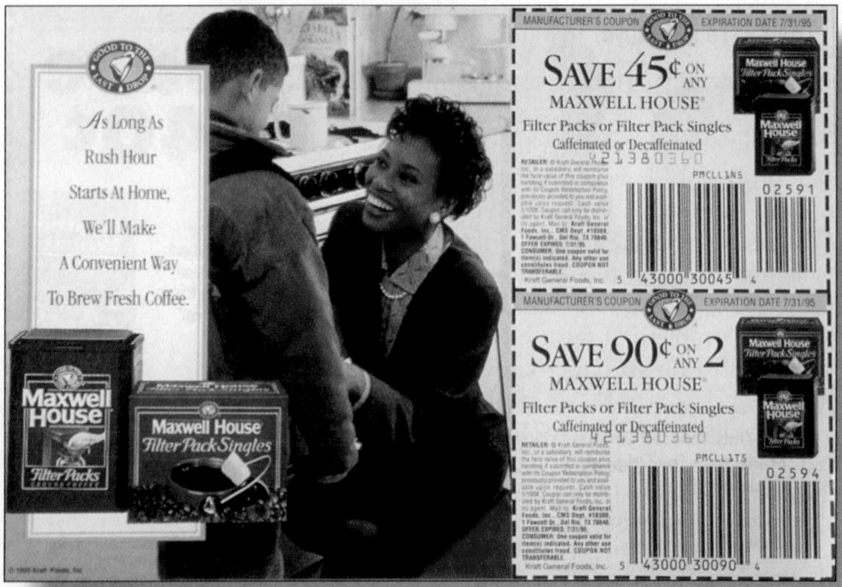

Figure 16.2

Illustration of Cents-Off Coupon Offers

© Michael Newman/Photo Edit

CPG marketers issue coupons. The use of coupons is not, however, restricted to packaged goods. For example, General Motors Corporation mailed coupons valued as high as $1,000 to its past customers in hopes of encouraging them to purchase new cars. Surveys indicate that virtually all American consumers use coupons at least on occasion, with redemption levels increasing during periods of economic downturns and declining when the economy is bustling.[26] Research has established that consumers vary greatly in terms of their *psychological inclination* to use coupons and that this coupon proneness is predictive of actual coupon redemption behavior. That is, some consumers are more inclined to use coupons because they are thriftier and receive greater psychological pleasure from saving money.[27]

Although vastly more coupons are distributed in the United States than elsewhere, *redemption rates* (the percentage of all distributed coupons that are taken to stores for price discounts) are higher in most other countries. However, couponing in some countries is virtually nonexistent or in the fledgling stage. For example, in Germany the government limits the face value of coupons to 1 percent of a product's value, which effectively eliminates couponing in Germany for low-priced CPGs. Only a small amount of couponing occurs in France because the few chains that control the retail grocery market in that country generally oppose the use of coupons. Couponing activity in Japan is in the early stages following the lifting of government restrictions.

Coupon Distribution Methods

The method of coupon distribution brand managers prefer is the *freestanding insert* (FSI). FSIs, which are inserts in Sunday newspapers, account for approximately 88 percent of all coupons distributed in the United States.[28] The other media for coupon distribution are handouts at stores and other locations (5%), direct mail (2%), magazines (1.8%), newspapers (1.5%), in- and on-packages (1.4%), the Internet (0.2%), and all other methods of distribution (0.3%).[29] These percentages vary slightly from year to year, but FSIs have dominated coupon distribution for a number of years.

Another major trend in coupon distribution has been the establishment of cooperative coupon programs. These are programs in which a service distributes coupons for a single company's multiple brands or brands from multiple companies. Two such service companies—Valassis and News Corp.'s SmartSource service—are responsible for distributing the billions of FSI coupons in separate inserts in newspapers around the United States. Both Valassis and SmartSource distribute coupons every Sunday throughout the year and represent literally hundreds of different brands and companies. Procter & Gamble, the leading issuer of FSIs, has its own FSI insert program (P&G brandSAVER) that is distributed in Sunday newspapers every four weeks. Valpak Direct Marketing Systems is a cooperative program for distributing coupons by direct mail.

Coupon Cost

The extensive use of couponing has not occurred without criticism. Some critics contend that coupons are wasteful and may actually increase prices of consumer goods. Whether coupons are wasteful and inefficient is debatable, but it is undeniable that coupons are an expensive proposition. For a better understanding of coupon costs, consider the case of a coupon with a $1 face value. (The *face value* is the amount paid to the consumer when he or she redeems the coupon at a retail checkout when purchasing the brand for which the coupon is offered.) The actual cost of this coupon is considerably more than $1. In fact, the actual cost, as shown in Table 16.3, is substantially more at $1.59. As can be seen from the table, the major cost element is the face value of $1 that is deducted from the purchase price. But the marketers offering this coupon incur several other costs: (1) a hefty distribution and postage charge (40 cents), (2) a handling fee that is paid to retailers for their trouble (8 cents), (3) a misredemption charge resulting from fraudulent redemptions (estimated at 7 cents), (4) internal preparation and processing costs (2 cents), and (5) a redemption cost (2 cents). The actual cost of $1.59 per redeemed coupon is 59 percent greater than the face value of $1. Assume a marketer distributes 40 million of these FSI coupons and that 2 percent, or 800,000, are redeemed. The total cost of this coupon "drop" would thus amount to $1,272,000. It should be apparent that coupon activity requires substantial investment to accomplish desired objectives.

Obviously, programs that aid in reducing costs, such as cooperative couponing and online delivery, are eagerly sought. Coupons are indeed costly, some are wasteful, and other promotional devices may be better. However, the extensive use of coupons suggests either that there are a large number of incompetent brand managers or that superior promotional tools are not available or are economically infeasible. The latter explanation is the more reasonable when considering how the marketplace operates. If a business practice is uneconomical, it will not continue to be used for long. When a better business practice is available, it will replace the previous solution. Conclusion: It appears that coupons are used extensively because marketers have been unable to devise more effective and economical methods for accomplishing the trial-generating objectives that coupons accomplish.

Is Couponing Profitable?

There is evidence that those households most likely to redeem coupons are also the most likely to buy the brand in the first place. Moreover, most consumers revert to their pre-coupon brand choice immediately after redeeming a competitive brand's coupon.[30] Hence, when consumers who redeem would have bought the brand anyway, the effect of couponing, at least on the surface, is merely to increase costs and reduce the per-unit profit margin. However, the issue is more involved than this. Although most coupons are redeemed by *current brand users,*

table 16.3

Full Coupon Cost

1. Face value	$1.00
2. Distribution and postage cost	0.40
3. Handling charge	0.08
4. Consumer misredemption cost	0.07
5. Internal preparation and processing cost	0.02
6. Redemption cost	0.02
Total Cost	$1.59

Source: Adapted from an analysis performed by the McKinsey & Co. consulting firm.

competitive dynamics force companies to continue offering coupons to prevent present consumers from switching to other brands that do offer coupons or other promotional deals.

Couponing is a fact of life that will remain an important part of marketing in North America and elsewhere. The real challenge for promotion managers is to seek ways to increase couponing profitability, to target coupons to consumers who may not otherwise purchase their brands, and to reward consumers for remaining loyal to their brands.

The following sections describe the major forms of couponing activity, the objectives each is intended to accomplish, and the innovations designed to increase couponing profitability. The presentation of couponing delivery methods follows the framework presented earlier in Table 16.1. It will be worthwhile to revisit Table 16.1 so as to better understand the specific couponing methods that follow.

Point-of-Purchase Couponing

As will be described later in the context of point-of-purchase advertising (Chapter 20), approximately 70 percent of purchase decisions are made while shoppers are in the store. It thus makes sense to deliver coupons at the point where decisions are made. Point-of-purchase coupons come in three forms: instant, shelf-delivered, and electronically delivered by optical scanner.

Instantly Redeemable Coupons

Most coupon distribution methods have delayed impact on consumers because the coupon is received in the consumer's home and held for a period of time before it is redeemed. *Instantly redeemable coupons* (IRCs) are peelable from the package and are designed to be removed by the consumer and redeemed at checkout when purchasing the brand carrying the coupon. This form of coupon represents an immediate reward that can spur the consumer to trial purchase the promoted brand (see cell 1 in Table 16.1). Instant coupons provide a significant price reduction and an immediate point-of-purchase incentive for consumers.

Although the instant coupon is a minor form of couponing, it has emerged in recent years as an alternative to price-off deals (in which every package must be reduced in price). The redemption level for instant coupons is considerably higher than the level for other couponing techniques. Whereas the dominant couponing method, FSIs, generates an average redemption level of approximately 1.5 percent (i.e., on average about 15 out of every 1,000 households that receive FSIs actually redeem them at stores), the average redemption rate for instant coupons has been estimated to be as high as 30 percent.[31] One would think that most purchasers would remove instant coupons at the time of purchase so as to receive the savings, but obviously the majority does not take advantage of these instant coupons.

A study compared the effectiveness of instantly redeemable coupons against freestanding inserts in generating sales for a brand of body wash. The FSI coupons and IRCs had 50-cent or $1 face values. Each coupon type and value combination (that is, 50-cent FSI coupon, $1 FSI coupon, 50-cent IRC, or $1 IRC) was placed on the body wash brand in each of two markets for a two-month period. Recorded sales data revealed that the IRCs outperformed FSI coupons of equal value. Moreover, the 50-cent IRC increased sales volume by 23 percent more than the $1 FSI coupon![32] This obviously is a counterintuitive finding that requires explanation.

A spokesperson for the research company said his company had no idea why the 50-cent IRC outperformed the $1 FSI coupon. However, research from the academic front offers an answer. One study found that a 75-cent coupon was not considered any more attractive than a 40-cent coupon.[33] A more directly relevant study determined that higher-value coupons *signal higher prices* to consumers.[34] This is especially true when consumers are *unfamiliar with a brand.* In this situation, high coupon values may scare off consumers by suggesting, or signaling, that these brands are expensive.

Perhaps the $1 FSI coupon for the body wash implied to prospective customers that the brand must be high priced or it could not otherwise justify offering such an attractive coupon. This being the case, they would not have removed the FSI coupon for later redemption. Comparatively, the 50-cent IRC was available to consumers at the point of purchase where the brand's actual price was also available. They had no reason to expect a high price; rather, they saw an opportunity to receive an attractive discount by simply peeling the coupon and presenting it to the clerk when checking out.

Ironically, higher-valued coupons may attract primarily current brand users who know the brand's actual price and realize the deal the attractive coupon offers, whereas a higher-valued coupon may discourage potential switchers from other brands if to them it signals a high price. This, of course, is particularly problematic with FSIs, which are received away from the point of purchase and, as a matter of practicality, include only the coupon value but not the brand's regular price. Such is not the case, however, with IRCs.

It would be unwise to draw sweeping generalizations from this single study based on only one product category (body wash), but the intriguing finding suggests that IRCs are capable of outperforming FSIs. Only with additional research will we know whether this finding holds up for other products.

Shelf-Delivered Coupons

Shelf-delivered coupon devices are attached to the shelf alongside coupon-sponsoring brands. A red device (referred to as the "instant coupon machine") is the best known among several shelf-delivered couponing services. Consumers interested in purchasing a particular brand can pull a coupon from the device and redeem it when checking out. The average redemption rate for shelf-delivered coupons is approximately 9 to 10 percent.[35]

Scanner-Delivered Coupons

© Susan Van Etten

There are several electronic systems for dispensing coupons at the point of purchase. Best known among these is a service from Catalina Marketing Corporation that is available in thousands of stores nationwide. Catalina offers two programs, one called Checkout Coupon and the other Checkout Direct. The *Checkout Coupon* program delivers coupons based on the particular brands a shopper has purchased. Once the optical scanner records that the shopper has purchased a competitor's brand, a coupon from the participating manufacturer is dispensed. By targeting competitors' customers, Catalina's Checkout Coupon program ensures that the manufacturer will reach people who buy the product category but are not currently purchasing the manufacturer's brand. The redemption rate is approximately 8 percent.[36]

Catalina's other couponing program, *Checkout Direct,* enables marketers to deliver coupons only to consumers who satisfy the coupon-sponsoring manufacturer's specific targeting requirements. The Checkout Direct program allows the coupon user to target consumers with respect to their purchase pattern for a particular product (e.g., direct coupons only to consumers who purchase toothpaste at least once every six weeks) or based on the amount of product usage (e.g., deliver coupons only to heavy users of the product). When shoppers who satisfy the coupon-sponsor's requirement make a purchase (as indicated by their check-cashing ID number), a coupon for the sponsoring brand is automatically dispensed for use on the shopper's next purchase occasion.

Frito-Lay used the Checkout Direct system to increase trial purchases when it introduced the Baked Lay's brand. Frito-Lay's brand managers targeted super-heavy users of healthier snack foods such as its own Baked Tostitos. Based on optical scanner data that records and stores consumers' past purchase data, the Checkout Direct system was programmed to issue coupons for Baked Lay's only to those consumers who purchased "better-for-you" snacks at least eight times during the past 12 months. When these consumers checked out, the scanner triggered a coupon for Baked Lay's. In excess of 40 percent of the coupons were redeemed, and the repeat-purchase rate was a very impressive 25 percent.[37]

Both Catalina programs are used to encourage trial purchasing or to induce retrial among those consumers who have not purchased a particular brand for a period of time. However, because coupons are distributed to consumers when they are checking out of a store and cannot be used until their next visit, the reward is *delayed*—unlike the instant or shelf-delivered coupons. Nevertheless, these scanner-delivered couponing methods are effective and cost-efficient because they provide a way to target coupon distribution carefully. Targeting, in the case of Checkout Coupon, is directed at competitive-brand users and, in the case of Checkout Direct, is aimed at users who satisfy a manufacturer's prescribed product-usage requirements.

Mail- and Media-Delivered Coupons

These coupon-delivery modes initiate trial purchase behavior by offering consumers *delayed* rewards. Mail-delivered coupons represent about 2 percent of all manufacturer-distributed coupons. Mass-media modes (newspapers and magazines) are clearly dominant, carrying about 90 percent of all coupons—the bulk of which is in the form of freestanding inserts in Sunday newspapers.

Mail-Delivered Coupons

Marketers typically use mail-delivered coupons to introduce new or improved products. Mailings can be either directed at a broad cross section of the market or targeted to specific geodemographic segments. Mailed coupons achieve the highest household penetration.

Coupon distribution via magazines and newspapers reaches fewer than 60 percent of all homes, whereas mail can reach as high as 95 percent. Moreover, direct mail achieves the highest redemption rate (3.5 percent) of all mass-delivered coupon techniques.[38] There also is empirical evidence to suggest that direct-mail coupons increase the amount of product purchases, particularly when coupons with higher face values are used by households that own their homes, have larger families, and are more educated.[39]

The major disadvantage of direct-mailed coupons is that they are relatively expensive compared with other coupon-distribution methods. Another disadvantage is that direct mailing is especially inefficient and expensive for brands enjoying a high market share. This is because a large proportion of the coupon recipients may already be regular users of the coupon brand, thereby defeating the primary purpose of generating trial purchasing. The inefficiencies of mass mailing account for the rapid growth of efforts to target coupons to narrowly defined audiences such as users of competitive brands.

FSIs and Other Media-Delivered Coupons

As earlier noted, approximately 88 percent of all coupons distributed in the United States are via freestanding inserts in Sunday newspapers. The cost per thousand for freestanding inserts is only about 50 percent to 60 percent of that for direct-mail coupons, which largely explains why FSIs are the dominant coupon-delivery mode. Another advantage of FSIs is that they perform an extremely important reminder function for the consumer who peruses the Sunday inserts, clips coupons for brands he or she intends to buy in the coming week, and then redeems these at a later date.[40] Finally, there is some evidence that FSIs also perform an advertising function. That is, when perusing the Sunday inserts, consumers are exposed to FSI "advertisements" and are somewhat more likely to purchase promoted brands even without redeeming coupons.[41] This comes as no great surprise because FSI coupons often are eye-catching "advertisements."

Research has shown that attractive pictures in FSIs are particularly effective when viewers of the FSI are loyal to a brand other than the one featured in the FSI. In this situation, consumers, loyal as they are to another brand, are not motivated to process arguments about a nonpreferred brand featured in the FSI. Hence, the use of attractive pictures (versus message arguments) is necessary to increase the odds that consumers will clip the FSI coupon.[42]

In addition to FSIs, coupons also are distributed in magazines and as part of the regular (noninsert) newspaper page. Redemption rates for coupons distributed in magazines and newspapers average less than 1 percent.[43] A second problem with magazine- and newspaper-delivered coupons is that they do not generate much trade interest. Finally, coupons delivered via magazines and newspapers are particularly susceptible to misredemption. The latter issue is so significant to all parties involved in couponing that it deserves a separate discussion later.

In- and On-Pack Coupons

In- and on-pack coupons are included either inside a product's package or as part of a package's exterior. This form of couponing should not be confused with the previously discussed instant, or peelable, coupon. Whereas IRCs are removable at the point of purchase and redeemable for that particular item while the shopper is in the store, an in- or on-pack coupon cannot be removed until it is in the shopper's home to be redeemed on a subsequent purchase occasion. This form of couponing thus affords consumers with a *delayed* reward that is designed more for encouraging repeat than trial purchases (see cell 4 in Table 16.1).

A coupon for one brand often is promoted by another brand. For example, General Mills promoted its brand of granola bars by placing cents-off coupons in cereal boxes. Practitioners call this practice *crossruffing,* a term borrowed from bridge and bridge-type card games where partners alternate trumping one another when they are unable to follow suit.

Although marketers use crossruffing to create trial purchases or to stimulate purchase of products, such as granola bars, that are not staple items, in- and on-pack coupons the *same brand* carries are generally intended to *stimulate repeat purchasing.* That is, once consumers have exhausted the contents of a particular package, they are more likely to repurchase that brand if an attractive inducement, such as a cents-off coupon, is available immediately. A package coupon has *bounce-back value,* so to speak. An initial purchase, the bounce, may stimulate another purchase, the bounce back, when an appealing inducement such as an in-package coupon is made available.[44]

A major advantage of in- and on-pack coupons is that there are virtually *no distribution costs.* Moreover, redemption rates are much higher because brand users receive most of the package-delivered coupons. The average redemption rate for in-pack coupons is around 6 to 7 percent, whereas the redemption rate for on-pack coupons is slightly less than 5 percent.[45] Limitations of package-delivered coupons are that they offer delayed value to consumers, do not reach nonusers of the carrying brand, and do not leverage trade interest due to the delayed nature of the offer.

Online Couponing

A number of Internet sites now distribute coupons. Although representing a very small percentage of all coupons distributed (less than 1 percent), online couponing is growing in popularity. Consumers print the coupons on their home (or work) printers, and then, as with other modes of coupon delivery, redeem the printed coupon along with the purchased item at checkout.

Allowing consumers to print their own coupons creates considerable potential for *fraud* because it leaves open the possibility that consumers will manipulate the face value and print multiple copies. Moreover, computer-savvy criminals download coupon files and scan coupons into their computers, and then change the bar codes, dates, amounts, and even the sponsoring brand.[46] To avoid this problem, some online couponing services allow the consumer to select the brands for which he or she would like to receive coupons, and then actual coupons are mailed. It is too early to predict whether online couponing will continue to grow in popularity, especially since some retailers such as Wal-Mart refuse to accept Internet coupons. However, unless companies are able to curtail the substantial amount of online couponing fraud, it is likely that online couponing will not experience significant growth.

The Special Case of Wireless Couponing

As described in Chapter 13 when discussing Internet marketing, distributing promotional offers via mobile phones is growing in popularity. For example, major package good companies such as Procter & Gamble, General Mills, and Kimberly-Clark are experimenting with coupon offers to mobile phone users. These companies have teamed up with the Kroger supermarket chain to test whether distributing coupons via mobile phones is an effective and efficient method. Here is how mobile couponing will work during this test: Consumers will download to their mobile phones a ringtone-like application called Cellfire, which will allow them to check Cellfire's electronic "shopping mall" to see which brands are offering coupons. They then cash in coupons by showing to cashiers at store checkouts their cell phone screens that display selected coupons.[47]

Cellfire is just one of many mobile phone organizations that are attempting to exploit the potential of cell phones (the "third screen") to distribute coupons and perform other marcom tasks. As mentioned in Chapter 13, only time will tell whether mobile couponing will work, but the prospects are promising considering coupon offers via cell phones are relatively inexpensive for marketers to offer and highly convenient for consumers—eliminating the need to clip coupons at home and to remember to take them to the store.

The Coupon Redemption Process and Misredemption

Coupon misredemption is a widespread problem. The best way to understand how misredemption occurs is to examine the redemption process. A graphic of the process is presented in Figure 16.3.

The Process

The process begins with a manufacturer distributing coupons to consumers via FSIs, direct mail, or any of the other distribution modes previously described (see *path A* in Figure 16.3). Consumers collect coupons, take them to the store, and present them to a checkout clerk, who subtracts each coupon's face value from the shopper's total purchase cost (*path B*). For the shopper to be entitled to the coupon discount, certain conditions and restrictions must be met: (1) he or she must buy the merchandise specified on the coupon in the size, brand, and quantity directed; (2) only one coupon can be redeemed per item; (3) cash may not be given for the coupon; and (4) the coupon must be redeemed before the expiration date. (Some coupon misredemption occurs because consumers present coupons that do not meet these requirements.)

Retailers, in turn, redeem the coupons they have received to obtain reimbursement from the manufacturers that sponsored the coupons. Retailers typically hire another company, called a *clearinghouse,* to sort and redeem the coupons in return for a fee (*path C*). Clearinghouses, acting on behalf of a number of retail clients, consolidate coupons before forwarding them. Clearinghouses maintain control by ensuring that their clients sold products legitimately in the amounts they submitted for redemption.

Clearinghouses forward the coupons to *redemption centers* (*path D*), which serve as agents of coupon-issuing manufacturers. A redemption center pays off on all properly redeemed coupons (*path E*) and then is compensated for its services by the manufacturer (*path F*). If a center questions the validity of certain coupons, it may go to its client, a manufacturer, for approval on redeeming suspected coupons.

The system is not quite as clear-cut as it may appear from this description. Some large retailers act as their own clearinghouses, some manufacturers serve as

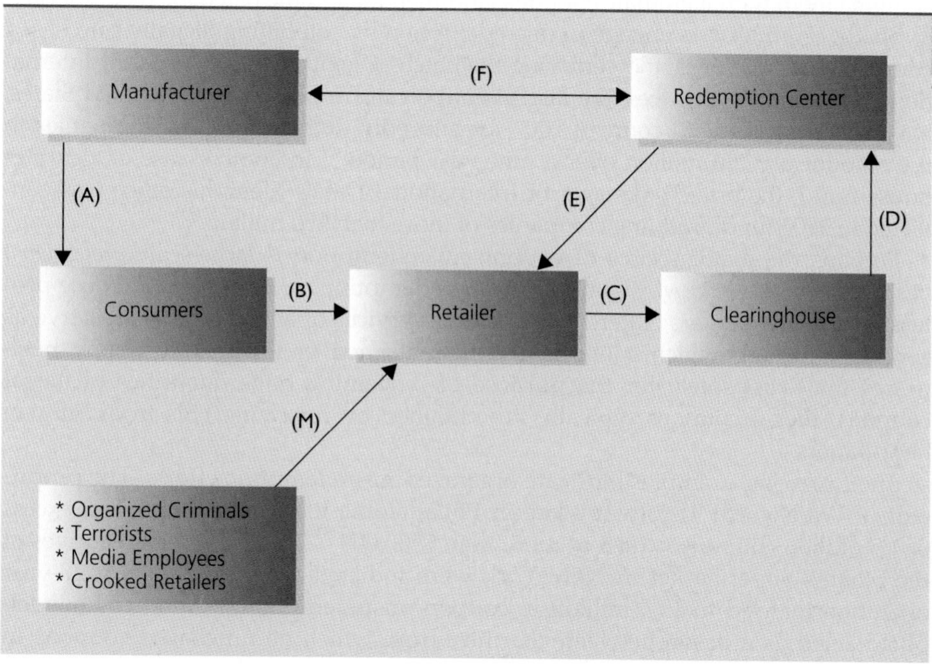

figure 16.3

Coupon Redemption and Misredemption Process

their own redemption centers, and some independent firms offer both clearinghouse and redemption-center services.

However, regardless of the specific mechanism by which a coupon is ultimately redeemed (or misredeemed), the retailer is reimbursed for the amount of the face value paid to the consumer and for payment of a handling charge, which currently in the United States is 8 cents per coupon. Herein rests the potential for misredemption: An unscrupulous person could earn $1.08 from redeeming a coupon that has a face value of $1. One thousand such misredeemed coupons would produce earnings of $1,080. Exacerbating the potential for misredemption is the fact that many coupons now have face values worth $1 or more.

The Consequences

Estimates of the misredemption rate range from a low of 15 percent to a high of 40 percent. Many brand managers have assumed a 20 to 25 percent rate of misredemption when budgeting for coupon events. However, it is likely that past estimates of coupon misredemption have been inflated; it now appears that fraudulent coupon redemption is, on average, closer to 3 or 4 percent rather than the 20 to 25 percent assumed previously.[48] Although imposing tighter controls at all stages of the coupon redemption process has reduced the magnitude of misredemption, a 3 to 4 percent misredemption level nevertheless represents millions of dollars lost by manufacturers.

The Participants

How does misredemption occur and who participates in it? Misredemption occurs at every level of the redemption process. Sometimes *individual consumers* present coupons that have expired, coupons for items not purchased, or coupons for a smaller-sized product than that specified by the coupon. Consumers also on occasion electronically alter the barcodes on computer-generated coupons to receive larger discounts than coupon-offering manufacturers intended.

Some *clerks* take coupons to the store and exchange them for cash without making a purchase. At the store level, *retailer managers* may boost profits by submitting extra coupons in addition to those redeemed legitimately. A dishonest retailer can buy coupons on the black market, age them in a clothes dryer (or even in a cement mixer) so that they appear to have been handled by actual consumers, combine them with legitimate coupons, and then mail in the batch for redemption.

Shady *clearinghouses* engage in misredemption by combining illegally purchased coupons with real ones and certifying the batch as legitimate. Texas-based International Outsourcing Services, the largest coupon clearinghouse in the United States, was indicted in federal court in 2007 for allegedly defrauding CPG companies in the amount of $250 million over a nine-year period.[49] In another case of clearinghouse fraud, the branch manager of International Data's Memphis office was convicted in 2004 for defrauding companies of more than $50 million.[50]

Perhaps the major source of coupon misredemption is large-scale *professional misredeemers* (see *path M*, standing for misredemption, in Figure 16.3). These professional misredeemers either: (1) recruit the services of actual retailers to serve as conduits through which coupons are misredeemed or (2) operate phony businesses that exist solely for the purpose of redeeming huge quantities of illegal coupons. Illegal coupons typically are obtained by removing FSIs from Sunday newspapers.

The following examples illustrate organized misredemption efforts. The proprietor of Wadsworth Thriftway store in Philadelphia illegally submitted in excess of 1.5 million coupons valued at more than $800,000.[51] The top three executives of the Sloan's Supermarket in New York were indicted for their role in a 20-year operation that led to $3.5 million in coupon misredemption.[52] Another Philadelphian acted as a liason between charities, from which he purchased coupons in bulk, and a supermarket employee, who submitted them for repayment by manufacturers or their redemption centers. The middleman earned $200,000 from the couponing scam before he was arrested.[53] Five operators of Shop n' Bag supermarkets in Philadelphia bought nearly 12 million coupons for only 20 percent to 30 percent of their face value and then redeemed them prior to being arrested.[54] And finally, according to the *New York Post,* Mideastern terrorists misredeemed perhaps up to $100 million by funneling illegally redeemed coupons through minimarts and Hispanic bodegas.[55]

The Role of Promotion Agencies

As discussed in Chapter 7, brand managers typically employ advertising agencies to create advertising messages, buy advertising media, and perform other services related to a brand's advertising function. Although less known than their ad agency counterparts, brand managers also hire specialized promotion agencies to perform sales promotion functions. These agencies—like their advertising agency counterparts—work with brand managers in formulating promotion strategies and implementing tactical programs.

Assume, for example, that a brand manager believes that a new brand needs to be sampled in trial-sized bottles to facilitate high levels of trial-purchase behavior. The promotion also will include coupons in the box containing the trial-size sample. Further, an introductory advertising campaign in magazines will include an attractive sweepstakes offer to draw attention to the ad and enhance consumer involvement with the brand. The brand manager determines that it will be best to use the services of a promotion agency that can expertly design a sampling program that efficiently targets sample distribution to young consumers and a sweepstakes program that would appeal to this age group.

The Rise of the Online Promotion Agency

In addition to conventional promotion agencies, which traditionally have emphasized programs using off-line media and in-store distribution, there is a new generation of promotion agencies that emphasize online promotions. The Internet has become an increasingly important venue for conducting promotions. Coupons, sweepstakes offers, online promotional games, free sample offerings, and online continuity programs are just some of the promotions that are virtually ubiquitous on the Web. These programs are effective because they enable marketers to target promotions to preferred consumers, to deliver the programs relatively inexpensively, and to measure results with greater precision than what is possible with other marketing programs. Promotion agencies are a valuable resource for brand managers in both planning strategically sound promotions and carrying through their implementation.

Summary

This chapter focused on consumer-oriented promotions. The various sales promotion tools available to marketers were classified in terms of whether the reward offered to consumers is immediate or delayed and whether the manufacturer's objective is to achieve trial impact, encourage repeat purchases, or reinforce brand images. Specific sales promotion techniques are classified as falling into one of six general categories (see Table 16.1).

The first and most critical requirement for a successful sales promotion is that it be based on clearly defined objectives. Second, the program must be designed with a specific target market in mind. It should also be realized that many consumers, perhaps most, desire to maximize the rewards gained from participating in a promotion while minimizing the amount of time and effort invested. Consequently, an effective promotion, from a consumer-response perspective, must make it relatively easy for consumers to obtain their rewards, and the size of the reward must be sufficient to justify the consumers' efforts. A third essential ingredient for effective sales promotions is that programs must be developed with the interests of retailers in mind—not just those of the manufacturer.

The bulk of the chapter was devoted to two of the major forms of consumer-oriented sales promotions: sampling and couponing. It was pointed out that sampling is the premier promotion for generating trial usage of a new brand. The various methods of distributing samples were presented, and it was emphasized that regardless of distribution method, three practices are necessary for sampling success: (1) targeting rather than mass distributing samples, (2) using innovative distribution methods where appropriate, and (3) undertaking efforts to measure sampling's return on investment. The specific circumstances when sampling is appropriately used were discussed, and various problems with sampling were identified.

The second major type of promotion, couponing, was described in terms of the magnitude of usage and types of distribution methods (via freestanding inserts, direct mail, and optical scanners, at the point of purchase, on the Internet, etc.). The growing role of online couponing was identified. A major section described the coupon-redemption process and in this context discussed the act of coupon misredemption.

Discussion Questions

1. Why are immediate (versus delayed) rewards more effective in inducing the consumer behaviors a brand marketer desires? Use a specific, concrete illustration from your own experience to support your answer.
2. One of the major trends in product sampling is selective sampling of targeted groups. Assume you work for a company that has just developed a candy bar that tastes almost as good as other candy bars but has far fewer calories. Marketing research has identified the target market as economically upscale consumers, ages primarily 25 to 54, who reside in suburban and urban areas. Explain specifically how you might selectively sample your new product to approximately two million such consumers.
3. Compare and contrast sampling and media-delivered coupons in terms of objectives, consumer impact, and overall roles in marketing communications strategies.
4. A packaged goods company plans to introduce a new bath soap that differs from competitive soaps by virtue of a distinct new fragrance. Should sampling be used to introduce the product?
5. A manufacturer of golf balls introduced a new brand that supposedly delivered greater distance than competitively priced balls. However, in accordance with restrictions the governing body that regulates golf balls and other golfing equipment and accessories established, this new ball when struck by a driver travels on average only a couple of yards farther than competitive brands. The manufacturer identified a list of three million golfers and mailed a single golf ball to each. In view of what you have learned about sampling in this chapter, comment on the advisability of this sampling program.
6. Present your personal views concerning the number of coupons distributed annually in the United States. Is widespread couponing in the best interest of consumers?
7. Rather than offering discounts in the form of coupons, why don't brand managers simply reduce the prices of their brands?
8. Using Table 16.3 as a rough guide, calculate the full cost per redeemed coupon given the following facts: (1) face value = 75 cents, (2) 20 million coupons distributed at $7 per thousand, (3) redemption rate = 3 percent, (4) handling cost = 8 cents, and (5) misredemption rate = 5 percent.
9. Go through a Sunday newspaper and select three FSIs. Analyze each in terms of what you think are the marketer's objectives in using this particular promotion. Do not restrict your chosen FSIs to just those offering coupons.
10. Assume you are brand manager of Mountain State Bottled Water. This new brand competes in a product category with several well-known brands. Your marketing communications objective is to

generate trial purchases among predominantly younger and better-educated consumers. Propose a promotion that would accomplish this objective. Assume that your promotion is purely experimental and that it will be undertaken in a small city of just 250,000 people. Also assume that: (1) you cannot afford product sampling; (2) you will not advertise the promotion; and (3) your budget for this experimental promotion is $5,000. What would you do?

11. A concluding section of the chapter indicated that promotion agencies have become an increasingly important resource for brand managers in planning and executing promotional programs. One could argue that the fees brand managers pay for the services of promotion agencies might better be spent elsewhere—for example, on increased advertising levels. Present arguments both in favor of and in opposition to hiring promotion agencies.

End Notes

1. Information about the college sample program offered by Alloy Media + Marketing is located at http://www.alloymarketing.com/media/college/sampling.htm (accessed May 3, 2008).
2. Tim Parry, "College Try," *Promo,* September 2004, 23–25.
3. Although the following discussion is based mostly on the author's prior writing and thinking on the topic, these points are influenced by descriptions obtained from various practitioners.
4. Pierre Chandon, Brian Wansink, and Gilles Laurent, "A Benefit Congruency Framework of Sales Promotion Effectiveness," *Journal of Marketing* 64 (October 2000), 65–81. The following discussion of benefits is based on a typology provided by these authors. See their Table 1 on pages 68–69.
5. The idea that consumer promotions perform an informational role receives prominent attention in Priya Raghubir, J. Jeffrey Inman, and Hans Grande, "The Three Faces of Consumer Promotions," *California Management Review* 46 (summer 2004), 23–42.
6. "Secret Weapon," *Promo,* December 2007, 44.
7. Jack Neff, "Viva Viva! K-C Boosts Brand's Marketing," *Advertising Age,* June 11, 2007, 4, 41.
8. Sarah Ellison and Carlos Tehada, "Young Couples Starting Out Are Every Marketer's Dream," *Wall Street Journal Online,* January 30, 2003, http://online.wsj.com.
9. For an interesting study of food sampling in grocery stores, see Stephen M. Nowlis and Baba Shiv, "The Influence of Consumer Distractions on the Effectiveness of Food-Sampling Programs," *Journal of Marketing Research* 42 (May 2005), 157–168.
10. Kate MacArthur, "Give It Away: Fast Feeders Favor Freebies," *Advertising Age,* June 18, 2007, 10.
11. Dan Hanover, "We Deliver," *Promo,* March 2001, 43–45.
12. "Sampling Wins Over More Marketers," *Advertising Age,* July 27, 1992, 12.
13. Lafayette Jones, "A Case for Ethnic Sampling," *Promo,* October 2000, 41–42.
14. David Vaczek, "Points of Switch," *Promo,* September 1998, 39–40.
15. Patricia Odell, "Firsthand Experience," *Promo,* May 2007, 19.
16. Betsy Spethmann, "Branded Moments," *Promo,* September 2000, 83–98.
17. Lorin Cipolla, "Instant Gratification," *Promo,* April 2004, AR35.
18. Amy Johannes, "Room Service," *Promo,* February 2008, 38–40.
19. Jack Neff, "P&G Brings Potty to Parties," *Advertising Age,* February 17, 2003, 22.
20. Adapted from Glenn Heitsmith, "Gaining Trial," *Promo,* September 1994, 108; and "Spend a Little, Get a Lot," *Trial and Conversion III: Harnessing the Power of Sampling Special Advertising Supplement* (New York: Promotional Marketing Association, Inc., 1996–1997), 18.
21. Charles Fredericks, Jr., "What Ogilvy & Mather Has Learned about Sales Promotion," *The Tools of Promotion* (New York: Association of National Advertisers, 1975). Although this is an old source, the wisdom still holds true today.
22. Lynn G. Reiling, "Consumers Misuse Mass Sampling for Sun Light Dishwashing Liquid," *Marketing News,* September 3, 1982, 1, 2.
23. Maciek Gajewski, "Samples: A Steal in Poland," *Advertising Age,* November 4, 1991, 54.
24. Different organizations arrive at varying estimates of actual coupon distribution numbers. For example, see Patricia Odell, "We've Been Clipped," *Promo,* September 2007, AR11.
25. "Clipping Path," *Promo,* April 2004, AR7.
26. Peter Meyers, "Coupons to the Rescue," *Promo,* April 2008, 63.
27. Donald R. Lichtenstein, Richard G. Netemeyer, and Scot Burton, "Distinguishing Coupon Proneness from Value Consciousness: An Acquisition-Transaction Utility Theory Perspective," *Journal of Marketing* 54 (July 1990), 54–67. For a detailed treatment of factors that influence consumers' coupon-redemption behavior, see also Banwari Mittal, "An Integrated Framework for Relating Diverse Consumer Characteristics to Supermarket Coupon Redemption," *Journal of Marketing Research*

31 (November 1994), 533–544. See also Judith A. Garretson and Scot Burton, "Highly Coupon and Sales Prone Consumers: Benefits beyond Price Savings," *Journal of Advertising Research* 43 (June 2003), 162–172.
28. Betsy Spethmann, "Clipping Slows," *Promo's 14th Annual Sourcebook*, 2007, 9.
29. Ibid.
30. Kapil Bawa and Robert W. Shoemaker, "The Effects of a Direct Mail Coupon on Brand Choice Behavior," *Journal of Marketing Research* 24 (November 1987), 370–376.
31. Daniel Shannon, "Still a Mighty Marketing Mechanism," *Promo*, April 1996, 86.
32. "Checkout: Instant Results," *Promo*, October 1998, 75.
33. Kapil Bawa, Srini S. Srinivasan, and Rajendra K. Srivastava, "Coupon Attractiveness and Coupon Proneness: A Framework for Modeling Coupon Redemption," *Journal of Marketing Research* 34 (November 1997), 517–525.
34. Priya Raghubir, "Coupon Value: A Signal for Price?" *Journal of Marketing Research* 35 (August 1998), 316–324.
35. Russ Bowman and Paul Theroux, *Promotion Marketing* (Stamford, Conn.: Intertec Publishing Corporation, 2000), 24.
36. Ibid.
37. "When the Chips Are Down," *Promo Magazine Special Report*, April 1998, S7.
38. Bowman and Theroux, *Promotion Marketing*.
39. Kapil Bawa and Robert W. Shoemaker, "Analyzing Incremental Sales from a Direct Mail Coupon Promotion," *Journal of Marketing Research* 53 (July 1989), 66–78.
40. Erwin Ephron, "More Weeks, Less Weight: The Shelf-Space Model of Advertising," *Journal of Advertising Research* 35 (May/June 1995), 18–23.
41. Srini S. Srinivasan, Robert P. Leone, and Francis J. Mulhern, "The Advertising Exposure Effect of Free Standing Inserts," *Journal of Advertising* 24 (spring 1995), 29–40.
42. France Leclerc and John D. C. Little, "Can Advertising Copy Make FSI Coupons More Effective?" *Journal of Marketing Research* 34 (November 1997), 473–484.
43. Bowman and Theroux, *Promotion Marketing*.
44. For a technical analysis of the role of crossruffing, see Sanjay K. Dhar and Jagmohan S. Raju, "The Effects of Cross-Ruff Coupons on Sales and Profits," *Marketing Science* 44 (November 1998), 1501–1516.
45. Bowman and Theroux, *Promotion Marketing*.
46. Karen Holt, "Coupon Crimes," *Promo*, April 2004, 23–26, 70; Jack Neff, "Internet Enabling Coupon Fraud Biz," *Advertising Age*, October 20, 2003, 3.
47. Alice Z. Cuneo, "Package-goods Giants Roll Out Mobile Coupons," *Advertising Age*, March 10, 2008, 3, 26.
48. "A Drop in the Crime Rate," *Promo*, December 1997, 12.
49. Jack Neff, "Package-goods Players Just Can't Quit Coupons," *Advertising Age*, May 14, 2007, 8.
50. "Pushing Back the Tide," *Promo*, April 2006, 81.
51. Cecelia Blalock, "Another Retailer Nabbed in Coupon Misredemption Plot," *Promo*, December 1993, 38.
52. Ibid.
53. Cecelia Blalock, "Tough Sentence for Coupon Middle Man," *Promo*, June 1993, 87.
54. "Clipped, Supermarket Owners Charged with Coupon Fraud," *Promo*, May 1997, 14.
55. "Report: Coupon Scams Are Funding Terrorism," *Promo*, August 1996, 50. This issue was also the subject of testimony before the Senate Judiciary Technology, Terrorism, and Government Information Subcommittee, February 24, 1998.

17

Premiums and Other Promotions

You may recall the section in Chapter 14 that discussed the value and importance of maintaining and managing databases of past and prospective customers. It was pointed out that an up-to-date database for a brand makes firms able (1) to direct advertising efforts to those individuals who represent the best prospects for that brand, (2) to enhance the brand's advertising productivity, and (3) to create long-term relationships with customers. The discussion in this insert describes the role of sales promotions in contributing to a useful and up-to-date database.

Volvo ran a *sweepstakes* promotion that was held in context of the Johnny Depp movie, *Pirates of the Caribbean.* The promotion collected names and addresses from 52,000 people. Volvo immediately e-mailed these entrants and offered $500 toward the purchase of a new Volvo. It also requested entrants to opt-in for future messages, and nearly 15,000 complied. These individuals now receive periodic e-mail newsletters and promotional offers.

Buick ran a *contest* that provided entrants with the opportunity to win a new Buick Lucerne. The ultimate purpose of the contest was to encourage people to visit Buick dealerships. Of the more than 500,000 entrants to the contest, 3,000 agreed to take a test drive—due in large part to an offer to receive a free hat autographed by famous golfer Tiger Woods. This promotion generated a large number of potential Buick purchasers and also contributed to Buick's large and expanding database.

Using promotions to build databases is a practice not limited to large, global brands such as Volvo and Buick. Consider the case of Kelly's Roast Beef, a small Massachusetts-based chain of fast-food restaurants. Kelly's database contained the names of just 700 people until it ran a successful *sweepstakes* offering a trip to Ireland. The promotion drew in excess of 10,000 entrants who provided name and address information. Kelly's now uses its expanded database to send postal mail and e-mail messages to people who live within five miles of any of its stores. These messages announce special promotions, introduce new menu items, and identify new store locations. A

© AP Images/PRNewsFoto/Checkers Drive-In Restaurants, Inc.

spokesperson for Kelly's noted that loyal customers are the company's lifeblood and that it is essential to acknowledge their loyalty, keep them informed, and demonstrate appreciation.

An up-to-date database is essential to achieve these objectives, and because people generally are reluctant to give up personal information, some form of incentive—a sweepstake, contest, or premium offer—is essential to overcome this reluctance and to collect names and addresses from willing customers.[1]

Chapter Objectives

After reading this chapter you should be able to:

1. Understand the role of premiums, the types of premiums, and the developments in premium practice.
2. Recognize the role of price-off promotions and bonus packages.
3. Be aware of the role of rebates and refund offers.
4. Know the differences among sweepstakes, contests, and games, and the reasons for using each form of promotion.
5. Understand the role of continuity promotions.
6. Appreciate retailer-driven promotions.
7. Evaluate the potential effectiveness of sales promotion ideas, and appraise the effectiveness of completed promotional programs.

>>Marcom Insight:

The Use of Promotions to Nurture Customer Loyalty

Introduction

This chapter picks up where Chapter 16 left off and discusses major forms of consumer-oriented promotions other than sampling and couponing. To frame the subsequent discussion again, Table 16.1 is repeated in this chapter as Table 17.1.

The presentation proceeds as follows: first discussed is the use of product *premiums* (cells 2, 3, and 6 in Table 17.1); second, *price-off promotions* (cell 3); third, *bonus packs* (cell 3); fourth, *games* (cell 3); fifth, *rebates and refunds* (cell 4); sixth, *continuity programs* (cell 4); and seventh, *sweepstakes and contests* (cell 6). Three additional topics will follow the discussion of specific promotional tools: (1) overlay and tie-in promotions, (2) retailer-driven promotions, and (3) techniques for evaluating sales promotion ideas and conducting postmortem analyses.

It is important to emphasize again that each of the various promotional techniques covered in this chapter performs a unique role and is therefore appropriately used to achieve limited objectives. This chapter conveys each tool's role and identifies, where appropriate, unique limitations or problems associated with using each tool. It will be useful to review Table 17.1 before studying the various types of promotions.

Premiums

Broadly defined, **premiums** are articles of merchandise or services (e.g., travel) manufacturers offer as a form of gift to *induce action* on the part of consumers and possibly also retailers and the sales force. Our focus in this chapter is on premiums' consumer-oriented role. Premiums represent a versatile promotional tool and—depending on the type of premium offer—are able to generate trial purchases, encourage repeat purchasing, and reinforce brand images. Brand

table 17.1

Major Consumer-Oriented Promotions

	Brand Management Objective		
Consumer Reward	**Generating Trial Purchases**	**Encouraging Repeat Purchases**	**Reinforcing Brand Image**
Immediate	**Cell 1** • Samples • Instant coupons • Shelf-delivered coupons	**Cell 3** • Price-offs • Bonus packs • In-, on-, and near-pack premiums • Games	**Cell 5** (No Promotions Match Cell 5's Conditions)
Delayed	**Cell 2** • Scanner-delivered coupons • Media- and mail-delivered coupons • Online coupons • Mail-in premiums • Free-with-purchase premiums	**Cell 4** • In- and on-pack coupons • Rebates and refunds • Phone cards • Continuity programs	**Cell 6** • Self-liquidating premiums • Sweepstakes and contests

managers' major reasons for providing premiums are to increase consumer brand loyalty and to motivate new purchases.[2]

Brand managers use several forms of premium offers to motivate desired consumer behaviors: (1) free-with-purchase premiums; (2) mail-in offers; (3) in-, on-, and near-pack premiums; and (4) self-liquidating offers. These forms of premiums perform somewhat different objectives. Free-with-purchase and mail-in offers are useful primarily for generating brand *trial* or *retrial.* In-, on-, and near-pack premiums serve *customer-holding purposes* by rewarding present consumers for continuing to purchase a liked or preferred brand. And self-liquidators perform a combination of *customer-holding* and *image-reinforcement* functions.

Free-with-Purchase Premiums

Both marketers of durable goods and consumer packaged goods (CPG) brands provide **free-with-purchase premiums** (also called *free-gift-with-purchase premiums*). As shown in Table 17.1, this form of premium typically represents a delayed reward to consumers that is primarily designed to generate *trial purchases.* Examples of this type of free-with-purchase premium include an offer from Michelin to receive a $100-retail-value emergency roadside kit with the purchase of four Michelin tires. Volkswagen gave away Apple iPods with purchases of New Beetle automobiles. Sun City, a nationwide developer of homes for retirees, offered a free golf cart to people who purchased a new home within 18 days from receiving the offer. Attractive premiums such as these might motivate indecisive consumers to purchase the premium-offering item rather than a competitive option.

Research has shown that the perceived value of a premium item, or gift, depends on the *value of the brand that is offering the gift.* In particular, the identical item was perceived to be of lower value when it was offered as a free gift by a lower- versus higher-priced brand.[3] This finding buttresses the point made in the previous chapter that sales promotions perform an *informational role* in addition to utilitarian and hedonic functions. This is to say that sales promotions provide signaling information consumers use to judge product quality and value. An important implication of this finding is that brands used as gift items must be cautious that their images are not damaged by the sponsoring brand. The adage "Beware of the company you keep" is as applicable in the premium-partners context as it is in social relations.

Mail-In Offers

By definition, a **mail-in offer** is a premium in which consumers receive a free item from the sponsoring manufacturer in return for submitting a required number of proofs of purchase. As shown in Table 17.1, this form of premium represents a *delayed reward* to consumers that is primarily designed to generate *trial purchases* (cell 2).

For example, Kellogg's brand of Smart Start cereal urged consumers to mail in for a free cholesterol and wellness kit, and its Frosted Flakes brand offered a children's book by mail with the purchase of two Kellogg's cereals (see Figure 17.1). Nestle's brand of Nesquik chocolate milk offered a free zip-up hoodie to consumers who provided six UPC bar codes from Nesquik items along with $6.99 for handling and shipping. Colgate-Palmolive offered a free SpongeBob powered toothbrush to those families that (1) purchased a regular Colgate toothbrush and (2) provided evidence of their child having visited a dentist.

Perhaps as few as 2–4 percent of consumers who are exposed to free mail-in offers actually take advantage of these opportunities. However, mail-in premiums

© AP Images/PRNewsFoto/United Through Reading

Figure 17.1

Illustration of a Mail-in Premium

can be effective if the premium item is appealing to the target market. (See the *Global Focus* insert for a really clever promotion that used a mail-in premium.)

In-, On-, and Near-Pack Premiums

In- and **on-pack premiums** offer a free item inside or attached to a package or make the package itself the premium item. In general, in- and on-package premiums offer consumers *immediate value* and thereby encourage increased product consumption from consumers who like or prefer the premium-offering brand (see Table 17.1, cell 3).

For example, Colgate toothpaste sometimes attaches a free Colgate toothbrush to the package, and Pantene shampoo is occasionally packaged with a unit of free Pantene conditioner. Ford Motor Company in conjunction with Target stores and various brands of Kellogg's cereal (Froot Loops, Apple Jacks, Frosted Flakes, and Cocoa Krispies) promoted its Fusion automobile by placing 600,000 toy Fusions into these cereal boxes. Among these 600,000 toy cars was one red model affixed with the Target logo. The person buying that particular box won a real Fusion. In a similar promotion, Ralston Purina offered tiny sports car models in about 11 million boxes of six cereal brands. Ten of these boxes contained scale-model red Corvettes. Lucky consumers turned in the models for real Corvettes.

Near-pack premiums provide the retail trade with specially displayed premium pieces that retailers then give to consumers who purchase the promoted product. Near-pack premiums are less expensive because additional packaging is not required. Furthermore, near-pack premiums can build sales volume in stores that put up displays and participate fully.

The Special Case of "Buy X, Get 1 Free" Offers

One of the most frequent promotions CPG companies use is the "Buy X, Get 1 Free" offer—where X stands for 1, 2, 3, or sometimes even 4 purchases that are needed to receive a free gift. The "gift" in this case is another unit of the same brand that is conducting the promotion or a unit of a different brand. For example, Oust air sanitizer offered a free aerosol can of that product with the purchase of another can (Buy 1, Get 1 Free). Crunch Crisp candy wafers ran a Buy 2 Get 1 Free promotion. Also in the candy category, M&M's had a Buy Any 3, Get Any 1 Free offer for the consumer to buy any three of M&M's brands (e.g., M&M's, Twix, 3 Musketeers, Snickers), and receive a free M&M's candy of choice. Little Debbie, a maker of sugar-based snack items, offered a free box of any type of Little Debbie snack (e.g., Honey Buns, Oatmeal Creme Pies) when purchasing four boxes of any type of Little Debbie snack (Buy 4, Get 1 Free).

The Buy X, Get 1 Free form of premium represents an *immediate reward* to consumers, and, for manufacturers, this type of premium serves the purpose primarily of *rewarding a brand's loyal customers* or *encouraging trial* from purchasers of competitive brands who are willing to switch in order to save money—availing oneself of a Buy 1, Get 1 Free offer is tantamount to paying half price for each

global focus

Barq's Root Beer and Russian Knickknacks

Barq's root beer is a regional soft drink brand that was founded in New Orleans. Nearly a hundred years after its founding, Barq's remained a small-share brand with a limited advertising and promotion budget. In the early 1990s Barq's decided to promote the brand in commemoration of the 15th anniversary of Elvis Presley's death. Barq's vice president of marketing thought up a great premium idea that would involve purchasing an old Cadillac that Elvis had owned, cutting it into thousands of small pieces, and offering each piece to a different consumer as part of a mail-in premium requiring multiple proofs of purchase of Barq's root beer. There was only one problem with this premium idea: The administrators of the Presley estate demanded a $1 million licensing fee, which exceeded tenfold Barq's budget for the promotion.

Unable to afford this, Barq's marketing vice president scrambled to find a replacement. Just about this time, the Soviet government collapsed. Seeing the news on TV, the vice president hit immediately on the idea of a replacement for the failed Elvis promotion: "The Soviet Union Going Out of Business Sale." Mind you, this had all taken place within a month or less—decision making on the run, so to speak. With a meager $70,000 in his possession, Rick Hill, Barq's marketing vice president, boarded a plane to Russia to purchase ex-Soviet Union memorabilia. Unable to find legitimate businesspeople from whom to purchase ex-Soviet items, Hill turned to members of the Soviet Mafia. Within two weeks he spent the $70,000 acquiring 4,000 pounds of ex-Soviet stuff (Russian nesting dolls, Lenin Day pins, military medals, etc.) that was shipped back to the United States.

Barq's offered one randomly chosen Soviet knickknack with a 12-pack proof of purchase and 50 cents postage and handling charge. This last-minute, desperate promotion achieved incredible results: 5 percent of all consumers eligible for the promotion actually took advantage of it, and sales increased 30 percent versus the comparable period the previous year. This mail-in premium promotion also received the industry's top promotion award for the year. The moral of the story: A creative promotion that is of high topical interest and captures the public's imagination can be extremely successful.

SOURCE: Adapted from Rod Taylor, "From Russia with Root Beer," *Promo,* June 2003, 143–144.

unit. Unlike other forms of premiums, which typically generate relatively low levels of consumer response, Buy X and Get 1 Free promotions are received heartily by consumers due to the immediacy of the reward and the attractive savings.

Self-Liquidating Offers

The name **self-liquidating offers** (known as SLOs by practitioners) reflects that the consumer mails in a stipulated number of proofs of purchase along with sufficient money to cover the manufacturer's purchasing, handling, and mailing costs of the premium item. In other words, consumers pay for the actual cost of the premium; from the manufacturer's perspective the item is *cost-free,* or, in other words, *self-liquidating.* Attractive self-liquidating premiums can serve to enhance a brand's image (cell 6 in Table 17.1)—by associating the brand with a positively valued premium item—and also can encourage repeat purchasing by requiring multiple proofs of purchase to be eligible for the premium offer. Brand managers often use SLOs as a complement to sweepstakes offers. The combination of these two promotions enhances consumer interest in and interaction with the brand.

Gerber employed an SLO promotion when offering the Gerber Keepsake Millennium Cup. With 12 Gerber baby food proofs of purchase and $8.95, consumers received a cup engraved with their child's name and birth date. This item at retail likely would have sold for around $25. Gerber projected that many parents would purchase Gerber products exclusively until they acquired the requisite number of proofs of purchase.

It is noteworthy that very few consumers ever send for a premium. Companies expect only 0.1 percent of self-liquidators to be redeemed. A circulation of 20 million, for example, would be expected to produce only about 20,000 redemptions. Industry specialists generally concur that the most important consideration in developing a self-liquidating offer is that the premium be appealing to the target audience and represent a meaningful value. It is generally assumed that consumers look for a savings of at least 50 percent of the suggested retail price. The *IMC Focus* insert provides an illustration of a valued and highly successful SLO.

Phone Cards

Phone cards represent a rather unique type of premium offer. This form of promotion incentive is classified in Table 17.1 as performing a *repeat-purchasing* objective and providing consumers with a *delayed reward* (cell 4). This is a bit of a simplification as phone cards also are capable of generating trial purchases and reinforcing brand images. Although a variety of phone cards are available, the most common type offers a preset amount of long-distance calling time. Phone cards are lightweight and easy to mail, provide an inexpensive promotional tool, and are

IMC >> i.m.c. focus

A Super-Successful Self-Liquidating Premium Promotion

Consumer goods giant Nabisco needed an exciting promotion that would enhance the image of its various brands among consumers and encourage retailers to provide special display space that would substantially increase sales volume. One of Nabisco's managers came up with the brilliant idea of using autographed baseball trading cards as a self-liquidating premium offer, or SLO. Trading cards are the most popular sports collectible in the United States, and thousands of people are willing to pay $50 or more to have the autograph of famous athletes signed to a trading card. In fact, sports autographs represent a half-billion-dollar business each year in the United States.

The SLO developed by Nabisco executives and its promotion agency was straightforward: Interested consumers were required to mail in two proofs of purchases of any of several Nabisco brands (Oreos, Chips Ahoy, Wheat Thins, and Ritz Crackers) along with $5 and they could get their pick of autographed cards from a lineup of famous Hall of Fame baseball players (Ernie Banks, Bob Gibson, Brooks Robinson, Willie Stargell, etc.). This was an incredible deal for consumers considering autographed cards from these players now are worth over six times the $5 cost.

Interestingly, Nabisco paid these Hall of Fame baseball players $2 for each signed card. However, Nabisco requested 90,000 cards per player, which thus provided them with $220,000 in income—a huge signing task indeed, but one that most people would gladly undertake for earning over $200,000! To assure that the signed cards contained authentic signatures from the player depicted on the card, participants to the promotion received a certificate of authenticity, which partially explains why the cards have increased six times in value.

At a $5 charge for each card, Nabisco was able to self-liquidate the cost of the promotion and to pay for the expense of two promotions that distributed hundreds of thousands of FSI coupons to prospective purchasers of the sponsoring Nabisco brands. The promotion also generated two months of special display space in retail stores for participating Nabisco brands. All in all, this was an extremely successful sales promotion that provided value to consumers and generated increased sales and profits for Nabisco's brands.

SOURCE: Adapted from Rod Taylor, "Signature Event," *Promo*, July 2006, 57–58.

perceived as useful by consumers. Marketers also are able to collect information from consumers, who typically are required to answer a few questions before their cards are activated.

What Makes a Good Premium Offer?

It is undeniable that consumers enjoy gifts, like to receive something for free, and are responsive to offers for premium objects that are attractive and valuable. However, brand managers must be careful to select premiums that are suitable in view of the objectives that are intended to be accomplished during the promotional period. In other words, as previously established, the various forms of premiums serve somewhat different objectives. As always, the choice of premium object and delivery method should be based on an explicit detailing of which objective is to be accomplished. Also, managers must be circumspect in choosing premium items that are compatible with the brand's image and appropriate for the target market.

Price-Offs

Price-off promotions (also called *cents-off* or *price packs*) entail a reduction (typically ranging from 10 to 25 percent) in a brand's regular price. A price-off is clearly labeled as such on the package. This type of promotion is effective when the marketer's objective is: (1) to reward present brand users; (2) to get consumers to purchase larger quantities of a brand than they normally would (i.e., to load them), thereby effectively preempting the competition; (3) to establish a repeat-purchase pattern after initial trial; (4) to ensure that promotional dollars do, in fact, reach consumers (no such assurance is possible with the trade-allowance promotions covered in Chapter 15); (5) to obtain off-shelf display space when such allowances are offered to retailers; or (6) to provide the sales force with an incentive to obtain retailer support. Although price-off promotions perform multiple objectives, this text classifies price-offs as primarily representing a form of *immediate reward* for consumers to encourage *repeat purchasing* (cell 3 in Table 17.1).

Price-offs are unable to reverse a brand's downward sales trend, produce a significant number of new users, or attract as many trial users as samples, coupons, or premium packs. Further, *retailers often dislike price-offs* because they create inventory and pricing problems, particularly when a store has a brand in inventory at both the price-off and the regular prices. Yet despite trade problems, price-offs have strong consumer appeal.

Federal Trade Commission Price-Off Regulations

Manufacturers cannot indiscriminately promote their brands with continuous or near-continuous price-off labeling. To do so would deceive consumers into thinking the brand is on sale when in fact the announced sale price is actually the regular price.

The Federal Trade Commission controls price-off labeling with the following regulations:[4]

1. Price-off labels may only be used on brands already in distribution with established retail prices.
2. There is a limit of three price-off label promotions per year per brand size.
3. There must be a hiatus of at least 30 days between price-off label promotions on any given brand size.
4. No more than 50 percent of a brand's volume over a 12-month period may be generated from price-off label promotions.

5. The manufacturer must provide display materials to announce the price-off label offer.
6. The dealer is required to show the regular shelf price in addition to the new price reflecting the price-off label savings.

Bonus Packs

Bonus packs are extra quantities of a product that a company makes available to consumers at the regular price. Listerine mouthwash provided consumers with a free 250-milliliter bottle along with the purchase of a 1.7-liter bottle. Carnation offered consumers 25 percent more hot cocoa mix at the regular price. Flex-A-Min, a product designed to enhance joint flexibility, offered 33 percent more tablets for free. Electrasol dishwashing powder provided 25 percent more of the product at the regular price. Golf ball manufacturers on occasion reward consumers with an extra pack of three balls when they purchase a dozen.

Table 17.1 classifies this form of promotion as providing consumers with an *immediate reward* and, for manufacturers, primarily serving a *repeat purchase* objective (cell 3). In other words, *present brand users* are the consumers most likely to avail themselves of a bonus offer; hence, receiving a bonus quantity (at no extra price) rewards these consumers for their purchase loyalty and encourages repeat purchasing.

Bonus packs are sometimes used as an *alternative to price-off deals* when the latter are either overused or resisted by the trade. The extra value offered to the consumer is readily apparent and for that reason can be effective in *loading current users* and thereby removing them from the market—a defensive tactic that is used against aggressive competitors.

Games

Promotional games represent a growing form of promotion that is being increasingly used in lieu of sweepstakes and contests. Games provide consumers with an *instant reward* and, for marketers, serve primarily to encourage *repeat purchasing* from existing brand users (cell 3 in Table 17.1). Promotional games are capable of creating excitement, stimulating brand interest, and reinforcing brand loyalty. Many varieties of instant-win games are available online. Simply google (instant-win games) and thousands of entries will appear. Playing games online requires that one provide an e-mail address and perhaps additional address information. These games are designed to increase consumer engagement with the sponsoring brand.

One of the many forms of instant-win games is the placement of winning numbers under package lids. Coca-Cola, for example, offered consumers a chance to win $1 million and a role in a movie from Universal Studios, along with thousands of other smaller prizes, if the consumer opened a can containing winning numbers. V8 vegetable juice had a look-under-the-cap contest in which winners received trips to famous resorts. Note that almost invariably, games are marketed with claims of "instant win" because consumers prefer instant gratification.

Avoiding Snafus

Brand managers and the promotion firms they recruit to execute games have to be extremely careful to ensure that a game does not go awry. There have been a number of celebrated snafus in the conduct of promotional games. For example, due to a printing error, 30,000 residents of Roswell, New Mexico received scratch-off tickets from their local Honda dealer that pronounced each of them a winner of the dealer's $1,000 grand prize. Because the dealer was unable to pay off on the full $30,000,000 liability, the 30,000 "winners" received an apology along with an opportunity to win a $5,000 grand prize or one of twenty $1,000 prizes.[5]

A Pepsi bottler in the Philippines offered a one-million-peso grand prize (which at the time was equivalent to approximately US$36,000) to holders of bottle caps with the number *349* printed on them. To the bottler's (and PepsiCo's) great chagrin, a computer error (by the printer that produced the game numbers) created 500,000 bottle caps with the winning number *349* imprinted—making PepsiCo liable for approximately $18 billion! The botched promotion created mayhem for PepsiCo, including attacks on Pepsi trucks and bottling plants and anti-Pepsi rallies. Pepsi's sales plummeted in the Philippines, and market share fell by nine points. To resolve the problem, PepsiCo paid consumers with winning caps $19 apiece. More than 500,000 Filipinos collected about $10 million. The Filipino justice department excused PepsiCo from criminal liability and dismissed thousands of lawsuits.[6]

The Beatrice Company's Monday Night Football promotion illustrates another failed game. Contestants scratched silver-coated footballs off cards to reveal numbers, hoping to win the prize offered if the numbers on the cards matched the number of touchdowns and field goals scored in the weekly Monday night National Football League game. Game planners intended the chances of getting a match to be infinitesimal. However, to Beatrice's great surprise, a salesman for rival Procter & Gamble (P&G) put in a claim for a great deal more money than Beatrice had planned on paying out. A computer buff, the salesman cracked the game code and determined that 320 patterns showed up repeatedly in the cards. By scratching off just one line, he could determine which numbers were underneath the rest. Knowing the actual number of touchdowns and field goals scored on a particular Monday night, he would start scratching cards until winning numbers were located. He enlisted friends to assist in collecting and scratching the cards. Thousands of cards were collected, mostly from Beatrice salespeople. The P&G salesman and friends identified 4,000 winning cards worth $21 million in prize money! Beatrice discontinued the game and refused to pay up.[7]

This section would be incomplete without discussing a major scandal that rocked the promotions industry in 2001. Brand managers for McDonald's restaurants and Simon Marketing, a company hired to run a summer promotion for McDonald's, created a Monopoly-type game that was to provide customers with millions of dollars in promotional prizes. Unfortunately, there was a major problem in the game's execution. An employee in charge of game security at Simon Marketing allegedly stole winning tickets and distributed them to various friends and accomplices, who obtained approximately $13 million in prize money. After learning of the theft and informing the Federal Bureau of Investigation, McDonald's immediately introduced a different promotional game run by another promotional agency so as to make good on its promise to customers and restore its credibility. Apparently, the Simon Marketing employee who ripped off McDonald's had for several years been stealing winning game tickets from other games.[8]

A spokesperson for the Promotion Marketing Association, the trade association for the industry, characterized this debacle as a "black eye" for the promotion marketing industry. The moral is clear: Promotional games can go awry, and brand managers must go to extreme lengths to protect the integrity of the games that are designed to build, not bust, relationships with customers.

Rebates and Refunds

A **rebate** (also called a *refund*) refers to the practice in which manufacturers give *cash discounts* or reimbursements to consumers who submit proofs of purchase. Unlike coupons, which the consumer redeems at retail checkouts, rebates are mailed to manufacturers (or their representatives) with proofs of purchase, and, unlike premiums, the consumer receives a cash refund with a rebate rather than a gift item. Marketers are fond of rebates because they provide an alternative to the use of coupons and stimulate increased consumer purchasing. Rebate offers can reinforce brand loyalty, provide the sales force with something to talk about, and enable the manufacturer to flag the package with a potentially attractive deal.

CPG companies are major users of rebates. For example, Campbell's offered a $5 rebate to customers who provided cash register receipts indicating they had bought 10 cans of Campbell's soups and had also purchased a DVD for the movie, *Shrek the Third.* Hartz Ultra Guard (for killing fleas and ticks) offered a $3 rebate on that item. For CPG brands, rebates require consumers to acquire rebate slips at retail sites or to go online to designated Web sites and download appropriate forms. There is some evidence indicating that consumers are more responsive to online than off-line (via traditional retail outlets) rebate and refund offers.[9]

Durable goods companies, especially manufacturers of electronic items, are increasing their use of rebates. Automobile companies are among the major users (Figure 17.2). For example, General Motors offered a $7,500 rebate on its premium-priced Cadillac XLR.[10] European manufacturers are increasingly using rebates when marketing their cars in the United States.

Rebates offer consumers *delayed* rather than immediate value, since the consumer must wait to receive the reimbursement. In using these programs, manufacturers achieve *customer-holding objectives* by encouraging consumers to make multiple purchases (in the case of CPG items) or by rewarding previous users with cash discounts for again purchasing the manufacturer's brand. Rebate offers also can attract switchers from competitive brands who avail themselves of attractive discount offers.

Phantom Discounts

Perhaps the major reason manufacturers are using rebates more now than ever is that many consumers *never bother to redeem them.* Thus, when using rebates, manufacturers get the best of both worlds—they stimulate consumer purchases of rebated items without having to pay out the rebated amount because most consumers do not mail in rebate forms. Hence, rebates can be thought of as a form of *phantom discount.*[11] It is for this reason consumer advocates often condemn manufacturers' use of rebates.

One may wonder why consumers purchase rebated items but then fail to take the time to submit forms to receive the rebate amount. Academic research offers an explanation. It appears that at the time of brand choice, consumers tend to exaggerate the benefit to be obtained from a rebate relative to the future effort required to redeem a rebate offer.[12] In other words, it seems that many consumers engage in a form of *self-deception* when purchasing rebated merchandise. They find rebate offers attractive and on that basis decide to purchase particular brands. Yet later on at home they are unwilling to commit the necessary time and effort to send in rebate forms, or simply forget to do so.

Are manufacturers exploiting consumers when offering rebates, or are consumers to be blamed for their own inaction? This should make for interesting class discussion.

Rebate Fraud

Rebate fraud occurs by manufacturers, retailers, and consumers. Manufacturers commit fraud when promoting rebate offers but then failing to fulfill them when consumers submit rebate slips with accompanying proof of purchase. Retailers sometimes advertise attractive rebates but then do not disclose (or disclose only in

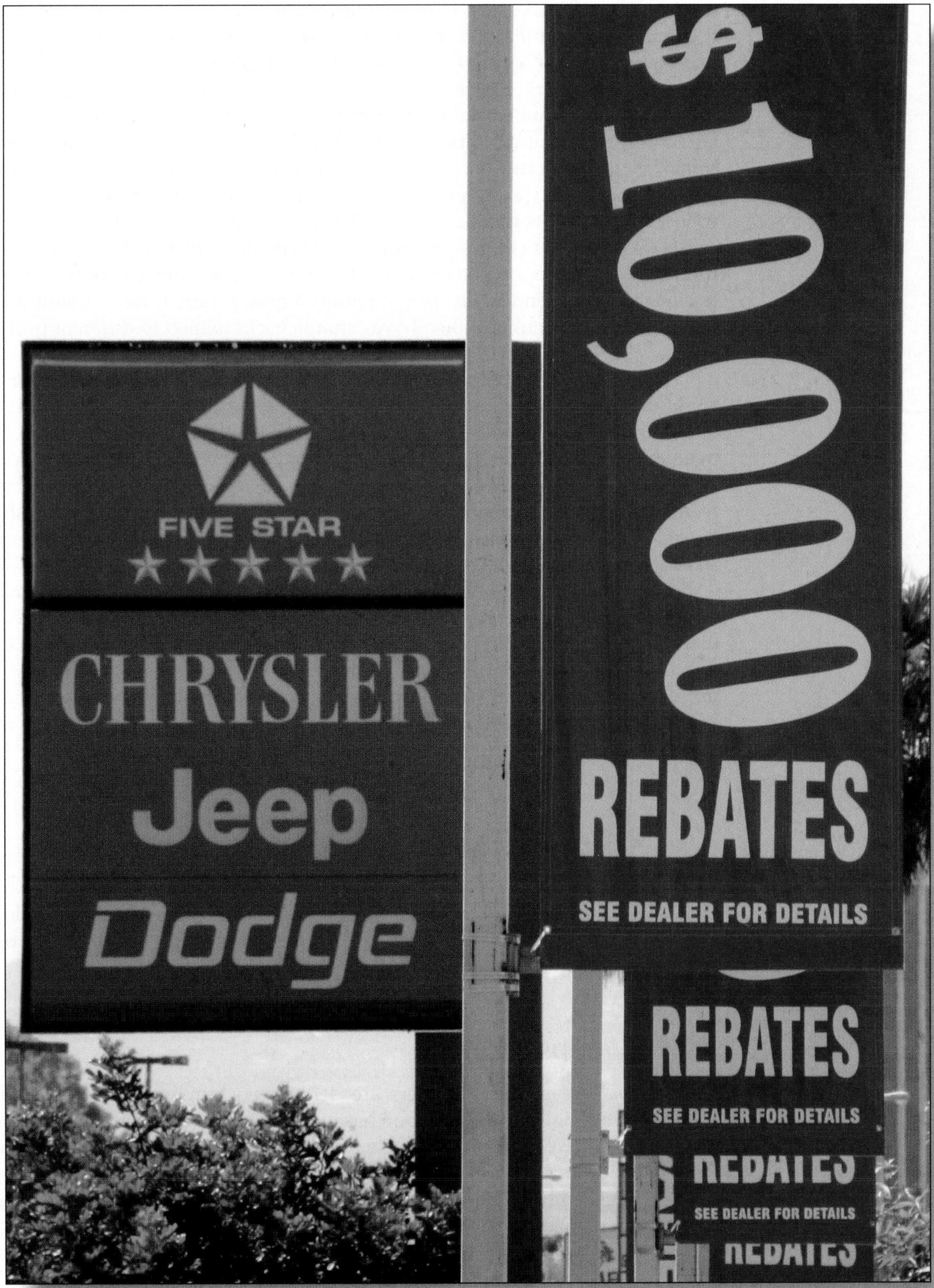

© AP Images/Reed Saxon

Figure 17.2

Automobile Rebate Offers

fine print) that the rebates will not arrive for several months or that the consumer must purchase another item to be eligible for the rebate. For example, a retail advertisement may claim that a computer has a $400 rebate offer but neglect to mention that the consumer must sign up for three years of Internet service to receive it.[13]

It is not just marketers that engage in misleading or fraudulent rebating practices. Consumers undertake their own form of rebate-related fraud. There is, in fact, a huge amount of fraud associated with bogus claims paid out to "professional" rebaters. Fraud occurs when professionals acquire their own cash registers, generate phony cash-register receipts, and send them on to manufacturers to collect refund checks without making the required product purchases. Other scam artists use computers to design phony UPC symbols, which they mail to manufacturers as evidence of purchases they actually have not made. Of course, these professionals do not send in just single refund requests; rather, they submit requests under multiple names and then have refund checks mailed to different post office boxes.

Two promotions illustrate this fraudulent practice.[14] One manufacturer ran a $3 refund offer requiring submission of a UPC to be eligible for the refund. Three out of four refund requests had the same misprinted UPC number on them. Investigators determined that *Moneytalk*, a former refunding magazine, had misprinted the product's UPC number in one of its issues. In a second case, a manufacturer's rebate forms were available in stores before its product reached store shelves. Nonetheless, this did not deter 2,200 rebate requests from flowing in immediately—all accompanied by bogus cash-register receipts and UPC numbers.

Postal authorities and marketers are taking aggressive efforts to curtail refunding fraud. Many marketers are beginning to state on their refund and rebate forms that they will not send checks to post office boxes. Others are stating that checks will be mailed only to the return address listed on the envelope. Because organized refund redeemers use computers to generate mailing and return address labels, manufacturers are further deterring fraud by stipulating on their refund and rebate forms that printed mailing labels are prohibited.

Figure 17.3

Illustration of a Sweepstakes Offer

© Courtesy of Bayer HealthCare LLC, Consumer Care Division

Sweepstakes and Contests

Sweepstakes and contests are widely used. Although sweepstakes (or sweeps) and contests differ in execution, both offer consumers the opportunity to win cash, merchandise, or travel prizes.

Sweepstakes

In a **sweepstakes,** winners are determined purely *on the basis of chance.* Accordingly, proofs of purchase *cannot* be required as a condition for entry. Two sweepstake offers are illustrative. A sweep from Continental Tire (Figure 17.3) encourages consumers to purchase four tires to get a Magellan RoadMate GPS unit and a chance to win a car, bike, camera, or other prizes. A sweep from Resolve carpet- and laundry-stain removing products (Figure 17.4) provides entrants the opportunity to win new appliances and house cleaning services for six months. Further details are available at Resolve's Web site. Note in both figures that coupon offers are provided in addition to the sweepstakes. As described later in this chapter, this form of dual promotion is known as an *overlay* promotion—one promotion "laid" on top of another.

Sweepstakes represent a very popular promotional tool. Approximately three quarters of packaged-goods marketers use sweepstakes, and nearly one third of households participate in at least one sweepstakes every year.[15] Compared with many other sales promotion techniques, sweepstakes are relatively inexpensive, simple to execute, and are able to accomplish a variety of marketing objectives. In addition to reinforcing a brand's positioning and image, well-designed sweepstakes can attract attention to advertisements, promote increased brand distribution at retail, augment sales-force enthusiasm, and reach specific groups through a prize structure that is particularly appealing to consumers in the group.

The effectiveness and appeal of a sweepstakes is generally limited if the sweepstakes is used alone. When tied in with advertising, point-of-purchase displays, and other promotional tools, sweepstakes can work effectively to produce significant results. However, consumer response to sweepstakes is very low, perhaps less than 0.5 percent.[16] Nonetheless, because sweeps require less effort from consumers and generate greater participation, brand managers greatly prefer this form of promotion over contests.

© Reprinted with permission of Reckitt Benckiser, Inc.

Figure 17.4

Illustration of another Sweepstakes Offer

Contests

In a **contest,** the participant must act according to the rules of the contest and may or may not be required to submit proofs of purchase. Illustrative of many contests is one conducted for Hershey's Syrup. Managers of this brand in conjunction with its promotion agency created a contest that appealed to soccer moms and their children. The contest required submission of an action photo of a 6- to 17-year-old child or teen playing soccer along with an original store receipt with the purchase price of a 24-ounce bottle of Hershey's Syrup circled. This promotion associated Hershey's Syrup with soccer, which is enjoyed by millions of families, and also encouraged brand purchasing so as to allow the consumer to participate in the contest and thus become eligible to win any of numerous prizes. A contest such as this fits with the brand's wholesome image and matches the interests of many consumers in its target market.

Contests sometimes require participants to do more than simply send in a photo. For example, in a contest for the Philadelphia Tribune (Figure 17.5), consumers were encouraged to visit the Philly Tribune Web site to enter the contest."[17] Three winners received Blackberry Curve smart phones, and a final winner received an Apple iPhone. No purchase or subscription was necessary to participate in this contest. Dickies, a manufacturer of work clothes, required entrants to nominate someone for the "American Worker of the Year" award and to explain in 100 words or less their reasons why the nominee deserved this recognition. A promotion for Sun-Maid raisins required entrants to create an original recipe that used at least one-half cup of raisins and could be prepared in 20 minutes or less. Pillsbury (maker of dessert baking mixes and frostings) required entrants to explain in 50 words or less, "What upcoming event would you like the Pillsbury Doughboy to help you celebrate and why?" The makers of Motrin IB ran an *Extreme Makeover: Home Edition* contest whereby participants could win an extreme makeover of their homes valued at $50,000. The contest required participants to send a photo of their homes and write an essay regarding why their homes were worthy of an extreme makeover. This contest appropriately related Motrin to the successful

Figure 17.5

Illustration of a Promotional Contest

© AP Images/PRNewsFoto/The Philadelphia Tribune

TV program *Extreme Makeover: Home Edition* in claiming that Motrin IB (Ibuprofen) is *Home Edition*'s "partner in pain relief."

Consumer response to contests is typically lower than even their very low response to sweepstake offers. Nonetheless, if a standard distribution of approximately 40 million FSIs announce a contest and if, say, 0.4 percent of recipients participate in the contest, there will be a total of 160,000 participants. By virtue of participating in the contest, these individuals will have interacted with the brand more than as mere recipients of advertising messages and thus will have an opportunity to bolster their attitude toward the brand.

Online Sweeps and Contests

Online promotional events are growing in importance. Most companies now direct consumers to register online to participate in a sweepstakes or contest. Online sweeps and contests (along with online games) appeal to consumers and also further the interest of brands by creating awareness, building consumer interaction with the brand, and enabling the expansion of a brand's opt-in e-mail database. You can go to the Web sites of some of your favorite brands and see that almost every one offers some form of online sweeps, contest, or game.

Continuity Promotions

Promotions sometimes reward consumers' repeat purchasing of a particular brand by awarding points leading to reduced prices or free merchandise. It is obvious from this description why continuity promotions also are referred to as *reward, loyalty,* or *point* programs. In general, continuity promotions reward consumers for purchasing a particular brand repeatedly or shopping regularly at a particular store. The program need not be based on point accumulation and instead may simply require a certain number of purchases to be eligible for prizes. For example, Budget Rent A Car ran a continuity promotion whereby renters received free Bollé ski goggles with five Budget car rentals.

Frequent-flyer programs by airlines and frequent-guest programs by hotels represent one form of loyalty program. Flyers and hotel guests accumulate points that can be redeemed eventually for free flights and lodging. These programs encourage consumers to stick with a particular airline or hotel to accumulate requisite numbers of points as quickly as possible. Renaissance Hotels, for example, provided 1,000 bonus miles per stay plus three extra miles for every U.S. dollar spent. These points were added to hotel guests' frequent-flyer point totals with designated airlines. Holiday Inn's Priority Club program rewards consumers for stays at Holiday Inn and at other hotels the company, InterContinental Hotels Group (IHG), owns. Priority Club members redeem these points for free stays at Holiday Inn or at other IHG hotels. IHG's Web site claims that in one 4-year period members redeemed over 50 billion points worth \$340 million.[18]

Consumer goods companies are increasingly using a variety of loyalty programs. For example, Purina, a marketer of pet foods, has a program aimed at its Pro Club members that enable them to earn Purina Points when clipping and mailing in "weight circles" from bags of participating Purina brand dog foods. These points can be redeemed for rewards such as rebate checks (used for future purchases of Purina products), checks for veterinary services, and gift certificates for restaurants and travel.[19]

Consumers who are already loyal to a brand that offers a point program or other continuity plan are rewarded for what they would have done anyway—namely, buy a preferred brand on a regular basis. In such a case, a point program does *not* encourage repeat purchasing, although it can serve to cement an already strong relation with the customer. Conversely, point programs can encourage consumers whose loyalty is divided among several brands to purchase more frequently the brand that awards promotion points or rewards repeat purchases in some other fashion. This is perhaps where continuity programs have the greatest value.

Overlay and Tie-In Promotions

Discussion to this point has concentrated on individual sales promotions. In practice, promotions often are used in combination to accomplish objectives that could not be achieved by using a single promotional tool. Furthermore, these techniques, individually or in conjunction with one another, are often used to promote simultaneously two or more brands either from the same company or from different firms.

The simultaneous use of *two or more sales promotion techniques* is called an **overlay,** or *combination,* program. The *simultaneous promotion of multiple brands in a single promotional effort* is called a **tie-in,** or *group,* promotion. *Overlay* refers to the use of multiple promotional tools, whereas *tie-in* refers to the promotion of multiple brands from the same or different companies. Overlay programs and tie-ins often are used together, as the following sections illustrate.

Overlay Programs

Media clutter, as noted repeatedly in past chapters, is an ever-present problem facing marketing communicators. When used individually, consumers may never notice promotion tools (particularly coupons). A combination of tools—such as the use of a coupon offer with another promotional device (e.g., a sweepstakes or contest as shown in Figures 17.3, 17.4, and 17.5)—increases the likelihood that consumers will attend to a message and process the promotion offer. In addition, the joint use of several techniques in a well-coordinated promotional program equips the sales force with a strong sales program and provides the trade with an attractive incentive to purchase in larger quantities (in anticipation of enhanced consumer response) and to increase display activity.

Tie-In Promotions

Growing numbers of companies use tie-ins (group promotions) to generate increased sales, to stimulate trade and consumer interest, and to gain optimal use of their promotional budgets. Tie-in promotions are cost-effective because the cost is shared among multiple brands. A tie-in involves two or more brands from the same company (Kellogg's cereals in Figure 17.6) (an *intra*company tie-in) or from different companies (*inter*company tie-ins). Figure 17.7 demonstrates an intercompany tie-in promotion between Caribou Coffee and Apple® iTunes® and iPod®.

Tie-in relationships between *complementary* brands from different companies are being used with increasing regularity. For example, the complementarity between Dole (Dole Food Company, Inc.) bananas

Figure 17.6

Illustration of an Intracompany Tie-In Promotion

© Lon C. Diehl/Photo Edit

© AP Images/PRNewsFoto/Caribou Coffee

Figure 17.7

Illustration of an Intercompany Tie-In Promotion

and Reese's (The Hershey Company) toppings can be shown with a coupon that might indicate purchasers of two bottles of Reese's peanut butter toppings can receive up to two pounds of Dole bananas free. In addition to achieving strategic marcom objectives, tie-ins represent a cost-efficient promotion because multiple brands—from the same company or from different companies—share the cost of producing and distributing the FSIs that promote the brands.

Implementation Problems

Tie-in promotions are capable of accomplishing useful objectives, but not without potential problems. Promotion *lead time*—the amount of time required to plan and execute a promotion—is lengthened because two or more entities have to coordinate their separate promotional schedules. Furthermore, creative conflicts and convoluted messages may result from each partner trying to receive primary attention for its product or service.

To reduce problems as much as possible and to accomplish objectives, it is important that: (1) the profiles of each partner's customers be similar with regard to pertinent demographic or other consumption-influencing characteristics; (2) the partners' images reinforce each other (e.g., Reese's and Dole both are well-known brands with images of consistent high quality); and (3) the partners be willing to cooperate rather than imposing their own interests to the detriment of the other partner's welfare.

Retailer Promotions

Discussion has thus far focused on manufacturer promotions that are directed at consumers. Retailers also design promotions for their present and prospective customers. These retailer-inspired promotions are created to increase store traffic, offer shoppers attractive price discounts or other deals, and build customer loyalty.

Retail Coupons

Couponing is a favorite promotion among many retailers in the grocery, drug, and mass-merchandise areas of business. Some grocery retailers hold special "coupon days" when they redeem manufacturer coupons at double or even triple their face value. For example, a grocery store on a "triple-coupon day" would deduct $1.50 from the consumer's bill when he or she submits a manufacturer's coupon with a face value of 50 cents. Retailers typically limit their double- or triple-discount offers to manufacturer coupons having face values of 99 cents or less.

Retailers outside the grocery industry frequently use coupons. For example, Bed Bath & Beyond, a well-known home accessories retailer, regularly offers coupons worth 20 percent off most items carried in the store. Ashley Furniture, which markets itself as the number-one home furniture brand in North America, offered coupons in one promotion ranging in value from $50 to $250. The $50-value coupon was redeemable on any purchase ranging from $499 to $999, whereas the $250-value coupon could be redeemed only on purchases of $2,500 or more.

Frequent-Shopper Programs

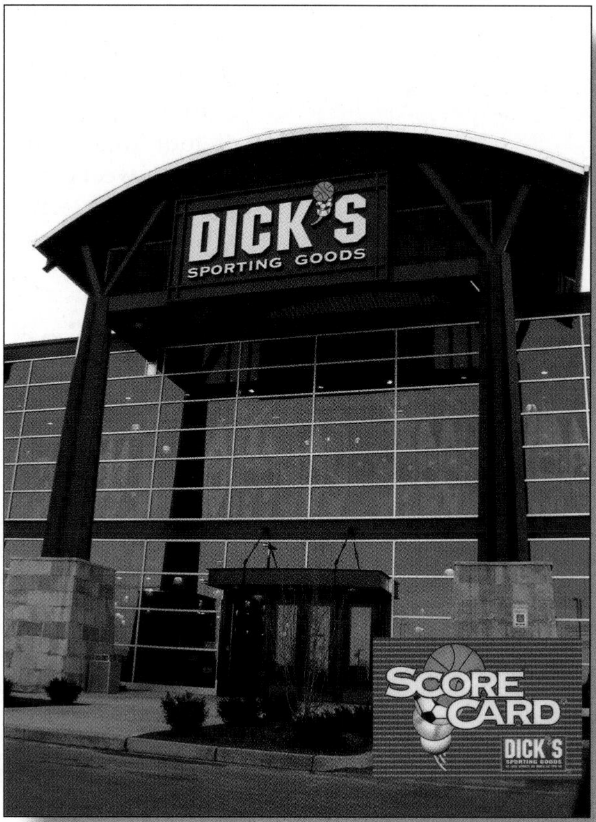

© Susan Van Etten

A number of retailers offer their customers frequent-shopper cards that entitle shoppers to discounts on select items purchased on any particular shopping occasion. For example, in a Wednesday advertising flyer, one grocery retailer offered its cardholders savings such as \$2.99 on the purchase of two Mrs. Paul's fish fillets, \$1.25 when buying two cans of Minute Maid juice, and \$1.70 with the purchase of Freschetta pizza. Customers receive these savings on submitting their frequent-shopper cards to checkout clerks, who scan the card number and deduct savings from the shopper's bill when discounted items are scanned. These frequent-shopper cards encourage repeat purchasing from a particular retail chain. Because they are designated with labels such as "VIC" (very important customer), they also serve to elevate the shopper's sense of importance to a store. Finally, frequent-shopper card programs provide retailers with valuable databases containing information on shopper demographics and purchase habits.

In another form of loyalty program, some retailers provide customers with plastic cards that are presented to clerks for automatic scanning with every purchase made from that particular store. For example, Dick's Sporting Goods is a retail chain that specializes, as the name suggests, in a wide variety of sporting goods products. Dick's has a "Score Card" program whereby customers submit their cards with every purchase and accumulate points enabling discounts on subsequent purchases. This is a perfect application of a loyalty, or rewards, program—one in which earning points fits perfectly with the point-scoring athletic games whose equipment and apparel is featured in this retail chain's stores.

Special Price Deals

Many retailers use a variety of creative ways of reducing prices on a temporary basis. For example, Goody's—a regional discount apparel chain—has run a price-discounting promotion in which paper shopping bags are mailed out to shoppers—paper bags of the sort that one sees in grocery stores. The bags are printed with statements such as, "20% off everything you can stuff in this bag." The deal is offered on a one-day-only basis and then repeated again at different times throughout the year. The value of a special-pricing program such as this is that it creates excitement on the part of customers, while at the same time not requiring blanket price reductions for all customers—just those who bring their bags to the store on the designated date.

Samples and Premiums

Sampling is another form of retailer-based sales promotion that is in wide use. Although many instances of store sampling represent joint programs between stores and manufacturers, retailers are sampling their own store or private label products increasingly. Club stores such as Costco are famous for providing a variety of food samples on any given purchase occasion. Such promotions serve to increase sales of the sampled items and also possess an entertainment-type value that enhances the shopping experience.

Stores also offer premiums to encourage purchases of select items. For example, Quiznos offered a free six-inch submarine sandwich when customers purchased chips and a medium fountain drink. Publix, a regional grocery chain known for its outstanding service, conducted a promotion in which consumers purchasing any of four well-known national brands (e.g., Heinz organic ketchup, Del Monte organic sweet peas) would receive a free equivalent item from Publix's GreenWise private label—e.g., buy Heinz organic ketchup and receive a free bottle of GreenWise organic ketchup.

Evaluating Sales Promotion Ideas

Numerous alternatives are available to manufacturers and retailers when planning sales promotions. There also are a variety of objectives that effective promotion programs can achieve. The combination of numerous alternatives and diverse objectives leads to a staggering array of possibilities. A systematic procedure for selecting the type of sales promotion is therefore essential. The following sections outline procedures for appraising potential promotions during the idea stage and then, after they have run, for evaluating their effectiveness.

A Procedure for Evaluating Promotion Ideas

The following straightforward, three-step procedure directs a brand manager in determining which promotion ideas and approaches have the best chance of succeeding.[20]

Step 1: Identify the Objectives

The most basic yet important step toward developing a successful promotion is the clear identification of the specific objective(s) to be accomplished. Objectives should be specified as they relate both to the trade and to ultimate consumers; for example, objectives may be to generate trial, to load consumers, to preempt competition, to increase display space, and so on.

In this first step, the promotional planner must commit the objectives to writing and state them specifically and in measurable terms. For example, "to increase sales" is too general. In comparison, "to increase display space by 25 percent over the comparable period last year" is a specific and measurable objective.

Step 2: Achieve Agreement

Everyone involved in a brand's marcom program must agree with the objectives developed. Failure to achieve agreement on objectives results in various decision makers (such as the advertising, sales, and brand managers) pushing for different programs because they have different goals in mind. Also, in line with the following step, a promotion program can more easily be evaluated in terms of a specific objective than can a vague generalization.

Step 3: Evaluate the Idea

With specific objectives established and agreement achieved, the following five-point evaluation system can be used to rate alternative sales promotion ideas:

1. *Is the idea a good one?* Every idea should be evaluated against the promotion's objectives. For example, if increasing product trial is the objective, a sample or a coupon would be rated favorably, whereas a sweepstakes would not.
2. *Will the promotion idea appeal to the target market?* A contest, for example, might have great appeal to children but for certain adult groups have disastrous

results. In general, it is critical that the target market be treated as the benchmark against which all proposals should be judged.

3. *Is the idea unique, or is the competition doing something similar?* The prospects of receiving interest from both the trade and consumers depend on developing promotions that are not ordinary. Creativity is every bit as important to the success of promotions as it is with advertising.
4. *Is the promotion presented clearly so that the intended market will notice, comprehend, and respond positively to it?* Sales promotion planners should start with one fundamental premise: Most consumers are unwilling to spend much time and effort figuring out how a promotion works. It is critical to a promotion's success that instructions be user-friendly. Let consumers know easily and clearly what the offer is and how to respond to it.
5. *Is the proposed idea cost-effective?* This requires an evaluation of whether the proposed promotion will achieve the intended objectives at an affordable cost. Sophisticated promotion planners cost out alternative programs and know in advance the likely bottom-line payoff from each promotion option.

Postmortem Analysis

The previous section described a general procedure for evaluating proposed promotion ideas while they are in the planning stage, before actual implementation. It is essential to have a way of evaluating a promotional program after it has been implemented as well. Such evaluation would be useful for future planning purposes, especially if the evaluation becomes part of brand management's "institutional memory" rather than discarded shortly after the evaluation is completed. A seasoned practitioner in the promotion industry has proposed judging completed promotion programs in terms of five characteristics: expense, efficiency, execution ease, equity enhancement, and effectiveness.[21]

Expense

A promotion program's expense is the sum of the direct outlays invested in the promotion. Typical cost elements include: the expense to create the promotion; costs to advertise it; and payouts for coupons redeemed, refunds paid, game prizes awarded, samples given away, and so on.

Efficiency

Efficiency represents a promotion's *cost per unit moved.* The efficiency metric is calculated simply by dividing the total cost of the completed promotion by the number of units sold during the promotional period.

Execution Ease

This represents the total time and effort that went into the planning and execution of a promotion. Obviously, everything else held constant, promotions that require less time and effort are preferred.

Equity Enhancement

This criterion involves a subjective assessment of whether a promotion has enhanced a brand's image or possibly even detracted from it. A sweepstakes offer, for example, may serve to enhance a brand's equity by associating it with, say, a prestigious grand prize. A self-liquidating premium may accomplish the same goal. Comparatively, a game may be inappropriate for some brands by virtue of appearing tacky. As always, the evaluation depends on the brand positioning and target-market situation.

Effectiveness

A promotion's effectiveness can best be assessed by determining the total units of the promoted item that were sold during the promotional period.

Combining the Individual Factors

Having evaluated a completed promotion program along the five "E" dimensions, it is desirable that the individual evaluations be combined into a *single score.* This can be done simply enough by using a straightforward model that weights each of the five factors in importance and then summates the products of each factor's score by its weight. A model such as the following could be used:

$$\textbf{Program } j\textbf{'s Score} = \sum_{i=1}^{5} (\mathrm{E}_{ij} \times \mathrm{W}_i)$$

where,

Program j = A just-completed promotional program (one of many potential promotional programs that have been run for a brand and subsequently evaluated).

E_{ij} = Evaluation of the jth promotional program on the ith evaluation factor (i.e., the efficiency factor, the executional ease factor, etc.).

W_i = Weight, or relative importance, of the ith factor in determining promotion success. (Note that the weight component is subscripted just with an i, and not also a j, because the weights are constant across program evaluations. Comparatively, evaluations of the individual factors, E_{ij}, require a j subscript to reflect the likelihood of varying evaluations across different promotional programs.)

Table 17.2 illustrates this straightforward model.[22] Consider a company that has run three promotional programs during a particular year. On completion, each program was evaluated with respect to the five evaluative criteria (expense, efficiency, etc.) on 10-point scales, with 1 indicating poor performance and 10 reflecting an excellent execution on each evaluative criterion. Notice also in Table 17.2 that the five criteria have been weighted as follows: Expense = .2, Efficiency = .1, Execution Ease = .1, Equity Enhancement = .3, and Effectiveness = .3. These weights sum to 1 and reflect the relative importance *to this particular brand manager* of the five factors. (Relative importance of these factors will obviously vary across different brands, depending on each brand's image, the company's financial standing, and so on.)

Given this particular set of weights and evaluations, it can be concluded that program 1 was the least successful of the three promotions, whereas program 3 was the most successful (see Table 17.2). Brand managers can thus archive these evaluations for reference. Eventually, norms can be established for specifying the average effectiveness level different types of promotions (samples, coupon programs, rebates, etc.) achieve.

Table 17.2

Evaluation of Three Completed Promotional Programs

Program *j*	Expense *Weight* = .2	Efficiency *Weight* = .1	Execution Ease *Weight* = .1	Equity Enhancement *Weight* = .3	Effectiveness *Weight* = .3	Total Score
Program 1	7	6	7	5	9	6.9
Program 2	9	8	8	7	8	7.9
Program 3	8	9	8	10	9	9.0

Of course, Table 17.2 is purely illustrative. However, in actual promotion situations it is possible for brand managers to evaluate promotions formally, provided that the procedure for evaluating each criterion is clearly articulated, systematically implemented, and consistently applied to all promotions that are appraised. The point to be appreciated is that the model on which Table 17.2 is based is suggestive of how promotional programs *can* be evaluated.

Intelligent brand managers must develop their own models to accommodate their brand's specific needs, but the point to be emphasized is that this can be accomplished with the application of thought and effort. The alternative to having a formalized evaluation system, such as the one proposed here, is simply to run promotion events and then never to evaluate their success. Can you imagine as a student what it would be like to take courses but never to receive grades, never to be evaluated? How would you know how well you have done? How would your institution know whether grading standards have changed over the years? How would prospective employers know how well you performed in college compared with other job applicants? Like it or not, evaluation is essential. Good business practice requires it. The issue is not whether to evaluate promotions but how to do it in a valid and reliable manner.

Summary

This chapter focused on consumer-oriented promotions other than sampling and couponing. Specific topics addressed included the use of product premiums, price-off promotions, bonus packs, games, rebates and refunds, sweepstakes and contests, and continuity programs.

The discussion of premiums included the various forms of premium offers: free-with-purchase premiums; mail-in offers; in-, on-, and near-pack premiums, including Buy X, Get 1 Free offers; self-liquidating offers; and phone cards as a special form of premium. Also described were the specific conditions necessary to execute a successful premium promotion.

Price-off promotions, which typically entail a reduction ranging from 10 to 25 percent of a brand's regular price, were described as a form of sales promotion that provides consumers with an immediate reward and serves marketers by encouraging repeat purchasing. The Federal Trade Commission's specific regulations regarding price-off promotions were presented.

Bonus packs provide consumers with extra quantities of a promoted brand for free (e.g., 25 percent more than the regular size). This form of promotion represents an immediate reward for consumers and serves to encourage repeat purchasing by rewarding consumers for their loyalty to a brand.

Games are frequently used as a means of increasing consumer enthusiasm and involvement with a brand, and in so doing perform a repeat-purchasing function by providing consumers with an instant reward. The implementation of games is fraught with the potential for snafus, so brand managers and their promotion agencies must exercise caution when using this form of promotion.

CPG and durable-goods companies use rebate and refund programs as a means of offering consumers a cash discount—but, of course, only if they go to the effort of redeeming the ebate offer. Marketers are fond of rebates because they provide an alternative to the use of coupons and stimulate consumer purchase behavior. Rebate offers can reinforce brand loyalty, provide the sales force with something to talk about, and enable the manufacturer to flag the package with a potentially attractive deal. Because most consumers never redeem rebates, this form of promotion is referred to as a phantom discount. Consumers, in a sense, self-deceive themselves in buying a brand to take advantage of the rebate offer but then do not undertake the necessary effort to redeem the rebate within the period allotted by the brand marketer.

Both sweepstakes and contests offer consumers the opportunity to win cash, merchandise, or travel prizes. Unlike other forms of sales promotions, sweeps and contests serve primarily image-enhancement purposes rather than generating trial usage or encouraging repeat-purchase behavior. Where sweeps require no effort on the part of the consumer other than mere entry via mail or more frequently online, contests necessitate that the consumer write an essay or perform another function. Sweeps generate higher responses from consumers than contests and thus are generally preferred by brand managers and promotion agencies.

Continuity promotions are used by many marketers to encourage brand loyalty and repeat-purchase behavior. These include the ubiquitous frequent-flyer programs offered by airlines, frequent-guest offerings from hotels, and many variants of these well-known programs that are offered to encourage consumers to continue purchasing a brand so as to accumulate points that eventually can be redeemed to receive some form of reward.

Overlay and tie-in promotions involve the use of two or more sales promotion techniques in combination with one another (an overlay, or combination, program) or the simultaneous promotion of multiple brands in a single promotional effort (a tie-in, or group, promotion). Both types of joint promotions are used as a means of spreading promotional dollars among multiple brands or multiple companies and achieving greater impact from every promotional offering.

The chapter concluded by discussing various forms of retailer-driven promotions and procedures for testing promotions, whether undertaken by manufacturers or retailers. First discussed was a three-step procedure for testing promotion ideas prior to their implementation; then described was a method for conducting a postmortem analysis of completed promotions. This latter analysis involves evaluating what can be referred to as the five "E" factors related to promotion success: expense, efficiency, execution ease, equity enhancement, and effectiveness.

Discussion Questions

1. Present a position on the following statement (voiced by a student who read a previous edition of this textbook): "I can't understand why in Table 17.1 mail-in premiums are positioned as accomplishing just a trial-impact function. It would seem that this form of promotion also accomplishes repeat-purchasing objectives."
2. Your company markets hot dogs, bologna, and other processed meats. You wish to offer a self-liquidating premium that would cost consumers approximately $25, would require five proofs of purchase, and would be appropriately themed to your product category during the summer months. Your primary market segment consists of families with school-age children crossing all socioeconomic strata. Suggest two premium items and justify your choices.
3. What is the purpose of the Federal Trade Commission's price-off regulations?
4. Compare bonus packs and price-off deals in terms of consumer impact.
5. How can sales promotion reinforce a brand's image? Is this a major objective of sales promotion?
6. Compare sweepstakes, contests, and games in terms of how they function and their relative effectiveness.
7. Your company markets antifreeze. Sales to consumers take place in a very short period, primarily September through December. You want to tie in a promotion between your brand and the brand of another company that would bring more visibility to your brand and encourage retailers to provide more shelf space. Recommend a partner for this tie-in promotion and justify the choice.
8. Have you participated in online promotions, and, if so, what has been your experience? Considering just a single online promotion that you participated in and considering yourself representative of the brand's target market, do you think the promotion accomplished its objective?
9. What are your thoughts regarding the future of online promotions?
10. Visit a local grocery store and identify five instances of sales promotions. Describe each promotion and comment on the objectives that promotion was intended to accomplish for the sponsoring brand or for the retailer.
11. Have you ever participated in some form of loyalty program? What has been your experience? For example, do you think the program served to increase your repeat business with the sponsoring brand?

End Notes

1. This description is adapted from Amy Johannes, "What Now?" *Promo,* April 2007, 30–34.
2. Patricia Odell, "Inventive Incentives," *Promo,* September 2006, 33–40.
3. Priya Raghubir, "Free Gift with Purchase: Promoting or Discounting the Brand?" *Journal of Consumer Psychology* 14 (1 & 2), 2004, 181–186.
4. *Code of Federal Regulations Title 16,* Volume 1, Part 502 Revised as of January 1, 2000, http://www.ftc.gov/os/statutes/fpla/part502.shtm (accessed May 5, 2008); *Consumer Promotion Seminar Fact Book* (New York: Association of National Advertisers, n.d.), 7.
5. Jean Halliday, "Honda Dealer Gets into Ad Accident," *Advertising Age,* July 23, 2007, 3.
6. Glenn Heitsmith, "Botched Pepsi Promotion Prompts Terrorist Attacks," *Promo,* September 1993, 10.
7. Laurie Baum, "How Beatrice Lost at Its Own Game," *BusinessWeek,* March 2, 1987, 66.
8. Bob Sperber and Karen Benezra, "A Scam to Go?" *Brandweek,* August 27, 2001, 4, 10; Kat MacArthur, "McSwindle," *Advertising Age,* August 27, 2001, 1, 22, 23; Donald Silberstein, "Managing Promotional Risk," *Promo,* October 2001, 57; "Arch Enemies," *Promo,* December 2001, 17.
9. "Walking the Tightrope," *Promo,* March 2001, 48–51.
10. Jonathan Welsh, "Auto Makers Pile on Buyer Incentives," *The Wall Street Journal,* September 11, 2007, D1.
11. William M. Bulkeley, "Rebates' Appeal to Manufacturers: Few Consumers Redeem Them," *Wall Street Journal Online,* February 10, 1998, http://www.online.wsj.com.
12. Dilip Soman, "The Illusion of Delayed Incentives: Evaluating Future Effort-Money Transactions," *Journal of Marketing Research* 35 (November 1998), 427–437.
13. Ira Teinowitz and Tobi Elkin, "FTC Cracks Down on Rebate Offers," *Advertising Age,* July 3, 2000, 29.
14. Kerry J. Smith, "Postal Inspectors Target Rebate Fraud," *Promo,* April 1994, 13.
15. "Healthy, Wealthy, and Wiser," *Promo's 8th Annual SourceBook 2001,* 38–39.
16. Shari Brickin, "Stupid vs. Strategic Sweeps," *Promo,* July 2007, 61–62.
17. For discussion of the consumer psychology underlying testimonials, see Terence A. Shimp, Stacy Wood, and Laura Smarandescu, "Self-generated Advertisements: Testimonials and the Perils of Consumer Exaggeration," *Journal of Advertising Research* 47 (December 2007), 453–461.
18. http://www.ihgplc.com/files/pdf/factsheets/factsheet_priorityclub.pdf (accessed May 7, 2008).
19. http://www.purinaproclub.com (accessed May 6, 2008).
20. Adapted from Don E. Schultz and William A. Robinson, *Sales Promotion Management* (Lincolnwood, Ill.: NTC Business Books, 1986), 436–445.
21. Sara Owens, "A Different Kind of E-marketing," *Promo,* May 2001, 53–54.
22. This table is an adaptation of ibid., 53.

CHAPTERS

18

Marketing-Oriented Public Relations and Word-of-Mouth Management

19

Event and Cause Sponsorships

20

Signage and Point of Purchase Communications

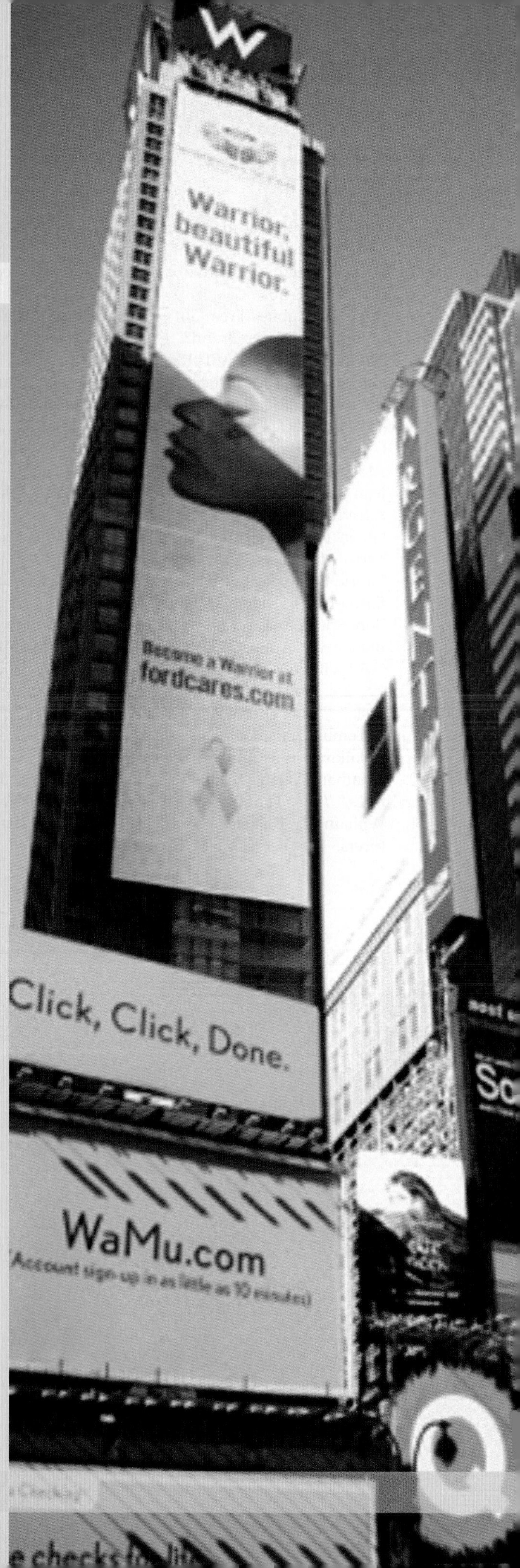

Part 5
Other Marcom Tools

Part Five includes three chapters that examine marcom tools that are less prominent than mass-media advertising and sales promotions but nonetheless play important roles in persuading consumers and influencing their behavior. *Chapter 18* examines the topic of marketing-oriented public relations along with word-of-mouth influence. Covered in this chapter is the historically entrenched practice of reactive public relations along with the more recent practice of proactive public relations. A special section is devoted to negative publicity, including the issue of how to handle rumors and urban legends. Also covered in Chapter 18 are the related topics of managing word-of-mouth influence and generating buzz for brands.

Chapter 19 examines event- and cause-oriented sponsorships. Coverage includes discussion of the specific factors that a company should consider when selecting an event to sponsor—factors such as image match-up, target audience fit, clutter, and economic viability. The benefits of cause-oriented marketing are detailed, and factors that should be considered when selecting a cause to support are reviewed.

Chapter 20 examines two important aspects of firms' marcom programs that typically receive little coverage in marketing communications texts: out-of-store signage (both off- and on-premises signage) and in-store signage in the form of point-of-purchase communications. Billboard advertising is the major out of home (OOH) medium, and chapter coverage presents the various strengths and limitations of this form of advertising. Also described is how OOH audience size and characteristics are measured along with a case study of billboard effectiveness. A unique section is devoted to the use of store signage to attract attention and draw customers to retail businesses.

The final topic treated in Chapter 20 is point-of-purchase (P-O-P) advertising. The point-of-purchase is the critical point where the brand name, logo, and package come face to face with the customer. Expanded investment in this marcom component is explained in terms of the valuable functions that P-O-P performs for consumers, manufacturers, and retailers. The chapter devotes considerable attention to the various forms of P-O-P communications, presents results from the POPAI Consumer Buying Habits Study, and provides evidence regarding the impact displays can have on increasing a brand's sales volume.

18

Marketing-Oriented Public Relations and Word-of-Mouth Management

There are few things in life people find more appalling than rats. Imagine the disgust experienced upon viewing a televised scene of multiple rats running around a restaurant. That restaurant happened to be a KFC/Taco Bell store located in the Greenwich Village section of New York City. Following a call to its tip line from a disgruntled consumer, New York television station WNBC first reported the rats-running-wild story on its early morning news program. The initial response in a joint statement issued by KFC and Taco Bell (both restaurant chains owned by Yum Brands) was that the incident is totally unacceptable but that it is isolated to a single restaurant that would not be allowed to reopen until it has been sanitized.

One might think: "That should do it. The company has acknowledged the problem and proposed a solution—close the store until it receives a clean bill of health." Unfortunately, in a world of YouTube and high-speed Internet connection, no problem is isolated and limited to a single store once it is broadcast worldwide through blogs linked to other blogs. A spokesperson for Nielsen BuzzMetrics, which monitors situations such as this, put it in these terms: "In the world of fast food, hygiene is the No. 1 talk driver, and rats take it to food-hygiene-on-steroids level. Rats are Defcon 5."[1] In fact, shortly after the story appeared on WNBC-TV more than 1,000 blogs had cited or spread the story along with the footage of rats scurrying around the restaurant.

Prior to the advent of the Internet, stories such as this would have died rather quickly in the absence of an efficient medium for their initial distribution and continuation. Nowadays, negative news about products and stores is quickly and widely disseminated—especially when it is as profoundly vivid and disgusting as a scene of rats in a restaurant. And, although company officials can claim that this is an isolated event, consumer psychology is such that people

© STEPHEN HILGER/Bloomberg News/Landov

generalize the negative scene to all KFC/Taco Bell restaurants, and all suffer some diminution in brand equity, which requires aggressive public relations efforts to restore KFC/Taco Bell's equity.[2]

Chapter Objectives

After reading this chapter you should be able to:

1 Appreciate the nature and role of marketing public relations (MPR).

2 Discern the differences between proactive and reactive MPR.

3 Comprehend the types of commercial rumors and how to control them.

4 Appreciate the importance of word-of-mouth (WOM) influence.

5 Understand the role of marketing public relations in creating favorable WOM and building brand buzz.

>>Marcom Insight:

Rats in KFC/Taco Bell Restaurant

Introduction

This chapter explores the multiple roles the public relations aspect of an integrated marketing communications program performs. Also examined are word-of-mouth influence and the role of marketing-oriented public relations in creating favorable word of mouth (WOM) and building brand buzz.

Public relations, or PR, is an organizational activity involved with fostering goodwill between a company and its various publics. PR efforts are aimed at various corporate constituencies, including employees, suppliers, stockholders, governments, the public, labor groups, citizen action groups, and consumers. As just described, PR involves relations with *all* of an organization's relevant publics. In other words, most PR activities do *not* involve marketing per se but rather deal with general management concerns. This more encompassing aspect of public relations can be called *general PR*.

Our concern in this chapter is only the narrow aspect of public relations involving an organization's interactions with actual or prospective customers. This marketing-oriented aspect of public relations is called *marketing public relations*, or MPR for short.[3]

MPR is performing an increasingly important marcom function for both B2C and B2B companies. Whereas advertising messages are regarded by consumers as direct attempts to influence their attitudes and behaviors, MPR messages come across not as advertisements but as unbiased reports from journalists. An MPR message in comparison with an advertisement assumes a mantle of *credibility*. MPR messages also are considerably less expensive than advertisements because the airtime or newspaper space is provided free of charge by the newspaper, magazine, radio, television station, or Internet site that transmits the message. Hence, for the dual reasons of high credibility and low expense, MPR messages (and thus the PR departments and PR agencies that produce them) have achieved a more prominent position in firms' IMC efforts.

MPR versus Advertising

The role that PR, or MPR, should play in a firm's marcom program has been a matter of no small debate over the years. Most marcom practitioners and brand managers have historically believed that MPR's role is specialized and limited. Some critics contend that MPR is too difficult to control and measure. However, a provocative book titled *The Fall of Advertising & the Rise of PR* has challenged prevailing beliefs and argued for an expanded role for PR.[4] The book's authors contend that public relations and its major tool, publicity, represent the most important instrument in the marketer's tool bag. The book's thesis is that new products can be introduced with little if any advertising and, instead, that a brand's marketing communicators can get the job done with creative and powerful public relations. The authors use as anecdotal evidence the success of well-known brands such as eBay, PlayStation, Starbucks, The Body Shop, Palm, and BlackBerry—all of which were introduced without large advertising budgets and focused instead on publicity and word-of-mouth buzz.

The authors of *The Fall of Advertising & the Rise of PR* have a point when stating that PR (or what we are calling *MPR*) is invaluable for introducing new products. However, two very important qualifications must be acknowledged: First, all new products cannot, contrary to the authors' omnibus claim, rely on publicity for successful introductions. Considering that most new products are *not* high in uniqueness or visibility, the news media are not interested in presenting free publicity for these mundane products. Only a small subset of products captures the imagination of the media.

Hence, widespread publicity simply is not an option for ordinary products. Marketing communicators therefore must create the news themselves, and that means investing in advertising to create brand awareness and build positive brand images. In short, brand-equity creation via MPR is restricted to that subset of truly unique products and brands. Second, even for those truly unique new products that can benefit from MPR, it is only a matter of time before free publicity no longer is available. At that point, the brand-equity-maintenance responsibility falls squarely on advertising's shoulders. After the newsworthiness wears off, advertising is absolutely necessary to maintain brand interest. MPR can be extremely effective and substantially less costly than advertising, but it is not a panacea. Let us turn now to a deeper exploration of MPR.

Marketing-Oriented Public Relations (MPR)

As noted, MPR is an increasingly important component in companies' marcom programs. A survey of senior marketing managers determined that MPR registers very high for purposes of increasing brand awareness, providing credibility, reaching purchase influencers, and educating consumers.[5]

MPR can be further delineated as involving both proactive and reactive initiatives. **Proactive MPR** is a tool for communicating a brand's merits and typically is used in conjunction with other marcom tools such as advertising and sales promotions. Dictated by a company's marketing objectives, proactive MPR is offensively rather than defensively oriented and opportunity seeking rather than problem solving. **Reactive MPR,** by comparison, describes the conduct of public relations in response to outside influences. It is undertaken as a result of external pressures and challenges brought by competitive actions, shifts in consumer attitudes, or other external influences. Reactive MPR deals most often with influences having *negative consequences* for an organization. Reactive MPR attempts to repair a company's reputation, prevent market erosion, and regain lost sales.

Proactive MPR

The major role of proactive MPR is in the area of product introductions or product revisions. Proactive MPR is integrated with other IMC tools to give a product additional exposure, newsworthiness, and credibility. This last factor, *credibility,* largely accounts for the effectiveness of proactive MPR. Whereas advertising is often suspect—because we question advertisers' motives, knowing they have a personal stake in influencing us—product announcements by a newspaper editor, a television broadcaster, or blogger are notably more believable.

Publicity is the major tool of proactive MPR. Like advertising, the fundamental purposes of marketing-oriented publicity are to enhance a brand's equity in a twofold manner: (1) facilitating brand awareness by increasing recognition and recall of publicity releases and (2) augmenting brand image by forging in customers' minds strong and favorable associations with the brand. Three widely used forms of publicity are product releases, executive-statement releases, and feature articles.

Product releases announce new products, provide relevant information about product features and benefits, and inform interested listeners and readers how to obtain additional information. Product releases are often published in the product section of trade magazines (i.e., publications that cater to specific industries) and in general interest business publications (such as *BusinessWeek, Forbes, Fortune,* and the *Wall Street Journal*), in electronic as well as hard-copy form. Product releases also are reprinted in local and national (e.g., *USA Today*) newspapers.

Increasingly, product releases are made available online via social media such as YouTube and MySpace and by means of blogs and podcasts.

Executive-statement releases are news releases quoting chief executive officers and other corporate executives. Unlike a product release, which is restricted to describing a new or modified product, an executive-statement release may address a wide variety of issues relevant to a corporation's publics, such as:

- Statements about industry developments and trends
- Forecasts of future sales
- Views on the economy
- Comments on research and development or market research findings
- Announcements of new marketing programs the company launches
- Views on foreign competition or global developments
- Comments on environmental issues

Whereas product releases are typically published in the business and product sections of newspapers and magazines along with their online versions, executive-statement releases are published in the news section. This location carries with it a significant degree of credibility. Note that any product release can be converted into an executive-statement release by changing the way it is written.

Feature articles are detailed descriptions of products or other newsworthy programs that a PR firm writes for immediate publication or airing by print or broadcast media or distribution via appropriate Internet sites. Materials such as these are inexpensive to prepare, yet they can provide companies with tremendous access to many potential customers.

Many newspapers often publish feature articles about new products that are of likely interest to the paper's readers. For example, the "do it yourself" section of a local newspaper published a product release for the Skil cordless screwdriver. Although this release appeared to be written by a local columnist, to the trained eye it obviously was a product release prepared by Skil's PR agency and likely was published in dozens, if not hundreds, of local newspapers. The opening paragraph and an accompanying photo of the product immediately captured the reader's attention when stating, "Don't be deceived by the size of Skil's palm-sized cordless screwdriver. The tool has a bigger punch than you'd expect." Later in the release, the do-it-yourselfer's interest was really piqued with the claim "But here's the real beauty of the tool: charge the battery, stick the screwdriver in a drawer, and it will hold the charge for two years. So it's ready to work whenever you are." It is easy to imagine that thousands of readers of this product release searched for a Skil cordless screwdriver on their next trip to their favorite store carrying products such as this.

Reactive MPR

Unanticipated marketplace developments—such as the rats-in-a-restaurant incident described in the chapter-opening *Marcom Insight*—can place an organization in a vulnerable position that demands reactive MPR. In simple terms, bad things happen and unanticipated events sometimes occur that require a public relations response. In general, the most dramatic factors underlying the need for reactive MPR are product defects and failures.

A Sampling of Celebrated Cases

Following is a sampling of negative events that have occurred over the last several decades and received widespread media attention. The ordering is chronological and ranges from the most recent events to an event occurring as far back as the early 1980s.

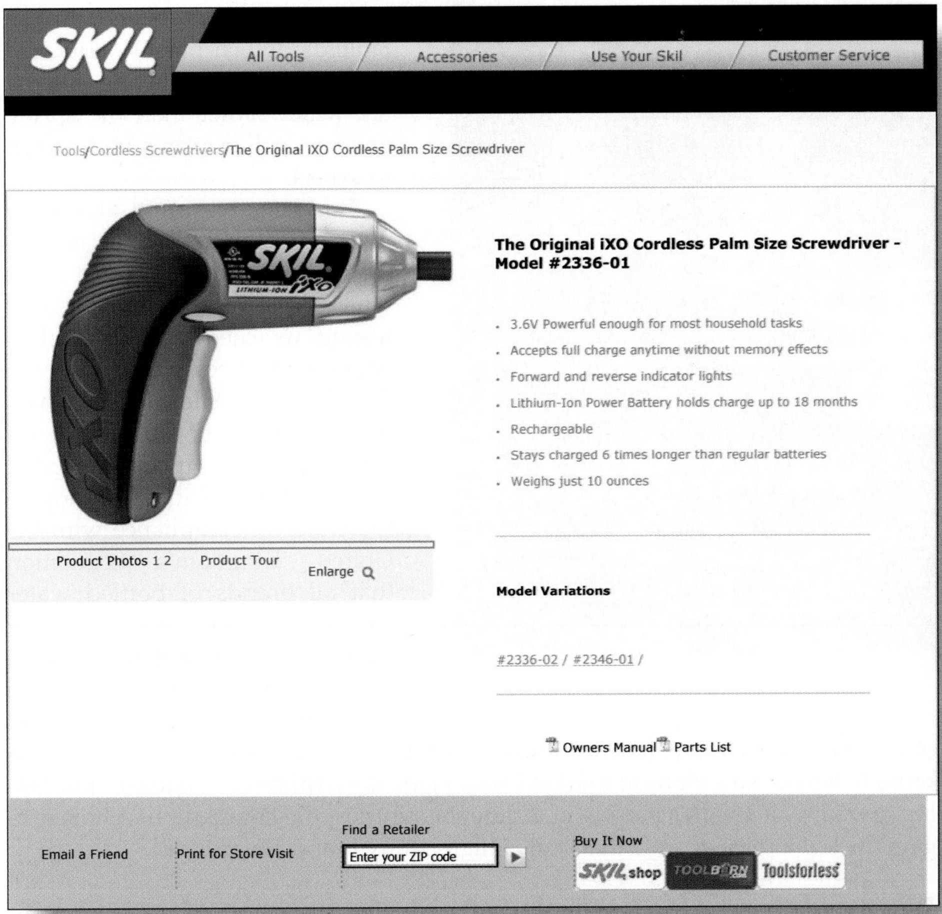

© Courtesy of Bosch

Mattel and Lead Paint In 2007 Mattel Inc. announced three major recalls involving products marketed under its brand names that were manufactured in China. For example, nearly 800,000 Barbie dolls were recalled due to unsafe levels of lead paint.[6]

Menu Brands and Rat Poisoning Another China-sourcing problem resulted in 2007 when over 60 million cans of pet food made by Canada's Menu Brands had to be recalled because they contained wheat imported from China that had traces of rat poison, resulting in the deaths of a number of cats and dogs and deeply disturbing pet owners.[7]

ReNu MoistureLoc Lens-cleaner In 2006 Bausch & Lomb withdrew its ReNu MoistureLoc lens-cleaner brand after allegations that the brand caused potentially blinding cornea infections. Bausch & Lomb was widely criticized after the American public learned that ReNu previously had been withdrawn from two key Asian markets. Crisis-management specialists anticipated that Bausch & Lomb's poor handling of the crisis would extend beyond the MoistureLoc brand and adversely affect other brands in the company's product portfolio.[8]

Dasani in the United Kingdom Unlike European brands of bottled water, such as Evian and Perrier that come from mineral springs, Coca-Cola's Dasani brand is tap water that undergoes a rigid filtering process to remove chlorine and mineral particles. After these are removed, a mineral mix is added to the purified water to provide a fresh taste. Although Dasani is a success in North America, it was new to the European continent as of 2004. Coca-Cola chose the United Kingdom as the launching point for its planned European "invasion." First off, the brand received

© ADAM ROUNTREE/Bloomberg News/Landov

negative press from British tabloids, which harshly criticized Coca-Cola for marketing filtered tap water rather than the spring water that Europeans had grown to expect.

This negative press may have doomed the brand from the outset, but the *coup de grâce* came when Coke recalled Dasani after testing revealed that its bottled water had excessive levels of a chemical (bromate) that increases the risk of cancer after long-term exposure. The problem resulted from adding calcium chloride to the water in compliance with the United Kingdom's regulation that all brands of bottled water contain calcium. Coke's batch of calcium chloride apparently contained unexpectedly high levels of bromide, and excessive levels of bromide's derivative, bromate, formed during production. This incident put a rapid halt to Coke's plans to market Dasani globally. Although capable of marketing a variety of smaller brands in different countries, the company had hoped to gain the economies of scale that only a high-equity brand can provide.[9]

Vioxx and Heart Attacks/Strokes Vioxx, the arthritis and acute-pain medication made by the pharmaceutical giant, Merck & Co., was withdrawn from worldwide distribution in late 2004 after a scientific study revealed that patients taking Vioxx for 18 months or longer had double the risk of suffering heart attacks or strokes compared to a control group taking a placebo. With 2003 Vioxx sales of $2.5 billion, this withdrawal had significant financial implications for Merck, and the negative publicity surrounding Merck's failure to withdraw the product even sooner could have damaging long-term implications for the Vioxx brand and for Merck overall.[10]

Coke, Pepsi, and Pesticide in India An Indian environmental group released a report in 2003 claiming that its laboratory tests revealed that pesticide residues in various soft-drink brands Coke and Pepsi bottled were at least 30 times higher than acceptable limits in Europe. Shortly after the report became public, sales of these two major soft-drink brands fell by over 30 percent. Officials at both companies denied that their pesticide-related standards are any different in India than elsewhere. Nonetheless, India's Supreme Court issued a ruling that both Coke and Pepsi must provide warning labels on their soft-drink containers that indicate the level of pesticide residue. In view of this publicity disaster, both companies faced the challenge of restoring the trust Indian consumers had in these high-equity brands.[11]

Firestone Tires and Vehicle Rollovers Firestone tires—made by Firestone, a U.S. subsidiary of Japan's Bridgestone Corporation—was the focus of negative publicity, especially in 2000, when Ford Explorer sport utility vehicles fitted with Firestone tires experienced numerous rollover accidents. The particular tire in question was eventually recalled, but both Firestone and the Explorer were subjected to intense public scrutiny and even scorn. More will be said about this event in a following section on crisis management.

Coca-Cola and Tainted Carbon Dioxide in Belgium An accident in a Coca-Cola bottling plant in Belgium in 1999 introduced some tainted carbon dioxide into bottles of Coke, and European consumers, mostly in Belgium, reported becoming ill after drinking the product. Coca-Cola's initial response was to deny that its product was at fault, which prompted a public outcry in reaction to this corporate denial and created feelings among consumers that Coca-Cola officials did not care about their health and safety.

Media throughout Europe wrote articles asserting that Coca-Cola products had poisoned consumers. Senior officers at Coca-Cola eventually got the message, and PR people were put to work to offset the considerable damage to Coke's brand equity and profitability. Among other initiatives, the company hired thousands of Belgians to distribute coupons to grocery store shoppers for free 1.5-liter bottles. This incident resulted in millions of dollars of lost revenue, much more than likely would have been lost had the company responded more quickly and apologetically.[12]

Syringes in Pepsi: A Hoax In 1993 a New Orleans man contacted the Cable News Network (CNN) and alleged that he had found a syringe in a can of Diet Pepsi. This was only the first of several reported contaminations from different geographical areas. PepsiCo officials, knowing the reports were false and that the Diet Pepsi bottling process was completely safe, reacted to the negative publicity by using the media. A video showing the bottling process of PepsiCo products was released shortly after the initial news broke and was seen by an estimated 187 million viewers. It demonstrated the remote possibility that a foreign object, especially something as large as a syringe, could be inserted in cans in the less than one second they are open for filling and capping. That same day, PepsiCo's president and chief executive officer appeared on ABC's *Nightline* along with the commissioner of the Food and Drug Administration (FDA). PepsiCo's chief executive officer assured viewers that the Diet Pepsi can was 99.9 percent safe, and the FDA commissioner warned consumers of the penalties for making false claims.

Two days later, the FDA commissioner noted at a news conference that "it is simply not logical to conclude that a nationwide tampering has occurred" and that the FDA was "unable to confirm even one case of tampering." These statements were later broadcast over national TV along with a video news release showing a consumer inserting a syringe into a Diet Pepsi can. She had been caught by the store's surveillance camera. With this exposure, the crisis was essentially over. Although volume case sales dropped slightly during the period immediately following the hoax, sales returned to normal in a matter of weeks.

Perrier Contaminated with Benzene Perrier was the leading brand of bottled water in the United States until 1990 when Source Perrier, the manufacturer, announced that traces of a toxic chemical, benzene, had been found in some of its products. Perrier recalled 72 million bottles from U.S. supermarkets and restaurants and subsequently withdrew the product from distribution elsewhere in the world. The total cost of the global recall was estimated to have exceeded $150 million. Perrier's sales in the United States declined by 40 percent, and Evian replaced it as the leading imported bottled water. Perrier's business has never fully recovered.

Tylenol and Cyanide Poisoning In 1982, seven people in the Chicago area died from cyanide poisoning after ingesting Tylenol capsules. Many analysts predicted that Tylenol would never regain its previously sizable market share. Some observers even questioned whether Johnson & Johnson ever would be able to market anything under the Tylenol name. Many pundits consider Johnson & Johnson's handling of the Tylenol tragedy as nearly brilliant. Rather than denying a problem existed, J&J acted swiftly by removing Tylenol from retail shelves. Spokespeople appeared on television and cautioned consumers not to ingest

Tylenol capsules. A tamperproof package was designed, setting a standard for other companies. As a final good-faith gesture, J&J offered consumers free replacements for products they had disposed of in the aftermath of the Chicago tragedy. Tylenol regained its market share shortly after this campaign began.

Parenthetically, in a tragic replay of the Tylenol case, two people in the state of Washington died in 1991 after ingesting cyanide-laced Sudafed capsules. Following Tylenol's lead, the Burroughs Wellcome Company, Sudafed's maker, immediately withdrew the product from store shelves, suspended advertising, established an 800-number phone line for consumer inquiries, and offered a $100,000 reward for information leading to the arrest of the product tamperer. Burroughs Wellcome's quick and effective response reportedly resulted in only a brief sales slump for Sudafed.

Crisis Management

As the previous examples illustrate, product crises and negative publicity can hit a company at any time and lead to strong negative reactions from consumers. It is important to note, however, that not all consumers are equally swayed by negative publicity. Unsurprisingly, consumers who hold more positive evaluations of a company are more likely to challenge negative publicity about that company and thus are less likely to experience diminished evaluations following negative publicity. In contrast, those who are less loyal are especially susceptible to the adverse effects of negative publicity.[13]

Companies often are slow to react to crises. The reason, according to one crisis-management expert, can be explained as follows:

© Associated Press/AP

> *When disaster strikes, the first instinct of leadership is often to worry about the company, or the stock price, or the management team, the production line, their own jobs or bonuses. The last thing they think about is, "What is that mom with two kids in the shopping cart thinking about my product right now?"*[14]

The lesson to be learned is that quick and positive responses to negative publicity are imperative. Negative publicity is something to be dealt with head-on, not denied. When done effectively, reactive MPR can virtually save a brand or a company. A corporate response immediately following negative publicity can lessen the damage that will result, damage such as a diminution in the public's confidence in a company and its brands or a major loss in sales and profits.

And in the era of the Internet, a company's brand image can be tarnished virtually immediately as the result of a product failure, defect, contamination problem, or any other form of negative marketing-related news.[15] Consider the Firestone/Ford Explorer debacle that was described previously. In the wake of news that its 15-inch tires fitted on Ford Explorer SUVs were responsible, at least in part, for hundreds of rollovers and more than 200 deaths, Bridgestone/Firestone issued a massive recall of more than 6.5 million Firestone tires.

Officials at Ford denied that that company was at fault and placed the blame squarely on the shoulders of Bridgestone/Firestone. Although Bridgestone/Firestone was incredibly slow to respond to the negative publicity being disseminated, Ford realized the power of the Internet and placed an ad on about 200 Web sites with the potential of reaching millions of people. The ad invited viewers to click through to Ford's recall site, which included information about the specific tire models included in the recall, the tire models that were appropriate for replacement, and locations of authorized replacement dealers. The site also provided press releases from Ford and a statement from the company's chief executive officer claiming that Ford does not take lightly its customers' safety and trust.

Whereas Bridgestone/Firestone was slow to react to the negative publicity, Ford adroitly took advantage of the speed and impact of the Internet to offset negative publicity directed toward it. Perhaps the Ford Explorer was itself not free of blame for the numerous rollover accidents, but due in large part to Ford's PR efforts, the general public placed the blame almost exclusively on Firestone. A consultancy firm reported that Firestone's score on a reputation index had plummeted by an amount never before registered in its research on company and brand reputations.[16]

Just as Ford used the Internet to its advantage in offsetting bad publicity about Firestone tires and the Explorer's rollover accidents, other companies faced with negative publicity must also avail themselves of the power of this medium. One observer has compared the spread of negative product news via the Internet as equivalent to "reverse viral marketing."[17] To offset this "virus," companies can use the Internet to convey their own news in hopes of partially offsetting the negative information about their brands. This is especially important in the present era of great skepticism, where consumers have grown increasingly cynical of corporations.

A crisis-management authority expressed the opinion that the first thing a company needs to do when a brand is in crisis is to go online immediately and investigate what the bloggers are saying about the brand. "You want to get into the dialogue and motivate your loyal users to help you."[18]

The Special Case of Rumors and Urban Legends

You have heard them and probably helped spread them since you were a child in elementary school. They are often vicious and malicious. Sometimes they are just comical. Almost always they are false. We are talking about rumors and urban legends. As a technical aside, urban legends and rumors capture slightly different phenomena. Whereas urban legends are a form of rumor, they go beyond rumor by transmitting a story involving the use of *irony;* that is, urban legends convey subtle messages that are in contradiction of what is literally expressed in the story context.[19] As a case in point, consider the "Gucci Kangaroo" legend:

> *Have you heard about the American tourists who were driving in the outback of Australia? They had been drinking, and it seems that their car hit a kangaroo. Thinking the kangaroo to be dead, the tourists decided to take a gag photograph. They hastily propped the kangaroo up against a fence and dressed it in the driver's Gucci jacket. They proceeded to take photographs of the well-dressed marsupial. Well, it seems that the kangaroo had merely been stunned rather than dead. All of a sudden he revived and jumped away wearing the man's jacket, which also contained the driver's license, money, and airline ticket.*[20]

Technical distinction noted, we need not get hung up differentiating between the more general case of rumors and the specific instance of urban legends. Hereafter we will refer simply to rumors in a sense that encompasses urban legends. It further is noteworthy that our interest involves only those rumors that involve products, brands, stores, or other objects of marketing practice.[21] A variety of Internet Web sites focus on rumors and urban legends, and many of these refer to products, technological developments, and even specific brands. For a review of many types of urban legends, go to Urban Legends Reference Pages (http://www.snopes.com) and see legends related to business and specific products such as automobiles and computers.

Commercial rumors are widely circulated but unverified propositions about a product, brand, company, store, or other commercial target.[22] Rumors are probably the most difficult problem public relations personnel face. What makes rumors so troublesome is that they spread like wildfire—especially via e-mail transmittal and blogs—and almost always state or imply something very undesirable, and possibly repulsive, about the target of the rumor.[23] For example, the rumor spread quickly around the United States that because Mountain Dew is colored with a dye (Yellow 5), drinking the product lowers a man's sperm count. Although untrue, this urban legend influenced teenager's soft-drink consumption behavior, with some actually consuming more Mountain Dew than normal as a means of birth control and others consuming less for fear that later in life they would not be able to have children.[24]

Consider also the case of the persistent urban legend that surrounded Procter & Gamble (P&G) for years. The rumor involved P&G's famous man-in-the-moon logo, which was claimed to be a symbol of the devil. According to the rumor-mongers, when the stars in the old logo were connected, the number *666* (a symbol of the Antichrist) was formed. Also, the curls in the man-in-the-moon's beard also supposedly formed *666* when held up to a mirror. Although nonsensical, this rumor spread throughout the Midwest and South. P&G eventually decided to drop the old logo and change to a new one. The new logo retains the 13 stars, which represent the original U.S. colonies, but eliminates the curly hairs in the beard that appeared to form the number *666*.

Following are some other rumors/urban legends you may have heard at one time or another.[25] Many of these are from the past and none are true, but all have been widely circulated:

- McDonald's Corporation makes sizable donations to the Church of Satan.
- Wendy's hamburgers contain something other than beef, namely red worms. (Other versions of this rumor have substituted McDonald's or Burger King as the target.)
- Pop Rocks (a carbonated candy made by General Foods) explode in your stomach when mixed with soda.
- Bubble Yum chewing gum contains spider eggs.
- A woman while shopping in a Kmart store was bitten by a poisonous snake when trying on a coat imported from Taiwan.
- A boy and his date stopped at a Kentucky Fried Chicken (KFC) restaurant on their way to a movie. Later the girl became violently ill, and the boy rushed her to the hospital. The examining physician said the girl appeared to have been poisoned. The boy went to the car and retrieved an oddly shaped half-eaten piece from the KFC bucket. The physician recognized it to be the remains of a rat. It was determined that the girl died from consuming a fatal amount of strychnine from the rat's body.
- In what is referred to as the "Gerber Myth," thousands of consumers sent letters to a post office box in Minneapolis following a rumor circulating on the Internet (as well as in church bulletins and day care centers) that Gerber, a baby food company, was giving away $500 savings bonds as part of a lawsuit settlement. Complying with the rumor's advice, parents mailed copies of their child's birth certificate and Social Security card to the Minneapolis address. For a period of time, the post office box received daily between 10,000 and 12,000 pieces of Gerber Myth mail.

The preceding examples illustrate two basic types of commercial rumors: conspiracy and contamination.[26] **Conspiracy rumors** involve supposed company policies or practices that are threatening or ideologically undesirable to consumers. For example, a conspiracy rumor circulated in New Orleans claiming that the founder of the Popeyes restaurant chain, Al Copeland, supported a reprehensible politician known to have Ku Klux Klan and Nazi connections. Copeland immediately called a press conference, vehemently denied any connections with the politician, and offered a $25,000 reward for information leading to the source of the rumor. This swift response squashed the rumor before it gained momentum.[27]

Another example of a conspiracy rumor involved the little-known Brooklyn Bottling Corporation. This company introduced an inexpensive line of soft drinks under the name Tropical Fantasy. Tropical Fantasy quickly gained sales momentum and was heading toward becoming the top-selling brand in small grocery stores in many northeastern markets. But then rumor peddlers went to work. Leaflets started appearing in low-income neighborhoods warning consumers away from Tropical Fantasy, claiming that the brand was manufactured by the Ku Klux Klan and contained stimulants that would sterilize African-American men. Angry Tropical Fantasy drinkers threatened distributors with baseball bats and threw bottles at delivery trucks. Some stores stopped accepting shipments. Sales of Tropical Fantasy plummeted.[28] One can only wonder whether an employee of a competitive brand may have started this malicious rumor.

Contamination rumors deal with undesirable or harmful product or store features. For example, a rumor started in Reno, Nevada, that the Mexican imported beer Corona was contaminated with urine. A beer distributor in Reno who handled Heineken, a competitive brand, actually had initiated the rumor. Corona sales fell by 80 percent in some markets. The rumor was hushed when an out-of-court settlement against the Reno distributor required a public statement declaring that Corona was not contaminated. See the *IMC Focus* insert for additional examples of contamination rumors involving the artificial sweetener ingredient aspartame and plastic water bottles.

What Is the Best Way to Handle a Rumor?

When confronted with a rumor, some companies believe that doing nothing is the best way to handle it. This cautious approach is apparently based on the fear that an antirumor campaign will call attention to the rumor itself. An expert on rumors claims that rumors are like fires, and, like fires, time is the worst enemy. His advice is not merely to hope that a rumor will simmer down but also to combat it swiftly and decisively to put it out![29] An antirumor media campaign needs to be launched as quickly as possible.

An antirumor campaign would minimally involve the following activities: (1) deciding on the specific points in the rumor that need to be refuted; (2) emphasizing that the conspiracy or contamination rumor is untrue and unfair; (3) picking appropriate media and vehicles for delivering the antirumor message; and (4) selecting a credible spokesperson (such as a scientist, a government official as in the case of the Pepsi hoax described previously, a civic leader, or a respected theologian) to deliver the message on the company's behalf.[30]

Word-of-Mouth Influence

The discussion to this point has been about marketing-oriented public relations and the activities of both proactive and reactive MPR, including dealing with urban legends and rumors and managing crises. Implicit in these discussions is

IMC >> i.m.c. focus

Two Cases of Contamination Rumors: Aspartame and Plastic Water Bottles

Aspartame is the key ingredient found in artificial (nonsugar) sweeteners such as NutraSweet and Equal and is used to sweeten diet drinks such as Diet Coke and Diet Pepsi along with literally hundreds of other products. Rumors have spread, for at least a decade, that aspartame is responsible for epidemic health problems. People responsible for circulating this rumor, some of whom are scientists or claim to be, assert that aspartame is responsible for an epidemic of multiple sclerosis and systemic lupus. Lupus is claimed to be especially rampant among drinkers of Diet Coke and Diet Pepsi. Other maladies attributed to aspartame include fibromyalgia, leg numbness, vertigo, tinnitus (ear ringing), joint pain, anxiety attacks, blindness, birth defects, acute memory loss (especially among diabetics), and depression. This urban legend/rumor has been declared false by Snopes.com—an organization that monitors and researches urban legends—based largely on the fact that the legend has been debunked by the American Council on Science and Health, and the U.S. Food and Drug Administration has failed to identify any reliable pattern of symptoms that can be attributed to aspartame usage.

Another widespread urban legend/rumor involves plastic water bottles, such as those used by millions of consumers when drinking bottled mineral water. The claim, in short, is that re-using plastic bottles is dangerous because these bottles contain a potentially carcinogenic element known by its chemical-composition initials as DEHA. Plastic bottles allegedly are safe only for one-time usage or, at most, up to a week maximum. Repeatedly washing and rinsing plastic bottles supposedly breaks down the plastic leading to the release of DEHA into the water that people drink. It also is claimed that leaving plastic water bottles in cars is particularly dangerous because the extreme heat resulting from the greenhouse effect in automobiles breaks down the plastic, releases DEHA, and causes breast cancer. Snopes.com has declared this rumor false as well based, in part, on the Food and Drug Administration's determination that DEHA does not pose a health risk.

SOURCES: Adapted from http://www.snopes.com/medical/toxins/aspartame.asp and http://www.snopes.com/medical/toxins/petbottles.asp.

the idea that proactive and reactive PR efforts are undertaken with the intention of influencing the conversations that take place among people about products, services, and other marketplace topics—conversations that transpire both "over the fence" (i.e., face to face) and over the Internet. In other words, marketing communicators desire to influence what people say about products and specific brands. The purpose of this section, then, is to better understand word-of-mouth influence in the marketplace and how marcom specialists can influence the dialogue in the best interests of the brands they manage.

Research has established that word-of-mouth influence (WOM) is both complex and difficult to control.[31] Nonetheless, it is critical that brand managers attempt to control WOM in the best interests of their brands. It has been estimated that the average American consumer participates in an excess of 120 WOM conversations over the course of a typical week, with conversations focusing most often on products and services such as food and dining, media and entertainment, sports and hobbies, beverages, and shopping and retail.[32] Sometimes the influence is negative, such as was described in the previous sections on crisis management and urban legends and rumors. On other occasions WOM is beneficial to a brand, and in such an event the objective is to facilitate as much positive information as possible and to build favorable "buzz" about a brand.[33] The following sections first present some conceptual ideas about word-of-mouth influence and then discuss the practice of buzz building.

global focus

Create a False Blog and Go to Jail

Bloggers often say great things about new products and particular brands. Unfortunately, one cannot always be certain of the blogger's authenticity. Is the blogger a real consumer who has used a product, really likes it, and wants to tell others about it, or is this a blog created by the company that markets the product or by someone who the company has paid to say favorable things about its product?

The problem of false blogs is worldwide. In the United States word-of-mouth marketers generally are of the opinion that self-regulation is mostly capable of preventing false blogging and that government regulation is unnecessary, at least for the time being, to prevent the problem. However, in the United Kingdom legislation went into effect in 2008 that made it a criminal offense to represent oneself falsely as a consumer when blogging about brands. This regulation was designed to prevent instances such as when Sony ran an online campaign ("All I want for Christmas is a PSP") that used what appeared to be amateurish video footage with a blog falsely attributed to one of the characters in the video. In another celebrated case of false blogging, the founder of Whole Foods wrote critical comments about his competitors under an assumed name.

Writing positive messages online without making the origin of the message clear is now illegal throughout Europe. Up to the time of this writing (mid-2008), the exact penalties for false blogging have not been specified. A test case will be necessary to establish a precedent. However, false bloggers are on alert that misrepresenting the source of a blog can lead to financial penalties and even jail time.

SOURCE: Adapted from Emma Hall, "U.K. Cracks Down on Word-of-Mouth with Tough Restrictions," *Advertising Age*, April 28, 2008, 132.

Strong and Weak Ties

People are connected in what can be referred to as *social networks* of interpersonal relationships. Family members and friends interact on a regular basis, and people intermingle with work associates daily. There also are interaction patterns that are less frequent and less strong. We thus can think of social relations in terms of *tie strength.* Consumers' interpersonal relations range along a continuum from very strong ties (such as frequent and often intimate communications between friends) to weak ties (such as rare interactions between casual acquaintances).[34] It is through these ties, both weak and strong, that information flows about new products, new restaurants, recently released movies and albums, and myriad other products and services.[35]

The important point to conclude from this brief discussion is that marketing communications—especially via advertising media—is critical for getting the information-dissemination ball rolling. Thereafter, it is social interactions between B2C consumers or B2B customers that drive the flow of information about products, services, and brands. That is, advertising represents the first step followed by WOM as the second step in a two-step flow of communications that ultimately leads to people talking about and advocating particular brands.[36] Hence, marketing communicators need to orchestrate the flow of information about products using advertising and "buzz" efforts (as discussed in a later section) and then the information ball will be propelled at an accelerating rate by social networks of people interacting with one another—through face-to-face interactions, via social media such as YouTube and MySpace, or by means of blogs. (See the *Global Focus* insert for description of how "false" blogging about products and brands is a crime in the United Kingdom.)

© iStockphoto.com/Alexander Hafemann

The Role of Opinion Leaders in WOM Dissemination

Although most everyone talks about products and services, people differ in how much they discuss these items and in terms of how much influence they have on others. The people who have the most influence are referred to as "influentials" or "opinion leaders," with the latter term being preferred in this chapter.

An **opinion leader** is a person within a social network of family, friends, and acquaintances who has particular influence on other individuals' attitudes and behavior.[37] Opinion leaders perform several important functions: They inform other people about products, they provide advice and reduce the follower's perceived risk in purchasing a product, and they offer positive feedback to support or confirm decisions that followers have already made. Thus, an opinion leader is an informer, persuader, and confirmer.

Opinion leadership influence is typically restricted to one or several consumption topics rather than applying universally across many consumption domains. That is, a person who is an opinion leader with respect to issues and products in one consumption area—such as, movies, computers, skiing, or cooking—is not generally influential in other unrelated areas. It would be very unlikely, for example, for one person to be respected for his or her knowledge and opinions concerning all four of the listed consumption topics.

Opinion leaders are motivated to engage in communications exchanges with others because they *derive satisfaction* from sharing their opinions and explaining what they know about products and services. Opinion leaders thus continually strive (and often feel obligated) to keep themselves informed. In general, *prestige* is at the heart of word-of-mouth influence, whether that influence is from opinion leaders or from those who follow in the information dissemination process. "We like being the bearers of news. Being able to recommend gives us a feeling of prestige. It makes us instant experts."[38]

Researchers have used the term "maven" to characterize people who are experts in marketplace matters.[39] (In dictionary terms, a maven is considered an expert in everyday matters.) *Market mavens* have information about many kinds of products, stores, and other facets of markets, and initiate discussions with consumers and respond to requests from others for market information. In other words, the market maven is looked upon as an important source of information and receives prestige and satisfaction from supplying information to friends and others. Opinion leaders are mavens!

Prevent Negative WOM

Positive word-of-mouth communication is a critical element in the success of new and established brands. In fact, research indicates that consumers are much more likely to have positive than negative things to say about brands.[40] Nonetheless, unfavorable WOM can have devastating effects on a brand's image, because consumers seem to place more weight on negative than positive information in forming evaluations.[41]

Marketing communicators can do several things to minimize negative word of mouth.[42] At a minimum, companies need to show customers that they are responsive to legitimate complaints. Manufacturers can do this by providing detailed warranty and complaint-procedure information on labels or in package inserts. Retailers can demonstrate their responsiveness to customer complaints through employees with positive attitudes, store signs, and inserts in monthly billings to customers. Companies also can offer toll-free numbers and e-mail addresses to provide customers with an easy way to voice their complaints and provide suggestions. By being responsive to customer complaints, companies can avert negative—and perhaps even create positive—WOM.

Creating Buzz

The preceding section applied traditional concepts such as opinion leadership to describe the process of word-of-mouth communication. That section may have given the impression that WOM is something that just happens and that marketing communicators are like spectators in a sporting event who passively enjoy the action but are not involved in its creation. The present section clarifies that marketing communicators are—or should be—active participants in the WOM process rather than merely idle bystanders.

Because interpersonal communications play such a key role in affecting consumers' attitudes and actions, brand marketers have found it essential to influence what is said about their brands proactively rather than merely hoping that positive word of mouth is occurring. Marketing practitioners refer to this proactive effort as creating the buzz. By definition, we can think of **buzz creation** as the systematic and organized effort to encourage people to talk favorably about a particular brand—either over the fence or over the Internet—and to recommend its usage to others who are part of their social network. (Terms other than buzz creation are used to refer to proactive efforts to spread positive WOM information; these include *guerrilla marketing, viral marketing, diffusion marketing,* and *street marketing.*)

Let us explore the practice of buzz creation and understand why this activity is used extensively, even now to the point that major advertising agencies have created buzz-generating units.

Some Anecdotal Evidence

Before formally examining the topic of buzz creation, it will be useful first to examine some illustrations of this practice:

- Microsoft's Halo2 game reached retail shelves several years ago just before the Christmas shopping season. However, prior to that time more than 1.5 million orders had already been placed. This early success and widespread buzz were accomplished by creating a Web site (http://halo2.com) that whetted the appetites of people who play games such as Halo2. The fascinating thing about the Web site is that it was written in the language of and from the viewpoint of aliens (the Covenant) who, in Halo2's story line, are prepared to attack Earth. Without a single word of English or any other Earth language, "gamers" were able to crack the Covenant's language within 48 hours, which

© SETH WENIG/Reuters/Landov

was about two weeks quicker than Microsoft personnel had anticipated. Apparently gamers worked as a community and divvied up responsibilities until the language code was broken. Intense excitement was created by this unique Web site, which generated enthusiasm for the new Microsoft game and stimulated early ordering.[43]

- In an effort to get young trendsetters to become brand evangelists, Toyota used guerilla tactics in launching its Scion model. So-called street teams were formed to distribute promotional items to large gatherings of young consumers in cities across the United States. People had the opportunity to test-drive Scion models fitted with video cameras and then e-mail copies of the drives to friends.[44]
- Mel Gibson produced a religious film, *The Passion of the Christ,* that chronicled the last 12 hours of Jesus's life. Gibson invested around $25 to $30 million of his own money in producing the movie. Gibson spent months on the road prior to the movie's launch, meeting with church leaders and giving speeches about the film. His production company advised theologians as to how to use the movie to promote churches and recruit new members. The huge amount of buzz resulted in a film that was highly successful at the box office.[45]
- Another movie, *Crouching Tiger, Hidden Dragon*—the Chinese-language martial arts film directed by Ang Lee—also used buzz-building techniques to achieve box office success. With a limited budget for promoting the film, the studio decided that word of mouth would be critical to the film's box-office success. In an effort to generate "cheerleading" by movie aficionados, special screenings of the film were presented to a variety of audiences deemed likely to spread positive commentary about the film. These screenings included audiences such as graduates of a women's leadership institute, an assemblage of female athletes, advertising agency executives, and representatives of magazines and television. It was expected that these various groups would subsequently share their delight with others and thus get the WOM "ball" rolling for the movie.[46]
- Lee jeans needed a way to encourage consumers to visit stores where they might try on and purchase the Lee brand. Toward this end, the brand's advertising agency created an online game that featured characters from an accompanying ad campaign. To move to level two of the game, consumers needed a special code they could obtain only by checking out a price tag for Lee jeans. To generate enthusiasm for the game, e-mail messages were sent to 200,000 consumers who were targeted with the intent of directing them to an online video clip designed to interest them in the game characters. These messages, described as "hip" and "intriguing," were widely disseminated by the original recipients to their friends, who in turn, in the best spirit of viral marketing passed the messages along to their friends, who forwarded it to their friends, and so on.[47]
- In an effort to establish Long Beach, a suburb of Los Angeles, as a hub for West Coast flights, marketing personnel at JetBlue undertook a buzz-building campaign. The campaign was designed to reach influential customers such as bartenders and hotel concierges in hopes they would spread the word about JetBlue Airways and its flights from the Long Beach airport. College interns were employed to visit bars, hotels, and other locales and to talk up JetBlue and provide "influentials" with bumper stickers, buttons, and tote bags that served as visible reminders of JetBlue's daily flights from the Long Beach airport. To generate further interest in JetBlue and initiate buzz, interns drove Volkswagen Beetles, painted in JetBlue's signature blue color, around the streets of Long Beach.[48]
- During the opening show of the 2004 season of Oprah Winfrey's popular daytime television program, every audience member—276 in total—received a new Pontiac G6 automobile worth over $28,000. Oprah did not provide these gifts from the goodness of her heart; rather, the cars were donated by the Pontiac division of General Motors in an effort to generate gobs of free publicity about the new G6. Winfrey devoted a half hour of airtime to the Pontiac G6 and

described the car as being "so cool!" Of course, Pontiac's marketing people arranged this stunt in coordination with producers of *The Oprah Winfrey Show.* As part of the arrangement, the G6 became sole sponsor of Winfrey's Web site (http://oprah.com) for 90 days. Pontiac's marketing director claimed that the car giveaway generated $20 million in unpaid media coverage and public relations—quite a bargain considering that the actual cost to Pontiac of the donated automobiles likely was less than $5 million.[49]

Formal Perspectives on Buzz Creation

To now more fully appreciate the concept of buzz, it will be useful to introduce the concepts of networks, nodes, and links. These concepts apply not just to buzz creation but also to any type of network—including brains (nerve cells connected by axons), the World Wide Web (Internet sites linked with other sites), transportation systems (cities linked with other cities via roads, highways, and interstate systems), societies (people linked with other people), and so on.[50] More specifically, consider, for example, a transportation network such as the airline system. The *nodes* in an airline system are the various airports that are located in cities served by airlines; these cities, in turn, are linked by the airline routes that emanate in one city and culminate in another. Most nodes (airports) in an airline system are linked to relatively few other nodes. However, some large airports (e.g., Chicago O'Hare, Atlanta Hartsfield, and New York JFK) are *hubs* (another name for large nodes) that are linked with numerous other airports.

The notion of an airline network is applicable to social systems. Each person within his or her own social system can be considered a node. Each person (node) is potentially linked with every other person (additional nodes). Although most of us are linked with relatively few individuals, some people are linked with numerous others. Due to the large number of contacts these highly connected people have, they sometimes are referred to as *influentials.* In comparison to major hubs in airline networks, influentials represent the hubs in social networks. It obviously follows that if you, as a marketing communicator, want people to disseminate positive WOM about your brand, then getting your message to influentials is critical to your success. This is what Jet Blue did when reaching out to bartenders and hotel concierges in hopes they would spread the word about JetBlue Airways and its flights from the Long Beach airport.

Hereafter, we will describe two perspectives on the notion of creating buzz. The first perspective equates buzz creation to an epidemic. The second originates from principles derived by the renowned consulting firm, McKinsey & Company, and is called explosive self-generating demand. Although there is some redundancy in these perspectives, each is sufficiently unique to warrant separate treatment.

Generating Buzz Is Akin to Creating an Epidemic

Marketplace buzz can be compared to an epidemic. By analogy, consider how the common influenza (flu) virus spreads. A flu epidemic starts with a few people, who interact with other people, who in turn spread it to others until eventually, and generally quickly, thousands or even millions of people have the malady. Needless to say, flu epidemics could not occur unless people—such as school children—were in close contact with one another. For an epidemic to occur there must be a *tipping point,* which is the moment of critical mass at which enough people are infected so that the epidemic diffuses rapidly throughout the social system.[51]

It has been conjectured that epidemics in a social context, including the spread of information about brands, can be accounted for by three straightforward rules—the law of the few, the stickiness factor, and the power of context:[52]

Law of the Few The first rule, the law of the few, suggests that it only takes a few well-connected people to start an epidemic. These people—variously referred to as connectors, influentials, or opinion leaders—are capable of starting "commercial epidemics" because (1) they know a lot of people, (2) they receive satisfaction from sharing information, and (3) they are innately persuasive in advocating products and brands. In short, buzz-building efforts require *messengers* who are willing to talk about products and share their usage experiences with others and who, by virtue of their inherent persuasiveness, influence others to become product users and perhaps "apostles" as well.[53]

Paid advertising initiates the two-step process, but it alone could never accomplish the results that informal social networks achieve. Advertising might inform, but it is common people who legitimize product and brand usage. Indeed, whereas advertisements lack complete credibility—because people realize that ads are designed to influence their behavior—personal messages from friends and acquaintances are readily accepted because no vested interest typically is involved. Even strangers providing online reviews of books, albums, and other items can be highly influential on product sales.[54]

Stickiness Factor The second rule, the stickiness factor, deals with *the nature of the message,* whereas the first rule involves the messenger. Messages that are attention catching and memorable (i.e., "sticky" messages) facilitate talk about brands. This explains why urban legends fly through the social system. Such messages are inherently interesting and thus are passed along with lightning speed. (It would be useful at this point to return to pp. 210 to 212 in Chapter 8 to review the six common features of messages that tend to stick.)

The point is that not all messages stick and are worth repeating, just those that are innately interesting and memorable. Millions of people talked about the giveaway of hundreds of Pontiacs on *The Oprah Winfrey Show* mentioned earlier, because that was a newsworthy and exciting event. Tens of millions of people discussed Janet Jackson's (unintentional?) breast-baring that occurred during the halftime program of the 2004 Super Bowl. The death of racehorse Eight Belles during the 2008 Kentucky Derby was the subject of widespread discussion after the filly completed the race but then broke two front ankles and had to be euthanized. Eight Belles represented the subject of a sticky message because (1) she had finished second in a race, the Kentucky Derby, that is regarded as the most prestigious of all horse races; (2) it is rare for a filly to perform so well; and (3) the manner in which she was injured was so dramatic—immediately after rather than during the race. Further flaming the WOM about Eight Belles was the controversy stirred by PETA (People for the Ethical Treatment of Animals), which claimed that horseracing is inherently inhumane.

In general, people must want to talk about a product or brand-related idea if it is to spread. Some topics, such as those just mentioned, are inherently fascinating. Most commercial messages, however, are not that interesting Hence, it is through clever advertising and viral-marketing efforts that otherwise mundane news can be made interesting, even exciting, and thus worthy of sharing with other people who are connected via strong or weak social ties.

Power of Context The third rule of epidemics, the power of context, simply indicates that the circumstances and conditions have to be right for a persuasive message a connector conveys to have its impact and initiate an epidemic. It does not sound very scientific to say it, but sometimes the "stars have to be properly aligned" for epidemics to occur. In other words, there is a chance factor involved that is difficult to predict or control, or even to explain. But whatever the exact reason, sometimes the circumstances are just right for word-of-mouth dissemination. For example, had Eight Belles sustained her disastrous injury during a preliminary race at Churchill Downs—the racetrack where the Kentucky Derby is run—it is doubtful that this context would have generated much interest and subsequent WOM discussion. However, given that she was injured during *the* Kentucky Derby race, that context provided the final ingredient for the rapid spread of conversation about her injury and subsequent euthanizing.

Consider also a situation where a student on your campus gets arrested for driving under the influence. This would not be particularly exciting news that would prompt discussion among the student body. However, envision that this student was the son or daughter of the university president or another senior administrator. In this context, discussion about his or her behavior would be rampant. When the context is right, WOM epidemics can occur.

Igniting Explosive Self-Generating Demand

The foregoing account has simply described the conditions that are congenial to the spread of commercial epidemics. The present account will examine how buzz generation can be managed to get the message about a brand rapidly diffused throughout a social network.

The well-known management consulting firm, McKinsey & Company, has formulated a set of principles for igniting positive WOM momentum for new brands. McKinsey's associates refer to word-of-mouth momentum as *explosive self-generating demand,* or ESGD for short. The following principles underlie the ignition of ESGD:[55]

Design the Product to be Unique or Visible Products and brands that are most likely to experience ESGD have two distinguishing characteristics. First, they are *unique* in some respect—in terms of appearance (e.g., vehicles such as the Hummer, the Mini Cooper, and the Smart car), functionality (e.g., Apple's iPhone), or in any other attention-gaining manner. Second, they are highly *visible* or *confer status* on opinion leaders and connectors, who are among the first to know about new products and services. For example, being among the first to own a new video game, to dine at an exciting new restaurant, to try an interesting new beverage, or to attend a provocative movie can confer a sense of status on the innovator, which explains why these topics command much time in our day-to-day discourse.

In general, not all products are worthy of buzz. Rather, people are interested in talking only about those products and brands that have some uniqueness, excitement, or some inherent "wow" factor.[56]

Select and Seed the Vanguard Every new product and service has a group that is out in front of the crowd in terms of the speed at which the group adopts the product. McKinsey & Company calls this group the *vanguard.* The challenge for the marketer of a new brand is identifying which consumer group will have the greatest influence over other consumers and then doing whatever it takes to get that group, the vanguard, to accept your brand. Athletic shoe companies often launch new brands by supplying advance pairs to local basketball heroes. In general, vanguards include basketball stars, Hollywood divas, the most popular kids in high schools, the coolest kids in "the hood," and so on. The vanguard for new business books are business leaders, such as those occupying corner offices in major corporations. When they read a new book and consider it relevant to their organization, they will encourage their subordinates to read the same book, and they, in turn, instruct their underlings to do the same, and so on.

Usually the vanguard is a carefully selected target group that is most likely to love a new movie, a new book, or other product or service. In the publishing industry, "cheerleading" is stimulated by giving free copies of a new book to a select group of opinion leaders. This practice is suitably referred to as "seeding" the market—plant a seed, watch it grow, and harvest the results (huge sales volume). For example, teenage girls in Japan play an extremely important cheerleading role (called *kuchikomi*) that has been recognized and cultivated by Japanese firms.

Kuchikomi refers to the swift network of word-of-mouth advertising that connects teenage girls in Japan. Never was kuchikomi more apparent than in the success of the Tamagotchi craze that first hit Japan and then spread globally. Because there is little space in Japan for people to own pets, the Tamagotchi toy provided a substitute outlet for the desire to own an animal. Meaning "cute little egg," Tamagotchi is a plastic toy with an embedded electronic chip that emits chirps of affection based on the owner's behavior. After an extraterrestrial creature hatches from the toy "egg," the owner presses select buttons on a tiny screen to feed, clean, and care for the virtual pet. Proper care is rewarded with affectionate chirps. Bandai Company Ltd., the innovator of this product, estimated initial sales of about 300,000 Tamagotchi at $16 each. However, without any advertising and relying primarily on the WOM generated by teenage girls and other owners, sales volume reached 23 million units in Japan in slightly over one year. Since then Bandai has exported the Tamagotchi to more than 25 other countries.

The Tamagotchi is just one example of the kuchikomi power of Japan's teenage girls. Many Japanese consumer product companies do not just wait for Japanese girls to engage in word-of-mouth behavior but also solicit their opinions during new-product development. Japanese companies recruit girl guides, as they are called, to test proposed new products and provide feedback on preliminary television commercials. They also are paid to cheerlead new products. For example, Dentsu Eye, a marketing consultancy, paid schoolgirls to talk up a previously unknown product at their schools. Brand awareness quickly grew to 10 percent of high school students. Dentsu Eye's executives estimated that using television advertising to achieve a comparable level of brand awareness would have cost at least $1.5 million compared with less than $100,000 actually paid to the schoolgirls.[57]

Ration Supply Scarcity is a powerful force underlying influencers' efforts to persuade. This is because people often want what they cannot have. Automobile companies frequently exploit this reality by producing insufficient supplies to meet immediate demand when a new model is launched, especially one that is unique in design. The supply of Apple's iPhones also was insufficient to meet initial demand. The thinking is that people will talk more about those things they cannot immediately have. Thus, by rationing supply at the outset of product introduction, the excitement level increases and the WOM network is set into action.

Use Celebrity Icons Perhaps there is no better means to generate excitement about a new product than to first get it into the hands of a celebrity. Hairstyles, clothing fashions, and product choices that celebrities adopt are often accepted by large numbers of people who emulate their behavior. In the world of golf, for example, celebrities often appear in advertisements or infomercials and tout the benefits of new balls, clubs, and self-help products. Oprah Winfrey's endorsement of new books and many other products (such as the Pontiac G6) virtually assures product success.

Tap the Power of Lists The media disseminate many kinds of lists that are designed to influence consumer behavior and direct action. For example, aspiring college students and their parents read magazines such as *U.S. News & World Report's* annual lists of top colleges and universities. Newspapers regularly provide lists of the best mutual funds. Radio stations and Web sites regularly announce the top-drawing movies over the weekend. It has been claimed that "lists are potent tools for creating buzz because they're effective road signs for information-besieged consumers who don't know where to focus their attention."[58] In short, appearing on a credible list is virtually tantamount to becoming the topic of widespread discussion among people who are interested in the list's contents.

Nurture the Grass Roots Similar to the concept of cheerleading described earlier, this tactic is based on the idea of getting adopters of a product to convert other people into users. Naturally, people who are satisfied with a product often will encourage others to use the same product. But rather than "letting it happen" (or fail to happen), the notion of nurturing the grass roots involves—as do all buzz-building tactics—some form of *proactive effort* to motivate present product adopters to recruit new members or customers. People who have achieved success with a new form of diet or exercise program, for example, can be encouraged with incentives to recruit others to adopt this same form of behavior. Exercise clubs sometimes provide discounts to current members when they attract additional members to the club. Brand communities can be formed (online or otherwise) so that present adopters of a product can share their enthusiasm and hopefully spread the word to others. In short, nurturing the grass roots involves a proactive effort to get existing customers more involved with the product and thus willing to become product disciples.

Summing Up

This section hopefully has provided you with an appreciation that WOM momentum can be managed in a proactive fashion rather than accepted as a *fait accompli.* Also, it should be clear that not all products and brands are appropriate for buzz-creation efforts. The principles identified here offer insight into when and why buzz creation is particularly likely and most effective.

Growing numbers of firms are turning to buzz creation as a low-cost and effective supplement for (or even an alternative to) mass media advertising. Hence, it will serve you well to study this topic in greater detail than has been possible in this text. A number of books on the topic have been written in recent years. Please refer to the following endnote for a list of several informative and well-written books on the topic.[59] (This list, in line with the ESGD principle about the value of lists, should further generate buzz for these books about buzz building.)

Summary

This chapter covered two major topics: marketing public relations and word-of-mouth management, including buzz creation. An important distinction was made between general public relations (general PR), which deals with overall managerial issues and problems (such as relations with stockholders and employees), and marketing public relations (MPR). The chapter focused on MPR.

MPR consists of proactive MPR and reactive MPR. Proactive MPR is an increasingly important tool in addition to advertising and sales promotions for enhancing a brand's equity and market share. Proactive MPR is dictated by a company's marketing objectives. It seeks opportunities rather than solves problems. Reactive MPR, conversely, responds to external pressures and typically deals with changes that have negative consequences for an organization. Handling negative publicity and rumors are two areas in which reactive PR is most needed.

Opinion leadership and word-of-mouth influence are important elements in facilitating more rapid product adoption and diffusion. Opinion leaders are individuals who are respected for their product knowledge and opinions. Opinion leaders inform other people (followers) about new products and services, provide advice and reduce the follower's perceived risk in purchasing a new product, and confirm decisions that followers have already made. Positive word-of-mouth influence is often critical to new-product success. It appears that people talk about new products and services because they gain a feeling of prestige from being the bearer of news. Marketing communicators can take advantage of this prestige factor by stimulating cheerleaders, who will talk favorably about a new product or service.

Buzz creation—also called viral marketing, guerrilla marketing, and street marketing—is a relatively recent phenomenon as a proactive marketing practice. Firms employ the services of buzz-creation units to generate new product adoption by recruiting the efforts of connected people (influentials, opinion leaders) who will both adopt and talk about new products. Buzz creation can be compared to a social epidemic. Online buzz generation is occurring at an increasingly rapid pace with the advent of chat rooms and blogs.

Discussion Questions

1. Assume you are the owner of a restaurant in your college or university community. A rumor about your business has circulated claiming that your head chef has AIDS. Your business is falling off. Explain precisely how you would combat this rumor.
2. What are the advantages of publicity compared with advertising?
3. Some marketing practitioners consider publicity to be too difficult to control and measure. Evaluate these criticisms.
4. Some marketing people claim that any news about a brand, negative or positive, is good as long as it enables the brand to get noticed and encourages people to talk about the brand. Do you agree that negative publicity is always good? Under what conditions might it *not* be good?
5. Assume you are the director of your college or university's athletic department. A major story hits the news claiming that several of your athletes received inappropriate assistance writing term papers. Supposing the story is untrue, that this is nothing but a rumor, how would you handle this negative publicity?
6. Faced with the rumor about Corona beer being contaminated with urine (see the discussion earlier in the chapter), what course of action would you have taken if the Heineken distributor in Reno had not been identified as starting the rumor? In other words, if the source of the rumor were unknown, what steps would you have taken?
7. Classify the various rumors presented in the text (e.g., P&G's logo and McDonald's/Church of Satan connection) as either conspiracy or contamination rumors.
8. Describe two or three commercial rumors, or urban legends, other than those mentioned in the chapter. Identify each as either a conspiracy or a contamination rumor. Describe how you think these rumors started and why people apparently consider them newsworthy enough to pass along. (You might want to locate an urban legend Internet site for ideas. See, for example, http://www.snopes.com.)
9. Suppose you are the owner of a new clothing store located in your college or university community that caters primarily to the campus population. Your fledgling store cannot yet afford media advertising, so the promotional burden rests on stimulating positive word-of-mouth communications. Present a specific strategy for how you might go about stimulating positive WOM.
10. With thoughts of the Toyota Prius in mind, if you were the brand manager for this brand, what would you do to generate explosive self-generating demand?
11. The researchers who conceived the concept of the market maven devised a scale to measure consumers' responses to the following six items:
    (1) I like introducing new brands and products to my friends.
    (2) I like helping people in providing them with information about many kinds of products.
    (3) People ask me for information about products, places to shop, or sales.

(4) If someone asked where to get the best buy on several types of products, I could tell him or her where to shop.

(5) My friends think of me as a good source of information when it comes to new products or sales.

(6) Think about a person who has information about a variety of products and likes to share this information with others. This person knows about new products, sales, stores, and so on, but does not necessarily feel he or she is an expert on one particular product. This description fits me well.

Respondents are asked to rate each item on a seven-point scale, from strongly disagree (1) to strongly agree (7); thus, total scores range from a low of 6 (strongly disagrees to all six items) to 42 (strongly agrees to all items). Administer the scale to two friends whom you regard as market mavens and to two friends who are not market mavens. See if the mavens receive predictably higher scores than the nonmavens.

12. With reference to the principles of explosive self-generating demand (ESGD), explain how you would go about seeding a new music CD in a particular market of your choice. Be specific regarding the nature of the target audience toward which your seeding efforts will be directed and the techniques/methods you will employ to seed the vanguard among your target audience.
13. Why do you think that marketing practitioners use the terms *guerilla marketing, viral marketing,* and *street marketing* in reference to efforts to create buzz for new products and brands?
14. With reference to the discussion of explosive self-generating demand, describe a current movie that *would* lend itself to buzz-creation efforts and another that would *not.* What is the difference between these movies that makes only one amenable to buzz-building efforts?

End Notes

1. DEFCON is short for Defense Readiness Condition, and DEFCON 5 designates normal peacetime military readiness.
2. Adapted from Kate MacArthur, "Taco Hell: Rodent Video Signals New Era in PR Crises," *Advertising Age,* February 26, 2007, 1, 46.
3. The dividing line between marketing PR and general PR is not perfectly clear, as described well by Philip J. Kitchen and Danny Moss, "Marketing and Public Relations: The Relationship Revisited," *Journal of Marketing Communications* 1 (June 1995), 105–118.
4. Al Ries and Laura Ries, *The Fall of Advertising & the Rise of PR* (New York: HarperBusiness, 2002).
5. Paul Holmes, "Senior Marketers Are Sharply Divided about the Role of PR in the Overall Mix," *Advertising Age,* January 24, 2005, C1.
6. Nicholas Casey, "Mattel Issues Third Major Recall," *The Wall Street Journal,* September 5, 2007, A3.
7. Jack Neff, "Pet-Food Industry Too Slow: Crisis-PR Gurus," *Advertising Age,* March 26, 2007, 29.
8. Rich Thomaselli, "Bausch & Lomb Shortsighted in Crisis," *Advertising Age,* May 22, 2006, 3, 39.
9. Chad Terhune and Deborah Ball, "Dasani Recall Hurts Coke's Bid to Boost Water Sales in EU," *Wall Street Journal Online,* March 22, 2004, http://www.online.wsj.com; Chad Terhune, Betsy McKay, and Deborah Ball, "Coke Table Dasani Plans in Europe," *Wall Street Journal Online,* March 25, 2004, www.online.wsj.com.
10. "FDA Public Health Advisory: Safety of Vioxx," September 30, 2004, http://www.fda.gov/cder/drug/infopage/vioxx/PHA_vioxx.htm (accessed May 15, 2008).
11. Joanna Slater, "Coke, Pepsi Fight Charges of Product Contamination," *Wall Street Journal Online,* August 15, 2003, http://online.wsj.com.
12. Amie Smith, "Coke's European Resurgence," *Promo,* December 1999, 91.
13. Rohini Ahluwalia, Robert E. Burnkrant, and H. Rao Unnava, "Consumer Response to Negative Publicity: The Moderating Role of Commitment," *Journal of Marketing Research* 37 (May 2000), 203–214. For another related finding, see Niraj Dawar and Madan M. Pillutla, "Impact of Product-Harm Crises on Brand Equity: The Moderating Role of Consumer Expectations," *Journal of Marketing Research* 37 (May 2000), 215–226.
14. Brian Quinton quoting Gene Grabowski, "Sticky Situations," *Promo,* October 2007, 31.
15. For theoretical treatment of consumer complaining behavior on Internet Web sites, see James C. Ward and Amy L. Ostrom, "Complaining to the Masses: The Role of Protest Framing in Customer-Created Complaint Web Sites," *Journal of Consumer Research* 33 (September 2006), 220–230.
16. Jean Halliday, "Firestone's Dilemma: Can This Brand Be Saved?" *Advertising Age,* September 4, 2000, 1, 54; William H. Holstein, "Guarding the Brand is Job 1," *U.S. News & World Report,* September 11, 2000; Karen Lundegaard, "The Web @ Work? Ford Motor Company," *Wall Street Journal Online,* October 16, 2000, http://online.wsj.com.

17. Dana James quoting PR man Jack Bergen in "When Your Company Goes Code Blue," *Marketing News*, November 6, 2000, 1, 15.
18. Quinton quoting Allen Adamson in "Sticky Situations," 34.
19. For an insightful discussion of urban legends and an interesting experiment testing factors influencing the likelihood that legends will be transmitted, see D. Todd Donavan, John C. Mowen, and Goutam Chakraborty, "Urban Legends: The Word-of-Mouth Communication of Morality through Negative Story Content," *Marketing Letters* 10 (February 1999), 23–34.
20. Ibid.
21. Donavan et al.'s content analysis of 100 urban legends revealed that 45 percent included product references, 12 percent involved warnings about innovations and technology, and 10 percent identified specific brands.
22. This definition is adapted from Fredrick Koenig, *Rumor in the Marketplace: The Social Psychology of Commercial Hearsay* (Dover, Mass: Auburn House, 1985), 2.
23. For a review of the academic literature related to rumors as well as inspection of three interesting studies, see Michael A. Kamins, Valerie S. Folkes, and Lars Perner, "Consumer Responses to Rumors: Good News, Bad News," *Journal of Consumer Psychology* 6, no. 2 (1997), 165–187.
24. Ellen Joan Pollock, "Why Mountain Dew Is Now Grist for Fertile Teen Gossip," *Wall Street Journal Online*, October 14, 1999, http://online.wsj.com.
25. These rumors, all of which are false, have been in circulation at one time or another since the 1970s. All are thoroughly documented and analyzed in Koenig's fascinating book, *Rumor in the Marketplace.*
26. Koenig, *Rumor in the Marketplace*, 19.
27. Amy E. Gross, "How Popeyes and Reebok Confronted Product Rumors," *Adweek's Marketing Week*, October 22, 1990, 27.
28. "A Storm over Tropical Fantasy," *Newsweek*, April 22, 1991, 34.
29. Koenig, *Rumor in the Marketplace*, 167.
30. These recommendations are adapted from ibid., 172–173.
31. Dee T. Allsop, Bryce R. Bassett, and James A. Hoskins, "Word-of-Mouth Research: Principles and Applications, *Journal of Advertising Research* 47 (December 2007), 398–411.
32. Ed Keller, "Unleashing the Power of Word of Mouth: Creating Brand Advocacy to Drive Growth," *Journal of Advertising Research* 47 (December 2007), 448–452.
33. For example, WOM for movies has been demonstrated to have a significant impact on box office revenues. See Yong Liu, "Word of Mouth for Movies: Its Dynamics and Impact on Box Office Revenue," *Journal of Marketing* 70 (July 2006), 74–89.
34. For further discussion, see Everett M. Rogers, *Diffusion of Innovations*, 5th ed. (New York: Free Press, 2003), chapter 8; and Jacqueline Johnson Brown and Peter H. Reingen, "Social Ties and Word-of-Mouth Referral Behavior," *Journal of Consumer Research* 14 (December 1987), 350–362.
35. In addition to Brown and Reingen's findings, ibid., see also Jacob Goldenberg, Barak Libai, and Eitan Muller, "Talk of the Network: A Complex Systems Look at the Underlying Process of Word-of-Mouth," *Marketing Letters* 12 (August 2001), 211–224.
36. For further discussion and research evidence, see Jeffrey Graham and William Havlena, "Finding the 'Missing Link': Advertising's Impact on Word of Mouth, Web Searches, and Site Visits," *Journal of Advertising Research* 47 (December 2007), 427–435.
37. Rogers, *Diffusion of Innovations*.
38. This quote is from the famous motivational researcher Ernest Dichter, in Eileen Prescott, "Word-of-Mouth: Playing on the Prestige Factor," *The Wall Street Journal*, February 7, 1984, 1.
39. Lawrence F. Feick and Linda L. Price, "The Market Maven: A Diffuser of Marketplace Information," *Journal of Marketing* 51 (January 1987), 83–97.
40. Keller, "Unleashing the Power of Word of Mouth."
41. Paul M. Herr, Frank R. Kardes, and John Kim, "Effects of Word-of-Mouth and Product-Attribute Information on Persuasion: An Accessibility-Diagnosticity Perspective," *Journal of Consumer Research* 17 (March 1991), 454–462; Richard J. Lutz, "Changing Brand Attitudes through Modification of Cognitive Structure," *Journal of Consumer Research* 1 (March 1975), 49–59; Peter Wright, "The Harassed Decision Maker: Time Pressures, Distractions, and the Use of Evidence," *Journal of Applied Psychology* 59 (October 1974), 555–561.
42. Marsha L. Richins, "Negative Word-of-Mouth by Dissatisfied Consumers: A Pilot Study," *Journal of Marketing* 47 (winter 1983), 76.
43. Kris Oser, "Microsoft's Halo2 Soars on Viral Push," *Advertising Age*, October 25, 2004, 46.
44. Jean Halliday, "Toyota Goes Guerilla to Roll Scion," *Advertising Age*, August 11, 2003, 4; Norihiko Shirouzu, "Scion Plays Hip-Hop Impresario to Impress Young Drivers," *The Wall Street Journal Online*, October 5, 2004, http://online.wsj.com.
45. T. L. Stanley, "Gibson on Mission to Market 'Passion,'" *Advertising Age*, February 16, 2004, 27; Merissa Marr, "Publicity, PR and 'Passion,'" *The Wall Street Journal Online*, February 20, 2004, http://online.wsj.com.
46. John Lippman, "Sony's Word-of-Mouth Campaign Creates Buzz for 'Crouching Tiger,'" *The Wall Street Journal Online*, January 11, 2001, http://online.wsj.com.
47. Ellen Neuborne, "Ambush," *Agency*, spring 2001, 22–25.
48. Chris Woodyard, "JetBlue Turns to Beetles, Beaches, Bars," *USA Today*, August 22, 2001, 3B.
49. Sholnn Freeman, "Oprah's GM Giveaway Was Stroke of Luck for Agency, Audience," *The Wall Street Journal Online*, September 14, 2004, http://online.wsj.com; Jean Halliday and Claire Atkinson, "Pontiac Gets Major Mileage Out of $8 Million 'Oprah' Deal," *Advertising Age*, September 20, 2004, 12.
50. Albert-László Barabási and Eric Bonabeau, "Scale-free Networks," *Scientific American*, May 2003, 60–69.
51. The idea of a "tipping point" is based on the popular book by journalist Malcolm Gladwell, *The Tipping Point* (Boston: Little, Brown and Company, 2000).
52. Ibid.
53. It is important to note that the notion that only a few influentials are sufficient to initiate a marketplace

epidemic is not without challenge. For a sophisticated treatment of this issue, see Duncan J. Watts and Peter Sheridan Dodds, "Influentials, Networks, and Public Opinion Formation," *Journal of Consumer Research* 34 (December 2007), 441–458.

54. For example, see Judith A. Chevalier and Dina Mayzlin, "The Effect of Word of Mouth on Sales: Online Book Reviews," *Journal of Marketing Research* 43 (August 2006), 345–354.
55. Renée Dye, "The Buzz on Buzz," *Harvard Business Review* (November/December 2000), 139–146.
56. This expression was attributed to a marketing practitioner and cited in Justin Kirby, "Online Viral Marketing: The Strategic Synthesis in Peer-to-Peer Brand Marketing," *Brand Channel White Paper*, 2004.
57. Aki Maita, "Tamagotchi," *Ad Age International*, December 1997, 10; Norihiko Shirouzu, "Japan's High-School Girls Excel in the Art of Setting Trends," *The Wall Street Journal Online*, April 24, 1998, http://online.wsj.com.
58. Dye, "The Buzz on Buzz."
59. Emanuel Rosen, *The Anatomy of Buzz: How to Create Word-of-Mouth Marketing* (New York: Doubleday, 2000); Marian Salzman, Ira Matathia, and Ann O'Reilly, Buzz: *Harness the Power of Influence and Create Demand* (New York: Wiley, 2003); Jon Berry and Ed Keller, *The Influentials: One American in Ten Tells the Other Nine How to Vote, Where to Eat, and What to Buy* (New York: Free Press, 2003); Greg Stielstra, *Pyro Marketing* (New York: HarperCollins, 2005).

19

Event and Cause Sponsorships

First, a primer: NASCAR, which stands for National Association for Stock Car Auto Racing, is the sanctioning body that oversees different types of vehicle races in the United States but is best known for the Sprint Cup Series. Each year there are approximately 35–40 Sprint Cup events that take place at different racetracks around the United States on a weekly basis from early February through mid-November. NASCAR is highly popular, second only to the National Football Association in terms of TV ratings for sporting events.[1]

NASCAR itself has many sponsors, and each of the 40 drivers who compete in Sprint Cup events has his own individual sponsors. Take the case of Unilever, the huge multinational corporation that manufactures and markets many well-known brands of beverages, cleaning products, food, and personal care items. Unilever began sponsoring NASCAR and individual drivers in the mid-1990s but discontinued after failing to achieve adequate results. In 2004 Unilever returned to sponsoring 13 NASCAR races for three brands in the food category (e.g., Ragu pasta sauce). By 2007 Unilever was sponsoring 25 races for a number of brands from its food, personal care, and cleaning products categories. Research by ACNielsen determined that Unilever brands were receiving excellent returns from their investments in NASCAR sponsorships.

NASCAR driver Kasey Kahne represents nine Unilever brands: Ragu, Hellmann's, Shedd's, Lipton, Lawry's, Wishbone, Wisk, Slim-Fast, and Klondike ice cream

© Jerry Markland/Getty Images for NASCAR

bars—the latest brand tied to NASCAR. The Klondike sponsorship is part of an integrated marcom program for this brand. Beyond simply sponsoring NASCAR, Unilever's brand managers have learned that they must support their brands with other marcom programs that activate sales at retail. For example, Klondike's brand manager invests in several IMC initiatives to activate profitable levels of retail sales: (1) Klondike's NASCAR sponsorship is promoted in TV spots and on Jumbotrons (huge TV screens) that are located at racetracks; (2) samples of Klondike are distributed from ice cream trucks at stores, race-related events, and camping facilities near NASCAR races; and (3) Kasey Kahne's image is included on Klondike packages and on point-of-sale materials. Unilever has learned that sales typically jump by an impressive 50 percent when the image of a well-liked driver appears on packages of its brands.

NASCAR fans are highly loyal to individual drivers and, consequently, are strongly inclined to purchase brands that sponsor these drivers. This explains why sponsorship spending on NASCAR events generates very attractive returns on investments—provided that at least two conditions are met: (1) sponsoring brands fit well with the demographics of NASCAR fans and (2) sufficient dollars are invested in other marcom tools (such as those described for Klondike) so that the sponsorship working together with these other IMC initiatives can activate retail sales.[2]

Chapter Objectives

After reading this chapter you should be able to:

1. Understand event sponsorships and how to select appropriate events.
2. Appreciate the reasons underlying the growth of event sponsorships
3. Know what factors a company should consider when selecting an event to sponsor.
4. Understand how and why companies ambush events.
5. Appreciate the importance of measuring sponsorship performance.
6. Recognize the nature and role of cause-related marketing (CRM).
7. Appreciate the benefits of CRM programs.
8. Understand that accountability is a key consideration for cause-oriented as well as event-oriented sponsorships.

>>Marcom Insight:
Unilever's Sponsorship of NASCAR

Introduction

This chapter explores the topic of sponsorship marketing and its two constituent elements: event and cause sponsorships. Sponsorships represent a growing aspect of marketing communications and are regarded as an important marketing tool by most marketing executives. More than two-thirds of chief marketing officers who responded to a recent survey indicated that event sponsorship is a vital marketing function.[3] Sponsorships involve investments in events or causes for the purpose of achieving various corporate objectives, especially ones related to enhancing brand equity and augmenting sales. The following definition captures the practice of sponsorship marketing:

> *[S]ponsorship involves two main activities: (1) an exchange between a sponsor [such as a brand] and a sponsee [such as a sporting event] whereby the latter receives a fee and the former obtains the right to associate itself with the activity sponsored and (2) the marketing of the association by the sponsor. Both activities are necessary if the sponsorship fee is to be a meaningful investment.*[4]

At least five factors account for the growth in sponsorships:[5]

1. By attaching their names to special events and causes, companies may be able to avoid the clutter inherent in advertising media. It is noteworthy that some extensively sponsored events, such as the Olympic Games and the National Association for Stock Car Auto Racing (NASCAR; see *Marcom Insight* for further discussion), have become highly cluttered. Sponsors desiring to associate their brands with relatively uncluttered events—i.e., events with few other sponsors—must either pay huge fees to obtain exclusive sponsorship rights or select smaller, lesser-known events to sponsor.
2. Sponsorships help companies respond to consumers' changing media habits. For example, with the decline in network-television viewing, sponsorships offer a potentially effective and cost-efficient way to reach customers.
3. Sponsorships help companies gain the approval of various constituencies, including stockholders, employees, and society at large. That is, these constituencies respond favorably when a brand associates itself with a desirable event or cause.
4. Relationships forged between a brand and a sponsored event can serve to enhance a brand's equity, both by increasing consumers' awareness of the brand and by enhancing its image.[6]
5. The sponsorship of special events and causes enables marketers to target their communications and promotional efforts to specific geographic regions or to specific demographic and lifestyle groups. For example, many well-known brands sponsor riders in professional bull-riding (PBR) events—brands such as Ford Truck, the U.S. Army, Cabela's (a sporting goods retailer), Carhartt work clothing, DeWalt tools, Wrangler jeans, Dickies work and casual clothing, and Jack Daniel's (a bourbon distiller). These and many other sponsors are attracted to PBR due to the demographic composition of PBR fans, who are predominantly male (60 percent), between the ages of 21 and 49, and mostly live west of the Mississippi River (71 percent). Marketers of these rugged masculine products find PBR sponsorship to fit well with their target markets' geographic and demographic characteristics.[7]

Now that we have provided an overview of the general features of sponsorship marketing, the following sections detail the practice of event and cause-oriented sponsorships, respectively.

Event Sponsorship

Event sponsorships include supporting athletic events (such as golf and tennis tournaments, college football bowl games, the Olympics, extreme sports such as snowboarding and professional bull riding); entertainment tours and attractions; arts and cultural institutions; and festivals, fairs, and annual events of various and sundry form.

Although relatively small compared to the two major components of the marcom mix—that is, advertising and sales promotions—expenditures on event sponsorship are increasing. Worldwide, brand marketers are estimated to spend close to $40 billion on event sponsorships.[8] U.S. marketers alone spent approximately $15 billion sponsoring events in 2008.[9] Well over half of that amount went toward sponsoring various sporting events such as motor sports (e.g., NASCAR), golf and tennis, professional sports leagues and teams, and the Olympics.

Thousands of companies invest in some form of **event sponsorship,** which is defined as a form of brand promotion that ties a brand to a meaningful athletic, entertainment, cultural, social, or other type of high-interest public activity. Event marketing is distinct from advertising, promotion, point-of-purchase merchandising, or public relations, but it generally incorporates elements from all these communications tools.

Selecting Sponsorship Events

Marketers sponsor events to develop relationships with consumers, enhance brand equity, and strengthen ties with the trade. Successful event sponsorships require a meaningful *fit* among the brand, the event, and the target market. For example, brands such as Dove and Salon Selectives sponsor Shecky's Girls Night Out (http://girlsnightout.sheckys.com). This is an annual series of 35 events that take place in a number of major American cities. The target audience for these events is trend-oriented professionals who earn more than $80,000 annually. Attendees pay a modest fee of $10 to see displays of the latest fashions from up-and-coming designers and receive free samples from event sponsors. Unilever's Dove brand, for example, sponsors the event as an opportunity to introduce attendees to its new brands.[10]

© AP Images/Alden Pellett

Factors to Consider

What specific factors should a company consider when selecting an event? The following points identify the key issues when evaluating whether an event represents a suitable association for a brand:[11]

1. *Image matchup*—Is the event consistent with the brand image and will it benefit the image? The Coleman Company, a maker of grills and other outdoor equipment, sponsors NASCAR races, fishing tournaments, and country-music festivals. All these events appropriately match Coleman's image and also represent appropriate venues for its target customers. Unionbay, a jeans and sportswear brand, along with soft-drink brand Mountain Dew and snowboard maker Burton, sponsored the U.S. Open Snowboarding Championships. It would seem that this event matches perfectly the images of all three brands.

2. *Target audience fit*—Does the event offer a strong likelihood of reaching the desired target audience? Wal-Mart stores and General Mills' Hamburger Helper brand have sponsored fishing competitions, which might seem like a limited event for these brands to sponsor until it is pointed out that there are more than 50 million Americans who are active fishermen and fisherwomen.[12] The Old Navy chain of retail clothing stores has sponsored Major League Soccer. The demographics of Old Navy's typical customer match well the characteristics of consumers who both participate in soccer and view it live or on television. H. J. Heinz Company's frozen pizza-topped snack, Bagel Bites, has sponsored ESPN's Winter and Summer X Games (*X* stands for *extreme sports*) in an appeal to teenagers. This event is just behind the Olympic Games in its appeal to 6- to 17-year-olds. And United Parcel Service (UPS) sponsored Triple Crown winning racehorse, Big Brown. Many of UPS's users undoubtedly had great interest in watching the last leg of the Triple Crown, the Belmont Stakes, after Big Brown previously had won the Kentucky Derby and Preakness Stakes. See the *IMC Focus* insert for further discussion.
3. *Sponsor misidentification*—Is this event one that the competition has previously sponsored, and therefore is there a risk of being perceived as "me-too-istic" and confusing the target audience as to the sponsor's identity? Sponsor misidentification is not a trivial issue.[13] For example, Coca-Cola paid $250 million to be the official soft drink of the National Football League (NFL) for a five-year period. After sponsoring the NFL for several years, a general survey (not about Coca-Cola per se) asked football fans to name brands that sponsor the NFL. Thirty-five percent of the respondents named Coke as an NFL sponsor. Unfortunately (for Coca-Cola), another 34 percent falsely identified Pepsi-Cola as a sponsor![14]
4. *Clutter*—As with most every marcom communications medium, an event sponsor typically competes for signage and attention from every other company that sponsors the event. It obviously makes little sense to sponsor an event unless live participants and television viewers are likely to notice your brand and associate it with the event that it is paying to sponsor. NASCAR, for example, attracts a large number of sponsors due to the extraordinary growth rate in fan interest. However, recognizing the problem with sponsorship clutter, one observer noted that unless a brand is a prime NASCAR sponsor it easily "can get lost on the bumper."[15]

   By comparison to NASCAR's sponsorship clutter, consider a clever sponsorship undertaken by Procter & Gamble's Prilosec brand of heartburn medication. Prilosec became a sponsor of the Bunco World Championship after research revealed that millions of women are regular bunco players and that about one third of women who play bunco suffer frequent heartburn.[16] Prilosec experienced an uncluttered sponsorship arena when it signed on to co-host the Bunco World Championship.[17]
5. *Complement other marcom elements*—Does the event complement existing sponsorships and fit with other marcom programs for the brand? Many brands sponsor multiple events. In the spirit of integrated marketing communications, it is important that these events "speak with a single voice." (Refer back to Chapter 1 for more on speaking with a single voice.)
6. *Economic viability*—This last point raises the all-important issue of budget constraints. Companies that sponsor events must support the sponsorships with adequate advertising, point-of-purchase materials, sales promotions, and publicity in order to activate retail sales.[18] One professional in the

IMC >> i.m.c. focus

Big Brown (the Thoroughbred Racehorse) and UPS

As with all aspects of life, luck plays a role in brand managers' sponsorship decisions. Consider the case of UPS and its sponsorship of the thoroughbred racehorse named Big Brown. Needless to say, the horse is a large brown stallion, and UPS, its sponsor, also is known by the nickname "big brown" due to the brown paint motif used on its fleet of trucks, airplanes, and personnel uniforms.

Why would anyone give a racehorse such a mundane name as Big Brown, the type of name a child might assign to a large dog? Well, the original owner of Big Brown also owned a Brooklyn, NY trucking company that hauls shipments for UPS. In gratitude after his company received a contract extension from UPS, the owner picked UPS's moniker as the name for his horse. This original owner of Big Brown later sold his controlling interest in the horse to a company called IEAH Stables.

A few weeks prior to the 2008 Kentucky Derby, IEAH Stables approached United Parcel Service with the proposition that UPS sponsor Big Brown in the Kentucky Derby. UPS accepted the offer and became the exclusive sponsor of Big Brown, who went on to win the Kentucky Derby (run in Louisville, Kentucky). Then, two weeks later, he won the Preakness Stakes race run in Baltimore, Maryland. The third Triple Crown race, the Belmont Stakes, was run three weeks later at Belmont Park outside New York City on Long Island. Big Brown was expected to become the twelfth racehorse to win America's Triple Crown. No racehorse had won all three races since 1978 when Affirmed accomplished that feat. Alongside Affirmed, Big Brown was expected to join the ranks of famous racehorses such as Seattle Slew, Secretariat, Citation, Count Fleet, and War Admiral that previously had won the Triple Crown.

Unfortunately (for Big Brown's owners), the horse was unable to pull off victory in the Belmont Stakes. After losing practice time due to sustaining a substantial crack in one of his hoofs that required veterinarian intervention, Big Brown ran a pathetic race and came in last in a field of just nine horses. Nonetheless, publicity was enormous, as news of Big Brown's failure to win the Triple Crown spread across all mass media outlets and the Internet. UPS's modest investment in this sponsorship undoubtedly paid for itself many times over. Although UPS would have gained even more had Big Brown won the Belmont Stakes to become the first horse in 30 years to win the Triple Crown, the company nevertheless obtained a vast amount of publicity during and after the race from its association with a race horse that shared its nickname.

SOURCE: Adapted from Corey Dade, "UPS Extends Its Pact to Sponsor Big Brown," *The Wall Street Journal*, May 17, 2008, A4.

sponsorship arena uses the rule of thumb that two to three times the cost of a sponsorship must be spent in properly supporting it and offers the following advice:

> *A sponsorship is an opportunity to spend money. But like a car without gasoline, sponsorship without sufficient funds to maximize it goes nowhere. Therein lies the biggest secret to successfully leveraging sponsorship: It's not worth spending money for rights fees unless you are prepared to properly support it.*[19]

Creating Customized Events

Some firms develop their own events rather than sponsoring existing events. For example, managers of the Kibbles 'n Bits brand of dog food developed the "Do Your Bit for Kibbles and Bits" tour that covered 33 U.S. cities during a three-month period. The event involved having consumers in each of these cities enter their dogs into a competition to determine which dog would be picked for the brand's next TV commercial based on the quality of tricks the dog would perform to receive

© Associated Press/AP

Kibbles 'n Bits food. More than 11,000 people attended the event, and 2,500 dogs were entered into the competition. The Kibbles 'n Bits brand gained anywhere from one to four share points in key markets during this event.[20]

In general, there are two major reasons that brand managers choose to customize their own events rather than sponsor events another organization conducts. First, having a customized event provides a brand total control over the event. This eliminates externally imposed timing demands or other constraints and also removes the problem of clutter from too many other sponsors. Also, the customized event is developed to match perfectly the brand's target audience and to maximize the opportunity to enhance the brand's image and sales. A second reason for the customization trend is that there is a good chance that a specially designed event is more effective but less costly than a preexisting event.

It would be simplistic to conclude that brand managers or higher-level marketing executives should eschew sponsoring well-known and prestigious events. Sponsoring the Olympics or another major sporting or entertainment event can greatly enhance a brand's image and boost sales volume. Indeed, successfully achieving a strong link with an event that is highly valued means that the event's stature may transfer at least in some small part to the sponsoring brand. However, achieving such an outcome requires that a strong, durable, and positive link be established between the sponsoring brand and the event. All too often individual brands are swamped by larger and better-known sponsoring brands and no solid or durable link is formed. This being the case, it is doubtful that the sponsorship represents a good return on investment.[21]

Ambushing Events

In addition to increased customization, a number of companies around the world engage in what is called *ambush marketing,* or simply *ambushing.*[22] **Ambushing** takes place when companies that are *not* official sponsors of an event undertake marketing efforts to convey the impression that they are.[23] For example, research following a past summer Olympics determined that 72 percent of respondents to a survey identified Visa as an official sponsor of the Olympic Games and that 54 percent named American Express as a sponsor. As a matter of fact, Visa paid $40 million to sponsor the Olympics, whereas American Express simply advertised heavily during the telecast of the Olympics.[24]

In a survey associated with the 2008 Olympics held in Beijing, nearly 1,600 consumers in 10 Chinese cities were polled to determine which brands they linked to the Olympics. Due to ambushing efforts, 5 of the top 12 brands cited were *not* Olympic sponsors, including PepsiCo, KFC, and Nike.[25] There is little doubt that ambushing efforts can be highly effective when done well.

One may question whether it is ethical to ambush a competitor's sponsorship of an event, but a counterargument can easily be made that ambushing is simply a financially prudent way of offsetting a competitor's effort to obtain an advantage over your company or brand. (The ethical aspects of ambushing would make for interesting class discussion.)

Measuring Success

Whether participating as an official sponsor of an event, customizing your own event, or ambushing a competitor's sponsorship, the results from all these efforts must be measured to determine effectiveness. As always, *accountability* is the key.

Sponsorships cannot be justified unless there is proof that brand equity and financial objectives are being achieved. However, sponsorships represent an area that among all marcom activities may be the least accountable in terms of conducting research to determine whether the sponsorship of a particular event has achieved brand equity and financial objectives. Two practitioners have stated the case for sponsorship measurement:

> *Sponsorships can be an enormous waste of money and a drain on the marketing budget without a well-structured business case and a measurement plan. When it comes to sponsorship, the key question marketers need to ask is: How do you do sponsorships that build brand equity and maintain fiscal responsibility?*[26]

Many critics have claimed that sponsorship arrangements often involve little more than managerial ego trips—that is, key executives sponsor high-profile events as a means of meeting famous athletes or entertainers and gaining great tickets and luxurious accommodations. Whether this cynical perspective is correct is beyond this text to resolve, but the point is that a brand's welfare cannot be compromised by executive caprice.

As always, measuring whether an event has been successful requires, first, that the brand marketer specify the objective(s) that the sponsorship is intended to accomplish. Second, to measure results, there has to be a baseline against which to compare some outcome measure. This baseline is typically a premeasure of brand awareness, brand associations, or attitudes prior to sponsoring an event. Third, it is necessary to measure the same variable (awareness, associations, etc.) after the event to determine whether there has been a positive change from the baseline level.

The metrics used to measure sponsorship effectiveness are straightforward. The measure companies most frequently use is a simple head count of how many people attended an event.[27] The total cost of the event is then divided by the number of attendees to obtain a measure of efficiency; this measure is useful for comparison against the per-capita costs of other sponsorships. Other frequently used measures include tracking sales volume following an event, determining how many hits to the brand's Web site occurred post-event, counting the number of samples or coupons that were distributed, or measuring changes in brand awareness and brand image.

Cause Sponsorships

A relatively minor but important aspect of overall sponsorships, cause-related marketing involves an amalgam of public relations, sales promotion, and corporate philanthropy. Cause-oriented sponsorships typically involve supporting causes deemed to be of interest to some facet of society, such as environmental protection and wildlife preservation. As of 2008, American marketers spent $1.5 billion on cause-related marketing.[28] **Cause-related marketing (CRM)** entails alliances that companies form with *nonprofit organizations* to promote their mutual interests. Companies wish to enhance their brands' images and sales, and nonprofit partners obtain additional funding by aligning their causes with corporate sponsors. Although CRM was initiated in the United States in the early 1980s, companies throughout the world have become active participants in supporting causes. The *Global Focus* insert describes the unique Product RED licensing program that was co-founded by Irish rocker Bono and Bobby Shriver (John F. Kennedy's nephew) and that supports the Global Fund to Fight AIDS, Tuberculosis and Malaria.

There are several varieties of cause-related practices, but the most common form of CRM arrangement involves a company *contributing to a designated cause every time the customer undertakes some action that supports the company and its brands.* The company's contribution is, in other words, contingent on the customer

global focus

The Product RED CRM Program

Cofounded by Irish band U2's lead vocalist Bono along with Bobby Shriver—John F. Kennedy's nephew—and launched in 2006, Product RED is a unique cause-related marketing (CRM) initiative. The typical CRM program involves a company contributing a portion of its *revenue* from the sales of a particular brand to a designated cause. Comparatively, the Product RED CRM program involves a different business model. First, the Product RED non-profit organization sells no products; rather, it lines up *licensees*—companies such as Apple, Converse, Gap, Giorgio Armani, and Motorola—who carry their own versions of RED products in their brick and mortar and online stores. (Many, but not all, of the licensees' products are the color red.) Licensees sign a five-year licensing deal with Product RED for which they obtain category exclusivity. Licensees commit to offering items that are the same or better quality than their regular (non-RED) products and to selling these items at non-premium prices.

Second—and this is an important distinction from the typical CRM program—licensees typically contribute a portion of their *profits* (rather than revenues) from selling RED products. The amount of profit contributed varies among the licensees. For example, Armani contributes 40 percent of its gross profits and Gap donates 50 percent of its profits after marketing costs. Some critics are dubious of the use of profit rather than revenue as the basis for determining the amount of contribution, arguing that revenue-based contributions are more transparent in comparison to donations based on profits that are a function of a company's accounting practices. Finally, all contributions go directly to the Global Fund to Fight AIDS, Tuberculosis and Malaria.

All said, the Product RED initiative has made substantial contributions to the Global Fund in its efforts to combat various maladies in Africa. In the program's first year customers in the United Kingdom purchased approximately $200 million worth of RED products, of which $10 million was donated to the Global Fund. The initial contributions from the United States amounted to somewhere between $6 and $7 million going to the Global Fund.

Some cynics have criticized the Product RED initiative on grounds that licensees such as Gap and Motorola have spent more money marketing their own brands than they have contributed to the Global Fund. Defenders of Product RED claim, in contrast, that the program is entirely sincere, effective, and sustainable. Moreover, all parties involved in Product RED are beneficiaries of this program: Licensees benefit from increased store traffic and from the positive associations that are reaped from participating in this worthy cause; consumers gain from achieving a sense of doing good when purchasing and using RED products; and, most important, recipients in Africa are assisted by funds to combat AIDS, tuberculosis, and malaria. As with all successful CRM programs, Product RED represents a winning situation for all involved parties.

SOURCES: Adapted from Betsy Spethmann, "The RED Brigade," *Promo,* January 2007, 18–25; Mya Frazier, "Costly Red Campaign Reaps Meager $18M," *Advertising Age,* March 5, 2007, 1, 43; Bobby Shriver, "CEO: Red's Raised Lots of Green," *Advertising Age,* March 12, 2007, 8.

performing a behavior (such as buying a product or redeeming a coupon) that benefits the firm. Obviously, firms aligning themselves with particular causes do so partially with philanthropic intentions but also with interest in enhancing their brands' images and, frankly, selling more products. As always, whether cause-related alignments accomplish these goals depends very much on the specifics of the situation—in this case, the nature of the product involved and the magnitude of the contribution offered.[29] The following examples illustrate how cause-related marketing operates.

- Whirlpool Corporation's KitchenAid division has been a supporter of the Susan G. Komen Breast Cancer Foundation. In a unique program, Whirlpool donated $50 to the foundation for every purchase of a pink mixer (pink being the symbol for breast cancer awareness) that was purchased via the company's Web site or a toll-free telephone number. The $50 donation represented a generous

17 percent of the revenue Whirlpool obtained for this special-colored mixer priced at $289.99. In a more recent cause-oriented initiative called Cook for the Cure, KitchenAid donated a minimum of $1,000,000 to Susan G. Komen for the Cure in conjunction with its pink product collection (see Figure 19.1).

- General Mills' Yoplait brand yogurt also has supported the Susan G. Komen Breast Cancer Foundation. In its Save Lids to Save Lives promotion, Yoplait made a 10-cent contribution to the Komen Foundation up to a total of $1.5 million for every lid that consumers mailed back to the company.
- Georgia-Pacific, the maker of Quilted Northern Ultra bath tissue (among many other products), contributed 50 cents for every Quilted Northern Ultra UPC that consumers mailed in. Georgia-Pacific promised to donate up to $500,000 annually to the Komen Foundation in its role to fight breast cancer.
- In support of the Share Our Strength program that is dedicated to reducing hunger and poverty, Tyson Foods donated more than 12 million pounds of chicken and other food products. For every package purchased, Tyson donated a pound of chicken, beef, or pork to the Share Our Strength program—up to three million pounds (see Figure 19.2).
- The Campbell Soup Company has for more than 30 years sponsored the Labels for Education program, which helps schools obtain classroom supplies by asking families to collect labels from various Campbell's brands. Since the program began, Campbell has contributed items worth over $100 million to schools and organizations in exchange for the millions of labels submitted.
- For each Heinz baby food label mailed in by consumers, H. J. Heinz Company contributed 6 cents to a hospital near the consumer's home.
- Nabisco Brands donated $1 to the Juvenile Diabetes Research Foundation for each certificate that was redeemed with a Ritz-brand proof of purchase (Figure 19.3).
- Retailer Tommy Bahama has raised significant funds for The Garden of Hope & Courage project by donating a percentage of the sale of designated items from its apparel and accessory collections.
- Reynolds Metals Company, a maker of aluminum foil and other food packaging products, contributed 5 cents to local Meals on Wheels programs every time any of three Reynolds brands was purchased.
- Brand managers of Pedigree (a brand of pet food) supported the cause of sheltering and feeding abandoned dogs. Pedigree matched each purchase of a 22-pound bag of its brand of dog food by donating another 22-pound bag of food to dog shelters.

© AP Photo/Aaron Tyler Anderson

Figure 19.1

KitchenAid's CRM Program

Figure 19.2

Tyson's Share Our Strength CRM Program

© Courtesy of Tyson Foods, Inc.

The Benefits of CRM

Cause-related marketing is corporate philanthropy based on profit-motivated giving. In addition to helping worthy causes, corporations satisfy their own tactical and strategic objectives when undertaking cause-related efforts. By supporting a deserving cause, a company can (1) enhance its corporate or brand image, (2) thwart negative publicity, (3) generate incremental sales, (4) increase brand awareness, (5) broaden its customer base, (6) reach

© Joe Raedle/Getty Images

Figure 19.3

Nabisco Brands CRM program required a Ritz-brand proof of purchase.

new market segments, and (7) increase a brand's retail merchandising activity.[30]

Research reveals that consumers have favorable attitudes toward cause-related marketing efforts. One study found that the vast majority of Americans (72 percent) think it is acceptable for companies to involve a cause in their marketing. Moreover, an even larger proportion of respondents to this survey (86 percent) indicated that they would be likely to switch from one brand to another of equal quality and price if the other brand associates itself with a cause. This latter percentage takes on added significance when noting that a decade earlier the percentage of consumers indicating they would switch brands to a brand supporting a cause was only 66 percent.[31]

On the downside, about one-half of the sample in another study expressed negative attitudes toward CRM; this negativity was due in large part to consumers' cynicism about the sponsoring firm's self-serving motive.[32] Research has revealed that brands may not benefit from CRM efforts if their support is perceived as having an ulterior motive rather than authentic concern about the sponsored cause.[33] This negative effect may be diminished when multiple organizations support a cause rather than a single sponsor.[34] Also, consumers are distrustful of CRM programs that are vague in terms of exactly how much will be donated to the cause, and, in fact, the majority of CRM offers are abstract and unclear about the amount of contribution (e.g., "a portion of the proceeds will be donated").[35]

The Importance of Fit

How should a company decide which cause to support? Although there are many worthy causes, only a subset is relevant to the interests of any brand and its target audience. Selecting an appropriate cause is a matter of fitting the brand to a cause that is naturally related to the brand's attributes, benefits, or image and also relates closely to the interests of the brand's target market. When there is a natural congruence between the sponsor and the cause, the sponsoring brand is looked upon more favorably and benefits from being perceived as more socially responsible.[36] Absence of a close fit can suggest to consumers that the brand is sponsoring a cause merely for self-serving reasons. Campbell Soup Company's Labels for Education program nicely matches the target audience of children and their parents who consume Campbell's branded products. In fact, the same can be said of all of the illustrative examples of CRM programs provided previously.

Accountability Is Critical

In the final analysis, brand marketers are obligated to show that their CRM efforts yield sufficient return on investment or achieve other important, nonfinancial objectives. Corporate philanthropy is wonderful, but cause-related marketing is not needed for this purpose—companies can contribute to worthy causes without tying the contribution to consumers' buying a particular brand.[37] However, when employing a cause-related marketing effort, a company intends to accomplish marketing goals (such as improved sales or enhanced image) rather than merely exercising its philanthropic aspirations. Hence, a CRM effort should be founded on specific objectives—just the same as any marcom campaign. Research—such as a pre- and posttest data collection, as described for event sponsorships—is absolutely essential to determine whether a CRM effort has achieved its objective and is thereby strategically and financially accountable.

Colgate-Palmolive applied a straightforward formula in measuring the effectiveness of one of its sponsorships in which the CRM program was based on consumers redeeming FSI coupons. Using scanner data, Colgate compared product sales in the three weeks following a coupon drop with the average sales for the preceding six months. The difference between these two sales figures was multiplied by the brand's net profit margin, and the event's cost on a per-unit basis was subtracted to determine the incremental profit.[38] This procedure has the virtue of being logically sound and easy to implement.

Summary

Sponsorship marketing was the subject of this chapter. Sponsorships involve investments in events and causes to achieve various corporate objectives. Event marketing is a rapidly growing facet of marketing communications. Although small in comparison with advertising and other major promotional elements, worldwide expenditures on event promotions exceeded $40 billion in a recent year. Event marketing is a form of brand promotion that ties a brand to a meaningful athletic, cultural, social, or other high-interest public activity. Event marketing is growing because it provides companies with alternatives to the cluttered mass media, an ability to target consumers on a local or regional basis, and opportunities for reaching narrow lifestyle groups whose consumption behavior can be tied to the event.

Cause-related marketing (CRM) is a relatively minor aspect of overall sponsorship but a practice that is important nonetheless. Although there are several varieties of CRM programs, the distinctive feature of the most common form of CRM is that a company's contribution to a designated cause is linked to customers engaging in revenue-producing exchanges with the firm. Cause-related marketing serves corporate interests while helping worthy causes. Well-conducted CRM programs represent a win-win-win situation for corporate sponsors, the causes that are sponsored, and the consumers who engage in behaviors that generate funds for a worthy cause.

Discussion Questions

1. Select a brand of your choice, preferably one that you really like and purchase regularly. Assuming that this brand is not presently involved in a cause sponsorship, propose a nonprofit organization with which your chosen brand might align itself. Also, recommend a specific CRM program for this brand that would enhance the brand's sales volume and contribute to the cause.
2. Is ambushing unethical or just smart, hard-nosed marketing?
3. In 1999, the year after Mark McGwire had slugged a record-smashing 70 home runs—a record broken three years later by Barry Bonds—the coffee chain Starbucks contributed $5,000 to child-literacy causes for each home run McGwire hit. Explain why this is or is not, in your opinion, a good CRM program from Starbucks' perspective.
4. With respect to the chapter-opening *Marcom Insight,* what are your views regarding sponsoring NASCAR events and specific race drivers? In general, what kinds of brands would or would not be appropriate for sponsoring NASCAR? Be specific in your response and clarify any assumptions necessary to formulate your response to these queries.
5. Research reported in *Advertising Age* reveals that the favorite brands of candy among American college students are Snickers and M&M's. Select either of these brands and propose (1) an appropriate *event* for that brand to sponsor and (2) an appropriate *cause* for it to sponsor. Justify your choices.
6. With respect to either of the brands, Snickers or M&M's, from Question 5, how specifically would you attempt to measure the success of the *event*

you proposed sponsoring in your response to that question?

7. Considering the Product RED program discussed in the *Global Focus* insert, what are your views on basing charitable contributions on profits rather than revenues?
8. Are your personal views concerning cause-oriented marketing positive or negative? Please offer explanation in support of your response.
9. As mentioned in the chapter, event sponsorship expenditures in the United States far exceed investments in cause-oriented sponsorships—basically a tenfold differential ($15 billion versus $1.5 billion in 2008). Why, in your opinion, is the difference so large? In other words, why do you think that brand marketers in the United States much prefer to allocate their marcom budgets to sponsoring events rather than causes?
10. The National Football League (NFL) does not permit players to wear logos of sponsoring brands. For discussion sake, let us assume that the NFL suspends its prohibition of players displaying brand logos on their uniforms. Now suppose that you are the event manager for a brand of your choice and you want to sponsor a specific NFL football player to represent your brand. What player would you sponsor and why? To justify your choice fully, you must describe your brand's target audience and indicate the image you desire to associate with your brand.

End Notes

1. These details are from Steve McCormick, "What is NASCAR?" http://nascar.about.com/od/nascar101/f/whatisnascar.htm (accessed May 18, 2008).
2. The information about Unilever's sponsorship of NASCAR is adapted from Patricia Odell, "Unilever's NASCAR Sponsorship Takes an Ice Cream Pit Stop," *Promo,* August 2007, 8–9. For an interesting report on the effectiveness of sponsoring NASCAR events, see Stephen W. Pruitt, T. Bettina Cornwell, and John M. Clark, "The NASCAR Phenomenon: Auto Racing Sponsorship and Shareholder Wealth," *Journal of Advertising Research* 44 (September/October 2004), 281–296.
3. Kate Maddox, "Report Finds Most CMOs View Events as 'Vital,'" *BtoB,* March 14, 2005, 6.
4. T. Bettina Cornwell and Isabelle Maignan, "An International Review of Sponsorship Research," *Journal of Advertising* 27 (spring 1998), 11.
5. The first three factors are adapted from Meryl Paula Gardner and Phillip Joel Shuman, "Sponsorship: An Important Component of the Promotions Mix," *Journal of Advertising* 16, no. 1 (1987), 11–17.
6. T. Bettina Cornwell, Donald P. Roy, and Edward A. Steinard II, "Exploring Managers' Perceptions of the Impact of Sponsorship on Brand Equity," *Journal of Advertising* 30 (summer 2001), 41–42. See also Angeline G. Close, R. Zachary Finney, Russell Z. Lacey, and Julie Z. Sneath, "Engaging the Consumer through Event Marketing: Linking Attendees with the Sponsor, Community, and Brand," *Journal of Advertising Research* 46 (December 2006), 420–433.
7. Patricia Odell, "Running with the Bulls," *Promo,* January 2007, 6–8.
8. "Events & Sponsorship," *Marketing News's 2007 Marketing Fact Book,* July 15, 2007, 31.
9. "The Growth of Cause Marketing," based on the IEG Sponsorship Report, 2008, http://www.causemarketingforum.com/page.asp?ID=188 (accessed May 20, 2008).
10. Amy Johannes, "Girl's Club," *Promo,* March 2008, 8–9.
11. Adapted from Mava Heffler, "Making Sure Sponsorships Meet All the Parameters," *Brandweek,* May 16, 1994, 16.
12. Robert Marich, "Hunters, Anglers Lure the Big Bucks," *Advertising Age,* February 14, 2005, S–8.
13. Gita Venkataramani Johar, Michel Tuam Pham, and Kirk L. Wakefield, "How Event Sponsors Are Really Identified: A (Baseball) Field Analysis," *Journal of Advertising Research* 46 (June 2006), 183–198.
14. James Crimmins and Martin Horn, "Sponsorship: From Management Ego Trip to Marketing Success," *Journal of Advertising Research* 36 (July/August 1996), 11–21.
15. Sam Walker, "NASCAR Gets Coup as Anheuser Is Set to Raise Sponsorship Role," *Wall Street Journal Online,* November 13, 1998, http://online.wsj.com.
16. Bunco is a simple dice game typically played in groups of four people each, that are seated at three tables. In recent years the game has spread across the United States. The simplicity of the game enables participants to eat and chat while playing. For further details, see http://www.buncorules.com/whatis.html.
17. Ellen Byron, "An Old Dice Game Catches on Again, Pushed by P&G," *The Wall Street Journal,* January 30, 2007, A1.
18. For one illustration of the importance of adequately promoting event sponsorships, see Pascale G. Quester and Beverley Thompson, "Advertising and Promotion Leverage on Arts Sponsorship Effectiveness," *Journal of Advertising Research* 41 (January/February 2001), 33–47.
19. Heffler, "Making Sure Sponsorships Meet All the Parameters."
20. Wayne D'Orio, "The Main Event," *Promo,* May 1997, 19.
21. You may want to examine the following two articles that address the issue of whether Olympic sponsorship is a prudent financial investment: Kathleen Anne Farrell and W. Scott Frame, "The Value of Olympic Sponsorships: Who Is Capturing the Gold?" *Journal of Market*

Focused Management 2 (1997), 171–182. For a more positive perspective, see Anthony D. Miyazaki and Angela G. Morgan, "Assessing Market Value of Event Sponsoring: Corporate Olympic Sponsorships," *Journal of Advertising Research* 41 (January/February 2001), 9–15.

22. For review, see Francis Farrelly, Pascale Quester, and Stephen A. Greyser, "Defending the Co-Branding Benefits of Sponsorship B2B Partnerships: The Case of Ambush Marketing," *Journal of Advertising Research* 45 (September 2005), 339–348.
23. Dennis M. Sandler and David Shani, "Olympic Sponsorship vs. 'Ambush' Marketing: Who Gets the Gold?" *Journal of Advertising Research* 29 (August/September 1989), 9–14.
24. David Shani and Dennis Sandler, "Counter Attack: Heading Off Ambush Marketers," *Marketing News*, January 18, 1999, 10.
25. Normandy Madden, "Ambush Marketing Could Hit New High at Beijing Olympics," *Advertising Age*, July 23, 2007, 22.
26. John Nardone and Ed See, "Measure Sponsorships to Drive Sales," *Advertising Age*, March 5, 2007, 20.
27. This is based on a survey of event marketing conducted by the magazine *Promo* and published in Patricia Odell, "Crowd Control," *Promo*, January 2005, 22–29.
28. "The Growth of Cause Marketing."
29. Michal Strahilevitz, "The Effects of Product Type and Donation Magnitude on Willingness to Pay More for a Charity-Linked Brand," *Journal of Consumer Psychology* 8, no. 3 (1999), 215–241.
30. P. Rajan Varadarajan and Anil Menon, "Cause-Related Marketing: A Coalignment of Marketing Strategy and Corporate Philanthropy," *Journal of Marketing* 52 (July 1988), 58–74.
31. "2004 Cone Corporate Citizenship Study Results," Cause Marketing Forum, December 8, 2004, http://www.causemarketingforum.com.
32. Deborah J. Webb and Lois a Mohr, "A Typology of Consumer Responses to Cause-Related Marketing: From Skeptics to Socially Concerned," *Journal of Public Policy & Marketing* 17 (fall 1998), 239–256.
33. Yeosun Yoon, Zeynep Gürhan-Canli, and Norbert Schwarz, "The Effect of Corporate Social Responsibility (CSR) Activities on Companies with Bad Reputations," *Journal of Consumer Psychology* 16, no. 4 (2006), 377–390; Lisa R. Szykman, Paul N. Bloom, and Jennifer Blazing, "Does Corporate Sponsorship of a Socially-Oriented Message Make a Difference? An Investigation of the Effects of Sponsorship Identity on Responses to an Anti-Drinking and Driving Message," *Journal of Consumer Psychology* 14, nos. 1&2 (2004), 13–20.
34. Julie A. Ruth and Bernard L. Simonin, "The Power of Numbers: Investigating the Impact of Event Roster Size in Consumer Response to Sponsorship," *Journal of Advertising*, 35 (winter 2006), 7–20.
35. John W. Pracejus, G. Douglas Olsen, and Norman R. Brown, "On the Prevalence and Impact of Vague Quantifiers in the Advertising of Cause-Related Marketing (CRM)," *Journal of Advertising* 32 (winter 2003–2004), 19–28.
36. Debra Z. Basil and Paul M. Herr, "Attitudinal Balance and Cause-Related Marketing: An Empirical Application of Balance Theory," *Journal of Consumer Psychology* 16, no. 4 (2006), 391–403; T. Bettina Cornwell, Michael S. Humphreys, Angela M. Maguire, Clinton S. Weeks, and Cassandra L. Tellegen, "Sponsorship-Linked Marketing: The Role of Articulation in Memory," *Journal of Consumer Research* 33 (December 2006), 312–321; Carolyn J. Simmons and Karen L. Becker-Olsen, "Achieving Marketing Objectives through Social Sponsorships," *Journal of Marketing* 70 (October 2006), 154–169; Satya Menon and Barbara E. Kahn, "Corporate Sponsorships of Philanthropic Activities: When Do They Impact Perception of Sponsor Brand?" *Journal of Consumer Psychology* 13, no. 3 (2003), 316–327; Nora J. Rifon, Sejung Marina Choi, Carrie S. Trimble, and Hairong Li, "Congruence Effects in Sponsorship: The Mediating Role of Sponsor Credibility and Consumer Attributions of Sponsor Motive," *Journal of Advertising* 33 (spring 2004), 29–42.
37. It has been argued that cause-related marketing may serve to enhance a company's goodwill but may not improve a company's ability to compete. See Michael E. Porter and Mark R. Kramer, "The Competitive Advantage of Corporate Philanthropy," *Harvard Business Review* (December 2002), 5–16.
38. Gary Levin, "Sponsors Put Pressure on for Accountability," *Advertising Age*, June 21, 1993, S1.

20

Signage and Point of Purchase Communications

The Stop & Shop Supermarket Company is a large and progressive supermarket chain in New England. Always alert to ways of increasing its financial performance and enhancing consumers' shopping experiences, the chain experimented with an "intelligent" shopping cart in 16 of its 300 stores. Affectionately referred to as Shopping Buddy, the carts were equipped with a wireless touch-screen IBM computer with a laser scanner to enable shoppers to check prices and to scan purchased products. The carts maintained a running total of how much the shopper was spending, which facilitated rapid self-checkout at the end of the shopping trip. As the shopper approached items in the aisle, the intelligent shopping cart alerted him or her to which items were on sale and for which items shelf-dispensed coupons were available. Equipped with radio frequency identification (RFID) technology, the consumer also could query Shopping Buddy for any item's location in the store and be directed via a path displayed on the computer screen to the exact location of that item.[1]

Stop & Shop's experiment with the Shopping Buddy ultimately failed—presumably due to financial nonviability—and the supermarket chain replaced the intelligent shopping cart with a handheld device called EasyShop. However, because intelligent shopping carts represent a technology capable of serving the interests of all parties—consumers, retailers, and manufacturers—Stop & Shop's experiment with intelligent shopping carts is not the last. In fact, an up-and-coming company named MediaCart Holdings has worked with Microsoft to develop an intelligent shopping cart that promises economic viability as well as functionality.

MediaCarts are mounted with video screens at the back of shopping carts to enable maximum visibility. Using RFID technology, in-store advertisements and promotions are broadcast to the video screens as the shopper approaches items in the aisle, thus enabling brand marketers to deliver messages very close to the time when shoppers are making product- and brand-selection decisions. Much like the Shopping Buddy cart, the MediaCart allows shoppers to scan purchased products and to maintain a running tally of how much has been purchased. Then, at the end of the shopping trip, rapid checkout is facilitated by simply uploading a shopper's purchases from MediaCarts to supermarket computers. Beyond these apparent advantages, the MediaCart affords invaluable market research data for retailers and manufacturers by analyzing the sales impact of in-store ads and by providing potential staffing efficiencies for retailers as the carts eliminate the need for clerks to key in every purchased item.[2]

© AP Images/PRNewsFoto/Microsoft Corp.

Chapter Objectives

After reading this chapter you should be able to:

1. Appreciate the role and importance of on-premise business signage.
2. Review the various forms and functions of on-premise signage.
3. Appreciate the role and importance of out-of-home, or off-premise, advertising.
4. Understand billboard advertising's strengths and limitations.
5. Appreciate the role and importance of point-of-purchase advertising.
6. Review evidence of P-O-P's role in influencing consumers' in-store decision making.
7. Examine empirical evidence revealing the effectiveness of P-O-P displays.
8. Appreciate the importance of measuring audience size and demographic characteristics for out-of-home as well as in-store advertising messages.

>>Marcom Insight:

Shopping Cart Advertising

Introduction

This chapter deals with topics that represent a form of advertising but not in the same sense typically thought of when considering media such as television, radio, magazines, newspapers, and the Internet. Rather, the material covered in this chapter examines communicating with consumers at the point of purchase or close to it. In particular, we explore three general forms of marketing communications: on-premise signage, out-of-home advertisements (e.g., billboards), and in-store point-of-purchase (P-O-P) messages. All of these communication modes attempt to influence consumers' store- or brand-selection decisions. On-premise store signage, out-of-home ads, and P-O-P messages represent important forms of communications that serve in very important ways to influence consumers' awareness and images of retail outlets and the brands they carry.

Topical coverage first examines forms of message delivery that literally are located outside retail stores. We distinguish two general forms of "outside" marcom messages and refer to these as (1) on-premise business signage and (2) out-of-home advertisements, or off-premise ads. The difference between on-premise business signage and out-of-home advertising (off-premise signage) is that the former communicates information about products and services in close proximity to the store, whereas the latter provides information about goods and services that are available somewhere else.[3] Following this coverage of "outside" communications, we then turn attention to "inside" forms of message presentation, which are referred to as point-of-purchase advertising, or, for short, P-O-P.

On-Premise Business Signage

This section deals with a topic—on-premise signage—that is commonplace and may therefore be considered trivial. We are indeed surrounded by store signs of one variety or another. Every reader of this text has been exposed to literally thousands of signs—many, if not most, of which have not much captured your attention or interest. However, we can place this topic in perspective when noting that on-premise signs (i.e., those located on or near retail stores) are considered the most cost-effective and efficient form of communication available to retail businesses. Beyond this generalization, the value of on-premise signs has been described in these optimistic terms:

> *No amount of money spent on other forms of communication media will equal the investment return of the well-designed and optimally visible on-premise sign. Surveys of new customers/clients disclose over and over that the on-premise business sign either: (1) provided the new customer with their first knowledge of the company, or (2) provided the new customer with their first impression of the company. This is true even if the customer originally learned of the business through some other communication medium, such as the Yellow Pages or "word of mouth." It is no longer [an] overstatement to assert that legible, conspicuous place-based signage, easily detectable and readable within the cone of vision of the motoring public, is essential to small business survival.*[4]

Types of On-Premise Signs

Although on-premise signs include an incredible diversity of signage that is limited only by designers' creativity and governmental regulations, we can identify two general categories, free-standing and building-mounted.[5] *Free-standing signs* include monument signs, pole signs, A-frame (a.k.a. sandwich-board) signs, portable signs, inflatable signs, and other forms of signs that are *unattached* to a retail building (see Figure 20.1 for illustration). *Building-mounted signs* are *attached* to buildings and include projecting signs, wall signs, roof signs, banners, murals, and canopy or awning signs (see Figure 20.2 for illustration).

© Judith K. Shimp

Figure 20.1

Illustration of Free-Standing Sign

The ABCs of On-Premise Signs

On-premise signs enable consumers to identify and locate businesses and can influence their store-choice decisions and prompt impulse purchasing. These functions are conveniently referred to as the *ABCs of store signage.* That is, an effective sign should minimally perform the following functions:[6]

- **A**ttract new customers
- **B**rand the retail site in consumers' minds
- **C**reate impulse buying decisions

Of course, the specific functions performed and the importance of having eye-catching and attractive signs depend on the nature of the business, whether it is a small retailer with a relatively fixed clientele—in which case, signage is relatively less critical—or a business that must constantly attract new customers. In this latter situation, signage performs a critical function because for retailers to stay in business and potentially thrive they must capture travelers, who are one-time or occasional customers.

Attracting new customers requires first and foremost that a store sign *capture the consumer's attention.* This is no small feat when considering that the retail landscape often is dense with competing signs that are attempting to achieve the same outcome: to capture attention and make a positive impression. Experts in the design of store signage use a concept, termed conspicuity, that refers to the ability of a sign to capture attention. By definition, **conspicuity** involves those signage characteristics that enable walkers or drivers and their passengers to distinguish a sign from its surrounding environment.[7] This requires that a sign be of sufficient size and the information on it be clear, concise, legible, and distinguishable from competing signage.

Figure 20.2

Illustration of Building-Mounted Sign

© JAY LAPRETE/Bloomberg News/Landov

Seek Expert Assistance

This section has merely touched on the topic of on-premise signage. Although the material presented is basic and descriptive, it cannot be overemphasized how important signage is to retail success. Signs perform an extremely important communication function, and one is well advised to seek the assistance of professionals when making such determinations as where best to locate a sign, how large it should be, what colors and graphics are best employed, and so on.

The old saying "He who represents himself has a fool for a lawyer" is likely as applicable to making an on-premise sign-selection decision as it is in all matters legal. Fortunately, a tremendous amount of experience and expertise has accumulated in the off-premise sign industry, and retailers can turn to professional sign companies for needed assistance. Large retail chains include professionals on their staffs who specialize in signage, but small retailers do not have this luxury and should seek the assistance of professionals. A wealth of accumulated information is available for ready access (see end notes 3 through 6).

Out-of-Home (Off-Premise) Advertising

The previous section dealt with on-premise advertising retailers undertake to attract attention and direct traffic to their stores. The present topic, off-premise advertising, is carried out by product and service retailers and by manufacturers of consumer-oriented brands.

Though out-of-home (OOH) advertising pales in significance compared to media such as television and is regarded as a supplementary advertising medium, OOH is nonetheless a very important form of marketing communications. The Outdoor Advertising Association of America, the industry's trade association, estimates that OOH advertising expenditures in the United States amounted to $7.3 billion in one recent year.[8]

Out-of-home, or outdoor, advertising is the oldest form of advertising, with origins dating back literally thousands of years. Although billboard advertising is the major aspect of out-of-home advertising, outdoor media encompasses a variety of other delivery modes: advertising on bus shelters and other street furniture; various forms of transit advertising (including ads on buses, taxis, and trucks); skywriting advertisements and advertisements on blimps; and advertising at special venues such as shopping-mall displays, at campus kiosks, and at airports. This last form of outdoor advertising is rapidly growing. For example, a new terminal (Terminal Five) at London's Heathrow Airport—the world's busiest international airport—is inundated with 333 billboards and posters and over 200 flat-screen monitors that air short, soundless ads. This number of outdoor ad vehicles may seem excessive in just a single airport terminal, but in its first year of operation Heathrow's Terminal Five is expected to have upwards of 27 million passengers passing through it.[9] A recent academic study offers an in-depth look at the functioning and effectiveness of airport advertising.[10]

The one commonality among the various OOH media is that consumers see them outside of their homes (hence the name) in contrast to television, magazines, newspapers, and radio, which typically are received in the home (or in other indoor locations). And reaching consumers with ad messages outside their homes is especially important when considering that most people spend much of their daily time at work or otherwise away from their homes. Americans report traveling an average of slightly over 300 miles in a vehicle during a typical week with an average round-trip commute totaling about 55 minutes.[11] It is obvious from these statistics that outdoor media reach millions of people in the United States as well as around the globe. In fact, global spending on outdoor advertising exceeded $23 billion in a recent year.[12] (See the *Global Focus* insert for discussion of billboard advertising trends in several countries outside the United States.)

Billboard advertising is the major outdoor medium and accounts for nearly two-thirds of total OOH advertising expenditures in the United States. Interestingly, the term billboard originates from the custom in colonial America of attaching a paper poster containing a message (known as a "bill") on a board for conveyance around town.[13] Advertising on billboards is designed with *name recognition* as the primary objective.

Forms of Billboard Ads

The major forms of billboard advertising are poster panels, painted bulletins, digital (electronic) billboards, and "specialty" billboards.

global focus

Billboard Advertising Trends in BRIC Countries

Brazil, Russia, India, and China—the so-called BRIC countries—are rapidly changing and economically advancing. Billboard advertising in these countries is changing alongside other economic transformations.

In a dramatic move in Brazil, the city of São Paulo recently imposed an outright ban on billboards, neon signs, and electronic panels with passage of its "Clean City" law. Rio de Janeiro is considering implementing a similar ban. São Paulo's billboard ban has resulted in a number of outdoor advertising companies going out of business. The ban, however, does not prevent advertising on "street furniture" such as bus shelters, newsstands, and public toilets. Brand marketers denied the opportunity to use billboard advertising are increasing usage of street-furniture advertising as well as radio and newspaper advertising.

A second BRIC country, Russia, is noted for the pervasive use of billboard advertising in its major city, Moscow. Moscow's city leaders have repeatedly discussed restricting outdoor ads, although a complete São Paulo-type ban is not in the works. Yet, many billboards have been downsized and others have been removed from prominent historic buildings such as the Lenin Library. Moscow remains one of the biggest markets in Europe for outdoor ads.

Turning to China, city leaders in Beijing also have imposed restrictions on the use of billboards and other forms of outdoor advertising. It seems that these restrictions have occurred because many of the billboard ads in Beijing are directed at the city's affluent class, and city officials desire to curtail appeals to self-indulgence and luxury—in keeping with the China's socialistic ideals and the desire to maintain harmony among its people.

Unlike the other BRIC countries, billboard advertising is booming in India. Billboard advertising is an outstanding medium for reaching consumers of all income levels in India. On the one hand, billboards represent one of the few media for reaching India's poor, who do not have TVs and rarely read newspapers or magazines. On the other hand, billboard ads reach the more affluent class of Indians who often ride in chauffeur-driven cars and spend hours stuck in traffic in India's clogged cities. Some restrictions have been imposed on billboard advertising in certain cities in India but nothing of the magnitude of restrictions in other BRIC countries.

Some interesting developments in outdoor advertising are occurring in India. For example, one outdoor advertising company has developed a mobile billboard truck that parks, raises a billboard 20 feet on a pole, and then rotates the ad message to face passing traffic. The company has an inventory of 25 trucks that move to locations where they will be seen by the most prospective purchasers of the advertised brands—e.g., at train stations in the morning and in the suburbs in the evening. In rural areas of India, outdoor ad companies are utilizing a rugged vinyl that can be glued on uneven surfaces such as concrete, brick, and wood.

SOURCE: Adapted from Claudia Penteado and Andrew Hampp, "A Sign of Things to Come?" *Advertising Age*, October 1, 2007, 1, 45; Jason Leow, "Beijing Mystery: What's Happening to the Billboards?" *The Wall Street Journal*, June 25, 2007, A1; Eric Bellman and Tariq Engineer, "More Signs of India's Growth," *The Wall Street Journal*, April 26, 2007, B2.

Poster Panels

These billboards are what we regularly see alongside highways and in other heavily traveled locales. Posters are silk-screened or lithographed and then pasted in sheets to the billboard. A few media conglomerates (Clear Channel Outdoor, CBS Outdoor, and Lamar Advertising) essentially control the U.S. billboard industry.

Posters can be either 8-sheet or 30-sheet, literally designating the number of sheets of paper required to fill the allotted billboard space. An 8-sheet poster is approximately 6 feet high by 12 feet wide, although the actual viewing area is slightly smaller—5 feet by 11 feet (in other words, 55 square feet of viewing space). The much larger 30-sheet poster is 12.25 feet high by 24.5 feet wide, with a viewing area of 9.6 feet by 21.6 feet (roughly 207 square feet).

Bulletins

Bulletins are either hand painted directly on billboards by artists billboard owners hire or are computer-generated vinyl images applied to the billboard space. Standard sizes for bulletins are 12 feet tall by 24 feet wide (288 square feet of viewing space) and 14 feet tall by 48 feet wide (672 square feet). Advertisers use bulletins for an extended period—from one to three years—to achieve a consistent and relatively permanent presence in heavily traveled locations. Compared to posters, bulletins are more permanent due to their rain-resistance and antifading qualities.

Electronic (Digital) Billboards

Electronic billboards (also known as digital billboards) represent the biggest development in billboard advertising in many decades, perhaps ever. This new form of billboard is reminiscent of a huge flat-screen television that rotates ads every four to 10 seconds in a manner similar to a PowerPoint slideshow presentation.

Major billboard companies such as Clear Channel Outdoor are elated over the prospects for digital billboards because advertisements on these electronic billboards are frequently rotated; traditional billboards are restricted to a single advertising message throughout the course of the contract period—typically from four weeks to a full year. This has enabled billboard companies to increase their revenues substantially—perhaps as much as 6 to 10 times greater than with traditional billboards based on results from the first generation of digital billboards.[14]

As of 2007, approximately 700 digital billboards were installed across the United States, and it is anticipated that as many as 4,000 electronic billboards will be standing within a decade.[15] At least two factors limit the growth of digital billboards. First, they are expensive to install and cost upwards of $250,000 each.[16] Second, a number of cities and even entire states are opposed to this form of billboard due to concerns that they distract drivers, produce too much light at night, and represent visual pollution. (Whether digital billboards are unsightly and unsafe should make for interesting classroom discussion.)

In addition to offering revenue advantages for billboard companies, individual advertisers also stand to benefit from the availability of the digital billboard medium. First, digital billboards make it possible to change ads as frequently as needed. For example, an advertiser could announce a sale or special promotion one week and then the following week return to a nonpromotional sales message. A second advantage of digital billboards is the ability to rotate messages throughout the day. For example, a fast-food restaurant might promote a breakfast item during the morning drive time and then advertise other menu items during later dayparts. A third advantage of digital billboards is that they enable integration—in the best spirit of the tenets of integrated marketing communications—with other digital ads that a consumer may be exposed to during the course of a day. For example, one may see a digital billboard ad for a particular brand on the way to work, then see the same digital ad later in the day on a computer, and perhaps then again on one's cellphone screen.

Figure 20.3

Neiman Marcus Interactive Media Wall

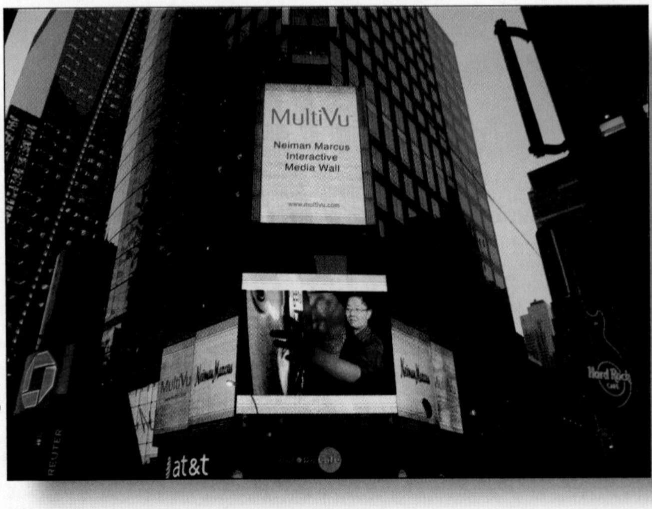

© AP Images/PRNewsFoto/PR Newswire Association LLC

Specialty Billboards

Resulting from the desire to attract consumer attention from the multitude of marketing messages that clutter the landscape in urban areas and along highways, specialty billboards represent different artistic and graphical techniques to present advertising messages in an especially engaging and creative way. Consider PR Newswire's interactive media wall in Times Square, used by leading consumer brands such as Pepsico and Neiman Marcus (Figure 20.3). The massive Reuters billboard is seen by about 1.5 million people every day. Figure 20.4, for a fitness center, provides another creative use of specialty billboards in showing a billboard tilted in the direction of an overweight man who appears to be in need of the advertised service.

© The Johnson Group, Chattanooga, TN

Figure 20.4

Specialty Billboard for a Fitness Center

Buying Billboard Advertising

Outdoor advertising is purchased through companies that own billboards such as the aforementioned Clear Channel Outdoor, CBS Outdoor, and Lamar Advertising. These companies are located in all major markets throughout the nation. To simplify the national advertiser's task of buying outdoor space in multiple markets, buying organizations, or agents, facilitate the purchasing of outdoor space at locations throughout the country.

Outdoor advertising suppliers have historically sold poster-advertising space in terms of so-called *showings.* A showing is the percentage of the population that is theoretically exposed to an advertiser's billboard message. Showings are quoted in increments of 25 and are designated as #25, #50, #75, and #100. The designation #50, for example, means that 50 percent of the population in a particular market is expected to pass daily the billboards on which an advertiser's message is posted. A showing of #100 is equivalent to saying that virtually the entire population in a given market has an opportunity to see (referred to as an OTS) an advertiser's message in that particular market.

In recent years outdoor advertising companies have converted to *gross rating points (GRPs)* as the metric for quoting poster prices. As is the case with mass advertising media (TV, magazines, etc.), GRPs represent the percentage and frequency of an audience an advertising vehicle is reaching. Specifically, one outdoor GRP means reaching 1 percent of the population in a particular market a single time. Outdoor GRPs are based on the daily duplicated audience (meaning that some people may be exposed on multiple occasions each day) as a percentage of the total potential market. For example, if four billboards in a community of 200,000 people achieve a daily exposure to 80,000 people, the result is 40 gross rating points. As with traditional showings, GRPs are sold in blocks of 25, with 100 and 50 being the two levels purchased most.

Billboard Advertising's Strengths and Limitations

Billboard advertising presents marketing communicators with several unique strengths and problems.[17]

Strengths

A major strength of billboard advertising is its *broad reach* and *high frequency levels.* Billboards are effective in reaching virtually all segments of the population. The number of exposures is especially high when signs are strategically located in heavy traffic areas. Automobile advertisers are heavy users of outdoor media because they can reach huge numbers of potential purchasers with high frequency. The same can be said for telecommunications companies (such as AT&T, Verizon, and Cingular) and fast-food restaurants.

Another advantage is *geographic flexibility.* Outdoor advertising can be strategically positioned to supplement other advertising efforts (e.g., TV, radio, and newspaper ads) in select geographic areas where advertising support is most needed.

Low cost per thousand is a third advantage. The cost-per-thousand metric (abbreviated as *CPM,* where *M* is the Roman numeral for 1,000) is literally the cost, on average, of exposing 1,000 people to an advertisement. Outdoor advertising is the least expensive advertising medium on a CPM basis. However, as emphasized in Chapter 12 when discussing the relative advantages of traditional advertising media, CPM comparisons across different media can be misleading. Because the various media perform different functions, it is inappropriate to use CPM as the sole basis of evaluation.

A fourth strength of billboard advertising is that *brand identification is substantial* because billboard ads are literally bigger than life. The ability to use large representations offers marketers excellent opportunities for brand and package identification. Also, billboard companies are becoming quite ingenious in designing billboards that attract viewers' attention through the use of creative techniques and eye-catching visuals—such as those shown in Figures 20.3 and 20.4. Consider also a creative billboard ad for promoting Adidas soccer products in Japan.

TBWA/Japan

Figure 20.5

Humans Playing Soccer on a Japanese Billboard

Outdoor media play a more prominent role in Japan than in countries such as the United States because the average resident in a city such as Tokyo has a 70-minute commute to work, which makes billboards and other outdoor media an attractive and relatively inexpensive way of reaching them. However, the heavy spending on outdoor ads has created a major clutter problem. Sports-equipment and apparel maker Adidas came up with a novel solution: It designed faux soccer fields on billboards and suspended (via dangling ropes; see Figure 20.5) two soccer players and a ball 12 stories above the ground. The two dangling soccer players played 10- to 15-minute matches at one-hour intervals during afternoons, while hundreds of pedestrians gathered below to watch. Of course, while they watched the soccer "matches," they were continuously exposed to the Adidas name and logo along with a message overlaid on the soccer "field" proclaiming, "Own the passion and you own the game." It is difficult to imagine a more attention-gaining billboard than Adidas's use of live soccer players.[18]

A fifth advantage of billboard advertising is that it provides an excellent opportunity to reach consumers as a *last reminder before purchasing*. This explains why restaurants and products such as beer are among the heaviest billboard users. (U.S. tobacco advertisers also were heavy outdoor advertisers; in 1999, as part of a legal settlement with the state attorneys general, tobacco brands stopped advertising in outdoor media.)

Limitations

A significant problem with outdoor advertising is *demographic nonselectivity*. Outdoor advertising can be geared to general groups of consumers (such as inner-city residents) but cannot pinpoint specific market segments (say, professional African-American men between the ages of 25 and 39). Advertisers must turn to other advertising media (such as magazines and radio) to better pinpoint audience selection. However, with technology that is under development, billboard advertising is in the process of improving its ability to target customers. For example, a California company, Smart Sign Media, introduced technology that adjusts digital billboards to the radio stations playing inside passing vehicles. Using radio-station selection as an indicator of income, Smart Sign's technology calculates the average income of people who pass by and then changes the message to target the biggest cluster of people who drive by a particular billboard location.[19]

Short exposure time is another drawback. "Now you see it, now you don't" appropriately characterizes the fashion in which outdoor advertising engages the consumer's attention. For this reason, outdoor messages that have to be read are less effective than predominantly visual ones. Bright colors, vivid images, and visual messages are essential in effective billboard advertising.

A third outdoor advertising limitation involves *environmental concerns.* Billboards, the so-called "litter on a stick," have been banned in some manner by several U.S. states and hundreds of local governments. Although some would argue that attractive billboards can enliven and even beautify neighborhoods and highways with attractive messages, others consider this advertising medium to be ugly and intrusive. This largely is a matter of personal taste. The articles cited in the following end note explore the issue in some depth, including a discussion of the value and potential hazards attendant to the growing use of changeable message signs—that is, digital billboards that vary the advertising message on a schedule of every 4 to 10 seconds.[20]

Measuring Billboard Audience Size and Characteristics

When placing ads in print (newspapers and magazines) and broadcast media (radio and TV), advertisers have access to so-called syndicated data sources that inform them about (1) the size of the audience to be reached when using these media, and (2) the demographic characteristics of audiences reached by media vehicles such as individual magazines (e.g., *Cosmopolitan*) or TV programs (e.g., *Saturday Night Live*). (Audience measurement techniques for the print and broadcast media were described in detail in Chapter 12.) This information is invaluable when planning for and making media buying decisions. In advance of making a media buy, an advertiser can estimate what percentage of a target audience is likely to be reached and the average frequency audience members will have an OTS (opportunity to see—or read or hear) an ad message during, say, a four-week media planning period. Print and broadcast media are, then, *measurable,* and advertisers have quite a lot of faith in the accuracy of the audience data for these media.

Comparatively, there has been no equivalent measurable audience data available for the out-of-home advertising industry. Historically, the outdoor industry has relied on traffic data the Traffic Audit Bureau collects that simply indicates how many people pass by an outdoor site such as a billboard. However, no information has been available regarding the demographic characteristics of the people who have an opportunity to see advertising messages on billboards. The lack of verified data regarding audience characteristics is widely regarded as a significant impediment that must be overcome if outdoor advertising is to become a more widely used advertising medium. Although traffic-flow data indicate the number of people who may have an opportunity to see a billboard message, it provides absolutely no information about people's demographic characteristics, which is the type of information advertisers need to make intelligent targeting decisions.

This lack of information has retarded the growth of the OOH industry and has prevented many advertisers from investing heavily in out-of-home media. Relatively few national advertisers spend large percentages of their advertising budgets on OOH advertising. This situation is unlikely to change until the OOH industry somehow develops accurate measures of audience size and demographic characteristics. To place ads in media without accurate knowledge of audience characteristics is equivalent to, in farmer's language, "purchasing a pig in a poke [a bag or sack]." In other words, it is unwise to purchase something that has been concealed without knowing in advance what you are acquiring.

Nielsen Personal Outdoor Devices (Npods)

Fortunately, Nielsen Media Research, a company that specializes in the measurement of advertising audiences, is making substantial strides toward developing ways to determine the *demographic characteristics of outdoor audiences.* Nielsen's service involves selecting a representative sample of individuals, collecting from them pertinent demographic information, and equipping them with battery-operated meters called *Npods* (Nielsen Personal Outdoor Devices). Using global positioning satellite (GPS) technology, these Npod meters automatically track individuals' movements from the time they leave their homes until they return. With knowledge of the demographic characteristics of sample members and knowing literally their geographical whereabouts, it is possible to connect these two data sets and draw conclusions about the demographic characteristics of the people who have had an opportunity to see an ad carried on any particular billboard location.

Armed with verifiable knowledge about the demographic characteristics of people who pass particular billboard locations or the sites of other outdoor ads, it is likely that advertisers will increase their use of OOH advertising. Initial research by Nielsen Outdoor in Chicago determined that men age 35 to 54 have the highest exposure to outdoor advertising and that full-time employed individuals in the upper income categories are especially likely to be exposed to outdoor ads.[21]

Figure 20.6

Illustrations from the Outhouse Springs Billboard Campaign

Cognetix Advertising/Adams Outdoor

A Case Study of Billboard Effectiveness

Adams Outdoor Advertising, a large Atlanta-based firm, undertook a creative campaign to demonstrate the effectiveness of billboard advertising. With the assistance of Cognetix—an advertising agency located in Charleston, South Carolina—a scheme was hatched to test the effectiveness of billboard advertising. Adams and Cognetix ran a billboard campaign for a fictitious brand of bottled water they named *Outhouse Springs.* Playing on the concept of incongruity (bottled water named Outhouse Springs?) and using potty-type humor, billboard advertisements for Outhouse Springs were located throughout the Charleston market and achieved a 75 showing at a four-week cost of approximately $25,000. Messages on the billboards included amusing, albeit incredulous, statements such as "America's First Recycled Water"; "Originally in Cans... Now in Bottles"; "L-M-N-O- ..."; and "It's #1, Not #2" (see Figure 20.6 for illustrations).[22]

To assess campaign effectiveness, brand awareness, attitudes, and purchase intentions were measured in weekly intervals. By week three, 67 percent of a large sample of consumers indicated awareness of the hypothetical Outhouse Springs brand, 77 percent had neutral or favorable attitudes toward this bottled water brand, and 85 percent indicated an intention to purchase Outhouse Springs.

Although admittedly a highly unique and buzzable product (recall the discussion on buzz-building in Chapter 19), this campaign for a fictitious brand of bottled water reveals that large numbers of people are exposed to billboard ads and can be favorably influenced. Part of the success was no doubt due to the fact that widespread buzz generated stories on TV, on radio, and in newspaper

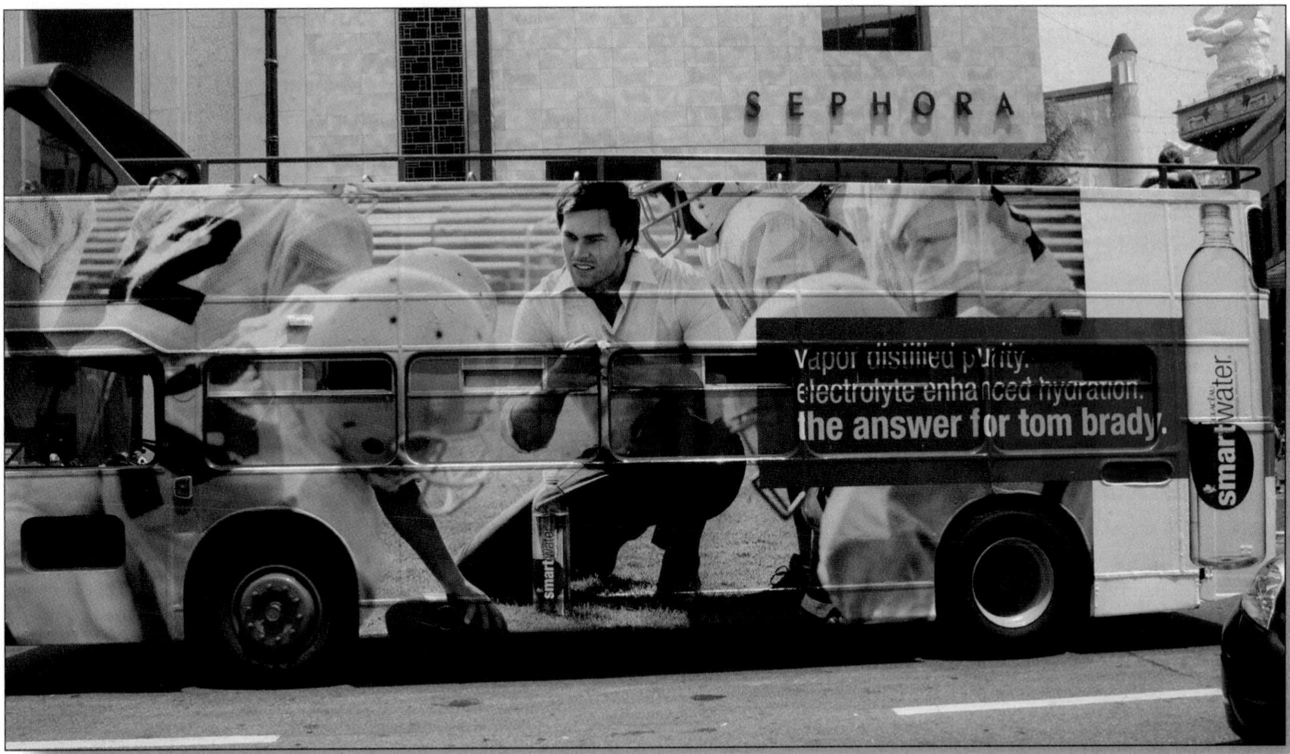

Figure 20.7

A Transit Advertisement for SmartWater

articles. Nonetheless, this test of a hypothetical brand illustrates that people are alert to billboard messages that are attention catching and memorable. For further discussion of the Outhouse Springs case along with other case studies of outdoor advertising effectiveness, go to the Outdoor Advertising Association of America's Web site: http://www.oaaa.org/outdoor/research/audience.asp.

Other Forms of OOH Advertising

The emphasis to this point has focused on billboards, which are the major form of OOH advertising. However, as alluded to earlier, OOH advertising also includes various forms of transit advertising (ads on buses, taxis, and trucks), advertising on bus shelters and other "street furniture," and various miscellaneous forms of outdoor advertising.

The creativity and potential effectiveness of these forms of nonbillboard OOH advertising is best illustrated with an examples. Figure 20.7 is a transit advertisement for SmartWater—a nutrient-enhanced vapor distilled European brand that seems to give Tom Brady his energy. The creativity and potential effectiveness of these forms of nonbillboard OOH advertising is best illustrated with examples. Figure 20.7 is a transit advertisement for SmartWater, a nutrient-enhanced, vapor-distilled European brand

Figure 20.8

Full-Wrap Bus Ad for Kodak

© Tony Freeman/Photo Edit

Figure 20.9

Bus Bench Ad for MADD

that seems to give Tom Brady his energy. Figure 20.8 shows another transit advertisement, this one for Kodak. As a sponsor of the 1998 Nagano Olympic Games, Eastman Kodak Company had marketing visibility with Japanese consumers who may never before have been exposed to Kodak products. A fleet of twelve full-sized city buses were completely "wrapped" with Kodak or Olympic imagery promoting Kodak's involvement in the Games, and served as attention-grabbing traveling billboards. Figure 20.9 is a bus bench ad for MADD and is another useful form of advertising directed at transit customers and passers-by.

Point-of-Purchase Advertising

Brand names and packages, topics of Chapter 3, confront head on at the point of purchase the ultimate arbiter of their effectiveness, the consumer. The point of purchase, or store environment, provides brand marketers with a final opportunity to affect consumer behavior. Brand managers recognize the value of point-of-purchase advertising; indeed, marketers in the United States are now spending in excess of $20 billion on various forms of point-of-purchase (P-O-P) communications.

The point of purchase is an ideal time to communicate with consumers because this is the time at which many product and brand-choice decisions are made. It is the time and place at which all elements of the sale (consumer, money, and product) come together.[23] The consumer's in-store behavior has been described in the following terms that highlight the importance of point-of-purchase advertising:

> *Shoppers are explorers. They're on safari, hunting for bargains, new products and different items to add excitement to their everyday lives. Three of every four are open to new experiences as they browse the aisles of supermarkets and search for bargains at drugstores and mass merchandisers.*[24]

Figure 20.10

Illustration of a Permanent Display

© POPAI, Point-Of-Purpose Advertising International

This translates into an opportunity to make a measurable impact just when shoppers are most receptive to new product ideas and alternative brands. Savvy marketers realize that the in-store environment is the last best chance to make a difference. P-O-P advertising often represents the culmination of a carefully integrated IMC program—at the point of purchase, consumers are reminded of previously processed mass media advertisements and now have the opportunity to benefit from a sales promotion offer.

The Spectrum of P-O-P Materials

Point-of-purchase materials include various types of signs, mobiles, plaques, banners, shelf ads, mechanical mannequins, lights, mirrors, plastic reproductions of products, checkout units, full-line merchandisers, various types of product displays, wall posters, floor advertisements, in-store radio and TV advertisements, electronic billboard advertising, and other items.[25] Industry representatives classify P-O-P materials into four categories:

- *Permanent displays:* These are displays intended for use for six months or more. (Note that the six-month dividing line is an arbitrary convention established by Point-of-Purchase Advertising International, which is known by its abbreviation, POPAI.) An illustration of a permanent display for BMW is presented in Figure 20.10.

- *Semipermanent displays:* Semipermanent P-O-P displays have an intended life span of less than six but more than two months. Figure 20.11 presents a semipermanent display for Listerine products.
- *Temporary displays:* Temporary P-O-P displays are designed for fewer than two months' usage. A temporary display for Kodak Inkjet products is presented in Figure 20.12.
- *In-store media:* In-store media include advertising and promotion materials such as in-store radio advertising, retail digital signage (TV-like screens at key locations), shopping cart advertising (such as discussed in the chapter-opening *Marcom Insight*), shelf advertisements (called shelf talkers), and floor graphics (advertisements placed on store floors; see illustration in Figure 20.13). A third-party company (i.e., a company other than the brand manufacturer or retailer) typically executes these in-store media. Brand marketers pay advertising rates to secure in-store radio time or shopping-cart and shelf-talker space on a nationwide basis or in specific markets.

© POPAI, Point-Of-Purpose Advertising International

Figure 20.11

Illustration of a Semi-Permanent Display

What Does P-O-P Accomplish?

Companies are increasingly investing in point-of-purchase advertising materials. As mentioned earlier, P-O-P advertising expenditures in the United States exceed $20 billion annually. This investment is justified because in-store materials provide useful services for all participants in the marketing process: manufacturers, retailers, and consumers.

Accomplishments for Manufacturers

For manufacturers, P-O-P keeps the company's name and the brand name before the consumer and reinforces a brand image that has been previously established through mass-media advertising or other outlets. P-O-P signage and displays also call attention to sales promotions and stimulate impulse purchasing.

Service to Retailers

P-O-P serves retailers by attracting the consumer's attention, increasing his or her interest in shopping, and extending the amount of time spent in the store—all of which lead to increased retail revenue and profits. Furthermore, P-O-P materials perform a critical merchandising function by aiding retailers in maximizing available space when, for example, various products are displayed in the same unit. P-O-P displays also enable retailers to better organize shelf and floor space and to improve inventory control and stock turnover.

Value to Consumers

Consumers are served by point-of-purchase units that deliver useful information and simplify the shopping process. Permanent, semipermanent, and temporary P-O-P units provide this value to consumers by setting particular brands apart from similar items and

Figure 20.12

Illustration of a Temporary Display

© Susan Van Etten/Photo Edit

© Susan Van Etten/Photo Edit

Figure 20.13

Illustration of Floor Advertisements

simplifying the selection process. Also, in-store media inform consumers of new products and brands. (See the *IMC Focus* for further discussion of in-store TV advertising.)

However, there is a downside to the growing use of in-store displays and advertising materials: consumers sometimes are overwhelmed with excessive P-O-P stimuli. A marketing commentator has even compared the widespread usage of in-store advertising materials with online spam.[26] Like all advertising media, the in-store environment suffers from ad *clutter*, which can irritate consumers and reduce the effectiveness of brand marketers' advertising efforts. This explains why a number of retailers are implementing "clean floor" policies by reducing the number, size, and appearance of displays in an effort to enhance consumers' shopping experience.[27]

In addition to benefiting all participants in the marketing process, point-of-purchase plays another important role: It serves as the capstone for an IMC program. P-O-P by itself may have limited impact, but when used in conjunction with mass-media advertisements and promotions, P-O-P can create a synergistic effect. Research has shown that when P-O-P reinforces a brand's advertising message, the increase in sales volume can be substantial. Illustrations of this synergism appear in a later section that presents empirical evidence of P-O-P's effectiveness.

P-O-P's Influence on Consumer Behavior

P-O-P materials influence consumers in three general ways: (1) by *informing* them about specific items; (2) by *reminding* them of information acquired from other advertising media; and (3) by *encouraging* them to select particular brands, sometimes on impulse.

Informing

Informing consumers is P-O-P's most basic communications function. Signs, posters, displays, in-store advertisements, and other P-O-P materials alert consumers to specific items and provide potentially useful information.

Motion displays are especially effective for this purpose. Motion displays, although typically more expensive than static displays, represent a potentially sound business investment if they attract significantly higher levels of shopper attention. Evidence from three studies shows that motion displays often are worth the extra expense.[28]

Researchers tested the relative effectiveness of motion and static displays for Olympia beer, a once successful but now bygone brand, by placing the two types of displays in a test sample of California liquor stores and supermarkets. Each of the sampled stores was stocked with either static or motion displays. Another sample of stores, serving as the control group, received no displays. More than 62,000 purchases of Olympia beer were recorded during the four-week test period. Static displays in liquor stores increased Olympia sales by 56 percent over stores with no displays (the control group). In supermarkets, static displays improved Olympia sales by a considerably smaller, although nonetheless substantial, amount (18 percent). More dramatic, however, was the finding that motion displays increased Olympia sales by 107 percent in liquor stores and by 49 percent in supermarkets.

A second test of the effectiveness of motion displays used S. B. Thomas' English muffins as the focal product. Two groups of 40 stores each were matched by store volume and customer demographics. One group was equipped with an

IMC >> i.m.c. focus

The Growth of In-Store TV

Each of the four major TV networks in the United States (ABC, CBS, Fox, and NBC) has affiliated stations throughout the country, thus representing attractive media for reaching millions of viewers for TV programs and the commercials carried therein. And now a number of retailers—Wal-Mart, Target, Borders, Kroger, etc.—are establishing their own in-store TV networks. Over 600,000 TV screens are now located in U.S. retail stores, with an expected annual growth rate of 20 percent. Unlike the four major (out-of-store) TV networks, which reach consumers in the comfort of their homes or at bars and other public venues, the in-store TV networks expose consumers to ads when they are shopping and thus as close as possible to the time when they make purchase decisions.

Unsurprisingly, Wal-Mart was one of the first retailers to recognize the potential of in-store TV as a means for exposing its customers to ads for brands carried in its stores. Nielsen Media Research estimates that the Wal-Mart network reaches 133 million viewers in a typical four-week period, which represents about one-third of Wal-Mart's customers during the same period. What advertising content is carried on the Wal-Mart TV network? You might think just ads placed by Wal-Mart itself. In actuality, the ads are placed by national advertisers who hope to reach consumers as close as possible to the point at which they make purchasing decisions. For example, Kellogg Co. reported a significant increase in sales from advertising two new products on Wal-Mart TV, Cheez-It Twists and Corn Flakes with bananas. TV spots on Wal-Mart TV cost anywhere from $50,000 to $300,000 per four-week period, with the actual cost depending on the frequency with which the ads appear.

Advertisers have learned that it is best to customize ads just for in-store TV rather than running the identical ads shown on conventional television. In-store ads must be particularly attention grabbing in order to divert consumers' attention away from the primary reason they are in the store, namely to shop rather than to watch TV ads. This calls for using shorter ads than what typically appears on out-of-store TVs and also positioning TV monitors at eye level to have an optimal opportunity of diverting the shopper's attention.

SOURCE: Amy Johannes, "Tuning In: In-store TV Finds Captive Audiences," *Promo,* January 2008, 11–12; Erin White, "Look Up for New Products in Aisle 5," *The Wall Street Journal Online,* March 23, 2004, http://online.wsj.com; Ann Zimmerman, "Wal-Mart Adds In-store TV Sets, Lifts Advertising," *The Wall Street Journal Online,* September 22, 2004, http://online.wsj.com.

S. B. Thomas' English muffin post sign that moved from side to side. The other 40 stores used regular floor displays with no motion. Sales of Thomas' muffins in the stores stocked with motion displays were more than 100 percent greater than in stores with static displays.

A third test of motion versus static displays involved Eveready batteries in tests conducted in Atlanta and San Diego. Six drugstores, six supermarkets, and six mass merchandise stores were divided into two groups, as with the Thomas' muffin study. For mass merchandisers, the static displays increased sales during the test period by 2.7 percent over the base period, but surprisingly, sales in the drug and food outlets using the static displays were slightly less (each 1.6 percent lower) than those not using the static displays. By comparison, the motion displays uniformly increased sales by 3.7 percent, 9.1 percent, and 15.7 percent in the drugstore outlets, supermarkets, and mass merchandisers, respectively.

All three sets of results demonstrate the relative effectiveness of motion displays compared to static displays. The consumer information-processing rationale (see Chapter 5) is straightforward: (1) Motion displays attract attention. (2) Attention, once attracted, is directed toward salient product features, including recognition of the displayed brand's name. (3) Brand name information activates consumers' memories pertaining to brand attributes previously processed from media advertising. (4) Information on brand attributes, when recalled, supplies a reason for the consumer to purchase the displayed brand. It also is possible that merely seeing a display intimates that the displayed brand is on sale, whether it is or not.[29]

Hence, a moving display performs the critical in-store function of bringing a brand's name to active memory. The probability of purchasing the brand increases, perhaps substantially (as in the case of S. B. Thomas' English muffins), if the consumer is favorably disposed toward the brand. The Eveready display was less effective apparently because the selling burden was placed almost exclusively on the display. Without prior stimulation of demand through advertising, the static display was ineffective, and the motion display was not as effective as it might have been.

Reminding

A second point-of-purchase function is reminding consumers of brands they have previously learned about via broadcast, print, or other advertising media. This reminder role serves to complement the job already performed by advertising before the consumer enters a store.

To appreciate the reminder role served by point-of-purchase materials fully, it is important to address a key principle from cognitive psychology: the **encoding specificity principle.** In simple terms, this principle states that information recall is enhanced when the context in which people attempt to retrieve information is the same as or similar to the context in which they originally encoded the information. (Encoding is the placing of informational items into memory.)

A non-marketing illustration—one that may bring back some unpleasant memories—will serve to clarify the exact meaning and significance of the encoding specificity principle. Remember a time when you were studying for a crucial exam that required problem-solving skills. You may have been up late at night trying to solve a particularly difficult problem, perhaps in accounting, calculus, or statistics. Eventually, the solution came to you, and you felt well prepared for the next day's exam. Sure enough, the exam had a problem very similar to the one you worked on the night before. However, to your dismay, your mind went blank, and you were unable to solve the problem. But after the exam, back in your room, the solution hit you like the proverbial ton of bricks.

Encoding specificity is the "culprit." Specifically, the context in which you originally encoded information and formulated a solution to the problem (i.e., your room) was different from the context in which you subsequently were asked to solve a similar problem (your classroom). Hence, contextual retrieval cues were unavailable in the classroom to readily facilitate your recall of how you originally solved the problem.

Returning to the marketplace, consider the situation in which consumers encode television commercial information about a brand and its unique features and benefits. The advertiser's expectation is that consumers will be able to retrieve this information at the point of purchase and use it to select the advertiser's brand over competitive offerings. It does not always work like this, however. Our memories are fallible, especially since we are exposed to an incredible amount of advertising information. Although we may have encoded advertising information at one time, we may not be able to retrieve it subsequently without a reminder cue at the point of purchase.

Consider, for example, the pink-bunny-pounding-a-drum advertising campaign. Most everyone is aware of this campaign, but many consumers have difficulty remembering the advertised brand. (Think for a moment; which brand is it?) When facing brands of Duracell, Eveready, and Energizer on the shelf, the consumer may not connect the pink-bunny advertising with any specific brand. Here is where point-of-purchase materials can perform a critically important role. Energizer (the pink-bunny brand) can facilitate encoding specificity by using shelf signs or packaging graphics that present the bunny and the Energizer name together, just as they appeared together in advertisements. Accordingly, by providing consumers with encoding-specific retrieval cues, chances are that consumers will recall from earlier advertisements that Energizer is the battery brand that powers the unceasing drum-pounding bunny.

The crucial point is that media advertising and P-O-P communications must be tightly integrated so that in-store reminder cues can capitalize on the background work media advertising accomplishes. Signs, displays, and in-store media provide the culmination for an IMC campaign and increase the odds that consumers will select a particular brand over alternatives.

Encouraging

Encouraging consumers to buy a specific item or brand is P-O-P's third function. Effective P-O-P materials influence product and brand choices at the point of purchase and encourage unplanned purchasing and even impulse buying. The following section elaborates on this critical role of P-O-P advertising.

Evidence of In-Store Decision Making

Studies of consumer shopping behavior have shown that a high proportion of all purchases are unplanned, especially in supermarkets, drugstores, and mass merchandise outlets (such as Wal-Mart and Target). *Unplanned purchasing* means that many product and brand choice decisions are made while the consumer is in the store rather than beforehand. Point-of-purchase materials play a role—perhaps the major role—in influencing unplanned purchasing. The following section discusses research on unplanned purchasing, and a subsequent section then presents impressive evidence on the role of P-O-P displays in increasing sales volume.

The POPAI Consumer Buying Habits Study

A trade association named Point-of-Purchase Advertising International (POPAI) conducted this important study, which confirms that in-store media, signage, and displays heavily influence consumers' purchase decisions.[30] The study collected data from 4,200 consumers who were shopping in the stores of 22 leading supermarket chains and 4 mass merchandisers—Bradlees, Kmart, Target, and Wal-Mart—located in 14 major markets throughout the United States. The study was conducted in the following manner:

- Researchers screened shoppers age 16 or older to determine that they were on a "major shopping trip."
- Researchers then interviewed qualified shoppers both before they began their shopping (entry interviews) and after they had completed their shopping trips (exit interviews). Interviews were conducted during all times of the day and every day of the week.
- During the preshopping entry interviews, researchers used an unaided questioning format to ask shoppers about their planned purchases on that particular occasion and probed for brand buying intentions. Then, during postshopping exit interviews, researchers gathered supermarket shoppers' register tapes or physically inventoried shoppers' carts at the four mass merchandise stores.
- By comparing shoppers' planned purchases obtained during entry interviews with actual purchases during exit interviews, it was possible to classify every brand purchase into one of four types of purchase behaviors: specifically planned, generally planned, substitute purchases, and unplanned purchases. Each group is defined as follows:

    1. *Specifically planned:* This category represents purchases of a brand that the consumer had indicated an intention to buy. For example, the purchase of Diet Pepsi would be considered a specifically planned purchase if during the entry interview a consumer mentioned her or his intention to purchase

table 20.1

Results from the POPAI Consumer Buying Habits Study

Type of Purchase	Supermarket	Mass Merchandising Store
1. Specifically planned	30%	26%
2. Generally Planned	6	18
3. Substiute	4	3
4. Unplanned	60	53
In-store decision rate (2+3+4)	70%	74%

Source: *The 1995 POPAI Consumer Buying Habits Study*, p. 18 (Washington, D.C.: Point-of-Purchase Advertising International). Reprinted by permission.

that brand and in fact bought Diet Pepsi. According to the Consumer Buying Habits Study (see Table 20.1), 30 percent of supermarket purchases and 26 percent of mass merchandise purchases were specifically planned.

2. *Generally planned:* This classification applies to purchases for which the shopper indicated an intention to buy a particular product (say, a soft drink) but had no specific brand in mind. The purchase of Diet Pepsi in this case would be classified as a generally planned purchase rather than a specifically planned purchase. Generally planned purchases constituted 6 percent of those in supermarkets and 18 percent in mass merchandise stores (see Table 20.1).
3. *Substitute purchases:* Purchases where the shopper does not buy the product or brand indicated in the entry interview constitute substitute purchases. For example, if a consumer said she or he intended to buy Diet Pepsi but actually purchased Diet Coke, that behavior would be classified as a substitute purchase. These represented just 4 percent of supermarket purchases and 3 percent of mass merchandise purchases.
4. *Unplanned purchases:* Under this heading are purchases for which the consumer had no prior purchase intent. If, for example, a shopper buys Diet Pepsi without having informed the interviewer of this intent, the behavior would be recorded as an unplanned purchase. Sixty percent of the purchases in supermarkets and 53 percent of those in mass merchandise stores were classified as unplanned.

Notice in Table 20.1 that the summation of generally planned, substitute, and unplanned purchases constitutes the *in-store decision rate.* In other words, the three categories representing purchases that are *not* specifically planned together represent decisions influenced by in-store factors. The in-store decision rates are 70 and 74 percent for supermarkets and mass merchandise stores, respectively. These percentages indicate that in-store factors influence approximately 7 out of 10 purchase decisions. It is apparent that P-O-P materials represent a very important determinant of consumers' product and brand choice behaviors!

It is important to recognize that not all purchases interviewers recorded as unplanned are truly unplanned. Rather, some purchases are recorded as unplanned simply because shoppers are unable or unwilling during the entry interview to inform interviewers of their exact purchase plans. This is not to imply that the POPAI research is seriously flawed but rather that the measurement of unplanned purchases probably is somewhat overstated due to the unavoidable bias just described. Other categories may be biased also. For example, by the same logic, the percentage of specifically planned purchases is probably somewhat understated. In any event, POPAI's findings are important even if they are not precisely correct.

The summary statistics in Table 20.1 represent types of purchases aggregated over literally hundreds of product categories. It should be apparent that in-store decision rates vary greatly across product categories. To emphasize this point, Tables 20.2 and 20.3 present categories with the highest and lowest in-store decision rates for supermarkets (Table 20.2) and mass merchandise stores (Table 20.3).

table 20.2

Product Categories with the Five Highest and Five Lowest In-Store Decision Rates: Supermarket Purchases

Category	In-Store decision Rate
Highest in-store decision rate [sans First aid]	
First aid	93%
Toys, sporting goods, crafts	93
Housewares/hardware	90
Stationery	90
Candy/gum	89
Lowest in-store decision rate [again, sans First aid]	
Produce	33
Meat, seafood	47
Eggs	53
Coffee	58
Baby food/formula	58

Source: "Product Categories with the Five Highest and Five Lowest In-Store Decision Rates: Supermarket Purchases," p. 19. *The 1995 POPAI Consumer Buying Habits Study* (Washington, D.C.: Point-of-Purchase Advertising International). Reprinted by permission.

table 20.3

Product Categories with the Five Highest and Five Lowest In-Store Decision Rates: Mass Merchandise Purchases

Category	In-Store Decision Rate
Highest in-Store decision rate	
Apparel accessories	92%
Foils, food wraps	91
Hardware, electric, plumbing	90
Infant/toddler wear	90
Garbage bags	88
Lowest in-store decision rate	
Disposable diapers	35
Baby food	35
Eyedrops and lens care	52
Prerecorded music, videos	54
Coffee, tea, cocoa	55

Source: "Product Categories with the Five Highest and Five Lowest In-Store Decision Rates: Mass Merchandise Purchases," p. 20. *The 1995 POPAI Consumer Buying Habits Study* (Washington, D.C.: Point-of-Purchase Advertising International). Reprinted by permission.

The data presented in Tables 20.2 and 20.3 make it clear that in-store decision rates vary substantially. Supermarket products that are virtual staples (e.g., produce) and mass merchandise products that are essential and regularly purchased items (e.g., disposable diapers) have the lowest in-store purchase rates because most consumers know they are going to purchase these items when they go to the store. Conversely, nonnecessities and items that generally do not occupy top-of-the-mind thoughts (e.g., first-aid supplies and garbage bags) are especially susceptible to the influence of in-store stimuli. It is clear that for these types of products, brand marketers must have a distinct presence at the point of purchase if they hope to sway purchase decisions toward their brands.

Factors Influencing In-Store Decision Making Academic researchers were provided access to data from POPAI's *Consumer Buying Habits Study.*[31] The researchers' objective was to determine what effect a variety of shopping-trip factors (e.g., size of shopping party, use of a shopping list, number of aisles shopped) and consumer characteristics (e.g., deal proneness, compulsiveness, age, gender, and income) have on unplanned purchasing.

table 20.4

Supermarket and Mass Merchandise Product Categories with Highest Average Brand Lifts from Displays

	Brand List Index
Supermarket categories	
Butter/margarine	6.47
Cookies	6.21
Soft drinks	5.37
Beer/ale	4.67
Mixers	4.03
Sour cream/cream cheese	3.79
Cereal	3.73
Hand and body soaps	3.62
Packaged cheese	3.57
Canned fish	3.55
Salty snacks	3.50
Mass merchandise categories	
Film/photofinishing	47.67
Socks/underwear/panty hose	29.43
Cookies/crackers	18.14
Small appliances	8.87
Foils, food wraps, and bags	7.53
Adult apparel	7.45
Pet supplies	5.55
Packaged bread	5.01

Source: "Supermarket and the Mass Merchandise Product Categories with Highest Average Brand Lifts from Displays," p. 24. *The 1995 POPAI Consumer Buying Habits Study* (Washington, D.C.: Point-of-Purchase Advertising International). Reprinted by permission.

The researchers determined that the rate of unplanned purchasing is elevated when consumers are on a major (versus fill-in) shopping trip, when they shop more of a store's aisles, when the household size is large, and when they are deal prone. Perhaps the major practical implication from this research is that retailers benefit from having consumers shop longer and traverse more of the store while shopping, thus increasing the odds of purchasing unintended items. One way of accomplishing this is by locating frequently purchased items (e.g., items such as bread and milk) in locations that require consumers to pass as many other items as possible.[32]

Brand Lift POPAI and a collaborating research company developed a measure—called the *brand lift index*—to gauge the average increase of in-store purchase decisions when P-O-P is present versus when it is not.[33] (The term *lift* is used in reference to increasing, or lifting, sales in the presence of P-O-P materials.) The brand lift index simply indicates how in-store P-O-P materials affect the likelihood that customers will buy a product that they had not specifically planned to buy.

Table 20.4 shows the products that enjoy the highest brand lift from displays. For example, the index of 47.67 for film and photofinishing products in mass merchandise stores indicates that shoppers are nearly 48 times more likely to make in-store purchase decisions for these products when advertised with displays than if there were no displays. (Note that the index of 47.67 does *not* mean that sales of film and other photofinishing items are over 47 times greater when a display is used. Rather, this index merely reveals that consumers are nearly 48 times more likely to make in-store decisions in the presence versus absence of displays.) And supermarket shoppers are 6.47 times more likely to make in-store decisions to purchase butter or margarine when these items are displayed compared to when they are not displayed. Needless to say, displays can have incredible influence on consumer behavior.

Evidence of Display Effectiveness

Practitioners are vitally interested in knowing whether the cost of special P-O-P displays is justified. Two important studies have examined the impact of displays and provided evidence that enlightens this issue.

The POPAI/Kmart/P&G Study

This notable study was conducted by a consortium of a trade association (POPAI), a mass merchandiser (Kmart), and a consumer-goods manufacturer (Procter & Gamble [P&G]).[34] The study investigated the impact that displays have on sales of P&G brands in six product categories: paper towels, shampoo, toothpaste, deodorant, coffee, and fabric softener. The test lasted for a period of four weeks, and P&G's brands were advertised in mass media outlets and sold at their regular prices throughout the test period. Seventy-five Kmart stores in the United States were matched in terms of brand sales, store volume, and shopper demographics and then assigned to three panels, or groups, of 25 stores each:

Control panel. The 25 stores in this group merchandised P&G brands in their normal shelf position *without any special displays.*

Test panel 1. These 25 stores carried the advertised brands on *display.*

Test panel 2. The 25 stores in this group carried the advertised brands on *display;* however, different displays were used than those in test panel 1, or the same displays were used as in test panel 1 but at different locations in the store.

Specific differences in displays/locations between test panels 1 and 2 are shown in Table 20.5. For example, paper towels were displayed in a mass waterfall display at two different (but undisclosed) store locations; shampoo was displayed in either a special shelf unit display or a floorstand display; and coffee was displayed either on a quarter pallet outside the coffee aisle or a full pallet at the end of the coffee aisle—called an endcap display.

Most importantly, the last column in Table 20.5 compares the percentage sales increase in each set of test stores (with displays) against the control stores

Table 20.5

Display Information for POPAI/Kmart/P&G Study

Product Category	Test Panels and Displays	Test Panel Sales versus Control Panel Sales (Percentage increase)
Paper towels	Test 1: Mass waterfall (MW) display	447.1%
	Test 2: MW display in a different location	773.5
Shampoo	Test 1: Shelf unit	18.2
	Test 2: Floorstand	56.8
Toothpaste	Test 1: Floorstand in toothpaste aisle	73.1
	Test 2: Quarter pallet outside toothpaste aisle	119.2
Deodorant	Test 1: Powerwing	17.9
	Test 2: Powerwing in a different store location	38.5
Coffee	Test 1: Quarter pallet outside coffee aisle	500.0
	Test 2: Full pallet on endcap of coffee aisle	567.4
Fabric softener	Test 1: Full pallet on endcap of laundry aisle	66.2
	Test 2: Quarter pallet outside laundry aisle	73.8

Source: "Display Information for POPAI/Kmart/P&G Study," from "POPAI/Kmart/Procter & Gamble Study" of P-O-P Effectiveness in Mass Merchandising Stores, p. 20. *The 1995 POPAI Consumer Buying Habits Study* (Washington, D.C.: Point-of-Purchase Advertising International). Reprinted by permission.

where P&G brands were sold in their regular (nondisplay) shelf locations. It is readily apparent that positive sales increases materialized for all products and under both set of display conditions versus the nondisplay control stores. In some instances the increases were nothing short of huge. P&G's brands of shampoo and deodorant experienced modest increases during the four-week test of only about 18 percent (test panel 1), whereas paper towels and coffee experienced triple-digit increases in both display conditions—sales increases of 773.5 percent for paper towels (test panel 2) and 567.4 percent for coffee (test panel 2)!

The POPAI/Warner-Lambert Studies

Two additional studies extend the POPAI/Kmart/P&G findings obtained from mass merchandise stores in the United States to drugstores in Canada.[35] POPAI and Warner-Lambert Canada jointly investigated the effectiveness of P-O-P displays on sales of health items in drugstores. Eighty stores from four major drugstore chains participated (Shoppers Drug Mart, Jean Coutu, Cumberland, and Pharmaprix), and testing was conducted in three major cities: Toronto, Montreal, and Vancouver. Two brands were involved in the testing: Benylin cough syrup and Listerine mouthwash.

The Benylin Study Stores were divided into four groups for the Benylin test: Stores in group 1 offered regularly priced Benylin in its normal (nondisplay) shelf position; stores in group 2 merchandised Benylin in the normal shelf position but at a feature (i.e., discounted) price; stores in group 3 displayed Benylin at a feature price on endcap displays; and group 4 stores used in-aisle floorstand displays of Benylin at a feature price. Sales data were captured during a two-week period in each store to gauge display effectiveness.

The effectiveness of both feature pricing and displays is determined simply by comparing sales volume during the test period in store groups 2 through 4 with sales in group 1—the baseline group. These comparisons reveal the following:

- Stores in group 2 (Benylin located at its regular shelf position but feature priced) enjoyed 29 percent greater sales volume of Benylin than the stores in group 1 (Benylin at its regular price and normal shelf location). This 29 percent increment reflects simply the effect of feature pricing as both store groups sold Benylin from its regular shelf location.
- Stores in group 3 (Benylin on an endcap display and feature priced) enjoyed 98 percent greater sales of Benylin than did stores in group 1. This increment reflects the substantial impact that the endcap display and feature price combination had on the number of units sold. The large percentage increase in comparison to group 2 (i.e., 98 percent versus 29 percent) reflects the incremental impact of the endcap display location over the effect of feature pricing per se.
- Stores in group 4 (Benylin displayed in-aisle and feature priced) realized 139 percent greater sales volume than the baseline stores, which indicates that this location, at least for this product category, is more valuable than is the endcap location.

The POPAI/Warner-Lambert Listerine Study Stores were divided into four groups for this test: group 1 stores offered regularly priced Listerine in its normal shelf position; group 2 stores offered Listerine in the normal shelf position but at a feature price; group 3 stores displayed Listerine at a feature price on endcap displays at the *rear* of the store; and group 4 stores displayed Listerine at a feature price on endcap displays at the *front* of the store. Sales data were captured during a two-week period in each store to gauge display effectiveness.

Again, the effectiveness of displays can be determined by comparing sales volume of groups 2 through 4 with sales in baseline group 1:

- Stores in group 2 (Listerine located at its regular shelf position but feature priced) enjoyed 11 percent greater sales volume of Listerine than the stores in group 1 (where Listerine was regular priced and located in its regular shelf position).
- Stores in group 3 (Listerine at a rear endcap display and feature priced) experienced 141 percent greater sales of Listerine than the stores in group 1.
- Stores in group 4 (Listerine at a front endcap display and feature priced) enjoyed 162 percent greater sales volume than the baseline stores.

Both sets of results reveal that these two drugstore brands, Benylin and Listerine, benefited greatly when feature priced and merchandised from prized locations. The Listerine study results came as a bit of surprise to industry observers, however, who expected the advantage of the front endcap location to be substantially greater in comparison to the rear endcap location. The premium price that manufacturers pay for front endcap placement (versus rear endcap positioning) may not be fully justified in light of these results. Additional research with other product categories is needed before any definitive answer is possible.

The Use and Nonuse of P-O-P Materials

Although P-O-P materials can be very effective for manufacturers and perform several desirable functions for retailers, the fact remains that perhaps as much as 40 to 50 percent of P-O-P materials supplied by manufacturers are never used by retailers or are used incorrectly.[36]

With the advent of radio frequency identification chips (RFID) attached to displays, manufacturers have acquired keen insight into retailers' use or nonuse of displays. The RFID technology enables manufacturers to track the exact location of displays and to know when display units are erected and taken down. Procter & Gamble learned in a study of display usage for its Braun's Cruzer electric razors that one third of retailers did not comply with their agreement to erect a display for this product. P&G also found that retailers erected displays correctly only 45 percent of the time.[37] Research by Kimberly-Clark determined that its retailers used the correct P-O-P displays only 55 percent of the time.[38] It is apparent that retailers do not always comply with manufacturers' display-usage instructions.

Reasons Why P-O-P Materials Go Unused

Five major reasons explain why retailers choose not to use P-O-P materials. First, there is no incentive for the retailer to use certain P-O-P materials because these materials are inappropriately designed and do not satisfy the retailer's needs. Second, some displays take up too much space for the amount of sales generated. Third, some materials are too unwieldy, too difficult to set up, too flimsy, or have other construction defects. A fourth reason many signs and displays go unused is because they lack eye appeal. Finally, retailers are concerned that displays and other P-O-P materials simply serve to increase sales of a particular manufacturer's brand during the display period, but that the retailer's sales and profits for the entire product category are not improved. In other words, a retailer has little incentive to erect displays or use signage that merely serves to transfer sales from one brand to another but that does not increase the retailer's overall sales and profits for the product category.

Encouraging Retailers to Use P-O-P Materials

Encouraging retailers to use P-O-P materials is a matter of basic marketing. Persuading the retailer to enthusiastically use a display or other P-O-P device means that the manufacturer must view the material from the retailer's perspective. First and foremost, P-O-P materials must satisfy the retailer's needs and the consumers' needs rather than just those of the manufacturer. This is the essence of marketing, and it applies to encouraging the use of P-O-P materials just as much as promoting the acceptance of the manufacturer's own brands. Hence, manufacturers must design P-O-P materials to satisfy the following requirements:

- They are the right size and format.
- They fit the store decor.
- They are user friendly—that is, easy for the retailer to attach, erect, or otherwise use.
- They are sent to stores when they are needed (e.g., at the right selling season).
- They are properly coordinated with other aspects of the marcom program (i.e., they should tie into a current advertising or sales promotion program).
- They are attractive, convenient, and useful for consumers.[39]

Measuring In-Store Advertising's Audience

Earlier in the chapter we concluded the section on OOH advertising by discussing the measurement of that medium's audience size and characteristics and noting that, unfortunately, accurate data have in the past been unavailable regarding OOH's audience characteristics. Historically, the same could be said for P-O-P advertising. However, in recent years the P-O-P's trade association—the Point of Purchase Advertising International (POPAI)—has undertaken a major initiative in conjunction with a consortium of major brand marketers and retailers (e.g., Coca-Cola, Kellogg, Kroger, Miller Brewing, P&G, and Wal-Mart), to develop a means of measuring the effectiveness of in-store advertising media.[40] This initiative, termed PRISM (Pioneering Research for an In-Store Metric) has devised a procedure for acquiring standard diagnostics (reach, frequency, gross ratings, etc.) for measuring the performance of in-store media. It is only a matter of time before brand marketers can plan and evaluate in-store advertising using the same procedures and discipline they have used for decades in planning for and evaluating advertising placed in print and broadcast media.

Summary

This chapter covered three relatively minor (vis-à-vis mass-media advertising) forms of marcom communications: on-premise business signage; out-of-home, or off-premise, advertising; and point-of-purchase advertising. The first two topics were covered somewhat briefly compared to P-O-P advertising, but the argument was made that both off- and on-premise messages perform important functions and are capable of influencing consumers' awareness of and perceptions of stores and brands. The various forms of off- and on-premise messages were described and illustrations provided. Primary emphasis was devoted to billboard advertising. This discussion included description of the forms of billboard advertising, explanation of billboard advertising's strengths and limitations, and discussion of how billboard ads are purchased and how the effectiveness of billboard advertising is measured.

Major chapter coverage was devoted to P-O-P advertising. The point of purchase is an ideal time to communicate with consumers. Accordingly, anything that a consumer is exposed to at the point of purchase can perform an important communication function. A variety of P-O-P materials—signs, displays, and various in-store media—are used to attract consumers' attention to particular brands, provide information, affect perceptions, and ultimately influence shopping behavior. P-O-P displays—which are distinguished broadly as permanent, semipermanent, or temporary—perform a variety of useful functions for manufacturers, retailers, and consumers.

Research has documented the high incidence of consumers' in-store purchase decision making and the corresponding importance of P-O-P materials in these purchase decisions. POPAI's *Consumer Buying Habits Study* classified all consumer purchases into four categories: specifically planned, generally planned, substitutes, and unplanned decisions. The combination of the last three categories represents in-store decisions that are influenced by P-O-P displays and other store cues. Importantly, it is estimated that in-store decisions represent as much as 70 percent of supermarket purchase decisions and 74 percent of the decisions in mass merchandise stores. Research on the effectiveness of displays—such as the joint undertaking by POPAI, Kmart, and Procter & Gamble—provides evidence that displayed brands sometimes enjoy gigantic, triple-digit increases in sales volume during the display period.

Discussion Questions

1. What are your personal views about the advantages and disadvantages of supermarket shopping with intelligent shopping carts such as the Shopping Buddy and the MediaCart (see *Marcom Insight*)?
2. During past decades, cigarette advertisements were responsible for a very large percentage of all billboard advertising in the United States. What explanation can you offer for why this product dominated the billboard medium? What is it about consumer behavior related to this product that would make billboards an especially attractive advertising medium?
3. Changeable message signs are billboards that vary the advertising message on a schedule of every 4 to 10 seconds. What, in your opinion, is the value of this technology to the advertiser, and what are the potential hazards to society?
4. The Outhouse Springs bottled water case illustrated an effective application of billboard advertising. With reference to the material on "buzz generation" covered in Chapter 18, what is it about this particular campaign that may make these results atypical and thus unrepresentative of more mundane products advertised via billboards?
5. Conduct an informal audit of on-premise business signage in your college or university community. Specifically, select five examples of on-premise signage that you regard as particularly effective. Using material from Chapter 5 on the CPM and HEM models, explain why your chosen illustrations likely stand a good chance of attracting consumer attention and influencing their behavior.
6. What functions can point-of-purchase materials accomplish that mass media advertising cannot?
7. Explain why the *POPAI Consumer Buying Habits Study* probably overestimates the percentage of unplanned purchases and underestimates the percentage of specifically planned and generally planned purchases.
8. Although not presented in the chapter, the *POPAI Consumer Buying Habits Study* revealed that the percentage of in-store decisions for coffee was 57.9 percent, whereas the comparable percentage was 87.1 percent for a group of "sauce" products (salsa, picante sauce, and dips). What accounts for the 29.2 percent difference in in-store decision making between coffee and the "sauce" products? Go beyond these two product categories and offer a generalization as to what factors determine whether a particular product category would exhibit a low or high proportion of in-store decision making.
9. The *POPAI Consumer Buying Habits Study* also revealed that the highest average brand lift index from signage (rather than displays) in mass merchandise stores was dishwashing soaps, with an index of 21.65. Provide an exact interpretation of this index value.
10. The discussion of the S. B. Thomas' English muffin study pointed out that in stores using motion displays, sales increased by more than 100 percent. By comparison, sales of Eveready batteries, when promoted with motion displays, increased anywhere from 3.7 percent to 15.7 percent, depending on the type of store in which the display was placed. Provide an explanation that accounts for the tremendous disparity in sales impact of motion displays for English muffins compared with batteries.
11. Why were motion and static displays considerably more effective at increasing Olympia beer sales in liquor stores than in supermarkets?
12. The MediaCart described in the chapter-opening *Marcom Insight* is subject to criticism on grounds that it will cost checkout clerks in supermarkets their jobs. What is your perspective on this matter?

End Notes

1. This description is based on several sources: "We 'Check Out' Latest Supermarket 'Smart' Cart," MSNBC.com, July 20, 2004, http://www.msnbc.com; "Stop & Shop to Roll Out New Intelligent Shopping Carts from IBM and Cuesol," *Yahoo! Finance*, October 13, 2004; Kelly Shermach, "IBM Builds High-Tech Grocery Cart," *CRMBuyer*, November 16, 2004.
2. This description of the MediaCart is based on Jack Neff, "A Shopping-Cart-Ad Plan That Might Actually Work," *Advertising Age*, February 5, 2007; "Microsoft Comes to Grocery Aisle," *The Wall Street Journal*, January 14, 2008; and personal correspondence from Jon Kramer, MediaCart Holdings' Chief Marketing Officer (July 17, 2006).
3. R. James Claus and Susan L. Claus, *Unmasking the Myths about Signs* (Alexandria, VA: International Sign Association, 2001), 16.
4. Claus and Claus, *Unmasking the Myths about Signs*, 9.
5. This distinction and the following details are from *The Signage Sourcebook: A Signage Handbook* (Washington, D.C.: U.S. Small Business Administration, 2003), 193.
6. Darrin Conroy, *What's Your Signage?* (Albany, N.Y.: The New York State Small Business Development Center, 2004), 8.
7. Ibid., 20.
8. This figure is for 2007, the last year available for advertising expenditures at the time of this writing; http://www.oaaa.org/outdoor/facts (accessed May 26, 2008).
9. Aaron O. Patrick, "Mass of Messages Lands at Heathrow," *The Wall Street Journal*, February 14, 2008, B3.
10. Rick T. Wilson and Brian D. Till, "Airport Advertising Effectiveness," *Journal of Advertising* 37 (spring 2008), 59–72.
11. Pierre Bouvard and Jacqueline Noel, "The Arbitron Outdoor Study," *Arbitron*, 2001, http://www.arbitron.com.
12. Aaron O. Patrick, "Technology Boosts Outdoor Ads as Competition Becomes Fiercer," *The Wall Street Journal*, August 28, 2006, A1.
13. Claus and Claus, *Unmasking the Myths about Signs*, 17.
14. "Digital Outdoor Advertising," http://www.wikinvest.com/concept/digital_outdoor_advertising (accessed May 26, 2008).
15. The estimate of 700 billboards is from Joseph Popiolkowski, "Digital Billboards Get Green Light," December 3, 2007, http://www.stateline.org/live/details/story?contentId=260259 (accessed May 26, 2008). The 4,000 figure is from Parick Condon, "Digital Billboards Face Challenges from Cities," *Marketing News*, March 15, 2007, 14.
16. Popiolkowski, "Digital Billboards Get Green Light."
17. For additional insights into why companies use billboard advertising, see Charles R. Taylor, George R. Franke, and Hae-Kyong Bang, "Use and Effectiveness of Billboards," *Journal of Advertising* 35 (winter 2006), 21–34.
18. Geoffrey A. Fowler and Sebastian Moffett, "Adidas's Billboard Ads Give Kick to Japanese Pedestrians," *The Wall Street Journal Online*, August 29, 2003, http://online.wsj.com; Normandy Madden, "Adidas Introduces Human Billboards," *Advertising Age*, September 1, 2003, 11.
19. Kimberly Palmer, "Highway Ads Take High-Tech Turn," *The Wall Street Journal Online*, September 12, 2003, http://online.wsj.com.
20. Myron Laible, "Changeable Message Signs: A Technology Whose Time Has Come," *Journal of Public Policy & Marketing* 16 (spring 1997), 173–176; Frank Vespe, "High-Tech Billboards: The Same Old Litter on a Stick," *Journal of Public Policy & Marketing* 16 (spring 1997), 176–179; Charles R. Taylor, "A Technology Whose Time Has Come or the Same Old Litter on a Stick? An Analysis of Changeable Message Boards," *Journal of Public Policy & Marketing* 16 (spring 1997), 179–186.
21. "First-ever U.S. Ratings Data from Nielsen Outdoor Show that Males 35-54 Have the Highest Exposure to Outdoor Advertising," *Nielsen Media Research*, December 6, 2005, http://www.nielsenmedia.com (accessed May 26, 2008).
22. A former graduate student, Ms. Brie Morrow, informed me of the Outhouse Springs billboard campaign. Brie and two of her colleagues, Jason Darby and Erin Vance, performed background work in writing a term paper for another class. I have referred to their term paper as well as additional source materials such as Jeremy D'Entremont, "Outhouse Springs and Piggly Wiggly Help Save the Light," *Lighthouse Digest*, http://www.lighthousedepot.com.
23. John A. Quelch and Kristina Cannon-Bonventre, "Better Marketing at the Point-of-Purchase," *Harvard Business Review* (November/December 1983), 162–169.
24. "Impact in the Aisles: The Marketer's Last Best Chance," *Promo*, January 1996, 25.
25. An inventory of P-O-P advertising materials is provided in Robert Liljenwall and James Maskulka, *Marketing's Powerful Weapon: Point-of-Purchase Advertising* (Washington, D.C.: Point-of-Purchase Advertising International, 2001), 177–180.
26. Kate Fitzgerald, "In-store Media Ring Cash Register," *Advertising Age*, February 9, 2004, 43.
27. "Retail Goes Feng Shui," *Promo*, October 2007, 16, 18.
28. *The Effect of Motion Displays on the Sales of Beer; The Effect of Motion Displays on Sales of Baked Goods; The Effect of Motion Displays on Sales of Batteries* (Englewood, N.J.: Point-of-Purchase Advertising Institute, undated).
29. J. Jeffrey Inman, Leigh McAlister, and Wayne D. Hoyer, "Promotion Signal: Proxy for a Price Cut," *Journal of Consumer Research* 17 (June 1990), 74–81.
30. *Measuring the In-Store Decision Making of Supermarket and Mass Merchandise Store Shoppers* (Englewood, N.J.: Point-of-Purchase Advertising Institute, 1995). Please note that POPAI has since changed its name from the Point-of-Purchase Advertising Institute to Point-of-Purchase Advertising International.

31. J. Jeffrey Inman and Russell S. Winer, "Where the Rubber Meets the Road: A Model of In-store Decision Making," *Marketing Science Institute Report* No. 98–122 (October 1998).
32. Ibid., 26.
33. *Measuring the In-Store Decision Making of Supermarket and Mass Merchandise Store Shoppers,* 23.
34. POPAI/Kmart/Procter & Gamble Study of P-O-P Effectiveness in Mass Merchandising Stores (Englewood, N.J.: Point-of-Purchase Advertising Institute, 1993).
35. *POPAI/Warner-Lambert Canada P-O-P Effectiveness Study* (Englewood, N.J.: The Point-of-Purchase Advertising Institute, 1992).
36. John P. Murry, Jr. and Jan B. Heide, "Managing Promotion Program Participation within Manufacturer-Retailer Relationships," *Journal of Marketing* 62 (January 1998), 58. *POPAI/Progressive Grocer Supermarket Retailer Attitude Study* (Englewood, N.J.: Point-of-Purchase Advertising Institute, 1994), 2.
37. Amy Johannes, "RFID Ramp-Up," *Promo,* March 2008, 14.
38. Amy Johannes, "Big Brother in the Aisles," *Promo,* May 2007, 14, 16.
39. Adapted from Don E. Schultz and William A. Robinson, *Sales Promotion Management,* 278–279. For further insights on gaining retailer participation in P-O-P programs, see Murry, Jr., and Heide (1998), "Managing Promotion Program Participation within Manufacturer-Retailer Relationships."
40. Doug Adams and Jim Spaeth, "In-store Advertising Audience Measurement Principles" (Washington, D.C.: Point-of-Purchase Advertising International, July 2003).

CHAPTER

21

Ethical, Regulatory, and Environmental Issues

Part 6
Marcom Constraints

Part Six consists of a single chapter, *Chapter 21.* It is important to examine the topics covered in this chapter—ethical, regulatory, and environmental issues—so as to appreciate fully that marketing communicators operate under constraints that limit certain actions yet ultimately benefit free markets and the businesses and customers who participate in them. The ethical issues discussed include targeting vulnerable groups, deceptive advertising, and unethical marcom practices. Also covered are governmental regulations, industry self-regulation of marcom practices, and environmental issues relevant to marcom decisions. In a world characterized by global warning, rapidly increasing petroleum costs, and accelerated depletion of natural resources, it is critical that marketing communicators play their part in sustaining resources and preserving the natural environment.

21

Ethical, Regulatory, and Environmental Issues

Equal, NutraSweet, and Splenda are well-known names of artificial sweeteners that are substitutes for sugar. Many consumers know these brands more by their package colors (blue, pink, and yellow) than by their brand names. Which one of these brands do you think has the largest market share in the United States? The leading brand has annual sales that are four times greater than any of the other well-known brands. The brand leader is Splenda.

Splenda was introduced to American consumers in 2000 and was advertised as being "Made from sugar, so it tastes like sugar" followed by "But it's not sugar." These claims resonated positively with consumers, and Splenda jumped to the top-selling sugar substitute in America. But the Merisant Company, maker of competitive brands Equal and NutraSweet, alleged in a lawsuit that the marketer of Splenda, McNeil Nutritionals, deliberately confused consumers by suggesting that Splenda is a natural product. Merisant's suit claimed that Splenda's sales increased substantially after McNeil's advertising approach tied Splenda to sugar by dropping the tagline statement "But it's not sugar" from ad messages and using other images implying that Splenda is a natural, non-artificial sugar-based product.[1]

Merisant lodged a complaint with the National Advertising Division (covered later in the chapter) and later filed a lawsuit in Pennsylvania against McNeil. The legal issues are technical, and the basis on which Merisant claimed that Splenda is not a natural sugar product requires a degree in chemistry to comprehend fully. Even McNeil, the maker of Splenda, acknowledged that Splenda's main ingredient is not natural. However, the clash between these artificial-sweetener competitors centered on the issue of whether Splenda's advertising and other marcom messages represented the brand as a "natural," sugar-based product.

The lawsuit between Merisant and McNeil came to a surprising culmination when the two parties arrived at a confidential settlement ending the court battle.[2] Interestingly, however, about the same time, a court in Paris determined that the marketing of Splenda in France is misleading to consumers and ordered that McNeil's advertising claims for Splenda cease. McNeil is appealing the court's decision at the time of this writing.[3]

© Richard B. Levine/Newscom

Chapter Objectives

After reading this chapter you should be able to:

1 Appreciate the ethical issues associated with advertising, sales promotions, and other marcom practices.

2 Understand why the targeting of marketing communications toward vulnerable groups is a heatedly debated practice.

3 Explain the role and importance of governmental efforts to regulate marketing communications.

4 Be familiar with deceptive advertising and the elements that guide the determination of whether a particular advertisement is deceptive.

5 Be acquainted with the regulation of unfair business practices and the major areas where the unfairness doctrine is applied.

6 Know the process of advertising self-regulation.

7 Appreciate the role of marketing communications in environmental (green) marketing.

8 Recognize the principles that apply to all green marcom efforts.

>>Marcom Insight:

Battle of the Sweeteners

Introduction

This chapter examines three major topics: (1) *ethical issues* in marketing communications, (2) the *regulation* of marcom practices, and (3) *environmental matters* and their implications for marketing communications. All three topics are interrelated: Ethical issues confronting contemporary marketing communicators sometimes occur over environmental marketing efforts, and regulation (from federal and state governments and by industry self-regulators) is needed due in large part to some unethical marketing communications practices.[4] The discussion of Splenda in the opening represents a situation where issues of advertising ethics and regulation were implicated.

Ethical Issues in Marketing Communications

Marketing communicators in their various capacities—as advertisers, sales promoters, package designers, public relations representatives, point-of-purchase designers, and so on—regularly make decisions that have ethical ramifications. Ethical lapses and moral indiscretions sometimes occur under pressures of trying to meet business goals and attempting to satisfy the demands of the financial community.

With an understanding of how marketing communications is ripe for assertions of unethical actions—because marcom practitioners sometimes *do* engage in unacceptable behaviors, although probably no more so than practitioners engaged in other societal pursuits—you will be better prepared to assess your own planned actions by taking a moral check and resisting the temptation to do something that may be expedient and rewarding in the short run but inappropriate and potentially costly in the long run. A respected educator has framed the importance of examining ethical issues in the following terms:

> *I think most people—and [college] students are no different—know right from wrong. I believe they care about doing right. But even those of us with a rudimentary moral sensibility aren't always able to evoke those basic principles when dealing with fairly routine business decisions. For instance, we may do an enthusiastic sales pitch and promise things our company isn't quite ready to deliver, or we might highlight the positive aspects of our products and downplay the negative ones. We might formulate financial projections to favor the outcome we advocate. We might overstep the boundaries when advertising to children or go overboard when we use personal data to target customers.... Ethical dilemmas do not arrive bathed in red lights. There is no sign that says, "You're about to enter an ethical zone." Therefore, ethics education is not about defining for students what is right and what is wrong. Ethics education should aim to raise our students' antennae for recognizing ethical implications, conflicts of interest, and exercises of asymmetric power when such dilemmas pop up without warning.*[5]

Ethics in our context involves matters of right and wrong, or *moral*, conduct pertaining to any aspect of marketing communications. For our purposes, the terms ethics and morality will be used interchangeably and considered synonymous with societal notions of *honesty, honor, virtue,* and *integrity.* Although it is relatively easy to define ethics, the field of marketing—as well as elsewhere in society—lacks consensus about what ethical conduct actually entails.[6] We nonetheless can identify marketing communications practices that are especially susceptible to ethical challenges. The following sections examine, in order, ethical issues in

(1) targeting marketing communications, (2) advertising, (3) public relations, (4) packaging communications, (5) sales promotions, and (6) Internet marketing.

The Ethics of Targeting

According to widely accepted dictates of sound marketing strategy, firms should direct their offerings at specific segments of customers rather than use a scatter or shotgun approach. Nevertheless, ethical dilemmas are sometimes involved when special products and corresponding marketing communications efforts are directed at particular segments. Especially open to ethical debate is the practice of targeting products and communications efforts to segments that, for various psychosocial and economic reasons, are vulnerable to marketing communications—such as children, teens, and economically disadvantaged groups.[7]

Targeting Children and Teens

In-school marketing programs, advertisements in traditional media, and messages on the Internet continually urge children to desire various products and brands. In fact, one study has estimated that U.S. businesses spent $15 billion in one year advertising and marketing their brands to children ages 12 and under.[8] Critics contend that many of the products targeted to children are unnecessary and that the communications are exploitative. Because it would involve debating personal values to discuss what children do or do not need, the following examples present the critics' position and allow you to draw your own conclusions.[9]

Targeting Food and Beverage Products. Consider a past advertising campaign that targeted Gatorade to children. Advertisements claimed that Gatorade is the "healthy alternative for thirsty kids." Nutritionists and other critics charged that Gatorade is unnecessary for children and no better than water—no harm or benefit arises from its consumption.[10] If indeed Gatorade does not benefit kids, is it ethical to urge them to encourage a parent to purchase this product?

Childhood obesity and the marketing of food products to children are especially hotly debated topics. According to the Centers for Disease Control and Prevention, nearly 1 in 6 children is considered obese, a rate that compares to 1 in 16 cases of childhood obesity only about 25 years ago.[11] Many critics consider it unethical to market food products to children, perhaps especially through cartoon characters touting sugared cereals and unhealthy snacks.[12]

Consider targeting efforts by the famous food company, Campbell Soup. Campbell historically marketed its soup and pasta brands primarily to mothers with the expectation that they would make appropriate choices for their children. But the company's market research revealed that direct appeals to children would increase sales volume. Accordingly, Campbell at one time used rapper Bow Wow and soccer player Freddy Adu as spokespeople to reach older children. To appeal to younger children, Campbell advertised its products during TV programs such as *Dora the Explorer* and *Jimmy Neutron*.[13] Soup and pasta are pretty good products in the nutritional scheme of things, so is targeting these products to children unethical?

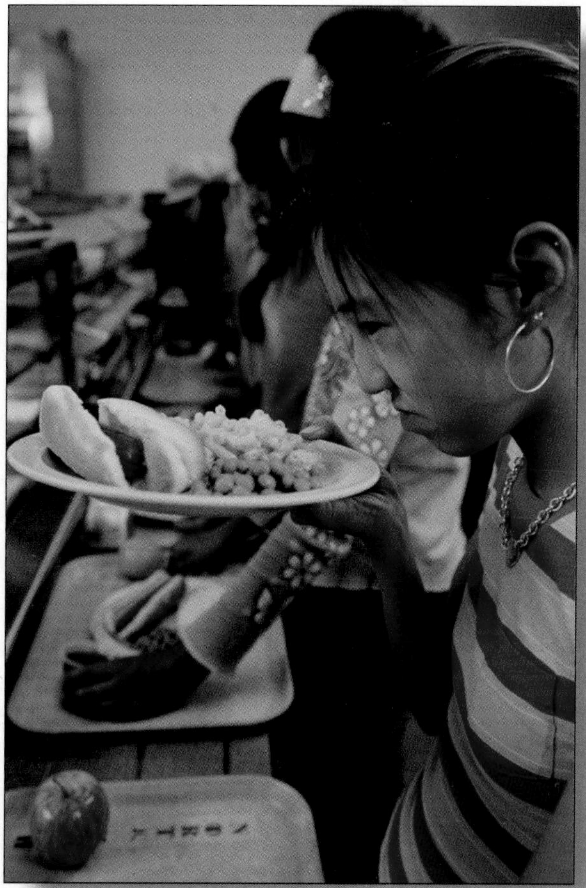

© Yellowdog Productions/The Image Bank/Getty Images

Consider also an advertising effort by the Subway sandwich chain, which, as you may recall, achieved much success using spokesman Jared Fogle, a once morbidly obese man who supposedly lost nearly 250 pounds by dieting on Subway sandwiches. Subway extended the campaign several years ago in an effort directed at children. In one commercial a preteen boy was overheard in the background saying, "When my brother had friends over, I would, like, stay up in my room because I was afraid they'd call me fat, or something. Now I'm not afraid of that at all. I started running and eating better stuff. I'm Cody. I'm twelve years old." After the child bared his soul, Jared Fogle came before the camera and declared, "More than anything, we [Subway] want your children to lead long and healthy lives." By implication, eating at Subway rather than at nutritionally challenged fast-food outlets is one means for children to reduce weight and increase the quality of their lives. Critics asserted that this campaign was exploitive.[14] Defenders of Subway's advertising countered by claiming that this type of advertising serves to raise children's awareness of the importance of eating more nutritious foods and undertaking exercise regimens. Did Subway cross the exploitation line with this advertising?

Due to a combination of pressure from critics, fear of more regulations from the Federal Trade Commission, and perhaps their own high moral standards, 11 of the largest food and beverage companies in the United States (e.g., Campbell Soup, General Mills, Kellogg, and PepsiCo) recently adopted self-imposed rules that limit advertising to children under 12. Among other rules, the companies pledged to discontinue use of licensed characters in ads (i.e., characters from popular TV shows and movies) unless they are to be used for promoting healthier products—such as General Mills' use of SpongeBob SquarePants on packages to promote its frozen vegetable mixes. Additionally, the companies agreed to stop advertising in elementary schools.[15]

Figure 21.1

Targeting Tobacco Products

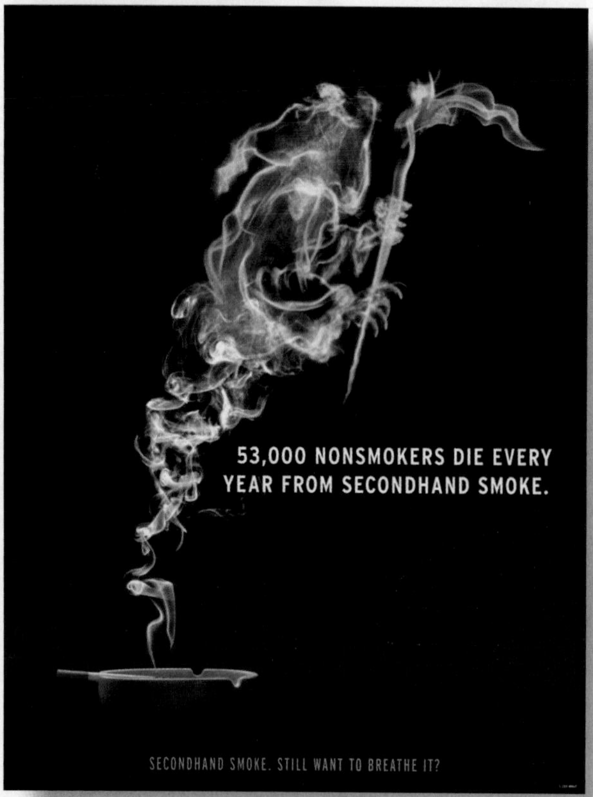

53,000 NONSMOKERS DIE EVERY
YEAR FROM SECONDHAND SMOKE.
SECONDHAND SMOKE. STILL WANT TO BREATHE IT?

© AP Images/PRNewsFoto/Minnesota Partnership for Action Against Tobacco

Targeting Tobacco and Alcohol Products. Marketers have been criticized for targeting adult products to teens and college students. The Miller Brewing Company, for example, was criticized for running a television commercial for its Molson Ice brand that focused on a label displaying 5.6 percent alcoholic content while an off-camera announcer uttered that Molson Ice is a "bolder" drink. A spokesperson for the Center for Science in the Public Interest asserted that the Molson Ice commercial appealed to children because they "drink to get drunk" and higher alcohol content is "what they want in a beer."[16] The beer industry itself would be expected to oppose such advertising because one of the brewing industry's advertising guidelines explicitly states that beer advertisements "should neither state nor carry any implication of alcohol strength."[17]

In general, there is considerable concern regarding the marketing of beer and other alcoholic beverages to teens and young adults. A study by a watchdog group at Georgetown University reported that one-quarter of alcohol advertising was more likely seen by youths than adults.[18] Research undertaken by the Centers for Disease Control and Prevention monitored over 67,000 radio spots in 104 markets in the United States and concluded that 49 percent of those ads were aired on programs that are youth oriented. The study concluded that beer and liquor companies are not abiding by a self-imposed ban on advertising to teens.[19]

Lawsuits have been filed against major brewers and other companies that market alcohol products on the basis that their advertising and marketing practices increase underage drinking.[20] A consumer advocacy group, the Center for Science in the Public Interest, initiated an effort to reduce the amount of alcohol advertising on televised sports. Coaching legends Dean Smith (ex-basketball coach at the University of North Carolina) and Tom Osborne (ex-football coach, now Athletic Director, at the University of Nebraska) participated in the program, and Ohio State University (OSU) became the first major school to get involved when it blocked its local media partners from airing any alcohol ads during the broadcast of OSU sporting events.[21]

By far the greatest recent controversy involved claims of unfair targeting of cigarettes to teens via advertisements and product placements in movies. This issue concerns many parents, consumer advocates, and academic researchers who have suggested that exposure to cigarette advertising leads youth to view cigarettes as a positive consumption symbol and to be more likely to smoke.[22] (Other researchers have challenged whether the scientific evidence does in fact permit the conclusion that advertising increases teenage smoking.[23]) A group of 41 members of the U.S. Congress sent a letter to 11 women's magazines (e.g., *Cosmopolitan, Glamour,* and *Vogue*) urging the magazines to stop accepting tobacco ads because, according to these Congressional members, young women represent a large proportion of these magazines' readership and that their health is being threatened.[24] Investigators also have studied whether antismoking campaigns are effective in lowering teenagers' attitudes toward smoking and their likelihood of beginning to smoke or discontinuing once the habit is started.[25]

Targeting Miscellaneous Products. Another criticized aspect of children-directed marketing communications is the practice of targeting posters, book covers, free magazines, and other so-called learning tools to children. Disguised as educational materials, these communications often are little more than attempts to persuade schoolchildren to want the promoted products and brands. Critics contend these methods are unethical because they use children's trust in educational materials to hawk merchandise.

Critics also are up in arms over the marketing of adult-oriented entertainment products to children and teens. The Federal Trade Commission (FTC) has issued a regular series of reports, titled *Marketing Violent Entertainment to Children,* that criticizes the entertainment industry for targeting children with advertisements for violent films, video games, and music. However, the FTC believes that its authority in regulating such advertising is limited in that it would have difficulty proving that such ads are deceptive or unfair, which, as we will cover in a subsequent section, are the two doctrines under which the FTC regulates advertising. The FTC has called on the entertainment industry to self-regulate and rigorously apply its own codes of conduct, although there are serious concerns that the industry is not much motivated or even capable of cleaning its own house.[26] An editor of *Advertising Age,* a publication widely read by advertising practitioners and a voice of reason in the ad industry, offers the following appropriate conclusion to this discussion:

> *This publication's editors ... almost always side with the advertising industry in preferring self-regulation to government intervention. But self-regulation is a privilege earned with responsible behavior and voluntary restraint. In the marketing of entertainment products to children, marketers have shown little restraint. If they continue to act irresponsibly, they will have invited the regulation they so desperately want to avoid.*[27]

Targeting Economically Disadvantaged Consumers

Makers of alcohol and tobacco products frequently employ billboards and other advertising media in targeting brands to economically disadvantaged consumers.

Although billboard advertising of tobacco products is restricted under the Master Settlement Agreement between the federal government and firms in the tobacco industry, in the past billboards advertising tobacco and alcohol were disproportionately more likely to appear in inner-city areas.[28]

Two old but nonetheless celebrated cases illustrate the concerns.[29] (The reason more current cases are not reported here is because none have appeared recently. Marketers have apparently gotten the message that targeting certain products to urban minorities and other economically disadvantaged groups will generate vast negative publicity.) A national uproar ensued when R. J. Reynolds (RJR) was preparing to introduce Uptown, a brand of menthol cigarette aimed at African-Americans and planned for test marketing in Philadelphia, where African-Americans make up 40 percent of the population. Because African-Americans have more than a 50 percent higher rate of lung cancer than whites, the product launch incensed many critics, including the U.S. government's secretary for Health and Human Services. In response to the public outcry, RJR canceled test marketing, and the brand died.[30]

Following in the wake of Uptown's demise, critics challenged another firm, the Heileman Brewing Company, for introducing its PowerMaster brand of high-alcohol malt liquor targeted to inner-city residents—a brand containing 5.9 percent alcohol compared with the 4.5 percent content of other malt liquors.[31] Brewing-industry supporters claimed that rather than being exploitive, PowerMaster and other malt liquors merely meet the demand among African-Americans and Hispanics, who buy the vast majority of malt liquor.[32] Nonetheless, the U.S. Treasury Department's Bureau of Alcohol, Tobacco, and Firearms (ATF), which regulates the brewing and liquor industries, would not permit the Heileman Brewing Company to market malt liquor under the name PowerMaster. The ATF considered the name PowerMaster as promoting the brand's alcoholic content, which violated federal regulations.

The R. J. Reynolds tobacco company was again widely criticized when preparing to introduce its Dakota brand of cigarettes to young, economically downscale women. RJR's plans to test market Dakota in Houston were squashed when critics created an outcry in response to what was considered to be exploitive marketing.[33]

Is Targeting Unethical or Just Good Marketing?

The foregoing discussion pointed out instances where advertising and other forms of marketing communications were criticized because they were directed at specific target markets. Proponents of targeting respond to such criticisms by arguing that targeting benefits rather than harms consumers. Targeting, according to the proponents, provides consumers with products best suited to their particular needs and wants. Not to be targeted, according to the advocates' position, is to have to choose a product that better accommodates someone else's needs.[34]

The issue is, of course, more complicated than whether targeting is good or bad. Sophisticated marketing practitioners and students fully accept the strategic justification for target marketing. There is the possibility, however, that some instances of targeting are concerned not with fulfilling consumers' needs and wants but rather with exploiting consumer vulnerabilities—so that the marketer gains while society loses. Herein rests the ethical issue that cannot be dismissed by claiming that targeting is sound marketing.[35]

Ethical Issues in Advertising

The role of advertising in society has been debated for centuries. Advertising ethics is a topic that has commanded the attention of philosophers, practitioners, scholars, and theologians. Even advertising practitioners are mixed in terms of their awareness of and concern for ethical issues in the day-to-day conduct of advertising.[36] The following is a succinct yet eloquent account of why advertising is so fiercely criticized:

> *As the voice of technology, [advertising] is associated with many dissatisfactions of the industrial state. As the voice of mass culture it invites intellectuals' attack. And as the most visible form of capitalism it has served as nothing less than a lightning-rod for social criticism.*[37]

A variety of ethical criticisms have been leveled against advertising. Because the issues are complex, it is impossible to treat each criticism in great detail. Thus, the following discussion introduces some illustrative issues with the expectation that each will prompt more in-depth thought and perhaps class discussion.[38]

Advertising Is Untruthful and Deceptive

Roughly two thirds of Americans think that advertising often is untruthful.[39] As will be discussed in a subsequent section, deception occurs when an advertisement falsely represents a product and consumers believe the false representation. By this definition, it is undeniable that some advertising *is* deceptive—the existence of governmental regulation and industry self-regulation attests to this fact. It would be naïve, however, to assume that *most* advertising is deceptive. The advertising industry is not much different than other institutions in a pluralistic society. Lying, cheating, and outright fraud are universal, occurring at the highest levels of government and in the most basic human relationships. Advertising is not without sin, but neither does it hold a monopoly on it.

Nonetheless, when advertising *is* deceptive, consumers are harmed and even competitors of deception perpetrators are negatively affected because deceived consumers become increasingly skeptical and develop diminished trust in the accuracy of subsequent advertising claims.[40] Advertisers of direct-to-consumer (DTC) pharmaceutical products have been scrutinized in recent years due to the magnitude of such advertising and the questionable honesty of some of the claims made for these products. For example, the cholesterol drug Vytorin—well known for its graphic advertising executions that characterized cholesterol as resulting from two sources, food and heredity, and portrayed images of older relatives dressed in apparel reminiscent of high-cholesterol food items—continued to advertise that it is an effective agent for reducing cholesterol even after a large scientific study the brand's manufacturer undertook revealed that Vytorin was ineffective for its claimed ability to reduce plaque buildup in the arteries. Due to cases such as Vytorin, it is possible that Congress will encourage the Food and Drug Administration to scrutinize pharmaceutical ads more closely.[41]

Advertising Is Manipulative

The criticism of manipulation asserts that advertising can influence people to do things they would not otherwise do were it not for exposure to advertising. Taken to the extreme, this suggests that advertising is capable of moving people against their free wills. But people, when *consciously aware* that attempts are being made to persuade or influence them, have the cognitive capacity to resist efforts to motivate them in a direction they wish not to be moved. That is, consumers know how marketing communicators attempt to persuade them and possess cognitive defenses for protecting themselves from coercion.[42] This is not to say that as consumers we never make bad decisions or are not sometimes led into buying things later regretted; however, being susceptible to persuasive influences and making bad decisions is not tantamount to being manipulated. We can thus conclude that individuals *who are cognitively aware* that an attempt is being made to persuade them are pretty good at protecting themselves from doing things that are counter to their best interests.

However (and it is a big however) there is growing evidence that much human behavior *is not under conscious control.* (This issue was previously discussed in Chapter 9 in the context of subliminal advertising.) Many of our actions occur virtually automatically (without cognitive intervention), as if we were on autopilot. Communicators can, for example, activate—or prime—subconscious thoughts in people using subtle techniques and subliminal messages. For example, people can be primed with the thought of "being cooperative," and without conscious awareness, these people are inclined to act more cooperatively, at least temporarily, in comparison with another group of people who have not been primed. For subconscious priming to be effective, the primed topic must be compatible with the individual's current need states. In other words, one cannot be subliminally induced to act more cooperatively unless she or he has a need to cooperate.[43]

Second, a primed goal state does not remain an active driver of judgments and behavior over the long run, but is limited in its length of influence. Hence, an advertiser may activate a certain thought, but the consumer would not act on that thought if she or he is not presently in the market to purchase a related product. It would be expected that mass-media advertising would have little effectiveness in this regard given that exposure to ads and purchase decisions typically occur separately. Perhaps, however, point-of-purchase advertising (e.g., in-store radio programming) would provide an opportune albeit unethical medium for subliminally priming consumers to purchase products and brands.

In sum, advertising practitioners (along with communicators in other aspects of life) *are* able to influence consumers in very subtle ways. It is unknown whether advertisers are indeed employing the subtle priming techniques known to modern psychologists, but techniques exist to influence consumers in ways unknown to them. In short, advertising practitioners have the wherewithal to manipulate if they so choose. Although marketing communicators theoretically can use subliminal cues and primes to influence consumer behavior subtly, priming is not like brainwashing or embedding electronic computer chips in brains to control people's behavior (as if they were automatons). The *Manchurian Candidate,* in the event you have read this classic book or have seen the movie, is *not* representative of the type of power that marketing communicators command (thankfully).

Advertising Is Offensive and in Bad Taste

Advertising critics contend that advertisements are sometimes insulting to human intelligence, vulgar, and generally offensive to the tastes of many consumers. The critics have in mind such practices as sexual explicitness or innuendo, outlandish humor, and excessive repetition of the same advertisements. Many consumers consider ads for erectile dysfunction drugs (brands such as Cialis and Viagra) as especially offensive, particularly when they appear on programs children view. The American Pediatrics Association has encouraged marketers to restrict such ads to after 10 PM so that children do not learn to view sex as a "recreational sport."[44]

Undeniably, quite a lot of advertising is disgusting and offensive.[45] Yet the same can be said for all forms of mass-media presentations. For example, many network television programs verge on the idiotic, movies are often filled with inordinate amounts of sex and violence, and videos "citizen journalists" produce and Internet sites such as YouTube carry often are nothing short of egregious. This certainly is not to excuse advertising for its excesses, but a balanced view demands that critical evaluations of advertising be conducted in a broader context of popular culture.

Advertising Creates and Perpetuates Stereotypes

At the root of this criticism is the contention that advertising tends to portray certain groups in a very narrow and predictable fashion. For example, minorities have historically been portrayed disproportionately in working-class roles rather than in the full range of positions they actually occupy; women have been stereotyped as sex objects; and senior citizens sometimes are characterized as feeble and forgetful. Although advertising *has* been guilty of perpetuating stereotypes, it would be unfair to blame advertising for creating these stereotypes, which, in fact, are perpetuated by all elements of society. Spreading the blame does not make advertising any better, but it does show that advertising is probably not any worse than the rest of society.

Advertising Persuades People to Buy Things They Do Not Really Need

A frequently cited criticism suggests that advertising causes people to buy items or services they do not need. This criticism is a value-laden judgment. Do you need another pair of shoes? Do you need a college education? Who is to say what you or anyone else needs?

Advertising most assuredly influences consumer tastes and encourages people to undertake purchases they may not otherwise make, but is this unethical? In my view, advertising is unethical only when it misleads, deceives, and takes advantage of vulnerable consumers. Otherwise, advertising's purpose *is* to sell, and responsible consumers in capitalistic societies are obliged to show self-restraint in avoiding purchasing items they do not "need" or cannot afford.

Advertising Plays on People's Fears and Insecurities

Some advertisements appeal to the negative consequences of not buying and using certain products—rejection by others, failure to have provided for the family if one should die without proper insurance coverage, not sending a contribution to save starving children in developing countries, and so on. Some advertisers are guilty of influencing consumer behavior by appealing to negative emotions such as fear, guilt, and humiliation.

However, once again, advertising possesses no monopoly on this transgression. For example, theologians sometimes threaten that non-believers will go to hell; politicians assert that our fate will be even worse if we vote for their opponent; teachers warn that our futures are in jeopardy if we do not get term papers in on time; and parents intimidate their children on a routine basis using a variety of "fear appeals." Looked at this way, it might be deduced that advertisers are rather innocent by comparison.

A Trade Association's Code of Ethical Standards

In sum, the institution of advertising is certainly not free of criticism, but advertising reflects the rest of society; any indictment of advertising probably applies to society at large. It is doubtful that advertisers and other marketing practitioners are any less ethical in their practices than are other elements of society.[46] Responsible advertising practitioners, knowing their practice is particularly susceptible to criticism, have a vested interest in producing legitimate advertisements. The advertising industry has an important stake in its members acting ethically so as to ward off public criticism and governmental regulation. Accordingly, advertising practitioners typically operate under ethical codes of conduct, such as the American Association of Advertising Agencies' (AAAA) code of ethical standards.

The AAAA is the national trade association that represents advertising agencies in the United States. Its members are responsible for creating approximately three-quarters of the total advertising volume placed nationwide by ad agencies. AAAA's mission is to improve and strengthen the ad agency business, to advocate advertising, to influence public policy, to resist advertising-related legislation that it regards as unwise or unfair, and to work with government regulators to achieve desirable social and civic goals. The AAAA promulgated a code of high ethical standards in 1924 and updated the code in 1990. It is presented here verbatim because it represents, on the one hand, a set of lofty goals for the advertising industry and, on the other, a framework for evaluating whether advertisements these agencies produce meet these high standards.

> *We, the members of the American Association of Advertising Agencies, in addition to supporting and obeying the laws and legal regulations pertaining to advertising, undertake to extend and broaden the application of high ethical standards. Specifically, we will not knowingly create advertising that contains:*
>
> a. *False, or misleading statements or exaggerations, visual or verbal*
> b. *Testimonials that do not reflect the real opinion of the individual(s) involved*
> c. *Price claims that are misleading*
> d. *Claims insufficiently supported or that distort the true meaning or practicable application of statements made by professional or scientific authority*
> e. *Statements, suggestions, or pictures offensive to public decency or minority segments of the population.*
>
> *We recognize that there are areas that are subject to honestly different interpretations and judgment. Nevertheless, we agree not to recommend to an advertiser, and to discourage the use of, advertising that is in poor or questionable taste or that is deliberately irritating through aural or visual content or presentation.*
>
> *Comparative advertising shall be governed by the same standards of truthfulness, claim substantiation, tastefulness, etc., as apply to other types of advertising.*
>
> *These Standards of Practice of the American Association of Advertising Agencies come from the belief that sound and ethical practice is good business. Confidence and respect are indispensable to success in a business embracing the many intangibles of agency service and involving relationships so dependent upon good faith.*
>
> *Clear and willful violations of these Standards of Practice may be referred to the Board of Directors of the American Association of Advertising Agencies for appropriate action, including possible annulment of membership as provided by Article IV, Section 5, of the Constitution and By-Laws.*[47]

Ethical Issues in Public Relations

Publicity, the aspect of public relations that relates primarily to marketing communications, involves disseminating positive information about a company and its products and handling negative publicity when things go wrong. Because publicity is like advertising in that both are forms of mass communications, many of the same ethical issues apply and need not be repeated. The one distinct aspect worthy of separate discussion is the matter of *negative publicity*.

A number of illustrious cases have surfaced in recent years in which companies have been widely criticized for marketing unsafe products. For example, as discussed in Chapter 18, Merck & Co. came under attack after a scientific study revealed that patients taking Vioxx—the arthritis and acute pain medication—for 18 months or longer had double the risk of suffering heart attacks or strokes compared to a control group taking a placebo. The way firms confront negative publicity has important strategic and ethical ramifications. The primary ethical issue concerns whether firms confess to product shortcomings and acknowledge problems or, instead, attempt to cover up the problems.

Ethical Issues in Packaging and Branding

Four aspects of packaging involve ethical issues: (1) label information, (2) packaging graphics, (3) packaging safety, and (4) environmental implications of packaging.[48] *Label information* on packages can mislead consumers by providing exaggerated information or by unethically suggesting that a product contains more of desired attributes (for instance, nutrition) or less of undesired attributes (such as trans fat) than is actually the case. *Packaging graphics* are unethical when the picture on a package is not a true representation of product contents (as when a children's toy is made to appear much bigger on the package than it actually is). Another case of potentially unethical packaging is when a store brand is packaged so that it looks virtually identical to a well-known national brand. *Unsafe packaging* problems are particularly acute when packaging is not tamperproof and contains dangerous products that are unsafe for children. Packaging information is misleading and unethical when it suggests environmental benefits that cannot be delivered.[49]

Related to packaging ethics is *brand naming*. A marketer's choice of brand name engages ethical considerations when the chosen name suggests the brand possesses product features that it does not, or will deliver benefits that it cannot. In other words, the brand is incapable of living up to the expectations the name signals and thus is potentially misleading. Consider, for example, a hypothetical children's toy carrying the name "PowerGlider." Because this name suggests that the toy (a plastic airplane) has an actual power source such as an engine, consumers would be deceived when purchasing the brand if in fact the only source of power is the person who has to throw it.

Another ethical violation occurs when a company borrows (or steals) a brand name from a better known and established brand. In effect, by using another company's well-known brand for its own product, the violator is capitalizing on the power of *leveraging* as described in Chapter 2. Stealing another company's established brand name is not only unethical but also illegal. A global form of brand-naming piracy occurs when marketers in one country use brand names for their products that are virtually the same as the names of established brands from another country.

Ethical Issues in Sales Promotions

Ethical considerations are involved with all facets of sales promotions, including manufacturer promotions directed at wholesalers and retailers and to consumers. As was discussed in Chapter 15, retailers have gained considerable bargaining power vis-à-vis manufacturers. One outcome of this power shift has been retailers' increased demands for deals. *Slotting allowances* illustrate the power shift. This practice (thoroughly discussed in Chapter 15) requires manufacturers to pay retailers a per-store fee for their willingness to handle a new stock unit from the manufacturer. Critics of slotting allowances contend this practice represents a form of bribery and is therefore unethical.

Consumer-oriented sales promotions (including practices such as coupons, premium offers, rebates, sweepstakes, and contests) are unethical when the sales promoter offers consumers a reward for their behavior that is never delivered—for example, failing to mail a free premium object or to provide a rebate check. Sweepstakes and contests are potentially unethical when consumers think their odds of winning are much greater than they actually are.[50]

As a matter of balance, it is noteworthy that marketers are not the only ones guilty of unethical behavior in the area of sales promotions. Consumers also engage in untoward activities such as submitting coupons at the point of checkout for items not purchased or tendering phony rebate claims.

IMC >> i.m.c. focus

A Rigged Promotion for Frozen Coke

Imagine that you are a mid-level marketing executive and that you are trying to increase your business with a major customer. You specifically are attempting to convince the customer that it should run a nationwide promotional contest featuring one of your products. This contest, if successful, will increase sales of your product and boost your customer's profits. However, the customer is not convinced the promotion will be effective and wants to conduct a trial run prior to undertaking the promotion nationally. The test will be conducted by comparing sales in a city where the promotion is run (the "test" city) against sales in another city that is not offering the promotion (the "control" city). Initial test results reveal your customer's business does not much increase in the test versus control city. The nationwide promotion is in jeopardy. Your job status is threatened. What to do?

This hypothetical situation actually occurred several years ago. The protagonists were Coke and its customer, Burger King. Mid-level executives at Coca-Cola Co. pitched the idea to Burger King to run a promotion offering a free Frozen Coke (a product consisting of crushed ice blended with Coke) when customers bought a "value meal" at a Burger King outlet. The argument presented to Burger King was that by offering free Frozen Cokes it could significantly increase customer traffic and thus the sales of value meals.

Burger King's executives were unwilling to commit to an expensive, nationwide promotion until they had some evidence that it would significantly increase sales. They decided to run a test in Richmond, VA (the test city), where free Frozen Cokes would be offered when a value meal was purchased, and compare the number of value meal purchases in Richmond during the test period against value meal volume in Tampa, FL (the control city), where free Frozen Cokes would *not* be provided when consumers purchased value meals. This test involved, in other words, a simple field experiment where the presence (Richmond) or absence (Tampa) of free Frozen Cokes was the experimental treatment.

Unfortunately, initial sales results at the start of the Richmond promotion were disappointing, as value meal volume in Richmond was not much different than in Tampa. Under pressure that Burger King might reject the concept of a nationwide promotion, which would have adverse effects for sales of Frozen Coke, a couple of mid-level Coca-Cola executives hatched a

Ethical Issues in Online Marketing

Ethical issues abound in the use of the Internet as a marcom medium, many of which overlap with the prior, general discussions involving the ethics of advertising and promotions. Aside from the general ethical issues already discussed, invasion of individuals' *privacy* is notable. Because online marketers can collect voluminous information about people's personal characteristics, online shopping behavior, and use of information, it is easy to invade individuals' privacy rights by selling information to other sources and divulging confidential information. It would take us too far afield to get into a detailed discussion of all the issues surrounding privacy invasion, but interested readers are encouraged to examine the articles listed in the following end note.[51]

Another ethical violation in online marketing relates to the use of blogs. Companies are unethical when their blogs include positive testimonials from falsified consumers. Unethical blogging practices also are evidenced when companies pay individuals to write blogs that provide positive evaluations of a company's products. Needless to say, there is great potential for information on blogs to be exaggerated if not outright erroneous.

scheme to boost sales of value meals in Richmond during the remainder of the test. They hired a freelance consultant and gave him $9,000 to distribute to Boys & Girls Clubs in the Richmond area. The freelancer distributed cash to leaders of these clubs, who were instructed to treat children to value meals at Burger King.

Although this $9,000 in cash contributed less than 1 percent of the total number of value meals purchased in Richmond during the test period, it played a role in demonstrating that sales of value meals in Richmond increased by 6 percent during the test period in comparison to a Tampa sales increase of only 2 percent. On the basis of this differential, Burger King decided to take the promotion nationwide.

Needless to say, the rigged promotion eventually came to Burger King's attention, but only after the fast-food chain had invested in the nationwide Frozen Coke promotion. Coca-Cola's corporate office acknowledged that its employees improperly influenced the test results in Richmond, but the company denied any corporate wrongdoing and laid the blame on the mid-level employees who devised the rigged sales results. Coca-Cola agreed to pay Burger King up to $21 million to compensate it and its franchises for any financial losses.

In explaining his behavior to a supervisor, one of the mid-level executives rationalized that the monetary giveaway was necessary in Richmond to "deseasonalize the data in order to have an accurate measure [of sales response]." His justification, in other words, was that the weather was warmer in Tampa compared to Richmond at the time of the test, which would, according to his logic, have biased business in favor of greater value meal sales in Tampa than Richmond. In short, this executive rationalized what appears to be unethical behavior, but his argument is self-serving and disingenuous. If he truly thought that seasonal differences would have biased test results, then he should have convinced Burger King's executives to pick a control city where the weather would have been comparable to Richmond's rather than selecting Tampa.

In sum, the mid-level executives at Coca-Cola got caught with their proverbial pants down. They engaged in what appears to be unethical behavior and were exposed. The corporation claimed no wrongdoing, but the executives apparently felt pressure to do whatever was necessary to produce results. This case is minor in comparison to past financial scandals at Enron and elsewhere, but it demonstrates yet again that businesspeople eventually pay for their (unethical) mistakes.

SOURCES: Christina Cheddar Berk, "Executive at Coke Gives Up His Post in Scandal's Wake," *The Wall Street Journal Online*, August 26, 2003, http://online.wsj.com (accessed August 26, 2003); Chad Terhune and Richard Gibson, "Coke Agrees to Pay Burger King $10 Million to Resolve Dispute," *The Wall Street Journal Online*, August 4, 2003, http://online.wsj.com (accessed August 4, 2003). Chad Terhune, "How Coke Officials Beefed Up Results of a Marketing Test," *The Wall Street Journal Online*, August 20, 2004, http://online.wsj.com (accessed August 20, 2004).

Fostering Ethical Marketing Communications

Primary responsibility for ethical behavior resides within each of us when we are placed in any of the various marketing communicator roles. We can take the easy route and do what is expedient, or we can pursue the moral high road and treat customers in the same honest fashion we expect to be treated. In large part, it is a matter of our own personal integrity. *Integrity* is perhaps the pivotal concept of human nature. Although difficult to define precisely, integrity generally means being honest and not acting in a deceptive or purely expedient manner.[52] Hence, marketing communications itself is not ethical or unethical—it is the degree of integrity communications practitioners exhibit that determines whether their behavior is ethical or unethical. As a case in point, see the *IMC Focus* dealing with a rigged promotion for Frozen Coke.

Placing the entire burden on individuals is perhaps unfair, because how we behave as individuals is largely a function of the organizational culture in which we operate. Businesses can foster ethical or unethical cultures by establishing *ethical core values* to guide marketing communications behavior. Two core values that would go a long way toward enhancing ethical behavior are (1) treating customers with respect, concern, and honesty—the way you would want to be treated or the way you would want your family treated—and (2) acting toward the environment as though it were your own property.[53]

Firms can foster ethical marcom behavior by encouraging their employees to apply each of the following tests when faced with an ethical predicament:[54]

1. Act in a way that you would want others to act toward you (the *Golden Rule test*).
2. Take only actions that an objective panel of your professional colleagues would view as proper (the *professional ethics test*).
3. Always ask, "Would I feel comfortable explaining this action on television to the general public?" (the *TV test*).

During your business career (and otherwise in life), you undoubtedly will be confronted with times of moral/ethical predicament calling for one decision versus another. Thoughts such as these will enter your mind: "My supervisor wants me to do such and such (fill in the blank), but I am not sure it is the right thing to do." "I could increase my brand's sales and profits if I were to (fill in the blank), but although doing that would be expedient, I am concerned that it is not the right thing to do." When confronted with such dilemmas, stop before you act. Apply the three tests. Imagine yourself standing before a television camera and justifying your behavior. Ask if this is how you would want someone to treat you. Ponder whether other professionals would endorse your behavior. In short, think before you act. Business can be tough. Living with your own bad decisions (those reflecting anything other than high integrity) can be miserable.

We conclude this section by presenting the thoughts of a marketing practitioner who has urged his fellow practitioners to conduct their marcom activities in a manner that lifts the human spirit rather than appeals to human nature's most base instincts. He urges marcom practitioners to contemplate four questions before creating and transmitting messages.[55] These questions deserve our careful consideration.

- *What lasting impact will this message have on our brand if we continue to communicate it over the long run?*
- *What lasting impact, if any, will my message have on society at large?*
- *Does my message appeal to the best in people and attempt to lift the human spirit?*
- *What response am I trying to elicit and what macro message does that send about our society?*

Regulation of Marketing Communications

Advertisers, sales promotion managers, and other marcom practitioners are faced with a variety of regulations and restrictions that influence their decision-making latitude. The past century has shown that regulation is necessary to protect consumers and competitors from unethical, fraudulent, deceptive, and unfair practices that some businesses choose to perpetrate. In market economies there is an inevitable tension between the interests of business organizations and the rights of consumers. Regulators attempt to balance the interests of both parties while ensuring that an adequate level of competition is maintained.

When Is Regulation Justified?

Strict adherents to the ideals of free enterprise would argue that government should rarely if ever intervene in the activities of business. More moderate observers believe that regulation is justified in certain circumstances, especially when consumer decisions are based on *false or limited information.*[56] Under such circumstances, consumers are likely to make decisions they would not otherwise make and, as a result, incur economic, physical, or psychological injury. Competitors also are harmed because they lose business they might have otherwise enjoyed when companies against whom they compete present false or misleading information. In theory, regulation is justified if the *benefits realized exceed the costs.* What are the benefits and costs of regulation?[57]

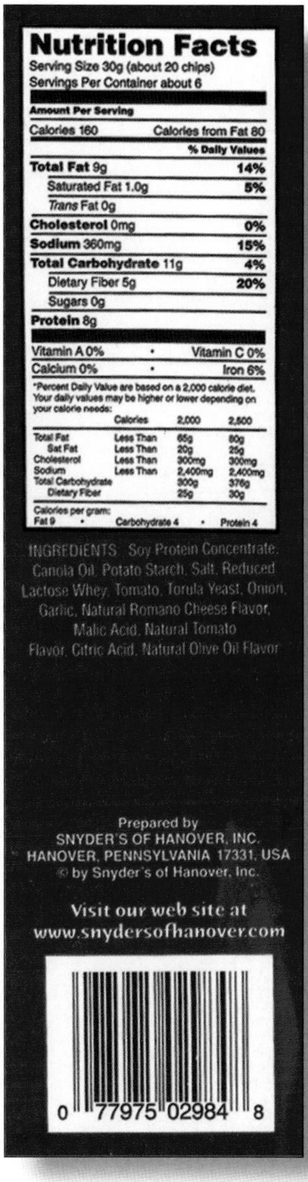

Snyder's of Hanover EatSmart All Natural Snacks

Benefits

Regulation offers three major benefits. First, *consumer choice* among alternatives is improved when consumers are better informed in the marketplace. For example, consider the Alcoholic Beverage Labeling Act, which requires manufacturers to place the following warning on all containers of alcoholic beverages:

> *GOVERNMENT WARNING: (1) According to the Surgeon General, women should not drink alcoholic beverages during pregnancy, due to the risk of birth defects. (2) Consumption of alcoholic beverages impairs your ability to drive a car or operate machinery, and may cause health problems.*[58]

This regulation informs consumers that drinking has negative consequences. Pregnant women can help themselves and especially their unborn children by heeding this warning to refrain from drinking alcoholic beverages, although it is unlikely that warning labels alone have a major impact in curbing drinking among pregnant women.[59]

A second benefit of regulation is that when consumers become better informed, *product quality tends to improve* in response to consumers' changing needs and preferences. For example, when American consumers began learning about the dangers of fat and cholesterol during the 1990s, manufacturers started marketing healthier food products that now are widely available in grocery stores. The same can be expected to occur in restaurants with legislation in some states that requires restaurants to make available nutritional information for the levels of calories, fat, and sodium contained in menu items.

A third regulatory benefit is *reduced prices* resulting from a reduction in a seller's "informational market power." For example, prices of used cars undoubtedly would fall if dealers were required to inform prospective purchasers about a car's defects, because consumers would not be willing to pay as much for automobiles with known problems.

Costs

Regulation is not costless. Companies often incur the *cost of complying* with a regulatory remedy. For example, U.S. cigarette manufacturers are required to rotate over the course of a year four different warning messages for three months each. This obviously is somewhat more costly than the previously required single warning message. *Enforcement costs* regulatory agencies incur and taxpayers pay represent a second cost category.

The *unintended side effects* that might result from regulations represent a third cost to both buyers and sellers. There are a variety of potential side effects that are unforeseen at the time legislation is written. For example, a regulation may unintentionally harm sellers if buyers switch to other products or reduce their level of consumption after regulation is imposed. The cost to buyers may increase if sellers pass along, in the form of higher prices, the costs of complying with a regulation. Both of these prospects are possible when food makers either choose to switch from hydrogenated oil or continue to make their products with hydrogenated oil, with the requirement that they must reveal the high levels of trans fat in their labeling. In sum, regulation is theoretically justified only if the benefits exceed the costs.

When regulation is justified, federal and state agencies, along with the industry, work to oversee the integrity of marketing communications. The following sections examine the two forms of regulation that affect many aspects of marketing communications: governmental regulation and industry self-regulation.

Regulation by Federal Agencies

Governmental regulation takes place at both the federal and state levels. All facets of marketing communications are subject to regulation, but advertising is the one area in which regulators have been most active. This is because advertising is the most conspicuous aspect of marketing communications. The discussion that follows examines federal governmental regulation of advertising in the United States as performed by two agencies: the Federal Trade Commission (FTC) and the Food and Drug Administration (FDA). Readers who wish to know more about advertising regulation in European Union countries are directed to the source cited in this end note.[60]

The FTC is the U.S. government agency with primary responsibility for regulating advertising at the federal level. The FTC's regulatory authority cuts across three broad areas that directly affect marketing communicators: deceptive advertising, unfair practices, and information regulation.

Deceptive Advertising

In a general sense, consumers are deceived by an advertising claim or campaign when (1) the impression left by the claim or campaign is false—that is, there is a *claim-fact discrepancy;* and (2) the false claim or campaign is *believed* by consumers. The important point is that a false claim is not necessarily deceptive by itself. Rather, consumers must believe a claim to be deceived by it: "a false claim does not harm consumers unless it is believed, and a true claim can generate harm if it generates a false belief."[61]

Although the FTC makes deception rulings case by case, it does employ some general guidelines in deciding whether deceptive advertising has occurred. Under current deception policy, the FTC will find a business practice deceptive if, to the consumer's detriment, an advertised claim has been made or an important fact is omitted, either of which is likely to mislead consumers who are acting reasonably under the circumstances. Thus there are three elements that provide the essence of the FTC's deception policy:[62]

1. Misleading. There must be a representation, omission, or a practice that is likely to mislead the consumer. The FTC defines a *misrepresentation* as an express or implied statement contrary to fact. For example, if a pharmaceutical company claimed that one of its prescription drugs did not contain a substance that it actually did, this would be considered a misrepresentation. A *misleading omission* is said to occur when qualifying information necessary to prevent a practice, claim, representation, or reasonable expectation or belief from being misleading is *not* disclosed. A misleading omission would exist, for example, if the same pharmaceutical company failed to disclose an important side effect of using its prescription drug.

2. Reasonable consumer. The act or practice must be considered from the perspective of the "reasonable consumer." The FTC's test of reasonableness is based on the consumer's interpretation or reaction to an advertisement—that is, the commission determines the effect of the advertising practice on reasonable members of the group to which the advertising is targeted. The following quote indicates that the FTC evaluates advertising claims case by case in view of the target audience's unique position—its education level, intellectual capacity, mental frame, and so on.

> *For instance, if a company markets a cure to the terminally ill, the practice will be evaluated from the perspective of how it affects the ordinary member of that group. Thus, terminally ill consumers might be particularly susceptible to exaggerated cure claims. By the same token, a practice or representation directed to a well-educated group, such as a prescription drug advertisement to doctors, would be judged in light of the knowledge and sophistication of that group.*[63]

3. Material. To be considered deceptive, the representation, omission, or practice must be "material." A *material representation* involves information that is important to consumers and that is likely to influence their *choice* or *conduct* regarding a product. In general, the FTC considers information to be material when it pertains to the central characteristics of a product or service (including performance features, size, and price). Hence, if an athletic-shoe company falsely claimed that its brand possesses the best shock absorption feature on the market, this would be a material misrepresentation to the many runners who make purchase choices based on this factor. In contrast, if this same company were to claim falsely that it has been in business for 28 years—when in fact it has been in business for only 25 years—this would not be regarded as material because most consumers would not be swayed much differently whether the company had been in business 25 or 28 years.

An important case involving the issue of materiality was brought by the FTC against Kraft Foods and its advertising of Kraft Single American cheese slices. The FTC challenged Kraft on grounds that advertisements for Kraft Singles falsely claimed that each slice contains the same amount of calcium as *five* ounces of milk. In fact, each slice of Kraft Singles begins with five ounces of whole milk, but during processing 30 percent, or 1.5 ounces of milk, is lost. In other words, each slice contains only 70 percent of the amount of calcium claimed in Kraft's advertisements.[64] Kraft responded that its $11 million advertising campaign did not influence consumer purchases. Kraft's legal counsel argued that the advertisements (1) did not convey the misleading representation the FTC claimed, but (2) even if this representation had been conveyed, it would not have mattered because calcium is a relatively unimportant factor in consumers' decision to purchase Kraft Singles. (Out of nine factors consumers rated in a copy test, calcium was rated no higher than seventh.)

Whereas the FTC's position was that Kraft's advertising *was* likely to mislead consumers, Kraft's defense was that its calcium claim, whether false or not, is nondeceptive because the difference between 5 ounces of milk and 3.5 ounces is an immaterial difference to consumers. Kraft's defense, in other words, amounted to the following: Yes, we (Kraft) made claims about the calcium benefits of Kraft Singles, but the issue of deceptiveness is moot because the difference in calcium content between what we claimed (a single slice contains the calcium equivalency of 5 ounces of milk) and what is reality (a single slice contains the calcium equivalency of 3.5 ounces of milk) is immaterial to consumers and hence not deceptive.

After hearing detailed testimony on the matter and following an appeal process, the commissioners of the FTC determined that Kraft's advertising claim was indeed material.[65] Accordingly, the FTC ordered Kraft to cease and desist (literally, "stop and go no more," or discontinue) further misrepresentations of Kraft Singles' calcium content. The Kraft case generated much discussion and controversy. The articles cited in the following end note are worth reading for this particular case, as well as for

Terri Miller/E-Visual Communications, Inc.

their broader significance to advertising practice and public policy involving deceptive advertising.[66]

Covert Marketing Practices and Deception. A particularly cunning form of advertising deception occurs when consumers are exposed to covert forms of marcom messages, or what also is referred to as "masked marketing." These are messages that appear *not* to be marketing communications but that actually are.[67] The slyness of masked messages makes them especially potent and potentially deceptive because unsuspecting consumers are inclined to accept messages that appear to be from a nonmarketing source, whereas if they knew these claims were from a marketer they would be somewhat skeptical and more inclined to reject their validity.[68]

There are various forms of masked marketing communications, but just two forms are described.[69] First, buzz-building or viral campaigns (see Chapter 18) are sometimes conducted in person-to-person settings (e.g., in bars) where people are hired to say positive things about a new brand. Unsuspecting recipients of such messages presume that the favorable word of mouth is from an actual consumer who really likes the brand, when in fact the "buzzer" has been hired to deliver a disguised sales message. Not all viral campaigns are deceptive, but some are.

Infomercials are a second form of masked message. These messages often come across to viewers as TV programs when in actuality they are nothing more than "long advertisements" that mask their real intent by including testimonials from presumed experts and actors posing as real product users. Of course, not all infomercials are phony, but some are.

False infomercials, misleading viral campaigns, and other forms of masked messages are deceptive when they satisfy the three precepts of the FTC's deception policy, namely, (1) when they are delivered to reasonable consumers, (2) when they are misleading, and (3) when the content of the messages is material.

Unfair Practices

The FTC has legal authority to regulate unfair as well as deceptive acts or practices in commerce. Unlike deception, a finding of unfairness to consumers may go beyond questions of fact and relate merely to public values.[70] The criteria used to evaluate whether a business act is unfair involve such considerations as whether the act (1) offends public policy as it has been established by statutes, (2) is immoral, unethical, oppressive, or unscrupulous, and (3) causes substantial injury to consumers, competitors, or other businesses.[71]

The FTC's right to regulate unfair advertising was a matter of considerable dispute for years because the precise meaning of "unfair" was not clear. The dispute ended when Congress devised a definition of unfairness that is satisfactory to all parties. **Unfair advertising** is defined as "acts or practices that cause or are likely to cause *substantial injury to consumers,* which is *not reasonably avoidable* by consumers themselves and *not outweighed by countervailing benefits to consumers or competition*" (emphasis added).[72] The italicized features of the definition point out Congress's intention to balance the interests of advertisers with those of consumers and to prevent capricious applications of the unfairness doctrine by the FTC.

The FTC has applied the unfairness doctrine in instances where questionable advertisements are aimed at children. Because children are more credulous and less well-equipped than adults to protect themselves, public-policy officials are especially concerned with protecting youngsters. The unfairness doctrine is especially useful in cases involving children because many advertising claims are not deceptive per se but are nonetheless potentially unethical, unscrupulous, or inherently dangerous to children. For example, the FTC considered one company's use of Spider-Man vitamin advertising unfair because such advertising was judged capable of inducing children to take excessive and dangerous amounts of vitamins.[73]

In recent years, the FTC has most actively applied the unfairness doctrine to numerous instances of telemarketing scams and Internet fraud.[74] Both technologies are ripe for fraudulent behavior by unscrupulous marketers, and such behavior can readily injure consumers (as well as competitors) because the tricks and scams cannot reasonably be avoided by consumers themselves. E-mail fraud is the most widely practiced abuse, and the FTC has brought over 200 enforcement actions under its unfairness power against such fraudulent behavior.[75]

Information Regulation

Although the primary purpose of advertising regulation is the prohibition of deceptive and unfair practices, regulation also is needed at times to provide consumers with information they might not otherwise receive. The corrective advertising program is the most important of the FTC's information provision programs.[76]

Corrective advertising is based on the premise that a firm that misleads consumers should have to use future advertisements to rectify the deceptive impressions it has created in consumers' minds. Corrective advertising is designed to prevent a firm from continuing to deceive consumers rather than to punish the firm.

Consider the corrective advertising order the FTC issued against the Novartis Corporation and its Doan's Pills (an over-the-counter medicine for minor backache pain). Doan's advertisements referred to the brand's special or unique ingredients, called itself the "back specialist," and depicted the brand against packages of competitors Advil, Bayer, and Tylenol. The FTC concluded that the advertising campaign created the false impression that Doan's was more effective than other over-the-counter (OTC) drugs for combating back pain. The FTC ordered Novartis to undertake an $8 million advertising campaign to correct the misimpression that Doan's Pills outperform other OTC analgesics in treating back pain. This order required Doan's packaging and advertising to carry the message, "Although Doan's is an effective pain reliever, there is no evidence that Doan's is more effective than other pain relievers for back pain." Novartis's legal counsel claimed the order was excessive, whereas others have appraised the order as an inadequate remedy in the face of compelling evidence that Doan's advertising was deceptive.[77]

The FTC walks a fine line when issuing a corrective advertising order and specifying the remedial action a deceptive advertiser must take. The objective is to restore the marketplace to its original position prior to the deceptive advertising so that a firm does not continue to reap the rewards from its past deception. However, there is always the possibility that the corrective advertising effort may go too far and severely damage the firm and perhaps, unintentionally, hurt other companies in the industry.[78]

Product Labeling

The FDA is the federal body responsible for regulating information on the packages of food and drug products. The FDA has become very active in regulating the type of nutritional information that must appear on food labels, as, for example, the requirement that labels must include the amount of trans fats contained in a single serving.

Prescription Drug Advertising

Whereas the FTC is responsible for regulating deceptive and unfair advertising for all products (including OTC drugs), the FDA is charged with regulating advertisements for *prescription drugs.* This has been a major challenge in recent years with the onset of direct-to-consumer (DTC) advertising. As the name suggests, this form of advertising involves messages for prescription drugs that are directed toward consumers. Pharmaceutical companies expect DTC ads to motivate consumers to urge their physicians to prescribe advertised drug brands. The FDA's role is, in this regard, to police the truthfulness of DTC ads and to ensure that any claims made are supported by scientific evidence.

The FDA requires prescription drug advertisers to present a *balanced perspective* when advertising drugs. That is, in addition to touting product benefits, they must also identify the side effects and risks of using particular drugs. You may have noticed that TV commercials for DTC drugs show how wonderful a drug is in treating arthritis, cholesterol levels, weight problems, or other health issues. It is only at the end of the commercial that consumers are informed that in using the drug one may experience nausea, diarrhea, reduced sexual functioning, or any of a number of other undesirable consequences. Drug companies would prefer not to mention these side effects, but doing so is required by the FDA—for the protection of consumers in the best spirit of regulation.

In magazine ads, pharmaceutical companies provide detailed information about their products' undesirable side effects, but this information typically is placed on the back pages of ads and in very small print. Critics have questioned the value of such information on grounds that it is too technical, too detailed, and difficult to read because it typically is printed in very small print. Accordingly, the FDA proposed that drug makers present less-detailed information about side effects in print ads, but that they explain the most serious problems in language accessible to typical consumers.

Regulation by State Agencies

Individual states have their own statutes and regulatory agencies to police the marketplace from fraudulent business practices. There is every indication that states will remain active in their efforts to regulate advertising deception and other business practices, which poses a potentially significant problem for many national advertisers who might find themselves subject to multiple, and perhaps inconsistent, state regulations.[79] It is somewhat ironic that many national companies would prefer to see a stronger FTC because these companies are better off with a single regulatory agency that institutes uniform national guidelines and keeps the marketplace as free as possible from the fly-by-night operators that tarnish the image of all businesses.

Advertising Self-Regulation

Self-regulation, as the name suggests, is undertaken by the advertising community itself (i.e., advertisers, industry trade associations, and ad media) rather than by governmental bodies. Self-regulation is a form of *private government* whereby peers establish and enforce voluntary rules of behavior.[80] Advertising self-regulation has flourished in countries such as Canada, France, the United Kingdom, and the United States.[81]

Media Self-Regulation

The *advertising clearance process* is a form of self-regulation ad media undertake that happens behind the scenes before a commercial or other advertisement reaches consumers. A magazine advertisement or television commercial undergoes a variety of clearance steps prior to its actual printing or airing, including (1) advertising agency clearance, (2) approval from the advertiser's legal department and perhaps also from an independent law firm, and (3) media approval (such as television networks' guidelines regarding standards of taste).[82] A finished ad that makes it through the clearance process and appears in advertising media is then subject to the possibility of post hoc regulation from federal (e.g., the FTC), state attorneys general, and self-regulators (e.g., the National Advertising Review Council).

The National Advertising Review Council

Self-regulation by the National Advertising Review Council (NARC) has been the most publicized and perhaps most effective form of self-regulation. NARC is an organization formed via a partnership among the Association of National Advertisers, the American Association of Advertising Agencies, the American Advertising Federation, and the Council of Better Business Bureau's National Advertising Division (NAD).

NARC consists of three review units: the Children's Advertising Review Unit (CARU), NAD, and the National Advertising Review Board (NARB). CARU monitors children's television programming and commercials, whereas the NAD and NARB were established to sustain standards of truth and accuracy in national advertising to adults. NARB is the umbrella-like term applied to the combined NAD/NARB self-regulatory mechanism; however, by strict definition, NARB is a court consisting of 50 representatives who are formed into five-member panels to hear appeals of NAD cases when an involved party is dissatisfied with the initial verdict.[83] NAD is the investigative arm of NARB and is responsible for evaluating, investigating, and holding initial negotiations with an advertiser on complaints involving truth or accuracy of national advertising. NAD only reviews advertisements that are national rather than local.

The number of cases investigated and resolved varies, but NAD often becomes involved in as many as 150 cases a year. Cases are brought to the NAD by competitors, initiated by the NAD staff itself, or originate from local Better Business Bureaus, consumer groups, and individual consumers.

For example, based on a challenge from the Colgate-Palmolive Company, the NAD investigated an advertising claim for Clorox's Pine-Sol brand that appeared in Spanish-language advertising. A TV commercial for Pine-Sol presented a scene in which a girl moves her bare feet across the floor and onto the white pants of a boy seated across from her. The annoyed boy stands up to reveal that the girl's dirty feet have soiled his pants. The commercial then suggests that Pine-Sol, but not Fabuloso (a competitive brand marketed by Colgate-Palmolive), would have done a better job in cleaning the floor. A particularly controversial claim in the Pine-Sol commercial was that "Nothing is more embarrassing than a dirty house. Use Pine-Sol instead which cleans all of your house better than Fabuloso." The NAD pointed out that "advertisers should exercise care to ensure that claims which implicitly disparage competitors are truthful, accurate and narrowly drawn."[84] NAD determined that the Clorox Company needed to discontinue permanently the comparative claim that Pine-Sol is superior to Fabuloso.

Another NAD case involved an advertisement by Lenovo Inc. that was challenged by Dell. Lenovo had claimed in its advertising that it has the world's "Best-Engineered PCs with the Awards to Prove It." NAD determined that Lenovo has in fact been the recipient of numerous awards but that there is as yet no single award for the "Best-Engineered PCs." The NAD recommended that the claim be discontinued. Lenovo indicated that it would appeal NAD's conclusion to the NARB.[85]

In a final illustration of NAD's self-regulatory process, the NAD examined advertising claims by Neutrogena's brand named Rapid Clear Acne Eliminating Spot Gel. Advertising for this brand had made a number of claims including that Rapid Clear will enable "Clearer skin in under 8 hours"; that the use of this product "Visibly reduces breakouts in 8 hours"; and that "It's clinically proven to visibly reduce pimple size, redness and swelling in under 8 hours. No dryness. No irritation. Just noticeable improvement." NAD determined that Neutrogena Corp.

had provided a reasonable basis for its product performance and efficacy claims.[86] This case demonstrates that not all of NAD's decisions go against the party accused of engaging in deceptive advertising.

In conclusion, advertising self-regulation reduces the need for government regulation and maintains the general integrity of advertising and, in so doing, protects both consumers and competitors. A president of NARC has succinctly captured self-regulation's value:

> *Self-regulation is smart business. It provides a level playing field. Continuing NAD improvements provide the quickest, least expensive and most effective way for advertisers to challenge one another's claims. A court case can take over a year (vs. NAD's 60 business days) and cost 10 times as much as a NAD case.*[87]

Environmental Marketing Communications

People around the world are concerned with the depletion of natural resources and the degradation of the physical environment. The world's carbon footprint has grown larger with the rapid economic development of China and India, added to huge petroleum consumption by highly industrialized countries such as the United States. Although skeptics remain, the scientific community generally agrees that global warming is largely a man-made reality and that corrective measures are required. (See the *Global Focus* insert for discussion of environmentally sustainable consumption in 14 countries.)

Many companies are responding to environmental concerns by introducing environmentally oriented products and undertaking marcom programs to promote them. These actions are referred to as *green marketing*.[88] Legitimate green marketing efforts must minimally accomplish two objectives: improve environmental quality and satisfy customers.[89] Anything short of meeting these objectives amounts to bogus environmental marketing, or what has been referred to as *greenwashing*—a takeoff on the word hogwash. The following section discusses illustrative marcom efforts that fall under the banner of credible green marketing.

Green Marketing Initiatives

Motivated for reasons such as achieving regulatory compliance, gaining competitive advantage, being socially responsible, and following the commitment of top management, some companies have made legitimate responses to environmental problems.[90] These responses mostly have been in the form of *new* or *revised products*. Perhaps the major environmentally responsive product initiative has been the introduction of electric-gas hybrid vehicles such as the Toyota Prius. The Prius has been in such great demand, partially due to rising gas prices and the fact that hybrid autos get much better mileage per gallon than conventional autos, that Toyota has had difficulty filling orders.

Compact fluorescent lightbulbs (CFL) are increasingly prevalent because they are longer lasting and more energy efficient than traditional incandescent bulbs. Even Nike has gone green with its introduction of Air Jordan XX3 sneakers that have an outsole made of recycled material and almost no chemical-based glues.[91]

Although these product innovations are important, of more direct relevance to this text are the marcom efforts that appeal to environmental sensitivities. The major green communications efforts involve (1) advertisements that promote green products, (2) environmentally friendly packaging, (3) seal-of-approval programs that promote green products, (4) cause- and event-oriented marcom efforts that support environmental consciousness, (5) point-of-purchase display materials that are environmentally efficacious, (6) direct marketing programs that reduce the amount

>> global focus

Environmentally Sustainable Consumption in 14 Countries

National Geographic magazine together with a global research firm measured consumer progress in 14 countries toward sustainable environmental consumption. The study included 14,000 consumers who were asked about their energy-use behavior, transportation choices, food usage, use of green versus traditional products, attitudes toward the environment, and knowledge of environmental issues. Answers to these questions led to the construction of a green consumer behavior index, or *Greendex,* for each of the 14 countries: Australia, Brazil, Canada, China, France, Germany, Great Britain, Hungary, India, Japan, Mexico, Russia, Spain, and the United States. The higher a country's average score on the Greendex, the more environmentally friendly, or sustainable, consumer behavior is in that country.

Results from the survey revealed that consumers in Brazil and India were tied for the highest Greendex score at 60 points. Consumers from China (56.1), Mexico (54.3), Hungary (53.2), and Russia (52.4) followed as the next highest-scoring countries on the Greendex. Considering consumers from wealthy countries, those in Australia, Germany, and Great Britain tied with scores of 50.2, and were followed closely on the Greendex by consumers from Spain (50) and Japan (49.1). The lowest-scoring consumers were from France (48.7), Canada (48.5), and—in last place—consumers from the United States (44.9).

You can calculate your personal Greendex score by going to http://event.nationalgeographic.com/greendex. Perusal of this site will enable you to see why each of the 14 countries scored high or low on the Greendex. For example, Brazil, the highest scoring country along with India, received its high score because Brazilian consumers (1) live in small residences, (2) rarely use home heating, (3) wash their clothes in cold water, (4) are far below average (compared to other countries) in ownership of vehicles, (5) use public transportation, and (6) are concerned more than consumers in other countries about environmental problems.

Comparatively, consumers in the United States scored the lowest on the Greendex because (1) heating and air-conditioning are commonplace and residences tend to be large, (2) a low percentage of American consumers use public transportation, (3) a small percentage of Americans walk or bike daily, (4) food consumption in the United States is the least environmentally sustainable of all countries (e.g., Americans are the least likely of all consumers in the 14 countries to consume locally grown foods, and over one-third of Americans drink bottled water daily), and (5) American consumers (along with Australian and European consumers) are much less concerned about environmental problems than those in emerging economies.

If this seems critical of American consumers, I should note that my personal score on the Greendex survey was an abysmal 42, which is almost three points below the American average. I mention this because I consider myself a very strong advocate of the environment and a good global citizen. However, as a reasonably well-to-do American, I live in a relatively large home that is heated and air-conditioned and drive a private vehicle rather than take public transportation. In effect, I am penalized on the Greendex because I have the good fortune of being economically advantaged. My wife and I have taken strides to reduce our carbon footprint by purchasing energy-efficient appliances, buying locally grown food products when available, reducing our amount of driving, using compact fluorescent lightbulbs throughout our home, installing energy-efficient windows, and buying "green" products whenever possible.

Fortunately or unfortunately, depending on perspective, those of us who live in wealthy countries and participate in the riches our countries offer will always generate more carbon and other greenhouse gases than will less economically fortunate consumers living elsewhere around the globe. Nonetheless, we all can do a better job in reducing our impact on the environment by altering consumption habits and making choices that may cost a little more in the short run but in the long run will benefit the environment and society at large.

SOURCE: Adapted from "Consumer Choice and the Environment—A Worldwide Tracking Survey," http://event.nationalgeographic.com/greendex/index.html (accessed May 14, 2008).

of resource usage by developing more efficient solicitations, and (7) outdoor advertising efforts that reduce the usage of environmentally damaging materials.

Courtesy, Shell International

Figure 21.2

Green Advertising Addressing the Biophysical Environment

Green Advertising

Environmental appeals in advertising were commonplace in American advertising for a short period in the early to mid-1990s, but the initial fervor toward the deteriorating physical environment waned. In fact, for 10 years following this period it was difficult to find examples of environmentally oriented advertising. Now, however, with a rising tide of interest in green marketing and green consumption, environmental appeals have reemerged. Green advertising represents a wise marcom strategy, but only if brand marketers have something meaningful to say about the ecological efficacy of their brands vis-à-vis competitive brands. More advertisers would undoubtedly jump on the green bandwagon if their brands had environmentally based relative advantages.

There are three types of green advertising appeals: (1) ads that address a relationship between a product/service and the biophysical environment (e.g., the ad for Shell in Figure 21.2); (2) those that promote a green lifestyle without highlighting a product or service (see Figure 21.3); and (3) ads that present a corporate image of environmental responsibility (see Figure 21.4).[92]

Environmentally Friendly Packaging Responses

Various efforts have been initiated to improve the environmental effectiveness of packaging materials. Early efforts included packaging soft drinks and many other products in recyclable plastic bottles, switching from polystyrene clamshell containers to paperboard packages for burgers and other sandwiches, and introducing concentrated laundry detergents to shrink packages and thus produce less waste disposal to be placed in already crowded landfills. More recently, we have seen efforts on the part of companies such as PepsiCo to reduce the amount of plastic used in bottles for some of its noncola beverages (e.g., Lipton iced tea and Tropicana juice drinks).[93] PepsiCo's Pepsi and Diet Pepsi cans are now made with 40 percent recycled aluminum,[94] and Coca-Cola has financially supported the world's largest bottle-to-bottle recycling plant and has promised to recycle 100 percent of its aluminum cans sold in the United States.[95]

In one of the major initiatives toward more ecologically friendly packaging, Wal-Mart introduced a package-reduction program that requires its 60,000 worldwide suppliers to rate themselves in terms of various packaging-related factors (e.g., product-to-package ratio, percent of recycled content, and packing tightness of shipping pallets). Suppliers report their scores to Wal-Mart and track the progress of their packaging-reduction efforts. Wal-Mart uses this information as input into its selection of suppliers in competitive product categories. Wal-Mart's objective is by 2013 to cut by 5 percent the amount of packaging on products carried in its stores. Packaging reduction of this magnitude would equate to savings of millions of trees and millions of barrels of oil that go into producing packaging materials.[96]

As counter to these positive packaging developments, there is evidence that package materials often are wasted due to a practice called *short filling*. For example, over 40 percent of juice containers, milk cartons, and other dairy products contain a smaller amount of product—from 1 to 6 percent less—than the package labels promise.[97] This short-filling problem is partially due to profit skimming and also results, more innocently, from poorly calibrated packing machines.

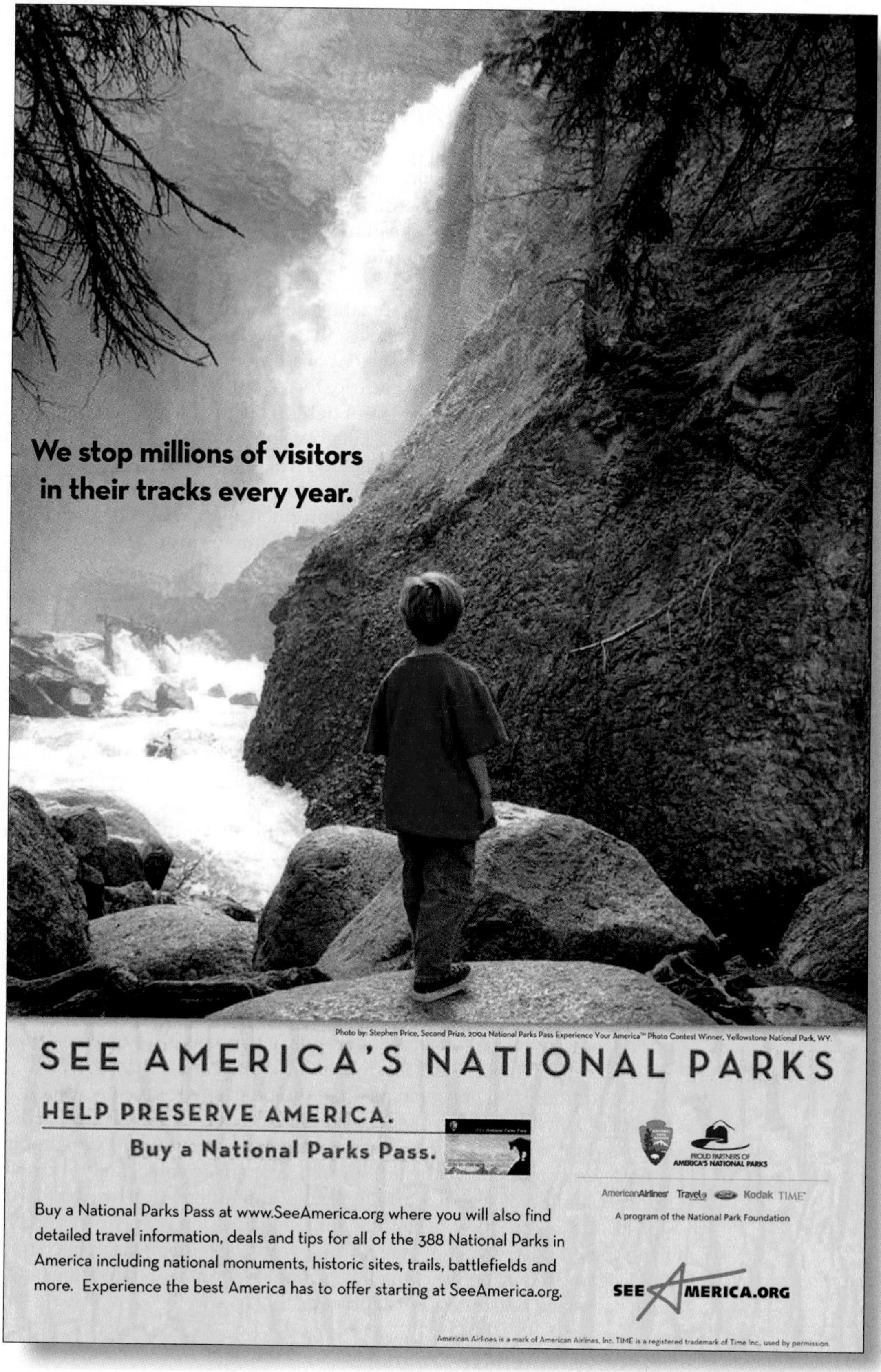

Figure 21.3

Green Advertising Promoting a Green Lifestyle

Whatever the reason, the fact remains that short filling results annually in thousands of tons of wasted packaging materials.

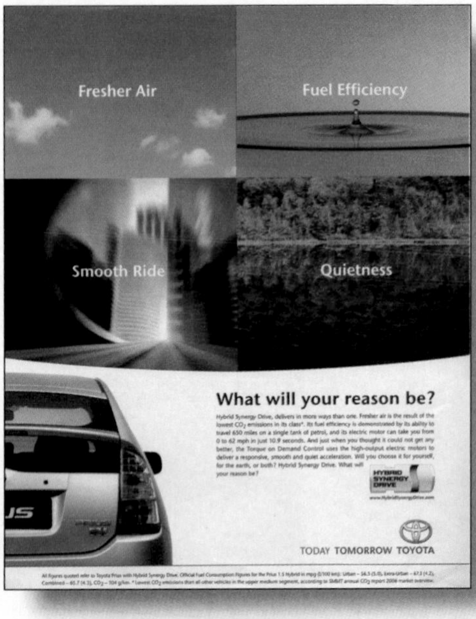

© Image courtesy of The Advertising Archives

Figure 21.4

Green Advertising Presenting an Image of Environmental Responsibility

Seal-of-Approval Programs

Organizations around the world have designed programs to assist consumers in identifying environmentally friendly products and brands. In Germany, for example, the Blue Angel seal represents a promise to consumers that a product carrying an environmental claim is legitimate. Three printer products from Samsung recently received Blue Angel certification. Green Seal, a Washington, DC., nonprofit organization, has developed standards and awarded seals to companies that meet environmental standards—which fewer than 20 percent of all products in the category are able to satisfy. General Electric, for example, received a seal for developing compact fluorescent lightbulbs. In addition to Green Seal, there are various product-category-specific seal programs. For example, the 100% Recycled Paperboard Alliance—a group of North American recycled paperboard manufacturers—allows participating members to identify their products with a logo that consists of a semicircle of small arrows pointing to the words *100% Recycled Paperboard.* More than 80 companies have received certification from the 100% Recycled Paperboard Alliance.[98] Programs such as these provide consumers with assurance that the products carrying these seals legitimately are environmentally friendly.

Cause- and Event-Oriented Sponsorship Programs

Cause-oriented marketing is practiced when companies sponsor or support worthy environmental or social programs (Chapter 19). In doing so, the marketing communicator anticipates that associating the company and its brands with a worthy cause will generate goodwill. It is for this reason that companies sponsor various environmental causes. For example, Bank of America introduced an eco-friendly credit card and promised to contribute $1 to an environmental organization for every dollar consumers using the card spent.[99] Absolut vodka encouraged consumers to visit its Web site and select one of three environmental charities (the Ocean Foundation, the Fruit Tree Planting Foundation, and the Environmental Media Association) that the company would contribute $1 to up to a total of $500,000 to each charity.[100] Cause-oriented programs can be effective if they are not overused and if consumers perceive a company's involvement in an environmental cause is sincere and not just raw commercialism.

In addition to sponsorships that promote environmental causes, companies also are employing event sponsorships related to the environment. For example, Ben & Jerry's sponsored a "Campus Consciousness Tour" by combining a rock show (with rock band Guster) and an ecology-oriented fair to further students' understanding of global warming issues. Interested students were provided with postcards to send to Congress encouraging emission-reduction efforts for vehicles, and Ben & Jerry's Web site (http://www.lickglobalwarming.com) featured a videogame requiring users to make sound environmental decisions toward receiving backstage passes to a Guster concert.[101]

Point-of-Purchase Programs

Billions of dollars are invested in plastic, wood, metal, paper, and other display materials. Many of the displays manufacturers send to retailers are never used and simply end up in landfills. Closer consultations with retailers regarding their point-of-purchase needs would lead to fewer unused and discarded displays. Also, increased use of permanent displays (those engineered to last at least six months) would substantially reduce the number of temporary displays that are quickly discarded. As a result, this would mean a major conservation effort and substantial savings to manufacturers. The use of recycled paper and plastic is another eco-friendly way to reduce the negative impact of the voluminous P-O-P displays consumer goods marketers use.

Direct Marketing Efforts

Direct marketing materials such as brochures, pamphlets, and especially catalogs are voluminous, requiring, of course, major consumption of trees and use of huge amounts of natural gas in their production. Unfortunately, recent research revealed that only 28 percent of the surveyed direct marketers said that the environment is a frequent factor in their decision making.[102] Companies that use direct marketing in their marcom programs can improve their stewardship of the environment by doing a better job in targeting customers and thereby cutting out waste circulation, by removing unlikely purchasers from their mailing lists, and by reducing the frequency of mailing catalogs and other solicitations to prospective customers.

Outdoor Advertising Responses

The highways and streets of America are inundated with tens of thousands of outdoor signs. With the exception of electronic signs (Chapter 20), nearly all of the billboards are covered either with banners made from polyvinyl chloride (PVC), a toxic petroleum-based product, or with thick paper that is impractical to reuse or recycle. Removal of these materials from billboards leads to massive waste that enters into landfills. CBS Outdoor, the second-largest billboard company in the United States, intends to discontinue using PVC vinyl sheets and replace them with a plastic that is reusable. Lamar Advertising, the third largest outdoor ad firm, is in the process of replacing thick paper panels with a thinner and lighter-weight material. Finally, the leader in outdoor advertising in the United States, Clear Channel Outdoor, is reducing energy usage in its hundreds of thousands of displays by using more energy-efficient lights.[103] All in all, the outdoor advertising industry is making important strides toward "going green."

Guidelines for Green Marketing

The significance of the environmental problem demands that marketing communicators do everything possible to ensure that green claims are credible, realistic, and believable. To assist companies in knowing what environmental claims can and cannot be communicated in advertisements, on packages, and elsewhere, the FTC promulgated guides for environmental marketing claims, commonly referred to as the Green Guides.[104] These guides outline four general principles that apply to all environmental marketing claims: (1) qualifications and disclosures should be sufficiently clear and prominent to prevent deception; (2) claims should make clear whether they apply to the product, the package, or a component of either; (3) claims should not overstate an environmental attribute or benefit, either expressly or by implication; and (4) comparative claims should be presented in a manner that makes the basis for the comparison sufficiently clear to avoid consumer deception. At the time of this writing, the FTC is in the process of updating the Green Guides.

In addition to these general guidelines, marcom practitioners are offered four general recommendations for making appropriate environmental claims: (1) make the claims specific, (2) use claims that reflect current disposal options, (3) make the claims substantive, and (4) only use supportable claims.[105]

1. **Make Specific Claims.** This guideline is intended to prevent marketing communicators from using meaningless claims such as "environmentally friendly" or "safe for the environment." The use of specific environmental claims enables consumers to make informed choices, reduces the likelihood that claims will be misinterpreted, and minimizes the chances that consumers will think that a product is more environmentally friendly than it actually is. In general, it is recommended that environmental claims be as specific as possible—not general, vague, incomplete, or overly broad. For example, a claim that a brand of washing detergent is "fully biodegradable" is more precise than an expression that this brand is "good for the environment."
2. **Reflect Current Disposal Options.** This recommendation is directed at preventing environmental claims that are technically accurate but practically unrealizable due to local trash-disposal practices. For example, most communities dispose of trash by burying it in public landfills. Because paper and plastic products do not degrade when buried, it is misleading for businesses to make environmental claims that their products are degradable, biodegradable, or photodegradable.
3. **Make Substantive Claims.** Some marketing communicators use trivial and irrelevant environmental claims to convey the impression that a promoted brand is environmentally sound. An illustration of a nonsubstantive claim is a company promoting its polystyrene foam cups as "preserving our trees and forests." Another trivial claim is when single-use products such as paper plates are claimed to be "safe for the environment." Clearly, a paper plate is not unsafe to the environment in the same sense that a toxic chemical is unsafe; however, paper plates and other throwaways do not actually benefit the environment but rather exacerbate the landfill problem.
4. **Make Supportable Claims.** This recommendation is straightforward: Environmental claims should be supported by competent and reliable scientific evidence. The purpose of this recommendation is to encourage businesses to make only those environmental claims that can be backed by facts. The injunction to businesses is clear: Do not claim it unless you can support it.

Summary

This chapter examined a variety of issues related to ethical marcom behavior, the regulation of marketing communications, and green marcom initiatives. The first major section looked at ethical marketing communications behavior. The ethics of each of the following marcom activities were discussed: the targeting of marketing communications efforts, advertising, public relations, packaging communications, sales promotions, and online marketing communications. A concluding discussion examined how firms can foster ethical behavior.

The second section examined the regulation of marcom activities. The regulatory environment was described with respect to both government regulation and industry self-regulation. The FTC's role was explained in terms of its regulation of deception and unfair practices. Self-regulation by the Council of Better Business Bureaus' National Advertising Division (NAD) and National Advertising Review Board (NARB) were discussed.

In the final section, environmental, or *green*, marketing was described, and implications for marketing communications were elaborated. Marketing communicators have responded to society's environmental interests by developing more environmentally friendly packaging and undertaking other communications initiatives. Recommendations provided to marketing communicators for making appropriate environmental claims are to (1) make the claims specific, (2) have claims reflect current disposal options, (3) make the claims substantive, and (4) make supportable claims.

Discussion Questions

1. Did Subway cross the exploitation line when it targeted its food products to obese children?
2. What is your opinion regarding the ethics of product placements in movies targeted to children? Identify the arguments on both sides of the issue, and then present your personal position.
3. Is targeting unethical or just good marketing? Identify the arguments on both sides of the issue, and then present your personal position.
4. What is your view regarding Anheuser-Busch's use in the early-to-mid 1990s of humorous TV commercials that portrayed animated characters Frank and Louie, and an accompanying cast of lizard and frog characters? Is this form of advertising simply a marvelous creative execution, or is it insidious in its potential to encourage children to like the concept of drinking beer, and perhaps Budweiser in particular? (Note: If you do not recall these commercials, ask your professor to provide a description.)
5. Are you in favor of the federal government requiring nutritional labeling, or do you consider such requirements an unnecessary intrusion into the free marketplace? Justify your position on this matter.
6. What is the distinction between a deceptive and an unfair business practice?
7. Give examples of advertising claims that, if found false, probably would be considered material and those that probably would be evaluated as immaterial.
8. What is your opinion of the defense Kraft used in claiming that calcium is an immaterial product attribute?
9. When discussing the criticism that advertising is manipulative, a distinction was made between persuasion efforts of which consumers are cognitively aware and those that fall below their conscious radar screens. First, explain in your own words the distinction between the potential for advertisers to manipulate consumers cognitively and unconsciously. Second, express your thoughts about the ethical ramifications of, say, retailers' potential use of in-store advertising to air subliminal messages.
10. What is your view of a proposal by Senator Hillary Clinton (Democrat, New York) that would ban all advertising and marketing in elementary schools?
11. In theory, corrective advertising represents a potentially valuable device for regulating deceptive advertising. In practice, however, corrective advertising must perform a very delicate balancing act by being strong enough without being too forceful. Explain the nature of this dilemma.
12. In the late 1990s, the Distilled Spirits Council of the United States voted to lift its voluntary ban on advertising "hard" liquor on television and radio, a self-imposed ban that had been in effect for nearly a half-century. In your opinion, what are the arguments on both sides of the issue regarding the removal of this ban? If you were an executive the Distilled Spirits Council employed, would you have urged a return to the airways? Is this return to advertising distilled spirits via electronic media unethical or, alternatively, is it a matter of a gutsy business decision by the Distilled Spirits Council that was long overdue?
13. Some consumers are more concerned about the physical environment than others. Provide a specific profile of what in your opinion would be the socioeconomic and psychographic (i.e., lifestyle) characteristics of the "environmentally concerned" consumer.
14. The text mentioned—in the context of discussing packaging ethics—that an ethical infraction may occur when marketers package store brands so that they look virtually identical to well-known national brands. What are your thoughts on this?
15. From your experience, are most green marketing claims legitimate or do they represent greenwash? Support your answer with examples.
16. Are the profit motive and green marketing inherently in conflict?

End Notes

1. The statements in this and the following paragraph are based on Avery Johnson, "How Sweet It Isn't," *The Wall Street Journal*, April 6, 2007, B1.
2. Lorraine Heller, "Merisant & McNeil Reach Quiet Settlement in Splenda Battle," *FoodUSA*, May 14, 2007, http://www.foodnavigator-usa.com (accessed June 3, 2008).
3. Lorraine Heller, "Splenda Ad Slogans Banned in France," *FoodUSA*, May 11, 2007, http://www.foodnavigator-usa.com (accessed June 3, 2008).
4. For an interesting discussion of the interrelation between ethical issues and regulation, see George M. Zinkhan, "Advertising Ethics: Emerging Methods and Trends," *Journal of Advertising* 23 (September 1994), 1–4.
5. Carolyn Y. Yoo, "Personally Responsible," *BizEd*, May/June 2003, 24.
6. O. C. Ferrell and Larry G. Gresham, "A Contingency Framework for Understanding Ethical Decision Making in Marketing," *Journal of Marketing* 49 (summer 1985), 87–96.
7. A provocative and informative discourse on the issue of consumer vulnerability is presented in N. Craig Smith and Elizabeth Cooper-Martin, "Ethics and Target Marketing: The Role of Product Harm and Consumer Vulnerability," *Journal of Marketing* 61 (July 1997), 1–20.
8. Sara Schaefer Munoz, "Nagging Issue: Pitching Junk to Kids," *The Wall Street Journal Online*, November 11, 2003, http://online.wsj.com (accessed November 11, 2003).
9. For those who are interested in learning more about how children and teenagers are influenced by marcom messages, the following articles, all in the same issue of one journal, are must reading: Louis J. Moses and Dare A. Baldwin, "What Can the Study of Cognitive Development Reveal about Children's Ability to Appreciate and Cope with Advertising?" *Journal of Public Policy & Marketing* 24 (fall 2005), 186–201; Cornelia Pechmann, Linda Levine, Sandra Loughlin, and Frances Leslie, "Impulsive and Self-Conscious: Adolescents' Vulnerability to Advertising and Promotion," *Journal of Public Policy & Marketing* 24 (fall 2005), 202–221; and Peter Wright, Marian Friestad, and David M. Boush, "The Development of Marketplace Persuasion Knowledge in Children, Adolescents, and Young Adults," *Journal of Public Policy & Marketing* 24 (fall 2005), 222–233.
10. Laura Bird, "Gatorade for Kids," *Adweek's Marketing Week*, July 15, 1991, 4–5.
11. Matthew Grimm, "Is Marketing to Kids Ethical?" *Brandweek*, April 5, 2004, 44–48.
12. Joseph Pereira and Audrey Warren, "Coming Up Next...," *The Wall Street Journal Online*, March 15, 2004, http://online.wsj.com (accessed March 15, 2004).
13. Stephanie Thompson, "Campbell Aims Squarely at Kids with Push for Pastas and Soups," *Advertising Age*, May 31, 2004, 62.
14. Janet Whitman, "Subway Weighs Television Ads on Childhood Obesity," *The Wall Street Journal Online*, June 16, 2004, http://online.wsj.com (accessed June 17, 2004); Bob Garfield, "Subway Walks Line between Wellness, Child Exploitation," *Advertising Age*, July 26, 2004, 29.
15. "U.S. Food Companies to Restrict Advertising Aimed at Children," July 18, 2007, http://online.wsj.com (accessed July 18, 2007); Andrew Martin, "Kellogg to Phase Out Some Food Ads to Children," June 14, 2007, http://www.nytimes.com (accessed June 17, 2004).
16. Eben Shapiro, "Molson Ice Ads Raise Hackles of Regulators," *The Wall Street Journal*, February 25, 1994, B1, B10.
17. Guideline 8 in the Industry Advertising Code. Published in an undated pamphlet distributed by the Department of Consumer Awareness and Education, Anheuser-Busch, Inc., St. Louis, MO.
18. Brian Steinberg and Suzanne Vranica, "Brewers Are Urged to Tone Down Ads," *The Wall Street Journal Online*, June 23, 2003, http://online.wsj.com (accessed June 23, 2003).
19. "Alcohol Radio Ads Still Air on Programs with Teen Audiences," September 1, 2006, http://online.wsj.com (accessed September 1, 2006).
20. Christopher Lawton, "Lawsuits Allege Alcohol Makers Target Youths," *The Wall Street Journal Online*, February 5, 2004, http://online.wsj.com (accessed February 5, 2004).
21. Stefan Fatsis and Christopher Lawton, "Beer Ads on TV, College Sports: Explosive Mix?" *The Wall Street Journal Online*, November 12, 2003, http://online.wsj.com (accessed November 12, 2003).
22. See, for example, Lawrence C. Soley, "Smoke-filled Rooms and Research: A Response to Jean J. Boddewyn's Commentary," *Journal of Advertising* 22 (December 1993), 108–109; Richard W. Pollay, "Pertinent Research and Impertinent Opinions: Our Contributions to the Cigarette Advertising Policy Debate," *Journal of Advertising* 22 (December 1993), 110–117; Joel B. Cohen "Playing to Win: Marketing and Public Policy at Odds over Joe Camel," *Journal of Public Policy & Marketing*, 19 (fall 2000), 155–167; Kathleen J. Kelly, Michael D. Slater, and David Karan, "Image Advertisements' Influence on Adolescents' Perceptions of the Desirability of Beer and Cigarettes," *Journal of Public Policy & Marketing* 21 (fall 2002), 295–304; Cornelia Pechmann and Susan J. Knight, "An Experimental Investigation of the Joint Effects of Advertising and Peers on Adolescents' Beliefs and Intentions about Cigarette Consumption," *Journal of Consumer Research* 29 (June 2002), 5–19; Marvin E. Goldberg, "American

Media and the Smoking-related Behaviors of Asian Adolescents," *Journal of Advertising Research* 43 (March 2003), 2–11; Marvin E. Goldberg, "Correlation, Causation, and Smoking Initiation among Youths," *Journal of Advertising Research* 43 (December 2003), 431–440.

23. See, for example, Claude R. Martin, Jr., "Ethical Advertising Research Standards: Three Case Studies," *Journal of Advertising* 23 (September 1994), 17–29; Claude R. Martin, Jr., "Pollay's Pertinent and Impertinent Opinions: 'Good' versus 'Bad' Research," *Journal of Advertising* 23 (March 1994), 117–122; John E. Calfee, "The Historical Significance of Joe Camel," *Journal of Public Policy & Marketing,* 19 (fall 2000), 168–182; Robert N. Reitter, "Comment: 'American Media and the Smoking-related Behaviors of Asian Adolescents,'" *Journal of Advertising Research* 43 (March 2003), 12–13; Charles R. Taylor and P. Greg Bonner, "Comment on 'American Media and the Smoking-related Behaviors of Asian Adolescents,'" *Journal of Advertising Research* 43 (December 2003), 419–430.
24. "Women's Magazines Are Urged to Stop Accepting Tobacco Ads," June 6, 2007, http://online.wsj.com (accessed June 6, 2007).
25. For an insightful review of the literature and a provocative study on this issue, see J. Craig Andrews, Richard G. Netemeyer, Scot Burton, D. Paul Moberg, and Ann Christiansen, "Understanding Adolescent Intentions to Smoke: An Examination of Relationships among Social Influence, Prior Trial Behavior, and Antitobacco Campaign Advertising," *Journal of Marketing* 68 (July 2004), 110–123.
26. Ira Teinowitz, "Filmmakers: Give Ad-practice Shifts a Chance to Work," *Advertising Age,* October 2, 2000, 6; David Finnigan, "Pounding the Kid Trail," *Brandweek,* October 9, 2000, 32–38; Betsy Spethmann, "Now Showing: Federal Scrutiny," *Promo,* November 2000, 17.
27. Scott Donaton, "Why the Kids Marketing Fuss? Here's Why Parents Are Angry," *Advertising Age,* October 16, 2000, 48.
28. "Fighting Ads in the Inner City," *Newsweek,* February 5, 1990, 46.
29. For further reading about these and other controversial cases, see Smith and Cooper-Martin, "Ethics and Target Marketing."
30. Dan Koeppel, "Insensitivity to a Market's Concerns," *Adweek's Marketing Week,* November 5, 1990, 25; "A 'Black' Cigarette Goes Up in Smoke," *Newsweek,* January 29, 1990, 54; "RJR Cancels Test of 'Black' Cigarette," *Marketing News,* February 19, 1990, 10.
31. Laura Bird, "An 'Uptown' Remake Called PowerMaster," *Adweek's Marketing Week,* July 1, 1991, 7.
32. "Fighting Ads in the Inner City."
33. For more discussion of this case, see Smith and Cooper-Martin, "Ethics and Target Marketing."
34. See John E. Calfee, "'Targeting' the Problem: It Isn't Exploitation, It's Efficient Marketing," *Advertising Age,* July 22, 1991, 18.
35. For additional insight on the issue, see Smith and Cooper-Martin, "Ethics and Target Marketing."
36. For an insightful treatment of practitioners' views of advertising ethics, see Minette E. Drumwright and Patrick E. Murphy, "How Advertising Practitioners View Ethics," *Journal of Advertising* 33 (summer 2004), 7–24. For additional coverage of practitioners' views on advertising morality, see Jeffrey J. Maciejewski, "From Bikinis to Basal Cell Carcinoma: Advertising Practitioners' Moral Assessments of Advertising Content," *Journal of Current Issues and Research in Advertising* 27 (fall 2005), 107–115.
37. Ronald Berman, "Advertising and Social Change," *Advertising Age,* April 30, 1980, 24.
38. The interested reader is encouraged to review the following three articles for an extremely thorough, insightful, and provocative debate over the social and ethical role of advertising in American society. Richard W. Pollay, "The Distorted Mirror: Reflections on the Unintended Consequences of Advertising," *Journal of Marketing* 50 (April 1986), 18–36; Morris B. Holbrook, "Mirror, Mirror on the Wall, What's Unfair in the Reflections of Advertising?" *Journal of Marketing* 51 (July 1987), 95–103; Richard W. Pollay, "On the Value of Reflections on the Values in 'The Distorted Mirror,'" *Journal of Marketing* (July 1987), 104–109. Pollay and Holbrook present alternative views of whether advertising is a "mirror" that merely reflects societal attitudes and values or a "distorted mirror" that is responsible for unintended and undesirable social consequences.
39. John E. Calfee and Debra Jones Ringold, "The 70% Majority: Enduring Consumer Beliefs about Advertising," *Journal of Public Policy & Marketing* 13 (fall 1994), 228–238.
40. Peter R. Darke and Robin J. B. Ritchie, "The Defensive Consumer: Advertising Deception, Defensive Processing, and Distrust," *Journal of Marketing Research* 44 (February 2007), 114–127.
41. Rich Thomaselli, "Vytorin Ad Shame Taints Entire Marketing Industry," *Advertising Age,* January 21, 2008, 1, 33.
42. Marian Friestad and Peter Wright, "The Persuasion Knowledge Model: How People Cope with Persuasion Attempts," *Journal of Consumer Research* 21 (June 1994), 1–31; Marian Friestad and Peter Wright, "Persuasion Knowledge: Lay People's and Researchers' Beliefs about the Psychology of Advertising," *Journal of Consumer Research* 22 (June 1995), 62–74.
43. For an accessible treatment on the issue of automatic, or noncontrolled motivation and behavior, see John A. Bargh, "Losing Consciousness: Automatic Influences on Consumer Judgment, Behavior, and Motivation," *Journal of Consumer Research* 29 (September 2002), 280–285. See also John A. Bargh and Tanya L. Chartrand, "The Unbearable Automaticity of Being," *American Psychologist* 54 (July 1999), 462–479; Johan C. Karremans, Wolfgang Stroebe, and Jasper Claus, "Beyond

Vicary's Fantasies: The Impact of Subliminal Priming and Brand Choice," *Journal of Experimental Social Psychology* 42 (November 2006), 792–798.

44. Avery Johnson, "New Impotence Ads Draw Fire–Just Like Old Ones," *The Wall Street Journal,* February 16, 2007, B1.
45. Terence A. Shimp and Elnora W. Stuart, "The Role of Disgust as an Emotional Mediator of Advertising Effects," *Journal of Advertising* 33 (spring 2004), 43–54.
46. Stephen B. Castleberry, Warren French, and Barbara A. Carlin, "The Ethical Framework of Advertising and Marketing Research Practitioners: A Moral Development Perspective," *Journal of Advertising* 22 (June 1993), 39–46. Indirectly, a similar argument is made in the following source that intimates that dishonesty is widespread in society: Nina Mazar and Dan Ariely, "Dishonesty in Everyday Life and Its Policy Implications," *Journal of Public Policy & Marketing* 25 (spring 2006), 117–126.
47. American Association of Advertising Agencies, http://www.aaaa.org.
48. These issues were identified by Paula Fitzgerald Bone and Robert J. Corey, "Ethical Dilemmas in Packaging: Beliefs of Packaging Professionals," *Journal of Macromarketing* 12 (No. 1, 1992), 45–54. The following discussion is guided by this paper. The authors identified a fifth ethical aspect of packaging (the relationship between a package and a product's price) that is not discussed here.
49. For an interesting discussion of perceptual differences among packaging professionals, brand managers, and consumers on the issue of packaging ethics, see Paula Fitzgerald Bone and Robert J. Corey, "Packaging Ethics: Perceptual Differences among Packaging Professionals, Brand Managers and Ethically-interested Consumers," *Journal of Business Ethics* 24 (April 2000), 199–213.
50. For an insightful discussion of sales promotion practices and related consumer psychology that result in exaggerated expectations of winning, see James C. Ward and Ronald Paul Hill, "Designing Effective Promotional Games: Opportunities and Problems," *Journal of Advertising* 20 (September 1991), 69–81.
51. A special issue of the *Journal of Public Policy & Marketing* 19 (spring 2000) is devoted to privacy and ethical issues in online marketing. See the articles on pages 1 through 73 by the following authors: George R. Milne; Eve M. Caudill and Patrick E. Murphy; Mary J. Culnan; Joseph Phelps, Glen Nowak and Elizabeth Ferrell; Ross D. Petty; Anthony D. Miyazaki and Ana Fernandez; and Kim Bartel Sheehan and Mariea Grubbs Hoy.
52. Jeffrey P. Davidson, "The Elusive Nature of Integrity: People Know It When They See It, but Can't Explain It," *Marketing News,* November 7, 1986, 24.
53. Donald P. Robin and R. Eric Reidenbach, "Social Responsibility, Ethics, and Marketing Strategy: Closing the Gap between Concept and Application," *Journal of Marketing* 51 (January 1987), 44–58. In this context, two additional articles that discuss ethical responsibilities of marketing practitioners are Rhoda H. Karpatkin, "Toward a Fair and Just Marketplace for All Consumers: The Responsibilities of Marketing Professionals," *Journal of Public Policy & Marketing* 18 (spring 1999), 118–122; Gene R. Laczniak, "Distributive Justice, Catholic Social Teaching, and the Moral Responsibility of Marketers," *Journal of Public Policy & Marketing* 18 (spring 1999), 125–129.
54. Based on Gene R. Laczniak and Patrick E. Murphy, "Fostering Ethical Marketing Decisions," *Journal of Business Ethics* 10 (1991), 259–271.
55. Dave Dolak, "Let's Lift the Human Spirit," *Brandweek,* April 28, 2003, 30.
56. Michael B. Mazis, Richard Staelin, Howard Beales, and Steven Salop, "A Framework for Evaluating Consumer Information Regulation," *Journal of Marketing* 45 (winter 1981), 11–21.
57. The following discussion is adapted from Mazis, et al.
58. Alcohol Beverage Labeling Act of 1988, S.R. 2047.
59. A thorough review of research pertaining to warning labels is provided by David W. Stewart and Ingrid M. Martin, "Intended and Unintended Consequences of Warning Messages: A Review and Synthesis of Empirical Research," *Journal of Public Policy & Marketing* 13 (spring 1994), 1–19. See also Janet R. Hankin, James J. Sloan, and Robert J. Sokol, "The Modest Impact of the Alcohol Beverage Warning Label on Drinking Pregnancy among a Sample of African-American Women," *Journal of Public Policy & Marketing* 17 (spring 1998), 61–69.
60. Ross D. Petty, "Advertising Law in the United States and European Union," *Journal of Public Policy & Marketing* 16 (spring 1997), 2–13.
61. J. Edward Russo, Barbara L. Metcalf, and Debra Stephens, "Identifying Misleading Advertising," *Journal of Consumer Research* 8 (September 1981), 120. For a thorough review of advertising deception, see also David M. Gardner and Nancy H. Leonard, "Research in Deceptive and Corrective Advertising: Progress to Date and Impact on Public Policy," *Current Issues & Research in Advertising* 12 (1990), 275–309.
62. For a more thorough discussion of these elements and other matters surrounding FTC deception policy, see Gary T. Ford and John E. Calfee, "Recent Developments in FTC Policy on Deception," *Journal of Marketing* 50 (July 1986), 82–103.
63. Public copy of a letter dated October 14, 1983, from FTC Chairman James C. Miller III to Senator Bob Packwood, Chairman of Senate Committee on Commerce, Science, and Transportation.
64. These facts are offered by Jacob Jacoby and George J. Szybillo, "Consumer Research in FTC Versus Kraft (1991): A Case of Heads We Win, Tails You Lose?" *Journal of Public Policy & Marketing* 14 (spring 1995), 2.
65. Ruling of the Federal Trade Commission, Docket No. 9208, January 30, 1991.
66. Jef I. Richards and Ivan L. Preston, "Proving and Disproving Materiality of Deceptive Advertising Claims," *Journal of Public Policy & Marketing* 11 (fall 1992), 45–56; Jacoby and Szybillo, "Consumer Research in

FTC Versus Kraft," 1–14; David W. Stewart, "Deception, Materiality, and Survey Research: Some Lessons from Kraft," *Journal of Public Policy & Marketing* 14 (spring 1995), 15–28; Seymour Sudman "When Experts Disagree: Comments on the Articles by Jacoby and Szybillo and Stewart," *Journal of Public Policy & Marketing* 14 (spring 1995), 29–34.

67. Ross D. Petty and J. Craig Andrews, "Covert Marketing Unmasked: A Legal and Regulatory Guide for Practices That Mask Marketing Messages," *Journal of Public Policy & Marketing* 27 (spring 2008), 7–18.
68. Ibid.
69. See ibid., p. 8, for a typology of six forms of masked marcom messages.
70. Dorothy Cohen, "The Concept of Unfairness as It Relates to Advertising Legislation," *Journal of Marketing* 38 (July 1974), 8.
71. Cohen, "Unfairness in Advertising Revisited," *Journal of Marketing* 46 (winter 2008), 8.
72. Christy Fisher, "How Congress Broke Unfair Ad Impasse," *Advertising Age,* August 22, 1994, 34.
73. Cohen, "Unfairness in Advertising Revisited," 74.
74. J. Howard Beales III, "The FTC's Use of Unfairness Authority: It's Rise, Fall, and Resurrection," *Journal of Public Policy and Marketing* 22 (fall 2003), 192–200.
75. Ibid.
76. The following discussion borrows liberally from the excellent review article by William L. Wilkie, Dennis L. McNeill, and Michael B. Mazis, "Marketing's 'Scarlet Letter': The Theory and Practice of Corrective Advertising," *Journal of Marketing* 48 (spring 1984), 11. See also Gardner and Leonard, "Research in Deceptive and Corrective Advertising."
77. See Michael B. Mazis, "FTC v. Novartis: The Return of Corrective Advertising?" *Journal of Public Policy & Marketing* 20 (spring 2001), 114–122; Bruce Ingersoll, "FTC Orders Novartis to Run Ads to Correct 'Misbeliefs' about Pill," *The Wall Street Journal Online,* May 28, 1999, http://online.wsj.com.
78. A study evaluating the effects of a corrective advertising order against STP oil additive determined that corrective advertising action in this case worked as intended: False beliefs were corrected without injuring the product category or consumers' overall perceptions of the STP Corporation. See Kenneth L. Bernhardt, Thomas C. Kinnear, and Michael B. Mazis, "A Field Study of Corrective Advertising Effectiveness," *Journal of Public Policy & Marketing* 5 (1986), 146–162. This article and the one by Mazis in the previous endnote are essential reading for anyone interested in learning more about corrective advertising.
79. Andrew J. Strenio, Jr., "The FTC in 1988: Phoenix or Finis?" *Journal of Public Policy & Marketing* 7 (1988), 21–39.
80. Jean J. Boddewyn, "Advertising Self-Regulation: True Purpose and Limits," *Journal of Advertising* 18, no. 2 (1989), 19–27.
81. Jean J. Boddewyn, "Advertising Self-Regulation: Private Government and Agent of Public Policy," *Journal of Public Policy & Marketing* 4 (1985), 129–141.
82. Avery M. Abernethy and Jan LeBlanc Wicks, "Self-regulation and Television Advertising: A Replication and Extension," *Journal of Advertising Research* 41 (May/June 2001), 31–37; Avery M. Abernethy, "Advertising Clearance Practices of Radio Stations: A Model of Advertising Self-Regulation," *Journal of Advertising* 22 (September 1993), 15–26; Herbert J. Rotfeld, Avery M. Abernethy, and Patrick R. Parsons, "Self-Regulation and Television Advertising," *Journal of Advertising* 19 (December 1990), 18–26; Eric J. Zanot, "Unseen but Effective Advertising Regulation: The Clearance Process," *Journal of Advertising* 14, no. 4 (1985), 44–51, 59.
83. Eric J. Zanot, "A Review of Eight Years of NARB Casework: Guidelines and Parameters of Deceptive Advertising," *Journal of Advertising* 9, no. 4 (1980), 20.
84. "Clorox, Colgate Participate in NAD Forum," *NAD News,* April 28, 2008, http://www.nadreview.org (accessed May 31, 2008).
85. "Lenovo, Dell Participate in NAD Forum," *NAD News,* April 8, 2008, http://www.nadreview.org (accessed May 31, 2008).
86. "Neutrogena Corporation Participates in NAD Forum," *NAD News,* May 27, 2008, http://www.nadreview.org (accessed May 31, 2008).
87. Jim Guthrie, "Give Self-regulation a Hand," *Advertising Age,* October 15, 2001, 16.
88. The concept of green marketing has various dimensions beyond this general explanation. For a review of the nuances, see William E. Kilbourne, "Green Advertising: Salvation or Oxymoron?" *Journal of Advertising* 24 (summer 1995), 7–20.
89. Jacquelyn A. Ottman, Edwin R. Stafford, and Cathy L. Hartman, "Avoiding Green Marketing Myopia," *Environment* 48 (no. 5, 2006), 23–36.
90. Subhabrata Bobby Banerjee, Easwar S. Iyer, and Rajiv K. Kashyap, "Corporate Environmentalism: Antecedents and Influence of Industry Type," *Journal of Marketing* 67 (April 2003), 106–122; Pratima Bansal and Kendall Roth, "Why Companies Go Green: A Model of Ecological Responsiveness," *Academy of Management Journal,* 43 no. 4 (2000), 717–736.
91. Nicholas Casey, "New Nike Sneaker Targets Jocks, Greens, Wall Street," *The Wall Street Journal,* February 15, 2008, B1.
92. This classification is based on Subhabrata Banerjee, Charles S. Gulas, and Easwar Iyer, "Shades of Green: A Multidimensional Analysis of Environmental Advertising," *Journal of Advertising* 24 (summer 1995), 21–32. For additional discussion of the types of environmental advertising claims and their frequency of use, see Les Carlson, Stephen J. Grove, and Norman Kangun, "A Content Analysis of Environmental Advertising Claims: A Matrix Method Approach," *Journal of Advertising* 22 (September 1993), 27–39.
93. Betsy McKay, "Pepsi to Cut Plastic Used in Bottles," *The Wall Street Journal,* May 6, 2008, B2.
94. "Coming around Again," *Marketing News,* May 15, 2008, 4.
95. Michael Bush, "Sustainability and a Smile," *Advertising Age,* February 25, 2008, 1, 25.

96. Betsy Spethmann, "How Would You Do?" *Promo,* February 2007, 18.
97. For review of a report on the short-filling problem, see http://www.ftc.gov/opa/1997/07/milk.htm.
98. For list, see http://www.rpa100.com/recycled/look-whos-using-the-rpa-100-symbol (accessed June 1, 2008).
99. Based on a Bank of America press release, http://newsroom.bankofamerica.com/index.php?s=press_releases&item=7697 (accessed June 1, 2008).
100. Brian Quinton, "Absolut Zero," *Promo,* April 2008, 10.
101. Stephanie Thompson, "Ben & Jerry's: A Green Pioneer," *Advertising Age,* June 11, 2007, S-8.
102. Carol Krol, "Direct Marketers Not Feeling 'Green,'" *BtoB,* May 5, 2008, 14.
103. Information in this section is adapted from Shira Ovide, "Can Billboard Trade Go Green?" *The Wall Street Journal,* September 19, 2007, B2.
104. Published in the *Federal Register* on August 13, 1992 [57 FR 36,363 (1992)]. These guides also available are online at http://www.ftc.gov/bcp/grnrule/green02.htm. See also, Jason W. Gray-Lee, Debra L. Scammon, and Robert N. Mayer, "Review of Legal Standards for Environmental Marketing Claims," *Journal of Public Policy & Marketing* 13 (spring 1994), 155–159.
105. Julie Vergeront (principal author), *The Green Report: Findings and Preliminary Recommendations for Responsible Environmental Advertising* (St. Paul: Minnesota Attorney General's Office, November 1990). The following discussion is a summary of the recommendations in *The Green Report.* The Federal Trade Commission's guidelines are similar in stating that environmental claims should (1) be substantiated; (2) be clear as to whether any assumed environmental advantage applies to the product, the package, or both; (3) avoid being trivial; and (4) if comparisons are made, make clear the basis for the comparisons.

glossary

A

Achievers One of eight VALS segments of American adult consumers. Motivated by the desire for achievement, Achievers have goal-oriented lifestyles and a deep commitment to career and family.See also **Believers, Experiencers, Innovators, Makers, Strivers, Survivors,** and **Thinkers.**

Account-specific marketing A descriptive term that characterizes promotional and advertising activity that a manufacturer customizes to specific retail accounts; also called *co-marketing*.

Active synthesis The second stage of perceptual encoding, active synthesis involves a more refined perception of a stimulus than simply an examination of its basic features. The context of the situation in which information is received plays a major role in determining what is perceived and interpreted.

Advertising strategy A plan of action guided by corporate and marketing strategies which determine the following: how much can be invested in advertising; at what markets advertising efforts need to be directed; how advertising must be coordinated with other marketing elements; and, to some degree, how advertising is to be executed.

Affordability method An advertising budgeting method that sets the budget by spending on advertising those funds that remain after budgeting for everything else.

Ambushing An activity that takes place when companies that are not official sponsors of an event undertake marketing efforts to convey the impression that they are.

Appropriateness An advertisement is appropriate to the extent that the message is on target for delivering the brand's positioning strategy and capturing the brand's relative strengths and weaknesses vis-à-vis competitive brands.

Associations The particular thoughts and feelings that consumers have linked in memory with a particular brand.

Attention A stage of information processing in which the consumer focuses cognitive resources on and thinks about a message to which he or she has been exposed.

Attractiveness An attribute that includes any number of virtuous characteristics that receivers may perceive in an endorser. The general concept of attractiveness consists of three related ideas: *similarity, familiarity,* and *liking*.

Attributes In the means-end conceptualization of advertising strategy, attributes are features or aspects of the advertised product or brand.

Awareness class The first step in product adoption. Four marketing-mix variables influence the awareness class: samples, coupons, advertising, and product distribution.

B

Baby boom The birth of 75 million Americans between 1946 and 1964.

Believers One of eight VALS segments of American adult consumers. Believers are motivated by ideals. They are conservative, conventional people with concrete beliefs based on traditional, established codes: family, religion, community, and the nation. See also **Achievers, Experiencers, Innovators, Makers, Strivers, Survivors,** and **Thinkers.**

Bill-back allowances A form of trade allowance in which retailers receive allowances for featuring the manufacturer's brand in advertisements (billback ad allowances) or for providing special displays (bill-back display allowances).

Bonus pack Is a form of sales promotion whereby extra quantities of the product are provided to consumers at the brand's regular price.

Brand Is a company's particular offering of a product, service, or other consumption object. Brands represent the focus of marcom efforts.

Brand image style A creative advertising style that involves psychosocial rather than physical differentiation. The advertiser attempts to develop an image for a brand by associating it with symbols.

Buzz creation The systematic and organized effort to encourage people to talk favorably about a particular item (a product, service, or specific brand) and to recommend its usage to others who are part of their social network.

C

Cause-related marketing (CRM) A relatively narrow aspect of overall sponsorship which involves an amalgam of public relations, sales promotion, and corporate philanthropy. The distinctive feature of CRM is that a company's contribution to a designated cause is linked to customers' engaging in revenue-producing exchanges with the firm.

Click fraud When a competitor or other party clicks on a sponsored link repeatedly in order to foul up advertising effectiveness.

Commercial rumor A widely circulated but unverified proposition about a product, brand, company, store, or other commercial target.

Comparative advertising The practice in which advertisers directly or indirectly compare their products against competitive offerings, typically claiming the promoted item is superior in one or several important purchase considerations. Comparative ads vary both with regard to the explicitness of the comparisons and with respect to whether their target of comparison is named or referred to in general terms.

Compatibility Is the degree to which an innovation is perceived to fit into a person's way of doing things; in general, a new product/brand is more compatible to the extent that it matches consumers' needs, personal values, beliefs, and past consumption practices.

Competitive parity method A budgeting method that sets the advertising budget by basically following what competitors are doing. Also called the **match-competitors method.**

Complexity The degree of perceived difficulty of an innovation. The more difficult an innovation is to understand or use, the slower the rate of adoption.

Comprehension The ability to understand and create meaning out of stimuli and symbols.

Concretizing A marketing approach based on the idea that it is easier for people to remember and retrieve *tangible* rather than *abstract* information.

Connectedness address whether an advertisement reflects empathy with the target audience's basic needs and wants as they relate to making a brand-choice decision in a product category.

Consequences In the means-end conceptualization of advertising strategy, consequences represent the desirable or undesirable results from consuming a particular product or brand.

Conspicuity The ability of a sign to capture attention; those signage characteristics that enable walkers or drivers and their passengers to distinguish a sign from its surrounding environment. This requires that a sign be of sufficient size and the information on it be clear, concise, legible, and distinguishable from the competing signage.

Conspiracy rumors Unconfirmed statements that involve supposed company policies or practices that are threatening or ideologically undesirable to consumers.

Contact Potential message delivery channels capable of reaching target customers and presenting the communicator's brand in a favorable light. Interchangeable term with **touch point.**

Contamination rumors Unconfirmed statements dealing with undesirable or harmful product or store features.

Contest A form of consumer-oriented sales promotion in which consumers have an opportunity to win cash, merchandise, or travel prizes. Winners become eligible by solving the specified contest problem.

Continuity A media planning consideration that involves how advertising should be allocated during the course of an advertising campaign.

Continuous advertising schedule In a continuous schedule, a relatively equal number of ad dollars are invested in advertising throughout the campaign.

Corrective advertising Advertising based on the premise that a firm that misleads consumers should have to use future advertisements to rectify any deceptive impressions it has created in consumers' minds. Its purpose is to prevent a firm from continuing to deceive consumers rather than to punish the firm.

Coupon A promotional device that provides cents-off savings to consumers upon redeeming the coupons.

CPM An abbreviation for cost per thousand, in which the *M* represents the Roman numeral for 1,000. CPM is the cost of reaching 1,000 people.

CPM-TM A refinement of CPM that measures the cost of reaching 1,000 members of the target market, excluding those people who fall outside of the target market.

Creative brief The work of copywriters is directed by this framework, which is a document designed to inspire copywriters by channeling their creative efforts toward a solution that will serve the interests of the client.

Customer lifetime value The net present value (NPV) of the profit that a company stands to realize on the average new customer during a given number of years.

D

Data mining Involves the process of searching databases to extract information and discover potentially hidden but useful facts about past, present, and prospective customers.

Deal Refers to any form of sales promotion that delivers a price reduction to consumers. Retailer discounts, manufacturer cents-off offers, and the ubiquitous coupon are the most common forms of deals.

Diverting Occurs when a manufacturer restricts a deal to a limited geographical area rather than making it available nationally, which results in retailers buying abnormally large quantities at the deal price and then selling off, at a small profit margin, the excess quantities through brokers in other geographical areas.

E

Effective rating points (ERPs) equal the product of effective reach, or 3+ exposures, times frequency.

Effective reach The idea that an advertising schedule is effective only if it does not reach members of the target audience too few or too many times during the media scheduling period, typically a four-week period. In other words, there is a theoretical optimum range of exposures to an advertisement with minimum and maximum limits. Also called *effective frequency*.

Elasticity Is a measure of how responsive the demand for a brand is as a function of changes in marketing variables such as price and advertising.

Encoding specificity principle A principle of cognitive psychology, which states that information recall is enhanced when the context in which people attempt to retrieve information is the same or similar to the context in which they originally encoded the information.

Encoding variability hypothesis A hypothesis contending that people's memories for information are enhanced when multiple pathways, or connections, are created between the object to be remembered and the information about the object that is to be remembered.

Ethics In the context of marketing communications involves matters of right and wrong, or *moral*, conduct.

Event sponsorship A form of brand promotion that ties a brand to a meaningful cultural, social, athletic, or other type of high-interest public activity.

Executive-statement release A news release quoting CEOs and other corporate executives.

Exit fee A *deslotting charge* to cover the handling costs for a chain to remove an item from its distribution center.

Experiencers One of eight VALS segments of American adult consumers. Experiencers are motivated by self-expression. As young, enthusiastic, and impulsive consumers, Experiencers quickly become enthusiastic about new possibilities but are equally quick to cool. See also **Achievers, Believers, Innovators, Makers, Strivers, Survivors,** and **Thinkers.**

Experiential needs Needs representing desires for products that provide sensory pleasure, variety, and stimulation.

Expertise The knowledge, experience, or skills possessed by an endorser as they relate to the communications topic.

Exposure In marketing terms, signifies that consumers come in contact with the marketer's message.

F

Feature analysis The initial stage of perceptual encoding whereby a receiver examines the basic features of a stimulus (brightness, depth, angles, etc.) and from this makes a preliminary classification.

Feature article A detailed description of a product or other newsworthy programs that are written by a PR firm for immediate publication or airing by print or broadcast media or distribution via appropriate Internet sites.

Flighting schedule refers to a schedule wherein the advertiser varies expenditures throughout the campaign and allocates zero expenditures in some months.

Forward buying The practice whereby retailers take advantage of manufacturers' trade deals by buying larger quantities than needed for normal inventory. Retailers often buy enough product on one deal to carry them over until the manufacturer's next scheduled deal; hence, forward buying also is called *bridge buying.*

Free-with-purchase premium This form of premium is typically provided by durable-good brands and involves free merchandise with the purchase of the brand.

Frequency The number of times, on average, within a four-week period that members of the target audience are exposed to the advertiser's message. Also called *average frequency.*

Functional needs Those needs involving current consumptionrelated problems, potential problems, or conflicts.

G

Galvanometer A device (also referred to as a psychogalvanometer) for measuring *galvanic skin response* or *GSR.* The galvanometer indirectly assesses the degree of emotional response to an advertisement by measuring minute amounts of perspiration.

Generation X (Gen X) To avoid overlap with the baby boomer generation and Generation Y, this text defines Generation X as people born between 1965 and 1981. See also **Baby boom and Generation Y.**

Generation Y (Gen Y) To avoid overlap with the preceding generation, Generation X, this text defines Generation Y as people born between 1982 and 1994. See also **Generation X.**

Generic style A creative advertising style in which the advertiser makes a claim about its brand that could be made by any company that markets the product.

Gross rating points (GRPs) A statistic that represents the mathematical product of reach multiplied by frequency. The number of GRPs indicates the total weight of advertising during a time frame, such as a four-week period. The number of GRPs indicates the gross coverage or duplicated audience that is exposed to a particular advertising schedule.

H

Hedonic needs Needs such as pleasure satisfied by messages that make people feel good. People are most likely to attend those stimuli that have become associated with rewards and that relate to those aspects of life that they value highly.

Hierarchy of effects A model predicated on the idea that advertising moves people from an initial stage of unawareness about a product/brand to a final stage of purchasing that product/brand.

I

Identification The process whereby the source attribute of attractiveness influences message receivers, that is, receivers perceive a source to be attractive and therefore identify with the source and adopt the attitudes, behaviors, interests, or preferences of the source.

Infomercial A form of television advertising that serves as an innovative alternative to the conventional form of short television commercial. Infomercials are full-length commercial segments run on cable (and sometimes network) television that typically last 30 minutes and combine product news and entertainment.

Innovators One of eight VALS segments of American adult consumers. Innovators are successful, sophisticated, takecharge people with high self-esteem. Because they have such abundant resources, they exhibit all three primary motivations (i.e., ideals, achievement, and self-expression) in varying degrees. See also **Achievers, Believers, Experiencers, Makers, Strivers, Survivors, and Thinkers.**

In-pack premium Is a premium item provided inside the package of the brand that offers the free item as a promotional inducement.

Integrated marketing communications (IMC) A communications process that entails the planning, integration, and implementation of diverse forms of marcom (advertisements, sales promotions, publicity releases, events, etc.) that are delivered over time to a brand's targeted customers and prospects.

Intense and prominent cues Cues that are louder, more colorful, bigger, brighter, and so on, thereby increasing the probability of attracting attention.

Internalization The source attribute of credibility influences message receivers via a process of internalization; that is, receivers perceive a source to be credible and therefore accept the source's position or attitude as their own. Internalized attitudes tend to be maintained even when the source of the message is forgotten and even when the source switches to a new position.

Interstitials A form of Internet advertising in which messages appear between two content Web pages rather than within a Web page as is the case with pop-up ads.

Involuntary attention One of the forms of attention that requires little or no effort on the part of the message receiver; the stimulus intrudes upon a person's consciousness even though he or she does not want it to. See also **Voluntary attention.**

Issue/advocacy advertising A form of corporate advertising that takes a position on a controversial social issue of public importance. It does so in a manner that supports the company's position and best interests. See also **Corporate image advertising.**

K

Keywords One of the features of search engine advertising (SEA), keywords are specific words and short phrases that describe the nature, attributes, and benefits of a marketer's offering.

L

Laddering A marketing research technique that has been developed to identify linkages between attributes, consequences, and values. It involves in-depth, one-on-one interviews using primarily a series of directed probes.

M

Mail-in offer Is a premium in which consumers receive a free item from the sponsoring manufacturer in return for submitting a required number of proofs of purchase.

Makers One of eight VALS segments of American adult consumers. Makers are motivated by self-expression. They express themselves and experience the world by working on it—building a house, raising children, fixing a car, or canning vegetables—and have enough skill and energy to carry out their projects successfully. See also **Achievers, Believers, Experiencers, Innovators, Strivers, Survivors,** and **Thinkers.**

Marcom objectives The goals that the various marcom elements aspire to individually or collectively achieve during a scope of time such as a business quarter or fiscal year. Objectives provide the foundation for all remaining decisions.

Mature people People who are 55 and older.

Meaning The set of internal responses and resulting predispositions evoked within a person when presented with a sign or stimulus object.

Media The general communication methods that carry advertising messages, that is—television, magazines, newspapers, and so on.

Media planning An approach that involves the process of designing a scheduling plan that shows how advertising time and space will contribute to the achievement of marketing objectives.

Message research Also known as *copy testing*, message research is a technique that tests the effectiveness of creative messages. Copy testing involves both pretesting a message during its development stages and posttesting the message for effectiveness after it has been aired or printed.

Metaphor A form of figurative language that applies a word or a phrase to a concept or an object, such as a brand, that it does not literally denote to suggest a comparison with the brand (e.g., Budweiser is "the king of beers").

Middle age Is the age range starting at age 35 and ending at age 54 at which point maturity is reached.

N

Near-pack premium A premium offer that provides the retail trade with specially displayed premium pieces that retailers then give to consumers who purchase the promoted brand.

Novel ads are (along with other forms of marcom messages) unique, fresh, and unexpected. Novelty draws consumers' attention to an ad so that they engage in more effortful information processing about the brand.

Novel messages Are those that are unusual, distinctive, or unpredictable. Such messages tend to produce greater attention than those that are familiar and routine.

O

Objective-and-task method A budgeting method that establishes the advertising budget by determining the communication tasks that need to be established. See also **Percentage-of-sales method.**

Observability The degree to which other people can observe one's ownership and use of a new product. The more a consumption behavior can be sensed by other people, the more observable it is and typically the more rapid is its rate of adoption.

Off-invoice allowance A deal offered periodically to the trade that literally permits wholesalers and retailers to deduct a fixed amount from the invoice.

Online video ads Also referred to as *streaming video*, these are audiovideo Internet ads that are similar to standard 30second TV commercials but are often shortened to 10 or 15 seconds and compressed into manageable file sizes.

On-pack premium Is a premium item that is attached to the package of the brand that offers the free item as a promotional inducement.

Opinion leader Is a person who frequently influences other individuals' attitudes and behavior related to new products. They inform other people (followers) about new products, reduce followers' perceived risk in purchasing new products, and confirm decisions that followers have already made.

Opt-in emailing Is the practice of marketers' asking for and receiving consumers' permission to send them messages on a particular topic. The consumer agrees (optsin) to receive messages on topics of interest rather than receiving messages that are unsolicited.

Overlay program The use of two or more sales promotion techniques in combination with one another; also called *combination program.*

P

Paper diaries ACNielsen's alternative data collection procedure (as opposed to the electronic people meter) for estimating TV program ratings in local markets throughout the United States. Participating households complete a 20page diary four times a year, during sweep months.

Pay-for-performance programs A form of trade allowance that rewards retailers for performing the primary function that justifies a manufacturer's offering a trade allowance—namely, selling increased quantities of the manufacturer's brands to shoppers.

Percentage-of-sales method A budgeting method that involves setting the budget as a fixed percentage of past or anticipated (typically the latter) sales volume. See also **Objective-and-task method.**

Perceptual encoding The process of interpreting stimuli, which includes two stages: feature analysis and active synthesis.

Phishing An illegal e-mailing practice related to spam in which criminals send e-mail messages appearing to be from legitimate corporations and direct recipients to phony Web sites that are designed to look like companies' actual Web sites. These phony Web sites attempt to extract personal data from people such as their credit card and ATM numbers.

Physical attractiveness Is a key consideration in many endorsement relationships and involves an endorser's beauty, athleticism, and sexuality.

Physiological testing devices measure any of several autonomic responses to advertisement. Because individuals have little voluntary control over the autonomic nervous system, researchers use changes in physiological functions to indicate the actual, unbiased amount of arousal resulting from advertisements.

Pop-up ads Are a form of Internet advertising in which ads appear in a separate window that materializes on the screen seemingly out of nowhere when a selected Web page is loading.

Positioning The key feature, benefit, or image that a brand stands for in the target audience's collective mind.

Positioning Advertising Copy testing (PACT) A set of nine copy testing principles developed by leading U.S. advertising agencies.

Positioning statement The key idea that encapsulates what a brand is intended to stand for in its target market's mind.

Preemptive style A creative advertising style in which the advertiser that makes a particular claim effectively prevents competitors from making the same claim for fear of being labeled a copycat.

Premiums Articles of merchandise or services offered by manufacturers to induce action on the part of the sales force, trade representatives, or consumers.

Price-off promotion Also called cents-off or price packs, this form of sales promotion entails a reduction, typically ranging from 10 to 25 percent, in a brand's regular price.

Proactive MPR A form of marketing PR that is offensively rather than defensively oriented and opportunity-seeking rather than problem solving. See also **Reactive MPR.**

Product release A publicity tool that announces a new product, provides relevant information about product features and benefits, and informs interested listeners/readers how additional information can be obtained.

Promotion Refers to any *incentive* used by a manufacturer to induce the *trade* (wholesalers, retailers, or other channel members) and/or *consumers* to buy a brand and to encourage the *sales force* to aggressively sell it.

Psychographics Information about consumers' attitudes, values, motivations, and lifestyles that relate to buying behavior in a particular product category.

Psychological reactance A theory that suggests that people react against any efforts to reduce their freedoms or choices. When products are made to seem less available, they become more valuable in the consumer's mind.

Pull Marketing efforts directed to ultimate consumers with the intent of influencing their acceptance of the manufacturer's brand. Manufacturers hope that the consumers will then encourage retailers to handle the brand. Typically used in conjunction with *push.*

Pulsing advertising schedule refers to a schedule wherein some advertising is used during every period of the campaign, but the amount of advertising varies from period to period.

Pupillometer is a device used to conduct pupillometric tests, which measure respondents' pupil dilation as they view a television commercial or focus on a printed advertisement. Responses to specific elements in an advertisement are used to indicate positive reaction (greater dilation) or negative reaction (smaller relative dilation).

Push A manufacturer's selling and other promotional efforts directed at gaining trade support from wholesalers and retailers for the manufacturer's product.

R

Rating points Ratings points are the foundation for concepts such as effective, gross, and target rating points. A single rating point simply represents one percent of a designated group or an entire population that is exposed to a particular advertising vehicle such as a TV program.

Reach The percentage of an advertiser's target audience that is exposed to at least one advertisement over an established time frame (a four-week period represents the typical time frame for most advertisers). Reach represents the number of target customers who see or hear the advertiser's message one or more times during the time period. Also called *net coverage, unduplicated audience,* or *cumulative audience (cume).*

Reactive MPR Marketing undertaken as a result of external pressures and challenges brought by competitive actions, changes in consumer attitudes, or other external influences. It typically deals with changes that have negative consequences for the organization. See also **Proactive MPR.**

Rebate Manufacturers give cash discounts or reimbursements to consumers who submit proofs of purchase when purchasing the manufacturer's brand. Unlike coupons, which the consumer redeems at retail checkouts, rebates/refunds are mailed with proofs of purchase to manufacturers.

Recency principle Known also as the shelf-space model for media planning, this principle is based on the idea that achieving a high level of weekly reach for a brand should be emphasized over acquiring heavy frequency.

Relationship An enduring link between a brand and its customers. Successful relationships between customers and brands lead to repeat purchasing and perhaps even loyalty toward a brand.

Relative advantage The degree to which an innovation is perceived as better than an existing idea or object in terms of increasing comfort, saving time or effort, and increasing the immediacy of reward.

Repeater class This third stage in the adoption process is influenced by four marketing-mix variables: advertising, price, distribution, and product satisfaction.

Resonant advertising seeks to present circumstances or situations that find counterparts in the real or imagined experiences of the target audience. Advertising based on this strategy attempts to match "patterns" in an advertisement with the target audience's stored experiences.

Respect Is an endorser characteristic that represents the quality of being admired or esteemed due to one's personal qualities and accomplishments.

Revenue premium The revenue differential between a branded item and a corresponding private labeled item.

ROMI The idea of *return on investment* (ROI), which is well known in accounting, finance, or managerial economics circles, is referred to in marketing circles as ROMI, or *return on marketing investment.*

S

Sales-to-advertising response function The relationship between money invested in advertising and the response, or output, of that investment in terms of revenue generated.

Sampling The use of various distribution methods to deliver actual- or trial-size products to consumers. The purpose is to initiate trial-usage behavior.

Self-liquidating offer Known as SLOs by practitioners, this form of premium requires consumers to mail in a stipulated number of proofs of purchase along with sufficient money to cover the manufacturer's purchasing, handling, and mailing costs of the premium item.

Self-regulation Regulation of advertising by advertisers themselves rather by state or federal government bodies.

Self-report measurement is a system wherein consumers' emotional reactions in response to advertisements are measured by asking them to self-report their feelings. Both verbal and visual self-reports are used for this purpose.

Semiotics The study of signs and the analysis of meaningproducing events. This perspective sees meaning as a constructive process.

Share of market (SOM) Represents a brand's proportion of overall product category sales.

Share of voice (SOV) Represents a brand's proportion of overall advertising expenditures in a product category.

Sign Something physical and perceivable by our senses that represents or signifies something (the referent) to somebody (the interpreter) in some context.

Similarity Represents the degree to which an endorser matches an audience in terms of characteristics such as age, gender, and ethnicity that are pertinent to the quality of an endorsement relationship.

Single-source data consist of household demographic information; household purchase behavior; and household exposure to (or, more technically, the opportunity to see) new television commercials that are tested under real-world, in-market test conditions.

Slotting allowance The fee a manufacturer pays a supermarket or other retailer to get that retailer to handle the manufacturer's new product. The allowance is called slotting in reference to the slot, or location, that the retailer must make available in its warehouse to accommodate the manufacturer's product.

Standardized Advertising Unit (SAU) system A system adopted in the 1980s, making it possible for advertisers to purchase any one of 56 standard ad sizes to fit the advertising publishing parameters of all newspapers in the United States.

Sticky ads are ads for which the audience comprehends the advertiser's intended message; they are remembered, and they change the target audience's brand-related opinions or behaviors.

Strivers One of eight VALS segments of American adult consumers. Strivers are trendy and fun loving. Because they are motivated by achievement, Strivers are concerned about the opinions and approval of others. Money defines success for Strivers, who don' t have enough of it to meet their desires. See also **Achievers, Believers, Experiencers, Innovators, Makers, Survivors**, and **Thinkers.**

Superstitials Are short, animated Internet ads that play over or on top of a Web page.

Survivors One of eight VALS segments of American adult consumers. Survivors live narrowly focused lives. With few resources with which to cope, they often believe that the world is changing too quickly. They are comfortable with the familiar and are primarily concerned with safety and security. Because they must focus on meeting needs rather than fulfilling desires, Survivors do not show a strong primary motivation. See also **Achievers, Believers, Experiencers, Innovators, Makers, Strivers,** and **Thinkers.**

Sweepstakes A form of consumer-oriented sales promotion in which winners receive cash, merchandise, or travel prizes. Winners are determined purely on the basis of chance.

Symbolic needs Internal consumer needs such as the desire for self-enhancement, role position, or group membership.

T

Target rating points (TRPs) An adaptation of gross rating points (GRPs), TRPs adjust a vehicle's rating to reflect just those individuals who match the advertiser's target audience.

Thinkers One of eight VALS segments of American adult consumers. Thinkers are motivated by ideals. They are mature, satisfied, comfortable, and reflective people who value order, knowledge, and responsibility. See also **Achievers, Believers, Experiencers, Innovators, Makers, Strivers,** and **Survivors.**

Three-exposure hypothesis This addresses the *minimum* number of exposures needed for advertising to be effective.

Tie-in The simultaneous promotion of multiple brands in a single sales-promotion effort; also called *joint promotion.*

Touch point See **Contact.**

Trade allowances Also called trade deals, these allowances are used by manufacturers to reward wholesalers and retailers for performing activities in support of the manufacturer's brand such as featuring the brand in retail advertisements or providing special display space.

Transformational advertising Brand image advertising that associates the experience of using an advertised brand with the unique set of psychological characteristics that would not typically be associated with the brand experience to the same degree without exposure to the advertisement.

Trialability The extent to which an innovation can be used on a limited basis. Trialability is tied closely to the concept of perceived risk. In general, products that lend themselves to trialability are adopted at a more rapid rate.

Trier class The group of consumers who actually try a new product; the second step in which an individual becomes a new brand consumer. Coupons, distribution, and price are the variables that influence consumers to become triers.

Trustworthiness The honesty, integrity, and reliability of a source.

U

Unfair advertising Is a legal term to define advertising acts or practices that cause or are likely to cause substantial injury to consumers, which is not reasonably avoidable by consumers themselves and not outweighed by countervailing benefits to consumers or competition.

Unique selling proposition (USP) style A creative advertising style that promotes a product attribute that represents a meaningful, distinctive consumer benefit.

V

Values In the means-end conceptualization of advertising strategy, values represent important beliefs that people hold about themselves and that determine the relative desirability of consequences.

Value proposition Is the essence of an advertisement or other marcom message and the reward to the consumer for investing his or her time attending the message.

Vehicles The specific broadcast programs or print choices in which advertisements are placed.

Voluntary attention One of three forms of attention that occurs when a person willfully notices a stimulus. See also **Involuntary attention.**

W

Wearout Refers to the ultimately diminished effectiveness of advertising over time.

Wi-Fi Short for *wireless fidelity,* this technology enables computers and other wireless devices such as cell phones to connect to the Internet via low-power radio signals instead of cables. Hence, users can have Internet access at base stations, or so-called hotspots, that are Wi-Fi equipped.

Z

Zapping occurs when viewers switch to another channel when commercials are aired.

Zipping takes place when ads that have been recorded along with program material using a digital video recorder are fast-forwarded when the viewer watches the prerecorded material.

name index

A

Aaker, David A., 238*n*
Aaker, Jennifer L., 57*n*
Abernethy, Avery M., 390*n*, 356*n*, 441*n*, 637*n*
Abraham, Magid M., 177*n*, 479*n*
Achenbaum, Alvin, 356*n*
Achenreiner, Gwen Bachmann, 91*n*
Adams, Anthony J., 315*n*
Adams, Doug, 601*n*
Adamson, Allen P., 92*n*, 558*n*
Adamy, Janet, 57*n*, 189
Aeppel, Timothy, 203*n*
Agassi, Andre, 216
Agins, Teri, 274*n*
Agrawal, Jagdish, 274*n*
Ahluwalia, Rohini, 273*n*, 557*n*
Ailawadi, Kusum L., 56*n*, 478*n*, 479*n*
Aksehirli, Zeynep, 57*n*
Alba, Joseph W., 91*n*
Alden, Dana L., 275*n*
Ali, Muhammad, 253
Allen, Chris T., 177*n*, 203*n*, 391*n*
Allsop, Dee T., 558*n*
Alpert, Frank H., 391*n*
Altsech, Moses B., 275*n*
Ambler, Tim, 31*n*, 176*n*, 177*n*
Amir, Sarit, 239*n*
Anderson, Paul F., 151*n*
Andrews, J. Craig, 93*n*, 635*n*, 637*n*
Ang, Swee Hoon, 238*n*
Angwin, Julia, 390*n*
Anholt, Simon, 57*n*
Applebaum, Michael, 441*n*
Arden, Elizabeth, 254
Ariely, Dan, 636*n*
Armstrong, Lance, 216
Arnold, Catherine, 93*n*
Arnould, Eric J., 313*n*
Ash, Stephen B., 277*n*
Assael, Henry, 356*n*
Atkinson, R. Claire, 31*n*, 152*n*, 558*n*
Avery, Rosemary J., 391*n*

B

Bagozzi, R. P., 277*n*
Baker, Lori, 356*n*
Baker, Michael J., 274*n*
Baker, Stephen, 418*n*
Balasubramanian, Siva K., 440*n*
Baldinger, Allan L., 313*n*
Baldwin, Dare A., 634*n*
Ball, Deborah, 557*n*
Baltas, George, 93*n*
Balto, David, 479*n*
Bamossy, Gary, 124*n*
Banerjee, Subhabrata Bobby, 637*n*
Bang, Hae-Kyong, 600*n*
Banks, Louis, 239*n*
Bansal, Pratima, 637*n*
Barabási, Albert-László, 558*n*
Bargh, John A., 277*n*, 635*n*
Barnard, Neil, 203*n*
Barnes, James, 278*n*
Barnett, Teresa, 93*n*
Baron, Robert S., 276*n*
Barone, Michael J., 277*n*, 278*n*
Barry, Thomas E., 176*n*
Basil, Debra Z., 573*n*
Bassett, Bryce R., 558*n*
Basu, Kunal, 275*n*
Batra, Rajeev, 92*n*, 239*n*
Baum, Laurie, 531*n*
Bawa, Kapil, 506*n*
Beales, J. Howard, III, 636*n*, 637*n*
Beatty, Sally Goll, 31*n*
Beatty, Sharon E., 124*n*, 238*n*, 276*n*
Becker-Olsen, Karen L., 573*n*
Belch, George E., 276*n*
Belch, Michael A., 276*n*, 440*n*
Bemmaor, Albert C., 203*n*
Benezra, Karen, 531*n*
Bergen, Jack, 558*n*
Berger, Paul D., 390*n*
Berlo, David K., 151*n*
Berman, Ronald, 635*n*
Bernhardt, Kenneth L., 637*n*
Berry, Jon, 479*n*, 559*n*
Berry, Lisette, 203*n*
Bettman, James B., 151*n*
Bettman, James R., 273*n*
Bevans, Michael, 419*n*
Bhat, Subodh, 419*n*
Bigné, J. Enrique, 177*n*
Bijmolt, Tammo H. A., 204*n*
Bird, Laura, 634*n*, 635*n*
Bittar, Christine, 274*n*
Blacker, Stephen M., 390*n*
Blackwell, Roger D., 124*n*
Blair, Margaret Henderson, 314*n*, 315*n*
Blalock, Cecelia, 506*n*
Blanchard, Sandy, 390*n*
Blasko, Vincent J., 177*n*, 237*n*
Blattberg, Robert C., 440*n*, 478*n*, 479*n*
Blazing, Jennifer, 573*n*
Block, Lauren Goldberg, 275*n*
Block, Martin P., 276*n*
Bloom, Helen, 203*n*
Bloom, Paul N., 479*n*, 573*n*
Boddewyn, Jean J., 637*n*
Bonabeau, Eric, 558*n*
Bonds, Barry, 257
Bone, Paula Fitzgerald, 390*n*, 479*n*, 636*n*
Bonner, P. Greg, 635*n*
Borden, Jeff, 440*n*
Borzekowski, Dina L. G., 57*n*
Boslet, Mark, 92*n*
Boulding, William, 57*n*, 91*n*
Boush, David M., 634*n*
Bouvard, Pierre, 600*n*
Bowman, Douglas, 478*n*
Bowman, Russ, 506*n*
Brasel, S. Adam, 57*n*
Brehm, Jack W., 276*n*
Brickin, Shari, 531*n*
Briesch, Richard, 479*n*
Brignell, Joanne, 30*n*
Britt, Bill, 238*n*
Brock, Timothy C., 274*n*
Brotherton, Timothy P., 276*n*
Brown, Jacqueline Johnson, 558*n*
Brown, Norman R., 573*n*
Brown, Steven P., 314*n*
Brown, Terence A., 203*n*
Brown, Tom J., 391*n*
Bruce, Gary Schroeder, 356*n*
Bruner, Gordon C., II, 277*n*, 418*n*
Bruzzone, Donald E., 314*n*
Bryant, Kobe, 257
Buchanan, Bruce, 278*n*
Buehler, Phil, 57*n*
Bulik, Beth Snyder, 57*n*, 124*n*
Bulkeley, William M., 531*n*
Burke, Joanne, 356*n*
Burnkrant, Robert E., 152*n*, 273*n*, 557*n*
Burns, Kelli S., 418*n*
Burns, William J., 274*n*
Burton, Scot, 93*n*, 274*n*, 505*n*, 506*n*, 635*n*
Bush, Michael, 637*n*
Busler, Michael, 274*n*
Butensky, Ave, 356*n*
Buzzell, D., 479*n*
Byers, Lee, 315*n*
Byron, Ellen, 572*n*

C

Cacioppo, John T, 273*n*, 315*n*
Cahill, Aileen M., 417*n*
Calfee, John E., 635*n*, 636*n*
Campbell, Leland, 275*n*
Campbell, Margaret C., 315*n*
Cannon, Hugh M., 356*n*
Cannon, Joseph P., 479*n*
Cannon-Bonventre, Kristina, 600*n*
Cantril, Hadley, 152*n*
Capriati, Jennifer, 257
Cardona, Mercedes M., 203*n*, 239*n*
Carlin, Barbara A., 636*n*
Carlson, Les, 274*n*, 637*n*
Carter, Vince, 255
Casey, Nicholas, 418*n*, 557*n*, 637*n*
Castleberry, Stephen B., 636*n*
Caudill, Eve M., 636*n*
Centlivre, Lou, 238*n*
Chakraborty, Goutam, 558*n*
Chakravarti, Dipankar, 275*n*
Champa, Paula, 238*n*
Chandon, Pierre, 93*n*, 478*n*, 505*n*
Chartier, Francis, 441*n*
Chartrand, Tanya L., 277*n*, 635*n*
Chattopadhyay, Amitava, 275*n*, 418*n*
Chaudhuri, Arjun, 56*n*, 177*n*
Chevalier, Judith A., 559*n*
Chevron, Jacques, 56*n*, 478*n*
Childers, Terry L., 152*n*
Chintagunta, Pradeep K., 418*n*
Choffray, Jean-Marie, 177*n*
Choi, Sejung Marina, 573*n*
Chow, Jay, 12
Chow, Simeon, 239*n*
Christiansen, Ann, 635*n*
Chura, Hillary, 58*n*, 160
Cialdini, Robert B., 276*n*
Cioffi, Jennifer, 314*n*
Cipolla, Lorin, 505*n*
Clancy, Kevin J., 151*n*, 390*n*
Clark, John M., 572*n*
Clark, Margaret, 152*n*
Clark, Monica M., 391*n*
Clarke, T. K., 277*n*
Claus, Jasper, 635*n*
Claus, R. James, 600*n*
Claus, Susan L., 600*n*
Cline, Thomas W., 275*n*
Close, Angeline G., 572*n*
Coe, Barbara J., 239*n*
Cohen, Dorothy, 637*n*
Cohen, Joel B., 239*n*, 634*n*
Cohen, Robert, 203*n*
Cole, Catherine A., 314*n*, 390*n*
Colley, Russell H., 177*n*
Condon, Parick, 600*n*
Conroy, Darrin, 600*n*
Cooper, Peter, 314*n*
Cooper-Martin, Elizabeth, 634*n*
Copeland, Al, 545
Corey, Robert J., 636*n*
Cornelissen, Joep P., 30*n*
Cornwell, Lisa, 418*n*
Cornwell, T. Bettina, 314*n*, 572*n*, 573*n*
Costley, Carolyn, 278*n*
Cote, Joseph A., 92*n*
Cotte, June, 276*n*
Coulter, Keith S., 313*n*
Coulter, Robin A., 276*n*, 313*n*
Coulter, Robin Higie, 276*n*, 313*n*
Cox, Anthony D., 277*n*
Cox, Dena, 277*n*
Craddock, Alyce Byrd, 238*n*
Crask, Melvin R., 238*n*
Creamer, Matthew, 56*n*
Crimmins, James, 572*n*
Crocker, Betty, 80
Cronin, John J., 390*n*
Cronley, Maria L., 278*n*
Crutchfield, Tammy Neal, 203*n*
Culnan, Mary J., 636*n*
Cuneo, Alice Z., 419*n*, 506*n*
Cuperfain, Ronnie, 277*n*

Curran, Catharine M., 203*n*
Cutler, Bob D., 239*n*

D

Dahl, Darren W., 275*n*
Dahlen, Micael, 418*n*
Dalton, Greg, 93*n*
Dana, Rebecca, 356*n*
Danzig, Fred, 276*n*
Darby, Jason, 600*n*
Darke, Peter R., 635*n*
Darmon, Rene Y., 277*n*
d'Astous, Alain, 440*n*–441*n*
Davidson, Jeffrey P., 636*n*
Davis, Joel J., 441*n*
Davis, John, 124*n*
Dawar, Niraj, 557*n*
Day, Ellen, 238*n*
De Avila, Joseph, 418*n*
Debbie, Little, 512
Deighton, John, 92*n*, 203*n*, 440*n*
Delaney, Kevin J., 419*n*
Denes-Raj, Veronika, 152*n*
DeNitto, Emily, 275*n*
D'Entremont, Jeremy, 600*n*
Deshpande, Rohit, 124*n*, 274*n*, 478*n*
Desrochers, Debra M., 479*n*
Dethloff, Clay, 239*n*
Dewitte, Siegfried, 314*n*
Dhar, Sanjay K., 506*n*
Dichter, Ernest, 558*n*
Dickson, Peter R., 92*n*
Dodd, Christopher A., 440*n*
Dodds, Peter Sheridan, 559*n*
Doden, Daniel L., 92*n*
Dolak, Dave, 636*n*
Dolbow, Sandra, 57*n*
Domzal, Teresa J., 151*n*
Donaton, Scott, 635*n*
Donavan, D. Todd, 558*n*
Donius, Jim, 315*n*
Donthu, Naveen, 277*n*, 391*n*, 418*n*
D'Orio, Wayne, 572*n*
Doyle, Peter, 56*n*
Dreze, Xavier, 479*n*
Droge, Cornelia, 277*n*
Drumwright, Minette E., 635*n*
D'Souza, Giles, 203*n*
Dubas, Khalid M., 276*n*
Dubé, Laurette, 91*n*
Dubitsky, Tony M., 92*n*, 313*n*, 314*n*
Dubow, Joel S., 314*n*
Duncan, Tim, 254
Dye, Renée, 559*n*
Dyer, David C., 278*n*
Dylan, Bob, 267, 269

E

Eagleson, Geoff, 313*n*
Ebenkamp, Becky, 91*n*, 124*n*
Edwards, Jim, 391*n*
Edwards, Steven M., 441*n*
Ehrenberg, A. S. C., 478*n*
Ehrenberg, Andrew, 203*n*
Elkin, Tobi, 531*n*
Elkind, Fred, 124*n*
Ellen, Pam Scholder, 390*n*
Elliott, Michael T., 152*n*, 390*n*, 391*n*
Elliott, Stuart, 203*n*
Ellison, Sarah, 391*n*, 505*n*
El-Murad, Jaafar, 237*n*
Elpers, Josephine L. C. M. Woltman, 275*n*
Engel, James F., 124*n*
Enright, Allison, 418*n*, 419*n*, 441*n*
Ephron, Erwin, 336, 390*n*, 419*n*, 506*n*
Eppright, David R., 275*n*
Epstein, Seymour, 152*n*
Erdem, Tülin, 56*n*, 57*n*
Erdogan, B. Zafer, 274*n*
Esteban, Gabriel, 277*n*

F

Farah, Samar, 30*n*
Farrell, Kathleen Anne, 572*n*
Farrelly, Francis, 573*n*
Fatsis, Stefan, 634*n*
Feick, Lawrence F., 274*n*, 558*n*
Feinberg, Fred, 57*n*
Feinberg, Richard, 277*n*
Fern, Edward F., 278*n*
Fernandez, Ana, 636*n*
Fernandez, Karen V., 441*n*
Ferraro, Rosellina, 391*n*
Ferrell, Elizabeth, 636*n*
Ferrell, O. C., 634*n*
Finney, R. Zachary, 572*n*
Finnigan, David, 635*n*
Fisher, Christy, 637*n*
Fisher, Robert J., 91*n*, 417*n*
Fitzgerald, Joan, 391*n*
Fitzgerald, Kate, 418*n*, 600*n*
Flaherty, Karen, 275*n*
Fogle, Jared, 608
Folkes, Valerie S., 93*n*, 558*n*
Foltz, Kim, 238*n*
Forbes, Thom, 356*n*
Ford, Gary T., 636*n*
Fournier, Susan, 57*n*
Fowler, Geoffrey A., 600*n*
Fox, Edward J., 479*n*
Fox, Karen F. A., 239*n*
Frame, W. Scott, 572*n*
France, Karen Russo, 479*n*
Frangos, Alex, 419*n*
Franke, George R., 600*n*
Frankenberger, Kristina D., 275*n*
Frazer, Charles F., 176*n*, 238*n*, 356*n*
Freberg, Stan, 237*n*
Fredericks, Charles, Jr., 478*n*, 505*n*
Freeman, Laura, 356*n*
Freeman, Sholnn, 558*n*
French, Warren, 636*n*
Friedmann, Roberto, 151*n*
Friestad, Marian, 634*n*, 635*n*
Frisby, Cynthia M., 390*n*
Frydlewicz, Rob, 356*n*
Furse, David H., 314*n*

G

Gable, Myron, 277*n*
Gajewski, Maciek, 505*n*
Garbarino, Ellen, 92*n*
Garber, Lawrence L., Jr., 92*n*
Gardner, David M., 636*n*
Gardner, Meryl Paula, 152*n*, 572*n*
Garfield, Bob, 30*n*, 237*n*, 238*n*, 634*n*
Garnett, Kevin, 254–255
Garretson, Judith A., 274*n*, 505*n*
Gatchel, Robert J., 314*n*
Gedenk, Karen, 478*n*
Geiger, Bob, 276*n*
Gelb, Betsy D., 314*n*
Gengler, Charles, 92*n*
Georgescu, Peter A., 30*n*
Gershman, Michael, 92*n*
Geyskens, Inge, 418*n*
Gibson, Bryan, 277*n*
Gibson, Lawrence D., 356*n*
Gibson, Mel, 550
Gielens, Katrijn, 91*n*
Giese, Joan L., 92*n*
Gillin, Paul, 418*n*
Gladwell, Malcolm, 558*n*
Gleason, Mark, 315*n*
Goldberg, Marvin E., 124*n*, 634*n*
Goldenberg, Jacob, 237*n*, 558*n*
Gómez, Miguel I., 479*n*
Goodhardt, G. J., 478*n*
Gorman, Bill, 390*n*
Gorn, Gerald J., 124*n*, 277*n*, 278*n*, 418*n*
Gould, Stephen J., 30*n*
Grabowski, Gene, 557*n*
Graham, Jeffrey, 558*n*
Grande, Hans, 505*n*
Graser, Marc, 30*n*
Gray-Lee, Jason W., 638*n*
Grayson, Mark W., 151*n*
Green, Andrew, 390*n*
Green, Heather, 418*n*
Greenleaf, Eric A., 93*n*
Grein, Andreas F., 30*n*
Gresham, Larry G., 634*n*
Grewal, Dhruv, 278*n*
Greyser, Stephen A., 573*n*
Grimm, Matthew, 30*n*, 634*n*
Gross, Amy E., 558*n*
Grove, Stephen J., 637*n*
Grover, Rajiv, 313*n*
Grunert, Klaus G., 152*n*
Gulas, Charles S., 275*n*
Gundlach, Gregory T., 479*n*
Gupta, Pola B., 441*n*
Gupta, Sunil, 57*n*, 177*n*, 478*n*
Gürhan-Canli, Zeynep, 239*n*, 573*n*
Gutchess, Angela H., 57*n*
Guthrie, Jim, 637*n*
Gutman, Jonathan, 238*n*

H

Ha, Louisa, 152*n*
Hackley, Christopher E., 238*n*
Hagan, Joe, 390*n*
Haley, Russell I., 313*n*
Hall, Bruce F., 313*n*
Hall, Emma, 441*n*
Halliday, Jean, 30*n*, 418*n*, 531*n*, 557*n*, 558*n*
Hammond, Kathy, 478*n*
Hankin, Janet R., 636*n*
Hanover, Dan, 30*n*, 505*n*
Hanssens, Dominique M., 478*n*, 479*n*
Harrington, H. James, 314*n*
Harris, Lynn, 277*n*
Harris, R. J., 152*n*
Hartley, Bob, 30*n*
Hartman, Cathy L., 637*n*
Hartman, Timothy P., 276*n*
Hastorf, Albert H., 152*n*
Hathcote, Jan M., 239*n*
Havlena, William, 558*n*
Hawkins, Del I., 276*n*
Hawkins, Scott A., 151*n*
Hayden, Steve, 208
Heath, Chip, 238*n*
Heath, Dan, 238*n*
Heckler, Susan E., 92*n*, 152*n*, 391*n*
Heffler, Mava, 572*n*
Heher, Ashley M., 127
Heide, Jan B., 601*n*
Hein, Kenneth, 441*n*
Heitsmith, Glenn, 505*n*, 531*n*
Heller, Lorraine, 634*n*
Henderson, Caroline M., 203*n*
Henderson, Pamela W., 92*n*
Henthorne, Tony L., 276*n*
Hernandez, Sigfredo A., 124*n*
Herr, Paul M., 274*n*, 558*n*, 573*n*
Hershberger, Edmund K., 418*n*
Higgins, Michelle, 124*n*
Higie, Robin A., 274*n*
Hill, Ronald Paul, 636*n*
Hill, Sam, 203*n*
Hilton, Paris, 257
Hirschman, Elizabeth C., 58*n*, 151*n*
Hoch, Stephen J., 151*n*, 479*n*
Hodgman, John, 240
Hogan, Paul, 148
Holbrook, Morris B., 56*n*, 151*n*, 177*n*, 635*n*
Hollier, E. Ann, 177*n*
Hollis, Nigel, 313*n*
Holmes, Paul, 557*n*
Holstein, William H., 557*n*
Holt, Karen, 506*n*
Homer, Pamela M., 274*n*, 239*n*
Honomichl, Jack, 314*n*
Horn, Martin, 572*n*
Horne, David A., 390*n*
Hoskins, James A., 558*n*
Houston, Michael J., 92*n*, 152*n*
Howard, Daniel J., 92*n*
Howard, Suzanne Gibbs, 238*n*, 313*n*
Howe, Neil, 124*n*
Hoy, Mariea Grubbs, 636*n*
Hoyer, Wayne D., 275*n*, 600*n*
Hoyt, Christopher W., 479*n*
Hughes, Arthur M., 440*n*
Huhmann, Bruce A., 276*n*
Hume, Scott, 315*n*
Humphreys, Michael S., 573*n*
Hung, C. L, 177*n*
Hung, Kineta, 277*n*
Hunt, H. Keith, 152*n*
Hunt, James B., 275*n*
Hutchinson, J. Wesley, 91*n*
Hwang, Jang-Sun, 417*n*
Hyatt, Eva M., 92*n*

I

Inman, J. Jeffrey, 505*n*, 600*n*
Isen, Alice M., 152*n*
Ishmael, Gwen S., 313*n*
Iverson, Allen, 254
Iyer, Easwar S., 637*n*
Izard, Carroll E., 276*n*

J

Jackson, Michael, 257
Jacoby, Jacob, 636*n*
Jain, Shailendra Pratap, 278*n*
James, Dana, 124*n*, 558*n*
James, LeBron, 254
Janiszewski, Chris, 92*n*
Jargon, Julie, 492
Jaworski, Bernard J., 151*n*, 273*n*, 417*n*
Jeanne Livelsberger, 177*n*
Jean-Pierre, Puneet Manchanda, 418*n*
Jedidi, Kamel, 478*n*
Jensen, Thomas D., 274*n*
Jewler, A. Jerome, 237*n*
Jianlian, Yi, 255
Johannes, Amy, 30*n*, 478*n*, 505*n*, 572*n*, 602*n*
Johar, Gita Venkataramani, 572*n*
John, Deborah Roedder, 57*n*, 91*n*, 124*n*
John, Elton, 267
Johnson, Avery, 634*n*, 636*n*
Johnson, Bradley, 203*n*, 237*n*, 356*n*, 418*n*
Johnson, Randy, 216
Johnson, Rebecca, 92*n*
Johnson, Robert, 274*n*
Johnstone, Emma, 440*n*
Jones, Graham Spickett, 30*n*
Jones, John Philip, 177*n*, 314*n*, 315*n*, 356*n*
Jones, Lafayette, 505*n*
Jones, Marion, 257
Jones, Roland, 356*n*
Joseph, W. Benoy, 274*n*
Jugenheimer, Donald W., 177*n*
Jun, Sung Youl, 57*n*

K

Kahle, Lynn R., 238*n*, 239*n*, 274*n*
Kahn, Barbara E., 573*n*
Kahne, Kasey, 560
Kahneman, Daniel, 273*n*
Kalmenson, Stuart, 177*n*
Kamakura, Wagner A., 239*n*, 274*n*
Kamins, Michael A., 274*n*, 558*n*
Kang, Stephanie, 391*n*
Kang, Yong-Soon, 274*n*
Kangun, Norman, 637*n*
Karan, David, 634*n*
Kardes, Frank R., 278*n*, 558*n*
Karp, Hannah, 124*n*
Karp, Lynn, 152*n*
Karpatkin, Rhoda H., 636*n*
Karpinski, Richard, 419*n*
Karremans, Johan C., 635*n*
Karrh, James A., 440*n*
Kashyap, Rajiv K., 637*n*
Kassarjian, H. H., 273*n*
Kastenholz, John J., 314*n*
Kavanoor, Sukuman, 278*n*
Keane, Bill, 390*n*
Kees, Jeremy, 93*n*
Keillor, Garrison, 217
Kellaris, James J., 275*n*, 277*n*
Keller, Ed, 558*n*, 559*n*
Keller, Kevin Lane, 57*n*, 92*n*, 152*n*, 315*n*
Keller, Punam Anand, 275*n*
Kelley, David, 239*n*
Kelly, Kathleen J., 634*n*
Kelman, Herbert C., 274*n*
Kennedy, Rachel, 203*n*
Kent, Robert J., 177*n*, 277*n*, 391*n*
Kerin, Roger A., 92*n*, 276*n*
Kernan, Jerome B., 151*n*
Kerr, Graham, 314*n*
Kesmodel, David, 418*n*
Key, Wilson B., 276*n*
Kilbourne, William E., 277*n*, 637*n*
Kim, John, 558*n*
Kim, Kyeongheui, 57*n*
Kim, Min Chung, 203*n*
King, Karen Whitehill, 275*n*, 356*n*, 390*n*
King, Steve, 203*n*
Kinnear, Thomas C., 152*n*, 238*n*, 390*n*, 637*n*
Kirby, Justin, 559*n*
Kirmani, Amna, 177*n*
Kitchen, Philip J., 30*n*, 557*n*
Klaassen, Abbey, 389*n*, 391*n*, 440*n*, 441*n*
Klebba, Joanne M., 314*n*
Klein, Robert E., III, 151*n*
Klink, Richard R., 92*n*
Kneale, Dennis, 390*n*
Knight, Susan J., 634*n*
Koenig, Fredrick, 558*n*
Koeppel, Dan, 635*n*
Kohli, Chiranjeev, 92*n*
Komen, Susan G., 569
Koslow, Scott, 238*n*
Kournikova, Anna, 257
Koval, Robin, 238*n*
Kover, Arthur J., 238*n*
Kozak, Randall P., 314*n*
Kozup, John, 93*n*
Kraemer, Helena C., 57*n*
Kramer, Jon, 600*n*
Kramer, Mark R., 573*n*
Krauss, Clifford, 58*n*
Kreshel, Peggy J., 356*n*
Krieg, Peter C., 151*n*
Krishnamurthi, Lakshman, 478*n*
Krishnan, H. Shanker, 177*n*, 275*n*
Krol, Carol, 31*n*, 419*n*, 638*n*
Krugman, Herbert E., 313*n*, 329, 356*n*
Kuhayda, John, 441*n*
Kulik, Robert L., 274*n*
Kulkarni, Mukund S., 203*n*
Kumar, Anand, 177*n*, 418*n*
Kurzbard, Gary, 276*n*

L

La Ferle, Carrie, 441*n*
LaBahn, Douglas W., 92*n*
Laband, David N., 441*n*
LaBarbera, Priscilla A., 314*n*
Lacey, Russell Z., 572*n*
Laczniak, Gene R., 636*n*
LaGesse, David, 418*n*
Laible, Myron, 600*n*
Lambiase, Jacqueline, 276*n*
Lamons, Bob, 56*n*, 151*n*
Lancaster, Kent M., 177*n*, 356*n*
Lannon, Judie, 314*n*
Laskey, Henry A., 238*n*
LaTour, Michael S., 276*n*
Laurent, Gilles, 478*n*, 505*n*
Lawrence, Jennifer, 203*n*
Lawton, Christopher, 91*n*, 634*n*
Lebar, Ed, 57*n*
Le Boutillier, John, 92*n*
Le Boutillier, Susanna Shore, 92*n*
Leckenby, John D., 356*n*
Leclerc, France, 91*n*, 506*n*
Lee, Ang, 550
Lee, Chol, 275*n*
Lee, Eunkyu, 57*n*
Lee, Yih Hwai, 238*n*
Leeflang, Peter S. H., 479*n*
Lefton, Terry, 238*n*, 418*n*
Lehmann, Donald R., 56*n*, 57*n*, 478*n*, 177*n*, 479*n*
Leigh, J. H., 151*n*, 177*n*, 237*n*, 239*n*, 275*n*, 276*n*, 314*n*, 390*n*
Lemon, Katherine N., 57*n*
Leonard, Nancy H., 636*n*
Leone, Robert P., 506*n*
Leong, Siew Meng, 238*n*
Lernan, Dawn B., 92*n*, 30*n*
Leslie, Frances, 634*n*
Letterman, David, 347
Levin, Gary, 440*n*, 573*n*
Levine, Linda, 634*n*
Levy, Doran J., 124*n*
Lew, William, 93*n*
Li, Hairong, 573*n*
Li, Tao, 30*n*
Libai, Barak, 558*n*
Lichtenstein, Donald R., 505*n*
Liesse, Julie, 418*n*
Light, Larry, 57*n*, 177*n*, 203*n*
Lilien, Gary L., 177*n*
Liljenwall, Robert, 600*n*
Lindgren, Jack, 356*n*
Lippman, John, 558*n*
Litman, Barry R., 152*n*
Little, John D. C., 506*n*
Liu, Yong, 558*n*
Liu, Yuping, 417*n*, 418*n*
Lloyd, Susan M., 418*n*
Lock, Andrew R., 30*n*
Lodish, Leonard M., 177*n*, 314*n*, 315*n*, 479*n*
Lohan, Lindsey, 257
Lohse, Gerald L., 441*n*
Lohtia, Ritu, 418*n*
Loken, Barbara, 57*n*
Long, Justin, 240
Longman, Kenneth A., 356*n*
Lord, Kenneth R., 441*n*
Loughlin, Sandra, 634*n*
Louie, Therese A., 274*n*
Lowrey, Tina M., 92*n*
Lubetkin, Beth, 177*n*
Lubliner, Murray J., 93*n*
Luce, Mary Frances, 273*n*
Lundegaard, Karen, 557*n*
Lutz, Richard J., 124*n*, 418*n*, 558*n*
Lutzky, Christian, 478*n*
Lynch, John G., 91*n*
Lysonski, Steven, 276*n*

M

MacArthur, Kate, 505*n*, 557*n*
Macé, Sandrine, 478*n*
Machleit, Karen A., 203*n*
Macias, Wendy, 356*n*
Maciejewski, Jeffrey J., 635*n*
MacInnis, Deborah J., 151*n*, 273*n*, 277*n*, 315*n*
MacKenzie, Scott B., 273*n*
Macklin, M. Carole, 92*n*
Madden, Normandy, 573*n*
Madden, Thomas J., 57*n*, 203*n*, 275*n*
Maddox, Kate, 30*n*, 203*n*, 356*n*, 417*n*, 418*n*, 572*n*
Magliozzi, Thomas L., 390*n*
Maguire, Angela M., 573*n*
Maheswaran, Durairaj, 278*n*
Maignan, Isabelle, 572*n*
Maita, Aki, 559*n*
Malaviya, Prashant, 274*n*
Manchanda, Rajesh V., 275*n*
Mandese, Joe, 390*n*
Mandhachitara, Rujirutana, 177*n*
Manning, Burt, 390*n*
Manning, Kenneth Craig, 277*n*, 278*n*, 479*n*
Mantese, Joe, 356*n*
Margulies, Walter P., 92*n*
Marich, Robert, 572*n*
Marks, Lawrence J., 390*n*
Marr, Merissa, 558*n*
Martin, Andrew, 634*n*
Martin, Claude R., Jr., 151*n*, 177*n*, 237*n*, 275*n*, 314*n*, 390*n*, 635*n*
Martin, Ingrid M., 636*n*
Maruggi, Albert, 418*n*
Maskulka, James, 600*n*
Matathia, Ira, 559*n*
Matheson, Donna M., 57*n*
Mathur, Anil, 124*n*
Matta, Shashi, 93*n*
Mayer, Robert N., 638*n*
Mayzlin, Dina, 559*n*
Mazar, Nina, 636*n*
Mazis, Michael B., 636*n*, 637*n*
Mazursky, David, 237*n*
Mazzon, Jose Afonso, 239*n*
McAlexander, James H., 58*n*
McAlister, Leigh, 203*n*, 600*n*
McClellan, Steve, 390*n*
McCormick, Steve, 572*n*
McCracken, Grant, 57*n*, 151*n*, 238*n*
McCracken, J. Colleen, 92*n*
McDonald, John P., 239*n*
McEnally, Martha R., 31*n*
McGrady, Tracy, 255
McGuire, William J., 151*n*
McKay, Betsy, 557*n*, 637*n*
McKee, Kathy Brittain, 440*n*
McLaughlin, Edward W., 479*n*
McLaughlin, Katy, 136
McLean, Don, 267
McMillan, Sally J., 417*n*
McNeill, Dennis L., 637*n*
McQuarrie, Edward F., 151*n*, 273*n*
Mela, Carl F., 177*n*, 478*n*
Menelly, Nancy E., 390*n*
Menon, Anil, 573*n*
Menon, Geeta, 92*n*
Menon, Satya, 573*n*

Metcalf, Barbara L., 636*n*
Meyers, Herbert M., 93*n*
Meyers, Peter, 505*n*
Meyers-Levy, Joan, 277*n*
Miciak, Alan R., 274*n*
Mick, David Glen, 151*n*, 152*n*, 273*n*
Middleton, Kent R., 239*n*
Miller, Amy, 314*n*
Miller, Darryl W., 390*n*
Miller, James C., III, 636*n*
Miller, Stephen, 203*n*
Milne, George R., 636*n*
Ming, Yao, 254
Mingus, Charlie, 208
Miniard, Paul W., 124*n*, 277*n*, 278*n*
Misra, Shekhar, 239*n*
Mitchell, Andrew A., 152*n*, 276*n*
Mittal, Banwari, 505*n*
Mittelstaedt, John D., 274*n*
Miyazaki, Anthony D., 573*n*, 636*n*
Moberg, D. Paul, 635*n*
Moffett, Sebastian, 600*n*
Mohammed, Rafi A., 417*n*
Mohr, Lois A., 573*n*
Mokwa, Michael P., 237*n*
Money, R. Bruce, 274*n*
Monga, Alokparna Basu, 57*n*
Moore, Elizabeth S., 124*n*
Moore, Melissa, 276*n*
Moore, Timothy E., 277*n*
Moorman, Christine, 273*n*
Moorthy, Sridhar, 203*n*
Morgan, Angela G., 573*n*
Morgan, Carol M., 124*n*
Morgan, Richard, 57*n*, 177*n*, 203*n*
Morgan, Robert M., 203*n*
Morgan, Ruskin, 91*n*
Morrison, Margaret, 390*n*
Morrison, Mary, 418*n*
Morrison, Van, 269
Moschis, George P., 124*n*
Moses, Louis J., 634*n*
Moss, Danny, 557*n*
Mouchoux, Dominique, 203*n*
Mowen, John C., 558*n*
Muehling, Darrel D., 239*n*, 277*n*
Mukherjee, Ashesh, 275*n*
Mulally, Alan, 60
Mulhern, Francis J., 506*n*
Muller, Eitan, 558*n*
Muniz, Albert M., Jr., 58*n*
Munoz, Sara Schaefer, 634*n*
Murphy, Patrick E., 635*n*, 636*n*
Murry, John P., Jr., 601*n*

N

Naik, Prasad A., 30*n*
Narasimhan, Chakravarthi, 91*n*, 478*n*
Nardone, John, 573*n*
Natarajan, Rajan, 276*n*
Neff, Jack, 30*n*, 58*n*, 314*n*, 389*n*, 418*n*, 441*n*, 478*n*, 505*n*, 506*n*, 557*n*
Nelson, Emily, 151*n*, 391*n*
Neslin, Scott A., 56*n*, 92*n*, 203*n*, 478*n*, 479*n*
Netemeyer, Richard G., 505*n*, 635*n*
Neu, D. M., 314*n*
Neuborne, Ellen, 558*n*
Nevett, Terence, 274*n*
Newman, Larry M., 124*n*
Noble, Stephanie M., 441*n*
Noel, Jacqueline, 600*n*
Nördfalt, Jens, 314*n*
Norman, Andrew T., 391*n*
Novak, Thomas P., 239*n*
Nowak, Glen, 636*n*
Nowlis, Stephen M., 479*n*, 505*n*

O

Oakes, Steve, 277*n*
Obermiller, Carl, 274*n*
O'Brien, John T., 356*n*
O'Connell, Vanessa, 277*n*
O'Connor, Terry, 56*n*
Odell, Patricia, 390*n*, 440*n*, 441*n*, 505*n*, 531*n*, 572*n*
O'Guinn, Thomas C., 58*n*
Ohanian, Roobina, 274*n*
O'Keefe, Daniel J., 274*n*
Oliver, Richard L., 177*n*
Oliver, Richard W., 417*n*
Olsen, G. Douglas, 573*n*
Olson, Jerry C., 152*n*, 238*n*, 239*n*
O'Malley, Gavin, 417*n*
O'Neal, Shaquille, 254
O'Reilly, Ann, 559*n*
Oser, Kris, 124*n*, 417*n*, 558*n*
Osler, Rob, 91*n*
Ostrom, Amy L., 557*n*
Ostrom, Thomas M., 274*n*
Ostrow, Joseph W., 31*n*
Ottman, Jacquelyn A., 637*n*
Ovide, Shira, 638*n*
Owens, Sara, 531*n*
Ozanne, Julie L., 92*n*

P

Painton, Scott, 277*n*
Paivio, Allan, 152*n*
Palan, Kay M., 124*n*, 278*n*
Palmer, Kimberly, 600*n*
Papatla, Purushottam, 478*n*
Pardun, Carol J., 440*n*
Park, C. Whan, 57*n*, 151*n*, 277*n*
Parmar, Arundhati, 441*n*
Parry, Tim, 505*n*
Parsons, Amy L., 275*n*
Parsons, Patrick R., 637*n*
Patrick, Aaron O., 418*n*, 600*n*
Patti, Charles H., 176*n*, 177*n*, 239*n*, 356*n*
Patwardhan, Hemant, 440*n*
Pauwels, Koen, 478*n*, 479*n*
Pawle, John, 314*n*
Payne, John W., 273*n*
Pechmann, Connie, 315*n*
Pechmann, Cornelia, 277*n*, 634*n*
Pedrick, James H., 390*n*
Penick, Harvey, 220, 238*n*
Peracchio, Laura A., 124*n*
Percy, Larry, 152*n*, 239*n*, 276*n*
Pereira, Joseph, 634*n*
Perner, Lars, 558*n*
Peter, J. Paul, 239*n*
Peterson, Robert A., 276*n*
Petit, Thomas A., 31*n*
Petty, Richard E., 273*n*, 274*n*, 315*n*
Petty, Ross D., 636*n*, 637*n*
Pham, Michel Tuam, 572*n*
Phelps, Joseph E., 636*n*
Phelps, Michael, 257
Phillips, Joanna, 441*n*
Pickton, Dave, 30*n*
Piercy, Nigel F., 31*n*
Pieters, Rik G. M., 204*n*
Pillutla, Madan M., 557*n*
Pinto, Mary Beth, 276*n*
Pitts, Robert E., 276*n*
Plessis, Erikdu, 314*n*
Poels, Karolien, 314*n*
Polk, Thad A., 57*n*
Poll, Harris, 56*n*
Pollack, Judann, 30*n*
Pollay, Richard W., 276*n*, 634*n*, 635*n*
Pollock, Ellen Joan, 558*n*
Polykoff, Shirley, 213
Porter, Michael E., 573*n*
Poulos, Basil, 238*n*
Power, Michael, 217
Pracejus, John W., 573*n*
Prendergast, Gerard, 177*n*
Prescott, Eileen, 558*n*
Preston, Ivan L., 177*n*, 636*n*
Price, Linda L., 91*n*, 313*n*, 558*n*
Priester, Joseph R., 274*n*
Pruitt, Stephen W., 572*n*
Purk, Mary E., 479*n*
Puto, Christopher P., 238*n*

Q

Quelch, John A., 479*n*, 600*n*
Quester, Pascale G., 572*n*, 573*n*
Quinton, Brian, 557*n*, 638*n*

R

Rabuck, Michael J., 315*n*
Raghubir, Priya, 93*n*, 505*n*, 506*n*, 531*n*
Raju, Jagmohan S., 506*n*
Raman, Kalyan, 30*n*
Randazzo, Sal, 152*n*
Rao, Ambar G., 315*n*
Rao, MacInnis, 315*n*
Rao, Murlidhar, 177*n*
Rao, Ram C., 203*n*
Rao, Vithala R., 479*n*
Ratneshwar, S., 277*n*
Raven, Peter, 277*n*
Ray, Michael L., 203*n*
Reichert, Tome, 276*n*
Reid, Leonard N., 275*n*, 356*n*, 390*n*
Reidenbach, R. Eric, 636*n*
Reiling, Lynn G., 505*n*
Reiman, Joey, 237*n*
Reingen, Peter H., 558*n*
Reitter, Robert N., 635*n*
Revson, Charles, 203*n*
Reyes, Sonia, 93*n*
Reynolds, Thomas J., 238*n*
Richards, Jef I., 203*n*, 636*n*
Richardson, Bruce, 177*n*
Richardson, C., 356*n*
Richey, Keith, 57*n*
Richins, Marsha L., 558*n*
Richmond, David, 276*n*
Rickard, Leah, 30*n*
Ridley, Danny, 277*n*
Ries, Al, 238*n*, 557*n*
Ries, Laura, 557*n*
Riesz, Peter C., 274*n*
Rifon, Nora J., 573*n*
Riley, Richard, 479*n*
Ringold, Debra Jones, 635*n*
Riordan, Edward A., 238*n*, 356*n*
Ripken, Cal, 255
Riskey, Dwight R., 315*n*
Ritchie, Karen, 124*n*
Ritchie, Robin J. B., 635*n*
Roan, Shari, 91*n*
Robertson, T. S., 273*n*
Robin, Donald P., 636*n*
Robinson, Thomas N., 57*n*
Robinson, William A., 478*n*, 531*n*, 601*n*
Rodgers, Shelly, 418*n*
Roehm, Michelle L., 277*n*
Rogers, Everett M., 91*n*, 558*n*
Rogers, Martha, 276*n*
Rose, Bill, 441*n*
Rose, Randall L., 277*n*, 278*n*
Rosen, Dennis L., 441*n*
Rosen, Emanuel, 559*n*
Rosenberg, Karl E., 315*n*
Rossiter, John R, 152*n*, 239*n*, 313*n*
Rotfeld, Herbert J., 275*n*, 637*n*
Roth, Kendall, 637*n*
Rothschild, Michael L., 391*n*
Roy, Donald P., 572*n*
Russell, Cristel Antonia, 391*n*, 440*n*
Russo, J. Edward, 636*n*
Rust, Roland T., 57*n*, 417*n*
Ruth, Julie A., 57*n*, 573*n*
Ryan, Bernard, Jr., 203*n*

S

Sable, David, 30*n*
Saegert, Joel, 277*n*
Sakano, Tomoaki, 274*n*
Salmon, Walter J., 479*n*
Salop, Steven, 636*n*
Salzman, Marian, 559*n*
Samiee, Saeed, 57*n*
Samuels, Jeffrey M., 92*n*
Samuels, Linda B., 92*n*
Sanders, Lisa, 30*n*, 124*n*, 238*n*, 314*n*, 441*n*
Sandler, Dennis M., 573*n*
Sankaralingam, Avu, 356*n*, 390*n*
Sasser, Sheila L., 238*n*
Sawicka, Monika, 57*n*
Sawyer, Alan G., 92*n*
Scammon, Debra L., 638*n*
Schewe, Charles D., 124*n*
Schibrowsky, John A., 124*n*
Schiller, Zachary, 479*n*
Schindler, Robert M., 478*n*
Schlosser, Ann E., 418*n*
Schmitt, Bernd H., 91*n*
Schouten, John W., 58*n*
Schroer, James C., 177*n*
Schultz, Don E., 30*n*, 124*n*, 237*n*, 238*n*, 440*n*, 478*n*, 531*n*, 601*n*
Schumann, David W., 239*n*

Schwartz, Shalom H., 239*n*
Schwarz, Norbert, 573*n*
Scott, Linda M., 92*n*, 151*n*, 277*n*
Seiler, Christine A., 276*n*
Selmants, Jodean, 93*n*
Sen, Sankar, 92*n*
Sen, Subrata K., 91*n*, 478*n*
Sengupta, Jaideep, 418*n*
Sengupta, Sanjit, 419*n*
Sethi, S. Prakash, 239*n*
Sethuraman, Raj, 204*n*, 479*n*
Severn, Jessica, 276*n*
Shalker, Thomas E., 152*n*
Shani, David, 573*n*
Shanklin, William L., 274*n*
Shannon, Daniel, 506*n*
Shapiro, Eben, 634*n*
Sharapova, Maria, 257
Sharma, Subhash, 57*n*
Sheehan, Kim Bartel, 636*n*
Shellenberg, R. Paul, 314*n*
Sheng, Ellen, 390*n*
Shepherd, Cybill, 257
Shermach, Kelly, 600*n*
Shi, Yi-Zheng, 177*n*
Shiffrin, Richard M., 152*n*
Shimp, Aubrey, 418*n*
Shimp, Terence A., 57*n*, 274*n*, 278*n*, 531*n*, 636*n*
Shirouzu, Norihiko, 558*n*
Shiv, Baba, 505*n*
Shocker, Allan D., 57*n*
Shoemaker, Robert W., 506*n*
Shrum, L. J., 92*n*, 417*n*
Shuman, Phillip Joel, 572*n*
Siddarth, S., 479*n*
Silberstein, Donald, 531*n*
Silk, Alvin J., 177*n*
Silva-Risso, Jorge, 478*n*
Simmons, Carolyn J., 573*n*
Simonin, Bernard L., 57*n*, 573*n*
Simonson, Itamar, 479*n*
Simpson, Jessica, 256
Singh, Surendra N., 314*n*, 390*n*
Sinisi, John, 204*n*
Sirdeshmukh, Deepak, 177*n*
Slater, Joanna, 557*n*
Slater, Michael D., 634*n*
Sloan, James J., 636*n*
Smarandescu, Laura, 531*n*
Smith, Amie, 478*n*, 557*n*
Smith, Kerry E., 479*n*
Smith, Kerry J., 531*n*
Smith, Kirk H., 276*n*
Smith, N. Craig, 634*n*
Sneath, Julie Z., 572*n*
Snook-Luther, David C., 276*n*
Sokol, Robert J., 636*n*
Soley, Lawrence, 276*n*
Soley, Lawrence C., 634*n*
Solomon, Sorin, 237*n*
Soman, Dilip, 531*n*
Soong, Roland, 391*n*
Spaeth, Jim, 203*n*, 601*n*
Spake, Deborah F., 203*n*
Spears, Britney, 257, 258
Speck, Paul Surgi, 152*n*, 275*n*, 390*n*, 391*n*
Sperber, Bob, 531*n*
Speros, James D., 58*n*
Spethmann, Betsy, 478*n*, 479*n*, 505*n*, 506*n*, 635*n*, 638*n*
Spotts, Harlan E., 274*n*, 275*n*
Spreng, Richard A., 273*n*
Srinivasan, Raji, 203*n*
Srinivasan, Shuba, 478*n*
Srinivasan, Srini S., 506*n*
Srinivasan, V., 479*n*
Srivastava, Rajendra K., 506*n*
Srull, Thomas K., 152*n*
Staelin, Richard, 57*n*, 91*n*, 636*n*
Stafford, Edwin R., 637*n*
Stanley, T. L., 558*n*
Stayman, Douglas M., 124*n*, 238*n*, 274*n*, 314*n*
Steel, Emily, 124*n*, 390*n*
Steenkamp, Jan-Benedict E. M., 91*n*, 418*n*
Steinard, Edward A., II, 572*n*
Steinberg, Brian, 30*n*, 441*n*, 634*n*
Stem, Donald E., Jr., 277*n*
Stephens, Debra, 636*n*
Stern, Barbara B., 151*n*, 440*n*
Stern, Judith A., 177*n*
Stevens, Mary Ellen, 177*n*
Stevenson, Julie S., 418*n*
Stewart, David W., 277*n*, 314*n*, 315*n*, 636*n*, 637*n*
Stewart, Ian, 276*n*
Stielstra, Greg, 559*n*
Strahilevitz, Michal, 573*n*
Strathman, Alan J., 273*n*
Strauss, William, 124*n*
Strenio, Andrew J., Jr., 637*n*
Stroebe, Wolfgang, 635*n*
Strong, James T., 276*n*
Stuart, Anne, 440*n*
Stuart, Elnora W., 636*n*
Stuart, Jennifer Ames, 57*n*
Sudhir, K., 479*n*
Sudman, Seymour, 637*n*
Sukhdial, Ajay, 238*n*
Sullivan, Laurie, 441*n*
Suri, Jane Fulton, 313*n*
Swait, Joffre, 56*n*, 57*n*
Swaminathan, Vanitha, 314*n*
Swinyard, William R., 203*n*
Szegedy-Maszak, Marianne, 275*n*
Szybillo, George J., 636*n*
Szykman, Lisa R., 573*n*

T

Tagg, Stephen, 274*n*
Talpade, Salil, 124*n*
Tannenbaum, Stanley I., 237*n*
Tarshis, Andrew M., 315*n*
Taylor, Charles R., 600*n*, 635*n*
Taylor, Ronald E., 238*n*
Tedesco, Richard, 274*n*
Tehada, Carlos, 505*n*
Teinowitz, Ira, 276*n*, 531*n*, 635*n*
Tellegen, Cassandra L., 573*n*
Tellis, Gerard J., 204*n*, 356*n*
Terhune, Chad, 557*n*
Thaler, Linda Kaplan, 238*n*
Theroux, Paul, 506*n*
Thomas, Jerry W., 313*n*
Thomaselli, Rich, 274*n*, 557*n*, 635*n*
Thompson, Beverley, 572*n*
Thompson, Stephanie, 30*n*, 634*n*, 638*n*
Thorson, Esther, 30*n*, 151*n*, 177*n*, 418*n*
Thottam, Jyoti, 418*n*
Till, Brian D., 274*n*, 278*n*, 600*n*
Tkacik, Maureen, 478*n*
Tom, Gail, 93*n*
Toomey, Margaret A., 356*n*
Trimble, Carrie S., 573*n*
Tripathi, Shashank, 418*n*
Tripp, Carolyn, 274*n*
Trout, Jack, 238*n*
Trump, Donald, 252
Tsui, Bonnie, 92*n*
Tucciarone, Joel D., 314*n*
Tucker, Lauren, 356*n*
Twedt, Dik Warren, 93*n*
Twitchell, James B., 237*n*
Tyagi, Rajeev K., 479*n*
Tybout, A. M., 277*n*
Tyson, Mike, 257

U

Underwood, Robert L., 92*n*
Unnava, H. Rao, 152*n*, 177*n*, 273*n*, 557*n*
Urbanski, Al, 478*n*

V

Vaczek, David, 505*n*
Vakratsas, Demetrios, 176*n*
van Heerde, Harald J., 204*n*, 479*n*
Van Osselaer, Stijn M. J., 92*n*
Vance, Erin, 600*n*
Vanden Bergh, Bruce G., 276*n*
Varadarajan, P. Rajan, 573*n*
Varki, Sajeev, 417*n*
Vence, Deborah L., 124*n*
Vergeront, Julie, 638*n*
Verhoef, Peter C., 30*n*
Vespe, Frank, 600*n*
Vicary, James, 265
Vick, Michael, 216, 257
Vora, Premal P., 203*n*
Vranica, Suzanne, 30*n*, 390*n*, 441*n*, 634*n*
Vriens, Marco, 313*n*

W

Wahlberg, David, 314*n*
Wakefield, Kirk L., 572*n*
Walker, Rob, 419*n*
Walker, Sam, 572*n*
Wallendorf, Melanie, 151*n*
Wansink, Brian, 93*n*, 203*n*, 238*n*, 478*n*, 505*n*
Ward, James C., 557*n*, 636*n*
Warlop, Luk, 239*n*
Warren, Audrey, 634*n*
Wassmuth, Birgit, 151*n*
Watson, Paul J., 314*n*
Watts, Duncan J., 559*n*
Webb, Deborah J., 573*n*
Webster, Cynthia, 124*n*
Wee, Chow-Hou, 277*n*
Weeks, Clinton S., 573*n*
Wehr, Lisa, 419*n*
Weilbacher, William M., 176*n*
Weinberg, Charles B., 278*n*
Weinberger, Marc G., 274*n*, 275*n*
Weinstein, Elizabeth, 418*n*
Weiss, Allen M., 315*n*
Weiss, Doyle L., 356*n*
Weiss, Michael J., 124*n*
Wells, William D., 238*n*
Welsh, Jonathan, 531*n*
Welty, Ward, 239*n*
Wentz, Laurel, 203*n*
West, Douglas C., 177*n*, 237*n*
West, Susan, 239*n*
Westberg, Steven J., 239*n*
White, Erin, 274*n*
White, Tiffany Barnett, 418*n*
Whitehead, Alfred North, 273*n*
Whitlark, David B., 239*n*
Whitman, Janet, 634*n*
Wicks, Jan LeBlanc, 637*n*
Wie, Michelle, 253
Wiles, Judith A., 314*n*
Wilkens, Henry T., 277*n*
Wilkes, Robert E., 124*n*
Wilkie, William L., 479*n*, 637*n*
Williams, Diane, 441*n*
Williams, Hank, 267
Williams, Serena, 216, 254
Wilson, Rick T., 600*n*
Winer, Russell S., 601*n*
Wingfield, Nick, 441*n*
Winters, Lewis C., 239*n*
Wittink, Dick R., 479*n*
Wood, Stacy, 531*n*
Woods, Tiger, 5, 250, 252, 256, 415, 508
Woodside, A., 239*n*
Woodyard, Chris, 558*n*
Wright, Peter, 275*n*, 558*n*, 634*n*, 635*n*
Wright-Isak, Chris, 356*n*

Y

YongGoh, Dubé Khim, 418*n*
Yoo, Boonghee, 177*n*
Yoo, Carolyn Y., 56*n*, 57*n*, 634*n*
Yoon, Yeosun, 573*n*
York, Emily Bryson, 124*n*
Yorkston, Eric, 92*n*
Young, Charles, 313*n*
Young, Chuck E., 314*n*
Young, James Webb, 203*n*
Young, Neil, 269
Yovovich, B. G., 356*n*

Z

Zackowitz, Margaret G., 124*n*
Zaltman, Gerald, 313*n*
Zanot, Eric J., 637*n*
Zarem, Jane E., 418*n*
Zeithaml, Valarie A., 57*n*
Zeta-Jones, Catherine, 254
Zhang, Shi, 278*n*
Zhang, Yong, 275*n*
Zhao, Hao, 203*n*
Zhu, Rui, 277*n*
Zimmer, Mary R., 151*n*
Zingery, Theresa A., 390*n*
Zinkhan, George M., 275*n*, 314*n*, 634*n*
Zufryden, Fred S., 177*n*, 390*n*, 418*n*

subject index

A

AAAA. *See* American Association of Advertising Agencies (AAAA)
ABC Premiere Events, 382t
Absolut vodka, 214, 224, 630
Accenture, 78
Account executives, 194
Account management, 194
Account managers, 194
Account planning, 219
Accountability
  in CRM, 570–71
  in event sponsorship, 566–67
  marketing communications, achieving of, 50–55
  perspective on, 165–66
  of P-mail advertising, 426
Account-specific marketing, 471–72
Accurate data, collecting of, in determining Marcom effectiveness, 52
Achievement
  defined, 229, 229t
  example of, 231, 233f
Achievers, in VALS framework, 104f, 105
ACNielsen, ScanTrack of, 302–03
ACP. *See* Association of Coupon Professionals (ACP)
Active synthesis, 143
Acura, 75
Adams Outdoor Advertising, 584
Adaptation, human, 245
Adidas, 38, 254–55, 402
Adoption
  brand, Marcom and, 62–71. *See also* Brand adoption
  product, 62
AdSense, 411–12
Advantage, relative, in facilitating brand adoption, 64–66, 66f
Advergaming, 435–36, 436f
Advertisement(s)
  processing of, enhancing consumers' motivation, opportunity, and ability in, 242–50
  sticky, 210–13
Advertising. . *See also* Newspaper advertising; Point-of purchase advertising; specific methods and types, e.g., Green marketing
  AAAA's code of ethical standards in, 613–14
  ad-investment considerations, 195–201
  advocacy, 235–36
  audiovisual, 427–28
  bad taste in, 612
  banner, on Internet, 398–99, 399t
  behavioral targeting in, 413–14
  billboard, 578–84. *See also* Billboard advertising
  brand-oriented, 234–35, 235f
  cable, 378
  catalog, 427–28
  celebrity endorsers in, 250–58. *See also* Endorsers, celebrity
  on cellular phones, in India, 408
  cinema, 436
  comparative, 269–71, 270f. *See also* Comparative advertising
  competitive, sales promotions in neutralizing, 456
  content-targeted, 411–12
  corporate, 235
  corporate issue, 235–36
  corrective, 623
  costs of, 183–88, 186t, 187t
  creative
    alternative styles of, 223–27, 223t, 225f, 226f
    brand image creative style, 224
    emotional creative style, 225, 226f
    generic creative style, 225–26
    guidelines for: laddering as, 233–34; means-end chaining as, 228–33
    preemptive creative style, 226–27
    resonance creative style, 225, 225f
    resonant, 225, 225f
    USP style, 223–24, 223t
    values in, nature of, 228–29, 229t
  deceptive, regulations against, 620–22
  defined, 182
  direct
    in movies, 432–33
    via postal mail, 422–31, 422t, 429t. *See also* P-mail advertising
  disinvesting in, case for, 196–97
  display, on Internet, 398–99, 399t
  DTC, regulation of, 624
  effective
    CAN elements in, 209–10
    creating, 208–19
    creation of, 208–19
  effectiveness of, measuring of, 192
  e-mail, 403–09. *See also* E-mail advertising
  emotional reactions to, measurement of, 297–99. *See also* Emotional reactions, measurement of
  ethical issues in, 610–14. *See also* Ethical issues, in advertising
  feature, in influencing sales of discounted brands, 474t, 476
  functions of, 188–90
    adding value, 190
    assisting other company efforts, 190
    increasing salience, 189
    influencing, 188–89
    informing, 188
    reminding, 189
  green, 628, 628f–30f
  green marketing, 626–32
  humor in, role of, 258–60, 259f
  in-store, measuring audience for, 598
  interactive, 394–95
  Internet, 392–419. *See also* Internet; Internet advertising
  investing in, case for, 196
  keyword-matching, 411
  lack of, effects of, 459
  magazine, 363–71, 364f, 365f, 366t, 369t
  magnitude of, 183–88, 186t, 187t
  management of, overview of, 180–205. *See also* Advertising management
  manager's role in, 199–200
  manipulation in, 611–12
  mass media, 11
  meaning transfer in, 130
  MECCAS Model of, 230–33, 230t, 231f–33f
  mistakes in, 217–19, 218f
  in movies, 432–33
  music in, functions of, 267–69
  newspaper, 360–63, 362t
  offensive, 612
  OOH, 352–53, 578–85. *See also* Out-of-home (OOH) advertising
  outdoor, in green marketing, 631
  in persuading people to buy things they do no really need, 613
  in playing on people's fears and insecurities, 613
  P-mail, 422–31, 422t, 429t. *See also* P-mail advertising
  P-O-P, 586–98. *See also* Point-of-purchase (P-O-P) advertising
  positioning in, 130
  prescription drug, regulation of, 623–24
  print, 4
  radio, 371–74, 372t
  reasons for, 482–83
  reinforcing of, sales promotions in, 458
  resonant, 225, 225f
  search engine, 409–13, 411f
  self-regulation of, 624–26
  sex in, 262–264, 264f. *See also* Sex, in advertising
  share of market in, 200–201, 200t
  slogans for, 222
  spending for, 200–201, 200t
    of top global marketers, 167
  stereotypes in, 612
  subliminal messages in, 264–67. *See also* Subliminal messages
  successes in, 217–19, 218f
  Super Bowl, rising cost of, 381
  symbolic embeds in, 264–67
  tattoo, 438
  transformational, 224
  transit, 585, 585f, 586f
  TV, 4, 304–11, 305f, 306t, 307t, 309f, 375–88, 376t, 379t, 382t, 386f. *See also* Television (TV) advertising
    network, 376t, 377
  in TV programs, 431–34
  uncertain effects of, 185, 188
  unethical, vs. good marketing, 610
  unfair, defined, 622

untruthfulness in, 611
usage expression, 188
values relevant to, 229–30
video-game, 435–36, 436f
vs. MPR, 536–37
vs. pricing elasticity, 197–201, 200t
wireless e-mail, 406–07
yellow-pages, 434–35
Advertising Age, 609
Advertising agencies
account management, 194
boutiques, 193
compensation for, 194–95
creative services, 194
full-service, 193–94
media services, 194
message research lessons learned by, 286
research services, 194
role of, 192–94
top-25 (U.S.) in ad revenue, 192, 193t
Young & Rubicam, 346
Advertising campaign, "Mac versus PC," 323
Advertising clearance process, 624–25
Advertising elasticity, 200, 200t
Advertising management, 180–205
introduction to, 182–83
process of, 190–95
advertising agencies in, 192–94. *See also* Advertising agencies
advertising strategies in, 191–92, 191f
client perspective on, 191–92, 191f
Advertising media, 316–59, 420–41, 422t. *See also* Radio; specific methods, e.g., Newspaper(s)
alternative, 437–38, 437f
buying of, 319–20
described, 318
magazines, 363–71, 364f, 365f, 366t, 369t
messages and, 318–19
newspapers, 360–63, 362t
traditional, 358–91
introduction to, 360
mass media, 358–91
types of, 360
vs. vehicles, 318
Advertising messages
concreteness in, 211–12
corporate image in, 234–35, 235f
credibility in, 212
effective and creative, 206–39
Aflac duck, 214–15, 216f
Albsolut vodka, 214
creative brief, 219–21. *See also* Creative brief
Guinness beer, 217
Honda, 216–17
illustrations of, 213–17
iPod, 217
Miss Clairol campaign, 213–14
Nike, 216
effectiveness of
measuring of, 280–315
recognition and, recall in, 289–97
emotionality in, 212
getting messages to "stick," 210–13
introduction to, 208
simplicity of, 211
storytelling in, 212–13
unexpectedness in, 211
Advertising research, 282–86
components of, 282–84
difficulty of, 282
forms of, 282–84
industry standards for, 284–86
introduction to, 282–86
Advertising Research Foundation (ARF), 28, 286
Advertising Research System (ARS) Persuasion Method, 300–02
Advertising Response Model (ARM), of BRC, 294, 295f
Advertising strategy, 320
described, 191
implementing of, 192
Advertising-to-sales ratios, 185, 187t
Advil, 623
Advocacy advertising, 235–36
AdWords, 411, 412
Affordability method, 175
Aflac duck, 214–15, 216f
African-Americans, demographic targeting to, 118t, 119, 119f
Age, as factor in demographic targeting, 109–17, 110t, 111f, 113f, 115f
Agency mistakes, 218–19
Agreement, in determining Marcom effectiveness, 52
Ailing Outgoers, 117
Aim, 37
AirJordan XX3, 626
Alcohol products targeting of, to children and teens, 608–09
Alcoholic Beverage Labeling Act, 619
Allowance(s)
bill-back, 464
bill-back and, 464
bill-back display, 464
deslotting, 466
off-invoice, 463
undesirable consequences of 467–69, 467t
slotting, 615
trade. *See* Trade allowances
Alloy Media + Marketing, 480
Allstate Insurance, 154
Altria Group, 119
America, world's perception of, 47–48
American Airlines, 73, 100
American Association of Advertising Agencies (AAAA), 28
code of ethical standards of, 613–14
American Council on Science and Health, 546
American Family Life Assurance Company (Aflac), 214–15, 216f
American households, ever-changing, demographic targeting and, 117–18
American Idol, 339, 376, 380, 382t, 385, 433, 434
American Music Awards, 352
American Pediatrics Association, 612
"American Worker of the Year" award, 521
ANA. *See* Association of National Advertisers (ANA)
Anacin, 248
Analysis(es)
feature, 143
lifetime-value, 429–31, 429t
Ancestral groups of U.S. residents, 109t
Anheuser-Busch, 121, 201, 294
"Animal Advice," 403
Animatics, 283
Appeal(s), 240–78
to consumer fears, 260–62
appropriate intensity, 260–61
fear appeal logic, 260
to consumer guilt, 262
emotional, in packaging, 85–86
introduction to, 242
to scarcity, related case of, 261–62
Apple, 66, 67–68, 71–73, 206, 207, 217, 240, 433, 511, 521, 523, 524f, 554
Appropriateness, in advertising, 210
Aquafina Alive, 100
Aquafresh, 83
Arbitron, 374, 387, 414
Ardberg, 423
ARF. *See* Advertising Research Foundation (ARF)
ARM. *See* Advertising Response Model (ARM)
Arm & Hammer, 37
Armor All, 83
ARS Persuasion scores, 300
predictive validity of, 301–02, 301t
Ashley Furniture, 524
ASI Market Research, 296–97
Asian-Americans, demographic targeting to, 121–22
Asics, 38
Aspartame, 546
Asset(s), long-term, 429
Association(s), mental, 39
described, 36–37
Association of Coupon Professionals (ACP), 28
Association of National Advertisers (ANA), 28, 52, 432
in self-regulation, 625
AT & T, 6–7, 80, 80f, 185, 186t, 226
Attention
conscious, 142
defined, 142
involuntary, 245, 245f, 246f
selective, in CPM, 142–43
Attitude(s)
forming of, 158f, 161
reinforcing of, 158f, 161
Attractiveness
in celebrity endorsement, 256
physical, 251t, 252–53
Attribute(s), 39
brand, 230t
defined, 228
endorsers, 251–54, 251t
Attribute positioning, 133f, 137
Audience(s)
of billboard advertising, measuring size and characteristics of, 583–84
for in-store advertising, 598
for magazine advertising, 367–68
radio, measurement for, 374
target
for creative brief, 219–20
fit for, in event sponsorship, 564
measurable characteristics of, 98
selecting of, 321–22
TV, measurement of, 385–88, 386f. *See also* Television (TV) advertising, audience measurement in
video-game, measuring of, 435
Audience fractionalization
in radio advertising, 372t, 374
in TV advertising, 379t, 380
Audience matchup, in celebrity endorsement, 254

Audiovisual advertising, 428
Auqafresh, 37
Automobile(s), hybrid, 65
Autonomic responses, 298
Average price, advertising elasticities and, 198–200
Avon, 384
Awareness
brand, 37–38, 37f, 38f, 259
top-of-mind, 38, 38f, 188
from unawareness to, advancing consumers from, 158, 158f
Awareness class, 62, 63f
Axe deodorant, 437

B

B2B. *See* Business-2-business (B2B)
B2C. *See* Business-2-consumer (B2C)
Baby-boom generation, 110, 115, 115f
Bad taste, in advertising, 612
Bagel Bites, 564
Balance-of-power shift, budgetary allocations related to, 449–50
Bandai Company Ltd., 554 554
Banner ads, on Internet, 398–99, 399t
Barq's root beer, 513
Bayer, 623
Bazooka bubble gum, 455
"Bazooka Super Treasure," 455
Beatrice Company, Monday Night Football promotion by, 517
Be-Bratz.com, 403
Bed Bath & Beyond, 524
Beef Checkoff Program, 231, 233f
Beefeater Gin, 432
Behavior(s), marketing communications effects on, 50–55
Behavior-affecting objective, 18–19
Behavioral targeting, online, 413–14
Behaviorographic(s), 98, 99f
Behaviorographic targeting, 98–101, 99f
online, 100
privacy concerns of, 101
BehaviorScan, of IRI, 303–04, 306, 307
Belief(s)
forming of, 158f, 161
reinforcing of, 158f, 161
Believers, in VALS framework, 104f, 105
Belmont Stakes, 564–65
Ben & Jerry's, 490, 492, 630
Benadryl anti-itch cream, 489
Benefit(s), 39
Marcom regulations of, 619
Benefit positioning, 133f–35f, 134–37
based on functional needs, 133f, 134, 134f
based on symbolic needs, 133f, 134
Benevolence, defined, 229, 229t
Benylin study, of display effectiveness, 596
Benzene, Perrier contaminated with, 541
"Best brands" survey, 32
Best Buy, 121
Better Business Bureaus, 625
Better Homes & Gardens, 366, 368
Betty Crocker brand, 80, 81f
Bic razors, specialty billboard for, 580, 580f
Big Brown, 564–65
Bill-back ad allowances, 463
Bill-back allowances, 463
Bill-back display allowances, 463
Billboard advertising, 578–84
in BRIC countries, 579
bulletin, 580
buying, 581
effectiveness of, case study, 584–85, 584f
electronic (digital) billboards, 580
forms of, 578–81, 581f
Japanese, humans playing soccer, 582, 582f
limitations of, 582–83
measuring audience size and characteristics of, 583–84
poster panels, 579
specialty, 580–81, 581f
strengths of, 581–82, 581f, 582f
Birch Scarborough Research, 374
BlackBerry, 536
Blackberry Curve smart phones, 521, 521f
Blockbluster, 488
Blog(s), 401–02
as advertising format, on Internet, 402
Bloggers, 547
Blue Angel seal, 630
BMW, 425
BMW Mini Cooper, 68
Bohemian Mix, 106–07
Bollé, 522
Bon Appétit, 366
Bonus packs, 516
Booz Allen Hamilton, 188
Borders, 589
Bottom-up (BU) budgeting, 22
Bottom-up/top-down (BUTD) process, 22
Bounty paper towels, 486, 491
Boutique(s), 193
Boys & Girls Clubs, 617
Bradlees, 591
Brain imaging, neuroscience and, 298
Brand(s). *See also* specific brands, e.g., Coca-Cola
characteristics of, in facilitating brand adoption, 64–69
described, 34
discounted, sales of, feature advertising and displays in, 474t, 474–76
familiar, 310, 398
higher- and lower-quality promotion of, asymmetric effects of, 474t, 476
higher-market-share, deal elasticity with, 474t, 475
leveraging associations from other brands, 44f, 45
mature, sales promotions in invigorating sales, 455
meaning of, in consumers' memories, 131
menu, rat poisoning and, 539
new adoption of, 62–71. *See also* Brand adoption
facilitating success of, 60–93
package for, 81–89. *See also* Packaging
repositioning of, 137, 139–40
selection of, subliminal stimuli influencing, 266–67
world-class, characteristics of, 48–49, 49t
Brand adoption
characteristics of, quantifying of, 69–71, 69f
facilitating
brand characteristics in, 64–69
compatibility in, 66–67
complexity in, 67–68
observability in, 68–69
relative advantage in, 64–66, 66f
steps in, 62–64, 63f
trialability in, 68
Marcom and, 62–71
Brand Adoption Process, 62, 63f
Brand Adoption Process Model, 63f, 64
Brand attributes, 230t
Brand awareness, 37–38, 37f, 38f, 259, 398
Brand choice
influencing, 336–37
subliminal priming and, 268
Brand consequences, 230t
Brand differentiation, 305, 305f
Brand equity, 34–49
customer-based perspective on, 36–41, 37f, 38f
defined, 34
enhancing of, 41–46, 44f
benefits from, 46, 48
by creating appealing messages, 42
by having brand speak for itself, 42
leveraging by, 42–46, 44f
firm-based perspective on, 35–36, 36t
Brand familiarity, 310, 398
Brand image, 37f, 39–41
creative style of, 224
Brand lift index, 594, 594t
Brand logo, 79–80, 79f, 80f
Brand loyalty
accomplishing, 158f, 161
reduced, budgetary allocations related to, 451
Brand management objectives, 483–84, 485t
Brand managers, message research lessons learned by, 286
Brand matchup, in celebrity endorsement, 254–55
Brand names
logos and, 79–80, 79f, 80f
made-up, 75
requirements for
achieve compatibility with desired image and product design or packaging, 75–76
be memorable and easy to pronounce, 76–77
distinguish from competitive offerings, 72–73
exceptions to "rules," 77
facilitate consumer learning of brand associations, 73–75
good, 71–77
suggestiveness of, 73–74
Brand naming, 71–80
in advertising, 615
empty-vessel philosophy of, 77
process of, 77–79, 77f. *See also* Brand-naming process
sound symbolism and, 75
Brand packaging, 81–89. *See also* Packaging
Brand parity, increased, budgetary allocations related to, 450–51
Brand placements
in cinema, 436
in TV programs, 384–85, 431–34
in yellow pages, 434–35
Brand positioning, framework for, 132–33, 133f

Brand positioning statement, 22
Brand recall, 38
Brand recognition, 38
Brand strengths, 243
Brand users, current, coupon redemption by, 495–96
Branded entertainments, 432
Branding
ethical issues in, 615
ingredient, 45
360-degree, touch points and, 14–16
Brand-level promotion targets, 447–48, 448f
Brand naming process, 77–79, 77f
create candidate brand names, 77f, 78
evaluate candidate names, 77f, 78
register trademark, 77f, 79
select brand name, 77f, 78–79
specify objectives for brand name, 77–78, 77f
Brand-oriented advertising, 234–35, 235f
Brand-related personality dimensions, 40–41
Bratz, 403
Braun, 384, 597
Brawny, 486
BRC. *See* Bruzzone Research Company (BRC)
BRIC countries, billboard advertising in, 579
Bridge buying, 466–68, 467t
Bridgestone Corporation, 540
Bridgestone/Firestone, 542–43
Brief, creative, construction of, 219–21. *See also* Creative brief
BriteVision, 15
Broad reach, 362, 362t
in newspaper advertising, 362, 362t
Brooklyn Bottling Corporation, 545
Brooks Brothers, 410
Bruzzone Research Company (BRC), 293–95, 294f–96f
BU budgeting, 22
Bubble Yum, 544
Bud Light, 160, 172t
Budget Rent A Car, 522
Budgeting, 22, 166–75
BU, 22
competitive interference in, 174–75
competitive parity method, 171–75, 172t, 173f
objective-and-task, 170–71
percentage-of-sales method, 169–70
in practice, 169–75, 172t, 173f
for promotions, increased allocations, 448–54, 451f, 449t, 450t, 453t
TD, 22
in theory, 166–69, 168t
Budweiser, 121, 172t, 173, 432
Buick, 508
Buick Rainer, 6
Building-mounted signs, 577, 577f
Bulletin(s), advertising on, 580
Bunco World Championship, 564
Bureau of Alcohol, Tobacco
and Firearms, of U.S. Treasury Department, 610
Firearms and Explosives, 465
Burger King, 616–17
Burroughs Wellcome Company, 542
Busch, 172t
Busch Light, 172t
Business consumers, representation of starting point for all marketing communicative activities by, 10–13, 10t
Business Week, 6
Business-2-business (B2B), 182, 183f, 185, 188
on Internet, 397
Business-2-business (B2B) companies, 170
Business-2-business (B2B) environment, 6
Business-2-business (B2B) marketing, on Internet, 394
Business-2-consumer (B2C), 182, 185, 188
Business-2-consumer (B2C) companies, 170
Business-2-consumer (B2C) marketing, 6
on Internet, 394, 397
BUTD process, 22
"Buy X, Get 1 Free" offers, 512–13
Buying
bridge, 466–68, 467t
forward, 466–68, 467t
Buzz creation, 549–55
anecdotal evidence of, 549–51
compared to epidemic, 551–52
described, 549
designing product to be unique or visible in, 553
igniting explosive self-generating demand in, 553–55
law of few in, 552
nurture grass roots in, 555
perspectives on, 551–55
power of context in, 552–53
ration supply in, 554
select and seed vanguard in, 553–54
stickiness factor in, 552
tap power of lists in, 555
use celebrity icons in, 554–55
Bystanders, 113

C

Cabela, 562
Cable advertising, 378
Cable News Network (CNN), 215, 541
CACI (ACORN), 106
Cadbury, 455
Cadillac XLR, 518
Caesars Palace, 432
Calculation(s), illustrative, in media planning, 339–40
Camera(s), digital, 65
Campaign(s)
advertising. *See* specific campaigns
successful, 218
Campbell Soup Company, 76, 225–26, 308–09, 309f, 464, 468, 518, 569, 607,
"Campus Consciousness Tour," 630
Campus Trial Paks, 480
Camry, 26
CAN. *See* Connectedness, appropriateness, and novelty (CAN)
Canada's Air Miles Reward Program, 18
Canon, 350
CAN-SPAM, 405
Carhartt, 562
Caribou Coffee chain, 17, 523, 524f
"Carne Asada Taquitos," 293, 294, 294f
CARU. *See* Children's Advertising Review Unit (CARU)
Cash flow, discounted, 190
Catalina Marketing Corporation, 497
Caterpillar 414E Industrial Loader campaign, 424
Cause sponsorships, 567–71. *See also* Cause-related marketing (CRM)
Cause-related marketing (CRM), 567–71
accountability in, 570–71
benefits of, 569–70
in green marketing, 630
importance of fit in, 570
CBS Outdoor, 631
CDC. *See* Centers for Disease Control and Prevention (CDC)
CD-ROMs, advertising by, 428
Celebrity(ies)
in advertising, 280
in buzz creation, 554–55
Celebrity endorsers, 250–58. *See also* Endorsers, celebrity
Cell phones
advertising on, in India, 408
Internet advertising on, 407–09
LG, 46
Cellfire, 409, 500
Census Bureau, 107, 116–17
Center for Science in the Public Interest, 608
Centers for Disease Control and Prevention (CDC), 607–08
Cents-off packs, 515–16
CEOs. *See* Chief executive officers (CEOs)
Certification, product, symbolism of, 136
CFL. *See* Compact fluorescent lightbulbs (CFL)
CFOs. *See* Chief financial officers (CFOs)
Characteristic(s), consumer, 242–43
Charmin, 490–92, 491f
Charmin Potty Palooza tour, 490, 491f
"Cheap seats," 447
Checkout Coupon, 497
Checkout Direct, 497
Cheerios, 82
Cheez-It Twists, 589
Chelada, 121
Chevrolet, 267
Chiat/Day, 206
Chicago Sun-Times, 361
Chicago Tribune, 361
Chief executive officers (CEOs), 50
Chief financial officers (CFOs), 50
Chief marketing officers (CMOs), 50
Children, targeting to, 111, 111f
ethics of, 607–09
Children's Advertising Review Unit (CARU), in self-regulation, 625
Chrysler, 384, 432
Cinema advertising, 436
Cingular, 80, 80f
Citibank, 226–27
Claim-fact discrepancy, 620
Clairol, 384
Clairol Herbal Essences shampoo, 480
Clamato, 121
Claritas (PRIZMNE), 106
Clear Channel Outdoor, 580
Clearasil, 480
Clearinghouses, in coupon redemption process, 501–03, 501f
Click fraud, 412–13

Click-through rates (CTRs), 398–99, 416
Clinique, 72
Clio Awards, in U.S., 209
Clorox, 55, 460, 625
Close-Up (toothpaste), 37, 82
Clutter, 208
 defined, 420
 in event sponsorship, 564
 in newspaper advertising, 362–63, 362t
 in radio advertising, 372t, 373
 in reducing message effectiveness, 142–43
 in TV advertising, 379t, 382–83
CMOs. *See* Chief marketing officers (CMOs)
CNN, 215, 541
Coca-Cola, 41–43, 75–76, 79, 79f, 82, 121, 188, 265, 267, 269, 385, 433, 434, 437, 437f, 516, 539–41, 564, 616–17, 628
Code of ethical standards, of AAAA, 613–14
Cognetix, 584
Coleman Company, 563
Colgate, 37, 512
Colgate-Palmolive Company, 511, 571, 625
College students, odor-fighting products for, 114
Color, in packaging, 82–83
Co-marketing, 472
Commercial(s). *See also* specific product, e.g., Pepsi
 characteristics of, 280
 differentiation among, 305, 305f
 testing of, prefinished form, 283
Commercial rumors, 544
Commerical(s), costs of, 316
Commissions from media, 194–95
Communication(s)
 described, 164
 integrated marketing, 3–31. *See also* Integrated marketing communications (IMC)
 marketing
  integrated, 3–31. *See also* Integrated marketing communications (IMC)
  tools of, 7–8, 7t
 P-O-P, 574–601. *See also* Point-of-purchase (P-O-P) communications
Communication objectives, 164
Communication outcomes, 27
Community, online gaming, profile of, 435
Compact fluorescent lightbulbs (CFL), 626
Compaq, 75
Comparative advertising, 269–71, 270f
 advantages of, 271
 considerations dictating use of, 271
 credibility issue in, 271
 effectiveness of, 270–71
  assessment of, 271
 situational factors in, 271
Compatibility, in facilitating brand adoption, 66–67
Compensation, advertising agency, 194–95
Competence, brand-related, 40
Competitive interference, 174–75
Competitive parity method, 171–75, 172t, 173f
Complexity, in facilitating brand adoption, 67–68
Comprehension, 144
 defined, 143
 of what is intended, in CPM, 143
Concreteness, in advertising, 211–12
Concretization(s), 248, 250, 250f
Concretizing, 211–12
Condé Nast, 364
Conditioned stimulus, 269
Conformity, defined, 229, 229t
Congress, U.S., 609, 611, 630
Connectedness
 in advertising, 209
 appropriateness, and novelty (CAN), elements of, 209–10, 242
Conscious attention, 142
Consciousness, ecology, in Mac owners' psychographic profiles, 323
Consequence(s)
 brand, 230t
 defined, 228
Consistent investment spending, 188
Conspiracy rumors, 545
Constructive process, 128
Consumer(s)
 advancing from unawareness to awareness, 158, 158f
 on brand equity, 42
 characteristics of, 242–43
 in control, 11
 economically disadvantaged, targeting of, 609–10
 knowledge about, in positioning, 140–49. *See also* Positioning
 loading of
  sales promotions in increasing product usage by, 457–58
  sales promotions in preempting competition by, 458
 "LOHAS," 136
 mature, targeting to, 116–17
 memories of, brand meaning in, 131
 middle-aged, targeting to, 114–16, 115f
 P-O-P advertising benefits for, 587–88
 processing advertisements by, enhancement of, 242–50
 product information trusted by, 184
 promotions oriented to, 510t
 reaching of, in TV advertising, 379, 379t
 representation of starting point for all marketing communicative activities by, 10–13, 10t
 responsiveness of, budgetary allocations related to, 452
 stockpiling by, 458–59
 targeting to, 96–125. *See also* Targeting
 trial purchases by, sales promotions in obtaining, 456–57
Consumer behavior, P-O-P's influence on, 588–91
Consumer Buying Habits Study, of POPAI, 591–94, 592t–94t
Consumer fears, appeals to, 260–62
Consumer guilt, appeals to, 262
Consumer packaged goods (CPGs) companies, 446, 482, 512, 518
Consumer processing model (CPM), 140–47, 141f, 143f, 146f, 147f
 agreement with what is comprehended, 144
 comprehension of what is intended, 143
 described, 141, 147–48
 exposure to information, 141–42
 paying attention, 142–43
 retention and search/retrieval of stored information, 145–47, 146f, 147f
Consumer rewards, 484–85, 485t
Consumercentric, 11
Consumer-oriented promotions, 482–506, 510t
 reasons for, 482–83
Contact(s)(s), 14
Contamination rumors 545, 546
Content-targeted advertising, 411–12
Contests 521–22, 521f
 online, 522
Contextual meaning, in V8 juice advertisements, 130, 131f
Continental, 73
Continental Tire, 520, 520f
Continuity, in media planning, 33–35, 335f
Continuity promotions, 522–23
Continuous advertising schedule, 334, 335f
Converse, 38
Cookies, 413
Coors Light, 172t
Copy research, 283
Copy Research Validity Project, of ARF, 286
Copy tests, 283
 vs. weight tests, 304
Corn Flakes, 589
Corona, 545
Corona Extra, 172t, 173
Corporate advertising, 235
Corporate image, advertising and, 234–35, 235f
Corporate issue (advocacy) advertising, 235–36
Corporate reward structures, budgetary allocations related to, 452
Corrective advertising, 623
Corvettes, 512
Cosmopolitan, 324, 366
Cost(s)
 advertising, 183–88, 186t, 187t
 celebrity endorsement–related, 256
 of commercials, 316
 coupon, 495, 495t
 in event sponsorship, 563–64
 exit, 466
 Marcom regulations of, 619–20
 in media planning, considerations related to, 339–40
 of sales promotion ideas, evaluation of, 527, 528t
 of SEA, 410
 sunk, 311
 of Super Bowl advertising, 381
 of TV advertising, 379t, 380
Cost per click (CPC), 411
Cost per thousand (CPM), 339–40
Cost per thousand impressions, 415
Costco, 485, 525
Cost-free, 513
Cost-per-action (CPA) metric, 415
Council of Better Business Bureau, NAD of, in self-regulation, 625
Country(ies), world's largest, 109t
Coupon(s)
 cost of, 495, 495t
 defined, 493
 distribution methods, 494
 as FSIs, 494–97, 499
 in-pack, 499–500
 instantly redeemable, 496–97
 mail-delivered, 498–99
 media-delivered, 499
 misredemption, 501–03, 501f
 on-pack, 499–500

redemption process, 495–96, 501–03, 501f
consequences of, 502
described, 501–02, 501f
participants in, 502–03
redemption rates for, 494
by current brand users, 495–96
for in-pack coupons, 500
retail, 524
scanner-delivered, 497–98
shelf-delivered, 497
"Coupon days," 524
Couponing, 493–503
background of, 493–96, 495t
online, 500
point-of-purchase, 496–98
IRCs, 496–97
scanner-delivered coupons, 497–98
shelf-delivered coupons, 497
profitability of, 495–96
wireless, 500
CPA metric, 415
CPC. *See* Cost per click (CPC)
CPG companies. *See* Consumer packaged goods (CPG) companies
CPGs. *See* Consumer packaged goods (CPGs)
CPM. *See* Consumer processing model (CPM)
CPM measure, in magazine advertising, 365–66
CPM-TM, 339–40
CPM-TM measure, in magazine advertising, 366
Creative brief
background of, 219
behavioral outcome of, 220–21
constructing of, 219–21
described, 219
measures of, 220
medium for, 221
message for, 221
nitty-gritty details related to, 221–22
objectives of, 220
positioning for, 221
strategy for, 221
target audience for, 219–20
thoughts and feelings related to, 220
Creative content, media weight and, relationship between, 309–10
Creative meaning, 128–31, 129f, 131f
Creative services, 194
Creative strategy, leverage point and, 230t
Credibility, 251t, 252
in advertising, 212
in celebrity endorsement, 255–56
in comparative advertising, 271
Credible, defined, 144
Crest, 37
Crocs (rubber shoes), 73, 74, 134, 134f, 135
Crouching Tiger, Hidden Dragon, 550
Crunch Crisp, 512
CTRs. *See* Click-through rates (CTRs)
Cue(s), intense and prominent, use of, 245, 245f, 246f
Culturally constituted world, 130
Current brand users, coupon redemption by, 495–96
Customer lifetime value, 42
Customer loyalty, 371
Customized publishing, 371
Cute things, in advertising, 280
Cyanide poisoning, Tylenol and, 541–42

D

Dakota brand, 610
Dasani, in United Kingdom, 539–40, 540f
Data
accurate, collecting of, in determining Marcom effectiveness, 52
single-source, 303
Data mining, practice of, 431
Database(s), uses of, 428–31, 429t
Database marketing, 428–31, 429t
data mining in, 431
lifetime-value analysis in, 429–31, 429t
Day-after recall testing, 295–97
Dayparts, programming, in TV advertising, 375–76, 376t
Daytime, in TV advertising, 375
DC, 437
DC210 zoom digital camera, 384
DCF. *See* Discounted cash flow (DCF)
Deal(s)
defined, 451
frequency of
consumer's reference price change due to, 474–75, 474t
height of deal spike related to, 474, 474t
retailers pass through less than 100 percent of, 475, 474t
special price, 525
trade, 462–68. *See also* Trade allowances
Deal or No Deal, 382t
Deception, in advertising, 611
Decision(s)
fundamental, 20
implementation, 20, 23–26, 25f
Decision making, in-store, 591–94, 592t–94t. *See also* In-store decision making
Decision-making process, of marketing communications, 20–27, 21f, 25f
DEHA, 546
Delayed rewards, 485
Dell, 69, 206, 625
Delta, 73
Demand
law of inverse, 198
primary, 188
secondary, 188
Demographers, defined, 110
Demographic(s), 98, 99f
Demographic targeting, 107–22
changing age structure and, 109–17, 110t, 111f, 113f, 115f
children, 111–12, 111f
ethnic population developments and, 120t, 118–22, 118t, 119f. *See also* Ethnic populations, demographic targeting to
ever-changing American household and, 117–18
mature consumers, 116–17
middle-aged consumers, 114–16, 115f
teenagers, 112–13, 113f
young adults, 113–14
Dentsu Eye, 554
Department of Commerce, 107
Department of Justice, 374
Design, in packaging, 83
Deslotting allowances, 465–66
DeWalt tools, 562
Dick Clark's Rockin' New Years Eve, 352 352
Dickies, 521, 562
Dick's Sporting Goods, 525, 525f
Diesel, 45
Diet Coke, 263, 546, 592
Diet Dr Pepper media plan, 49t, 346–47, 348t
Diet Pepsi, 248, 546, 591–92, 628
Digital billboards, advertising on, 580
Digital cameras, 65
Digital video recorder (DVR), effect on TV advertising viewing, 380, 382
Direct, defined, 420
Direct advertising
in movies, 432–33
via postal mail, 422–31, 422t, 429t. *See also* P-mail advertising
Direct marketing, in green marketing, 631
Direct Marketing Association (DMA), 28 28
Direct-to-consumer (DTC) advertising, regulation of, 624
DirecTV, 388
Disaster(s), complete, 219
Discount(s), phantom, 518
Discounted cash flow (DCF), 190 190
Disinvesting, in advertising, 196–97
Disney-ABC Domestic Television Company, 378
Display(s), in influencing sales of discounted brands, 474t, 476
Display (banner) advertisements, on Internet, 398–99, 399t
Distribution, frequency, concept of, 325–26, 325t
Distribution methods, creative, 489–91, 491f
Diverting, 467t, 468
DKNY, 45
DMA. *See* Direct Marketing Association (DMA)
Doan's Pills, 623
Dodger Stadium, 447
Dogmatism, in Mac owners' psychographic profiles, 323
Dole, 523–24
Donnelly Marketing (ClusterPlus), 106
Don't Forget the Lyrics, 382t
Door-to-door sampling, 487
Dora the Explorer, 607
Dove, 135, 135f, 563
Dr Pepper, 83
Drifters, 113, 114
DTC advertising. *See* Direct-to-consumer (DTC) advertising
Dual-coding theory, 147
Dunkin' Donuts, 121, 136, 432, 437
DuPont, 45, 247
Duracell, 590
Dutch Boy paint, 87
DVDs, advertising by, 428
DVR. *See* Digital video recorder (DVR)

E

Eastman Kodak Company, 586, 585f
EasyShop, 574
"Eat My Dust," 424
eBay, 536
EBoost, 490
Ecology consciousness, in Mac owners' psychographic profiles, 323

Economically disadvantaged consumers, targeting of, 609–10
Economy, in radio advertising, 372t, 373
EDLP. *See* Everyday low pricing (EDLP)
Effective advertising
  CAN elements in, 209–10
  creation of, 208–19
Effective rating points (ERPs), 330–31
Effective reach
  concept of, 328–29
  planning for, 330–31, 331t
Effectiveness, of sales promotion ideas, evaluation of, 528, 528t
Efficiency
  of P-mail advertising, 426
  of sales promotion ideas, evaluation of, 527, 528t
Einstein's theory, 483
Elasticity
  advertising, 200, 200t
  defined, 197
  pricing, vs. advertising, 197–201, 200t
Electronic (digital) billboards, advertising on, 580
Element(s), mixing, 23–24, 25f
Elementary school-age children, targeting to, 111
Eligible reader, 290
E-mail, opt-in, vs. spam, 404–05
E-mail advertising, 403–09
  e-zines, 405–06
  opt-in e-mailing vs. spam, 404–05
  phishing, 405
  wireless, 406–07
E-mail magazines (e-zines), 405–06
eMarketer, 400
Emerging Issues Task Force, 452
Emotional appeal, in packaging, 85–86
Emotional creative style, 225, 226f
Emotional reactions, measurement of, 297–99
  galvanometer in, 299
  neuroscience and brain imaging in, 298
  physiological testing in, 298–99
  pupillometer in, 299
  self-report measurement in, 298
Emotionality, in advertising, 212
Empty-vessel philosophy, of brand naming, 77
Encoding, perceptual, 143
Encoding information, 246–47
Encoding specificity, 85
Encoding variability hypothesis, 174
Encouraging, by P-O-P advertising, 591
Endorsers, 240–78
  celebrity, 250–58
    attractiveness and, 256
    attributes of, 251–54, 251t
    audience matchup and, 254
    brand matchup and, 254–55
    cost considerations and, 256
    credibility and, 255–56
    Q scores and, 257–58
    saturation factor and, 256
    selection considerations, 254–57
    trouble factor and, 256–57
    working ease vs. difficulty factor and, 256
  introduction to, 242
Energizer, 83, 590–91
Entertainment
  branded, 432
  in TV advertising, 379, 379t
Environment, B2B, 6
Environmental issues, 626–32
  green marketing–related initiatives, 626–32. *See also* Green marketing
Environmental Media Association, 630
Environmentally friendly packaging, responses to, 628, 630
Environmentally sustainable consumption, in 14 countries, 626
Envy, 77
Epidemic(s), rules of, 552–53
Equal, 546, 604
EquiTrend survey, 48
Equity, brand, 34–49. *See also* Brand equity
Equity enhancement, of sales promotion ideas, evaluation of, 528t, 528–29
ERPs. *See* Effective rating points (ERPs)
ESGD. *See* Explosive self-generating demand (ESGD)
ESPN, 564
Estée Lauder, 384
Esuvee-H, media-scheduling software for, hypothetical illustration, 342t, 343–46, 344t
Ethic(s), defined, 606–07
Ethical core values, in Marcom, 617–18
Ethical issues, 606–18
  in advertising, 610–14
    AAAA code of ethical standards, 613–14
    bad taste, 612
    deceptiveness, 611
    manipulation, 611–12
    offensiveness, 612
    persuade people to buy things they do no really need, 613
    play on people's fears and insecurities, 613
    stereotypes, 612–13
    untruthfulness, 611
  in branding, 615
  in Marcom, 606–18
    fostering of, 617–18
    introduction to, 606–07
  in online marketing, 616
  in packaging, 615
  in public relations, 614
  in sales promotions, 615
  targeting-related, 607–10. *See also* Targeting
Ethnic populations
  demographic targeting to, 118–22, 118t, 119f, 120t
    African-Americans, 118t, 119, 119f
    Asian-Americans, 121–22
    Hispanic Americans (Latinos), 118t, 119–21, 120t
  population representation in U.S., 118–19, 118t
Event sponsorship, 563–67
  ambushing events in, 566
  creating customized events in, 565–66
  events selection for, factors in, 563–65
  in green marketing, programs for, 630
  measuring success in, 566–67
Everready, 589
Every Day with Rachel Ray, 486–87
Everyday low pricing (EDLP), 469–70
Evian, 539
Excedrin Migraine pills, 246, 246f
Excitement
  brand-related, 40
  in TV advertising, 379, 379t
Execution ease, of sales promotion ideas, evaluation of, 527, 528t
Executives(s), account, 194
Exemplar, defined, 247–48
Exemplar-based learning, 247–48, 249f
Exit fees, 466
Expectation(s), creating of, 158f, 160
Expenses. *See* Cost(s)
Experian (MOSAIC), 106
Experiencers, in VALS framework, 104f, 105
Experiential marketing programs, 18
Experiential needs, positioning-based, 133f, 134–36, 135f
Expertise, 251t, 252
Explosive self-generating demand (ESGD), 553–55
Exposure(s)
  defined, 141
  effective, number of, 329–30
  to information, in CPM, 141–42
Extreme Makeover: Home Edition, 382t, 521–22
E-zines, 405–06

F

Face value, 495
Facebook, 113, 114, 403
Fair trading, symbolism of certifying products in, 136
Familiar brands, 310, 398
Family Circus, 367
FASB. *See* Financial Accounting Standards Board (FASB)
Fashion, goal-oriented, 397
Fat Free Pringles, 492
FDA. *See* Food and Drug Administration (FDA)
Fear(s)
  advertising playing on, 613
  consumer, appeals to, 260–62
Fear appeal logic, 260
Feature analysis, 143
Federal agencies, regulation by, 620
Federal Aviation Administration, 78
Federal Bureau of Investigation, 406–07, 517
Federal Communications Commission, 374
Federal Trade Commission (FTC), 405, 608, 609
  price-off regulations by, 515–16
  regulation by, 620–24
Federal Trademark Dilution Act of 1995 73 73
Fee(s). *See* Cost(s)
FHM Comedy Fest, 481
Fiat Automobiles of Brazil, 454
Financial Accounting Standards Board (FASB), 452–53
Financial incentive, in trade promotion program, 462
Firestone tires, vehicle rollovers and, 540
Firestone/Ford Explorer, 542–43
First exposure, powerful, 336
First Flavor, 487
Fishful Thinking, 235, 235f
Flat-screen, plasma TVs, 65
Flexibility
  in newspaper advertising, 362, 362t

of P-mail advertising, 426
Flighting schedule, 334–35
fMRI. *See* Functional magnetic resonance imaging (fMRI)
Food and beverage products, targeting of, to children and teens, 607–08
Food and Drug Administration (FDA), 70, 541, 546, 611, 620–24, 623
Foot Locker, 444–45, 444f
Football stadium's cup holders, as advertising medium, 437, 437f
Forbes, 6
Ford Explorer, 540, 542–43
Ford F-150 truck, 434
Ford Five Hundred, 60
Ford Motor Company, 32, 119, 185, 186t, 433, 512
Ford Taurus, 60
Ford Truck, 562
Forrester Research, 397
Fortune, 6
Forward buying, 467–68, 467t
Fractionalization, audience
  in radio advertising, 372t, 374
  in TV advertising, 379t, 380
Frail Recluses, 117
Framing, verbal, 247
Fraud
  click, 412–13
  rebate, 518, 520
Free eats, 447
Free-gift-with-purchase premiums, 511
Free-standing inserts (FSIs), 494–97, 499, 524
Free-standing signs, 576–77, 577f
Free-with-purchase premiums, 511
Frequency
  defined, 326
  described, 324
  in media planning, 324–26, 325t
Frequency distribution, concept of, 325–26, 325t
Frequency value planning, 331–33, 332t
Frequent-shopper program, 525, 525f
Freschetta pizza, 525
Fresh Step, 259, 259f
Fringe time, in TV advertising, 375
Frito-Lay, 498
Frito-Lay copy tests, evidence from, 305–06, 306t
Frozen Coke, 616–17
Fruit Tree Planting Foundation, 630
Fruit$_2$O, 62, 63f
FSIs. *See* Free-standing inserts (FSIs)
FTC. *See* Federal Trade Commission (FTC)
Full-service advertising agencies, 193–94
Functional magnetic resonance imaging (fMRI), 298
Functional needs, positioning-based, 133f, 134, 134f
Fundamental decisions, 20

G

Galvanic skin response (GSR), 299
Galvanometer, 299
Game(s), promotional, 516–17
Gatorade, 83
GE. *See* General Electric (GE)
Geico, 154, 437
Gen Xers, targeting to, 113–14
General Electric (GE), 6, 108, 630
General Mills, 80, 86–87, 188, 408, 490, 499, 500, 564, 569, 608
General Motors (GM), 119, 185, 186t, 235, 319, 402, 494, 518, 519f
Generation X (Gen Xers), targeting to, 113–14
Generation Y, 112
Generic creative style, 225–26
Gentlemen's Quarterly (GQ), 366
Geodemographic(s), 98, 99f
Geodemographic targeting, 106–07
Georgetown University, 608
Georgia-Pacific, 569
Gerber, 513–14
Gerber Keepsake Millennium Corp., 513–14
"Gerber Myth," 544
Gerber Products, 426
Gestalt, 247, 247f
GfK Custom Research North America, 289–93, 291f
Gillette, 70–71
Gillette Sensor razor, 223
Glad products, 460
Glad trash bags, 437
GlaxoSmithKline, 185, 186t
Glen Moray, 423
Glenmorangie Distillery, 423
Global Fund to Fight AIDS, Tuberculosis and Malaria, 567–68
Global marketers' advertisement spending, 167
GM. *See* General Motors (GM)
Goal-oriented fashion, 397
Go-Gurt yogurt, 86–87
Goldfish, 235
Golf, 170
Golf Digest, 364–65, 364f
Goody's, 525
Google, 402, 404, 410–12
"Got Milk?", 264, 264f
GQ, 366
Grease, 269
Great Pyramids, 83
Green advertising, 628, 628f–30f
Green Guides, 631–32
Green marketing
  CRM in, 630
  defined, 626
  direct marketing efforts in, 631
  environmentally friendly packaging responses, 628, 630
  event-oriented sponsorship programs in, 630
  guidelines for, 631–32
  initiatives for, 626–32
  outdoor advertising in, responses to, 631
  P-O-P programs in, 630–31
  seal-of-approval programs in, 630
Green Seal, 630
Greendex score, 627
GreenWise, 75
Grey Poupon, 432
Gross rating points (GRPs), 307–08, 326–28
GRPs. *See* Gross rating points (GRPs)
GSR. *See* Galvanic skin response (GSR)
Gucci, "Gucci Kangaroo" legend, 432, 543
Guilt, consumer, appeals to, 262
Guinness beer, in Africa, 217
Guinness Import Company, 490

H

Hall of Fame baseball players, 514
Hamburger Helper, of General Mills, 564
Hanes Smooth Illusions, 226
Hanger Network, 15
Harley-Davidson, 54, 115
Harris Interactive, 48
Hartz Ultra Guard, 518, 519f, 256
"Hassle factor," in celebrity endorsement, 256
Health and Human Services, 610
Healthy Choice, 73
Healthy Hermits, 117
Heathrow's Terminal Five, 578
Hedonic, experiential model (HEM), 140, 141f, 147–49, 148f
Hedonic needs, appeals to, 243f, 244–45, 244f
Hedonism
  defined, 229, 229t
  example of, 231, 232f
Heileman Brewing Company, 610
Heineken, 437
Heinz, 85–86, 245, 245f, 526
Hellmann's, 250, 250f, 400
HEM. *See* Hedonic, experiential model (HEM)
Hershey Foods Corporation, 15
Hershey's Kisses, 15
Hershey's Syrup, 521
Hewlett-Packard (HP), 75, 206, 350, 472
Hidden Valley Ranch, 248, 249f
Hispanic Americans (Latinos), demographic targeting to, 118t, 119–21, 120t
H.J. Heinz Company, 564, 569
Holiday Inn's Priority Club program, 522
Home Depot, 231, 233f
Honda Accord, 60, 130
Honda Motor Company, 130, 216–17, 516–17
Hoover, 384
Horizontal lines, in packaging, 83
Hormel Foods, 472–73
Hot Wheels, 111
Hotspots
  defined, 406
  locating of, 406
HP. *See* Hewlett-Packard (HP)
Huggies (diapers), 73
Human adaptation, 245
Hummer, 68, 553
Hummer Alpha, 231, 233, 233f
Humor, in advertising, 280
  role of, 258–60, 259f
  TV, 379, 379t
Hybrid automobiles, 65
Hypothesis(es)
  encoding variability, 174
  three-exposure, 329–30

I

I Can't Believe It's Not Butter (margarine), 73
I Can't Believe It's Not Chicken (a faux-chicken soy-based product), 73
IAB. *See* Internet Advertising Bureau (IAB)
Identification, process of, 251t, 252–53
IHG. *See* InterContinental Hotels Group (IHG)
Ill-structured problem, 23

Illustrative calculations, in media planning, 339–40
iMac, 67–68
Image(s)
brand, 37f, 39–41
corporate, advertising and, 234–35, 235f
Image matchup, in event sponsorship, 563
Image reinforcement purposes, 484
Imagery
usage, 137, 139f
user, 137, 139f
IMC. *See* Integrated marketing communications (IMC)
Implementation decisions, 20, 23–26, 25f
IMRA. *See* Incentive Manufacturers and Representatives Alliance (IMRA)
IMUs. *See* Internet marketing units (IMUs)
"In Search of Real Food," 400
Incentive(s)
defined, 446
financial, in trade promotion program, 462
Incentive Manufacturers and Representatives Alliance (IMRA), 28
Individualization, of Internet, 394–95
Infiniti, 425
Influence, WOM, 546–49. *See also* Word-of-mouth (WOM) influence
Influencing, advertising for, 188–89
Infomercials, 383–84
Information
encoding of, opportunity for, 246–47
exposure to, in CPM, 141–42
in packaging, 85
stored, retention and search/retrieval of, 145–47, 146f, 147f
Information dissemination, Marcom in, 547
Information regulation, 623
Information Resources, Inc. (IRI), BehaviorScan of, 303–04, 306, 307
Informational needs, appeals to, 243f, 244–45, 244f
Informing, by advertising, 188
P-O-P, 588–90
Ingenuity, defined, 420, 421
Ingredient branding, 45
In-house advertising operation, 192
Innovator(s), in VLAS framework, 104, 104f
In-pack coupons, 499–500
In-pack premiums, 512
Insecurities, advertising playing on, 613
Insert(s), free-standing, 494–97, 499, 524
Instantly redeemable coupons (IRCs), 496–97
In-store advertising, audience for, measuring of, 598
In-store decision making
brand lift and, 594, 594t
evidence of, 591–94, 592t–94t
factors influencing, 593–94
POPAI Consumer Buying Habits Study of, 591–94, 592t–94t
In-store sampling, 488
In-store TV, growth of, 589
Integrated marketing communications (IMC), 3–31. *See also* Marketing communications (Marcom)
defined, 10
examples of, 6
features of, 10–20, 10t
build relationships rather than engage in flings, 10t, 17–18
consumer/business consumer representing starting point for all marketing communications activities, 10–13, 10t
focus on ultimate objective, 10t, 18–19
multiple messages must speak with single voice, 10t, 16–17
obstacles to implementing, 20
360-degree branding, 14–16
touch points, 14–16
use all tools available, 10t, 13–16
introduction to, 6–7
overview of, 4–31
reduced dependence on mass media in, 11–13
skeptics of, 9
synergy and, 9–10
Integrity, in Marcom, fostering of, 617
Intense cues, use of, 245, 245f, 246f
Intensity, appropriate, 260–61
Interactive advertising, 395
Interactivity, of Internet, 394–95
Interbrand's Top 20 Global Brands, 2007, 49, 49t
InterContinental Hotels Group (IHG), 522
Interference, competitive, role of, 174–75
Internalization, process of, 251t, 252
International Advertising Awards, in London, 209
International Data, 502
Internet, 534. *See also* Internet advertising
as advertising medium, 394
compared with other ad media, 395–96
individualization of, 394–95
interactivity of, 394–95
interstitials on, 400
introduction to, 394–97, 396t
pop-up ads on, 399–400
superstitials on, 400
Webisodes on, 400, 401
Internet advertising, 392–419. *See also* specific types, e.g., E-mail advertising
behavioral targeting in, 413–14
blogs in, 402
display (banner) ads, 398–99, 399t
effectiveness of, measuring of, 414–15
e-mail advertising, 403–09
formats, 396–97, 396t
introduction to, 394–97, 396t
measuring performance of, metrics for, 414–15
mobile phones in, 407–09
podcasts in, 402–03
rich media on, 399–400
search engine, 409–13, 411f. *See also* Search engine advertising (SEA)
social networks in, 403
on Web sites, 397–98
Internet Advertising Bureau (IAB), 28, 399
Internet marketing units (IMUs), types and sizes of, 399, 399t
Internet sampling, 488
Interpersonal relationships, social networks of, 547
Interpretation, 143
Interpreter, 129
Interstitial(s), on Internet, 400
Intimacy, in radio advertising, 372–73, 372t
Intrusion value, in TV advertising, 379, 379t
Investing, in advertising, 196
Investment(s)
marketing, return on, 50, 52
returns on, 165
Involuntary attention, 245, 245f, 246f
iPhone, 521, 554
iPod, 66, 73, 217, 511, 523, 524f
Ipsos-ASI, Next*TV Method, 296–97, 300
IRCs. *See* Instantly redeemable coupons (IRCs)
IRI. *See* Information Resources, Inc. (IRI)
iTunes, 523, 524f

J

Jack Daniel's, 562
Japanese billboard, humans playing soccer on, 582, 582f
JELL-O pudding, 14–15
JetBlue, 73, 78, 79, 550
Jetta, 170
Jif (peanut butter), 83
Jimmy Neutron, 607
J&J. *See* Johnson & Johnson (J&J)
John Deere, 68
Johnson & Johnson (J&J), 185, 186t, 248, 401, 541–42
Jose Cuervo Especial tequila, 290, 293, 299
JP Morgan Chase, 226
Junkyard Wars, 182
Juvenile Diabetes Research Foundation, 569

K

Kaplan Thaler Group, 214–15
Kellogg Co., 82, 188, 511, 512, 589
Kelly's Roast Beef, 508–09
Kentucky Derby, 552, 553, 564–65
Kentucky Fried Chicken (KFC), 488, 534, 534f, 544, 566
Keyword(s)
defined, 410
in increasing odds that ready consumers encounter your ad, 410, 411f
Keyword search, 410–11
Keyword-matching advertising, 411
KFC/Taco Bell restaurants, 535
Kia Sorento, 290, 291f
Kibbles 'n Bits, 565–66
Kidon Media-Link, 318
Kimberly-Clark, 409, 500, 597
KitchenAid, 568–69, 569f
Kmart, 544, 591
Knowledge structures, 145
accessing of, ability for, 247
creation of, ability for, 247–50, 249f, 250f
described, 247
KOA Kampground, 489
Kodak, 82, 350, 384, 585, 586f
Kool-Aid, 472
Kraft Foods, 62, 319, 426, 464–66, 492, 621–22
Kroger, 500, 589
K-Swiss, 38
KFC. *See* Kentucky Fried Chicken (KFC)

Ku Klux Klan connections, 545
Kuchikomi, 554

L

Label information, in advertising, 615
Labeling, product, regulations for, 623
Labels for Education program, 569
Labor-based fee system, 195
Laddering, 233–34
  defined, 233
Lamar Advertising, 631
Land Rover, 68
Landor Associates, 78, 79
Latinos, demographic targeting to, 118t, 119–21, 120t
Laundry hanger, as advertising touch point, 15
Law and Order, 382t
Law of inverse demand, 198
Law of the few, in buzz creation, 552
Lead times
  in magazine advertising, 366t, 367
  short, in radio advertising, 372t, 373
Learning
  exemplar-based, 247–48, 249f
  types of, 145–46, 147f
Lee jeans, 550
Lenovo, Inc., 625
Lever Brothers, 493
Leverage point, creative strategy and, 230t
Leveraging, brand equity via, 42–46, 44f
Levi Strauss & Co., 45, 437
Levi Strauss Dockers, 9–10
Lexicon Branding, Inc., 72
Lexus, 425
Lexus Magazine, 371
LG cell phone, 46
LG's VX series, 73
Lifetime-value analysis, 429–31, 429t
Limited processing capacity, 145
Linkage(s), strengthening of, 145–46, 147f
Lions International Advertising Festival, in Cannes, France, 209
Lipton Ice brand, 268
Liquid-Plumr, 73
Listerine PocketPaks, 88
Little Debbie, 512
Liveamatics, 283
L.L. Bean, 427–28
Local personalities, in radio advertising, 372t, 373
Logic, fear appeal, 260
Logo(s), 79–80
  role of, 79–80, 79f, 80f
  updating of, 80, 81f
"LOHAS" consumers, 136
Longevity, in magazine advertising, 366, 366t
Long-term asset, 429
Long-term memory (LTM), 145 145
L'Oreal's Absolute, 115, 116
Los Angeles Dodgers baseball organization, 447
Lost, 382t
Louis Vuitton, 432
Loyalty
  brand
    accomplishing, 158f, 161
    reduced, budgetary allocations related to, 451
  customer, 371
Loyalty programs, 17–18
LTM. *See* Long-term memory (LTM)
Lucent Technologies, 77, 78
Lycra, 45

M

Mac computers, owners of, personalities of, 323
"Mac versus PC" advertising campaign, 323
MacIntosh, 206, 207
Macy's Thanksgiving Day Parade, 352
Mad TV, 14
MADD, 586, 586f
Magazine(s), 363–71, 364f, 365f, 366t, 369t
  buying space in, 363–66, 364f, 365f
  customized, 371
  e-mail, 405–06
  sampling by, 486–87
Magazine advertising, 363–71, 364f, 365f, 366t, 369t
  audience measurement for, 367–68
  limitations of, 366t, 367
  strengths of, 366–67, 366t
Magellan RoadMate GPS unit, 520, 520f
Mail, postal, direct advertising via, 421–31, 421t, 428t. *See also* Direct advertising, via postal mail; P-mail advertising
Mail-delivered coupons, 498–99
Mail-in offers, 511–12, 512f
Major League Soccer, 564
Maker(s), in VALS framework, 104f, 105
Management, advertising, overview of, 180–202. *See also* Advertising management
Management supervisors, 194
Manager(s)
  account, 194
  role in advertising, 199–200
Manchurian Candidate, 612
Mantra, defined, 22
Manufacturer(s), P-O-P advertising benefits for, 587
Marcom. *See* Integrated marketing communications (IMC); Marketing communications (Marcom)
Marea, 454
Market(s), share of, 200–201, 200t
Marketing
  account-specific, 472–73
  audiovisual, 427–28
  B2B, on Internet, 394
  B2C, 6
    on Internet, 394, 397
  catalog, 427–28
  cause-related, 567–71, 630. *See also* Cause-related marketing (CRM)
  database, 428–31, 429t
    data mining in, 431
    lifetime-value analysis in, 429–31, 429t
  direct, in green marketing, 631
  online, ethical issues in, 616
  sponsorship, 560–73. *See also* Sponsorship(s); Sponsorship marketing
Marketing communications (Marcom). *See also* Integrated marketing communications (IMC)
  brand adoption and, 62–71. *See also* Brand adoption
  challenges facing, 32–58. *See also* specific challenge topics, e.g., Brand equity
    accountability, 50–55
    behavior effects, 50–55
    brand equity enhancement, 34–49
  decision-making process in, 20–27, 21f, 25f
  effectiveness of, measurement of
    calibrating specific effects in, 53
    collecting accurate data in, 52
    difficulty in, 51–53
    gaining agreement in, 52
    metrics in, 51–52
    MMM in, 53–55
  effects of, hierarchy of, 157–62, 158f, 159f
  elements of, 7–8, 7t
  environmental, 626–32. *See also* Green marketing
  ethical issues in, 606–18. *See also* Ethical issues
  evaluation of, 27
  implementation decisions, 23–26, 25f
  information-dissemination ball rolling by, 547–48
  integrated, 3–31. *See also* Integrated marketing communications (IMC)
  integration of, 8–10
    reasons for, 8–9
  objectives of, 156–66
    setting of, 156–66. *See also* Objective setting
  outcomes of, 26–27
  regulation of, 618–26. *See also* Regulation of Marcom
  tools of, 7–8, 7t
  types of, 7
Marketing communications decisions
  fundamental, 21–23
  targeting, 21–22
Marketing evaluations, 257–58
Marketing investment, return on, 50, 52
Marketing mistakes, 218
Marketing mix modeling (MMM), in determining Marcom effectiveness, 53–55
Marketing programs, experiential, 18
Marketing public relations (MPR), 534–59
  crisis management by, 542–43
  defined, 536
  described, 537
  introduction to, 536–37
  proactive, 537–38, 539f
  reactive, 538–42, 540f
  rumors and, 543–45
  urban legends, 543–456
  vs. advertising, 536–37
Marketing strategy, 320
Marketing Violent Entertainment in Children, 609
Marlboro, 224, 472
Mars, Inc., 16–17
Martha Stewart brand, 35
Marvel, 437

Mass audience coverage, 362, 362t
Mass market, splintering of, budgetary allocations related to, 451–52
Mass media, reduced dependence on, 11–13
Mass media advertising, 11, 358–91
Master Settlement Agreement, 610
MasterCard, 14
Material representation, 621–22
Mattel, Inc., 111, 403
  lead paint and, 539
Mature consumers, targeting to, 116–17
Maxima, 226
Maxwell House coffee, 493, 494f
Mazola, 82
McCann Worldgroup, 12
McDonald's, 35–36, 36t, 39, 121, 126, 136, 360, 488, 517, 544
McKinsey & Company, 551, 553
McNeil Nutritionals, 604
MeadWestvaco Corporation, 137
Meaning
  brand, in consumers' memories, 131
  contextual, V8 advertisements advertising, 130, 131f
  creative, 128–31, 129f, 131f
  defined, 129
  meaning of, 129
Meaning transfer, 44, 129–31, 131f
Means-end chains, 228–33
  advertising applications of, 230–33, 230t, 231f–33f
  identifying of, 233–34
    practical issues in, 234
Measurability, of P-mail advertising, 425–26
Measurement(s), self-report, of emotional responses, 298
MECCAS Model, of advertising, 230–33, 230t, 231f–33f
Media. *See also* Advertising media
  advertising, 316–59, 420–40, 422t
  alternative, potpourri of, 436–38, 437f
  commissions from, 194–95
  defined, 24
  described, 318
  mass
    advertising by, 11, 358–91
    reduced dependence on, 11–13
  messages and, 318–19
  objectives of, specifying of, 322–31
  "other," 420–41
  reduced effectiveness of, budgetary allocations related to, 452
  rich, on Internet, 399–400
  selection of, 24, 319–20
Media planners, 194
Media planning
  brand choice influencing in, 336–37
  continuity in, 33–35, 335f
  cost considerations in, 339–40
  described, 320
  Diet Dr Pepper plan, 49t, 346–47, 348t
  first exposure in, 336
  frequency in, 324–26, 325t
  illstrative calculations in, 339–40
  Olympus camera plan, 350, 352–54, 353t
  optimizing weekly reach in, 337
  process of, 320–21, 321f
  reach in, 322–24
  recency planning, 335–38
  Saab 9-5's plan, 348–50, 351t
  shelf-space model, 335–38
  software for, 341–46, 342t, 344t
  specifying media objectives in, 322–31
  target audience in, 321–22
  toward reconciliation in, 338
  trade-offs in, necessity of making, 340–41
  weight, 326–33, 331t, 332t
Media self-regulation, 624–25
Media services, 194
Media Sexploitation, 265
Media strategy, 321, 321f
Media weight, creative content and, relationship between, 309–10
MediaCart Holdings, 574
Media-delivered coupons, 498–99
Mediamark Research, Inc. (MRI), 414, 365, 368–71, 369t
Media-neutral approach, 12–13
Media-scheduling software, 341–46, 342t, 344t
Memory
  elements of, 145
  long-term, 145
  short-term, 145
  working, 145
Memory organization packets, 145
Mentadent, 37
Mental associations, 39
  described, 36–37
Menu brands, rat poisoning and, 539
Mercedes, 425
Mercedes Benz, 142
Merchandising space, on- and off-shelf, sales promotions in increasing, 455–56
Merck & Co., 540, 614
Merisant Company, 604
Message(s), 206–39. *See also* Advertising messages, effective and creative
  attention to, motivation in, 243f–46f, 244–46. *See also* Motivation, to attend to messages
  creating of, 24
  effectiveness of, measuring of, 280–315
    recognition and recall in, 289–97
  novel, 245, 245f
  posttesting of, 284
  pretesting of, 284
  processing of, motivation in, 246, 247f
  sky, 437
  subliminal, 264–67. *See also* Subliminal messages
Message appeals, 240–78. *See also* Appeals
Message endorsers, 240–78. *See also* Endorsers
Message research
  background of, 282
  forms of, 286–88, 289t
  industry standards for, 284–86
  lessons learned from, for brand managers and ad agencies, 286
  qualitative, 287
  quantitative, 287–88, 289t
  reasons for, 283
Message-driven approach, in brand equity enhancement, 42
Metric(s), in determining Marcom effectiveness, 51–52
Metrics
  CPA, 415
  defined, 414
  for measuring Internet advertising performance, 414–15
MGA Entertainment, Inc., 403
Michelin tires, 261, 511
Microsoft, 71–72, 75, 574
  Halo2 game of, 549–50, 549f
Middle-aged consumers, targeting to, 114–16, 115f
Millennial Generation, 112
Miller beer, 201
Miller Brewing Company, 160, 608
Miller Genuine Draft, 172t
Miller High Life, 172t
Miller Lite, 160, 165–66, 172t, 264
Mindset Media, 323
Mini Cooper, 553
Minute Maid juice, 525
Miscomprehension, 144
Misleading omission, defined, 620
Misredeemer(s), professional, 501f, 502
Misredemption, coupon, 501–03, 501f
Misrepresentation, defined, 620
Miss Clairol campaign, 213–14
MMA. *See* Mobile Marketing Association (MMA)
MMM. *See* Marketing mix modeling (MMM)
MMS. *See* Multimedia Messaging Service (MMS)
M&M's, 512
MOA (motivation, opportunity, and ability) factors, 243–44, 243f
Mobile Campus, 408
Mobile Marketing Association (MMA), 28
Mobile phones, Internet advertising on, 407–09
Mobium Creative Group, 139
Modern Marvels, 182
Molson, 18
Molson Ice, 608
Momentum
  defined, 26
  establishing of, 26
Monday Night Football promotion, by Beatrice Company, 517
Money, street, 464–66
Moneytalk, 520
Motion, use of, 245–46, 246f
Motion displays, 588
Motivation
  to attend to messages, 243f–46f, 244–46
    appeals to informational and hedonic needs, 243f, 244–45, 244f
    intense or prominent cues, 245, 245f, 246f
    motion, 245–46, 246f
    novel stimuli, 245, 245f
  enhancement of, in processing advertisements, 242–50
  opportunity, and ability (MOA) factors, 243–44, 243f
  to process messages, 246, 247f
Motivational Response Method (MRM), 299
Motorola, 46, 73, 77
Motrin IB, 521–22
Mott's, 121
Mountain Dew, 8, 544, 563
Movies, direct advertising in, 432–33
MPR. *See* Marketing public relations (MPR)
Mr. Clean Magic Eraser, 66, 66f
MRI. *See* Mediamark Research, Inc. (MRI)
MRM. *See* Motivational Response Method (MRM)

Mrs. Paul's fish fillets, 525
MSN Search, mtvU Campus Invasion Tour, 410, 481
Multimedia Messaging Service (MMS), 407
Music, in advertising, 280
functions of, 267–69
Music enthusiasts, in Mac owners' psychographic profiles, 323
MySpace, 113, 403, 538
Mythbusters, 382

N

1998 Nagano Olympic Games, 586, 586f
NAB. *See* Newspaper Advertising Bureau (NAB)
Nabisco, 16–17, 514, 569
NAD. *See* National Advertising Division (NAD)
Naming, brand, 71–80. *See also* Brand naming
NARB. *See* National Advertising Review Board (NARB)
Narrowcasting, 378
NASCAR (National Association for Stock Car Auto Racing), 560–64
National Advertising Division (NAD), 604
of Council of Better Business Bureau, in self-regulation, 625
National Advertising Review Board (NARB), in self-regulation, 625
National Advertising Review Council (NARC), in self-regulation, 625–26
National Association for Stock Car Auto Racing (NASCAR), 560–64
National Basketball Association (NBA), 254
National Collegiate Athletic Association (NCAA) March Madness basketball tourney, 438
National Football League (NFL), 517, 564
National Geographic, 368, 627
National Merit Semifinalists, 447
Nations Brand Index (NBI), 47
Natural Light, 172t
Natural searches, 410
Nazi connections, 545
NBA. *See* National Basketball Association (NBA)
NBI. *See* Nations Brand Index (NBI)
Near-pack premiums, 512
Need(s). *See also* specific needs, e.g., Symbolic needs experiential, positioning-based, 133f, 134–36, 135f
hedonic, appeals to, 243f, 244–45, 244f
informational, appeals to, 243f, 244–45, 245f
positioning-based, 133f–35f, 134–36
symbolic, positioning-based, 133f, 134
Neosporin, 233
Nescafé, 404
Nestle, 402–03, 511
Net present value (NPV), 429–30, 429t
Network(s), social, of interpersonal relationships, 547
Network TV advertising, 376t, 377
Neuromarketing, 43
Neuroscience, brain imaging and, 298
Neutrogena, 625–26
"New Air," 78
New Balance, 38
New Beetle automobiles, 511
New brands. *See* Brand(s), new
"New York City tough," 437
New York Post, 503
News Corp., SmartSource of, 494
Newspaper(s), 360–63, 362t
buying space in, 361
percentage of households reading, 360
percentage of households receiving, 360
sampling by, 486–87
Newspaper advertising, 360–63, 362t
buying space, 361
limitations of, 362–63, 362t
local, 360
strengths of, 362, 362t
Newspaper Advertising Bureau (NAB), 360
NFL. *See* National Football League (NFL)
Nielsen, new challenger to, 387–88
Nielsen BuzzMetrics, 402, 534
Nielsen Cinema, 436
Nielsen GamePlay Metrics, 436
Nielsen Media Research, 385, 436, 584, 589
Nielsen Personal Outdoor Devices (Npods), 584
Nielsen's Diary Panels, 386–87
Nielsen's local people meters, 387
Nielsen's people meter(s), 414
Nielsen's People Meter technology, 385–86, 386f
Nightline, 541
Nike, 11–12, 38, 68–69, 216, 444–45, 566, 626
Nikon, 350
Nintendo, 66
Nissan, 226
Nissan Altima Coupe, 148–49, 148f
Nivea, 490
"No Tears" approach, to endorser selection, 254–57
Nokia, 46
Non-wasted weight, 328
Nordstrom, 410
Northwest Airlines, 73
Novartis Corporation, 623
Novel messages, 245, 245f
Novelty, in advertising, 210
Now What? campaign, 4
Npods, 584
NPV. *See* Net present value (NPV)
NutraSweet, 546, 604
NyQuil, 269, 270f, 271, 480
NyQuil Cold & Flu medicine, 247, 247f

O

Objective(s)
behavior-affecting, 18–19
brand management, 483–84, 485t
communication, 164
focusing on, 18–19
pre-sales, 164
repeat-purchase, 484
setting of, 22, 154–66. *See also* Objective setting
Objective setting, 154–66
accomplishing brand loyalty, 158f, 161
accountability perspective, 165–66
advancing consumers from unawareness to awareness, 158, 158f
affordability method, 175
creating expectation, 158f, 160
criteria for, 162–63, 162f
encouraging trial purchases, 158f, 160–61
forming beliefs and attitudes, 158f, 161
heretical view, 164–65, 165f
in hierarchy of Marcom effects, 157–62, 158f, 159f
introduction to, 156
objective-and-task method, 170–71
reinforcing beliefs and attitudes, 158f, 161
requirements for, 162–63, 162f
stated in terms of sales, 164–66, 165f
traditional view, 164
Objective-and-task budgeting, 170–71
Observability, in facilitating brand adoption, 68–69
Ocean Foundation, 630
Odor-fighting products, 114
Offensive advertising, 612
Offer(s), mail-in, 511–12, 512f
Off-invoice allowances, 462–63
diverting due to, 467t, 468
foward buying due to, 466–67, 467t
retailers blamed for, 468
undesirable consequences of, 466–68, 467t
Oil of Olay, 139–40
Old Navy, 564
Olympia beer, 588
Olympic Games, 562, 566
Olympus camera media plan, 350, 352–54, 353t
Omission(s), misleading, defined, 620
On- or in-pack sampling, 487
100% Recycled Paperboard Alliance, 630
Online behavioral targeting, 100
Online contests, 522
Online couponing, 500
Online gaming community, profile of, 435
Online marketing, ethical issues in, 616
Online promotion agencies, 503
Online sweeps, 522
Online video advertisements, 400
On-pack coupons, 499–500
On-pack premiums, 512
On-premise sign(s)
ABCs of, 577, 577f
types of, 576–77, 577f
On-premise signage, 576–78, 577f
expert assistance related to, 577–78
OOH. *See* Out of home (OOH)
OOH advertising, 578–85. *See also* Out-of-home (OOH) advertising
Openness, in Mac owners' psychographic profiles, 323
Opinion leader(s), defined, 548
Opportunity(ies), enhancement of, in processing advertisements, 242–50
Opportunity to see (OTS), 329–33
Oprah's Big Give, 382t
Opt-in e-mailing, vs. spam, 404–05
Orbit White Melon Breeze, 245, 245f
Oreos, in China, 492
Orientation, value, 230, 230t
"Other" media, 420–41
OTS. *See* Opportunity to see (OTS)
Oust air sanitizer, 512
Outcome- or performance-based programs, 195
Outdoor advertising, in green marketing, 631
Outdoor Advertising Association of America, 578
Outhouse Springs, 584–85

Out-of-home (OOH) advertising, 352–53, 578–85
billboard ads, 578–84. *See also* Billboard advertising
described, 578
transit advertising, 585, 585f, 586f
Overlay programs, 523
Overlay promotions, 523

P

Pace, in advertising, 280
Packaging, 81–89
color in, 82–83
defined, 81
design and shape cues in, 83
designing of, 88–89, 88f
conduct product category analysis in, 88f, 89
determine communication priorities in, 88f, 89
identify silent brand attributes or benefits in, 88f, 89
perform competitive analysis in, 88f, 89
specify brand-positioning objectives in, 88–89
ethical issues in, 615
evaluation of
emotional appeal in, 85–86
information in, 85
VIEW model, 84–87, 85f, 86f
visibility in, 84, 85f
workability in, 86–87, 86f
expressions related to, 81
graphics for, 615
physical materials in, 84
requirements for, 87
size of, 83–84
structure of, 81–84
unsafe, 615
PACT. *See* Positioning Advertising Copy Testing (PACT)
Palm, 536
Palomar Medical Technologies, Inc., 70
Pampers diapers, 491
Paper diaries, of TV viewing behavior, 387
Parker Hannifin, 182
Parmalat brand, 67
Pay-for-performance programs, 470–72
"Paying attention," in CPM, 475, 142–43
Pedigree, 569
Pennzoil, 82
People, 352, 487
People, leveraging associations from, 44f, 45
People for the Ethical Treatment of Animals (PETA), 552
Pepsi Challenge, 43
Pepsi Creative Challenge contest, 12
PepsiCo, 12, 41–43, 48, 100, 121, 188, 267, 269, 432, 472, 517, 540, 564, 566, 628
syringes in, hoax, 541
Pepsodent, 37
Percentage-of-sales budgeting, 169–70
Perception, 143
selective, 143, 143f
Perceptual encoding, 143
Perceptual field, 129
Perrier, 539
contaminated with benzene, 541
Personality(ies)
local, in radio advertising, 372t, 373
matching products to, 323
Personality dimensions, brand-related, 40–41
Persuasion, measures of, 299–302, 301t
ARS method of, 300–02
IpSOS-ASI Next*TV Method, 296–97, 300
Pesticide(s), 540
PETA (People for the Ethical Treatment of Animals), 552
Pfizer, Inc., 88
P&G. *See* Proctor & Gamble (P&G)
Phantom discounts, 518
Philadelphia Extra Light cream cheese, 147
Philadelphia Tribune, 521, 521f
Philips Lighting, 457
Phishing, 405
Phone(s), mobile
advertising on, in India, 408
Internet advertising on, 407–09
LG, 46
Phone cards, 514–15
Phony UPC symbols, 520
Photomatics, 283
Photosmart, 472
Physical attractiveness, 251t, 252–53
Physiological testing, of emotional responses, 298–99
Picnic, 265
Pillsbury, 521
Pine-Sol, 625
Pioneer, 384
Pioneering Research for In-Store Metric (PRISM), on measuring effectiveness of in-store advertising media, 598
Pirates of the Caribbean, 508
"Pity to Waste It," 423
Pizza Hut food chain, 17
Place(s), leveraging associations from, 44f, 46, 47
Planner(s), media, 194
Planning
account, 219
frequency value, 331–33, 332t
media. *See* Media planning
reach, effective, 330–31, 331t
recency, 335–38
Playboys, 113
PlayStation, 536
PMA. *See* Promotion Marketing Association (PMA)
P-mail, defined, 422
P-mail advertising, 422–31, 422t, 429t
accountability of, 426
audiovisual advertising, 428
catalog marketing, 427–28
data mining in, 431
database marketing, 428–31, 429t
efficiency of, 426
features of, 425–26
flexibility of, 426
functions of, 426–27
lifetime-value analysis in, 429–31, 429t
measurability of, 425–26
successful campaigns with, illustrations of, 423–25
targetability of, 425
users of, 426–27
widespread use of, factors accounting for, 423
Podcast(s), 402–03
Podcasting, 402–03
PodNova, 402
Point-of-purchase (P-O-P) advertising, 586–98
accomplishments with, 587–88
couponing in, 496–98
display effectiveness in
Benylin study, 596
evidence of, 595–97, 595t
POPAI/Kmart/P&G study, 595–96, 595t
POPAI/Warner-Lambert Listerine study, 596–97
POPAI/Warner-Lambert studies, 596–97
influence on consumer behavior, 588–91
informing, 588–90
reminding, 590–91
in-store decision making, 591–94, 592t–94t
materials for, 586–87, 587f, 588f
materials in, use and nonuse of, 597–98
Point-of-Purchase Advertising International (POPAI), 29, 591–94, 592t–94t
Consumer Buying Habits Study of, 591–94, 592t–94t
Point-of-purchase (P-O-P) communications, 574–99. *See also* specific types, e.g., Out-of-home (OOH) advertising
billboard advertising, 578–84
introduction to, 576
on-premise signage, 576–78, 577f
OOH advertising, 578–85
Point-of-purchase couponing, 496–98
Point-of-purchase (P-O-P) programs, in green marketing, 630–31
Poisoning, cyanide, Tylenol and, 541–42
Pontiac G6, 550–52, 551f
Pony, 432
P-O-P advertising, 586–98. *See also* Point-of-purchase (P-O-P) advertising
P-O-P communications, 574–99. *See also* Point-of-purchase (P-O-P) communications
P-O-P materials, use and nonuse of, 597
P-O-P programs, in green marketing, 630–31
Pop Rocks, 544
POPAI. *See* Point-of-Purchase Advertising International (POPAI)
POPAI Consumer Buying Habits Study, 591–94, 592t–94t
POPAI/Kmart/P&G study, of display effectiveness, 595–96, 595t
POPAI/Warner-Lambert Listerine study, of display effectiveness, 596–97
POPAI/Warner-Lambert studies, of display effectiveness, 596–97
Popeyes restaurant chain, 545
Pop-up advertisements, on Internet, 399–400
Portable People Meter, 374
Positioning, 22, 126–53
actions in, 131–32
in advertising, 130
attribute, 133f, 137
based on experiential needs, 133f, 134–36, 135f
based on functional needs, 133f, 134
benefit, 133f–35f, 134–37. *See also* Benefit positioning
brand, framework for, 132–33, 133f

CPM in, 140–47. *See also* Consumer processing model (CPM)
described, 132
HEM in, 147–49, 148f
interrelated ideas in, 131–132
introduction to, 128
non–product-related, 133f, 137, 139f
nuts and bolts of, 131–40
in practice, 131–40
product-related, 133f, 137, 138f
proposed outcomes of, 132, 132f
in theory, 128–31, 129f, 131f
usage imagery in, 137, 139f
user imagery in, 137, 139f
Positioning Advertising Copy Testing (PACT), 284
Positioning statement, 132
brand, 22
defined, 17
Postal mail (P-mail) advertising, 422–31, 422t, 429t. *See also* P-mail advertising
Poster panels, advertising on, 579
Post-it (notepads), 73, 437, 437f
Potty Palooza facilities, of P&G, 491
Power
defined, 229, 229t, 444
example of, 231, 233, 233f
Power of context, in buzz creation, 552–53
PowerMaster, 610
PowerPoint, 580
PPAI. *See* Promotional Products Association International (PPAI)
Prairie Home Companion, 217
Preakness Stakes, 564–65
Precisely wrong thinking, vs. vaguely right thinking, logic of, 165f
Precision, defined, 420, 421
Predictive validity, of ARS Persuasion scores, 301–02, 301t
Preemptive creative style, 226–27
Premium(s), 508–15, 525–26
defined, 510
free-gift-with-purchase, 511
free-with-purchase, 511
good offers, components of, 515
in-, on-, or near-pack, 512
introduction to, 510
mail-in offers, 511–12, 512f
phone cards, 514–15
revenue, defined, 35
self-liquidating offers, 513–14
Pre-sales objectives, 164
Preschoolers, targeting to, 111, 111f
Prescription drug advertising, regulation of, 623–24
Price(s), average, advertising elasticities and, 198–200
Price packs, 515–16
Price reductions, retail, temporary, 472–74, 474t
Price sensitivity, increased, budgetary allocations related to, 450–51
Price-offs, 515–16
FTC regulations on, 515–16
Pricing elasticity, vs. advertising, 197–201, 200t
Prilosec, 564
Primary demand, 188
Prime time, in TV advertising, 375–76, 376t
Priming, subliminal, 266
Pringles, 82
Print advertising, 4
Prison Break, 14
Proactive MPR, 537–38, 539f
Processing time, reducing of, opportunity for, 247, 247f
Procter & Gamble (P&G), 14, 55, 66, 87, 96, 114, 119, 121, 136, 139–40, 148, 185, 186t, 188, 195, 384, 403, 408, 426, 460, 469, 490–94, 500, 517, 544, 564, 597
Product adoption, 62
Product certification, symbolism of, as fair traded, 136
Product information, consumers' trust related to, 184
Product labeling, regulations for, 623
Product RED licensing program, 567–68
Product usage, increasing, by loading consumers, 458–59
Professional misredeemers, 501f, 502
Profile(s), psychographic
customized, 102, 102t
general purpose, 102–06, 103t, 104f
Program evaluation, 20
Programming dayparts, in TV advertising, 375–76, 376t
Progressive Insurance, 154
Progresso Soup, 490
Prominent cues, use of, 245, 245f, 246f
Promotion(s), 508–15. *See also* Sales promotions; specific types and Rebates/refunds
advertised, increased store traffic due to, 474t, 475
bonus packs, 516
capabilities of, 454–59, 454t, 457f
consumer-oriented, 482–504, 485t, 510t
reasons for, 482–83
continuity, 522–23
customizing of, 471–72, 473f
defined, 446
games, 516–17
generalizations about, 472–76, 474t
increased budgetary allocations to, 448–54, 451f, 449t, 450t, 453t
balance-of-power shift and, 450
consumer responsiveness and, 452
corporate reward structures and, 452
factors accounting for, 448–52, 451f, 449t, 450t
increased brand parity and price sensitivity and, 450–51
new accounting rules related to, 452–53, 453t
push and pull strategies in, 449–52, 449t
reduced brand loyalty and, 451
reduced media effectiveness and, 452
short-term orientation and, 452
splintering of mass market and, 452
methods of, classification of, 485–86, 485t
in one product category affecting sales of brands in complementary and competitive categories, 474t, 476
overlay, 523
premiums, 508–15
price-off, 515–16
push and pull strategies in, 449, 449t
reasons for, 482–83
rebates/refunds, 517–20, 519f
retailer, 524–26, 525f
sales, 444–59. *See also* Sales promotions
targets of, 447–48, 448f
tie-in, 523–24, 523f, 524f
implementation problems related to, 524
trade, role of, 459–61. *See also* Trade promotions
users of, 446–47
uses of, 446
Promotion agencies
online, 503
role of, 503
Promotion Marketing Association (PMA), 29, 517
Promotional Products Association International (PPAI), 29
Proposition(s), value, 218
Psychographic(s), 98, 99f
described, 101
Psychographic profiles
customized, 102, 102t
general purpose, 102–06, 103t, 104f
Psychographic segmentation scheme, Yankelovich MindBase, 102, 103t
Psychographic targeting, 98, 99f, 101–06
customized profiles in, 102, 102t
Psychological reactance, 261–62
Public relations
ethical issues in, 614
marketing-oriented, 534–59. *See also* Marketing public relations (MPR)
Publishing, customized, 371
Publix, 75, 526
GreenWise label, 526
Pull, 449, 449t
Pull strategies, 449–52, 451f
Pulsing advertising schedule, 334
Puma, 15, 38
Pupillometer, 299
Purchase(s)
repeat, encouraging, 457
trial, encouraging of, 158f, 160–61
Purchasing
unplanned, 591–94, 592t–94t
unwise, 613
Purina, 248, 426, 512, 522
Purina Points, 522
Push, 449, 449t
Push strategies, 449–52, 451f, 449t

Q

Q scores, role of, 257–58
Quaker Oats, 426
Qualitative message research, 287
Quality, in magazine advertising, 366, 366t
Quantitative message research, 287–88, 289t
Quick results, in trade promotion program, 461
Quilted Northern Ultra bath tissue, 569
Quiznos, 526

R

RADAR. *See* Radio's All Dimension Audience Research (RADAR)
Radio, 371–74, 372t
buying time on, 372, 374
prevalence of, 371
Radio advertising, 371–74, 372t
audience measurement for, 374

buying time in, 372, 374
limitations of, 372t, 373–74
strengths of, 372–73, 372t
Radio audiences, measurement for, 374
Radio frequency identification (RFID) chips, 597
Radio's All Dimension Audience Research (RADAR), 374, 414
"Rainforest Alliance Certified," 136
Ralph Lauren brand, 35, 137, 139f
Ralston Purina, 248, 426, 512, 522
Rapid Clear Acne Elimination Spot Gel, 625
Rating(s), described, 326
Rating point(s)
described, 326
effective, 330–31
gross, 307–08, 326–28
target, 328
Ratio(s), advertising-to-sales, 185, 187t
RAZR, 73, 77
Reach
broad, 362, 362t
described, 322
determinants of, 323–24
effective
concept of, 328–29
planning for, 330–31, 331t
in media planning, 322–24
weekly, optimizing of, 337
Reach planning, effective, 330–31, 331t
Reactance, psychological, 261–62
Reaction(s), emotional, measurement of, 297–99. *See also* Emotional reactions, measurement of
Reactive MPR, 538–42, 540f
Reader(s), eligible, 290
Reader's Digest, 486
"Reasonable consumer," 620–21
Rebates/refunds, 517–20, 519f
defined, 517–18
phantom discounts, 518
rebate fraud, 518, 520
Recall, 414
brand, 38
controversy related to, 297
measures of, 289–97, 291f, 294f–96f
Recency planning, 335–38
Recency principle, 336
Recognition
brand, 38
measures of, 289–97, 291f, 294f–96f
Reconciliation, in media planning, 338
Redemption centers, 501–03, 501f
Redemption of coupons, 495–96
process of, 501–03, 501f
Redemption rates
for coupons, 494
in-pack, 500
by current brand users, 495–96
Reebok, 38
Reese, 524
Referent, 129
Refund(s), 517-20, 519f. *See also* Rebates/refunds
Regulation of Marcom, 618–26
of benefits, 619
of costs, 619–20
against deceptive advertising, 620
of DTC advertising, 624
by federal agencies, 620
information, 623
justification for, 618–20
of prescription drug advertising, 623–24
in product labeling, 623
by state agencies, 624
against unfair practices, 622–23
Relationship(s), building of, 10t, 17–18
Relative advantage, in facilitating brand adoption, 64–66, 66f
Reminding, by advertising, 189
P-O-P, 590–91
Renaissance Hotels, 522
ReNu MoistureLoc Lens-cleaner, 539
Repeat purchases, encouraging, sales promotions in holding current usage by, 457
Repeater class, 63f, 64
Repeat-purchase objective, 484
Repositioning, of brands, 137, 139–40
Research
advertising, 282–86. *See also* Advertising research; Message research
copy, 283
qualitative message, 287
quantitative message, 287–88, 289t
Research services, 194
Resolve, 520, 521f
Resonant advertising, 225, 225f
Respect, 251t, 252–53
Response(s)
autonomic, 298
sales, 302–04
Retail price reductions, temporary, sustantial increase in sales due to, 473–74, 474t
Retailer(s)
minimizing effort and cost of, in trade promotion program, 462
P-O-P advertising benefits for, 587
Retailer performance, improvement in, in trade promotion program, 462
Retailer promotions, 524–26
coupons, 524
frequent-shopper program, 525, 525f
premiums, 525–26
samples, 525–26
special price deals, 525
Retention, search/retrieval and, of stored information, in CPM, 145–47, 146f, 147f
Return on investment (ROI), 165
estimating of, 491, 491t
Return on marketing investment (ROMI), 50, 52
Revenue, premium, defined, 35
Revenue Science, 100
Reward(s)
consumer, 484–85, 485t
delayed, 485
Reynolds Metals Company, 569
RFID chips. *See* Radio frequency identification (RFID) chips
Rich media, on Internet, 399–400
Right thinking, vaguely, vs. precisely wrong thinking, logic of, 165f
Ripomatics, 283
Ritz, 569, 570f
R.J. Reynolds (RJR) tobacco company, 609–10
Road & Track, 425
Rocket science, 180
ROI. *See* Return on investment (ROI)
Rolex watches, 231, 231f
Rolling Stone magazine, 367
ROMI. *See* Return on marketing investment (ROMI)
Ruggedness, brand-related, 41
Rumor(s), 543–46
commercial, 544
conspiracy, 545
contamination, 545, 546
handling of, 545
Russian knickknacks, 513
Ryder, 434

S

Saab 9-5 campaign, 348–50, 351t, 425
Saatchi & Saatchi, 14, 217
Safeguard soap, 491
Sale(s), Marcom objectives stated in terms of, 164–66, 165f
Sales force
poorly trained, effects of, 459
TV advertising effects on, 379, 379t
Sales promotions, 444–59. *See also* specific types and Promotion(s)
capabilities of, 454–58, 454t
facilitate introduction of new products to trade, 455
hold current users by encouraging repeat purchases, 457
increase on- and off-shelf merchandising space, 455–56
increase product usage by loading consumers, 457–58
invigorate sales of mature brand, 456
neutralized competitive advertising and sales promotions, 455
obtain trial purchases from consumers, 456–57
preempt competition by loading consumers, 459
reinforce advertising, 459
customizing of, 471–72, 473f
ethical issues in, 615
generalizations about, 472–76, 474t
ideas' evaluation, 526–29, 528t
postmortem analysis, 527–29, 528t
procedure, 526–27
incentives in, 446
increased budgetary allocations to, 448–54, 448f, 449t, 450t, 453t
introduction to, 446–48, 448f
limitations of, 454t, 458–59
inability to compensate for poorly trained sales force or lack of advertising, 459
inability to give trade or consumers any compelling long-term reason to continue purchasing brand, 459
inability to permanently top established brand's declining sales trend or change basic nonacceptance of undesired product, 459
nature of, 446–47
push and pull strategies in, 449, 449t
short-term orientedness of, 446
stimulate sales force enthusiasm for new, improved, or mature product, 454–55, 454t

targets of, 447–48, 448f
Sales response, measures of, 302–04
ACNielsen's ScanTrack in, 302–03
IRI's BehaviorScan, 303–04
testing procedure, 304
Sales-to-advertising response function, 167–68, 168t
Salience, increasing, advertising for, 189
Salon Selectives, 563
Sample(s), 525–26
Sampling, 486–93, 525–26
defined, 486
by direct mail, 486
door-to-door, 487
effectiveness of, 486
of food and beverage products with taste strips, 487
at high-traffic locations and events, 487
indications for, 491–92
in-store, 488
Internet, 488
by magazines, 486–87
by newspapers, 486–87
on- or in-pack, 487
practices in, 488–91, 491f, 491t
estimating ROI, 491, 491t
targeting sample recipients, 488–89
using creative distribution methods, 489–91, 491f
problems related to, 492–93
at unique venues, 487–88
Sam's Club, 485
Samsung, 630
Samsung Hue, 73
Samsung M300, 73
Samsung Sync, 73
Samuel Adams, 432
Sanka, 82
Sara Lee, 426
Saturation factor, in celebrity endorsement, 256
SAU system. *See* Standardized Advertising Unit (SAU) system
Save Lids to Save Lives, 569
S.B. Thomas' English muffins, 588–90
SBC Communications, 6
Scanner-delivered coupons, 497–98
ScanTrack, of ACNielsen, 302–03
Scarcity, appeals to, related case of, 261–62
Schemata, "Score Card" program, 145, 525, 525f
SEA. *See* Search engine advertising (SEA)
Seal-of-approval programs, in green marketing, 630
Search(es)
keyword, 410–11
natural, 410
Search engine advertising (SEA), 409–13, 411f
costs of, 410
described, 409–10
fundamentals of, 409–10
problems with, 412–13
purchasing keywords in, 410–12
selecting content-oriented Web sites in, 410–12
Search/retrieval, retention and, of stored information, 145–47, 146f, 147f
Sears, 35, 121, 384
Second Life, 403
Secondary demand, 188
Secret Clues, 455
Security
defined, 229, 229t
example of, 233
Seer, 402
Selective perception, illustration of, 143, 143f
Selectivity, in magazine advertising, 366, 366t
Self-direction
defined, 229, 229t
example of, 231, 231f
Self-liquidating, defined, 513
Self-liquidating offers (SLOs), 513–14
Self-regulation
advertising, 624–26
media, 624–25
Self-report(s), visual, of emotional responses, 298
Self-report measurement, of emotional responses, 298
Sensory stores (SS), 145
ServiceMaster, 434
Sex
in advertising, 262–64, 264f
potential downside of, 263–64, 264f
role of, 263
stopping-power role of, 263
Shape, in packaging, 83
Share of market (SOM), 172–74, 172t, 173f, 200–201, 200t
Share of voice (SOV), 172–74, 172t, 173f
Share Our Strength program, 569, 569f
Shecky's Girls Night Out, 563
Shelf-delivered coupons, 497
Shelf-space model, 335–38
Shell Oil, 79, 79f
Shop n' Bag supermarkets, 503
Shopping Buddy, 574
Short filling, 628, 630
Short Message System (SMS), 407
Short-term (working) memory (STM) 145
Short-term orientation, budgetary allocations related to, 452 "Short-term solution," 24
Shrek the Third, 518
Sign(s)
defined, 128–29
described, 129
free-standing, 576–77, 577f
meanings of, 129
on-premise
ABCs of, 577, 577f
types of, 576–77, 577f
thumbs-up, 129f
Signage, 574–99
on-premise, 576–78, 577f
Signify, 128
Similarity, 251t, 253–54
Simmons Market Research Bureau (SMRB), 365, 368–71, 414
Simon Marketing, 517
Simplicity, in advertising, 211
Sincerity, brand-related, 40
Single voice principle, 10t, 16–17
Single-source data, 303
Single-source systems (SSSs), 302–04
Sirius Satellite Radio, 374
Situational factors, in comparative advertising, 271
60 Minutes, 382t
Skil cordless screwdriver, 538, 539f
SKUs. *See* Stock-keeping units (SKUs)
Sky messages, 437
Skytypers, 437
Slanted lines, in packaging, 83
Slingbox, 382, 383
Sloan's Supermarket, 502
Slogan(s), advertising, 222
SLOs. *See* Self-liquidating offers (SLOs)
Slotting allowances, 464–66, 615
Smart car, 320, 321, 322f, 553
Smart Fortwo, 320–21, 324
Smart Sign Media, 583
Smart Solid, 15
Smart Start, 511
SmartWater, 585, 586f
SMRB. *See* Simmons Market Research Bureau (SMRB)
SMS. *See* Short Message System (SMS)
Social networking sites, on Internet, 403
Social networks, of interpersonal relationships, 547
Social Security, 544
Softone bulbs, 456
Software, media-scheduling, 341–46, 342t, 344t
SOM. *See* Share of market (SOM)
Song Airways, 73, 437
Sonic, 488
Sony, 350, 547
Sony Ericsson's W300, 73
Sony Pictures Television, 378
Sony PlayStation, 432
Sophistication, brand-related, 40–41
Sound symbolism, brand naming and, 75
Source Perrier, 541
Southwest Airlines, 73
SOV. *See* Share of voice (SOV)
Spam
defined, 405
vs. opt-in e-mailing, 404–05
"SPAM Stuff" continuity program, 472, 473f
Special price deals, 525
Specialty billboards, 580–81, 581f
Specific effects, calibrating of, in determining Marcom effectiveness, 53
Specificity, encoding, 85
Spending, consistent investment, 188
Spider-Man, 622–23
Spirit Airlines, 73
Splenda, 604
SpongeBob, 511
SpongeBob SquarePants, 608
SpongeBob SquarePants boxes, 480
Sponsor misidentification, in event sponsorship, 564
Sponsorship(s), 560–73
cause, 567–71. *See also* Cause-related marketing (CRM)
event, 563–67
growth in, reasons for, 562
introduction to, 562
Sponsorship marketing, 560–73. *See also* Sponsorship(s)
defined, 562
features of, 562
Sports Illustrated, 290, 293, 352, 365, 365f, 367
Sprint Cup Series, 560
SRDS. *See* Standard Rate and Data Service (SRDS)
SRDS Media Solution, 363, 365
SRI Consulting Business Intelligence's (SRIC-BI's) VALS system, 102, 104f

SRIC-BC (GeoVALS), 106
SRIC-BI's VALS system, 102, 104f
SS. *See* Sensory stores (SS)
SSSs. *See* Single-source systems (SSSs)
Stacy's Pita Chip campaign, 424, 424f
Standard Rate and Data Service (SRDS), 363, 365
Standardized Advertising Unit (SAU) system, 361
Starbucks, 48, 126, 136, 189, 406, 536
Starch Readership Service, 289–93, 291f
State agencies, regulation of, 624
State Farm Insurance, 4, 154, 434
  Now What? campaign of, 4–5
Statement(s), positioning, 132
  brand, 22
  defined, 17
Steal-o-matics, 283
Stereotype(s), in advertising, 612
Stickiness factor, in buzz creation, 552
Sticky advertisements, 210–13
Stimulation, defined, 229, 229t
Stimulus(i)
  conditioned, 269
  novel, 245, 245f
  unconditioned, 269
STM. *See* Short-term (working) memory (STM)
Stocking allowance, 463–66
Stock-keeping units (SKUs), 455, 463–64
Stockpiling, 457–58
Stop & Shop Supermarket Company, 574
Stopping-power role, of sex, 263
Stored information, retention and search/retrieval of, 145–47, 146f, 147f
Storyboards, 283
Storytelling, in advertising, 212–13
Strategy(ies)
  advertising, 320
    described, 191
    implementing of, 192
  creative, leverage point and, 230t
  described, 221
  market, 320
  media, 321, 321f
Street money, 463–66
Strength(s), brand, 243
Strengthening of linkages, 145–46, 147f
Strivers, in VALS framework, 104f, 105
Stylus Verve, 352
Subaru, 74
Subaru Outback, 148
Subliminal, defined, 264
Subliminal messages, 264–67
  brand choice and, 268
  embedded-symbol variety of, 266
  influence on brand choice, 266–67
  unlikely success of, 265–67
Subliminal priming, 266
Subliminal Seduction, 265
Suburban Pioneers, 107
Subway, 212, 608
Sudafed, 542
Suggestive brand names, 73–74
Sun Light dishwashng liquid, 493
Sunk costs, 311
Sun-Maid raisins, 521
Super Bowl advertising, 293, 352
  costs of, 316–17, 381
Super Bowl XVIII, 206
Superiority, in Mac owners' psychographic profiles, 323
Superstitials, on Internet, 400
Supervisor(s), management, 194
Supply, rationing of, in buzz creation, 554–55
Survivor, 385, 433
Survivor(s), in VALS framework, 104f, 105
Susan G. Komen Breast Cancer Foundation, 568–69, 569f
Sweepstakes, 520–21, 520f, 521f
  online, 522
Swerve, 75–76
Symbolic embeds, 264–67
Symbolic needs, positioning-based, 133f, 134
Symbolism, sound, brand naming and, 75
Syndicated programming, 378
Synergy
  defined, 3
  IMC and, 9–10
Synthesis(es), active, 143

T

Tachistoscope, 265
Taco Bell, 293, 294, 294f, 534
Tacoda track, 100
Tamagotchi, 554
Target(s), 512, 589, 591
  promotion, 447–48, 448f
Target audience
  for creative brief, 219–20
  in event sponsorship, 564
  measurable characteristics of, 98
  selecting of, 321–22
Target rating points (TRPs), 328
Targetability, of P-mail advertising, 425
Targeting, 21–22, 96–124. *See also* specific types, e.g., Behaviorographic targeting
  behavioral, online, 100, 413–14
  behaviorographic, 98–100, 99f
    online, 100
    privacy concerns of, 101
  characteristics of, classification of, 98, 99f
  of children and teens, 607–09
  demographic, 107–22
  of economically disadvantaged consumers, 609–10
  ethics of, 607–10
  geodemographic, 106–07
  introduction to, 98
  psychographic, 98, 99f, 101–06
    customized profiles in, 102, 102t
Tarrant Apparel Group, 256
Taste, bad, in advertising, 612
Tattoo advertising, 437
Taxi, 78
TD budgeting, 22
TDBU process, 22
TEARS Model, 251–54, 251t
Ted Airlines, 72–73
Teenage Research Unlimited, 112
Teenagers, targeting to, 112–13, 113f
  ethics of, 607–09
Television (TV), 375–88, 376t, 379t, 382t, 386f
  flat-screen, plasma, 65
  imagery from, transferred to radio advertising, 372t, 373
  in-store, growth of, 589
  prevalence of, 375
Television (TV) advertising, 375–88, 376t, 379t, 382t, 386f
  ad copy distinctions, 305, 305f
  all good things must end, 310–11
  audience erosion effects on, 379t, 380–83, 382t
  audience measurement in, 385–88, 386f
    local, 386–87
    measuring away-from-home viewers (and listeners), 387
    national (network), 385–86, 386f
  cable, 378
  conclusions about, 304–11, 305f, 306t, 307t, 309f
  DVR effects on, 380, 382
  infomercials, 383–84
  limitations of, 379t, 380–83, 382t
  local, 378–79
  more is not necessarily better, 306–10, 307t, 309f
  network, 377, 376t
  programming dayparts in, 375–76, 376t
  quick effects of, 311
  spot, 377–78
  by State Farm Insurance, 4
  strengths of, 379, 379t
  stubbornness in, 311
  syndicated, 378
  in TV programs, 431–34
Television (TV) programs
  brand placements in, 384–85
  direct advertising in, 431–34
  top-10 prime-time broadcast, 382t
Television (TV) viewing, 383
Television (TV) viewing audiences, erosion of, effect on TV advertising, 379t, 380–83, 382t
Tequila marketers, 292
"Test Drive a Macintosh" promotion, 68
TexCover II, 137, 139
"Thanking the Troops," 294–95, 295f, 296f
The Apprentice, 252, 433
The Body Shop, 536
The Clam Plate Orgy, 265
The Fall of Advertising & the Rise of PR, 536
The Fruit Label Company, 437
The Garden of Hope & Courage, 569, 570f
The Grammys, 352
The Little Brown Book, 371
The Martin Agency, 352
The Oprah Winfrey Show, 551, 551f, 552
The Passion of the Christ, 550
"The People's Choice" site, 403
The Pillsbury Company, 490
"The Relationship Company," 226
The Wall Street Journal, 72, 100, 354
Thing(s), leveraging associations from, 44f, 45
Thinkers, in VALS framework, 104, 104f
Three Olives vodka, 263
3M Company, 437, 437f
360-degree branding, touch points and, 14–16
Three-exposure hypothesis, 329–30
Thrifty-Rent-A-Car, 78–79
Thumbs-up sign, 129f
Tide detergent, 14
Tie-in promotions, 523–24, 523f, 524f
  implementation problems related to, 524
Time, 352
Time Warner, 185, 186t

Timeliness, in newspaper advertising, 362, 362t
Timing, in trade promotion program, 460
Tinactin, 248
TNS Media Research, 387–88
Tobacco products, targeting of, to children and teens, 608–09
TOMA. *See* Top-of-mind awareness (TOMA)
Tommy Bahama brand, 569, 570f
Tooth Tunes, 74
Toothbrush, muscial, 74
Top-down (TD) budgeting, 22
Top-down/bottom-up (TDBU) process, 22
Top-of-mind awareness (TOMA), 38, 38f, 188, 398
Touch points
  effectiveness of, 16
  examples of, 14–16
  laundry hanger as, 15
  360-degree branding and, 14–16
Toyota, 121, 550
Toyota Camry, 60
Toyota Cressida, 226
Toyota Highlander, 137, 138f
Toyota Motor Corporation, 26
Toyota Motor Sales U.S.A., 14
Toyota Prius, 65, 626
Toys "R" Us, 488
Trade allowances, 462–68
  bill-back allowances, 463
  efforts to rectify problems related to, EDLP, 468–72
    customize promotions, 471–72, 473f
    pay-for-performance programs, 470–71
  exit fees, 465
  forms of, 463–66
  objectives of, 462
  off-invoice allowances, 462–63
  slotting allowances, 463–65
  uses of, 462–63
Trade associations, in Marcom field, 28–29
Trade deals, 462–68. *See also* Trade allowances
Trade promotions
  objectives of, 460–62
  role of, 460–62
  scope of, 461
  spending related to, altered organization at P&G to better manage, 461
  successful, ingredients for, 460–61
Trademark(s), registration of, 77f, 79
Trade-off(s), in media planning, necessity of making, 340–41
Trading, fair, symbolism of certifying products in, 136
Tradition, defined, 229, 229t
Traffic Audit Bureau, 583
Transfer, meaning, 44, 129–31, 131f
Transformational advertising, 224
Transit advertising, 585, 585f, 586f
Transmeta Corp., 73–74
Trial purchases, encouraging of, 158f, 160–61
Trialability, in facilitating brand adoption, 68
Trier class, 63f, 64
"Triple-coupon day," 524
Tropical Fantasy, 545
Trouble factor, in celebrity endorsement, 256–57
TRPs. *See* Target rating points (TRPs)
True Blue, 78–79
Trustworthiness, 251t, 252
Tums, 248, 250
TV. *See* Television (TV)
TWA, 73
Tweens, targeting to, 111–12
20th Century Fox, 15 24, 434
Twinkies, 432
2004 Super Bowl, 552
Tylenol, 82, 541–42, 623
Tylenol Cold Multi-Symptom Nighttime Liquid, 269, 270f
Tyson, 569

U

U-Haul, 434
Ultimate objective, focusing on, 18–19
Uncle Ben's (rice), 82
Unconditioned stimulus, 269
Unexpectedness, in advertising, 211
Unfair advertising practices
  defined, 622
  regulations against, 622–23
Unilever, 185, 186t, 319, 437, 560, 563
Unique selling proposition (USP) style, 223–24, 223t
United Airlines, 73
United Parcel Services (UPS), 564
Universal Studios, 516
Universalism, defined, 229, 229t
University National Merit Scholarship, 447
University of Florida, 408
University of Texas, 408
Unplanned purchasing, 591–94, 592t–94t
Unsafe packaging, 615
Untruthfulness, 611
Unwise purchasing, 613
UPC symbols, phony, 520
UPS (United Parcel Services), 564
Uptown, 609–10
Urban legends, 543-46 "Urban Pasture" motif, 490
U.S. Army, 562
U.S. Census Bureau, 107, 116–17
U.S. Congress, 609, 611, 630
U.S. News & World Report, 555
U.S. Open Snowboarding Championships, 563
U.S. Trade Association, in marcom field, 28–29
U.S. Treasury Department, Bureau of ATF of, 610
US Open, 18, 354, 437
USA Today, 354
Usage expression advertising, 188
Usage imagery, 137, 139f
User imagery, 137, 139f
USP style. *See* Unique selling proposition (USP) style
USTA National Tennis Center, 18

V

V8 juice, 130, 131f, 463, 516
Vaguely right thinking, vs. precisely wrong thinking, logic of, 165f
Valassis, 494
Validity, predictive, of ARS Persuasion scores, 301–02, 301t
Valpak Direct Marketing Systems, 494
Value(s)
  adding, advertising for, 190
  in advertising, 190
  customer lifetime, 429
  defined, 228
  ethical core, in Marcom, 617–18
  face, 495
  intrusion, in TV advertising, 379, 379t
  nature of, 228–29, 229t
  net present, 429
  relevant to advertising, 229–30
  universal, 229, 229t
Value orientation, 230, 230t
Value proposition, 218
Vans, 38
Vehicle(s)
  buying of, 319–20
  described, 318
  selecting of, 319–20
  vs. media, 318
Verbal framing, 247
Verizon, 78, 185
Vertical lines, in packaging, 83
Very important customer ("VIC"), 525
Vicks NyQuil, 269, 270f, 271
Victoria's Secret, 267
Vidal Sassoon Wash & Go shampoo, 493
Video advertisements, online, 400
Video-game advertising, 435–36, 436f
Video-game audiences, measuring of, 435–36
VIEW model, in packaging evaluation, 84–87, 85f, 86f
Vioxx, heart attacks/strokes and, 540
Visa, 566
Visibility, in packaging, 84, 85f
Visine, 226
Visual self-reports, of emotional responses, 298
Visualizations, lack of, in radio advertising, 372t, 373–74
Viva, 486
Vodka marketers, 292
Voice-overs, in advertising, 280
Volkswagen (VW), 170–71, 511
Volkswagen (VW) Beetle, 145, 146f
Volvo, 425, 508
VW. *See* Volkswagen (VW)
Vytorin, 611

W

Wadsworth Thriftway store, 502
Wal-Mart, 46, 119, 500, 564, 589, 591, 628
Walt Disney Company, 111, 185, 186t
Walt Disney World, 18
Warner-Lambert, 489
Washing machines, for masses, 65
Wearout, defined, 310
Web sites, for Internet advertising, 397–98
Webisode(s), on Internet, 400, 401
Weekly reach, optimizing of, 337
Weight
  media, creative content and, relationship between, 309–10
  in media planning, 326–33, 331t, 332t
  non-wasted, 328
Weight tests, vs. copy tests, 304
Wendy's, 211, 488, 544
Wet Ones, 224
Wheaties, 82
Whirlpool Corp., 65, 115, 568–69, 569f
White Picket Fence, 107

Whitman's Sampler, 84, 85f
WiFi, 406
WiFi Seeker, 406
Wii, 66
Wireless couponing, 500
Wireless e-mail advertising, 406–07
Wisk detergent, 12, 13
WOM influence, 545–49. *See also* Word-of-mouth (WOM) influence
Word-of-mouth (WOM) influence, 545–49. *See also* specific elements
  creating Buzz, 549–55. *See also* Buzz creation
  described, 545–46
  dissemination process, 548
  negative, prevention of, 548–49
  opinion leaders' role in, 548
  strong and weak ties related to, 547
Workability, in packaging, 86–87, 86f
Working memory, 145
World Series, 352
World Wide Web, 394, 395, 551
World-class brands, characteristics of, 48–49, 49t
Wrangler jeans, 562
Wrong thinking, precisely, vs. vaguely right thinking, logic of, 165f

X

Xbox 360 owners, online gaming by, 435
XM Satellite Radio, 374

Y

Yahoo!, 400, 403, 410
Yankelovich MindBase psychographic segmentation scheme, 102, 103t
Yellow-pages advertising, 434–35
YMS. *See* "Youth materialism scale" (YMS)
Yoplait, 569
Yoplait Express, 87
Young & Rubicam advertising agency, 346
Young adults, targeting to, 113–14
"Your World Delivered," 6
"Youth materialism scale" (YMS), 112
YouTube, 538, 612
Yup & Comers, 113–14

Z

Zaltman Metaphor Elicitation Technique (ZMET), 287
Zapping, in TV advertising, 379t, 380
Zero sum, 392
Zipping, in TV advertising, 379t, 380
ZMET. *See* Zaltman Metaphor Elicitation Technique (ZMET)
Zune, 71–72, 75
Zune Marketplace, 71–72